THE CRIMINAL LAW OF SCOTLAND

THE CRIMINAL LAW
OF SCOTLAND

by

SIR GERALD H. GORDON

C.B.E., Q.C., LL.D.

*Formerly Sheriff of Glasgow and Strathkelvin
and
Formerly Professor of Scots Law
at the University of Edinburgh*

THIRD EDITION

Volume II

Edited by

MICHAEL G. A. CHRISTIE

M.A., LL.B, Solicitor

*Formerly Lecturer in Law
at the University of Aberdeen*

Nemo sine crimine vivit
Dicta Catonis, i.5

Published under the auspices of
SCOTTISH UNIVERSITIES LAW INSTITUTE LTD

W. GREEN
EDINBURGH
2001

First published 1967
Second Impression 1968
Second Edition 1978
Third Edition, Vol. I 2000

Published in 2001 by W. Green & Son Ltd
21 Alva Street
Edinburgh EH2 4PS

Typeset by J. P. Price, Chilcompton, Somerset

Printed and bound in Great Britain by MPG Books Ltd, Bodmin, Cornwall

No natural forests were destroyed to make this product;
only farmed timber was used and replanted

A CIP catalogue record of this book is available from the British Library

ISBN 0 414 013999

PREFACE TO VOLUME II

The editor's aim has been the revision of the text of Book II (with the exception of original Chapters 46, 52 and 53) of the second edition of Sir Gerald Gordon's *Criminal Law* so that the revised text will reflect the state of Scots criminal law as of August 1, 2001. Sir Gerald has read and commented upon drafts of all third edition chapters; but responsibility for the final form of these, and for any errors and omissions, is entirely that of the editor.

Since the publication of the First Volume, some important decisions of the Appeal Court have altered what appears there. In particular, Chapter 7 ("The Criminal Mind") should now be read subject to the opinions of the Court in *Drury v. H.M. Advocate*, 2001 S.L.T. 1013 (see Chapter 23 of this Volume), where the *mens rea* for murder, the distinction between murder and culpable homicide, and the operation of provocation were all re-examined. The discussion of diminished responsibility, in Chapter 11 of Volume I, must also now be read subject to the opinion of the Court in *Galbraith v. H.M. Advocate (No. 2)*, 2001 S.L.T. 953 (see paragraph 25.08 of this Volume).

The editor would wish to acknowledge the considerable debt he owes to those who assisted in, and encouraged, the preparation of this edition. In particular, he would wish to express his gratitude to Sir Gerald Gordon for his close, efficient and invariably good-humoured attention, often at very short notice, to material intended for publication here.

He would also wish to thank Professor Bill McBryde, Professor George Gretton, and Professor Joe Thomson for their patience and enduring encouragement over the considerable period of time which the preparation of this edition has occupied. Thanks are also due to Karen Taylor and Neil McKinlay for their unfailing encouragement and support as commissioning editors to W. Green. Contributions by Sarah McMillan, especially in relation to the revision of Chapter 28 of this Volume, and Natalya Paul Cowan, relative to matters of law in New Hampshire, are also gratefully acknowledged.

The editor bears a particular debt of gratitude to Margaret R. Christie, who not only word-processed the entire text of the second edition but also proofread the manuscript for both Volumes. Her encouragement, patience and unflagging support have been of inestimable value.

Michael Christie
October, 2001

CONTENTS

BOOK II: SPECIFIC CRIMES

PART I: OFFENCES OF DISHONESTY

PART II: OFFENCES OF DAMAGE TO PROPERTY

PART III: NON-SEXUAL OFFENCES AGAINST THE PERSON

SECTION 1 — Homicide

SECTION 2 — Concealment of Pregnancy and Abortion

PART VII: OFFENCES AGAINST PUBLIC ORDER AND WELFARE

PART VIII: OFFENCES AGAINST THE COURSE OF JUSTICE

TABLE OF CASES

TABLE OF STATUTES

ACTS OF THE PARLIAMENT OF SCOTLAND

STATUTES OF THE PARLIAMENT OF ENGLAND

STATUTES OF THE PARLIAMENT OF GREAT BRITAIN

ACTS OF THE SCOTTISH PARLIAMENT

TABLE OF STATUTORY INSTRUMENTS

LIST OF ABBREVIATIONS
(Excluding standard journals and law reports)

Alison

Principles and Practice of the Criminal Law of Scotland, A.J. Alison (2 Vols: Vol. i, *Principles* (Edin., 1832); Vol. ii, *Practice* (Edin., 1833).

Anderson

The Criminal Law of Scotland, A.M. Anderson (2nd ed., Edin., 1904).

Burnett

A Treatise on Various Branches of the Criminal Law of Scotland, J. Burnett (Edin., 1811).

D

The Digest of Justininan, T. Mommsen (ed.) with P. Krueger, with English translation ed. by A. Watson (University of Pennsylvania Press, 1985).

Draft English Code

Law Commission, *A Criminal Code for England and Wales*, Vol. 1 (Report and Draft Criminal Code Bill); Vol. 2 (Commentary): Law Com. No. 177, H. of C. No. 299, 1989.

Ersk.Inst.

An Institute of the Law of Scotland, J. Erskine, J.B. Nicolson (ed.), 2 Vols (Edin., 1871).

Gill

The Crime of Fraud: A Comparative Study. Unpublished Ph.D. thesis by Dr (now Lord) B.J. Gill, University of Edinburgh, 1975.

Gl. Williams

Criminal Law: The General Part, Glanville L. Williams (2nd ed., London, 1961).

Hall

General Principles of Criminal Law, J. Hall (2nd ed., Indianapolis, 1960).

Hall and Glueck

Cases on Criminal Law and its Enforcement, L. Hall and S. Glueck (St. Paul. Minn., 1st ed., 1940; 2nd ed., 1958). (References are to 2nd ed., unless otherwise stated.)

Hume

Commentaries on the Law of Scotland Respecting Crimes, Baron Hume, 4th ed., B.R. Bell (ed.), 2 Vols. (Edin., 1844).

Inst.

Institutiones Justiani, J.B. Moyle (ed.) (12th ed., Oxford, 1912).

Kenny

Kenny's Outlines of Criminal Law, C.S. Kenny, 19th ed., J.W.C. Turner (ed.) (Cambridge, 1966).

L.C.W.P.

Law Commission Working Paper. Series of Working Papers published for the English Law Commission (H.M.S.O.).

Macaulay

Notes on the Indian Penal Code, Lord Macaulay (published in *Collected Works of Lord Macaulay*, Lady Trevelyan (ed.) (London, 1866, Vol. VII)).

Macdonald

A Practical Treatise on the Criminal Law of Scotland, J.H.A. Macdonald (Lord Kingsburgh), (1st ed., Edin., 1867); 3rd ed., by the author assisted by N.D. Macdonald (Edin., 1894); 5th ed., J. Walker (later Lord Walker) and D.J. Stevenson (eds) (Edin., 1948). (References are to 5th ed. unless otherwise stated.)

Mackenzie

The Laws and Customs of Scotland in Matters Criminal, Sir G. Mackenzie, (2nd ed., Edin., 1699).

Model Penal Code, T.D.	American Law Institute: Model Penal Code — Tentative Drafts (Philadelphia, 1956-61).
Model Penal Code, P.O.D.	American Law Institute: Model Penal Code — Proposed Official Draft (Philadelphia, 1962).
Model Penal Code, O.D.	American Law Institute: Model Penal Code, Official Draft (Philadelphia, 1985).
Modern Approach	*The Modern Approach to Criminal Law*, L. Radzinowicz and J.W.C. Turner (eds) English Studies in Criminal Science, Vol. IV (London, 1945).
N.E.D./O.E.D.	*Oxford English Dictionary*, J.A.H. Murray (ed.); 2nd ed., J.A. Simpson and E.S.C. Weiner (eds) (Oxford, 1989).
R.C.	Report of Royal Commission on Capital Punishment, 1953, Cmd. 8932.
R.C.Evid.	Report of Royal Commission on Capital Punishment: Minutes of Evidence, London, 1949-51.
Renton & Brown	*Criminal Procedure according to the Law of Scotland*, by R.W. Renton and H.H. Brown, 6th ed., G.H. Gordon (ed.) assisted by C.H.W. Gane (Edin., 1996).
Sayre	*A Collection of Cases on Criminal Law*, F.B. Sayre (Rochester, N.Y., 1927).
Smith and Hogan	*Criminal Law*, J.C. Smith and B. Hogan, 9th ed., Sir John C. Smith (ed.), (London, 1999).
T.B. Smith	*A Short Commentary on the Law of Scotland*, T.B. Smith (Edin., 1962).
Stair Inst.	*The Institutions of the Law of Scotland*, by Viscount Stair, ed., J.S. More, 2 Vols (Edin., 1832).
StGB	Strafgesetzbuch (German Penal Code).
1995 Act	Criminal Procedure (Scotland) Act 1995.

Note: For the penalties available for common law crimes, and explanation of the terms "prescribed sum", "statutory maximum" and "standard scale", see Nigel M.P. Morrison (ed.), *Sentencing Practice* (W. Green/Sweet & Maxwell, Edinburgh 2000), Chap. A3. Currently, the prescribed sum and the statutory maximum are both set at £5,000; and levels 1, 2, 3, 4 and 5 of the standard scale are set at £200, £500, £1,000, £2,500 and £5,000 respectively.

VOLUME II

SPECIFIC CRIMES

PART I

Offences of Dishonesty

CHAPTER 14

THEFT

Hume's account of stealing, which might be described as the tradi- **14.01** tional way of looking at the crime, has in many respects not survived into modern times. Whereas the core of traditional stealing lay in: (a) the unauthorised taking and carrying away of moveable goods owned by someone other than the thief[1]; and (b) the intention to deprive the owner permanently of those goods,[2] the modern law makes unauthorised appropriation the essential characteristic.[3] Indeed, appropriation now informs both the *actus reus* and *mens rea* elements, in that the former consists (for example) of conduct which deprives the complainer temporarily or permanently of "possessory rights" in the property, and the latter of the intention so to deprive him. Possessory rights here seem to refer, in a non-technical sense, to the complainer's right to physical enjoyment of the property, and would include the rights to use, control, (possibly) have re-delivered (as, for example, in the case of lost property) or, more simply but vaguely, "possess" that property.[4] Since the basic emphasis is applied to physical enjoyment and its loss to the complainer,[5] property which is the subject of theft must, it is thought, have actual existence and, as under the traditional account of theft, be physically moveable.

There are certainly advantages in using appropriation as the essential feature of theft, since, for example, it simplifies the way in which the *actus reus* of the crime may be described: instead of having to discuss the traditional account of theft in detail and later developments as exceptions to or modifications of that account, Scots law has through the concept of appropriation acquired a single concept with which to describe the various modes of stealing: thus taking and removing property, certain conduct following on the finding of property, and actings in contravention of the complainer's right to use or control property are all simply ways of showing the required appropriation.

It is tempting to imagine that depriving a person of his possessory rights, *i.e.* his rights to use and control property at the relevant time, exhausts the concept of appropriation; but this would risk over-simplifying the law and might also decriminalise situations which have for long been regarded as thefts. For example, it has been accepted for some time that those who have property of another on loan or under a

---

[1] Hume, i, 57. See also Alison, i, 265.

[2] An assumption made from Hume, i, 75. See also Alison, i, 270–271.

[3] See in particular *Carmichael v. Black; Carmichael v. Penrice*, 1992 S.C.C.R. 709, L.J.-G. Hope at 719A; *Iqbal v. Annan*, 1983 S.C.C.R. 332, Lord Cameron at 335.

[4] More extensive deprivations, as where the accused destroys the property completely or sells it to a scrap merchant, still seem to involve the assumption by the accused of one or other of the complainer's possessory rights.

[5] See *Carmichael v. Black; Carmichael v. Penrice*, 1992 S.C.C.R. 709, L.J.-G. Hope at 720C, Lord Allanbridge at 721D, and Lord Cowie at 722C.

hire-purchase agreement can steal that property, although they can hardly do so by conduct which excludes the owner from exercising his rights to use and control that property, for the owner is already excluded from exercising them by contract and not by any conduct on the part of the person who has the property on hire.[6] Appropriation, therefore, certainly includes the deliberate depriving an owner of his possessory rights in property; but it must also extend to situations where a person already in authorised possession of the property deprives its owner of rights to the property by acting towards that property as if he was its owner.[7]

The modern approach to stealing does, however, promote a much wider conception of the crime than would have been accepted by the institutional writers. The most obvious complainer is the owner of the property in question; but at least some of the rights protected by theft conceived in terms of appropriation may be rights which, as stated above, the owner is not entitled to have at any particular time, through contract or otherwise. This raises the question whether theft primarily protects the owner (as was always assumed to be the case under the traditional account of the law) or whether that protection now extends to a possessor who is not the owner. If the latter is now the case, theft arguably extends to *furtum possessionis*,[8] and it is possible to envisage that an owner might be convicted of stealing his own property (although there might be good reasons why such a conclusion should be avoided).[9] In the leading case of *Carmichael v. Black; Carmichael v. Penrice*,[10] where the appeal court first made clear that simple deprivation of possessory rights was sufficient for appropriation in theft, Lord Justice-General Hope stated: "I am not persuaded that this approach involves an extension of theft beyond the limits which have already been recognised. While the act [of immobilising a vehicle allegedly unauthorisedly parked in a private car park] cannot be described as theft by taking away, I consider that it can properly be described as theft by appropriation of the car in the car park."[11] It may be, therefore, that as mere possessors were not protected (as against the owner, at least) under the traditional law of theft, they would continue not to be under the law as laid down in *Carmichael v. Black*: but the matter is not free from doubt.

---

[6] See paras 14.07 and 14.08, *infra*. Hume's account of theft, in terms of an unauthorised and felonious *taking of possession* of property from its owner, excluded the subsequent dishonest actings of those who were already in possession under, for example, contracts of loan, hire or carriage — unless it could be proved that their intentions had been dishonest *from the outset of their possession* (Hume, i, 58–62, 68–69). This account was regarded even in the 19th century as too narrow in that it sheltered many who popularly were, and thus should legally be, regarded as thieves (such as the hirer of a horse who subsequently sold it to meet a pressing debt): see paras 14.02 *et seq.*, *infra*. Thus the more modern account, in terms of appropriation, must seek to avoid sheltering those whom 19th and 20th century authorities declared (notwithstanding Hume's views) to be guilty of theft.

[7] This carries the potential objection that what is apparently stolen is not the property itself but rather a right in or to that property — *i.e.* an incorporeal right (see para. 14.13, *infra*).

[8] *cf.* Alison, i, 271; Burnett, p. 115; and see Hume, i, 73. Also *cf.* Mackenzie, I, 19,1. *Cf. furtum usus*, which has never been recognised in Scots law: see para 15.47, *infra*.

[9] See para. 14.29, *infra*.

[10] 1992 S.C.C.R. 709.

[11] *ibid.*, at 720A.

More generally, the more modern authorities[12] *can* be read as driving a coach and four through many concepts, if not the whole structure, of the traditional law of theft as that was understood at the time of the second edition of this book. These authorities certainly contain dicta which are difficult to reconcile with what were thought to be settled rules; and yet there is little to suggest that the judges who delivered those dicta considered themselves to be involved in any fundamental reformulation of the crime. With certain exceptions,[13] therefore, the following exposition will proceed on the basis that that traditional law of theft continues to apply in Scotland — with the caveat that appropriate regard must be had to modern judicial opinions which are at apparent variance with the rules of the traditional scheme.

It should also be noted that the modern authorities make the distinction between theft and certain other crimes (for example, clandestine taking and using,[14] and taking and driving away a motor vehicle[15]) very difficult to draw, if indeed it can be drawn at all; for it now seems that all deliberate and unauthorised borrowing of property belonging to another is theft, and the fact that some other offence may be charged in the same circumstances does not alter the position at all.

THE ACTUS REUS OF THEFT

From "taking" to "appropriating"

Theft was traditionally defined, both in legal and in lay usage, as the **14.02** dishonest taking of the goods of another,[16] and the typical theft situation is indeed one in which A takes something belonging to B from B's house, or desk, or pocket. Continental law, and English law before the Theft Act 1968, regard an unlawful taking as an essential feature of theft, and distinguish cases of theft from cases in which, for example, A decides to treat as his own property goods which came into his possession with the consent of their original owner. The latter situation tends to be regarded not as theft but as a breach of trust.[17] Historically,

---

[12] Especially *Carmichael v. Black; Carmichael v. Penrice*, 1992 S.C.C.R. 709.

[13] Particularly relative to *mens rea* — see paras 14.47 *et seq., infra.*

[14] See paras 15.29–15.32, *infra.*

[15] See paras 15.33–15.37, *infra.*

[16] See *e.g.* Hume, i, 57; Alison, i, 250; Macdonald, p. 16; Nouveau Code Pénal, Art. 311–1, which states "Le vol est la soustraction frauduleuse de la chose d'autrui"; StGB, Art. 242 which refers to someone who "eine fremde bewegliche Sache einem anderen wegnimmt"; Larceny Act 1916, s.1 (now replaced by Theft Act 1968 which abandons the need for an unlawful taking), which stated "a person steals who . . . takes and carries away anything capable of being stolen." *Cf.* N.E.D., which gives the meaning of "steal" as "to take dishonestly or secretly", and defines theft as the "felonious taking away" of another's property.

[17] *cf.* Nouveau Code Pénal, Art. 314; StGB, Art. 246; Larceny Act 1916, s.20. The American Model Penal Code and South African law treat theft by taking, embezzlement and at least some types of fraud all as forms of the one crime of theft, but have been unable to dispense with separate treatment of the various forms: see Model Penal Code P.O.D., s.223; J. Burchell and J. Milton, *Principles of Criminal Law* (2nd ed., Cape Town, 1997) Chaps 62 and 63 (*cf.* Chaps 66 and 67). The provisions of the 1995 Act allowing a conviction for embezzlement or fraud on a charge of theft, etc., produce much the same result in Scotland although they retain theft, fraud, etc., as distinct offences, a distinction perhaps more important in civil law than in criminal law, because of the civil doctrine of *vitium reale.*

breach of trust[18] can be regarded as a later and more sophisticated type of crime than theft, and at any rate in the United Kingdom it was regarded as a less serious crime. Serious cases of theft were at one time capital offences in Scotland, but breach of trust was never capital.

As indicated above,[19] Scots law does not now regard an unlawful taking as a prerequisite of theft, and indeed has not done so for over a hundred and fifty years.[20] In one of the more recently reported cases, the matter was put thus:

> "[T]he essential feature of the physical act necessary to constitute theft is the appropriation, by which control and possession of the thing is taken from its owner or custodier. In principle, therefore, the removal of the thing does not seem to be necessary, if the effect of the act which is done to it is its appropriation by the accused."[21]

14.03 *The development of Scots law.* Hume subscribed to the classical doctrine that theft required an unlawful taking. He defined theft as "the felonious taking and carrying away of the property of another, for lucre", following the Roman law definition: *contrectatio fraudulosa rei alienae, lucri faciendi gratia.*[22] In Hume's opinion, it was not theft for a borrower to appropriate goods lent to him, for a carrier to appropriate goods given him for carriage, or for anyone to appropriate goods he had found since he was to be presumed to have taken possession of them originally with the intention of returning them to the owner.[23] Theft for Hume was accordingly a crime of fairly narrow compass, a situation which was probably felt to be desirable at a time when any substantial or aggravated theft was a capital offence. Theft, just because it was capital, was restricted to acts exhibiting profligacy and daring,[24] qualities which were absent in those cases in which the accused did not have to go and take the goods from their owner. The activities of what would be today called "white-collar criminals", the dishonest bank clerks, carriers, factors, watchmakers, pawnbrokers, and so on, were regarded as "very different in moral turpitude and individual daring"[25] from the activities of those who actually broke into people's houses or picked their pockets in order to steal their belongings. The latter deserved hanging, and so were convicted of theft; the former did not, and so were convicted only of breach of trust.

Hume himself found his own definition of theft too narrow. It meant, for example, that a butler could not steal his master's plate, since it came into his hands with his master's consent, but it was felt that a man was

---

[18] Sometimes called breach of trust and embezzlement, and in modern times usually called embezzlement.

[19] See para. 14.01, *supra.*

[20] See *John Smith* (1838) 2 Swin. 28; *Geo. Brown* (1839) 2 Swin. 394; para. 14.05, *supra.*

[21] *Carmichael v. Black; Carmichael v. Penrice*, 1992 S.C.C.R. 709, L.J.-G. Hope at 719A.

[22] Hume, i, 57. *Cf.* Alison, i, 250; "the secret and felonious abstraction of the property of another". Alison's treatment of theft follows Hume's closely and as it too was published before the decisions in *Smith* and *Brown, supra,* is not of great importance in this connection. Mackenzie's treatment of the matter is not very clear, although he himself seems to have preferred not to restrict theft to cases of unlawful taking: Mackenzie, I, 19, 2. Burnett, who traces the requirement of unlawful taking to the *Regiam Majestatem,* is in the same position as Hume: see Burnett, p.111.

[23] Hume, i, 58, 62. Burnett apparently did not share Hume's charitable view of finders, but the cases he cites — *Scott* (1802) and *Mitchell* (1713) — seem to support Hume: Burnett, pp. 123–124.

[24] Hume, i, 59.

[25] *Hugh Climie* (1838) 2 Swin. 118, L.J.-G. Hope at 123.

entitled to exact the full rigours of the law against a dishonest servant[26]; it meant that if a traveller put his case down in the hall of an inn to await the porter who was to carry it to his carriage and someone else picked it up and made off with it that was theft, but if the porter picked it up and made off with it that was only breach of trust, which seemed absurd. So Hume took the view that the butler and the porter were not given possession of the goods by the owner, but only custody of them; the first time they obtained possession was when they made off with them, and that constituted an unlawful taking of possession and was accordingly theft.[27] In short, Hume substituted "felonious taking of possession of goods" for "felonious taking of goods".

This solution depended upon there being a clear way of distinguishing custody from possession; but the cases demonstrate that there was no consistent or satisfactory way of making such a distinction.[28]

Hume's restricted and restrictive views of theft met with some initial **14.04** success in the courts[29]; but it appears from the leading cases of 1838 and 1839[30] that his views had occasionally been rejected prior to 1838. It was also significant that by the mid-1830s theft had ceased to be a capital crime in practice.[31] Thereafter it was easier for the courts to accept the common sense judgment that dishonest hirers, repairers, finders and storekeepers were as much thieves as dishonest porters.[32]

JOHN SMITH[33] AND GEORGE BROWN.[34] The first full discussion of the **14.05** question in a reported case is in *John Smith*. *Smith* was a case of theft by finding, but it contains a number of general observations which show

---

[26] Mackenzie regarded "domestic theft", as he called theft by servants, as an aggravated form of theft: Mackenzie, I, 19, 2.

[27] Hume, i, 63–65.

[28] The labelling of an accused as a "mere" custodier, rather than a possessor, and thus capable of stealing that of which he has "custody" often seemed simply a rationalisation of the court's desire to convict him of theft rather than of breach of trust, and the technique was similar to that used in employing causal concepts as rationalisations of responsibility judgments: see Vol. I, para. 4.01. For examples of the large variety of attempts to distinguish between custodiers and possessors, see Hume, i, 61, 63–65; Alison, i, 251–254; Macdonald, pp. 32–37; *Duncan Macintosh* (1835) Bell's Notes 15; *Geo. Brown* (1839) 2 Swin. 394, L.J.-C. Boyle at 425, Lord Moncreiff at 430; *Robt Smith and Jas Wishart* (1842) 1 Broun 342, Lord Moncreiff at 349–350; *Wm Rodger* (1868) 1 Couper 76, Lord Ardmillan at 84–85; *Elder v. Morrison* (1881) 4 Couper 530; *O'Brien v. Strathern*, 1922 J.C. 55 in which it was held that a soldier could steal his kilt, although such an offence would normally be dealt with under military law.

[29] See, *e.g.*, *Baird and Manson* (1810) Burnett 114; *Archibald McKain* (1830) Bell's Notes 9; *Peter Campbell* (1833) *ibid.*; *Thos. E. Pearse* (1832) *ibid.* 10; and other cases cited in Bell's Notes pp. 9–18. *Cf. Mitchell* (1829) Bell's Notes 10, in which a carrier was convicted of theft.

[30] See para. 14.05, *infra*.

[31] Aggravated theft and theft of large amounts, which were classed as *furta gravia*, remained technically capital until the Criminal Procedure (Scotland) Act 1887, s.56: but the Crown invariably restricted the pains of law. The last death sentence for simple theft noted by Bell is that in *John Tweddal* (1829) Bell's Notes 27 and was followed by a reprieve; the last for aggravated theft was *Wm Den*, for theft by housebreaking in 1833: Bell's Notes 41.

[32] That the virtual abolition of capital punishment for rape did not prevent the court adopting a restrictive definition of that crime: see *Wm Fraser* (1847) Ark. 280 and *Chas Sweenie* (1858) 3 Irv. 109, is probably due to the inherent seriousness of rape, a plea of the Crown, and to the fact that unlike theft it had been capital in all cases.

[33] (1838) 2 Swin. 28.

[34] (1839) 2 Swin. 394.

clearly that Hume's insistence on an illegal taking had been abandoned in cases other than theft by finding. Lord Justice-Clerk Boyle said that "the later practice of the court . . . undoubtedly, has not required a felonious first-taking to constitute theft",[35] and Lord Mackenzie and Lord Moncreiff both remarked that Hume's requirement of such a taking had already been departed from in the cases of carriers and hirers.[36] Lord Meadowbank said that: "It is of no consequence of what character the original possession of the property is. The moment the intention of appropriating the property of another is formed, then the theft is committed."[37]

14.06   The accused in *Geo. Brown*[38] was a jeweller who was charged with having appropriated on a date in January 1839 a number of watches he had been given for repair between August and December 1838, and with having stolen them. The Crown argued that Hume was wrong in insisting on an unlawful taking as an essential element in theft, and pointed out that Hume himself had been obliged "to raise a new distinction, which goes far to break down his general rule" to provide for theft by a servant, where he was content "to adopt a figurative, instead of an actual, *taking*."[39] The Crown relied on Mackenzie[40] and on Roman Law,[41] and argued that the distinction between theft and breach of trust was one between cases of persons "holding property [as] the mere hand for detaining or transmitting it" and the case where the holder has "a right of management — a power to exchange", and had nothing to do with the way in which the property came into the accused's hands.[42]

Although this argument represents the modern distinction between theft and breach of trust (in the sense of embezzlement) fairly accurately it was too radical for even the majority of judges in *Brown,* and was not accepted in terms by the court. All the judges agreed that the law had changed since Hume, but they also agreed that the distinction between theft and breach of trust depended on the nature of the "possession" transferred to the accused. The majority[43] held that Brown's possession was so limited and temporary as to amount only to custody and so to make his crime theft; the minority[44] that it was sufficiently unlimited and lengthy to render him guilty only of breach of trust. The effect of *Brown,* therefore, was to replace Hume's unsatisfactory distinction between custodiers and possessors with an equally unsatisfactory distinction between limited and unlimited possessors.[45]

---

[35] (1838) 2 Swin. at 50.

[36] At 54.

[37] At 52.

[38] (1839) 2 Swin. 394.

[39] At 398.

[40] Mackenzie, I, 19, 1, 2.

[41] Inst. 4,1,6: "Furtum autem fit, non solum cum quis intercipiendi causa rem alienam amovet; sed generaliter cum quis alienam rem invito domino contrectat."

[42] 2 Swin. at 400.

[43] L.J.-G. Hope, Lords Meadowbank, Mackenzie, Moncreiff and Cockburn.

[44] L.J.-C. Boyle and Lord Medwyn.

[45] See, *e.g., Thos Paterson* (1840) 2 Swin. 521; *Robt Smith and Jas Wishart* (1842) 1 Broun 342; *Jas Dalziel* (1842) 1 Broun 425; *Eliz. Anderson* (1858) 3 Irv. 65; *Philip Kneen* (1858) 3 Irv. 161; *John Martin* (1873) 2 Couper 501; *Alex. Boyd* (1874) 2 Couper 541; *Wormald v. Lord Advocate* (1875) 3 Couper 191; *Potter and Ors v. H.M. Advocate* (1878) 4 Couper 135; *H.M. Advocate v. John Anderson* (1887) 1 White 475; *O'Brien v. Strathearn,* 1922 J.C. 55; — all examples of possession deemed so limited as to allow conviction for theft: and see, *e.g., Catherine Crossgrove or Bradley* (1850) J. Shaw 301; *W.T. Keith* (1875) 3 Couper 125 — both examples where possession was considered sufficiently extensive to preclude theft.

THEFT BY A HIRER. Discussions of limited possession or custody are, **14.07** however, quite pointless once it is accepted, as it is in Scotland, that the hirer of goods can steal them, even where the original hire is undertaken bona fide and the felonious intention does not arise until after the contract has started to operate. The idea of limited possession depends for its meaning on the existence of a class of unlimited possessors who are incapable of stealing the goods they possess. But the concept of such a class was quietly exploded even before the decision in *Geo. Brown*[46] by the recognition that a bona fide hirer could steal. The whole point of a contract of hire is to transfer possession, and not merely custody, whatever meanings are given to these terms.[47]

THEFT BY A HIRE-PURCHASER. Furthermore, although there is no **14.08** reported authority on the subject, the prosecution of hire-purchasers for theft is of common occurrence, and the hire-purchaser cannot be regarded as a limited possessor since he is a hirer with an option to purchase. Indeed, he is sometimes treated by the law as if he were an owner,[48] and is usually regarded by lay people as an owner. But he can steal, and the reason he can steal is that until he has exercised his option to purchase he is only a hirer, only a possessor, of the goods.[49] It is true that some hire-purchase contracts place limitations on the hirer's use of the subjects by providing, for example, that he must keep them in a certain place, or that he must not pledge them during the continuance of the contract, but a breach of such a condition is no more than evidence of appropriation. Whether a hirer who pawns the subjects is guilty of theft does not depend on whether the contract contains a clause prohibiting pledging, it depends on whether the pawning exhibits an intention to appropriate the goods during the currency of the hire. And it would be theft to appropriate hire-purchase goods even if the contract contained no limitation on the hirer's use of them.

Macdonald retains the concept of possession for a limited purpose, **14.09** but defines it so as to render it meaningless. He states that, "[t]he felonious appropriation of goods by the person to whom they have been entrusted for a limited and specified purpose constitutes theft. A purpose will be regarded as limited when it excludes exercise of the powers of ownership, and where the purpose is left unspecific the crime is embezzlement rather than theft."[50] This can mean only that unless ownership is transferred to the accused his appropriation is theft. The idea of "limited purpose" has been borrowed from the cases which discuss the distinction between theft and embezzlement in circumstances where A is given goods by B in order to do something with them on B's

---

[46] (1839) 2 Swin. 394. Lord Mackenzie and Lord Moncreiff, at 428 and 430 respectively, both include the example of the hirer of a horse along with those of the carrier and finder as cases in which the courts had disagreed with Hume.

[47] This discussion is concerned, of course, solely with non-fungible property. So far as fungibles are concerned the position is quite different — a hire or loan of fungibles effects a transfer of property and so excludes theft: Stair, Inst. 1, 11, 2; Ersk., Inst. 3, 1, 18–20; Bell's Commentaries, i, 275.

[48] For example, Road Traffic Act 1988, s.192(1); Hire-Purchase Act 1964, Pt III, as substituted by Consumer Credit Act 1974, Sched. 4, para.22.

[49] See *R. v. Campher*, 1961 (2) S.A. 401 (T), where A in order to borrow money from B sold to and then hire-purchased a car from B; A subsequently sold the car to C and was convicted of theft.

[50] Macdonald, p.32.

behalf, such as to deliver them to C — a specific purpose, or to invest or
sell them and account to B for the proceeds — an unlimited purpose: it
has no proper place in the context of hire, where A possesses the goods
for his own benefit, very often without any purpose being specified, and
where he never has power to sell the goods or otherwise deal with them
on B's behalf.

Briefly, the distinction between theft and embezzlement has nothing to
do with whether A has possession (limited or unlimited), or only
custody, of the property. Scots law requires neither a taking of the
property nor a taking of the possession of the property to constitute
theft; all it requires is appropriation relative to the property, and
appropriation by (probably) someone other than the owner.[51]

14.10 *Appropriation.* It is now clear that the essential element of the *actus reus*
of theft is appropriation.[52] The leading case of *Carmichael v. Black;
Carmichael v. Penrice*[53] makes plain that what matters in theft is not the
offender's gain, but the owner's loss.[54] This serves to underline that an
unathorised taking of goods from their owner is no longer essential
(although sufficient, of course) and that appropriation involves conduct
which without authorisation deprives the owner of one or more of those
rights, for example possessory rights, which his ownership of the
property in question would in the circumstances entail. Thus in *Carmichael v. Black; Carmichael v. Penrice* itself, the accused were held to
have been relevantly charged with theft in that they had not moved but
immobilised motor-cars unauthorisedly parked in a private car-park with
the result that the motorists in question were deprived of the use of their
vehicles. It was specifically noted (on authority) that it did not matter
whether the intentions of the accused were to deprive the motorists

---

[51] The decision in *Carmichael v. Black; Carmichael v. Penrice* (1992 S.C.C.R. 709), that
theft consisted in depriving the complainer of the use and possession of his motor-car by
wheel-clamping, might be used to support an argument leading to the conclusion that an
owner can steal his own property at a time when the possession of that property is
legitimately with another; but such a conclusion is contrary to all authoritative writings (see
Hume, i, 77–78; Alison, i, 273; Burnett, p.120: see also Macdonald, p.16), was plainly not
contemplated by any of the judges in *Carmichael v. Black*, and is open to theoretical and
practical objection (see para. 14.28, *infra*).
[52] See *Iqbal v. Annan*, 1983 S.C.C.R. 332, where Lord Cameron at 335 did not doubt the
soundness of the proposition that "appropriation is a necessary element in proof of theft",
and *Carmichael v. Black; Carmichael v. Penrice*, 1992 S.C.C.R. 709, at 719A where L.J.-G.
Hope said that "the essential feature of the physical act necessary to constitute theft is the
appropriation". See also, *e.g.*, the styles of complaint used in *McMillan v. Lowe*, 1991
S.C.C.R. 67, and *Kane v. Friel*, 1997 S.C.C.R. 207.
[53] 1992 S.C.C.R. 709.
[54] *ibid.*, L.J.-G. Hope at 720B-C, and Lord Allanbridge at 722C. Their opinions endorse
Hume's proposition at i, 75. For convenience, "owner" is used here to describe the
motorist whose loss was under consideration: it is moot, however, whether only an owner
as such can be deprived in the way contemplated by the court, since those having lesser
interests than ownership may be within the *ratio* of the decision. As the case is concerned
with the relevancy of a complaint for theft, it was not known whether the complainers were
owners or not of the vehicles they had parked. Nor would it have mattered in the
circumstances of this case — since the vehicles clearly had owners who were other than the
accused, and there was no question of consent having been granted to, or believed to have
been granted to, the accused. Had consent been an issue, then the question as to who
could grant consent had the complainers not been owners might well have been important;
it is submitted, however, that the accused would have been protected provided they acted
in the reasonable belief that whoever had the necessary power had consented or, perhaps,
would have consented to what was done (see para. 14.54, *infra*).

temporarily or permanently[55] or what the motives of the accused were in acting as they did, provided "the purpose and effect of the wheel clamp was to immobilise the vehicle and to deprive the motorist of his possession and use of it as [a] motor-car."[56] It was emphasised that such deprivation must be deliberate — *i.e.* accompanied by *mens rea* since "entrapment of another's motor-car by accident or as a result of some legitimate act, such as the closing or locking of a gate for security, will not constitute theft."[57]

It must be plain, therefore, that what is looked for in theft cases is evidence of appropriation, *i.e.* deliberate, unauthorised deprivation of the owner's rights and that there are no particular restrictions on how such appropriation may be shown. It must also be plain that it is difficult to keep "appropriation" (in terms of the *actus reus*) entirely separate from the *mens rea* for theft, especially in cases (such as that of *Geo. Brown*[58]) where the accused already has lawful possession of the property in question and where a change in mental attitude is as likely to mark his appropriation as any particular outward conduct.

Under the English Theft Act 1968, a person is guilty of theft if he dishonestly appropriates property belonging to another with the intention of premanently depriving the other of it[59]; and any assumption by a person of the rights of an owner amounts to appropriation.[60] In *R. v. Morris*,[61] the House of Lords unanimously decided that appropriation would be satisfied if *any* of the rights of an owner were to be assumed by the defendant, and, although now doubted and subjected to critical comment in later authority,[62] that: "the concept of appropriation . . . involves not an act expressly or impliedly authorised by the owner but an act by way of adverse interference with or usurpation of those rights."[63] Such an account may be a useful way of referring to appropriation in Scots law, always provided that it is borne in mind that the act of "adverse interference" or "usurpation" need not (and need not be intended to) deprive the owner of his possessory rights permanently.

---

[55] *ibid.*, L.J.-G. Hope at 719B-C, referring to *Milne v. Tudhope*, 1981 J.C. 53 and to L.J.-C. Wheatley's opinion there at 57–58, and to *Kidston v. Annan*, 1984 S.C.C.R. 20. *Cf.* the (English) Theft Act 1968, s.1(1).

[56] *ibid.*, L.J.-G. Hope at 720A. See also his opinion from 719C-G.

[57] *ibid.*, L.J.-G. Hope at 720B, who then continued: "To deprive another of the possession and use of his property can only be described as theft if there is appropriation — whether by taking it away or doing something else to it to this effect — and this is done deliberately."

[58] (1839) 2 Swin. 394.

[59] s.1(1).

[60] s.3(1).

[61] [1984] A.C. 320, Lord Roskill at 332A.

[62] See *R. v. Gomez* [1993] A.C. 442, HL, Lord Keith of Kinkell at 459–464; Lord Browne-Wilkinson at 495–6: *R. v. Hinks* [2000] 3 W.L.R. 1590, Lord Steyn (expressing the opinion of the majority of the House of Lords) at 1597G–1598C. The criticism, at least in part, concerns the fact that s.1(1) of the Theft Act 1968 does not state that the appropriation is to be without the consent of the owner, and that the interpretation of appropriation proffered in *R. v. Morris (supra)* illegitimately rewrites s.1(1) so that appropriation is qualified by such lack of consent. In other words, appropriation should be construed in England independently of any consent expressed or implied by the owner — but, where such consent exists (or is believed by the defendant to exist), the element of dishonesty will prevent the appropriation amounting to theft (see s.2(1) of the 1968 Act). This line of thought depends entirely on the specific wording of the Theft Act 1968 and has no necessary application to Scots law.

[63] [1984] A.C. 320, Lord Roskill at 332D.

14.11 *Appropriation and attempted theft.* As appropriation is the unifying essential factor for all types of theft in Scotland, there is no need to divide the *actus reus* of the crime into different categories for separate analysis. It is thus as much a deprivation of an owner's possessory rights to remove and make off with his property[64] as it is to find his lost property and treat it as one's own,[65] or to assume rights of ownership over property given to one for repair[66] or on loan,[67] or for delivery to another,[68] or to prevent another having the use and enjoyment of his property.[69] But there is probably no appropriation, at least in the Scottish sense, where a customer in a self-service store removes articles placed on shelves within that store: such removal is with the implied (if not express) consent of the owner — although such consent is probably conditional on the customer's being "honest", in the sense of proposing "to take the articles to the check-out to pay the proper price"[70] — and thus he does not effect or intend any adverse interference with or usurpation of the rights of the owner of the articles in question. It is to be noted that the essence of appropriation is deprivation, not acquisition, of such rights.[71] If, of course, the "honest" customer changes his mind and decides not to pay for the goods he has removed, then there will be appropriation from the moment of his changed attitude.

There may be no conduct which indicates the accused's intent prior to his passing the last possible check-out and failing to tender the articles

---

[64] See, *e.g. Fowler v. O'Brien*, 1994 S.C.C.R. 112 (removal and use of a bicycle against the owner's express wishes); *Valentine v. Kennedy*, 1985 S.C.C.R. 89 (catching and retaining fish which should have been recognised as the property of another and returned to their owner); *Milne v. Tudhope*, 1981 J.C. 53 (unauthorised removal of parts of a house).

[65] See, *e.g.*, *John Smith* (1838) 2 Swin. 28 (finding a wallet and other property in the street and failing to take any measures to return it to the owner); *McMillan v. Lowe*, 1991 S.C.C.R. 113 (finding cheque books and cheque cards in a telephone box, failing to take any steps to hand the property to the owner or her bank, and concealing the property from the police). *Cf. Angus McKinnon* (1863) 4 Irv. 398; *Campbell v. McLennan* (1888) 1 White 604.

[66] See, *e.g.*, *Geo. Brown* (1839) 2 Swin. 394 (assumption of owner's rights over watches handed over for repair); *Kidston v. Annan*, 1984 S.C.C.R. 20 (refusal to return television set handed over for repairs estimate).

[67] See, *e.g.*, *Jane McMahon or McGraw* (1863) 4 Irv. 381 (theft of a shawl received on loan).

[68] See, *e.g.*, *Iqbal v. Annan*, 1983 S.C.C.R. 332 (packages of tobacco and cigarettes retained by person who had undertaken to accept them on behalf of a neighbouring shopkeeper).

[69] See, *e.g.*, *Carmichael v. Black; Carmichael v. Penrice*, 1992 S.C.C.R. 709 (clamping of a motor vehicle found to be unauthorisedly parked in a private car park). *Cf.* the English view in the civil case of *Arthur v. Anker* [1996] 2 W.L.R. 602, and especially the opinion of Sir Thomas Bingham, M.R., at 611G–612F, where the above Scottish case is considered and its conclusions rejected.

[70] *Barr v. O'Brien*, 1991 S.C.C.R. 67, L.J.-G. Hope at 69G. It is believed to be a requirement of theft in Scotland that the appropriation be without the owner's consent. see paras 14.36 *et seq.*, *infra*.

[71] *cf.* English law as set out in *R. v. Gomez* [1993] A.C. 492, HL, where the view appears to be taken that all customers in self-service stores appropriate items by the simple act of removing these items from the shelves on which they are displayed. See also *R. v. Hinks* [2000] 3 W.L.R. 1590, where the majority of the House of Lords held that gifts of money and a television set made to the defendant by a man of limited intellectual capacity nevertheless constituted appropriations of property belonging to another in terms of ss. 1(1) and 3(1) of the Theft Act 1968. In England, therefore, appropriation seems to be compatible with both honesty and dishonesty: it is a descriptive rather than a normative concept — unlike the situation in Scotland.

for payment[72]; but equally, there may be evidence to support a charge of theft prior to that stage being reached. In *Barr v. O'Brien*,[73] for example, the accused took two computer tapes from the display in a self-service store and put them into his pocket (rather than into a trolley or basket supplied by the store for customers' use); but, apart from the fact that he made no attempt to pay for the tapes (itself rather neutral as evidence, since he had at no stage in the scenario passed the last possible check-out point), he behaved in a suspicious fashion when he became aware that he was being watched by the store detective. The court had no difficulty in holding that he had properly been convicted of a completed theft in the circumstances. Where a customer in such a store destroys an article (for example, by eating it) after he has taken it from a shelf or cabinet or whatever, but long before he has reached the check-out, this presents a potentially awkward problem. It probably raises a presumption of appropriation of the article in question; but facts, circumstances and common sense will ultimately decide whether a charge of theft can be sustained in such a case. (This may be one of those situations where the perception of the accused's overall behaviour as either honest or dishonest may be decisive.[74])

It was a peculiarity, however, of the law as understood by Hume[75] and indeed as understood throughout the nineteenth century into modern times, that where theft involved "taking" the goods of another, a removal or "amotio" of those goods was required. They had to be removed from "their place". But, since attempted theft was not indictable until 1887, the tendency was to treat the slightest removal as sufficient to satisfy the *actus reus* element of the crime.[76] In modern times, such a removal of goods may be thought too slight to qualify as a sufficient deprivation for theft, although, now that any attempt to commit any offence is criminal,[77] it may suffice for attempt; it is likely, however, that the older cases will continue to provide authority for treating the slightest removal (without consent of the owner) as sufficient conduct to satisfy the *actus reus* of theft rather than the attempted theft which modern theory might otherwise favour.[78] Thus it is probably still sufficient for theft if goods in a container (such as a drawer or pocket) are simply taken out of that container, even if the accused never manages to carry them off; but mere movement of the goods within that container will not suffice.[79] It would not be sufficient, therefore, for a pickpocket to touch or move about or take hold of articles in the victim's pocket[80]: there would be no "amotio" until each article was withdrawn

---

[72] *cf. Petrovich v. Jessop*, 1990 S.L.T. 594, where the accused was seen to conceal inside a plastic bag two books he removed from the shelf of a book-store. No attempt was made to detain him, however, until he had actually left the store without attempting to pay for them.

[73] 1991 S.C.C.R. 67.

[74] See paras 14.23 and 14.51, *infra*.

[75] Hume, i, 71–73. See also Alison, i, 265: "It is essential in theft that there be not only a taking, but a carrying away; but it is sufficient to complete the crime if the thing be removed for the shortest time, and for a small distance from its proper place and state of keeping." *Cf.* Burnett, p.121: "This may be said, that any *amotion* of the goods from what is considered *their proper place of keeping*, and which clearly evinces the purpose of the taker, is a *carrying away*, and a sufficient completion of the act."

[76] *Cornelius O'Neil* (1845) 2 Broun 394, L.J.-G. Hope at 396.

[77] 1995 Act, s.294(1), (2).

[78] See Vol. I, Chap. 6.

[79] See Macdonald, p.22.

[80] Hume, i, 70; Alison, i, 265–266; *Wm Cameron* (1851) J. Shaw 526.

from its pocket, although, once it was out, it would not matter if the article was still attached to the pocket by, for example, a chain or strap.[81] Similar considerations apply where the goods are on a limited space such as a desk, a table-top, or a shelf. It was (and presumably still is) a sufficient removal to take something out of a till,[82] or off a shelf,[83] or to take a package off a truck even if it were then left lying in the roadway.[84]

The choice in such cases prior to 1887 was that between theft and (most probably) no crime at all; nowadays, as indicated above, attempted theft would be available to deal with cases of limited removal — such as moving a thing out of one room into another or moving it but a few paces out of premises,[85] or pulling a pile of clothing towards a window by someone standing outside with a stick,[86] or placing an item in or on a container with a view to carrying the item off more easily.[87] But it is likely, as indicated above, that in similar cases today, the older authorities will be followed, to the extent that the minimal "amotio" formerly sufficient will suffice also for the purposes of appropriation under the modern law. As Lord Cowie has put the matter: "amotio . . . may [now] only be important in establishing the completed act of theft as opposed to an attempt."[88] In brief, wherever the extended notion of "removal" would have been inadequate under the older law, the case can then be considered for prosecution as an attempted theft; but where that extended notion was formerly adequate, it probably remains so for the purposes of appropriation.

PROPERTY WHICH CAN BE STOLEN

14.12   The type of property which could be stolen under the traditional conception of theft was restricted by the requirement that there had to be an unlawful *removal* of goods belonging to another. There had, therefore, to be "something" which might physically be "taken away". In brief, that "something" had to be both corporeal and moveable. The modern development of the crime in terms of appropriation, under which an unlawful physical taking of the property in question is no longer essential, may appear to open the way to a more extensive view of what may be stolen[89]; but the general emphasis still lies on physical action (for example, clamping, removing, destroying) relative to the property even though there may be exceptions to this, and no reported case in Scotland provides any basis for suggesting any movement towards

---

[81] *Wm Lyndsey* (1829) Bell's Notes 19; *Jas Macdougal* (1843) Macdonald, 22; *Jas Purves and Geo. McIntosh* (1846) Ark. 178; *Wm Cameron* (1851) J. Shaw 526; *John Reilly* (1876) 3 Couper 340.

[82] *Peter Anderson* (1800) Hume, i, 72.

[83] *Macqueen and Baillie* (1810) Hume, i, 72; *Jas Smart* (1837) Bell's Notes 19.

[84] *John Pray and Ors* (1819) Hume, i, 72.

[85] *John Welsh* (1808) Hume, i, 72; *John M. Carter* (1832) Bell's Notes 19; *John Paterson and Alex. Glasgow* (1827) Syme 174.

[86] *Cornelius O'Neil* (1845) 2 Broun 394.

[87] *John Welsh* (1808) Hume, i, 72; *Robt Philips and David Simpson* (1832) Bell's Notes 19; *Wm Sharpe McCaughie* (1836) 1 Swin. 205.

[88] *Carmichael v. Black; Carmichael v. Penrice*, 1992 S.C.C.R. 709, at 722B.

[89] *cf.* The (English) Theft Act 1968, s.4(1): "'Property' includes money and all other property, real or personal, including things in action and other intangible property."

a relaxation of the former restrictions.[90] It is submitted, therefore, in the absence of any contrary authority, that stealable property remains limited to things which are corporeal and moveable; such property will include, however, money whether in the form of coin, note, postal order or other order or negotiable instrument, so that theft of notes to the value of £220, for example, is theft of £220 and not merely of a number of pieces of paper. Also in accordance with the traditional concept, property for obvious reasons must be owned by someone before it can be stolen (since there can be no rights at all in ownerless property), and (probably) owned by a person other than the person accused of stealing it.[91]

Corporeal property

Stealable property must have physical existence. There must in theft **14.13** be a "thing" to which one can point and say, "[t]hat is what A stole".[92] Accordingly, incorporeal property cannot be stolen.[93] One cannot steal a right to an accounting, a privilege, a debt, or a *spes successionis*. One can, however, steal the corporeal document embodying the right, such as a written contract, a ticket, an I.O.U., a trust deed or a will. But in such a case what one is stealing is just the piece of paper and not the right, and strictly speaking the value of the stolen article is its value as paper and ink, although no doubt the court would take the whole circumstances into account in passing sentence, and would regard the theft of a will or of a decree as more serious than the theft of a magazine.[94]

Information. A document or computer disk containing information, such **14.14** as valuable trade secrets, may be taken from the owner with the intention of copying and using that information and then returning the document or disk. Were it the case, as in modern English law, that theft required an intention to deprive the owner permanently of his property,[95] there could be no theft in such circumstances: the document or disk would have been temporarily borrowed only, and the information itself would remain unchanged. In Scotland, however, now that it is plain that an intention to appropriate property temporarily is sufficient for theft,[96] there could at least be a relevant charge of theft in respect of the

---

[90] See in particular *Grant v. Allan*, 1987 J.C. 71, where a charge of clandestinely taking (in the sense of "making") and, without lawful authority, detaining copies of computer printouts containing confidential information belonging to another, the copies actually having been offered to trade rivals of the owner for the financial benefit of the accused, was conceded by the prosecution not to be a charge of theft. The appeal court then held that what was charged did not amount to a relevant crime at all in Scotland; but it seems that it was the absence of anything corporeal which had been taken without authority which disqualified the charge from being one of theft.

[91] See para. 14.28, *infra*.

[92] *cf.* attempted theft where, of course (see Vol. I, para. 6.56), it is not essential to show what the accused intended to steal (see styles for attempted theft in the 1995 Act, Sched. 2): indeed there may have been in the event nothing for him to steal or it may have been uncertain what had been the object of his theftuous intention (see, *e.g.*, *Lamont v. Strathern*, 1933 J.C. 33; *McLeod v. Mason and Ors*, 1981 S.C.C.R. 75).

[93] Hume, i, 75n.

[94] Hume, i, 80; Alison, i, 279; *Wm Mitchell* (1811) and *Wm Swan and Duncan Hunter* (1815) both Hume, i, 80; Macdonald, p.21; *Jas Dunipace* (1842) 1 Broun 506; *Henderson v. Young* (1856) 2 Irv. 414.

[95] See Theft Act 1968, s.1(1), and *R. v. Lloyd* [1985] Q.B. 829.

[96] *Milne v. Tudhope*, 1981 J.C. 53; *Kidston v. Annan*, 1984 S.C.C.R. 20; *Carmichael v. Black; Carmichael v. Penrice*, 1992 S.C.C.R. 709: see paras 14.48 and 14.49, *infra*.

document or disk itself.[97] The owner would have been deprived of control, possession and use of it during the time it was in the hands of the "thief". From the point of view of the modern law, the treatment of the case against *Dewar*[98] is, therefore, somewhat curious. The accused there broke into his master's office, carried off a book containing trade secrets, had them copied, and returned the book. He was charged with theft by housebreaking in that he broke in and carried off the book, and with fraudulently copying the secrets "with a view to making unlawful gain". The court in Alison's words "did not consider this as a case of proper theft, the paper having been fraudulently abstracted, with a view only to copy and return it; but they held it an irregular and punishable act".[99] Since the accused had no authority whatsoever to have possession of the book, his conduct amounted to a clear appropriation and he would certainly have been convicted of stealing the book were such a charge to come before the courts today.[1]

Where, however, the accused does have the owner's authority to have the document or disk (or to create it[2]), as might well be the case in the course of the accused's employment, and where he uses the information it contains for his own benefit, there is no appropriation of anything corporeal and, therefore, in terms of the law as it is believed to be in Scotland, no theft[3] — although unlawful use of the information may be, for example, a breach of patent or copyright, and as such a statutory offence.[4]

14.15 *Non-solid objects.* Air and other gases, as well as water and other fluids, are not normally thought of as corporeal but they are capable of being stolen, provided they are owned, have been brought into a definite place, and are of measurable quantity. Water in a private pond, oxygen in a cylinder, milk in a cow, even perhaps air in a car tyre, can be stolen at common law.[5]

14.16   ENERGY. The most common example of a theft of energy is where the electricity supplier cuts off A's supply for non-payment of his account and he contrives to reconnect the supply and so obtains electricity. In

---

[97] See the first charge in *H.M. Advocate v. Mackenzies* (1913) 7 Adam 189; *cf. John Deuchars* (1834) Bell's Notes 20, which proceeded on a plea of guilty.

[98] (1777) Burnett 115; Hume, i, 75; Alison, i, 271.

[99] Alison, i, 271. Dewar was imprisoned for 14 days and banished for three years from Dunbartonshire and Lanarkshire, and also had to pay damages and compensation.

[1] The case may provide some authority for an alternative charge of an innominate offence: see para. 15.52, *infra*.

[2] For example, by printing it out, as in *Grant v. Allan*, 1987 J.C. 71, or by copying files to it, in the case of a disk.

[3] See *Grant v. Allan*, 1987 J.C. 71, as also the comments made by the court therein relative to the second charge in *H.M. Advocate v. Mackenzies* (1913) 7 Adam 189.

[4] See also the offences of selling or offering to sell personal data under s.55(4) and (5) of the Data Protection Act 1998: the penalty is a fine not exceeding the statutory maximum on summary conviction, and a fine of any amount on conviction on indictment.

[5] *cf.* Macdonald, 20. So far as domestic gas is concerned the Gas Act 1986, Sched. 2B (added by Gas Act 1995, Sched. 2), para. 10(1)(c) makes it an offence to prevent any meter from duly registering the quantity of gas supplied; para. 11 makes it an offence to restore without the consent of the Gas Supplier supplies which have been cut off: maximum penalty in either case is a fine of level 3 on the standard scale. Similar provisions are made for the unlawful taking or using of water supplied by a public authority: Water (Scotland) Act 1980, Sched. 4, para. 31; see also para. 32 (prevention of meters from registering quantity of water): maximum penalty in either case is a fine of level 2 on the standard scale. *Cf. R. v. Rothery* (1946) 63 Cr.App.R. 71 (theft of a specimen of blood provided by person suspected of a drink-driving offence).

such a case A is normally charged with common law theft of the number of units unlawfully obtained. There is no authority on the relevance of such a charge, but it is in common use and has never been challenged in the High Court. It must therefore be accepted that Scots law, unlike many other systems, is prepared to regard electricity as corporeal for the purpose of the law of theft.[6] Where it is not possible to measure the amount of electricity dishonestly obtained recourse may be had to statutory provisions prohibiting any interference with electricity supplies,[7] although some prosecutors charge theft of an "unknown quantity" of electricity.[8]

SERVICES. The mere obtaining of a service without the consent of the **14.17** provider is not theft. If A's telephone line is disconnected by the provider, but he manages to reconnect it, his use of the line will not in itself be theft. If he makes an outgoing call he may be guilty of stealing the electricity involved, and of making a telephone call without paying and intending not to pay, but if he only receives incoming calls he will not, it is thought, be guilty of theft at all.[9]

Animate objects. Animate objects may be stolen in the same way as any **14.18** other corporeal moveables.[10]

Value irrelevant. Any article which has value, however small, can be **14.19** stolen, and this means in effect that anything which can be said to have an owner can be stolen. Although in practice attention may be paid to the *de minimis* rule it is theft to steal articles even of derisory value like used envelopes or old receipts. In *Larg and Mitchell*[11] the accused were convicted of stealing two forged notes, in *Wm Wilson*[12] of stealing a

---

[6] *cf.* Nouveau Code Pénal, Art. 311–2: "La soustraction frauduleuse d'énergie au préjudice d'autrui est assimilée au vol."

[7] Paragraph 5(2) of Sched. 6 (as substituted by the Utilities Act 2000, s.51(2) and Sched. 4) to the Electricity Act 1989 makes it an offence to restore a supply of electricity by an electricity supplier or distributor which has been cut off, and para. 11(1) of Sched. 7 to that Act makes it an offence to alter the register of any electricity meter or to prevent it duly registering the quantity of electricity supplied by any supplier: max. pen. in each case a fine of level 3 on the standard scale.

[8] The Atomic Energy Act 1946, s.10, enables the responsible Minister to prohibit the working of minerals from which radio-active substances can be obtained, and also the "acquisition, production, treatment, possession, use, disposal, export or import" of any such minerals or substances, except under Government licence: maximum penalty five years' imprisonment and a fine on indictment, three months' and prescribed sum on summary conviction.

[9] If the call is made via a human operator, he may be guilty of a peculiar kind of fraud on that operator; if he is on an automatic exchange the fraud, if any, will be even more peculiar and can probably be disregarded in practice. It is an offence under s.42 of the Telecommunications Act 1984 (as am. by the Telecommunications (Fraud) Act 1997, s.2(1)) dishonestly to obtain a service provided by means of a licensed telecommunication system with intent to avoid payment of any applicable charge: maximum penalty five years and a fine on indictment, six months and a fine of the statutory maximum on summary conviction. That section does not apply to the dishonest receipt of a television or sound broadcasting service provided from a place in the U.K., such receipt being an offence under s.297 of the Copyright, Designs and Patents Act 1988: maximum penalty a fine of level 5 on the standard scale: see *infra*, para. 15.55. (See also s.42A of the Telecommunications Act 1984, as inserted by the Telecommunications (Fraud) Act 1997, s.1.)

[10] Hume, i, 81; Alison, i, 279; Burnett, p.124; Macdonald, p.16. This extends even to human beings, which means in effect that live human beings can be stolen if they are under the age of puberty, since over that age they cannot be "owned".

[11] (1817) Hume, i, 76–77.

[12] (1827) Alison, i, 275.

cotton bag worth less than a halfpenny, in *Wm Higgins and Thos Harold*[13] of robbery of a memorandum book, and in *Thos Donaldson and Ors*[14] of robbery of a pair of old boots not worth one shilling.

Even though an article would be generally regarded as valueless it is capable of being stolen if someone rightly regards himself as owning it.[15] It would not normally be theft to take crumbs out of a man's pocket but, if the victim or the accused were a collector of crumbs and regarded them as of value, that would be theft although it might not be prosecuted.[16] Less fanciful examples might be found in the theft of a philatelist's collection of used stamps, or perhaps even of a collection of used theatre tickets. As a general principle it may be said that anything which is thought of by someone as sufficiently valuable to be regarded as "his", can be stolen from him.

Moveable property

14.20   Only moveable property can be stolen,[17] but "moveable" in this context means only "capable of being moved" and does not mean that an object which is "heritable" cannot be stolen. It is theft to take fruit from a tree, potatoes from a field,[18] grass from a lawn,[19] lead from a roof, or a sash from a window frame.[20] Anything which can be severed from the heritage and taken away can be stolen,[21] so that it is possible to steal a house, either by dismantling it and removing it piecemeal, or by lifting it up in a giant crane.

In *Alex. Robertson and Ors*[22] the accused were charged with pasturing their sheep on M's turnip field and stealing the turnips eaten by the sheep. The charge was held to be irrelevant for technical reasons (because it failed to specify whether the accused or the sheep had taken the turnips), and Lord Neaves expressly reserved the question whether it was theft to pasture one's sheep on someone else's ground.[23] Macdonald is of opinion that there is no good reason why such pasturing should not be theft,[24] and it is submitted that it is theft, the sheep being merely the innocent agents of their owner in appropriating the turnips. The only difficulty is whether the charge ought to be one of malicious mischief since the turnips are taken and consumed all at once; but since the object is clearly to use the turnips for the sheep owner's benefit and in the way turnips are normally used and not to destroy them to injure the victim or out of sheer destructiveness, the crime is properly theft and not malicious mischief.

---

[13] (1814) Alison, i, 234.

[14] (1823) *ibid.*

[15] Hume, i, 76; Alison, i, 275. Hume is concerned mainly with whether the article is of any value to the thief so that it can be said to have been taken for lucre — *cf.* Macdonald, p.20.

[16] And it might be a defence for the thief to show that he thought the articles useless and of no value to himself, pecuniary or otherwise — *cf.* Hume, i, 76.

[17] Ersk., Inst. 4, 4, 58; Hume, i, 79; Alison, i, 278. Although the opinions in *Carmichael v. Black; Carmichael v. Penrice* (1992 S.C.C.R. 709) may arguably be read as opening the way to a wider conception of "stealable property", the factual basis of the case concerned only the immobilisation of motor-cars (see para. 14.10, *supra*).

[18] *Andrew Young* (1800) Hume, i, 79–80.

[19] Hume, i, 79.

[20] *Jas Watson and John O'Brien* (1828) Alison, i, 278.

[21] Hume, i, 79; Macdonald, p.20; see also the items which were stolen in *Milne v. Tudhope*, 1981 J.C. 53.

[22] (1867) 5 Irv. 480.

[23] At 482.

[24] Macdonald, p.21n.

Owned property

Res nullius. That which has never had an owner cannot be stolen, but **14.21** belongs rightfully to the first taker by *occupatio*. Wild animals which have been neither killed nor confined cannot be stolen, because no one has any property rights in them.[25] An owner of land does not thereby become owner of wild animals on the land, but if he creates an enclosure into which he places captured animals these animals and their issue are his property as much as a parrot in a cage or a rabbit in a hutch. The position is the same with regard to fish.[26] While in the sea they have no owner,[27] but once caught in a fisherman's net they belong to him, and can be stolen from him.[28] To take wild game or fish may be a breach of the incorporeal rights of the Crown or the landowner and may be a statutory offence, but it is not theft, and at common law the poacher owns his unlawful haul.[29]

Similarly, air and sea water are unowned but can be stolen from anyone who has become owner of quantities of them by enclosing them. To take water out of a private pond is as much theft as to take grass from a private field, although it is unlikely to be prosecuted.[30]

Lost and abandoned property. Even property which has been lost or **14.22** abandoned by its owner continues to be owned. Obviously property which has been mislaid continues to be owned by its owner for as long as

---

[25] Hume, i, 81–82; Alison, i, 279–280; Macdonald, pp. 16–17. See *Wilson v. Dykes* (1872) 2 Couper 183.

[26] See *Valentine v. Kennedy*, 1985 S.C.C.R. 89 (Sh.Ct).

[27] Unless they are part of the regalia — *cf. Parker v. Lord Advocate* (1904) 6 F., HL 37.

[28] *John Huie* (1842) 1 Broun 383.

[29] *Scott v. Everitt* (1853) 15 D. 288.

[30] The Theft Act 1607 provides that "Quhasoeuir Stellis Beis and fisches in propir stankis and loches Shall be callit and convenit thairfoir as a braker of the Law befoir ony ordinar magistrat" and fined 40 pounds Scots. In *Pollok v. McCabe and Anr* (1909) 6 Adam 139, a reservoir belonging to a local authority was stocked with fish by the coterminous proprietor who had sold the reservior to the authority under reservation of his fishing rights. This reservoir was held to be a stank within the meaning of the Act. It may well be, however, that to take such fish is a common law theft — the fish being brought into ownership by being enclosed in the pond which had no outlet or inlet except a pipe covered by a grating.

The Oyster Fisheries (Scotland) Act 1840 provides that to "wilfully and knowingly take and carry away any oysters or oyster brood from any oyster bed, laying, or fishery, being the property of any other person . . . and sufficiently marked or known as such shall be deemed theft and punishable by one year's imprisonment": s.1. The Act goes on to provide that it shall be deemed to be attempted theft, punishable by three months' imprisonment, to "unlawfully and wilfully use any dredge, or any net, instrument, or engine whatsoever, within the limits of any such oyster fishery . . . for the purpose of taking oysters . . . although none shall be actually taken, or . . . with any . . . instrument . . . drag upon the ground or soil of any such fishery": s.2; see *Robt Thomson and Geo. Mackenzie* (1842) 1 Broun 475. Section 3 of the Act makes an exception for the catching of floating fish with instruments adapted to take such fish only. Where A has a licence to take oysters of a certain size, or under certain conditions, and exceeds his licence, he is guilty of an offence against the Act: *Wm Garrett and Thos Edgar* (1866) 5 Irv. 259.

The Mussel Fisheries (Scotland) Act 1847 makes similar provision for mussel beds, scalp layings and fisheries: see *Chisholm v. Black and Morrison* (1871) 2 Couper 49.

The Sea Fisheries (Shellfish) Act 1967, s.7, which applies to shellfish in or on beds in an area with respect to which a right of several fishery has been granted under the Act and to oysters in or on a private oyster bed, provides that such shellfish and oysters are the absolute property of the grantee or owner. Section 7(4) (as am. by the Sea Fisheries (Shellfish) Amendment (Scotland) Act 2000 (asp 12) s.1) prohibits *inter alia* the use of any implement of fishing except a line and hook or a net adapted to catch flat fish and so used as not to disturb or injure the shellfish.

he maintains a hope of recovering it; once that hope has been given up, the status of the property becomes that attached to things which have been deliberately thrown away. Property is not abandoned, however, when the owner gives it up for a specific purpose, as where rubbish is put out for collection by the local authority,[31] or in the quite different case where a coffin is handed over for cremation[32] or burial at sea[33]; but truly abandoned property falls to the Crown in accordance with the principle — *quod nullius est fit domini regis*.[34] Any person who takes possession of (*i.e.* finds) lost or abandoned property may, therefore, steal it if he appropriates it. There may be a particular act, such as selling[35] or destroying the property, which provides evidence of appropriation; but in the absence of such an act, appropriation may be inferred from the facts and circumstances.[36] It is axiomatic that the mere finding of lost or abandoned property can never effect any transfer of ownership to the finder,[37] and it seems clear in law that appropriation of such property must be theft irrespective of whether the appropriation takes place immediately on the accused's finding the property or at some later time[38] and irrespective of whether the identity of the owner is known or not to the accused.[39] But what is clear to a lawyer is not necessarily appreciated by members of the public. In particular, it is not necessarily widely known that the Crown falls heir to property which has been "thrown away", and that property which has once had an owner never becomes *res nullius*. In short, the question lies whether there can ever be innocent appropriation of lost of abandoned property or whether one is always committed to conclude that "if a person finds a £1 note and appropriates it to his own use . . . that is plainly theft and nothing else."[40] Modern authority suggests that appropriation of found property is not necessarily conclusive of theft unless the prosecutor can show that the circumstances reek of dishonesty. In *Kane v. Friel*[41] the accused was charged with theft in terms that having found a quantity of copper pipe and a sink he did, without attempting to find the owner, appropriate the same to his own use. It seems that he admitted to the police that he had found the goods behind the premises of a store, and that he had been on his way to sell

---

[31] *Williams v. Philips* (1957) 121 J.P. 163. *Cf. R. v. Pace* (1965) 48 D.L.R. (2d.) 532: sale of leftover food by army cook instead of putting it out as garbage is theft. See also *Hibbert v. McKiernay* [1948] 2 K.B. 142: lost golf balls become the property of the golf club.

[32] *Dewar v. H.M. Advocate*, 1945 J.C. 5.

[33] *Herron v. Diack and Newlands*, 1973 S.L.T. (Sh.Ct.) 27.

[34] Bell's Principles, para. 1291 (3); *Lord Advocate v. University of Aberdeen and Budge*, 1963 S.C. 533.

[35] See, *e.g.*, the form of the charge in the 1995 Act Sched 5: "having found a watch, you did, without trying to discover its owner, sell it on . . . at . . ., to O.R., and steal it."

[36] See, *e.g., John Waugh* (1873) 2 Couper 424, finding straying calves, taking them and keeping them on one's farm without trying to trace the owner; *Paterson v. H.M. Advocate* (1901) 3 Adam 490, finding sheep and placing one's own identification mark on them; *Peter Connelly* (1864) and *McLaughlin v. Stewart* (1865), both Macdonald, p.32, pawning goods the day after finding them and without trying to trace their owner; *MacMillan v. Lowe*, 1991 S.C.C.R. 113, concealing (and making no attempt to hand to the police, the owner or the owner's bank) cheque books and cheque cards found by the accused in a telephone box.

[37] See Civic Government (Scotland) Act 1982, s.73 (no ownership created in finder by mere act of finding).

[38] See *John Smith* (1838) 2 Swin. 28; *MacMillan v. Lowe*, 1991 S.C.C.R. 113; *cf., Kane v. Friel*, 1997 S.C.C.R. 207.

[39] See *John Waugh* (1873) 2 Couper 424; *MacMillan v. Lowe*, 1991 S.C.C.R. 113.

[40] *Campbell v. Maclennan* (1888) 1 White 604, Lord Rutherfurd Clark (diss.) at 607.

[41] 1997 S.C.C.R. 207.

them to a scrap merchant. There appeared to be clear appropriation of the various items. His appeal against conviction was, however, successful. The advocate-depute accepted at the appeal that the prosecution had to show that there was dishonest appropriation and thus an intention to appropriate the items dishonestly, and the Appeal Court, in accepting these propositions, held that there had been insufficient evidence from which to infer such "a dishonest intention to appropriate".[42] The Court noted that the advocate-depute had not placed reliance on the "somewhat technical doctrine"[43] (that abandoned property falls to the Crown) in order to argue that the *mens rea* could be inferred in this case. A rehearsal of the facts then demonstrated that there was no sufficient evidence to suggest that the appellant must have known that the property was something that someone would have wanted to retain. There was no evidence as to the condition or value of the goods or as to the circumstances in which they had been found; there was no evidence that any such goods had been reported as "stolen". The implication of the decision in this case is that appropriating found property is not theft unless the prosecutor can convince the court that the accused must have known that that property was not "abandoned" — where "abandoned" is used in a popular, non-technical sense. This really is a matter of *mens rea* rather than *actus reus*, for the person who, for example, takes and sells (or spends) what he has found lying in the street clearly as a matter of law deprives the owner (since there always is an owner) of rights in the property; but he cannot be said to intend to so deprive the owner if it was not reasonable for him to have considered that there might have been an owner, given all the circumstances of the case. Thus, in this sense, there is no dishonest intention to steal. Alternatively, the decision might mark the recognition that the rule concerning Crown ownership of abandoned property does not apply in the criminal law, or, at least, not to the crime of theft; but there is insufficient indication in the case that the Appeal Court had considered or were prepared to accept such a proposition. The case does, however, give rise to two further but related issues: (a) whether "dishonesty" can be used to inform a broader concept of "innocent" appropriation; and (b) the significance of failing to attempt to trace the owner of found property.

(a) INNOCENT APPROPRIATION. Under modern English law, the appro- **14.23** priation of property in theft must be *dishonest*.[44] This vague and difficult concept[45] has not been the subject of much forensic discussion in Scotland, but has been appealed to in some modern cases, particularly where application of the strict letter of the law might appear to work injustice.[46] This may be particularly apt in relation to the finding of property which has been lost or abandoned, where, if the appropriation

---

[42] *ibid.*, L.J.-G. Rodger at 210C.

[43] *ibid.*, p.209A.

[44] Theft Act 1968, s.1(1). The term is not defined other than by way of three examples of non-dishonest appropriation — see s.2(1).

[45] For the current English "test" for dishonesty, see *R. v. Ghosh* [1982] Q.B. 1053, CA, Lord Lane C.J., at 1064D-F.

[46] See, *e.g.*, *Mackenzie v. Maclean*, 1981 S.L.T. (Sh.Ct.) 40; *Kane v. Friel*, 1997 S.C.C.R. 207: *cf. Iqbal v. Annan*, 1983 S.C.C.R. 332, where Lord Cameron said at 336 that the conduct of the accused had been "indicative of a dishonest appropriation of the goods".

does not show the wickedness normally associated with theft, an acquittal may be achieved on the basis that the facts do not show "dishonesty". This is a question of circumstances[47]; and even where the accused can be in no doubt that what he finds has not been abandoned by its owner, if he does all that can reasonably be expected of him and retains the property for a considerable time with a view to the owner recovering it from him, it may well be that his subsequent appropriation will not be considered dishonest for the purposes of theft. One of the most important circumstances to be considered would be the value of the property. A person who finds a £1 coin in the street and who makes a few enquiries[48] of bystanders or local shopkeepers as to its ownership before using it to fund his homeward bus journey may justifiably be considered not to have dishonestly appropriated it. It must be accepted that respectable people who would never dream of shoplifting or housebreaking do regard it as quite proper to retain found property in certain circumstances; and there is a distinct feeling that what such people do cannot be theft.[49] The question lies, however, whether lack of wickedness or dishonesty is really just a useful guide in deciding whether to prosecute rather than a criterion for determining whether the act in question amounts to theft: but if it is to be employed as such a criterion, it can hardly be confined to cases of finding and appropriating lost or abandoned property.[50] It is probably true that notions of dishonesty have underpinned most accounts of common law theft and may inform many decisions reached in court; but if it is to be given a more forward role in the definition of the crime, what dishonesty means and whether it is to be received in a subjective sense (for example, where the accused must be shown to have believed he was not acting honestly) or, as is more likely in Scotland, objective sense (for example, where the accused's actions were in accordance with reasonable persons' views of dishonesty) will have to be considered with greater precision than has hitherto been the case.

14.24   (b) DUTIES OF A FINDER. A significant factor in deciding whether a person has stolen property found by him may concern what action he took to trace the identity of the owner. This assumes that at common law there is a duty on a finder to do what is reasonable to identify the owner, with a view to redelivery of the property to that owner. The statutory style of charge for theft of found property contains the phrase "without trying to discover its owner",[51] and similar wording can be found in actual charges for thefts of this nature.[52] Where, of course, it would not be reasonable for the accused to have considered that there was an owner, it can hardly be significant at all that he did not seek to identify the owner of the property; conversely, where the circumstances should have suggested to him the existence of an owner who would wish to

---

[47] *Kane v. Friel*, 1997 S.C.C.R. 207; see para. 14.22, *supra*.
[48] See para. 14.24, *infra*.
[49] *cf.* Vol. I, paras 1.12, 1.13.
[50] *cf. Mackenzie v. Maclean*, 1981 S.L.T. (Sh.Ct.) 40 — a case rather loosely related to the finding and appropriating of abandoned property.
[51] See 1995 Act, Sched. 5.
[52] See, *e.g.*, *Kane v. Friel*, 1997 S.C.C.R. 207 ("without attempting to find the lawful owner thereof"); *MacMillan v. Lowe*, 1991 S.C.C.R. 113 ("without trying to discover the true owner").

recover the property, it will depend on the circumstances what importance should be attached to the efforts (if any) made to trace that owner.
Thus, failure to make any attempt to trace him is not necessarily
consistent with, let alone determinative of, theft; whilst efforts made to
identify him may in the circumstances be so inadequate as to be not
inconsistent with theft. In the same way, it may or may not be significant
what efforts the accused made to ensure the safety and security of the
property he found.

Duties are certainly imposed on finders, however, under Part VI of the
Civic Government (Scotland) Act 1982. Under the Act, a person who
takes possession of property without the authority of the owner, in such
circumstances as to make it reasonable to infer that the property is lost
or abandoned, must take reasonable care of that property and must
without unreasonable delay deliver it, or report that he has taken
possession of it, to a police constable, the owner of the property, a
person with the right to possess it, the owner or occupier of the land or
premises where it was found, or any person having apparent authority to
act on behalf of any of those stated persons.[53] It will be noted that there
is no specific obligation on a finder to take steps to trace the owner[54]; but
it is an offence to fail without reasonable excuse to comply with any of
the duties which are imposed.[55] It may or may not be a significant factor
in a charge of theft where the accused is alleged to have appropriated
found property that he had failed to obtemper his duties under the

---

[53] s.67(1), (3).

[54] *cf.* the obligation on a chief constable under s.68(3) to take reasonable steps to
ascertain the identity of the owner or person having right to possession of property which
has been delivered up to the police by the finder, or which has been reported to them as
having been found.

[55] s.67(6): maximum penalty a fine of level 2 on the standard scale. The statutory rules
in the Civic Government (Scotland) Act do not apply, for example, to property found on
premises, vehicles, vessels or aircraft of public transport service undertakers, provided
separate provision is made for such lost or abandoned property in or under any other
enactment (see the *Stair Memorial Encyclopaedia*, Vol. 18, para. 552, for a complete list of
exclusions). Thus, for instance, an airport operator is empowered to make byelaws
covering (*inter alia*) the safe custody and redelivery of property found within the airport or
in any aircraft which happens to be at that airport (Airports Act 1986, s.63(2)(j)) and it is
an offence to contravene such byelaws (s.64: maximum penalty a fine of level 4 on the
standard scale). Under s.83(4) and Sched. 5, para. 11(2) of that 1986 Act, former
regulations applying to airports may have effect as if they were such byelaws under
s.63(2)(j): thus the British Airports Authority (Lost Property) Regulations 1972 (S.I. 1972
No. 1027) remain in force, and provide by reg. 4 that if a person finds lost property, he
must immediately hand it to an airport officer or a constable, and inform him of the
circumstances in which it was found. Similar rules apply to buses and tramcars — see
Public Passenger Vehicles Act 1981, s.60 (as amended by the Transport and Works Act
1992, s.61), and regulations made under or preserved by it, including the Public Service
Vehicles (Lost Property) Regulations 1978 (S.I. 1978 No. 1184) and in particular reg. 5
(which provides that any person finding property accidentally left on a public service
vehicle must hand it at once to the conductor). Under s.67 of that Act of 1981, it is an
offence to contravene such a regulation: max. pen. a fine of level 2 on the standard scale.

Part VI of the Civic Government (Scotland) Act 1982 also contains provision for the
disposal of unclaimed lost property — under which the finder may be offered the property
(see ss. 68(4) and 70(2)) and thus acquire ownership of it (s.71(1)). Part VI applies to the
Crown and to any interests it may have in the property (s.78). It has been held that Pt VI
does not apply to stolen or fraudulently acquired property in the hands of the police, and
also that the rules for identifying the owner and disposing of property are inapplicable to
such property: *Fleming v. Chief Constable of Strathclyde*, 1987 S.C.L.R. 303 (Sh.Ct); but
provision has now been made for such property under Pt VIIA, which was added to the
1982 Act by the Police Property Act 1997, s.6.

Act: the problem was noted by Lord Justice-General Rodger in *Kane v. Friel*[56]; but he reserved his opinion in the absence of any argument on the issue from either side during the appeal. Again, it seems that the significance of such a failure will depend on the facts and circumstances rather than on any substantive rule.

14.25 WRECKS. It is accepted that a wreck and its cargo are never regarded as abandoned,[57] and to appropriate them would be theft by finding. Hume, who did not recognise theft by finding, treated this as a separate common law crime, that of plundering wrecks, sometimes known as "wrecking".[58] Although the crime of wrecking is still referred to by Macdonald,[59] there is no reported case of a common law charge of wrecking later than 1842,[60] and wrecking may now be regarded simply as an aggravated form of theft[61] or, where the only motive is destruction, of malicious mischief.

Certain types of wrecking, however, are punishable by statute. The Merchant Shipping Act 1995 makes it a crime to take any vessel stranded in United Kingdom waters, or any part of its cargo, or anything belonging to it, to a foreign port and sell it there.[62] The Act further makes a person guilty of an offence if he "wrongfully carries away or removes any part of any vessel stranded . . . or . . . in distress . . . or any part of the cargo or equipment thereof, or any wreck",[63] and to fail to deliver up any articles washed up on shore.[64] Those provisions also apply to wrecked aircraft.[65] Historic wrecks may be protected by an order under the Protection of Wrecks Act 1973.

14.26 *Human beings.* Living persons over the age of puberty cannot be stolen. A child under that age is regarded as the property of a person having at the relevant time the parental rights of custody[66] and can, therefore, be stolen, the theft being called *plagium*.[67] The consent of the child, whether given freely or induced by fraud, is as irrelevant as the

---

[56] 1997 S.C.C.R. 207, at 209B.

[57] Hume, i, 485.

[58] Alison, i, 640. As long as anyone remains on the wreck the taking of anything from it will be either simple theft or robbery, depending on the circumstances: *Robt Graham* (1792) Hume, i, 486.

[59] Macdonald, p.44.

[60] *John Balfour* (1842) 1 Broun 372, where the accused was acquitted on charges including one of "plundering, pillaging, or destroying goods . . . belonging to a wreck or stranded vessel."

[61] *Geo. McKay and Ors* (1839) 2 Swin. 344; *cf.* Bell's Notes 115.

[62] s.245. Maximum penalty five years' imprisonment.

[63] s.246(3)(d). Maximum penalty a fine of level 4 on the standard scale.

[64] s.237(2). Maximum penalty a fine of level 4 on the standard scale.

[65] Aircraft (Wreck and Salvage) Order 1938, S.R. & O. No. 136, Rev. I. 1329, Art. 2.

[66] *Hamilton v. Wilson*, 1993 S.C.C.R. 9, at 13D-E, where L.J.-G. Hope stated: "the essence of the crime of plagium is the deliberate taking of a child from the custody of a parent or other person who has for the time being the parental right of custody in terms of the statute [Law Reform (Parent and Child) (Scotland) Act 1986, s. 2(1); see now Children (Scotland) Act 1995, ss. 1–4, 11] or under an order made by the court. The matter does not depend upon the natural relationship between a father and his child." *Cf. Downie v. H.M. Advocate*, 1984 S.C.C.R. 365. A parent who is excluded from such custody can be guilty of stealing his own child: see *Hamilton v. Mooney*, 1990 S.L.T. (Sh.Ct) 105.

[67] Hume, i, 84; Alison, i, 280; Macdonald, p.21.

"consent" of a stolen dog or sheep,[68] although if a child were taken by force the taker would be guilty of a crime against the person of the child as well as against the property of the person having parental custody. Although child stealing goes by the name of *plagium*, or sometimes of "Man-stealing", it is not a separate offence, but only an aggravated form of theft.[69]

It may be a defence to *plagium* that it was done to protect the child from harm, but the circumstances would probably have to be such that the child was in danger of death or serious injury and there was no other way of dealing with its situation.[70]

Human remains. The position of human remains in the law of theft is not **14.27** altogether clear. It is settled that to remove a body from its grave is not theft, but the separate crime of violating sepulchures.[71] It is said also to be settled that to take a body before burial from those entitled to deal with it is theft. This rule is said by the institutional writers and by Macdonald to rest on the authority of the case of *McKenzie*[72] where the accused broke into a house at night and removed a corpse; but the charge was not one of theft, but of "Ryot and Violence".[73] The latter would provide sufficient protection for an unburied body, and avoid the theoretical difficulty of having to regard such a body as the property of the deceased's executors prior to burial, and not property at all after burial. In *Dewar v. H.M. Advocate*,[74] however, it was held to be theft to appropriate coffin lids delivered for cremation, the court basing their decision partly on the fact that the lids were removed before cremation, a stage they regarded as the equivalent of interment. As they tended to equate the position of the coffins with that of the bodies they contained so far as the question of ownership was concerned, *Dewar* may be said to offer some support for the view that a body can be stolen before burial. Lord Moncrieff, in particular, seems to have assumed that an unburied body can be stolen. He spoke of things being "as remote from human guardianship and as unsusceptible of claims of property as is a body which had finally and conclusively been interred", and said that, "[a] body, once it has been interred, can no longer be protected by the law [of] theft."[75] The law may be that to appropriate an unburied body is theft, while to deal with it in any other unauthorised way is an innominate offence of the kind exemplified in *McKenzie.*[76]

The approach of the court in *Dewar,* therefore, confirms the view that a human body, as such, can be owned, and so can be stolen. If that is so, it is possible to hold that it is theft to steal a body which instead of being buried has been gifted to a laboratory, or placed in a museum, or even

---

[68] *H.M. Advocate v. Cairney or Cook and Anr* (1897) 2 Adam 471; *Mary Millar or Oates* (1861) 4 Irv. 74; *cf. Helen Wade* (1844) 2 Broun 288. Alison, i, 630, suggests that to entice a child away is an innominate offence, but the later cases make it clear that it is theft.

[69] Hume, i, 84; *Rachel Wright* (1809) Hume, i, 84; *Janet Douglas* (1817) *ibid.*, 85; *Marion Rosmond or Skeoch* (1855) 2 Irv. 234.

[70] See *Downie v. H.M. Advocate*, 1984 S.C.C.R. 365, Sheriff Young at 367, 370–371.

[71] Hume, i, 85; Alison, i, 461; Macdonald, pp. 21 and 52. See *infra*, para. 42.01.

[72] (1733) Burnett 124. See Hume, i, 85; Alison, i, 282; Macdonald, p.21. Anderson, too, states at 175 that: "A dead body not yet buried may be stolen."

[73] See record in Books of Adjournal quoted in *H.M. Advocate v. Coutts* (1899) 3 Adam 50, 57–58n.

[74] 1945 J.C. 5.

[75] At 14.

[76] *supra.*

embalmed and kept in a glass case in the widow's living-room. Indeed, the need to protect specimens in laboratories and exhibits in museums is itself a strong argument for treating a body as capable of being owned, particularly as there is no specific legislation to cover such cases in Scotland.[77] It seems unreasonable to suggest that a museum has no property in its mummies, or that an anatomical laboratory has no property in parts of a body it has dissected, and which it has preserved for exhibition.[78]

---

[77] The Anatomy Act 1984 appears only to confer possessory rights. In the English case of *R. v. Kelly* [1999] 2 W.L.R. 384, CA, the conviction for theft of a man who had unauthorisedly taken various body parts from the Royal College of Surgeons was upheld. The parts were anatomical specimens which had been preserved and dissected, and the intention of the appellant (an artist) was to make casts of them for artistic display. He had had no intention of returning the specimens; and his sole defence was that such specimens could not he stolen. Lord Justice Rose, delivering the opinion of the Court, confirmed that neither a corpse nor its parts was or were capable of being stolen (at 392H) and if that legal position were to be changed it would require Parliamentary sanction: but he also held that parts of a body which had "acquired different attributes by virtue of the application of skill, such as dissection or preservation techniques, for exhibition or teaching purposes" were distinguishable, and were items of property capable of being stolen (at 393C-D). He also suggested that it would not be impossible for the common law to develop this principle by recognising that body parts on which no work had been done but which were set apart for transplantation or extraction of DNA or exhibition at a legal trial should be regarded as stealable property (at 393D-E).

For a case involving theft of a specimen of blood, see *R. v. Rothery* (1976) 63 Cr.App.R. 231.

[78] *cf.* Model Penal Code, T.D. 1, 77. There is also the question whether a body which has been interred and then exhumed can be stolen. Lord Moncrieff spoke in *Dewar, supra,* at 14, of the "undisputed proposition" that a body once it has been interred is not protected by the law of theft, but there is no authority dealing specifically with exhumed remains. The answer depends on the reason for the rule that a buried body cannot be stolen. If the reason is that it becomes incapable of being owned then it would be equally impossible to own an exhumed body, although persons acting under an exhumation warrant would have possessory rights in the body. But if the reason is that the buried body is deemed to be abandoned, however reverentially, the exhumed body will be the property of the Crown, and so can be stolen. *Dewar* rather suggests that the latter is the correct reason, although it does not decide the question. The court in *Dewar* defined the point at which interference with a body ceases to be theft by reference to the beginning of the process of destruction of the body, which they fixed as the time of burial. Lord Moncrieff said, "It is when a step has conclusively been taken to set agoing the process of dissolution of the bodies of the dead that the law ceases to protect the body from acts of theft": at 14. The analogy with abandonment appears even more clearly in some remarks of Lord Normand who said: "It may be argued that the ashes are capable of being stolen, and that it is not until the ashes are interred or disposed of in accordance with the wishes of the relatives that the crime of violation of sepulchres can take place": at 11. On that view a body committed for burial or cremation can be stolen, but once the original owner's directions have been carried out he has no further interest in the matter. The relative who asks for the ashes to be returned to him in a casket would retain his property in them, but the relative who simply hands over a body for cremation or burial without further instructions has no property rights in the body once it has been buried or cremated. This solution has the merit of protecting exhumed bodies but it is not free from difficulties. If, as has been argued — *cf. Weir* (1710) quoted in *H.M. Advocate v. Coutts* (1899) 3 Adam 50, 55n — the owner of a cemetery cannot be guilty of violating sepulchres, this may be because a man may do as he will with his own, and the bodies buried in his ground belong to him. Lord Moncrieff in *Dewar* suggested that the whole question was one of expediency and policy rather than of the legal possibility of owning a body. In speaking of the stage at which dissolution starts, he said, "At that stage such acts [of theft] are not to be anticipated. It is clear, on the other hand, that there is no stage in the history of a body at which it is more subject to be misappropriated or mishandled than in the privacy of the antechamber which leads to the furnace of a crematorium": at 14. If expediency is to be taken as the criterion, then it is submitted that the law should be that while a body in a grave cannot be stolen, an unburied body and an exhumed body can be stolen, as can

Must the property be owned by someone other than the accused?

The modern case authority of *Carmichael v. Black; Carmichael v.* **14.28**
Penrice[79] contains dicta which suggest that appropriation extends to
deprivation of the owner's possessory rights[80]; but the opinions also refer
more vaguely to depriving the motorist or complainer of the use of his
motor-car.[81] There is clearly little significance in the exact terminology
used in the case, and it did not matter there whether or not the
complainers actually owned the vehicles they had left in the private car
park: they were owned by someone other than the accused, and that was
all that mattered. But the rights of which the complainers had been
allegedly deprived in the case were those of use and control.

These certainly are rights usually enjoyed by an owner of moveable
property; but, of course, an owner without losing ownership may cede
such rights in his property to another, for example by contract of hire or
by way of pledge. The question then arises whether theft may be
committed in a case where the owner without consent (and without
other lawful authority) recovers the property before such recovery is
legally due. If theft is possible in such a situation, then an owner of
property can steal that property (his own property) from a person having
a lesser right to the property than himself. The concept of being able to
steal property that one owns seems somewhat paradoxical and strange[82];
it would permit, for example, a pledgor and a pledgee, and a person who
hires and a person who hires from him, to steal from one another; it
might also be the case that an owner who steals his own property would
find himself restricted in what he might legitimately do with that
property since it might be argued that the *vitium reale* which the civil law
attaches to stolen goods would prevent him passing a good title to a
third party who takes in good faith.[83] Further, the owner (for example, a
person who has hired property to A under a hire-purchase agreement)
might not have been aware that the car he has clamped in his private car
park in fact belongs to him in terms of the contract with the complainer.
It is submitted, therefore, that there are sound theoretical and practical
reasons for retaining the view of the institutional writers who all agree
that a man cannot steal his own property. Hume says, "I see no reason
to believe that in our practice, a person shall in any case be held guilty of
theft, though he may of some inferior wrong, for irregularly taking that
which is his own."[84] Alison states simply, "No one can commit theft of
his own goods."[85] Burnett, too, points out that one cannot steal one's
own property, even if one acts in the mistaken belief that it belongs to
someone else.[86] Even Macdonald, who wavers considerably on this
matter, does say at one point that "The thing taken must at the time be
the property of another than the thief, because a person is not guilty of

---

bodies which are not buried but preserved in institutions or even in private places.
[79] 1992 S.C.C.R. 709.
[80] See, *e.g.*, *ibid.*, L.J.-G. Hope at 719A; Lord Allanbridge at 721D.
[81] See, *e.g.*, *ibid.*, L.J.-G. Hope at 719F, and 720A; Lord Allanbridge at 721D.
[82] Stealing one's own property is nevertheless what is contemplated expressly under
English law: see The Theft Act 1968, s.5.
[83] See para. 14.29, *infra*.
[84] Hume, i, 77.
[85] Alison, i, 273.
[86] Burnett, p.120.

theft for irregularly taking that which is his own although he may thereby commit some offence other than theft."[87]

The case law on the subject is, however, very old and unsatisfactory. It concerns goods which had been seized by customs officers but not yet formally condemned, so that ownership had not vested in the Crown.[88] In so far as these cases can be received as authority at all, they tend to suggest that where the Crown had become owner of the property in question, the correct charge would be one of theft, but prior to that stage having been reached an innominate offence would be the only possibility in the case of an accused who had succeeded in extracting "his" goods from the relevant repositories of the customs authorities. In short, these cases do not detract from the view taken by the institutional writers.[89] It is submitted, therefore, that the law continues to be that a person cannot be convicted of the theft of property which he owns, and that there is no warrant for defining "owner" so as to include a possessor or the holder of any other lesser right in the thing.[90] The concept of theft as limited to the stealing of goods belonging to someone else is a simple one, and one which makes it possible to develop and apply the law consistently and without recourse to ingenuity and paradox. If the goods do not belong to the accused it does not matter to whom they belong, or that the prosecution cannot show whose they are.[91] There is probably a presumption of fact that they do not belong to the accused, so that it will be for him to set up the defence that they are his own.[92]

14.29 *Furtum possessionis.* In South Africa, following Roman law, an apparent exception is recognised to the general rule that an owner cannot steal his own property. Where the owner has given possession of property he owns to A, but retains the ownership of that property, he commits *furtum possessionis* if he takes his property from A before he is entitled to do so and without consent or other lawful authority. But Burchell and Milton point out that he is not guilty of theft of the property — for the property is his own.

Rather he is guilty of stealing the possessory interests which A was entitled to enjoy.[93]

This suggests that the offence is one *sui generis* or certainly one which is different from ordinary theft, and which possibly thus avoids the difficulty posed by a *vitium reale* attaching to the property itself. It may be that Scots law would recognise a similar exception in a suitable case,

---

[87] Macdonald, p.16. *Cf.* Mackenzie who adopts the definition of theft in *Justinian's Institutes*, and concludes that, "Theft may be described, to be a fraudulent away-taking, or using what belongs to another man, without the owner's consent": Mackenzie, I, 19, 1.

[88] See *Williamson* (1767) Burnett 118; *Lockhart* (1800) *ibid.*, 119; *Macdonald and Chisholm* (1814) Hume, i, 77; *Jas Munro and Ors* (1833) Bell's Notes 23.

[89] Macdonald, at p.16, gives the impression that there are circumstances in which a person may be guilty of stealing his own property; but there are no authorities to support his view.

[90] *cf.* Theft Act 1968, s.5; J. Burchell and J. Milton, *Principles of Criminal Law* (2nd ed., Cape Town, 1997), pp. 548–9.

[91] Hume, i, 77–78; Alison, i, 277; Macdonald, p.17.

[92] Hume, i, 78. It was, however, necessary before 1887 to specify from whose possession the goods were taken, and usual to specify who was the owner: see Hume, ii, 200; Bell's Notes 203. Since 1887 this has no longer been the practice, and all that is done is to specify the time and place of the theft, and the nature of the goods: Criminal Procedure (Scotland) Act 1887, Sched. A. (See now 1995 Act, Scheds 2 and 5.)

[93] J. Burchell and J. Milton, *Principles of Criminal Law* (2nd. ed., Cape Town, 1997), at p. 548.

given that *Carmichael v. Black; Carmichael v. Penrice*[94] in essence makes appropriation in theft satisfied by a deprivation of the complainer's possessory rights of use and control; but there was no suggestion in that case that the accused had any right of property in the vehicles which were clamped by them, and there is nothing in the judicial opinions to suggest that their Lordships had any such situation in contemplation. In any event, the case decides that in the unusual circumstances which pertained, a deprivation of the complainer's possessory rights of use and control *can* be sufficient to make a charge of *stealing* a motor-car a relevant one — it having been apparently assumed for the purposes of the decision that the complainer was the owner.[95]

Limited ownership. Unfortunately the simple principle that one cannot **14.30** steal one's own property has been somewhat obscured by the introduction of the concept of "limited ownership" into the discussion of the distinction between theft and breach of trust.[96] The idea is that a "limited owner" such as a pawnbroker, or even someone who has goods on a prolonged loan, cannot steal the goods but can only commit a breach of trust in respect of them. This, it is submitted, is wrong. If anyone can be described as a limited owner in the pledgor-pledgee situation, or in the context of long loan or hire-purchase for that matter, it is the pledgor, lender or finance company. They are owners of the goods whose enjoyment of their ownership is very much limited by the rights of the other parties to the respective contracts. The latter are not owners at all, they are persons having some lesser right in the goods of another person.[97] Nor does the fact that the right of the pawnbroker includes a right to dispose, or become owner, of the goods under certain statutory conditions affect the matter until these conditions have been purified and the requisite procedure gone through.

The concept of "limited ownership" indicates a realisation that a lawful possessor can steal. It is an attempt to relieve people in the position of pawnbrokers of liability for theft by treating them as a kind of owner, but it is submitted that the attempt is misconceived.

The case usually cited in support of the concept of limited ownership is *Catherine Crossgrove or Bradley*[98] in which it was held that a pawnbroker could not steal goods pledged to him, because he had "a title to the goods themselves, which, by lapse of time, became absolute, and enabled the party to sell, and give a valid right to all the world."[99] It is submitted that this is a clear misconception of the pawnbroker's position, and that the case was wrongly decided.[1]

---

[94] 1992 S.C.C.R. 709.

[95] Both Burnett (at p.115) and Alison (at i, 271), however, specifically deny that *furtum possessionis* (as defined in Roman law — see para. 14.30, n.6, *infra*) is part of Scots law. See also Hume, i, 59.

[96] For example, Macdonald (3rd ed.) p.58: the phrase does not appear in the 5th ed.; Anderson, p.179; T.B. Smith, p.193.

[97] That neither pledge, loan nor hire-purchase effects the transfer of property in the goods except of course where fungibles are concerned, is clear: Ersk., Inst. 3, 1, 33 and 3, 3, 14; Bell's Commentaries, i, 278; *Helby v. Matthews* [1895] A.C. 471.

[98] (1850) J. Shaw 301.

[99] Lord Moncreiff at 305.

[1] It is discussed in detail *infra*, para. 17.08. It is sufficient to note here that the contract of pledge does not affect ownership, and that the pawnbroker's right to sell the goods is hedged round by statutory restrictions: Consumer Credit Act 1974, ss. 120, 121.

Apart from *Bradley* there is no authority for the view that the Scots law of theft recognises a limited ownership in a pledgee[2] and accordingly, if *Bradley* is regarded as wrongly decided, the concept of "limited ownership" can be discarded. It follows that a pawnbroker *can* steal goods pledged with him, but that the pledgor who takes the goods back in breach of pledge is not guilty of theft. Similarly, agents of a hire-purchase company who repossess goods in breach of contract but before the hirer has exercised his option to purchase are not guilty of theft.[3] Hume says that "the owner would be guilty of a crime, and, as some allege, guilty of theft even in certain circumstances, if he should secretly withdraw the thing from [the pledgee's] possession",[4] but it is clear from his views on the customs cases[5] that his own opinion is that such an act is not theft.[6] Burnett, too, says that it is a necessary consequence of the rule *neminem rei suae propriae furtum facere posse* that "no one can steal, though he clandestinely takes from the occupier, goods that he had given to him on loan, or in pledge", but that such acts may constitute an innominate offence.[7]

14.31 *Transfer of ownership.* Whether or not A is the owner of a thing at the relevant time falls to be decided by the civil law of property. The borrower of a non-fungible, for example, does not become the owner of the thing, while the borrower of a fungible does, which is why it is not theft to fail to repay a financial loan.[8] In contracts of sale or return, or of sale on approval, property will normally pass to the prospective buyer either on his approval of the article, on his disposal of it to a third party, or on his adoption of the sale in any other way such as his retention of the thing beyond the time fixed for approval or return without signifying his rejection of it.[9] It is, of course, open to parties to make their own arrangements about the passing of property, and in any particular situation the question of theft or no theft will depend on whether or not property has passed in terms of the particular contract.

The rather tricky situation which can arise in the ordinary cash sale over the counter where the buyer goes out with the goods without paying

---

[2] The question was raised in circumstances similar to those of *Bradley* in *Agnes McGinlay or Docherty and William Docherty* (1841) 1 Broun 548, and certified to the High Court by Lord Cockburn on an objection to the relevancy of the charge, but there were no further proceedings.

[3] *cf.* Hume, i, 77n.

[4] Hume, i, 59.

[5] Hume, i, 77. See para. 14.28, *supra.*

[6] In Roman law pledgor and pledgee can each steal from the other: Inst. 4, 1, 1 and 4, 1, 14, but the Roman law of theft is mainly concerned with civil action, and also recognises unauthorised use as theft. Moreover, the Roman contract of pledge unlike the Scots included a mandate to sell — see Bell's Principles, para. 207. It would be highly paradoxical in Scots law to say that pledgor and pledgee, or finance company and hire-purchaser, can steal from each other. Moreover, stolen goods have a *vitium reale* so that the thief cannot pass a good title but the finance company have and can pass a good title, as indeed can a pledgor subject to the pledgee's rights, but the dishonest pawnbroker or hire-purchaser has no title to give. See now, however, Hire-Purchase Act 1964, Pt III, as substituted by Consumer Credit Act 1974, Sched. 4. *Cf.* South African law relative to *furtum possessionis* — see para. 14.29, *supra.*

[7] Burnett, p.120. There are also two cases which indicate that the possession of a lien over goods does not prevent the possibility of theft: *Craig v. Ponton* (1829) 2 S.J. 31, a lodging-house keeper stealing his guests' luggage; and *Fraser v. Anderson* (1899) 2 Adam 705, an unpaid seller reselling goods still in his possession.

[8] Stair, Inst. 1, 11, 2; Ersk. Inst. 3, 1, 18–20; Bell's Commentaries, i, 275.

[9] Sale of Goods Act 1979, s.18, r.4; *cf. Brown v. Marr, Barclay, etc.* (1880) 7 R. 427; *Cowan v. McMinn* (1859) 3 Irv. 312.

for them has not been considered in Scotland. It would probably be dealt with broadly, without any attempt being made to analyse the position closely.[10] The situation would probably be equiparated with that where A just snatches goods from a counter without entering into any form of "contract" or discussion at all, and so be treated as theft, but it could probably also be dealt with as a form of fraud — obtaining goods without paying and intending not to pay for them.[11] Where the sale is a credit sale there can clearly be no theft, and the only possible crime involved in a failure to pay would be fraud.

John Mooney[12] concerns the slightly different situation where the cus- **14.32** tomer hands over money — in that case a £1 note — in payment for an article costing less and the shopkeeper keeps the money and does not give any change. Mooney was charged alternatively with theft of £1 and theft of 19s. 9^1/₂d., the change due to the customer. The report is very brief and indicates only that Lord Justice-Clerk Hope directed the jury that if there was theft at all it was theft of the £1 note. Presumably the crime was treated as theft rather than embezzlement because, in the words of the charge, the note was given to Mooney for the purpose of procuring change and of his taking 2^1/₂d. and paying the balance to the customer. It is difficult to see how Mooney could be guilty of stealing the £1 and not merely 19s. 9^1/₂d. since both parties intended him to keep the note, and he was entitled to 2^1/₂d. out of the £1 in payment of the goods he supplied. But it can be argued that he was not guilty of stealing the 19s. 9^1/₂d. either, or indeed of any crime at all. His dishonesty consisted in a failure to give change, and it is doubtful if this is criminal. What Mooney did looked like theft because of the proximity in space of the parties and the very short time which elapsed between the handing over of the note and the failure to give change. In principle, however, the situation is similar to that where B knows that he owes A less than £5 for goods supplied but does not know the exact amount; he sends A a cheque for £5 with a request to return the change; A cashes the cheque and either gives no change at all or gives short change. It is difficult to envisage A being charged with theft of the cheque in such a situation.

In the South African case of *R. v. Scoulides*[13] the facts were similar to *Mooney* except that the shopkeeper handed over part of the change due, and the court held that the shopkeeper had stolen the note. Schreiner J.A. rejected the argument that property in the note passed to the shopkeeper and, after some discussion of whether the note was held by

---

[10] See *infra*, para. 14.37. There are two cases whose facts resemble this situation but both were decided by reference to the absence of *mens rea* and both related to very special circumstances which the court obviously felt were unsuitable for prosecution whatever the technical position. In *Clyne v. Keith* (1887) 1 White 356, where a customer snatched goods from a shop assistant without paying, the court seem to have felt that property had not passed to the customer but held, in a typically idiosyncratic judgment by Lord Young, that there was no theftuous intent. In *Greig v. Finlay* (1901) 3 Adam 316 the appellants were in a group of men who ordered fish suppers, and then left with them without paying for them after a quarrel had broken out in which they did not wish to become involved: they returned two days later and paid for them. The conviction was quashed on formal grounds and not on the merits, but L.J.-G. Balfour remarked *obiter* that there had been no theft.

[11] *infra*, para. 18.12.

[12] (1851) J. Shaw 496.

[13] 1956 (2) S.A. 388 (A.D.); see also *S. v. Graham* 1975 (2) S.A. 569 (A.D.), and J. Burchell and J. Milton, *Principles of Criminal Law* (2nd ed., Cape Town, 1997), pp. 554–560; *cf. R. v. Lawrence* [1972] A.C. 626.

him in trust, concluded that he became owner only if and when the goods and the correct change were tendered to the customer in exchange. The learned judge remarked that, "the law would indeed be gravely deficient if it treated the seller, not as a thief, but only as a contract breaker".[14] A South African writer has commented that this decision exhibits "an extensive interpretation . . . justified in the interest of criminal justice even if not strictly in accordance with legal principle."[15]

Schreiner J.A. was anxious that customers in such situations should be protected by the criminal law, no doubt envisaging systematic cheating of this kind on the part of a dishonest shopkeeper. But in such a case it is submitted that in Scotland it would be possible to convict the shop-keeper of fraud by inducing the customers to hand over their notes on the pretence that he would behave like an honest shopkeeper and give proper change. Such a charge could also be brought in an isolated case, but it would be easier to prove that the shopkeeper's intention had been dishonest from the outset, *i.e.* before he received the note, where it could be shown that he systematically refused to give proper change in this way.

14.33 *Trust property.* The legal ownership of trust property is in the trustees,[16] so that unless the beneficiary is also in some way an owner he will commit theft if he takes property from the trust estate, even if he takes only property to which he has a vested right.[17] In view, however, of the special nature of the situation, it is unlikely that a charge of theft would often be brought against a beneficiary, at any rate if the goods were not taken until after the appointed period of division; and if any charge were brought the beneficiary might often be able to plead that he acted under a *bona fide* claim of right.

If, however, he acted patently in *mala fide*, it is submitted that he could be convicted of theft. Cases of this kind are very rare, and there is no decision on the matter. In *John McRae*[18] a bankrupt was charged with theft of assets which were the subject of a trust deed for creditors. Among the arguments against the relevancy of the charge was one that the trust deed had not been delivered and that there was nothing to show that the property had been transferred to the trustee. It was also argued that in any event the bankrupt retained a radical right in property which had been transferred under such a trust deed. The theft charge was rejected as irrelevant but no reasons were given, and the case merely illustrates the questions which arise in such a situation.

---

[14] At 394–395.

[15] E.M. Burchell, "Recent Developments in South African Criminal Law", *Acta Juridica*, 1959, 99 at 108. The same writer remarks that the decision may have been motivated by the impossibility of preferring a charge of embezzlement in the circum-stances. It might be possible to charge embezzlement of the change in Scotland, but only by inventing some sort of trust in the shopkeeper so that he could be said to hold the note on behalf of the customer. This would be a rather strained extension of embezzlement, and it is submitted that the facts do not really come within the scope of that crime.

[16] Stair Inst. 1, 13, 7; Ersk. Inst., 3, 1, 32.

[17] There is some authority for the view that a beneficiary has more than a *jus crediti* and has indeed a form of ownership, or in any event has a right which is *sui generis* and akin to the English equitable ownership: see *e.g. Allen v. McCombie's Trs*, 1909 S.C. 710; but his right is probably ultimately only a personal one and not a form of ownership: see T.B. Smith, 569 *et seq.*; Wilson and Duncan, *Trusts, Trustees and Executors* (2nd ed., Edin., 1995) pp. 15–17 (paras 1–42 to 1–50).

[18] (1867) 5 Irv. 463.

In *Chisholm and Ors v. Black and Anr*[19] some fishermen were charged with the statutory offence of taking fish from a scalp held by the magistrates of the area for behoof, *inter alia*, of the accused. The accused were clearly acting in *mala fide*, as their conduct was in breach of an interdict and in excess of the trust rights. Lord Ardmillan, however, observed that "it is quite possible for the inhabitants of the town to commit a theft upon property belonging to the Magistrates in trust for the community."[20]

All that can be said of these two cases is that they show that the concept of theft by a beneficiary from his trustee is not one wholly alien to Scots law; it is not possible to say what attitude the law will take in any given case of this kind.

The converse proposition, that a trustee cannot be convicted of stealing trust property is undoubtedly true.[21]

Joint and common property. Where property is held by a number of **14.34** people each of whom has the right to dispose of his own share, it is said to be held in common.[22]

In such a situation each co-owner can be said to own his own share, so that any co-owner who takes the share of another is guilty of theft.[23]

Where property is held inseparably by a number of people, as in the case of property held by partners or co-trustees, the property is said to be held jointly.[24] Normally, dishonest partners and trustees are charged with embezzlement and not with theft, and in view of the difficulties involved in joint ownership it is preferable to take this course.[25]

HUSBAND AND WIFE. The *ratio* of *Harper v. Adair*[26] lends some support **14.35** to the view that joint owners cannot steal from each other. *Harper* held that a wife could steal from her husband because, following on the Married Women's Property (Scotland) Acts 1881 and 1920, spouses no longer held their property under the *communio bonorum*, and were accordingly to be regarded as strangers to each other in the law of theft.[27] It was further argued that in any event there was a presumption that the stolen goods, which consisted of furniture bought by the husband, had been bought as joint property. The court refused to accept

---

[19] (1871) 2 Couper 49; *cf. R. v. Bonner* [1970] 1 W.L.R. 838.

[20] At 56.

[21] See Lord Walker, "The Growth of the Criminal Law", 1958 J.R. 230, 238.

[22] *Magistrates of Banff v. Ruthin Castle*, 1944 S.C. 36 L.J.-C. Cooper at 68; T.B. Smith pp. 479–480.

[23] Where the shares are not readily distinguishable a co-owner who did not take funds or goods in excess of the value of his own share would be presumed to have taken, or at any rate to have intended to take, the part of the property belonging to him.

[24] *supra*, n. 22. The nomenclature has not been consistently used in the past.

[25] A charge of embezzlement by a partner of funds received by him for the partnership was upheld by the High Court in *Peter Anthony Sumner*, Nov. 1983, unrep'd. Mackenzie, however, suggests that it is theft for a member of a "society" to use the common property other than according to the rules of the society, since this is an employment of it for one's own use: Mackenzie, I, 19, 2. The Larceny Act 1916, s.40(4) provided that a co-partner who stole should be dealt with as if he was not a co-partner, and a co-partner who takes dishonestly with intent to acquire another co-partner's share is clearly guilty of theft under the wide provisions of the Theft Act 1968. Burnett, however, adopts the converse view that theft can be committed only of goods which are the exclusive property of another: at p.117.

[26] 1945 J.C. 21.

[27] L.J.-G. Normand at 27–28; Macdonald, p.18, is, it is submitted, wrong in saying that the decision depended on the fact that the spouses were living separate.

this presumption, and regarded the goods as the husband's exclusive property.[28] The case suggests that had the property been held jointly there would bave been no theft, but the point cannot be said to have been decided.[29]

The goods must be appropriated without the owner's consent

14.36   It is part of the definition of theft that it is an unauthorised appropriation of the goods of another, *i.e.* that the appropriation is without the other's consent, and it is the absence of consent which distinguishes theft from fraud. There can be no theft if the owner agreed to transfer property in the goods to the accused, even although the consent was impetrated by fraud.[30] The distinction between theft and fraud has declined in importance since the Criminal Procedure (Scotland) Act 1887 which provided that an accused who is charged with theft may be convicted of fraud, and vice versa,[31] but it remains of cardinal importance in the civil common law of property — for a person who buys an article from someone who obtained it by fraud obtains a good title if he acts bona fide and without knowledge of the fraud, but he cannot obtain a title to the article if it has been stolen.[32]

14.37   Where the owner agrees to transfer possession to the accused but not to transfer ownership, as happens in loans of non-fungibles, it is, as has been argued, theft for the borrower to appropriate the goods,[33] and this is so whether or not the original consent to transfer of possession was fraudulently obtained. Hume, who did not regard it as theft to appropriate hired goods, made an exception for the case in which the accused had all along intended to appropriate the goods, and had only pretended to want to hire them. He argued that in such a case there had been no *consensus in idem* between the accused and the owner, since the one intended to transfer possession and the other to obtain ownership. Accordingly, Hume argued, there was no valid contract, and so no consent to the transfer of possession which would prevent the hirer being guilty of theft.[34]

This argument must be dismissed as ingenious, and in any event is one to which there is no need to resort once it is accepted that a bona fide hirer can steal.[35] But the principle involved in the argument is still

---

[28] L.J.-G. Normand at 28.

[29] It is far from clear that spouses did hold property jointly under the old law, the true position being probably that it all belonged to the husband: see E.M. Clive, *Husband and Wife* (4th ed., Edinburgh, 1997), pp. 219–220; *Joseph Kilgour* (1851) J. Shaw 501, Lord Wood at 505. Nor was the question of theft by a spouse ever settled in the old law: see *Yuill or Muirhead v. Mackintosh* (1889) 1 White 105, L.J.-C. Moncreiff at 110; *Kilgour, supra; Donald Macleod* (1832) 2 Swin. 190; *Janet Becket* (1831) Shaw 217. Mackenzie's view was that spouses could steal from each other: Mackenzie, I, 19, 14.

[30] Hume, i, 57–58; Alison, i, 259.

[31] s.59; see now 1995 Act, Sched. 3, para. 8(3),(4). It has almost disappeared in England: *R. v. Lawrence* [1972] A.C. 626; *R. v. Gomez* [1993] A.C. 442; *R. Hinks* [2000] 3 W.L.R. 1590, HL.

[32] Bell's Principles, para. 527. But see Hire-Purchase Act 1964, Pt III, as substituted by Consumer Credit Act 1974, Sched. 4, for the special situation in relation to motor-cars in certain circumstances.

[33] *cf. supra*, para. 14.07.

[34] See Hume, i, 69.

[35] Hume himself was none too happy about it, nor was Burnett who preferred to regard the *mala fide* hirer as guilty of fraud: at pp. 113–114, but it was accepted by the court in *Wm Barr* (1832) 5 Deas and Anderson 260 where Barr induced a horse owner to hire him a horse on the pretence that he wished to visit a sick father, and immediately took the horse away and sold it.

important. Where the contract by which the owner consents to transfer ownership to the accused is void, and not merely voidable, the consent can be disregarded, and the accused is guilty of theft.[36] Where Hume is wrong, it is submitted, is in regarding the horse-hiring contract as void, and not as only voidable.[37]

Where A does obtain possession by fraud, for example by giving a false account of his financial situation, and subsequently appropriates the goods, he is, strictly speaking, guilty of two crimes, fraud and theft.[38] There is some authority for the proposition that it is competent to charge both crimes cumulatively, since the two charges do not concern the same *species facti* — the fraud consists in A's inducing B to part with the goods and the theft in his subsequent appropriation of them — but such cumulative charges were not encouraged by the courts.[39]

In *Jas Hill*[40] the accused pretended to various merchants that he had been sent on behalf of another person to obtain goods for him "on sight or loan" and then appropriated the goods they gave him. He was originally charged with fraud, but Lord Young indicated that in his view the crime was not fraud, and that charge was dropped and another indictment was raised charging him with theft. In holding the theft charge relevant Lord Justice-Clerk Moncreiff said, "I have no doubt that where the possession of articles is libelled as having been obtained . . . by means of false pretences . . . and these are said to have been subsequently appropriated to the prisoner's own use, that that constitutes theft."[41] What Lord Moncreiff said is indisputable, but Lord Young's view that it is not fraud to obtain possession by false pretences if the goods are subsequently appropriated is wrong. It stands alone,[42] and is contrary to authority and practice.[43]

---

[36] *infra*.

[37] Hume argued that it was void for essential error as to the nature of the contract. But there is no error as to the nature of the contract: both parties intend to enter a contract of hire, the difference between them is that one intends to abide by it and the other does not. The rogue enters the contract with a dishonest motive, but it is a contract of hire into which he enters. The situation is wholly different from that in which, *e.g.* A signs a contract of sale in the belief that it is a contract of hire, or a bond of caution in the belief that it is a petition for the abolition of income tax: see *Fletcher v. Lord Advocate*, 1923 S.C. 27, Lord Sands at 31. On error in contract see *Gloag on Contract* (2nd ed., Edinburgh, 1929), Chap. 26; T.B. Smith, Chap. 37; W.W. McBryde, *The Law of Contract in Scotland* (Edinburgh, 1987), Chap. 9.

[38] See *e.g. Henry Hardinge* (1863) 4 Irv. 347; *Jas. Chisholm* (1849) J. Shaw 241; *cf. Margt Sharp* (1874) 2 Couper 543. See also H.H. Brown, "The Distinction Between Fraud and Fraudulent Theft", 1908 S.L.T (News) 43.

[39] *Jas. Chisholm* (1849) J. Shaw 241, 251, but cumulative charges of this kind were upheld in *Chisholm*. In *Margt Grahame* (1847) J. Shaw 243n the accused went to a shop and fraudulently induced them to send goods to a certain address; she then went to the address and pretended that the goods had been sent there by mistake and were really intended for her, and so obtained possession of and appropriated them. She was charged with inducing the shop to deliver the goods which she "received and appropriated as after libelled", and then with the theftuous appropriation of them from the address to which they were sent.

[40] (1879) 4 Couper 295.

[41] At 300.

[42] Except for a dictum of Lord Young himself in *Dingwall v. H.M. Advocate* (1888) 2 White 27 at 39–40.

[43] *Margt Grahame, supra*; *Jas Chisholm, supra*; *Alex. Boyd* (1874) 2 Couper 541; *Wm Rodger* (1868) 1 Couper 76; *Henry Hardinge* (1836) 4 Irv. 347; *John Menzies* (1842) 1 Broun 419; *Jas Maitland* (1842) 1 Broun 57. There is, however, this to be said for Lord Young: where possession only is obtained by fraud and the goods are later appropriated, it is strictly speaking wrong to charge the accused with fraudulent appropriation of the goods

The reason that in practice someone who gets goods by saying falsely he has been sent to collect them is charged with theft, and the hire-purchaser with fraud, is probably that the more elaborate the fraud the less resemblance the facts have to the typical case of theft, the case in which A literally takes something away from B without his consent.[44]

At one end of the scale is the man who fraudulently induces a shopkeeper to let him take a tie to the front door to see how it looks in daylight and runs off with it, and at the other the man who obtains valuable possessory rights in goods by a complex scheme. The former would certainly be charged with theft — the possession which the owner consents to his having is only fleeting, there is no articulated pretence, and his behaviour is next door to that of a shoplifter; the latter would probably be charged with fraud because his conduct looks much more like a swindle than a snatch. Intermediate situations are allocated with more or less consistency to one category or the other.[45]

14.38 *Can fraud exclude consent?* The proposition that there can be no theft where the original owner consents to transfer property in the goods to the accused, even if the consent is impetrated by fraud, does not appear

---

as was done in *Henry Hardinge, supra*; but there is no reason for not charging him with fraudulently obtaining possession of them.

The modern practice is to charge either theft or fraud. Where the pretence is a simple one used only to enable the accused to lay hands on the goods, as where he pretends he has been sent to collect them for someone else, it will probably be regarded as the *modus* of a theft, and be libelled in the charge only to give fair notice of the Crown case. Such cases can be described as "thefts by false pretences": *cf. Jas Hill* (1879) 4 Couper 295, L.J.-C. Moncreiff at 300. The 1995 Act, Sched. 5, contains a charge of this kind which reads: "You did steal a coat which you obtained from R.O. on the false representation that you had been sent for it by her husband." Where, however, the fraud is more elaborate, and particularly where A obtains some right of his own in the goods such as a right under a hire-purchase contract, the practice is to treat the crime as fraud even if A subsequently appropriates the goods. In such a case the charge may read that A pretended to B that he was in regular employment with a particular firm and wished to obtain goods on hire-purchase, that he thereby induced B to hand over the goods to him on hire-purchase, and on payment by A of the due deposit, and that "he forthwith appropriated them to his own use without paying and intending not to pay therefor, and did thereby defraud B thereof." This charge is an omnibus one — it includes the fraud of inducing delivery of the goods by the pretence that A was in regular employment, the fraud of inducing delivery by the pretence of an honest intention to pay for them, and the theft of appropriating goods held on hire-purchase. But as the last part of the charge shows, it is meant to be a charge of fraud. The intention not to pay is included in case it is shown that B was not influenced by the pretences of regular employment and would have delivered the goods in any event; the averment of appropriation is included in case the Crown fail to prove any fraudulent pretence at all, so that they can then obtain a conviction for theftuous appropriation, and also to show that B was not merely induced to incur a bad debt but lost his goods altogether, a factor which might affect the question of sentence.

[44] In *Carmichael v. Black; Carmichael v. Penrice* (1992 S.C.C.R. 709) there was, of course, no question of anything being literally taken away from the complainer since his motor-car was simply immobilised where it had been left by him; but it was not the court's intention to suggest there that stealing by taking away no longer qualified as *the* typical case of theft (see L.J.-G. Hope at 718F).

[45] In *R. v. Lawrence* [1972] A.C. 626 a foreign student allowed a taxi-driver to take money out of his wallet for his fare. The driver took more than the fare, and was convicted of theft of the excess which amounted to £6. A similar result would follow in Scotland (although absence of the owner's consent is still essential to theft in Scotland) because of the similarity to a theft by taking and because no consent was given to the taking of the excess money, and perhaps also because of the absence of any false statement inducing the student to pass property in the excess money. It would be possible to frame a charge of fraudulently inducing the student to permit all the money taken to be taken by pretending that it was due, but the Scots definition of fraud cannot easily encompass representations so "contemporaneous" with the taking. The theft—fraud distinction is clearly artificial in this kind of case.

to be accepted by Macdonald. He says, "When it is said that if the taker believed he had the owner's concurrence he is not guilty of theft, this does not cover the case of the concurrence being obtained by fraud . . . If a person by fraudulent misrepresentations induce tradesmen to part with goods on sale or return, the fraud excludes contract, and the property does not pass."[46] The meaning of these passages is not clear: what is at issue is not the defence of the effect of a consent which has been given but has been obtained by fraud. Again, what is at issue is not a consent to part with the goods on sale or return, but a consent to transfer ownership. It does appear, however, that what Macdonald means is that even a consent to the transfer of property in the goods is invalid if obtained by fraud, and that the appropriation of goods so obtained is theft. If that is what he means, it is submitted that he is wrong in principle, and is unsupported by authority except for one case which, it will be argued, was wrongly decided.

The passages cited by Macdonald from Hume and Alison are con- **14.39** cerned only with obtaining possession by fraud, and both writers specifically restrict themselves to cases in which consent to transfer property has not been obtained.[47]

In *John Menzies*[48] the accused went to persons to whom a certain tradesman had delivered goods and pretended that he had been sent by that tradesman "to get them back, on account of an alleged mistake, which he wished to rectify." Lord Cockburn held that this was theft and not fraud, but gave no reason for his decision beyond saying that the matter had been clearly settled by recent decisions — presumably the cases which had held that theft did not require an unlawful taking of the goods.[49] There is nothing in the report to indicate that there was any intention to pass property to the accused, or indeed to the tradesman for whom the accused pretended to be acting, since the articles were only to be taken back to be rectified.

Wm Barr[50] has already been discussed,[51] and is the classic case of what was known in England as larceny by a trick, where the accused obtains possession of goods by fraud and then appropriates them. Whether or not the contract of hire is invalid in such a situation, there is no question of any consent by the owner to transfer property to the accused.[52]

In *Margt Grahame*[53] the accused went into a shop and ordered goods to be sent to a Miss P at a certain address "for inspection, with a view to purchase" knowing that the address was occupied not by a Miss P, but by a Mr P She then called at the address, pretended she had been sent by Miss P for goods delivered there in error, and obtained possession of the goods which she appropriated. She was charged with stealing the goods and no objection was taken to the relevancy of the indictment.

In *Jas Hill*[54] the accused pretended to merchants that he had been sent on behalf of another person to obtain goods "on sight or loan" and was convicted of theft.

---

[46] Macdonald, pp.18–19.

[47] Hume, i, 68–69; Alison, i, 259–260.

[48] (1842) 1 Broun 419.

[49] *John Smith* (1838) 2 Swin. 28; *Geo. Brown* (1839) 2 Swin. 394.

[50] (1832) 5 Deas and Anderson 260.

[51] *supra*, para. 14.37.

[52] *cf.* also *Robt Nicolson* (1842) 1 Broun 370, where the accused, who was given a horse to show it off for sale, but was not empowered to sell it, was convicted of stealing the horse by selling it and appropriating the proceeds; *Walter Tyrie* (1827) Alison, i, 259, and *John Smith* (1829) *ibid.* 260.

[53] (1847) J. Shaw 243n.

[54] (1879) 4 Couper 295.

These cases have two features in common. In all of them there was no intention by the owner to transfer property in the goods to anyone, and there was no intention to transfer any right in the goods at all to the accused.[55] The second feature is by far the more important, because it means that if A pretends to B that he has been sent by C to collect goods the property in which B intends to transfer to C, A is guilty of theft if he appropriates the goods, there being no intention by B to transfer property to A. Such situations are essentially the same as that in *Morrison v. Robertson*,[56] in which T pretended to the pursuer that he was the son of W and wished to buy some cattle for W, thereby inducing the pursuer to give him cattle on credit which he promptly sold to the defender. As Professor Smith has pointed out,[57] the decision that the pursuer was entitled to recover the cattle from the defender, *i.e.* that the contract with T was void, can be reached independently of any question of error induced by T's fraud, on the simple ground that the pursuer never intended to deal with T or to transfer any property to him.[58]

14.40   In *Jas Chisholm*[59] the accused was the person to whom a transfer of property in the goods had been contemplated. He had ordered some potatoes, to be paid for on delivery. When the messenger arrived with

---

[55] See also *Janet Lawrie* (1849) Macdonald 33, in which the accused obtained an article from a shop on the pretence that she wanted to show it to her sister for whom she was buying it, and then pawned it: she was convicted of theft.

[56] 1908 S.C. 332. See also *Macleod v. Kerr,* 1956 S.C. 253.

[57] T.B. Smith, p.816. T. was in fact convicted of theft. See also W.W. McBryde, *The Law of Contract in Scotland* (Edinburgh, 1987), para. 9–84.

[58] *cf.* 1908 S.C. 332, Lord McLaren at 336–337. Reference should also be made to three other cases which are in themselves indecisive. In *Wm Robertson* (1835) Bell's Notes 18, the accused got possession of goods by pretending he had been sent for them by a tailor, and then appropriated them. He was charged cumulatively with fraud and theft, and the charge of theft was dropped after objection. The case preceded the development of the law of theft in *John Smith* and *Geo. Brown, supra,* and is in any event not authority for the proposition that the charge of theft was irrelevant. In *Sam. Michael* (1842) 1 Broun 472, the accused ordered and took delivery of goods in a false name and character. He was charged with theft and fraud, but the court indicated that they were doubtful of the relevancy of the theft charge, and it was dropped. This case raises the very difficult question of the validity of a contract made with A in the belief that he is B, or at any rate that he is not A, but the question was neither decided nor discussed in *Michael*. In *Brown v. P.F. Dumfries* (1846) Ark. 62, Brown had asked S. for a loan of £20. Just as S was about to hand over four £5 notes his candle went out and he went to relight it. On his return he found Brown with the notes in his hand, and on his asking for them Brown handed over three, claiming he had not received the fourth. When the police were called, Brown handed over the fourth note and said that the whole thing had been a joke. He was charged with stealing £5 from S. who "was about to lend him a larger sum of money, of which the stolen note formed a part." The whole affair was highly peculiar and somewhat of a storm in a teacup and it is not surprising that Brown's conviction for theft was quashed. The ground given by the appeal court was that the loan had been completed and the property in all four notes had passed to Brown before he hid the fourth note. The Crown argument that Brown had never intended to accept the money as an honest loan, an argument inspired by *Wm Barr* (1832) 5 Deas and Anderson 260, *supra,* was rejected. Lord Moncreiff said that there could be no theft as the property had passed, and that there was no proof of any fraudulent intent at the time the loan was requested. This remark cannot, however, be regarded as authority for the proposition that had there been such an original fraudulent intent no property would have passed and there would have been theft. A loan induced by a fraud is still a loan, and a loan of money passes property. Macdonald does not cite this case in this connection at all, but uses it as his authority for the proposition that a man cannot steal his own property: Macdonald, p.16. In any case the facts are too special and the reported opinions too short for the case to be regarded as an authority for any proposition.

[59] (1849) J. Shaw 241.

the potatoes he asked him to deliver them to certain other persons, and promised payment after delivery. The potatoes were delivered as instructed by the accused but no payment was made. Chisholm was charged with stealing each lot of potatoes as it was delivered, as well as with fraud. The theft charge was objected to on the ground that the property in the potatoes had passed to the accused, but the court repelled the objection and held that the passing of property was conditional on payment on delivery, and that in the absence of such payment the potatoes remained the property of the merchant.[60] Whatever one may think of the court's interpretation of the contract, it is clear that the theft charge was upheld on the view that the potato merchant had not consented to pass the property to Chisholm in the circumstances which obtained.

In *Henry Hardinge*[61] the accused pretended to a railway porter that he **14.41** had been sent by G to collect G's luggage, and so induced the porter to hand him the luggage. He was charged alternatively with theft and fraud, and was convicted of theft. There was no question in *Hardinge* of any consent to pass property to the accused, for the railway porter was not the owner of the goods, and had no authority from the owner to dispose of the property in them to anyone. *Hardinge* is authority not for the view that fraud excludes consent to change of ownership, but for the independent proposition that "If a man went to a person in possession of the property of another, and by any false pretext whatever obtained it from the custodier, carried it off, and appropriated it to his own purposes, that was theft",[62] and it is theft simply because it is the appropriation of another's property without his consent.

There remains *Wm Wilson*.[63] Wilson was a retail jeweller who induced **14.42** a wholesaler to send him goods on approval by making false statements and exhibiting business books with false entries purporting to show that he was engaged in a large and genuine business; in fact he systematically pawned the goods he obtained. He was charged with fraud, theft and contraventions of the Debtors (Scotland) Act 1880.

It was argued on Wilson's behalf that a sale on approval passed property, and that accordingly the theft charges were bad. The court did not dispute that a sale on approval could pass property, but they held that where the owner's consent to the passing of the property had been obtained by fraud it was invalid and the goods remained his, so that Wilson's crime was theft. Lord Justice-Clerk Moncreiff said that where goods were obtained by fraud, "that of course could pass no property, because without a legal contract entered into without fraud — which was not the case here — the property in the goods could not pass to the panel. The goods therefore remained the property of [the wholesaler], who had been thus cheated out of them, until they were pawned, and thereby stolen."[64] Lord Craighill went so far as to say that the proposition that property could pass in the circumstances of the case was "almost a contradiction in terms, because it involves this proposition, that goods obtained by falsehood, fraud and wilful imposition, which is

---

[60] At 252. The Crown then accepted a plea of guilty to fraud.
[61] (1863) 4 Irv. 347.
[62] L.J.-C. Inglis at 350–351.
[63] (1882) 5 Couper 48.
[64] At 60–61.

itself a substantive offence, become upon delivery the property of the person to whom they are sent, and exclude the possibility of his commission of the crime of theft."[65]

It might be possible to argue that all that *Wilson* decided was that property could not pass unless there had been a valid consent by the original owner to its passing, and that the question of whether the consent in any case was valid was a question for the law of contract,[66] but the judgments in *Wilson* are so widely framed as to make it clear that the court was of opinion that no fraudulently-induced consent could ever be valid.

It is difficult to understand the attitude of the court in *Wilson* particularly as the House of Lords had clearly laid down only three years earlier that a person who obtained goods by fraud acquired a property in them which he could pass to a bona fide third party, although the goods could be recovered from the cheat before they had been transferred to the third party. As Lord Chancellor Cairns said in the case in question, *Tennent v. City of Glasgow Bank,*[67] "a contract induced by fraud is not void, but only voidable at the option of the party defrauded; . . . this does not mean that the contract is void till ratified, but that the contract is valid till rescinded."[68]

The proposition regarded by Lord Craighill as almost contradictory in terms is accepted by Hume, Burnett and Alison.[69] Hume himself cites a case similar to *Wilson* as an example of fraud: *Thos Hall,*[70] and indeed the "long-firm fraud" has always been regarded as fraud, and not as theft: *Wilson* stands alone among reported cases in holding that it is theft to obtain the ownership of goods by fraud. *Wilson* would turn every fraudulent appropriation into a theft, and however reasonable this might be it is not the law of Scotland. It conflicts with the principle that theft and fraud are different crimes, and that their difference lies in this, that "in the one case, the proprietor has agreed to transfer the property, therefore he has only been *imposed upon* in the transfer; in the other, he has never agreed to part with his property, and therefore the subsequent appropriation is theft."[71] Furthermore, if *Wilson* is correct in equating theft with fraud, all goods fraudulently appropriated bear a *vitium reale* so that a bona fide third party can never obtain a good title to them, and this is inconsistent with the principle that some fraudulent contracts are only voidable and not void; unless one is to say that theft for the purposes of the law of *vitium reale* has a different meaning from theft in the criminal law, which would introduce a new and unnecessary confusion into the law.

---

[65] At 62.

[66] A view supported by the version of Lord Moncreiff's judgment in the report at 19 S.L.R. 772, 774, where he is reported as saying: "Now, there was not here any legal contract, and the property therefore could not pass."

[67] (1879) 6 R. (H.L.) 69, 70.

[68] Whether fraud can ever render a contract void and not merely voidable in Scots law on the ground that the error induced by the fraud is "essential" is a very difficult question: see T.B. Smith, Chap. 37, but it is clear that where the error induced by the fraud is of the kind present in *Wilson*, an error as to the financial standing of a party, it could never render a contract void: *cf.* Bell's Principles, para. 11; *Stewart v. Kennedy* (1890) 17 R. (H.L.) 25, Lord Watson at 28–29. See also W.W. McBryde, *The Law of Contract in Scotland* (Edinburgh, 1987), Chaps 9 and 10.

[69] Hume, i, 68–69; Burnett, p.114; Alison, i, 250, 259, 261. The proposition that a person who obtains property by a fraud which renders the contract voidable is not a thief is also supported by the most recent civil case on the subject: *MacLeod v. Kerr*, 1965 S.C. 253.

[70] (1789) Hume, i, 172.

[71] Alison, i, 259.

It is accordingly submitted that *Wilson* was wrongly decided and should be overrruled, if an opportunity of doing so ever arises.[72]

VOID CONTRACTS. There remains the possibility of a fraud which goes **14.43** so to the heart of the contract as to vitiate completely the apparent consent to the transfer of ownership. In such a case there would be no consent, and any subsequent appropriation might be theft. Whether or not a contract is void and not merely voidable for error does not, however, depend on whether the error was fraudulently induced, but on whether the error however made, is what is sometimes called "essential error",[73] and this is a question for the law of contract whose decision on the matter the criminal law would probably follow.[74] Unfortunately the law of contract is far from clear on this point, and it is not even clearly settled that any error can render a contract void in Scots law.[75]

There are no Scots criminal cases which deal with this question, but the sort of situation which might arise can be illustrated by reference to an English case. In *Cundy v. Lindsay*[76] a man called Blenkarn sent an order for goods to the plaintiffs representing that he was Blenkiron & Co., a reputable firm which had an office in the same street as that in which he lived. The plaintiffs sent him the goods under the impression that they were sending them to Blenkiron & Co. Blenkarn sold the goods to the defendants who took them bona fide. The plaintiffs were held entitled to recover the goods on the ground that their contract with Blenkarn was void and had accordingly given him no title which he could pass to the defendants. If *Cundy v. Lindsay* were to be accepted in Scotland, a person in the position of Blenkarn could perhaps be charged with stealing the goods, but it is unlikely that such a charge would in practice be brought. The charge would be fraud, because the facts clearly disclose a fraud, and such a charge would avoid any difficulties about the existence of a contract.[77]

A parallel situation arises where an over-payment is made to A in **14.44** error and A retains this payment in the knowledge of the error. Whether A is guilty of theft depends on whether it can be said that the payer

---

[72] It is unlikely to arise since in practice *Wilson* is not followed, and it is contrary to the civil case of *MacLeod v. Kerr, supra.* See also *Young v. D.S. Dalgleish & Son (Hawick)*, 1994 S.C.L.R. 696 (Sh.Ct), in which *MacLeod v. Kerr* was followed. *Cf. O'Neill v. Chief Constable of Strathclyde Police*, 1994 S.C.L.R. 253 (Sh.Ct), where a contract of barter was declared void since the rogue had offered a stolen car in exchange, and the view was taken that such a contract is void if one of the parties is to receive property of which he cannot become the owner.

[73] Bell's Principles, para. 11; *Stewart v. Kenedy* (1890) 17 R. (H.L.) 25.

[74] But see the observations of L.P. Clyde in *MacLeod v. Kerr, supra,* at 255–256. In that case B advertised a car for sale and A, using a false name, answered the advertisement and bought the car with a stolen cheque; he thereafter sold the car to an innocent third party from whom B unsuccessfully sought to recover it. The contract in *MacLeod* was only voidable, so that Lord Clyde's observations on the position where the contract is held to be void are *obiter*, and the case in any event is not technically binding on the High Court. Lord Clyde's view appears to be that where A pretends to be X so as to induce B to enter into a contract with him which is void for essential error as to identity, A is not guilty of theft, provided B intended to transfer property in the article, although in fact since the contract is void no property is transferred. If Lord Clyde is correct there is no theft in Scotland in the *Cundy v. Lindsay* situation, *infra*, although there is no contract either. See also Scottish Law Commission Memorandum No. 27.

[75] See T.B. Smith, Chap. 37; W.W. McBryde, *The Law of Contract in Scotland* (Edinburgh, 1987), Chaps 9 and 10. But see *MacLeod v. Kerr, supra.*

[76] (1878) 3 App. Cas. 459. See also *Morrisson v. Robertson*, 1908 S.C. 332, *supra; MacLeod v. Kerr, supra.*

[77] See n.72, *supra.*

intended him to receive the money he did receive. In *Moynes v. Coopper*[78] for example, a wages clerk gave A a pay envelope containing more than A was entitled to; A discovered the mistake but kept all the money in the packet. A's guilt here depends on whether one is to say that the employer through his clerk intended to transfer to A the contents of the envelope in which case there is no theft, or intended to give A the wages he was due in which case A is guilty of theft.[79]

There is one old Scots case whose facts are similar to those in *Moynes v. Coopper* but the question of the effect of error was not considered by the court. It is *Robert Potter*.[80] It was alleged that Potter had gone into a bank, or sent someone in on his behalf, to cash a bill for £120, and that the bank clerk had miscalculated the amount due and paid over £1,053. Potter was charged with theft of the overpayment and this charge was held relevant, but the only question argued was whether it would still have been theft had the money been given to someone on Potter's behalf and handed by him to Potter some time later, a question the court answered affirmatively. It was conceded that had Potter himself received the parcel of money from the bank and retained it he would have been guilty of theft. The reason for the concession is not given, and in view of the concession the case cannot be regarded as authority for the proposition that the retention of an overpayment is theft. Macdonald regards such a retention as theft, by analogy with theft by finding,[81] and that is the position where the error is such as to vitiate any intention to transfer property in the money handed over to A. But suppose the error is not such as to vitiate this intention, and property is transferred to A. In such a case the overpayer may have a civil remedy, but it is difficult to see what crime A has committed. The court in *Potter* also held a charge of fraudulently retaining the overpayment to be relevant and no doubt felt that such retention was dishonest and ought to be criminal, but there is no other authority for saying that it is criminal to take advantage of an uninduced error.[82]

The whole subject of error is of great interest and also of great confusion, and belongs to the civil law of contract and restitution.[83] So far as the law of theft is concerned it is sufficient to say that where the error is such as to vitiate an apparent consent to the transfer of property by B to A, A's appropriation of the goods may be theft, although it would not normally be so charged, but where the error does not have this effect A is not guilty of theft since he cannot steal goods the property in which has been transferred to him, whether or not in error, and whether or not the error has been fraudulently induced by him.

---

[78] [1956] 1 Q.B. 439.

[79] The question which troubled the English courts — that A's intention to keep the over-payment was not contemporaneous with his taking the money — does not arise in Scotland.

[80] (1844) 2 Broun 151.

[81] At p.31. Similarly, Anderson, p.177.

[82] An overpayment made under a factual error or an error as to general law may, however, be recovered by civil process: *Morgan Guaranty Trust Co. of N.Y. v. L.R.C.*, 1995 S.C. 151, over-ruling *Glasgow Corporation v. Lord Advocate*, 1959 S.C. 203.

[83] See, *e.g.* T.B. Smith, Chap. 37; A.L. Goodheart, "Mistake as to Identity in the Law of Contract" (1941) 57 L.Q.R. 228; *R. v. Middleton* (1873) 2 C.C.R. 38; *Russell v. Smith* [1958] 1 Q.B. 27; *Ingram v. Little* [1961] 1 Q.B. 31; *Lewis v. Averay* [1972] 1 Q.B. 198.

Consent must be to permanent appropriation[84]

It is implicit in the principles already discussed that the only consent **14.45** with which the law of theft is concerned is a consent by an owner to transfer property in his goods to A. If a person leaves his watch lying unguarded in the expectation that A will come and take it and be caught *in flagrante delicto*, he has not consented to A's appropriation of the watch; *a fortiori* there is no consent if the owner has merely failed to look after his goods properly and left them where they are a temptation to any potential thief.[85] It is accordingly undisputed that a theft can be committed under the eye of a police officer, owner or anyone else, who stands by and waits for the theft to be completed before intervening to arrest the thief.[86] A distinction appears to be drawn in England between passively allowing a theft to take place and actively assisting in the theft. As Lord Goddard put it in *R. v. Turvey*,[87] if an owner says to his servant who has been approached with a request for assistance from the thief " 'Let [the appellant] come in and take the goods' that would have been one thing, but he was told to take the goods and hand them to [the appellant], and that makes all the difference."[88] In *R. v. Chandler*,[89] however, the accused was convicted of theft where the owner's servant gave him the key he had asked for, and then told the police. This is, of course, quite different from the situation where the whole theft is initiated by the police who obtain the key from the owner and give it to an informer who then solicits the thief to break in — in such a case it would probably be held in Scotland as it was in Canada that there should be no conviction for theft.[90]

Macdonald cites a case in 1862 in which the lessees of a theatre employed a detective to act as a check-taker in order to trap other check-takers who were suspected of stealing money handed to them. The other employees were ultimately convicted of the theft of money taken

---

[84] Where the *actus reus* of theft is satisfied by conduct which deprives the owner of the use of his property on a temporary basis (as in *Carmichael v. Black; Carmichael v. Penrice*, 1992 S.C.C.R. 709 — see para. 14.10, *supra*), it ought to follow that the owner's consent to such temporary deprivation will elide theft, at least in so far as the accused does no more than, for example, immobilise a car at the exact spot where it had been left by its owner. If this is correct, then such consent would be an exception to the stated orthodox rule — an exception which is applicable perhaps only to the sort of unusual situation which pertained in *Carmichael v. Black*.

The issue of consent was not explored by the court in that case: two of the judges (Lords Allanbridge and Cowie at pp. 721C–D and 722B respectively) considered that the charge in question was truly one of theft by finding — which would appear to make consent an irrelevant issue; but the notice which the accused applied to car windscreens allegedly contained the assertion that "having parked . . . and having seen the notice [*i.e.* the notice displayed in the car park] you [*i.e.* the owners] have consented to the risk of immobilisation and the levy of £45 for release." The difficult issue of implied consent was, therefore, a possible argument for the accused at their subsequent trial; but the matter is further complicated in that the theft charges, unlike the alternative charges of extortion, made no mention of any windscreen notices, although these were referred to in a joint minute of agreed facts lodged by one of the accused at the appeal on relevancy. All of this underlines that *Carmichael v. Black* is a difficult case to reconcile with the authorities which preceeded it, and suggests that it may be a decision which at least in some respects is confined to its own unusual facts.

[85] Macdonald, p.19; *cf.* Hume, i, 63.
[86] Macdonald, p.19; *Wm Vair* (1835) Bell's Notes 14.
[87] (1946) 31 Cr.App.R. 154, 157.
[88] See also *R. v. Miller and Page* (1965) 59 Cr.App.R. 241.
[89] [1913] 1 K.B. 125.
[90] *R. v. Lemieux* [1967] S.C.R. 492.

with the connivance of this detective. It is submitted that Macdonald is correct in stating that, "A person . . . may . . . employ another to obtain the confidence of the thief, pretending to join in his crime, and so secure proof of guilt" without being held to have consented to the thief's crime.[91] But Macdonald is talking in the context of the above case, and he goes on to say, "It often occurs that when police-officers see a theft about to be committed, they wait until it has been completed, but it has never been maintained that the offence on that ground ceases to be theft." The Scots position on the distinction taken in England must be regarded as still unsettled, but the requirement of consent to *permanent* appropriation supports the view that there is always theft, subject perhaps to an independent defence of entrapment in appropriate cases.[92]

There may, however, be cases in which an owner genuinely wishes his goods to be stolen. Suppose that B, who is short of money, owns a valuable picture for which he has no liking but which is heavily insured. If B employs A to steal the picture, and is willing to let A keep the picture as his share of the bargain, then although A may be guilty art and part of defrauding the insurance company, he will not be guilty of theft since he will have obtained the picture with the owner's consent. The situation would be otherwise if B had agreed with A that he should secretly recover the picture from him, and A failed to honour the bargain — but in that case A's theft would consist in his failure to return the picture and not in his original taking of it.[93]

The consent must be that of the owner

14.46 It is also implicit in the preceding discussion that the only relevant consent is that of the owner, or at least of someone entitled to transfer property in the goods. Where B's goods are in C's hands, it is theft to appropriate them with C's consent, unless C is empowered by B to transfer property in the goods, or the situation is one in which the law gives C a right to transfer property in the goods, as where C is a mercantile agent,[94] and A takes the goods bona fide.

Where A wrongly believes that C is the owner of the goods or is empowered to transfer property in them, an *actus reus* of theft will be created, but A will be entitled to rely on his error as a defence.[95]

It was formerly the practice in Scotland to aver that the goods were at the time of the theft "the property of or in the lawful possession of", or

---

[91] Macdonald, p.19. But see *R. v. Miller and Page* (1965) 49 Cr.App.R. 241.

[92] On which again there is no authority.

[93] In the case of *Kay and Strain*, High Court at Glasgow, May 1952, unrep'd, F. pretended to enter into a conspiracy with the accused to steal Mrs. F.'s coat and make a claim on the insurance company. F. then arranged with the police to catch the accused in the act of removing the coat. The accused were charged with the theft of the coat and with an attempted conspiracy to defraud. As the coat was Mrs. F.'s there was no difficulty in obtaining a conviction for theft, there being no defence pled that the accused believed F. had authority to deal with his wife's property. Had the coat been F.'s there would still have been a theft, since F. only pretended to agree to the accused taking the coat, but the accused might have successfully pleaded that they believed they were acting with F.'s approval. If, however, F. had been a genuine conspirator and the coat had been his, there would have been no theft at all, but only a conspiracy to defraud.

[94] See Factors Act 1889; Sale of Goods Act 1979, ss. 24, 25. See also Hire-Purchase Act 1964, Pt III, as substituted by Consumer Credit Act 1974, Sched. 4, in relation to motor-cars.

[95] *cf.* Gl. Williams, "Mistake as to Quantity in the Law of Larceny" [1958] Crim.L.R. 221, and J.C. Smith, "Larceny and False Pretences", *ibid.*, p.92.

even just "in the possession of",[96] the person from whom they were stolen. This averment has not been in use since 1887,[97] but even before then it was of no significance except as giving notice to the accused of the evidence to be led against him regarding the circumstances of the theft. It does not matter to whom the goods belonged at the time of the theft, provided they did not belong to the accused, and it matters not at all from whose possession they were taken, nor indeed, as has been shown,[98] whether they were "taken" from anyone's possession at all. It is the owner, and not the possessor, who is protected by the Scots law of theft. It is theft for A to take from B goods which B himself has stolen from C: in such a case A has stolen from C just as much as B has, and just as much as if he had taken the property out of C's hands, or had found it lying in the street where C had dropped it accidentally.[99] The situation is essentially the same as that in which B finds goods and hands them to A so that A may trace and return them to the owner, but A instead appropriates the goods himself, in which case A is clearly guilty of theft.[1] The only difference between taking goods in someone's lawful possession, and taking goods already stolen, is that where the goods are taken from a prior thief with his consent the crime of the second taker is not theft but reset.

A difficult issue relates to cases where the owner is a corporation. It is trite law that a corporation, such as a limited liability company, has a separate persona from the shareholders and directors, and that the corporation as such is capable of owning property. A corporation can, therefore, be the victim of theft — provided it has not consented to the appropriation. But if those who control it, *e.g.* the board of directors, dishonestly authorise the appropriation of some or all of the company's property to their personal use, it would appear that the owner has consented and that there can be no theft.[2] *A fortiori*, there would be no theft where the company in question has the minimum number of directors required by law and those directors are also the shareholders. There seems little difference between the directors' acts and those of the company in such circumstances. In England, an opposite view was taken by the Court of Appeal in *Attorney-General's Reference (No. 2 of 1982)*,[3] and this is now the favoured view there.[4]

But the English law of theft does not require an appropriation to be "without the consent of the owner",[5] so that there can be appropriation in England even where the owner has consented.[6] The matter can then be determined as theft or not according to whether the appropriation was dishonest or not.[7] This argument is not open in Scotland, and it

---

[96] *Eliz. Beggs or Tonner* (1846) Ark. 215.

[97] See Criminal Procedure (Scotland) Act 1887, Sched. A, and now 1995 Act, Scheds 2 and 5.

[98] *supra*, para. 14.07 *et seq.*

[99] *John Smith* (1838) 2 Swin. 28, Lord Cockburn at 57; *cf. Sam. Wood and Agnes Marshall* (1842) Bell's Notes 23; *Eliz. Beggs or Tonner, supra*; Macdonald, p.17.

[1] *Blackies v. Gair* (1859) 3 Irv. 425, L.J.-C. Inglis at 431. Lord Neaves' remark at 430 that, "It is at least very doubtful whether one thief can steal from another" is somewhat ambiguous, he does not steal from the other thief, but from the owner.

[2] See *McHugh and Tringham* (1988) 88 Cr. App.R. 385.

[3] [1984] Q.B. 624.

[4] See J.C. Smith, *The Law of Theft* (7th ed., London, 1993) at p.31 (para. 2-49); Smith and Hogan, pp. 531–533.

[5] See Theft Act 1968, s.1(1).

[6] See *R. v. Gomez* [1993] A.C. 442; *R. v. Hinks* [2000] 3 W.L.R. 1590, HL.

[7] See Theft Act 1968, s.2(1)(b).

seems unlikely that theft can be made out under Scots law in such circumstances.

THE MENS REA OF THEFT

The intention to deprive

14.47 *The orthodox rule.* Until the case of *Milne v. Tudhope*,[8] it was thought that the *mens rea* of theft required an intention to deprive the owner permanently of his property and that an intention to deprive temporarily would not do.[9] Macdonald, however, states in the 5th edition that: "The crime is properly one of theft if the owner of the property is clandestinely deprived of possession of it even although the deprivation be temporary, and so the taking of a book to copy its contents for an illegitimate purpose was held to be theft although there might be no intention to retain the book."[10] Until recently, however, Macdonald was not followed, to the extent that in *Kivlin v. Milne*,[11] where a car was taken away without authority and driven about before being abandoned, the appeal court sustained a conviction for theft by finding that an intention to deprive the owner permanently of his vehicle could be inferred from the fact that it was left in a place where the owner was unlikely to discover it by his own investigations. Because theft was thought to be confined to situations where such intention could be proved (or more likely inferred), the courts were moved to invent the crime of "clandestine taking and using" in order to criminalise situations which they thought should be criminal but were not chargeable as theft since no intent to deprive permanently could be shown.[12] A similar reason was thought to underlie the enactment of the statutory offence contained now in section 178 of the Road Traffic Act 1988.[13] In short, unauthorised borrowing of goods was considered to be either no crime at all, or a crime *sui generis*: it was certainly not theft, since there was no intent to deprive permanently.

14.48 *An exception to the orthodox rule.* In *Milne v. Tudhope*,[14] Macdonald's view that intention to deprive temporarily would sometimes suffice for theft[15] was accepted by the sheriff and not challenged on appeal. The

---

[8] 1981 J.C. 53; see para. 14.48, *infra*.

[9] Hume, i, 75 refers to "a purpose of never returning it to the owner". See also Alison, i, 270, where he states that the accused in taking and carrying away goods from the owner must intend "to deprive him of his property" and contrasts that (at 271) with examples of unlawful borrowing for a temporary purpose, which he does not consider to be theft at all — for "we do not admit the *furtum usus* or *possessionis* of the Roman law". See also *Herron v. Best*, 1976 S.L.T. (Sh.Ct.) 80.

[10] At p.20. The authorities relied on by Macdonald are *H.M. Advocate v. Mackenzies* (1913) 7 Adam 189, at 194–195 where there are *obiter* remarks by L.J.-C. Macdonald himself to much the same effect as the statement in his book, save that the taking on a temporary basis appeared to require that there be a nefarious purpose to it; *Dewar* (1777) Burnett 115, where the court apparently refused to recognise as theft the sort of circumstances narrated by Macdonald; and *John Deuchars* (1834) Bell's Notes 20, which, proceeding as it did on a plea of guilty, is of little consequence as an authority. *Cf.* Macdonald (3rd ed.) at p.23; Anderson, p.176.

[11] 1979 S.L.T. (Notes) 2.

[12] See *Strathern v. Seaforth*, 1926 J.C. 100, and paras 15.29 to 15.32, *infra*.

[13] See paras 15.33 to 15.37, *infra*.

[14] 1981 J.C. 53.

[15] See para. 14.47, *supra*.

accused, along with others, had been executing a contract for the extensive renovation of a house owned by the complainer. The complainer had been dissatisfied with the workmanship and required that certain modifications be carried out at no extra cost to himself. The accused then removed articles (such as radiators, doors and glazing units) from the house, partly (as was alleged) out of anger but mainly since he was anxious to secure a personal meeting with the complainer at which he hoped to persuade the complainer to allow him to carry out the extra work on the basis of extra payment for it. The accused was convicted of theft even though it was accepted that he did not intend to keep the articles permanently. The sheriff took the view that in law a clandestine taking, aimed at achieving a nefarious purpose, constituted theft, even if the taker intended all along to return the thing taken when his purpose had been achieved.[16] At the subsequent appeal, Lord Justice-Clerk Wheatley noted that, as that account of the law had not been challenged as incorrect by counsel for the appellant, the sole matter for discussion was the extent to which the facts found showed "clandestinity" and a "nefarious" purpose. With respect to the former, the Lord Justice-Clerk held that a clandestine taking meant simply that the removal of the property had been secret so far as the owner was concerned[17] — however "open" it might otherwise have been; and, with respect to the latter, that holding goods to ransom after they had been taken without authority constituted a "nefarious purpose", and that it did not matter for the purposes of the case whether nefarious meant "criminal" or "unlawful", since the conduct of the accused was both criminal (as extortion) and unlawful. Perhaps the most significant point to emerge from the case, however, was that intention to appropriate permanently was still regarded as the orthodox *mens rea* for theft: it was only in exceptional circumstances that an intent to deprive temporarily of possession was acceptable.[18]

The exception becomes the rule? Subsequent cases give the impression **14.49** that the type of *mens rea* accepted by default in *Milne v. Tudhope*[19] was a legitimate alternative to an intent to deprive permanently although, of course, it had never been discussed or debated at appeal court level at all. Thus, for example, the jury was directed by Lord Stewart in *Sandlan v. H.M. Advocate*[20] that the temporary removal and concealment of (*inter alia*) jewellery as part of a fraudulent scheme[21] was a nefarious purpose and sufficiently secret to be clandestine, and that that was what was required to constitute this "rather unusual" type of theft. The slightly later case of *Kidston v. Annan*[22] was similar to that of *Milne v. Tudhope* save that the accused was given possession of the property (a television set) but refused to return it unless the cost of repairs (which

---

[16] 1981 J.C. 53, at 55. Macdonald's textbook rule (see para. 14.47, *supra*) and L.J.-C. Macdonald's *obiter dictum* in *H.M. Advocate v. Mackenzies* (1913) 7 Adam 189 at 194–195, were referred to as the sheriff's main authorities.

[17] 1981 J.C. 53, at 57.

[18] Perhaps it is also significant, if not prophetic, that the advocate-depute at the appeal argued that the facts showed either an intention to deprive permanently or an intention to deprive *indefinitely*. See para. 14.50, *infra*.

[19] See para. 14.48, *supra*.

[20] 1983 S.C.C.R. 71.

[21] On the assumption that there had been such a scheme, which was not accepted by one of the accused.

[22] 1984 S.C.C.R. 20.

had not been authorised) was first met. Lord Justice-General Emslie had
no difficulty in finding that this was a case of "holding goods to
ransom"[23] just as in the earlier case. There was, however, no taking —
clandestinely or otherwise: nor was "clandestinity" involved in the facts
found at the trial. Finally, in *Carmichael v. Black; Carmichael v.
Penrice*,[24] Lord Justice-General Hope stated: "It has been held, in a
case[25] where there was undoubtedly amotio . . . that an intention to
deprive an owner permanently of his property is not essential to the
crime and accordingly that an intention to deprive temporarily will
suffice."[26] The theft charge in that case was couched in simple terms and
made no mention of any purpose (nefarious or otherwise) that the
accused may have had in immobilising the complainer's motor-car. It is
plain that the absence of such a purpose was not regarded as important
by the court. As Lord Justice-General Hope put it, in the course of the
Crown appeal against a finding that such a theft charge was irrelevant:
"The appropriation in that case [*Kidston v. Annan*] was for an unlawful
purpose, which amounted in effect to extortion. But the libel of the
charges in the present case does not state that it was the intention to
hold the car to ransom for payment of a sum of money or for any other
purpose whether temporary or otherwise. The proposition is simply that
it was theft to detain the vehicle with the intention of depriving the
motorist of the use of it, albeit temporarily, against his will."[27] It was that
proposition which the appeal court seems to have accepted as a correct
statement of the law; and if that is so, then an intention to deprive the
complainer temporarily of his possessory rights in property is sufficient
for theft. Indeed, one might go further and conclude that such an
intention is now the minimum level of *mens rea* — and that an intention
to deprive the owner permanently of his property is sufficient but no
longer necessary. Whilst that latter proposition is almost certainly correct
in the modern law,[28] it is open to doubt whether a bare intention to
deprive temporarily will suffice. The cases which favour a temporary
intent to deprive have all on their facts involved a "nefarious" purpose,
whether that purpose be extortion or fraud[29]; and such judicial authority
as has ever been quoted in favour of the acceptance of an intention to
deprive temporarily apparently requires there to be a "nefarious" or
illegitimate purpose behind such an intention.[30]

---

[23] *ibid.*, at 23.

[24] 1992 S.C.C.R. 709.

[25] The case was, of course, *Milne v. Tudhope*, 1981 J.C. 53.

[26] *ibid.*, at 719B. It is not significant that in the former case there was amotio, since the
same rule was applied in the instant case, where there was no amotion of the property at
all.

[27] 1992 S.C.C.R. 709, at 719C.

[28] *cf.* R.A.A. McCall Smith and D. Sheldon, *Scots Criminal Law* (2nd ed., Edinburgh,
1997), at pp. 256–257 where the authors argue in favour of the traditional view that the
mens rea of theft is an intention to deprive the owner permanently of this goods.

[29] *Milne v. Tudhope*, 1981 J.C. 53 (extortion); *Sandlan v. H.M. Advocate*, 1983 S.C.C.R.
71 (fraud); *Kidston v. Annan*, 1984 S.C.C.R. 20 (extortion); *Carmichael v. Black;
Carmichael v. Penrice*, 1992 S.C.C.R. 709 (extortion — since although the appeal
proceeded as a matter of relevancy, a joint minute of agreement revealed that the
unauthorisedly parked car had been immobilised and a notice attached to it stating that it
would not be released until a sum of money had been paid; in addition, the primary
charge, which the appeal court upheld as relevant, was one of extortion).

[30] See *H.M. Advocate v. Mackenzies* (1913) 7 Adam 189, L.J.-C. Macdonald at 194–195.

Intention to deprive indefinitely. In *Fowler v. O'Brien*,[31] it became clear **14.50** that there was some confusion, at least in the lower courts, as to the required *mens rea* for theft. The accused had taken away a bicycle after its owner had refused him permission to ride it. He did not return it, and it was some days before the owner was able to retrieve it after receiving a "tip-off". It was difficult to distinguish the facts of this case from those of *Kivlin v. Milne*,[32] save that the latter dealt with a motor vehicle. The district court convicted the accused of theft of the cycle, stating that this was not a case of ordinary temporary deprivation, since the taking was not clandestine and there was no nefarious purpose — the accused not having set any conditions precedent to its return. Indeed it was an exceptional case, in which an intention to deprive temporarily would suffice for conviction. At the subsequent appeal, the advocate-depute supported the conviction on the basis of what was decided in *Kivlin v. Milne*; but the appeal court decided that the case was not one where there was either an intention to deprive permanently or even temporarily — since the accused had indeed not stated when or under what conditions he would return the bicycle. Instead, it was said to be a case where there was an intention to deprive the owner indefinitely. Consequently, it was not necessary to consider the clandestinity of the taking or the purpose of the accused in doing so.

The result is that it is now very difficult to find any principle to which the *mens rea* of theft conforms. It is also very difficult even to describe the various types (for there are clearly several types) of *mens rea* which the courts have identified. There is an intention to deprive the owner permanently of his property — which accords better with the traditional conception of theft[33] than its modern counterpart; there is what might be described as a conditional intention to deprive, where the accused sets some condition which, when or if purified, will limit the complainer's deprivation, although it is uncertain if the condition set must be of any particular type; there is an intention to deprive indefinitely — which differs from the other types of *mens rea* in some unarticulated way[34]; and there may be other exceptional types of acceptable mental element which are as yet unformulated. It clearly does not matter whether the accused profited by his conduct or whether or not he intended to; but if an intention to deprive temporarily does require the accompaniment of a nefarious purpose, then the accused's motives cannot completely be dismissed as irrelevant.[35]

Dishonesty. It is far from certain that "dishonesty" has any part to play in **14.51** the substantive law of theft. If it does have such a part, dishonesty can be regarded simply as a characteristic of appropriation determined objectively from the facts and circumstances.[36] In English law, theft is committed by one who "dishonestly appropriates property belonging to

---

[31] 1994 S.C.C.R. 112.

[32] 1979 S.L.T. (Notes) 2; see para. 14.47, *supra*.

[33] See para. 14.01, *supra*.

[34] McCall Smith and Sheldon, *op. cit.*, at pp.256–257, regard the distinction between it and an intention to deprive permanently as linguistic only.

[35] *cf.* Hume, i, 75–76; Alison, i, 273–274; Burnett, pp.115–116; Macdonald, p.20.

[36] See para. 14.23, *supra*.

another",[37] but dishonesty is regarded as a *mens rea* element.[38] There
may be a similar development at common law in Scotland, since in
Kane v. Friel[39] Lord Justice-General Rodger, in narrating that the
advocate-depute had accepted that it was for him to prove that the
appropriation had been dishonest, concluded that what that meant was
that the Crown had to prove that the "intention must have been to
appropriate the items dishonestly."[40] In the context of that case, it may
be that dishonesty meant knowledge that items which had been found
were "property that someone intended to retain" — a matter of
reasonable inference from the value and condition of the property, and
the circumstances in which it had been found. But it seems impossible to
suggest any more definite significance for "dishonesty" other than its
context-related effect on the interpretation of the facts and circumstances.[41] It is thought, however, that its use[42] is likely to be confined to
the more marginal cases of theft, where the view might be taken that
prosecution had been unjustified. Where, for example, an office worker
unauthorisedly borrows from the petty cash to pay for a taxi so that he
may visit his sick child in hospital, he is technically guilty of theft; but if
he intended to replace the money, and was in a position to do so, his
case might turn on the issue of his dishonesty.

Error in theft

14.52   The law of error applies to theft as it does to all common law crimes,
but error in theft has certain special features because theft requires
intention to appropriate property, probably "dishonestly" and certainly
without the owner's consent. It is, generally speaking, not theft for A to
take goods to which he believes himself entitled, and an erroneous belief
that he is entitled to take goods may take one of four forms. It may be
an error as to the identity of the goods, an error as to whether the owner
has consented to A's having the goods, an erroneous belief that A is the
lawful owner of the particular goods, or an erroneous belief that A's
actings are not unlawful.

14.53   (a) *Error as to identity.* It is clearly not theft if A takes B's coat because
he mistakes it for his own. It is, however, probably theft if A takes B's
coat knowing that it might be B's and intending to keep it whether it

---

[37] Theft Act 1968, s.1(1).

[38] *R. v. Ghosh* [1982] Q.B. 1053, CA, Lord Lane C.J. at 1064A. The other *mens rea*
element is "the intention of permanently depriving the other of it"; Theft Act 1968, s.1(1).

[39] 1997 S.C.C.R. 207.

[40] *ibid.*, 209G.

[41] In *R. v. Ghosh* [1982] Q.B. 1053, CA, a two-part test is laid down for English law:
first, it is necessary to determine (objectively) whether what the defendant did was
dishonest according to the standards of reasonable and honest people; if the conduct was
dishonest by those standards, then secondly, the question lies whether the defendant
himself must have realised that what he was doing was dishonest by the standards of
reasonable and honest people. If he did know that, then he meets the dishonesty
requirements — even though he might genuinely believe himself justified in the action he
took.

[42] See, *e.g.*, *Mackenzie v. Maclean*, 1981 S.L.T. (Sh.Ct) 40, where in effect the theft
consisted in selling to the public damaged beer cans which the accused had been instructed
to throw away; the sums obtained were small, were probably not solicited, and were
probably devoted to "acceptable" purposes.

turns out to be B's or his own,[43] although there is no authority on the question.[44]

(b) *Error as to consent.* It is equally clearly not theft if A wrongly, but **14.54** (probably) reasonably, believes that B has consented to his having the goods. As Macdonald puts it, "if the person takes, believing that what he is taking is his own, or that he has the owner's concurrence, he is not guilty of theft."[45] So, for example, if A is employed as a salesman and given goods to sell on behalf of B, it is theft for him to sell any goods which may remain in his hands after his appointment has been terminated,[46] but it would not be theft if A reasonably believed that he was entitled, in terms of his contract of employment, to sell these goods and retain the proceeds against any commission or salary due to him by B. It is probably now the law that a reasonable but mistaken belief that the owner (or any other person having power to do so) did consent to what one did with the property, or would have so consented had he known of the circumstances, will provide a defence.

Recklessness is probably a sufficient *mens rea* in this connection.[47]

(c) *Claim of right.* Errors as to the identity of the goods or the consent **14.55** of the owner are essentially errors of fact. The defence of claim of right arises where A is aware of the true identity of the goods and knows that the person who presently has them is not prepared to consent to his obtaining them, but believes that he has a legal right to them. The defence of claim of right may of course arise where A is correct in his belief as to his legal rights, but it may also arise where A's belief has been arrived at because of an error of law in interpreting the situation. There is hardly any Scots authority on claim of right, erroneous or otherwise, but the typical claim of right case is one where A wrongly believes that on a proper interpretation of a will, or the proper operation of the laws of intestacy, the property in question belongs to him.

It is difficult to say how extensive the scope of this defence is in Scots law, and in particular it is difficult to say whether it applies only where A believes the goods are at the time of the taking his legal property, or

---

[43] See Vol. I, paras 7.65 and 9.03.

[44] A different situation arises where A intends to steal *x* and in error steals *y* instead, where neither *x* nor *y* belong to him. Suppose that A breaks into B's house knowing that B has a particular jewel of special value, but takes another jewel which he mistakes for the valuable one, he would probably be convicted of theft on the ground that what he intended to steal was the object he took, and his error as to its nature, quality or value is irrelevant. It might be argued that if A went to B's house for the sole purpose of stealing the valuable jewel his error would be relevant but it is unlikely that this argument would be accepted. Suppose now that the valuable jewel is in a closed box which A cannot open until he gets away from the house, and he takes the wrong box, or the box happens at the time to contain some other article and not the desired jewel. It is misleading to say just that "removal of a box . . . completes the theft of its contents": Macdonald, p.24; Anderson, p.177; it does not, it completes only the removal of its contents. If A takes the box intending to appropriate whatever may be in it he is guilty of stealing whatever is in it, whether or not he hoped it to contain a particular thing: Hume, i, 76. But if his only purpose was to steal the particular jewel, and he returns the box and its contents when he discovers his mistake, it certainly used to be arguable that there was no theft at all; but now that a temporary deprivation of another's property is sufficient for theft, he would probably be convicted of stealing the box and sentenced according to what was in it, without much discussion of the matter. *Cf. R. v. Easom* [1971] 2 Q.B. 315.

[45] Macdonald, p.18. See also *Dewar v. H.M. Advocate*, 1945 J.C. 5, L.J.-C. Cooper at 8.

[46] Macdonald, p.36; *Alex. Mitchell* (1874) 3 Couper 77.

[47] See Vol. I, para. 7.65.

whether it is enough that he believes he has a legal right to have them transferred to him.

Hume quotes a number of very old cases dealing with disputes regarding property which may be said to indicate that a belief that one is entitled to the goods is sufficient[48] but, as Alison says, "the change of manners has rendered them now rather matter of curiosity than use."[49] Hume also states that, "If John carry off James's goods by a poinding, here, however irregular soever the diligence, nay, though John's proceedings be unconscientious even and oppressive, still the taking in this form can never infer theft . . . but at most a spulzie only or oppression."[50] This, however, is rather a different point. The defence here is not that John believed he was entitled to the goods, indeed if he was acting oppressively he may have lacked such a belief, but simply that the taking of the goods was not unlawful, since it proceeded on a warrant of court. In such a case the crime does not consist in the execution of the warrant, but in the oppressive means used to obtain it.

14.56 The case which is usually regarded as the leading case on claim of right is *Ker and Stables*,[51] but it is not helpful. It appears that Ker had quarrelled with his brother about the distribution of their father's estate, and had carried off certain articles without his brother's consent. He was charged with theft and pleaded that he believed he was entitled to the articles, and had merely chosen to go and carry them off rather than take legal proceedings to recover them. The court agreed to a form of verdict which acquitted the accused on the ground that there was "no sufficient evidence that the articles he carried away were the property" of his brother.[52] The jury included in their verdict a finding that Ker was "highly culpable", and this suggests that Ker acted wrongly in taking the law into his own hands, but, because of his belief that what he was taking was rightfully his, did not act dishonestly. *Ker* may, therefore, be authority for the view that it is not theft for A to take goods from B in the belief that B is under a legal duty to transfer them to him, although it may amount to some other crime.[53]

The only other reported case on claim of right is *John Sanders*[54] where A took articles which had belonged to his deceased sister, and pleaded in his defence that he believed that he, and not the sister's children, was her lawful heir, a defence which was held relevant but rejected by the jury.

14.57 (d) *Entitlement*. In claim of right the accused proceeds on his view of the legal effect of a particular situation which he believes makes him the true legal owner of the goods. What is here called the defence of "entitlement" arises where A's error is more general and consists in believing merely that his behaviour is not unlawful. Such a belief is offered as a defence on the ground that it shows that his actings were not "felonious" or that they lacked "theftuous intention"; it may co-exist with knowledge that the original owner of the goods has not consented to A's appropriation.

---

[48] Hume, i, 74.
[49] Alison, i, 271–272.
[50] Hume, i, 73–74.
[51] (1792) Burnett 118; see Hume, i, 73; Alison, i, 271.
[52] Burnett, p.118.
[53] *infra*, para. 15.46.
[54] (1833) Bell's Notes 20.

The case of *Fraser v. Anderson*[55] falls partly into this category and partly into the category of claim of right. The facts were that A sold some heifers to B on the 16th of the month, payment to be made into A's bank account within a few days. The heifers, which had become B's property on the 16th, were left with A for grazing. B in fact paid the price on the 22nd, but A did not know this and he resold the cattle on the 28th. He was convicted of theft but his conviction was quashed on appeal on the ground that the facts found by the sheriff did not make it clear that he had acted with felonious intent. The view of the High Court was that if A believed he was entitled to sell the cattle and merely "acted as he did in ignorance of his legal remedy in the circumstances, and that he thought that the money not having reached him, he had a right to proceed to sell the cattle at his own hand" there was no theft.[56]

Dewar v. H.M. Advocate,[57] where a crematorium manager was charged **14.58** with stealing coffin lids, is more complex. Dewar's general line of defence (which was left to the jury by Lord Justice-Clerk Cooper but regarded as irrelevant by the Appeal Court) could be expressed in two ways. One, which is clearly relevant, is that he believed that the original owners of the coffins had made them over to him to do as he pleased with them when they gave them to him for cremation. The other is that because of his belief as to the practice in other crematoria he thought he was entitled to do as he liked with the coffins. This latter was the defence which Lord Moncrieff characterised trenchantly as amounting to the proposition that, "One who has committed a theft claims to be entitled to say that his theft is not to be regarded as theft and is not criminal because it is in constant repetition by others."[58] The defence could be expressed more favourably as being that the accused believed that what he was doing was something he was entitled to do, and that therefore he acted without "felonious intent". The real difficulty about this form of defence is that it involves an error of law of a kind not normally accepted by the courts — a belief that the accused's conduct was not criminal — and can therefore be considered as being as irrelevant as the belief of an English uncle who sleeps with his niece in Scotland that his behaviour is not incestuous, or that of a driver that it is not an offence to drive through an amber light when he could safely stop. But it is arguable that such a defence is relevant in theft in so far as it excludes the felonious intent which is part of the definition of the crime.[59]

The law regarding the defence of entitlement cannot be said to be wholly settled, but *Dewar* at least indicates that the courts will not be sympathetic to such a defence, and it may be confined to cases like *Fraser v. Anderson*[60] where there is some legal dispute between the parties as to their rights in relation to the goods, and where the accused believes that he has some kind of claim to the goods. It will apparently not do for A to say merely that he thought he was acting lawfully

---

[55] (1899) 2 Adam 705.
[56] Lord Kinnear at 709. Lord Adam's dissent was because he thought the sheriff had inferred the existence of felonious intent, while the majority held that the sheriff had not found such an intent and so had failed to justify his verdict.
[57] 1945 J.C. 5.
[58] At 16.
[59] A belief that A's crime constituted fraud or embezzlement and not theft would certainly be irrelevant.
[60] (1899) 2 Adam 705.

because he was following a common practice which he did not regard as dishonest.[61]

It will not, of course, do for an employee who takes money out of the till to say that he thought he was entitled to do so because his employer owed him wages. The claim of right or entitlement must relate to the actual things taken. It must also relate to a legal and not merely a moral claim.[62]

14.59 RECKLESSNESS. There is no authority on whether a recklessly formed belief as to claim of right or legal entitlement is sufficient to exclude guilt.[63]

Necessity

14.60 Necessity of hunger is not generally accepted as a defence to theft[64] although it may be a mitigation. But it is submitted that it is not theft to take B's property in order to save C's life or in order to save a greater amount of property belonging either to B or C.[65] This may be justified by reference to necessity, or to a lack of "felonious intent".

14.61 *Criminal Law (Consolidation) (Scotland) Act 1995.* Section 8(5) of this Act provides that a woman detained in a brothel who takes away any clothes she needs to enable her to leave, or is found with any clothes taken for that purpose, is not liable to any criminal proceedings in respect of her taking or possession thereof.

---

[61] But see *Allenby v. H.M. Advocate*, 1938 J.C. 55, *infra*, para. 17.33. *Cf. Watts and Gaunt v. The Queen* [1953] 1 S.C.R. 505; *R. v. Shymkowich* [1954] S.C.R. 606. In Scots law it appears that this type of belief must be reasonable rather than merely honest; but see Vol. I, paras 9.31 and 9.32. In other systems it is enough that it be honestly held: *e.g. R. v. Turner (No. 2)* [1971] 1 W.L.R. 901; *R. v. Howson* [1966] 3 C.C.C. 348. (Ont.) But see also *Morissette v. U.S.*, 246 (1952).

[62] *cf.* Gl. Williams, p.322; *Harris v. Harrison* [1963] Crim.L.R. 497.

[63] See Vol. I, para. 9.31.

[64] Hume, i, 55.

[65] See Vol. I, para. 13.04.

CHAPTER 15

AGGRAVATED THEFTS AND ALLIED OFFENCES

AGGRAVATED THEFTS

Theft by Housebreaking

Housebreaking is the most common of all aggravations of theft, and **15.01** was at one time sufficient to render any theft capital.[1] Although it is still regarded as an important aggravation, and indeed theft by housebreaking is thought of as almost a distinct crime, the only necessary practical effect of the aggravation is that it takes the crime out of the jurisdiction of the district court.[2]

Housebreaking is an aggravated way of committing theft and accordingly it must precede the theft, and be the means by which the theft is carried out. Where A enters premises without housebreaking, steals something, and then breaks out of the premises, he is not guilty of theft by housebreaking, since the theft was completed before the breaking occurred. Although there is no reported case which can be said to decide this proposition, it is generally accepted as correct,[3] and there is no contrary authority.[4]

Alison states that theft followed by a breaking out of premises is an **15.02** aggravated form of theft, but there are no reported cases in which this aggravation has been sustained.[5]

The meaning of "house". Scots law does not distinguish among different **15.03** types of building, and housebreaking can take place against any roofed building.[6] All that is necessary is that the place "can properly be considered, and in common speech would be called, a house, or a shut and fast building, and not a mere open shed, booth, or temporary place for lumber."[7] Housebreaking can also be committed against an

---

[1] Hume, i, 98.

[2] 1995 Act, s.7(8)(b)(ii).

[3] Alison, i, 288; Macdonald, pp. 29–30; *Edward Kennedy* (1831) Alison, i, 288. *Cf.* Hume, i, 101; *Wm Barclay and Eliz. Temple* (1830) Bell's Notes 39; *Mary Ann Webster* (1831) *ibid.*

[4] Lord Mackenzie remarked in *Christian Duncan* (1849) J. Shaw 225, that breaking out had been held sufficient to constitute housebreaking, but his Lordship decided the contrary in *Edward Kennedy, supra.*

[5] Alison, i, 288.

[6] For example *Jas Donnelly and Wm Wood* (1824) Alison, i, 292: a wash house; *Robt and Martin Macgregor* (1825) *ibid.* and *David Millar and John Macdonald* (1831) Macdonald 24: a church; *Chas. Macdonald* (1826) Alison, i, 292: a stable loft; *John Fraser* (1831) Bell's Notes 41: a henhouse; *Jas Easton and Ors* (1832) *ibid.*: a cellar.

[7] Hume, i, 103. *Cf.* Alison, i, 291; Burnett, p.138.

unfinished building, provided it is roofed and closed up.[8] Where, however, a number of buildings are enclosed in a locked yard, it is not housebreaking to break into the yard, since it is not a building.

15.04 ROOMS SEPARATELY OCCUPIED. Once a house has been entered any forcible entry of rooms inside the house is not housebreaking, but the separate aggravation of opening lockfast places. If A walks into an hotel by an open front door, or is himself a guest in the hotel, and breaks into the locked room occupied by another guest, that is not housebreaking. *A fortiori* if A and B are lodgers in one house, it is not housebreaking for A to break into B's bedroom.[9]

On the other hand, "Where a house is occupied in distinct floors by separate tenants or proprietors, each floor is a separate house; and where a floor is subdivided among different poor persons, who inhabit one or two rooms each, each room is a separate house, and entitled to the protection of such."[10] This rule is intended to cover the common Scots urban tenement (or, where the tenants are of a higher social class, "block of flats") which is entered by a common passage which is often open to the street; but the same rule applies where the passage itself has a locked door. What is important is not that the access to each flat is by a common passage, but that each flat is occupied as a separate dwelling. If A comes through the door of the common passage without housebreaking and then breaks into one of the "flats", that is housebreaking.

There are situations which fall between the case of the hotel and the case of the block of flats. Suppose that a house is let out in rooms to lodgers without being "converted" into a block of flats, that each lodger has a key to the main door and to his own room, that each lodger does his own cooking and cleaning, but that they share a common kitchen and bathroom. It is suggested that in view of the prevalence of this type of arrangement each room should be regarded as a separate dwelling by an extension of the rule regarding the urban tenement in which the various "householders" often share certain amenities. Such a situation can be distinguished from that of the hotel, or the house whose owner "takes in lodgers", by the fact that in the latter cases services are provided by the owner of the building for all the "lodgers" in common.[11]

The question is not of great importance. In practice any doubtful case will probably be charged as theft by opening lockfast places and it is extremely unlikely that objection will be taken on the ground that the charge should have been one of theft by housebreaking.[12]

---

[8] Hume, i, 103; *John Wright and David Johnstone* (1837) Bell's Notes 41. *Cf. John Boax* (1827) Syme 248, where the accused broke into an addition to a house, which was being constructed at the time.

[9] Alison, i, 287; Macdonald, p.25. *Cf.* Hume, i, 101; Burnett, p.138.

[10] Alison, i, 293; *Alex. Cowie* (1824) *ibid.*

[11] In *Christian Duncan* (1849) J. Shaw 225, the accused was charged with breaking into an attic room occupied by a lodger, and the charge was held to be relevant. The Crown argued that the attic door formed the entrance to the lodger's "habitation" and constituted its only safeguard.

[12] See *John Sutherland* (1941) Macdonald 30, which suggests that even if it were taken such an objection would be unsuccessful, on the ground that the Crown are not precluded from charging the minor aggravation, at any rate in doubtful cases.

The meaning of "breaking". "Housebreaking" originally meant what it **15.05** said and involved effraction of the building concerned, but early in its history the term was extended to include what might be called "constructive" housebreaking.[13] Every important case on housebreaking except *Peter Alston and Alex. Forrest*[14] has been decided in favour of the Crown, and constructive housebreaking covers a very wide field indeed. It can probably be said now that any unauthorised entry, other than by an unlocked door or open ground floor window or by turning a key found in a lock, is housebreaking. The original idea of housebreaking as an act of violence[15] has now been wholly departed from. The idea that the aggravation of housebreaking is intended as a protection to careful householders[16] has also been departed from: it is housebreaking to open a locked door with a key which has been left hidden under a stone near the door[17] or even, it is submitted, hanging on a hook near the door.[18] All that is left is the idea of overcoming the security of the building[19] or, as Hume puts it, "the ordinary obstacles provided against entry,"[20] but this can be achieved without any force, and it might be better to speak of "avoiding" the ordinary obstacles to entry. It is housebreaking to enter a house by a way which the householder would not expect to be used, such as a chimney,[21] even if the householder had left his door open so that the thief could have entered by it without housebreaking.

SECURITY. It is not housebreaking to enter by an ordinary opening, **15.06** such as a door which is unsecured. A secured opening is one which is fastened, whether by a lock or in any other way such as, for example, by a bar of wood placed across the inside of a door.[22] In *Ann Mackenzie*[23] the housebreaking was alleged to have consisted in pushing open a door which had been secured by a heavy chest placed against it, but the relevancy of these averments was not decided. Macdonald is probably correct in saying that in such a situation it depends on whether the weight placed against the door was intended merely to prevent it from swinging open, or was intended to secure the door against being pushed open and was heavy enough to require more than an ordinary push to disturb it — *i.e.* on whether the householder relied on it as part of the security of the building.[24] If, of course, the thief were to break the door down and climb over the obstacle, that would be clearly housebreaking. The weight of a door itself might even be sufficient security, particularly if it is placed in a position making it difficult to enter, as where it is a cellar door which lies flat on the roadway.[25]

---

[13] Hume, i, 98; *John Pringle* (1715) Hume, i, 99: use of false keys; *Geo. Robertson* (1672) Hume, i, 100: creeping in at a window.
[14] (1837) 1 Swin. 433.
[15] *cf.* Hume, i, 98.
[16] Hume, i, 98; *Alston and Forrest, supra*, Lord Gillies at 466.
[17] *Alex. Macdonald* (1826) Alison, i, 285; *Alston and Forrest*, L.J.-C. Boyle at 465.
[18] Although this has not been expressly decided: *infra*, para. 15.09.
[19] Alison, i, 282; Macdonald, p.25, where he talks of "violating" the security.
[20] Hume, i, 98.
[21] *Rendal Courtney* (1743) Hume, i, 99.
[22] *John Allan* (1774) Hume, i, 100; *cf. Jas Arcus* (1844) 2 Broun 264. *McIntosh and Murray* (1846) Ark. 133 raised but did not decide the question whether it was housebreaking to enter by opening the shutter or wooden blind on a window.
[23] (1845) 2 Broun 669.
[24] Macdonald, pp. 25–26.
[25] *Angus Sutherland* (1874) 3 Couper 74, which is a rather special case: see *infra*, para. 15.12.

It has been authoritatively decided that a burglar alarm is clearly an integral part of the security of a building, and that to disconnect it constitutes attempted housebreaking.[26]

With respect to other devices such as security lights[27] and surveillance cameras,[28] however, it is a question of fact and circumstance whether they can be accorded the same status as burglar alarms.

15.07   ENTRY. Housebreaking is not committed unless the security of the building is overcome, but the accused need not enter the premises.

It is not housebreaking to break through some external safeguard, so long as the security of the building itself is not overcome. In *Thos. Sinclair and Jas. McLymont*[29] the accused broke a pane of glass in a window and then tried to push up a shutter on the inside of the window. They were charged with breaking the glass with intent to enter and steal, and this charge was held irrelevant, on the ground that the security of the building had not been overcome, since the true protection of the building was provided not by the window but by the shutters. The case was distinguished from *Jas. Monteith*[30] in which a charge of "breaking the door of a House for the purpose of entering and Stealing therefrom" had been upheld on the ground that once the door had been broken there was no further obstacle to entry.[31] More recently, in *McClung v. McLeod*[32] where the accused had broken the windows of the premises but there was no finding that he had entered them, the High Court upheld a conviction for housebreaking with intent to steal, on the ground that the essence of the crime was the violation of the security of the premises.

In a charge of theft by housebreaking it is not necessary to show that A entered the premises himself, but it is necessary to show that he extracted goods by way of the breach he had made.[33] It is theft by housebreaking to break a window and put one's hand or a stick through the gap and take something out.[34]

---

[26] *Burns v. Allan*, 1987 S.C.C.R. 449.

[27] See *Heywood v. Reid*, 1995 S.C.C.R. 741.

[28] *cf. Bett v. Brown*, 1997 S.L.T. 1310, where moving an exterior surveillance camera so that it no longer provided protection for the premises it was meant to serve was charged (unsuccessfully) as malicious mischief. Depending on the precise facts, there seems no particular reason to distinguish a device which provides visual warning from one which provides audible warning of intrusion, and, therefore, no reason in principle why interference with a surveillance camera should not be regarded as an attempt to overcome the security of premises which that camera is intended to protect.

[29] (1864) 4 Irv. 499.

[30] (1840) 2 Swin. 483.

[31] *Sinclair and McLymont, supra,* at 501. In *Monteith, supra,* the indictment libelled attempted housebreaking with intent to steal, as well as the charge of breaking the door for that purpose. The charge of attempted housebreaking was dropped by the Crown because it was regarded as a new crime, but no comment seems to have been made on the relevancy of the alternative charge. Lord Neaves in *Sinclair* seems to have regarded both cases as charges of housebreaking with intent to steal. The circumstances in these cases could now be charged as attempted housebreaking with intent to steal.

[32] (1974) 38 J.C.L. 221.

[33] Hume, i, 101–102; Alison, i, 288–289; Macdonald, p.29.

[34] *Margt Fitton and Ors* (1830) Bell's Notes 39; *W.H. Wightman* (1832) *ibid.; Wm Harvey* (1833) *ibid.; Wm Vair and Anr* (1834) *ibid., cf. Wm. Vair and Ors* (1835) *ibid.; Cornelius O'Neil* (1845) 2 Broun 394. *Cf. Alex. Rose and John Taylor* (1842) 1 Broun 437.

Modes of housebreaking. The following are the most common modes of **15.08**
housebreaking:

(1) By actual effraction of the building. It is housebreaking to force a
door or break through a wall or roof. Housebreaking may also be
committed by breaking the floor or ceiling of an adjoining flat[35] or by
breaking through an inside wall from neighbouring premises.

(2) By using skeleton keys, false keys, or other forms of picklock.[36] It is
probably also housebreaking for A to use a key of his own which
happens also to fit B's lock. Since the key was not meant to be used for
B's lock it can be regarded as analogous to a skeleton key when it is so
used.

(3) By using a stolen key.[37]

(4) By using a found key. Where a key is found at a distance from the **15.09**
entry in time and place the case is analogous to the use of a stolen key,
and in some such cases A may indeed be held to have stolen it.[38] But it is
also housebreaking to use a key found at the premises at the time of
entry. In *Alex Macdonald*[39] the charge was of "unlocking the outer door
of the said house by means of the key thereof, which you found
concealed in a hole, or under a stone near the said door", and this was
held to be housebreaking. Alison says, "It is equally housebreaking if the
entry has been effected by taking the key out of a hole or hiding place
where it had been secreted, as is very frequently the case with the
labouring classes, when they leave the house to go to their work",[40] so
that is it housebreaking to use a key left under the mat so that the child
of the house can enter on his return from school. Macdonald says, "It
has not yet been decided whether in the case of a key taken out of the
door, but left hanging on a nail in sight of the thief, housebreaking is
committed if he take down the key and use it",[41] but there are dicta
which indicate that this is housebreaking, and it is submitted that they
are correct.[42]

---

[35] *Jas Prior* (1830) Alison, i, 284.

[36] Hume, i, 98; Alison, i, 284; *John Stewart* (1826) Syme 2; *Christian Duncan* (1849) J.
Shaw 225.

[37] Hume, i, 99; *Colin Fraser and Daniel Gunn* (1827) Alison, i, 284–285; *A. Thomson and
Ors* (1827) Syme, 187; *Archd Mackenzie* (1832) Bell's Notes 37. *cf. John Farquharson*
(1854) 1 Irv. 512, L.J.-G. McNeill at 517.

[38] In *John Farquharson*, (1854) 1 Irv. 512 at 517, L.J.-G. McNeill said: "Perhaps the
strongest of the decided cases is that which has been alluded to on the part of the
prosecution, where a key hid at some little distance, having been taken from its place of
concealment, and the door opened thereby, that was held to constitute housebreaking,
though it seems to be very little removed from the case of the key left in the door." (The
case referred to was that of *Alexr Macdonald* (1826) Alison, i, 285.) His Lordship went on
to say that "although a person who has thus got access to [premises] should afterwards
restore the key to its proper place of deposit, and intended from the first to do so, I should
still hold that he had committed housebreaking, and with reference to that act, had stolen
the key."

[39] (1826) Alison, i, 285.

[40] Alison, i, 285.

[41] Macdonald, p.27.

[42] *Peter Alston and Alex. Forrest* (1837) 1 Swin. 433, L.J.-C. Boyle at 465, Lord Moncreiff
at 470, *contra* Lord Mackenzie at 469; *Henry Voigts Jardine* (1858) 3 Irv. 173, Lord Deas at
175. Anderson, however, says that it is not housebreaking: Anderson, pp.180–181. *Cf.
Galloway and Sutherland* (1829) Bell's Notes 35, where it was held to be opening lockfast
places to open a drawer with a key left on top of the chest of drawers.

A key which has been left in the lock is regarded as the equivalent of a handle, and it was held in *Peter Alston and Alex. Forrest*[43] that it is not housebreaking to unlock the door by turning it.[44]

Where entry is gained by lifting a latch or undoing a bolt, the principle of *Alston and Forrest* applies, and there is no housebreaking.[45] There are some cases cited in Bell's Notes in which it was held to be housebreaking to put a hand through a hole in the door and so gain access to and pull back a bolt,[46] but they precede *Alston and Forrest*. The only subsequent reported case which deals with this situation is *Ann Ashton*[47] in which it was held that if the mode of entry used — "putting her hand through a hole in the . . . door, and therby turning . . . the inside handle of the check-lock" — was the normal mode of entry there would be no housebreaking, but that "if the hole was accidental, or made for some other purpose, using it will show a degree of contrivance, which may perhaps amount to the aggravation."[48]

15.10   (5) By an unauthorised use of a key in one's possession. In *John Farquharson*[49] the accused was given the key of premises to take to the owner's home after the premises had been locked up. Instead of doing so he came back and used the key to enter the premises. This was held to be housebreaking by analogy with the use of a stolen key. In *Henry Voigts Jardine*[50] the accused was an ex-employee of a bank who had failed to return his key on being dismissed, and had later used it to enter the bank, and this was regarded as housebreaking.[51] In both these cases the court laid stress on the unlawfulness of the accused's possession of the key at the time of entry, but it might be better to concentrate on the unlawfulness of his use of the key as a means of entry. Suppose A is given a key to hand to B in a few days' time, and instead uses the key to gain entry during that time, when his possession of the key is lawful. It is submitted that that would be housebreaking, being an unauthorised use of the true key. On the other hand, if A is given a key to enable him to open a shop in the mornings and uses that key to enter and steal at night, it is submitted that that would not be housebreaking — it is true that his nocturnal entry is not authorised, but he is in possession of the key for the purpose of using it to enter the premises, and is therefore a person authorised to enter with that key.[52]

---

[43] (1837) 1 Swin. 433.

[44] This decision was reached by a bare majority of the court, indeed by the casting vote of L.J.-G. Hope, who said (at 472) that he had paid little attention to the practice of criminal law since he had last sat in the High Court, *i.e.* probably since 1811. His reason for voting as he did was that he had "always been an enemy to constructive crimes".

[45] *John Smith or Stevenson* (1834) Bell's Notes 36; *Janet Wilson* (1837) *ibid.* 37; *John Anderson* (1862) 4 Irv. 235.

[46] *John Maclean* (1828), *John Devin and Francis Polin* (1829), *John Grant* (1835), all Bell's Notes 36.

[47] (1837) 1 Swin. 478.

[48] L.J.-G. Hope at 479.

[49] (1854) 1 Irv. 512.

[50] (1858) 3 Irv. 173.

[51] No objection was taken to the relevancy of this charge although Lord Deas expressed his dislike of it, particularly as it was not averred that Jardine had no right to retain the key. The jury were directed that there would be housebreaking if the accused had no right to have the key but had been under a duty to return it: L.J.-C. Inglis at 176.

[52] Macdonald, p.26. *Cf. John Farquharson, supra,* L.J.-G. McNeill at 518: "We, however, expressly reserve our opinion as to the case of a shopman who is entrusted with the ordinary keeping and custody of the key."

(6) By windows. The law regarding entry by a window is not free from **15.11**
doubt. It has been said that it is not housebreaking to enter by an open
window, any more than by an open door,[53] but this is true only where the
window is at or near ground level[54] and where it is so placed that there is
no special risk in leaving it open.[55] Probably the position is that it is
housebreaking to enter by a window through which entry was not to be
expected, which means in effect that entry by a window is housebreaking,
except where the window is a french window and so equivalent to a door,
or where it is so near to the ground that one can easily step through it.
Where the window is out of ordinary reach entry through it is
housebreaking.[56]

Where the window is normally used as an entry it is not housebreaking
to enter by it. In *Jas. Davidson*[57] the aggravation of housebreaking was
dropped after it had been shown that the owner and the accused, who
was his lodger, often entered by the window in question.[58]

There is one very important difference between windows and doors
which makes the question of entry by an open window of little practical
importance. It is not housebreaking to turn the handle of an unlocked
door or to push open a door which is slightly ajar, but it is housebreaking
to push up a closed but unsecured window, or even to open further a
window which is already open,[59] even although to do so does not involve
breaking or by-passing any lock or catch.

(7) By any unusual opening. It is said to be housebreaking to enter by **15.12**
any unusual or unintended mode of entrance,[60] and one can probably go
so far as to say that any entry other than by a door, or perhaps an open
ground floor window, is housebreaking unless it can be shown that the
particular mode of entry was in fact usual in the particular case. It has
been held to be housebreaking to enter by a chimney,[61] a sewer,[62] a
water wheel[63] and an opening in a roof.[64]

In *Angus Sutherland*[65] entry was gained to a workshop by means of a
trap door in the pavement and a ladder. The trap door was a heavy one,
but this was the way in which employees normally entered the premises.
Nonetheless it was held to be housebreaking on the ground that, unlike a

---

[53] Hume, i, 98; Alison, i, 283; *Jas Hamilton and Ors* (1833) Bell's Notes 38; *John Carrigan and Thos. Robinson* (1853) 1 Irv. 303.

[54] Hume, i, 98; Alison, i, 283; *Wm Anderson* (1840) Bell's Notes 199.

[55] Macdonald, p.27.

[56] *cf. Wm Cameron* (1832) 4 S.J. 591. *Cf. Robt Clapperton* (1833) Bell's Notes 36.

[57] (1841) 2 Swin. 630.

[58] *cf. Wm Martin and Ors* (1832) Bell's Notes 38.

[59] Macdonald, p.27; *John Watson* (1773) Hume, i, 100; *John Dick and John Jeffrey* (1829) Alison, i, 283–284; *Wm Vair and Anr* (1834) Bell's Notes 39, *cf. Wm Vair and Ors* (1835) *ibid.*; *Cornelius O'Neill* (1845) 2 Broun 394; *John Munro and John Gillon* (1834) Bell's Notes 38.

[60] Alison, i, 282.

[61] *Rendal Courtney* (1743) Hume, i, 99; *Geo. Scott Middleton* (1824) Alison, i, 282; *John Mann* (1837) Bell's Notes 37.

[62] Hume, i, 99.

[63] *John Hunter* (1801) Hume, i, 99.

[64] Macdonald, p.29. See *John Carrigan and Thos Robinson* (1853) 1 Irv. 303, Lord Cowan at 304.

[65] (1874) 3 Couper 74.

house door, it was "a mode of access which none except those belonging to the shop were expected to enter".[66]

15.13 (8) By trickery. (a) The writers agree that it is housebreaking for A to induce B who is inside a building to open the door to him, and then to gain entry by pushing his way in past B,[67] but it is submitted that Alison is correct in indicating that such cases are more properly regarded as cases of robbery.[68]

(b) The writers also agree that it is housebreaking if A acts in concert with C, a servant of the house, and C opens the door to A in pursuance of their common plan to steal from the house.[69] It may, however, be argued that if C is entitled to enter the house himself by the way in which he permits A to enter, *e.g.* by unlocking the front door, this is not housebreaking any more than it would be housebreaking for C to let himself in with a key to the front door and then steal something.

(c) Although it is not housebreaking to break out of a house, it is housebreaking if A is admitted to the house, say as a guest one afternoon, and undoes the bolt of a door so that he will be able to return later by that door.[70]

Shipbreaking

15.14 This is an independent aggravation of theft,[71] but there are very few cases of it.[72] The essence of the charge is the breaking into locked cabins and other parts of the ship, and there are cases in which the crime has been charged as theft by opening lockfast places.[73] It appears to be incompetent to libel both shipbreaking and opening lockfast places,[74] and in modern practice the charge would almost certainly be one of theft by opening lockfast places.

---

[66] L.J.-C. Moncreiff at 77. There are also some cases concerning openings which were unusual in the sense that they were not within ordinary reach, as in the case of openings some distance above ground level. In *Helen Dott* (1829) Bell's Notes 35, the Crown dropped a charge of housebreaking by climbing through an opening in a shed door six feet above ground, and in *Archd Duncan and Chas Mackenzie* (1831) Bell's Notes 35, the jury were directed that it was not housebreaking to enter by a loft window 12 feet above ground which was used for taking in goods. In *Wm Cameron* (1932) 4 S.J. 591 a charge of housebreaking by climbing over a railing and entering a window was dropped on the ground that it was not alleged that the window was out of ordinary reach. On the other hand it has been said to be housebreaking to enter through an opening in the roof accessible only by ladder: see *John Carrigan and Thos. Robinson* (1853) 1 Irv. 303, Lord Cowan at 304. In that case itself the Crown, on Lord Cowan's invitation dropped a charge of housebreaking by entering through an open bole four feet from the ground. In *Wm Boyd and Ors* (1845) Macdonald 29, it was held to be housebreaking to extract articles through the openings in the side of an upper drying shed, which were constructed like a Venetian blind.

These cases are all special and give little general guidance. The law probably is that entry by any opening to which access is difficult is housebreaking. It would be housebreaking, it is submitted, to enter by a six-foot-high opening which could be reached only by climbing a wall, but not to enter by a higher opening which could be reached by an unprotected stair.

[67] Hume, i, 100; Burnett, p.138; Alison, i, 287; Macdonald, p.25. *Alston and Forrest, supra,* Lord Moncreiff at 470.

[68] Or, as he terms it, "stouthrief": Alison, i, 287.

[69] Hume, i, 101; Burnett, p.138; Alison, i, 287; Macdonald, p.25.

[70] Hume, i, 99; Burnett, p.138; Alison, i, 287; *cf. Wm Brown* (1715) Hume, i, 99, in which the question was not decided.

[71] Macdonald, p.30.

[72] *Nathanael Scott* (1844) 2 Broun 184; *Wm Inglis and Kenneth Gilvear* (1848) Ark. 461; *Thos Guthrie and Jas Convery* (1867) 5 Irv. 368.

[73] *Robt Miller* (1838) Bell's Notes 35; *John Henderson and Wm Craig* (1836) 1 Swin. 300.

[74] *Inglis and Gilvear, supra.*

Theft by opening lockfast places

This aggravation is analogous to housebreaking and the rules applicable **15.15** to housebreaking apply to it, *mutatis mutandis*.[75] It is opening lockfast places to break down the door or window of a locked room,[76] or the side or lid of a locked chest,[77] to pick a lock or use a false,[78] stolen or found key.[79] It is not opening lockfast places to turn a key left in the lock.[80] It is not opening lockfast places to open an unlocked drawer or closed door, or to open further one which is partly open.[81]

LOCKFAST PLACE. The term "lockfast place" extends to anything other **15.16** than buildings which is secured by a lock, including a room,[82] a ship's cabin, a safe, a drawer, a box or a motor-car. So far as the few reported cases go there is no authority for extending "lockfast places" to cover things secured other than by locks.

"BY". As in theft by housebreaking, the opening of the lockfast place **15.17** must precede the away-taking of the goods. Since to remove a container is to remove its contents,[83] it is not theft by opening lockfast places to take a box or safe away from a house and thereafter force it open and abstract its contents.

THE EFFECT OF THE AGGRAVATION. Prior to the coming into effect of **15.18** the relevant parts of the Criminal Justice (Scotland) Act 1963, charges of theft by opening lockfast places could not be tried in inferior courts, but that Act removed the restriction.[84] As a result, charges of theft by opening lockfast places can now be dealt with in district courts, so the aggravation has no necessary technical effect at all.

EXPLOSIVES. In modern practice the most serious aggravation of theft **15.19** is the opening of lockfast places by means of explosives, a crime which has, however, become much less common than it once was. Although theoretically this is just a form of opening lockfast places and can be tried in a district court, the modern practice is to take almost all such cases in the High Court, and to impose severe penalties.[85] Although it might be competent to lead evidence of the use of explosives on a charge merely libelling the forcing open of a lockfast safe, the practice is to libel

---

[75] Hume, i, 98; Burnett, p.136; Alison, i, 295; Macdonald, p.30. Hume and Burnett seem to regard opening lockfast places and housebreaking as different forms of a more general aggravation of "violence", but opening lockfast places is now clearly accepted as a specific aggravation in its own right, despite *Jas Anderson* (1852) 1 Irv. 93.

[76] *John Henderson and Wm Craig*; *Robt Miller, supra*.

[77] *Jas Gray* (1824) Alison, i, 296.

[78] *F. Jordan* (1826) Syme, 13; *E. Hall* (1826) *ibid*. 47.

[79] *Galloway and Sutherland* (1829) Bell's Notes 35, where the key had been left on top of the chest; *Robt Horn and Jas Maclaren* (1831) *ibid*., where the key had been left in a nearby open drawer. *Cf. Samuel Inglis* (1824) and *Geo. and John Beath* (1827) Alison, i, 296.

[80] Burnett's statement to the contrary: Burnett, p.136, was made before *Alston and Forrest supra*. See also Alison, i, 296.

[81] Alison, i, 296.

[82] For examnple, *Mary Young or Gilchrist and Cecilia Hislop*, Bell's Notes 34; *Houston Cathie* (1830) *ibid*.

[83] Macdonald, p.24; *Jas Smart* (1837) Bell's Notes 19; *Jas Stuart and Alex. Low* (1842) 1 Broun 260. *Cf. David Walker* (1836) 1 Swin. 294.

[84] See now 1995 Act, s.7(8)(b).

[85] Sentences of five years for "safe-blowing" are quite common where the accused has any significant criminal record at all. See also Explosive Substances Act 1883.

that the safe was forced open by means of explosives when this is the case.

Theft by drugging

15.20   This is recognised by Macdonald as an aggravated mode of theft.[86] There are only two cases which deal with it, and both of these are old, and important only because they indicate that it is theft and not robbery for A to prevail on B to take drink or drugs which render him insensible and then steal from him.[87] Drugging is not regarded as a special aggravation like housebreaking or opening lockfast places, and probably need not be specifically libelled. In the common case in which A plies B with drink so as to make him drunk but not unconscious and then picks his pocket, he is charged simply with theft from the person of B. The court is, of course, entitled to take A's *modus operandi* into account along with the other circumstances of the case in passing sentence.

Child stripping[88]

15.21   This again is only one of the circumstances of the offence which the court are entitled to take into account in passing sentence, and is not a special aggravation which must be libelled, or which has any necessary effect on sentence or jurisdiction. Stealing clothes from the person of a child was at one time punished with great severity.[89] There are no reported cases of child stripping since 1834.[90]

Theft of articles of value

15.22   In Hume's day the theft of an article of substantial value was regarded as capital, even though the theft was otherwise unaggravated.[91] In modern practice the value of the property stolen is still of great importance in considering sentence or in deciding in what court a charge should be brought, but it is no longer the practice to libel the value of the stolen articles. The only necessary effect is that charges of stealing, resetting or embezzling goods valued at more than level 4 on the standard scale cannot be tried in district courts.[92]

Thefts of animals will be more or less serious according to the value of the animal involved. Sheep, cattle or horse stealing is no longer regarded as an aggravated theft as such.[93]

---

[86] Macdonald, p.31.

[87] *David Wilson and Ors* (1828); *John and Catherine Stuart* (1829) both Bell's Notes 22, see *infra*, para. 16.06.

[88] See R.S. Shiels, "Theft by Child Stripping", 1998 Jur.Rev. 119.

[89] *Janet Irvine* (1832): transportation for life; *Jean McBeath* (1828): transportation for 14 years: Hume, i, 91n. See also *Ann Dunlop* (1828) Alison, i, 309, where the children were decoyed to the place of the theft and left there after their clothing had been removed, and *Ann Collins or Macdonald* (1834) Bell's Notes 28, a charge of theft by stripping and of exposing and deserting the child.

[90] Recent research has located 10 unreported "theft by child stripping" cases between 1847 and 1872 in the Justiciary Records maintained in the Scottish Record Office. It may be that the value of what was taken from the victims was of less importance than the enticing of the children away from their home localities and the subsequent abandoning of them to their fate: see R.S. Shiels, "Theft by Child Stripping", 1998 Jur.Rev. 119.

[91] Hume, i, 91.

[92] 1995 Act, s.7(8)(b)(iii). For the standard scale, see 1995 Act, s.225(2); level 4 is presently £2,500.

[93] *cf.* Hume, i, 88 *et seq.*; Alison, i, 309 *et seq.*; Macdonald, p.39.

Theft by a habit and repute thief

It was formerly the law that theft by a person who was a known thief, a **15.23** thief by habit and repute, was capital.[94] Theft by a habit and repute thief may still be a specific form of aggravated theft, and it may still be relevant to libel that the accused is such a thief,[95] but in practice this is never done.

Prior to the coming into force of the Criminal Justice (Scotland) Act 1980,[96] theft (as also reset, fraud and embezzlement) could not be tried in a district court if the accused had a previous conviction for dishonest appropriation of property[97]; but now that that restriction no longer applies,[98] this aggravation has no necessary technical effect at all.

Theft by persons in a position of trust

It has always been recognised as proper to take into account in **15.24** considering sentence that A was a servant of B or had been entrusted by B with the articles he stole from him.[99] Generally speaking this is not regarded as a specific aggravation in modern practice, except in the case of a policeman or post office official. Where a theft is alleged to have been committed by a policeman in the course of his duty, that should probably be specifically libelled.[1] This aggravation does not, however, affect the jurisdiction of any court to try the case.

Theft of mail

Theft of mail was recognised by Hume as an example of capital theft **15.25** at common law,[2] and is no doubt still an aggravated theft at common law.[3] This is possibly the assumption made in the "Note" to Schedule 9 of the Postal Services Act 2000. That note indicates that, notwithstanding the repeal of the Post Office Act 1953, "[t]he repeal of section 52 of the Post Office Act 1953 (which extends only to Scotland) does not affect any liability at common law in respect of any offence described in that section." What that section described, therefore, continues to be of some relevance. As amended by the Theft Act 1968 and the Post Office Act 1969, it provided:
"If any person —
    (a) steals a mail bag;
    (b) steals any postal packet in course of transmission by post;
    (c) steals any chattel, money or valuable security out of a postal packet in course of transmission by post; or

---

[94] Hume, i, 92; Alison, i, 296–297.

[95] *H.M. Advocate v. Hunter* (1890) 2 White 501; *H.M. Advocate v. Browne* (1903) 6 F.(J.) 24.

[96] See Sched. 8.

[97] See Criminal Procedure (Scotland) Act 1975, s.285(b)(iv).

[98] See now 1995 Act, s.7(8).

[99] Mackenzie, I, 19, 2; Macdonald, p.39; *A. Elliot or Alexander* (1826) Syme 1; *Watt v. Home* (1851) J. Shaw 519, L.J.-C. Hope at 522; *Hugh Climie* (1838) 2 Swin. 118, L.J.-G. Hope at 124.

[1] Macdonald, p.38; Anderson, p.49; *Archd McCallum* (1846) Macdonald 38. *Cf. Robt Ferrie and Wm Banks* (1831) Bell's Notes 34; *Brown v. Hilson*, 1924 J.C. 1.

[2] Hume, i, 80–81; *cf.* Alison, i, 342 *et seq.*

[3] *cf. Holmes and Lockyer* (1869) 1 Couper 221, L.J.-C. Patton at 237.

(d) stops a mail with intent to rob or search the mail,[4]
he shall be guilty of [an offence]".

The following definitions, which form part of the descriptions of the
various offences, were given in section 87(1) of the Act:

" 'mail bag' includes any form of container or covering in which
postal packets in course of transmission by post are conveyed,
whether or not it contains any such packets;
'postal packet' means a letter, postcard, reply postcard, newspaper,
printed packet, sample packet, or parcel, and every packet or article
transmissible by post, and includes a telegram;"

Section 87(2) provided that for the purposes of the Act:

"(a) a postal packet shall be deemed to be in course of transmission by post from the time of its being delivered to any post
office to the time of its being delivered to the addressee;
(b) the delivery of a postal packet of any description to a letter
carrier or other person authorised to receive postal packets of
that description for the post or to an officer of the Post Office
to be dealt with in the course of his duty shall be a delivery to
a post office:
(c) the delivery of a postal packet at the premises to which it is
addressed or redirected (except they be a post office from
which it is to be collected), or to the addressee's servant or
agent or to some other person considered to be authorised to
receive the packet, shall be a delivery to the addressee."

15.26   TRANSMISSION BY POST. A post office letter box was included in the
meaning of "post office",[5] so that a postal packet was in course of
transmission as soon as it was put into a letter box. A letter put into the
post in this way by post office investigators as a "test letter" was a postal
packet in course of transmission by post even if the addressee was
fictitious and the letter's only purpose was to enable the investigators to
catch a suspected postman *in flagrante delicto*.[6]
    In two old English cases it was held that a letter put into the suspect
postman's bag or sorting tray without going through the usual channels
was not a post letter.[7] The Post Office Act 1953 gave a definition of
postal packet which was wide enough to cover such letters, but there is
also the question of when a letter is "in course of transmission by post."
In *Hood v. Smith*[8] a test letter with a country postmark addressed to
London was put in a post office letter box in the district to which it had
been addressed, from which it was taken by a post office official who
kept it overnight and then placed it with the suspect's delivery. This
elaborate performance was presumably designed to evade the difficulties
of the earlier cases, and it was held that the letter had been in course of

---

[4] Sections 52(b) and 52(c) created distinct offences and might have been charged
cumulatively, but this was unlikely to occur in practice — see *Alex. McKay* (1861) 4 Irv. 88.
[5] Section 87(1) of the 1953 Act.
[6] *H.M. Advocate v. McVean* (1930) 10 S.L.T. 648 (Lord McLaren), following *Reg. v.
Young* (1846) 2 Car. & K. 466.
[7] *R. v. Rathbone* (1841) 2 Mood. 242: test letter put in a bundle of letters being sorted
by suspect; *R. v. Shepherd* (1856) Dears. 606: test letter handed in at window in hall of post
office to an inspector who gave it to another inspector who gave it to a sorter to give to the
suspect to sort.
[8] (1933) 150 L.T. 477.

post throughout. Avory J. pointed out that in any event its receipt by the suspect was sufficient in terms of the Post Office Act 1908 to make it a letter in course of transmission by post thereafter, and the same result was achieved by section 87(2)(b) of the 1953 Act.

CHATTEL. "Chattel" in Scotland meant a corporeal moveable.[9]   **15.27**

VALUABLE SECURITY. "Valuable Security" was defined as meaning "any **15.28** document creating, transferring, surrendering or releasing any right to, in or over property, or authorising the payment of money or delivery of any property, or evidencing the creation, transfer, surrender or release of any such right, or the payment of money or delivery of any property, or the satisfaction of any obligation."[10]

For modern postal services offences, see *infra*, paragraph 15.38.

KINDRED OFFENCES

Taking and using the property of another

According to Burnett, "A taking merely for use, or for some tempo- **15.29** rary purpose, and then to restore the thing, is not theft, thought it is an irregular and punishable act."[11] Hume and Alison both agree that it is not theft, for example, for a servant to borrow his master's horse for an unauthorised ride and then to return it, but do not indicate clearly whether they regard it as criminal at all.[12] Burnett and Alison both go on to say that Scots law does not recognise the *furtum usus* of Roman law, but the question here is not merely one of unlawful use, but of unlawful taking and using.

The only authority cited by Burnett and Alison for the proposition that unlawful taking and using is ever criminal is the case of *Dewar*[13] which is very special in its facts, since it concerned the taking of a book of secrets in order to copy them and return the book.

Dewar itself cannot be regarded as authority for any more than the innominate offence constituted by its own particular circumstances.[14] There are, however, indications that in some circumstances it may be criminal to take unlawful possession of one's own property,[15] and if that is so it would be a crime to take unlawful possession of someone else's property in similar circumstances. There is no authoritative general description of these circumstances nor is it clear how they are related to

---

[9] Section 87(1) of the 1953 Act.
[10] Theft Act 1968, Sched. 2, para. 12.
[11] Burnett, p.115.
[12] Hume, i, 73; Alison, i, 270.
[13] (1777) Burnett 115; Hume, i, 75.
[14] For a discussion of the case of *Dewar* see *supra*, para. 14.14. There are dicta in the case of *H.M. Advocate v. Mackenzies* (1913) 7 Adam 189, *per* L.J.-C. Macdonald at 149, to the effect that to take an article for a serious purpose of obtaining something of value through the possession of it is theft, but the dicta are *obiter*, and suggest in any event that the crime is theft and not a separate crime of taking and using.
[15] See *infra*, para. 15.40. The Scottish Law Commission's suggestion that it is clandestine taking and using surreptitiously to copy, or even read, a secret document was always doubtful, particularly as there was in such a case no taking of the thing itself (see Memorandum No. 40, para. 69); but their suggestion cannot now be correct following the decision in *Grant v. Allan*, 1987 S.C.C.R. 402. See para. 15.46, *infra*.

the obsolescent civil wrong of spuilzie which involved taking unlawful possession of moveables.[16]

15.30   STRATHEARN V. SEAFORTH. The general crime of unlawfully taking and using the property of another rests entirely on the case of *Strathern v. Seaforth*,[17] at any rate so far as modern law is concerned. In that case the charge read "you did . . . at B farm . . . clandestinely take possession of a motor car, the property of M.R. . . . you well knowing that you had not received permission from, and would not have obtained permission from, said M.R. to your so doing, and did drive and use said motor car in the streets . . . aftermentioned." The Crown argued that this was a relevant charge and that its criminality consisted in "clandestinely taking possession in the knowledge that permission would be refused." They also argued that in any event "the common law was elastic enough to cover acts which were criminal though perpetrated in a novel way." The defence argued that the Crown were attempting to introduce *furtum usus*, which "was quite well known and was not recognised as a crime," and that the crime in *Dewar*,[18] which was a very special case, was theft of incorporeal property. The opinions of the judges are very short.[19] Lord Justice-Clerk Alness said that the authorities cited by the Crown supported their argument,[20] and went on to say that even without authority he would have been convinced of the criminality of the charge, his reason being that otherwise an article "may be taken from its owner, and may be retained for an indefinite time by the person who abstracts it and who may make profit out of the adventure, but that, if he intends ultimately to return it, no offence . . . has been committed . . . if that were so, in these days . . . [when] motor cars are openly parked in the public street, the result would be not only lamentable but absurd."[21]

The following observations may be made on the case:

(1) "Clandestine" is not a term of art in Scots law. It was used by Hume and Erskine to distinguish theft from robbery, the former being clandestine in the sense that it was unaccompanied by violence,[22] but it appears to have been intended to mean more than that in *Strathern v. Seaforth*. Although it was regarded as an important element of the charge the only definition offered was one by Lord Anderson who said it implied "a certain degree of secrecy", and that the accused had acted without authority.[23] But if the former is its meaning it is difficult to see what relevance the practice of parking cars in public places has to the case. It is clear that the reason behind *Strathern v. Seaforth* (whatever its *ratio decidendi*) was a desire to punish people for unlawfully driving cars away from their parking places in public streets, although that was not the situation in the case and the case itself may not be authority for such

---

[16] Stair Inst. 1,9,16; Ersk. Inst. 3,7,16. *Cf.* T.B. Smith, p.649; *Stove v. Colvin* (1831) 9 S. 633; *cf. Mackintosh v. Galbraith* (1900) 3 F. 66. For a detailed discussion of spuilzie see D.M. Walker, "Spuilzie", 1949 S.L.T. (News) 136, and Chap. 28 of the same learned author's *The Law of Delict in Scotland* (2nd ed., Edinburgh, 1981).

[17] 1926 J.C. 100.

[18] (1777) Burnett 115; Hume, i, 75.

[19] Contrast the elaborate and scholarly approach of the South African court to the same question in *R. v. Sibiya*, 1955 (4) S.A. 247 (A.D.).

[20] These were Burnett, p.115; Alison, i, 270; Hume, i, 73, 75; *Dewar, supra*, and *Mackenzies, supra*.

[21] At 102.

[22] Hume, i, 77; Ersk. Inst. 4,4,58.

[23] At 103.

punishment. The application of the case to such a situation has never been tested and may never be tested, since taking and driving away motor vehicles without authority is now a statutory offence.[24]

(2) Lord Alness spoke of the accused making a profit out of his unlawful possession, but no question of profit arose in the sense in which the accused in *Dewar*,[25] or even a housebreaker who borrows the owner's keys to effect entry, can be said to profit from his possession. It does appear, however, that there must be both a taking and a using,[26] and it may be that if A unlawfully and clandestinely borrows B's book and finds he has no time to read it and returns it he is not guilty of the crime created in *Strathern v. Seaforth*,[27] but that he will be guilty if he reads it before returning it.[28]

(3) Lord Alness also spoke of taking for "an indefinite time" with the intention "ultimately" to return,[29] which suggests that the unlawful use must be for an extended time, but there is nothing in the reported circumstances of *Strathern v. Seaforth*[30] or in the typical joyriding cases to indicate that the time involved was more than a few hours.

(4) It is clear that it is a good defence to the crime that A had or believed he had or would have obtained on request the consent of the owner to what he did.

MURRAY V. ROBERTSON. The only reported discussion of *Strathern v.* **15.31** *Seaforth*[31] is in *Murray v. Robertson.*[32] The accused was a fish merchant in Ardrossan who was charged with clandestinely taking possession of a number of fish boxes belonging to other merchants and using them to transport his own fish to Glasgow. The boxes had been used by their owners to send fish to buyers in Ardrossan or elsewhere and should have been returned by these buyers. There was evidence that boxes were often not returned properly, and these had somehow found their way into the accused's yard, having perhaps been left there by buyers of the fish who had no further use for them. The accused's explanation for his use of them to send fish to Glasgow was that he wanted to return them but was unwilling to pay carriage on them as empties, and there was evidence that the owners would be able to recover them once they reached the Glasgow market. There was, however, no question of any lack of *mens rea*, as it was found as a fact that the accused knew he would not have received the owners' permission for his use of the boxes.

The accused's conviction was quashed on the ground that, "[i]f the charge sounds in crime at all, it is because possession was alleged to have been taken clandestinely", and that in the absence of any evidence as to how the boxes came into the accused's possession the Crown had failed to prove that he had taken them clandestinely.[33] The case was argued and decided on the ground that a clandestine taking was required, but it would have been sufficient to say that the crime required a "taking" and

---

[24] Road Traffic Act 1988, s.178, originally Road Traffic Act 1930, s.28.
[25] (1777) Burnett 115; Hume, i, 75.
[26] See esp. Lord Anderson at 103. The editors of Macdonald treat *Strathern v. Seaforth* as a recognition of *furtum usus*: Macdonald, p.20, but this is wrong: see T.B. Smith, p.194.
[27] 1926 J.C. 100.
[28] See Scottish Law Commission, *op. cit., loc. cit.*
[29] At 102.
[30] 1926 J.C. 100.
[31] 1926 J.C. 100.
[32] 1927 J.C. 1.
[33] L.J.-C. Alness at 4–5.

the Crown had failed to prove that the accused had "taken" the boxes, clandestinely or otherwise. The Crown argued that a clandestine taking occurred whenever property was appropriated temporarily by someone who knew he was acting without authority, but the court rejected this argument and relied for their decision on the fact that the boxes had for some time lain in the open in the accused's yard, and that he had used them openly.

The reason for the difference between *Strathern v. Seaforth* and *Murray v. Robertson* may well have been that the court in the former case wanted to protect car owners, while the court in the latter case felt, as Lord Anderson said,[34] that the accused was "a man of substance, presumably a respectable member of society," who had acted reasonably in sending the boxes to Glasgow rather than putting them in the street. Indeed, from a social point of view, it would have been enough to say that *Strathern v. Seaforth* provided a necessary protection for car owners in modern conditions while the likelihood and effect of unlawful use of fish boxes was not such as to require the intervention of the criminal law. But the legal effect of *Murray v. Robertson* seems to be that the crime in *Strathern v. Seaforth* is limited to the *clandestine* abstraction of another's property.[35] *Strathern v. Seaforth* is therefore not authority for the proposition that taking and using the property of another without his consent is in itself a crime in Scotland. The Crown argued in *Murray v. Robertson* that *Strathern v. Seaforth* did not create any differentiation between a man openly walking into a garage and taking a car and someone doing the same thing by means of a disguise or subterfuge, but although the court did not refer to that argument their decision impliedly rejects it.

In practical terms, however, the effect of *Murray v. Robertson* has probably been to discourage any extension of *Strathern v. Seaforth* beyond vehicles like boats or cycles, rather than to limit the criminal taking of such vehicles to takings by stealth.

15.32   Despite *Murray v. Robertson*[36] it is submitted that it is a crime at common law to take and use the property of another without his consent and that the crime is committed whether or not the taking is secretive. There can be no good reason for making it a crime to take and ride off on a pedal cycle from a cul de sac at midnight but not to do the same thing in a main street at high noon. A reading of *Strathern v. Seaforth*[37] itself gives the impression that the court would have held the latter criminal.

Murray v. Robertson can be treated as a very special case in which the court were anxious to avoid conviction and found the element of clandestinity a useful way of distinguishing *Strathern v. Seaforth* although, as has been argued, this was not necessary in order to avoid convicting the accused in *Murray v. Robertson*. It is unfortunate that instead of saying either that the Crown had failed to prove any taking of possession, or even that as they had averred clandestinity in that case they were bound to prove it, Lord Alness said that without the adverb "clandestinely" the charge would have been irrelevant, and that the other

---

[34] At 6.
[35] L.J.-C. Alness at 1927 J.C. 5.
[36] 1927 J.C. 1.
[37] 1926 J.C. 100.

judges agreed that clandestinity was essential. But it is submitted, albeit with some misgiving, that these observations on clandestinity can and should be treated as *obiter*. Charges of taking and using are not very common and always include an averment of clandestinity but they are not in practice restricted to secret takings.

Road Traffic Act 1988, section 178. This section provides that: **15.33**

"(1) A person who in Scotland —
  (a) takes and drives away a motor vehicle without having either the consent of the owner thereof or other lawful authority, or
  (b) knowing that a motor vehicle has been so taken, drives it or allows himself to be carried in or on it without such consent or authority, is, subject to subsection (2) below, guilty of an offence."[38]

TAKES. The section appears to require an unlawful physical taking of a **15.34** motor vehicle, and this would correspond well with the paradigm case for which the crime was believed to be intended. As was said in *Mowe v. Perraton*,[39] the section[40] "is intended to deal with the case of people who take motor cars which do not belong to them, drive them away, and then abandon them, because it is difficult to say that they intended to deprive the owner permanently of the possession".[41] In short, the crime was designed to plug a perceived gap[42] in the criminal law caused by the (then) inflexibility of the *mens rea* of theft[43]; but it shared with theft, however, the concept of "taking". Although the statutory offence may well have been "intended in its very nature to deal with takings made without any reference to the owner",[44] cases soon arose in which persons employed to drive motor vehicles about their employers' businesses undertook unauthorised journeys in those vehicles — either during or

---

[38] Maximum penalty on indictment 12 months' imprisonment and a fine, on summary conviction three months' and the statutory maximum: see Road Traffic Offenders Act 1988, Sched. 2, Pt. I.

[39] [1952] 1 All E.R. 423.

[40] The crime first appeared in s.28 of the Road Traffic Act 1930, and (for Scotland at least) remains more or less in its original form — as set out in para. 15.33, *supra*. English law departed from the Road Traffic Act's version of the crime in 1968 — see the Theft Act 1968, s.12(1). There are differences in wording, therefore, as between the current Scottish and English versions of the statutory crime: in particular, a "taking and driving away of a motor vehicle" is required in Scotland, whereas English law requires the "taking of a conveyance for the defendant's own or another's use." Both versions require a taking "without the consent of the owner or other lawful authority", and to that extent at least, English authority has been found persuasive in Scotland — see *Barclay v. Douglas*, 1983 S.C.C.R. 234, considered *infra*.

[41] Lord Goddard C.J. at 424. The advent of the Theft Act 1968 has made little difference to what is perceived as the basic rationale for the offence: "Now there is no doubt about the mischief towards which this provision (like its predecessors, sections 28(1) and 217(1) of the Road Traffic Acts, respectively) is directed. It is directed against persons simply taking other persons' vehicles for their own purposes, for example, for use in the commission of a crime, or for a joyride, or just to get home, without troubling to obtain the consent of the owner, but without having the *animus furandi* necessary for theft": *Whittaker v. Campbell* [1984] Q.B. 318, Goff L.J. at 328 E-F.

[42] *Strathern v. Seaforth*, 1926 J.C. 100, notwithstanding: see paras 15.30–15.32, *supra*.

[43] The modern flexible approach to the *mens rea* of theft would permit at least paradigm cases under s.178 of the Road Traffic Act 1988 to be prosecuted as theft: see paras 14.47–14.51, *supra*. The modern practice seems to be to confine prosecution under s.178 to cases where the owner of the car is related, or at least known, to the offender, and to treat cases of taking strangers' cars as theft.

[44] *R. v. Peart* [1970] 2 Q.B. 672, Sachs L.J. at 675D.

following their official working hours. Initially, the correspondence with the paradigm case was maintained by drawing potentially difficult and not-wholly-convincing distinctions between unauthorised use during authorised periods of possession (when there could be no fresh "taking" of what was already possessed)[45] and such use after the vehicle should have been returned to the employer's yard or garage — preferably with a time gap between authorised and unauthorised driving, so that an actual unauthorised taking could be pointed out.[46] It was not entirely clear, however, that a physical taking of the vehicle was an essential matter; and the more modern English authorities have confirmed that it is unauthorised *use* which is of prime importance. For example, in *R. v. Phipps*,[47] A was allowed to borrow B's car in order to take A's wife to the railway station, but A continued to use the car thereafter: he was convicted principally on the basis that the failure to return the car coupled with subsequent unauthorised use constituted the statutory offence. In *McKnight v. Davies*,[48] the matter was finally clarified. The case concerned a truck driver who had an accident on his way to return the truck to its depot at the end of his day's work. As a result he panicked, drove to a public-house for a drink after which he drove some friends home, drove back to another public-house for a drink, drove home, and parked the truck. He drove it to its depot next day. The court preferred *Phipps* to the earlier cases[49] and upheld the conviction. It was said, however, that, "Not every brief, unauthorised diversion from his proper route by an employed driver in the course of his working day will necessarily involve a 'taking' of the vehicle for his own use", but any appropriation to his own use "which repudiates the rights of the true owner, and shows that he has assumed control of the vehicle for his own purposes" is enough.[50] Although the court regarded the offence as committed when the vehicle was driven off from the first public house, *McKnight v. Davies* does not in principle require any specific taking at all; and this also now seems to be law in Scotland.

In *Barclay v. Douglas*,[51] the complainer left his car outside A's house and was driven to a public-house by A in A's father's vehicle. En route, A enquired whether the complainer wished his car to remain where he had left it, and it was eventually agreed that A should drive the complainer's car the 100 yards or so to the complainer's home where it was to be left. A was given the keys to the complainer's car. On A's way to the complainer's car, he decided not to drive that car the short distance as had been agreed upon, but to take it on a ten mile round-trip. He was, therefore, authorised to "take" the car, but not to use it for the journey he eventually chose to undertake. Although there was an appeal against conviction in this case, A's counsel conceded that the appeal was without substance: no opinion was, therefore, delivered by the Appeal Court. In following *McKnight v. Davies* Sheriff Macphail said this: "[A]n employee or borrower may intelligibly be said to 'take' a vehicle which has been entrusted to him if the word 'take' is understood to have its usual or ordinary meaning which signifies merely a physical

---

[45] See *Mowe v. Perraton* [1952] 1 All E.R. 423.
[46] See *R. v. Wibberley* [1966] 2 Q.B. 214.
[47] (1970) 54 Cr. App.R. 300.
[48] [1974] R.T.R. 4.
[49] *Mowe v. Perraton* [1952] 1 All E.R. 423; *R. v. Peart* [1970] 2 Q.B. 672.
[50] [1974] R.T.R., Lord Widgery C.J. at 8A.
[51] 1983 S.C.C.R. 224.

act. He may take it lawfully or unlawfully, and he does so unlawfully where he intends to use it for a purpose entirely different from that for which it has been entrusted to him."[52] Although it is true that in this case A had decided to go on an unauthorised journey before he entered the complainer's car, it seems clear from the sheriff's opinion as a whole that the decision is based on the general principle that it is a contravention of section 178 for a person entrusted with a motor vehicle to make an unauthorised journey in that vehicle. It is probably the law in Scotland, therefore, that section 178 extends well beyond conventional "joy-riders" and relates to anyone who is entrusted with a vehicle (whether as hirer, borrower or employee) and who decides at any time whilst the vehicle is in his possession to drive the vehicle on a journey not authorised by the owner.[53]

It was held in *Tolley v. Giddings*[54] that knowledge that a vehicle has **15.35** been stolen and not merely taken away is no defence to a charge of allowing oneself to be carried without the owner's consent. It is submitted that this would be followed in Scotland, and that equally it is no defence to a charge of taking and driving away that the crime was truly theft.[55]

"DRIVES". "MOTOR VEHICLE". For the meaning of these terms see *infra*, **15.36** paragraphs 30.04 and 30.06.

DEFENCES. Section 178(2) provides that: **15.37**

"If . . . the jury . . . or the court, is satisfied that the accused acted in the reasonable belief that he had lawful authority, or in the reasonable belief that the owner would, in the circumstances of the case, have given consent if he had been asked for it, the accused shall not be liable to be convicted of the offence."

It has been said that the section was "not meant to deal with the case where a person is moving a vehicle simply for his convenience, because, for example, it is blocking his doorway."[56]

Postal services offences. The Postal Services Act 2000 creates the **15.38** following offences in connection with unlawful dealing with mail:

---

[52] *ibid.*, at 229–230.

[53] Minor deviations from authorised use may be subject to a *de minimis* principle — but that would be a matter for prosecutorial discretion rather than substantive law. Sheriff Macphail intimated that his opinion was not intended to cover deviations from authorised routes, nor cases involving fraud (*ibid.*, 230). Where fraud induces an owner to allow A to hire or borrow his vehicle, then, provided the fraud does not vitiate consent (as it usually does not in criminal law), the principle used in *Barclay v. Douglas* should continue to determine whether an offence under s.178 has been committed: see *Whittaker v. Campbell* [1984] Q.B. 318; *cf. R. v. Peart* [1970] 2 Q.B. 672.

[54] [1964] 2 Q.B. 354.

[55] It is competent to convict of a contravention of s.178 on a charge of theft on indictment but not, for some unexplained reason, on a summary complaint: Road Traffic Offenders Act 1988, s.3(3).

[56] *Shimmel v. Fisher and Ors* [1951] 2 All E.R. 672, Lord Goddard C.J. at 673. But see also *R. v. Bow* [1977] R.T.R. 6.

"**83**. — (1) A person who is engaged in the business of a postal operator[57] commits an offence if, contrary to his duty and without reasonable excuse, he —

    (a) intentionally delays or opens a postal packet[58] in the course of its transmission by post,[59] or

    (b) intentionally opens a mail-bag.[60]

(2) Subsection (1) does not apply to the delaying or opening of a postal packet or the opening of a mail-bag under the authority of—

    (a) this Act or any other enactment (including, in particular, in pursuance of a warrant issued under any other enactment), or

    (b) any directly applicable Community provision.

(3) Subsection (1) does not apply to the delaying or opening of a postal packet in accordance with any terms and conditions applicable to its transmission by post.

(4) Subsection (1) does not apply to the delaying of a postal packet as a result of industrial action in contemplation or furtherance of a trade dispute.

(5) In subsection (4) 'trade dispute' has the meaning given by section 244 of the Trade Union and Labour Relations (Consolidation) Act 1992 . . . ; and the reference to industrial action shall be construed in accordance with that Act . . . .

(6) A person who commits an offence under subsection (1) shall be liable —

    (a) on summary conviction, to a fine not exceeding the statutory maximum or to imprisonment for a term not exceeding six months or to both,

    (b) on conviction on indictment, to a fine or to imprisonment for a term not exceeding two years or to both.

84.—(1) A person commits an offence if, without reasonable excuse, he—

    (a) intentionally delays or opens a postal packet[61] in the course of its transmission by post,[62] or

    (b) intentionally opens a mail-bag.[63]

---

[57] Under s.125(1), " 'postal operator' means a person who provides the service of conveying postal packets from one place to another by post or any of the incidental services of receiving, collecting, sorting and delivering such packets".

[58] Under s.125(1), " 'postal packet' means a letter, parcel, packet or other article transmissible by post".

[59] Under s.125(3), "(a) a postal packet shall be taken to be in course of transmission by post from the time of its being delivered to any post office or post office letter box to the time of its being delivered to the addressee, (b) the delivery of a postal packet of any description to a letter carrier or other person authorised to receive postal packets of that description for the post or to a person engaged in the business of a postal operator to be dealt with in the course of that business shall be a delivery to a post office, and (c) the delivery of a postal packet — (i) at the premises to which it is addressed or redirected, unless they are a post office from which it is to be collected, (ii) to any box or receptacle to which the occupier of those premises has agreed that postal packets addressed to persons at those premises may be delivered, or (iii) to the addressee's agent or to any other person considered to be authorised to receive the packet, shall be a delivery to the addressee".

[60] Under s.125(1), " 'mail-bag' includes any form of container or covering in which postal packets in the course of transmission by post are enclosed by a postal operator in the United Kingdom or a foreign postal administration for the purpose of conveyance by post, whether or not it contains any such packets".

[61] See n.58, *supra*.

[62] See n.59, *supra*.

[63] See n.60, *supra*.

(2) Subsections (2) to (5) of section 83 apply to subsection (1) above as they apply to subsection (1) of that section.

(3) A person commits an offence if, intending to act to a person's detriment and without reasonable excuse, he opens a postal packet which he knows or reasonably suspects has been incorrectly addressed to him.

(4) Subsections (2) and (3) of section 83 (so far as they relate to the opening of postal packets) apply to subsection (3) above as they apply to subsection (1) of that section.

(5) A person who commits an offence under subsection (1) or (3) shall be liable on summary conviction to a fine not exceeding level 5 on the standard scale or to imprisonment for a term not exceeding six months or to both."

Customs offences. The unlawful removal of goods from customs ware- **15.39** houses and of spirits from distilleries is penalised by section 100 of the Customs and Excise Management Act 1979 and section 17 of the Alcoholic Liquor Duties Act 1979 respectively.[64]

Unlawfully taking one's own property

Burnett says at one point, in dealing with the *mens rea* of theft, "The **15.40** felonious purpose implies, that the taker knew that the thing taken was the exclusive property of another, and that he had no right to meddle with it. If he knew or believed that he had a right to take it, . . . he cannot be guilty of *theft*, however punishable he may be for an irregular act, or for a delinquency sui generis,"[65] This view is supported by the case of *Ker and Stables*,[66] which referred to guilt of carrying off property, "in a clandestine and illegal manner", where the accused removed some property which one of them claimed belonged to him as part of his inheritance but which was being retained by his brother.

Ker and Stables is not a satisfactory authority on general principles, and the only other authorities are equally unsatisfactory. They concern persons accused of unlawfully taking their goods out of customs ware-houses after the goods had been seized but before they had been formally condemned. In three of these cases the taking was accompanied by violence,[67] and in the fourth[68] the court had doubts as to the relevancy of charges of theft and "felonious taking and carrying away goods regularly seized by the officers of the revenue." The most that these cases can be said to have decided is that it is a common law offence to remove one's goods from the lawful possession of revenue officers. Hume says of these cases that a person may be guilty "of some inferior wrong, for irregularly taking that which is his own"[69] and that there is no indication that the Customs authorities are in a different position from other lawful possessors, but it is by no means clear in what circumstances it is a crime to behave in this way, and there is no authoritative decision on the matter at all. Presumably a situation which does not constitute the

---

[64] *infra*, paras 38.18 and 38.19.
[65] Burnett, p.117.
[66] *ibid*. 118, discussed *supra*, para. 14.56.
[67] *Adam* (1710) Burnett 151; *Alex. Williamson* (1767) Burnett 118; *Macdonald and Chisholm* (1814) Hume, i, 77.
[68] *Lockhart* (1800) Burnett 119. *Jas Graham and Ors* (1824) Alison, i, 238 is unhelpful.
[69] Hume, i, 77; Macdonald, p.16; see *supra*, para. 14.28.

delict of spuilzie[70] will not constitute a crime, but there may be spuilzies which are not criminal. The absence of any reported cases on this question since 1814 suggests that prosecutions for unlawfully taking one's own property are unlikely in the absence of violence or breach of the peace.

15.41 *Furtum usus.* In Roman law it was theft for a person in the position of pledgee, depositary of borrower, to make any use of the goods which was contrary to the contract under which he held them.[71] Both Burnett and Alison state that Scots law does not recognise *furtum usus*.[72] It would appear to follow from *Murray v. Robertson*[73] that to use goods lawfully in one's possession in a way to which one knows the owner of the goods will not agree is quite different from using goods one has taken from the owner without his consent, and Lord Justice-Clerk Alness indicated that mere use of goods is not criminal.[74] It is thought that it would not be a common law crime, for example, to go into an open car in order to sleep in it.[75]

15.42   The only suggestion to the contrary is that contained in the indictment in *H.M. Advocate v. Mackenzies*[76] which included a charge of copying secrets from a book which, for aught said in the charge, was lawfully in the accused's possession. The court did not discuss the relevancy of this charge except from the point of view of the law of attempt, and it is in any event concerned with the use of incorporeal property. But it does suggest that there might be circumstances in which unlawful use of corporeal moveables would be criminal. These circumstances would be where A was either a public servant entrusted with an article in the course of his duty, or where he had been entrusted with the article under a contract involving a special obligation of trust on his part. So far as the public servant is concerned, his case is best dealt with under the heading of breach of duty by a public servant.[77] The position of the private employee is more difficult. The lorry driver who uses his employer's vehicle to take his wife to the cinema instead of leaving it overnight in the garage would not, it is submitted, be guilty of any common law crime. But a research worker who used one of his firm's new and expensive inventions for his private advantage might conceivably be guilty of a form of breach of trust which would consist essentially in his making an unauthorised use of the article.

In the ordinary case, however, *furtum usus* is not a crime. A borrower or hire-purchaser who pawns goods without the owner's consent with the intention of redeeming them before the end of the hire may be in breach

---

[70] *supra*, para. 15.29, n. 16.

[71] Inst. 4,1,6. *Cf.* Mackenzie, I, 19,1.

[72] Burnett, p.115; Alison, i, 271. But *contra* Macdonald, p.20, relying on *Strathern v. Seaforth, supra.*

[73] 1927 J.C. 1.

[74] *ibid.*, at p.5.

[75] But see Road Traffic Act 1988, s.25, which makes it a crime to get on to or tamper with the mechanism of a motor-vehicle without lawful authority or reasonable excuse: Max. pen. level 3 on the standard scale (Road Traffic Offenders Act 1988, Sched. 2, Pt I).

[76] (1913) 7 Adam 189.

[77] *infra*, para. 44.01.

of contract, but that does not affect the common law position so far as *furtum usus* is concerned, and he is guilty of no common law offence.

A fortiori A cannot be found guilty of a crime by breaking a contractual undertaking restricting his use of his own goods. He may be in breach of trust if he holds the goods as a trustee for a beneficiary, but even then is not guilty of a crime so long as he does not commit embezzlement. There can, of course, be no *furtum usus* of money, since money cannot be used without being appropriated.[78]

Trespass on heritage

Although Alison uses the word "trespass" to describe unlawful taking **15.43** and using of moveables, his references are all to English cases[79] and the term is of no significance in Scots criminal common law. There are a number of statutes dealing with trespass in pursuit of game,[80] but the only statute dealing with criminal trespass in itself is the Trespass (Scotland) Act 1865. That Act (as amended by the Statute Law (Repeals) Act 1973 and the Roads (Scotland) Act 1984) provides:

> "**3.** Every person who lodges in any premises, or occupies or encamps on any land, being private property, without the consent and permission of the owner or legal occupier of such premises or land, and every person who encamps or lights a fire on or near any road or enclosed or cultivated land, or in or near any plantation, without the consent and permission of the owner or legal occupier of such road, land, or plantation, shall be guilty of an offence."[81]

"Premises" are defined as meaning and including "any house, barn, stable, shed, loft, granary, outhouse, garden, stackyard, court, close, or inclosed space."[82]

In *Paterson v. Robertson*[83] a tenant gave her sub-tenants notice to quit, **15.44** and when they refused to go she removed her own furniture from the house, locked the house up, and delivered the key to the owner's factor. The sub-tenants returned to the house using a key obtained from a neighbour and remained after being warned to leave. They were convicted of a contravention of the Trespass Act. Lord Justice-General Normand said that the Act was not intended as a way of settling a disputed lease, and that no crime had been committed up to the time that the tenant locked the house up, but that after that they had no legal or ostensible title, having been actually dispossessed, and were in the position of "squatters who had effected a lodgment in the house at their

---

[78] *supra*, para. 14.31.

[79] Alison, i, 275.

[80] See also Firearms Act 1968, s.20 (trespassing in a building [subs.(1)] or on land [subs.(2)] without reasonable excuse, whilst having a firearm, or imitation firearm, with one. The reference to "imitation firearm" was added by the Firearms (Amendment) Act 1994, s.2(1). Maximum penalty under s.20(1) are seven years (see Criminal Justice and Public Order Act 1994, Sched. 8) and a fine on indictment, and six months and the prescribed sum on summary conviction; and maximum penalty under s.20(2) is three months and level 4 on the standard scale.

[81] Maximum penalty level 1 on the standard scale.

[82] Section 2.

[83] 1944 J.C. 166.

own hands."[84] Lord Moncrieff agreed regretfully, observing that it was rather a legal difference than a difference in fact which broke the continuity of the sub-tenants' occupation.[85] This case shows that "lodges" in the Act is an active verb and requires the taking possession of the heritage, in much the same way as clandestine taking and using requires a taking of the goods. The Trespass Act is not contravened by someone who outstays his lease; there must be a taking and a taking without ostensible right. It would therefore be a defence to a charge under the Act that A believed he was entitled to be in possession of the heritage, at any rate if his belief was based on some colourable title.

Trespass on ships

15.45   It is an offence to go to sea in a United Kingdom ship without the consent of the master or other authorised person.[86]

It is also an offence for an unauthorised person to go on board a ship in a United Kingdom port without the consent of the master or other authorised person, or to remain on board after being requested to leave by the master, a constable, or an officer authorised by the Secretary of State or an officer of Customs and Excise.[87]

Incorporeal property

15.46   It is not a crime as such at common law to make use for one's own purposes of information to which one has access through one's employment in a position of trust. In *Grant v. Allan*[88] the complaint was in the following terms:

> "While employed [by certain employers] . . . and having access in the course of your employment to materials, the property of your said employers, and confidential information of value to the business of your said employers and in particular to computer printouts containing lists of your said employers' business customers, setting forth information in relation to dealings between your said employers and their customers, you did . . . at [the premises of those employers], clandestinely take and without lawful right or authority, given by your said employers or otherwise, detain copies of a quantity of said computer printouts with intent to dispose of said computer printouts to trade rivals of your said employers for valuable consideration, and [in the course of a telephone call and at a meeting] . . . attempt to induce [the manager and a director of a trade rival of the said employers] to hand over £400 in exchange [for the copy computer printouts], and all this you did feloniously."

The Crown argued that this charge amounted to a known innominate offence, namely "the dishonest exploitation of confidential information of another person",[89] and cited the cases of *Dewar*[90] and *H.M.*

---

[84] At 169–170.
[85] At 170.
[86] Merchant Shipping Act 1995, s.103. Maximum penalty level 3 on the standard scale.
[87] *ibid.*, s.104. Maximum penalty level 5 on the standard scale.
[88] 1987 J.C. 71.
[89] *ibid.*, L.J.-C. Ross's account of the advocate-depute's arguments, at 74.
[90] (1777) Burnett 115; Hume, i, 75; *supra*, para. 14.14.

Advocate v. Mackenzies[91] as authorities. In *Dewar*, the accused had broken into a locked room in order physically to remove what he was not in the course of his employment entitled to have, *i.e.* his employers' book of secret "receipts"; the receipts were then copied outwith his employers' premises, the copies kept and the book itself returned. In *Grant v. Allan*,[92] however, it was conceded by the Crown both before the Sheriff and on appeal that the word "take" in the complaint did not signify appropriation of the copy printouts containing the confidential information: indeed, the meaning of "take" in this context was intended to be "make". It was not suggested, therefore, that the accused did not have authority to make or possess the copies in the course of his employment; and thus a clear distinction could be drawn between *Dewar* and the instant case — unless the accused in *Dewar* had been punished not so much for the unauthorised taking of the book as for the copying of the confidential information. *Grant v. Allan*, however, leaves the matter in no doubt and confirms that unauthorised copying of confidential information and disposing (or attempting to dispose) of that information to a business rival of the owner of the information (even in breach of a duty of confidentiality to the owner in respect of that information) is not a crime at common law.[93] Of course, the accused in *Dewar* was convicted for some offence or other, since he was punished in terms of the jury's verdict: but he was not convicted of theft, nor of any broad offence of "dishonestly exploiting confidential information belonging to another".[94]

The indictment in *H.M. Advocate v. Mackenzies*[95] contained a charge of theft, but also a separate charge not unlike the one set down in the complaint in *Grant v. Allan*.[96] Indeed the later charge seemed *a fortiori* of the one in *Mackenzies*,[97] since the court had held there that the accused had never left the stage of preparation and had thus not done enough to be convicted of an attempt. But Lord Justice-Clerk Macdonald in *Mackenzies* expressed no concluded view on whether the non-theft charge in the indictment had itself been a relevant one under Scots law. His view that the charge fell short of what was needed for an attempt was based on a non-committal assumption that there existed a crime to be attempted.[98] Lord Salvesen was prepared to go further, it seems, and to deny that that part of the indictment disclosed any offence at all.[99] As Lord Justice-Clerk Ross put it in *Grant v. Allan*: "So far as the issue raised in this appeal is concerned . . . the case of *Mackenzies* is

---

[91] (1913) 7 Adam 189.

[92] 1987 J.C. 71.

[93] The owner or employer's remedy lies in contract, it seems: *Grant v. Allan*, 1987 J.C. 71, L.J.-C. Ross at 77, Lord McDonald at 78–79.

[94] L.J.-C. Ross emphasises that in *Dewar* the accused took possession of the book by unlawful means (*ibid.*, at 76), but otherwise joins with Lords McDonald and Wylie in suggesting that it is unclear what crime had been committed in that 18th century case.

[95] (1913) 7 Adam 189.

[96] 1987 J.C. 71

[97] The complaint in *Grant v. Allan*, however, lacked (unlike the indictment in *Mackenzies*) any express statement that the accused had acted in breach of an obligation of confidentiality to his employers.

[98] (1913) 7 Adam 189, at 195. *Cf.* the version of his opinion recorded at 1913 S.C. (J) 107 at 111 (quoted by L.J.-C. Ross in *Grant v. Allan*, 1987 J.C. 71, at 76).

[99] In his view, there was nothing disclosed there beyond a civil wrong — (1913) 7 Adam 189, at 199–200. Lord Dundas simply concurred in the opinion of the Lord Justice-Clerk.

neutral."[1] There being no authority to support the advocate-depute's contention, therefore, the court found that no relevant crime at common law was disclosed in the complaint.[2] *Grant v. Allan* represents a failed attempt to criminalise the dishonest use by an employee of incorporeal property belonging to his employer, in the absence of any unlawful physical taking of the thing in which or on which that information resides. *Dewar*,[3] however, was not over-ruled; it is probably, therefore, a crime at common law for an employee to take possession by unlawful means of the physical medium wherein his employer's valuable trade secrets are to be found, to take that medium away, to copy (and detain) the trade secrets it contains for some dishonest purpose, and thereafter to return it unchanged, in accordance with his original intention, to the exact location from which it was abstracted. This innominate offence is distinguished (if at all) from theft by the accused's intention to return the thing quickly — there being no intention at any time to deprive the owner of his corporeal property permanently, indefinitely or temporarily (in the sense of holding it to ransom)[4]; it is also probably distinguished from "taking and using" by the fact that the physical thing itself has not been "used", in the sense that a car is used, for example, by a joy-rider.[5]

Where A has obtained information in the course of his duty as a public official, his use of it may amount to the common law crime of breach of duty by a public official, and may also amount to a contravention of the Official Secrets Acts, or other statutory provisions.

15.47 *Copyright.* Copyright[6] is protected by the criminal law by virtue of the following provision of the Copyright, Designs and Patents Act 1988:

> Section 107
>
> "(1) A person commits an offence who, without the licence of the copyright owner—
> (a) makes for sale or hire, or
> (b) imports into the United Kingdom otherwise than for his private and domestic use, or
> (c) possesses in the course of a business with a view to committing any act infringing the copyright, or
> (d) in the course of a business—
>   (i) sells or lets for hire, or
>   (ii) offers or exposes for sale or hire, or
>   (iii) exhibits in public, or
>   (iv) distributes, or
> (e) distributes otherwise than in the course of a business to such an extent as to affect prejudicially the owner of the copyright an article which is, and which he knows or has reason to believe is, an infringing copy[7] of a copyright work,

---

[1] 1987 J.C. 71, at 76.

[2] The court was invited to exercise the declaratory power (see Vol. I, para. 1.15 *et seq.*) but declined to do so on the basis (amongst other reasons) of the difficulty of showing when and how confidential information might be exploited by an employee or ex-employee: see, *e.g.*, *ibid.*, L.J.-C. Ross at 77.

[3] (1777) Burnett 115; Hume, i, 75.

[4] See paras 14.47 *et seq.* (the *mens rea* of theft), *supra*.

[5] See paras 15.30 *et seq.*, *supra*.

[6] "Publication right" is also protected by the section. This right was introduced by the Copyright and Related Rights Regulations 1996 (S.I. 1996 No. 2967), regs 16 and 17.

[7] See s.27 (as am.) for definition of "infringing copy".

(2) A person commits an offence who—

(a) makes an article specifically designed or adapted for making copies of a particular copyright work, or

(b) has such an article in his possession,

knowing or having reason to believe that it is to be used to make infringing copies for sale or hire or for use in the course of a business.

(3) Where copyright is infringed (otherwise than by reception of a broadcast or cable programme)—

(a) by the public performance of a literary, dramatic or musical work, or

(b) by the playing or showing in public of a sound recording or film,

any person who caused the work to be so performed, played or shown is guilty of an offence if he knew or had reason to believe that copyright would be infringed.

(4) A person guilty of an offence under subsection (1)(a), (b), (d)(iv) or (e) is liable—

(a) on summary conviction to imprisonment for a term not exceeding six months or a fine not exceeding the statutory maximum, or both:[8]

(b) on conviction on indictment to a fine or imprisonment for a term not exceeding two years, or both.

(5) A person guilty of any other offence under this section is liable on summary conviction to imprisonment for a term not exceeding 6 months[9] or a fine not exceeding level 5 on the standard scale, or both.

(6) Sections 104 to 106 (presumptions as to various matters connected with copyright) do not apply to proceedings for an offence under this section; but without prejudice to their application in proceedings for an order under section 108 below."

In terms of section 1 of the Act, copyright subsists in original literary, dramatic, musical or artistic works, in sound recordings, films, broadcasts or cable programmes, and in the typographical arrangement of published editions.[10]

Unauthorised exploitation of illicit recordings and performance rights. **15.48** Protection from the unauthorised exploitation of illicit recordings[11] and performance rights[12] is provided by section 198 of the Copyright, Designs and Patents Act 1988 as follows:

"(1) A person commits an offence who without sufficient consent—

(a) makes for sale or hire, or

---

[8] Where "publication right" is the subject matter of the offence, the maximum penalty on summary conviction is three months' imprisonment and a fine of level 5 on the standard scale, S.I. 1996 No. 2967, reg. 17(3)(a).

[9] Where "publication right" is involved, the maximum prison sentence is three months: S.I. 1996 No. 2967, reg. 17(3)(a).

[10] See ss. 1–8, as amended, for definitions of these various terms.

[11] See s.197 for definition.

[12] See s.180 *et seq.*

    (b) imports into the United Kingdom otherwise than for his private and domestic use, or

    (c) possesses in the course of a business with a view to committing any act infringing the rights conferred by this Part [Part II], or

    (d) in the course of a business—

        (i) sells or lets for hire, or

        (ii) offers or exposes for sale or hire, or

        (iii) distributes,

a recording which is, and which he knows or has reason to believe is, an illicit recording.

    (2) A person commits an offence who causes a recording of a performance made without sufficient consent to be—

    (a) shown or played in public, or

    (b) broadcast or included in a cable programme service, thereby infringing any of the rights conferred by this Part, if he knows or has reason to believe that those rights are thereby infringed.

    (3) In subsections (1) and (2) 'sufficient consent' means—

    (a) in the case of a qualifying performance subject to an exclusive recording contract—

        (i) for the purposes of subsection (1)(a) (making of recording), the consent of the performer or the person having recording rights, and

        (ii) for the purposes of subsection (1)(b), (c) and (d) and subsection (2) (dealing with or using recording), the consent of the person having recording rights.

The references in this subsection to the person having recording rights are to the person having those rights at the time the consent is given or, if there is more than one such person, to all of them.

    (4) No offence is committed under subsection (1) or (2) by the commission of an act which by virtue of any provision of Schedule 2 may be done without infringing the right conferred by this Part.

    (5) A person guilty of an offence under subsection (1)(a), (b) or (d)(iii) is liable—

    (a) on summary conviction to imprisonment for a term not exceeding six months or a fine not exceeding the statutory maximum, or both;

    (b) on conviction on indictment to a fine or imprisonment for a term not exceeding two years or both.

    (6) A person guilty of any other offence under this section is liable on summary conviction to a fine not exceeding level 5 on the standard scale or imprisonment for a term not exceeding six months, or both."

It is also an offence under section 201 of the Act for any person "to represent falsely that he is authorised by any person to give consent for the purposes of this Part [Part II] in relation to a performance, unless he believes on reasonable grounds that he is so authorised."[13]

---

[13] Maximum penalty on summary conviction is imprisonment for six months and a fine of level 5 on the standard scale.

Fraudulent receipt of transmissions. Section 297 of the Copyright, Designs **15.49** and Patents Act 1988 makes it an offence dishonestly to receive a programme included in a programme service (as defined in the Broadcasting Act 1990) provided from a place in the United Kingdom with intent to avoid payment of any applicable charge.[14]

PREVENTIVE OFFENCES

Housebreaking with intent to steal

In *Chas. Macqueen and Alex. Baillie,*[15] a charge of "feloniously **15.50** breaking into any house or shop, with the felonious intent of stealing therefrom" was held relevant, and housebreaking with intent to steal became a recognised crime in the law of Scotland. In *Jas Monteith*[16] a charge of "breaking the door of a House for the purpose of entering and Stealing therefrom" was upheld, but in *Thos Sinclair and Jas McLymont*[17] an averment of "break[ing] a pane of glass in a window . . . and . . . endeavour[ing] to force or push up the shutter on the inside of said window" with intent to steal was held insufficient since the security of the house had not been overcome. The distinction, if any, between the two cases is no longer important as attempted housebreaking with intent to steal is now a crime like any other attempted crime.[18]

The meaning of "housebreaking" is the same as in its use in "theft by housebreaking".[19]

The housebreaking must be with intent to commit theft. Housebreaking itself is not a crime as such although it may be a form of malicious mischief. There is no authority for treating housebreaking with intent to commit any crime other than theft as itself a substantive crime,[20] and indeed in *H.M. Advocate v. Forbes*[21] the appeal court confirmed that a charge of housebreaking with intent to commit assault and rape was irrelevant on the ground that there was no authority to support it. The court did affirm, however, that the accused's alleged conduct would relevantly support a charge of breach of the peace.

"THEREFROM". The common form of charge libels the breaking into **15.51** premises with intent to steal therefrom. The crime may however be committed by breaking into one set of premises with intent to steal from another. In *Wm Thomson and Ors*[22] the court upheld a charge of housebreaking with intent to break into and steal from an adjoining house,[23] the two premises being under one roof and separated by a wall.

---

[14] Maximum penalty on summary conviction is a fine of level 5 on the standard scale.
[15] (1810) Hume, i, 102; Burnett, pp.142–143.
[16] (1840) 2 Swin. 483.
[17] (1864) 4 Irv. 499.
[18] 1995 Act, s.294.
[19] See *supra*, paras 15.05 *et seq.*
[20] Alison lists "Any violent invasion of personal freedom, or of the security of private houses, though not done for the purposes of theft or spoliation" as an innominate offence but the cases to which he refers deal with forcibly entering a house and assaulting the occupants: Alison, i, 633–634. See *infra*, paras 29.08, 29.09.
[21] 1994 S.C.C.R. 163.
[22] (1845) 2 Broun 389.
[23] *cf. Jas Bell* (1830) 2 Broun 391n.

Lord Cockburn reserved his opinion on the position where "the house-breaking was committed with intent to steal from an open house adjoining that broken into."[24] Macdonald is of opinion that this would be housebreaking with intent to steal[25] on the ground that the violation of the security of the one is a violation of the security of both. He cites the case of *Jas Hall and Wm Donnelly*[26] where the charge was of breaking into "a byre immediately adjoining the said house, and the passing over a bedstead which formed the division between the said house and byre."

There appear to be three different types of situation which may occur:

(1) A breaks into *a* with intent to break through a wall or other obstacle separating *a* from *b* and securing *b* against access from *a*, with intent to steal from *b*. This constitutes housebreaking with intent to steal on the authority of *Thomson*.

(2) A breaks into *a* with intent to enter and steal from *b* which adjoins *a* and can be entered without further violence, *e.g.* by crossing a corridor or going through an open door, or climbing a bench or bedstead dividing the two places. This, too, constitutes housebreaking, on the authority of Macdonald, and *Hall and Donnelly*: *a* and *b* can be regarded as one building, and so to break in to *a* is to break into *b*.

(3) In *Jas Ross and Jas Stewart*[27] the charge was of theft by house-breaking committed by breaking into a barn, the *modus* libelled being a break-in to a building from which A climbed over a wall separating the building from the barn, and entered the barn without further violence. Lord Cockburn declined to hold the charge relevant without certifying it for the opinion of the High Court, and the Crown did not press the matter further. The question remains undecided.

Opening lockfast places with intent to steal

15.52   In *Allan Lawrie*[28] objection was taken to the relevancy of a charge of opening lockfast places with intent to steal. The High Court seem to have been of opinion that it was relevant, but reluctant to decide the matter in the absence of any precedent, and the Crown withdrew the charge. Again, in *Wm Mickel*[29] the charge was dropped after Lord Medwyn had declined to uphold it when sitting alone on circuit. Macdonald refers to these two cases and goes on to say, "There appears to be no reason why it should not be relevantly charged."[30] In fact charges of opening lockfast places with intent to steal, and of attempting to do so, are of daily occurrence, and have been taken in both sheriff courts and the High Court without objection. Macdonald suggests that opening lockfast places with intent to steal might be charged as attempted theft,[31] but in view of the difficulties involved in defining

---

[24] At 391.
[25] Macdonald, p.50n.
[26] (1835) Macdonald 50.
[27] (1842) 1 Broun 294.
[28] (1837) 2 Swin. 101n; Bell's Notes, 40.
[29] (1844) 2 Broun 175.
[30] Macdonald, p.51.
[31] *ibid.*, *cf. McLeod v. Mason and Ors*, 1981 S.C.C.R. 75, where two charges of attempted theft of motor vehicles were predicated upon forcing open (or attempting to force open) lockfast motorcars with intent to steal: nevertheless, the Appeal Court was of the opinion that in charges of opening lockfast vehicles with intent to steal, it was not necessary for the prosecutor to specify whether the intent was to steal from the vehicles or to steal the vehicles themselves. That being so, the Scots common law crime seems to cover much the same ground as the English statutory offence of "vehicle interference" (see Criminal Attempts Act 1981, s.9).

attempted theft[32] the practice is to charge the crime as one of opening or attempting to open lockfast places with intent to steal.

Civic Government (Scotland) Act 1982

(a) *Being in or on a building etc. with intent to commit theft.* Section 57 **15.53** of this Act provides:

"(1) Any person who, without lawful authority to be there, is found in or on a building or other premises, whether enclosed or not, or in its curtilage or in a vehicle or vessel so that, in all the circumstances, it may reasonably be inferred that he intended to commit theft there shall be guilty of an offence and liable, on summary conviction, to a fine not exceeding [level 4 on the standard scale] or to imprisonment for a period not exceeding 3 months or to both.

(2) In this section 'theft' includes any aggravation of theft including robbery."

FOUND IN OR UPON PREMISES ETC. The accused must be "found phys- **15.54** ically on the premises at the relevant moment" in the sense of being seen or heard to be there. Circumstantial evidence from which it can be inferred that he had been on premises is insufficient. It has been held sufficient, however, for an accused person to have been "found" in the curtilage of a house where the occupier of that house (immediately after the burglar alarm on his own property had been activated) saw someone whom he could not then identify climbing over a fence into a neighbouring garden, set off at once in hot pursuit and found the accused hiding in that garden.[33]

WITHOUT LAWFUL AUTHORITY. Although it would be normal (and **15.55** prudent) to lead evidence from relevant witnesses to establish that the accused had no lawful authority to be where he was found,[34] it has been held that the onus upon the Crown to show such lack of authority may be discharged by inference from the facts and circumstances.[35]

INFERENCE OF THEFTUOUS INTENT. This inference is to be drawn from **15.56** all the circumstances and will depend on the precise facts proved.[36] The time of day when the accused was found on premises has been considered of some importance,[37] as has, of course, the accused's behaviour at those premises at the relevant moment[38] or even at other places prior to that moment.[39]

---

[32] See Vol. I, Chap. 6.

[33] *Marr v. Heywood*, 1993 S.C.C.R. 441 — partly approving, partly distinguishing the earlier case of *MacLean v. Paterson*, 1968 J.C. 67 (which was decided under the now repealed s.7 of the Prevention of Crime Act 1871).

[34] See, *e.g.*, *McBurnie v. McGlennan*, 1991 S.C.C.R. 756, where the officer in charge of a nursery school gave such evidence.

[35] *Moran v. Jessop*, 1989 S.C.C.R. 205.

[36] See, *e.g.*, *McBurnie v. McGlennan*, 1991 S.C.C.R. 756, L.J.-G. Hope at 758F.

[37] See, *e.g.*, *McClung v. McGlennan*, 1990 S.C.C.R. 163; *cf. Cameron v. Normand*, 1993 S.C.C.R. 308.

[38] See, *e.g.*, *Fulton v. Normand*, 1995 S.C.C.R. 629.

[39] See *Frail v. Lees*, 1997 S.C.C.R. 354, Lord Sutherland at 355 D-E.

15.57 *Convicted thief in possession of tool or object.* Section 58 of the Act provides:

> "(1) Any person who, being a person to whom this section applies—
> (a) has or has recently had in his possession any tool or other object from the possession of which it may reasonably be inferred that he intended to commit theft or has committed theft; and
> (b) is unable to demonstrate satisfactorily that his possession of such tool or other object is or was not for the purposes of committing theft
> shall be guilty of an offence and liable, on summary conviction, to a fine not exceeding [level 4 on the standard scale] or to imprisonment for a period not exceeding 3 months or to both.
>
> (2) For the purposes of subsection (1) above, a person shall have recently had possession of a tool or other object if he had possession of it within 14 days before the date of—
> (a) his arrest without warrant for the offence of having so possessed it in contravention of subsection (1) above; or
> (b) the issue of a warrant for his arrest for that offence; or
> (c) if earlier, the service upon him of the first complaint alleging that he has committed that offence.
>
> . . .
>
> (4) This section applies to a person who has two or more convictions for theft which are not, for the purposes of the Rehabilitation of Offenders Act 1974, spent convictions.
>
> (5) In this section 'theft' includes any aggravation of theft including robbery."

15.58 REASONABLE INFERENCE OF THEFT OR INTENTION TO COMMIT THEFT. This inference may be drawn not only from the nature of the tools or objects possessed but also from "the time, place or other circumstances casting light on the nature of the possession."[40]

15.59 INABILITY TO DEMONSTRATE THAT POSSESSION WAS NOT FOR THEFTUOUS PURPOSE. Since being unable satisfactorily to demonstrate that possession is or was not for the purposes of theft is a material part of the offence, it is not justifiable for the police to charge a person under section 58 unless they have given that person the opportunity to provide an appropriate explanation[41] and either no such explanation or an unsatisfactory one has been given. Nevertheless, it is for the court finally to determine the adequacy of any explanation tendered by the accused: and although the accused's explanation must relate to the time when he had possession of the object, there is no rule that an explanation must be given at or close

---

[40] *Newlands v. MacPhail*, 1991 S.C.C.R. 88, L.J.-G. Hope at 94F. *Newlands* disapproved the earlier sheriff court decision of *Allan v. Bree*, 1984 S.C.C.R. 228, which restricted what could be used to make the necessary inference to the nature of the objects possessed on the ground that a narrow interpretation of such statutory offences was generally to be preferred.

[41] *Phillips v. MacLeod*, 1995 S.C.C.R. 319, L.J.-G. Hope at 322 B; *Docherty v. Normand*, 1996 S.C.C.R. 701, L.J.-G. Hope (giving the opinion of a court of five judges) at 706D-F.

to the time he was found in possession of it; consequently, an explanation may be tendered for the first time at the trial and does not then come too late.[42]

Explosive Substances Act 1883

Section 4 of this Act provides that: **15.60**

"(1) Any person who makes or knowingly has in his possession or under his control[43] any explosive substance, under such circumstances as to give rise to a reasonable suspicion that he is not making it or does not have it in his possession or under his control for a lawful object, shall, unless he can show that he made it or had it in his possession or under his control for a lawful object, be . . . liable to [14 years' imprisonment]."

It has been held in England that an accused person must be shown to have had knowledge that what he made, possessed or controlled was an explosive substance — especially so where the physical object in question is considered to be an explosive substance by virtue of the extended definition of such set out in section 9.[44]

It has also been held in England that it is a defence to a charge under section 4 that the object of making the explosive was to protect the accused or his family or property against imminent apprehended attack by means he believed to be reasonably necessary for the purpose, but that such a defence will rarely succeed where, as in the relevant case, the explosives are petrol bombs.[45] Where, however, the crown lead evidence giving rise to a suspicion of an unlawful object, it does not matter whether that object is intended to be achieved in the United Kingdom or abroad.[46]

---

[42] *Docherty v. Normand*, 1996 S.C.C.R. 701 (court of five judges) overruling *Mathieson v. Crowe*, 1993 S.C.C.R. 1100. L.J.-G. Hope, giving the opinion of the court in *Docherty*, said at 705A: "All that can be said is that the explanation must have been one which the person could have provided at the time when he was found. It will not do if he were to state at his trial that he had now discovered one which he could not have given earlier." Presumably this restriction would apply to the accidental discovery of a reason which was unknown to the accused at the relevant time and not the true reason why he was in possession of the object(s) when he was found.

[43] See *Black v. H.M. Advocate*, 1974 S.L.T. 247, *infra*, para. 22.23.

[44] See *R. v. Berry (No. 3)* [1994] 2 All E.R. 913. Lord Taylor of Gosforth at 918g-h acknowledged that s.4 of the Act attaches the word "knowingly" only to possessors and controllers, but stated: "The word 'knowingly' [there] simply emphasises that where possession or control is relied upon, the defendant must know the substance is in his possession, for example in his house or his car. No person who makes the substance can be unaware that he had done so". This was a different type of knowledge, however, from knowing that the thing in question was an explosive substance. Section 9(1) of the Act narrates: "In this Act, unless the context otherwise requires — The expression 'explosive substance' shall be deemed to include any materials for making any explosive substance; also any apparatus, machine, implement, or materials used, or intended to be used, or adapted for causing, or aiding in causing, any explosion in or with any explosive substance; also any part of any such apparatus, machine, or implement." In *Berry*, the alleged 'explosive substance' consisted of electronic timers which might or might not have been used in connection with the detonation of bombs.

[45] *Attorney-General's Reference (No. 2 of 1983)* [1984] Q.B. 456; see in particular Lord Lane C.J. at 471 B.

[46] *R. v. Berry* [1985] A.C. 246.

CHAPTER 16

ROBBERY

Robbery may be defined as theft accomplished by means of personal **16.01**
violence or intimidation.[1] It is sometimes said that robbery must be
against the will of the victim, as opposed to theft in which the goods are
taken *without his consent*,[2] but this is not a satisfactory distinction. It
leads to theoretical difficulties in cases where the victim is rendered
unconscious or even killed before his property is taken, circumstances
which clearly amount to robbery,[3] or where the robbery is accomplished
so speedily that the victim does not realise what has happened until it is
all over.[4] A more important objection to the distinction is that it lays
stress on the will of the victim, whereas what matters is the will of the
accused. If, for example, the victim erroneously believed that he was
being attacked for reasons of revenge or lust and consequently disregarded the safety of his wallet, the assailant who had intended all along
only to take the wallet would be as guilty of robbery as if the victim had
exerted all his efforts to retain the wallet.[5]

Robbery implies theft. Technically, robbery is a distinct crime from theft **16.02**
and not an aggravation of it,[6] but logically it is theft aggravated by
personal violence or intimidation. There can accordingly be no robbery
unless there is a theft, and the law regarding appropriation,[7] things
capable of being stolen,[8] and the *mens rea* of theft,[9] apply equally in
robbery.[10] It follows that it is not robbery to take one's own property

---

[1] *cf.* Alison, i, 227: "Robbery consists in the violent and forcible taking away the
property of another." See also Anderson, p.183. In the modern law of theft, it is not
necessary (although sufficient) for property to be "taken away" by the thief: see
paras 14.01, 14.10–14.11, *supra*. Nevertheless, theft involving a taking away of property
from the victim remains the most likely basis for robbery.

[2] Macdonald, p.39, n.8. *Cf.* Hume, i, 106.

[3] *James Blair* (1830) Bell's Notes 43–44; *Isabella Welsh or Hollands and John Macginnis*
(1832) Bell's Notes 44.

[4] *William Adams or Reid* (1829) Bell's Notes 43.

[5] The term "stouthrief", which was never clearly distinguished from "robbery", but
which seems to have been used mainly for robbery or theft aggravated by housebreaking or
by mob violence, is now in desuetude: see Ersk. Inst., 4,4,64; Hume, i, 110; Burnett, p.145;
Alison, i, 227; Macdonald, p.39, n.5; Anderson, p.183; *Geo. Smith and Ors* (1848) Ark. 473,
480; *Edward Murray* (1879) 4 Couper 315.

[6] Alison, i, 227. *Isabella Cowan and Ors* (1845) 2 Broun 398; *Falconer and Ors* (1852) J.
Shaw 546. There was considerable agitation in the 1860s for the abolition of robbery as a
specific offence, partly to facilitate its being tried by the sheriff and partly to avoid the now
superseded problem of acquitting on a charge of theft if robbery were proved, and vice
versa: see Evidence to Royal Commission on Law Courts in Scotland, 1868–1870, *passim*.

[7] See paras 14.10 and 14.11, *supra*.

[8] See paras 14.12–14.35, *supra*.

[9] See paras 14.47–14.51, *supra*.

[10] Hume, i, 104–105.

from another by force[11] although it will usually be assault, and may constitute a specific innominate offence related to the crime of unlawfully taking one's own property as robbery is to theft.[12] It follows also that claim of right should be a good defence to a charge of robbery, although again not necessarily to any assault that might be involved.[13] It would, however, be robbery for A to use violence to force B to sell him an article B did not wish to sell, even if A offered a fair price for it.[14]

It is not robbery forcibly to exact an incorporeal right. Burnett refers to a case of forcing someone to sign and deliver a writ, in which the accused was convicted of an innominate offence and not of robbery.[15] If, however, the paper containing the writ is the property of the victim the accused may be convicted of robbing him of it.[16]

16.03   APPROPRIATING. The type of theft in robbery is most likely to involve a physical taking away (*amotio*) of the property from the victim. This form of theft is assumed by the authoritative writers, who did not, of course, consider theft to have any other manifestation and who could hardly have anticipated modern development of that crime.[17] It must now be the case that any deprivation of the owner or custodier's possessory or proprietary rights in stealable property achieved by appropriate violence or intimidation is probably robbery: thus, if the accused in *Carmichael v. Black*; *Carmichael v. Penrice*[18] had used violence or intimidation to prevent the complainer from entering and driving off his vehicle whilst they affixed a wheel clamp to it, robbery would have been an appropriate charge, even though the vehicle had not been moved at all and the accused's intention was to deprive the complainer of his vehicle but temporarily. Even in the more likely case of robbery where the accused physically takes property from the victim, appropriation in the form of "taking" is widely construed. It is thus robbery to pick up an article which the victim has dropped, or even which has fallen in the course of the struggle.[19] It is robbery if the accused pulls out the victim's watch and then drops it on the ground and leaves it, because the *amotio*[20] is completed when the watch leaves the pocket.[21] If the article is not taken by the accused but falls from the victim in the course of the struggle and is left lying, there is only an attempted robbery.[22]

---

[11] Provided the submission made in para. 14.28, *supra*, is accepted.

[12] And similarly it may be a specific innominate offence to take someone else's property by force and use it: see Burnett, p.151; Alison, i, 239. Alison accepts that *res sua* is a defence to robbery, but immediately goes on to make an exception for the case where the property is in the "lawful possession" of another, an exception for which he cites no authority.

[13] Macdonald, p.42 refers to *Donald McInnes and Malcolm McPherson* (1836) 1 Swin, 198 as a case of "trial for robbery by forcibly taking payment of a debt due to the assailant himself". The accused were acquitted on the robbery charge, and no arguments or opinions are quoted, so the case cannot be regarded as authority for any proposition.

[14] Burnett, p.152.

[15] *Geo. Adam* (1791) Burnett 153; *cf. John Milne* (1805) Burnett 151.

[16] *Jas Dunipace* (1842) 1 Broun 506.

[17] See paras 14.02–14.11, *supra*, for the development of theft.

[18] 1992 S.C.C.R. 709.

[19] Hume, i, 105; Burnett, 149; Alison, i, 234.

[20] See Hume i, 104–106 on *amotio*; see also para. 14.11, *supra*.

[21] *Purves and McIntosh* (1846) Ark. 178.

[22] Burnett, p.148. *Cf.* Hume, i, 105 quoting Hale's *Pleas of the Crown*, and *Jas Holland* (1808) Buch. Pt II, 66.

It is robbery to compel the victim to hand over the thing. The classic "highway robbery" situation of "Your money or your life" is a robbery — a consent elicited by force and fear is irrelevant in robbery.[23]

Robbery implies personal violence. Where there is actual violence and not **16.04** merely intimidation the violence must be directed to the person; where the violence is done to property as in housebreaking or forcing lockfast places there is only an aggravated theft. But the theft in robbery need not be a theft *from* the person. It is robbery to attack a watchman and so gain entry to premises and steal; it is robbery to attack a householder and force him to open his safe and hand over the contents.[24] Hume says that robbery applies "to anything which is under the immediate care and protection of the person invaded; so that unless by force or terror applied to him, it cannot be taken away."[25] The requirement of immediacy has not come under discussion in any reported Scots cases.[26] The type case of robbery is that in which goods are taken from the person of the victim. The situation where they are taken from his care is an extension of this, and the idea of immediacy is introduced because the more immediately the thing is under his care the nearer the situation approaches the type case. To assault a man and take his keys to open a safe beside which he is standing is clearly robbery. But suppose A robs B in Glasgow and takes from him keys which he uses to enter and steal from a house in Edinburgh — is what happens in Edinburgh robbery? It is thought not. There is a robbery in Glasgow, but all that happens in Edinburgh is a theft by housebreaking by means of a stolen key.

THE NATURE OF THE VIOLENCE. Alison says that the degree of violence **16.05** necessary for robbery varies with the condition of the victim, that a smaller degree of violence will be sufficient in the case of a woman in a remote place than in the case of a robust man in a frequented one.[27] There is, however, no authority for suggesting that A cannot be convicted of robbery if B's resistance is overcome more easily than that of the average man of his build. Burnett, in a passage cited by Alison,[28] is concerned only to show that any violence which in fact puts the victim in fear is sufficient and he refers to the case of a woman accosted on the highway as an example of this. It is quite clear that any violence used to effect a theft converts that theft into robbery. It is robbery to grip a man by his waist in order to pick his pocket,[29] to pull a man's watch out of his pocket with such violence that he falls to the ground[30] or for A to grip B's hand in order to prevent B interfering with A's accomplice's efforts to pick his pocket.[31] All that is necessary is that there should be sufficient

---

[23] Hume, i, 107; Alison, i, 231. *Wm Macmillan and Spence Gordon* (1829), *ibid. Cf. Harrison v. Jessop*, 1991 S.C.C.R. 329.

[24] *Wm Macmillan and Spence Gordon* (1829) Alison, i, 231; *Matthias Little* (1830), *ibid.*: Macdonald, p.40.

[25] Hume, i, 106.

[26] But see *Smith v. Desmond; R. v. Desmond, R. v. Hall* [1965] A.C. 960.

[27] Alison, i, 229.

[28] *ibid.*; Burnett, p.146.

[29] *John and Alex. Givan* (1846) Ark. 9, L.J.-C. Hope at 11, rejecting as inaccurate Alison's report of the case of *Alex. Smith* (1833) at Alison, i, 237: the case is accurately reported at Bell's Notes 43.

[30] *Jas Fegen* (1838) 2 Swin. 25; *O'Neill v. H.M. Advocate*, 1934 J.C. 98.

[31] *Helen Melville and Ors* (1832) Bell's Notes 43.

force used to take the crime out of the category of a theft by surprise, and so to distinguish it from theft by snatching or pickpocketing. If A sets out to commit theft by pickpocketing, and the victim notices this and a struggle develops before A has completed the theft, that will be enough to turn the pickpocketing into a robbery.[32]

16.06   DRUGGING. It is not altogether clear whether it is robbery or merely aggravated theft to overcome a person's resistance by means of drugs, except where the drugs themselves are forcibly administered. Bell cites two cases in which the accused gave the victim drugs in order to steal from him after he had become unconscious, in both of which the charges were of administering the drugs with intent to steal and of theft,[33] and himself suggests that by analogy with the law of rape this should be robbery and not theft. The matter has not been authoritatively decided, but it is submitted that these are not cases of robbery. The analogy with rape is a plausible one, but it is not exact. The act of intercourse is prima facie an assault rendered innocent by the consent of the woman; the act of picking a man's pocket is not in itself an act of violence and must be accompanied by violence before it becomes a robbery. The question is whether the administration of drugs is to be regarded as an act of violence for this purpose. To force a man to take a drug, or forcibly inject him with a drug, and then steal from him, is as much a robbery as to knock him down and then steal from him. But to slip a drug into a drink he is taking voluntarily smacks more of subterfuge than of violence, and theft by subterfuge is not robbery.[34]

16.07   THE VIOLENCE MUST PRECEDE THE THEFT. Robbery is theft by means of violence, so the violence must precede the theft, *i.e.* precede the stage at which appropriation occurs. It is therefore not robbery to use force against an owner in order to retain an article one has just snatched from him,[35] or to use force to escape after a successful pickpocketing operation, or after any theft.

16.08   THE VIOLENCE MUST BE WITH INTENT TO ROB. The type-case of robbery is that in which A attacks B in order to steal from him. But there may be robbery where the attack was not originally made with intent to rob, provided that that intent developed in the course of the attack and was present at the time the thing was appropriated. If A assaults B out of revenge and in the course of the struggle notices that B is carrying a wallet and decides to take it, he will be guilty of a simple assault, and also of a robbery, part of the attack being referable to an intention to rob B of the wallet.

Suppose now that A assaults B and renders him unconscious, and then for the first time notices B's wallet, and decides to steal it. Is that assault

---

[32] Hume, i, 105; *John Wishart* (1845) 2 Broun 445.

[33] *David Wilson and Ors* (1828) and *John Stuart and Anr* (1829) Bell's Notes 22: in the latter case the victim was killed.

[34] The 2nd Sched. to the Firearms Act 1968 lists "administration of drugs with intent to enble or assist the commission of a crime" as a crime, probably under the influence of the Offences against the Person Act 1861, s.22. See also *infra*, paras 29.48, 33.07.

[35] *Daniel Stuart* (1829) Bell's Notes 42; *Thos Innes and Ann Blair* (1834), *ibid.*; *Joan Reid and Helen Barnet* (1844) 2 Broun 116, L.J.-C. Hope at 118.

and theft, or assault and robbery? It is submitted that it is assault and theft, since the wallet was not taken by force. If A left B unconscious and C came along and stole the wallet, C would not be guilty of robbery, and it is submitted that where A's attack on B was not motivated by an intention to rob, his subsequent taking of the wallet is on all fours with C's.[36] There is little or no authority on the question. It is almost certainly the law that if A assaults B with intent to rob him of an article *x*, and after the conclusion of the assault notices and steals *y*, he will be convicted of robbery. It is probably the case that where A assaults B and also steals from him there is a presumption that the assault was embarked on with the intention of committing the theft. But it is submitted that Burnett and Alison are incorrect when they say that there can be robbery where the intention to steal first arises after the conclusion of the assault.[37] Bell raises the question but does not answer it, and the case he quotes is of no assistance as it does not suggest that the intent to steal first arose after the attack was over.[38] Macdonald says that, "if a person has been treated violently, but the taking has been subsequent to and disconnected from the violence, the offence is not robbery".[39] "Disconnected" suggests some interval in time, but the time interval is not important — what is important is that the taking is disconnected from the violence in the sense that it was not the object of the violence.[40]

Burnett also remarks that it is robbery to accept money offered by a **16.09** woman as an inducement to desist from rape.[41] A charge of robbery was brought in these circumstances in *Jas. Templeton*,[42] but its relevancy was attacked, and when the court expressed doubts on the matter and offered to certify the case to the High Court for decision the Crown dropped the charge. Macdonald says, "[t]here can be no doubt that such a taking is not robbery",[43] and it is submitted that that is correct. In such

---

[36] In other words there is not robbery every time an assault is followed by theft. This is now a purely technical matter. Prior to the Criminal Justice (Scotland) Act 1963, s.44, now the 1995 Act, s.5(4), robbery could be tried only on indictment, and in practice where the circumstances did not merit such treatment and it was desired to try the case summarily, the accused was charged with two separate offences of assault and theft. In many cases this was on the facts a piece of legal fiction since the circumstances clearly amounted to robbery. But if every assault followed by stealing were robbery it would have been impossible for this fiction to be applied. The charge of assault and theft proceeded on a fictitious assumption that the intent to steal arose after the completion of the assault. Although it is competent to convict of theft on a charge of theft even if the evidence discloses that the facts amount to robbery: 1995 Act, Sched. 3, para. 8(4), it would not be good practice to charge theft alone where the Crown knew that on any assumption the facts amounted to robbery. Indeed even if assault and theft were charged and the evidence showed clearly that the crime was robbery the conviction for assault might be technically bad, since in such circumstances the charge should have been of assault-and-robbery, *i.e.* of robbery aggravated by assault, and not of two separate crimes: *cf. Abraham McGinnes* (1842) 1 Broun 231.

[37] Burnett, p.150; Alison, i, 238; *Young* (1801) Burnett, p.150, is inconclusive.

[38] *Jas Blair* (1830) Bell's Notes 44.

[39] Macdonald, p.41.

[40] The case to which Macdonald refers: *John Dawson* (1835) Bell's Notes 41, is very confused in its facts, and is unhelpful.

[41] Burnett, p.150.

[42] (1871) 2 Couper 140.

[43] Macdonald, p.41.

a situation the assault is committed with intent only to ravish and no force is used for the purpose of obtaining money.[44]

16.10 *Robbery and assault and robbery.* In most cases of robbery the appropriating of the goods is preceded by a distinct assault, as where A knocks B down, or binds and gags him, and then takes his property. In such a situation it might be said that there are two crimes — the assault, and the taking which, because it is preceded by the assault, is robbery, and the situation is in modern practice called "assault and robbery." But despite this nomenclature the legal position is that there is only one crime — robbery, and "assault and robbery" is robbery aggravated by the preceding assault.[45]

There are, however, cases in which the taking is not preceded by any assault, but is itself so violent as to constitute robbery, in which the charge is just "You did rob A.B. of . . ." and not, "you did assault A.B. . . . and rob him . . ."[46] Although this type of "simple robbery" is not common, there are a number of examples of it, and its existence is well settled.[47] These cases have to be distinguished from cases of pickpocketing or bag-snatching, which are thefts and not robberies, because they are committed by surprise and not by violence.[48] Whether a case is one of theft or robbery is always a question of fact, and is often a very difficult question.[49] Where, however, the victim falls or sustains any

---

[44] This would seem to be so in modern English law (see Theft Act 1968, s.8(1); J.C. Smith, *The Law of Theft* (7th ed., 1993), para. 3-05: *cf.*, the common law position, which favoured robbery on the ground that the money is handed over under the influence of terror inspired by the accused, as shown in *R. v. Blackham* (1787) 2 East P.C. 711, where the accused took the money and continued his attempt at rape). That there is no robbery in such a situation also seems to be the case in modern South African law: see J. Burchell and J. Milton, *Principles of Criminal Law* (2nd ed., Cape Town, 1997), p.570 at 3.

[45] *O'Neill v. H.M. Advocate*, 1934 J.C. 98. It should be noted, however, that in modern practice it is competent to convict the accused of any part of what is charged in an indictment provided it constitutes in itself a crime: 1995 Act, Sched.3, para.9(2), so that it would be competent to convict of assault on a charge of assault and robbery if the Crown proved the attack but failed to prove the stealing. But if both are proved the assault is subsumed in the robbery and the accused cannot be convicted of the two as separate crimes: *cf. Abraham McGinnes* (1842) 1 Broun 231.

[46] 1995 Act, Sched. 2: it is usual to libel "did assault A.B. . . . and rob (*or* attempt to rob) him of . . . ", but the schedule gives a style "did assault . . . and attempt to take from him . . ." as, presumably, a style for attempted robbery.

[47] For example, *Jas Campbell* (1824) Hume, i, 107; *Abraham McGinnes* (1842) 1 Broun 231.

[48] Hume, i, 106. See *Cromar v. H.M. Advocate*, 1987 S.C.C.R. 635, where a tug, sufficiently strong to break the handles of a plastic bag the victim was carrying, was in the circumstances considered adequate to disclose robbery rather than theft. (The Crown had originally charged assault and robbery; but the allegations of assault were departed from during the trial.)

[49] In *McGinnes, supra*, the accused apparently knocked off the victim's hat with one blow, and this was held to be robbery. In *John and Alex. Givan* (1846) Ark. 9 it was held to be robbery to pick a man's pocket by seizing him round the waist — but it would not be robbery just to place one's hand in his pocket and abstract something. On the other hand, it has been held to be theft to snatch something out of a man's hand: *Walter Monro* (1828) Bell's Notes 21; *Robert Edmonston and Jas Brown* (1834), *ibid.* at 22, or out of a wallet he is holding in his hand: *John Millar* (1829) *ibid.* at 21, or to edge the victim into a passage and put one's hands into his pocket: *Mary Robertson* (1837) *ibid.*; *cf. Wm Duggin and John Ketchen* (1828), *ibid.* In *Ann Watt or Ketchen* (1834) Bell's Notes 21, the victim's money was in his neckcloth, and the accused snatched the neckcloth and got hold of the money although the victim managed to retain the neckcloth, and the Crown dropped the charge of robbery. Bell also cites a number of cases of theft which might nowadays be regarded as robbery, *e.g. Wm Cummings* (1830) Bell's Notes 21–22 where the snatch was preceded by a kick which "would not have injured a child", and *Neil Macgilvray and Thos Macmillan* (1841) Bell's Notes 22, where the victim was caught round the middle and his watch torn from its guard chain.

injury as a result of the crime it will be robbery and not theft. In *James Fegen*,[50] in which the charge narrated that Fegen threw the victim to the ground, the evidence was that he had only pulled the victim's watch out of his pocket by seizing its chain but that the victim had fallen, either accidentally or by being tripped, and that while he was falling his chain had been broken by another pull. His only injury was a very slight one to his knee. In these circumstances the court held that the violence was sufficient to establish the charge of robbery.

Fegen[51] was followed in *O'Neill v. H.M. Advocate*.[52] O'Neill was **16.11** charged with "assault and robbery" by knocking a woman's head against a wall and taking her handbag. The jury convicted him of robbery but acquitted him of assault, and their verdict was appealed as being perverse. The court upheld the verdict on the ground that although the jury had negatived the specific assault libelled, there was sufficient evidence of violence to justify the conviction for robbery. Lord Justice-Clerk Aitchison said, "It is well settled that in robbery there must be violence. On the other hand, it is not necessary to robbery that there should be actual physical assault. It is enough if the degree of force used can reasonably be described as violence."[53] He went on to hold that the injuries which the victim had been proved to have sustained were ascribable to the snatching of her handbag, and indicated a degree of force sufficient for robbery even without any prior assault. The position is a little peculiar, and it may be that the difference between assault and robbery, and robbery, is merely that in the former case there is more violence, and therefore a more serious offence is committed. After all, there cannot be a robbery unless there is an assault (or, of course, intimidation).[54] It appears that where the assault and the appropriating of the goods are one and the same act, as where a man's hat is knocked off and taken, or a woman's handbag pulled so hard that she falls to the ground, there is simple robbery, but that where there is any assault in addition to that contained in the act of appropriating or where the act of appropriating is not itself an assault but is made possible by an earlier assault, there is aggravated robbery, known as assault and robbery.

---

[50] (1838) 2 Swin. 25.

[51] (1838) 2 Swin. 25.

[52] 1934 J.C. 98.

[53] At 101.

[54] See, *e.g.*, *Flynn v. H.M. Advocate*, 1995 S.C.C.R. 590, where a conviction for robbery was quashed in that the jury had negatived the allegations of violence against the victim contained in the charge. *Cf.* the curious case of *MacKay v. H.M. Advocate*, 1997 S.C.C.R. 743, where the jury were directed that there was insufficient evidence of assault due to lack of corroboration; they thus deleted the words "you did assault" from the indictment, but apparently left undisturbed the specific allegations which had constituted the modus of the assault in the charge: as these allegations had been uncorroborated, it is strange that the Appeal Court accepted them as part of the evidence of violence or intimidation against the complainer, and thus as evidence favourable to the conviction for robbery. It is difficult to reconcile this decision with what was decided in the earlier case of *Flynn*; but it seems that the evidence of the complainer as to what happened to him does not itself have to be corroborated if it is part of the narrative of the crime of robbery and is consistent with other evidence suggestive of violence or intimidation towards him.

Intimidation

16.12   It is settled that actual violence is not necessary to robbery. "Such behaviour, as justly alarms for the personal and immediate consequences of resistance or refusal" is sufficient.[55] The development from violence to intimidation is clear — it is robbery to shoot B and steal from him; it is also robbery, because it is technically an assault, to present a weapon at B and intimidate him into handing over his goods; and from there it is but a short step to say that it is robbery to threaten to shoot B without actually producing a weapon.

16.13   *Need that threat be of personal violence?* There is no dispute that a threat of immediate personal violence constitutes robbery. Whether threats of any other kind are sufficient is unsettled. Hume indicates that they are not, unless accompanied by threats of personal violence or made in circumstances which "beget a reasonable fear of immediate violence though not expressly threatened, in case of refusal to comply."[56] Alison is not clear, but indicates that threats to set B's house on fire or to drag him off to gaol would constitute robbery if they amounted to threats of personal danger, as by binding B and taking him to gaol by force.[57] Macdonald says merely that the threat must induce reasonable fear of coercion or bodily injury.[58] The sole modern reported case which raises, but does not decide, the issue is *Harrison v. Jessop*,[59] where, as a means to obtaining part payment of a debt owed by the tenant of restaurant premises, the accused told the complainers (an employee and a relative of the tenant) that they would not be allowed to leave the premises until they had handed over the contents of the till. The subsequent conviction for robbery was upheld by the Appeal Court, but on the rather loose basis that the money from the till had been handed over against the will of the complainers.[60] It is submitted, therefore, that any threat of immediate injury, personal or otherwise but including physical restraint, will constitute robbery, the only question being whether B was induced to hand over his property as a result of the threat. As Burnett says, "it may reasonably be maintained, that whatever operates as a terror in the mind from near and immediate danger, and which may reasonably be supposed to subdue the power of resistance, and to compel the person to part with his property, is an act of force sufficient to constitute robbery."[61] It is accordingly submitted that the definition of robbery given in Gardiner and Lansdown's *South African Criminal Law*[62] is applicable to Scotland on this point: "Robbery is theft, from the person of another . . . accompanied by actual violence or threats of violence to

---

[55] Hume, i, 107; *Sim.* Burnett, pp.146–147; Alison, i, 230–232. *Wm Macmillan and Spence Gordon* (1829), *Matthias Little* (1830), both Alison, i, 231; Anderson, pp.183–184; Macdonald, p.41.

[56] Hume, i, 108.

[57] Alison, i, 231.

[58] Macdonald, p.40.

[59] 1991 S.C.C.R. 329.

[60] The case for the appellant was also argued on the untenable basis that the *mens rea* of the appellant had been insufficient for theft, since he had not at the time intended to deprive the complainers permanently of the money: see paras 14.47–14.51, *supra*, as to the modern *mens rea* for theft.

[61] Burnett, p.147.

[62] (Cape Town, 1946), at 1706. This definition is not accepted in J. Burchell and J. Milton, *Principles of Criminal Law* (2nd ed., Cape Town, 1997), where, at pp. 569–570, it is argued that robbery requires physical violence: *cf.* Theft Act, s.8(1).

such person or his property or reputation". It follows that if A picks up B's telephone and threatens that he will inform the police or even the press of something detrimental to B unless B hands over a sum of money, and B hands over the money because his will to refuse has been overcome by the threat, A is guilty of robbing B of the money.[63] Threats to property, and threats of personal injury to other persons, for example to B's children, will also constitute robbery on this definition.[64]

Robbery and extortion. Robbery by threats is distinguished from **16.14** extortion by the immediacy of the threat and of the obtaining of the money. For A to threaten B that unless he immediately gives him £*x* A will immediately telephone the police is robbery: for A to threaten B that unless he immediately gives him £*x* A will telephone the police tomorrow is extortion. And likewise for A to threaten B that unless he promises to give him £*x* tomorrow A will immediately telephone the police is extortion and not robbery. For robbery the threat must be of immediate injury and the demand must be for immediate delivery of the money or goods.[65] It follows that robbery cannot be committed by correspondence — it is not robbery for A to write to B demanding money by return of post under threat of violence. Nor is it robbery for A to send C to threaten B that unless he gives him money to take back to A, A will injure B. But it would be robbery for C to threaten B that unless B handed money over to C for A, C would then and there injure B.

Aggravations, kindred offences, etc.

Robbery can be aggravated by the same circumstances as operate to **16.15** aggravate theft.

Housebreaking with intent to rob has not appeared as a charge in any reported case, but it might be a competent charge.

Section 52(d) of the Post Office Act 1953 made it an offence punishable with 10 years' imprisonment to "stop a mail with intent to rob or search the mail." Although the whole of the 1953 Act was repealed by the Postal Services Act 2000, a note to Sched. 9 of the latter Act indicates that the repeal of section 52 of the former Act does not affect any liability at common law "in respect of any of the offences described in that section".

To obtain unlawful possession of one's own or another's goods by violence or threats would probably constitute only an aggravated assault, or perhaps a species of oppression or extortion.[66]

---

[63] This was recognised at common law in England only in respect of threats to accuse of sodomy and threats to injure property: see *Pollock v. Divers* [1967] 2 Q.B. 195, but there is no reason for such a restriction.

[64] Threats of injury to C may constitute robbery even if robbery is restricted to threats of personal injury: see Theft Act 1968, s.8(1); J.C. Smith, *The Law of Theft* (7th ed., 1993), paras 3–1 to 3–15.

[65] Hume, i, 108; Alison, i, 231 *et seq.*; Burnett, p.147; Macdonald, p.41; Anderson, pp.183–184; see also J. Burchell and J. Milton, *Principles of Criminal Law* (2nd ed., Cape Town, 1997), at p.570.

[66] *cf.* Hume, i, 74; Alison, i, 239, where he suggests that in the case of one's own goods it is only a *spuilzie*; Burnett, pp.151–152.

16.16 *Mock robbery*. If A goes into a shop and presents a gun at the assistant and forces her to hand over the contents of the till, all for a joke, and then returns the money, this is now almost certainly robbery. Alison and Burnett describe it as "a high outrage, and severely punishable"[67] rather than robbery; but their views have been overtaken by modern developments such as that evil intent in assault means merely that the conduct of the accused was deliberate (irrespective of motive),[68] and that an intention to deprive temporarily will suffice for theft — at least where a nefarious purpose is involved.[69]

Piracy

16.17 Piracy is essentially robbery on the high seas. It is distinguished from privateering by the absence of any authorisation of the pirate's actings by a recognised State. Piracy can be committed not only by one ship against another, but also by persons on a ship against that ship by taking forcible possession of the ship from its master.[70] An actual robbery is not necessary, a frustrated attempt being sufficient.[71]

As is the case with modern robbery, piracy requires only the forcible taking of possession so that an intention to appropriate the ship permanently is not necessary. In *Cameron v. H.M. Advocate*[72] the charge was of, *inter alia*, unlawfully depriving the skipper of his command, threatening him, robbing him of his keys, putting him ashore, and navigating the vessel on to the high seas, whereby it was alleged that the accused "did . . . take masterful possession" of the vessel, and appropriate it to their own use. According to the trial judge, Lord Cameron, intention to appropriate temporarily was enough. Lord Wheatley, on appeal, held that the facts set out in the dittay disclosed a number of offences and that it was not necessary to decide whether or not they constituted piracy. He did, however, say:

> "The offence of piracy is part of the municipal law of Scotland, and even if internationally accepted principles have been incorporated therein, it still remains our own municipal law. The prerequisites of the offence of piracy according to the law of Scotland are those set out in the presiding judge's opinion on relevancy to which I refer and which I adopt *brevitatis causa* subject to what immediately follows. In particular, I consider that he conveniently summarises the position when he says in his opinion: 'There is enough . . . in the authorities to make it possible to say that, when a ship is feloniously taken out of the possession of the owner or those in whose charge the vessel has been placed, against their will and by means of violence or threats of violence and, so taken, thereafter appropriated to the use of those who have done so, the crime so committed

---

[67] Alison, i, 239; Burnett, p.150.

[68] See *Lord Advocate's Reference (No.2 of 1992)*, 1993 J.C. 43, where the accused was charged, *inter alia*, with assault with intent to rob and attempted robbery, in circumstances similar to those postulated in the text, *supra*, save that he ran off before obtaining any money.

[69] See paras 14.47–14.49, *supra*.

[70] For example, *Peter Heaman and Francois Gautier* (1821) Hume, i, 483. See Hume, i, 480–485; Alison, i, 638–640; Anderson, pp.68–69; Macdonald, pp.43–44; *Re Piracy Jure Gentium, infra*.

[71] *Re Piracy Jure Gentium* [1934] A.C. 586.

[72] 1971 J.C. 50.

is piracy *jure gentium*.' The use of more glamorous terms or Latin phrases in no way expands in effect these basic requirements."[73]

Piracy is also an international crime, and persons guilty of piracy *jure* **16.18** *gentium* may be tried wherever they are caught, irrespective of the place of the piracy, or the nationality of the accused or the victim.[74]

Piracy in international law is now defined in the Merchant Shipping and Maritime Security Act 1997 as follows:

> "(a) Any illegal acts of violence or detention, or any act of depredation, committed for private ends by the crew or the passengers of a private ship or a private aircraft, and directed—
>> (i) on the high seas, against another ship or aircraft, or against persons or property on board such ship or aircraft;
>> (ii) against a ship, aircraft, persons or property in a place outside the jurisdiction of any State;
> (b) any act of voluntary participation in the operation of a ship or of an aircraft with knowledge of facts making it a pirate ship or aircraft;
> (c) Any act of inciting or of intentionally facilitating an act described in sub-paragraph (a) or sub-paragraph (b) of this article.
>
> The acts of piracy as defined . . ., committed by a warship, government ship or government aircraft whose crew has mutinied and taken control of the ship or aircraft are assimilated to acts committed by a private ship or aircraft.
>
> A ship or aircraft is considered a pirate ship or aircraft if it is intended by the persons in dominant control to be used for the purpose of committing one of the acts referred to . . . The same applies if the ship or aircraft has been used to commit any such act so long as it remains under the control of the persons guilty of that act."[75]

That definition does not, however, affect Scots municipal law, and where the acts complained of occur in Scottish territorial waters or in other circumstances giving the Scottish courts jurisdiction to enforce Scots law,[76] the case is determined solely by reference to the municipal law.[77]

Hijacking. Section 1 of the Aviation Security Act 1982 provides: **16.19**

> "(1) A person on board an aircraft in flight who unlawfully, by the use of force or by threats of any kind, seizes the aircraft or exercises control of it commits the offence of hijacking, whatever his nationality, whatever the State in which the aircraft is registered and whether the aircraft is in the United Kingdom or elsewhere, but subject to sub-section (2) below.

---

[73] 1971 J.C. 50, 61.
[74] Hume, i, 480.
[75] Sched. 5, Arts 101–103.
[76] As for example under the Merchant Shipping Act 1995, s.281.
[77] *Cameron v. H.M. Advocate*, 1971 J.C. 50.

(2) If —

    (a) the aircraft is used in military, customs or police service; or

    (b) both the place of take-off and the place of landing are in the territory of the State in which the aircraft is registered;

subsection (1) above shall not apply, unless—

    (i) the person seizing or exercising control of the aircraft is a United Kingdom national[78]; or

    (ii) his act is committed in the United Kingdom; or

    (iii) the aircraft is registered in the United Kingdom or is used in the military or customs service of the United Kingdom or in the service of any police force in the United Kingdom.

(3) A person who commits the offence of hijacking shall be liable, on conviction on indictment, to imprisonment for life.

(4) If the Secretary of State by order made by statutory instrument declares —

    (a) that any two or more States named in the order have established an organisation or agency which operates aircraft; and

    (b) that one of those States has been designated as exercising, for aircraft so operated, the powers of the State of registration,

the State declared under paragraph (b) of this subsection shall be deemed for the purposes of this section to be the State in which any aircraft so operated is registered; but in relation to such an aircraft subsection (2)(b) above shall have effect as if it referred to the territory of any one of the States named in the order.

(5) For the purposes of this section the territorial waters of any State shall be treated as part of its territory."

---

[78] Under s.38(1) of the Aviation Security Act 1982 (as amended by the Schedule to the Hong Kong (British Nationality) Order 1986 (S.I. 1986 No. 948)), a United Kingdom national is someone who is: (a) a British Citizen, a British Dependent Territories citizen, a British National (Overseas), or a British overseas citizen; or (b) a person who under the British Nationality Act 1981 is a British subject; or (c) a British protected person, within the meaning of that 1981 Act.

CHAPTER 17

EMBEZZLEMENT

Breach of trust and embezzlement

"Breach of trust and embezzlement" is a composite name for what is **17.01**
now regarded as a single crime[1] whose modern name is "embezzlement".[2] The word "embezzlement" suggests the misappropriation of a
particular sum and emphasises the similarity between embezzlement and
theft, but this is rather misleading since one of the distinctions between
the two crimes is that it is not necessary to be able to point to a
particular sum or thing which has been embezzled in the way in which it
is necessary to be able to point to a stolen thing. On the other hand,
embezzlement is restricted to the misappropriation of things capable of
being stolen,[3] whereas "breach of trust" may have a wider connotation.
It may be possible to commit breach of trust with regard to things other
than corporeal moveables or money, for example by revealing secrets
imparted to one in confidence,[4] but if such a form of breach of trust does
exist it is undeveloped and virtually unformulated, except in those cases
in which it comes under the category of breach of duty by public
officials.[5]

Embezzlement, theft and fraud

Hume deals with embezzlement only in the context of theft, and is **17.02**
concerned to point out that certain situations which might look like theft
are truly only cases of breach of trust.[6] As has been seen,[7] Hume
confined theft to cases of unlawful taking; where A dishonestly appropriated things of which he had lawful possession, his crime was only breach
of trust. Hume makes only one reference to the type of case which is
today regarded as typical of embezzlement, and he regards that case as
essentially the same as that of the footman who appropriates his livery

---

[1] Although this was not always so: see *Wm McGall* (1849) J. Shaw 194. *Cf. Geo. Smith*
(1836) 1 Swin. 301.
[2] *Taylor v. Maitland* (1879) 4 Couper 262, 266; *Agnew v. Addison* (1892) 3 White 368,
372; Criminal Procedure (Scotland) Act 1887, Sched. A (now Sched. 2 of the Criminal
Procedure (Scotland) Act 1995).
[3] *cf. Guild v. Lees*, 1994 S.C.C.R. 745, where it was unsuccessfully argued that what was
appropriated by the appellant was incorporeal property and thus incapable of being
embezzled. The appellant had had authority to draw cheques on his employer's bank
account for expenses incurred relative to his employment, but had in fact drawn a cheque
on that account to meet his own domestic electricity bill.
[4] *H.M. Advocate v. Mackenzies* (1913) 7 Adam 189; see also Scottish Law Commission
Memorandum ("Confidential Information") No. 40 (1977).
[5] See *infra*, para. 44.01.
[6] Whatever the modern view, and it is not altogether consistent, there was no doubt in
Hume's day that breach of trust was a lesser crime than theft, since it could never be
capital.
[7] *supra*, para. 14.01.

and who, according to Hume, was guilty not of theft but only of breach of trust. He says, immediately after dealing with the footman, "[u]nder the same rule falls the case of a factor, who runs off with his employer's rents, after receiving them from the tenants, or even (which is stronger) the case of an overseer or steward, entrusted with the management of a farm, who privately disposes of the grain and other commodities, the produce of the land, and applies the price to his own behoof."[8] "The wrong" in such a case, he explains, "does not lie in the disposal of the things; for this falls under the powers of the steward's office: Neither does the clandestine manner of the disposal make him a thief; because his master has put the produce out of his own hands, into those of the steward, to be administered at his discretion, so he faithfully account for the value. The trespass lies, therefore, in the short accounting, and concealment of his receipts, not in the withdrawing of the species or *corpus*; and this, though criminal, is however a fraud only, or breach of trust, and not an act of theft."[9]

In this short passage Hume has set out the essential features of the modern embezzlement with much greater clarity than has any modern judge or writer, but he does not develop the matter, and indeed is not clear whether the crime is breach of trust or fraud. In particular, he does not seem to have appreciated that the steward's crime was very different from that of the dishonest footman, carrier or hirer, and was also distinguishable from that of the rent collector. The only case to which he refers in speaking of the steward is *Rosebery v. Tait*[10] in which it was held that such a steward was guilty not of theft, but of "fraudulent conceal-ments of the proceeds of his master's goods, and by false contrivances endeavouring to prevent those proceeds from coming to his master's knowledge",[11] an innominate offence which sounds more like fraud than anything else.[12]

Burnett likewise treats of breach of trust when dealing with theft, and seems to regard it as essentially a form of fraud — he talks of "that species of trust, the breach of which is punishable only as fraud."[13]

Alison follows Hume fairly closely, although he gives a number of additional examples of embezzlements by factors, managers, and the like, which were heard in the 1820s, and most of which were charged as "breach of trust, fraud and embezzlement."[14] Such embezzlements appear to have been regarded as essentially frauds committed by false accounting and perhaps aggravated by breach of confidence, rather than as a form of theft like the breach of trust committed by the carrier or hirer.[15]

---

[8] Hume, i, 60.

[9] *ibid.*

[10] (1776) Hume, i, 60.

[11] Hume, i, 61.

[12] *cf. Reid v. Gentles* (1857) 2 Irv. 704, where a similar charge was withdrawn after objection.

[13] Burnett, pp.111–113; *Andrew Webster* (1783) Burnett 113, a charge of "fraudulent embezzlement in breach of trust."

[14] Alison, i, 345, 355–358.

[15] *cf. Geo. Smith* (1836) 1 Swin. 301 where a partner indorsed promissory notes in the firm's signature in breach of the trust reposed in him by his partner and then discounted the notes and embezzled the proceeds; he was charged with breach of trust and embezzlement.

It can now be regarded as accepted that breach of trust or embezzlement is not a species of fraud,[16] but is a crime of its own with more affinities to theft than to fraud.[17]

Embezzlement and theft. Hume did not offer a definition of embezzle-   **17.03** ment to cover all the situations he regarded as falling under that head but if he had done it would probably have been "the felonious appropriation of the goods of another of which the accused had lawful possession." This definition ceased to be easily applicable after the cases of *John Smith*[18] and *Geo. Brown*[19] which decided that an unlawful taking was not a necessary ingredient of theft in Scots law. The ideal result of these cases would have been that all cases of breach of trust other than those of the type represented by Hume's steward should be treated as cases of theft, and the category of breach of trust or embezzlement should be reserved for cases like that of the steward. The judges were, however, reluctant to take this course, and tried to cling to the old rules despite the fact that it was impossible to make them consistent with what had been said in *Smith* and in *Brown*, and despite the fact that as theft had ceased in practice to be a capital offence it was no longer necessary to define it restrictively or to have resort to breach of trust for cases of theft which did not deserve hanging.[20] As a result the judges had great difficulty in distinguishing between theft and embezzlement; indeed they often professed themselves unable to do so, and described the distinction as artificial and technical.[21] This was partly the result of a refusal to jettison Humean concepts altogether,[22] and as late as 1879, for example, Lord Young distinguished the two crimes by reference to the distinction

---

[16] See *e.g. Guild v. Lees*, 1994 S.C.C.R. 745, at 747 D, where the Appeal Court held that the actings of the appellant excluded fraud but "fell clearly within the scope of the crime of embezzlement as described by Macdonald on the Criminal Law of Scotland at pp. 45–47." See also *H.M. Advocate v. Wishart* (1975) S.C.C.R. (Supp.) 78.

[17] It is not necessary in a charge of embezzlement, for example, to prove that any false entries were made in the accused's books, or any false statements made by him: *Walter Duncan* (1849) J. Shaw 270; Macdonald, p.47.

[18] (1838) 2 Swin. 28.

[19] (1839) 2 Swin. 394.

[20] See *supra*, paras 14.03, 14.06.

[21] See *e.g. Hugh Climie* (1838) 2 Swin. 118 — decided just before *Brown, supra* — in which Lord Mackenzie said "theft and breach of trust may be committed at the same time": at 125, and Lord Cockburn described the distinction as "the most evanescent and slimmest known in our criminal law": at 127; *Robt Smith and Jas Wishard* (1842) 1 Broun 342, in which Lord Moncreiff said that the difference between the two crimes "certainly turns upon very nice distinctions": at 349; *Watt v. Home* (1851) J. Shaw 591, in which Lord Colonsay said, "Perhaps there is no part of our law which is more involved in obscurity, as propounded by our elementary writers, than the distinction between breach of trust and theft": at 521 — his Lordship went on to say that matters had been rendered more distinct of late, but that, alas, was no more than a pious hope; *Elder v. Morrison* (1881) 4 Couper 530, in which Lord Young said that breach of trust was merely a species of theft: at 535; *H.M. Advocate v. City of Glasgow Bank Directors* (1879) 4 Couper 161, in which L.J.-C. Moncreiff said, "the distinction between theft and breach of trust is a very fine and subtle one, and, I think, depends more upon words than upon substance": at 190; *H.M. Advocate v. Richd Laing* (1891) 2 White 572, in which Lord Kincairney said that the distinction was technical rather than substantial: at 576; *cf.* L.J.-C. Boyle's confident statement in *David Walker* (1836) 1 Swin. 294, three years before *Brown, supra*, that the two crimes were "totally different": at 296, which must be ascribed either to rashness or to a lack of prescience.

[22] After all, Hume, and Alison who just repeats Hume, are still the only available books of authority, other than Macdonald, dealing with the subject.

between seizing property from another's possession, and appropriating property already in one's own possession.[23]

17.04 *Theft, theft-embezzlement and embezzlement.* One of the factors which adds to the difficulties involved in discussing embezzlement is that there appear to be not two, but three, classes of cases involved. At one extreme are the cases of the butler and the porter and the like which are clearly cases of theft[24] and were indeed so recognised by Hume; at the other are cases like those of Hume's steward which are almost equally clearly not cases of theft.[25] In between there is a large number of cases which Hume would have regarded as breach of trust but which since *Brown*[26] can be regarded as theft. This class, which might be described as the class of theft-embezzlement cases, is not clearly distinguishable from either of the other two classes, but it does seem to exist. It is true that the courts were often called upon in such cases to decide between theft and embezzlement, and succeeded in doing so, but they used a number of different criteria, and it may well be that their choice of criterion depended on whether on first impression the case looked more like theft or embezzlement, more like Hume's butler or his steward.

If the case looked like theft it was easy enough to apply a criterion which showed it to be theft, and the same was true for embezzlement.[27] It is mainly for this reason that it is necessary to talk of "theft-embezzlement". It is impossible to deduce a consistent definition of embezzlement from the cases, because the cases are not themselves consistent with each other.[28] Macdonald's definition, "the felonious appropriation of property which is in the possession of the offender as trustee, agent, factor, or other administrator; or which is in his possession with a view to his becoming beneficial owner in certain contingencies, as *e.g.* under a contract of pledge, or of sale or return; or which is in his custody for a purpose left unspecific",[29] is not so much a definition as a catalogue, and is in any event incorrect.

---

[23] *Wm Scott* (1879) 4 Couper 227, 234. Lord Young's appreciation of the position was probably not helped by his efforts to compare it with the old English crime of embezzlement which was a very limited and special crime most if not all instances of which would be regarded in modern Scots law as theft — in so far as there was an English equivalent for the Scots embezzlement it was fraudulent conversion, but it was not a satisfactory equivalent either.

[24] For example, *Philip Kneen* (1858) 3 Irv. 161, where a ship's master sold his cargo.

[25] And which would never have been so regarded, except perhaps in Mackenzie's day when the crime of "breach of trust" was hardly recognised: Mackenzie, I, 19, 1–2. *Cf.* the information for the Crown in *Geo. Brown* (1839) 2 Swin. 394, 395.

[26] (1839) 2 Swin. 394.

[27] *cf.* the approach to the problem of causality and responsibility, Vol. I, para. 4.01, although judicial attitudes are much more disinterested in the sphere of theft and embezzlement. L.J.-C. Thomson's comments on a quite different problem in the case of *British Oxygen Co. v. South West Scotland Electricity Board*, 1958 S.C. 53, 67, describe the situation in theft-embezzlement cases aptly: "The interesting debate to which we listened showed that one can speculate endlessly about the solution to this problem. On which side one comes down seems to depend largely on one's line of approach or rather from which end one approaches. Each view starts from a different premise. Grant that premise and a strong case can be made for either [view]."

[28] Indeed any attempt to discuss the Scots law of embezzlement leaves one in the state of mind described by T.S. Eliot in *Burnt Norton*: "Words strain . . . Under the tension, slip, slide, perish. Decay with imprecision, will not stay in place, Will not stay still."

[29] Macdonald, p.45.

It is true that in practice the distinction between theft and embezzlement is not now as important as it once was, since it is now competent to convict of embezzlement on a charge of theft and vice versa.[30] But the distinction still has some importance,[31] and some attempt must be made to define it, or at any rate to set out the features of embezzlement proper, *i.e.* of those embezzlements which would not be regarded as theft on any criterion. And the category of theft-embezzlement cases still exists — there are still cases which one prosecutor would charge as embezzlement while another would charge them as theft, although in view of the provisions of the 1995 Act the prosecutor rarely has to justify his choice of crime.

In this situation, it is proposed to discuss the various criteria used by the courts to distinguish theft from embezzlement, and then to consider the special characteristics of embezzlement proper.

The distinction between theft and embezzlement

The following are the most important of the criteria used in the cases. **17.05**

(1) *The relationship between the accused and the complainer.* Hume distinguished persons "who are in a responsible state as officers", such as cashiers, tellers, collectors of taxes, treasurers and judicial factors, whose crimes he regarded as breach of trust, from "an ordinary menial", but he did so mainly in order to show that the latter did not have possession of the goods in his hands, but only custody, and could for that reason be guilty of theft.[32] Even after *Geo. Brown*[33] this criterion retained some force, and it is still used, although it is now divorced from the Humean concepts of custody and possession.

It is not however of great importance in itself, and often serves only to emphasise the limited authority the accused has to deal with the money he holds, and so to show that he lacked that power to administer the money which is an essential feature of embezzlement proper. The more menial the accused's position the less likely is he to have any administrative authority and the more likely to be charged with theft. As Macdonald says, "[a] person employed to assist the owner in his business — not as an agent taking a general charge, or superintending a local branch, but as an assistant under the master's eye, and on the master's premises — taking his employer's goods, or money he receives from customers" will be guilty of theft.[34]

This criterion may help to explain why a traveller sent by a firm to collect their debts is often charged with embezzlement, while a bank teller was held to be guilty of theft as early as 1842,[35] at least partly on the ground that his position resembled that of a servant and not, as Hume had indicated, that of a tax collector. But there have been cases in which charges of theft against branch managers[36] and even company

---

[30] Criminal Procedure (Scotland) Act 1887, s.59. The earlier practice was to charge both crimes alternatively. See now 1995 Act, Sched. 3, para. 8(3) and (4).

[31] In *Kent v. H.M. Advocate,* 1950 J.C. 38, the jury convicted of embezzlement on a charge of embezzlement, and the Appeal Court who held that the crime was theft declined to substitute a verdict of theft, and instead quashed the conviction. It also appears that it may be a defence to a charge of reset of theft to show that the goods were embezzled: *O'Brien v. Strathern*, 1922 J.C. 55, L.J.-G. Clyde at 57.

[32] Hume, i, 61.

[33] (1839) 2 Swin. 394.

[34] Macdonald, pp.36–37.

[35] *Robt Smith and Jas Wishart* (1842) 1 Broun 342, L.J.-C. Hope at 351.

[36] *H.M. Advocate v. Smith* (1887) 1 White 413, Lord Craighill at 415.

directors[37] have been found relevant. Conversely, it is not uncommon for cashiers and clerkesses to be charged with embezzlement.

17.06   The accused's rank in his employment may also be of importance from what might be called the sociological aspect of the distinction between theft and embezzlement. Embezzlement is typically a white-collar crime. Message-boys and railway porters steal, while the defalcations of solicitors, stockbrokers or company directors are usually dignified by the less crude term "embezzlement". It is true that embezzlement is often regarded as a more serious crime than theft because of the breach of trust involved and because most white-collar embezzlers misappropriate substantial sums before they are caught, but the old idea that theft is a "lower-class" crime persists: it is more easy to imagine a member of one's club embezzling even the club funds than it is to imagine him picking the pocket of the hall porter or breaking into the club. It is true that the City of Glasgow Bank Directors were charged with theft, but this charge was eventually dropped.[38] In *H.M. Advocate v. John Smith*[39] Lord Craighill commented that, "[t]he fact that a man is a manager does not prevent him stealing,"[40] but the Crown charged theft and embezzlement alternatively. Again, in *H.M. Advocate v. Laing*[41] a law agent was charged with theft of money given him by a client to discharge a bond, but the jury exercised their statutory power to convict him only of embezzlement.

17.07   "ENTRUSTED". It is sometimes said that there can be no embezzlement unless the accused is in a position of trust *vis-à-vis* the money embezzled,[42] but "trust" is nowhere defined in this connection, and there is ample authority that a person entrusted with money can steal it.[43] Indeed "theft under trust" has been said to be a "known crime".[44] Every person who receives the property of another under some duty in respect of it, whether to employ it on behalf of that other or merely to retain it and return it after a certain time, can be said to receive it under trust; whether his misappropriation of it is theft or embezzlement depends on other considerations.

17.08   (2) *The nature of the accused's possession.* This is a survival from the Humean doctrine that a custodier can steal but a possessor cannot.[45] The only important appearance of this criterion subsequent to *Geo. Brown*[46] is in *Catherine Cossgrove or Bradley*.[47] The accused was a pawnbroker

---

[37] *Potter and Ors v. H.M. Advocate* (1878) 4 Couper 135.
[38] *Potter and Ors v. H.M. Advocate, supra*; *H.M. Advocate v. City of Glasgow Bank Directors* (1879) 4 Couper 161.
[39] (1887) 1 White 413.
[40] At 415.
[41] (1891) 2 White 572.
[42] For example, *Ronald Gordon* (1846) Ark. 196, L.J.-C. Hope at 200; *John McLeod* (1858) 3 Irv. 79, 86.
[43] For example, *Hugh Climie* (1838) 2 Swin. 118; *Robt Smith and Jas Wishart* (1842) 1 Broun 342.
[44] *Watt v. Home* (1851) J. Shaw 519, L.J.-C. Hope at 522; *cf. Hugh Climie* (1838) 2 Swin. 118, L.J.-G. Hope at 124.
[45] *supra*, para. 14.03; see Hume, i, 58–61.
[46] (1839) 2 Swin. 394.
[47] (1850) J. Shaw 301; a similar charge was brought in *Agnes McGinlay or Docherty and Wm Docherty* (1843) 1 Broun 548, but its relevancy was not decided.

who was charged with the theft of goods given to her in pledge, and the charge was held irrelevant. Lord Moncreiff distinguished *Brown* on the ground that to give goods in pledge, unlike giving them for repair, "not merely gave a right of possession, but a title to the goods themselves, which, by lapse of time, became absolute, and enabled the party to sell, and give a valid right to all the world."[48]

This, it is submitted, is a false view, and ignores the crucial factor that the pawnbroker's right to sell the goods is the creature of statute and is circumscribed by statutory rules which make him very much the trustee of the pledgor when he does sell them.[49] Furthermore, the pawnbroker's title does not become absolute by mere lapse of time, but is subject to the pledgor's right of redemption — and the pledgor usually hopes that the contract will be terminated by redemption and not by sale.

Lord Ivory spoke of the pawnbroker having "legal possession *proprio jure*", and claimed to be unable to distinguish between appropriation by the pawnbroker of the goods during the currency of the pledgor's right of redemption and the pawnbroker's unlawful retention of any of the proceeds of a lawful sale after the expiry of the period,[50] a distinction which, it is submitted, is clear.[51]

Lord Wood thought that if Mrs Bradley were guilty of theft there could be no such crime as breach of trust since the latter required an original lawful possession.[52] There are several answers to this point. One is that perhaps there should be no such crime as breach of trust; another is that although the court in *Brown* did try to distinguish possession and custody, they recognised that a bona fide hirer could steal[53]; a third is that it is possible to distinguish theft and breach of trust otherwise than by reference to lawful possession, although the latter is an essential ingredient in breach of trust.

Lord Justice-Clerk Hope thought that the "criminal violation of a contract of trust" was embezzlement,[54] but he did not say what he meant by "contract of trust", and pledge is no more a contract of trust than repair, hire or deposit. Lord Hope also distinguished *Bradley* from cases of "limited and temporary custody, unaccompanied with any title of property in the things themselves",[55] but no title of property is given in pledge.

It has already been submitted[56] that *Bradley* was wrongly decided. It proceeded on a misapprehension of the law of pledge, as well as on a misapprehension of the law of embezzlement. It may be that it is relevant to charge a pawnbroker with embezzlement, but it is submitted that it is clearly relevant to charge him with theft if he appropriates the pledge during the time that the pledgor is entitled to redeem it. If he appropriates it after that time he is still guilty of theft since he has no

---

[48] J. Shaw at 305.

[49] See Consumer Credit Act 1974, ss.120, 121; similar legislation existed in 1850 and replaced the earlier procedure of applying to the court for a warrant to sell: see Ersk. Inst. 3,1,33.

[50] J. Shaw at 306.

[51] In any event Lord Ivory's views on the matter are suspect since he apparently believed that pledge involved a transfer of property: *Watt v. Home* (1851) J. Shaw 519, 521.

[52] J. Shaw at 305.

[53] See *supra*, para. 14.06.

[54] J. Shaw at 306.

[55] *ibid.*

[56] *supra*, para. 14.30.

authority to do so.[57] If he sells the article in the way authorised by the Consumer Credit Act and then appropriates more than his share of the proceeds, his crime may well be embezzlement, but that is entirely different from taking the article itself while it still belongs to the pledgor.[58]

17.09   (3) *"Limited and specified time or purpose."* This again is a relic of Humean ideas of custody and possession, although it still appears in Macdonald who says: "The felonious appropriation of goods by the person to whom they have been entrusted for a limited and specified purpose constitutes theft",[59] and was relied on by the court as a criterion for distinguishing theft and embezzlement as late as 1922 when it was held that a soldier could steal his kilt.[60]

There are some cases in which the Crown specifically averred in a charge of theft that the accused had been given possession of the goods for a short time,[61] but the only important case which depends on this criterion to any great extent is *Wm Taylor Keith.*[62]

The accused was an auctioneer who was instructed to sell a piano at a private house, on the understanding that if he did not succeed in doing so he should be "entrusted with it" for sale at a public roup. He was charged that having failed to sell it at the house he took it to an auction room and "thus having obtained the temporary custody" of it, and having again failed to sell it at the auction room, he pawned it and appropriated the money advanced on it, and so stole it.[63] Lord Ardmillan held that this was not a good charge of theft, on the ground that it was not specifically averred that the accused's custody was for a short time or a specific purpose, and said that: "Where the custody is not for a short time and not for a specified purpose, and the article is appropriated, a sort of trust is constituted, and the crime is breach of trust."[64]

It is, however, arguable that an auctioneer's possession is as limited and specified as a watchmaker's, since he has the goods for a definite purpose — to sell them by auction.

What can be said is that where A receives goods merely for delivery to a certain place, or to look after them for the owner, he is likely to be charged with theft; whereas if the purpose for which he receives them is more complex, and particularly if he is entitled to use any money he receives, he is likely to be charged with embezzlement. But the distinction is not easily expressed in terms of specificity of purpose. Indeed, where A receives goods on an unqualified loan for a term, *i.e.* where

---

[57] Indeed he is prohibited by the Consumer Credit Act 1974 which prescribes the way in which he is to deal with the pledge: ss.120–121 (as amended by S.I. 1983 No. 1568, S.I. 1998 No. 997 and S.I. 1998 No. 998). Where the debt does not exceed £75 the position is different since such articles become the broker's property if not redeemed within the statutory period: s.120(1), as amended by Consumer Credit (Further Increase of Monetary Amounts) Order 1998 (S.I. 1998 No. 997), Art. 3, Sched.

[58] It may be noted also that the pawnbroker holds the goods for his own benefit rather than for the benefit of the pledgor, and that is an indication that his crime is theft rather than embezzlement: see *infra*, para. 17.29.

[59] Macdonald, p.32.

[60] *O'Brien v. Strathern* 1922 J.C. 55, L.J.-G. Clyde at 57, although it should not have been necessary to resort to this criterion for what appears to have been an indisputable proposition for over a century.

[61] *Wm Rodger* (1868) 1 Couper 76; *Jane McMahon or McGraw* (1863) 4 Irv. 381.

[62] (1875) 3 Couper 125.

[63] At 132.

[64] At 133.

there is nothing said at all about the purpose of his possession, he will almost certainly be charged with theft; while if he receives them for the "specified purpose" of doing business with them on B's behalf, he will almost certainly be charged with embezzlement.

In any event, embezzlement proper probably cannot arise until after the accused has embarked upon the purpose for which he was given the goods. If B gives A a horse to sell and return with the price there may be some question whether A is guilty of theft or embezzlement if he sells the horse and pockets the price; but if he appropriates the horse before selling it he is clearly guilty of theft, and indeed his crime is very like a theft by taking.

(4) *The source of A's possession.* If B gives A his watch to repair, or a **17.10** £10 note to get changed, and A appropriates the watch or the £10, there is little difficulty in holding that this is theft.[65] Suppose, now, that A receives £10 from B with which to buy an article from C for B, and appropriates the article; or is sent by B with an article to sell to C for him, and appropriates the price — can it be said that A has stolen the article or the price which he has received, not from B but from C, and which has never been in B's possession?

Alison says that a carrier who appropriates goods put into his hands for delivery to a particular person is guilty of embezzlement in the same way as is a clerk who appropriates money received on behalf of his master, and one of the reasons he gives is that "in such a case, the money has never been properly in his master's possession."[66] Again in *Wm Scott*[67] Lord Young described embezzlement as the appropriation of money "lawfully received . . . on account of the owner (into whose possession it has never passed)".[68] Both Alison and Lord Young were, however, strong Anglicisers, and indeed Lord Young went on to indicate in *Scott* that the only difference between Scots and English law was that Scots law extended embezzlement to cover agents as well as servants. In England it was settled that "the dishonest servant commits larceny of the chattel which he takes *out* of his master's possession, but embezzlement of the chattel which he intercepts *before* it has reached his master's possession",[69] but English embezzlement was essentially a quite different crime from Scots embezzlement.[70]

Macdonald is of opinion that, "A servant would be guilty of theft if, being sent with an article to market for the purpose of selling it and bringing back the price, he kept the money; or if he were sent with an article to pawn, and appropriated the amount advanced."[71] His authorities are both *obiter dicta*. One is a statement by Lord Wood that if a

---

[65] *Geo. Brown* (1839) 2 Swin. 394; *Robt Michie* (1839) 2 Swin. 319.

[66] Alison, i, 358, the owner in the case of the carrier being presumably taken to be the consignee and not the consignor.

[67] (1879) 4 Couper 227.

[68] At 234.

[69] Kenny, para. 229. The crime no longer exists in England: Theft Act 1968.

[70] The case of *Strathern v. Caisley*, 1937 J.C. 118, in which an employer who failed to account to the appropriate Ministry for statutory insurance deductions made by him from his employees' wages was convicted of embezzlement, is not helpful in this connection since the relevant statute provided that the deductions were to be deemed to have been entrusted to him for payment by him to the Ministry, which is sufficient to justify a charge of embezzlement, albeit perhaps also one of theft, and to elide any theoretical difficulties that might otherwise arise.

[71] Macdonald, p.35.

servant is given a horse to sell and deliver the price to his master, and he appropriates the horse or the price, that is equally theft,[72] and the second[73] is not really in point at all, as it is a remark by Lord Justice-Clerk Hope to the effect that if A is sent with a gown to pawn and forms the intention of appropriating the advance *before* he pawns the gown, that might be theft *of the gown.*[74]

It is submitted that the passage quoted from Macdonald is correct, but not for the reason that the master never had possession of the goods. It is correct because in these cases the goods or money were received by A under a duty to deliver them to his master *in forma specifica.* That is the proper criterion, and not whether they were ever in the master's possession.[75]

17.11 (5) *The duty to deliver goods in forma specifica.* This is the simplest and therefore the most attractive of the criteria used to distinguish theft and embezzlement. It means that where A holds B's property with a duty to deliver it to C or to return it to B *in forma specifica*, and not merely to deliver a like amount or value, A's appropriation of the property is theft and not embezzlement. This offers a definite yardstick which can be easily applied. It also emphasises that in theft one must be able to point to the particular thing which has been stolen. Where the accused's obligation is only to deliver an equivalent amount, one cannot do this — he is not bound to deliver the thing he received, or any particular thing at all; indeed, in the true embezzlement cases his obligation will be to

---

[72] *Watt v. Home* (1851) J. Shaw 519, 521.

[73] *Daniel Fraser* (1850) J. Shaw 365, 367.

[74] It would be theft of the gown by appropriation at the time that intention was formed, since the gown would be pawned as A's property and not as that of the owner. See also *Robt Stevenson* (1854) 1 Irv. 571.

[75] If this submission is correct it is possible to reconcile two apparently contradictory views expressed by Lord Cockburn. In *John Smith*, 2 Swin. at 58, he specifically referred to property *"never received"* (his italics) by the owner, such as property in a porter's hands for delivery to the owner, or found property, and held that the appropriation of that property was theft. In *Robt Michie, ibid.*, at 321, he indicated that if a shop boy were sent with a note for change and changed the note and appropriated the change, that might be not theft but embezzlement. That suggestion is probably wrong, see *infra*, but it can be explained by reference to Lord Cockburn's view that "no man ever desires money to be delivered *in forma specifica*": *Hugh Climie* (1838) 2 Swin. 118, 127, which can be interpreted to mean that money can be stolen only by an unlawful taking, or by a person in the shop boy's position appropriating it *before* carrying out his instruction to hand the specific note to the bank to be changed, an instruction which would take the case out of the general statement that money is never desired to be delivered *in specie*. In theory there may be difficulty in cases where it is not clear that the goods belong to B. Where A discloses to C that he is buying or selling on B's behalf the goods are transferred from C to B, and A is only a messenger. But if A does not disclose his agency, C's intention will be to transfer the goods to A, and it is unlikely that A could ever be charged with theft from C. But although A may appear to be an owner to C and indeed to all the world except B, he is not the owner *vis-à-vis* B, which is what matters. This is rather like saying that A is a sort of legal owner, and B only an equitable one, so that A cannot be guilty of theft. In practice, however, it is very doubtful if A would be regarded as having any sort of title in the goods, unless he were B's mercantile agent. In any other situation the criminal law would not bother itself with the niceties of the civil law, but simply convict A of stealing B's property. Put another way, one might say that it would be thought exaggerated to call the message boy who eats the apples he is sent to buy for his employer an embezzler, and obvious to call him a thief. It is true that collecting agents and cashiers are often charged with embezzlement, but this has nothing to do with the fact that their employers never came into possession of the money — they could be charged with embezzlement whether they pocketed the money before putting it in the till, or put it in the till and then took it out again, and in any event could usually in either case be charged with theft just as easily as with embezzlement.

account for his intromissions and hand over a true balance, rather than any specific sum.[76] The case law as a whole, however, does not allow the distinction between theft and embezzlement to be stated in terms of a duty to deliver *in forma specifica*, although it has been so stated in a number of cases.[77]

It will be convenient to discuss this criterion separately in regard to things other than money, and in regard to money.

(a) THINGS OTHER THAN MONEY. Generally speaking the appropriation **17.12** of things other than money is theft, the article stolen being that received by the accused and not delivered by him at the due time to the person entitled to delivery. If B gives A his watch to repair, or his washing to launder, and A appropriates it, he is guilty of theft.[78] Similarly, if B sends A to collect or buy for him an article from C and A appropriates the article, A is guilty of theft.[79] These cases are all distinguishable from the case where A borrows an article from B for his, A's own use, but the mere fact that in the former cases A holds the article on behalf of B does not in itself make his crime embezzlement. Although one can perhaps say that in modern law there can be no embezzlement unless A holds the goods on behalf of B, it is not the case that if he does so hold the goods there can be no theft. What matters is the duty of the watchmaker to return the watch he was given, or of the messenger to hand to B the article he was given or sold by C.[80] It is true that where B sends A with money to buy goods from C, A's duty is not to return the money B gave him, but its "proceeds", but this is a strained use of "proceeds". B knows from the outset what he is to receive, and at the moment of appropriation A's duty is quite specific — it is to deliver the "article" in his possession either to B or C, depending on whether the appropriation takes place before or after he has dealt with C. If A appropriates the money before he goes to C, he is clearly guilty of theft[81]; and it is submitted that he is guilty of theft if he appropriates what he receives from C, since that is an appropriation of an article given him to deliver to B *in forma specifica*.

It is submitted that this is a satisfactory criterion in the case of things other than money, and indeed charges of embezzlement of things other than money are very rare.[82] This may be due partly to the change in

---

[76] *cf. H.M. Advocate v. John Geo. Bell* (1892) 3 White 313; *Alex. Gilruth Fleming* (1885) 5 Couper 552; *Wm Scott* (1879) 4 Couper 227; *John Rae* (1854) 1 Irv. 472.

[77] For example, *Hugh Climie* (1838) 2 Swin. 118; *Elder v. Morrison* (1881) 4 Couper 530; *H.M. Advocate v. Laing* (1891) 2 White 572.

[78] *supra*, para. 14.06.

[79] Macdonald, pp.34–35.

[80] One can, of course, envisage awkward cases. Suppose A is sent by B, C and D, to buy each of them a kilo of the same brand of butter. It cannot be said that it matters which kilo he gives to B, which to C, and which to D, and in that sense there is no duty to deliver in specific form. But there is a duty to deliver butter to the three men, and to deliver the butter purchased from the grocer with their money. A has no right to use B's butter himself, and buy B another pound the following week, or to sell B's butter at a profit and give B his money back, or even his money plus the profit. The only difficulty in this situation is in saying which of three identical articles belongs to which of the three buyers. But in the situation in which the criminal law is interested, the situation where A fails to deliver one or more kilos of butter, this difficulty is not important — if he gives only C his butter, he will be convicted of stealing B's and D's.

[81] *cf. Daniel Fraser* (1850) J. Shaw 365.

[82] The relevancy of a sheriff court charge of embezzling a number of sheep left by the owners in the accused's charge was not challenged in *Taylor v. Maitland* (1879) 4 Couper 262. In fact the sheep had belonged to the accused and had been made over to the owners in security by an *ex facie* absolute deed, which may have been why the charge was laid as embezzlement and not theft. And see *Kent v. H.M. Advocate*, 1950 J.C. 38; *infra*, para. 17.23.

terminology from "breach of trust" to "embezzlement". To use the word "embezzle" in respect of things other than money seems an incursion into metaphor.

17.13   SPECIFICATIO. The only difficulty that might arise would be where B gave A materials to make into an article and the process affected the materials to such an extent as to bring into operation the doctrine of *specificatio*, whereby the finished article would belong to A. As Bell says: "if the materials, as a separate existence, be destroyed *in bona fide*, the property is with the workman; the owner of the materials having a personal claim for a like quantity and quality, or for the price of the materials."[83] Where A acts *in mala fide, i.e.* where he has decided to appropriate the result before he starts the operation, he does not become the owner of the finished article.[84] Where A is given materials to manufacture and appropriates them without carrying out the manufacturing process at all, he is guilty of theft.[85]

There is no authority on the operation of *specificatio* in the criminal law, but Bell's phraseology indicates that the result would be to make the subsequent appropriation of the manufactured article embezzlement and not theft. The question was raised but not decided in *Watt v. Home*[86] where the accused was a weaver who was convicted of theft of yarn given him for weaving. Lord Wood expressly reserved his opinion on whether it would have made any difference if he had woven the yarn before appropriating it,[87] and Lord Colonsay referred to the fact that the yarn had not been subjected to the operation for which it had been given to the accused.[88] Macdonald regards it as undecided "whether it would be theft if the tailor had made the coat, or the weaver had made the web, before the appropriation", but thinks it probably is. His reason is that, "If a journeyman receive cloth from his master to make a coat, and after making it carry it off, he is guilty of stealing the coat," and he regards the tailor making a coat for his customer as hired by him in the same way as the journeyman is hired by his master.[89] The short answer to this is that the customer-tailor relationship is not the same as that of the tailor-journeyman. But it is necessary to consider why the journeyman is guilty of theft. The answer is that the finished coat is not his property, it belongs either to his master or to his master's customer. If the finished coat made by the master himself can be said to belong to the customer and not to the tailor, then the tailor is guilty of theft. Whether or not it can be so regarded depends on the law of property: all that is argued here is that if the tailor becomes owner by *specificatio* he cannot be guilty of theft.[90]

---

[83] Bell's Principles, para. 1298; *International Banking Corporation v. Ferguson, Shaw & Sons,* 1910 S.C. 182; *Wylie and Lochhead v. Mitchell* (1870) 8 M. 552.

[84] *McDonald v. Provan (of Scotland Street) Ltd,* 1960 S.L.T. 231, criticised in a note at 1961 J.R. 60.

[85] Macdonald, pp. 35–36. *Cf. Eliz. Anderson* (1858) 3 Irv. 65, Lord Ardmillan at 68; *Peter Littler* and *Peter Campbell,* both (1833) Bell's Notes 9, in which tailors were convicted of embezzling materials given them to make up suits are impliedly overruled by *Geo. Brown, supra.*

[86] (1851) J. Shaw 519.

[87] At 520.

[88] At 521.

[89] Macdonald, p.36.

[90] In *Richard Gibbons,* High Court at Glasgow, Sept. 1856, unrep'd, the accused had

(b) MONEY. The most important feature of money in this connection is **17.14** that "no man ever desires money to be delivered *in forma specifica*",[91] except in those rare cases where the coins or notes have a *pretium reale*. That being so one might think that the appropriation of money was always embezzlement, except in cases of theft by taking. That, however, is not the law.[92] Alternatively, one might apply the criterion of delivery *in forma specifica* to money, and adopt a rule that a mere change in denomination is to be disregarded in deciding whether or not delivery was to be made in that form. On that view, whenever A's duty was to deliver the precise amount of money received by him, his crime would be theft. And this, to some extent, is the position. If A is given £10 to buy an article or just to hand to B,[93] and appropriates the £10, he is guilty of theft.[94] And *Robt Smith and Jas Wishart*,[95] in which it was held that a bank teller who misappropriated money entrusted to him in the course of his duties was guilty of theft, suggests that if B sends A to C to obtain money from him for B, it is theft for A to keep the money obtained from C, although in such a case it is immaterial to B whether or not he receives the precise notes and coins C gave to A.

The situation is more complicated where A is given £10 with which to buy a number of articles for B and return with them and the change. It is possible to regard each step as a separate transaction; and at each step it will be possible to say just what A is bound to deliver to B or to someone else on B's instructions. That something will always be definite, so that at

---

been employed "as an agent . . . for the purpose of making up shirts, or getting the same made up, from cloth and other materials furnished by [your employers] to you," and was charged that "having received from and been entrusted . . . with cloth and other necessary materials for the making of shirts" and it being his "duty and according to [his] trust faithfully to transmit" the shirts to his employers he embezzled the shirts made from the cloth or alternatively stole them, the shirts being described in each alternative as "the property or in the lawful possession" of the employers. Similarly, in *Wm Hay*, High Court at Edinburgh, Feb. 1861, unrep'd, the accused who was a miller who had been entrusted with wheat to be made into flour and had failed to deliver the flour, was charged with embezzling or alternatively stealing the wheat, or the said flour made therefrom, "the property or in the lawful possession of" the person who had given it to him to make into flour. Gibbons did not appear at his trial and Hay offered a plea of guilty to embezzlement which was accepted, so that there was no challenge to the relevancy of either indictment — see Macdonald, p.36. Although the circumstances raise the point under discussion, the alternative charges of theft and embezzlement may have been brought as a matter of form, as they frequently were. The argument that while the cloth or wheat might be stolen the shirts or flour could only be embezzled does not appear to have been in the minds of the framers of the indictments since Gibbons was charged only with stealing or embezzling the shirts, presumably because it was known he had made up the shirts, and Hay charged with embezzling or stealing either wheat or flour since it was not known whether he had made up the flour.

Burnett refers to a case of *Stewart* in 1806 and a case of *Ritchie* in 1807, where the accused were charged with fraudulently selling and appropriating yarn given them to manufacture, in his chapter on fraud: Burnett, p.174, but although there may be fraud on the buyer of such yarn, the mere appropriation by the workman could not nowadays be regarded as fraud.

[91] *Hugh Climie* (1838) 2 Swin. 118, Lord Cockburn at 127.

[92] Although one might go even further and say that, except in theft by taking, what is "stolen" is not the corporeal coin or note but an incorporeal right to a debt or an accounting, so that theft does not come into it at all. But the law tends to treat the dishonest appropriation of money as the appropriation of something corporeal: see, *e.g.*, *Guild v. Lees*, 1994 S.C.C.R. 745.

[93] Criminal Procedure (Scotland) Act 1995, Sched. 5: "having received from G.R. £6 to hand to E.R., you did . . . steal the said sum."

[94] *David Field* (1838) 2 Swin. 24; and the same is true if he is given the £10 to get it changed at a bank: *Robt Michie* (1839) 2 Swin. 319; *cf. Margt Mills* (1865) 5 Irv. 196.

[95] (1842) 1 Broun 342.

the moment of appropriation it is possible to point to what has been appropriated. If A appropriates the £10 at the outset, he has stolen the £10; if he buys a £5 article as instructed by B and appropriates the change he has stolen the £5 change, since the moment the change came into his possession it was his duty either to deliver it to B, or to deliver it to C in exchange for, say, a £2.50 article and £2.50 change.

17.15   In *Hugh Climie*[96] the accused was given £17 in notes and cash for the purpose of paying £9 to C and £8 to D; he appropriated the money and was charged with theft. This charge was held to be irrelevant for a number of reasons. Lord Justice-General Hope confessed himself unable to form a "consistent opinion" on the subject, but thought that the use of the word "intrusted" in the indictment and the absence of a "fraudulent contrectation" were important[97]; Lord Justice-Clerk Boyle relied on the fact that the accused was given one parcel of £17 which he had to divide between C and D, and was not given separate parcels of £9 and £8 to deliver *in forma specifica*[98]; Lord Mackenzie placed no importance on the word "intrusted", but relied on the absence of any duty to deliver particular coins or notes *in forma specifica*, and on the suggestion that it would have been a good defence for Climie to show that he had paid over the moneys a week after the due date[99]; Lord Medwyn agreed with Lords Boyle and Mackenzie; Lords Moncreiff, Cockburn and Meadowbank, all had serious doubts on the matter. *Climie* is perhaps best regarded as a decision based solely on the particular wording of the indictment, and on the Crown's failure to state sufficiently clearly a duty to deliver the £17 handed to A between C and D, and not just to pay them £9 and £8, respectively.[1] It seems to have been accepted that where a duty to hand over *in forma specifica* is clearly averred, the crime is theft.

17.16   It cannot, however, be said that wherever such a duty exists, the crime can be only theft. In *John McLeod*[2] the accused, who was a sub-postmaster who was given £1 to issue a postal order and send it to a named person, was charged alternatively with theft and breach of trust, and the theft charge was successfully attacked on the ground that the money had been handed over for "agency and negotiation",[3] although even buying and sending a postal order by someone not employed in the Post Office can hardly be properly described as involving agency or negotiation. In *Jas Macdonald*[4] a policeman who appropriated money given him by a convicted person in payment of a fine instead of handing

---

[96] (1838) 2 Swin. 118.
[97] At 123–124: they are, of course, trivial.
[98] At 124–125.
[99] At 125.
[1] See especially Lord Mackenzie at 125, Lord Moncreiff at 126 and Lord Meadowbank at 127–128.
[2] (1858) 3 Irv. 79.
[3] At 86.
[4] (1860) 3 Irv. 540.

it over to the authorities was charged with breach of trust, and the court indicated that "the case laid was clearly one of breach of trust. The accused had received the money in trust for the purpose stated. He was bound to carry out the trust so committed to him by paying the money as directed. This he had not done, but had appropriated it to his own uses."[5]

If the quotation from *Jas Macdonald*[6] were correct there would be no room for theft at all, except in cases of theft by taking, but that is clearly not the position. There can be little doubt that a policeman who did not hand over money given to him for delivery to the authorities would today be charged with theft, and equally little doubt that a person in the position of the accused in *Climie*[7] would today be charged with theft. But a sub-postmaster might still be charged with embezzling money given him to send a postal order, because postmasters are the kind of people who are usually charged with embezzlement. In the same way, if the fine had been handed to a sheriff clerk, who is the person who deals with fines and through whose hands many fines pass on their way to Exchequer, the sheriff clerk might well be charged with embezzlement for putting the fine in his pocket. He would certainly be so charged if he carried on a course of dishonest conduct with regard to the fines he received.

Most of the cases which involve a duty to hand over a specific amount **17.17** of money are theft-embezzlement cases, and many of them are usually charged as embezzlement. Schedule 2 of the 1995 Act gives the following style for a charge of embezzlement: "did, while acting as a commercial traveller to Brown and Co., . . . receive from the persons . . . set forth the respective sums of money . . . specified for the said Brown and Co., and did embezzle the same." "Commercial traveller" covers a large variety of relationships, but a similar style might well be used in charging a dishonest collector employed to call on the customers of a credit draper. What is the difference between his case, and the case where A appropriates £10 given to him by C to take to B? Mainly, it seems, a difference in size and complexity. The message boy who appropriates the note given him to deliver to B looks like a thief, and the situation looks like that of the porter who steals the traveller's baggage. But the collector who receives a large number of sums of money from different people in the same day looks much more like an embezzler. In order to prove his guilt it is usually necessary to lead evidence about the way he keeps his books, or gives receipts; it may even be necessary to employ an accountant, and the Crown will have to bring into play the typical

---

[5] At 541. The point at issue in the appeal, however, was not directed to the distinction between theft and embezzlement. There have also been charges of embezzlement against sheriff officers for failing to account for the proceeds of a sale following on a poinding: *Malcolm McKinlay* (1836) 1 Swin. 304; *Jas Campbell* (1845) 2 Broun 412, and similar charges might be brought today because of the complication of the officer's right to a fee for carrying out the sale, although strictly his duty is to pay over a specific sum — the money raised at the sale less his taxed fee: see Debtors (Scotland) Act 1987, s.38. (It should be noted that poindings and warrant sales are to be abolished when the Abolition of Poindings and Warrant Sales Act 2001 (asp 1) comes into force on December 31, 2002. Prior to its commencement, it is anticipated that the Scottish Parliament will substitute some alternative procedure: see G.L. Gretton, "Striking the Balance. Warrant Sales: at the Turning Point", 2001 S.L.T. (News) 255.)

[6] *supra*.

[7] (1838) 2 Swin. 118.

paraphernalia of an embezzlement case. All this, together with the fact that since money is involved one can say that there was a duty to account only, and not to deliver *in forma specifica*, makes it easy to treat the matter as an embezzlement. If one wished to be cynical one might say that one appropriation makes a thief, but many make an embezzler. But the duty to hand over a specific sum is the same in both cases, and in neither case has the accused any right to administer the fund for his employer. The collector may be entitled to keep the money for longer than the message boy, and be obliged only to hand it in each week, but this makes no difference in principle — if settlement day is Friday it will not be said that the collector stole what he collected that day but only embezzled what he collected on the Wednesday. The collector, like the message boy, receives the money for the specific purpose of delivering it to his employers. The same is true of a cashier, although there again the crime charged is often embezzlement. A bank teller who misappropriated any substantial amount of money might well be charged with embezzlement, despite the decision in *Robt Smith and Jas Wishart*[8] that his crime is theft.

In practice the position appears to be much as follows. Persons who are in a position in which they habitually handle money and engage in numerous transactions are usually charged with embezzlement; persons who are given money to deliver on an isolated occasion are usually charged with theft. Persons in responsible positions like managers, solicitors, factors and so on, are usually charged with embezzlement; persons in menial positions like message boys are usually charged with theft.

17.18   On the other hand, persons who belong to the class of potential embezzlers, so to speak, rather than to the class of potential thieves, may be charged with theft if it is possible to isolate a specific occasion on which one can say that they received a specific sum of money for the purpose of delivering it to a specific person.

This is shown by a number of examples. Treasurers of societies are normally charged with embezzlement since they usually have powers of disbursement as well as of collection, but Macdonald is correct in pointing out that a treasurer whose sole duty was to retain money collected in a locked box to which he did not even have a key, would not be charged with embezzlement today, and that *David Walker*,[9] in which such a charge was brought, must be regarded as overruled by *Geo. Brown*.[10]

In *H.M. Advocate v. City of Glasgow Bank Directors*[11] it was even held that bank directors who were given bills for collection would be guilty of theft if they used them for the purpose of settling debts of the bank, and in *H.M. Advocate v. Smith*[12] Lord Craighill pointed out that a shop

---

[8] (1842) 1 Broun 342.
[9] (1836) 1 Swin. 294.
[10] (1839) 2 Swin. 394; Macdonald, p.48. In *Elder v. Morrison* (1881) 4 Couper 530, the treasurer's duties were apparently to retain the members' weekly subscriptions and to divide them out at the end of a term, the club being really a private savings group. He was charged with embezzlement and theft in the sheriff court and convicted of embezzlement. The High Court upheld the conviction, mainly on the ground that it would have been unjust to set him free, but they indicated that they regarded the case as properly one of theft.
[11] (1879) 4 Couper 161, 190.
[12] (1887) 1 White 413.

manager might be guilty of theft "if it was his duty to hand over to his employers the very sums he received, and instead of doing so he kept them."[13]

In *Alex. Gilruth Fleming*[14] the accused was a factor who was charged **17.19** with stealing certain sums received by him "under the trust and duty that you should forthwith hand over the same" to certain other persons. The court dismissed this charge as irrelevant, saying that a factor was "not a servant who receives money for the sake of custody; he is one doing business for another for hire. The moneys he receives are in his possession, and these, though they may be embezzled, cannot be stolen, because the circumstances and the power over that which he receives prevent such taking as is necessary for theft."[15] This may well be so, but it goes in the teeth of the specific averment that Fleming received the moneys in question for the purpose of handing them directly to certain persons: it is clear from the indictment that so far as the subject of the charge was concerned Fleming had no such power, but only a duty of immediate delivery.

In *H.M. Advocate v. Laing*[16] the accused was a solicitor who was **17.20** alleged to have received certain sums from H., "as his law agent", for the purpose of paying the balance of a bond held by J. over H.'s property, and of discharging the bond. He failed to carry out H.'s instructions and in fact paid some of the money given him directly into his own bank account. He was charged with theft, and Lord Kincairney directed the jury that "If one receives money merely to pass it on to another, his crime, if he feloniously appropriates the money, would be theft. If he gets it under an obligation to account for the like amount, the felonious appropriation would be embezzlement. The distinction nowadays is rather technical than substantial."[17] The jury exercised their statutory power of convicting of embezzlement, but it is doubtful if they acted properly in doing so, since Laing did not even begin to carry out his instructions from H. He was in the position of the message boy sent with a coat to pawn who appropriates the coat, and not in that of the boy who pawns the coat and appropriates the advance.

The reason for the jury's verdict in *Laing*[18] may well have been a **17.21** feeling that solicitors are more aptly described as embezzlers than as thieves, and that seems to be the view of the law today. In *Edgar v. Mackay*[19] a solicitor was instructed to recover an account on behalf of a client; he received some payments from the debtor but did not tell his

---

[13] At 415.

[14] (1885) 5 Couper 552.

[15] Lord Craighill at 569: his Lordship referred to Lord Young's definition of embezzlement in *Wm Scott* (1879) 4 Couper 227, 234, in terms of the appropriation of property lawfully received by the accused on account of the owner into whose possession it had never passed, which is criticised *supra*. Scott himself was a bill broker who was charged with theft of the proceeds of bills given him by the City of Glasgow Bank to get discounted and pay them the proceeds. The theft charge was withdrawn at the court's suggestion, a course which can be justified by reference to the fact that Scott, unlike the Glasgow Bank directors, was alleged to have appropriated not the bills but their proceeds.

[16] (1891) 2 White 572.

[17] At 576.

[18] (1891) 2 White 572.

[19] 1926 J.C. 94.

client and did not pay the moneys over, even after the client had terminated his agency. This, on the face of it, looks like theft, but the charge was that "you did, while acting as agent for . . . receive £x . . . and did embezzle the same."[20]

17.22   (6) *Power of administration.* This criterion, which was mentioned as early as *Robt Smith and Jas. Wishart* in 1842,[21] and which is usually referred to by saying that the accused had only a "liability to account"[22] is the only one which enables one to define those cases in which embezzlement is always charged and theft never.

A power of administration involves a right to use a fund or any other capital stock for the benefit of someone else, with a duty to account for one's administration and make over at the due time not merely the fund, indeed perhaps not the fund at all, but the proceeds of one's administration. If A is given a block of shares and told to "play the market" with them on B's behalf, he is under no duty to give B back the same shares; if he is given stock with which to start a business on behalf of B he will not be expected to return that stock to B. If A makes a profit for B he is liable to account for that profit; if he makes a loss he is under no duty to return to B the value of the fund originally given him, all he has to do is show that the loss was honestly incurred. In effect this means that he has to show that he administered B's capital for B's benefit, and did not use any of it for his own purposes.

Another feature of this situation is that B cannot know at any time prior to the date of accounting how much A is liable to pay over to him. Unlike the employer of a cashier or collector he cannot find out how much A owes him by simply adding up the sums A has received on his behalf up to that time. He must also know what A has had to expend on his behalf, and what profits or losses are likely to occur before the accounting date.

This criterion is much vaguer than any of the others, and is by no means free from difficulty. It is not easy to say, for example, whether a cashier becomes an administrator because she is entitled to use the money paid in at the cash desk to give the message boy his 'bus fares. In practice, the doubtful cases will be charged as embezzlement, and the most one can say is that a full-blown administrator will not be charged with theft.[23]

17.23   UNAUTHORISED ACTINGS. An administrator is guilty of embezzlement only and not of theft, because of the mandate given him by his principal to deal with the goods or money entrusted to him.[24] If, therefore, he exceeds this mandate, he ceases to be an administrator, and his

---

[20] It may be that embezzlement was charged because the Crown could not show what had happened to the money, but only that the accused had not accounted for it. But nonetheless they had to prove appropriation in either event and, once they had shown that the proper inference to be drawn from the facts was that the accused had appropriated the money, there seems no reason why he could not have been convicted of theft.

[21] 1 Broun 342, Lord Medwyn at 350.

[22] For example, *H.M. Advocate v. John Smith* (1887) 1 White 413; *H.M. Advocate v. Laing* (1891) 2 White 572; *cf. Alex. Gilruth Fleming* (1885) 5 Couper 552.

[23] In *R. v. Hall* [1973] 1 Q.B. 126, it was held that a travel agent who received money from customers for holidays which he did not provide and who put the money into his trading account, was not guilty of theft, there being no obligation to deal with the money in any particular way: *cf.* Theft Act 1968, s.5(3).

[24] Hume, i, 60.

misappropriations will be reckoned as theft and not as embezzlement. Such at any rate appears to be the import of *Kent v. H.M. Advocate*.[25] K. was the buyer and office manager of X Co. at Glasgow; he ordered a consignment of goods from Y Co. to be delivered to X Co. at Edinburgh; the goods were rejected at Edinburgh, and K. was charged that thereafter, "having been authorised" by X Co. and by Y Co. to dispose of the goods and account to them for the proceeds, he sold the goods but failed to account for the price. His conviction for embezzlement was quashed on appeal on the ground that the Crown case had been put to the jury on the basis that the sale of the goods had been authorised, and that they had failed to prove this.[26] The Crown argued that the jury must have been satisfied on four points — that the goods did not belong to K., that they were sold by him, that he had been authorised to sell them, and that he had failed to account for the proceeds — and that as the third had not in fact been proved, what the Crown *had* proved was that K. had stolen the goods,[27] but the Court declined to substitute a verdict of theft since the jury's minds had not been applied to the view of the facts presented on appeal.

The court in *Kent* took an atomistic view of the facts, and treated the sale of the goods by K. as an isolated and unauthorised transaction, similar in kind to a sale by A of goods given him by B for safe-keeping. If the court had looked at the sale in the context of the whole transaction, they might have regarded it as constituting an embezzlement by K. of the goods viewed as the proceeds of his authorised purchase from Y Co.

Kent itself can be regarded as a somewhat special case: its actual *ratio decidendi* depended on a strict interpretation of the particular evidence led; it was unusual in that it was concerned with goods and not with money, and so looked more like theft than embezzlement; it was concerned with only one transaction, so that again it was easy to see the case as one of theft; and finally it appears from the reports that no authority was cited to the court on the law of embezzlement — certainly none was referred to in the judgments. But *Kent* does highlight what may be a fatal flaw in the whole concept of embezzlement. It is at least logically possible to disentangle the facts of even the most complicated embezzlement and consider each incident separately, and if this is done it will be clear that in every case the accused dealt with his principal's property in an unauthorised way. The administrator's authority is limited to administering the fund on his principal's behalf. If he takes money out of the principal's bank account and puts it on a horse, that is an unauthorised use of the money, and on the analogy of *Kent* could be said to constitute theft whether or not he had authority to operate the bank account on the principal's behalf. *A fortiori*, if he takes money paid to him as an agent and pays it straight to his bookmaker without ever putting it into the principal's bank account or showing it in his books, that is theft. Every time A uses goods or money on his own behalf, every time he misappropriates them, he is, so to speak, acting *ultra vires* and not as an administrator. It might be possible to distinguish between the appropriation of the result of an authorised transaction which would be

---

[25] 1950 J.C. 38.

[26] The case leaves one with the impression that had the Crown simply averred and proved that K. had sold the goods and kept the price the court might have upheld a conviction for embezzlement.

[27] 1950 J.C. 38, L.J.-G. Cooper at 42.

embezzlement, and the appropriation of the result of an unauthorised transaction which would be theft, but such a distinction would be very difficult to apply. *Kent* itself can be regarded as the appropriation of goods acquired by an authorised transaction or, if only the last stage in the process is taken into account, as the appropriation of the proceeds of an unauthorised sale.

Kent suggests that there is no such thing in Scotland as embezzlement proper, that if any embezzlement is scratched hard enough a theft will appear, and that the only reason this has not yet been fully appreciated is that Scots lawyers have been too lazy mentally to do the necessary scratching. This, however, goes too far. *Kent* was a very special case, and a case in which only one transaction was involved, so that it was easy to disentangle the facts and point to what had been stolen and to when and where it had been stolen. In most cases of embezzlement proper that is not possible, and it is impossible, if only for that reason, to frame a charge of theft.[28] Embezzlement, it is submitted, does exist as a crime in Scotland, although its scope is much more limited today than it was in Hume's day. There are, that is to say, cases which no prosecutor would regard as other than embezzlement; and there may also be cases in which a charge of theft would be out of the question because the goods belonged to the accused, but in which a charge of embezzlement could be brought.[29]

The special features of embezzlement

17.24   The following features distinguish embezzlement proper from theft.

(1) It is essential for embezzlement that the goods which, or the proceeds of which, are appropriated should have been in the possession of the accused with the authority of the person to whom he is bound to account. In *J.D. Wormald*[30] W. was a solicitor who was instructed by a client to find him a heritable security and invest some money in it for him.

The client gave W. a deposit receipt to enable him to uplift the money from the bank.

W. uplifted the money before he had found a security in which to invest it, and appropriated it himself. This was held to be theft on the ground that W. had no authority to uplift the money before he had obtained a security in which to invest it. Macdonald says of this case and of the similar case of *J.B. Walker Lee*[31] that, "Appropriation by a solicitor

---

[28] There are many cases of theft-embezzlement which are charged as embezzlement because it is easier to frame such a charge than to break the facts down into a number of thefts.

[29] See *infra*. It should also be noted that the continued existence of the crime of embezzlement received statutory recognition in the Criminal Procedure (Scotland) Act 1887, Sched. A of which includes two forms of embezzlement charge of which the first, "You did, while in the employment of J.P. . . . embezzle £40 . . . of money" may be a charge of embezzlement proper, while the second, "You did, while acting as commercial traveller to B and Co. . . . at the times and places specified in the inventory hereto subjoined, receive from the persons therein set forth the respective sums of money therein specified for the said B and Co., and did embezzle the same (*or* did embezzle £47 of money, being part thereof)" is clearly a charge, or rather a group of charges, of theft-embezzlement. (These forms of charge, with some trivial amendments, have been rolled forward into the Criminal Procedure (Scotland) Act 1995, Sched. 2.)

[30] (1876) 3 Couper 246.

[31] (1884) 5 Couper 492.

of funds entrusted to him by his client for investment has been held to be theft, but the practice now is to regard such appropriation as embezzlement."[32] This, however, misses the point of *Wormald* which is that (as was explained in the later case of *Alex. Gilruth Fleming*[33]) W.'s obtaining of the money before finding a security was treated by the court as a felonious taking — *i.e.* as a theft by taking and not as a theft involving any wider conception of appropriation at all. *Wormald* is still authority for the proposition that embezzlement cannot be charged where the accused took possession of the money or goods initially without his principal's consent.[34]

(2) There can be no embezzlement unless A has already embarked **17.25** upon a course of dealing with B's goods, and has already exchanged some of the goods and appropriated the proceeds of that exchange. If B gives A an article to sell for him and A sells it and appropriates the price, he may be guilty of theft-embezzlement or of embezzlement proper, depending on whether or not A is an administrator *quoad* the goods; but if A appropriates the goods before selling them in accordance with his contract with B that appropriation is theft whether or not A is an administrator.[35] If A never enters into administration, so to speak, his appropriation of the goods is of the same kind as an appropriation of luggage by a porter.

Again, if A continues to have goods in his possession after his administration has been ended, his appropriation of these goods should be theft and not embezzlement. In *Alex. Mitchell*[36] an agent who had been given gods to sell was charged with stealing some that he had sold after the termination of his agency, and this was held to be a relevant charge of theft.[37] A bank manager who walks out with the funds of the bank after he has been dismissed should be in no better position than a stranger who walks into the bank and puts the contents of the safe in his pocket. In *Edgar v. Makay*[38] however, a solicitor who had collected some money for a client which he failed to hand over, and who was found to have appropriated the money after the client had terminated his agency,[39] was charged with and convicted of embezzlement, no doubt out of deference to his profession as well as because the Crown could not point to any specific act of appropriation.[40]

(3) The appropriation must take place in the course of a transaction **17.26** which the accused is authorised to conduct, or must at any rate be the appropriation of the proceeds of such a transaction. Appropriation in the course of or by way of an unauthorised transaction is theft.[41]

---

[32] Macdonald, p.34.

[33] (1885) 5 Couper 552, Lord Craighill at 570–571.

[34] It may be that Wormald should have been charged with obtaining the money from the bank by fraudulently pretending that he was entitled to uplift it, but the fraud on the bank would not affect the contemporaneous theft of it from the client, a theft of which the deceit practised on the bank would be the *modus*. If, of course, W's intention had been to keep the money in his own safe until he found a security, he would have a good defence to the charge of theft, although he might still be technically guilty of a fraud on the bank.

[35] See Macdonald, p.34; *Daniel Macdonald* (1829) Bell's Notes, 15 and *Janet Drummond* (1832) Bell's Notes, 14; *Robt Nicolson* (1842) 1 Broun 370; *cf. Robt Stevenson* (1854) 1 Irv. 571; *Ronald Gordon* (1846) Ark. 196.

[36] (1874) 3 Couper 77.

[37] A verdict of not proven was eventually returned by the jury.

[38] 1926 J.C. 94.

[39] See *ibid.*, Lord Anderson at 99.

[40] *supra*, para. 17.21.

[41] *Kent v. H.M. Advocate*, 1950 J.C. 38, see *supra*, para. 17.23.

17.27   (4) Macdonald states that embezzlement may be committed "although
the trust which is broken was itself created by a fraud on the part of the
accused", as in the case of a person pretending to be a sheriff-officer
who induces a debtor to entrust him with the execution of a decree and
fails to account to the creditor for the proceeds of the execution,[42] but a
case of that kind would nowadays be charged as fraud or theft.

But the law does appear to regard A as guilty of embezzlement if he
retains any funds received in his capacity as B's agent, although the
funds were obtained fraudulently and in pursuance of a criminal course
of action to which B was not a party. In *George Smith*[43] the accused was a
partner of a firm who endorsed the firm's name on promissory notes
given him in his private capacity, without any authority to do so. He was
charged with embezzling the money he received by discounting the
notes. The relevancy of the charge was not challenged as the accused
failed to appear, but Macdonald[44] thinks it was relevant.[45]

The most recent example of this type of situation arose in *Frank v.
H.M. Advocate.*[46] The facts of the case were rather complicated, but can
be briefly described as follows. F. was instructed by B. to sell B.'s stock of
jewellery and *objets d'art* by auction; F. approached R. and fraudulently
induced him to pay the grossly inflated sum of £498 for the articles he
was supposed to be auctioning, of which he handed over only £298 to B.

He was charged with defrauding R., and also that having received
£498 from R. on behalf of B., he pretended that he had received only
£298 "for which amount you accounted to [B.] . . . and did . . .
appropriate £200, being part of said £498, to your own use and did
embezzle the same." F. was convicted on both charges, and although his
conviction was quashed on appeal it was not suggested at any stage that
the second charge was irrelevant or that it was improper to charge him
with both crimes cumulatively. The only reference to the matter was a
remark by Lord Justice-Clerk Aitchison that if the goods sold by F.
belonged to B., "then the rest of the case became clear, because it is
admitted that of the £498 actually received from [R.], £200 was
unaccounted for".[47]

The idea behind these cases is this — A receives the money in his
capacity as B's agent, therefore he is bound to account for it to B,
therefore his failure to do so constitutes embezzlement.[48] But this may
be an over-simplified approach. The difficulty is that the money allegedly
embezzled from B in such cases is not money to which B has any right,
nor is it money in respect of which A has any duty to account to B. It is
money obtained by A as the result of a crime to which B is not even a
party. The embezzlement in *Frank* was of the type which might have
been charged as theft, in which case the difficulty would have been more
obvious — for A could hardly be convicted of stealing from B money
which had been obtained by A from C by fraud.

---

[42] *Malcolm McKinlay and David Macdonald* (1836) 1 Swin. 304; Macdonald, p.47.
[43] (1836) 1 Swin. 301.
[44] Macdonald, p.47.
[45] See also *John Reeves* (1843) 1 Broun 612.
[46] 1938 J.C. 17.
[47] At 21.
[48] *Frank* might almost be regarded as the converse of *Lloyd v. Grace, Smith and Co.*
[1912] A.C. 716, in which it was held that an employer was liable to a client for money
embezzled by an employee.

It might, indeed, be easier to justify a charge of embezzlement against A if B had been a party to the fraud. Suppose A and B conspire to sell B's property by fraud and A, who does the actual selling, does not account properly to B for what he receives from the dupe. In such a situation it can be said not only that A received the money as B's agent, but that as between himself and B he was bound to account for the money he received from C. Yet it can hardly be supposed that A would be charged with embezzlement.[49]

Except perhaps *John Reeves*[50] there is no earlier authority to support the charge of embezzlement in *Frank* and despite the apparent indication given by *Frank* as to modern practice, it is unlikely that should such a situation recur the accused would be charged with embezzlement — for one thing, to charge both fraud and embezzlement is arguably a contravention of the principle that two common law crimes cannot be charged on the basis of the same *species facti*.

(5) As has been argued, a man cannot steal goods of which he is the **17.28** legal owner,[51] but he can, it is thought, embezzle them. This is a question which has not been decided in Scotland.[52] Lord Young in *Wm Scott*[53] described embezzlement as the appropriation of money belonging to someone else, but his Lordship was thinking in terms of Humean concepts and his observations were not directed to the possibility of embezzling one's own property. It seems that in at least one case A can embezzle his own property, that is to say property of which he is the legal owner, and that is the case of misappropriation of trust funds by a trustee.[54]

In situations where A is a trustee, there may be embezzlement even where A is not in the fullest sense an administrator. If a trustee appropriates property which he holds for the sole purpose of retaining it until a certain date and then distributing it in terms of the trust, he could be charged with embezzlement, although the situation looks more like a theft by a custodier. The trustee's misappropriation may be regarded as embezzlement for one of two reasons — (a) because the mere fact of his being a trustee gives him a "right" of administration since it makes him an owner, or (b) because he cannot be guilty of theft since he is an owner, but is clearly guilty of a breach of his trust, and it is not worthwhile adding another crime to the group of theft, theft-embezzlement, and embezzlement.

---

[49] The application of the maxim *ex turpi causa non oritur actio* in the criminal law is uncertain. While it seems clear that one member of a fraudulent conspiracy would not be charged with embezzling from the others, or *e.g.* one member of a kidnapping gang with embezzling part of the ransom money which he failed to hand over to his colleagues, there may be situations in which persons who engage in criminal activities will be charged with embezzlement. There have, for instance, been cases in which street bookmakers' runners have been charged with embezzling bets received by them in contravention of the Betting Acts. In *H.M. Advocate v. Hodkinson & Morton* (1903) 4 Adam 219, at 227–228, Lord Young expressed the opinion that the law would not take account of betting frauds, but frauds on bookmakers are commonly prosecuted: see *Claytons v. H.M. Advocate* (1906) 5 Adam 12, at 16 where L.J.-C. Macdonald disapproved of Lord Young's opinion.

[50] (1843) 1 Broun 612.

[51] *supra*, paras 14.28, 14.33.

[52] It has been decided that a partner may be convicted of embezzlement from his firm: *Peter Anthony Sumner*, High Court on appeal, Nov. 1983, unrep'd.

[53] (1879) 4 Couper 227, at 234.

[54] *Heritable Reversionary Co. v. Millar* (1892) 19 R.(H.L.) 43. Lord Herschell at 43–44, Lord Watson at 49–50, where he talks of "committing a fraud".

17.29   (6) A cannot be guilty of embezzlement unless he holds the goods on behalf of B. This proposition is necessary in order to distinguish that failure to account which constitutes embezzlement from mere failure to repay a loan, which is not a crime at all. If A borrows money from B he becomes the owner of that money and cannot steal it; furthermore he is owner for his own behoof and not on befalf of or in trust for B or anyone else, and so he cannot embezzle it.

Appropriation in embezzlement

17.30   The treatment of appropriation in cases of embezzlement is complicated by two factors — (a) the subject-matter of most embezzlements is money, and a loan of money involves a transfer of property to the borrower, so that no distinction can be drawn between appropriation and unlawful borrowing; but (b) in embezzlement proper, A has a general power to act as if he were owner of the money concerned, and may even be the owner, so that it can be argued that provided he produces the proper amount of money at the end of the accounting period, it does not matter that he has "borrowed" some of it for himself during that period. As a result there has been a certain amount of confusion on this matter, and the cases lead to the rather vague conclusion that A is guilty of embezzlement only if he has acted "dishonestly".[55] The position can be clarified if the *actus reus* and the *mens rea* of embezzlement are distinguished as far as possible.

17.31   *The actus reus of embezzlement.* Embezzlement consists in the unlawful appropriation of goods due to another by a person in such a situation that his acts constitute embezzlement rather than theft. So far as money is concerned embezzlement consists in the unauthorised use of money by a person in such a position. The fact that A is able to account fully at the end of a fixed period is not inconsistent with embezzlement during that period. In *John Lawrence*[56] the accused was an executor who misappropriated money given him in that capacity by a co-executor. He was charged with embezzling the money within six months of the death of the deceased, *i.e.* before the date at which he became liable to account to the beneficiaries. There may be some question whether on the facts Lawrence was guilty of a breach of trust *quoad* his co-executor rather than *quoad* the beneficiaries, but Lord Neaves' judgment makes it clear that embezzlement can be committed prior to the end of the accounting period, and can be committed by someone who is nonetheless able to account fully in the sense that he has at his disposal funds with which to pay his principal. Lord Neaves defined embezzlement as the employment of funds "in any business at any time contrary to the trust". "The executor", he added, "may be as flourishing as a bay tree; but if, contrary to the terms of the trust he employ them in such a manner as to put them to any risk, he commits a wrong. The *animus* with which he does so may or may not be of importance in estimating the crime, . . . but is of no importance in a question of relevancy."[57]

It is true that Lord Neaves seems to require an element of risk in the use of the fund, but at the same time his example of the rich executor suggests that the crime is committed even when there is no risk to the

---

[55] *J.B. Walker Lee* (1884) 5 Couper 492; *Allenby v. H.M. Advocate,* 1938 J.C. 55.
[56] (1872) 2 Couper 168.
[57] At 173.

beneficiary. One could argue that any use of money involves some risk, but it is submitted that it is preferable to hold simply that any use of money by an administrator in breach of trust constitutes an *actus reus* of embezzlement.

Lord Neaves' next sentence can be "translated" as, "the *mens rea* with which he acts may be of importance in deciding whether he should be convicted of embezzlement, but does not affect the existence of the *actus reus* of the crime."

"APPROPRIATION". As in theft, what constitutes appropriation in **17.32** embezzlement is a question of fact. In some cases it is easy to point to an act of appropriation, such as the transfer of money to A's private account.[58] In other cases it is not possible to point to any act of appropriation, and all the Crown can show is that A held money on behalf of B with a duty to pay it to B at a certain time, and that he failed to do so. It is then a question of fact whether the circumstances lead to the necessary inference that A's failure to pay B was due to his having embezzled the money at some earlier unascertainable date.[59] Where no time is fixed for payment by A, appropriation may be inferred from a failure to pay within a reasonable time.[60] Moreover, if A once appropriates B's money, whether the evidence is of an actual act of appropriation or merely of a failure to make due payment, the fact that A pays B after the appropriation is as irrelevant as the return of stolen property by a repentant thief.[61]

The mens rea of embezzlement. This is essentially the same as the *mens* **17.33** *rea* of theft, and can be said to consist in an intention to appropriate money or goods due to another without his consent. It follows that a belief by A that he was acting with the consent of the appropriate person, or that for any other reason he was acting within the limits of his authority as an administrator, is a good defence to a charge of embezzlement. In practice, however, this defence is usually described in terms of the absence of "criminal" or "felonious" intent, *i.e.* in terms of the absence of general *mens rea*.[62] The most significant case on this point is *Allenby v. H.M. Advocate*.[63] A. was a fish salesman who acted as

---

[58] *H.M. Advocate v. Richd Laing* (1891) 2 White 572, Lord Kincairney at 575. On the special position of interest accruing on money held by a solicitor in a general clients' account, see Solicitors (Scotland) Act 1980, s.36 (as amended by Law Reform (Miscellaneous Provisions) (Scotland) Act 1980, s.25 and Solicitors (Scotland) Act 1988, Sched. 1, para. 10, Sched. 2).

[59] *H.M. Advocate v. D.T. Colquhoun* (1899) 3 Adam 96.

[60] *Edgar v. Mackay*, 1926 J.C. 94.

[61] *Edgar v. Mackay*, 1926 J.C. 94, where the payment was made immediately after the accused's arrest. This no doubt made it easier to infer that the original non-payment was due to embezzlement and not merely to inefficiency, but it would still have been open to the court to infer embezzlement had the payment been made before arrest.

[62] *H.M. Advocate v. City of Glasgow Bank Directors* (1879) 4 Couper 161, 187, where L.J.-C. Moncreiff required "bad faith, some corrupt motive, some guilty knowledge, some fraudulent intent", and *J.B. Walker Lee* (1884) 5 Couper 492, 496, where Lord Young required that the accused should act "with the mind of a thief or a knave, and intending to take his neighbour's property." But despite this, it is submitted that in Scotland as in England (prior to the Theft Act 1968, at least) "claim of right" involves belief in a legal and not just a moral right: *Harris v. Harrison* [1963] Crim.L.R. 497; Gl. Williams, p.322: *cf.* the wording of the Theft Act 1968, s.2(1)(a) and the opinion of Smith and Hogan, at p.535 as to its interpretation; see also *R. v. Close* [1977] Crim.L.R. 107.

[63] 1938 J.C. 55.

manager for certain trawl owners whose fish he sold. He paid all moneys received by him for the sale of fish into a common fund out of which he met his running costs, and paid over the balance to the respective owners. He was charged with applying money for behoof of one owner which he had received and credited in his books on behalf of another owner. The sheriff directed the jury that this constituted embezzlement,[64] and A. was convicted. The High Court quashed the conviction on the ground that the jury should have been directed that they must acquit unless they were satisfied that A. had acted dishonestly. The *ratio* of *Allenby* is the somewhat narrow one that in the special circumstances of the case, which were that A. had followed common trade practice,[65] and had not himself benefited from his irregular actings, the jury were not given sufficiently explicit directions on *mens rea*.[66] The reason for the court's decision was no doubt that the judges felt that A. had not acted dishonestly, but honesty and dishonesty are rather vague concepts in this type of case. Lord Wark remarked that the sheriff-substitute had almost given the jury a sufficient direction when he told them to "consider whether or not the man did what he did, believing he was entitled to do it."[67]

This suggests that the defence in *Allenby* should be regarded as a form of the defence of claim of right or entitlement,[68] that A.'s defence was not just a vague denial of dishonesty but the specific defence that he believed he was acting in a way he was entitled to act, that he was acting within his agency. This formulation can be used to separate the honest from the dishonest without recourse to circular arguments about "honesty", or to vague notions of general *mens rea*.[69] What the court seem to be saying is that whether or not conduct falls on the wrong side of the line separating a bad accounting or business practice from embezzlement depends on whether the jury think it "criminal", but there is a danger here of abandoning legal definitions of crime in favour of the *ad hoc* feelings of the jury.[70]

---

[64] *cf. H.M. Advocate v. Richd Laing* (1891) 2 White 572, where Lord Kincairney said, "if an agent receives money on behalf of a client and uses it for his own purposes, he is guilty of theft or of embezzlement, whether he lodges it in his bank account, or employs it in his business, or pays it on account of other clients": at 574–575. The position of interest accruing on funds held by a solicitor in a general clients' account is regulated by Solicitors (Scotland) Act 1980, s.36 (as amended by Law Reform (Miscellaneous Provisions) (Scotland) Act 1980, s.25 and Solicitors (Scotland) Act 1988, Sched. 1, para. 10, Sched. 2.

[65] But see *Dewar v. H.M. Advocate*, 1945 J.C. 5; Vol. I, para. 9.31; and *supra*, para. 14.58.

[66] 1938 J.C., L.J.-C. Aitchison at 58.

[67] At 60.

[68] *supra*, paras 14.55 to 14.58.

[69] See Vol. I, para. 7.05. The defence of claim of right or legal entitlement when applied to embezzlement resolve themselves into a belief that A was acting in an authorised way.

[70] *cf. R. v. Feely* [1973] 1 Q.B. 530 and the more modern two-stage test for dishonesty given out by Lord Lane C.J. in *R. v. Ghosh* [1982] Q.B. 1053, at 1064D–F.

CHAPTER 18

COMMON LAW FRAUD

Simple fraud and practical cheating

Fraud, which was formerly known as "falsehood, fraud, and wilful **18.01** imposition",[1] is a crime of very wide denotation in modern Scots law. Macdonald describes it as the bringing about of some definite practical result by means of false pretences,[2] and this is a good working description.[3] Where, however, the pretence involved is of the kind known as "practical cheating",[4] it is not necessary that it should have brought about any result, it is enough that it should have been made. If A writes a letter to B in which he makes a false statement, that is a simple fraud and the crime is not completed until B has been induced to do or refrain from doing something by the falsehood[5]; if, however, A writes a letter to B in imitation of C's handwriting and signs it in C's name, that is practical cheating and there is a completed crime, the crime of uttering, as soon as the letter is put in the post.[6] The uttering of forged documents is the commonest example of practical cheating, but there may be other kinds of cheat which fall under this head. The important feature of practical cheating is that it involves the passing off of an article or writing which itself pretends to be other than it is, which tells a lie about itself, so to speak, as in the case of a forged document, and does not merely contain a written falsehood as in the case of a begging letter containing lies.[7]

SIMPLE FRAUD

Every case of simple fraud must contain three elements: (1) a false **18.02** pretence; (2) a definite practical result; (3) a causal link between the pretence and the result.

---

[1] *cf. Jas Maitland* (1842) 1 Broun 57; *Elizabeth McWalter or Murray* (1852) J. Shaw 552. For the historical background, and the way in which "public" falsehoods such as counterfeiting and forgery became confused with a general crime of defrauding individuals, see Gill, Chap. 1.

[2] Macdonald, p.52.

[3] But see *infra*, para. 18.15 *et seq.*

[4] See Macdonald, p.58, for this term.

[5] *cf. Jas Shepherd* (1842) 1 Broun 325; *Michael Hinchy* (1864) 4 Irv. 561. The suggestions to the contrary in *Geo. Kippen* (1849) J. Shaw 276 cannot be accepted as correct.

[6] Hume, i, 150; Alison, i, 401; Macdonald, pp.64–65.

[7] See Kenny, para. 387; Smith and Hogan, pp. 659 *et seq.*; *R. v. Dodge*; *R. v. Harris* [1972] 1 Q.B. 417, CA; *R. v. More* [1987] 1 W.L.R. 1578, HL, especially Lord Ackner at 1585A and 1585F: *cf. R. v. Donnelly* (1984) 79 Cr.App.R. 76, CA, where the court appears to have taken a view contrary to that accepted in *More*. (Sir John Smith, *op.cit.* at pp. 660–661, takes the view that *Donnelly* is wrongly decided, although the modern English decisions depend, of course, on interpretations of ss. 1 and 9 of the Forgery and Counterfeiting Act 1981.) Bankruptcy frauds, frauds involving perversion of the course of justice, and certain insurance frauds, are all special and do not require a practical result: see Macdonald, p.58.

The false pretence

18.03   False pretences may be of many kinds, and it would be pointless to enumerate even the reported examples. The two most common are: (1) the assumption of a false character, *e.g.* inducing B to hand over goods by pretending to be, or to be acting on behalf of, a particular person or type of person to whom B would be willing to give the goods,[8] or a person of credit and good business repute,[9] by falsely assuming an official character such as that of a notary,[10] clergyman,[11] revenue officer,[12] sheriff officer[13] or official of any private organisation,[14] by pretending that one is authorised to carry out the duties of an office from which one has been suspended,[15] or that one belongs to a class of persons such as that of army pensioners or unemployed persons who are entitled to certain payments,[16] or that one is possessed of special skills, whether for example that one is a skilled surgeon, or craftsman of any kind, or a sorcerer,[17] or is in a position of influence whereby one can obtain a benefit for the dupe,[18] or by telling a false "hard luck" story to obtain charity[19]; and (2) the ascription of a false character to goods one is selling, *e.g.* by pretending that a worthless painting or manuscript is an Old Master or a Burns fragment,[20] that a preparation has certain valuable properties or is of a certain recognised kind,[21] or that an article one is selling belonged to a person reputed for his judgment of that type of article.[22]

18.04 *Express and implied pretences.* The simplest and most common type of pretence is an express statement made orally or in writing. But a

---

[8] Hume, i, 174–176; *Jas Clerk* (1834) *ibid.* 176; *Adam Fraser* (1801) Alison, i, 364; *Andrew Harvey* (1811) Hume, i, 174; *Bethia Hamilton* (1814) Hume, i, 174; *Geo. Scott* (1828) Alison, i, 365; *Geo. Walker* (1839) Bell's Notes 64; *Jas Maitland* (1842) 1 Broun 57; *Robt Meldrum and Catharine Reid* (1838) 2 Swin. 117; *Sam. Michael* (1842) 1 Broun 472; *John Menzies* (1842) *ibid.* 419; *Margt Grahame* (1847) J. Shaw 243n; *Henry Hardinge* (1863) 4 Irv. 347; *Margt Sharp* (1874) 2 Couper 543; *Spence v. Neilson* (1892) 3 White 309.

[9] *Thos Hall* (1789) Hume, i, 172–173; *Nicholas Kirby* (1799) Hume, i, 174; *John Harkins or Harkisson* (1842) 1 Broun 420; *Macgregor and Inglis* (1846) Ark. 49; *Adolph Kronacher* (1852) 1 Irv. 62; *Wm Rodger* (1868) 1 Couper 76; *Wm Edward Bradbury* (1872) 2 Couper 311; *John Thos Witherington* (1881) 4 Couper 475; *John Hall* (1881) *ibid.* 500; *Wm Wilson* (1882) 5 Couper 48; *Dingwall v. H.M. Advocate* (1888) 2 White 27; *H.M. Advocate v. Simon Macleod and Roderick Geo. Macleod* (1888) *ibid.* 71; *H.M. Advocate v. Swan* (1888) 2 White 137.

[10] *Thos Marjoribanks* (1597) Hume, i, 159.

[11] *Geo. Craighead* (1750) Hume, i, 159.

[12] *Alex. Reid* (1802) *ibid.*; *Wm Cruickshank* (1829) Shaw 227.

[13] *Donald MacInnes and Malcolm Macpherson* (1836) 1 Swin. 198.

[14] *John Campbell* (1822) Hume, i, 175; *Neilson v. Stirling* (1870) 1 Couper 476.

[15] *Robt Millar* (1843) 1 Broun 529.

[16] *Jas Munro and John MacFarlane* (1809), *Alex. Kinnaird* (1810) and *Patrick Branan and Ors* (1820) all Hume, i, 174; *Murdoch Beaton* (1794) and *Chas Grant* (1813) both Hume, i, 172; *Townsend v. Strathern* 1923 J.C. 66.

[17] *Mary Hutchison or Arrol* (1818) Hume, i, 174.

[18] *Neil Douglas* (1816) Hume, i, 174.

[19] *Joan Rickaly* (1824) Hume, i, 175.

[20] *Frank v. H.M. Advocate*, 1938 J.C. 17; *H.M. Advocate v. A.H. Smith* (1893) 1 Adam 6.

[21] *J. and P. Coats Ltd v. Brown* (1909) 6 Adam 538.

[22] *Frank v. H.M. Advocate, supra*; *Turnbull v. Stuart* (1898) 2 Adam 536. Another common type of fraud is fraud upon bookmakers perpetrated by pretending that bets dispatched after the running of a race had been sent before the race, for example, by putting a false postmark on the envelope containing the bet, *e.g. Claytons v. H.M. Advocate* (1906) 5 Adam 12; *H.M. Advocate v. Hodkinson and Morton* (1903) 4 Adam 219; *Wood and Wight v. H.M. Advocate* (1899) 3 Adam 64.

pretence may also be made by implication. Many situations involve an implied representation as to the genuineness of an article. In *Jas Paton*[23] A. inflated the skins of some cattle he had entered in a competition, and put false horns on them; in *Alex. Bannatyne*[24] A sold a mixture of oats and other grain made up to look like pure oats; in both cases there was an implied representation that the articles were genuine — that the cows' skins and horns were natural, and that the grain was pure oats. A's conduct, again, may be such as to indicate that he is entitled to certain privileges as where he enters a club to which he does not belong by using someone else's membership card, or merely by adopting an air of self-possession sufficiently convincing to deceive the porter. It is fraud to get in to a married woman's bed and act in such a way as to make her believe it is her husband who is in the bed.[25]

If A orders a specific article or a specific quantity from B and B hands over something different B will be held to have pretended that he was fulfilling A's order even if the article delivered bears a disclaimer on its wrapping such as "Not sold by weight."[26]

There is also an implied statement of intention to pay on the part of anyone who obtains goods on credit.[27]

A situation may itself be fraudulent. If A and B pretend to be **18.05** committing adultery in order that C, an innocent party who sees them, may give evidence to enable one of their spouses to obtain a divorce, A and B will be guilty of fraud.[28] Again, anyone who engages in a card game represents that the game will be played fairly. In *Steuart v. Macpherson*[29] A and B induced C to play cards with them by pretending to be unknown to each other, a pretence made indirectly by their behaviour towards each other.[30] Burnett gives as an example of fraud the situation where A lends an article to B, takes it back clandestinely, and then claims it or its value from B.[31] Another unusual case is *Geo. Kippen*[32] in which B had obtained a warrant on a decree against A, and A raised a false summons against B in a false name and arrested the debt due to B by himself on the dependence of the fictitious action.

Cheques. It is clear that a cheque implies a representation that it will be **18.06** honoured.

This, however, is a representation as to the future, and not as such a relevant basis for a charge of fraud. A cheque is regarded as the equivalent of ready money,[33] and to give a cheque is thus to represent that it is as good as cash. This probably involves a representation that the giver of the cheque is authorised to draw it by the bank on which it is drawn, *i.e.* that there is an existing arrangement between him and the

---

[23] (1858) 3 Irv. 208.

[24] (1847) Ark. 361.

[25] *Wm Fraser* (1847) Ark 280; *infra*, para. 18.15.

[26] *Galbraith's Stores Ltd v. McIntyre* (1912) 6 Adam 641, esp. Lord Salvesen at 649.

[27] See *infra*, para. 18.12.

[28] *cf. Nicol Muschet and Campbell* (1721) Hume, i, 170; *Margt Boyle and Ors* (1859) 3 Irv. 440.

[29] 1918 J.C. 96.

[30] *cf. Wm Clark and Ors* (1859) 3 Irv. 409.

[31] Burnett, p.120.

[32] (1849) J. Shaw 276.

[33] See the civil case of *D. and C. Builders Ltd v. Rees* [1966] 2 Q.B. 617, Lord Denning M.R. at 623C.

bank for the honouring of the cheque.[34] In most cases this will involve a representation that the drawer has an account at the bank which is in sufficient credit to meet the cheque or that he has been granted overdraft facilities to meet the cheque. There is probably also an implied statement of intention by the drawer not to alter his bank account so as to prejudice the holder of the cheque.

There is little Scots authority on this important question. Macdonald says: "If a person obtains goods or money by using a cheque, he having no funds in the bank and knowing that the cheque will not be honoured, he commits fraud."[35]

In *Rae v. Linton*[36] Lord Neaves said:

> "The having money at his credit with a bank is not the only ground on which a man may draw a cheque. He may be directly authorised by the bank to draw on credit, either by reason of having granted a cash credit bond, or by reason merely of his undoubted solvency; or, being obliged to overdraw his account in a temporary emergency, he may be as morally certain that the bank will honour his draft as he would be if he know that he had money at his credit; or he may even be in ignorance that he is overdrawing his account at all . . . Suppose that it is proved that he drew and presented the cheque when there was nothing at his credit with the bank . . . : is that a crime? If so, I am afraid many very respectable persons are in danger daily of having a criminal charge laid against them. The simple use of the words 'falsely and fraudulently' are not enough to convert this innocent act into a crime. Some additional statement is necessary, to the effect that he had neither money nor credit, nor any right to believe that his cheque would be honoured, or that he knew that it would not be honoured."

The position regarding a post-dated cheque is even less clear. It probably represents only that the drawer has a current account, and that he has reason to believe the cheque will be met in due course.[37]

In England it has been said that:

> "[T]he familiar act of drawing a cheque (a document which on the face of it is only a command of a future act) is held to imply at least three statements about the present: (1) that the drawer has an account with that bank; (2) that he has authority to draw on it for that amount; (3) that the cheque, as drawn, is a valid order for the payment of that amount (*i.e.* that the present state of affairs is such that, in the ordinary course of events, the cheque will on its future presentment be duly honoured). It may be well to point out, however, that it does not imply any representation that the drawer now has money in this bank to the amount drawn for, inasmuch as he may well have authority to overdraw, or may intend to pay in (before the cheque can be presented) sufficient money to meet it."[38]

---

[34] *cf. R. v. Charles* [1977] A.C. 177, Lord Diplock at 182.
[35] pp. 55–56.
[36] (1874) 3 Couper 67, 72.
[37] See *R. v. Maytum-White* (1957) 42 Crim.App.R. 165.
[38] *R. v. Page* [1971] 2 Q.B. 330n., 333, citing Kenny (18th ed.), p.347.

The crux of the matter, however, lies in statement (3): "[T]he real representation made is that the cheque will be paid . . . that the existing state of facts is such that in ordinary course the cheque will be met."[39]

Although in the end of the day it may be that, as Dr (now Lord) Gill says,[40] rules of this kind are no more than canons of evidence, the courts will in practice assume that the generally implied representation was implicitly made on any occasion, subject to evidence to the contrary by the accused, and of course to any questions of *mens rea*, so that it is of some importance to establish what it is that is generally implied.[41]

There are no reported Scots cases on the use of cheque cards or credit cards. It has been held in England that the unauthorised use of a cheque card by a customer of the bank constitutes an additional false representation to the trader that the customer is authorised to draw the cheque, and a fraud thereby on the bank who are "induced" to allow the customer to overdraw to the extent required to meet the cheque.[42] Similar reasoning has been applied to credit card transactions, in that the presentation of a credit card (where to the knowledge of the presenter authority to use it has been withdrawn) constitutes a false representation of actual authority from the card company to use that card relative to the transaction in question. In England it is for the jury to decide in cheque card and credit card transactions whether it was that false representation which induced the dupe to hand over the goods; but it is to be expected that in practice they will decide that it was.[43]

FRAUDULENT SILENCE. Fraud may be committed by omission in cases **18.07** where A has a duty to disclose the truth to B. This duty may arise from a contractual relationship between A and B which obliges A to disclose the whole truth to B; in such cases any concealment of truth will amount to a fraudulent representation, since there will be implied in all A's statements a representation that he has disclosed the whole truth. The most common example of this type of fraud is the failure by company promoters or directors to make full disclosures in prospectuses or balance sheets,[44] which is usually dealt with today as a statutory offence.

Where A is under a statutory duty to make disclosures to B his failure to do so may also ground a charge of common law fraud. In *Strathern v. Fogal*[45] the accused falsified returns to the local assessor by failing to disclose certain premiums received by him from his tenants, as a result of which he evaded payment of the rates due on them, and this was held to be a good charge of common law fraud.

There may also be cases in which A innocently makes a statement to B which he subsequently realises has created a false impression on B from which A stands to benefit. In such circumstances he probably has a duty

---

[39] *R. v. Hazelton* (1874) L.R., 2 C.C.R. 134, Pollock B. at 140; quoted with conditional approval (since a cheque card was also involved — see *infra*) by Lord Edmund-Davies in *R. v. Charles* [1977] A.C. 177, at 191B.

[40] Gill, p.47.

[41] Whether for example, an honest belief that the cheque will be met is a defence may depend on what representations were impliedly made: *cf. R. v. Miller* [1955] N.Z.L.R. 1038, 1049; *R. v. Kuff* [1962] V.R. 578.

[42] *R. v. Kovacs* [1974] 1 W.L.R. 370; *R. v. Charles* [1977] A.C. 177.

[43] *R. v. Lambie* [1982] A.C. 449, HL. See the discussion of this case and the case of *Charles* (see n.42, *supra*) in Smith and Hogan, pp. 553–556.

[44] *H.M. Advocate v. City of Glasgow Bank Directors* (1879) 4 Couper 161; *H.M. Advocate v. Pattisons* (1901) 3 Adam 420.

[45] 1922 J.C. 73.

to rectify this impression.[46] Again, a person who sells reconditioned goods which look new has a duty to disclose the true nature of the goods, otherwise their appearance will constitute a representation that they are new.[47] Similarly, to present books of incomplete accounts without explanation in a situation in which the person shown the books would expect them to be offered as complete accounts is a misrepresentation that they are complete.[48]

According to Gill there is fraud where the accused knew that disclosure would have led the dupe to act otherwise than he did and otherwise than the accused wished him to act.[49]

18.08 *Statements of opinion.* A fraudulent pretence must be one as to a fact, and not merely an opinion. But a statement of opinion does involve a representation that the opinion is indeed held by its maker.[50]

18.09   PUFFING. A false pretence that one's goods are of "excellent quality" will not found a charge of fraud, however dishonestly it is made, but a pretence that, for example, the cutlery one is selling is silver when in fact it is electro-plated nickel silver would be a relevant ground of charge. The line between opinion and fact is necessarily not a definite one, and it is a question for the jury in each case whether the alleged representation falls within the class struck at by the law. A considerable latitude is allowed to sellers to "puff" their goods in advertisements, and it is unlikely that, for example, "Brand X removes grease instantly" would be regarded as a fraudulent representation if it were false.

This latitude extends even to businessmen making false or exaggerated statements of fact in the ordinary course of business dealings, for example, by holding themselves out falsely as able to benefit the other party to a proposed contract. In *Tapsell v. Prentice*[51] Lord Ardwall spoke of statements which were "just the ordinary lies which people tell when they want to induce credulous members of the public to purchase goods,

---

[46] *cf.* the civil law duty to rectify a statement which has been falsified by subsequent events: *With v. O'Flanagan* [1936] Ch. 575.

[47] *cf. Gibson v. National Cash Register*, 1925 S.C. 500; *Patterson v. Landsberg* (1905) 7 F. 675.

[48] *H.M. Advocate v. Pattisons.* (1901) 3 Adam 420, L.J.-G. Balfour at 470.

[49] Gill, p.69n, where the author quotes Lord Fraser's charge to the jury in *H.M. Advocate v. Livingston* (1888) 1 White 587, 592:

"[F]raud . . . may be any deception by which one man makes another believe, to the latter's injury, something that really does not exist. It might be done either by direct assertion, or by a suggestion not amounting to direct assertion, of something which was untrue. What did the prisoner do in this case? He went to various people and ordered goods without saying one word about his being an undischarged bankrupt . . . There was no assertion, certainly, that he was not an undischarged bankrupt; but, on the other hand, he kept back the important fact that he was an undischarged bankrupt. He knew perfectly well that if he had told that fact he would not have got credit for a single sixpence."

Cf. Buchmann v. Normand, 1994 S.C.C.R. 929, where an accused, who in fact had previous convictions, was found to have made a false statement recklessly in that he had failed to disclose those convictions by omitting to make any answer (in an application form for a particular licence) to a question which asked him to disclose them. He had also signed a declaration to the effect that the particulars given by him on the form were true; the charge was not, however, one of common law fraud, but rather of contravening the Civic Government (Scotland) Act 1982, s.7(4). (For the *mens rea* of fraud relative to the representation, see para. 18.31, *infra*.)

[50] *H.M. Advocate v. Pattisons* (1901) 3 Adam 420. L.J.-G. Balfour at 471–472; *Bisset v. Wilkinson* [1927] A.C. 177, PC.

[51] (1910) 6 Adam 354.

or to do something for them."[52] The position in such cases is probably
that if the accused does not go beyond what is recognised as permissible
in the business circles in which he moves, provided these circles are what
is known as "reputable", he will be regarded as lacking in any fraudulent
mens rea. This latitude does not, however, extend to false statements of
fact about the goods themselves as distinguished from statements of
opinion or advertising puffs.[53] Gill's view is that where the puffing has in
fact caused the susceptible buyer to buy on the faith of a misleading or
exaggerated advertisement "published in the expectation that few will be
deceived by it, but in the hope that at least some will" there should be
fraud.[54]

Representations about the future. A pretence about the future cannot **18.10**
form the basis of a charge of fraud — the law of fraud is concerned only
with representations regarding present or past facts.[55] A false prediction
is therefore not a relevant misrepresentation except in so far as it
misrepresents the predictor's state of mind.[56] But many statements
apparently about the future contain implied statements about the
present. If, for example, A tenders a post-dated cheque, that is not
merely a representation that the cheque will be met at a future date, it is
also a representation regarding A's present relationship with the bank on
which the cheque is drawn.[57] Again, if A says to B, "Give me £5 and I'll
get you some duty-free whisky," in certain circumstances that may be not
merely a promise about A's future conduct, but may also imply that A is
presently in a position to sell B whisky, perhaps that he has the whisky in
his possession or at any rate that he has access to smuggled supplies. A
representation that one will receive a payment at a future date may
imply a representation that one is presently entitled to the payment.[58]
And if these implied statements about a present state of affairs are false
they will be sufficient ground for a charge of fraud whether or not A
hopes and intends that he will be able to fulfil his undertaking. If A
presents B with a post-dated cheque drawn on a bank with which he has
no account and B acts on the faith of the cheque A is guilty of fraud
even if he honestly intended to pay B the amount of the cheque or even
to open an account in the bank in time for the cheque to be honoured.

Representations of intentions. Statements of intention, and particularly of **18.11**
intention to pay, raise two problems, which in turn arise out of the desire
to limit the crime of fraud so that it does not extend (a) to promise-
breaking, or (b) to a mere failure to pay one's debts.

---

[52] At 357.
[53] *ibid. Cf.* New Zealand Crimes Act 1961, s.245(4) and (5):
"Exaggerated commendation or depreciation of the quality of anything is not a false
pretence unless it is carried to such an extent as to amount to a fraudulent
misrepresentation of fact.
It is a question of fact whether such commendation or depreciation as aforesaid
does or does not amount to a fraudulent misrepresentation of fact."
[54] See pp.63–65. Most such cases can now be dealt with under the Trade Descriptions
Act 1968, *infra*, para 19.21, and a statement not caught by that Act is unlikely to be treated
as a common law fraud.
[55] T.B. Smith, p.202. *John Hall* (1881) 4 Couper 438; *Strathern v. Fogal*, 1922 J.C. 73.
[56] *infra*, para. 18.11 *et seq.*
[57] *cf. Rae v. Linton* (1874) 3 Couper 67; *Nicolas Kirby* (1799) Hume, i, 174; *supra*,
para. 18.06.
[58] Gill, p.57; *cf. Meldrum and Reid* (1838) 2 Swin. 117.

A promise is not in itself, strictly speaking, a statement of intention or of anything else at all, nor is it, therefore, capable of being true or false.[59] It is what Professor J.L. Austin has called a "performative utterance",[60] a ritual performance which effects a change in the relationship of the parties. The most striking example is the "I will" of the marriage ceremony, but any promise creates a moral obligation, and some promises create legal obligations. These obligations depend on the fact that the promise was made, irrespective of whether the maker intended to perform it. But there is something outrageous about saying "I promise to do *x*, but I haven't the least intention of doing it",[61] and the person to whom the promise is made is entitled to take it as including an implied statement of intention to carry it out.[62] Where that implied statement is false, there is a fraudulent representation. In such cases the intention represented is the intention at the time of the representation. There may well be an implied undertaking not to change one's intention, but that is not a representation except in so far as it itself implies a statement of intention not to change one's intention.

18.12 THE PRETENCE OF INTENTION TO PAY. In cases where it is alleged that A obtained something intending not to pay for it, the representation involved is a representation that at the time the contract was made A intended to pay on delivery, or at the expiry of a stated or reasonable term of credit. In order to prove such a charge the Crown must show that from the outset A did not intend to pay, whether or not he was ever in a position to pay, and whether or not any reasonable man in A's position would have expected to be able to pay. As Lord Justice-Clerk Moncreiff said in *John Thomas Witherington*,[63] "An honest man will not of course order goods from a dealer unless he knows, or has the best reason to believe, that he can pay for them; but men are sanguine, or careless, or speculative, and may be unable to pay when the day of reckoning comes round, although quite honest in their intention to fulfil their obligation", and such men are not guilty of fraud.

In *John Hall*[64] Lord Young, who held that statements of intention could not found a charge of fraud, pointed out that someone who starts off with the intention of not paying may later change his mind and pay, while someone who starts with the intention of paying may later decide not to pay, and asked, "Shall the former (who in fact pays) be punished as a criminal, and the latter (who does not) go free? A crime committed cannot thereafter be uncommitted." As Lord Young realised, if fraud may be committed by such statements the answer to both his questions is "Yes". The crime is not that of obtaining goods and failing to pay for them but of inducing the seller to hand over the goods by pretending one will pay, and once the goods are obtained the crime is complete and

---

[59] *cf. R. v. Sunair Holidays Ltd.* [1973] 1 W.L.R. 1105, 1109F–1110B. Some Australian states do, however, provide by legislation for "wilfully false promises": see, *e.g.*, the New South Wales Crimes Act 1900 (No. 40), ss.178C (obtaining credit by fraud), 179 (obtaining property by false pretence or wilfully false promise) and 180 (causing payment to be made (etc.) by false pretence or wilfully false promise).

[60] See Urmson, J.O. and Sbisa, Marina (Eds), J.L. Austin, *How to do Things with Words* (2nd ed., Oxford, 1976, revised 1980); and Chap. 10 of the same author's *Philosophical Papers* (2nd ed., Oxford, 1970).

[61] J.L. Austin, *Philosophical Papers*, p.248.

[62] But *cf. British Airways Board v. Taylor* [1976] 1 W.L.R. 13, Lord Wilberforce at 17.

[63] (1881) 4 Couper 475, 499–500.

[64] (1881) 4 Couper 438, 447.

cannot be "uncommitted".[65] Suppose, now, that A intended to pay at the time he ordered the goods or services and then changed his mind. In such a case the goods or services are not provided as a result of any false statement. The only ways in which a charge of fraud could be made would be by showing (a) that some subsequent and by then false repetition of the representation induced the dupe to disregard any doubts he might have formed about A's honesty, and to decide on the faith of the repeated statement that he would provide the goods or services; or (b) that a subsequent false statement made after the provision of the goods or services induced the dupe to do some other prejudicial act, such as allow A further credit. The mere fact that A changes his mind and defaults on his obligation does not make him guilty of fraud. For so to hold would mean that every representation of intention is a continuing one, and that there is therefore a duty to disclose that it has become false. And however morally praiseworthy such disclosure would be the criminal law cannot require it without running the risk of treating every defaulting debtor as guilty of fraud where it can be shown that but for his non-disclosure of his change of mind the creditor would have taken steps to try to secure payment.[66]

ARE SUCH PRETENCES RELEVANT? There was for a long time, up to and **18.13** including the publication of the first edition of this book in 1967, considerable doubt whether and if so to what extent Scots law recognised statements of intention as a basis for a charge of fraud. Hume did not deal with the matter. Alison did not deal with it explicitly but he stated that any charge of "swindling" required "a false representation of some sort, which occasions the giving credit, the most extensive fraud committed by merely ordering goods on credit, and not paying for them, without any such false representation, not falling under this species of crime",[67] which suggests that he would not have regarded a mere pretence of intention to pay as sufficient. It was not disputed that a pretence that one has funds, or that one is an established businessman,[68] or is in receipt of a wage or pension due to be paid at a certain future date[69] was relevant; the question was whether there could be fraud in the absence of any pretence of this kind. Macdonald was clearly of the view that there could, saying that "it is a crime to obtain goods . . . with the preconceived intention not to pay for them, although no false inducement have been held out",[70] although many of the cases he cited did contain other inducements. Anderson stated equally categorically that "False representations made to obtain goods must, in order to be criminal, have reference to past or present, and not solely to future time",[71] and his reference to *John Hall*[72] as authority makes it clear that he was excluding statements of intention. Professor Smith stated that "A

---

[65] *Pace*, Lord McLaren in *Simon Macleod and Roderick Geo. Macleod* (1888) 2 White 71, 76.

[66] *cf.* the difficult English case of *Ray v. Sempers* [1974] A.C. 370; G.H. Gordon, "English Criminal Law: Two Recent Developments" (1975) 20 J.L.S. 4.

[67] Alison, i, 362.

[68] *cf. John Hall* (1881) 4 Couper 438, 448.

[69] *Robt Meldrum and Catharine Reid* (1838) 2 Swin. 117. *Cf. H.M. Advocate v. Jas Swan* (1888) 2 White 137; *Patrick Thomas Caulfield* (1840) 2 Swin. 522.

[70] Macdonald, p.56.

[71] Anderson, p.195.

[72] (1881) 4 Couper 438.

man's intention . . . is an existing fact",[73] but his only authority was the strange case of *Macleod v. Mactavish*.[74]

It is now clear that a false statement of intention is a relevant misrepresentation. This was established in *Richards v. H.M. Advocate*[75] where the representation was one of an intention by a nominee of the accused to purchase and use for a certain purpose property which would not have been sold to him had the sellers known that it was not to be acquired by the nominee for the purposes represented. In rejecting an attack on the relevancy of the charge Lord Justice-Clerk Grant said:

"[F]or it seems to me that a man's present intention is just as much a fact as his name or his occupation or the size of his bank balance. Quite apart from general principle, however, we find as far back as 1849 the case of *Chisholm*,[76] in which Lord Justice-Clerk Hope sat with Lords Wood and Ivory. The main question in that case related to the relevance of a cumulative charge of fraud and theft on the same *species facti*. There was a further question, however, as to the relevancy of the fraud charge *per se*. The misrepresentation libelled was that the accused had promised to pay the price of certain goods at specified places at a future time. On the amendment of the libel (at the suggestion of the Court) by the insertion of a statement that the accused had entered upon the transactions with the intention of not paying for the goods, the libel was held relevant. This decision seems to me to be directly in point here, as does that in the later case of *Macleod v. Mactavish*.[77] There the sole misrepresentation was that the accused intended to remain in his employer's service for another half year. On a bill of suspension being taken the complaint was held to be relevant and the conviction upheld. One may also take into account the "board and lodging" cases (*cf.* Macdonald, at p. 56) and the specimen form of complaint set out in the Summary Jurisdiction (Scotland) Act, 1908, and repeated with one small amendment in the Second Schedule to the consolidating Act of 1954, thus: 'You did obtain from C.D. board and lodging to the value of 12s. without paying and intending not to pay therefor.' (The phrase 'and intending not' was originally 'or intending.') If the appellant is right, it is difficult to see how such a complaint could be relevant. We were also referred to Gordon on Criminal Law, in which the authorities are reviewed at pp. 546-548. His conclusion that 'a statement of present intention as to future conduct can ground a charge of fraud' is, in my opinion, fully justified by authority."[78]

It follows from *Richards* that it is an offence to obtain anything, including goods, services or credit, by a false representation that one intends to pay for them. Scots law therefore has no need of any special provision, statutory or otherwise, for the fraudulent obtaining of credit

---

[73] T.B. Smith, p.202.
[74] (1897) 2 Adam 354.
[75] 1971 J.C. 29.
[76] J. Shaw 241.
[77] (1897) 2 Adam 354.
[78] 1971 J.C. at 32–33. The statutory style for "board and lodging" cases now appears in the 1995 Act, Sched. 5.

or of such services as restaurant meals or board and lodgings, or for travelling in trains, etc., without paying.[79]

The result

Fraudulent appropriation. Mackenzie quotes the civilian definition of **18.14** fraud, which he refers to as falsehood, as "A fraudulent suppression, or imitation of Truth, in prejudice of another".[80] But he himself discusses fraud almost entirely from the point of view of the manner in which the fraud is perpetrated, distinguishing falsehood by writ, by witness, by coining and by false weights.[81] By Hume's time, however, fraud was thought of as consisting of the fraudulent appropriation of property.[82] For Hume fraud is committed "by some false assumption of name, character, commission, or errand, for the purpose of obtaining goods or money, or other valuable thing, to the offender's profit."[83] Burnett cites the civilian definition of falsehood as being "in a broad and comprehensive sense", "any 'fraudulent imitation or suppression of truth, to the prejudice of others'", but goes on to say that that does not describe "that species of falsehood, which is the proper object of criminal justice", the

---

[79] For examples of obtaining credit, see *Jas Smith* (1839) 2 Swin. 346; *Jas and Robert Mackintosh* (1840) 2 Swin. 511; *Jas Chisholm* (1849) J. Shaw 241; *Jas Hall and Ors.* (1849) J. Shaw 254: *Isadore Toitz*, High Court at Glasgow, Feb. 15, 1962, on remit from Glasgow Sheriff Court, unrep'd; *John Hall* (1881) 4 Couper 438; *Drew v. H.M. Advocate*, 1995 S.C.C.R. 647. Lord Ashmore's observations in *Strathern v. Fogal*, 1922 J.C. 73, 82, cannot stand with *Richards*. There are also many cases of "long-firm" frauds where the representation of intention not to pay was joined to representations as to the character of the accused or his business: see para. 18.03, n.9, *supra*.

For examples of board and lodging fraud see *Jas Wilkie* (1872) 2 Couper 323; *Jas Wilkie or McQuilkan* (1875) 3 Couper 102. The statutorily approved form of charge: did obtain board and lodgings without paying and intending not to pay therefor (1995 Act, Sched. 5) may just be a statutory shorthand for "did pretend to B that you intended to pay for board and lodgings and did induce him to provide them", but if so, this has been lost sight of in practice. In railway cases, for example, it is common to charge A with travelling from London to Edinburgh without paying and intending not to pay the fare, although such a charge could be said to libel a fraud in London by inducing the railway operator to permit A to board the train there, and if it is to be tried in Scotland should aver a further pretence and inducement to allow A to continue his journey beyond Berwick. The absence in practice of such an averment is unusual in a system which even today lays great stress on specification, and is an indication of the extent to which this type of fraud is treated in practice as being in a class of its own. The Regulation of Railways Act 1889, s.5(3), makes it an offence to travel or attempt to travel on a railway without previously paying one's fare, or to travel beyond one's station without previously paying the additional fare, if either is done "with intent to avoid payment": maximum penalty, level 2 [level 3, in the unlikely event of the Channel Tunnel Rail Link Act 1996, Sched. 9, Pt II, para. 8 being applicable to a Scottish case] or three months' imprisonment: see Transport Act 1962, s.84(2) as modified by the Criminal Procedure (Consequential Provisions) (Scotland) Act 1995, Sched. 1. But contrary to the usual practice with regard to statutory frauds, this section is rarely invoked and such frauds are prosecuted at common law, and sometimes punished with a sentence of imprisonment. It is also an offence under the subsection for a person who has not paid his fare to give a false name and address to a railway official.

[80] *cf.* D. 4.3.1.2. — "*omnem calliditatem fallaciam machinationem ad circumveniendium fallendum decipiendum alterum adhibitam.*"

[81] Mackenzie I, 27, pr.

[82] Or what is known is South Africa as "theft by false pretences," which is there restricted to the appropriation of things capable of being stolen: see J. Burchell and J. Milton, *Principles of Criminal Law* (2nd ed., 1997), pp. 553–554. *Cf.* the crime of "theft by deception" in the Model Penal Code, O.D. s.223.3. Frauds of this kind are regarded in South Africa and by the Model Penal Code as a species of theft (although Burchell and Milton, *op. cit.*, *loc.cit.*, doubt the need for such a crime given the reach of theft and fraud).

[83] Hume, i, 172.

crimen falsi, and himself restricts the crime to "all those falsehoods and frauds by which another is deprived of his property."[84]

Alison, too, talks of "All those falsehoods and frauds by which another is deprived of his property."[85]

Fraudulent appropriation of property includes obtaining property on loan by fraud and subsequently appropriating it, obtaining it on credit, and evading an obligation to pay money or deliver property by, for example, submitting a tax return containing fraudulent understatements of assets, or pretending that one has already paid a debt which is still due. It can also be extended to include the obtaining from B of an obligation to pay money or deliver goods, although the obligation is not carried out.[86]

18.15 *Fraud.* As Dr, now Lord, Gill has shown in his analysis of the cases, the result requirement in fraud was given an extensive interpretation in the nineteenth century, in order to make up for the absence of any crime of attempted fraud.[87] In particular, cases like *Jas Paton*[88] and *Hood v. Young*[89] extended fraud to cover cases where there was not merely an absence of economic loss, but no payment of money or delivery of goods at all, only a coming under an obligation to pay or deliver.

This extension of the law was no longer necessary after section 61 of the Criminal Procedure (Scotland) Act 1887 made all attempts to commit a crime indictable, but the courts continued to follow the earlier cases in situations where there had been payment for and delivery of goods, but the victim had not suffered economic loss.[90]

These cases, although they go beyond the idea of fraud as requiring the appropriation of something, do deal with economic interests.[91] Mention must, however, be made of *Wm Fraser*[92] where the accused had intercourse with a married woman by "deceiving her into the belief" that he was her husband. He was charged alternatively with rape, with assault with intent to ravish, and with "Fraudulently and Deceitfully obtaining Access to and having Carnal Knowledge of a Married Woman, by pretending to be her husband, or otherwise conducting himself, and behaving towards her so as to deceive her into the belief that he was her husband." The charges of rape and assault were held irrelevant by the majority of the court, mainly because of a disinclination to extend the scope of the then capital crime of rape, but no attack seems to have been made on the relevancy of the fraud charge which read in the minor, "did,

---

[84] Burnett, pp. 164–165. For a discussion of the confusion in the nineteenth century between "falsehood" and "fraud", see Gill, Chap. I.

[85] Alison, i, 362.

[86] *Jas Paton* (1858) 3 Irv. 208; *Hood v. Young* (1853) 1 Irv. 236. The idea that fraud consists in dishonestly appropriating the property of another was also expressed in the wording of the now repealed s.63 of the Criminal Procedure (Scotland) Act 1887, which was entitled "Previous convictions of dishonesty" and went on to talk of previous convictions of "robbery, theft . . . falsehood, fraud, and wilful imposition . . . and of all other crimes inferring dishonest appropriation of property."

[87] Gill, Chaps VII and VIII.

[88] (1858) 3 Irv. 208.

[89] (1853) 1 Irv. 236; see also *Alex. Bannatyne* (1847) Ark. 361, *infra*, para. 18.50.

[90] *H.M. Advocate v. A.H. Smith* (1893) 1 Adam 6; *Turnbull v. Stuart* (1898) 2 Adam 536; *J. & P. Coats Ltd v. Brown* (1909) 6 Adam 19.

[91] *cf.* the Crown argument in *MacLeod v. MacTavish* (1897) 2 Adam 354, 356 that "The essence of fraud was that one person should, by deceit, induce another to part with some patrimonial right or interest, not necessarily money."

[92] (1847) Ark. 280.

wickedly and feloniously, fraudulently and deceitfully, introduce yourself into the bed in the said house where the said M.S. or F. was then lying . . . and lie down . . . beside her, and lay your hand or hands upon her person, and pretend to be her husband, or otherwise conduct yourself and behave towards her so as to deceive her into the belief that you were her husband, . . . and thereby obtain access to, and have carnal knowledge of, her person." Lord Cockburn observed that this was clearly fraud because "Any deceit that injures and violates the rights of another, is clearly punishable."[93]

It may be that the other majority judges treated the crime as an innominate offence,[94] and it would certainly be nowadays charged as a statutory offence and not as fraud[95]; but Lord Cockburn's definition was more or less repeated in later cases,[96] although it was not again made the *ratio decidendi* of any case until *Adcock v. Archibald* in 1925[97] which may be said to have gone even further than *Fraser*.[98]

There are also a number of cases concerned with attempts to defeat the ends of justice which were charged as fraud,[99] but such cases are now dealt with as attempts to defeat the ends of justice and not as frauds. The same is true of making false accusations to the police.[1]

Adcock v. Archibald.[2] Adcock was a miner who put his own identification **18.16** pin on a hutch of coal worked by another miner and in this way pretended to his employers that he had worked the coal in the hutch.[3] Both Adcock and the other miner worked on a contract

---

[93] Ark. at 312. Where the fraud causes death as by inducing someone to take poison by pretending it is harmless the charge is not fraud but murder: *M. Elder or Smith* (1827) Syme 71.

[94] See Gill, pp. 137–140.

[95] The circumstances of *Fraser* were statutorily declared to be rape in the Criminal Law Amendment Act 1885, s.4, now Criminal Law (Consolidation) (Scotland) Act 1995, s.7(3): see Vol. I, para. 1.24; *infra*, para. 33.18.

[96] For example, *H.M. Advocate v. John Livingstone* (1888) 1 White 587, a case of bankruptcy fraud, where Lord Fraser said that fraud "may be any deception by which one man makes another believe, to the latter's injury, something that really does not exist": at 592, and *H.M. Advocate v. Pattisons* (1901) 3 Adam 420, in which L.J.-G. Balfour spoke of "a false representation which leads a man to do something which may be, and probably will be, to his hurt": at 473.

[97] 1925 J.C. 58.

[98] *supra.* In *Geo. Kippen* (1849) J. Shaw 276, B obtained decree against the accused who then raised a fictitious action in a false name against B on the dependence of which he arrested the debt due by himself to B. He was charged with fraud and an objection that the Crown had not averred that the fraudulent summons had had any result was repelled. Lord Moncreiff said simply that the accused had acted for an unlawful design, but that would not be enough, except in so far as the case belongs to the special class of frauds on the course of justice. Lord Cockburn, however, pointed to the fact that the arrestments were carried out and so had obstructed B in his efforts to do diligence on his decree against the accused, and L.J.-C. Hope said that the accused's object was not to cheat but to delay diligence, and he had succeeded in that.

[99] See *Rae and Little* (1845) 2 Broun 476.

[1] *Elliot Millar* (1847) Ark. 355. For the modern law see *infra*, paras 47.38 *et seq*.

[2] 1925 J.C. 58.

[3] The terms of the complaint were that "on 16th January 1925 . . . in the . . . Hartley Seam of Coal in . . . Bannockburn Colliery . . . you . . . did from a hutch loaded with coal which had been worked by W.W. . . . fraudulently remove the pin indicating that the coal therein had been so worked and substitute a pin indicating that the said coal had been worked by you, and did thus induce the . . . Alloa Coal Co . . . on 23rd January 1925, at the pay office at said colliery, to pay to you . . . instead of to the said W.W. . . . 1/3½ for working said coal."

entitling them to a minimum weekly wage plus a bonus of 1s. 3¹/₂d. for every hutch worked over a certain number. During the week in question neither Adcock not the other miner exceeded this number and each received only the guaranteed minimum wage. Adcock's pretence accordingly did not affect his wage or the other miner's, and did not cause any loss to the employers.

Adcock was convicted and his conviction was upheld on appeal on the ground that he had induced his employers to do something which but for his fraud they would not have done, namely, to credit him with the 1s. 3¹/₂d. for the hutch which should have been credited to the other miner. The court held that this was sufficient to justify a conviction for fraud. The *ratio* of *Adcock* is usually taken as being that, in Lord Justice-General Clyde's words, "Any definite practical result achieved by the fraud is enough."[4] Lord Hunter gave a more specific although perhaps not any less extensive statement of the law when he said that, "The essence of the offence consists in inducing the person who is defrauded either to take some article he would not otherwise have taken, or to do some act he would not otherwise have done, or to become the medium of some unlawful act."[5]

---

[4] 1925 J.C., at 61.

[5] *ibid.* Although the statements of the law in *Adcock* are generally accepted as correct (see, *e.g. H.M. Advocate v. Wishart* (1975) S.C.C.R. Supp. 78, Lord McDonald at 85) and the case itself is the leading case on fraud in Scots law it is by no means a satisfactory case and it is arguable that on its own facts it was wrongly decided. It is open to the following criticisms:

(1) It may be that all that occurred in *Adcock* was an attempted fraud. In *H.M. Advocate v. Camerons* (1911) 6 Adam 456, the accused staged a mock robbery and then made an informal claim on an insurance company, and the court found difficulty in deciding whether even an attempted fraud had been committed: see Vol. I, paras 6.21, 6.43. The cases cited to the court in *Adcock* although not referred to in the judgments dealt with the separate question of whether economic loss was essential for fraud: these were *Turnbull v. Stuart* (1898) 2 Adam 536; *H.M. Advocate v. A.H. Smith* (1893) 1 Adam 6; and *J. & P. Coats Ltd v. Brown* (1909) 6 Adam 19. The true authorities for the decision: *Wm Fraser* (1847) Ark 280, and perhaps *Geo. Kippen* (1849) J. Shaw 276, *Hood v. Young* (1853) 1 Irv. 236 and *Jas Paton* (1858) 3 Irv. 208, were not referred to.

(2) The accused was in effect convicted of a crime with which he was not charged: he was charged with inducing the employers to pay him 1s 3d. on January 23 and convicted in effect of inducing them to make a book entry sometime between January 16 and 23.

(3) The "result" in *Adcock* may have been practical, but it was surely trivial. Suppose *Adcock* had made the credit entry in his own hand; that would surely have been a deceit without any defrauding.

(4) *Adcock* could perhaps have been more satisfactorily decided on the ground that the employers had been induced to undertake an obligation, or to incur potential damage. But the obligation was incurred in the prior contract of employment and all that Adcock's fraud did was to deceive them about the effect of that obligation in a contingency which did not in fact arise. There is little or no Scots law on the element of potential prejudice in fraud; references to it appear in two cases where persons were induced to retain shares in a company which was in financial difficulties: *H.M. Advocate v. City of Glasgow Bank Directors* (1879) 4 Couper 161; *H.M. Advocate v. Pattisons* (1901) 3 Adam 420, but in each case the indictment libelled actual prejudice, and there is clearly actual economic loss involved in retaining falling shares as well as actual benefit to the company.

(5) *Adcock* could perhaps have been justified as a case of practical cheating — making B's hutch look like A's, but this possibility was never canvassed: see *Alex. Bannatyne* (1847) Ark. 361, *infra*, para. 18.50.

(6) It is unfortunate that a leading case of this nature should have been decided without a full canvassing of authority, and that the brief judgments delivered give the impression that the court was no more aware that it was deciding a leading case than it was apparently aware that it was supporting a conviction for a crime with which the accused had not been

The nature of the result. Although *Adcock v. Archibald*[6] indicates that **18.17** virtually any practical result is sufficient for fraud it is submitted that the scope of the crime is not as wide as that. The result must be not only practical, it must also involve some legally significant prejudice.

PRACTICAL. This requirement means no more than that the dupe must **18.18** have been induced to do something, and not merely to form a mistaken opinion or an intention based on a mistaken opinion. Fraud involves more than just deceit, although it does not involve very much more.[7]

PREJUDICE. The dupe must be induced to do something which places **18.19** him in a worse position than he would otherwise have been in.[8] This does not necessarily mean that he must suffer actual or potential economic loss. It is probably a crime to induce B to pay a fair price for an article by making false statements.[9] The range of situations which are regarded as prejudicial is very wide,[10] but to do away completely with the requirement of prejudice or disadvantage would lead to surprising results. Suppose B who is poor but proud asks A to sell a ring for him. A agrees but only obtains a very small price for the ring. A wants to help B but knows that he will not accept a gift or any form of charity so he tells him that he sold the ring for a good price and induces him to accept a large sum of money. Here A's deliberate deceit may have had a practical result, but it surely cannot be said that A is guilty of fraud.[11]

Again, it is probably also the law that the prejudice must be more than trivial.[12] If A writes to his insurance company with a false statement of loss and induces them to send him a claim form which he does not complete, there has been a practical result, and the company have lost the value of the paper on which they wrote to him and the postage of the letter, but it appears that A is not guilty of fraud, but at most of attempted fraud.[13]

---

charged.

Reference may be made to the South African case of *R. v. Steyn*, 1927 O.P.D. 172, although it is distinguishable from *Adcock*. In *Steyn* a police constable who was entitled to a government grant of £2 10s. 0d. to bury his child irrespective of the actual cost, altered the undertaker's receipt from £1 17s. 6d. to £2 17s. 6d. and presented the receipt to an official in order to obtain payment of his grant. It was held that his alteration of the document could not have caused prejudice and that therefore there was no forgery.

[6] 1925 J.C. 58.

[7] *cf. Welham v. D.P.P.* [1961] A.C. 103.

[8] *cf. Mackenzie v. H.M. Advocate*, 1988 S.L.T. 483, where it was held to be a fraud to induce a solicitor to raise a civil action against a third party by giving him false instructions.

[9] *cf.* the South African case of *R. v. Kinsella*, 1961 (3) S.A. 519 (C), where it was held that where A takes and sells B's goods with the intention of applying the proceeds to B's benefit but in the absence of any consent by B to his actings, or any approval by B of the proposed benefit, A is guilty of theft.

[10] See *infra.*

[11] *cf. Holmes and Lockyer* (1869) 1 Couper 221, L.J.-C. Patton, at 237: "[I]f the act itself were not criminal, the misrepresentation by which the panel got the power to do it could not make it a crime."

[12] In *Welham v. D.P.P.* [1961] A.C. 103, Lord Radcliffe at 128, this requirement is put down to the *de minimis* rule; but it is doubtful whether and to what extent such a rule operates in Scots criminal law except at the stage of deciding to prosecute; *cf.* Renton & Brown, para. 4-01.

[13] *cf. H.M. Advocate v. Camerons* (1911) 6 Adam 456.

In *John Andrew Geddes*[14] the indictment contained a charge which alleged that the accused had pretended to be a police officer and asked drivers to show him their driving licences, and did "fraudulently induce [them] to do acts which they would otherwise not have done, namely to accept you as a police officer and to answer questions put by you to them and to produce to you the documents". No objection was taken to the relevancy of this charge, presumably as it was merely included in order to enable evidence to be led in support of a murder charge on the same indictment. But the only practical result libelled is the showing of documents to the accused, and it might have been argued that that is hardly practical enough, and is in any event too trivial to ground a common law fraud charge; on the other hand, however, it might have been argued by the Crown that impersonation of a police officer is always criminal, but there is no authority for this, the crime of impersonating the police being treated in practice as only a statutory summary offence.[15]

Again, the crime of inducing the police to make unnecessary investigations by giving them false information is probably not regarded as a form of fraud,[16] and it is probably not the case that calling out a doctor or the fire brigade by a false report is regarded as a common law crime.[17]

These examples indicate that the crime of fraud is not in practice so extensive as *Adcock*[18] seems to indicate. It may well be that fraudulent conduct is criminal, or at any rate would be prosecuted, only where there is some potential pecuniary or personal injury, unless in very exceptional circumstances when it might be used to punish some significant piece of dishonesty which obviously merited being treated as criminal but did not fall within the normal scope of any common law crime.

It is submitted that merely to induce B to do something trivial like taking a cheque into his hands or even presenting it to his bank[19] is not enough. For this is hardly more than inducing him to believe a lie, and the crime is one of fraud and not one of deceit.[20] It is true that little if anything more than this happened in *Adcock*, and that it is unrealistic to distinguish between e.g. the facts in *Adcock* and the case where the book-entry is made by the workman himself.[21] The best that can be said for *Adcock* however is that while the Lord Justice-General's dictum has been accepted as the law,[22] it does not follow that it was properly applied

---

[14] High Court at Edinburgh, June 1963, unrep'd.

[15] Police (Scotland) Act 1967, s.43, *infra,* para. 19.98.

[16] See Vol. I, para. 1.37; and see also *infra*, para. 47.38.

[17] These situations may constitute statutory offences: Telecommunications Act 1984, s.42 (as amended by the now repealed Cable and Broadcasting Act 1984, Sched. 5: by the Broadcasting Act 1990, Sched. 20: and by the Telecommunications (Fraud) Act 1997, s.2); Fire Services Act 1947, s.31(1): see also Criminal Law Act 1977, s.51: bomb hoaxes. There is, of course, no rule of law in Scotland that conduct which constitutes a statutory offence cannot form the basis of a relevant common law crime: see *Waddell v. MacPhail*, 1986 S.C.C.R. 593.

[18] 1925 J.C. 58.

[19] The contrary view in *R. v. Turner* [1974] A.C. 357, Lord Reid at 367E, depends on the wording of the Theft Act 1968, s.16.

[20] It may be, however, that to induce B to take delivery of goods under a contract is a sufficient result: *J. & P. Coats Ltd v. Brown* (1909) 6 Adam 19, L.J.-C. Macdonald at 40; *Alex. Bannatyne* (1847) Ark. 361; see *infra*, para. 18.50.

[21] See Gill, p.134.

[22] It was, incidentally, challenged in the sheriff court in *Richards v. H.M. Advocate,* 1971 J.C. 29, on the ground that the indictment did not aver any loss by the seller, but merely the acceptance of a nominee as the real purchaser. The sheriff principal refused to accept this argument because it was "not in accord with the long-established case" of *Adcock*, and this part of his decision was not challenged on appeal.

to the facts of *Adcock*. That it has been accepted cannot now be denied, but its precise boundaries are as yet unsettled.[23]

LEGAL SIGNIFICANCE. The result must probably have some legal signifi- **18.20** cance — that is to say, involve loss of a value which is protected by law. It would hardly be a criminal fraud to induce A to fail to attend a dinner party to which he had been invited, unless the party also had a business purpose. Nor is it criminal fraud to induce someone to refrain from carrying out a crime.

Types of relevant result. The following are types of result which may form **18.21** the basis of a charge of fraud.

(1) The parting with possession or property in goods or money. Any pretence by A which induces B to hand over goods or money to A or C is a fraud, whether B is induced to sell, give, lend or hire, and whether or not B receives a fair price for the goods or a fair bargain for his money.[24] It is fraud to induce B to buy an article by false pretences even if B later makes a profit by reselling the article.[25] If A induces B to hire him a car by pretending that he is C and producing C's driving licence, he is guilty of fraud, even if he pays for the hire and returns the car at the due time. Such a transaction is on the whole to B's advantage since he makes his profit on the hire, but he has handed over the car by virtue of the false pretence, and that is sufficient.

(2) The sustaining of personal injury. Kenny objects to the definition **18.22** of fraud in terms of inducing B to act to his injury, and points out that such a definition would include fraudulently inducing a person to touch a

---

[23] It may have been, as Gill says, a "neglected treasure from the Crown's point of view" for a long time, but it is now much used. It was, for example, applied to a case of trade union ballot-rigging by uttering forged returns and ballot lists to a returning officer, and thereby inducing him to credit certain candidates with a certain number of votes; the indictment concluded "and this you did by fraud": *Macleod and Dunn*, High Court at Glasgow, Nov. 1974; Gill, pp.148–150. The charge was described on the backing of the indictment as "fraud". In charging the jury L.J.-C. Wheatley pointed out that the fact that the fraud had affected the result of the election did not really matter; it would equally have been a fraud if the results from the branch concerned had had no effect on the overall result: "the fraud consisted not in the fact that [C] was elected, the fraud consisted in the fact that [C] was credited with a large number of votes as against [B], these votes of course being quite illegitimate" (Transcript of Judge's charge, 16). In another case a solicitor was alleged to have engaged in a complicated scheme (involving cheques which were the subject of a separate embezzlement charge) aimed at enabling the accounts of a firm to appear to have been properly kept when they were inspected by Stock Exchange inspectors. The whole scheme was averred to have been carried out "with the intention of deceiving any person who examined the books, records or accounts" of the firm, but the charge, after a complicated narrative, libelled only that the inspectors "were thus induced . . . to accept" the firm's accounts as genuine, "and so to report thereon to [the Stock Exchange]". A number of charges of this kind were listed in charge 2 of the indictment, and at the end there was appended the averment, "and all this you did . . . in pursuance of said intention and by fraud and did thus defraud the members of [the firm engaged as Stock Exchange inspectors]." There was no averment that anyone suffered any loss as a result. Another charge narrated a pretence that a certain property was not the subject of a heritable security, and "you did thus induce" an accountant to report to the inspectors that he had satisfied himself that the assets in the balance sheet were free of any charge: *H.M. Advocate v. Wishart* (1975) S.C.C.R. (Supp.) 78; see Gill, pp. 150–151.

[24] *Turnbull v. Stuart* (1898) 2 Adam 536.

[25] *cf. H.M. Advocate v. A.H. Smith* (1893) 1 Adam 6. It appears also to be a completed fraud for A to induce B to post a sum of money to A although A never receives it: *Daniel Taylor* (1853) 1 Irv. 230, but this might now be charged as attempted fraud.

live electric wire.[26] Whatever the present position in England,[27] there is
no reason why such an inducement should not be a fraud in Scotland in
the same way as it is fraud to induce a woman to have intercourse by
pretending to be her husband.[28]

18.23   (3) The granting of a right or privilege. It is fraud to induce B to grant
a right or privilege. It is fraud to obtain entry to a meeting of a private
body by pretending to be a member or to be otherwise entitled to be
present, or to use fraudulent representations to obtain a licence to trade,
or to practice as a solicitor or doctor, or to drive a car, or to exercise any
other privilege.[29] It is also fraud to induce B to enter into an obligation
even although the obligation will be reducible on the ground of fraud.[30]
In *Hood v. Young*[31] A. put up some horses for auction which he falsely
stated were sound, and had been worked for a year by a farmer who was
about to emigrate, and so induced certain people to bid for them: this
was held to be a completed fraud although there was no averment that
any money passed.

18.24   (4) Inducing B to refrain from exercising a right or privilege. This is
the converse of (3) but there are some situations which can best be
described in this negative way. It is fraud for a debtor against whom
decree has passed to use false pretences to induce the creditor to refrain
from enforcing it.[32] It is also fraud to induce shareholders to refrain from
selling their shares,[33] but such retention will normally involve economic
loss. It would be fraud for a jeweller who received a gem to be set in a
brooch to return the brooch with a false gem in it in order to conceal his
loss of the true one.[34] It is probably sufficient that the fraud should have
induced B to delay in enforcing his rights, at any rate if it can be shown
that the delay made it more difficult for him ultimately to obtain what he
was entitled to.[35]

18.25   (5) Inducing B to render himself liable to prosecution. It is not clear
what Lord Hunter had in mind when he spoke in *Adcock v. Archibald*[36]
of inducing someone to become the medium of an unlawful act, but it
would be fraud to induce someone to commit a crime, or what would be
a crime if the necessary *mens rea* were present, although the facts might
often be treated as constituting instigation rather than fraud. It would be

---

[26] Kenny, para. 377.
[27] See *Welham v. D.P.P., supra*; Theft Act 1968, ss. 15, 16 (as amended by Theft Act
1978, s.5(5)), 20; Theft Act 1978, ss.1 and 2; and Smith and Hogan, pp. 552 *et seq.*
[28] *Wm Fraser* (1847) Ark. 280, *supra*. Dr. Gill argues that it is an assault, by analogy with
the murder cases. But assault is not a result-crime, and the facts described are not an
"attack" on the person. There might, however, be a charge of real injury: see *infra*,
para. 29.47.
[29] See *Wm Duncan and Alex. Cumming* (1850) J. Shaw 334.
[30] It is probably not a completed fraud merely to induce B to enter into a void
obligation, although the circumstances might well include some other prejudicial result.
[31] (1853) 1 Irv. 236.
[32] Or to take fraudulent steps to delay its enforcement: *Geo. Kippen* (1849) J. Shaw 276.
[33] *H.M. Advocate v. City of Glasgow Bank Directors* (1897) 4 Couper 161; *H.M.
Advocate v. Pattisons* (1901) 3 Adam 420.
[34] *cf. Anderson v. Stuart* (1836) 1 Swin. 35.
[35] *cf. R. v. Turner* [1974] A.C. 357 (although s.16(2)(a) of the Theft Act 1968,
interpreted in this case, was repealed by the Theft Act 1978, s.5(5)); *R. v. Abberton* [1931]
V.L.R. 237.
[36] 1925 J.C. 58, 61.

fraud for a 15-year-old girl to induce a man to have intercourse with her contrary to section 5(3) of the Criminal Law (Consolidation) (Scotland) Act 1995 by pretending she was 16.

The causal link between the representation and the result

It is axiomatic that the fraudulent representation must have induced **18.26** the dupe to do the act or make the omission which constitutes the result.[37] In *Mather v. H.M. Advocate*[38] A bought and obtained delivery of cattle from B, and thereafter tendered a cheque in payment, which was dishonoured. He was charged with fraud and the charge was dismissed as irrelevant because nothing had been obtained by the fraud implied in the bad cheque. The cattle had been delivered before the cheque was tendered so that it could not be alleged that A had obtained them *by* passing the cheque, and this was described by Lord Justice-General Strathclyde as the fatal flaw in the charge.[39]

It follows that it is a defence to a charge of fraud to show that the false pretence did not influence B in his actings, or to show that B knew the pretence was false. In order to convict A it is necessary to show that B believed the pretence and that this belief was a *sine qua non* of his action.[40] If that cannot be shown A may be convicted of attempted fraud, but he cannot be convicted of fraud.

Collateral statements. It is sometimes said that at any rate in commercial **18.27** matters the false pretence must relate to the subject-matter of the transaction, and not to any collateral matters,[41] but it is submitted that this means only that the representation must be shown to have induced the result complained of.

The two cases which are regarded as authority for the proposition that representations about collateral matters are irrelevant are both unsatisfactory. The first is *Tapsell v. Prentice*.[42] A was charged with pretending to a shopkeeper that she was the manageress of a group of gipsies about to camp in the neighbourhood, that she intended to buy provisions for them to the value of £30 from the shopkeeper, and that

---

[37] *Peter Gibb* (1833) Bell's Notes 64; *Jas Wilkie* (1872) 2 Couper 323; Macdonald, p.56.

[38] (1914) 7 Adam 525.

[39] At 528. Had the cheque been a forgery there would of course have been a completed crime of uttering. But in any event a relevant charge of fraud could probably have been made by averring that the tendering of the cheque induced B to refrain from taking other steps to recover the price: *cf. Geo. Kippen* (1849) J. Shaw 276; *R. v. Nader*, 1935 T.D.P. 97; *R. v. Turner* [1974] A.C. 357 (noting that s.16(2)(a) of the Theft Act 1968, which is interpreted in this case, was repealed by the Theft Act 1978, s.5(5)); *cf.* G.H. Gordon, "English Criminal Law: Two recent developments" (1975) 20 J.L.S. 4. It might also be possible to use the cheque as evidence that A had never intended to pay: *cf. supra*, para. 18.06; Gill, p.183.

[40] A may defraud B by means of a pretence made to C. Such a situation is common where C is B's servant, *e.g.* his salesman: *Gallagher v. Paton* (1906) 6 Adam 62, but there is no reason for confining it to such a case. If A makes a pretence to C with the intention of inducing a course of action by B, that, if successful, is a fraud on B. The fraudulent use of a cheque or credit card is an important example of this: a false representation is made to the trader that the rogue is entitled to use the card and the bank or credit company is obliged to pay out to the trader: see *R. v. Charles* [1977] A.C. 177; *R. v. Lambie* [1982] A.C. 449; *supra*, para. 18.06.

[41] Macdonald, p.55; *Strathern v. Fogal*, 1922 J.C. 73; *H.M. Advocate v. Macleods* (1888) 2 White 71, Lord McLaren at 76–77; *cf. R. v. Roebuck* (1856) 7 Cox C.C. 126; Gill, pp.183–184.

[42] (1910) 6 Adam 354.

"relying solely on the truth of said representation, did thus induce [the shopkeeper] to purchase from you a rug in excess of its proper value." The charge was dismissed as irrelevant principally on the technical ground that there was no averment of the true value of the rug or of the price actually paid for it.[43] Lord Justice-Clerk Macdonald also pointed out that the misrepresentation averred was not about the article sold,[44] and Lord Ardwall said that "these representations are not directly connected with the rug, which may have been a perfectly good one. Now there can be no crime in such a sale as is here alleged unless the fraudulent misrepresentations relate directly to the articles to be sold."[45]

It is apparent that the court was anxious not to inhibit what one might call the sales technique of intending sellers,[46] particularly where this technique was not directed to making false statements about the goods to be sold. It is also true that shopkeepers often give bargains in the hope that it will improve their goodwill, and that purchasers may indicate their intention to patronise a particular shop in the future in the hope of receiving a present bargain, without there being any fraud, since both parties know the value to be placed on such statements — if the shopkeeper gives a bargain he does so in the hope of obtaining custom, not in return for any representation that the customer firmly intends to give him more business. But the situation set out in the complaint in *Tapsell v. Prentice*[47] is different from this: it is that the shopkeeper bought the rug solely because of A's representations that she was in charge of the gipsies and that they would spend £30 in the shop, and it is implied, although it is not explicitly stated, that he knew he was paying an excessive price for it. In that situation it is difficult to see why the Crown could not have relevantly charged fraud had they given proper specification. It cannot be because the representations were about A and not about his goods. Suppose A knows that B will buy rugs only from natives of the country formerly known as Persia, and induces B to buy from him by pretending to be a native of that country: this is fraud, whether or not he overcharges B. The "assumption of a false character" has been the most clearly recognised form of fraud since the days of Hume[48]; nor, it is submitted, can it be because part of the pretence related to the future,[49] although this may have helped to induce the court to reject the charge, since charges of fraud involving statements of intention are more difficult to sustain than other kinds of fraud.[50]

18.28 The second case is *Strathern v. Fogal*[51] The accused were a landlord, F., and his sons. It was alleged that F. pretended to his tenants that he had let the premises to his sons and that unless the tenants made certain payments the sons would not renew their tenancies. It is not clear why

---

[43] Lord Salvesen said, at 357, that if there had been only a purchase and no payment made there could be no fraud because there would then be no advantage to the accused or injury to the shopkeeper, but the undertaking by the shopkeeper of an obligation to buy the rug would probably be a sufficient injury: *Hood v. Young* (1853) 1 Irv. 236.

[44] 6 Adam at 356.

[45] *ibid.*, at 357.

[46] See esp. *ibid.*, L.J.-C. Macdonald at 356, Lord Ardwall at 375.

[47] (1910) 6 Adam 354.

[48] Hume, i, 172; Alison, i, 362; Burnett, p.165; Anderson, p.193; Macdonald, p.54.

[49] *supra*. In any event the representation of intention was coupled with the representation about the gipsies.

[50] *supra*, para. 18.11.

[51] 1922 J.C. 73.

this elaborate subterfuge was indulged in, but the court held that the charge of fraudulently inducing the tenants to make the payments was irrelevant. Lord Hunter concentrated on the representation that the lease had been transferred to the sons, and said that, "The misrepresentation . . . did not in any real sense affect the subject of the bargain, but was essentially collateral, though it might be material and induce the contract;"[52] and relied on *Tapsell v. Prentice*[53] as authority.[54] Lord Hunter was probably influenced by the consideration, to which he referred, that F. was lawfully entitled to require the payments concerned from the tenants and to terminate their tenancies and put his sons in possession if the tenants refused to pay. That consideration itself suggests that the representation did not in the circumstances induce the contract, but it is submitted that it is wrong to go on to say that if they did induce the contract they were still irrelevant because they were collateral. It is difficult to see why a deliberate falsehood which is intended to induce and does induce a certain course of action should not be regarded as a relevant fraudulent representation; and it is also difficult to see why a representation as to the identity of the landlord should be regarded as collateral in a matter affecting the lease.

Lord Ashmore[55] referred to *Turnbull v. Stuart*[56] and *Hood v. Young*[57] which concerned false statements about horses sold at an auction, and to the reluctance with which the court had upheld the convictions in these cases, and particularly in *Turnbull* and concluded that the principle of these cases should not be extended to collateral matters but should be restricted to statements about the articles sold.[58] But these two cases were quite different on their facts from *Strathern v. Fogal*[59] and were cases in which the court's reluctance to convict was due to the absence of any economic injury. Lord Ashmore then went on[60] to express the opinion that the tenants might have agreed to make the payments because of the possibility of non-renewal, irrespective of the representation that the lease had been transferred to the sons, and referred to *Mather v. H.M. Advocate.*[61] In other words, he regarded the representation as irrelevant because it did not induce the payments, and this, it is submitted, is the best *ratio* for the decision.[62] In any event it is submitted that the case is special, and that Lord Hunter's statement of the law cannot be regarded as sufficient authority for the proposition that a false representation which induces B to make a payment to A can be disregarded on the ground that it relates to a "collateral" matter.

In *Richards v. H.M. Advocate*,[63] an averment of a representation as to **18.29** the future use of a house was challenged as irrelevant because collateral in the context of an inducement to enter missives. In rejecting this challenge Lord Justice-Clerk Grant said:

---

[52] At 79–80.

[53] (1910) 6 Adam 354.

[54] 1922 J.C. 73 at 80.

[55] At 81.

[56] (1898) 2 Adam 536.

[57] (1853) 1 Irv. 236.

[58] Although the law allows a certain latitude by way of "puffing" goods in order to induce a sale: *supra*, para. 18.09.

[59] 1922 J.C. 73.

[60] *ibid.*, at 82.

[61] (1914) 7 Adam 525.

[62] Lord Ashmore set aside the representations that the sons would refuse to renew the lease as irrelevant because they related to the future.

[63] 1971 J.C. 29.

"In his argument of subhead (iii) Mr. Macarthur relied mainly on the cases of *Tapsell v. Prentice*[64] and *Strathern v. Fogal*.[65] On their facts, however, these cases are clearly distinguishable from the present. No doubt there are many cases where the future use of heritable subjects is of no moment to the seller and may be a matter extraneous to the actual contract for the sale of those subjects. Here, however, on the face of the indictment (and I am not, of course, concerned at this stage with what may or may not have been established in evidence) the future use of the subjects was of crucial importance and was an essential governing factor in the completion of the contract for the sale of those same subjects. It cannot in my opinion, be treated merely as a matter collateral to the contract."[66]

18.30 *The mens rea of fraud.* The crime of fraud consists in making a false representation "falsely and fraudulently",[67] and these qualifications must apply both to the representation itself and to the result.

18.31 *The representation.* The only question here is whether it is necessary to show that A knew that the representation he was making was false, or whether it is sufficient to show that he made it recklessly. So far as civil law is concerned the position is probably as set out in the English case of *Derry v. Peek*[68] where Lord Herschell said, "[F]raud is proved when it is shewn that a false representation has been made (1) knowingly, or (2) without belief in its truth, or (3) recklessly, careless whether it be true or false."[69] The position in criminal law is not settled. There can be no fraud where the statement is made with an honest belief in its truth even if that belief is arrived at through gross carelessness,[70] but it is not clear whether fraud can be committed recklessly, *i.e.* whether it is fraud if A makes a representation which he knows to be necessary for the securing of a result, and which he realises may be false. In South Africa, the accused must have known or foreseen that the representation might be false.[71] It seems, therefore, to be the case there that it is fraudulent to make a statement in whose truth A does not honestly believe, and it has been held that A is not regarded as having an honest belief where he had wilfully abstained from any inquiry which might throw doubt on the truth of the statement.[72]

There is no Scots authority on the question, perhaps because in practice prosecutions for fraud are not brought unless the authorities

---

[64] (1910) 6 Adam 354.

[65] 1922 J.C. 73.

[66] At 33.

[67] See 1995 Act, Sched. 3, para. 3; *Dingwall v. H.M. Advocate* (1888) 2 White 27; *H.M. Advocate v. Jas Swan* (1888) 2 White 137.

[68] (1889) 14 App.Cas. 337; see also *Lees v. Tod* (1882) 9 R. 807.

[69] At 374; see T.B. Smith, p.834; Stair Memorial Encyclopaedia, Vol. 15, para. 603: *cf.* W.M. McBryde, *The Law of Contract in Scotland* (1987), paras 10–04 to 10–10.

[70] *Brander v. Buttercup Dairy Co.*, 1921 J.C. 19, Lord Hunter and Lord Anderson at 22; *Mackenzie v. Skeen*, 1971 J.C. 43. Dr, now Lord, Gill states that an honest belief recklessly arrived at also necessarily excludes fraud: Gill, p.81. It is not clear what the learned author is envisaging, but it is probably correct to say that the genesis of the belief does not matter provided it is at the material time held to be true. This does not affect the problematic nature of a representation which A at the material time realises may be false. *Cf. R. v. Mackinnon* [1959] 1 Q.B. 150.

[71] See J. Burchill and J. Milton, *Principles of Criminal Law* (2nd ed., 1997), p.588: *Ex p. Lebowa Development Corporation Ltd*, 1989 (3) S.A. 71 (T), at 101–105.

[72] *R. v. Myers*, 1948 (1) S.A. 375 (AD), which approved *Derry v. Peek, supra*.

take the view that A knew of the falsity of his representation. In principle Scots law might accept a false statement made recklessly as sufficient,[73] but would probably regard the requirement of an "honest belief" as too severe, since it suggests that an unconsidered statement can be fraudulent. It is unlikely that a situation in which A does not apply his mind at all to the truth or falsity of the statement would be regarded as fraudulent, and it may be that fraud requires a realisation on A's part that his statement might be false.

The representation must, of course, be made intentionally, and with a knowledge of the meaning it conveys to B. It is unlikely that the criminal law would adopt the rule that a man must be taken as intending the conventional meaning of the words he uses, except of course as a rule of evidence. If A can show that he used "glory" to mean a "knock down argument," and that he believed that that was how B would understand the word, then for the purposes of the case that is what "glory" does mean. This means that A must intend to deceive B by his lie, and intend that B should as a result do whatever it is that he was allegedly induced to do.[74]

The result. Fraud is a "crime of intent", and A cannot be guilty of **18.32** fraudulently inducing B to do *x* unless he intended to produce such a result by his falsehood.[75]

"Dishonestly". It is sometimes said that the pretence must be "dishon- **18.33** estly" made[76] and this raises the question of claim of right or entitlement as a defence to fraud. There is no authority on this matter.[77] Hume rejects claim of right as a defence in uttering[78] but the position there is not necessarily the same as in simple fraud. The authors of the Indian Penal Code specifically stated, "However immoral a deception may be, we do not consider it as an offence against the rights of property if its object is only to cause a distribution of property which the law recognizes as rightful",[79] and this seems cogent. It may be said that a fraud of this kind is dishonest — A knows that B will not return his property willingly, so he deliberately indulges in deceit in order to recover it — but dishonesty in the sense of telling lies is not in itself criminal; it becomes so only when it induces a result regarded by the law as prejudicial. The question thus comes to be whether a result which does no more than give the liar his lawful rights is to be regarded as prejudicial, and it is thought that it is not.[80]

---

[73] *cf.* Vol. I, para. 7.66.

[74] *cf.* Gill, pp. 88–91.

[75] *cf.* Vol. I, para. 7.12.

[76] For example, Macdonald, p.52.

[77] *Jas Johnston* (1848) Ark. 528, is quite inconclusive.

[78] Hume, i, 154–155.

[79] See Ratanlal Ranchhoddas and D.K. Thakore, *The Indian Penal Code* (3rd ed., Bombay, 1959), p.343. See also the discussion in Gl. Williams, para. 113.

[80] In *Paterson v. Ritchie*, 1934 J.C. 42, the accused applied for a widow's pension although she was at the time living with another man. The sheriff-substitute acquitted her of fraud on the ground that she was entitled to a pension under the relevant Act. The High Court held that on a proper interpretation of the Act she was not entitled to be classed as a widow for pension purposes. They declined, however, to disturb the sheriff's verdict, since the language of the Act was ambiguous, and the sheriff was entitled to find that the accused shared his view, in which case there would have been no fraud. The case is one in which what was at issue was the accused's belief in the truth of the pretence rather than

The motive with which the pretence is made is, of course, irrelevant. A fraud carried out in order to perpetrate a practical joke is a fraud in the same way as a threat perpetrated for the same purpose is a threat[81]; but it seems that a policeman who induces someone to commit a crime, such as selling him drugs, or liquor out of hours, but concealing his identity or assuming a false identity, will have a defence of public duty, provided he acted within the bounds set by the law of entrapment.[82]

PRACTICAL CHEATING

Forgery and uttering

18.34   The "type case" of practical cheating is the uttering of forged documents, and almost all the reported cases of practical cheating are cases of such uttering. Uttering may be regarded as a preventive crime designed to protect the sanctity of writing in the law, and particularly the sanctity of signed documents: it was because of the special status of signed writ in the law that the uttering of certain forged documents was made a capital crime at a time when attempted fraud was not a crime at all. Forgery appears originally to have been just one form of the general crime of falsehood, the *crimen falsi*, the form known as falsehood by writ, and indeed falsehood by writ was not strictly confined to forgery, but extended to certain forms of written lie even in the absence of any false subscription.[83] By the time of Hume and Alison, however, forgery was recognised as a nominate offence, although there was still a certain amount of confusion between forgery and other forms of falsehood by writ,[84] and although traces of this confusion may still linger, it is now the law that the uttering of forged documents is distinct from fraud, and constitutes in itself a completed crime.[85]

18.35   *Uttering and fraud.* Now that the crime of uttering forged documents can be tried summarily[86] and attempted fraud is a crime, the scope of the crime of uttering can be much reduced. Most cases of uttering have a practical result so that they can be treated as cases of simple fraud, and even when no practical result is achieved, the uttering itself will usually amount to an attempted fraud. It is often just a matter of convenience

---

her belief that she was entitled to the money obtained as a result of a false pretence. In *Nimmo v. The Lanarkshire Tramways Co.* (1912) 6 Adam 571, the accused was charged under the Tramways Act 1870 with knowingly travelling on a tramway beyond the distance for which he had paid. He had travelled on a special workman's vehicle and had paid the special reduced workmen's rate. It was the contention of the company that he was not eligible for the special rate, and his contention that he was. He had accordingly refused to pay any more. Lord Salvesen pointed out that he would be guilty if he had acted with intent to obtain a benefit to which he knew he was not entitled, but that in fact the element of fraud was totally absent, as "He was maintaining, as every citizen is entitled to do, a civil right on his part": at 577–578. It seems that the accused made no pretence to being other than what he was, a teacher, so that the question of dishonesty did not arise at all.

[81] *Eliz. Edmiston* (1866) 5 Irv. 219. And the same is true where the motive is "to keep his wife and family from starvation, or to pay more than twenty shillings in the pound": *H.M. Advocate v. Livingstone* (1888) 1 White 587, Lord Fraser at 592.

[82] See *Weir v. Jessop (No. 2)*, 1991 S.C.C.R. 636, L.J.-C. Ross at 644D-E.

[83] Mackenzie, I,27,2. *Cf.* Burnett, p.176.

[84] Hume, i, 137, 158; Alison, i, 380–381: see *infra*, para. 18.45.

[85] On whether the uttering of false documents is likewise a completed crime, see *infra*, paras 18.45 *et seq.*

[86] 1995 Act, s.5(4)(a); originally the Criminal Justice (Scotland) Act 1949, s.43.

whether the charge is framed as one of uttering or one of fraud. Where A obtains money from B by using a cheque on which C's name has been forged the charge can be either that he "uttered as genuine a cheque bearing to be signed 'C' said signature being forged by presenting it to B",[87] or that he "pretended to B that a cheque bearing to be signed by C was genuine the truth being that said signature was forged and did induce B to pay him £x." The latter form is preferable since it sets out A's offence more fully.[88]

There may, however, be situations in which only uttering and neither fraud nor attempted fraud can be charged. These are: (1) where the stage of attempt has not been reached. Since uttering involves putting the document out of the control of the utterer it will usually coincide with the stage of attempted fraud, but one cannot say *a priori* that this will always be so — there may be cases in which a forged document is uttered at such an early stage in a fraudulent scheme that the court would not be prepared to treat it as an attempted fraud. (2) Where the pretence involved in the forgery does not and was not intended to induce any practical result. Again, since *Adcock v. Archibald*[89] it will usually be possible by the use of sufficient ingenuity to point to some relevant result, but this may not always be so. If it is still the case that no fraud is involved in giving B a forged cheque in payment of goods already received,[90] such a situation will be an example of a criminal uttering which cannot be charged as fraud. (3) Where an uttering is committed in Scotland in pursuance of a scheme to commit a fraud abroad. If A forges C's signature to a letter sent to B in England purporting to be a request to B to give A a sum of money in England, and A posts the letter in Scotland and then goes to England for the money it can be argued that A is not guilty of fraud in Scotland,[91] but he is certainly guilty of uttering there.[92]

Forgery and uttering. Forgery itself is not a crime: anyone may amuse **18.36** himself by counterfeiting signatures; it is only when the forgery is uttered that the crime is committed.[93] In Hume's day and for some time thereafter the crime seems to have been regarded as essentially forgery,

---

[87] Criminal Procedure (Scotland) Act 1995, Sched. 2.

[88] See *e.g. H.M. Advocate v. Hardy*, 1938 J.C. 144, a charge of attempted fraud which included averments that the accused pretended that certain fabricated documents were genuine. It is competent to charge uttering and add an averment that B was induced to do something as a result, but only by treating the averment of inducement as narrative and not as an additional offence: see *Jas More* (1845) 2 Broun 442. It is no longer the practice to charge both uttering and fraud on the basis of the same transaction: see *e.g. Daniel Taylor* (1853) 1 Irv. 230. The practice of charging uttering as fraud seems to go back to the 1860s: see evidence of J.H.A. Macdonald, as he then was, to the Royal Commission on the Courts of Law in Scotland, 3rd Rep. 1870, C.36, Q. 16, 891.

[89] 1925 J.C. 58.

[90] *Mather v. H.M. Advocate* (1914) 7 Adam 525, *supra*, para. 18.26.

[91] But see Vol. I, paras 3.46 and 3.47.

[92] *Wm Jeffrey* (1842) 1 Broun 337. *Cf. R. v. Owen* [1957] 1 Q.B. 174, in which the accused were charged with forming a conspiracy in England to defraud a German government department and with uttering forged documents in London in pursuance of the fraud: the conspiracy charge was dismissed because there was no conspiracy against English law but the uttering charge was upheld because that crime was completed when the documents were posted in London. (It should be noted, however, that the law relating to conspiracies to commit offences outside the United Kingdom is now to be found in the Criminal Justice (Terrorism and Conspiracy) Act 1998, ss. 5–7.)

[93] Hume, i, 148; Macdonald, p.64. Contrast the English position: Forgery and Counterfeiting Act 1981, ss. 1–5.

and the uttering merely as an element necessary to its completion. The importance of the element of forgery was emphasised by the consideration that it was the nature of the document concerned which determined whether or not the crime was capital.[94] It was common to charge both "forgery and uttering" and "uttering" in order to provide for the situation where the utterer had not himself forged the writ.[95] Hume himself suggested at one stage that the utterer was *ipso facto* art and part with the forger,[96] but that conflicts with the rule that there is no accession after the fact in Scotland[97]: there is only a presumption of fact that the utterer of a forged document was also involved in its forging. The precise relation between forgery and uttering caused a certain amount of difficulty in a number of nineteenth-century cases,[98] but the matter is now clearly settled. There is only one crime involved, and that is the crime of uttering forged documents, and the question who forged the documents is strictly speaking irrelevant.[99] As a matter of fair notice, where it is proposed to lead evidence that it was the accused this should be libelled in the charge, but failure to do so will not vitiate the indictment.[1] Where such evidence is led it is evidence only that the accused knew the document was forged, it is not evidence of a separate crime, or even of an aggravation of the uttering charged.[2]

Forgery

18.37   A forged document is one which pretends to be genuine in the sense that it pretends to be authenticated by a particular person.[3]

18.38   *Signature*. The commonest form of authentication is by signature, and the commonest type of forgery is the imitation of a signature. Probably the uttering of any forged signature is criminal whether or not the signature is necessary in order to authenticate the document on which it appears[4]; it is sufficient that it is uttered, so to speak, as an authentic signature. In *John Henderson*[5] A stole from his master a bill of exchange which had been indorsed in blank; he forged his master's signature as indorsee and tendered the bill for payment: this was held to be an uttering although the bill could have been negotiated without the forged signature. The uttering of a deed on which the signature of a witness has been forged is undoubtedly a forgery, even though the deed itself and the granter's signature are genuine.[6] There is a suggestion that this may be so only where the deed is one which requires witnessing

---

[94] Hume, i, 158–162; Alison, i, 384.

[95] See *Michael Hinchy* (1864) 4 Irv. 561, Lord Neaves at 565.

[96] Hume, i, 155.

[97] Hume, i, 281; see Vol. I, para. 5.59.

[98] See *e.g. Reuben Brooks and Fredk Wm Thomas* (1861) 4 Irv. 132; *Duncan Stalker and Thos Wilson Cuthbert* (1844) 2 Broun 70; *Martin Walker and Ors* (1872) 2 Couper 328; *John Hutchison* (1872) 2 Couper 351; *Michael Hinchy* (1864) 4 Irv. 561.

[99] *cf.* Lord Walker, "The Growth of the Criminal Law", 1958 J.R. 230, 239–240.

[1] *H.M. Advocate v. Barr*, 1927 J.C. 51; *cf. Griffen v. H.M. Advocate*, 1940 J.C. 1.

[2] *H.M. Advocate v. Barr, supra*, L.J.-G. Clyde at 54.

[3] Hume, i, 140; Alison, i, 371; Macdonald, p.59.

[4] See the Requirements of Writing (Scotland) Act 1995, esp. ss. 1 and 2.

[5] (1830) 5 D. & A. 151.

[6] Alison, i, 381; *Simon Fraser* (1859) 3 Irv. 467.

for its validity[7]; but in general, witnessing is not now required in order that documents should be formally valid,[8] and, in any event, if *John Henderson*[9] is correct, the mere presentation of the deed with a forged signature will be sufficient whether or not the signature is necessary to make the deed valid.[10]

It is not necessary that the forged signature be a colourable imitation of the genuine one[11] or indeed that there be any imitation at all.[12] All that is necessary is that the document appears to be the authentic document of someone other than the person whose document it is. It is forgery to sign one's own name with the intention that it should pass as the signature of someone else of the same name.[13] It is also forgery to sign the name of a person who cannot write,[14] or to append a false authentication by initials,[15] or by mark.[16] In the same way, it would be forgery to use a company seal or stamp as a means of authentication. Again, if a typewritten "signature" is recognised as an authentication[17] it will be forgery to type another person's name.

---

[7] *Simon Fraser, supra*, L.J.-C. Inglis at 474.

[8] See the Requirements of Writing (Scotland) Act 1995, ss. 1, 2, 3, 5, 8 and 9; *cf.* s.6.

[9] (1830) 5 D. & A. 151, *supra*.

[10] The Subscription of Deeds Act 1681, made it an offence for anyone to sign a deed as witness unless he fulfilled the necessary qualifications for acting as such: that Act was repealed, however, by the Requirements of Writing (Scotland) Act 1995, Sched. 5, and no similar offence is substituted. The Scottish Law Commission (Report No. 112: "Report on Requirements of Writing"), recommended (in paras 5.28 and 5.29) that it should be an offence for a person to cause another to sign as witness when that other did not see the granter sign or was under 16 years of age or was mentally incapable of acting as a witness; but no such offence is created under the said Act of 1995.

[11] Hume, i, 141; *John McLennan and Kenneth Mackenzie* (1840) Bell's Notes 56; Macdonald, p.59.

[12] Hume, i, 141; Alison, i, 373; Macdonald, p.62.

[13] Hume, i, 142; Alison, i, 376; Macdonald, p.62. *Jas Hendry* (1839) Bell's Notes 49. *cf. Alex. J.P. Menzies* (1849) J. Shaw 153; *Jas Hall and Ors* (1849) *ibid.* 254.

[14] Hume, i, 141; Alison, i, 374; Macdonald, p.62.

[15] *Alex. Humphreys or Alexander* (1839) Bell's Notes 50.

[16] *Robt Gillies* (1831) Bell's Notes 50; *Duncan Cattanach* (1840) 2 Swin. 505; *Arch. McMillan* (1859), 3 Irv. 317.

[17] See *McBeath's Trs v. McBeath*, 1935 S.C. 471. It seems unlikely, however, in terms of the Requirements of Writing (Scotland) Act 1995, s.7(2) that typescript will now be acceptable as a method of signing by or on behalf of the granter of a document to which that Act relates; and in terms of s.7(5) of that Act, a witness is denied any informal method of signing his name.

In relation to electronic communications or data, however, the Electronic Communications Act 2000 provides as follows:

"**7.**—(1) In any legal proceedings —

(a) an electronic signature incorporated into or logically associated with a particular electronic communication or particular electronic data, and

(b) the certification by any person of such a signature,

shall each be admissible in evidence in relation to any question as to the authenticity of the communication or data or as to the integrity of the communication or data.

(2) For the purposes of this section an electronic signature is so much of anything in electronic form as—

(a) is incorporated into or otherwise logically associated with any electronic communication or electronic data; and

(b) purports to be so incorporated or associated for the purpose of being used in establishing the authenticity of the communication or data, the integrity of the communication or data, or both.

(3) For the purposes of this section an electronic signature incorporated into or associated with a particular electronic communication or particular electronic data is certified by any person if that person (whether before or after the making of the

18.39 *Vicarious execution.* It is forgery for a "relevant person" to execute on behalf of the granter any document which requires subscription for its formal validity where the granter is blind or unable to write but has given no authority to that person to do so, since the document will then falsely bear to be the granter's authentic deed, just as much as if his signature had been forged.[18] The same applies where a less formal document bears to be signed on the granter's behalf. In *Daniel Taylor,*[19] T. wrote a begging letter purporting to be from one A.M. to his sister narrating that A.M. had hurt his hand and bearing the words "Yours A.M. signed for me, I cannot", and this was held to be forgery, because it involved "misleading a person to believe that to be a genuine document which is not so".[20]

18.40 *Fictitious signatures.* Macdonald states definitely that it is forgery to sign in the name of a fictitious person, saying that the cases illustrating the point are too numerous to quote.[21] Macdonald is supported also by Alison[22] and Burnett.[23] In *Andrew Ovens*[24] Lord Justice-Clerk Boyle said "that it ought to be known that if persons put fictitious names of fictitious individuals or firms on bills and passed them, they were guilty of forgery." In *Jas Hall and Ors*[25] it was said to be forgery for a bankrupt called James Stevenson to sign "J. Stevenson & Co. Manchester", the name of a non-existent firm, as this would lead the recipient to rely on the credit of what appeared to be a bona fide firm in Manchester. In Lord Justice-Clerk Hope's words, any person taking such a bill "would infer the existence of such a firm there, and consequently suppose himself possessed of double security."[26] On the other hand Lord Justice-

---

communication) has made a statement confirming that—
    (a) the signature,
    (b) a means of producing, communicating or verifying the signature, or
    (c) a procedure applied to the signature,
is (either alone or in combination with other factors) a valid means of establishing the authenticity of the communication or data, the integrity of the communication or data, or both."
In terms of s.15(1), an electronic communication "means a communication transmitted (whether from one person to another, from one device to another or from a person to a device or vice versa) — (a) by means of a telecommunications system (within the meaning of the Telecommunications Act 1984); or (b) by other means but while in electronic form"; and under s.15(2), "(a) references to the authenticity of any communication or data are references to any one or more of the following — (i) whether the communication or data comes from a particular person or other source; (ii) whether it is accurately timed or dated; (iii) whether it is intended to have legal effect; and (b) references to the integrity or any communication or data are references to whether there has been any tampering with or other modification of the communication or data." Wide powers are granted under s.8 to modify existing enactments "for the purposes of authorising or facilitating the use of electronic communications."

[18] Hume, i, 143; Alison, i, 377–378; Macdonald, p.62; *Jas Doucherty and Ors* (1844) 2 Broun 159; *Wm Galloway* (1857) Macdonald, p.62. The modern law on subscription on behalf of those who are blind or unable to write is contained in the Requirements of Writing (Scotland) Act 1995, s.9 and Sched. 3; "relevant person" is defined in s.9(6).

[19] (1853) 1 Irv. 230.

[20] Lord Cockburn at 234.

[21] Macdonald, p.63 — see *Jas Hall and Ors* (1849) J. Shaw 254; *Andrew Ovens* (1828) Macdonald 63; *Alex. Cameron* (1839) Bell's Notes 49; *Wm Macgilvray* (1835), *B. Pender* (1836), and *Alex. Humphreys or Alexander* (1839), all Bell's Notes 50.

[22] Alison, i, 374.

[23] Burnett, p.179.

[24] (1828) Macdonald 63.

[25] (1849) J. Shaw 254.

[26] At 261.

Clerk Aitchison and Lord Wark both expressed doubts on the matter in the case of *Griffen v. H.M.* Advocate,[27] but their remarks were *obiter* and no authorities were quoted on the point.

The position probably is that merely to sign a name other than that on one's birth certificate is no more a crime than it is to use an assumed name in any other circumstances. But where a fictitious name is used in order to make it appear that a document is the document of some person other than its maker, that is forgery.[28]

It is of course forgery to use the name of a dead person.[29]

Use of true signature. Since a forged document is one which bears falsely **18.41** to be the authentic document of a certain person, forgery is committed equally whether the signature or the document is false. It is forgery to cut a true signature off a genuine document and affix it to a false one.[30] It is also forgery to write unauthorised matter above a true signature on a blank paper.[31] As Lord Neaves said in *Simon Fraser*,[32]

> "As there were two ways in which Mahomet and the mountain might be brought together, so there are two ways in which a forged bond may be made, either by signing a false name below the bond, or by writing the bond above the genuine signature without permission, and in that way fabricating the thing as a whole, it not being the genuine instrument of the party."

It is likewise forgery to make an unauthorised addition to, or deletion or alteration on, an authenticated document.[33] The alteration must be one which affects "some element essential to the character of the particular document by which he who signed it was bound",[34] or, where the document is not obligatory in nature, something which "make[s] it of other import and effect than when the genuine signature was affixed."[35] The commonest example is the alteration of the amount in a receipt,[36] bill of exchange[37] or cheque.[38] It is forgery to alter the date on a bill of

---

[27] 1940 J.C. 1, L.J.-C. Aitchison at 4, Lord Wark at 8.

[28] *cf. Clark v. Chalmers*, 1961 J.C. 60, in which it was held that although a person could change his name, if he pretended that his name was other than it in fact was at the time he was guilty of making a false statement under the Road Traffic Act 1960, s.235 (now s.174 of the Road Traffic Act 1988).

[29] Macdonald, p.63; *Jas Aitchison* (1833) Bell's Notes 56.

[30] Macdonald, p.64; Alison, i, 379.

[31] Hume, i, 145; Alison, i, 379; *Robt Brown* (1833) Bell's Notes 51 — there may of course be circumstances in which the bearer of a blank or incomplete document is authorised explicitly or by implication of law to complete the document in which case there is no forgery.

[32] (1859) 3 Irv. 467, 494.

[33] Hume, i, 159–160; Alison, i, 384; Macdonald, p.64; 1995 Act, Sched. 2. In *Duncan Stalker and Thos Wilson Cuthbert* (1844) 2 Broun 70, it was held to be "falsehood" and uttering to insert a testing clause with a false date, but it can be argued that this is not forgery, since a testing clause is always inserted after the document is authenticated — a false testing clause may be just a written lie, unless it be said that the implied authorisation is not to insert *a* testing clause, but to insert a correct testing clause.

[34] *Wm Mann* (1877) 3 Couper 376, L.J.-C. Moncreiff at 379.

[35] *Thos Mackenzie* (1878) 4 Couper 50, Lord Young at 52.

[36] *John Hutchison* (1872) 2 Couper 351. The court treated this as a crime analogous to forgery — at 359; but whether Hume so regarded it, or regarded it as a non-capital forgery — see Hume, i, 160 — it is certainly forgery today.

[37] *Thos Mackenzie* (1878) 4 Couper 50.

[38] *Wm Mann* (1877) 3 Couper 376. The Criminal Procedure (Scotland) Act 1995, Sched. 2. gives the following style: "did utter a cheque signed by H.S. for [£8] which had been altered without his authority by adding . . . the figure '0' . . . so as to make it read as a cheque for [£80]."

exchange and to cut out a reference to a second drawee who has
declined to accept it.[39]

18.42 *"Authorised forgeries"*. It is submitted that it is not forgery for A to sign
B's name to a deed at B's request or with B's authority. Hume says that,
"it is not a forgery, that to accommodate another who cannot write, and
at his desire, one signs a draught or receipt in the name of that other . . .
There is no imposition here, either done or intended."[40] There seems no
reason to confine the rule to cases of persons who cannot write — the
question is one of authenticity, and if A signs at B's request, the deed is
truly B's.[41] Macdonald appears to take the view that there is forgery in
such a case, but that the uttering may not be "felonious", and quotes
Lord Cockburn as saying in a case involving the uttering of the
document by A to a bank that if A consciously misled the bank by not
informing them of the circumstances of the "signing," it was no defence
that he had signed with B's permission.[42] But provided that what matters
in the circumstances is that the deed is B's authentic deed, and not that
it was written in B's own hand, it is submitted that B's permission
negatives forgery. There remains, however, the strange case of *Wm
Duncan and Alex. Cumming.*[43] The two accused, D. and C., formed a
scheme to obtain the diplomas of the Edinburgh Royal College of
Surgeons for D., the scheme being that C. should impersonate D. at the
examination. As a preliminary to sitting the examination candidates had
to complete and sign a certificate setting our their qualifications and
experience. D. made out such a form and it was signed by C. in D.'s
name: C. then attended at the examination which appears to have been
an oral one, and passed in D.'s name. Both were charged with forgery,
uttering, fraud and conspiracy. The forgery and uttering charge related
to the signature on the certificate, and it is submitted that the court were
wrong in holding it relevant. Lord Mackenzie, who gave the leading
opinion on this point, seems to have been somewhat carried away by the
fact that there had clearly been a fraud on the College of Surgeons (who
would not have regarded C. as eligible to sit their examination because
unlike D. he lacked the necessary preliminary qualifications), and he
also, like Lord Wood and Lord Justice-Clerk Hope, appears almost to
have been prepared to consider the certificate a forgery if it had been
signed by D. himself. Lord Mackenzie said that the authority of the
person whose name is signed was not always a defence, and instanced
the case of A giving B authority to sign his name to a the certificate a
forgery if it had been signed by D. himself. Lord Mackenzie said that the
authority of the person whose name is signed was not always a defence,
and instanced the case of A giving B authority to sign his name to a
draft, on the understanding that B would abscond with the money and A
escape liability by pleading forgery. But in such a case A would be liable
on the draft just because it was *not* a forgery, and the whole scheme
would fail.[44] It is submitted that an authorised authentication cannot

[39] *cf. Thos Forgan* (1871) 2 Couper 30.
[40] Hume, i, 154.
[41] *cf. Wm Waiters* (1836) 1 Swin. 273.
[42] *David Ross* (1844) Macdonald 66. Macdonald also refers to a more modern
unreported case: *David Anderson* (1923) where the point was taken in defence to a charge
of uttering, but the jury did not accept that A had been authorised: *ibid.*
[43] (1850) J. Shaw 334.
[44] Lord Mackenzie went on to say, "So in this case the charge of fabrication and
conspiracy runs throughout the whole, and whatever difficulty there might be in reducing
to rule the definitions which have been usually given for forgery, that only shows that the
ingenuity of bad men is greater than that of lawyers": at 340.

constitute forgery whether or not what is authenticated is true. It might be different if the examination had been a written one and the paper submitted by C. bore to be that of D. — that might be practical cheating since it is the authorship and not the authentication of an examination paper which is important — but an application form does not depend for its validity on being holograph of the applicant.[45]

What documents can be forged. There was at one time considerable **18.43** dispute as to whether forgery was restricted to obligatory writs, or at any rate to writs which in themselves operated to the prejudice of another,[46] but there is now no doubt that forgery extends to any authenticated document. In *Wm Rhind*[47] a charge of forging a certificate that the accused was a fit object of public charity was upheld as "one of those lesser [*i.e.* non-capital] forgeries which law recognises",[48] and even earlier, in *Daniel Taylor*[49] it was held to be forgery to write a begging letter in the name of another asking his sister to send money to a post office where the accused intended to collect it.[50] Any lingering doubts that might have remained[51] were finally laid to rest by Schedule A to the Criminal Procedure (Scotland) Act 1887, which included the following charge, "did utter as genuine a letter bearing to be a certificate of character . . . what was written above the signature . . . having been written there by some other person without . . . authority by handing it to . . . to whom you were applying for a situation."[52] All forgeries are today in the same rank, so to speak, and there is no distinction between the greater and lesser, a distinction which had in any event lost its purpose when forgery ceased to be capital in 1832.[53]

Historical documents and manuscripts. Macdonald says that where a **18.44** document is of purely historical interest, *e.g.* as being the manuscript of a particular person, its sale as genuine is fraud rather than uttering.[54] He refers to *H.M. Advocate v. A.H. Smith*[55] in which the accused was charged with pretending that certain documents were manuscript letters of Scott and Burns and thereby inducing certain persons to buy them from him and so defrauding them. But the fact that the successful use of the letters was charged as fraud does not mean that it could not have been charged as uttering. Literary forgeries may not, strictly speaking, be legal forgeries, but they might constitute a form of practical cheating.[56]

---

[45] *Quaere* the position where A is allowed to dictate his examination answers to B, and C comes along and impersonates A: this is probably just a conspiracy to defraud.

[46] Hume, i, 140; Alison, i, 381–383; Macdonald, pp. 60–62. *Cf. Jas Myles* (1848) Ark. 400.

[47] (1860) 3 Irv. 613.

[48] At 616.

[49] (1853) 1 Irv. 230.

[50] And see also *Wm Foodie and John Campbell* (1837) 1 Swin. 509: forging false death certificates to obtain benefits from a friendly society; *Walter H. Smith* (1840) 2 Swin. 525: a certificate of poverty to obtain charity; *John Neil* (1845) 2 Broun 368: a subscription list; *Arch. McMillan* (1859) 3 Irv. 317: a begging letter; *Wm Cregan* (1879) 4 Couper 313: an army certificate; *H.M. Advocate v. John Daniel* (1891) 3 White 103: a certificate under the Anatomy Act 1832.

[51] See *e.g. Henry Imrie* (1863) 4 Irv. 435.

[52] See now the 1995 Act, Sched. 2.

[53] Forgery, Abolition of Punishment of Death Act 1832.

[54] Macdonald, p.60.

[55] (1893) 1 Adam 6.

[56] See *infra*, para. 18.48.

18.45 *False documents*. As has been mentioned, Mackenzie divided falsehood into four categories, one of which was "Falsehood by writ",[57] and he did not distinguish between writs which were forged and writs which were false because they contained false statements, at any rate where they were instruments, or perhaps even probative writs, and the same is largely true of Burnett.[58] Even Hume is not altogether clear on this point. He deals first with capital forgeries, then he goes on to talk of the case of the notary signing a false instrument as "a different species of crime",[59] after which he discusses as a third species those cases in which the accused alters what has been written above a genuine signature, which today is regarded as forgery.[60] It is difficult therefore to say whether Hume considered false instruments and the like as a form of non-capital forgery, or whether he regarded them as a form of fraud.[61] Alison talks of false instruments as "one of the worst kinds of forgeries" but is thinking of cases involving the forgery of signatures of fictitious witnesses.[62]

18.46   The leading case on this question is *Simon Fraser*[63] in which the accused was a sheriff officer who was charged with forging the signature of a witness to an execution — a charge which was clearly relevant, and also with forgery by inducing a person to sign a blank paper as a witness, and then filling up a false execution of citation. It was not alleged that the execution was filled in without the witness's authority. It was held that the second charge was irrelevant since there had been no forgery but only the making of an untrue document. Lord Justice-Clerk Inglis described the charge as being "unquestionably a charge of falsehood; and the falsehood consists in knowingly making and uttering a formal writing containing a false statement", but not a relevant charge of forgery.[64] Lord Inglis defined forgery as the "making and uttering a writing, falsely intended to represent and pass for the genuine writing of another person", and added that, "*forged* and *genuine* are precisely opposite and contradictory terms."[65] His Lordship went on to say that although forgery had not originally been a *nomen juris*, the modern position was that the crime was restricted to "making and uttering . . . a writing falsely intended to represent and pass for the genuine writing of another person",[66] so that it did not extend to what had been done by Fraser.

Earlier statements that false executions or instruments are to be deemed forgeries[67] cannot stand with *Fraser*.[68] There remains the

---

[57] Mackenzie, I,27, pr.
[58] Burnett, p.177.
[59] Hume, i, 158.
[60] Hume, i, 159–160.
[61] *cf. Simon Fraser* (1859) 3 Irv. 467, Lord Deas at 487, L.J.-G. McNeill at 497.
[62] Alison, i, 380–381.
[63] (1859) 3 Irv. 467.
[64] At 475.
[65] *ibid.*
[66] At 476–477.
[67] For example, Stair, *Inst.*, 4,39,16. In *John Smith* (1852) 1 Irv. 125, a sheriff officer pleaded guilty to falsehood "by fabricating and uttering as genuine a false service copy of a summons and citation, purporting to be issued under the warrant or authority of a court of law", but there the document was "forged" in the sense that it was not genuinely issued by the court.
[68] *supra*. In *Fraser* Lord Cowan tried to distinguish the case of the notary executing a

question whether the uttering of false writs of this kind is, as Lord Inglis's opinion suggests, a completed crime, in which case the distinction between such false writs and forgeries would be merely verbal. It is submitted that the reasoning of *Fraser*[69] itself leaves no room for any special class of false writs, and that false executions and instruments are in the same position as other written falsehoods, so that the uttering of them is not in itself a completed crime.[70] To put them in a special position would introduce an unnecessary complication into the law, for which there is no practical justification now that attempted fraud is in any event criminal.[71]

There are a number of cases which might suggest that the law does recognise the uttering of false documents as criminal, but it is submitted that they do not necessarily lead to this conclusion. Two of them, *Reuben Brooks and Fredk Wm Thomas*[72] and *Martin Walker and Ors*,[73] concern the concoction of false affidavits intended to enable a confederate of a bankrupt to appear and use his influence in the sequestration, and bankruptcy frauds form a special class which would in any event today be prosecuted as offences against the Bankruptcy (Scotland) Act 1985 and not at common law.[74]

The next case is *Thos Black Webster*,[75] where a doctor was charged **18.47** with fabricating a false vaccination certificate, and uttering it to a registrar "with intent that [a] child should, in respect of such false certificate, be registered . . . and in respect whereof such child is . . . registered", as vaccinated. But although the Crown argued that the charge was not one of forgery or fraud but a special crime similar to the crime committed by a notary who uttered a false instrument, the accused's deceit had the result that the child was wrongly registered, and that would certainly be today regarded as sufficient to complete the crime of fraud.[76] The judge, Lord Neaves, who had been in the majority in *Simon Fraser*,[77] regarded the crime as belonging to a different class

---

false instrument — at 482 — but it is submitted that his position is indistinguishable at common law. The now repealed Act 1621, c. 22, which declared that the makers and users of false writs should be punished with the pains of falsehood, was passed before forgery became a *nomen juris*.

[69] *supra*.

[70] *Michael Hinchy* (1864) 4 Irv. 561.

[71] This is not to say of course that the use of false instruments or executions should not be more severely punished than other types of fraud — nor that the uttering or even the making of false executions might not be punishable as an attempt to pervert the course of justice. Anderson says in his section on fraud that, "If a document is fabricated, such as a certificate of character, the crime is completed the moment the document is uttered", and cites *Daniel Taylor* (1853) 1 Irv. 230 and *Thos Black Webster* (1872) 2 Couper 339, *infra*, as authorities: Anderson, p.196. He also deals in his section on forgery with "Falsehood by fabricating writings where the crime does not come up to forgery" in which he includes false certificates of marriage or banns, signatures to executions by absent witnesses, placing a false date on writs, fabricating letters which are expressed in the third person, fraudulently using as true falsified balance-sheets, vitiating bills, erasures, interlineations on deeds, and destruction of documents, a heterogeneous hotchpot of different types of written lies and forgeries: Anderson, pp. 199–200.

[72] (1861) 4 Irv. 132.

[73] (1872) 2 Couper 328.

[74] So far as *Reuben Brooks, supra,* is concerned there was an averment that the confederate had protected the bankrupt from imprisonment and the case can be regarded as a fraud which produced a result.

[75] (1872) 2 Couper 339.

[76] *supra*.

[77] (1859) 3 Irv. 467.

altogether as a breach of public duty by the accused in his capacity as a medical practitioner obliged to carry out the requirements of the vaccination legislation honestly.[78] The case is in any event special, and of a type which is usually prosecuted as a statutory offence in modern practice.

In *H.M. Advocate v. City of Glasgow Bank Directors*[79] and the similar case of *Jas Nicol Fleming,*[80] as well as in *H.M. Advocate v. Pattisons,*[81] there were charges of uttering false balance sheets, but these charges went on to aver that shareholders and others were induced by the balance sheets to buy or retain shares to their prejudice, and the charges were really charges of fraud although they contained a narrative of uttering. In *Hamilton and Ors v. H.M. Advocate*[82] there was a charge of uttering false business records as genuine by presenting them to inspectors of a statutory board as true, and no challenge was made to its relevance. The charge was one of a number grouped under a narrative of a fraudulent scheme, but it was libelled as an independent charge. It is submitted that the charge was irrelevant, and that the mere uttering of false books is no more than the telling of a written lie, and cannot be a crime in itself at common law.[83]

False articles

18.48 Cases of uttering false articles as genuine can be divided into two groups. In the first the article is tendered as authentic, as the creation of a person other than its maker; in the second it is tendered as being a different thing from what it truly is.

18.49 *Tendering as authentic.* This can be distinguished from forgery on the ground that the authenticity of a writ, or "signed instrument", does not depend on who wrote it but on who authorised it and made it his writ in law, while the authenticity of an article like a painting, or a piece of furniture, or even a manuscript, depends on who created it. The authenticity of a writ is a legal authenticity[84]; that of an Old Master a factual one. But it is easy to apply the analogy of forgery to things like fake Vermeers or Sheratons and *a fortiori* to fake manuscripts, and to hold that the uttering of counterfeit articles is an example of practical cheating. The position is the same whether the article pretends to be that of a particular person, living or dead, or whether it merely pretends to be that of someone other than its true maker. It does not matter whether the modern fake is uttered as a genuine Giorgione or merely as a genuine painting of the late fifteenth century — it would be popularly described as a forgery in both cases, and its uttering is, it is submitted, criminal in both cases.

There is no specific authority for this type of uttering but it is *a fortiori* of the uttering of articles as having a particular quality; it is popularly

---

[78] 2 Couper at 344. Lord Neaves also referred to the accused's deceit as involving danger to the public safety, but this does not appear to be the *ratio* of his decision. *Cf. David Gibson* (1848) Ark. 489, where a doctor who falsely certified that a convict was fit to be moved was charged *inter alia* with "granting a false certificate he being a public officer".

[79] (1879) 4 Couper 161.

[80] (1882) 5 Couper 36.

[81] (1901) 3 Adam 420.

[82] 1938 J.C. 134.

[83] *Michael Hinchy* (1864) 4 Irv. 561, Lord Neaves at 566.

[84] Which may be why forgery was once thought to be restricted to obligatory writs.

thought of as forgery; and it seems reasonable to expect the law to regard it in the same way as it regards forgery.[85]

Tendering as other than it is. According to Macdonald there is practical **18.50** cheating "where an article is made over to others as being that which it is not".[86] The authority for this type of offence is *Alex. Bannatyne*[87] in which the accused entered into a contract to sell B oatmeal and in pretended compliance therewith delivered a mixture of oatmeal, barleymeal and bran, and rendered an account for pure oatmeal which was not paid. He was charged with cheating and defrauding B, and it was argued on his behalf that as the meal supplied had been neither used[88] nor paid for there had been only an attempted fraud. The court rejected this argument and held that the fraud had been completed when the meal was received by B.

Four things should be noted about *Bannatyne.*[89]

(1) Historically, as Dr, now Lord, Gill has shown in his argument that there is no authority for the crime of practical cheating, *Bannatyne* can be explained by the absence of the offence of attempted fraud: the question at issue was whether there had been a completed fraud, and the case held only that what happened in *Bannatyne* was a sufficient result to complete the crime.[90] This view is supported by the fact that the defence argument was directed to the absence of economic loss, and that Lord Justice-Clerk Hope told the jury that fraud did not require unlawful gain, since "If a party furnished an article which was not what he professed it to be — and although when detected he did not claim the price — it was still a fraud."[91] Lord Hope drew an analogy with obtaining goods without intending to pay, where receipt of the goods completes the offence,[92] but this is a false analogy and confuses the parting with possession and the receipt of possession.

Dr, now Lord, Gill's view is also supported by the fact that *Bannatyne* was relied on in *J.& P. Coats Ltd v. Brown*,[93] although in the *Coats* case the article was paid for and the fraud charge was directed to the inducement of that payment.

One difficulty about this approach, however, is that it requires one to accept that the receipt of goods is a sufficient result for simple fraud. If *Bannatyne* is regarded as a case of practical cheating this can perhaps be avoided, although it must be said that given the existence of attempted fraud this may not be of great practical significance.

(2) But *Bannatyne*[94] goes further than this. For there are statements which indicate that what the court were relying on was the giving and not the receiving of the goods.[95] Lord Justice-Clerk Hope said, "But if

---

[85] Where the fake bears a signature or other authenticating mark the similarity with forgery is even greater, since there is an explicit false authentication.

[86] Macdonald, p.58.

[87] (1847) Ark. 361.

[88] There was evidence of partial use — at 368 — but use was not libelled.

[89] *supra*.

[90] Gill, Chap. VII, esp. pp. 116–117.

[91] (1847) Ark., at 380.

[92] *ibid.*, at 364.

[93] (1909) 6 Adam 19, L.J.-C. MacDonald at 40.

[94] (1847) Ark. 361.

[95] The indictment talks of a fraudulent intention that the goods be "received by the [buyers] as 'Oatmeal' ", and narrates that they were "received and shipped and delivered"

oatmeal was undertaken to be furnished, and if, when furnished, it was not oatmeal, then the Buyers were defrauded."[96]

Again, in charging the jury, Lord Hope said[97]:

> "The falsehood and fraud consisted in doing a thing against another's right and interest without the party's knowledge, and to that party's detriment, giving him an article which he had not expected to receive, and which he did not contract for; and such had been the circumstances of this case. For the commission of the crime of Fraud and Wilful Imposition, it was not requisite that the party made any unlawful gain from it. If a party furnished an article which was not what he professed it to be — and although when detected he did not claim the price — it was still a fraud."

Admittedly, Lord Hope talks throughout of fraud, and the charge was one of fraud, but the delivery of an article which is disconform to contract is not a "definite practical result", nor is it in itself a crime. It was said in a later case that the crime in *Bannatyne* depended on the fact that "an article was delivered as genuine when it was adulterated."[98]

If that is so, *Bannatyne* depends on being an example of a crime analogous to uttering and not to simple fraud. The article itself must be disguised so as to appear genuine. It is simple fraud and not practical cheating to sell margarine with a butter label, or a piece of glass acccompanied with a valuation describing it as a diamond, and the uttering of such an article is not a common law crime.[99] But it might be practical cheating to supply a piece of chrome with a false silver hall-mark,[1] or water dyed to look like whisky. Probably the disguise must affect the essential character of the article, but what its essential character is will depend on circumstances, and in particular on what characteristic of the article it was which led the dupe to want it. It is probably not a crime to tender mutton dressed as lamb, but it may be one to tender beef or rabbit so dressed.

(3) *Bannatyne*[2] is the only reported case which is authority for this type of practical cheating. *Jas Paton*,[3] in which the circumstances — the inflating of cattle skins and putting false horns on them before entering them in a competition — look like practical cheating, was not decided on this point, and is, if anything an authority contrary to *Bannatyne*. For *Paton* was argued on the question of whether the awarding of a prize which was not actually paid over was a sufficient practical result, and it was assumed that if it was not the charge would have to be dismissed. Had the case been thought of as one of practical cheating it would

---

as "Oatmeal", but it contains no clear averment that the buyers were ever induced to do anything, or indeed that they did anything except enter into the contract of sale, in pursuance whereof the goods were received by the shippers to be stored to the use of the buyers.

[96] At 366.

[97] At 380.

[98] *Thos Forgan* (1871) 2 Couper 30, Lord Neaves at 33.

[99] It may be an offence against the Trade Descriptions Act: see *infra*, para. 19.21.

[1] *Quaere* if this example is not a true forgery.

[2] (1847) Ark. 361.

[3] (1858) 3 Irv. 208.

not have mattered whether any result had been achieved.[4]

(4) *Bannatyne*[5] itself could today be charged as attempted fraud, since the accused claimed the price of the goods, but the decision is concerned with a completed crime, and would apply where there was no attempted fraud.

Bannatyne is a difficult case, and its application in any particular situation will involve the difficulty of deciding what form or degree of adulteration or disguise is necessary to bring a set of facts within its scope. For these reasons, and because of the modern law of attempted fraud and the existence of numerous statutory frauds, particularly under the Trade Descriptions Act 1968,[6] it is highly unlikely that *Bannatyne* will ever be followed.

But it does, with the support of Macdonald and Anderson, provide authority for a crime of practical cheating, and it would be rash to assume that it will never be resurrected by the Crown.

Personation. In the normal case where A assumes a false character or **18.51** even a false "personality" there is only simple fraud — A tells lies to the effect that he is a man of wealth, or a deserving army pensioner, a long-lost relative of the dupe, a police officer, or even a specific individual like the dupe's husband or the Lord Provost of Edinburgh. But if A dresses up as a policeman or a general or any other character of that kind, it is arguable that his impersonation constitutes practical cheating and that it is a complete crime for him to "utter" or present himself as such. There is no common law authority on this point,[7] and the most common forms of impersonation have been made statutory offences.[8]

Uttering

Two things are required for a criminal uttering: (1) The document or **18.52** article must be uttered as genuine, and (2) the uttering must be towards the prejudice of someone.[9]

(1) The utterer must intend to deceive the person to whom the document[10] is tendered as to its genuineness.[11] If, therefore, A delivers a forged document to B, as forged, so that B may utter it as genuine to C, A will be art and part in B's uttering to C, but his own giving of the document to B will not amount to a criminal uttering. Again, there is no uttering if A hands B a forgery so that B may admire the counterfeiter's skill.

---

[4] Macdonald (3rd ed.) recognises this but goes on to say that "it is thought that the crime was complete when the cattle were entered in the competition": at 88. That may be so, but it was not the view of the court. Anderson cites both *Paton* and *Bannatyne* as authority for the crime of practical fraud which he describes as occurring where an article is fraudulently displayed as genuine when it is not, which again ignores the *ratio* of *Paton*: Anderson, p.196.

[5] (1847) Ark. 361.

[6] *infra*, para. 19.21.

[7] The charge in *John Andrew Geddes,* High Court, June 1963, unrep'd, *supra,* para. 18.19, libelled an alleged result.

[8] See *infra*, paras 19.95 *et seq.*

[9] Hume, i, 150; Alison, i, 401–403; Macdonald, p.64.

[10] What is said about forged documents applies also to any other form of common law uttering.

[11] *John Smith* (1871) 2 Couper 1, L.J.-G. Inglis at 9.

If A obtains a writ which has been signed genuinely by B, and utters it to C as the writ of another person of the same name as B, that is a criminal uttering, although in a sense there has been no forgery.[12]

18.53   VENDING FORGED NOTES. Because of the danger involved in the existence of forged banknotes, and perhaps also because it is difficult to imagine anyone going to the trouble to forge notes unless he means to use them criminally, the common law has buttressed the preventive crime of uttering with a further preventive crime, that of selling forged notes as forged. The existence of this crime was settled in the case of *John Horne* in 1814.[13] H. was charged with "feloniously delivering, vending, or disposing of any . . . forged or counterfeited notes or obligations, as forged or counterfeited, for a valuable consideration less than the nominal value thereof, and for the fraudulent and felonious purpose of the same being used, uttered, or vended as genuine." It was held that although this did not constitute capital forgery and uttering, it was a crime. It is not clear whether this was because it was regarded as attempted uttering or a form of conspiracy, or because it was regarded as an independent crime, but later writers have treated it as an independent crime.[14] Alison describes the crime as "to utter or vend forged notes, knowing them to be forged, to an associate, at less than their nominal value, for the purpose of their being passed as genuine upon the public", Macdonald merely as "to vend [notes] at less than their face value even where they are vended as fabrications and so not uttered as genuine." It is submitted that Alison's definition is the correct one in that it is necessary to show that the vending was done in the course of a scheme to have the notes passed ultimately as genuine. This is clear from the discussion in *Horne*[15] which was much occupied with the law of attempt, and with the difference between acts of remote preparation and "important steps of a deep and an advanced conspiracy against the safety of trade,"[16] and in which it was stressed that the circumstances disclosed a "*traffic* in forged documents, — a *dealing* in them for profit, and for the precise purpose of their being afterwards uttered as genuine, the only purpose for which anyone would buy them."[17] On the other hand it should not be necessary to show that the notes were sold at less than face value although this will in practice almost always be the case.

18.54   (2) The uttering must be *towards the prejudice* of another.[18] It is not necessary that any prejudice should actually have followed, but the uttering must be calculated, objectively, to lead to prejudice. The term

---

[12] *cf. Jas Hendry* (1839) Bell's Notes 49, which suggests that A must have intended to use the signature fraudulently at the time of B's signing, but there seems no reason for insisting on this restriction.

[13] Hume, i, 150.

[14] Alison, i, 406; Macdonald, p.69.

[15] (1814) Hume, i, 150.

[16] Hume, i, 152.

[17] *ibid.* See also *Wm Cooke* (1833) Bell's Notes 58, which was a charge of vending notes "as counterfeit, at an under-value, to be afterwards used as genuine", and two cases reported by Alison: *Patrick Hendrie, Jun.* (1828), *Henry Macmillan* (1831), Alison, i, 407.

[18] Hume, i, 150; Macdonald, p.64; *John Smith* (1871) 2 Couper 1 L.J.-G. Inglis at 10. Lord Inglis suggests that the prejudice must be that of the person whose signature is forged, but there seems no reason in principle for any such restriction, and it could not apply in cases of practical cheating: see, *e.g.*, *Macdonald v. Tudhope*, 1983 S.C.C.R. 341, where the accused (the treasurer of a club) forged on certificates the signatures of persons who had not actually been present when he withdrew cash from gaming machines and then presented those certificates to the honorary secretary of the club as genuine documents of account.

"towards the prejudice" has not been defined, and it is usually presumed that any uttering is towards the prejudice of the "forgee". It probably includes any "use towards making the document available for what could be its natural and proper purpose if it were genuine"[19]; it probably excludes just showing the document to someone.[20] Macdonald says that it has not been decided whether registration for preservation only is uttering.[21] It is submitted that it is. Such registration is a formal act intended to preserve the document as formal evidence, and it puts the document out of the control of the utterer, in the sense that it makes it irrevocably public for all time.

It is not clear whether it is uttering for A to hand B a paper with a forged signature in order that B should fill in something above the signature and return the document to A for A to utter the completed document. Suppose A asks B to write something on a blank piece of paper, or to fill in a cheque form, and A then adhibits C's signature and utters the writ. In such a case there is clearly no uttering to B. Suppose now that A first of all puts on C's signature and then asks B to fill in the writ — is this any different from the first case? It is submitted that it is, and that in the second case there is an uttering to B. It is true that in neither case is the document or the cheque uttered to B, but in the second case a forged signature is uttered, whereby B is induced to fill in the cheque form, and this is "taking a forged subscription and using it" and is therefore uttering.[22] The question was raised in one case in which signed blank bill forms were handed to a bank teller for completion, but it was left undecided and the difficulty avoided by adding an averment that the forms were handed over for completion and discounting.[23]

Modes of uttering. (1) By presenting the document[24] as genuine to the **18.55** public or to a particular person. If A tries to get past a doorman by showing him a forged pass, that is uttering, although the pass never leaves A's hands. Similarly, if A sets up as a doctor and puts a forged diploma in his window, that is uttering, since it is a use of the document which may prejudice anyone who passes by looking for a doctor. It would probably not be uttering to hang the diploma in a private room, just as it would not be uttering to keep it in a drawer, but it would probably be uttering to hang it in a waiting or consulting room.

(2) By putting the document out of the utterer's control. If A gives a forged document to B without telling him it is forged, and with instructions to give it to C, that is an uttering to B. It does not matter

---

[19] *John Smith, supra,* Lord Deas at 11. See also *Macdonald v. Tudhope,* 1983 S.C.C.R. 341 at 347, where the Court stated: "Presentation of forged vouchers of expenditure is in our view clearly intended towards prejudice of a recipient, who is intended to accept them as genuine documents of account and make use of them accordingly."

[20] Macdonald, p.64.

[21] Macdonald, p.65: *cf.* at 66 — "It might be a relevant defence [to uttering by posting] that the sending of the document was only for preservation". See also Alison, i, 403. *Jas Shepherd* (1842) 1 Broun 325 is indecisive.

[22] See Lord Cockburn in *Michael Steedman* (1854) 1 Irv. 369 at 373.

[23] *Michael Steedman, supra* and at 1 Irv. 363; *John Reid* (1841) 2 Swin. 562. Macdonald says that, "it has not been decided whether the crime is complete if it be merely handed to another to be written out; and it is difficult to see how this alone could complete the crime": Macdonald, p.65.

[24] In *R. v. Harris* [1966] 1 Q.B. 184 it was held that to make and send to the dupe a photostatic copy of a forged receipt with intent to defraud was a "use" of the forgery and therefore an uttering of it in terms of the Forgery Act 1913, s.6(2).

whether or not B gives the document to C.[25] It is, for example, uttering to hand a forged document to one's solicitor with instructions to lodge it in process,[26] even although the solicitor refuses to do so.[27] If B does utter it to C then that uttering is also A's uttering, B being his innocent agent, and in such a case there are two utterings by A, that to B and that to C.[28] If B is art and part with A, then of course A's uttering to B is not criminal since it is not an uttering as genuine.[29]

The most common example of this type of uttering is posting a letter, which is in itself a complete uttering.[30] It could also in certain circumstances be uttering to place the writ where it is likely to be discovered, *e.g.* to place a forged will or other writ in a person's repositories with the intention that it would be discovered on his death.[31]

The mens rea of uttering

18.56 (1) *The uttering must be intentional.* A cannot utter a document by losing it, or letting it drop involuntarily from his hand.[32]

18.57 (2) *The accused must know that the writ is not genuine.* Since "it is not a forgery, that to accommodate another who cannot write, and at his desire, one signs a draught or receipt in the name of that other",[33] it is not uttering to pass a writ which has been, or which A believes has been, made with the authority of the person whose writ it bears to be.

18.58 (3) *"Fraudulent intent".* It is said that the uttering must be "felonious" and with "intent to injure" or "intention to defraud",[34] but this means little if anything more than that the uttering must be intended to have a prejudicial effect.

Claim of right is not available as a defence to uttering. As Hume said, "it is forgery (though the excuse might possibly be considered in the sentence), to frame a false bill, bond, or other voucher for a debt, be it ever so just, or a discharge for money which was truly paid, but the payment forgotten to be vouched: For still the offender has made a false deed, and is thus far benefited, and the other party prejudiced, as he has now written evidence of the state of the transaction, and enjoys therein that security which he coveted, and thought worth attaining at such a hazard."[35] An accused will not be heard to say that he thought he was legally entitled to forge a writ.

---

[25] *Jas Aitchison* (1835) Bell's Notes 57; *Wm Harvey* (1835) *ibid.*; *Wm Jeffrey* (1842) 1 Broun 337; *John Smith* (1871) 2 Couper 1; Alison is wrong in saying that it is necessary to show that B delivered the writ to C: see Alison, i, 403–406.

[26] *Hector McLean* (1838) 2 Swin. 183.

[27] *Geo. Wilson, Jr.* (1861) 4 Irv. 42, suggests that this may not be so, but the question was not decided and the suggestion is clearly wrong: *John Smith* (1871) 2 Couper 1.

[28] See *John Reid* (1842) 1 Broun 21.

[29] *Robt Meldrum and Catherine Reid* (1838) Bell's Notes 57, which suggests that the uttering to B is criminal, must be wrong.

[30] *Wm Harvey, supra, Wm Jeffrey, supra, Daniel Taylor* (1853) 1 Irv. 230; *John Smith, supra.*

[31] See *Duncan Stalker and Thos Wilson Cuthbert* (1844) 2 Broun 70.

[32] Macdonald, p.65; Alison, i, 402; *Jas Devlin* (1828) *ibid.* in which apparently the writ was dropped while the panel was handing it over to the person to whom he intended to utter it — such a situation might now be treated as attempted uttering.

[33] Hume, i, 154.

[34] Hume, i, 154; Alison, i, 394 (intent to injure): *Wm Waiters* (1836) 1 Swin. 273, Lord Medwyn at 275 (intention to defraud).

[35] Hume, i, 154–155.

The purpose of the uttering is irrelevant.[36] It is uttering to use a forged diploma in order to disprove a charge of perjury, or a forged bill to enable a creditor to apply for sequestration, although such are not the normal uses of the documents concerned.[37]

Destruction of documents

The converse of putting a false document into circulation is the **18.59** destruction of a genuine one, the act being completed by the mere fact of destruction, and there is authority that it is a crime merely to destroy a deed with fraudulent intent.[38] The crime is probably much narrower in scope than uttering, and may be limited to documents which are legally effective like wills[39] or decrees.[40] Where other kinds of documents are destroyed in order to prevent their use as evidence the matter can be dealt with as an attempt to pervert the course of justice; and in other cases the destruction of a document may form an element in a simple fraud.

In *Geo. Malcom*[41] M. was a bankrupt who was charged with destroying receipts he had given for payments made to him by a debtor of his prior to the sequestration. The crime was libelled as "Tearing, Destroying, or Mutilating any Account, Passbook, or other Writing containing vouchers or acknowledgements for the payment of money, with intent to Defraud or Injure Creditors, or the parties to whom the said account ... belongs." There was a plea of guilty and no discussion on relevancy. The facts would today be charged as an offence against the Bankruptcy (Scotland) Act 1985, section 67(2),[42] and must in any event be regarded as falling within the special class of bankruptcy frauds. The mere destruction of an account book cannot be regarded as any different from the use of a false account book, which is only the telling of a written lie.[43]

Setting fire with intent to defraud insurers

It is an independent and completed crime wilfully to set fire to one's **18.60** own property with intent thereby to defraud those who have insured the property against fire, at any rate in the case of buildings[44] or stock-in-trade.[45] This crime differs from ordinary fraud in that neither a practical result nor even the making of a fraudulent pretence by way of a claim on the insurers is necessary to complete it; and it differs from ordinary fire-raising in that it can be committed on one's own property.[46] It is not necessary to show that the accused himself derived or was likely to derive any benefit from the insurers; it is enough that the purpose of his action was to enable the insured person to benefit.[47]

---

[36] Macdonald, p.66.
[37] *ibid.*; *Jas Myles* (1848) Ark. 400; *Jas Bonella* (1843) 1 Broun 517.
[38] Macdonald, p.58.
[39] *John Rattray and Ors* (1848) Ark. 406.
[40] *Jas Dunipace* (1842) 1 Broun 506.
[41] (1843) 1 Broun 620.
[42] *infra*, para. 19.03.
[43] *supra*, para. 18.47.
[44] Hume, i, 134; Alison, i, 438; Macdonald, pp. 81–82; *Chas Little* (1857) 2 Irv. 624; *H.M. Advocate v. Paterson* (1890) 2 White 496.
[45] *Alex. Pollock* (1869) 1 Couper 257; *Hannah McAtamney or Henry and John McAtamney* (1867) 5 Irv. 363; *Wm McCreadie* (1862) 4 Irv. 214.
[46] See Hume, i, 134; Alison, i, 438, 641; Macdonald, pp. 81–82.
[47] *John Malcolm Brown* (1886) 1 White 243; *Hannah McAtamney or Henry, supra*, was decided on specification and in so far as it can be read as contradicting the above proposition is, it is submitted, wrong.

Where property is not destroyed but only, for example, hidden in order that a pretence might be made that it has been stolen or destroyed, the ordinary rules of fraud apply, and it is necessary to show a practical result,[48] and the same is probably the case where property other than ships is destroyed otherwise than by setting fire to it, or where small articles of property are burned in circumstances which do not involve any of the dangers inherent in a substantial fire.

It is probably not a common law crime to burn one's own property in order to defraud creditors, even where the property has itself been attached by sequestration or diligence.[49]

18.61 *Sinking ships.* It is also a crime to sink and destroy a ship, by fire or otherwise, with intent to defraud insurers.[50]

---

[48] *cf. H.M. Advocate v. Camerons* (1911) 6 Adam 456.

[49] *Robt Lawson* (1865) 5 Irv. 79; Macdonald, p.82.

[50] Hume, i, 176, 486; Alison, i, 641; Macdonald, p.83. *John Malcolm Brown, supra*; *H.M. Advocate v. Louis le Bourdais and Anr* (1888) 2 White 161. *Cf. Hobbs v. H.M. Advocate* (1893) 3 White 487.

CHAPTER 19

STATUTORY FRAUDS

BANKRUPTCY FRAUDS

Frauds in connection with bankruptcy were recognised as criminal in **19.01** two seventeenth century statutes, the Bankruptcy Act 1621 and the Bankruptcy Act 1696; both Acts are now repealed,[1] and bankruptcy frauds are currently dealt with under the Bankruptcy (Scotland) Act 1985.

Common law

Bankruptcy frauds are also criminal at common law. Originally the **19.02** common law probably recognised only those frauds which were directed against rights which had become vested in the bankrupt's creditors by sequestration[2] or the granting of a trust-deed,[3] but certain types of common law bankruptcy frauds may also be committed by persons who have not yet been divested of their estates.

Generally speaking "any act fraudulently conceived and carried out by a debtor for the purpose of deceiving his creditors or depriving them of their just rights" constitutes a bankruptcy fraud.[4] A bankruptcy fraud is complete when the accused has done or omitted to do certain specified things, whether or not his creditors have in fact suffered any loss, and whether or not the debtor's behaviour has produced any practical result.[5]

The commonest type of common law bankruptcy fraud is the "away-putting", or concealing, of assets.[6] This crime may be committed by a person whose estates have been sequestrated, or who has granted a trust deed for creditors, by a person who is insolvent, in the sense of "absolute insolvency", *i.e.* a person whose total realisable assets are less than his debts, even although no rights to his estate have been vested in his creditors,[7] and also by a person "on the eve of" or "in contemplation of" bankruptcy.[8] It is necessary that the "away-putting" should have been done with intent to defraud creditors.

---

[1] See Bankruptcy (Scotland) Act 1985, Sched. 8.

[2] Alison, i, 567; *David Morrison* (1817) and *John Carter* (1831), *ibid.*

[3] *Clendinnen v. Rodger* (1875) 3 Couper 171, L.J.-C. Moncreiff at 179.

[4] *Goudy on Bankruptcy*, (4th ed., Edinburgh, 1914), p.608.

[5] Macdonald, p.58; *Chas McIntyre* (1837) 1 Swin. 536; *R.F. Dick and Alex. Lawrie* (1832) 5 D. & A. 513.

[6] Macdonald, p.74; *Wm Thiele or Cornelius* (1884) 5 Couper 443; *Clendinnen v. Rodger, supra; Jas Henderson* (1862) 4 Irv. 208; *John McKay* (1866) 5 Irv. 329.

[7] *Clendinnen v. Roger, supra*, which overrules *Thos Sneden* (1874) 2 Couper 532; *John McRae* (1867) 5 Irv. 463; *Sangster and Ors v. H.M. Advocate* (1896) 2 Adam 182; Goudy, *op. cit.* pp. 608–609; Macdonald, p.74.

[8] *Clendinnen v. Roger, supra*, Lord Deas at 181; *Margt Smith or Eccles* (1866) 3 Couper 180n; *Wm and Catherine Inglis* (1863) 4 Irv. 418. Lord Neaves at 422–423. *Cf. Duffus v. Whyte* (1866) 1 S.L.R. 124; Goudy, *op. cit.* p.608; Macdonald, p.74.

It is a crime at common law for a bankrupt to destroy or mutilate accounts or other books with intent to defraud his creditors.[9]

It is also a common law crime to obtain sequestration by fraudulent means,[10] to present a fraudulent petition for sequestration,[11] or for a solvent debtor to conceal his effects from his creditors as part of a fraudulent design to make himself appear to be insolvent[12] or to obtain sequestration.[13]

The Bankruptcy (Scotland) Act 1985

19.03 Bankruptcy frauds are currently dealt with under section 67 of the Bankruptcy (Scotland) Act 1985 which provides, *inter alia*:

"(1) A debtor who during the relevant period makes a false statement in relation to his assets or his business or financial affairs to any creditor or to any person concerned in the administration of his estate shall be guilty of an offence, unless he shows that he neither knew nor had reason to believe that his statement was false.

(2) A debtor, or other person acting in his interest whether with or without his authority, who during the relevant period destroys, damages, conceals or removes from Scotland any part of the debtor's estate or any document relating to his assets or his business or financial affairs shall be guilty of an offence, unless the debtor or other person shows that he did not do so with intent to prejudice the creditors.

(3) A debtor who is absent from Scotland and who after the date of sequestration of his estate fails, when required by the court, to come to Scotland for any purpose connected with the administration of his estate, shall be guilty of an offence.

(4) A debtor, or other person acting in his interest whether with or without his authority, who during the relevant period falsifies any document relating to the debtor's assets or his business or financial affairs, shall be guilty of an offence, unless the debtor or other person shows that he had no intention to mislead the permanent trustee, a commissioner or any creditor.

(5) If a debtor whose estate is sequestrated—

    (a) knows that a person has falsified any document relating to the debtor's assets or his business or financial affairs; and

    (b) fails, within one month of the date of acquiring such knowledge, to report his knowledge to the interim or permanent trustee,

he shall be guilty of an offence.

(6) A person who is absolutely insolvent[14] and who during the relevant period transfers anything to another person for an inadequate consideration or grants any unfair preference to any of his creditors shall be guilty of an offence, unless the transferor or

---

[9] Macdonald, p.58; *Geo. Malcom* (1843) 1 Broun 620.

[10] Macdonald, p.74.

[11] *Robt and John Moir* (1842) 1 Broun 448.

[12] Macdonald, p.74; *Clendinnen v. Rodger, supra*, L.J.-C. Moncreiff at 178, Lord Ardmillan at 183.

[13] *Robert Gibson Neill* (1873) 2 Couper 395.

[14] For instance, a person whose liabilities are greater than his assets: see s.73(2) of the Act.

grantor shows that he did not do so with intent to prejudice the creditors.

(7) A debtor who is engaged in trade or business shall be guilty of an offence if at any time in the period of one year ending with the date of sequestration of his estate, he pledges or disposes of, otherwise than in the ordinary course of his trade or business, any property which he has obtained on credit and has not paid for unless he shows that he did not intend to prejudice his creditors.

(8) A debtor who is engaged in trade or business shall be guilty of an offence if at any time in the period of 2 years ending with the date of sequestration, he has failed to keep or preserve such records as are necessary to give a fair view of the state of his assets or his business and financial affairs and to explain his transactions, unless he shows that such failure was neither reckless nor dishonest:

Provided that a debtor shall not be guilty of an offence under this subsection if, at the date of sequestration, his unsecured liabilities did not exceed the prescribed amount[15]; but, for the purposes of this proviso, if at any time the amount of a debt (or part of a debt) over which security is held exceeds the value of the security, that debt (or part) shall be deemed at that time to be unsecured to the extent of the excess.

(9) If a debtor, either alone or jointly with another person, obtains credit to the extent of [£250][16] (or such other sum as may be prescribed) or more without giving the person from whom he obtained it the relevant information about his status he shall be guilty of an offence.[17]

(10) for the purposes of subsection (9) above—

(a) 'debtor' means—

    (i) a debtor whose estate has been sequestrated, or

    (ii) a person who has been adjudged bankrupt in England and Wales or Northern Ireland,

and who, in either case, has not been discharged.

(b) the reference to the debtor obtaining credit includes a reference to a case where goods are hired to him under a hire-purchase agreement or agreed to be sold to him under a conditional sale agreement; and

(c) the relevant information about the status of the debtor is the information that his estate has been sequestrated and that he has not received his discharge or, as the case may be, that he is an undischarged bankrupt in England and Wales or Northern Ireland.

(11) In this section—

(a) 'the relevant period' means the period commencing one year immediately before the date of sequestration of the debtor's estate and ending with his discharge;

---

[15] For instance, £20,000: see Bankruptcy (Scotland) Regulations 1985 (S.I. 1985 No. 1925), reg. 9.

[16] Sum in square brackets substituted by Bankruptcy (Scotland) Regulations 1985 (S.I. 1985 No. 1925), reg. 13 (added by Bankruptcy (Scotland) Amendment Regulations 1986 (S.I. 1986 No. 1914), reg. 3).

[17] Where the debtor, who fails to give the relevant information as to his status, is an employee of a company and obtains credit ostensibly for that company, he nevertheless commits an offence under this subsection if the company was no more than a device to conceal the true situation — *viz.*, that the business run by the company was the employee's own business: *Drew v. H.M. Advocate*, 1995 S.C.C.R. 647.

(b) references to intent to prejudice creditors shall include references to intent to prejudice an individual creditor.

(12) A person convicted of any offence under this section shall be liable—

(a) on summary conviction, to a fine not exceeding the statutory maximum or—

    (i) to imprisonment for a term not exceeding 3 months; or

    (ii) if he has previously been convicted of an offence inferring dishonest appropriation of property or an attempt at such appropriation, to imprisonment for a term not exceeding 6 months,

or (in the case of either sub-paragraph) to both such fine and such imprisonment; or

(b) on conviction on indictment to a fine or—

    (i) in the case of an offence under subsection (1), (2), (4) or (7) above to imprisonment for a term not exceeding 5 years,

    (ii) in any other case to imprisonment for a term not exceeding 2 years,

or (in the case of either sub-paragraph) to both such fine and such imprisonment."

19.04 *Submission of false claims*. Section 22 of the Act provides (*inter alia*):

"(1) For the purposes of voting at the statutory meeting, a creditor shall submit a claim in accordance with this section to the interim trustee at or before the meeting.

(2) A creditor shall submit a claim under this section by producing to the interim trustee—

(a) a statement of claim in the prescribed form; and

(b) an account or voucher (according to the nature of the debt) which constitutes *prima facie* evidence of the debt:

Provided that the interim trustee may dispense with any requirement under this subsection in respect of any debt or any class of debt.

. . .

(5) If a creditor produces under this section a statement of claim, account, voucher or other evidence which is false—

(a) the creditor shall be guilty of an offence unless he shows that he neither knew nor had reason to believe that the statement of claim, account, voucher or other evidence was false;

(b) the debtor shall be guilty of an offence if he —

    (i) knew or became aware that the statement of claim, account, voucher or other evidence was false; and

    (ii) failed as soon as practicable after acquiring such knowledge to report it to the interim trustee or permanent trustee.

. . .

(10) A person convicted of an offence under subsection (5) above shall be liable—

(a) on summary conviction to a fine not exceeding the statutory maximum or—

    (i) to imprisonment for a term not exceeding 3 months; or

(ii) if he has previously been convicted of an offence inferring dishonest appropriation of property or an attempt at such appropriation, to imprisonment for a term not exceeding 6 months,

or (in the case of either sub-paragraph) to both such fine and such imprisonment; or

(b) on conviction on indictment to a fine or to imprisonment for a term not exceeding 2 years or to both."

Company Directors Disqualification Act 1986. Section 11 of the Company **19.05** Directors Disqualification Act 1986 makes it an offence for an undischarged bankrupt to act as director of, or directly or indirectly to take part in or be concerned in the promotion, formation or management[18] of a company, except with the leave of the court which awarded seqestration.[19]

COMPANY FRAUDS

The Companies Act 1985, the Insolvency Act 1986, the Financial **19.06** Services Act 1986 and the Banking Act 1987 provide a number of offences in connection with the liquidation and operation of companies, which are analogous to fraud.

Insolvency Act 1986

Offences in connection with liquidation. The Act includes several offences **19.07** concerning liquidation which are similar to offences contained in the Bankruptcy (Scotland) Act 1985, section 67. These several offences are found in sections 206, 208, 210 and 211 which provide as follows:

"**206.**—(1) When a company is ordered to be wound up by the court or passes a resolution for voluntary winding up, any person, being a past or present officer of the company, is deemed to have committed an offence if, within the 12 months immediately preceding the commencement of the winding up, he has—

(a) concealed any part of the company's property to the value of [£500][20] or more, or concealed any debt due to or from the company, or

(b) fraudulently removed any part of the company's property to the value of [£500][21] or more, or

(c) concealed, destroyed, mutilated or falsified any book or paper affecting or relating to the company's property or affairs, or

(d) made any false entry in any book or paper affecting or relating to the company's property or affairs, or

(e) fraudulently parted with, altered or made any omission in any document affecting or relating to the company's property or affairs, or

---

[18] See *Drew v. H.M. Advocate*, 1995 S.C.C.R. 647.
[19] Maximum penalty: on indictment, two years' and a fine; and on summary conviction, six months' and fine of the statutory maximum (see s.13).
[20] Sum in square brackets substituted by Insolvency Proceedings (Monetary Limits) Order 1986 (S.I. 1986 No. 1996), art. 2, Sched., Pt I.
[21] See n.20, *supra.*

    (f) pawned, pledged or disposed of any property of the company which has been obtained on credit and has not been paid for (unless the pawning, pledging or disposal was in the ordinary way of the company's business).

    (2) Such a person is deemed to have committed an offence if within the period above mentioned he has been privy to the doing by others of any of the things mentioned in paragraphs (c), (d) and (e) of subsection (1); and he commits an offence if, at any time after the commencement of the winding up, he does any of the things mentioned in paragraphs (a) to (f) of that subsection, or is privy to the doing by others of any of the things mentioned in paragraphs (c) to (e) of it.

    (3) For the purposes of this section, 'officer' includes a shadow director.

    (4) It is a defence—

    (a) for a person charged under paragraph (a) or (f) of subsection (1) (or under subsection (2) in respect of the things mentioned in either of these two paragraphs) to prove that he had no intent to defraud, and

    (b) for a person charged under paragraph (c) or (d) of subsection (1) (or under subsection (2) in respect of the things mentioned in either of those two paragraphs) to prove that he had no intent to conceal the state of affairs of the company or to defeat the law.

    (5) Where a person pawns, pledges or disposes of any property in circumstances which amount to an offence under subsection (1)(f), every person who takes in pawn or pledge, or otherwise receives, the property knowing it to be pawned, pledged or disposed of in such circumstances, is guilty of an offence.

    (6) A person guilty of an offence under this section is liable to imprisonment or a fine, or both.[22]

    (7) The money sums specified in paragraphs (a) and (b) of subsection (1) are subject to increase or reduction by order under section 416 in Part XV."

    "**208.**—(1) When a company is being wound up, whether by the court or voluntarily, any person, being a past or present officer of the company, commits an offence, if he—

    (a) does not to the best of his knowledge and belief fully and truly discover to the liquidator all the company's property, and how and to whom and for what consideration and when the company disposed of any part of that property (except such part as has been disposed of in the ordinary way of the company's business), or

    (b) does not deliver up to the liquidator (or as he directs) all such part of the company's property as is in his custody or under his control, and which he is required by law to deliver up, or

    (c) does not deliver up to the liquidator (or as he directs) all books and papers in his custody or under his control belonging to the company and which he is required by law to deliver up, or

---

[22] Under Sched. 10, the maximum penalties are seven years' and a fine on indictment, and six months' and a fine of the statutory maximum on summary complaint.

(d) knowing or believing that a false debt has been proved by any person in the winding up, fails to inform the liquidator as soon as practicable, or

(e) after the commencement of the winding up, prevents the production of any book or paper affecting or relating to the company's property or affairs.

(2) Such a person commits an offence if after the commencement of the winding up he attempts to account for any part of the company's property by fictitious losses or expenses; and he is deemed to have committed that offence if he has so attempted at any meeting of the company's creditors within the 12 months immediately preceding the commencement of the winding up.

(3) For the purposes of this section, 'officer' includes a shadow director.

(4) It is a defence—

(a) for a person charged under paragraph (a), (b) or (c) of subsection (1) to prove that he had no intent to defraud, and

(b) for a person charged under paragraph (e) of that subsection to prove that he had no intent to conceal the state of affairs of the company or to defeat the law.

(5) A person guilty of an offence under this section is liable to imprisonment or a fine or both."[23]

"**210.**—(1) When a company is being wound up, whether by the court or voluntarily, any person, being a past or present officer of the company, commits an offence if he makes any material omission in any statement relating to the company's affairs.

(2) When a company has been ordered to be wound up by the court, or has passed a resolution for voluntary winding up, any such person is deemed to have committed that offence if, prior to the winding up, he has made any material omission in any such statement.

(3) For the purposes of this section, 'officer' includes a shadow director.

(4) It is a defence for a person charged under this section to prove that he had no intent to defraud.

(5) A person guilty of an offence under this section is liable to imprisonment or a fine, or both."[24]

"**211.**—(1) When a company is being wound up, whether by the court or voluntarily, any person, being a past or present officer of the company—

(a) commits an offence if he makes any false representation or commits any other fraud for the purpose of obtaining the consent of the company's creditors or any of them to an agreement with reference to the company's affairs or to the winding up, and

(b) is deemed to have committed that offence if, prior to the winding up, he has made any false representation, or committed any other fraud, for that purpose.

(2) For the purposes of this section, 'officer' includes a shadow director.

---

[23] See n.22, *supra*, for the actual maximum penalties.
[24] See n.22, *supra*, for the actual maximum penalties.

(3) A person guilty of an offence under this section is liable to imprisonment or a fine or both."[25]

19.08 *Destroying or falsifying books*. Section 209 provides:

"(1) When a company is being wound up, an officer or contributory of the company commits an offence if he destroys, mutilates, alters or falsifies any books, papers or securities, or makes or is privy to the making of any false or fraudulent entry in any register, book of account or document belonging to the company with intent to defraud or deceive any person.

(2) A person guilty of an offence under this section is liable to imprisonment or a fine, or both."[26]

19.09 *Defrauding creditors*. Section 207 provides:

"(1) When a company is ordered to be wound up by the court or passes a resolution for voluntary winding up, a person is deemed to have committed an offence if he, being at the time an officer of the company—

(a) has made or caused to be made any gift or transfer of, or charge on, or has caused or connived at the levying of an execution against, the company's property, or

(b) has concealed or removed any part of the company's property since, or within 2 months before, the date of any unsatisfied judgment or order for the payment of money obtained against the company.

(2) A person is not guilty of an offence under this section—

(a) by reason of conduct constituting an offence under subsection (1)(a) which occurred more than 5 years before the commencement of the winding up, or

(b) if he proves that, at the time of the conduct constituting the offence, he had no intent to defraud the company's creditors.

(3) A person guilty of an offence under this section is liable to imprisonment or a fine, or both."[27]

Companies Act 1985

19.10 *Fraudulent trading*. Section 458 of the Companies Act 1985 provides:

"If any business of a company is carried on with intent to defraud creditors of the company or creditors of any other person or for any fraudulent purpose, every person who was knowingly a party to the carrying on of the business in that manner is liable to imprisonment or a fine or both.[28]

This applies whether or not the company has been, or is in the course of being wound up."

It has been held that the collection and distribution of assets constitutes "carrying on business", which is not the same as carrying on

---

[25] See n.22, *supra*, for the actual maximum penalties.

[26] See n.22, *supra*, for the actual maximum penalties.

[27] Maximum penalty on indictment is two years' and a fine, and on summary conviction six months' and a fine of the statutory maximum: Insolvency Act 1986, Sched. 10.

[28] Maximum penalty is, on indictment, seven years' and a fine, and, on summary conviction, six months' and a fine of the statutory maximum.

trade, and that merely to prefer one creditor to another is not fraudulent.[29] It has also been held that the offence applies to an intent to defraud any customers of the company who are not creditors at the relevant time.[30]

"Intent to defraud" includes an intention to prejudice creditors in receiving payment by getting further credit when there is no good reason for expecting money to become available for payment, even without proof of knowledge at the time the debt was incurred that it was not likely to be paid.[31]

It has also been held that not everyone who works for a company is necessarily a person who is knowingly a party to the carrying on of the business of the company; thus, those with a controlling or managerial function certainly fall within the meaning of the section, but a mere salesman acting under orders may not be included.[32]

Reduction of capital. Section 141 of the Companies Act 1985 provides: **19.11**

"If any officer of the company—
  (a) wilfully conceals the name of a creditor entitled to object to the reduction of capital; or
  (b) wilfully misrepresents the nature or amount of the debt or claim of any creditor; or
  (c) aids, abets or is privy to any such concealment or misrepresentation as is mentioned above,
he shall be guilty of an offence and liable to a fine."[33]

Fraudulent use of "limited" or "public limited company". Section 33 **19.12** provides:

"(1) A person who is not a public company is guilty of an offence if he carries on any trade, profession or business under a name which includes, as its last part, the words 'public limited company' [or their equivalent in Welsh].[34]

(2) A public company is guilty of an offence if, in circumstances in which the fact that it is a public limited company is likely to be material to any person, it uses a name which may reasonably be expected to give the impression that it is a private company.

(3) A person guilty of an offence under subsections (1) or (2) and, if that person is a company, any officer of the company who is in default, is liable to a fine and, for continued contravention, to a daily default fine."[35]

Section 34 provides:

---

[29] *Re Sarflax Ltd.* [1979] Ch. 592, relative to the similarly worded offence contained in s.332 of the now repealed Companies Act 1948.

[30] *R. v. Kemp* [1988] Q.B. 645, CA, again relative to the similarly worded offence contained in the now repealed s.332 of the Companies Act 1948.

[31] *R. v. Grantham* [1984] 1 Q.B. 675, again relative to the similarly worded offence contained in the now repealed s.332 of the Companies Act 1948.

[32] See *R. v. Miles* [1992] Crim. L.R. 657, CA. The concept of art and part guilt may, however, ensnare, *e.g.*, a mere salesman, where he is fully aware of the truth.

[33] Maximum penalty (see Sched. 24) on indictment, a fine, and on summary conviction a fine of the statutory maximum.

[34] See s.26.

[35] Maximum penalties (see Sched. 24) are on summary conviction a fine of one-fifth of the statutory maximum and a daily default fine of one-fiftieth of the statutory maximum.

"If any person trades or carries on business under a name or title of which 'limited' [or its equivalent in Welsh][36], or any contraction or imitation of either of those words, is the last word, that person unless duly incorporated with limited liability[37], is liable to a fine and, for continued contravention, to a daily default fine."[38]

19.13 *Forged share warrants, etc.* Section 189 of the Companies Act 1985 provides:

"(1) If in Scotland a person—

(a) with intent to defraud, forges or alters, or offers, utters, disposes of, or puts off, knowing the same to be forged or altered, any share warrant or coupon, or any document purporting to be a share warrant or coupon, issued in pursuance of this Act; or

(b) by means of any such forged or altered share warrant, coupon, or document, purporting as aforesaid, demands or endeavours to obtain or receive any share or interest in any company under this Act, or to receive any dividend or money payable in respect thereof, knowing the warrant, coupon, or document to be forged or altered;

he is on conviction thereof liable to imprisonment or a fine or both.[39]

(2) If in Scotland a person without lawful authority or excuse (proof whereof lies on him)—

(a) engraves or makes on any plate, wood, stone, or other material, any share warrant or coupon purporting to be—

(i) a share warrant or coupon issued or made by any particular company in pursuance of this Act; or

(ii) a blank share warrant or coupon so issued or made; or

(iii) a part of such a share warrant or coupon; or

(b) uses any such plate, wood, stone, or other material, for the making or printing of any such share warrant or coupon, or of any such blank share warrant or coupon, or any part thereof respectively; or

(c) knowingly has in his custody or possession any such plate, wood, stone, or other material;

he is on conviction thereof liable to imprisonment or a fine or both."[40]

19.14 *Accounts.* Section 221 of the Companies Act 1985[41] requires a company to keep accounting records which are sufficient to disclose with reasonable accuracy the financial position of the company at any particular time and to enable balance sheets and profit and loss accounts to comply with the provisions of the Act. If a company fails to comply with this requirement, every officer of the company who is in default is guilty of an offence[42] unless he shows that he acted honestly and that, in the

---

[36] See s.26.

[37] "[I]ncorporated with limited liability" is to be construed as a reference to "registered as a company with limited liability" for the purposes of the Commonwealth Development Corporation (see Commonwealth Development Corporation Act 1999, Sched. 2, para. 8).

[38] For maximum penatlies, see n.35, *supra.*

[39] Maximum penalty (see Sched. 24) on indictment seven years' and a fine, or on summary conviction six months' and a fine of the statutory maximum.

[40] For maximum penalties, see n.39, *supra.*

[41] As substituted by the Companies Act 1989, s.2.

[42] See s.221(5).

circumstances in which the company's business was carried on, the default was excusable."[43]

Frauds in relation to investments

Investors are principally protected against fraud by the Financial **19.15** Services Act 1986.[44]

Financial Services Act 1986

Misleading statements. Section 47 of the Financial Services Act 1986 **19.16** provides:

"(1) Any person who—
   (a) makes a statement, promise or forecast which he knows to be misleading, false or deceptive or dishonestly conceals any material facts; or
   (b) recklessly makes (dishonestly or otherwise) a statement, promise or forecast which is misleading, false or deceptive,
is guilty of an offence if he makes the statement, promise or forecast or conceals the facts for the purpose of inducing, or is reckless as to whether it may induce, another person (whether or not the person to whom the statement, promise or forecast is made or from whom the facts are concealed) to enter or offer to enter into, an investment agreement or to exercise, or refrain from exercising, any rights conferred by an investment.
   (2) Any person who does any act or engages in any course of conduct which creates a false or misleading impression as to the market in or the price or value of any investments is guilty of an offence if he does so for the purpose of creating that impression and of thereby inducing another person to acquire, dispose of, subscribe for or underwrite those investments or to refrain from doing so or to exercise, or refrain from exercising, any rights conferred by those investments.
   (3) In proceedings brought against any person for an offence under subsection (2) above it shall be a defence for him to prove that he reasonably believed that his act or conduct would not create an impression that was false or misleading as to the matters mentioned in that subsection.
   (4) Subsection (1) above does not apply unless—
   (a) the statement, promise or forecast is made in or from, or the facts are concealed in or from, the United Kingdom;
   (b) the person on whom the inducement is intended to or may have effect is in the United Kingdom; or
   (c) the agreement is or would be entered into or the rights are or would be exercised in the United Kingdom.

   (5) Subsection (2) above does not apply unless—

---

[43] Maximum penalty (see Sched. 24, noting that the offence reference there has been altered from the original "s.223(1)" to "s.221(5)": see Companies Act 1989, Sched. 10, para. 24) on indictment two years' and a fine, or on summary conviction six months' and a fine of the statutory maximum.

[44] There are special provisions relating to insurance companies: see the Insurance Companies Act 1982, ss. 2, 14, 71 and 81. See also the Financial Services Act 1986, s.133 *et seq.*

(a) the act is done or the course of conduct is engaged in in the United Kingdom; or

(b) the false or misleading impression is created there.

(6) A person guilty of an offence under this section shall be liable—

(a) on conviction on indictment, to imprisonment for a term not exceeding seven years or to a fine or to both;

(b) on summary conviction, to imprisonment for a term not exceeding six months or to a fine not exceeding the statutory maximum or to both."

19.17 *Misleading statements — contracts of insurance.* In relation to contracts of insurance, section 133 of the Financial Services Act 1986 provides:

"(1) Any person who—

(a) makes a statement, promise or forecast which he knows to be misleading, false or deceptive or dishonestly conceals any material facts; or

(b) recklessly makes (dishonestly or otherwise) a statement, promise or forecast which is misleading, false or deceptive,

is guilty of an offence if he makes the statement, promise or forecast or conceals the facts for the purpose of inducing, or is reckless as to whether it may induce, another person (whether or not the person to whom the statement, promise of forecast is made or from whom the facts are concealed) to enter into or offer to enter into, or to refrain from entering or offering to enter into, a contract of insurance with an insurance company (not being an investment agreement) or to exercise or refrain from exercising, any rights conferred by such a contract.

(2) Subsection (1) above does not apply unless—

(a) the statement, promise or forecast is made in or from, or the facts are concealed in or from, the United Kingdom;

(b) the person on whom the inducement is intended to or may have effect is in the United Kingdom; or

(c) the contract is or would be entered into or the rights are or would be exercisable in the United Kingdom.

(3) A person guilty of an offence under this section shall be liable—

(a) on conviction on indictment, to imprisonment for a term not exceeding seven years or to a fine or to both;

(b) on summary conviction, to imprisonment for a term not exceeding six months or to a fine not exceeding the statutory maximum or to both."

Banking Act 1987

19.18   The Banking Act 1987 provides some measure of protection for persons who deposit money with deposit-taking businesses such as finance companies. Section 3 of the Act provides (*inter alia*):

"(1) Subject to section 4 [exempted persons and exempted transactions] . . ., no person shall in the United Kingdom accept a deposit[45] in the course of carrying on (there or elsewhere) a

---

[45] As defined in s.5. See para. 19.19, *infra*.

business which for the purposes of this Act is a deposit-taking business unless that person is an institution . . . authorised by the [Financial Services Authority][46] . . ."

It is an offence under subsection (2) for an unauthorised institution to accept a deposit in contravention of subsection (1).[47]

FRAUDULENT INDUCEMENT TO INVEST. Section 35 of the Banking Act **19.19** 1987 provides:

"(1) Any person who—
    (a) makes a statement, promise or forecast which he knows to be misleading, false of deceptive, or dishonestly conceals any material facts; or
    (b) recklessly makes (dishonestly or otherwise) a statement, promise or forecast which is misleading, false or deceptive,
is guilty of an offence if he makes the statement, promise or forecast or conceals the facts for the purpose of inducing, or is reckless as to whether it may induce, another person (whether or not the person to whom the statement, promise or forecast is made or from whom the facts are concealed)—
    (i) to make, or refrain from making, a deposit with him or any other person; or
    (ii) to enter, or refrain from entering, into an agreement for the purpose of making such a deposit.
(2) This section does not apply unless—
    (a) the statement, promise or forecast is made in or from, or the facts are concealed in or from, the United Kingdom or arrangements are made in or from the United Kingdom for the statement, promise or forecast to be made or the facts to be concealed;
    (b) the person on whom the inducement is intended to or may have effect is in the United Kingdom; or
    (c) the deposit is or would be made, or the agreement is or would be entered into, in the United Kingdom.
(3) A person guilty of an offence under this section shall be liable—
    (a) on conviction on indictment, to imprisonment for a term not exceeding seven years or to a fine or to both;
    (b) on summary conviction, to imprisonment for a term not exceeding six months or to a fine not exceeding the statutory maximum or to both.
(4) For the purposes of this section the definition of deposit in section 5 [*infra*] shall be treated as including any sum that would be otherwise excluded by subsection (3) of that section."
"Deposit", referred to above, is defined in section 5 of the Act, which provides:

---

[46] The original wording referred to "the Bank", meaning the Bank of England under s.1 of the 1987 Act. That section was amended by the Bank of England Act 1998, Sched. 5, para. 2, such that in most provisions of the 1987 Act, "the Bank" was replaced by "the Authority" — meaning the Financial Services Authority.

[47] Maximum penalty, on indictment two years' and a fine, or on summary conviction six months' and a fine of the statutory maximum.

"(1) Subject to the provisions of this section, in this Act 'deposit' means a sum of money [whether denominated in a currency or in ecus][48] paid on terms—

   (a) under which it will be repaid, with or without interest or a premium, and either on demand or at a time or in circumstances agreed by or on behalf of the person making the payment and the person receiving it; and

   (b) which are not referable to the provision of property or services or the giving of security;

and references in this Act to money deposited and to the making of a deposit shall be construed accordingly.

   (1A) . . .

   (2) For the purposes of subsection (1)(b) above, money is paid on terms which are referable to the provision of property or services or to the giving of security if, and only if—

   (a) it is paid by way of advance or part payment under a contract for the sale, hire or other provision of property or services, and is repayable only in the event that the property or services is not or are not in fact sold, hired or otherwise provided;

   (b) it is paid by way of security for the performance of a contract or by way of security in respect of loss which may result from the non-performance of a contract; or

   (c) without prejudice to paragraph (b) above, it is paid by way of security for the delivery up or return of any property, whether in a particular state of repair or otherwise.

   (3) Except so far as any provision of this Act otherwise provides, in this Act 'deposit' does not include—

   (a) a sum paid by the Bank[49] or an authorised institution;

   (b) a sum paid by a person for the time being specified in Schedule 2 to this Act;

   (c) a sum paid by a person, other than a person within paragraph (a) or (b) above, in the course of carrying on a business consisting wholly or mainly of lending money;

   (d) a sum which is paid by one company to another at a time when one is a subsidiary of the other or both are subsidiaries of another company or the same individual is a majority or principal shareholder controller of both of them; or

   (e) a sum which is paid by a person who, at the time when it is paid, is a close relative of the person receiving it or who is, or is a close relative of, a director, controller or manager of that person.

   (4) In the application of paragraph (e) of subsection (3) above to a sum paid by a partnership that paragraph shall have effect as if for the reference to the person paying the sum there were substituted a reference to each of the partners.

   (5) In subsection (3)(e) 'close relative,' in relation to any person means—

---

[48] Words within square brackets added by the Credit Institutions (Protection of Depositors) Regulations 1995 (S.I. 1995 No. 1442), reg. 45. These regulations also add subs.(1A) to s.5, in order to define what is meant by "ecu".

[49] This means the Bank of England — see s.106 (interpretation) of the 1987 Act, the definition offered there of "the Bank" not having been amended by the Bank of England Act 1998.

(a) his spouse;
(b) his children and step-children, his parents and step-parents, his brothers and sisters and step-brothers and step-sisters; and
(c) the spouse of any person within paragraph (b) above."

TRADE DESCRIPTIONS FRAUDS

The Trade Descriptions Act 1968 replaces the Merchandise Marks **19.20** Acts 1887 to 1953[50] and also contains provisions about statements of price and descriptions of services. Its principal effect is to penalise false statements made about goods or services supplied in the course of a trade or business.[51]

False descriptions of goods

Section 1(1) provides: **19.21**

"Any person who, in the course of a trade or business—

(a) applies a false trade description to any goods; or
(b) supplies or offers to supply any goods to which a false trade description is applied;

shall, subject to the provisions of this Act, be guilty of an offence."

"In the course of a trade or business". The Act does not apply to the **19.22** activities of a private members' club or to "domestic bodies or households".[52] It may, however, cover professional activities if carried on with a view to gain and profit.[53] It has been held that section 1 does not cover a description of goods made incidentally in the course of performing a service or giving advice in some matter affecting the goods; and it has been doubted whether acting as a nominee of the government in administering M.O.T. tests is a business.[54]

The concept of "trade or business" involves a degree of regularity such as to make the activity involved part of the normal practice of a business[55]: thus, a car hirer who regularly sold at trade prices his hire vehicles after a two year period of use (in order to fund the purchase of new vehicles) was considered to be acting in the course of trade or business in relation to such sales, although no profit was realised thereby and his business was principally one of hiring rather than selling cars.[56] On the other hand, the "need for some degree of regularity does not . . .

---

[50] See the preamble to the 1968 Act; *McNab v. Alexanders of Greenock*, 1971 S.L.T. 121; *Hall v. Wickens Motors* [1972] 1 W.L.R. 1418; *Cottee v. D. Seaton Ltd* [1972] 1 W.L.R. 1408.

[51] Maximum penalty for offences against ss. 1, 11–14 is a fine of the prescribed sum on summary conviction, a fine and two years' imprisonment on indictment.

[52] *John v. Matthews* [1970] 2 Q.B. 443, Lord Parker C.J. at 449A.

[53] *cf. R. v. Breeze* [1973] 1 W.L.R. 994; *infra*, para. 19.31.

[54] *Wycombe Marsh Garages v. Fowler* [1972] 1 W.L.R. 1156.

[55] *cf. Davies v. Sumner* [1984] 1 W.L.R. 1301, HL: no regular practice established in the case of a self-employed individual who sold the car he used for his courier services in part exchange for a new vehicle, but who had previously hired vehicles for the purposes of his business.

[56] *Havering L.B.C. v. Stevenson* [1970] 1 W.L.R. 1156.

involve that a one-off adventure in the nature of trade, carried through with a view to profit, would not fall within section 1(1) because such a transaction would itself constitute a trade . . . .[57] But the occasional sale of some worn out piece of shop equipment would not fall within the enactment."[58] It has also been held that a person who buys, works on and sells cars as a hobby does not sell them in the course of a trade or business.[59]

A dealer who makes a false statement regarding the worth of a car he is buying is guilty of an offence under the section.[60]

The section does not apply to statements made in answer to a customer's complaint made after the article has been supplied.[61] It may apply to a statement made after a sale in answer to a query made at the time of sale.[62]

It may also apply to a statement made by someone interested in a sale even if he is not himself a contracting party.[63]

19.23 *Application.* Section 4 of the Act provides:

"(1) A person applies a trade description to goods if he—
   (a) affixes or annexes it to or in any manner marks it on or incoporates it with—
      (i) the goods themselves, or
      (ii) anything in, on or with which the goods are supplied;
      or
   (b) places the goods in, on or with anything which the trade description has been affixed or annexed to, marked on or incorporated with, or places any such thing with the goods;
      or
   (c) uses the trade description in any manner likely to be taken as referring to the goods.

(2) An oral statement may amount to the use of a trade description.

(3) Where goods are supplied in pursuance of a request in which a trade description is used and the circumstances are such as to make it reasonable to infer that the goods are supplied as goods corresponding to that trade description, the person supplying the goods shall be deemed to have applied that trade description to the goods."

It was held in a case under the Merchandise Marks Acts that where a manufacturer sold an article with a certain description to a retailer who subsequently sold it to a customer the manufacturer could not be convicted of applying the description at the time of the sale by the retailer.[64]

---

[57] See *Elder v. Crowe*, 1996 S.C.C.R. 38.

[58] *Davies v. Sumner* [1984] 1 W.L.R. 1301, HL, Lord Keith of Kinkel at 1305G and 1306B. See also *Devlin v. Hall* [1990] R.T.R. 320; and *cf.* the civil case of *Buchannan-Jardine v. Hamilink and Anr*, 1981 S.L.T. (Notes) 60.

[59] See *Blakemore v. Bellamy* [1983] R.T.R. 303. See also I. Lloyd, "Consumer Protection: Sales 'in the course of a business' " (1984) 29 J.L.S. 147.

[60] *Fletcher v. Bugden* [1974] 1 W.L.R. 1056.

[61] *Hall v. Wickens Motors* [1972] 1 W.L.R. 1418.

[62] *R. v. Haesler* [1973] R.T.R. 486.

[63] *Fletcher v. Sledmore* [1973] R.T.R. 371, where the accused was a car repairer who sold the car to a dealer and then misdescribed it to the dealer's customer; *cf. Banbury v. Hounslow L.B.C.* [1971] R.T.R. 1.

[64] *Shulton (Great Britain) Ltd v. Slough B.C.* [1967] 2 Q.B. 471.

In *Norman v. Bennett*[65] it was said that "is applied" in section 1(1)(b) means "is applied at the time of supply or has been so applied in the course of negotiations leading to such supply."[66]

A person who sells a defective article such as a rusty car where he neither misdescribes the article nor knows of nor conceals the defect is not guilty of an offence. The Act is concerned with the misleading of buyers and not with the nature of the goods as such; but an alteration of the goods which causes them to tell a lie about themselves is a false description.[67]

The seller of a car applies to it the description of its mileage which appears on its odometer.[68]

The offence of applying a false trade description contrary to section 1(1)(a) is a continuing offence, such that the date of the offence may be any date when the goods had that description attached to them.[69]

ADVERTISEMENTS. Where a trade description is used in an advertise- **19.24** ment it will be taken to refer to all goods of the class in relation to which it is used, for the purpose of offences against section 1(1)(a), or, where the goods are supplied or offered by the publisher of the advertisement, for the purpose of offences against section 1(1)(b).[70] Section 5(3) provides:

> "In determining for the purposes of this section whether any goods are of a class to which a trade description used in an advertisement relates regard shall be had not only to the form and content of the advertisement but also to the time, place, manner and frequency of its publication and all other matters making it likely or unlikely that a person to whom the goods are supplied would think of the goods as belonging to the class in relation to which the trade description is used in the advertisement."

If A advertises "a lorry", and has only one lorry at the time, the advertisement is held to be a written description of that lorry at the time of the advertisement.[71]

Supply. This has been interpreted as occurring at the time of delivery.[72] **19.25** It seems, however, that an auctioneer does not "supply" the goods he auctions, for the purposes of section 1(1)(b), but if he misdescribes them he may be guilty of an offence under section 1(1)(a).[73]

---

[65] [1974] 1 W.L.R. 1229 at 1233A; see also *R. v. Hammertons Cars Ltd* [1976] 1 W.L.R. 1243.

[66] See also *Swithland Motors v. Peck* [1991] R.T.R. 322, at 328, where it is stated that: "The words 'is applied' do not describe the act. They merely describe a state of affairs."

[67] *Cottee v D. Seaton Ltd* [1972] 1 W.L.R. 1408. *cf. R. v. Ford Motor Co.* [1974] 1 W.L.R. 1220: the repair of minor damage caused during transit does not make it false to describe a car as "new". See also *Phillips v. Cycle and General Finance* [1977] 1 C.L. 24.

[68] *MacNab v. Alexanders of Greenock*, 1971 S.L.T. 121.

[69] *Hamilton v. H.M. Advocate*, 1996 S.C.C.R. 744.

[70] Section 5(1), (2).

[71] *Rees v. Munday* [1974] 1 W.L.R. 1284.

[72] *Rees v. Munday, supra.* See also *Normand v. D.M. Design Bedrooms Ltd*, 1996 S.C.C.R. 457, Sh.Ct, where it was held that it did not matter that at the time of a contract of sale the goods in question had yet to be manufactured, since once a trade description had been attached it was carried forward to the point of supply by delivery (unless the position was altered by actings of the parties during the interim period): it was further held that the offence under s.1(1)(b) was not affected by the existence of a contractual term which allowed the sellers to vary as they thought fit the specification of those goods.

[73] *Aitchison v. Reith and Anderson (Dingwall and Tain) Ltd*, 1974 S.L.T. 282.

19.26   OFFER TO SUPPLY. A person who exposes goods for supply, or has goods in his possession for supply, is deemed to offer to supply them.[74]

19.27   *Trade description.* Section 2 provides:

> "(1) A trade description is an indication, direct or indirect, and by whatever means given, of any of the following matters with respect to any goods or parts of goods, that is to say—
>
> (a) quantity, size or guage:
> (b) method of manufacture, production, processing or reconditioning;
> (c) composition[75];
> (d) fitness for purpose, strength, performance, behaviour or accuracy;
> (e) any physical characteristics not included in the preceding paragraphs;
> (f) testing by any person and results thereof[76];
> (g) approval by any person or conformity with a type approved by any person;
> (h) place or date of manufacture, production, processing or reconditioning;
> (i) person by whom manufactured, produced, processed or reconditioned;
> (j) other history, including previous ownership or use.[77]
>
> (2) The matters specified in subsection (1) of this section shall be taken—
>
> (a) in relation to any animal, to include sex, breed or cross, fertility and soundness;
> (b) in relation to any semen, to include the identity and characteristics of the animal from which it was taken and measure of dilution.
>
> (3) In this section 'quantity' includes length, width, height, area, volume, capacity, weight and number."

Descriptions which are governed by other legislation such as the Food Safety Act 1990, Medicines Act 1968, Agriculture Act 1970 and Plant Varieties Act 1997 are not included in the meaning of trade description under the 1968 Act.[78]

19.28   OPINION, ETC. The section has been said to apply only to statements of fact, and not to statements of intention or opinion.[79]

The words "extra value" appearing on a chocolate wrapper have been held not to be a trade description.[80]

---

[74] s.6; *cf. John v Matthews* [1970] 2 Q.B. 443, 448.

[75] Including the description of a package of goods, as where it is stated that "Torch supplied with cooker": *British Gas Corporation v. Lubbock* [1974] 1 W.L.R. 37.

[76] Including a statement that a test has been carried out: *Wycombe Marsh Garages v. Fowler* [1972] 1 W.L.R. 1156.

[77] Including the mileage of a car: *MacNab v. Alexanders of Greenock*, 1971 S.L.T. 121; *Tarleton Ltd v. Nattrass* [1973] 1 W.L.R. 1261.

[78] See the remaining subsections of s.2 of the Act and the Medicines Act 1968, Sched. 5, para. 16; Agriculture Act 1970, ss. 6(4), 87(3) and Sched. 5 (Pt X); Food Safety Act 1990, Sched. 3; Plant Varieties Act 1997, s.51. There are special provisions for trade marks: 1968 Act, s.34, as amended by the Trade Marks Act 1994.

[79] *Wycombe Marsh Garages v. Fowler* [1972] 1 W.L.R. 1156; *British Gas Corporation v. Lubbock* [1974] 1 W.L.R. 37.

[80] *Cadbury Ltd v. Halliday* [1975] 1 W.L.R. 649.

FALSITY. A trade description is or is deemed to be false in any of the **19.29** following cases[81]:

> "(1) A false trade description is a trade description which is false to a material degree.
>
> (2) A trade description which, though not false, is misleading, that is to say, likely to be taken for such an indication of any of the matters specified in section 2 of this Act as would be false to a material degree, shall be deemed to be a false trade description.
>
> (3) Anything which, though not a trade description, is likely to be taken for an indication of any of those matters and, as such an indication, would be false to a material degree, shall be deemed to be a false trade description.
>
> (4) A false indication, or anything likely to be taken as an indication which would be false, that any goods comply with a standard specified or recognised by any person or implied by the approval of any person shall be deemed to be a false trade description, if there is no such person or no standard so specified, recognised or implied."

It is therefore no answer to a charge that on its correct interpretation the description was true, if it was likely to be taken as meaning something else.[82]

It has been held in the sheriff court that "the concept of 'falsity' must surely import the idea of something deceptive or at least misleading being done in order to obtain an advantage" and that thus a glaring disconformity with contractual specification, which would immediately have been obvious to those supplied with the goods in question, was not an apt matter for prosecution under the Act.[83]

The meaning a description is likely to bear is normally a question of fact, and the trial court's decision will be overturned only if it is unreasonable.[84]

False indications as to price

Section 11 of the Act originally contained the provisions relevant to **19.30** this issue; but that section was repealed by the Consumer Protection Act 1987,[85] which substituted the following provisions contained in sections 20 to 24:

> "**20.**—(1) Subject to the following provisions of this Part [*i.e.*, Part III], a person shall be guilty of an offence if, in the course of any business of his, he gives (by any means whatever) to any consumers an indication which is misleading as to the price at which any goods,

---

[81] Section 3.

[82] *Robertson v. Dicicco* [1972] R.T.R. 431: "beautiful car" refers to performance as well as appearance; *cf. Doble v. David Greig Ltd* [1972] 1 W.L.R. 703.

[83] *Normand v. D.M. Design Bedrooms Ltd*, 1996 S.C.C.R. 457, Sh.Ct, 463A-B, following *Cavendish Woodhouse Ltd v. Wright* (1985) 149 J.P. 497.

[84] *Furniss v. Scholes* [1974] R.T.R. 133; *Kensington L.B.C. v. Riley* [1973] R.T.R. 122.

[85] See Sched. 5.

services, accommodation or facilities are available (whether generally or from particular persons).[86]

    (2) Subject as aforesaid, a person shall be guilty of an offence if—

    (a) in the course of any business of his, he has given an indication to any consumers which, after it was given, has become misleading as mentioned in subsection (1) above; and

    (b) some or all of those consumers might reasonably be expected to rely on the indication at a time after it has become misleading; and

    (c) he fails to take all such steps as are reasonable to prevent those consumers from relying on the indication.[86a]

    (3) For the purposes of this section it shall be immaterial—

    (a) whether the person who gives or gave the indication is or was acting on his own behalf or on behalf of another;

    (b) whether or not that person is the person, or included amongst the persons, from whom the goods, services, accommodation or facilities are available; and

    (c) whether the indication is or has become misleading in relation to all the consumers to whom it is or was given or only in relation to some of them.

    (4) A person guilty of an offence under subsection (1) or (2) above shall be liable—

    (a) on conviction on indictment, to a fine;

    (b) on summary conviction, to a fine not exceeding the statutory maximum.

    (5) No prosecution for an offence under subsection (1) or (2) above shall be brought after whichever is the earlier of the following, that is to say—

    (a) the end of the period of three years beginning with the day on which the offence was committed; and

    (b) the end of the period of one year beginning with the day on which the person bringing the prosecution discovered that the offence had been committed.

    (6) In this Part —

'consumer' —

    (a) in relation to any goods, means any person who might wish to be supplied with the goods for his own private use or consumption;

    (b) in relation to any services or facilities, means any person who might wish to be provided with the services or facilities otherwise than for the purposes of any business of his; and

    (c) in relation to any accommodation, means any person who might wish to occupy the accommodation otherwise than for the purposes of any business of his.

'price', in relation to any goods, services, accommodation or facilities, means—

---

[86] For an example of an alleged contravention of s.20(1), as also of s.21(1), see *Clydesdale Group plc. v. Normand*, 1993 S.C.C.R. 958, charge (10) of the complaint.

[86a] It has been held that the provisions of subs. (2) limit the offence to price indications which were misleading and relied upon at the time of purchase; consequently, refusal to honour a "price-refund promise" after the conclusion of a sale did not constitute an offence under s.20: *Link Stores Ltd v. Harrow L.B.C.* [2001] 1 W.L.R. 1479.

    (a) the aggregate of the sums required to be paid by a consumer
for or otherwise in respect of the supply of the goods or the
provision of the services, accommodation or facilities; or

    (b) except in section 21 below, any method which will be or has
been applied for the purpose of determining that aggregate.

21.—(1) For the purposes of section 20 above an indication given to
any consumers is misleading as to a price if what is conveyed by the
indication, or what those consumers might reasonably be expected
to infer from the indication or any omission from it, includes any of
the following, that is to say—

    (a) that the price is less than in fact it is;

    (b) that the applicability of the price does not depend on facts or
circumstances on which its applicability does in fact depend;

    (c) that the price covers matters in respect of which an additional
charge is in fact made;

    (d) that a person who in fact has no such expectation—

        (i) expects the price to be increased or reduced (whether
or not at a particular time or by a particular amount);
or

        (ii) expects the price, or the price as increased or reduced,
to be maintained (whether or not for a particular
period); or

    (e) that the facts or circumstances by reference to which the
consumers might reasonably be expected to judge the validity
of any relevant comparison made or implied by the indication
are not what in fact they are.

(2) For the purposes of section 20 above, an indication given to
any consumers is misleading as to a method of determining a price
if what is conveyed by the indication, or what those consumers
might reasonably be expected to infer from the indication or any
omission from it, includes any of the following, that is to say—

    (a) that the method is not what in fact it is;

    (b) that the applicability of the method does not depend on facts
or circumstances on which its applicability does in fact
depend;

    (c) that the method takes into account matters in respect of
which an additional charge will in fact be made;

    (d) that a person who in fact has no such expectation—

        (i) expects the method to be altered (whether or not at a
particular time or in a particular respect); or

        (ii) expects the method, or that method as altered, to
remain unaltered (whether or not for a particular
period); or

    (e) that the facts or circumstances by reference to which the
consumers might reasonably be expected to judge the validity
of any relevant comparison made or implied by the indication
are not what in fact they are.

(3) For the purposes of subsections (1)(e) and (2)(e) above, a
comparison is a relevant comparison in relation to a price or
method of determining a price if it is made between that price or
that method, or any price which has been or may be determined by
that method, and—

    (a) any price or value which is stated or implied to be, to have
been or to be likely to be attributed or attributable to the

goods, services, accommodation or facilities in question or to
any other goods, services, accommodation or facilities; or
(b) any method, or other method, which is stated or implied to
be, to have been or to be likely to be applied or applicable for
the determination of the price or value of the goods, services,
accommodation or facilities in question or of the price or
value of any other goods, services, accommodation or
facilities.

22.—(1) Subject to the following provisions of this section,
references in this Part to services or facilities are references to any
services or facilities[87] whatever including, in particular—
(a) the provision of credit or of banking or insurance services
and the provision of facilities incidental to the provision of
such services;
(b) the purchase or sale of foreign currency;
(c) the supply of electricity;
(d) the provision of a place, other than on a highway, for the
parking of a motor vehicle;
(e) the making of arrangements for a person to put or keep a
caravan on any land other than arrangements by virtue of
which that person may occupy the caravan as his only or main
residence.

(2) References in this Part to services shall not include references
to services provided to an employer under a contract of
employment.

(3) References in this Part to services or facilities shall not
include references to services or facilities which are provided by an
authorised person or appointed representative in the course of the
carrying on of an investment business.

(4) In relation to a service consisting in the purchase or sale of
foreign currency, references in this Part to the method by which the
price of the service is determined shall include references to the rate
of exchange.

(5) In this section—
'appointed representative', 'authorised person' and 'investment
business' have the same meanings as in the Financial Services Act
1986;
'caravan' has the same meaning as in the Caravan Sites and
Control of Development Act 1960;
'contract of employment' and 'employer' have the same meanings as in the Employment Rights Act 1996;
'credit' has the same meaning as in the Consumer Credit Act
1974.

23.—(1) Subject to subsection (2) below, references in this Part to
accommodation or facilities being available shall not include references to accommodation or facilities being available to be provided

---

[87] This section is to have effect as if the services or facilities mentioned there did not
include services or facilities provided by a European institution in the course of carrying on
home-regulated investment business in the United Kingdom: see the Banking Coordina-
tion (Second Council Directive) Regulations 1992 (S.I. 1992 No. 3218), Sched. 10,
para. 27; and as if these services or facilities did not include services or facilities provided
by a European investment firm in course of carrying on home-regulated investment
business in the United Kingdom: see the Investment Services Regulations 1995 (S.I. 1995
No. 3275), Sched. 10, para. 11.

by means of the creation or disposal of an interest in land except where—
  (a) the person who is to create or dispose of the interest will do so in the course of any business of his, and
  (b) the interest to be created or disposed of is a relevant interest in a new dwelling and is to be created or disposed of for the purpose of enabling that dwelling to be occupied as a residence, or one of the residences, of the person acquiring the interest.

(2) Subsection (1) above shall not prevent the application of any provision of this Part in relation to—
  (a) the supply of any goods as part of the same transaction as any creation or disposal of an interest in land; or
  (b) the provision of any services or facilities for the purposes of, or in connection with, any transaction for the creation or disposal of such an interest.

(3) In this section—
  'new dwelling' means any building or part of a building in Great Britain which—
  (a) has been constructed or adapted to be occupied as a residence; and
  (b) has not previously been so occupied or has been so occupied only with other premises or as more than one residence,

and includes any yard, garden, out-houses or appurtenances which belong to that building or part or are to be enjoyed with it;
  'relevant interest'—

  (a) in relation to a new dwelling in England and Wales, means the freehold estate in the dwelling or a leasehold interest in the dwelling for a term of years absolute of more than twenty-one years, not being a term of which twenty-one years or less remains unexpired;
  (b) in relation to a new dwelling in Scotland, means the [ownership][88] of the land comprising the dwelling, or a leasehold interest in the dwelling where twenty-one years or more remains unexpired.

24.—(1) In any proceedings against a person for an offence under subsection (1) or (2) of section 20 above in respect of any indication it shall be a defence for that person to show that his acts or omissions were authorised for the purposes of this subsection by regulations made under section 26 below.

(2)[89] In proceedings against a person for an offence under subsection (1) or (2) of section 20 above in respect of any indication published in a book, newspaper, magazine or film or in a programme included in a programme service (within the meaning of the Broadcasting Act 1990), it shall be a defence for that person to show that the indication was not contained in an advertisement.

(3) In proceedings against a person for an offence under subsection (1) or (2) of section 20 above in respect of an indication published in an advertisement it shall be a defence for that person to show that—

---

[88] Word substituted by the Abolition of Feudal Tenures etc. (Scotland) Act 2000 (asp 5), Sched. 12, para. 49.
[89] As amended by the Broadcasting Act 1990, Sched. 20, para. 48(a).

(a) he is a person who carries on a business of publishing or arranging for the publication of advertisements;

(b) he received the advertisements for publication in the ordinary course of that business; and

(c) at the time of publication he did not know and had no grounds for suspecting that the publication would involve the commission of the offence.

(4) In any proceedings against a person for an offence under subsection (1) of section 20 above in respect of any indication, it shall be a defence for that person to show that—

(a) the indication did not relate to the availability from him of any goods, services, accommodation or facilities;

(b) a price had been recommended to every person from whom the goods, services, accommodation or facilities were indicated as being available;

(c) the indication related to that price and was misleading as to the price only by reason of a failure by any person to follow the recommendation; and

(d) it was reasonable for the person who gave the indication to assume that the recommendation was for the most part being followed.

(5) The provisions of this section are without prejudice to the provisions of section 39 below.

(6)[90] In this section—

'advertisement' includes a catalogue, a circular and a price list."

False statements as to services

19.31   Section 14 provides:

"(1) It shall be an offence for any person in the course of any trade or business—

(a) to make a statement which he knows to be false; or

(b) recklessly to make a statement which is false;

as to any of the following matters, that is to say,—

(i) the provision in the course of any trade or business of any services, accommodation or facilities;

(ii) the nature of any services, accommodation or facilities provided in the course of any trade or business;

(iii) the time at which, manner in which or persons by whom any services, accommodation or facilities are so provided;

(iv) the examination, approval or evaluation by any person of any services, accommodation or facilities so provided; or

(v) the location or amenities of any accommodation so provided.

(2) For the purposes of this section—

(a) anything (whether or not a statement as to any of the matters specified in the preceding subsection) likely to be taken for such a statement as to any of those matters as would be false shall be deemed to be a false statement as to that matter; and

---

[90] As amended by the Broadcasting Act 1990, Sched. 20, para. 48(b), and Sched. 21.

(b) a statement made regardless of whether it is true or false shall be deemed to be made recklessly, whether or not the person making it had reasons for believing that it might be false.

(3) In relation to any services consisting of or including the application of any treatment or process or the carrying out of any repair, the matters specified in subsection (1) of this section shall be taken to include the effect of the treatment, process or repair.

(4) In this section 'false' means false to a material degree and 'services' does not include anything done under a contract of service."[91]

This section is not confined to pre-contractual statements which induce entry into a contract, but extends to such things as a description of what has been done by way of repair after the contract has been completed.[92] Nor is it limited to statements by a contracting party.[93] A description of oneself as, *e.g.* an architect is a statement as to the likely quality of the services offered, and so is covered by the section.[94]

"Facilities" has been held to include a guarantee of goods sold, as being the provision of the customer with the wherewithal to arrange for the repair of the goods.[95] But the term does not normally include the supply of goods, nor does section 14 apply to statements regarding price; where, therefore, a video recorder is offered "free" to anyone who buys a car, but in fact any customer taking advantage of the offer will receive a reduced trade-in allowance or discount, the offer is not a statement as to the provision of a facility, although it might be a false indication of price, contrary to section 20 of the Consumer Protection Act 1987.[96]

A person may be guilty of knowingly making a false statement if he knows of the falsity of the statement at the time it was read by the customer, even if he did not know of its falsity at the time it was made, as when a travel agent learns after the publication of a brochure that it contains a false statement.[97]

Promises and predictions. The main difficulty created by this section has **19.32** been that of distinguishing false statements as to existing facts (such as that a seat on an aircraft or a room in a hotel has been reserved[98]) which are criminal, and unfulfilled promises or predictions which are not.[99]

In *R. v. Sunair Holidays Ltd*[1] in a passage approved by the House of Lords in *British Airways Board v. Taylor*,[2] MacKenna J. said:

---

[91] Maximum penalty, on indictment two years' and a fine, and on summary conviction a fine of the prescribed sum: s.18.

[92] *Breed v. Cluett* [1970] 2 Q.B. 459.

[93] *Bambury v. Hounslow L.B.C.* [1971] R.T.R. 1.

[94] *R. v. Breeze* [1973] 1 W.L.R. 994.

[95] *Smith v. Dixons Ltd.*, 1986 S.C.C.R. 1, Sh.Ct.

[96] See *Newell v. Hicks* [1984] R.T.R. 135.

[97] See *Wings Ltd v. Ellis* [1985] A.C. 272, HL.

[98] *British Airways Board v. Taylor* [1976] 1 W.L.R. 13, HL.

[99] It does seem, however, that a false statement of intention to provide services may be covered by the Act, and if that is so there is no difference between false promises under the Act and false promises in the context of common law fraud, or for that matter between dishonest predictions in the respective contexts: see *R. v. Sunair Holidays Ltd* [1973] 1 W.L.R. 1105; *cf. supra*, paras 18.06, 18.10 *et seq.*

[1] *supra*, at 1109.

[2] *supra*.

"The section deals with 'statements' of which it can be said that they were, at the time when they were made, 'false'. This may be the case with a statement of fact, whether past or present. A statement that a fact exists now, or that it existed in the past, is either true or false at the time when it is made. But it is not the case with a promise or a prediction about the future. A prediction may come true or it may not. A promise to do something in the future may be kept or it may be broken. But neither the prediction nor the promise can be said to have been true or false at the time when it was made. We conclude that section 14 of the Trade Descriptions Act 1968 does not deal with forecasts or promises as such. We put in the qualifying words 'as such' for this reason. A promise or forecast may contain by implication a statement of present fact. The person who makes the promise may be implying that his present intention is to keep it or that he has at present the power to perform it. The person who makes the forecast may be implying that he now believes that his prediction will come true or that he has the means of bringing it to pass. Such implied statements of present intention, means or belief, when they are made, may well be within section 14 of the Act of 1968 and therefore punishable if they were false and were made knowingly or recklessly. But, if they are punishable, the offence is not the breaking of a promise or the failure to make a prediction come true. It is the making of a false statement of an existing fact, somebody's present state of mind or present means."

A travel agent is therefore not guilty of an offence if in January he honestly and without recklessness describes the expected state of a hotel in May, at least where the failure of the hotel to reach the expected standard is not his fault.[3] Whether a given statement is or is not one as to existing fact is a jury question.[4]

In *Herron v. Lunn Poly (Scotland) Ltd*[5] the travel agents had issued a brochure in October 1969 offering certain facilities for July holidays in a hotel due to open in April 1970. They continued to issue the brochure after March 1970 by which time the statements in it were false, since the hotel was uncompleted and the facilities unavailable.

They were convicted of a contravention of the section during the period April to July 1970. There was evidence that the brochure was shown to a client in May 1970, but the sheriff took the view that it was not necessary to show that anyone had read the brochure after April, provided it was issued and displayed.

In *Beckett v. Cohen*[6] an agreement to build a garage in 10 days, of the same kind "as existing garage" on a neighbour's land, was held to be merely a promise as to the future. Lord Widgery C.J. pointed out that where a person makes a promise as to what he will do, unrelated to an existing fact, nobody at the date of the promise can say that it is true or false, and added, "Parliament never intended or contemplated for a moment that the Act of 1968 should be used in this way, to make a criminal offence out of what is really a breach of warranty."[7]

---

[3] See also *Sunair Holidays v. Dodd* [1970] 1 W.L.R. 1037; *R. v. Clarksons Holidays Ltd* (1972) 57 Cr.App.R. 38.

[4] *R. v. Clarksons Holidays Ltd, supra; British Airways Board v. Taylor, supra.*

[5] 1972 S.L.T. (Sh.Ct.) 2.

[6] [1972] 1 W.L.R. 1593.

[7] At 1596–1597; appr'd. in *British Airways Board v. Taylor* [1976] 1 W.L.R. 13, 17E, 23D.

Other false descriptions

Section 12 makes false representations as to royal approvals and **19.33**
awards an offence. Section 13 penalises false representations by A that
any goods or services supplied by him are of a kind supplied "to any
person", presumably any named or otherwise identified person, such as
but not necessarily a well-known public figure.

Mens rea

The offences in sections 1, 12 and 13 of the Trades Descriptions Act **19.34**
1968, are offences of strict liability, subject only to the defences provided
in sections 24 and 25.[8] It follows, too, that subject to section 24 the
principal contracting party will be responsible for acts of supply and
application by his employees in the course of his trade or business.[9]

Section 14 requires either knowledge or recklessness, as well as being
subject to sections 24 and 25.

There has been some discussion as to the meaning of "recklessly" in
section 14(1)(b). In *Sunair Holidays v. Dodd*[10] Lord Parker C.J. said that
the statute imposed the common law definition as laid down in *Derry v.
Peek*,[11] which requires the absence of an honest belief in the truth of the
statement. But in *M.F.I. Warehouses v. Natrass*[12] the court took a wider
view of recklessness, holding that it did not require wilful blindness or
even dishonesty, but not making it clear what degree of inadvertence, if
any, would suffice. Lord Widgery C.J. said[13]:

> "I have much sympathy with the view of Salmon J. that where a
> criminal offence is being created and an element of the offence is
> 'recklessness', one should hesitate before accepting the view that
> anything less than '*Derry v. Peek* recklessness' will do. On the other
> hand, it is quite clear that this Act is designed for the protection of
> customers and it does not seem to me to be unreasonable to
> suppose that in creating such additional protection for customers
> Parliament was minded to place upon the advertiser a positive
> obligation to have regard to whether his advertisement was true or
> false.
>
> I have accordingly come to the conclusion that 'recklessly' in the
> context of the Act of 1968 does not involve dishonesty. Accordingly
> it is not necessary to prove that the statement was made with that
> degree of irresponsibility which is implied in the phrase 'careless
> whether it be true or false'. I think it suffices for present purposes if
> the prosecution can show that the advertiser did not have regard to
> the truth or falsity of his advertisement even though it cannot be
> shown that he was deliberately closing his eyes to the truth, or that
> he had any kind of dishonest mind."

---

[8] *MacNab v. Alexanders of Greenock*, 1971 S.L.T. 121; *Clode v. Barnes* [1974] 1 W.L.R.
544. The offences under s.20(1) and (2) of the Consumer Protection Act 1987 (see
para. 19.30, *supra*) are also of strict liability, subject to the defences set out in s.24 (see also
para 19.30, *supra*) and, in respect of s.20(1), s.39 (due diligence) of that Act.

[9] *ibid.*; s.20 makes the usual provision for the responsibility of the directors, etc., of a
company through whose consent, connivance or neglect an offence is committed by the
company.

[10] [1970] 1 W.L.R. 1037, at 1040H.

[11] (1889) 14 App.Cas. 337.

[12] [1973] 1 W.L.R. 307.

[13] At 313F.

In *Herron v. Lunn Poly (Scotland) Ltd*[14] (which was heard before *M.F.I. Warehouses v. Natrass*[15]) the sheriff accepted *Sunair Holidays v. Dodd*,[16] and applied *Derry v. Peek*,[17] and its Scottish equivalent *Lees v. Tod*,[18] and treated shutting one's eyes to the facts or purposely abstaining from enquiring into them as sufficient. He held that the accused were guilty of recklessness since they knew that the hotel they had advertised between April and July for July holidays was not ready by mid-May, and any inquiry would have shown that the facilities offered would not be ready for July holidaymakers. The sheriff also said of *Sunair Holidays v. Dodd*[19]:

> "There the charge was of recklessly making a statement as here, and his Lordship said: 'This was not the typical case of a brochure advertising accommodation which did not exist, having a swimming bath that was not constructed, or of hotel accommodation where a hotel was not opened.' The inference from these remarks is that a brochure containing such statements which were false, would be struck at by s.14(1)(b)."[20]

It may be noted that the earlier cases assume that section 14(1)(b) is restricted to statements which would constitute common law fraud, but it is submitted that there is no warrant for such an assumption, and that the whole tenor of the Act, including its definition of "false" in section 3 and its aim of consumer protection, supports an approach at least as wide as that in *M.F.I. Warehouses v. Natrass.*[21]

It has been held in England that the recklessness of an employee cannot be attributed to his employer so as to make the latter guilty of a contravention of the section.[22] This is probably also the case in Scotland, but is confused by the lack of clear decisions on the responsibility of employers.[23]

It may be doubted whether the Scots courts will follow the views expressed *obiter* by the House of Lords in *British Airways Board v. Taylor*[24] that it is a defence to a charge of recklessly making a false statement that one knew it was false.[25]

Defences

19.35 *Disclaimer.* A person may avoid responsibility for a false description, such as the mileage recorded on an odometer, by disclaiming any representation of its accuracy. To be effective the disclaimer must probably be made at the same place and time as the description: a disclaimer at a check-out point in a supermarket can probably not avoid responsibility for a statement on the article itself or on the shelves.[26] The

---

[14] 1972 S.L.T. (Sh.Ct.) 2.
[15] *supra.*
[16] *supra.*
[17] *supra.*
[18] (1882) 9 R. 807, 854.
[19] *supra.*
[20] 1972 S.L.T. (Sh.Ct.) 2, at 5, col. 1–2.
[21] *supra.*
[22] *Coupe v. Guyett* [1973] 1 W.L.R. 669.
[23] See Vol. I, paras 8.55 *et seq.*
[24] [1976] 1 W.L.R. 13. All the references to the interpretation of s.14 in this case are in a sense *obiter*, but the point discussed here was not argued at all.
[25] *cf.* Vol. I, para. 7.11.
[26] *Doble v. David Greig Ltd* [1972] 1 W.L.R. 703.

disclaimer must also be made prior to the supply, and must be as "bold, precise and compelling" as the description and as effectively brought to the customer's notice: a disclaimer "in the small print" is of no avail.[27] It may, however, be brought home where the buyer knew because of a prior course of dealing that the particular seller did not give any representations as to the matter in question.[28]

Statutory defences. Section 24(1) of the Trades Descriptions Act 1968 **19.36** provides:

"(1) In any proceedings for an offence under this Act it shall . . ., be a defence for the person charged to prove—

(a) that the commission of the offence was due to a mistake or to reliance on information supplied to him or to the act or default of another person, an accident or some other cause beyond his control; and

(b) that he took all reasonable precautions and exercised all due diligence to avoid the commission of such an offence by himself or any person under his control."[29]

"Mistake" in section 24(1) has been held to refer to a mistake by the person charged.[30]

There is a general duty on traders, including auctioneers, to make their own inquiries and not to rely on statements made to them by their suppliers.[31] It is no defence to a charge of applying a false description as to the mileage of a car to show reliance on the information contained on the odometer.[32]

It has been said that a defence of due diligence cannot succeed unless the precaution of making a disclaimer has been taken.[33] On the other hand, it has been pointed out that a disclaimer is not a defence in terms of section 24, but evidence that no representation was made.[34] It has also been suggested that to wind down an odometer to nought might be a way of avoiding making any representation as to mileage, since no one would be misled by it into believing it to be a true record.[35] Case authorities reveal, however, the very considerable difficulty in succeeding at all under a section 24 defence.[36]

Section 24(3) is limited to offences under section 1(1)(b), and applies where what is in issue is some defect in the goods rather than a representation about them. It provides a defence that the accused did

---

[27] *Norman v. Bennett* [1974] 1 W.L.R. 1229; *Zawadski v. Sleigh* [1975] R.T.R. 113; *R. v. Hammertons Cars Ltd* [1976] 1 W.L.R. 1243; *Amag Ltd v. Jessop*, 1989 S.C.C.R. 186.

[28] *Norman v. Bennett, supra.*

[29] See Vol. I, paras 8.68, 8.70.

[30] *Birkenhead and District Co-op Society v. Roberts* [1970] 1 W.L.R. 1497.

[31] *Herron v. Lunn Poly (Scotland) Ltd*, 1972 S.L.T. (Sh.Ct.) 2; *Aitchison v. Reith and Anderson (Dingwall and Tain) Ltd*, 1974 S.L.T. 282; *Sherrat v. Gerald's (The American Jewellers) Ltd* (1970) 68 L.G.R. 256; *Richmond-upon-Thames L.B.C. v. Motor Sales (Hounslow) Ltd* [1971] R.T.R. 116; *Wandsworth L.B.C. v. Bentley* [1980] R.T.R. 429.

[32] *MacNab v. Alexander's of Greenock*, 1971 S.L.T. 121; *Tarleton Ltd v. Nattrass* [1973] 1 W.L.R. 1261; *Simmons v. Potter* [1975] R.T.R. 347.

[33] *Simmons v. Potter* [1975] R.T.R. 347; *Crook v. Howells Garages (Newport) Ltd* [1980] R.T.R. 434.

[34] *Wandsworth L.B.C. v. Bentley* [1980] R.T.R. 429.

[35] *Lill Holdings v. White* [1979] R.T.R. 120, Lord Widgery C.J. at 123 J-K.

[36] See, *e.g.*, *Amag Ltd v. Jessop*, 1989 S.C.C.R. 186; *Ford v. Guild*, 1990 J.C. 55; *Costello v. Lowe*, 1990 J.C. 231.

not know and could not with reasonable diligence have ascertained that the goods did not conform to the description or that the description had been applied to the goods. It may not be available where the real defence is that the offence was due to the act or default of another person.[37]

19.37 ADVERTISEMENTS. It is a defence to a charge relating to an advertisement that the accused was in the business of advertising, and that having received the advertisement in the course of business he neither knew nor had reason to suspect that its publication would contravene the Act.[38]

19.38 PROCEDURE. Section 23 provides:

> "Where the commission by any person of an offence under this Act is due to the act or default of some other person that other person shall be guilty of the offence, and a person may be charged with and convicted of the offence by virtue of this section whether or not proceedings are taken against the first-mentioned person."

This section has been interpreted as applying to cases when the first mentioned person has no defence other than one under section 24(1). Where he has any other defence no offence has been committed and section 23 cannot come into play.[39]

Section 23 cannot be used where the offence was committed independently of anything done or omitted by the other person.[40] Where a defence under section 24(1) involves an allegation against another person or reliance on information supplied by another person, it cannot be advanced without leave of the court unless the Crown has been given, at least seven days before the trial, such information as the accused has as to the identity of that other person.[41]

It has been said that the act or default must be an unlawful one[42]; and it has been held that section 23 is not limited to persons acting in the course of a trade or business, such that a private individual who sells a car to a garage with what he knows to be a false odometer reading may be guilty of an offence in terms of the section when the garage subsequently sells the car to a customer.[43]

False information to officials

19.39 Section 29(1) penalises the wilful obstruction of officers acting in pursuance of the Act, and section 29(1)(c) specifically refers to failure without reasonable cause to give such an officer any assistance or information he may reasonably require.[44]

Section 29(2) makes it an offence to make a statement known to be false in giving information under section 29(1).[45]

---

[37] *Naish v. Gore* [1972] R.T.R. 102, O'Connor J. at 107.
[38] Section 25.
[39] *Coupe v. Guyett* [1973] 1 W.L.R. 669.
[40] *Tarleton Ltd v. Nattrass* [1973] 1 W.L.R. 1261.
[41] s.24(2). Relative to the Consumer Protection Act 1987, s.20(1) (see para. 19.30, *supra*), see s.39(2)(5) and s.40 of that Act for equivalent provisions.
[42] *Lill Holdings v. White* [1979] R.T.R. 120, Wien J. at 125 G-H.
[43] *Olgeirsson v. Kitching* [1986] 1 W.L.R. 304.
[44] Maximum penalty level 3 on the standard scale.
[45] Maximum penalty the prescribed sum on summary conviction, two years' imprisonment and a fine on indictment: s.18.

There is no obligation to give any information which might incriminate the giver.[46]

Customs offences

Section 50(6) of the Customs and Excise Management Act 1979 **19.40** penalises the importation of goods concealed in a container holding goods of a different description or which do not correspond with the entry made thereof on customs forms.[47]

Safety Helmets

Section 17 of the Road Traffic Act 1988 empowers the making of **19.41** regulations prescribing types of helmet recommended as offering protection to persons on motor-cycles, and section 17(2) makes it an offence to sell or offer for sale a helmet as a helmet affording such protection if it is not of an authorised type.[48] The section does not apply to helmets sold or offered for sale for export. "Helmet" includes any head-dress and the section applies to hiring as well as to sale.[49]

Patents and registered designs

Section 110 of the Patents Act 1977 provides: **19.42**

"(1) If a person falsely represents that anything disposed of by him for value is a patented product he shall, subject to the following provisions of this section, be liable on summary conviction to a fine not exceeding [level 4 on the standard scale].

(2) for the purposes of subsection (1) above a person who for value disposes of an article having stamped, engraved or impressed on it or otherwise applied to it the word 'patent' or anything expressing or implying that the article is a patented product, shall be taken to represent that the article is a patented product.

(3) Subsection (1) above does not apply where the representation is made in respect of a product after the patent for that product or, as the case may be, the process in question has expired or been revoked and before the end of a period which is reasonably sufficient to enable the accused to take steps to ensure that the representation is not made (or does not continue to be made).

(4) In proceedings for an offence under this section it shall be a defence for the accused to prove that he used due diligence to prevent the commission of the offence."

It is also an offence falsely to represent that a patent has been applied for in respect of an article disposed of for value where no application has been made, or where any application made has been withdrawn or refused: there is again a defence of due diligence.[50]

---

[46] Section 29(3).

[47] Maximum penalty three times the value of the goods, or a fine of level 3 on the standard scale, whichever is the greater.

[48] Maximum penalty level 3 on the standard scale; see Road Traffic Offenders Act 1988, Sched. 2, Pt I. See also Motor Cycles (Protective Helmets) Regulations 1998 (S.I. 1998 No. 1807) as amended by Motor Cycles (Protective Helmets) (Amendment) Regulations 2000 (S.I. 2000 No. 1488).

[49] Section 17(5).

[50] Patents Act 1977, s.111: maximum penalty, a fine of level 4 on the standard scale.

Section 112 of the 1977 Act provides:

"If any person uses on his place of business, or on any document issued by him, or otherwise the words 'Patent Office' or any other words suggesting that his place of business is, or is officially connected with, the Patent Office, he shall be liable on summary conviction to a fine not exceeding [level 5 on the standard scale]."

Section 35 of the Registered Designs Act 1949[51] provides:

"(1) If any person falsely represents that a design applied to any article sold by him is registered in respect of that article, he shall be liable on summary conviction to a fine not exceeding level 3 on the standard scale.

(2) If any person, after the right in a registered design has expired, marks any article to which the design has been applied with the word 'registered,' or any word or words implying that there is a subsisting right in the design under the Act, or causes any article to be so marked, he shall be liable on summary conviction to a fine not exceeding level 1 on the standard scale."

Trade marks

19.43   Section 95 of the Trade Marks Act 1994 provides:

"(1) It is an offence for a person—
    (a) falsely to represent that a mark is a registered trade mark, or
    (b) to make a false representation as to the goods or services for which a trade mark is registered,
knowing or having reason to believe that the representation is false.

(2) For the purposes of this section, the use in the United Kingdom in relation to a trade mark—
    (a) of the word 'registered', or
    (b) of any other word or symbol importing a reference (express or implied) to the registration,
shall be deemed to be a representation as to registration under this Act unless it is shown that the reference is to registration elsewhere than in the United Kingdom and that the trade mark is in fact so registered for the goods or services in question.

(3) A person guilty of an offence under this section is liable on summary conviction to a fine not exceeding level 3 on the standard scale."

Section 99 of that Act provides:

"(1) A person shall not without the authority of Her Majesty use in connection with any business the Royal arms (or arms so closely resembling the Royal arms as to be calculated to deceive) in such manner as to be calculated to lead to the belief that he is duly authorised to use the Royal arms.

(2) A person shall not without the authority of Her Majesty or of a member of the Royal family use in connection with any business any device, emblem or title in such a manner as to be calculated to lead to the belief that he is employed by, or supplies goods or services to, Her Majesty or that member of the Royal family.

---

[51] As amended by the Copyright, Designs and Patents Act 1988, Sched. 3, para. 24. (The amended text is set out in Sched. 4 of that Act.)

(3) A person who contravenes subsection (1) commits an offence and is liable on summary conviction to a fine not exceeding level 2 on the standard scale.

. . .

(5) Nothing in this section affects any right of the proprietor of a trade mark containing any such arms, device, emblem or title to use that trade mark."

Fertilisers and Feeding Stuffs

Part IV of the Agriculture Act 1970 deals with information contained **19.44** in the "statutory statement" supplicd along with fertilisers and feedingstuffs. Section 68(4)(b)(ii)[52] penalises the provision of particulars which are false to the prejudice of the purchaser.[53]

FOOD SAFETY FRAUDS[54]

Food Safety Act 1990

Food. "Food" under this Act includes drink, and articles and substances **19.45** of no nutritional value which are used for human consumption, chewing gum and like products and ingredients used to prepare food as so defined.[55] It does not include live animals or birds, or live fish which are not eaten while live, feeding stuffs for animals, birds or fish, controlled drugs, or medicines not specified by order.[56]

Sale. Section 14 of this Act provides: **19.46**

"(1) Any person who sells to the purchaser's prejudice any food which is not of the nature or substance or quality demanded by the purchaser shall be guilty of an offence.[57]

(2) In subsection (1) above the reference to sale shall be construed as a reference to sale for human consumption; and in proceedings under that subsection it shall not be a defence that the purchaser was not prejudiced because he bought for analysis or examination."[58]

"SELLS". The section applies not only to sales as defined by the Sale of **19.47** Goods Act 1979[59] but also to "the supply of food, otherwise than on sale, in the course of a business and . . . any other thing which is done with

---

[52] As substituted by the Agriculture Act 1970 Amendment Regulations 1982 (S.I. 1982 No. 980), reg. 5(2).

[53] Maximum penalty a fine of level 5 on the standard scale and three months' imprisonment.

[54] The sale of medical products is governed by the Medicines Act 1968, s.64.

[55] Section 1(1).

[56] Section 1(2).

[57] Maximum penalty on indictment two years' and a fine, and on summary conviction six months' and a fine of £20,000.

[58] "Nature", "substance" and "quality" do not represent true alternatives, and it is the practice to charge them cumulatively: *Miller v. French* [1948] C.L.Y. 4345. See J.S.C., "Food and Drugs Act Prosecutions", 1952 S.L.T. (News) 233.

[59] *cf. Thornley v. Tuckwell (Butchers) Ltd* [1964] Crim.L.R. 127; *Appleby v. Sleep* [1968] 1 W.L.R. 948 (Chemist dispensing N.H.S. prescription does not sell to the Health Service). It has been held that 'sale' includes a sale *to* a retailer, and sales by manufacturers or wholesalers: *Burrell v. T. Walls and Sons (Meat and Handy Foods) Ltd*, 1972 S.L.T. (Sh.Ct.) 27.

respect to food and is specified in an order made by the Secretary of State."[60] It does not apply, however, to the offering or exposing of food for sale.

19.48 PREJUDICE. A customer is prejudiced if, for example, he does not get what he asked and paid for.[61] Where, therefore, the customer is sold an inferior article, it is for the seller to show that he suffered no prejudice, or rather that the "reasonable customer" possessing no special knowledge would have suffered no prejudice.[62] It appears to be a defence for the seller to tell the buyer that he cannot vouch for the goods being of the quality demanded.[63] If the seller pleads that he displayed a notice indicating that the article was not of the nature, substance, or quality one would expect from such an article he must show both that the notice was seen by the particular customer,[64] and also that it was unambiguous in its terms, and was not one "which yields its meaning and intent only to study and reflection, which it is unreasonable to expect from the ordinary customers of a shop."[65]

In *Brander v. Kinnear*[66] whisky which was more than 35 per cent under proof (*i.e.* below the permitted standard) was sold in premises where a notice was displayed reading "All spirits sold . . . are diluted. No strength guaranteed", and the sale was held to be in contravention of the Act then in force,[67] on the ground that the notice was ambiguous and might be read to mean that although the whisky was diluted it was still within the statutory 35 per cent.[68]

In *Robertson v. McKay*[69] margarine to which a little butter had been added was sold as "Butter mixture". A customer entered the shop and asked for "1 lb. of that butter in the window", pointing to the mixture, and was sold the mixture. It was held that an offence had been committed as "butter mixture" would have conveyed to the ordinary customer that he was receiving a mixture of butters and not a mixture of butter and margarine.[70]

19.49 STANDARDS. It is a question of fact whether an article is of the nature, quality or substance demanded.[71] It is not an offence to sell an inferior quality of article provided the article sold is still entitled to the name under which it was demanded. In *Morton v. Green*[72] a dairyman sold two brands of cream at different prices, and he was charged with selling the cheaper brand in answer to a demand for "cream." It was held that as

---

[60] See s.2(1)(a),(b) as amended by the Food Standards Act 1999, Sched. 5, para. 2.

[61] *Souter v. Lean* (1903) 4 Adam 280, Lord Trayner at 283. *Cf. Preston v. Grant* [1925] 1 K.B. 177, Lord Hewart C.J. at 181.

[62] *Preston v. Grant, supra.*

[63] *Frew v. Gunning* (1901) 3 Adam 339, where the relevant disclaimer was made at the point of sale. It has been held, however, that *Frew v. Gunning* is a very special case, and that where a sale is made in error and the error later brought to the attention of the buyer, the seller's responsibility is not affected: *Skinner v. MacLean*, 1979 S.L.T. (Notes) 35.

[64] *Preston v. Grant, supra; Patterson v. Findlay*, 1925 J.C. 53.

[65] *Brander v Kinnear*, 1923 J.C. 42.

[66] 1923 J.C. 42

[67] Sale of Food and Drugs Act 1875, s.6.

[68] *cf. Patterson v Findlay*, 1925 J.C. 53; *Rodbourn v. Hudson* [1925] 1 K.B. 225.

[69] 1924 J.C. 31.

[70] Lord Cullen at 36, Lord Sands at 37.

[71] *Wilson and McPhee v. Wilson* (1903) 4 Adam 310, where expert evidence was led on whether the liquor provided in answer to a request for brandy was truly brandy.

[72] (1881) 4 Couper 457.

the cheaper brand was pure although inferior no offence had been committed. The mere fact that an article fails to conform to statutory regulations as to its composition does not mean that it is not of the nature and quality demanded.[73] In *MacLean v. G. and W. Riddell*[74] the accused sold mince which contained preservative at a time when preservatives were prohibited by statutory regulations. It was held that as the addition of the preservative did not render the mince harmful, affect its value or taste, or prevent it being still mince as demanded by the purchaser, there had been no contravention of the then relevant legislation[75] although there would have been a contravention of the regulations.

Labels and advertisements. Section 15 of the Act provides: **19.50**

"(1) Any person who gives with any food sold by him, or displays with any food exposed by him for sale[76] or in his possession for the purpose of sale, a label, whether or not attached to or printed on the wrapper or container, which—
(a) falsely describes the food; or
(b) is likely to mislead as to the nature or substance or quality of the food, shall be guilty of an offence.

(2) Any person who publishes, or is a party to the publication of, an advertisement (not being such a label given or displayed by him as mentioned in subsection (1) above) which—
(a) falsely describes the food; or
(b) is likely to mislead as to the nature or substance or quality of any food,
shall be guilty of an offence.

(3) Any person who sells, or offers or exposes for sale, or has in his possession for the purpose of sale, any food the presentation of which is likely to mislead as to the nature or substance or quality of the food shall be guilty of an offence.

(4) In proceedings for an offence under subsection (1) or (2) above, the fact that a label or advertisement in respect of which the offence is alleged to have been committed contained an accurate statement of the composition of the food shall not preclude the court from finding that the offence was committed.

(5) In this section references to sale shall be construed as references to sale for human consumption."[77]

---

[73] See also *Goldup v. John Manson Ltd* [1982] Q.B. 161, where it was held that the court is not obliged to accept uncontradicted expert evidence as to what the standard should be in relation to the fat content of beef. It is for the prosecution to show that the customer was demanding mince containing signifcantly less fat than was supplied: the court referred to and applied *Morton v. Green*, *supra*.

[74] 1960 S.L.T. (Sh.Ct.) 35.

[75] Food and Drugs (Scotland) Act 1956, s.2.

[76] Exposure for sale includes the offering of food as a prize in connection with any entertainment: s.2(2).

[77] The penalty for a contravention of this section is the same as that for a contravention of s.14.

General defence

19.51   A general defence of due diligence[78] is enacted by section 21,[79] which provides:

> "(1) In any proceedings for an offence under any of the preceeding provisions of this Part (in this section referred to as "the relevant provision"), it shall, subject to subsection (5)[80] below, be a defence for the person charged to prove that he took all reasonable precautions and exercised all due diligence to avoid the commission of the offence by himself or by a person under his control.
>
> (2) Without prejudice to the generality of subsection (1) above, a person charged with an offence under section . . . 14 or 15 above who neither—
>
> (a) prepared the food in respect of which the offence is alleged to have been committed; nor
>
> (b) imported it into Great Britain,
>
> shall be taken to have established the defence provided by that subsection if he satisfies the requirements of subsection (3) or (4) below.
>
> (3) A person satisfies the requirements of this subsection if he proves—
>
> (a) that the commission of the offence was due to an act or default of another person who was not under his control, or to reliance on information supplied by such a person;
>
> (b) that he carried out all such checks of the food in question as were reasonable in all the circumstances, or that it was reasonable in all the circumstances for him to rely on checks carried out by the person who supplied the food to him; and
>
> (c) that he did not know and had no reason to suspect at the time of the commission of the alleged offence that his act or omission would amount to an offence under the relevant provision.
>
> (4) A person satisfies the requirements of this subsection if he proves—
>
> (a) that the commission of the offence was due to an act or default of another person who was not under his control, or to reliance on information supplied by such a person;
>
> (b) that the sale or intended sale of which the alleged offence consisted was not a sale or intended sale under his name or mark; and
>
> (c) that he did not know, and could not reasonably have been expected to know, at the time of the commission of the alleged offence that his act or omission would amount to an offence under the relevant provision. . . ."

---

[78] For an example of an unsuccessful defence of this nature, argued in reply to a charge under the now repealed s.8(1)(a) of the Food and Drugs (Scotland) Act 1956, see *Alex Munro (Butchers) Ltd v. Carmichael*, 1990 S.C.C.R. 275.

[79] *cf.* the defence provided under the Medicines Act 1968, s.121.

[80] Subsection (5) refers to procedural matters, *i.e.* where the defence provided by s.21(1) involves the act or default of or information supplied by another person, the accused cannot rely on that defence without leave of the court unless he has given prior written notice thereof to the prosecutor giving such information as he has of the identity of the other person.

WEIGHTS AND MEASURES FRAUDS

Weights and Measures Act 1985

The law regarding weights and measures is consolidated in the **19.52** Weights and Measures Act 1985 which replaces a number of earlier statutes on the subject and provides a uniform code for the whole country.[81]

Units of weight and measure. The Act sets out and defines the weights **19.53** and measures which may be lawfully used for trade and with some minor exceptions prohibits the use for trade of any unit of weight or measure, or the use or possession for use for trade of any weight or measure, not included in the Schedules[82] to the Act.[83]

Use for trade. Section 7 provides: **19.54**

"(1) In this Act 'use for trade' means, subject to subsection (3) below, use in Great Britain in connection with, or with a view to, a transaction[84] falling within subsection (2) below where—
   (a) the transaction is by reference to quantity or is a transaction for the purposes of which there is made or implied a statement of the quantity of goods to which the transaction relates, and
   (b) the use is for the purpose of the determination or statement of that quantity.
(2) A transaction falls within this subsection if it is a transaction for—
   (a) the transferring or rendering of money or money's worth in consideration of money or money's worth, or
   (b) the making of a payment in respect of any toll or duty.
(3) Use for trade does not include use in a case where—
   (a) the determination or statement is a determination or statement of the quantity of goods required for dispatch to a destination outside Great Britain and any designated country,[85] and
   (b) the transaction is not a sale by retail, and

---

[81] The Act is long and complicated and what follows in the text is only a selective summary of its provisions.

[82] See s.1 and Scheds 1–3 of the 1985 Act. The Act has been much amended by regulations and orders, particularly pursuant to E.U. directives on metrication: see, *e.g.*, the Weights and Measures Act 1985 (Metrication) (Amendment) Order 1994 (S.I. 1994 No. 2866).

[83] Section 8(4). Maximum penalty a fine of level 3 on the standard scale and forfeiture: s.84(1).

[84] This may well overrule such cases as *Dickie v. White* (1878) 4 Couper 113, which held that it was not unlawful for a baker to use non-standard weights to determine the amount of ingredients for his wares. It will however still be lawful to have non-standard weights and measures in one's possession for one's private purposes: *Hood v. Malcolm* (1887) 1 White 491, but the onus of proof lies on the accused where he is a trader or the goods are on trading premises: s.7(5).

[85] These are such of Northern Ireland, the Channel Islands or the Isle of Man as the Secretary of State may designate at any time: s.94(2) of the 1985 Act.

(c) no transfer or rendering of money or money's worth is involved other than the passing of the title to the goods and the consideration for them.

(4) The following equipment, that is to say—

(a) any weighing or measuring equipment which is made available in Great Britain for use by the public, whether on payment or otherwise, and

(b) any equipment which is used in Great Britain for the grading by reference to their weight, for the purposes of trading transactions by reference to that grading, of hens' eggs in shell which are intended for human consumption,

shall be treated for the purposes of this Part of this Act as weighing or measuring equipment in use for trade, whether or not it would apart from this subsection be so treated.[86]

(5) Where any weighing or measuring equipment is found in the possession of any person carrying on trade or on any premises which are used for trade, that person or, as the case may be, the occupier of those premises shall be deemed for the purposes of this Act, unless the contrary is proved, to have that equipment in his possession for use for trade."

19.55 *Stamping.* It is unlawful to use for trade any weighing or measuring equipment of a prescribed class, unless it has been passed by an inspector or approved verifier and bears a stamp showing that it has been so passed.[87]

19.56 *Forging, etc.* Section 16[88] provides:

"(1) Subject to subsection (2) below, any person who, in the case of any weighing or measuring equipment used or intended to be used for trade—

(a) not being an inspector or approved verifier or a person acting under the instructions of an insector or approved verifier, marks in any manner any plug or seal used or designed for use for the reception of a stamp,

(b) forges, counterfeits or, except as permitted by or under this Act, in any way alters or defaces any stamp,

(c) removes any stamp and inserts it into any other such equipment,

(d) makes any alteration in the equipment after it has been stamped such as to make it false or unjust, or

(e) severs or otherwise tampers with any wire, cord or other thing by means of which a stamp is attached to the equipment,

shall be guilty of an offence.[89]

---

[86] The use of false scales in connection with customs or excise is penalised by s.169 of the Customs and Excise Management Act 1979 — *infra*, para. 38.11.

[87] Section 11(2); see the Deregulation (Weights and Measures) Order 1999 (S.I. 1999 No. 503), arts 2 and 3, which amend s.11 and insert new ss. 11A and 11B. Section 11(3) creates the offence for which the maximum penalty is a fine of level 3 on the standard scale: s.84(1), (2).

[88] As modified by the Deregulation (Weights and Measures) Order 1999 (S.I. 1999 No. 503), art. 2.

[89] Maximum penalty on summary conviction a fine of level 5 on the standard scale: s.84(6).

(2) Paragraphs (a) and (b) of subsection (1) above shall not apply to the destruction or obliteration of any stamp, plug or seal, and paragraph (e) of that subsection shall not apply to anything done, in the course of the adjustment or repair of weighing or measuring equipment by, or by the duly authorised agent of, a person who is a manufacturer of, or regularly engaged in the business of repairing, such equipment."

It is also an offence, punishable as above, to use for trade, sell, or expose or offer for sale any equipment bearing a stamp which has been unlawfully made or treated as above or which is false or unjust as a result of an alteration made after stamping.[90]

Possession and use of false weights. Section 17 provides: **19.57**

"(1) If any person uses for trade, or has in his possession for use for trade, any weighing or measuring equipment which is false or unjust he shall be guilty of an offence[91] and the equipment shall be liable to be forfeited.

(2) Without prejudice to the liability of any equipment to be forfeited, it shall be a defence for any person charged with an offence under subsection (1) of this section in respect of the use for trade of any equipment to show—

(a) that he used the equipment only in the course of his employment by some other person; and

(b) that he neither knew, nor might reasonably have been expected to know, nor had any reason to suspect, the equipment to be false or unjust.

(3) If any fraud is committed in the using of any weighing or measuring equipment for trade, the person committing the fraud and any other person party to it shall be guilty of an offence and the equipment shall be liable to be forfeited."[92]

The offence of possession under this section is one of strict responsibility, but can be committed only by a person who has actual control of the weights; the mere fact that a licensee is the only person who can lawfully use liquor measures in a sale does not make him their possessor,[93] although if short measure is actually sold he is liable as the seller.[94]

Sales by weight or measure

Authorised quantities, etc. Certain of the Schedules to the Act require **19.58** particular classes of goods to be sold only in particular quantities or only in quantities expressed in a particular manner, and it is an offence to sell, offer, or expose for sale, or agree to sell, such goods on one's own behalf or on behalf of another, or to cause or suffer any other person to do so on one's own behalf, otherwise than in that quantity or in a quantity expressed in that manner.[95]

---

[90] Section 16(3): maximum penalty as for s.16(1).

[91] Maximum penalty a fine of level 5 on the standard scale: s.84(6).

[92] Maximum penalty six months' and a fine of level 5 on the standard scale: s.84(4).

[93] *Bellerby v. Barle* [1983] 2 A.C. 101.

[94] *MacDonald v. Smith*, 1979 J.C. 55.

[95] Section 25(1). The maximum penalty for all the offences connected with the sale of goods is a fine of level 5 on the standard scale: s.84(6). On the question of the "head" on a glass of beer, see *Dean v. Scottish and Newcastle Breweries*, 1977 J.C. 90; but *cf.* s.43 of the 1985 Act.

19.59 *Pre-packed goods.* The Act requires certain goods when pre-packed[96] to be made up for sale or for delivery after sale only in particular quantities, or in a container marked[97] with particular information, and section 25(2) makes it an offence to sell or have in possession for sale,[98] or agree to sell or cause or suffer any other person to have for sale or delivery after sale, or agree to sell on his behalf, any such goods unless they are packed or made up as required by the relevant Schedule. It is also an offence for anyone to have goods which do not comply with these requirements in his possession for delivery after sale unless he has them in the course of carrying goods for reward.

19.60 *Failure to give information.* Where the Act requires the quantity of the goods sold as expressed in a particular manner to be made known to the buyer the person by whom and anyone on whose behalf the goods are sold is guilty of an offence if the quantity is not so made known.[99] It is also an offence to sell or offer or expose for sale goods in a vending machine in breach of any requirements made by the Act in relation to such sales.[1]

19.61 *Written information.* Section 26 provides that unless a statement of the quantity of any goods sold expressed in the manner required by the Act is made known to the buyer at the seller's premises and the goods are delivered at these premises on the same occasion as, and at or after the time of the giving of, the information, there must be delivered to the consignee a statement of quantity in writing at or before delivery of the goods. Failure to do so renders the seller and any person on whose behalf the goods are sold guilty of an offence.[2]

This section applies to any sale of goods:

> "(a) which is required by or under this Part of this Act to be a sale by quantity expressed in a particular manner;
> (b) in the case of which the quantity of the goods sold expressed in a particular manner is so required to be made known to the buyer at or before a particular time;
> (c) which, by being a sale by retail not falling within paragraph (a) or (b) above, is, or purports to be, a sale by quantity expressed in a particular manner other than by number."[3]

The section does not apply to sales (other than retail sales) where there is an agreement with the buyer for determining the quantity of goods sold after delivery.[4] Nor does it apply to the sale of liquids by capacity if the quantity is measured in the buyer's presence at the time of delivery elsewhere than at the seller's premises.[5]

The Secretary of State is given power to grant exemptions from the requirements of section 26, and in the meantime the section does not apply to a number of sales, including certain retail sales of fuel from

---

[96] See *Lucas v. Rushby* [1966] 1 W.L.R. 814.
[97] "Mark" in the Act includes a label: s.94(1).
[98] See *Ben Worsley Ltd v. Harvey* [1967] 1 W.L.R. 889.
[99] Section 25(4).
[1] Section 25(5).
[2] Section 26(2), (3).
[3] Section 26(1).
[4] Section 26(5).
[5] Section 26(6).

vehicles, sales by retail of bread, sales of intoxicating liquor for consumption on the seller's premises, and sales by vending machines.[6]

Short weight. Section 28(1) provides: **19.62**

"Subject to sections 33 to 37 below, any person who, in selling or purporting to sell any goods by weight or other measurement or by number, delivers or causes to be delivered to the buyer— (a) a lesser quantity than that purported to be sold, or

(b) a lesser quantity than corresponds with the price charged, shall be guilty of an offence."

A licensee is responsible for such a sale by a barman even if they are fellow employees.[7]

Marked quantities. Where goods which are pre-packed in a container **19.63** with a statement of quantity are deficient in quantity any person having them in his possession for sale, and (if it is shown that the deficiency cannot be accounted for by anything occurring after the goods have been sold by retail and delivered) any person by whom or on whose behalf they have been sold or agreed to be sold at any time when they were pre-packed in the container, is guilty of an offence.[8] In the case of goods which are not pre-packed but are made or made up for sale or delivery after sale in a container with a statement of quantity, or have a written statement of quantity associated with them in connection with a sale or agreement to sell, and which are deficient in quantity, the person by whom or on whose behalf they are sold or agreed to be sold is guilty of an offence if it is shown that the deficiency cannot be accounted for by anything occurring after delivery to the buyer.[9] It is a defence for anyone charged under these provisions to show that the deficiency arose after the goods were packed or made up, and the container marked or statement of quantity completed, as the case may be, "and was attributable wholly to factors for which reasonable allowance was made" in stating the quantity or making up the goods.[10]

These provisions apply where the quantity is stated as being the quantity at a time earlier than the time of the alleged offence, or with any other qualification, unless the goods are not of a type required under the Act to be sold with information as to their quantity.[11] Where, however, goods are sold in a marked container, then if it was marked in Great Britain the person who marked it, or on whose behalf it was marked, and in other cases the person by whom or on whose behalf the goods were first sold in Great Britain, is guilty of an offence if the deficiency is greater than can be reasonably justified on the ground justifying the qualification.[12] In the case of goods sold with an associated statement of quantity the seller is not entitled to rely on any qualification if the deficiency is greater than can be reasonably justified on the ground justifying the qualification.[13]

---

[6] Section 27.
[7] *MacDonald v. Smith*, 1979 J.C. 55.
[8] Section 30(1); see *F.W. Woolworth & Co. Ltd v. Gray* [1970] 1 W.L.R. 764; *Paterson v. Ross Poultry Ltd*, 1974 S.L.T. (Sh.Ct.) 38.
[9] Section 30(2).
[10] Section 35(2).
[11] Section 30(3).
[12] Section 30(4)(a).
[13] Section 30(4)(b).

19.64 *False statements of weight.* Section 29 contains the following provisions regarding false statements:

> "(2) Subject to sections 33 to 37 below, any person[14] who—
>   (a) on or in connection with the sale or purchase of any goods,
>   (b) in exposing or offering any goods for sale,
>   (c) in purporting to make known to the buyer the quantity of any goods sold, or
>   (d) in offering to purchase any goods,
> makes any misrepresentation whether oral or otherwise as to the quantity of the goods, or does any other act calculated to mislead a person buying or selling the goods as to the quantity of the goods, shall be guilty of an offence."

It will be noted that this section applies equally to buyers and sellers.

Where a customer asks for a certain quantity there is an implied representation that what he is given corresponds to the quantity asked for. In *Galbraith's Stores Ltd v. McIntyre*[15] the customer asked for a quarter pound of butter and was given a packet on which was printed "NOT sold by weight"; it was held that there was nonetheless an implied representation that the packet weighed a quarter pound.

> "(7) Without prejudice to section 30(2) to (4) above,[16] if in the case of any goods required by or under this Part of this Act to have associated with them a document containing particular statements, that document is found to contain any such statement which is materially incorrect, any person who, knowing or having reasonable cause to suspect that statement to be materially incorrect, inserted it or caused it to be inserted in the document, or used the document for the purposes of this Part of this Act while that statement was contained in the document, shall be guilty of an offence."

All statements as to weight are deemed to be statements as to net weight unless the contrary is expressed.[17]

19.65 *General exemptions.* Sections 28 and 29 do not apply to goods exempted by the Department of Trade at any time, and the Act exempts goods intended for the Forces, and goods in the case of which written notice is given to the seller that they are bought for dispatch outside Great Britain and any designated country,[18] or for use as stores within the meaning of the Customs and Excise Management Act 1979 in a ship or aircraft with an eventual destination outside the United Kingdom or Isle of Man.[19]

19.66 *General defences.* The following defences are available in proceedings for offences under Part IV of the Act, which deals with transactions in goods, *i.e.* for any offence under sections 25, 26 and 28 to 30 inclusive.

19.67 (1) *Warranty.* Where the offence relates to the quantity or pre-packing of any goods it is a defence for the accused to prove that he bought the goods from someone else as being of the quantity represented by the

---

[14] Whether or not he is a contracting party: *Collett v. C.W.S.* [1970] 1 W.L.R. 250.
[15] (1912) 6 Adam 641.
[16] *supra.*
[17] Section 28(2), which also applies to ss. 29, 30 and 31. See *McIntyre and Son v. Laird*, 1943 J.C. 96; *Paterson v. Ross Poultry Ltd.*, 1974 S.L.T. (Sh.Ct.) 38.
[18] These are such of Northern Ireland, the Channel Islands or the Isle of Man as the Secretary of State may designate at any time: s.94(2) of the 1985 Act.
[19] Section 24(2)(a), and (b)(i) and (ii).

accused or marked on any container or stated in any document to which the proceedings relate or as conforming with the statements marked on the container to which the proceedings relate, or with the requirements of the Act in relation to pre-packing, and that he had a written warranty to that effect. He must also show that at the time of the offence he had no reason to believe the warranty inaccurate, that he in fact believed in its accuracy, and, where the warranty was given by someone resident outside Great Britain and any designated country,[20] that he himself took reasonable steps to check its accuracy. Where the proceedings relate to quantity, he must also show that he took reasonable steps to see that the quantity remained unchanged while the goods were in his possession, and in all proceedings he must show that apart from any change in quantity the goods were in the same state as when he bought them.[21] Where a servant is charged he can plead this defence, provided the other conditions set out were fulfilled by or in relation to his employer and he personally had no reason to believe the warranty false.[22]

FALSE WARRANTIES. It is an offence for a person charged in any **19.68** proceedings under Part IV of the Act wilfully to attribute to any goods a warranty given in relation to any other goods.[23] It is also an offence for a seller to give a false warranty in respect of any goods in respect of which warranty might be pleaded under section 33, unless he proves he took all reasonable steps to ensure the statements were accurate and would continue to be so at all relevant times.[24]

MEANING OF WARRANTY. Any statement with respect to any goods **19.69** which is contained in any document required by Part IV of the Act to be associated with the goods or in any invoice, or where goods are made up in a container for sale or delivery any statement marked on the container, is deemed a written warranty of the accuracy of the statement.[25]

(2) *Due diligence*. Section 34 provides: **19.70**

"(1) In any proceedings for an offence under this Part of this Act or any instrument made under this Part, it shall be a defence for the person charged to prove that he took all reasonable precautions and exercised all due diligence to avoid the commission of the offence.[26]

(2) If in any case the defence provided by subsection (1) above involves an allegation that the commission of the offence in question was due to the act or default of another person or due to reliance on information supplied by another person, the person charged shall not, without the leave of the court, be entitled to rely on the defence unless, before the beginning of the period of seven

---

[20] For instance, such of Northern Ireland, the Channel Islands or the Isle of Man as the Secretary of State may designate at any time.

[21] Section 33(1); *F W Woolworth & Co. Ltd v. Gray* [1970] 1 W.L.R. 764. Notice of the warranty must be given to the prosecutor and the person who gave the warranty three days before the hearing: s.33(2).

[22] Section 33(3).

[23] Section 33(5).

[24] Section 33(6). The maximum penalties are the same as in other offences in connection with sale — *supra*.

[25] Section 33(8).

[26] See Vol. I, paras 8.68–8.70.

days ending with the date when the hearing of the charge began, he
served on the prosecutor a notice giving such information identifying or assisting in the identification of the other person as was then
in his possession."[27]

In the case of goods made up for sale or delivery in or on a container
marked with an indication of quantity, or goods which in connection
with their sale have associated with them a document purporting to state
their quantity, or goods required under Part IV of the Act to be pre-
packed or made up for sale only in particular quantities, and where the
quantity is "less than that marked on the container or stated in the
document in question or than the relevant particular quantity, it is a
defence that the deficiency in quantity arose after the marking of the
container, the completion of the document, or the making up of the
goods, as the case may be, and was "attributable wholly to factors for
which reasonable allowance was made in stating the quantity of the
goods in the marking or document or in making up or making the goods
for sale".[28]

19.71   (a) EVAPORATION. Where a charge is made that an amount of food
delivered is less than that purported to be sold it is a defence to show
that the deficiency was due wholly to unavoidable evaporation or
drainage since the sale, and that due care and precaution were taken to
minimise any such evaporation or drainage. This defence is not open in
the case of food pre-packed in a container required by the Act to be
marked with its quantity.[29]

19.72   (b) SUBSEQUENT TREATMENT. Where it is shown that between the time
of sale and the time of discovery of a deficiency the goods were
subjected with the buyer's consent to treatment which could result in a
reduction in quantity of the goods for delivery to the buyer or anyone on
his behalf, the person charged cannot be convicted of the offence of
selling a deficient quantity unless it is shown that the deficiency cannot
be accounted for by the treatment.[30]

19.73   (c) EXCESS. Where proceedings are brought in respect of any excess in
quantity it is a defence to prove that the excess was attributable to the
taking of measures reasonably necessary in order to avoid committing an
offence in respect of a deficiency in relation to the goods which are the
subject of the charge or of any other goods.[31]

19.74   (3) *Sample testing.* Where proceedings are brought in respect of excess
or deficiency in quantity of goods made up for sale in marked containers
or of pre-packed goods or goods otherwise made up or made for sale
which are required to be pre-packed or made up or made in particular
quantities, then if at the time and place the offending article was tested
there were other articles of the same kind which had been sold by the
accused or were in his possession for sale or delivery after sale and which

---

[27] When the commission by A of an offence is due to the act or default of B, B may be
dealt with whether or not proceedings are taken against A: s.32 of the 1985 Act.
[28] Section 35(1), (2) of the 1985 Act.
[29] Section 35(3).
[30] Section 35(4).
[31] Section 36.

were available for testing, a reasonable number of these articles must also be tested, and in any proceedings the court:

> "(a) if the proceedings are with respect to one or more of a number of articles tested on the same occasion, shall have regard to the average quantity in all the articles tested,
>
> (b) if the proceedings are with respect to a single article, shall disregard any inconsiderable deficiency or excess, and
>
> (c) shall have regard generally to all the circumstances of the case."[32]

False statements to inspectors

19.75 It is an offence wilfully to obstruct an inspector acting in pursuance of the 1985 Act,[33] and an offence to fail to comply with a requirement properly made by such an inspector, to fail to give him information, or to give him information which the accused knows to be false.[34]

COINAGE, BANKNOTE AND STAMP OFFENCES

Coinage and banknote offences

19.76 *Forgery and Counterfeiting Act 1981.* It is a crime at common law to utter a forged banknote,[35] and also to sell such a note as a forged note.[36] Coining was punishable at common law and under a number of old Scots statutes[37]; but offences relating to the coin and banknotes are now dealt with under the Forgery and Counterfeiting Act 1981. That Act provides for the following offences.

COUNTERFEITING. Section 14: **19.77**

> "(1) It is an offence for a person to make a counterfeit of a currency note or of a protected coin, intending that he or another shall pass or tender it as genuine.
>
> (2) It is an offence for a person to make a counterfeit of a currency note or of a protected coin without lawful authority or excuse."[38]

PASSING COUNTERFEIT NOTES OR COINS. Section 15: **19.78**

> "(1) It is an offence for a person—

---

[32] Section 37(1), (2); *Paterson v. Ross Poultry Ltd*, 1974 S.L.T. (Sh.Ct.) 38.

[33] Section 80: maximum penalty a fine of level 5 on the standard scale (s.84(6)).

[34] Section 81(1), (2); under subs. (3), there is no obligation to provide to an inspector information which is self-incriminating: maximum penalty a fine of level 5 on the standard scale (s.84(6)).

[35] Macdonald, p.69; *Archd and Susan Miller* (1850) J. Shaw 288; *John Henry Greatrex* (1867) 5 Irv. 375.

[36] *John Horne* (1814) Hume, i, 150 *et seq.*, *Wm Cooke* (1833) Bell's Notes 58; Alison, i, 406.

[37] Mackenzie I,27,9; Hume, i, 561; Alison, i, 451; *Mary White* (1841) 2 Swin. 568.

[38] Maximum penalty, for an offence under subs. (1) is on indictment 10 years' and a fine, and on summary conviction six months' and a fine of the statutory maximum (s.22(1), (2)); and the maximum for an offence under subs. (2) is on indictment two years' and a fine, and on summary conviction six months' and a fine of the statutory maximum (s.22(3), (4)). For definitions of terms used in this section, see para. 19.82, *infra*.

(a) to pass or tender as genuine any thing which is, and which he knows or believes to be, a counterfeit of a currency note or of a protected coin; or

(b) to deliver to another any thing which is, and which he knows or believes to be, such a counterfeit, intending that the person to whom it is delivered or another shall pass or tender it as genuine.

(2) It is an offence for a person to deliver to another, without lawful authority or excuse, any thing which is, and which he knows or believes to be, a counterfeit of a currency note or of a protected coin."[39]

19.79　POSSESSION OF COUNTERFEIT NOTES AND COINS. Section 16:

"(1) It is an offence for a person to have in his custody or under his control any thing which is, and which he knows or believes to be, a counterfeit of a currency note or of a protected coin, intending either to pass or tender it as genuine or to deliver it to another with the intention that he or another shall pass or tender it as genuine.

(2) It is an offence for a person to have in his custody or under his control, without lawful authority or excuse, any thing which is, and which he knows or believes to be, a counterfeit of a currency note or of a protected coin.

(3) It is immaterial for the purposes of subsections (1) and (2) above that a coin or note is not in a fit state to be passed or tendered or that the making or counterfeiting of a coin or note has not been finished or perfected."[40]

19.80　POSSESSION OF COUNTERFEITING MATERIALS AND IMPLEMENTS. It is an offence to make or have in one's custody or control "any thing" intended for use by oneself or others to make a counterfeit note or coin intended to be passed as genuine.[41]

It has been held that use of the words "any thing" allows the widest possible construction to be given to the offence, and in particular allowed the inclusion of things which were not part of the direct process of producing counterfeit $50 bills but which were used simply to check the quality of the film from which it was intended that counterfeiting plates should be created.[42]

It is also an offence to make or have in one's custody or control, without lawful authority or excuse, any thing one knows to be specially designed or adapted for making a counterfeit currency note.[43] It is further an offence to make or have in one's custody or control any thing

---

[39] Maximum penalties for s.15(1) and (2) are the same as those for ss.14(1) and 14(2) respectively: see n.38, *supra*. Such offences are always regarded as serious: see, *e.g.*, *McLeod v. Allan*, 1986 S.C.C.R. 666, where a custodial sentence of three months' (for passing a counterfeit Bank of England, £50 note) was upheld by the Appeal Court. For definitions of terms used in s.15, see para. 19.82, *infra*.

[40] Maximum penalties for s.16(1) and (2) are the same as those for s.14(1) and (2) respectively: see n.38, *supra*. For definitions of the terms used in s.16, see para. 19.82, *infra*.

[41] Section 17(1): maximum penalty 10 years' and a fine on indictment, and six months' and a fine of the statutory maximum on summary conviction (s.22).

[42] *R. v. Maltman* (1995) 1 Cr.App.R. 239, CA.

[43] Section 17(2): maximum penalty two years' and a fine on indictment, and six months' and a fine of the statutory maximum on summary conviction (s.22).

one knows to be capable of imparting to any thing a resemblance to all or part of either side of a protected coin or of the reverse of the image on either side of a protected coin.[44]

REPRODUCTION OF IMITATIONS. It is an offence to reproduce any British **19.81** currency note[45] or any part of such a note on any substance or scale without written permission from the relevant authority.[46] It is also an offence to make, sell or distribute, or have custody or control of, an imitation British coin[47] in connection with a scheme intended to promote the sale of any product or the making of contracts for the supply of any service, without prior Treasury consent in writing to such sale or distribution.[48]

General definitions. "Currency note" is defined by section 27(1) as **19.82** follows:

"(a) any note which—
(i) has been lawfully issued in England and Wales, Scotland, Northern Ireland, any of the Channel Islands, the Isle of Man or the Republic of Ireland; and
(ii) is or has been customarily used as money in the country where it was issued; and
(iii) is payable on demand; or
(b) any note which —
(i) has been lawfully issued in some country other than those mentioned in paragraph (a)(i) above; and
(ii) is customarily used as money in that country."

"Protected coin" is defined by section 27(1) as any coin customarily used as money in any country, or any coin specified in the Forgery and Counterfeiting (Protected Coins) Order 1981.[49]

"Counterfeiting is defined by section 28 as follows:

"(1) For the purposes of this Part of this Act a thing is a counterfeit of a currency note or of a protected coin—
(a) if it is not a currency note or a protected coin but resembles a currency note or protected coin (whether on one side only or on both) to such an extent that it is reasonably capable of

---

[44] Section 17(3): maximum penalty as for s.17(2). It is a defence to an offence under s.17(3) for the accused to prove that he acted with Treasury permission or with other lawful authority or excuse — s.17(4). (For definitions of the terms used in the offences dealt with in this paragraph, see para. 19.82, *infra*.)

[45] Under s.18(2), a British currency note is "any note which — (a) has been lawfully issued in England and Wales, Scotland or Northern Ireland; and (b) is or has been customarily used as money in the country where it was issued; and (c) is payable on demand".

[46] Section 18(1). Under s.18(2), "relevant authority" means, relative to British currency notes of any particular description, "the authority empowered by law to issue notes of that description".

[47] "British coin" means any coin which is legal tender in any part of the United Kingdom; and "imitation British coin" means any thing which resembles a British coin in shape, size and the substance of which it is made: s.19(2). For "legal tender", see the Coinage Act 1971, s.2, as amended by the Currency Act 1983, s.1(3).

[48] Section 19: maximum penalty for offences under ss. 18 and 19 is, on indictment a fine, and on summary conviction a fine of the statutory maximum (s.22(5)). (For definitions of the terms used in the offences mentioned in this paragraph, see para. 19.82, *infra*.)

[49] S.I. 1981 No. 1505.

passing for a currency note or protected coin of that description; or

(b) if it is a currency note or protected coin which has been so altered that it is reasonably capable of passing for a currency note or protected coin of some other description.

(2) For the purposes of this Part of this Act—

(a) a thing consisting of one side only of a currency note, with or without the addition of other material, is a counterfeit of such a note;

(b) a thing consisting—

(i) of parts of two or more currency notes; or

(ii) of parts of a currency note, or of parts of two or more currency notes, with the addition of other material,

is capable of being a counterfeit of a currency note.

(3) References in the Part of this Act to passing or tendering a counterfeit note or a protected coin are not to be construed as confined to passing or tendering it as legal tender."

Stamps

19.83   The forgery, and fraudulent printing or altering, of revenue dies and stamps is prohibited by section 13 of the Stamp Duties Management Act 1891.[50] The Act also prohibits the making of any paper in imitation of stamp duty paper[51] and the possession of paper, plates or dies used for stamp duty stamps, without lawful authority.[52]

ROAD TRAFFIC FRAUDS

Road Traffic Act 1988

19.84 *Forged documents.* Section 173 of the Road Traffic Act 1988 provides:

"(1) A person who, with intent to deceive—

(a) forges, alters or uses a document or other thing to which this section applies, or

(b) lends to, or allows to be used by, any other person a document or other thing to which this section applies, or

(c) makes or has in his possession any document or other thing so closely resembling a document or other thing to which this section applies as to be calculated to deceive,

is guilty of an offence.[53]

The section applies[54] to the following documents:

(a) any licence (including a counterpart of a licence to drive) under the Act,

---

[50] Maximum penalty: 14 years' imprisonment.

[51] Section 14, maximum penalty: seven years' imprisonment.

[52] Section 15, maximum penalty: two years' imprisonment.

[53] Maximum penalty is two years' on indictment, a fine of the statutory maximum on summary conviction: Road Traffic Offenders Act 1988, Sched. 2, Pt I.

[54] The following list is intended merely as an introductory guide; for the full statutory list see s.173(2), as amended: see R. Ward (Ed.), *The Encyclopaedia of Road Traffic Law and Practice* (1970, Sweet & Maxwell), Vol. 2, *sub.* "Road Traffic Act 1988", for current amendments and derivations.

(aa) the counterpart of a Community licence;
 (b) any test certificate;
 (c) any certificate necessary for any exemption from the require-
     ment to wear a seat belt;
(cc) any seal required under regulations relating to speed limiters;
 (d) any plate containing particulars which are required to be
     marked on vehicles or goods vehicles;
(dd) any prescribed document evidencing the appointment of an
     examiner;
 (e) any prescribed records required to be kept by operators
     relative to inspections of goods vehicles;
 (f) any prescribed document issued as evidence of the result of a
     test of competence to drive;
(ff) any prescribed certificate pertaining to completion of a
     training course for motor cyclists;
 (g) any prescribed badge or certificate relating to those qualified
     to offer driving instruction;
 (h) any prescribed certificate of insurance or security relating to
     third party risks;
 (j) any prescribed document produced as evidence of insurance
     relating to third party risks;
 (k) any prescribed document produced in lieu of a certificate of
     insurance or a certificate of security relating to third party
     risks;
 (l) any international road haulage permit[55]; and
 (m) a prescribed certificate of completion of a course by those,
     convicted of certain road traffic offences, who stand to
     benefit thereby from a reduced period of disqualification."

It has been held in England that "use" is confined to use in connection with the driving of a vehicle, and that it is not an offence against section 173 to send a false licence to an authority for renewal,[56] but this seems an unnecessarily narrow interpretation.

In proving an intention to deceive it is not necessary to show that the accused gained anything by his act.[57] It has been held that "calculated to deceive" in section 173(1)(c) means "likely to deceive" and that there is such likelihood where bogus uncompleted insurance certificates are found in the possession of the defendant.[58]

In *R. v. Cleghorn*[59] it was held that a certificate of insurance which related to a policy which had been cancelled was a document "so closely resembling" a valid certificate of insurance as to come within the corresponding section of the Road Traffic Act 1930.

LOG SHEETS, ETC. Section 99(5) of the Transport Act 1968 penalises the **19.85** making of false records relating to the hours of driving of drivers of goods vehicles under sections 97 and 98 of that Act or Community or international rules, where the maker makes an entry known to be false or an alteration in a record with intent to deceive.[60]

---

[55] See s.192(1) of the 1988 Act for the definition of such a permit.
[56] *R. v. McCardle* [1958] Crim.L.R. 50.
[57] *Jones v. Meatyard* [1939] 1 All E.R. 140.
[58] *R. v. Aworinde* [1996] R.T.R. 66, CA.
[59] [1938] 3 All E.R. 398.
[60] Maximum penalty, a fine of the prescribed sum on summary conviction, two years' on indictment.

19.86 *False statements and withholding information.*[61] Section 174 of the Road Traffic Act 1988 provides:

> "(1) A person who knowingly makes a false statement[62] for the purpose—
>
> > (a) of obtaining the grant of a licence under any Part of this Act to himself or any other person, or
> >
> > (b) of preventing the grant of any such licence, or
> >
> > (c) of procuring the imposition of a condition or limitation in relation to any such licence, or
> >
> > (d) of securing the entry or retention of the name of any person in the register of approved instructors maintained under Part V of this Act, or
> >
> > (dd) of obtaining the grant to any person of a certificate under s.133A of this Act, or
> >
> > (e) of obtaining the grant of an international road haulage permit to himself or any other person
>
> is guilty of an offence. . . .[63]
>
> (5) A person who makes a false statement or withholds any material information for the purpose of obtaining the issue—
>
> > (a) of a certificate of insurance or certificate of security under Part VI of this Act, or
> >
> > (b) of any document issued under regulations made by the Secretary of State in pursuance of his power . . . to prescribe evidence which may be produced in lieu of a certificate of insurance or a certificate of security is guilty of an offence."[64]

19.87 *Issue of false documents.* Section 175 provides:

> "If a person issues—
>
> > (a) any such document as is referred to in section 174(5)(a) or (b)[65] of this Act, or
> >
> > (b) a test certificate or certificate of conformity (within the meaning of Part II of this Act),
>
> and the document or certificate so issued is to his knowledge false in a material particular, he is guilty of an offence."[66]

19.88 *Personation of examiner.* Section 177[67] provides:

> "If a person, with intent to deceive, falsely represents himself to be, or to be employed by, a person authorised in accordance with regulations made under section 41[68] of this Act with respect to the checking and sealing of speed limiters or a person authorised by the

---

[61] For offences concerned with withholding information from the police see *infra*, para. 47.42 *et seq.*

[62] This includes the used of a false name: *Clark v. Chalmers*, 1961 J.C. 60.

[63] Subsections (2) to (4) deal with matters relating to goods vehicles, vehicle type approvals, test certificates and goods vehicle inspections.

[64] Maximum penalty, a fine of level 3 on the standard scale: Road Traffic Offenders Act 1988, Sched. 2, Pt I. Knowledge that the statement is false is not required on a charge of making a false statement under s.174(5); but the offence of withholding may require *mens rea*: *R. v. Cummerson* [1968] 2 Q.B. 534, CA.

[65] See para. 19.86, *supra.*

[66] Maximum penalty a fine of level 4 on the standard scale: Road Traffic Offenders Act 1988, Sched. 2, Pt I.

[67] As amended by the Road Traffic Act 1991, Sched. 4, para. 75.

[68] As amended by the Road Traffic Act 1991, Sched. 4, para. 50.

Secretary of State for the purposes of section 45[69] of this Act, he is guilty of an offence."[70]

The Vehicle Excise and Registration Act 1994

Forgery and fraud. Section 44 provides: **19.89**

"(1) A person is guilty of an offence if he forges, fraudulently alters, fraudulently uses, fraudulently lends or fraudulently allows to be used by another person anything to which subsection (2) applies.
    (2) this subsection applies to—
    (a) a vehicle licence,
    (b) a trade licence,
    (c) a nil licence,[71]
    (d) a registration mark,
    (e) a registration document, and
    (f) a trade plate (including a replacement trade plate).
    (3) A person guilty of an offence under this section is liable—
    (a) on summary conviction, to a fine not exceeding the statutory maximum, and
    (b) on conviction on indictment, to imprisonment for a term not exceeding two years or to a fine or (except in Scotland) to both."

It has been held in England that the word "forges" entails an intent to deceive but does not require an intent to defraud.[72]

The word "fraudulently" obviously entails an intent to defraud, but means no more than that the accused's actions were intended to deceive a person responsible for a public duty into doing something which he would not have done but for the deceit, or into not doing something which he would otherwise have done: there is no requirement of a purpose to achieve economic gain at the expense of another's loss, such as a purpose to evade payment of, for example, a vehicle licence fee.[73]

False or misleading declarations and information. Section 45 of the Act **19.90** provides:

"(1) A person who in connection with—
    (a) an application for a vehicle licence or a trade licence,
    (b) a claim for a rebate under section 20,[74] or
    (c) an application for an allocation of registration marks,

---

[69] Section 45 deals with vehicle testing.

[70] Maximum penalty a fine of level 3 on the standard scale: Road Traffic Offenders Act 1988, Sched. 2, Pt I.

[71] Paragraph (c) substituted by the Finance Act 1997, s.18 and Sched. 3, para. 6. "Nil licence" is defined in s.62(1) of the 1994 Act (as inserted by the 1997 Act, Sched. 3, para. 7(3)) as being a document in the form of a vehicle licence issued by the Secretary of State in respect of a vehicle which is an "exempt vehicle" — *i.e.* one which is exempt from payment of duty: see 1994 Act, Sched. 2.

[72] *R. v. Clayton* (1980) 72 Cr.App.R. 135.

[73] *R. v. Terry* [1984] A.C. 374, HL, following *Welham v. D.P.P.* [1961] A.C. 103, HL but overruling *R. v. Manners-Astley* [1967] 1 W.L.R. 1505, CA.

[74] Claims for rebates, where a vehicle becomes subject to a lower rate of duty than had originally been paid owing to fiscal changes during the year in question, are also covered by s.45: see, *e.g.*, the Finance Act 2000, s.20(10).

makes a declaration which to his knowledge is either false or in any material respect misleading is guilty of an offence.

(2) A person who makes a declaration which—

    (a) is required by regulations under this Act to be made in respect of a vehicle which is an exempt vehicle under paragraph 19 of schedule 2, and

    (b) to his knowledge is either false or in any material respect misleading,

is guilty of an offence.

(2A)[75] A person who makes a declaration or statement which—

    (a) is required to be made in respect of a vehicle by regulations under section 22[76], and

    (b) to his knowledge is either false or in any material respect misleading,

is guilty of an offence.

(3) A person who—

    (a) is required by virtue of this Act to furnish particulars relating to, or to the keeper of, a vehicle,[77] and

    (b) furnishes particulars which to his knowledge are either false or in any material respect misleading,

is guilty of an offence.

(3A)[78] A person who in supplying information or producing documents for the purposes of regulations made under section 61A[79] or 61B[80]—

    (a) makes a statement which to his knowledge is false or in any material respect misleading or recklessly makes a statement which is false or in any material respect misleading, or

    (b) produces or otherwise makes use of a document which to his knowledge is false or in any material respect misleading,

is guilty of an offence.

(3B) A person who—

    (a) with intent to deceive, forges, alters or uses a certificate issued by virtue of section 61A or 61B,

    (b) knowing or believing that it will be used for deception lends such a certificate to another or allows another to alter or use it, or

    (c) without reasonable excuse makes or has in his possession any document so closely resembling such a certificate as to be calculated to deceive,

is guilty of an offence.

(4) A person guilty of an offence under this section is liable—

    (a) on summary conviction, to a fine not exceeding the statutory maximum, and

    (b) on conviction on indictment, to imprisonment for a term not exceeding two years or to a fine or (except in Scotland) to both."

---

[75] Inserted by the Finance Act 1996, Sched. 2, para. 11.

[76] Section 22 relates to vehicle registration.

[77] As amended by the Finance Act 1996, Sched. 2, para. 11.

[78] Subsections (3A) and (3B) were inserted by the Finance Act 1995, Sched. 4, para. 24.

[79] This section deals with certification as to vehicle weight, and was inserted by the Finance Act 1995, Sched. 4, para. 28.

[80] This section deals with reduced pollution certification, and was inserted by the Finance Act 1998, Sched. 1, para. 2; see also para. 15 of that Sched.

COMPUTER MISUSE

Computer Misuse Act 1990. Section 1 provides: **19.91**

"(1) A person is guilty of an offence if—
(a) he causes a computer to perform any function with intent to secure access to any program or data held in any computer;
(b) the access he intends to secure is unauthorised; and
(c) he knows at the time when he causes the computer to perform the function that that is the case.
(2) The intent a person has to have to commit an offence under this section need not be directed at—
(a) any particular program or data;
(b) a program or data of a particular kind; or
(c) a program or data held in any particular computer.
(3) A person guilty of an offence under this section shall be liable on summary conviction to imprisonment for a term not exceeding six months or to a fine not exceeding level 5 on the standard scale or to both."

The computer used to perform the function in section 1(1) may be the same machine which held the data or program to which access was sought.[81]

"Unauthorised" access is defined in section 17(5) as follows:

"Access of any kind by any person to any program or data held in a computer is unauthorised if—
(a) he is not himself entitled to control access of the kind in question to the program or data; and
(b) he does not have consent to access by him of the kind in question to the program or data from any person who is so entitled . . ."

Where a person was entitled to access only those customers' computer files which were assigned to her, it was held that this did not entitle her to access non-assigned files on the basis that these further files were of the same kind, or at the same level, as the ones to which she did have authorised access.[82]

Where the offence is committed with intent to commit or to facilitate the commission on the same or any future occasion of an offence for which the sentence is fixed by law or which may be punishable by five years' imprisonment, the maximum penalty is five years and a fine on indictment, and six months and a fine of the statutory maximum on summary conviction.[83]

MISCELLANEOUS STATUTORY FRAUDS

There are a great number of statutory frauds of differing kinds, as well **19.92** as a great number of statutes which penalise the giving of false information in registers, returns and other documents required to be

---

[81] *Att.-Gen.'s Reference (No. 1 of 1991)* [1992] 3 W.L.R. 432, CA.
[82] *R. v. Bow Street Metrop. Mag., ex p. U.S. Govt* [2000] 2 A.C. 216, HL, which disapproved dicta to the contrary in *D.P.P. v. Bignell* (1998) 1 Cr.App.R. 1.
[83] See s.2. For the offence under s.3 of unauthorised modification of computer material, see para. 22.25, *infra*.

made under statute, some of which fall under sections 44–46 of the Criminal Law (Consolidation) (Scotland) Act 1995.[84] Indeed, most statutes which provide for the collection of information, or for the making of applications for or the issue of money or licences, contain sections imposing penalties for false statements, fraud or forgery.

The following are some of the more notable or more common enactments dealing with fraud.

Documentary evidence

19.93 The Documentary Evidence Act 1868 provides for the proving of Government orders and regulations by producing authorised copies of the order or regulation. Section 4 provides:

> "If any person . . .
> (1) Prints any copy of any proclamation, order, or regulation which falsely purports to have been printed by the Government printer, or to be printed under the authority of the legislature of any British colony or possession, or tenders in evidence any copy of any proclamation, order, or regulation, which falsely purports to have been printed as aforesaid, knowing that the same was not so printed; or
> (2) Forges or tenders in evidence, knowing the same to have been forged, any certificate by this Act authorized to be annexed to a copy of or extract from any proclamation, order, or regulation; he shall be guilty [of an offence and liable to imprisonment.]."

The Documentary Evidence Act 1882, section 3, makes similar provision with regard to copies of any Acts, orders, etc., falsely purporting to be printed under the superintendence or authority of the stationery office.[85]

Fraudulent mediums

19.94 Section 1 of the Fraudulent Mediums Act 1951 provides:

> "(1) Subject to the provisions of this section, any person who—
>
> > (a) with intent to deceive purports to act as a spiritualistic medium or to exercise any powers of telepathy, clairvoyance or other similar powers, or
> > (b) in purporting to act as a spiritualistic medium or to exercise such powers as aforesaid, uses any fraudulent device,
> shall be guilty of an offence.[86]
> (2) A person shall not be convicted of an offence under the foregoing subsection unless it is proved that he acted for reward; and for the purposes of this section a person shall be deemed to act for reward if any money is paid, or other valuable thing given, in respect of what he does, whether to him or to any other person."

---

[84] Formerly the False Oaths (Consolidation) (Scotland) Act 1933. See *infra*, para. 47.23.

[85] Maximum penalty: seven years' imprisonment.

[86] Maximum penalty, two years' and a fine on indictment, a fine of the prescribed sum and three months' on summary conviction.

Personation

A considerable number of statutes deal with various types of imper- **19.95**
sonation, the more important of which are referred to below.[87]

Personation in connection with the Forces and state officials. UNIFORMS **19.96**
AND DECORATIONS. It is an offence for anyone not serving in Her
Majesty's military forces to wear the uniform of any of those forces or
any dress having the appearance or bearing of any such uniform without
the Queen's permission, except in a licensed stage play, music hall,
circus, or bona fide military representation.[88]

It is also an offence to wear a decoration "so nearly resembling" one
supplied or authorised by the Defence Council as to be calculated to
deceive, or to represent oneself falsely as a person entitled to wear any
such decoration.[89]

It is an offence under section 57(1) of the Merchant Shipping Act
1995 to wear merchant navy uniform or any part of it without being
entitled to do so.[90]

Unauthorised use of uniforms is in certain circumstances a contravention of section 1 of the Official Secrets Act 1920.[91]

CERTIFICATES. It is an offence under the Seamen's and Soldiers' False **19.97**
Characters Act 1906[92] to forge a service or discharge certificate, or to
utter or seek advantage by means of any such forged certificate, or to
personate the holder of such a certificate.[93] It is also an offence to make
use of a forged or counterfeit statement or certificate as to character or
previous employment or a statement known to be materially false to
enlist in the Forces. Any person who makes a written statement he
knows to be materially false and which he allows or intends to be so used
also commits an offence.[94] Section 8 of the Armed Forces Act 1966
provides a penalty of three months' imprisonment or a fine of level one
on the standard scale for anyone who makes a false answer to any
question put to him in connection with enlistment in the Navy.[95]

The Police. THE POLICE (SCOTLAND) ACT 1967. Section 43 provides: **19.98**

"(1) Subject to the provisions of this section, any person who—
  (a) takes the name, designation or character of a constable for
    the purpose of obtaining admission into any house or other

---

[87] Personation at elections is dealt with along with other election offences, *infra*,
para. 38.26.

[88] Uniforms Act 1894 (applied to the Royal Air Force by the Air Force (Application of
Enactments) Order (No. 2) 1918, S.R. & O. No. 548, Rev. I., 896) s.2: maximum penalty a
fine of level 3 on the standard scale. Section 3 of the Act makes it an offence for
non-service personnel to wear naval or military uniform so as to bring contempt on that
uniform: maximum penalty a fine of level 3 on the standard scale or one month's
imprisonment.

[89] Army Act 1955, s.197; Air Force Act 1955, s.197 (see S.I. 1964 No. 488): maximum
penalty three months' imprisonment and a fine of level 3 on the standard scale.

[90] Maximum penalty a fine of level 1 on the standard scale, or, if worn in such a manner
as to be likely to bring contempt on the uniform, to such a fine and one month in prison:
see also s.57 (4).

[91] *infra*, para. 37.44.

[92] Applied to the Air Force by S.R. & O. 1918/548, *supra*.

[93] Section 1. Maximum penalty on summary conviction three months' imprisonment.

[94] Section 2. Maximum penalty a fine of level 3 on the standard scale.

[95] For similar provisions see Army Act 1955, s.19; Air Force Act 1955, s.19.

place or of doing or procuring to be done any act which such person would not be entitled to do or procure to be done on his own authority, or for any other unlawful purpose, or

   (b) wears any article of police uniform without the permission of the police authority for the police area in which he is, or

   (c) has in his possession any article of police uniform without being able to account satisfactorily for his possession thereof,

shall be guilty of an offence[96] . . .

   (2) Nothing in [the preceding subsection] shall make it an offence to wear any article of police uniform in the course of taking part in a stage play, or music hall or circus performance, or of performing in or producing a cinematograph film or television broadcast.

   (3) In this section 'article of police uniform' means any article of uniform or any distinctive badge or mark usually issued by any police authority to constables, or any article having the appearance of such article, badge or mark."

19.99 *Customs officers.* Personation of Customs officers is dealt with together with other Customs offences.[97]

19.100 *Personation in connection with professions.* DOCTORS. It is an offence under the Medical Act 1983 for any person wilfully and falsely to pretend to be, or to use any description implying that he is, registered under the Act or recognised by law as a medical practitioner or apothecary.[98]

19.101   DENTISTS. It is an offence under the Dentists Act 1984 to use the title of dentist unless one is a registered dentist or a registered medical practitioner, and it is an offence to use any description falsely implying that one is a registered dentist.[99]

19.102   VETERINARY SURGEONS. It is an offence under section 20(1) of the Veterinary Surgeons Act 1966 for any person who is not a registered veterinary surgeon to use any description implying that he is so registered.[1] Section 20(2) of the same Act further makes it an offence for anyone not registered as a veterinary surgeon to use the title of veterinary practitioner, or any title or description implying that he is qualified to practise veterinary surgery to a greater extent than is allowed to students under the Act. It is also an offence for any person to use, in connection with any business or premises, any name or description implying that he or anyone acting for the purposes of the business possesses veterinary qualifications which he does not in fact possess.[2]

---

[96] Maximum penalty a fine of level 4 on the standard scale or three months' imprisonment: see Criminal Procedure (Consequential Provisions) (Scotland) Act 1995, Sched. 2, Pt III.

[97] *infra*, para. 38.15.

[98] Section 49. Maximum penalty a fine of level 5 on the standard scale, payable to the General Medical Council and recoverable by any person in the sheriff court or district court together with expenses. *Cf. Eastburn v. Robertson* (1898) 2 Adam 607; *Younghusband v. Luftig* [1949] 2 K.B. 354; *Wilson v. Inyang* [1951] 2 K.B. 799.

[99] Section 39(1), (2). Maximum penalty a fine of level 5 on the standard scale, on summary conviction (s.39(3)). *Cf. Emslie v. Paterson* (1897) 2 Adam 323.

[1] Maximum penalty under s.20, a fine of the prescribed sum on summary conviction, and a fine on indictment.

[2] Section 20(3).

CHEMISTS. It is an offence under the Medicines Act 1968 to use the **19.103** title of chemist, pharmacist or druggist, or any emblem or description calculated to suggest a qualification in regard to drugs, unless one is duly qualified and entitled to do so.[3] It is an offence under section 20 of the Pharmacy Act 1954 to exhibit, forge, use or allow to be used with intent to deceive, a certificate of membership of the pharmaceutical society to which one is not entitled, or to possess any document so closely resembling such a certificate as to be calculated to deceive.[4]

OPTICIANS. It is an offence under the Opticians Act 1989 for any **19.104** individual to use the title of optometrist, or ophthalmic or dispensing optician or registered optician when he is not in fact registered as such, or to use any description falsely implying that he is registered, or for any body corporate to use any name or description falsely implying that it is enrolled in one of the lists kept under the Act.[5]

NURSES, MIDWIVES AND HEALTH VISITORS. Section 14 of the Nurses, **19.105** Midwives and Health Visitors Act 1979 makes it an offence for any person, by any conduct and with intent to deceive, falsely to represent himself as possessing qualifications in nursing, midwifery or health visiting or falsely to represent himself to be registered as a nurse, midwife or health visitor. It is also an offence for him, with intent that any person should be deceived, to cause or permit another person to make representations about him which if made by himself with such intent would have amounted to the offence last mentioned above. Similarly it is an offence for him to make any such representations, with intent to deceive, relative to another person if he knows them to be false.[6]

SOLICITORS. It is an offence under section 31 of the Solicitors **19.106** (Scotland) Act 1980 for any person (including a body corporate) who lacks the relevant qualifications wilfully and falsely to pretend to be a solicitor or notary public or a registered European lawyer, or to use any name or description implying that he is qualified to act as such, or that he is recognised by the law as so qualified.[7] It is also an offence for any person or body corporate wilfully and falsely to pretend to be an incorporated practice or to use any name or description implying that he or it is an incorporated practice.[8]

---

[3] Section 78: maximum penalty a fine of level 3 on the standard scale; *cf. Bremridge v. Turnbull* (1895) 2 Adam 29; *Bremridge v. Hume* (1895) *ibid.*, 24.

[4] Section 20: maximum penalty a fine of level 1 on the standard scale.

[5] Section 28: maximum penalty on summary conviction a fine of level 4 on the standard scale.

[6] Maximum penalty a fine of level 4 on the standard scale.

[7] Subsection (1), as amended by the Law Reform (Miscellaneous Provisions) (Scotland) Act 1985, Sched. 1, Pt I, para. 8; and as amended also by the European Communities (Lawyer's Practice) (Scotland) Regulations 2000 (S.S.I. 2000 No. 121), Sched. 1, para. 1(8). "Registered European lawyer" is defined in reg. 2(2) and (3) of S.S.I. 2000 No. 121. Maximum penalty a fine of level 4 on the standard scale: s.63(1) of the 1980 Act, as amended by the Law Reform (Miscellaneous Provisions) (Scotland) Act 1990, Sched. 8, para. 29(14).

[8] Solicitors (Scotland) Act 1980, s.31(2), as inserted by Sched. 1, Pt I, para. 8(b) to the Law Reform (Miscellaneous Provisions) (Scotland) Act 1985.

Mental Health (Scotland) Act 1984

19.107   Section 104 of this Act provides:

> "(1) Any person who makes any statement or entry which is false in
> any material particular in any application, recommendation, report,
> record or other document required or authorised to be made for
> any of the purposes of this Act or, with intent to deceive, makes use
> of any such entry or statement which he knows to be false, shall be
> guilty of an offence."[9]

Consumer Credit Act 1974

19.108   It is an offence under section 46 of this Act to convey false or
materially misleading information in certain advertisements published
for the purpose of the advertiser's business which indicates a willingness
to provide credit or to enter into an agreement for hiring goods.[10]
"Information stating or implying an intention on the advertiser's part
which he has not got is false."[11]

Section 165, which is similar to section 29 of the Trade Descriptions
Act 1968, creates the offences of obstructing and giving false information
to officers of authorities enforcing the Act. There is no duty to give
information which might incriminate the giver or his spouse.[12]

Section 168(1) provides a defence in the same terms as section 24 of
the Trade Descriptions Act 1968.[13]

Firearms

19.109   Section 3(5)[14] of the Firearms Act 1968 provides:

> "A person commits an offence if, with a view to purchasing or
> acquiring, or procuring the repair, test or proof of, any firearm or
> ammunition to which section 1 of this Act applies, or a shot gun, he
> produces a false certificate or a certificate in which any false entry
> has been made, or personates a person to whom a certificate has
> been granted, or knowingly or recklessly makes a statement false in
> any material particular."[15]

---

[9] Maximum penalty on indictment two years' imprisonment and a fine, on summary
conviction six months' and a fine of the statutory maximum: s.104(2).

[10] See s.43 of the Act. The maximum penalty is a fine of the prescribed sum on
summary conviction, two years and a fine on indictment: Sched. 1.

[11] Section 46(2). For offences by publishers and others, see s.47.

[12] Maximum penalty as above. For an example of an offence against s.165, see
Aitchison v. Rizza, 1985 S.C.C.R. 297.

[13] *supra*, para. 19.36.

[14] As amended by the Firearms (Amendment) Act 1997, Sched. 2, para. 2(1).

[15] Maximum penalty the prescribed sum and six months on summary conviction, five
years and a fine on indictment: Sched. 6, Pt I, as amended by the Criminal Justice and
Public Order Act 1994, Sched. 8, Pt III.

Social Security etc.

Section 112[16] of the Social Security Administration Act 1992 provides **19.110** that:

"(1) If a person for the purpose of obtaining any benefit or other payment under the relevant social security legislation[17] whether for himself or some other person, or for any other purpose connected with that legislation—
(a) makes a statement or representation which he knows to be false; or
(b) produces or furnishes, or knowingly causes or knowingly allows to be produced or furnished, any document or information which he knows to be false in a material particular,
he shall be guilty of an offence.

(2) A person guilty of an offence under this section shall be liable on summary conviction to a fine not exceeding level 5 on the standard scale, or to imprisonment for a term not exceeding 3 months, or to both."

Section 111A of that Act[18] also provides that:

"(1) If a person knowingly[19]—
(a) makes a false statement or representation;
(b) produces or furnishes, or causes or allows to be produced or furnished, any document or information which is false in a material particular;
(c) fails to notify a change of circumstances which regulations under this Act require him to notify; or
(d) causes or allows another person to fail to notify a change of circumstances which such regulations require the other person to notify,

with a view to obtaining any benefit or other payment or advantage under the relevant social security legislation[20] (whether for himself or some other person), he shall be guilty of an offence."[21]

---

[16] As amended by the Social Security Administration (Fraud) Act 1997, Sched. 1, para. 4(2) and (3), and by the Child Support, Pensions and Social Security Act 2000, Sched. 6, para. 6. It was held (in *Barrass v. Reeve* [1981] 1 W.L.R. 408) under similarly worded prior legislation that it was an offence under the equivalent section to make any statement known to be untrue, even if the statement was not made with intent to obtain benefit to which one was not entitled, but only in order to deceive an employer: as Waller L.J. said, at 413C-D, "the plain words of the subsection are covered if a person, for the purpose of obtaining any benefit or other payments under this Act, knowingly makes any false statement. . . . There are no words to say 'with intent to obtain money' or anything of that sort." *Cf.* s.111A, *infra*.
[17] See the Child Support, Pensions and Social Security Act 2000, Sched. 6, para. 8, which inserts s.121DA into the 1992 Act.
[18] Inserted by the Social Security Administration (Fraud) Act 1997, s.13, and as amended by the Child Support, Pensions and Social Security Act 2000, Sched. 6.
[19] The subsection narrates "dishonestly" instead of "knowingly" in the application of the offence to England and Wales: see s.111A(4). *Cf. Clear v. Smith* [1981] 1 W.L.R. 399.
[20] See n.17, *supra*.
[21] Maximum penalty on indictment, seven years' and a fine, and on summary conviction, six months' and fine of the statutory maximum: s.111A(3).

Water meters

19.111   It is an offence to alter a water meter fraudulently, or to prevent it recording accurately.[22]

Aviation Security Act 1982

19.112   Section 3(3) of this Act makes it an offence intentionally to communicate false, misleading or deceptive information where to do so endangers or is likely to endanger the safety of an aircraft in flight.[23] It is a defence to show that the accused believed on reasonable grounds that the information was true, or that he communicated the information in good faith while lawfully employed to perform duties which included the communication of information.[24]

It is also an offence for the operators of aircraft, the managers of aerodromes, occupiers of land forming part of an aerodrome, or persons permitted access to a restricted zone of an aerodrome for the purpose of their businesses knowingly or recklessly to make false statements in response to a request by the Secretary of State for information under section 11 of the Act.[25]

Falsification of registers

19.113 *Births, marriages and deaths.* Section 53 of the Registration of Births Deaths and Marriages (Scotland) Act 1965 provides:

"(1) If any person commits any of the following offences, that is to say—
 (a) if he knowingly gives to a district registrar information which is false in a material particular;
 (b) if he falsifies or forges any extract, certificate or declaration issued or made, or purporting to be issued or made, under this Act; or
 (c) if he knowingly uses, or gives or sends to any person, as genuine any false or forged extract, certificate or declaration issued or made, or purporting to be issued or made, under this Act,
he shall be liable—
 (i) on conviction on indictment, to a fine or to [two years' imprisonment] or both;
 (ii) on summary conviction, to [a fine of the prescribed sum or three months' imprisonment] or to both.

---

[22] Water (Scotland) Act 1980, Sched. 4, para.32: maximum penalty a fine of level 1 on the standard scale. *Cf.* gas and electricity meters, in respect of which the equivalent statutory offences are to be committed "intentionally or by culpable negligence" but without specific reference to fraud; it is difficult, however, to conceive of intentional alteration of such meters which would not be done for some fraudulent purpose: see the Gas Act 1986, Sched. 2B, inserted by the Gas Act 1995, Sched. 2, and as amended by the Utilities Act 2000, Sched. 6, para. 2(1): maximum penalty a fine of level 3 on the standard scale; and the Electricity Act 1989, Sched. 7, para. 11(1): maximum penalty also a fine of level 3 on the standard scale.

[23] Maximum penalty life imprisonment: s.3(7).

[24] Section 3(4).

[25] Section 11(5)(b): maximum penalty a fine of the statutory maximum on summary conviction, two years and a fine on indictment. (Section 11 as a whole has been amended by the Aviation and Marine Security Act 1990, Sched. 1, para. 2.) See also the offences involving (*inter alia*) the making of false statements in ss. 21A and 21B of the 1982 Act, inserted by the Aviation and Maritime Security Act 1990, s.5.

(2) If any person commits any of the following offences, that is to say—

    (a) if he wilfully or negligently destroys, obliterates, erases or injures any entry in any register kept under this Act, or causes or permits the register or any part thereof to be destroyed, obliterated, erased or injured; or

    (b) if he knowingly gives to a district registrar, for the purpose of registration in a register, particulars of a birth or of a death which have already been registered in that or any other register,

he shall be liable on summary conviction to a fine [of level 3 on the standard scale].

(3) If any person commits any of the following offences, that is to say— . . .

    (e) if he passes as genuine any reproduction of an extract or certificate if such reproduction has not been authorised in accordance with section 41(1) of this Act,

he shall be liable on summary conviction to a fine [of level 1 on the standard scale]."

MARRIAGE SCHEDULE. Section 24(1) of the Marriage (Scotland) Act **19.114** 1977 provides:

"Any person who—

    (a) falsifies or forges any Marriage Schedule, certificate or declaration issued or made, or purporting to be issued or made, under this Act; [or]

    (b) knowingly uses, or gives or sends to any person as genuine, any false or forged Marriage Schedule, certificate declaration or other document issued or made, or purporting to be issued or made, or required, under this Act . . . shall be guilty of an offence."[26]

Professional registers. It is an offence under section 44 of the Criminal **19.115** Law (Consolidation) Act 1995 to make false statements to procure registration in any register kept in pursuance of a public Act of Parliament.[27]

Statutory certificates

In addition to the Road Traffic, Merchant Shipping, and Companies **19.116** Acts, and the Acts dealing with professional bodies, there are a number of statutes which provide for the issue of licences or certificates and prohibit the fraudulent obtaining or the forgery of the relevant documents.[28]

Telephones. Dishonest use of a service provided by a licensed telecom- **19.117** munication system, other than a service broadcast from the United Kingdom,[29] with intent to avoid payment is an offence under section 2 of the Telecommunications Act 1984.[30]

---

[26] Maximum penalty a fine of the prescribed sum and three months on summary conviction, two years and a fine on indictment.

[27] *infra*, para. 47.30.

[28] For example, Pedlars Act, 1871, s.12; Firearms Act 1968, s.39 (as amended by the Firearms (Amendment) Act 1997, Sched. 2, para. 2); Consumer Credit Act 1974, s.7.

[29] See Copyright, Designs and Patents Act 1988, s.297(1), *supra*, para. 15.49.

[30] Maximum penalty (as amended by the Telecommunications (Fraud) Act 1997, s.2) on indictment, five years' and a fine, on summary conviction, six months and a fine of the prescribed sum. See also s.42A, inserted by the Telecommunications (Fraud) Act 1997, s.1.

Property Misdescriptions

19.118 *Property Misdescriptions Act 1991.* Section 1 of this Act provides:

> "(1) Where a false or misleading statement about a prescribed matter is made in the course of an estate agency business or a property development business,[31] otherwise than in providing conveyancing services,[32] the person by whom the business is carried on shall be guilty of an offence under this section.
>
> (2) Where the making of the statement is due to the act or default of an employee the employee shall be guilty of an offence under this section; and the employee may be proceeded against and punished whether or not proceedings are also taken against his employer.
>
> (3) A person guilty of an offence under this section shall be liable—
>
> (a) on summary conviction, to a fine not exceeding the statutory maximum, and
>
> (b) on conviction on indictment, to a fine.
>
> . . .
>
> (5) For the purposes of this section—
>
> (a) "false" means false to a material degree,
>
> (b) a statement is misleading if (though not false) what a reasonable person may be expected to infer from it, or from any omission from it, is false,
>
> (c) a statement may be made by pictures or any other method of signifying meaning as well as by words and, if made by words, may be made orally or in writing,
>
> (d) a prescribed matter is any matter relating to land which is specified in an order made by the Secretary of State".[33]

A person accused of a contravention of section 1 may avail himself of the "due diligence" defence provided under section 2.

---

[31] See subs. (5), paras (e) and (f).
[32] See *ibid.*, para. (g).
[33] See the Property Misdescriptions (Specified Matters) Order 1992 (S.I. 1992 No. 2834), Sched.

CHAPTER 20

RESET

COMMON LAW RESET

Reset is the retention of goods obtained by theft, robbery, fraud or **20.01**
embezzlement, with the intention of keeping them from their true
owner. The goods must have been obtained from the true owner by
someone other than the resetter, and must have been obtained by the
resetter with the consent of the person from whom he received them.
The most common type of reset is the purchase by A from B of goods
which B has stolen from C, and such a case presents little difficulty,
except from the point of view of evidence. Reset does, however, raise
some difficult problems because of the necessity of distinguishing it from
art and part guilt in theft, and because of the understandable tendency to
use it as a substitute for accession after the fact in cases of theft.

Reset was originally limited to reset of theft, and later, when robbery
was recognised as a distinct crime, of robbery.[1] It now extends to fraud
and embezzlement as well,[2] but such cases of reset as appear in the
reports are cases of reset of theft, and the law of reset was formed in the
context of theft. The principles of reset will therefore be discussed with
reference to reset of theft.[3]

Retention. "Retention" means "retention of possession", and it is **20.02**
submitted that there should be no reset without possession by the
accused.[4] "Possession" is not used in any technical sense, and is probably
best described as "having in one's keeping", or "having under one's
control". It is not necessary for the resetter actually to handle the goods
himself. If A owns a warehouse into which B puts stolen goods with A's
knowledge, or if A has a servant who receives stolen goods for him from
B, A is guilty of reset even if he never sees the goods. Macdonald says,
"If the first offender with his knowledge hide the property, even in a
hole in a wall, and he connive at this, he is guilty",[5] and it is submitted
that this is correct provided the goods are hidden there for him and not
for the thief. It is probably also the case that A may have constructive
possession of goods by coming into possession of a delivery note or other
document making him their possessor in law.

The law of art and part applies in reset as in other crimes, so that if A
sends B out to collect stolen goods from a thief, A is guilty of reset from

---

[1] *Isabella Cowan and Ors* (1845) 2 Broun 398; *Melville Anderson* (1846) Ark. 203; *Daniel Clark* (1867) 5 Irv. 437.
[2] Criminal Law (Consolidation) (Scotland) Act 1995, s.51.
[3] The 1995 Act, s.7(4)(a), permits a district court to try cases of "reset of theft" but not, by implication, cases involving other forms of reset.
[4] Hume, i, 113 — but see *infra*, paras 20.17–20.19.
[5] Macdonald, p.68.

the moment B comes into possession of the goods. Similarly, if a number of men go out to collect stolen goods from a thief, they are all guilty of reset, even although only one of them actually handles the goods.[6]

It is the possessing and not the receiving which is important. It does not matter whether A receives the goods from the thief or from someone who has himself received them from the thief, either innocently or as himself a resetter.[7] If A himself originally receives the goods innocently and subsequently keeps them after learning that they are stolen, he becomes guilty of reset when he acquires the guilty knowledge.[8]

Once A has received the goods any period of retention, however slight, is sufficient to complete the crime,[9] which means in effect that the receiving is in itself sufficient retention. In *Robt Finlay and Ors*[10] the thieves threw the goods on a bed in the accused's house, and one of the accused who threw a cover over the goods and then jumped out of the window was convicted of reset. Alison says:

> "Although, therefore, it would be hard to fix on a prisoner a charge of reset, merely because goods are thrown in at his window, or thrust in at his door, before he is well aware what is going forward; yet if he once acquiesce in the placing of the goods there under circumstances inferring his guilty knowledge, and still more if he lend any aid towards their concealment, even though it be only to screen the thief from detection, or extricate him from pursuit, his guilt is incurred."[11]

20.03   Reset is a continuing crime and is committed throughout the time that A is in possession of the goods with guilty knowledge, and wherever he goes with them or has them in possession.[12] If, therefore, A helps B, who is a resetter, either to obtain, or to keep, or to dispose of, the goods, A is guilty of reset art and part.

20.04   The common law position where the reset occurs in a different country from the theft is unsettled.[13] So far as thefts in England and Northern Ireland are concerned the matter is regulated by section 11(4)(b) of the 1995 Act, which curiously provides that: "Any person

---

[6] See, *e.g.*, *McRae v. H.M. Advocate*, 1975 J.C. 34, where two men accompanied a woman when she used a stolen cheque book to obtain goods: all three were considered to have been in possession of the cheque book at the relevant time. *Cf. McAttee and Ors v. Hogg* (1903) 4 Adam 190, a case on the meaning of "have in . . . possession" under the Salmon Fisheries (Scotland) Act 1868, s.21. But in *Purcell v. Brown* (1967) 31 J.C.L. 135 there was held to be no reset where the resetter bought but did not take delivery of goods from the thief who then hid them without the knowledge of the resetter.

[7] Hume, i, 114; Alison, i, 329; Burnett, p.156; Macdonald, pp. 67–68.

[8] Burnett, p.157; *Helen Russell and Ors* (1832) Bell's Notes 46; *Gold v. Neilson* (1907) 5 Adam 423, L.J.-C. Macdonald at 431.

[9] Alison, i, 333; Macdonald, p.68.

[10] (1826) Alison, i, 333.

[11] Alison, i, 333. See also *Wm Boyd and Ors* (1823) Alison, i, 329 where the thieves laid a bundle of stolen goods on the floor, and these were looked at by the accused, and "some communing [had] taken place about their purchase, which, however, was not finally concluded." The accused were convicted of reset, but it is submitted that that goes too far, as there does not appear to have been any possession at all by them (and, assuming this to be relevant, no sufficient connivance either — see para. 20.19, *infra*), so that at most there could be only attempted reset, or perhaps only attempted incitement to reset.

[12] *Gold v. Neilson* (1907) 5 Adam 423; *Gracie v. Stuart* (1884) 5 Couper 379.

[13] But *cf. Joseph Taylor* (1767) Hume, ii, 54, *Maclaurin's Cases*, No. 76; see Vol. I, para. 3.50.

who . . . in Scotland receives property stolen in any other part of the United Kingdom may be dealt with, indicted, tried and punished in Scotland in like manner as if he had stolen it in Scotland." This probably amounts to an unfortunate drafting error, since the final phrase should have read, "as if it had been stolen in Scotland"[14]; but whether or not property has been "stolen" would probably fall to be decided by reference to the law of the place of the alleged taking.

HUSBAND AND WIFE. A wife who receives or conceals goods stolen by **20.05** her husband and brought by him to their common abode, will not be convicted of reset unless she takes an active part in disposing of the goods, or, perhaps, makes a practice of resetting from her husband.[15] Alison gives the reason for the rule as "that the wife is considered as bound, by the humanity of the law, to cherish and protect her husband, and, so far from informing against him, to conceal his delinquencies, and protect him from punishment."[16] Anything which falls outwith Alison's description or rationale will fall outwith the privilege: it has thus been held that a wife had no privileged position where she retained the proceeds of a robbery carried out by her husband, those proceeds having been posted through her letter box by a third party some little time after her husband had begun to serve a sentence of imprisonment for the robbery itself.[17] Alison holds that a husband is not excused for resetting from his wife, saying that he cannot claim to have acted *ex reverentia mariti*,[18] and that probably remains the legal position.[19] This privilege is, therefore, of very limited application.

HARBOURING. Reset must be distinguished from the separate offence **20.06** of harbouring thieves.[20] It is not reset to allow a thief and his booty to come into one's house, so long as the thief remains in exclusive possession of the goods. But if the thief takes refuge in A's house and leaves his goods there, A may have joint possession of them with the thief, and be guilty of reset.

The goods. In reset of theft the goods must be stolen[21] and whatever can **20.07** be stolen can be resetted,[22] and it is submitted further that only goods which have been stolen can be resetted. That is to say, it is submitted that the proceeds of theft, the surrogate of stolen goods, cannot be the subject of reset. This submission is supported by Macdonald,[23] by the

---

[14] *cf*. Criminal Procedure (Scotland) Act 1975, ss. 7(2) and 292(2), now replaced by s.11(4)(b) of the 1995 Act: see Vol. I, para. 3.50, n.7.

[15] Alison, i, 338–339; Macdonald, p.68; *Boyd and Mary Maccormick* (1827) Alison, i, 339; *Thos Mallach and Anr* (1828) *ibid.*; *John and Mary Hamilton* (1849) J. Shaw 149.

[16] Alison, i, 339.

[17] *Smith v. Watson*, 1982 J.C. 34.

[18] Alison, i, 339.

[19] *Smith v. Watson*, 1982 J.C. 34.

[20] Hume, i, 113; Alison, i, 328; Macdonald, p.67. The authority for a common law crime of harbouring thieves appears to be an incidental reference to it by Hume in this context: if it exists it probably falls under the heading of offences against the course of justice. For statutory harbouring see *infra*, para. 20.26.

[21] *Donaldson v. Buchan* (1861) 4 Irv. 109.

[22] Including a child, since *plagium* is only a type of theft, although in *H.M. Advocate v. Cairney or Cook and Anr* (1897) 2 Adam 471, the reset charge was libelled in language suggesting that it was considered to be an innominate offence: as a charge of detaining and secreting a child known to be stolen, "for the purpose and with the effect of preventing [her mother] . . . obtaining [her] custody."

[23] Macdonald, p.68.

general tenor of Hume's treatment of the subject with its emphasis on the idea of detaining property from the owner,[24] and by Anderson who says, "Reset applies only to specific articles dishonestly obtained. If stolen property has been sold or pledged, it is not reset to receive the proceeds."[25] No *vitium reale* attaches to .the surrogate of stolen goods, and it is suggested that reset should be restricted to those cases in which the owner would have a real action against the resetter for his property.[26] In *Helen Blair*[27] the accused was charged with resetting 32 £1 notes which were said to be the balance of two £20 notes which had been stolen and changed into smaller notes. It was objected that this could not be reset because the single notes were not stolen property, but the question was not decided.[28] It is submitted that Macdonald is correct when he says that reset of money must be treated in the same way as reset of any other article[29]; indeed it is submitted that the case of money is here *a fortiori* of other types of article, because of its negotiable nature.[30]

20.08   "REGAINED GOODS". In *Alexander Hamilton*[31] the thief was caught by the police in possession of the stolen goods which were handed back to him so that he might take them to the resetter, which he did. The resetter was then prosecuted, and objected that at the time he received the goods they were no longer in the power of the thief, but had reverted to the owner, and so were no longer "stolen goods". The question was left undecided[32] and has not since been raised in a reported case. Macdonald expresses no opinion on the matter: he refers to a case[33] in which a solicitor who bought stolen goods from a thief on the owner's behalf was acquitted, but the acquittal in that case depends on the absence of any intention by the accused to detain the goods from the owner, and the question raised in *Hamilton*[34] does not enter into the case. Anderson indicates that in his view the charge in *Hamilton* was bad, saying that, "as the thief honestly acquired the goods from the police . . . the charge was dropped."[35] The matter is not an easy one. In the situation posited A does receive the goods with the intention of detaining them from the owner, and receives them from the thief. It can also be argued that the "consent" of the owner should be of no more effect in this situation than is the "consent" of an owner who sets a trap for a thief by leaving marked notes for him to steal. It is, however, possible to distinguish the "theft-trap" from the "reset-trap" by reference to the requirement of "stolen goods" as part of the *actus reus* of

[24] Hume, i, 113.

[25] Anderson, p.187.

[26] English law adopts the contrary view: Theft Act 1968, s.24(2).

[27] (1848) Art. 459.

[28] Lord Moncreiff said that he was not prepared to say that the objection was sound: at 461.

[29] Macdonald, p.68.

[30] The obsolete and now repealed Frauds by Workmen Act 1748 provided that anyone who received certain materials from persons employed or hired to prepare them or make up articles from them without the employer's or hirer's consent, should be guilty of an offence, "whether the same be or be not first . . . made up" if he knew that the employee or hired person had purloined or embezzled them: s.2.

[31] (1833) Bell's Notes 46.

[32] The court having "intimated, that, as the point had occurred on a sudden and was one certainly of novelty, they thought, without expressing a definite opinion on it, that it was so doubtful as to render it proper not to allow that charge to go to the jury": Bell's Notes 46.

[33] *Cook's Case* (1917) Macdonald 67.

[34] (1833) Bell's Notes 46, *supra*.

[35] Anderson, p.186.

reset, which brings one back to the meaning of that phrase. The important question is "When do stolen goods cease to have that character?" It is clear that goods which were stolen last year and recovered by the owner six months ago cannot now be regarded as stolen goods, and it is impossible to fix any time after recovery at which they cease to be stolen goods, so that one must probably hold that they lose that character as soon as the owner recovers them and whatever he does with them thereafter.[36] It is not, however, necessary to regard them as no longer "stolen goods" at any time before the owner recovers them, and it may be argued that if the police recover them from the thief and immediately return them to him to give to the resetter, they remain stolen goods.[37] This has the advantage of making it possible for resetters to be caught in traps, but there is force in the argument that when the police hold recovered property they do so on behalf of the owner. The position where a private individual recovers the property and hands it back to the thief to give to a resetter with the intention of trapping the resetter is more difficult, but it can perhaps there be said that the goods retain their character unless the private individual happens to be acting as the agent of the owner.

On the whole matter it is suggested that the best course is to regard the goods as ceasing to be "stolen" when they have been recovered by anyone acting on behalf of the owner, and to regard the police as acting on his behalf.[38]

Mens rea. There are two distinct elements in the *mens rea* of reset: guilty **20.09** knowledge and an intention to detain the goods from the owner.

GUILTY KNOWLEDGE. There can be no reset unless the person in possession of the goods knows that they have been stolen. "Bare suspicion . . . or reasons of hesitation and conjecture on the subject, are no sufficient grounds of conviction."[39] The presence or absence of knowledge, however, is usually ascertained objectively, and "it is sufficient, if circumstances are proved, which, to persons of an ordinary understanding, and situated as the pannel was, must have led to the conclusion that they were theftuously acquired."[40] No doubt, if an accused's explanation of ignorance is believed he will be acquitted whatever the state of the objective evidence, but equally an accused will rarely be believed in the face of strong objective evidence of knowledge.

---

[36] *cf.* the current position in English law under the Theft Act 1968, s.24(3): "no goods shall be regarded as having continued to be stolen goods after they have been returned to the person from whom they were stolen or to other lawful possession or custody, or after that person and any other person claiming through him have otherwise ceased as regards these goods to have any right to restitution in respect of the theft." See also Smith and Hogan, pp. 632–634.

[37] The existence of this distinction between recovery by the police and recovery by the owner was left open in the South African case of ex *p. Minister of Justice: In Re R. v. Maserow*, 1942 A.D. 164.

[38] In England property which has come into the hands of the police ceases to be stolen when, as a question of fact, the policeman "reduces the goods into his possession": *Att.-Gen.'s Reference (No. 1 of 1974)* [1974] Q.B. 744. If the goods have ceased to be stolen, this does not, of course, rule out attempted reset of them: see Vol. I, paras 6.55 and 6.56.

[39] Hume, i, 114. *Cf.* Alison, i, 328–331; Burnett, p.156; Macdonald, p.67; *Jas. Johnie* (1775) Hume, i, 114; Burnett, p.156; *cf. Watson and Gray* (1799) Hume, ii, 444, Burnett, p.156, where Hume and Burnett suggest that even "reason to believe" the goods stolen is not enough; *Isabella Stark or Mould* (1835) Bell's Notes 46.

[40] Alison, i, 330. *Cf.* Hume, i, 114.

In *Herron v. Latta*[41] the sheriff spoke in his stated case of wilful blindness,[42] but in sentencing the accused he said, "You did not really care whether the goods were honestly acquired or otherwise so long as you had them at a price substantially below the price you would have to pay otherwise." This is similar to the approach of the Rhodesian Appellate Division in *R. v. Ushewokunze*[43] where it was said to be enough to prove that the accused must have foreseen the real possibility that the goods were stolen and did not care, and not necessary to consider why he made no inquiry, and so not necessary to show that he deliberately refrained from making inquiries.[44]

20.10   The extreme requirements of the substantive law are very much weakened by the rule of evidence that where A is in possession of recently stolen goods in criminative circumstances he must displace the inference of guilt raised by these circumstances, a displacement very difficult to achieve in practice.[45]

20.11   The Criminal Procedure (Scotland) Act 1887, in extending reset to cover fraud and embezzlement, provided that "it shall be sufficient to set forth" in the charge that the goods were dishonestly appropriated "by theft or robbery, or by breach of trust and embezzlement, or by falsehood, fraud, and wilful imposition, as the case may be,"[46] which suggests that there are three distinct crimes: reset of theft or robbery, reset of embezzlement, and reset of fraud, and that if the Crown charge reset of theft they will fail if it turns out that the goods were obtained by

---

[41] Glasgow Sheriff Court, May 1967; (1968) 32 J.C.L. 51. The subsequent, unsuccessful, appeal is reported as *Latta v. Herron*, 1967 S.C.C.R. (Supp.) 18.

[42] *cf.* Vol. I, para. 7.64.

[43] 1971 (2) S.A. 360.

[44] In England, where the Theft Act 1968, s.22, talks of "knowing or believing" the goods are stolen, it is necessary to be satisfied that the defendant actually knew or believed that the goods in question were stolen. Consequently, it is insufficient that there were grounds for great suspicion such that the only reasonable conclusion was that the goods were stolen — if the defendant did not in fact believe that conclusion and closed his eyes to the obvious: *R. v. Forsyth* (1997) 2 Cr.App.R. 299, Beldam J.J. at 321A-E, disapproving *R. v. Hall* (1985) 81 Cr.App.R. 260, Boreham J. at 264, but upholding *R. v. Mays* (1984) 79 Cr.App.R. 72, Lord Lane C.J. at 75–76. See also *R. v. Grainge* [1974] 1 All E.R. 928; *R. v. Griffiths* (1974) 60 Cr.App.R. 14, both disapproving *Atwal v. Massey* [1971] 3 All E.R. 881, Lord Widgery C.J. at 882g-h; Smith and Hogan, pp. 645–646.

[45] *cf.* Vol. I, para. 7.27. It would be a misdirection, however, for a trial judge to tell a jury that it is for the accused to prove his innocence if they consider all the components of "the doctrine of recent possession" to be present: *McDonald (J. McF.) v. H.M. Advocate*, 1989 S.C.C.R. 559. Such a direction might also now contravene Art. 6(2) of the European Convention on Human Rights.

The Model Penal Code makes a belief that property has "probably been stolen" sufficient, and this would clearly not be so in Scotland: see Model Penal Code, O.D., s.223.6 (1). The Code also provides that knowledge or belief is to be presumed where a dealer has property stolen from separate persons on separate occasions, has received stolen property in another transaction within the preceding year, or being a dealer in that sort of property buys for a consideration he knows to be far below its reasonable value: *ibid.* s.223.6 (2). There are no such rules in Scotland although a low price is a circumstance tending to prove a "thieves' bargain," and so a criminative circumstance. If anything, a dealer in Scotland is in a better position than persons who are not dealers: *cf. Fox v. Patterson*, 1948 J.C. 104. In practice the possession of the proceeds of more than one theft, or the payment of a low price, a "rogue's bargain", is a strong element in proof of knowledge. It is also competent in a reset trial to lead evidence of previous convictions and evidence of possession by the accused within the preceding year of other stolen property: Prevention of Crimes Act 1871, s.19, but this is never done.

[46] Section 58, now 1995 Act, Sched. 3, para. 8(1).

fraud or embezzlement.[47] If that is so, it will be a good defence to the accused to show in a charge of reset of theft that he believed that the goods were only embezzled or fraudulently obtained, although such a defence would not be received with much sympathy. It would, however, be sufficient for the Crown to show that he knew them to have been obtained in the way charged without showing that he knew any of the details of the original appropriation.[48]

THE INTENTION. The *mens rea* of reset is said to require an intention to **20.12** conceal and withhold the goods from the owner.[49] But although the accused must mean to prevent the owner recovering the goods, he need not mean to keep them for himself, or to keep them for any length of time. If A takes possession of goods in order to hide them for a few minutes while the police search the place where B, the thief or another resetter, has placed them, A is guilty of reset since he is in possession of the goods with the intention of preventing their recovery by the owner. Again, A is equally guilty of reset whether he has the goods in order to assist the thief, or in order to make some profit for himself.[50] Where, however, he obtains the goods on behalf of the owner[51] or, like a policeman, with the intention of returning them to the owner, there can be no question of reset, whether or not he obtains them directly from the thief, and whether or not he pays the thief for them.

Reset of embezzlement. There are no reported cases of this kind and reset **20.13** of "proper embezzlement"[52] is probably impossible, since the essence of "proper embezzlement" is the absence of any duty to deliver any specific articles to the true owner, so that in such cases there are no "stolen goods" to reset.[53] Reset of embezzlement will therefore in practice be restricted to cases where the goods were originally obtained by theft-embezzlement.[54]

Reset of fraud. Here again there are no reported cases, but there are no **20.14** practical difficulties in charging A with resetting goods fraudulently appropriated by B. It might be argued, however, that since B has a voidable title to the goods, A should really be charged with theft from the original owner.[55]

---

[47] *cf. O'Brien v. Strathern*, 1922 J.C. 55, where the underlying assumption was that it was a defence to a charge of reset of theft to show that the goods were embezzled. See also *D.P.P. v. Neiser* [1959] 1 Q.B. 254.

[48] There is old authority that it is no defence to a charge of reset of theft that the goods were obtained by robbery, but that in a charge of reset of robbery it must be shown that the accused knew they were obtained by violence: *Melville Anderson* (1846) Ark. 203. *Cf. Jas Denholm and Thos Mill* (1858) 3 Irv. 101. The phraseology of the 1995 Act suggests that theft and robbery are equivalent for the purposes of reset, so that it would not now be a defence to a charge of reset of robbery to plead that one believed there had been only theft.

[49] Hume, i, 113. *Cf.* Alison, i, 328; Macdonald, p.68; *Clark v. H.M. Advocate*, 1965 S.L.T. 250.

[50] Hume, i, 113.

[51] *Cook's Case* (1917) Macdonald 67.

[52] See *supra*, para. 17.04.

[53] The defaulting solicitor's mistress is not guilty of resetting her weekly dress allowance because she knows it has been taken out of a trust fund administered by her lover!

[54] See *supra*, para. 17.04.

[55] The idea of reset of fraud is strongly attacked as unreal by Gill.

Reset and art and part theft

20.15   Reset and theft are mutually exclusive crimes. A thief cannot be guilty of resetting the goods he has stolen,[56] and equally a person who is art and part in the theft cannot be guilty of reset.[57] Fagin was not a resetter but a thief. Alison suggests that a resetter who receives the goods immediately after the theft may thereby become art and part in the theft,[58] but although such "immediate reset" may be evidence of art and part guilt in the theft, it cannot in itself constitute such guilt or amount to theft.[59] There can, of course, be art and part guilt in theft by assistance at the time without previous concert, but if the theft is completed before the receiver becomes involved, he cannot be guilty of theft.[60]

In *Blackies v. Gair*[61] a child found an article in the street and took it home to her parents who appropriated it. It was held that this might be either theft or reset by the parents — reset if the child had formed the intention to steal the thing before she gave it to her parents, theft if she had not. In *Robert and Agnes Black*,[62] Mrs B found a pocket book and took it home to her husband. Both were convicted of theft on the ground that the intention to appropriate the book had been formed in concert after Mrs B had taken it home. Had she appropriated it herself and then brought it home that would have been a completed theft, and Mr B could have been guilty only of reset.

20.16   *Reset and accession after the fact.* Unlike certain other systems Scots law does not distinguish between the person who receives stolen goods for the purpose of assisting the thief, and the person who receives them for his own benefit[63]: both are guilty of reset. Since a person who is art and

---

[56] Hume, i, 116; Alison, i, 331; Macdonald, p.67: *Backhurst v. MacNaughton*, 1981 S.C.C.R. 6; *Druce v. Friel*, 1994 S.C.C.R. 432. In Canada, it has been held that a man may be guilty of unlawful possession of goods after his release from prison following on conviction for stealing them: *Côté v. R.* [1975] 1 S.C.R. 303

[57] *cf. Wilson v. McFadyean*, 1945 J.C. 42, L.J.-G. Normand at 45. In *Harris v. Clark*, 1958 J.C. 3, the accused had invited a youth to steal certain articles which the accused had then bought from him. He was charged and convicted of reset without any objection being taken that the crime proved was theft. It is submitted that such an objection should have been successful, since his previous concert with the thief made him guilty of the theft, and in such circumstances "the charge of reset cannot with propriety be made use of": Hume, i, 116; *Anderson and Marshall* (1728) *ibid.*; *Wright and Ors* (1803) Burnett 275; *Walker* (1801) Burnett 555; *Macdonald and Wilson* (1818) Hume, i, 116.

It is competent to convict of reset on a charge of theft: 1995 Act, Sched. 3, para. 8(2), and common to do so, but incompetent to convict of theft on a charge of reset. It may also be argued that the 1995 Act merely implies an alternative charge of reset in every indictment or complaint for theft, and that in order to obtain a conviction for reset the Crown must prove reset, and so must exclude theft, which would often mean that the Crown would fail and the accused escape between two stools. In practice, however, where it is clear that the accused is either thief or resetter, and the Crown cannot prove theft, he is convicted of reset. But when he is charged with reset and is proved to have been a thief or art and part in theft it is submitted that the law still is that he must be acquitted: see *Backhurst v. MacNaughton*, 1981 S.C.C.R. 6.

[58] Alison, i, 333.

[59] *cf.* Hume, i, 116. In *People v. Egan* [1989] I.R. 681, A was asked by some people to let them use his premises to hide the proceeds of what he said he thought was going to be a minor theft, "a small stroke". They then brought the proceeds of an armed robbery to his premises. He was convicted of the robbery, and acquitted of a charge of reset.

[60] *Mackenzie and Johnston* (1846) Ark. 135.

[61] (1859) 3 Irv. 425.

[62] (1841) Bell's Notes 46.

[63] *cf.* J. Burchell and J. Milton, *Principles of Criminal Law* (2nd ed., 1997), p.552; see also *R. v. von Elling*, 1945 A.D. 234.

part with the thief cannot be guilty of reset it follows that, whatever the position with regard to jurisdiction,[64] theft is not regarded as a *crimen continuum* in this connection; for if it were, someone who received goods for the purpose of helping the thief would be guilty of theft. His innocence of theft depends on the absence of accession after the fact in Scots law, and on the fact that the theft is completed once the goods have been appropriated by the thief.

Now, if it is "the fundamental circumstance" of reset that the goods must come into the resetter's possession,[65] then this, taken in conjunction with the considerations just mentioned, can lead to some unwelcome results. It means, for one thing that if A helps B to dispose of goods stolen by B, A is guilty of no crime[66] so long as he does not have the goods in his possession. The desire to avoid this result has led to the recognition of the most minimal possession as sufficient for reset.[67] For example, it was not receiving in England for A to help a thief to carry goods out to his, the thief's, car,[68] but it would probably be reset in Scotland. This, however, only accentuates the paradoxical nature of the Scots position. For in Scotland if A arranges for the disposal by the thief B of stolen goods to C and accompanies B to C's house, and even obtains payment from B for his help, he may not be guilty of reset, but if he happens to help B to carry the goods to C's house he is guilty of reset. Moreover, if A were to come into the matter at a later stage and assist C to dispose of the goods to D he would be guilty of reset whether or not he ever had possession of the goods, since he would then be art and part with a resetter. Scots law suffers from the absence of accession after the fact, and has tried to use reset to make good the deficiency: but reset cannot serve this purpose completely so long as reset can be invoked only against a possessor. There can be no reset so long as the thief remains in exclusive possession of the goods,[69] and he cannot be said to share possession with A just because A tells him where he can find a buyer, or even acts as his agent in approaching the buyer.[70]

"PRIVY TO THE RETENTION". In an attempt to close the gap in the law **20.17** which results from the above considerations, Macdonald extended reset to cover "being privy to the retaining of property . . . dishonestly come by", even where the accused "never laid a finger on the property stolen."[71] If, as Macdonald suggests at one stage, this is confined to connivance at the retention of the property by a third party, it merely

---

[64] See Hume, ii, 54; *Joseph Taylor* (1767) Hume, ii, 54; Alison, ii, 77–78; *Robt Hay* (1877) 3 Couper 491; *Jas Stevenson* (1853) 1 Irv. 341.

[65] And the authoritative writers entertain no doubts that it is: see Hume, i, 113; Burnett, p.155; Alison, i, 328: *cf*. paras 20.17–20.19, *infra*.

[66] Unless, perhaps, of some form of attempt to pervert the course of justice, but this is highly dubious.

[67] Alison, i, 333, *supra*.

[68] *Hobson v. Impett* (1957) 41 Cr.App.R. 138.

[69] Hume, i, 113.

[70] If A were the buyer's agent he would be art and part in the reset which commences when the buyer obtains possession. But in the case posited, A is the thief's agent, and cannot fairly be said to be in concert with the buyer. In any event there will be cases where A drops out of the picture before the buyer obtains possession, or where there is no buyer but A merely tells the thief of a good hiding place.

[71] Macdonald, p.67; 3rd ed., p.90.

applies the ordinary law of art and part guilt to reset and is unexceptionable.[72] But in *H.M. Advocate v. Browne*[73] the author of Macdonald in his capacity as Lord Justice-Clerk discarded the requirement of possession altogether. The case itself was very simple — two accused were charged with theft and the evidence consisted of recent possession, a situation in which a jury might have convicted them either of theft or of reset — but Lord Justice-Clerk Macdonald gave the following direction:

> "If a man steals a bundle of notes out of a man's pocket, and after that informs another man that he has got these notes, that he has stolen them, or if the other man saw him stealing them and knew that they were stolen, then if the other man connived at it remaining in the possession of the thief or being put in any place for safe custody, such as hiding it in a cupboard, he is guilty of receiving feloniously even although he never puts his fingers on the notes at all. Reset consists of being privy to the retaining of property that has been dishonestly come by."[74]

This statement has been accepted by Anderson[75] and is given by the editors of the 5th edition of Macdonald as the authority for the statement that it is reset to connive at a third (*sic*) party retaining the goods. It was also approved by the High Court in *McCawley v. H.M. Advocate*,[76] where the accused who was a passenger in a stolen car when it was intercepted by the police was convicted of reset on the ground that he was privy to the driver's retention of the vehicle.[77] Lord Justice-General Clyde considered that there was sufficient evidence of privity since the accused had travelled "for some little distance at least in the stolen car", had run away when the police stopped the vehicle, and had otherwise "sought to evade capture".[78] It is difficult to see, however, the way in which the accused's escape from the scene and his subsequent efforts to evade capture contributed to his being "privy to the retention of the vehicle".

20.18   Macdonald's views were criticised by the Criminal Appeal Court in *Clark v. H.M. Advocate*[79] but were not overruled. The accused in *Clark* had accompanied the thief to a meeting at which the thief had handed

---

[72] Macdonald also says (at p.67) that "there must be an actual receiving, either by taking the property into possession, or by being privy to its being retained from the owner," which becomes more self-contradictory than at first appears if it is to be read as applying where neither the accused not his fellow-resetters have actual possession.

[73] (1903) 6 F. (J) 24 — its omission from Adam's Justiciary Reports may be significant.

[74] At p.26.

[75] Anderson, p.185.

[76] 1959 S.C.C.R. (Supp.) 2. The case is discussed by J.F. Wallace in "Reset without Possession" (1960) 5 J.L.S. 55. See also *Hoy v. MacLeod*, High Court appeal, Feb., 1967, unrep'd: (1967) 31 J.C.L. 135, where the accused merely rode pillion on a scooter stolen by the driver the day before.

[77] It is arguable that a passenger is in joint possession of the vehicle with the driver but the argument is very tenuous, and in any event the decision in *McCawley* proceeded on the basis of *Browne* and on the view that possession was unnecessary.

[78] *ibid*., at p. 4. *Cf. Hipson v. Tudhope*, 1983 S.C.C.R. 247 (where a conviction for reset was quashed, in that the accused — a passenger in a stolen car — made no attempt to escape and said no more than "not guilty" after the car crashed as a result of a police chase) and *Girdwood v. Houston*, 1989 S.C.C.R. 578 (where a conviction for reset was upheld on the basis that the accused, having originally denied all knowledge of the theft of goods, eventually and voluntarily admitted that he knew they were stolen and led the police to their place of concealment). See also para. 20.19, *infra*.

[79] 1965 S.L.T. 250.

over some of the stolen property to one W. who agreed to try to sell the property for the thief. The accused took no part in the meeting and was not present later the same day when W. gave the thief the money he had obtained from the sale of the property. The sheriff charged the jury in terms of *Browne*[80] and then, when they asked for further direction on the meaning of "connivance", told them that they:

> "[w]ould be entitled to draw an inference from the fact that he did nothing whatever to inform the police or anyone of that sort that stolen property was being disposed of, and that might raise an inference of connivance, but you have got to find this thing called connivance or whatever it is first of all, the mere fact that the accused was in company with the thief is not by itself sufficient."

It was this additional direction which was attacked in Clark's appeal against his conviction, and the court held that it constituted a misdirection, and that connivance could not be inferred from mere inactivity. Lord Justice-Clerk Grant and Lord Strachan went on, however, to comment on Macdonald's definition of reset, although neither the defence nor the Crown had attacked it. Lord Grant said he did not fully understand the direction in *Browne* and had difficulty in reconciling it with the principle that possession is fundamental to reset. Lord Grant also pointed out that Hume's reference to privity and connivance was restricted to the case where the goods are found in the accused's premises. Lord Strachan shared Lord Grant's difficulty in reconciling *Browne* and the requirement of possession, but said that Macdonald's views "appear to have remained unquestioned for more than sixty years and they could not be overruled without hearing adequate argument on both sides. I content myself therefore with the observation that in an appropriate case they may have to be reconsidered."[81]

Reconsideration may, however, have been ruled out by the appeal **20.19** court's reassertion and specific approval of *McCawley*[82] in *McNeil v. H.M. Advocate.*[83] It was a case in which the accused introduced the thief to the resetter to whom the goods were being taken in a car in which the accused was a passenger. The only point in the appeal, however, was the correctness of a direction to the jury in terms of *Browne*,[84] and the court held that, "if an accused is privy to the retention of property dishonestly come by he may be guilty of reset, although he is not in actual possession of the goods." Presumably this means "although he is not art and part in possession either". But there remains a difficulty in reconciling *McCawley* with *Clark's*[85] insistence on active connivance, and it is submitted that it is inconsistent with *Clark* to convict of reset simply on evidence that the accused was a passenger in a car he knew to have been stolen.[86]

---

[80] (1903) 6 F.(J) 24: see para. 20.17, *supra*.

[81] 1965 S.L.T., at p. 253: L.J.-C. Grant's views are set out on p.252.

[82] 1959 S.C.C.R. (Supp.) 2: see para. 20.17, *supra*.

[83] 1968 J.C. 29, heard by the same "Division" as decided *McCawley*.

[84] (1903) 6 F.(J) 24: see para. 20.17, *supra*.

[85] 1965 S.L.T. 250: see para. 20.18, *supra*.

[86] *cf.* an interesting French case where this was held to be reset on the basis of a general provision in the (then) Code Pénal making it an offence to benefit from the "produit" of a crime: Art. 460; the decision was strongly criticised because of the absence of possession or any positive act: see Recueil Dalloz 1971, 3.

STATUTORY OFFENCES

Army and Air Force Stores

20.20   Section 195 of the Army Act 1955 provides:

"Any person who, whether within or without Her Majesty's dominions, acquires any military stores or solicits or procures any person
to dispose of any military stores, or acts for any person in the
disposing of any military stores, shall be guilty of an offence . . .
unless he proves either—

(a) that he did not know, and could not reasonably be expected
to know, that the chattels in question were military stores, or

(b) that those chattels had (by the transaction with which he is
charged or some earlier transaction) been disposed of by
order or with the consent of the [Defence] Council or of
some person or authority who had, or whom he had reasonable cause to believe to have, power to give the order or
consent, or

(c) that those chattels had become the property of an officer who
had retired or ceased to be an officer, or of a warrant officer,
non-commissioned officer or soldier who had been discharged, or of the personal representatives of a person who
had died."[87]

"Acquire" is defined as meaning "buy, take in exchange, take in pawn
or otherwise receive", and "dispose" means "sell, give in exchange,
pledge or otherwise hand over", whether or not, in either case, the
transaction would be lawful but for the Act.

The Air Force Act 1955, section 195, makes the same provisions with
regard to Air Force Stores, and similar provision is made for naval stores
by the Naval Discipline Act 1957, section 98. Illegal dealings in official
documents are penalised by section 196 of the Army Act 1955, section
196 of the Air Force Act 1955, and section 99 of the Naval Discipline
Act 1957.[88]

Value added tax

20.21   Section 72(10) of the Value Added Tax Act 1994 provides:

"If any person acquires possession of or deals with any goods . . .
having reason to believe that value added tax on the supply of the
goods . . ., on the acquisition of the goods from another member
State or on the importation of the goods from a place outside the
member States has been or will be evaded, he shall be liable on
summary conviction to a penalty of level 5 on the standard scale or
three times the amount of the value added tax, whichever is the
greater."

Second-hand dealing

20.22   Since resetting and dealing in second-hand goods may be linked, there
are certain provisions of the Civic Government (Scotland) Act 1982
which are concerned, albeit indirectly, with this problem. Second-hand

---

[87] Maximum penalty on indictment two years' imprisonment and a fine, the prescribed
sum and three months' on summary conviction. *Cf. O'Brien v. Strathern,* 1922 J.C. 55.
[88] Maximum penalty, level 3 on the standard scale and three months' imprisonment.

dealers are required to hold a licence,[89] and must keep such records in relation to their stock in trade as the licensing authority may require.[90] They are also generally required not to dispose of any item of stock in trade until 48 hours have passed since that item was acquired.[91] It is an offence for any person who sells anything to a second-hand dealer to give a false name or address to the dealer[92]; and such a dealer is empowered to detain any person who offers him anything which he has reason to believe is "stolen or otherwise unlawfully obtained" — the detention to be no longer than is "reasonably necessary for obtaining the attendance of a constable".[93]

Metal dealing

Dealing in metal may be linked with resetting, and to discourage this, **20.23** "metal dealers" and "itinerant metal dealers" are required to be licensed under the Civic Government (Scotland) Act 1982.[94] Records of metal acquired by such dealers must be kept[95]; and dealers must not dispose of any metal until 48 hours have passed since the time of its acquisition.[96]

Counterfeit notes and coins

Section 16 of the Forgery and Counterfeiting Act 1981 provides: **20.24**
   "(1) It is an offence for a person to have in his custody or under his control any thing which is, and which he knows or believes to be, a counterfeit of a currency note or of a protected coin, intending either to pass or tender it as genuine or to deliver it to another with the intention that he or another shall pass or tender it as genuine.[97]
   (2) It is an offence for a person to have in his custody or under his control, without lawful authority or excuse, any thing which is,

---

[89] See s.24(1). A definition of "second-hand dealer" is provided in s.24(2). Exemptions from the requirement are listed in s.24(3), and include pawnbrokers, certain wholesalers, and charitable businesses.

[90] It is an offence to operate, without reasonable excuse, as such a dealer if no licence is held: maximum penalty on summary conviction, a fine of level 4 on the standard scale; and it is also an offence under s.7(2) not to comply with any condition attached to a licence (although there is a defence of due diligence under s.7(3)): maximum penalty on summary conviction, a fine of level 3 on the standard scale.

[91] See s.25(1); exceptions are narrated in subss. (2) and (3). It is an offence under s.25(7) to fail to comply with this requirement: maximum penalty on summary conviction, a fine of level 3 on the standard scale.

[92] See s.26(1): maximum penalty on summary conviction, a fine of level 3 on the standard scale.

[93] See s.26(2), (3).

[94] See ss. 28(1) and 32(1). Definitions of "metal dealer" and "itinerant metal dealer" are provided in s.37(1); and "carrying on business as a metal dealer" is defined in s.37(2). It is an offence to operate, without reasonable excuse, as such a dealer if no licence is held: maximum penalty on summary conviction, a fine of level 4 on the standard scale.

[95] See ss. 30(2) and (5), and 33(3). It is an offence to fail to comply with this requirement — see ss. 30(6) and 33(5) — maximum penalty on summary conviction, a fine of level 3 on the standard scale.

[96] See s.31(1). Failure to comply with this requirement is an offence under s.31(5): maximum penalty on summary conviction, a fine of level 3 on the standard scale. For other offences by metal dealers or itinerant metal dealers, see s.34.

[97] Under s.22(1) the maximum penalty is on indictment 10 years and/or a fine, and on summary conviction six months and/or a fine of the statutory maximum. "Currency note" and "protected coin" are defined in s.27(1), where it is made plain that Scottish and English bank notes, as well as notes customarily used as money in other countries, and coins customarily used as money in any country are included within the offence.

and which he knows or believes to be, a counterfeit of a currency note or of a protected coin."[98]

It is also an offence at common law to vend forged bank notes for less than their nominal value.[99]

Insolvency Act 1986

20.25   Section 206(5) of this Act provides:

"When a person pawns, pledges or disposes of any property in circumstances which amount to an offence under sub-section (1)(f), every person who takes in pawn or pledge, or otherwise receives, the property knowing it to be pawned, pledged or disposed of in such circumstances, is guilty of an offence."[1]

Harbouring

20.26   Section 80 of the Licensing (Scotland) Act 1976 provides:

"If any person who occupies or keeps any premises in respect of which a licence is held—
    (a) knowingly suffers thieves or reputed thieves . . . to remain in those premises, or knowingly premits thieves or reputed thieves . . . to meet or assemble in the premises; or
    (b) knowingly permits to be deposited in the premises goods which he has reasonable grounds for believing to be stolen goods;
he shall be guilty of an offence."[2]

---

[98] Under s.22(3) the maximum penalty is on indictment two years and/or a fine, and on summary conviction six months and/or a fine of the statutory maximum. For relevant definitions, see n.97, *supra*.

[99] *John Horne* (1814) Hume, i, 150; *Wm Cooke* (1833) Bell's Notes 58; Alison, i, 406; Macdonald, p.69.

[1] Maximum penalty on indictment seven years' imprisonment and a fine; on summary conviction six months' and a fine of the statutory maximum (see Sched. 10). Section 206(1)(f) provides that it is deemed to be an offence for any past or present officer of a company, within the 12 months prior to commencement of winding up of that company, to have "pawned, pledged or disposed of any property of the company which has been obtained on credit and has not been paid for (unless the pawning, pledging or disposal was in the ordinary way of the company's business)."

[2] Maximum penalty on summary conviction a fine of level 3 on the standard scale.

CHAPTER 21

EXTORTION AND CORRUPTION

EXTORTION

Extortion is the crime of obtaining money or any other advantage[1] by **21.01**
threats, and is known in non-technical language as blackmail.[2] Hume
uses the term "blackmail" for the extortion of ransom or "protection
money" by gangs, in return for their forbearing to attack the payer,[3] but
extortion has a much wider scope than this.[4]

Extortion and theft. It may be that one particular form of theft, where the **21.02**
accused unlawfully detains property belonging to another on a temporary
basis,[5] requires the making of an extortionate demand (as a condition for
the property's return); but the case law is uncertain as to the precise
requirements of such thefts.[6] In any event, such thefts entail the
appropriation of property A until (if ever) the person entitled to it
provides the accused (or his employer or principal) with property B, or
some other advantage. It should be clear, therefore, that what is stolen is
property A, and that if property B is handed over by the victim such
property is obtained by extortion. There *may* be a symbiotic relationship
between theft and extortion (or at least attempted extortion) in such
cases, but the two crimes remain distinct.[7]

Extortion and robbery. Robbery is the obtaining of property by violence, **21.03**
or by threats of immediate violence. Where the threatened violence is
not immediate, the crime is extortion. It is robbery to make B hand over
money by a threat to kill him instantly, but extortion to make him hand
it over by a threat that if he does not do so he will be killed next week.[8]
Again, it is not robbery to force A to execute a deed surrendering an

---

[1] See, *e.g.*, *Rae v. Donnelly*, 1982 S.C.C.R. 148, where, in a case of attempted extortion,
the managing director of a company demanded that one of his former employees abandon
a case of unfair dismissal which she had commenced against his company before an
industrial tribunal.

[2] This is still the term used by English law in s.21 of the Theft Act 1968: "blackmail" in
England is, however, rather different from extortion in Scots law; see Smith and Hogan,
pp. 605–611.

[3] Hume, i, 476–477.

[4] See "Blackmail" (1893) 1 S.L.T. 344.

[5] See paras 14.10, and 14.48–14.49, *supra*.

[6] See *Milne v. Tudhope*, 1981 J.C. 53; *Kidston v. Annan*, 1984 S.C.C.R. 20: *cf. Black v.
Carmichael*; *Penrice v. Carmichael*, 1992 S.C.C.R. 709.

[7] It probably goes too far to conclude that the two crimes could then be charged
cumulatively — see, *e.g.*, *Black v. Carmichael*; *Penrice v. Carmichael*, 1992 S.C.C.R. 709,
where theft and extortion (or attempted extortion) were charged in the alternative.

[8] Hume, i, 108, 439–440; Alison, i, 232.

incorporeal right by threatening him either with personal violence or in any other way, but it is submitted that to do so would amount to extortion.[9]

21.04 *Extortion and fraud.* To induce a course of action in B by deceit is fraud; to induce such a course by threats is extortion.[10] Although extortion is more closely connected in the popular mind with robbery than with fraud, and although it is historically a development of the crime of threats, its kinship with fraud is more important than that with robbery. For it follows from the former that extortion is not confined to the sphere of economic advantage, but extends to obtaining by threats any result which it would be fraud to obtain by deceit. It would accordingly be extortion for A to induce a woman to have sexual intercourse with him by threatening her that unless she did so he would tell her husband of her adultery with B, or for A to induce a police constable not to report a crime by threatening to use his influence to impede the constable's promotion.[11]

21.05 *Extortion and threats.* Certain forms of threat are illegal in themselves, and are merely aggravated by being accompanied with a demand for money or for anything else to which the threatener is not entitled. These include threats of violence to person or property.[12] It has also been said that threats to injure a man's reputation are criminal in themselves,[13] but this, it is submitted, is too widely expressed. False accusation of crime is itself criminal[14] and threats of such false accusation are probably also criminal, but it is doubtful whether a threat to expose a man's criminal, immoral or improper behaviour would be a crime where the threat was to expose the truth and it was unaccompanied by any demand.[15]

21.06   *ALEX. F. CRAWFORD.*[16] There are a number of nineteenth century cases which dealt with threats by A that unless B paid him money he would

---

[9] *cf. John Milne* (1805) Burnett 151, where the charge was "the . . . enticing and inveigling any person into a remote place, and there intimidating, concussing, and assaulting and compelling him by threats, to deliver up, contrary to his will, any writing" — the accused had executed a trust deed in G.'s favour and delivered some bills to him: he forced G. to sign a deed prepared by the accused importing a voluntary renunciation by him of the trust. Although this was charged as an innominate offence there seems no reason why a similar situation should not today be charged as extortion.

[10] *Silverstein v. H.M. Advocate*, 1949 J.C. 160, L.J.-C. Thomson at 163.

[11] *cf.* Canadian Criminal Code, s.346(1), which talks of "intent to obtain anything"; a previous version of this offence, in similar broad terms, has been applied to sexual intercourse: *R. v. Bird* [1970] 3 C.C.C. 340.

[12] Hume, i, 135, 439–422; Anderson, p.164; Macdonald, pp.128–129; *Geo. Smith* (1846) Ark. 4. In *Alex. Findlater and Jas McDougall* (1841) 2 Swin. 527 there was a charge of "Assault, especially . . . by an officer of the law upon a prisoner . . . and more especially still when committed . . . for the purpose of extorting from such prisoner a confession of guilt." See also *Geo. Jeffrey* (1840) 2 Swin. 497 where a police officer instituted or threatened prosecutions against persons from whom he then extorted money as consideration for abandoning the prosecutions. For more modern examples of extortion charges see *Fielding v. H.M. Advocate*, 1959 J.C. 101; *Hopes and Lavery v. H.M. Advocate*, 1960 J.C. 104; *Rae v. Donnelly*, 1982 S.C.C.R. 148 (a case of attempted extortion); and *Black v. Carmichael; Penrice v. Carmichael*, 1992 S.C.C.R. 709.

[13] *Jas Miller* (1862) 4 Irv. 238, L.J.-C. Inglis at 244.

[14] *infra*, para. 47.36.

[15] *cf. Rae v. Donnelly*, 1982 S.C.C.R. 148, where such a threat (which may or may not have been true) was accompanied by a demand to drop proceedings for unfair dismissal.

[16] (1850) J. Shaw 309.

falsely accuse him of something to his discredit,[17] but the first reported case which considers the situation where the allegations are true is *Alex. F. Crawford*. Crawford had written letters to the complainer alleging that the complainer had agreed to pay him £1,000 for some work he had done in connection with an estate he was concerned in administering, and threatening that unless he were paid £200 he would make known certain malpractices of the complainer in connection with the estate. He was charged with sending threatening letters "particularly for the purpose of extorting money", and the charge was held relevant. The court rejected the argument that it was necessary to show (a) that the accusations were false,[18] and (b) that the money demanded was not due to the accused. Lord Justice-Clerk Hope summed up the matter by saying that "The crime charged . . . is, his having endeavoured to extort money, by means of threats, and that crime is equally committed, whether the party using the threat has a good or a bad debt, and whether he uses a threat of personal violence, or such threats as here."[19]

The charge in *Crawford* is essentially a charge of making threats, and represents a development of the earlier cases on threats of personal violence. The crime is complete when the threat and the demand are made, even if no money is in fact obtained.[20]

OTHER CASES. In *Marion Macdonald and Anr*[21] it was made clear that **21.07** the ratio of *Crawford*[22] applied to threats to expose sexual immorality as well as to expose crime or dishonesty.[23]

In *Priteca v. H.M. Advocate*[24] the accused sent the victim a threatening letter with a request for money. He then sent him a copy of a circular asking people not to call at his shop as he was taking liberties with female customers. He was charged with sending a threatening letter "intended to induce the belief" that unless money was paid the circular would be issued and the victim's business paralysed, all of which was alleged to be done "(1) with intent to put [him] in a state of alarm and of apprehension of injury to his fortune and reputation, and (2) for the purpose of extorting money from him."

SILVERSTEIN v. H.M. ADVOCATE.[25] This case deals with a quite different **21.08** type of situation from that involved in *Crawford*,[26] or in any of the other reported cases. S. was the managing director of a landlord company who approached the manager of their tenant company, and told him that unless a certain sum of money was paid to him he would arrange for the landlords to "take the appropriate steps to dispossess" the tenants. He was charged with making this threat to the tenants' manager, inducing him to pay the money, and thus extorting the payment by threats, and this conviction was upheld on appeal. It will be seen that in form this is

---

[17] *Geo. Jeffrey* (1840) 2 Swin. 479; *John Ledingham* (1842) 1 Broun 254; *Euphemia Robertson and Ors* (1842) 1 Broun 295; *Margt Gallocher or Boyle and Ors* (1859) 3 Irv. 440.
[18] See also *McEwan v. Duncan and McLean* (1854) 1 Irv. 520.
[19] J. Shaw at 324.
[20] Macdonald, p.128. *Cf. Margt McDaniel and Anr* (1876) 3 Couper 271, where the demand was not for money but that the victim should commit perjury.
[21] (1879) 4 Couper 268.
[22] (1850) J. Shaw 309. See para. 21.06, *supra*.
[23] L.J.-C. Hope had expressed doubts about this in *Crawford, supra*, at 328.
[24] (1906) 5 Adam 79.
[25] 1949 J.C. 160.
[26] (1850) J. Shaw 309; see para. 21.06, *supra*.

more like a fraud charge than a charge of making threats, and that the crime is said to be the extortion of money, and not the making of a threat for the purpose of extorting money. *Silverstein* is the first reported instance of any such charge, and the defence went so far as to say that the crime of extortion was unknown to Scots law.[27] It was accepted by the court that the threat was not criminal in itself, but they held that "the demand for money to buy off the threatened action is of the essence of the charge."[28]

The *ratio* of *Silverstein*[29] was expressed by Lord Justice-Clerk Thomson as follows:

"This threat to use his influence to their hurt to his own personal advantage is a crime. The extraction of money from people by certain means is criminal. Fraud is the obvious example. There the perpetrator induces the victim to part with his money by deception. In the case of threats the inducement is some form of pressure. Where the pressure consists in creating in the victim fear that, unless he yields, his position will be altered for the worse, it is criminal unless the pressure sought to be exerted is recognised by the law as legitimate. Legal process is such a form of pressure. So too, in the light of the Solicitor-General's concession, is the pressure exerted by one contracting party on another contracting party . . . the threat to use one's own position and influence as a lever to alter the position of another to his detriment, unless that other buys immunity, is a relevant ground of charge. What brings about this result is that the payment demanded is not a payment to which the claimant has any right arising out of his legal relationship to the victim."[30]

21.09 *When can money be lawfully demanded under threat?* Lord Thomson indicated in *Silverstein*[31] that to demand money under threat was criminal unless the threat used was regarded as legitimate. This is to some extent circular — threats are criminal unless they are legitimate — but it serves to emphasise that the use of threats to obtain money is generally criminal, and will be so regarded unless it can be shown that in the particular case it was legitimate. Some Scots judges have gone further than this and suggested that any threat by A that unless B pays him money he will act to B's detriment constitutes the crime of

---

[27] A not dissimilar situation had been unsuccessfully charged as fraud in *Strathern v. Fogal* 1922 J.C. 73.

[28] L.J.-C. Thomson at 163.

[29] 1949 J.C. 160.

[30] At 163. Too much stress should not be placed on the concept of "influence" although it seems that the court were influenced by a general dislike of it — there may be business situations in which it is legitimate to use influence, and to charge for its use. S.'s crime was not that he tried to make use of his influence but simply that he threatened to injure the tenants unless they paid him money to which he had no claim recognised by law or business practice: *infra*. It should also be noted that S.'s threat was in itself illegal in that it involved a breach of his own fiduciary duty to advise the landlord company in its and not his interest, and that his demand was likewise illegal in that he had a duty to account to the company for any money received by him in virtue of his position as its agent: *cf. Frank v. H.M. Advocate*, 1938 J.C. 17.

[31] 1949 J.C. 160; see para. 21.08, *supra*.

extortion.[32] This, however, goes too far, and it is necessary to consider in what circumstance money can be legitimately demanded under threat.[33] Generally speaking, one may say that if either the threat or the demand is in itself illegitimate, there will be extortion; if both are legitimate in themselves the use of the threat to enforce the demand may not be criminal, provided that threat and demand are linked in a way recognised by the law as appropriate. It is, for example, extortion to back up a legitimate demand for payment of a due debt by a threat to expose the debtor's criminal activities,[34] or to use a legitimate threat to report a crime to the police in order to obtain money which is not due to the threatener: but it is not extortion to threaten to sue for a due debt if it is not paid.[35]

CONTRACT. It is clearly not extortion to threaten a course of action to **21.10** which B has agreed beforehand. If B belongs to a club whose rules provide that the committee may expel or fine a member who does certain things it will not be extortion for the committee to threaten B that in view of what he has done they will expel him unless he pays a fine of an amount permitted by the rules.[36]

LEGAL PROCESS. Legal process is a recognised form of pressure,[37] but **21.11** there are circumstances in which a threat by A to sue B may amount to extortion. It is suggested that it is extortion for A to threaten to sue B for a non-existent debt unless B pays him £x, whether or not A is entitled to £x from B. A threat of legal process is legitimate only where the threatened action is directly related to a legitimate demand.[38]

It is, of course, extortion to threaten to institute criminal proceedings, or report a matter to the criminal authorities, in order to obtain payment of a debt.[39] But suppose that B has stolen some goods from A, and A threatens to report him to the police unless he pays A £5 which A considers a reasonable estimate of the loss he has suffered by the theft. It is submitted that this would be extortion. A is entitled to recovery of

---

[32] *Alex. F. Crawford* (1850) J. Shaw 309, L.J.-C. Hope at 324; *Jas Miller* (1862) 4 Irv. 328, L.J.-C. Inglis at 246; *Silverstein v. H.M. Advocate, supra*, Lord Mackay at 164, Lord Jamieson at 166.

[33] This matter has never been fully discussed in Scotland (but *cf.* the opinion of L.J.-G. Hope in *Black v. Carmichael*; *Penrice v. Carmichael*, 1992 S.C.C.R. 709, at 716C–717B), and what is said here must be regarded as to some extent speculative. Reference may be made to two English articles: A.H. Campbell, "The Anomalies of Blackmail" (1939) 55 L.Q.R. 382, and Glanville Williams, "Blackmail" [1954] Crim. L.R. 79.

[34] *cf. Alex. F. Crawford, supra.*

[35] See *Black v. Carmichael*; *Penrice v. Carmichael*, 1992 S.C.C.R. 709, L.J.-G. Hope at 717A-B.

[36] *cf. Thorne v. Motor Trade Assocciation* [1937] A.C. 797, where the "club" was an association of traders whose rules permitted them to place a member on a "blacklist" and cease to deal with him if he infringed their rules regarding price maintenance, or to fine him in lieu of blacklisting.

[37] *Silverstein v. H.M. Advocate, supra*, L.J.-C. Thomson at 163.

[38] It may even be that if A is injured by B's fault, and the damage suffered by him does not at the most liberal estimate exceed £10, it is extortion for A to threaten to sue B for £500 unless B pays him £50, in the hope that B will pay up rather than face the expense of defending the threatened action. There are no cases of prosecution in such circumstances, but this may be because of the difficulty of proving that A knew his demand was, in the non-technical sense, extortionate, and because of a reluctance to interfere with the basic liberty to raise an action subject only to liability for expenses in the event of failure, so long as the Vexatious Actions (Scotland) Act 1898 has not been invoked.

[39] *supra.*

his goods, and it would hardly be regarded as extortion for him to agree not to report the matter if the goods were returned,[40] nor, it is thought, to threaten to report it if they are not returned.

But A is not entitled to "compensation" for the theft. It may even be the law that where B has stolen an article priced at £5 from a shop it is extortion for the shopkeeper to demand £5 under threat of reporting the matter to the police since, although the shopkeeper is entitled to his article back, he is not entitled to force B to buy the article from him.[41]

21.12   OTHER FORMS OF RECOVERY OF DEBT. In addition to threatening legal action to recover debts, a creditor is probably entitled to use, and so to threaten to use, any other means which are regarded as proper for the recovery of the debt in question.[42] Gambling debts are not recoverable by legal process but there is an arrangement among bookmakers whereby they can publish or "post" the names of any defaulters to other bookmakers, the result of such posting being of course to injure the reputation of the debtor and make it unlikely that bookmakers who have seen the notice will continue to do business with him. In *Hill v. Wm Hill (Park Land) Ltd*[43] Lord Normand rejected the suggestion that it was blackmail to threaten such a "posting" unless a debt was paid, "on the unanswerable ground that no wrong is done if an aggrieved party makes use of the ordinary means allowed by society to compel the loser to pay his debt of honour."[44] It may be said therefore that it is legitimate to use threats which are regarded as proper in the social or commercial group to which the parties belong.

In all cases involving recovery of a debt it is, of course, necessary that the threat invoked should bear some reciprocal relation to the debt — it would be extortion to threaten to post B as a defaulter if he did not pay a non-gambling debt, even if his gambling conduct had merited such posting.[45]

---

[40] Although it might be some form of criminal interference with the course of justice; *cf. infra*, para. 47.01.

[41] There is only one case known to the author whose facts fall into this category — it is *Samuel Smith*, June 23, 1959, a summary complaint in Stornoway Sheriff Court, where the complaint libelled that the manager of a store there "did threaten S.M. . . . that unless she paid to you as an individual, or to your employers . . . £5 . . . you would inform the police that she had stolen three tins of peas in [the store], and you did put said S.M. in such a state of alarm for her reputation that she delivered to you £5 . . . and you did extort said money from her." Compare this with *Hill v. McGrogan*, 1945 S.L.T. (Sh.Ct.) 18 where it was held not to be a crime to threaten to report a cleaner to her employers for theft if she did not resign. It is true that the element of extorting a benefit to the threatener was absent, but it may be arguable that there was a criminal inducement and that Sheriff-substitute A.M. Hamilton, K.C.'s comment that as it is not a crime to say that one is going to do what one is entitled to do without warning, it does not make it worse "to add that if the person attacked chooses to put the matter right to your satisfaction you will not further pursue him", is too widely expressed. There may be a difference between the employer making such a "bargain" and someone else making it.

[42] See *Black v. Carmichael; Penrice v. Carmichael*, 1992 S.C.C.R. 709, L.J.-G. Hope at 717B: "To use due legal process, such as an action in a court of law or a right of lien or retention available under contract, or to threaten to do so, is no doubt legitimate. It is not extortion if the debtor pays up as a result."

[43] [1949] A.C. 530.

[44] [1949] A.C. at 562. See Farwell L.J. in *Hyams v Stuart King* [1908] 2 K.B. 696 at 726.

[45] *cf.* Receuil Dalloz, 1957 186: an employee, who threatened to denounce his employers to the revenue authorities unless they paid him money allegedly due to him, was convicted of embezzlement, the court holding that "le délit de chantage existe lorsque les révélations dont est menacé le débiteur portent sur des faits étrangers à la cause de la dette."

BUSINESS COMPETITION. Although it may be extortion for A to threaten **21.13**
to damage B's business unless B buys him off,[46] the common law accepts
that ". . . tradition/Approves all forms of competition," and as Lord
Atkin said in *Thorne v. Motor Trade Association*,[47] "if a man may
lawfully, in the furtherance of business interests, do acts which will
seriously injure another in his business he may also lawfully, if he is still
acting in furtherance of his business interests, offer that other to accept a
sum of money from that other as an alternative to doing the injurious
acts. He must no doubt be acting not for the purpose of putting money
in his pocket, but for some legitimate purpose other than the mere
acquisition of money." A threat and demand of this kind — I will do x
which will harm your business unless you pay me £y — will be regarded
as legitimate only if the threat is reasonably related to the demand so
that the demand can be regarded as a fair price for A's forbearance, if it
is made bona fide, *i.e.* if A truly wishes to advance his own business and
is not concerned merely to force B to pay him money, and if the use of
the threat is recognised as a reputable business practice.

ENTERING INTO A CONTRACT. It is probably the law that A is entitled to **21.14**
charge any sum he wishes as the price for his entering into a contract
with B. He can refuse to sell his goods, to lease his property,[48] or to offer
his services, to B, unless B pays him £x, even though £x is what would be
called an "extortionate" price, and even though A's demand for it is
made because he knows that B has an unusually great need for the
goods, property or service. It would be very difficult not to accept this
situation in a society in which, by and large, the price of anything is what
one can get for it. Moreover, the idea that extortion involves a threat to
do something to the victim's detriment suggests that a "negative threat",
a threat not to grant a benefit, is insufficient to constitute the crime.
Where special conditions, such as general scarcity of necessities, make it
necessary to depart from this principle, the solution is by legislation
fixing maximum prices, or rendering certain payments such as premiums
required as a condition for entering into a lease, illegal, and making it a
statutory offence to demand more than the permitted amount.[49]

The need for a threat. It is essential in extortion that A should create the **21.15**
situation by a threat. If B hears that A is about to report him to the
police and offers to buy him off, there is no extortion if A accepts B's
offer. If B learns that C is about to act to his, B's detriment, and offers A
money to use his influence with C on B's behalf, A is not guilty of
extortion in accepting B's offer. Indeed, if A learns of C's intentions and
offers his services to B at a price, A is not guilty of extortion. A

[46] *Priteca v. H.M. Advocate* (1906) 5 Adam 79, *supra*, para. 21.07.

[47] [1937] A.C. 797, 807, an English case but one involving a branch of the law common
to both England and Scotland, that concerning A's right to injure B in furtherance of A's
business, and developed in such cases as *Quinn v. Leathem* [1901] A.C. 495; *Sorrell v. Smith*
[1925] A.C. 700; and *Crofter HandWoven Harris Tweed Co. v. Veitch*, 1942 S.C. (H.L.) 1.
See also K.W.B. Middleton, "Blacklist and Blackmail", 1937 S.L.T. (News) 137; L.H.
Hoffman, "*Rookes v. Barnard*" (1965) 81 L.Q.R. 116. The law is now complicated by
restrictive practices and competition legislation: see, *e.g.*, Stair Memorial Encyclopaedia,
Vol. 4, paras 1101 *et seq*.

[48] *Silverstein v. H.M. Advocate, supra*, para. 21.08.

[49] If such a statutory offence were not created, but the excess payment simply declared
illegal, that might be sufficient to make a demand for it under threat into a common law
extortion since the demand would be illegal.

distinction must be drawn between "B is going to act to your detriment: I can help you but it will cost you £x" which is an offer of help, and "Unless you pay me £x I will arrange for B to act to your detriment" which is a threat of injury.[50]

Claim of right

21.16   There is no Scots authority on claim of right as a defence to extortion. In England the corresponding crime of blackmail cannot be committed by a person who believes that he has reasonable grounds for his demand and that the use of malice is a proper means of reinforcing that demand.[51] Scots law is unlikely to leave the decision whether menaces are appropriate to the subjective judgement of the accused. It is more likely to adopt the approach of the Canadian Criminal Code which talks simply of making threats "without reasonable justification or excuse",[52] so that not merely the demand but the reasonableness of the use of the particular threat to back it up must be accepted by the law, and not just believed in by the accused.[53]

THE RENT ACTS

21.17   The most important statutory offences involving extortion are those concerned with the exacting of premiums as consideration for the lease of controlled property. The law is now codified in the Rent (Scotland) Act 1984. The following are the principal provisions.

21.18 *Section 82*:

> "(1) Any person who, as a condition of the grant, renewal or continuance of a protected [or assured[54]] tenancy, requires, in addition to the rent, the payment of any premium or the making of any loan (whether secured or unsecured) shall be guilty of an offence".[55]

Section 83 makes it an offence to require a premium as a condition of or receive a premium in connection with the assignation of such a tenancy, subject to a number of exceptions.[56]
A premium is defined as including "any fine or other like sum and any other pecuniary consideration in addition to rent."[57] The term does not include, however, a returnable deposit given by the tenant as surety for

---

[50] *H.M. Advocate v. Donoghue*, 1971 S.L.T. 2.

[51] Theft Act 1968, s.21.

[52] See s.346(1) of the Code.

[53] *The Queen v. Natarelli* [1967] S.C.R. 539, interpreting the similarly worded offence in a previous version of the Code.

[54] See Housing (Scotland) Act 1988, s.12 (definition of "assured tenancy") and s.27 (which applies, with some exceptions, ss. 82, 83 and 86–90 of the Rent (Scotland) Act 1984 to such a tenancy).

[55] Maximum penalty, level 3 on the standard scale; and the court may order repayment of the premium or loan: s.82(4). The receipt of such moneys is also an offence: s.82(2).

[56] Maximum penalty in each case level 3 on the standard scale. For a more detailed account of the law regarding premiums see *Stair Memorial Encyclopaedia*, Vol. 13, paras 689–695.

[57] Section 90(1). It does not include a sum paid in return for the consent of the landlord to a sublease: *Strathern v. Beaton*, 1923 J.C. 59.

domestic utility supplies and damage to the fabric or contents of the premises in question, provided the deposit does not exceed the amount of two months' rent.[58]

In considering whether any arrangement constitutes a premium the courts will look to the substance and not the form of the transaction, and a transaction may constitute a premium even although no money passes directly between the parties. So it is illegal for A to require B to sell his house to C at a price below its market value in return for the granting by A of a lease to B.[59] In *Macdonald v. John Laing and Sons*[60] the payment by the tenant was expressed as being in security of certain obligations under lease, but this was held to be a premium, even although absolute property in the money did not pass to the landlord. It was held to be enough that he acquired the use of it — the provision for paying interest to the tenant was described as elusory.[61] It is equally an offence to accept a premium offered by the tenant, as in *Meldrum v. Craven*[62] where the tenant advertised for the "key of a house" and offered £40. The landlord then offered a key for £40 and shortly afterwards granted a lease, and the £40 was held to be a premium.

It does not matter whether the payment is made to the landlord or to his nominee, or to anyone else, provided that it is paid in consideration of the grant of the tenancy.[63] A payment to a true third party like a payment to a sitting tenant in consideration of his giving up his tenancy may be legal, provided it is not in the circumstances a condition of the grant of the tenancy.[64]

Section 16(1). This section makes it an offence for a statutory tenant to **21.19** ask or receive payment of any sum, or the giving of any other consideration, by anyone other than the landlord, as a condition of giving up possession.[65]

Section 87(1): **21.20**

> "Any person who, in connection with the proposed grant, renewal, continuance or assignation of a protected [or assured[66]] tenancy on terms which require the purchase of furniture—
>
> (a) offers the furniture at a price which he knows or ought to know is unreasonably high, or otherwise seeks to obtain such a price for the furniture; . . .
>
> shall be liable to a fine not exceeding level 3 on the standard scale."

---

[58] Rent (Scotland) Act 1984, s.90(3).
[59] *Elmdene Estates Ltd v. White* [1960] A.C. 528.
[60] 1954 S.L.T (Sh.Ct.) 77.
[61] The deposit in the case amounted to more than 15 times the monthly rent: *cf.* s.90(3) of the Rent (Scotland) Act 1984.
[62] 1950 S.L.T. (Sh.Ct.) 20.
[63] *Elmdene Estates Ltd v. White, supra.*
[64] *Gourley v. Robertson*, 1931 S.L.T. (Sh.Ct.) 7; see now the Rent (Scotland) Act 1984, s.82.
[65] Maximum penalty, level 3 on the standard scale.
[66] Section 27 of the Housing (Scotland) Act 1988 makes s.87 of the Rent (Scotland) Act applicable to assured tenancies: see n.54, *supra.*

Harassment

21.21 *Section 22* provides:

"(2) If any person with intent to cause the residential occupier of any premises—

(a) to give up the occupation of the premises or any part thereof; or

(b) to refrain from exercising any right or pursuing any remedy in respect of the premises or part thereof;

does acts [likely[67]] to interfere with the peace or comfort of the residential occupier or members of his household, or persistently withdraws or withholds services reasonably required for the occupation of the premises as a residence, he shall be guilty of an offence.

(2A)[68] [Subject to subsection (2B) below] the landlord of any premises or an agent of the landlord shall be guilty of an offence if

(a) he does acts [likely] to interfere with the peace or comfort of the residential occupier or members of his household; or

(b) he persistently withdraws or withholds services reasonably required for the occupation of the premises in question as a residence, and (in either case) he knows, or has reasonable cause to believe, that the conduct is [likely] to cause the residential occupier to give up the occupation of the whole or part of the premises or to refrain from exercising any right or pursuing any remedy in respect of the whole or part of the premises.

(2B) A person shall not be guilty of an offence under subsection (2A) above if he proves that he had reasonable grounds for doing the acts or withdrawing or withholding the services in question."[69]

It has been held in England that conduct may constitute harassment even if it does not constitute a breach of contract or other civil wrong.[70]

It has also been held there that in terms of section 1(3) of the Protection from Eviction Act 1977[71] it is necessary for the Crown to prove a specific intent to harass a person believed to be a residential occupier, but that no offence will be committed where the defendant believes *on reasonable grounds* that the person harassed is a squatter.[72] A requirement of reasonable grounds for such a belief may accord with the general approach of Scots law; but it sits uneasily with the current

---

[67] Word substituted by Housing (Scotland) Act 1988, s.38(1), as itself amended by the Housing Act 1988, Sched. 17, para. 87.

[68] Subsections (2A) and (2B) were added by s.38 of the Housing (Scotland) Act 1988, and the words in brackets substituted by the Housing Act 1988, Sched. 17, para. 87.

[69] Maximum penalty for offences against s.22(2), (2A) or (2B), six months' imprisonment and the statutory maximum on summary conviction, two years' and a fine on indictment. Section 22(1) makes it an offence to evict or attempt to evict a residential occupier in the absence of reasonable belief that he had ceased to reside there.

[70] See *R. v. Burke* [1991] 1 A.C. 135, HL, which deals with the equivalent English legislation: Protection from Eviction Act 1977, s.1(3), as amended by the Housing Act 1988, s.29.

[71] The English equivalent of s.22(2) of the Rent (Scotland) Act 1984. *Cf.* the requirements under s.22(2A).

[72] See *R. v. Phekoo* [1981] 1 W.L.R. 1117, CA, Hollings J. at 1128D.

orthodoxy in England, where simple honesty of belief in such situations is the favoured view.[73]

UNSOLICITED GOODS AND SERVICES

Sections 2 and 3 of the Unsolicited Goods and Services Act 1971 **21.22** provide:

"**2.**—(1) A person who, not having reasonable cause to believe there is a right to payment, in the course of any trade or business makes a demand for payment, or asserts a present or prospective right to payment, for what he knows are unsolicited goods sent (after the commencement of this Act) to another person with a view to his acquiring them, shall be guilty of an offence and on summary conviction shall be liable to a fine not exceeding level 4 on the standard scale.

(2) A person who, not having reasonable cause to believe there is a right to payment, in the course of any trade or business and with a view to obtaining any payment for what he knows are unsolicited goods sent as aforesaid—
   (a) threatens to bring any legal proceedings; or
   (b) places or causes to be placed the name of any person on a list of defaulters or debtors or threatens to do so; or
   (c) invokes or causes to be invoked any other collection procedure or threatens to do so,
shall be guilty of an offence and shall be liable on summary conviction to a fine not exceeding level 5 on the standard scale.[74]

3.—(1) A person shall not be liable to make any payment, and shall be entitled to recover any payment made by him, by way of charge for including or arranging for the inclusion in a directory of an entry relating to that person or his trade or business, unless there has been signed by him or on his behalf an order complying with this section or a note complying with this section of his agreement to the charge and, in the case of a note of agreement to the charge, before the note was signed, a copy of it was supplied, for retention by him, to him or to a person acting on his behalf.

(2) A person shall be guilty of an offence punishable on summary conviction with a fine not exceeding the prescribed sum[75] if, in a case where a payment in respect of a charge would, in the absence of an order or note of agreement to the charge complying with this section, be recoverable from him in accordance with the terms of subsection (1) above, he demands payment, or asserts a present or prospective right to payment, of the charge or any part of it, without

---

[73] In *R. v. Phekoo* [1981] 1 W.L.R. 1117, at 1127H, Hollings J. took the view that the "honesty of belief even in the absence of reasonable grounds" approach was confined to the crime of rape: see *R. v. Morgan* [1976] A.C. 182; but that approach has subsequently been applied generally in English criminal law: see, *e.g.*, *R. v. Kimber* [1983] 1 W.L.R. 1118, CA; *R. v. Beckford* [1988] A.C. 130, PC; and the current academic opinion seems to be that what was said in *Phekoo* was not only *obiter* but also wrong: see Smith and Hogan, pp. 86–87.

[74] See *Readers' Digest Ltd v. Pirie,* 1973 J.C. 42.

[75] Or an unlimited fine on indictment: Unsolicited Goods and Services (Amendment) Act 1975, s.3(1).

knowing or having reasonable cause to believe that the entry to which the charge relates was ordered in accordance with this section or a proper note of agreement has been duly signed."

CORRUPTION

21.23   Corruption of public officials is an offence at common law and also under the Public Bodies Corrupt Practices Act 1889.[76] The Prevention of Corruption Act 1906 applies to public officials, but is also and principally directed against corruption of agents of private persons and bodies.[77]

Section 1 of the 1906 Act provides:

"(1) If any agent corruptly accepts or obtains, or agrees to accept or attempts to obtain, from any person, for himself or for any other person, any gift or consideration as an inducement or reward[78] for doing or forbearing to do, or for having . . . done or forborne to do, any act in relation to his principal's affairs or business, or for showing or forbearing to show favour or disfavour to any person in relation to his principal's affairs or business; or

If any person corruptly gives or agrees to give or offers any gift or consideration to any agent as an inducement or reward for doing or forbearing to do, or for having . . . done or forborne to do, any act in relation to his principal's affairs or business, or for showing or forbearing to show favour or disfavour to any person in relation to his principal's affairs or business; or

If any person knowingly gives to any agent, or if any agent knowingly uses with intent to deceive his principal, any receipt, account, or other document in respect of which the principal is interested, and which contains any statement which is false or erroneous or defective in any material particular, and which to his knowledge is intended to mislead the principal:

he [shall be liable—

(a) on summary conviction, to imprisonment for a term not exceeding 6 months or to a fine not exceeding the statutory maximum, or to both; and

(b) on conviction on indictment, to imprisonment for a term not exceeding 7 years or to a fine, or to both.][79]

(2) For the purposes of this Act the expression 'consideration' includes valuable consideration of any kind; the expression 'agent' includes any person employed by or acting for another; and the expression 'principal' includes an employer.

---

[76] See *infra*, para. 44.04. See also Customs and Excise Management Act 1979, *infra*, para. 38.16.

[77] It probably does not extend to the payment of gratuities and discounts in accordance with accepted commercial practice: see "Bribery and Secret Commissions" (1928) 44 Sc.Law Rev. 45.

[78] Including the receipt of money for past favours without any antecedent agreement: *R. v. Andrews-Weatherfoil Ltd* [1972] 1 W.L.R. 118.

[79] Words substituted by the Criminal Justice Act 1988, s.47(2), made applicable to Scotland by s.172(2).

(3) A person serving under the Crown or under any corporation or any municipal, borough, county, or district council, . . . is an agent within the meaning of this Act."[80]

"CONSIDERATION". Under the Prevention of Corruption Act 1916,[81] **21.24** where in proceedings under the Public Bodies Corrupt Practices Act 1889 or the Prevention of Corruption Act 1906, it is proved that any money, gift or other consideration has been paid or given to or received by a person in the employment of (*inter alia*) a public body by or from a person, or an agent of a person, holding or seeking to obtain a contract from (*inter alia*) any public body, the money, gift or consideration is deemed to have been paid or received corruptly until the contrary is proved on the balance of probabilities by the recipient. It has been held in this context that "consideration" is not a synonym for "gift" but presupposes the existence of a contract or bargain where something is given or done in return, and that if the Crown succeeds in proving the receipt of consideration it will have the advantage of the deeming provision without the necessity of further proving that the consideration was for less than full value or involved a gratuitous element.[82]

"CORRUPT". On the meaning of "corrupt", see the discussion of the **21.25** Public Bodies Corrupt Practices Act 1889, *infra*, paragraph 44.08.

"AGENT". It has been said that the meaning of "agent" in the Act is **21.26** "designedly very wide", and should not be interpreted restrictively by the courts.[83] If A is employed by a firm to sell engines and takes bribes from a customer for arranging an order for small tools, this is struck at by the Act even though the order is not strictly within the scope of his agency.[84] It is also an offence for an employee who is also a trade union official to take money for persuading the union not to object to the giver's being granted a contract by the offender's employers.[85] It has been held that a police constable is an agent for the purposes of the Act.[86]

ACTION UNNECESSARY. The offence is constituted by the offer or **21.27** acceptance of the bribe, and it does not matter whether the agent did or refrained from doing the action in respect of which the bribe was offered or accepted.[87]

---

[80] *R. v. Barrett (George)* [1976] 1 W.L.R. 946.

[81] Section 2.

[82] *Beaton v. H.M. Advocate*, 1993 S.C.C.R. 48, L.J.-G. Hope at 54D-G, following *R. v. Braithwaite* [1983] 1 W.L.R. 385. The question of whether s.2 of the 1916 Act contravenes Art. 6 (presumption of innocence) of the European Convention on Human Rights has been raised in an English case, *R. v. Att.-Gen., ex p. Rockall* [2000] 1 W.L.R. 882; but the case (an application for judicial review) was disposed of on a different issue: *cf. R. v. D.P.P., ex p. Kebilene* [1999] 3 W.L.R. 972, HL, esp. the opinion of Lord Hope of Craighead at pp. 991H-996C.

[83] *R. v. Dickinson and Anr* (1948) 33 Cr.App.R. 5, 9; *Morgan v. D.P.P.* [1970] 3 All E.R. 1053. But it has been held not to apply to a member of a licensing court: *Copeland v. Johnston*, 1967 S.L.T. (Sh.Ct.) 28; see *infra*, para. 44.06.

[84] *R. v. Dickinson, supra.*

[85] *Morgan v. D.P.P., supra.*

[86] *Graham v. Hart* (1908) 5 Adam 457.

[87] *R. v. Carr* [1957] 1 W.L.R. 165.

21.28　　FALSE DOCUMENTS. The third paragraph of section 1(1) is not concerned with corruption, and there can be an offence under it in the absence of any corruption. In *Sage v. Eicholz*,[88] A gave a false claim for a water rate rebate to an agent of the water board who was unaware of the falsity, and A was convicted under that paragraph. The court also pointed out that where the paragraph speaks of "his knowledge" it refers either to the agent or to the person who gives him the document, according to circumstances, so that the innocence of the agent was irrelevant since the document was false to the knowledge of the giver. It has been held in England, however, that no offence is committed under this paragraph where the document is an internal one passing only between an employee and his employers.[89]

21.29 *Employment Agencies Act 1973.* Section 6 of this Act[90] makes it an offence for a person carrying on an employment agency or business[91] to require, directly or indirectly, any fee[92] from (for example) a person seeking employment for providing services (including information) to him, in connection with finding employment for him.[93]

---

[88] [1919] 2 K.B. 171.

[89] *R. v. Tweedie* [1984] 2 Q.B. 729.

[90] As amended by the Employment Relations Act 1999, Sched. 7, para. 3.

[91] As defined in s.13(2) and (3) of the 1973 Act.

[92] As defined s.13(1) of the 1973 Act, it includes any charge however described.

[93] Maximum penalty on summary conviction level 3 on the standard scale. A court before which a person is convicted may also order him to pay to the Secretary of State a sum which appears to the court not to exceed the costs of the investigation which resulted in the prosecution (s.11B, added by the Employment Relations Act 1999, Sched. 7, para. 5).

PART II

OFFENCES OF DAMAGE TO PROPERTY

CHAPTER 22

DAMAGE TO PROPERTY

MALICIOUS MISCHIEF

Malicious mischief is confined by Hume to cases of killing or maiming **22.01** animals,[1] and cases of "great and wilful damage done to the property of another . . . done . . . with circumstances of tumult and disorder"[2] Hume appears to have considered the crime as a form of riot, saying that what the law is interested chiefly in "is not so much the patrimonial damage . . . as the insult to the public and the individual, by the violence and tumult attending the execution".[3] It is no longer necessary to show that an act of malicious mischief either involved gross damage or was accompanied by riot[4]; nor is it always necessary to show that physical damage was caused to corporeal property.[5] The modern crime, therefore, consists in destruction of or damage to the property of another[6] (whether by destroying crops,[7] killing or injuring animals,[8] knocking down walls or fences,[9] or in any other way) or the causing of economic loss in the absence of damage to any corporeal property (provided, it seems) that the loss is caused by unauthorisedly interfering with, in the sense of doing something positive to, another's property, such as turning on or off a switch which activates or prevents the operation of machinery[10]).

Malicious mischief and theft

The difference between malicious mischief and theft by destruction is **22.02** that in malicious mischief the destruction is carried out without any prior asportation. If A drives B's sheep on to his own land and kills them there, that is theft, even if he did so out of malice to B and not for any profit to himself; but if he kills the sheep in their own field that is

---

[1] Hume, i, 124.

[2] Hume, i, 122; similarly Alison, i, 449.

[3] Hume, i, 124.

[4] *Forbes v. Ross* (1898) 2 Adam 513.

[5] *H.M. Advocate v. Wilson*, 1983 S.C.C.R. 420 (Lord Stewart, diss.); *Bett v. Hamilton*, 1997 S.C.C.R. 621.

[6] Macdonald, p.84. In the recent case of *Lord Advocate's Ref. (No. 1 of 2000)* 2001 S.L.T. 507, the opinion of the court refers to the crime as "malicious damage" rather than malicious mischief, but the case was concerned with actual damage to property.

[7] *Rigg v. Trotter* (1714) Hume, i, 123; *Ward v. Robertson*, 1938 J.C. 32.

[8] *Archd Thomson* (1874) 2 Couper 551; *Andrew Steuart* (1874) *ibid.* 554; *Clark v. Syme*, 1957 J.C. 1.

[9] *Forbes v. Ross, supra.*

[10] *H.M. Advocate v. Wilson*, 1983 S.C.C.R. 420. Altering the aim of a security camera was not considered insufficient activity in *Bett v. Hamilton*, 1997 S.C.C.R. 621, although the prosecution failed on the ground that no financial loss was occasioned by the accused's actions. Deflating a tyre was considered sufficient in *Peter Penman*, High Court on appeal, March 1984, unrep'd.

malicious mischief even if the result is to profit A.[11] It is not malicious mischief to damage or destroy property one has originally stolen for gain, presumably because once the goods have been appropriated, however wrongfully, they are regarded as belonging to the thief for the purposes of this crime; but if C destroys property A has stolen from B, C is guilty of malicious mischief. The reason it is not theft to destroy property without first removing it from its owner's possession is that in this context the law still regards theft as consisting not merely in appropriation, for destruction is appropriation,[12] but in taking and appropriating.[13]

The mens rea of malicious mischief

22.03 *"Malicious"*. Malicious mischief can be committed only "wilfully" and this means that where damage has been caused it must have been inflicted either intentionally or recklessly. In *Ward v. Robertson*[14] the accused was a trespasser who trampled down grass in a field and damaged it so as to render it useless for grazing, the purpose for which it had been intended by the owner. His conviction for malicious mischief was quashed on the ground that there was no evidence that he knew or should have known that what he had done was likely to cause damage. Lord Justice-Clerk Aitchison said, "I am prepared to take the case upon the footing, although it may involve some departure from the law as laid down by Hume, that it is enough if the damage is done by a person who shows a deliberate disregard of, or even indifference to, the property or possessory rights of others", but held that in the particular case there was no evidence from which the court could infer that the accused knew or should have known that by crossing the field "he was doing, or even was likely to do" damage.[15]

Where there is no actual damage to corporeal property but economic loss caused to another as a result of the accused's unauthorised interference with the other's property, it may be that the loss must have been intended by the accused. In *H.M. Advocate v. Wilson*,[16] Lord Justice-General Emslie said, "The Crown properly conceded that consequential injury has to be intended by the initial act." But he also stated as follows: "It is clear from the words used in the libel that the Crown seek to establish that the act of the respondent founded upon was deliberate and malicious.[17] The Crown further seek to prove that this act resulted in a generating turbine being brought to a halt for an extended period of time with a consequential loss of generated electricity . . .

---

[11] Alison, i, 273–274; Burnett, p.116n.; *Anderson* (1809) Burnett 116; *Gilchrist* (1741) *ibid.*; *Wm and Jas Wilson* (1827) Alison, i, 274.

[12] *supra*, paras 14.10 and 14.12.

[13] The position where A destroys B's property while it is in his — A's — lawful possession has not been decided. It would probably be regarded as malicious mischief because of the absence of any unlawful taking and by analogy with the damaging of such property which would clearly be malicious mischief.

[14] 1938 J.C. 32.

[15] At 36. By "disregard of possessory rights" Lord Aitchison presumably referred to the destruction of property in another's possession; the accused was acting in disregard of possessory rights in that he was a trespasser; but this was disregarded as irrelevant. See also *Lord Advocate's Ref. (No. 1 of 2000)* 2001 S.L.T. 507, opinion of the court at para. [30].

[16] 1983 S.C.C.R. 420, at 423.

[17] "Malice" was taken to connote, "the evil intention deliberately to do injury or damage to the property": *ibid*.

[T]his would be an interference with the employer's property and the wording of the libel is such as to be habile to carry the inference that the initial positive, wilful, reckless and malicious act was intended to harm the employer by causing patrimonial injury."[18] Since *Ward v. Robertson*[19] was referred to by both the Lord Justice-General and Lord Macdonald[20] as authority for the proposition that the *mens rea* of malicious mischief extends to wilful disregard of or indifference to the rights of others, it is submitted that recklessness of that nature is a sufficient form of *mens rea* in all modes of the crime, and that *Wilson* is simply a case where the Crown elected to prove that the accused intended to cause the economic loss which occurred.

SPITE. It seems to have been thought at one time that malicious **22.04** mischief required malice in the sense of spite against the owner of the property. In *Wm Reid*[21] a charge of malicious mischief was dismissed as irrelevant because the damage was alleged to have been done with a view to increasing the accused's claim for compensation against the owner, his landlord, which made it impossible to describe the mischief as *malicious*. This must now be regarded as wrong. Malice in this sense is a matter of motive, and there is no need to show that it was present in order to establish the crime of malicious mischief.[22] In *Archibald Thomson*[23] the charge was of malicious mischief by injuring a cow "wilfully, and with the malicious intent and purpose of injuring [the owner] in his property and estate", but the conviction was only of malicious mischief without the malicious intention libelled, and this conviction was sustained.

Claim of right. The defence of claim of right in malicious mischief may **22.05** take one of two forms. It may be a claim that the damaged goods belonged to the accused, or that the accused was entitled to damage the goods and was acting in vindication of his rights.

RES SUA. This is clearly a defence to malicious mischief the *actus reus* **22.06** of which requires that the damage be done to the property of another. It follows that a belief that the goods are one's own is also a good defence, provided it is not held recklessly.

VINDICATION OF RIGHT. Discussions of this aspect of the matter tend to **22.07** confuse two separate ideas. The first is that some situations can be more suitably determined in the civil courts and, at any rate where the damage is trivial, should not be made the subject of a criminal charge.[24] It is a recognised administrative principle that in such cases prosecutions should not be brought,[25] but it is submitted that that does not mean that they should fail if they are brought in circumstances where a crime, however technical, has been committed.

---

[18] *ibid*.

[19] 1938 J.C. 32.

[20] 1983 S.C.C.R. at 424 and 426 respectively.

[21] (1833) Bell's Notes 47.

[22] *Clark v. Syme*, 1957 J.C. 1; *Lord Advocate's Ref. (No. 1 of 2000)* 2001 S.L.T. 507, opinion of court at para. [31].

[23] (1874) 2 Couper 551.

[24] *cf.* Alison, i, 449; *John and Wm Black v. Laing* (1879) 4 Couper 276; *Speid v. Whyte* (1864) 4 Irv. 584.

[25] Renton and Brown, para. 4-01.

The second idea is that it is a defence to a charge of malicious mischief to show that the accused believed that he was entitled to act as he did. It is submitted that such a belief is not a relevant defence although it may operate in mitigation.[26] It is clearly irrelevant in cases involving riotous damage[27] or the killing of animals,[28] and it is submitted that now that malicious mischief is no longer confined to such cases, the defence is not open even where the damage is slight and unaccompanied by riot.

22.08   The leading case on the matter is *Clark v. Syme*[29] and, although it happens to be a case involving the killing of a sheep, it was argued and decided in general terms. The accused was a farmer who had been having trouble with a neighbour because the latter's sheep were eating his turnips. He warned the neighbour that if he did not fence his sheep in he would kill the next one which came to his turnips, and he did kill a sheep which he found coming away from the turnips. The sheriff-substitute acquitted him of malicious mischief, holding that there had been no malice but a genuine misconception by the accused of his legal rights, and that his desire to vindicate his property in the face of provocation was excusable. The High Court reversed this decision and held that malicious mischief had been committed. Lord Justice-General Clyde said:

> "A misconception of legal rights, however gross, will never justify the substitution of the law of the jungle for rules of civilised behaviour or even of common sense . . . The respondent in this case acted deliberately. He knew what he was doing and he displayed in his actings a complete disregard of the rights of others . . . A desire to vindicate his own rights of property is all very well in its proper place, but, when that involves the deliberate destruction of the property and the invasion of the rights of others, it ceases, in my view, to be excusable."[30]

Lord Sorn pointed out that a man was not entitled to take the law into his own hands instead of applying to the civil courts for a remedy,[31] which supports the argument that the presence of a civil dispute does not excuse resort to wilful damage.

22.09 *Clark v. Syme*[32] was appealed by the Crown partly in order to clarify the situation created by two earlier cases. The first of these was *John and Wm Black v. Laing*.[33] There G. had become the tenant of a part of a Town Green which adjoined the Blacks' garden and over which the Blacks had a right of way. This right of way was closed by a fence and the Blacks tore down some five feet of fence in order to restore their access to their own property. Their conviction for malicious mischief was quashed. No opinions are reported, but the court's decision was based

[26] *cf. McDonald and Ors v. Mackay* (1842) 1 Broun 435.
[27] Hume, i, 122, where he speaks of damage "whether done from malice, or misapprehension of right."
[28] *Clark v. Syme* 1957 J.C. 1.
[29] 1957 J.C. 1.
[30] At 5.
[31] At 7.
[32] 1957 J.C. 1.
[33] (1879) 4 Couper 276.

on the view that although what the Blacks had done "was not to be commended, yet in the circumstances they were, on the whole, justified in removing the fence." This case was distinguished in *Clark v. Syme*[34] by reference to the remark about justification, but that is in itself circular. What was at issue was not the Blacks' right of way but their right to destroy the fence, and it is submitted that in acting as they did they behaved as Lord Sorn said in *Clark v. Syme*[35] a man was not entitled to behave. *Black v. Laing*[36] cannot easily stand with *Clark v. Syme* and it is submitted that it should be regarded as wrongly decided.

In *Speid v. Whyte*[37] A had a sale of wood, the articles of roup providing **22.10** that the wood had to be removed on certain days only and had to be paid for before removal. Two lots of wood were not bid for and the auctioneer sold them to B who agreed to buy them on condition he could remove them immediatedly. When B sent men with carts to remove the wood the next day A prevented them from doing so and cut their horses' harness straps. His conviction was quashed on the ground that the wood was still his property since the conditions of sale had not been implemented,[38] and that "although he may not have acted judiciously, or even legally, in the course he adopted to vindicate his property, still he did act in vindication of his supposed rights, and not merely from a desire to injure or destroy the property of another."[39] This, it is submitted, confuses motive and intent, it cannot stand with *Clark v. Syme*,[40] and must be regarded as wrongly decided. *Speid v. Whyte*[41] was distinguished in *Clark v. Syme* on the ground that the damage in the former was too trivial to disclose the degree of recklessness and wilful destruction of property essential for malicious mischief,[42] but this point was not referred to by Lord Neaves in *Speid v. Whyte* and is an unfortunate throwback to the obsolete idea that the damage in malicious mischief must be gross.

Forbes v. Ross[43] also falls to be considered in this connection, although it **22.11** was not cited in *Clark v. Syme*.[44] In *Forbes v. Ross* it was held to be malicious mischief to break down a wall which had been standing for some time and where there was no claim to property in the wall, although the damage was done in purported vindication of a right of way. *Black v. Laing*[45] was distinguished on the not very satisfactory ground that in it the fence had not been in existence for a long time. Although the decision in *Forbes v. Ross* accords with *Clark v. Syme*, *Forbes v. Ross* contains statements recognising a class of invasions of civil right which should not be dealt with as crimes and of which *Black v. Laing* is presumably an example. It also contains a dictum that for malicious mischief to exist without the element of riotous conduct there

---

[34] 1957 J.C. 1.
[35] See para. 22.08, *supra*.
[36] (1879) 4 Couper 276.
[37] (1864) 4 Irv. 584.
[38] It is not clear in just what way they had not been implemented.
[39] Lord Neaves at 586.
[40] 1957 J.C. 1.
[41] (1864) 4 Irv. 584.
[42] 1957 J.C. 1, L.J.-G. Clyde at 6.
[43] (1898) 2 Adam 513.
[44] 1957 J.C. 1.
[45] (1879) 4 Couper 276: see para. 22.09, *supra*.

must be a "total disregard of other people's rights and a knowledge that what you are doing is not within your own rights,"[46] which is inconsistent both with *Clark v. Syme* and with *Ward v. Robertson*[47] and must be regarded as erroneous.

22.12 *Defence.* The argument by counsel in *Clark v. Syme*[48] raised the question of justifiable defence of one's own property in malicious mischief, but this point was not dealt with by the court. The most common circumstances in which this point arises is where a farmer kills a dog which is worrying his sheep, and it is recognised that he is entitled to do this.[49] Beyond that one can only say that the general principles of self-defence apply and it is a question for the court to decide whether it was reasonable for A to act as he did in defence of his property. All that *Clark v. Syme* indicates is that it is not justifiable to kill a sheep in order to save one's turnips.

Necessity is a defence to malicious mischief as it is to other crimes, provided that the legal requirements for necessity are met[49a]; it is not a defence, however, under domestic law or customary international law, to content that damage was done to another's property in order to prevent the commission of another offence.[49b]

Special forms of malicious mischief

22.13 *Ships.* Macdonald treats the destruction of ships as a specific offence, and is concerned mainly with the destruction of one's own or one's principal's ship with intent to defraud insurers.[50] This is best regarded as a form of fraud.[51] There seems no good reason why the damage or destruction of a ship without any fraudulent intent should not be charged as malicious mischief.[52]

22.14 *Vandalism.* The Criminal Law (Consolidation) (Scotland) Act 1995, section 52, provides:

"(1) Subject to subsection (2) below, any person who, without reasonable excuse, wilfully or recklessly destroys or damages any property belonging to another shall be guilty of the offence of vandalism.

(2) It shall not be competent to charge acts which constitute the offence of wilful fire-raising as vandalism under this section."[53]

This provision was probably designed to single out the kinds of malicious mischief commonly referred to as vandalism; but the statutory offence

---

[46] L.J.-G. Robertson at 518.

[47] 1938 J.C. 32.

[48] 1957 J.C. 1.

[49] *cf. Farrell v. Marshall*, 1962 S.L.T. (Sh.Ct.) 65, a charge under the Protection of Animals (Scotland) Act 1912. See also K.H.O., "Civil Liability for Loss, Injury and Damage Caused by Animals", 1964 S.L.T (News) 65.

[49a] *Lord Advocate's Ref. (No. 1 of 2000)* 2001 S.L.T. 507, See also Vol. I, Chap. 13.

[49b] *ibid.,* opinion of the court at paras [36] and [99].

[50] Macdonald, p.83.

[51] Hume, i, 134, 176; Alison, i, 641; *supra*, para. 18.61.

[52] But see *John Martin* (1858) 3 Irv. 177.

[53] Maximum penalty, in the District Court, 60 days and a fine of level 3 on the standard scale; and in the Sheriff Court, three months and a fine of the prescribed sum for a first such offence, and six months and a fine of the prescribed sum for any subsequent such offence. The offence was first created by the Criminal Justice (Scotland) Act 1980, s.78.

obviously does not extend to the sort of malicious mischief where economic loss is caused without physical damage to property.[54] In *Black v. Allan*,[55] Lord Justice-General Emslie emphasised that vandalism was not the same as the common law crime but was "an offence standing on its own language." He also held that to convict of vandalism on the ground of reckless destruction or damage, it was necessary for a court to apply the test set down in the road traffic case of *Allan v. Patterson*[56] and be satisfied that the conduct was reckless in the sense that it created an obvious and material risk of the damage which occurred.[57] This may present another point of distinction between the statutory and common law offences, since in the absence of intention, malicious mischief requires that the accused should have known he was likely to cause damage or that he showed "a deliberate disregard of, or even indifference to, the property of others"[58]; but this distinction may be more apparent than real.[59] Vandalism requires that the accused's conduct be "without reasonable excuse"; and it is plain that once the issue of excuse is raised, the onus is upon the Crown to show that the relevant explanation was not a reasonable one[60]; the final decision on the matter is one of fact and circumstance for the court to determine.[61]

Postal installations. The Submarine Telegraph Act 1885, which applies **22.15** the Submarine Telegraph Convention of 1884, provides by section 3:

"(1) A person shall not unlawfully and wilfully, or by culpable negligence, break or injure any submarine cable [under the high seas or any pipe-line under the high seas or under the territorial sea adjacent to the United Kingdom[62]] in such manner as might interrupt or obstruct in whole or in part telegraphic [or telephonic[63]] communication . . . [64]

(3) Where a person does any act with the object of preserving the life or limb of himself or of any other person, or of preserving the vessel to which he belongs or any other vessel, and takes all reasonable precautions to avoid injury to a submarine cable, such person shall not be deemed to have acted unlawfully and wilfully within the meaning of the section.[65]

(4) A person shall not be deemed to have unlawfully and wilfully broken or injured any submarine cable, where in the bona fide attempt to repair another submarine cable injury has been done to such first-mentioned cable, or the same has been broken; but this shall not apply so as to exempt such person from any liability under this Act or otherwise to pay the cost of repairing such . . . injury."

---

[54] See para. 22.01, *supra*.

[55] 1985 S.C.C.R. 11, at 13.

[56] 1980 J.C. 57.

[57] 1985 S.C.C.R. at 13.

[58] *Ward v. Robertson*, 1938 J.C. 32, at 36: see para. 22.03, *supra*.

[59] See Vol. I, paras 7.58 and 7.61.

[60] See *Murray v. O'Brien*, 1994 S.L.T. 1051; *John v. Donnelly*, 1999 S.C.C.R. 802.

[61] See, *e.g.*, *McDougall v. Ho*, 1985 S.C.C.R. 199.

[62] See Continental Shelf Act 1964, s.8, and the Petroleum Act 1998, Sched. 4, para. 2(4); damage to high-voltage power cables and pipelines is criminal whether or not it affects communications.

[63] See Continental Shelf Act 1964, s.8.

[64] Under subs. (2), both acts and attempts are punishable; the maximum penalty is five years' imprisonment and a fine where the act was wilful, and three months' and a fine of level 3 on the standard scale where it was negligent.

[65] *Quaere*, if in such a case he could ever be said to act negligently.

The Postal Services Act 2000 provides by section 85:

"(1) A person commits an offence if he sends by post a postal packet which encloses any creature, article or thing of any kind which is likely to injure other postal packets in course of their transmission by post or any person engaged in the business of a postal operator."[66]

Section 86(2) of the same Act provides:

"A person commits an offence if without due authority, he paints or in any way disfigures any [universal postal service post] office, box or property."[67]

22.16 *Aircraft.* Section 2 of the Aviation Security Act 1982 provides:

"(1) It shall, subject to subsection (4) below, be an offence for any person unlawfully and intentionally—
(a) to destroy an aircraft in service or so to damage such an aircraft as to render it incapable of flight or as to be likely to endanger its safety in flight; or
(b) to commit on board an aircraft in flight any act of violence which is likely to endanger the safety of the aircraft.

(2) It shall also, subject to subsection (4) below, be an offence for any person unlawfully and intentionally to place, or cause to be placed, on any aircraft in service any device or substance which is likely to destroy the aircraft, or is likely so to damage it as to render it incapable of flight or as to be likely to endanger its safety in flight; but nothing in this subsection shall be construed as limiting the circumstances in which the commission of any act—
(a) may constitute an offence under subsection (1) above, or
(b) may constitute attempting or conspiracy to commit, or aiding, abetting, counselling or procuring, or being art and part in, the commission of such an offence.

(3) Except as provided by subsection (4) below, subsections (1) and (2) above shall apply whether any such act as is therein mentioned is committed in the United Kingdom or elsewhere, whatever the nationality of the person committing the act and whatever the State in which the aircraft is registered.

---

[66] Under subs. (2), an exception is made for any postal packet which encloses anything permitted by the postal operator concerned. Any necessary definitions relevant to subss. (1) and (2) are provided by s.125(1) and (3). On summary conviction, the maximum fine is one of the statutory maximum; and on conviction on indictment, the maximum penalty is 12 months' and a fine (see subs. (5)). The carriage of dangerous goods on ships is regulated by the Merchant Shipping (Dangerous Goods and Marine Pollutants) Regulations 1997 (S.I. 1997 No. 2367), and on aircraft by the Air Navigation Order 1995 (S.I. 1995 No. 1038), arts 51, 52 and 111, and Sched. 12.
[67] Words in brackets are imported from subs. (1). Under s.86(4), "universal postal service post office" includes any house, building, room, vehicle or place used for the provision of any postal service in connection with the provision of a universal postal service or a part of such a service; "universal postal service letter box" means "any box or receptacle provided by a universal service provider [see s.4(3) and (4)] for the purpose of receiving postal packets or any class of postal packets, for onwards transmission in connection with the provision of a universal postal service." Under s.86(3), the maximum penalty on summary conviction is a fine of level 3 on the standard scale. A "universal postal service" is a service which normally on every working day collects and delivers postal packets, not exceeding 20 kg in weight, on a United Kingdom-wide basis and at "affordable prices" set according to a public tariff — see s.4(1) and (7).

(4) Subsections (1) and (2) above shall not apply to any act committed in relation to an aircraft used in military, customs or police service unless—

(a) the act is committed in the United Kingdom, or

(b) where the act is committed outside the United Kingdom, the person committing it is a United Kingdom national.

(5) A person who commits an offence under this section shall be liable, on conviction on indictment, to imprisonment for life.

(6) In this section 'unlawfully'—

(a) in relation to the commission of an act in the United Kingdom, means so as (apart from this Act) to constitute an offence under the law of the part of the United Kingdom in which the act is committed, and

(b) in relation to the commission of an act outside the United Kingdom, means so that the commission of the act would (apart from this Act) have been an offence under the law of England and Wales if it had been committed in England and Wales or of Scotland if it had been committed in Scotland.

(7) In this section 'act of violence' means—

(a) any act done in the United Kingdom which constitutes the offence of murder, attempted murder, manslaughter, culpable homicide or assault or an offence under section 18, 20, 21, 22, 23, 24, 28 or 29 of the Offences against the Person Act 1861 or under section 2 of the Explosive Substances Act 1883, and

(b) any act done outside the United Kingdom which, if done in the United Kingdom, would constitute such an offence as is mentioned in paragraph (a) above."[68]

It is also an offence for any person "by means of any device, substance or weapon unlawfully and intentionally — (a) to destroy or seriously to damage — (i) property used for the provision of any facilities at an aerodrome serving international civil aviation . . ., or (ii) any aircraft which is at such an aerodrome but is not in service . . . in such a way as to endanger or be likely to endanger the safe operation of the aerodrome or the safety of persons at the aerodrome."[69]

Ships and fixed platforms. Intentionally destroying or damaging a ship or **22.17** a fixed platform, and intentionally damaging such property or a ship's cargo so as to endanger the safe navigation of the ship or the safety of

---

[68] See also s.3 (which penalises the destruction of, damage to, or interference with, property used for the purposes of air navigation, and carries a maximum penalty of life in prison) and s.4 (which makes it an offence to have with one in an aircraft, aerodrome in the United Kingdom or air navigation installation there, certain dangerous articles — including firearms and explosives: maximum penalty, on indictment five years in prison and a fine, and on summary conviction three months' and a fine of the statutory maximum). Part II of the 1982 Act contains provisions to protect aircraft, aerodromes and air navigation installations against "acts of violence", which include any act constituting in Scotland "the offence of malicious mischief" (see s.10(2)).

[69] See Aviation and Maritime Security Act 1990, s.1(2): maximum penalty is life in prison (s.1(5)). "Unlawfully" carries the same meaning as it does under s.2 of the Aviation Security Act 1982 (*supra*): see s.1(9) of the 1990 Act.

the platform, are offences under the Aviation and Maritime Security Act 1990.[70]

22.18 *Wrecks and military remains.* Under the Protection of Wrecks Act 1973, it is an offence if in a restricted area a person without a licence "tampers with, damages or removes any part of a vessel lying wrecked on or in the sea bed, or any object formerly contained in such a vessel."[71] Wrecks outside United Kingdom waters are protected by provisions made by the Secretary of State under the Merchant Shipping and Maritime Security Act 1997.[72] Tampering with or damaging military remains[73] without a licence is an offence under the Protection of Military Remains Act 1985.[74]

22.19 *Ancient monuments.* Under section 28 of the Ancient Monuments and Archaeological Areas Act 1979, it is an offence for a person without lawful excuse to destroy or damage any protected monument[75] "(a) knowing that it is a protected monument; and (b) intending to destroy or damage the monument or being reckless as to whether [it] would be destroyed or damaged."[76]

---

[70] See s.11(1): "Ship" and "fixed platform" are defined in s.17(1). Under s.11(2), it is an offence intentionally to place, or cause to be placed, on a ship or fixed platform any device or substance likely to destroy or damage that ship or platform. See also the offence under s.12, which relates to the intentional damaging or destroying, or intentional interference with, property used for the provision of maritime navigation facilities where "the destruction, damage or interference is likely to endanger the safe navigation of any ship": maximum penalty for an offence under s.11(1) or (2), or s.12, is life in prison (see ss. 11(6) and 12(7)). Provision for the protection of ships, and property on board ships and harbour areas, from (*inter alia*) acts of malicious mischief is made under Pt III of the Aviation and Maritime Security Act 1990: see esp. s.18, as amended by the Merchant Shipping (Maritime Security) Act 1997, Sched. 4, para. 2. See also the offence involving a deliberate act or omission (or an act or omission amounting to a breach or neglect of duty, or committed under the influence of drink or drugs) by a seaman employed in, or the Master of, a U.K. ship (or any ship in a U.K. port or in U.K. waters proceeding to or from such a port) where the act or omission causes or is likely to cause destruction or serious damage to (*inter alia*) his ship or its machinery or its navigational or safety equipment: Merchant Shipping Act 1995, s.58: maximum penalty, on indictment two years in prison and a fine, and on summary conviction a fine not exceeding the statutory maximum.

[71] See s.1(3). A "restricted area" is one designated under s.1(1) as an area where there is or may be a wreck and which, from a number of considerations, ought to be protected from unauthorised interference. Under s.3(3), defences are set out which include "necessity, due to stress of weather or navigational hazards". The maximum penalty is a fine on indictment, and, on summary conviction, a fine of level 5 on the standard scale (see s.3(4)).

[72] See s.24. Contraventions of requirements imposed under the authority of that section may be made offences carrying maximum penalties of a fine on indictment, and a fine of the statutory maximum on summary conviction.

[73] These refer to aircraft which have crashed or vessels which have been sunk or stranded while on military service, and which are either in a protected place or in part of a "controlled site" (as designated by the Secretary of State acting under s.1). "Aircraft" include hovercraft, gliders and balloons (s.9(1)); and "remains" include any cargo, munitions, apparel or personal effects which were on board during the final flight or voyage, as also any human remains associated with the aircraft or vessel (s.9(1)).

[74] See s.2(1) and (2). It is a defence under s.2(5) for the accused to show that he believed on reasonable grounds that the circumstances were such that the place would not have been a protected place; it is also a defence under s.2(6) for him to show that what was done was "urgently necessary in the interests of safety or health, or to prevent or avoid serious damage to property". The maximum penalty is a fine on indictment, and a fine of the statutory maximum on summary conviction (s.2(7)).

[75] See s.28(3). The reference there to "local authority" now includes "National Park Authority": see National Parks (Scotland) Act 2000 (asp 10), Sched. 5, para. 7.

[76] Maximum penalty, two years' and a fine on indictment, and six months' and a fine of the statutory maximum on summary conviction.

Electricity, gas and water. The Electricity Act 1989 provides by paragraph **22.20**
6(1) of Schedule 6[77]:

> "A person who intentionally or by culpable negligence damages or
> allows to be damaged—
> (a) any electric line or electrical plant provided by an electricity
>   distributor; or
> (b) any electricity meter provided by an electricity supplier,
>   shall be liable on summary conviction to a fine not exceeding
>   level 3 on the standard scale."

The Gas Act 1986 provides by paragraph 10(1) of Schedule 2B[78]:

> "If any person intentionally or by culpable negligence—
> (a) injures or allows to be injured any gas fitting provided by a
>   public gas transporter or gas supplier, or any service pipe by
>   which any premises are connected to such a transporter's
>   main;
> (b) alters the index to any meter used for measuring the quantity
>   of gas conveyed or supplied by such a transporter or supplier;
>   or
> (c) prevents any such meter from duly registering the quantity of
>   gas conveyed or supplied,
> he shall be . . . liable on summary conviction to fine not exceeding
> level 3 on the standard scale."

The Water (Scotland) Act 1980 provides by paragraph 32(1) of
Schedule 4:

> "If any person wilfully or negligently injures, or suffers to be
> injured, any water fitting belonging to the undertakers, or fraudu-
> lently alters the index of any meter used by them for measuring the
> water supplied by them, or prevents any such meter from registering
> correctly the quantity of water supplied, . . . he shall . . . be liable to
> a fine not exceeding [level 2 on the standard scale]."[79]

The use of explosives. The Explosives Act 1875 lays down rules designed **22.21**
to avoid the dangers associated with the making and keeping of
explosives[80] and prohibits their manufacture in unauthorised places.
Section 77 of the Act provides that:

---

[77] As substituted by Sched. 4 of the Utilities Act 2000 (see s.51(2)).

[78] Schedule 2B is inserted by the Gas Act 1995, s.9(2), and appears as Sched. 2 of the
1995 Act: the original "Gas Code" under Sched. 5 of the 1986 Act ceased to apply by
virtue of s.9(3) of the 1995 Act.

[79] See also para. 33: "If any person either — (a) wilfully and without the consent of the
undertakers, or (b) negligently, turns on, opens, closes, shuts off or otherwise interferes
with any valve, cock or other work or apparatus belonging to the undertakers and thereby
causes the supply of water to be interfered with, he shall be liable to a fine not exceeding
[level 4 on the standard scale]".

[80] "Explosive" is defined in s.3 of the 1875 Act as including substances "used or
manufactured with a view to produce a practical effect by explosion or pyrotechnic effect",
and includes petrol bombs: *R. v. Bouch* [1983] Q.B. 246.

"Any person other than the occupier of or person employed in or about any factory, magazine, or store who is found committing any act which tends to cause explosion or fire in or about such factory, magazine, or store, [shall be guilty of an offence]."[81]

22.22   The criminal use of explosives is dealt with mainly in the Explosive Substances Act 1883. This Act provides[82]:

> *Section 2.* "A person who in the United Kingdom or (being a citizen of the United Kingdom and Colonies) in the Republic of Ireland, unlawfully and maliciously[83] causes by any explosive substance an explosion of a nature likely to endanger life or to cause serious injury to property shall, whether any injury to person or property has been actually caused or not . . . be liable to imprisonment for life."

> *Section 3.* "(1) A person who in the United Kingdom or a dependency[84] or (being a citizen of the United Kingdom and Colonies) elsewhere unlawfully and maliciously—
>
> (a) does any act with intent to cause, or conspires to cause, by an explosive substance an explosion of a nature likely to endanger life or cause serious injury to property, whether in the United Kingdom or the Republic of Ireland, or
>
> (b) makes or has in his possession or under his control an explosive substance with intent by means thereof to endanger life, or cause serious injury to property, whether in the United Kingdom or the Republic of Ireland, or to enable any other person so to do,
>
> shall, whether any explosion does or does not take place, and whether any injury to person or property is actually caused or not, be . . . liable to imprisonment for [life]."[85]

"Explosive" has the same meaning in the Explosive Substances Act 1883 as in the Explosives Act 1875,[86] and includes a petrol bomb made in a milk bottle whose main effect is to produce a fireball.[87] Although the ingredients of a mixture of air and petrol in a bottle may not in themselves be in such proportions as to be an explosive substance, the fact that the bottle will become a fireball when it is broken makes the petrol, bottle and accompanying wick, materials for making an explosive substance as defined in section 9.[88]

---

[81] As amended by the Explosives Acts 1875 and 1923, etc. (Repeals and Modifications) Regulations 1974 (S.I. 1974 No. 1885), Sched. 2, para. 19(a). The section also prohibits trespassing in any factory, magazine or store or adjoining land. For enforcement, see Health and Safety at Work etc., Act 1974, s.33(3) and (4)(c), and Sched. 1.

[82] Sections 2 and 3, as substituted by Criminal Jurisdiction Act 1975, s.7.

[83] In *McIntosh v. H.M. Advocate*, 1993 S.C.C.R. 464, the Appeal Court seems to have accepted that 'maliciousness' is satisfied by 'recklessness' for the purposes of this section; but the Court reserved its opinion as to whether English authority favouring a subjective view of recklessness was to be applied here, the appeal in the case having been disposed of on other grounds.

[84] For instance, the Channel Islands, the Isle of Man and any colony other then one for whose external relations a country other than the U.K. is responsible: s.3(2), added by Criminal Jurisdiction Act 1975.

[85] "Life" substituted by Criminal Law Act 1977, s.33, Sched. 12.

[86] *R. v. Wheatley* [1979] 1 W.L.R. 144.

[87] *R. v. Bouch* [1983] Q.B. 246.

[88] See para. 22.24, *infra*.

It has been held at first instance in England that the words "A person who in the United Kingdom or a dependency" in section 3(1) serve to delineate where the relevant acts occurred or were to take place, and do not require the defendant physically to have been present in the United Kingdom or a dependency at the time of those acts.[89]

POSSESSION.   **22.23**

> *Section 4.* "(1) Any person who makes or knowingly has in his possession or under his control[90] any explosive substance, under such circumstances as to give rise to a reasonable suspicion that he is not making it or does not have it in his possession or under his control for a lawful object, shall, unless he can show that he made it or had it in his possession or under his control for a lawful object, be [liable to imprisonment for fourteen years]."

It has been held by the Court of Appeal in England that a defence of "lawful object" may in exceptional circumstances be available to a defendant charged with an offence under section 4 if he can satisfy the jury on a balance of probabilities that "his object was to protect himself or his family or his property against imminent apprehended attack and to do so by means which he believed were no more than reasonably necessary to meet the force used by the attacker."[91] The "lawful object" is not, however, confined to objects intended to be achieved in the United Kingdom, or to ones which would be lawful there. Where, therefore, there was evidence that the accused had manufactured electronic timing devices in England for use abroad, he had to show that they were meant for a lawful object abroad.[92]

DEFINITION.   **22.24**

> *Section 9.* "(1) The expression 'explosive substance' shall be deemed to include any materials for making any explosive substance; also any apparatus, machine, implement, or materials used, or intended to be used, or adapted for causing, or aiding in causing, any

---

[89] See *R. v. Ellis (Desmond)* (1992) 95 Cr.App.R. 52.

[90] Which requires actual possession or, where the explosives are found on premises occupied or controlled by the accused, knowledge of their presence together with acceptance of them into the premises or at least permission for or connivance at their remaining there: *Black v. H.M. Advocate*, 1974 J.C. 43. The Crown must also prove that the accused had knowledge that the substance in question was an 'explosive substance' (see para. 22.24, *infra*): *ibid.* See also *R. v. Berry (No. 3)* [1994] 2 All E.R. 913, where the English Court of Appeal held that knowledge of the character of the substance is required in the case of a defendant who is alleged to have made the substance, notwithstanding that subs. (1) confines the word "knowingly" to a person who has the substance in his possession or under his control: as Lord Taylor of Gosforth said at 918g-h "in our judgment all three categories of person must be shown to have known that the substance was an explosive substance. We cannot read the section as requiring proof of such knowledge in a possessor or controller, but not in the maker. The word 'knowingly' simply emphasises that where possession or control is relied upon, the defendant must know the substance is in his possession, for example in his house or his car. No person who makes the substance can be unaware that he had done so."

[91] *Att.-Gen.'s Reference (No. 2 of 1983)* [1984] 2 W.L.R. 465, Lord Lane C.J., at 478E-F. In the case, the defendant acted primarily with a view to defending his business premises.

[92] See *R. v. Berry* [1985] A.C. 246, HL. See also *R. v. Berry (No. 3)* [1994] 2 All E.R. 913, CA.

explosion in or with any explosive substance; also any part of any such apparatus, machine, or implement."[93]

22.25 *Computer misuse.* Section 3 of the Computer Misuse Act 1990 provides:

"(1) A person is guilty of an offence if—
  (a) he does any act which causes an unauthorised modification of the contents of any computer; and
  (b) at the time when he does the act he has the requisite intent and the requisite knowledge.

(2) For the purposes of subsection (1)(b) above the requisite intent is an intent to cause a modification of the contents of any computer and by so doing—
  (a) to impair the operation of any computer;
  (b) to prevent or hinder access to any program or data held in any computer; or
  (c) to impair the operation of any such program or the reliability of any such data.

(3) The intent need not be directed at—
  (a) any particular computer;
  (b) any particular program or data or a program or data of any particular kind; or
  (c) any particular modification or a modification of any particular kind.

(4) For the purposes of subsection (1)(b) above the requisite knowledge is knowledge that any modification he intends to cause is unauthorised.

(5) It is immaterial for the purposes of this section whether an unauthorised modification or any intended effect of it of a kind mentioned in subsection (2) above is, or is intended to be, permanent or merely temporary . . .

(7) A person guilty of an offence under this section shall be liable—
  (a) on summary conviction, to imprisonment for a term not exceeding six months or to a fine not exceeding the statutory maximum or to both; and
  (b) on conviction on indictment, to imprisonment for a term not exceeding five years or to a fine or to both."[94]

FIRE-RAISING

22.26 The most serious form of criminal injury to property is by fire-raising, which consists in setting fire to the property of another person.[95] Fire is "set" or "raised" whenever the property in question has started to burn, that is to say, whenever any part of it, however small, has been consumed by fire.[96] What amounts to consumption by fire in any case is a question

---

[93] The following statutory provision may also be noted: the Trade Union and Labour Relations (Consolidation) Act 1992, s.240, *infra*, para. 39.31.

[94] For definitions of "modification of the contents of any computer" and "unauthorised modification", see s.17(7) and (8): see also *R. v. Bow Street Magistrate, ex. p. U.S. Govt* [1999] Q.B. 847.

[95] *cf. John Mackirdy* (1856) 2 Irv. 474.

[96] *John Arthur* (1836) 1 Swin. 124, L.J.-C. Boyle at 152; *William Sutherland* (1825) Alison, i, 430.

of fact — in one case it was held that the fact that a door was charred did not necessarily mean that it had been set on fire.[97]

The fire need not be set directly to the property in the charge, provided, of course, that the burning of the property is causally connected with the accused's act.[98] If, therefore, A sets fire to his own house with the intention that the fire should spread to B's house, and it does so spread, A is guilty of setting B's house on fire[99]; if A sets fire to furniture and the fabric of the building is damaged, A may be guilty of setting fire to the building wilfully or culpably as the case may be,[1] since it has recently been decided, in a case which considerably simplifies the law, that there are two distinct crimes of fire-raising — wilful fire-raising, and culpable and reckless fire-raising.[2]

Wilful fire-raising, and culpable and reckless fire-raising

Wilful fire-raising. Where B's property is set on fire as a result of A's **22.27** conduct and it can be shown beyond reasonable doubt that A intended that result, A is guilty of wilful fire-raising in respect of that property; the subject matter of the offence may be any type of corporeal property belonging to B.[3] If A intentionally sets fire to property x and the fire spreads to property y belonging to B, but it cannot be shown that A intended to set fire to y, A cannot be convicted of wilful fire-raising in respect of y since the doctrine of transferred intent does not apply in fire-raising[4]; nor can he be convicted of culpable and reckless fire-raising relative to y, supposing that the requirements of that separate offence can be established, unless that offence has specifically been included in the charge[5]; and where recklessness rather than intention is applicable to the fire-raising, the Appeal Court has emphasised that intention cannot be inferred from that recklessness[6] (although it may, of course, be inferred from the whole circumstances of the case). It should perhaps be noted that it is not possible to charge acts constituting wilful fire-raising as the statutory offence of vandalism,[7] and that it is not possible to try a

---

[97] *Peter Grieve* (1866) 5 Irv. 263.

[98] *Alex. Pollock* (1869) 1 Couper 257.

[99] Hume, i, 129–130.

[1] *ibid.*; Alison, i, 433; *Margaret Fallasdale or Drysdale or Anderson* (1826) Hume, i, 130; *Janet Hamilton and Jas Campbell* (1806) Hume, i, 129. See also *Byrne v. H.M. Advocate,* 2000 S.C.C.R. 77 (Court of five judges), opinion of the Court (Lord Coulsfield) at 90G–91C.

[2] *Byrne v. H.M. Advocate,* 2000 S.C.C.R. 77 (Court of five judges), opinion of the Court (Lord Coulsfield) at 91G. For an account of the complexities and difficulties of the older law of fire-raising, see the 2nd edition of this book at paras 22–23 to 22–26; see also J. Chalmers, "Fire-raising: From the Ashes?", 2000 S.L.T. (News) 57.

[3] *Byrne v. H.M. Advocate,* 2000 S.C.C.R. 77 (Court of five judges), opinion of the Court (Lord Coulsfield) at 92A.

[4] *ibid.*, 89F–90A, approving *Blane v. H.M. Advocate,* 1991 S.C.C.R. 576 on this point. Hume, i, 24; Alison, i, 433 and 439; and Anderson, p.212, who all favour the application of transferred intent, must now be considered wrong to have done so, whilst Burnett, *per contra*, at 221, must be considered to be correct. For "transferred intent", see Vol. I, para. 9.10.

[5] *Byrne v. H.M. Advocate,* 2000 S.C.C.R. 77 (Court of five judges), opinion of the Court (Lord Coulsfield) at 89D–E, thus disapproving of the verdict substituted by the Appeal Court in *McKelvie v. H.M. Advocate,* 1997 S.L.T. 758.

[6] *ibid.*, at 90G–91D, disapproving on this point the charge to the jury in *H.M. Advocate v. Boyd,* High Court at Ayr, March 1997, unrep'd, and the opinion of the Appeal Court in *Blane v. H.M. Advocate,* 1991 S.C.C.R. 576, in so far as *Boyd* was followed there.

[7] See Criminal Law (Consolidation) (Scotland) Act 1995, s.52(2). For details of the offence of vandalism, see para. 22.14, *supra.*

person for wilful fire-raising, or attempted wilful fire-raising, in a district court.[8]

22.28 *Culpable and reckless fire-raising.* Unlike malicious mischief,[9] fire-raising is not a single offence with alternative forms of *mens rea*; instead, it is now clear that there are two separate fire-raising offences, and that these are distinguished according to the form of *mens rea* which can be shown in the circumstances. Where A's conduct recklessly, but not intentionally, causes damage to B's property[10] by fire, A is guilty of culpable and reckless fire-raising[11]; and thus, if A was charged with wilful fire-raising and nothing else, he cannot alternatively be convicted of culpable and reckless fire-raising.[12] If A's conduct shows an "utter disregard for the likelihood of the fire spreading to the subjects"[13] in question, or displays "a reckless disregard as to what the result of his act would be",[14] there is sufficient recklessness for conviction of this crime; but proof only of a lack of care (negligence) on his part will not suffice.[15] In *Archibald Phaup*[16] it was suggested that it might be culpable and reckless fire-raising to drop a match into a bush as a result of which a house was burnt, but something much more than this is necessary,[17] and it was said in *Robert Smillie*[18] that carelessness of that kind was insufficient. Where the material into which the match is dropped is obviously inflammable, like a tin of petrol, there may of course be recklessness.

22.29   CONSTRUCTIVE RECKLESSNESS. In *Robert Smillie*,[19] Lord Young described culpable and reckless fire-raising as *inter alia*, setting fire "while engaged in some illegal act",[20] which suggests that as in culpable homicide it is criminal to cause accidental harm of one kind while

---

[8] Criminal Procedure (Scotland) Act 1995, s.8(b)(i). See also *ibid.*, s.5(4)(b), which permits wilful fire-raising to be tried summarily in a sheriff court.

[9] See para. 22.03, *supra*. The width of malicious mischief, however, is such that it could include either of the fire-raising offences within its ambit.

[10] Any form of corporeal property will suffice: see *Byrne v. H.M. Advocate*, 2000 S.C.C.R. 77 (Court of five judges), opinion of the Court (Lord Coulsfield) at 92B. In the curious case of *Withers v. Addie*, 1986 S.L.T. (Sh.Ct.) 32, a charge in terms that the accused "recklessly set fire to shoelaces worn by [B] to his danger while he was dozing and [that] the fire took effect thereon and on his trousers to the injury of his leg" was found relevant, an objection that the crime was truly one of assault having been repelled: it seems that the Crown's contention, that what was set fire to was shoe laces and trousers (items of corporeal property) and that the reference to personal injury was an aggravation of reckless fire-raising, was upheld by the sheriff, who also held that the absence of the word "culpably" from the charge was of no moment. The Crown conceded that it could not show the necessary intent for assault. It is difficult to appreciate why the whole charge was not one of reckless injury in these circumstances.

[11] For the separate offence of wilful fire-raising, see para. 22.27, *supra*.

[12] *Byrne v. H.M. Advocate*, 2000 S.C.C.R. 77 (Court of five judges), opinion of the Court (Lord Coulsfield) at 90G to 91C. It would be necessary for culpable and reckless fire-raising specifically to have been charged in the alternative for such a conviction to be possible.

[13] *ibid.*, at 91B.

[14] *ibid.*, at 92B.

[15] *ibid.* See also *Carr v. H.M. Advocate*, 1994 S.C.C.R. 521.

[16] (1846) Ark. 176.

[17] In one early case, reckless fire-raising was described as fire-raising "in such a state of reckless excitement, as not to know or care" what one was doing: *Geo. MacBean* (1847) Ark. 262, L.J.-C. Hope at 263.

[18] (1883) 5 Couper 287, Lord Young at 291.

[19] (1883) 5 Couper 287.

[20] At 291.

intending to commit harm of another. But this dictum is *obiter*, there is no other authority in support of it and the analogy with culpable homicide cannot be pressed too far, if only because culpable homicide unlike culpable fire-raising was a crime of negligence. In *Jas Stewart*[21] the accused carelessly set fire to a truck while stealing whisky from it. He was charged with culpable and reckless fire-raising, and Lord Justice-General McNeill asked: "Is it more illegal to burn when the man is stealing than when he is not? This may be, but I should wish more authority on the point."[22] No authority was produced and the Crown dropped the case, so that it is not itself an authority on the matter. It is submitted, however, that the answer to the question is in the negative, and that there is no room for constructive recklessness in fire-raising.

Motive. The motive with which the fire is raised is irrelevant. The **22.30** suggestion in *Jean Gordon or Bryan and Ors*[23] that it is not fire-raising to burn a door in order to escape from prison and without any intention to burn the prison cannot be accepted.[24]

Res sua. Res sua is a good defence to a charge of fire-raising,[25] although **22.31** not to the separate crime of setting fire to property with intent to defraud insurers.[26] Where, however, A sets fire to property which is in the possession of a tenant or liferenter, he is guilty of fire-raising even if the property is uninhabited,[27] and it is, of course, fire-raising for a tenant in occupation to set fire to the subject of the lease.[28] It is probably not fire-raising to set fire to one's own property over which someone else has a heritable security.[29]

Where A sets fire to his own property in such a way as to harm or endanger B's property the important feature is the harm or danger to B's property, and it is irrelevant that A's initial act was directed against his own property.[30]

Creating danger to property by fire

Macdonald states that it is an offence "to set fire to combustibles in or **22.32** near buildings in a reckless manner, so as to cause danger of injury to life or property",[31] and there was a conviction on such a charge in *Jas B. Fleming.*[32] But, as was pointed out in *Jas Martin*,[33] to set fire to

---

[21] (1856) 2 Irv. 359.
[22] At 365.
[23] (1841) 2 Swin. 545, Lord Mackenzie at 546–547.
[24] Hume, i, 131.
[25] *cf. John Mackirdy* (1856) 2 Irv. 474.
[26] *supra*, para. 18.60. *Cf. Daniel Black* (1856) 2 Irv. 575.
[27] Hume, i, 133; Alison, i, 437; Burnett, p.216. References in these authorities to the category of "capital wilful fire-raising" can now be ignored: see *Byrne v. H.M. Advocate*, 2000 S.C.C.R. 77 (Court of five judges), opinion of the Court (Lord Coulsfield) at 86D.
[28] Alison, i, 435–436; *Margt Drysdale* (1826) Alison, i, 435; *Malcolm Gillespie and Ors* (1827) *ibid.*; *Wm Sutherland* (1825) *ibid.* 436; Alison is unclear whether this is restricted to cases where the tenant acts with intent to defraud insurers, but it is submitted that on principle it must be fire-raising for A to set fire to B's property whether or not A is a tenant: a right of possession is not a licence to burn.
[29] Alison, i, 437; Burnett, p.217; and this was arguably so even if the security had been in the form of an *ex facie* absolute disposition.
[30] Hume, i, 130; Macdonald, p.81.
[31] Macdonald, p.82.
[32] (1848) Ark. 519.
[33] (1876) 3 Couper 274.

combustibles is itself a crime, apart from the danger to other property which constitutes only an aggravation. An additional charge of "culpably and recklessly placing and leaving a light in close proximity to highly inflammable articles or vapours, without precaution taken to prevent their ignition, to the imminent risk and danger of the building, the property of others, in which they are contained, and to the great peril of the lives of the lieges" was rejected mainly because of lack of specification of the circumstances. Lord Ardmillan said, however, that "The mere leaving a light in a situation of possible or even probable danger, is . . . not quite sufficient to constitute a criminal offence."[34] The matter can be tested in the situation in which A sets fire to his own property and in so doing endangers B's property. Macdonald says, "A person may even be liable to punishment for setting fire to his own property, to the danger of his neighbour, although the fire was not intended to spread, and did not in fact spread to his neighbour's property."[35] The only case which may be said to be authority for this proposition is *John Arthur*,[36] which is unsatisfactory for a number of reasons. The circumstances were that A was a tenant who set fire to his furniture and almost set fire to the building itself in pursuance of an insurance fraud. He was charged, *inter alia*, with "wilfully and feloniously attempting to set fire to any furniture . . . in any shop . . . to the great risk and danger of the said shop, being the property of another person, and of the neighbouring tenement . . . and also of the lives of the lieges, more especially when committed with the felonious intent of defrauding [insurers]." Some of the judges regarded this as a charge of attempted wilful fire-raising, but there are dicta to the effect that it is an offence to set fire to one's own property in such a way as to endanger others.[37] The case is not a clear authority for any proposition, and it should further be noted that as in *Martin*[38] danger to both life and property was libelled, so that it cannot be said to support the view that it is a crime to endanger property by fire where there is no danger to life.[39]

Nevertheless, there is nothing unreasonable in making it criminal to cause such danger by fire in view of the essentially dangerous nature of fire although it may be that, as in the case of muirburn and explosives, this is a matter for legislation. If such a crime does exist, it may be restricted to deliberately setting fire to one's own property with reckless indifference to the danger thereby created to the property of others.

22.33 *Breach of the peace.* Hume states that if a man burns his own house, "If it is a house in a town, or is so situated that some degree of danger or alarm to the vicinage is occasioned by burning it, the offender shall be liable to punishment . . . as for a high breach of good neighbourhood and public police,"[40] and it is no doubt still competent to treat such a case as one of breach of the peace. Hume seems to be concerned with danger to persons, but to cause alarm to persons by endangering their property would constitute a breach of the peace.[41]

---

[34] At 278.
[35] Macdonald, p.81.
[36] (1836) 1 Swin. 124.
[37] See 128–129. In the event Arthur was convicted of attempted wilful fire-raising.
[38] (1876) 3 Couper 274.
[39] For the offence of endangering life, see *infra*, para. 29.58.
[40] Hume, i, 133–134.
[41] *infra*, para. 41.04.

Muirburn

This crime involves the setting fire to moorland, or to land covered **22.34** with heath. The crime is completed by setting fire to a moor whether or not any of the vegetation growing on it is burnt, and whether or not the moor is covered by heath.[42] The crime is statutory and is governed by the Hill Farming Act 1946. This Act prohibits the making of muirburn except during a specified season (normally from April 16 to September 30), and regulates the permitted making of muirburn by the following provisions:

> "Any person who—
>   (a) commences to make muirburn between one hour after sunset and one hour before sunrise; or
>   (b) fails to provide at the place where he is about to make muirburn, or to maintain there while he is making muirburn, a sufficient staff and equipment to control and regulate the burning operations so as to prevent damage to any woodland on or adjoining the land where the operations are taking place or to any adjoining lands, march fences or other subjects; or
>   (c) makes muirburn on any land without having given to the proprietors of the lands or woodlands adjoining the land and, if he is a tenant, to the proprietor of the land, not less than twenty-four hours' notice of his intention to make muirburn and of the day on which, the places at which, and the approximate extent to which, he intends to make muirburn; or
>   (d) makes muirburn on any land without due care so as to cause damage to any woodlands on or adjoining the land or any adjoining lands, woodlands, march fences, or other subjects,
> shall be guilty of an offence."[43]

The Act defines making muirburn as including "setting fire to or burning any heath or muir."[44]

---

[42] *Rodger v. Gibson* (1842) 1 Broun 78.

[43] Section 25. Maximum penalty for any offence in connection with muirburn, a fine of level 4 on the standard scale and 30 days' imprisonment: s.27 (as amended by the Wildlife and Countryside Act 1981, s.72(3)).

[44] Section 39(f).

PART III

Non-Sexual Offences Against the Person

SECTION 1 — *HOMICIDE*

CHAPTER 23

MURDER

HOMICIDE IN GENERAL

Homicide is the destruction of a self-existent human life.[1] It is not **23.01** homicide to take one's own life.[2]

"Self-existent". It is not settled in Scotland whether a child who has **23.02** breathed but has not been completely born is to be regarded as self-existent in the law of homicide. In *Jean McAllum*[3] Lord Justice-Clerk Inglis directed the jury that it was not homicide to destroy a child before it was fully born.[4] In *H.M. Advocate v. Scott*[5] Lord Young gave a direction that it did not matter that the injuries were inflicted on the child while it was still partly in its mother's body.[6] Lord Inglis is supported by English law,[7] but Lord Young's view is accepted by Macdonald,[8] and it is submitted that it is correct. There is a gap between abortion which consists in inducing a miscarriage, and the murder of a living child, a gap which is bridged in England by the statutory crime of killing a child capable of being born alive before it has an independent

---

[1] Hume, i, 186; Alison, i, 71; Macdonald, p.87.

[2] Alison, i, 1. Mackenzie, I, 13, and Anderson, p.148, say that it is a crime. Hume deals with it only from the point of view of the now obsolete penalty of escheat which followed on suicide: at i, 300. The modern view is that suicide is not criminal: T.B. Smith, p.182; R.C., para. 167; *cf. Jessie Webster* (1858) 3 Irv. 95, 98 where it was argued that attempted abortion should not be a crime, because it was analogous to attempted suicide which was not a crime. If the circumstances warrant it attempted suicide may be prosecuted as a breach of the peace, but although such charges are sometimes brought by the police they are hardly ever prosecuted in the sheriff court. The survivor of a suicide pact may however be guilty of homicide if he himself killed the deceased, since the consent of the victim is no defence: see "Suicide Pacts", 1958 S.L.T. (News) 209, and N. Gow, "Legal Aspects of Suicide", 1958 S.L.T. (News) 141; see also D.J. Lanham, "Murder by Instigating Suicide" [1980] Crim.L.R. 215.

[3] (1858) 3 Irv. 187.

[4] At 201.

[5] (1892) 3 White 240.

[6] At 244.

[7] See Smith and Hogan, at p. 338; see also Law Commission No. 177, 1989, *A Criminal Code for England and Wales*, Vol. I, Draft Code, cl. 53 (a), and Vol. II, paras 14.2 and 14.3.

[8] Macdonald, p.87. There is a presumption in South African law that a child which has breathed is born alive, whether or not at the time of its death it had been entirely separated from the body of its mother; the rule is, however, statutory — see Criminal Procedure Act 51 of 1977, s.239(1). Whether the presumption is rebuttable or not appears to be unsettled: see J. Burchell and J. Milton, *Principles of Criminal Law* (2nd ed., 1997), pp. 469–470.

existence,[9] and this gap can be shortened although not completely closed by adopting Lord Young's view which avoids the necessity of distinguishing between destroying a viable child the moment before it completely leaves the mother's body and destroying it a moment later, a distinction that appears to be without a difference.

A child is considered to be alive once it has breathed,[10] and it would probably be regarded as undisputed that it can have a separate existence before the severing of the umbilical cord.

It is homicide in Scotland as well as in England to injure a child in the womb so as to cause its death after it has been born alive.[11] 'Injury' in this context, might include the induction of grossly premature birth by (as in England) any "unlawful and dangerous act [which] changed the natural environment of the foetus in such a way that when born the child died when she otherwise would have lived."[12]

23.03 *The dying victim.* It is no answer to a charge of homicide that the victim would have died anyway at or about the time he was killed, provided of course that it can be shown that it was the accused's act which in fact caused the death. This is so whether the victim was suffering from an incurable disease, or whether it can be shown that he would necessarily have been involved in a fatal accident had the accused not killed him.[13]

23.04 *The actus reus of homicide.* Homicide can be committed by any act or culpable omission resulting in death. Macdonald says that the injury inflicted must be "real",[14] and that "Frightening a person, so as to bring

---

[9] Infant Life (Preservation) Act 1929. *Cf.* the civil case of *Rance and Anr v. Mid-Downs Health Authority* [1991] 2 W.L.R. 159, where it was opined that abortion under the Abortion Act 1967 would be illegal where s.1 of the 1929 Act applied and the Abortion Act 1967, s.5(1), as substituted by the Human Fertilisation and Embryology Act 1990, s.37(4), which rules that no offence under the 1929 Act is committed where a registered medical practitioner carries out an abortion in accordance with the provisions of the 1967 Act.

[10] Macdonald, p.87.

[11] See *McCluskey v. H.M. Advocate*, 1988 S.C.C.R. 629, where a child was caused injury whilst *in utero* as a result of the accused's reckless driving, was born alive, but then succumbed to that injury. (The case concerned the now repealed offence of causing death by reckless driving. For the modern offences of causing death by dangerous or, in some instances, careless driving, see the Road Traffic Act 1988, ss. 1, 2A and 3A, as added or amended by the Road Traffic Act 1991, ss. 1 and 3.) For the rule in English law, see *Att.-Gen.'s Reference (No. 3 of 1994)* [1998] A.C. 245, HL, Lord Mustill, at 254E to 255A, "established rule 5". In that case, it was held that injury to a woman (but not to the foetus she was carrying), which caused the foetus to be born so grossly prematurely that it died shortly after its birth, was capable of supporting a homicide charge against the person who had injured the mother. This was not, however, because injury to the mother was to be regarded also as injury to the foetus, on the argument that the foetus was as much part of the mother as one of her limbs: indeed, the House of Lords held that the relationship between mother and foetus is one of bond rather than identity, since the mother and foetus are genetically distinct. As Lord Mustill put the matter: "The mother and the foetus are two distinct organisms living symbiotically, not a single organism with two aspects."

[12] *Att.-Gen.'s Reference (No. 3 of 1994)* [1998] A.C. 245, HL, Lord Mustill at 264H: there the defendant stabbed a pregnant woman causing her, but not the foetus, significant injury. The foetus was subsequently born grossly prematurely due to the injuries and trauma suffered by the woman.

[13] Hume, i, 183; Alison, i, 71; Macdonald, pp. 87–88. There is, however, an exception in practice for the case of the doctor who prescribes pain-killing drugs in the knowledge that they will shorten life, provided they are given with the intention of easing pain and not as a measure of euthanasia. This exception has no legal basis but is an example of the law turning a blind eye for sympathetic reasons. It does not extend to acts intended to accelerate death.

[14] As does Anderson at p.145.

on fever and cause death, is not homicide."[15] But the cases to which he refers[16] are dealt with by Hume and Alison as cases in which it could not be proved that the accused's act had caused the death. Hume's own view was that "no distinction seems to be known to the law, with respect to the way in which the person is destroyed."[17] It is true that he excludes death caused by unkindness and ingratitude leading to a broken heart, but that is because of the difficulty of proof in such cases.[18]

There are two reported cases from the nineteenth and twentieth **23.05** centuries in which death from shock was treated as homicide. In *Wm Brown*[19] the deceased was an old woman whose bag was snatched by the accused and who died a fortnight later from "nervous shock acting upon a weak, diseased heart", and from the slight injuries she had received. In *Bird v. H.M. Advocate*[20] Lord Jamieson directed the jury that:

> "It is not necessary that the death should result from physical injuries. If the result of the treatment that the deceased person has received has been to cause shock and that person dies of shock, then the crime has been committed. If a person is assaulted, although to a slight degree, but is put in fear of serious bodily injury and dies as a result, then the crime has been committed".[21]

It is true that in these cases the shock was caused by a physical assault, but it is submitted that provided it was caused by the accused it does not matter how it was caused. In *Bird* itself Lord Jamieson pointed out to the jury that a gesture can constitute an assault,[22] and it is submitted that if such a gesture caused a fatal shock the *actus reus* of homicide would be present. In *Robertson and Donoghue*[23] Lord Justice-Clerk Cooper directed the jury that "it would not suffice for the purposes of a charge . . . of . . . homicide if the victim died merely of excitement; there must be a real injury",[24] but it is submitted that this is too broadly stated. If it can be shown that the fatal excitement was caused by the accused there is a homicide, although it may be very difficult to prove this, and even more difficult to go on to prove *mens rea* where *mens rea* is necessary. A thrombosis is just as much a real injury as a broken neck, a fatal attack of indigestion caused by poison, or the results of exposure to wind and weather, and it is indisputably homicide to cause death in any of these ways.[25]

---

[15] Macdonald, p.87.

[16] *Patrick Kinninmonth* (1697) Hume, i, 183; *Duff of Braco* (1707) Hume, i, 183–183; *cf.* Alison, i, 146.

[17] Hume, i, 189. See also *Boog* (1732) Burnett 7, in which a charge of causing death by ordering a constable to arrest a person known to be in bad health was held to be a relevant charge, although not murder, but then deserted.

[18] Hume, i, 189.

[19] (1879) 4 Couper 225.

[20] 1952 J.C. 23.

[21] At 25.

[22] *ibid.*

[23] High Court at Edinburgh, Aug. 1945, unrep'd. See C.H.W. Gane and C.N. Stoddart, *A Casebook on Scottish Criminal Law* (3rd ed., 2001), at paras 4.05 and 10.25.

[24] Transcript of L.J.-C. Cooper's charge, 18.

[25] Hume, i, 189–190; *cf.* also *John Robertson* (1854) 1 Irv. 469 where it was suggested that it might be homicide to terrify someone into committing suicide. In *Lourie v. H.M. Advocate*, 1988 S.C.C.R. 634, it was alleged that an elderly woman, who suffered from heart disease, had died of a heart attack brought on by the alarm and distress generated by the accused, who were alleged to have entered her house uninvited and there stolen a handbag in her presence; their convictions for culpable homicide were quashed, however, since there was no sufficient proof that the entry to the victim's house had been uninvited or that the deceased had witnessed the theft of the bag.

23.06 FRAUD. Cases of poisoning indicate that homicide can be committed by fraud: there is an implied false pretence every time A gives B cocoa laced with arsenic or a cake into which strychnine has been injected. In *John Ewing*[26] this pretence was made explicit, and the indictment read, "did . . . culpably and recklessly persuade or induce W.S. . . . to drink a quantity of a poisonous solution . . . by giving him a whisky bottle containing the said solution and pretending to him that the said bottle contained whisky or wine . . . and, the said W.S. having drunk . . . said solution in the belief that it was whisky or wine, . . . in consequence of which he died, you did kill the said W.S."

23.07 THIRD PARTY HOMICIDE. A may kill B by inciting an accomplice to carry out the fatal act, or by arranging things so that B dies at the hand of an innocent agent. Hume and Macdonald both regard it as homicide to cause death by giving false evidence at a capital trial,[27] and Macdonald also gives the example of an officer maliciously giving a soldier a false password so that a sentry kills him in the exercise of his duty.[28]

23.08 "CAUSE". The act of the accused must be shown to have caused the death of the victim.[29] Where death is caused by an omission it may be

---

[26] High Court at Glasgow, Dec. 1940, unrep'd.

[27] Hume, i, 190; Macdonald, pp. 92–93. Alison inclines to the contrary English view: i, 73.

[28] Macdonald, p.92.

[29] The following are examples of the way in which homicide may be committed: smothering someone by lying on his chest and covering his nose — *Wm Burke and Helen McDougal* (1828) Syme 345; a blow with the fist — *Peter Jafferson and Geo. Forbes* (1848) Ark. 464; *Shaw*, High Court at Edinburgh, Jan. 1959, unrep'd; setting a spring gun in which a marauder is caught and killed — *Jas Craw* (1826) Syme, 188; wrenching a gas meter from its supply pipes so as to cause an escape of gas which kills someone in the adjoining house — *Wm Finnigan*, High Court at Glasgow, March 1958, unrep'd; employing an unskilled person to carry out dangerous work such as dispensing medicine — *Robert Henderson and Wm Lawson* (1842) 1 Broun 360; working machinery — *Thos Hamilton and Henry Hutchison* (1874) 3 Couper 19; or organising the running of railway trains — *Wm Baillie and Jas McCurrach* (1870) 1 Couper 442; cutting a rope supporting the victim — *John McCallum and Wm Corner* (1853) 1 Irv. 259; or tilting a board in which he is standing — *John Campbell* (1836) 1 Swin. 309; exposing persons to inclement weather — *Catherine McGavin* (1846) Ark. 67; *Eliz. Kerr* (1860) 3 Irv. 645; *H.M. Advocate v. McPhee*, 1935 J.C. 46; failing to call for help at a birth — *Isabella Martin* (1877) 3 Couper 379; *H.M. Advocate v. Scott* (1892) 3 White 240; compelling someone to leave a ship and make his own way with insufficient food or clothes over an ice-pack — *cf. Robt Watt and Jas Kerr* (1868) 1 Couper 123; forcing persons to leave a trawler and enter a boat and then towing the boat in bad weather so that the boat is swamped and the occupants drowned — *Fredk Geo. Thomsett*, High Court at Edinburgh, Feb. 1939, unrep'd; pursuing a woman escaping from an attempted rape and chasing her over a cliff — *Patrick Slaven and Ors* (1885) 5 Couper 694; *John Robertson* (1854) 1 Irv. 469 in which it was suggested that it might be culpable homicide to terrify someone into committing suicide; pulling a woman's handbag and so causing her to fall — *Wm Brown* (1879) 4 Couper 225; assaulting a woman so as to cause her to squeeze and kill the child in her arms — *Hugh Mitchell* (1856) 2 Irv. 488; setting off a firework which frightens a horse which runs away knocking down and killing someone in its flight, or even leaving a horse unattended as a result of which it panics at the sound of a firework set off by someone else — *Geo. Wood Jnr and Alex. King* (1842) 1 Broun 262; causing a heart attack by threatening gestures — *Bird v. H.M. Advocate*, 1952 J.C. 23, Lord Jamieson at 25; folding up a bed with a child in it — *Williamina Sutherland* (1856) 2 Irv. 455; locking a person in a dirty closet without clothing — *Geo. Fay* (1847) Ark. 397; or in a cell with a lunatic or dangerous criminal — Hume, i, 190; failure by a poor law inspector to attend to an application for relief — *Wm Hardie* (1847) Ark. 247; the granting of a false certificate by a doctor whereby a prisoner is subjected to treatment which his health makes dangerous for him — *David Gibson* (1848) Ark. 489; luring a ship

necessary to show that but for the omission the victim would have lived,[30] but in the ordinary case of an act it is enough to show that it was a relevant cause of death whether or not the victim would have died anyway.[31] It is irrelevant that the victim would have survived had he received better medical attention than he did, unless the circumstances are such as to substitute something in the later medical history as the relevant cause of death.[32]

It does not matter how long the victim survives the accused's act or omission, although the longer he does survive the more difficult it will be to show that the death was caused by the accused, particularly if the victim apparently recovered from the accused's act and then sustained a fresh injury.[33]

Classes of homicide

Homicide is divided into criminal and non-criminal homicide. Non-criminal homicide is either casual or justifiable. Casual homicide is homicide by accident or mischance[34] and is said to be restricted to cases in which the accused was lawfully employed and not culpably careless[35]: it is important only in relation to involuntary culpable homicide.[36] Criminal homicide is divided into murder and culpable homicide. Culpable homicide can itself be divided into two crimes: (a) involuntary culpable homicide, which may be distinguished from murder by reference to *mens rea*, involuntary culpable homicide being, roughly speaking, homicide which is neither intentional nor grossly reckless, and (b) voluntary culpable homicide which is probably best described by saying that voluntary culpable homicide is intentional or reckless killing which lacks the wickedness required for murder.[36a] **23.09**

---

to destruction by setting false navigation lights — Macdonald, p.92; injecting a person with poison — Macdonald, p.91; turning on coal gas so that it is inhaled by the victim — *Wm Park and Anr*, High Court at Glasgow, Dec., 1948, R.C. App. 4, para. 38, unrep'd; walking into the path of a car so as to cause the driver to take action to avoid a collision, and then hitting the car, shouting, swearing, opening the driver's door, struggling with him, trying to let one of the tyres down, and placing the driver who had a weak heart in such a state of fear, alarm and exhaustion that he died there and then — *John Mason Taylor*, Criminal Appeal Court, June 1975, unrep'd; pushing someone who falls against another person who falls and sustains an injury from which she dies — *R. v. Mitchell* [1983] Q.B. 741; injecting a dangerous drug into the body of another person at his request where that person subsequently dies in consequence — *Finlayson v. H.M. Advocate*, 1979 J.C. 33; supplying, but not administering, a dangerous drug to another at her request where the person supplied administers the drug to herself and dies in consequence: *Lord Advocate's Reference (No. 1 of 1994)*, 1995 S.C.C.R. 177. There is also a form of manslaughter known as "manslaughter by flight" which occurs when the victim dies as a result of, *e.g.*, tripping while running away from an attack from which he fears imminent injury, the fear being caused by the conduct of the accused: *D.P.P. v. Daley* [1980] A.C. 237.

[30] *Isabella Martin* (1877) 3 Couper 379, L.J.-C. Moncreiff at 381.

[31] Hume, i, 183; Alison, i, 71–72; Macdonald, pp. 87–88; see Vol. I, para. 4.22. Cf. *Robertson and Donoghue*, para. 23.05, supra: "It is nonetheless homicide to accelerate or precipitate the death of an ailing person than it is to cut down a healthy man who might have lived for fifty years": Transcript of Judge's charge, 20.

[32] On causality, see Vol. I, paras 4.45 *et seq.*

[33] Hume, i, 181; *Patrick Kinninmonth* (1697) Hume, i, 181; Alison, i, 150; Macdonald, p.88; *Daniel Houston* (1833) Bell's Notes 70; cf. *Tees v. H.M. Advocate*, 1994 S.C.C.R. 451.

[34] Hume, i, 194–5; Alison, i, 139–144.

[35] Alison, i, 139; *H.M. Advocate v. Rutherford*, 1947 J.C. 1, L.J.-C. Cooper at 5.

[36] See *infra*, para. 26.19.

[36a] cf. *Drury v. H.M. Advocate*, 2001 S.L.T. 1013.

MURDER

Voluntary murder

23.10   Voluntary murder is murder committed with a wicked intention to kill.[37] It is not restricted to premeditated killing,[38] although premeditation may help to convince a jury that the intention was indeed wicked. In *Chas McDonald*[39] the jury returned a verdict of guilty of murder together with a recommendation to mercy on the ground of want of premeditation. There seems to have been some doubt as to whether this was a proper verdict of murder and the jury were sent back by Lord Justice-Clerk Patton to consider whether it was their view "that the panel did not premeditate the offence at all, . . . or . . . that he was not guilty of malice aforethought, in the sense of having settled and arranged beforehand to commit the murder." They were told that if they found there had been no premeditation at all they should convict of culpable homicide. It is not clear what Lord Patton meant by "premeditation", but it appears to have been no more than "intention", and probably something less, since the jury had been directed that recklessness was a sufficient *mens rea* for murder. The jury eventually brought in a recommendation to mercy on the ground of absence of malice aforethought. The defence argued that that was inconsistent with the verdict of murder and quoted a passage in Hume which stated that "The peculiar character of this sort of homicide is, that it is done wilfully, and out of malice aforethought".[40] This argument was rejected, and Lord Patton said that it was not necessary to prove premeditation in a murder charge.[41] Despite the confusion in terminology, *McDonald* is not authority for the requirement of premeditation in murder, and indeed is, if anything, authority for the accepted view that such premeditation is unnecessary.

23.11   The accused's intention may be inferred from his actings without recourse to any expression of intention by him. A jury would, for instance, be well entitled to hold that if A shot B in a vital organ, or stuck a bayonet in his stomach, or throttled him to death, he intended to kill. The alleged maxim that a person is presumed to intend the natural results of his actions does not, however, apply in murder — if it did every homicide in which death was a natural, or at any rate a foreseeable, result of A's act would be voluntary murder (unless the jury

---

[37] See *Drury v. H.M. Advocate*, 2001 S.L.T. 1013 (five judges), in which L.J.-G. Rodger, under reference to Hume, i, 254, held that Macdonald's familiar definition of murder — "Murder is constituted by any wilful act causing the destruction of life, whether intended to kill, or displaying such wicked recklessness as to imply a disposition depraved enough to be regardless of consequences" (Macdonald, p.89) — was generally incomplete and misleading in that: "In truth, just as the recklessness has to be wicked, so also must the intention be wicked." (see his Lordship's opinion at para. [11]; see also para. [10]). See also the supporting opinions of Lords Johnston, Nimmo-Smith and Mackay of Drumadoon of their respective opinions at paras [18], [2]-[3], and [8]. Lord Cameron of Lochbroom refers in a slightly different way to "wickedness of heart" as being an essential element in voluntary murder: see his opinion at para. [6].
[38] Hume, i, 254; Macdonald, p.89; Burnett, p.4.
[39] (1867) 5 Irv. 525.
[40] Hume, i, 254.
[41] 5 Irv. at 529.

were unable to find the necessary wickedness), which is clearly not the case. An intention to kill will be inferred only where the facts are such that the only reasonable explanation of A's behaviour is that he intended to kill, either in the sense of desiring to do so, or in the sense that he must have known that death was a necessary consequence of his conduct.[42]

Mens rea in voluntary murder. Until the recent decision of *Drury v. H.M.* **23.12**
Advocate,[43] the standard way of describing murder in Scots law invariably followed the "classic" definition given by Macdonald.[44] As far as voluntary murder was concerned, the required *mens rea* was established on satisfactory proof of an intention to kill. In *Drury*, however, Lord Justice-General Rodger expressed dissatisfaction with that standard description since it was plainly possible for there to have been an intention to kill without any ensuing guilt of murder, as, for example, where the accused had been acting in self-defence (which is a justification for the accused's intentional conduct), or under provocation or with diminished responsibility (both of which being excuses resulting in convictions for culpable homicide).[45] The appeal in *Drury* was actually concerned with whether proportionality was required as a matter of law in a particular (and exceptional) form of provocation; but what was said concerning murder there cannot be dismissed as an *obiter dictum*, since it was declared that the substance of the appeal could not be answered without consideration (indeed, reconsideration[46]) of criminal homicide as a whole.[47] In particular it was declared that the *mens rea* for voluntary murder (although that term was not used by the Court) was not merely an intention to kill, but rather a wicked intent to do so; this, it was said, had been the approach of Hume and Alison,[48] and was in any event preferable on principle since it enabled provocation and diminished responsibility, where in particular there was intention to kill, to be reconciled with the general law of criminal homicide. It was not so much that such factors as provocation and diminished responsibility "reduced" intentional murder to culpable homicide, but rather that those factors were to be weighed by a jury in deciding whether the accused's intent to

---

[42] See Vol. I, para. 7.18.

[43] 2001 S.L.T. 1013 (five judges).

[44] At p.89; see n.37, *supra*. This was usually the way in which juries were charged in murder cases: see *e.g.*, *H.M. Advocate v. Pearson* (1967) S.C.C.R. (Supp.) 20, Lord Cameron at 21; *Brown v. H.M. Advocate*, 1993 S.C.C.R. 382, where, at 389E, L.J.-G. Hope opined that the trial judge had given the jury a correct statement of the law by reading to them Macdonald's definition of murder; and *Scott v. H.M. Advocate*, 1995 S.C.C.R. 760, where the trial judge's quotation to the jury of the same definition (see 761B) was described by L.J.-C. Ross (at 674E) as entirely accurate and appropriate since it was the "classic" account of the crime. See also the Report of the Select Committee of the House of Lords on Murder and Life Imprisonment, Paper 78 (Session 1988–89), Vol. I, p.16, para. 38; Vol. III, p. 466, "Memorandum by the Lord Justice-General and Lord Justice Clerk" (which was representative of the views of the High Court of Justiciary as a whole).

[45] For self-defence, see Chap. 24, *infra*; for provocation, see Chap. 25, *infra*; and for diminished responsibility, see *Galbraith v. H.M. Advocate, (No. 2),* 2001 S.L.T. 953 (five judges): *cf.* Vol. I, Chap. 11.

[46] See the opinion of Lord Mackay of Drumadoon, at para. [2], where he states that the Court has a duty to reassess, and if necessary reformulate, the way in which the general principles of the criminal law are expressed.

[47] See the opinion of L.J.-G. Rodger at para. [8].

[48] See Hume, i, 254; Alison, i, 1–2.

kill had been wicked or not.[49] In short, if to the satisfaction of the jury, provocation or diminished responsibility[50] is established according to the legal requirements, it must follow that the wickedness of the intent cannot be shown and murder will not be a legitimate verdict.

23.13   It may readily be accepted that murder cannot be committed in the absence of wickedness, and it was probably always implicit that this was so in relation to an intent to kill. Hume indeed says as much: "The malice is implied *prima facie* in the act itself of intentional killing, which is the highest possible injury; and it lies therefore with the pannel to overcome this presumption by evidence on his part, of some of those circumstances of necessity, or excusable infirmity, which may serve him for a defence."[51] The opinions in *Drury*[52] may be read, however, as suggesting that such wickedness as is required is not to be presumed even rebuttably from a proved or admitted intention to kill, but rather is to be considered independently in each case by the jury according to the whole of the relevant evidence and the jury's moral judgment of the accused's intentional conduct in the circumstances of the case.[53] If the latter is correct, then the prosecutor's task at a murder trial will have been significantly increased by virtue of his having to address the issue of wickedness,[54] whilst the accused will have an enhanced opportunity for acquittal of murder since his ability to convince the jury that his intention had not been wicked would now appear to be at large.[55] It can hardly, however, have been the Court's intention in *Drury* to create a situation in which, for example, whether a man who sacrifices his child from religious motives is guilty of murder or not is to be determined upon a jury's unlimited view of his wickedness in the specific circumstances of his case.

Although the state of a man's mind may be as much a matter of fact as the state of his digestion,[56] the law has always claimed the right to decide what may or may not be relevant to that determination: thus, for example, self-induced intoxication may not, it seems, be pled in answer to a murder charge,[57] and there is no suggestion in *Drury* that any relaxation of that rule is contemplated. The law also sets limits to those factors which are considered relevant to the determination of *mens rea*, and *Drury* accepts, for example, that there are rules as to the availability of provocation. The Lord Justice-General also accepts of course in *Drury* that a jury's determination of factual issues (which, *ex hypothesi*, include

---

[49] See L.J.-G. Rodger's opinion at paras [8], [11], [17], [18] and [34]; Lord Johnston's opinion at para. [18] (*cf.* para. [17]); Lord Nimmo Smith's opinion at paras [2]-[3], and [7]; and Lord Mackay of Drumadoon's opinion at paras [8] and [14]. *Cf.* Lord Cameron of Lochbroom's opinion at paras [6] and [10].

[50] The precise way in which diminished responsibility operates to merit a conviction for culpable homicide was not explored by the Court, since the appeal was concerned with provocation: but see now *Galbraith v. H.M. Advocate (No. 2)*, 2001 S.L.T. 953 (five judges).

[51] Hume, i, 254.

[52] *Drury v. H.M. Advocate*, 2001 S.L.T. 1013 (five judges).

[53] See, *e.g.*, L.J.-G. Rodger's opinion, paras [17] and [34].

[54] *cf.* the opinion of L.J.-G. Rodger at para. [18].

[55] If this is so, then, *e.g.*, it can scarcely continue to be argued convincingly that coercion or necessity cannot be pled in answer to a voluntary murder charge, since such factors might plausibly be said to have an obvious bearing on whether the accused's intentions have the necessary wickedness for conviction.

[56] See the opinion of L.J.-G. Rodger at para. [21], quoting Bowen L.J. in *Edgington v. Fitzmaurice* (1885) 29 Ch.D. 459, at 483.

[57] *Brennan v. H.M. Advocate*, 1977 J.C. 38.

the accused's state of mind) depends on the drawing of inferences from the evidence.[58] With respect to these various points, as also the very great difficulty of deciding what wickedness means, in general or in specific circumstances,[59] it is submitted that a jury should be advised that, in voluntary murder, the *mens rea* of which they require to be satisfied is indeed a wicked intent to kill the deceased, but that if they are satisfied that intention to kill is proven or admitted on the part of the accused they may (but not must) infer that such intention is wicked in the absence of any legally relevant factor (such as provocation) which would cast doubt on the correctness or fairness of that inference. This would perhaps preserve the common sense view that most accused who intentionally kill deserve to be treated as murderers (which is ultimately what a requirement of "wickedness" must mean[60]) — at least in the absence of any legally relevant factor which would suggest otherwise[61] — whilst emphasising that murder, whether voluntary or involuntary, is a crime characterised by wickedness.[62]

Involuntary murder

It is undisputed that murder can be committed unintentionally, that is **23.14** to say, without any intention to kill the deceased,[63] but the principles of the law of involuntary murder and the way in which they have been applied, are very difficult to state clearly. They are not easily susceptible of logical analysis, and very few if any of the judicial dicta on the matter

---

[58] See, *e.g.*, his opinion at para. [15], in relation to recklessness, and para. [18], in relation to the *mens rea* of voluntary and involuntary murder: *cf.* para [32] where he states: "Where . . . the accused has reacted to provocation in a way in which no ordinary man or woman would have been liable to react, a jury can rightly conclude that he acted with that wickedness which justifies a conviction for murder." This statement is somewhat at odds, it has to be conceded with the Lord Justice-General's views at para. [34], where it is said: "If [the jury] concludes that the accused's reaction was more extreme than was to be expected of the ordinary man, then . . . the plea of provocation will fail and the jury will have to consider, on the basis of all the rest of the evidence, whether the appropriate verdict is one of murder or culpable homicide.

[59] See, *e.g.*, the opinion of Lord Mackay of Drumadoon at para. [10], where he indicates that in a murder charge involving an assault, it would be confusing for the jury to be told that the *mens rea* for assault involved an "evil intent". As his Lordship states: "Murder requires a wickedness, over and above the evil intent that may suffice for an assault or culpable homicide. Therein lies a possible difficulty. Depending upon the circumstances of a particular case, explaining to a jury the difference between 'wickedness' and 'evil intent' may not be straightforward." (The Lord Justice-General refers to this statement with seeming approval in his own opinion: at para. [10].)

[60] *cf.* para. 23.21, *infra*.

[61] *cf. Gray v. H.M. Advocate*, 1994 S.C.C.R. 225, L.J.-C. Ross's approach to the *mens rea* of murder and the effect of provocation at 235F.

[62] *cf. Boyle v. H.M. Advocate*, 1992 S.C.C.R. 824, where at 830B-C, L.J.-C. Ross refers to "murderous" rather than "wicked" intent; *cf.* Lord MacLean's interpretation of "murderous intention" in *Salmond v. H.M. Advocate*, 1991 S.C.C.R. 43, at 43F.

[63] Macdonald, pp. 89, 91; Hume, i, 256 *et seq.*; Alison, i, 1 *et seq.* The case of *Mary Horn alias Muckstraffick* (1824) Hume, i, 259, is special in that the Crown specifically libelled an intent to murder which was negatived by the jury whose verdict was accordingly construed as one of culpable homicide. In *Eliz. Kerr* (1860) 3 Irv. 645, a charge of murder by exposure of a child, the Crown accepted a plea to culpable homicide, and L.J.-C. Inglis' observation in passing sentence that he was bound to proceed on the basis that what he called recklessness amounting to such a desire or wilful intention to get rid of the child as to involve murder was absent and that the accused had only been "reckless and unthinking", should be treated as an attempt to rationalise the Crown's humanitarian acceptance of the plea and not as a statement of the distinction between murder and culpable homicide.

are the result of such an analysis.[64] The principles are vague and flexible, or perhaps one should say commonsense and non-technical, and their application has tended to be very much an *ad hoc* matter. Any attempt to rationalise them or subject them to analysis runs the risk of distorting them or of presenting a general attitude as if it were a system of legal rules, but it must be made in order to discover what the law is.

23.15 *Causation in involuntary murder.* Before A can be convicted of murdering B it must be shown that A's act caused B's death, and in this context an act *c* causes an event *e* if and only if *e* is a foreseeable result of *c*, or, as it is sometimes put, if *e* is within the range of "natural and probable consequences" of *c*.[65] Where *e* is a direct result of *c* it will be regarded as a foreseeable consequence of *c* unless the accused can show that it was caused "in some strange and unexpected way",[66] or by a minor injury "from which, according to the ordinary course of things, there was no reason to apprehend any material danger of the person's life."[67] To put it shortly, the accused can escape responsibility for murder only if he can show that death was "a sort of mischance".[68] Examples of mischance are where A jostles B or strikes him with his hand,[69] throws a snowball at him,[70] snatches at his watch so that B falls and breaks his skull,[71] or pushes B down intending only to dirty his clothes and B unexpectedly falls into a pool and drowns.[72]

In *Robertson and Donoghue*[73] Lord Justice-Clerk Cooper referred to the situation where "death was due to, say, natural causes, or to some subsequent accident or maltreatment or neglect, which broke the chain of causation between the so-called crime and the death" as one where death would be "an act of God or a mischance" and not attributable to the accused at all.[74] This is a different use of "mischance" from that in the cases cited in the preceding paragraph. "Mischance" was applied in those cases to the type of homicide which is only culpable homicide even when committed in the course of a robbery; it was applied in *Robertson and Donoghue*, also a robbery case, to the situation where there is no criminal homicide at all. There are three possible situations: (a) where death is a foreseeable result of A's act, in which case the crime may be murder or culpable homicide, depending on A's *mens rea*; (b) where death is a direct but unforeseeable result of A's act, in which case the

---

[64] For an attempt to construct a logical definition of the *mens rea* of murder, see Morris and Howard, *Studies in Criminal Law* (Oxford, 1964), Chap. 2. For discussion of the general English position, see (Lord) R. Goff, "The Mental Element in the Crime of Murder" (1988) 104 L.Q.R. 30; and Gl. Williams, "The Mens Rea for Murder: Leave it Alone" (1989) 105 L.Q.R. 387.

[65] For example, *Miller and Denovan*, High Court at Glasgow, Nov. 1960, unrep'd: Transcript of Lord Wheatley's charge, 30.

[66] Hume, i, 256.

[67] *ibid.* 258.

[68] *H.M. Advocate v. Fraser and Rollins*, 1920 J.C. 60, Lord Sands at 63; *Miller and Denovan*, High Court of Justiciary on Appeal, Dec. 1960, Opn. of L.J.-G. Clyde, 6: Lord Clyde's opinion appears as an appendix to *Parr v. H.M. Advocate*, 1991 S.L.T. 208, at 211–213, and is also set out in C.H.W. Gane and C.N. Stoddart, *A Casebook on Scottish Criminal Law* (3rd ed., 2001) at para. 10.38.

[69] Hume, i, 256.

[70] *Fraser and Rollins, supra*, Lord Sands at 63.

[71] *ibid.*; *cf. Wm Brown* (1879) 4 Couper 225.

[72] *John McCallum and Wm Corner* (1853) 1 Irv. 259. L.J.-G. McNeill at 270.

[73] High Court at Edinburgh, Aug. 1945, unrep'd.

[74] Transcript of L.J.-C. Cooper's charge, 16–17; see C.H.W. Gane and C.N. Stoddart, *A Casebook on Scottish Criminal Law* (3rd ed., 2001), at para. 4.05.

crime can never be more than culpable homicide; and (c) where death is not a direct result of A's act, as where A inflicts minor injury on B who is killed in an accident on his way to hospital in an ambulance, in which case neither murder nor culpable homicide is committed, because the causal link is absent.

Mens rea in involuntary murder. It is almost trite law that negligence is **23.16** not in itself a sufficient *mens rea* for murder. It is often said that murder requires either intent or recklessness, but recklessness itself in the sense of gross negligence or in the sense of actual foresight and acceptance of the risk of death is not a satisfactory criterion in the Scots law of murder. Recklessness is neither a necessary nor a sufficient *mens rea* for murder. If A kills B in the course of robbery he may be convicted of murder although his *mens rea* regarding the death was only one of negligence.[75] If A kills B "with such gross and wicked recklessness that his conduct ought properly to be regarded as criminal conduct,"[76] he will not be guilty of murder unless he caused death while committing another crime, or by an assault.[77]

INTENT TO HARM. Now that it is accepted that a drunken motorist who **23.17** drives his car at 70 miles an hour in a built-up area and kills a pedestrian on a pedestrian crossing or on the pavement is guilty (at common law) only of culpable homicide, it is submitted that the law can be accepted as being that murder cannot be committed unless the accused intended to cause some personal injury.[78] In *Patrick McCarron*[79] Lord Wheatley directed the jury that if the accused fired at his victim "not intending to kill or injure her but merely to frighten her, but acted with such gross and wicked negligence that he in fact killed her, [that] would be not murder but culpable homicide."[80] Hume's view that it is murder to shoot "at random among a multitude", or let a mad dog loose in the street[81] would not, it is thought, be followed today, unless there was at least an intention to injure someone, although not necessarily the deceased.[82]

Assault. The most common criminal intent involved in involuntary **23.18** murder is the intent to commit an assault, and assault cases are the most difficult to analyse. There are passages in Hume which suggest that an intention to commit any assault of which death is a foreseeable result is sufficient for murder,[83] but the examples he gives conjure up a picture of someone transported by rage, beating his victim repeatedly and violently,

---

[75] See *infra*, paras 23.26 *et seq.*

[76] *H.M. Advocate v. Sheppard*, 1941 J.C. 67, 69.

[77] *infra*. Unlike Australian law — *Hughes v. The King* (1951) 84 C.L.R. 170 — Scots law regards death caused by assault as a death caused in the course of another crime, and treats the assault as constituting both the unlawful context of the death and the reckless act causing death.

[78] *cf. R. v. Hyam* [1975] A.C. 55, Viscount Hailsham L.C. at 77–78.

[79] High Court at Perth, Feb. 1964, approved High Court of Justiciary on Appeal, Mar. 1964, unrep'd.

[80] Transcript of Judge's charge at 29.

[81] Hume, i, 23.

[82] In *Jos. Rae* (1817) Hume, i, 258, a chimney sweep whose apprentice had become stuck in a vent and who fastened ropes to his legs and pulled at them until he died was charged with murder, but the jury convicted of culpable homicide against the advice of the judge. A case of this kind would not today be charged as murder.

[83] Hume, i, 256, 258.

so carried away that he does not heed the injury he is causing, or else of someone engaging in "brinkmanship" and beating the victim to within an inch of his life.[84] They suggest that Hume would have accepted Lord Jamieson's description of the murderer as one who administers blows "with complete callousness and with an utter and reckless disregard of the consequences, and in a spirit of hatred".[85] It was in cases of that kind that Hume held that there had been murder, because "[i]n those great injuries and violences there is no wounding by rule, so as with certainty not to kill," and because there is displayed in them a "*corrupt disregard* of the person and life of another, [which] is precisely the dole or malice, the depraved and wicked purpose, which the law requires and is content with."[86]

Alison expresses the same ideas by saying that, "Murder . . . consists in the act which produces death, in consequence either of a deliberate intention to kill, or to inflict a minor injury of such a kind as indicates an utter recklessness as to the life of the sufferer, whether he live or die."[87] "Minor injury" must be read as "non-fatal", and not as synonymous with the "slight violence" which Hume talks of when referring to violence which is not foreseeably fatal.

Lord Cooper was asked by the Royal Commission on Capital Punishment if the scope of murder included cases where "violence is inflicted under circumstances which a reasonable man might infer would result in death."[88] He replied:

> "That is becoming a narrow point . . . That is the sort of point you leave to the jury, whether the circumstances on the evidence as a whole carry to your mind the conviction beyond reasonable doubt that the man, if he did not intend to kill, did not care whether he killed or not. That is not so much a legal question as a question for the jury, and dependent upon a narrow examination of the circumstances . . . If a man fires a revolver at another man's head and hits him, the law will infer that he intends to kill or does not care whether he kills or not.
>
> But I can figure types of assault in regard to which the law would make no assumption, and it would leave it to a jury to make a decision what the inference was."[89]

---

[84] For example, *Griffith Williams* (1800) Hume, i, 257: beating at intervals throughout the day, and declaring a resolution "to beat her so as just to leave life in her"; *John Cowie or Cowan* (1803) *ibid*.: beating with a stick and trampling to death, declaring that he would beat her, "though he should hang . . . for it"; *Maccraw* (1806) *ibid*. 260, Burnett, p.4: tearing the private parts of a ten-year-old girl; *Jas Anderson and Ors* (1823) Hume, i, 255; knocking to the ground and continuing to assault, punch on the head, and kick on the belly. Compare *Colin Telfer* (1815) Hume, i, 257, a single blow with a leg of beef, where the Crown sought only a verdict of culpable homicide, although the court thought it murder because of the "degree of malignity" exhibited by the blow.

[85] *H.M. Advocate v. Kizileviczius*, 1938 J.C. 60, Lord Jamieson at 63, cited with approval by L.J.-C. Cooper in *Robertson and Donoghue, supra*, p.27 of charge. See also Anderson, pp. 148–149 where he talks of "malicious purpose" and "abandoned depravity", and *H.M. Advocate v. Marshall* (1896) 4 S.L.T. 217.

[86] Hume, i, 257–258.

[87] Alison, i, 1.

[88] Q. 5456.

[89] Q. 5457–5458.

WICKED RECKLESSNESS. The intention to commit an assault is, there- **23.19** fore, not in itself sufficient *mens rea* for murder: it is necessary to go further and find some additional quality in the accused's intent. This additional quality is called "wicked recklessness", or "depravity", or "wicked disregard of consequences". The accepted modern statement of the law is contained in the following passages from Macdonald:

"Murder is constituted by any wilful act causing the destruction of life, whether [wickedly] intended to kill, or displaying such wicked recklessness as to imply a disposition depraved enough to be regardless of consequences . . .[90]

When death results from the perpetration of any serious and dangerous crime, murder may have been committed, although the specific intent to kill be absent.

This is so where the crime perpetrated involves either wilful intent to do grave personal injury, or the wilful use of dangerous means implying wicked disregard of consequences to life."[91]

Murder is the most heinous of all crimes, and cannot be present in the absence of wickedness and depravity. It has been submitted above that generally the necessary wickedness may be inferred where the killing was intentional.[92] Where the killing was unintentional but caused by an assault, wickedness and depravity must be found in the nature of the assault, which must exhibit "wicked recklessness". Recklessness is therefore not so much a question of gross negligence as of wickedness. Wicked recklessness is recklessness so gross that it indicates a state of mind which falls to be treated as being as wicked and depraved as the state of mind of a deliberate killer.[93]

The matter is confused by a loose use of "intent" which is satisfied by **23.20** recklessness.

When Lord Cooper spoke in *H.M. Advocate v. Rutherford*[94] of the choice between murder and culpable homicide depending entirely on the quality of intent, and stressed that he meant "intent" and not "motive", he did not mean only intent to kill, but "intent to kill, or at least with reckless indifference."[95] Nor is it the case that recklessness is merely evidence of intention, albeit Lord Cooper said in the same passage that "intent must always be a matter of inference — inference mainly from what the person does, but partly also from the whole surrounding circumstances of the case." The confusion of "intent", "intention" and "recklessness", and the tendency to talk of reckless conduct as evidence

---

[90] Macdonald, p.89, as modified (see word in square brackets) by *Drury v. H.M. Advocate*, 2001 S.L.T. 1013: see paras 23.12 and 23.13, *supra*. For a discussion of recklessness, see Vol. I, paras 7.45–7.68.

[91] Macdonald, p.91.

[92] See para. 23.13, *supra*.

[93] (This sentence, carried forward from the 2nd ed. of this work, is given out here in the form considered acceptable by L.J.-C. Ross in *Scott v. H.M. Advocate*, 1995 S.C.C.R. 760.) To the philosopher it may be that no state of mind which does not include an intention to kill can be equated with one which does include such an intention. But the law is concerned rather with an equivalence in the emotional attitude, the indignation, of the average man, judge or juryman, who regards the wickedly reckless man in the same way as he regards the intentional killer.

[94] 1947 J.C. 1, 6.

[95] *ibid*.

of "intent", can be seen in *Cawthorne v. H.M. Advocate.*[96] Lord Guthrie,
for example, rejected the defence argument that a jury could not infer
"intent to murder" from "utter and wicked recklessness, as to the
consequences"[97]; but "intent to murder" is not necessarily the same as
"intention to kill". And the court approved the trial judge's direction
that it is murder "if a man dies as a result of another acting with utter
and wicked recklessness . . . because . . . the very nature of the attack,
the utter and wickedly reckless attack displays a criminal intention."
Lord Guthrie does seem to favour the view that the only *mens rea* is
intention and that recklessness is only relevant as evidence. But the value
of his Lordship's view is difficult to assess as he talked of "the
fundamental rule of our criminal law that dole may be presumed from
the perpetration of the wicked act."[98] Lord Cameron said that "the
necessary criminal intent" could be established by proof of deliberate
intention to cause death or by inference from the nature and quality of
the acts themselves as displaying wicked recklessness. "Such reckless
conduct, intentionally perpetrated, is in law the equivalent of a deliberate intent to kill and adequate legal proof of the requisite mens rea."[99]
This appears to indicate that the "intention" required is satisfied by
proof that the acts done were not done accidentally or by mistake, but
that it is not necessary to show that they were done with intent to kill, or
even to do serious harm.[1] It was submitted in the second edition of this
work that the law was correctly, and more clearly, stated in Lord Justice-
General Clyde's opinion where he said: "The mens rea which is essential
to the establishment of [murder] may be established by satisfactory
evidence of a deliberate intention to kill or by evidence of such wicked
recklessness as to imply a disposition depraved enough to be regardless
of consequences",[2] and generally the more modern decisions support
this.[3]

---

[96] 1968 J.C. 32; see G.H. Gordon, "*Cawthorne* and the Mens Rea of Murder", 1969
S.L.T. (News) 41. The case itself concerned the *mens rea* of attempted murder, but this was
held to be the same as that of murder, see Vol. I, para. 7.81.

[97] At 37.

[98] At 38.

[99] At 38.

[1] *cf.* the interpretation of the statutory offence of wilful child neglect in *Clark v. H.M.
Advocate*, 1968 J.C. 53; Vol. I, para. 7.34. In *Scott v. H.M. Advocate*, 1995 S.C.C.R. 760,
L.J.-C. Ross, giving the opinion of the court, said of the passage from Lord Cameron's
opinion in *Cawthorne* quoted above: "Lord Cameron was . . . doing no more than holding
that wickedly reckless conduct was in law the equivalent of a deliberate intent to kill, and
. . . was not holding that such wickedly reckless conduct was in fact the equivalent of a
deliberate intent to kill. He was not saying that there was only one level of wickedness in
all cases of murder." This was said in the context of a submission (in part founded on what
was stated in the last sentence in para. 23–17 of the 2nd ed. of this work) that the
wickedness for wicked recklessness in murder had to be the same as the wickedness of a
deliberate killer. The court in *Scott* held that it was not normally appropriate to direct
juries on the level of wickedness appropriate for "either branch of the classic definition of
murder" as given out in Macdonald at p.89, and that it would serve only to confuse if juries
were to be directed that "they were required to consider such philosophical questions as to
whether the same level or wickedness must be attained according to whether a particular
case falls under the first or second branch of the definition of murder." (L.J.-C. Ross, at
765C.) The recent case of *Drury v. H.M. Advocate*, 2001 S.L.T. 1013, holds that wickedness
is an essential element in both "branches" of the definition of murder, and suggests, but
does not decide, that wickedness should mean the same in each "branch". *Scott* is not
referred to in *Drury*, however, and the issue must be regarded as moot.

[2] At 35.

[3] See, *e.g.*, *Scott v. H.M. Advocate*, 1995 S.C.C.R. 760; *Drury v. H.M. Advocate*, 2001
S.L.T. 1013.

There are therefore two[4] distinct forms of the *mens rea* of murder: **23.21**
wicked intent to kill and wicked recklessness.[5] To say that, "A is guilty of
murder when he kills with wicked recklessness" means only "A is guilty
of murder when he kills with such recklessness that he deserves to be
treated as a murderer." The main claim to acceptance which this circular
formula has is that it recognises that when it comes to a choice between
murder and culpable homicide the result does not depend on mathe-
matical assessments of probability measured against the standard of
reasonable foreseeability, but depends on a moral judgment which, so far
as capital murder was concerned, and the law grew up when all murders
were capital, could be summed up in the question: "Does A deservc
hanging?" It may be quite fitting that a murder conviction should in the
end of the day depend on this kind of moral consideration rather than
on the application of a legal definition of *mens rea*. It makes for great
flexibility and makes it possible for both the court and the Crown to
substitute culpable homicide for murder in cases where the strict letter
of the law would not allow this were murder to be defined without
reference to wickedness. On the other hand, it makes the law vague and
impossible to state in general terms. One cannot say that a certain
degree of carelessness in a fatal assault always makes it murder, one
must look to all the circumstances of each particular case and ask
whether they display such wickedness as to make a conviction for murder
appropriate. The absence of an academically satisfactory definition of
murder is, however, perhaps but a small price to pay for the practical
advantages of flexibility.

The present situation does, of course, mean that it is still the law that
murder is not restricted either to intentional killing or to cases where
there is an actual acceptance of the risk of death.[6] But as this seems to
be unavoidable at present,[7] the flexible "moral" approach has much to
commend it. There is always a danger, of course, that the courts may
take the decision between murder and culpable homicide away from the
jury and so substitute the moral attitude of a particular judge for that of
15 ordinary persons.[8] It has been argued that what is in issue is objective
recklessness as evidence of subjective intention and not as a criterion in
itself[9] but that is not how it is usually put to juries.[10]

It may be thought that the existence of wicked recklessness is
essentially a jury question and there is some support for this in the old
Scots idea that murder required a certain "malice" (or "wickedness"[11])
which might be negatived by a verdict of culpable homicide (an idea
which made the doctrine of diminished responsibility possible) as well as
in Lord Cooper's evidence to the Royal Commission.[12] There is also

---

[4] Or perhaps three: *infra*, para. 23.22.

[5] *cf. R. v. Hyam* [1975] A.C. 55, Viscount Hailsham L.C. at 77–78, though the meaning
of recklessness is different in England: Vol. I, para. 7.45.

[6] Nor is it so restricted in England: see, *e.g.*, the remarks of Lord Mustill in *Att.-Gen.'s
Reference (No. 3 of 1994)* [1998] A.C. 245, at 250D-F.

[7] *Pace*, Prof. Smith: see T.B. Smith, p.182.

[8] The recent decision of *Drury v. H.M. Advocate*, 2001, S.L.T. 1013, suggests that this
danger may be less apparent in future.

[9] See *ibid.*

[10] It was almost so put at one stage by Lord Walker in *John Currie and Ors*, High Court
at Glasgow, Dec. 1962, unrep'd, but Lord Walker seems to have meant only that the
reason objective recklessness was enough was the difficulty of proving intention.

[11] See *Drury v. H.M. Advocate*, 2001 S.L.T. 1013.

[12] See esp. R.C. Evid. of Lord Cooper, Q. 5457, 5458.

some support to be found in the recent decision of *Drury v. H.M. Advocate*,[13] although wicked recklessness was not a particular issue in the case; but there have been many cases in which juries have been directed that they are bound to find that wicked recklessness was present.[14]

23.22   INTENT TO DO SERIOUS INJURY. The existence of wicked recklessness in assault cases usually depends on the nature of the violence used — the more blows struck, the more dangerous the weapon, the more vital the parts of the body attacked, the more likely is the accused to be regarded as wicked and reckless. It is sometimes said that intention to do "grave personal injury" or "grievous bodily harm", to use an English technical term,[15] is sufficient *mens rea* for murder, but this is misleading. Evidence of an intention to do serious bodily harm will usually be enough to show wicked recklessness, provided the intention is carried out to the extent of inflicting severe injury, but such an intention is not necessary for murder. If A in fact assaults B with great violence the absence of any intention to do serious injury will not necessarily save him from a conviction for murder — he might indeed be so wild and reckless as to have no fixed intention at all and yet be convicted of murder.

There is now, however, some authority that intent to do serious or grievous bodily harm, or indeed bodily harm, is an independent *mens rea* of murder. In *Cawthorne v H.M. Advocate*[16] the trial judge divided the *mens rea* of murder into three "legs": intent to kill, intent to do bodily harm, and recklessness. It seems to have been conceded that intent to do serious bodily harm is sufficient, and this aspect of the case was not really argued.[17]

It is submitted that intent to do bodily harm is clearly in itself insufficient for murder; and that the only criterion of seriousness or grievousness in "intent to do serious or grievous bodily harm" is whether the degree of harm intended exhibits wicked recklessness.

---

[13] 2001 S.L.T. 1013.

[14] For example, *H.M. Advocate v. McGuinness*, 1937 J.C. 37; *Jeannie Donald*, High Court at Edinburgh, July 1934, unrep'd: see J.G. Wilson (ed.), *Trial of Jeannie Donald*, (Edinburgh and London, 1953), pp. 263–264, L.J.-C. Aitchison's charge to the jury; *Parr v. H.M. Advocate*, 1991 S.C.C.R. 180; *Broadley v. H.M. Advocate*, 1991 S.C.C.R. 416: but *cf. Brown v. H.M. Advocate*, 1993 S.C.C.R. 381, where L.J.-G. Hope (at 391A-B) said that the option of culpable homicide should be withdrawn from a jury only with great caution, since normally the determination of whether the necessary wicked recklessness had been established should be left to the jury.

[15] Which is sometimes used in Scotland: *e.g. Grant v. H.M. Advocate*, 1938 J.C. 7, a charge of putting carbolic in a baby's milk "with intent to do her grievous bodily harm," but was disapproved of by the High of Court of Justiciary on Appeal in *Somervilles*, Nov. 1964, unrep'd: see *infra*, para. 29.23, n.86. See also Children and Young Persons (Scotland) Act 1937, s.57(2), although now repealed (see Criminal Procedure (Scotland) Act 1975, Sched. 10) and re-enacted in a different form (see 1995 Act, s.208); *H.M. Advocate v. Donaldson*, 1970 S.L.T. 2, where "grievous bodily harm" was said to be synonymous with severe injury.

[16] 1968 J.C. 32.

[17] In *Surman v. H.M. Advocate*, 1988 S.C.C.R. 93, Lord Morison considered that there were three types of *mens rea* for murder — including an intention to do grave injury; but the subsequent appeal was not concerned with this issue. Again, in *H.M. Advocate v. Hartley*, 1989 S.L.T. 135, Lord Sutherland directed the jury that murder might be constituted by an intentional act causing the destruction of life with intent to kill or cause grievous bodily harm: that direction was criticised, however, by L.J.-G. Emslie in his evidence to the House of Lords Select Committee on Murder and Life Imprisonment (Report, H.L. Paper 78, Session 1988–89, Vol. III, para. 2017). See also T.H. Jones and S. Griffin, "Serious Bodily Harm and Murder", 1990 S.L.T. (News) 305.

LETHAL WEAPONS. In *H.M. Advocate v. McGuinness*[18] Lord Justice- **23.23**
Clerk Aitchison directed the jury that "People who use knives and
pokers and hatchets against a fellow citizen are not entitled to say 'We
did not mean to kill,' if death results. If people resort to the use of
deadly weapons of this kind, they are guilty of murder, whether or not
they intended to kill,"[19] and similar directions have been given in other
cases.[20] If the purport of these directions is that the use of "lethal
weapons" is itself sufficient to constitute the *mens rea* of murder, it is
submitted that they are unsatisfactory. For one thing, the term "lethal
weapon" is not helpful: murder can be committed by kicking[21] or
punching[22] without the use of any weapons at all. The question is not
"Did A use a lethal weapon?" but "Did A act with wicked recklessness?"
Burnett rightly remarks that "As a circumstance indicative of *intention*,
the nature of the instrument employed is material . . . To any other
effect than this, the Law regards not the nature of the instrument
employed. If death follows by the use of [an instrument], it is a *lethal
weapon* in the sense of law."[23] Similarly, Macdonald said that, "The
expression 'lethal' is vague, as it may depend upon the hand that uses it
whether a weapon is deadly or not."[24]

KNOWLEDGE. In considering a murder charge it is necessary to take **23.24**
into account the accused's state of knowledge, because without doing so
it is impossible to assess his wickedness. This means that his "recklessness" is determined, not by reference to the reasonable man in general,
but by reference to the reasonable man possessing the accused's
knowledge. Error regarding the circumstances, even negligent error, is a
defence to a murder charge. In *John Campbell*,[25] a charge of murder by

---

[18] 1937 J.C. 37. *McGuinness* was considered, apparently with approval in *Broadley v. H.M. Advocate*, 1991 S.C.C.R. 416, at 421E.

[19] At 40.

[20] Similar directions, where it was stated that there was no room for culpable homicide in lethal weapons cases, were approved by the High Court of Justiciary on Appeal in *Parr v. H.M. Advocate*, 1991 S.C.C.R. 180, and *Broadley v. H.M. Advocate*, 1991 S.C.C.R. 416. See also *Kennedy v. H.M. Advocate*, 1944 J.C. 171, where Lord Carmont told the jury that as a lethal weapon — a knife — had been used, they need not waste time considering the issue of murder or culpable homicide: at 174; *Crosbie and Ors*, High Court at Glasgow, Dec. 1945, unrep'd, a case involving bayonets and other weapons in which Lord Mackay refused a request by the Crown that he leave culpable homicide to the jury; *Harris and Ors*, High Court at Glasgow, Sept. 1950, approved in High Court of Justiciary on Appeal, Oct. 1950, unrep'd, an assault with a bottle. In *Crosbie* and *Harris* there were in each case more than one accused but no suggestion was made that the *mens rea* of each should be considered separately, or that one might be guilty of murder and others of culpable homicide: see Vol. I, paras 5.53 and 5.54: *cf. Brown v. H.M. Advocate*, 1993 S.C.C.R. 382, where a direction excluding culpable homicide was considered a misdirection on appeal, in that the jury should have been told to consider not only whether each accused contemplated that lethal weapons were to be used, but also whether each had in contemplation that such weapons might be used "with the necessary degree of wicked recklessness, such as that the deceased would be stabbed by plunging a knife into his heart" (L.J.-G. Hope at p. 391F). This opinion, which entailed that a purpose to use lethal weapons to cause serious injury to the deceased was not necessarily sufficient for murder, was challenged by the Crown in *Coleman v. H.M. Advocate*, 1999 S.C.C.R. 87, but the case was not considered a suitable one in which to review what Lord Hope had said in *Brown*: see Vol. I, paras 5.56 and 5.57.

[21] *Gallacher and Ors*, High Court at Glasgow, Nov 1950, unrep'd; rep'd on another point as *Gallacher v. H.M. Advocate*, 1951 J.C. 38 — culpable homicide was left to but rejected by the jury: Vol. I, para. 5.55.

[22] *Hamilton* (1807) Burnett 7; *Melvin v. H.M. Advocate*, 1984 S.C.C.R. 113.

[23] Burnett, p. 6.

[24] Macdonald (3rd ed.) p.157.

[25] (1836) 1 Swin. 309.

upsetting a platform on which the deceased was working, the jury were told that they could not convict of murder unless they were satisfied that the accused was aware of the distance the deceased would fall, and careless of the result.[26]

It follows that in murder, at any rate where no other crime except assault is involved, an attacker does not take his victim as he finds him, so far as latent conditions are concerned. It is not murder to kill a man by slapping him if he dies as a result because he had a weak heart, unless his condition was known to the accused. Where the weakness of the victim is patent, it must of course be taken into account in assessing the accused's guilt — what would be slight violence in the case of a healthy adult may be foreseeably fatal violence in the case of a child or a frail old man.[27]

23.25 *Other forms of personal injury.* The law applicable to assault applies equally where the accused intended to cause personal injury by some method other than assault, such as the administration of poison.

23.26 *Assault and robbery.* According to Hume, "if a person goes out armed, to rob on the highway, and he attacks a passenger, who resists, and in the struggle his pistol discharges, and the passenger is killed, this, without a doubt is murder . . . Nay further, though the robber do not carry out any mortal weapon, it seems still to be murder if a struggle takes place with the party assaulted, and in the course of this he falls and breaks his neck."[28] This statement is adopted by Alison in a passage headed "It is murder if death ensue from an intention not to kill, but to do some other highly wicked and felonious act",[29] and it may be that Alison regarded any death in the course of robbery as murder whether or not it was foreseeable. Macdonald states that, "if, in a struggle with a robber, the victim is dashed against the wall, or to the ground, and has his skull fractured, and dies, the crime is murder."[30]

23.27 Modern practice prior to *Miller and Denovan*[31] was not altogether uniform, but on the whole supported the view of the textbooks. In *H.M. Advocate v. Fraser and Rollins*[32] Lord Sands told the jury that where death was caused in perpetration of a robbery it was murder unless the death was "a sort of mischance",[33] although he also told them that "if a man uses reckless violence that may cause death, and uses that violence in perpetrating a crime, it is murder . . . you must have reckless use of force without any consideration of what the results of that use of force

---

[26] L.J.-C. Boyle at 315–316.

[27] Hume, i, 238; Alison, i, 5–6; Macdonald, p.89; *Thos Breckinridge* (1836) 1 Swin. 153, Lord Meadowbank at 160; *Robertson and Donoghue*, High Court at Edinburgh, Aug. 1945, unrep'd, Transcript of Judge's charge, 23. In *Edward Evans and Anr* (1873) 2 Couper 410, it was objected to an indictment charging murder by assault and exposure of a sick sailor that the accused's knowledge of his sickness was not libelled, and the objection was repelled. But this was just a question of specification and the court agreed that knowledge or ignorance of the victim's condition might affect the merits of the case.

[28] Hume, i, 24–25.

[29] Alison, i, 51 and 53.

[30] Macdonald, pp. 91–92.

[31] High Court at Glasgow, Nov. 1960; High Court of Justiciary on Appeal, Dec. 1960, unrep'd See *Parr v. H.M. Advocate*, 1991 S.L.T. 208, app. at 211.

[32] 1920 J.C. 60.

[33] 1920 J.C. 60, 63.

may be".[34] The jury were left to decide between murder and culpable homicide and convicted of murder, not surprisingly, as the deceased had suffered a broken nose, a broken jaw, brain injuries, and a ruptured liver.

In *Wm and Helen Harkness*[35] Lord Hunter quoted Macdonald's passage about dashing one's victim against a wall, and indicated that to cause death in the course of a robbery was always murder.

In *McCudden and Cameron*[36] Lord Blackburn accepted that the accused had no intention to injure the victim to the extent to which they did, but he directed the jury that where a housebreaker assaults the house-owner in an attempt to complete his illegal purpose "without intending to kill him but inflicts such injury that he does, that is murder and nothing else, and in no circumstances would such a crime be regarded by the law as culpable homicide."[37]

In *Jas Cunningham,*[38] a case where death was caused by repeated blows on the head, Lord Moncrieff directed the jury that unless they accepted the defence of diminished responsibility they must convict of murder.[39] In *Henry B. Parker,*[40] where death was caused by shooting, the same judge left culpable homicide to the jury who convicted of that crime.

In *Robertson and Donoghue,*[41] where the injuries inflicted were slight the jury were left to decide between murder and culpable homicide, and invited to choose the latter. Lord Cooper told the jury that "in this or in any other case" they must find that the accused acted with wicked and reckless indifference before convicting of murder.[42]

In *Chas Templeman Brown,*[43] an armed hold-up in which two people were shot dead, Lord Carmont gave no specific direction on this question, presumably because the case was fought mainly on the issue of diminished responsibility.

In his evidence before the Royal Commission on Capital Punishment Lord Cooper did not distinguish between assault and assault and robbery, and said that if a burglar presented a loaded firearm at a householder without any intention of injuring him but meaning only to intimidate him, then "in a moment of excitement presses the trigger without meaning to", if the accused could show that he acted without murderous intent, that would be a case of "culpable homicide pure and simple",[44] a view which might not be followed by the courts today.

The most significant treatment of the question is in *Miller and* **23.28** *Denovan,*[45] and it reverses the trend exhibited in Lord Cooper's evidence to the Royal Commission. The accused were two singularly depraved

---

[34] *ibid.*

[35] High Court at Glasgow, Jan 1922, unrep'd.

[36] High Court at Glasgow, April 1932, unrep'd.

[37] Transcript of proceedings, 304–305. Such an attack would, of course, convert the housebreaking into a robbery.

[38] High Court at Ayr, April 1939, unrep'd; rep'd on another point as *H.M. Advocate v. Cunningham,* 1939 J.C. 61.

[39] Transcript of Judge's charge, 35.

[40] High Court at Dundee, Dec. 1943, unrep'd.; rep'd on another point as *H.M. Advocate v. Parker,* 1944 J.C. 49.

[41] High Court at Edinburgh, Aug. 1945, unrep'd.

[42] Transcript of Judge's charge, 21.

[43] High Court at Glasgow, Dec. 1946, unrep'd. See also *Shaw v. H.M. Advocate* 1953 J.C. 51.

[44] Q. 5427.

[45] High Court at Glasgow, Nov. 1960; High Court of Justiciary on Appeal, Dec. 1960, unrep'd; but see *Parr v. H.M. Advocate,* 1991 S.L.T. 208, app. at 211.

youths who committed a series of robberies in the same public park
where Fraser and Rollins had committed their crime. But whereas
Fraser and Rollins used a woman as a decoy, the *modus operandi*
employed by Miller and Denovan was that they themselves decoyed men
they took to be homosexuals to a part of the park where they could be
attacked and robbed. In the course of one of these crimes the victim who
was wearing a cap was killed by being struck once on the head with a
three-foot-long piece of wood which fractured his skull. Lord Wheatley
read to the jury most of Macdonald's treatment of involuntary murder,
including his references to wickedness and depravity. But he went on to
direct them as follows:

> "Ladies and Gentlemen, it was put to you that the fact that the blow
> might not have resulted in death — and that was established in
> cross-examination — would entitle you to return a lesser verdict.
> Ladies and Gentlemen, the fact that the blow might not have
> resulted in death, although in point of fact it did, is in itself no
> answer to a charge of murder if the blow displayed such wicked
> recklessness as to imply a disposition depraved enough to be
> regardless of the consequences. In that situation it is murder. If
> Miller hit Cremin over the head with this large piece of wood to
> overcome his resistance in order to rob him, was that not such
> wicked recklessness as to imply a disposition depraved enough to be
> regardless of the consequences? If in perpetrating this crime of
> robbery a person uses serious and reckless violence which may cause
> death without considering what the result may be, he is guilty of
> murder if the violence results in death although he had no intention
> to kill. Ladies and Gentlemen, in view of the evidence in this case,
> and particularly the medical evidence as to the nature of the blow, if
> you came to the conclusion that the blow was delivered as the result
> of Miller hitting Cremin over the head with this large piece of wood
> in order to overcome his resistance in order that robbery might take
> place, then I direct you in law that there is no room for culpable
> homicide in this case. If there was homicide at all, in that situation
> it was murder. . .
>   . . . it is no answer to a murder charge to say, 'I hit the deceased
> in such a reckless manner that I had no regard for the con-
> sequences, but I had no idea that he would die.' If the degree of
> violence was such that death was within the range of the natural and
> probable consequences of the blow, then it becomes murder. We
> have heard in evidence . . . that this must have been a severe blow,
> and you are entitled to have regard to the nature of these injuries in
> assessing this — the area of the fracture and the degree of the
> haemorrhage. And I repeat what I said before: if in a struggle with a
> robber the victim is dashed against the wall, or to the ground, and
> has his skull fractured — and to that may I add, if he is hit over the
> head with a weighty object such as a plank of wood of this nature —
> and he dies, the crime is murder."[46]

Lord Wheatley's charge was approved by the Criminal Appeal Court
who affirmed that in certain circumstances a judge had a duty to
withdraw culpable homicide from the jury. Lord Justice-General Clyde
said:

---

[46] Transcript of Judge's charge, 30–31.

"If, for instance, the issue between these two possible verdicts depended on the amount of violence used, or upon a question whether death might have been in that particular case a mischance, there may be room for leaving both murder and culpable homicide to the jury for their decision. But it is no part of the function of a judge at a trial to avoid his responsibility by leaving the issue in all cases to the jury to work out for themselves".[47]

Although the statements of the law made in *Miller and Denovan* are not altogether free from the ambiguity which occurs throughout the authorities on this subject, the case indicates clearly that the criterion for distinguishing between murder and culpable homicide is an objective one.[48] This appears even more in what Lord Wheatley did than in what he said — he did not leave it to the jury to decide whether or not there had been wicked recklessness, and in particular, except for one reference to using violence "without considering what the result may be", he did not discuss Miller's actual mental state: it is also noteworthy that although Lord Wheatley discussed at length the question whether Denovan had been shown to be accessory to the use of the type of violence involved in the assault he did not suggest that the jury should consider whether he foresaw or accepted that the violence might prove fatal — he left the jury the option of acquitting him altogether of homicide, but not of convicting him of culpable homicide.

It is again not altogether clear whether the same objective test would have been applied had there been no context of robbery — the judgement of the Appeal Court can be read as approving the earlier "lethal weapon" cases in which culpable homicide was withdrawn from the jury. It was submitted in the second edition of this work that *Miller and Denovan* should be restricted to robbery — the robbery aspect having loomed large in the case and in Lord Wheatley's charge, and earlier cases having shown that robbery did occupy a special place in this branch of the law. It was argued in support of that submission that there was no sufficient warrant in earlier statements of the law for treating the wicked recklessness in simple assault cases so objectively as to make it a question of law for the judge in each case,[49] and concluded that the *ratio* of the lethal weapons cases must be that the evidence so overwhelmingly pointed to wicked recklessness that the jury could not but convict of murder. But in *Broadley v. H.M. Advocate*,[50] the Appeal Court did not agree that *Miller and Denovan* should be so restricted, and in effect held that there were cases, although each case would ultimately depend on its own facts, where as a matter of law the jury, if satisfied that the accused had carried out the assault in question, would be bound by the judge's direction to convict him of murder.[51]

---

[47] Opinion of L.J.-G. Clyde, at 6. See also *Robt Paul Dunn*, High Court of Justiciary on Appeal, Jan. 1980, unrep'd. *Cf. D.P.P. v Stonehouse* [1978] A.C. 55.

[48] See also *Broadley v. H.M. Advocate*, 1991 S.C.C.R. 416, L.J.-C. Ross at 423C–D.

[49] *cf. Att.-Gen. for N.I.'s Reference* 1975 [1977] A.C. 105.

[50] 1991 S.C.C.R. 416.

[51] *cf. Brown v. H.M. Advocate*, 1993 S.C.C.R. 382, at 391B, where L.J.-G. Hope said that, "[t]he alternative verdict of culpable homicide is one which should be withdrawn from the jury only with great caution, because the onus is on the Crown to prove its case and all questions as to the weight or quality of the evidence are for the jury and not for the trial judge. The correct approach to the questions raised by the direction as to what constitutes murder should normally be to leave it to the jury to decide whether the necessary degree of wicked recklessness has been established by the Crown." But he also stated (at 391B–D:

23.29   HOMICIDE BY AN ESCAPING ROBBER. An assault committed by a robber in an endeavour to escape after the completion of a robbery is not one committed for the purpose of robbery, and *a fortiori* an assault by an escaping housebreaker is not in the same category as one committed with robbery as its aim. It is possible that *Miller and Denovan*[52] does not apply in such situations, and that Lord Blackburn was wrong when he said in *McCudden and Cameron*[53] that, "It is perfectly well settled in our law that if a man breaks into the house of another with the intent to steal or anything else and is interfered with by the owner of the house, and in the attempt either to complete his illegal purpose or to cover up his tracks and escape he assails the owner of the house without intending to kill him but inflicts such injury that he does, that is murder and nothing else",[54] not merely because this does not take foreseeability into account, but because it treats the situation as on all fours with that of assault and robbery. In *John Caldwell*[55] Lord Stevenson told the jury that it was for them to decide whether wicked recklessness was present in a case where an escaping housebreaker shot a friend of the householder.[56]

It was submitted in the second edition of this work that that approach was the correct one and that such assaults should be treated in the same way as other cases of assault; but it is doubtful if the submission can be supported today, given the views expressed in *Broadley v. H.M. Advocate*.[57]

23.30   *Abortion*.[58] Hume,[59] Alison,[60] Burnett[61] and Macdonald[62] all state that to cause death by abortion is murder, but this is not supported by the reported cases, and is not in accordance with practice. Hume refers only to a case in 1785[63] in which the victim was poisoned by abortifacient drugs and the accused were charged alternatively with murder or culpable homicide by poison, without reference to the abortion, and which is not authority for any view.

In *Wm Reid*[64] the question of murder or culpable homicide was left to the jury, and the accused was acquitted of homicide altogether as the jury held that it had not been proved that death had resulted from the

---

"Nevertheless there may be cases where the number or nature of the blows struck or the weapons used are of such a character that there is no room for a verdict of culpable homicide . . . [but] every case depends on its own facts, and for this reason no precise guidance can be given as to when a direction to this effect will be appropriate. The best that can be said is that the question is ultimately one of fact, and that the trial judge should not take this course unless he is satisfied that there is no basis at all for the verdict in the evidence."

[52] High Court at Glasgow, Nov. 1960; High Court of Justiciary, Dec. 1960, unrep'd.
[53] High Court at Glasgow, Apr. 1932, unrep'd.
[54] Transcript of proceedings, 304–305.
[55] High Court at Glasgow, June 1946, unrep'd.
[56] Transcript of Judge's charge, 8. There was a question of culpable homicide on the issue of diminished responsibility, but the jury convicted of murder.
[57] 1991 S.C.C.R. 416.
[58] The cases all relate to a time when all abortions were regarded as criminal and must now, of course, be read as referring to abortions which are not permitted under the Abortion Act 1967: *infra*, para. 28.01.
[59] Hume, i, 263–264.
[60] Alison, i, 52.
[61] Burnett, pp. 5–6. Burnett also thinks it murder if death ensues from the giving of a drug "to produce unnatural desire".
[62] Macdonald, p.91.
[63] *Robt Dalrymple and Robt Joyner* (1785) Hume, i, 264.
[64] (1858) 3 Irv. 235.

abortion. *H.M. Advocate v. Chas Rae*[65] had the same result. In that case, Lord Shand gave the only reported direction on the point at issue. He said:

> "To constitute murder you must be satisfied that the instrument was a dangerous one, that it was used for an unlawful purpose, and that its use caused death . . . if the instrument was used not with any intention to destroy life, and was not a dangerous instrument, though used for an unlawful purpose, and death resulted, that would reduce the crime to one of culpable homicide."[66]

He went on to say that while it was for the jury to say whether the instrument was dangerous the medical evidence had been entirely to the effect that it was, and if that were so there would be no room for culpable homicide. *Rae* indicates that the question of murder or culpable homicide in abortion cases is a jury question, depending on the dangerous nature of the instrument used, and that it remains a jury question even where all the evidence is that the instrument is dangerous. "Dangerous" has not been defined, but it may be taken to denote an instrument of a kind whose use would imply wicked disregard of fatal consequences.

Homicide caused by illegal abortion is invariably charged as culpable homicide in modern practice[67] and although it may still be theoretically the law that death caused in this way is murder if wicked recklessness is present it is unlikely that a murder charge would ever now be brought in an abortion case.

Rape. Macdonald says that, "If, as the result of rape, the woman dies . . . **23.31** the crime murder",[68] but his authority is *D.P.P. v. Beard*,[69] which proceeded on a peculiarly English form of constructive malice and has no application to Scots law.[70] There is no Scots authority on the question.[71] In his evidence to the Royal Commission on Capital Punishment Lord Keith said that in such a situation, "If extraneous violence was used, if she was hit on the head with a stone to overcome resistance, that would be a very different case, but if the death resulted merely from the commission of the rape, I am not satisfied that in Scotland that would be murder."[72] Lord Cooper was asked:

> "A man may rape a child and that child may die from the violence thereby involved and the shock to its system. Another man may rape a girl or a woman of mature years, but may render his crime easier to commit by committing upon her body what I will call extraneous violence, such as hitting her on the head with a brick. Would you regard both cases as murder?"

---

[65] (1888) 2 White 62.
[66] At 69.
[67] For example, *Willis v. H.M. Advocate*, 1941 J.C. 1, where the police charged murder but the crime was indicted as culpable homicide. In one case a charge of culpable homicide was brought where one of the accused had a previous conviction for abortion and culpable homicide: *Malcolm Sinclair Johnstone and Ors*, High Court at Edinburgh, April 1943, unrep'd. See also R.C. Evid., Crown Agent's Memo., App. (a), para. 7.
[68] Macdonald, pp. 91–92.
[69] [1920] A.C. 479.
[70] *Brennan v. H.M. Advocate*, 1977 J.C. 38.
[71] In *H.M. Advocate v. Logan*, 1936 J.C. 100, the Crown restricted the charge to culpable homicide in the course of the trial.
[72] Q. 5127.

and he replied:

> "I think the second would be charged as, and might lead to a conviction of, murder. It would depend on circumstances whether the first one would either be charged or go to the jury as murder."[73]

Lord Cooper and Lord Keith clearly did not hold the view that any homicide in the course of rape was murder. It is submitted that murder is committed only where the violence used is such as to imply wicked recklessness and that such recklessness will not normally be present where the violence used is inseparable from the act of rape itself.

23.32 *Fire-raising.* One of the examples Hume gives of the operation of dole is where A sets fire to a house and kills B in consequence, which he regards as murder.[74] Burnett holds it to be murder where A sets fire to a house and kills someone who happens to be inside, even although he acted without intending any corporal injury to anyone and had every reason to believe the house empty.[75] Macdonald also says it is murder "if by an act of wilful fire-raising, persons in the house or neighbouring houses are killed."[76] There are no reported cases of this kind,[77] and the statements in the textbooks can be disregarded as deriving from a doctrine of constructive malice of a kind no longer accepted in Scots law. It is submitted that death caused by a fire-raiser cannot be murder unless the fire-raising displayed wicked recklessness. It may be that in view of the serious nature of fire-raising this case forms an exception to the suggested rule that murder also requires an intention to cause physical injury, but in the absence of any authority it cannot be asserted that this is so. Fire-raising is certainly a very serious and potentially dangerous crime, but so also is driving a car recklessly and under the influence of drink, and to cause death in the latter way is not murder in modern law.[78]

23.33 *Summary.* The Royal Commission on Capital Punishment said that "the law of Scotland does not recognise any doctrine of constructive malice or anything akin to it",[79] but this must be read subject to considerable qualification: there may not be such a doctrine in Scots law, but there is certainly something very akin to it. Historically, the position is probably that murder like every other common law crime required *mens rea* or

---

[73] Q. 5416.
[74] Hume, i, 24.
[75] Burnett, p.6.
[76] Macdonald, p.91. See also Alison, i, 52.
[77] *cf.* the peculiar case of *Sutherland (No.1) v. H.M. Advocate*, 1994 S.C.C.R. 80, where the accused was charged with, and convicted of the culpable homicide of the person who had assisted him in the intentional setting of fire to the accused's own house, apparently in an attempt to defraud insurers: there was no suggestion in the case that the homicide could or should have been charged as one of murder.
[78] Macdonald also refers to exposure, wrecking and scuttling as examples of crimes which are such that deaths caused in the course of them are murder: Macdonald, pp. 91–92. The exposure cases indicate that exposure is in the same position as assault — see *Eliz. Kerr* (1860) 3 Irv. 645, and *H.M. Advocate v. McPhee*, 1935 J.C. 46 where the exposure was preceded by a brutal assault and the jury convicted of culpable homicide. In practice cases involving the desertion of children are charged as culpable homicide: R.C. Evid., Crown Agent's Memo., App. (a), para. 14. There are no cases on wrecking or scuttling, which may be regarded as equivalent to fire-raising.
[79] R.C. para. 92.

dole in the sense of a wicked disposition,[80] or "general mens rea".[81] Where A killed B while intending to commit another crime, the wickedness exhibited by the intent to commit that crime would be a sufficient dole for murder, at any rate if the crime were a serious one, so that A would always be guilty of murder, since both the *actus reus* and the *mens rea* of murder were present. Dole was also present where A acted recklessly in the sense in which it is reckless to beat a man to within an inch of his life, fire a gun at him, or stick a bayonet in his stomach.[82] The law might then have developed so that murder could be committed intentionally, or recklessly, or by causing death in the commission of another dangerous crime such as fire-raising, rape or robbery. But this possible development was affected by two factors. In the first place there was a reluctance to invoke the concept of transferred intent to hang a man, so that the feeling grew up that even where death occurred in the course of another crime it was murder only if actual recklessness was exhibited: this would account for the way in which Macdonald states the law when he says that murder is constituted by an act displaying wicked recklessness, and then goes on to say that murder is committed when death results form the perpetration of a serious crime where that crime involves wicked disregard of consequences.[83] At the same time, however, the idea that the recklessness in murder had to be wicked and involve moral depravity led to the view that involuntary murder could be committed only in the course of committing another crime, or at least by an assault. The acceptance of this view was aided by the absence of any definition of recklessness in Scots law, and also by the development of the law as a result of which motorists and other "non-criminal" persons who cause death recklessly are not charged with murder, however gross their lack of care or rash their behaviour.

Although this suggested development is in line with Lord Cooper's remark that "we have practically reached the position where only intentional killing is murder",[84] the actual situation is that there is murder wherever death is caused with wicked intention to kill or by an act intended to cause physical injury and displaying a wicked disregard of fatal consequences. Now that capital punishment has been abolished forensic discussion of the *mens rea* of murder is less common than formerly.[85] Judges often content themselves with citing Macdonald's definition to juries, thus rendering their directions unassailable. Any future development is more likely to be by way of abolishing the distinction between murder and culpable homicide[86] than by any refinement of the *mens rea* requirement for murder; but of such development there is as yet little sign. The High Court have affirmed in fairly recent cases, however, that a judge is entitled to withdraw culpable homicide from the jury in any case in which the evidence is such that no reasonable jury could hold that wicked recklessness was not present, and

---

[80] Hume, i, 23 *et seq.*
[81] See Vol. I, para. 7.05.
[82] Hume, i, 254 *et seq., supra.*
[83] Macdonald, pp. 89, 91, *supra*, at para. 23.19.
[84] R.C. Evid., Q. 5417.
[85] But see *Drury v. H.M. Advocate*, 2001 S.L.T. 1013.
[86] *cf. R. v. Hyam* [1975] A.C. 55, Lord Kilbrandon at 98E; *McAdam v. H.M. Advocate* 1960 J.C. 1, L.J.-G. at 4; *Drury v. H.M. Advocate*, 2001 S.L.T. 1013.

have made it clear that *Miller and Denovan*[87] is not limited to robbery cases.[88]

JUSTIFIABLE HOMICIDE

23.34 Homicide is justifiable in the following circumstances:
1. In the execution of public justice, of which the only example is the carrying out of a death sentence.[89]

23.35	2. In the furtherance of public justice:
(a) *In the execution of a warrant*. Hume was of opinion that an officer executing the order of a criminal court was entitled to kill in order to carry out his task,[90] even in circumstances not amounting to ordinary self-defence. Officers executing the warrant of a civil court were in Hume's view entitled to kill in the execution of a warrant only where there was a prospect of danger to life.[91] Their case was different from that of private persons acting in self-defence in that:

> "The latter . . . must be in actual and immediate danger of his life *as at the moment of killing*, and so situated, that, unless by sacrificing the assailant, he cannot escape alive. But the officer shall be acquitted, if, at the time of killing, such danger be *in or near and manifest preparation for him*, so as to let him see that *he shall come to be in peril of his life*, if he persevere in the prosecution of his duty, and although, by deserting the service, he might at once put an end to the hazard."[92]

There are no modern Scottish cases on the subject (and those quoted by Hume do not unequivocally support his view on the position of the criminal officer), but the law today is probably that neither civil nor criminal officers are entitled to kill except in self-defence.[93] The civil officer is almost certainly in no better situation than a private citizen, except that if he causes death by using force which he is entitled to use the death will be treated as caused by a lawful act, and not by an assault. The modern criminal officer is probably still privileged to some degree: he would not, it is submitted, be bound to save himself by flight but be entitled to go ahead and try to carry out his duty, even although it appear that it will be necessary to kill in order to do so with safety to his own life. But he would not be entitled to kill in anticipation of danger to himself. A police officer who notices that the criminal has a gun in his pocket is entitled to go ahead and try to arrest him, but is not entitled to kill him until it appears that the criminal is on the point of using the gun.

---

[87] High Court at Glasgow, Nov. 1960; High Court of Justiciary on Appeal, Dec. 1960, unrep'd: but see *Parr v. H.M. Advocate*, 1991 S.L.T. 208, app. at 211.
[88] See, *Parr v. H.M. Advocate*, 1991 S.L.T. 208; *Broadley v. H.M. Advocate*, 1991 S.C.C.R. 416, both cases involving multiple blows with weapons.
[89] Hume, i, 195; Alison, i, 127.
[90] Hume, i, 197–200; *cf.* Alison, i, 131; Burnett, pp. 62 *et seq.*
[91] Hume, i, 203–204; *cf.* Alison, i, 129 *et seq.*; Burnett, pp. 67 *et seq.*
[92] Hume, i, 204
[93] Macdonald, p.95. See J.C. Macdonald, "Justifiable Homicide" (1897) 4 S.L.T. (News) 225.

(b) *In the suppression of a riot.*[94] A magistrate is bound, and so is **23.36** entitled, to use force where necessary in order to suppress a riot:

> "If, therefore, in his lawful and laudable exertions towards this end, he shall be opposed or resisted by the rioters, who will not desist, or disperse, or suffer themselves to be taken, but make head against the magistrate, and his *posse*, and violently molest and hinder him therein, certainly he may make good his purpose by force, and at the hazard of their lives; so he do not employ such means unnecessarily, or before the proper season. This is the clear doctrine of the common law, founded in reason and necessity, and indispensable for the ends of government".[95]

Since the magistrate is entitled to use force only so far as necessary, he would be bound to use all other available means first, such as entreaty, firing over the heads of the mob, using tear gas, and so on. If it is clear from the outset that only homicidal force will stop the mob, the magistrate may use such force immediately.

A riot or mob in this connection is any disorderly assembly which is proceeding "to outrageous deeds of violence against property and person",[96] and which has reached such proportions and created such a breach of public order, that it cannot be dealt with by ordinary police action. The magistrate is in a favourable position in that he is entitled to kill to protect property from the mob, in order to protect the safety and not merely the lives of persons, and in that he is not limited to killing a particular assailant who has put the life of a particular person in danger, but may order troops to fire on the mob as a whole in the event of a general disturbance.

3. Homicide by a member of the armed forces in the exercise of his **23.37** duty.[97] It may be doubted whether the same privilege would now extend to revenue officers.[98]

4. Homicide in obedience to a lawful command, that is to say to a **23.38** command falling within one of the above groups. The hangman who carries out the judge's sentence, the constable or soldier who kills on the lawful order of a superior or magistrate, have the same protection as the person who gave the order. The position of the subordinate who carries out an unlawful order is discussed separately.[99]

---

[94] See "Quelling Riot" (1894) 1 S.L.T. 245.

[95] Hume, i, 197.

[96] Hume, i, 197. It is uncertain whether homicidal force could nowadays be justifiable in defence of property, even against a mob: *cf.* P.W. Ferguson, *Crimes Against the Person* (2nd ed., 1998), para. 2.06.

[97] Hume, i, 205; Burnett, p.71; Alison, i, 39, 132; Macdonald, pp. 105–106; *McKenzie and Ors* (1803) Burnett 75; *Henry Lloyd* (1810) *James Henry* (1813) both Hume, i, 209; *Robt Hawton and Wm Geo. Parker* (1861) 4 Irv. 58; *H.M. Advocate v. Sheppard*, 1941 J.C. 67; see Vol. I, paras 13.32 *et seq.*

[98] See Hume, i, 214–217.

[99] See Vol. I, para. 13.31.

23.39   5. Homicide in cases of justifiable necessity other than self-defence. There is no Scots authority on this matter and the question is discussed separately.[1]

23.40   6. Homicide in self-defence. This is the most important form of justifiable homicide in practice, and deserves a chapter to itself.

---

[1] See Vol. I, paras 13.08 *et seq.*

CHAPTER 24

SELF-DEFENCE

The term "self-defence"

Two things require to be said at the outset about the term "self- **24.01** defence". First, it is a misleading term. Its literal meaning would confine it to situations in which a man acted in order to defend his own person; but it is used to cover acts in defence of persons other than oneself,[1] and also acts in defence of things other than personal safety, such as chastity or property. Secondly, it is used both to describe a fact and to make a legal judgement. "He acted in self-defence" may mean only "He acted for the purpose of defending himself", or it may mean "He acted for the purpose of defending himself and was justified in doing so, having regard to all the circumstances". Whether any situation is one of self-defence in the first meaning is a question of fact; whether any situation is one of self-defence in the second meaning involves questions of law, and depends on the rules regarding self-defence in the legal system in the context of which the statement is made. A Scots and an American lawyer might agree that in a particular situation a man was acting in self-defence in the first sense, and disagree about whether he was justified in so doing. A man has no absolute legal right to act in self-defence; his only right is to act in justifiable self-defence; and the justification of his act in law depends on rules of law.

Types of situation in which a man may act in self-defence

It is convenient to consider self-defence in a number of different types **24.02** of situation:

(a) *Self-defence against a justifiable attack.* The condemned man who tries to kill his executioner is acting in self-defence; so is the robber who defends himself against his victim while the latter is acting in justifiable self-defence against the robber's initial attack. This type of case can be dealt with briefly, as self-defence in such situations is clearly unjustifiable. Whatever the moral rights and wrongs in any case, a man cannot be legally entitled to interfere to prevent an executioner carrying out the law. And if the law allows a person to defend himself against an

---

[1] *John Forrest* (1837) 1 Swin. 404; *H.M. Advocate v. Carson and Anr*, 1964 S.L.T. 21, an assault case; *Boyle v. H.M. Advocate*, 1992 S.C.C.R. 824. Partly for the reason that one may defend persons other than oneself, some text writers have abandoned the use of "self-defence" in favour of "private defence", *i.e.* "the right to use force in defence of oneself or another", which is then contrasted with "public defence", *i.e.* the right to use force "in the course of preventing crime or arresting offenders": see Smith and Hogan, pp. 259 *et seq. Cf.* the Law Commission No. 177, 1989, *A Criminal Code for England and Wales*, Vol. I, Draft Code, cl. 44: "Use of force in public and private defence". See also E.M. Burchell and P.M.A. Hunt, *South African Criminal Law & Procedure* (3rd ed., 1997), Vol. I., *General Principles of Criminal Law* (by J.M. Burchell), pp. 72 *et seq.*; *cf. ibid.*, Chap. 13 "Public Authority", pp. 120 *et seq.*

assailant it cannot allow the assailant to kill him just because he exercised his right of self-defence and so put the assailant's life in danger. It must be as criminal to kill someone who is resisting the attempt to kill him as it is to kill someone who offers no resistance. The fact that the resistance may endanger the life of the attacker is irrelevant unless the resistance ceases to be justifiable.

(b) *Self-defence against an unjustified and unprovoked attack.* This is the situation of the man who defends himself against an attack for which he is in no way responsible, as where he is set upon by robbers. This is what Hume, Burnett and Alison describe as self-defence against a felon.[2]

(c) *Self-defence against an unjustified but provoked attack,* i.e. *self-defence where both parties are to some extent to blame for the situation in which the attack occurs.* Hume calls this "self-defence in a quarrel,"[3] and Burnett, "self-defence on provocation".[4] This is the most common situation in practice, and may be further divided into the following types of situation: (1) Where the victim initiated the situation by a wrongful act of a minor nature, by "some offence of word or deed, real or conceived, which has kindled anger on the spot, and led at last, to a mortal strife."[5] (2) Where the accused initiated the situation by a wrongful act, but the victim retaliated in an unjustifiable way and put the accused's life in danger. The facts in such situations will approximate to one of the two following examples: (i) The accused slaps the victim's face and the latter retaliates by attacking the accused with a lethal weapon and the accused kills him in order to save his own life; (ii) A robber attacks a shopkeeper and the latter retaliates in self-defence. The shopkeeper, however, goes beyond what is necessary for his own safety and in so doing puts the robber's life in danger, and the robber kills him in self-defence. A legal system may treat the homicide in: (i) as justifiable, and in (ii) as unjustifiable, or treat both as justifiable or unjustifiable, but it cannot, it is submitted, hold that (ii) is justifiable and (i) is not.[6]

HUME'S TREATMENT OF SELF-DEFENCE

Self-defence against a felon

24.03 *The rules.* Hume is favourably disposed to this type of self-defence, and deals quite fully with it.[7] He does not look on the man who defends himself against a felon as doing something the law grudgingly permits, but as exercising his rights as a citizen, in that he is not only entitled but even encouraged to kill his assailant. Hume takes as an example the man who "being on the highway, and alone, is suddenly thrust at with a sword from behind, or has a pistol fired in his face, by one who springs out on

---

[2] Hume, i, 217–222; Burnett, p.39; Alison, i, 132–136.
[3] Hume, i, 218, 222 *et seq.*
[4] Burnett, p.40.
[5] Hume, i, 222.
[6] There is a further situation where A defends himself against an attack by a person who is not criminally responsible. This will be treated as defence against a "felon", since the attack is a criminal one although the attacker is not punishable.
[7] Hume, i, 217–222.

him from the side of the way."[8] Such a man, being innocent of all blame, has no duty to try to escape from the assault, but "is rather called on, instantly, and without shrinking, to stand on his defence, that the assailant may not continue to have the advantage of him, but be straight way deterred from the prosecution of his felonious purpose."[9] He is entitled to suppose the worst of his attacker, and even "though the assailant give back on the resistance, yet still the innocent party is not for this obliged immediately to desist (since it may be only a feigned retreat, or to call his associates); and . . . he may pursue nevertheless, and use his weapon, until he be completely out of danger."[10]

The accused in this situation need show only that he acted for the purpose of defending himself, without showing also that what he did was *necessary* for that purpose. His plea will not be defeated just because he continued his defence after it was no longer necessary to preserve himself from imminent danger; nor because he could have saved himself from danger by escape. He must not, of course, continue his "defence" once the assailant is secured and he himself completely out of all danger, since he can then no longer be said to be defending himself at all, but is acting out of "deliberate cruelty or revenge".[11] But so long as he is genuinely defending himself, he is not bound to use only the minimum force necessary to preserve his life from imminent danger, but is entitled to go some length to "mak siccar" that he is free from any possible danger.

These rules are different from the rules laid down by Hume for self-defence in a quarrel, where he restricts the right of self-defence to the use of the minimum force necessary to save one's life, and where "the survivor must have given back, and done all that in him lay to take himself out of the affray."[12]

What may be defended. According to Hume a person may kill to save his **24.04** own life or that of others, to prevent rape, and, in some circumstances, to preserve his property.[13]

As Hume points out,[14] both Roman and Jewish law permit the killing of a housebreaker; but they both regard this as an application of the right to kill in defence of life. A nocturnal thief may be killed because one cannot see whether or not he is armed or what his intentions are,

---

[8] Hume, i, 218.

[9] *ibid.*

[10] *ibid.*

[11] *ibid.*; *cf. Joseph and Maxwell Allison* (1838) 2 Swin. 167; *H.M. Advocate v. Graham*, 1958 S.L.T. 167.

[12] Hume, i, 217–218; *cf.* Macdonald, p.106.

[13] Hume, i, 218–219. Similarly Burnett, p.53; Alison, i, 132–139. Hume does not specifically mention the prevention of sodomy, and it can be distinguished from rape both because the definition of the latter requires resistance from the woman before she can complain to the criminal law, or, presumably, evade the civil consequences of adultery, and because of the historical veneration of female virginity. Killing in defence of male chastity seems to have been regarded as justifiable in Roman Law: *cf.* D. 48.8 1 (4): "Item, divus Hadrianus rescripsit eum, qui stuprum sibi vel suis per vim inferentem occidit, dimittendum." See also Donnedieu de Vabres, 230: "Tout le monde admet qu'il peut s'agir d'une aggression contre la santé, la pudeur ou l'honneur." It was explicitly declared to be justifiable in Rabbinic law: Mishna, Sanhedrin, 8.7. Neither Roman nor Jewish law was quoted in the relatively modern case of *McCluskey v. H.M. Advocate*, 1959 J.C. 39, where it was held that such killing was not justifiable; and *McCluskey* was followed in *Elliott v. H.M. Advocate*, 1987 S.C.C.R. 278.

[14] Hume, i, 220.

and because it is reasonable to fear that he will use violence.[15] Killing a nocturnal housebreaker was explicitly recognised as justifiable homicide by the Scots Act of 1661, c.217,[16] and Hume accepts this as being the law. But he explains it, in line with the Roman and Jewish attitudes, on the ground that the householder is entitled to assume that the intruder intends to commit murder, rape, hamesucken, or to set fire to the house, all dangers which go beyond a mere threat to property. Again, Hume considers it justifiable to kill a daylight thief where there is reasonable apprehension of similar danger. The difference between the nocturnal and daylight thief is that the mere fact of daylight stealing does not make it reasonable for the owner to apprehend such dangers.[17]

It must be said, however, that Hume is not altogether clear on this matter. He seems to be moving towards the view that only danger to life can justify killing, but he does not explicitly state this as his opinion. At one point he says that the householder invaded by night cannot be absolutely enjoined by law not to kill the invader, although "[t]enderness for the life of another may indeed suggest to one to endeavour, by cries and otherwise, to deter him from his purpose, before proceeding to make use of higher means",[18] but he thinks that a man may have a right to kill an escaping thief in order to rescue his property.[19]

In *William Williamson*[20] the accused lay in wait for a thief who had robbed his bleachfield on earlier occasions, and killed him as he was entering an outhouse. He was acquitted, and Hume considered that the case went further than his view of the law. Alison considers it "hardly reconcileable with the principles of law".[21] The rule that there is no right to kill merely in defence of property can be regarded as having been finally settled by the case of *Jas Craw*[22] where a charge of murder was held relevant against a game-keeper in relation to the death of a poacher who had been killed by a spring-gun set by the accused.[23] The position regarding housebreakers, however, remains unclear.[24]

---

[15] *cf.* D. 48.8.9: "Furem nocturnum si quis occiderit, ita demum impune feret, si parcere ei sine periculo suo non potuit." *Cf.* also Rashi's Commentary on Exod. 22.2 which prohibits the killing of a thief "if the sun shone upon him": Rashi treats the phrase as metaphorical, and as meaning that it is illegal to kill a thief if it is clear that the latter did not intend to kill the owner even if the owner resisted him, whatever the time of day.

[16] A.P.S. VII, 203, cited by Hume, at i, 220, as c. 22: the Act was repealed by the Statute Law Revision (Scotland) Act 1906.

[17] Hume, i, 221.

[18] *ibid*. 220.

[19] *ibid.* 222; Burnett, p.57.

[20] (1801) Hume, i, 220–221.

[21] Alison, i, 105.

[22] (1826) Syme 188 and 210.

[23] See also *John McBryde* (1843) 1 Broun 558.

[24] See *infra.* In *John Forrest* (1837) 1 Swin. 404 the deceased was involved in an attack on a house where a number of women servants were living in the charge of the accused, and self-defence was based in part on apprehension for the safety of the women, and fear that the attackers intended forcibly to carry them off: Lord Moncreiff at 418, and this aspect of the case can be classed with self-defence against rape. In the not dissimilar case of *John Fordyce* (1804) Burnett, 55, the attack was designed in part to remove the accused's mistress from his house and there was evidence that he was afraid for his safety at the hands of the mob led by his wife whom he killed, as well as being afraid they would burn his house. *Edward Lane* (1830) Bell's Notes 77 may support the view that it is justifiable to kill an escaping housebreaker in defence of property but there was some question of personal violence there too. *Wm Wright* (1835) 1 Swin. 6 was rather different: the deceased forced his way into the accused's house and assaulted him, apparently because of non-repayment of a loan, and the accused retaliated excessively and was convicted of culpable homicide.

Hume's reasons

Although Hume's tendency to restrict the right of self-defence to the **24.05** defence of life — and of chastity which is widely recognised as equivalent to life in this connection — shows that there is some similarity between his views on self-defence and the law of necessity, Hume does not base the right of defence against a felon on necessity. He talks of "the necessary defence of one's life, against an attempt feloniously to take it away",[25] but he allows the person who is attacked to exceed what is necessary in order to save himself from imminent peril. The right of self-defence is thought of as an independent right, grounded in the law of nature.[26] This right exists where the assailant "is no true man, to be contended with on equal terms, but a foul criminal, found in the commission of a high felony, and the fit object, therefore, of extreme and summary justice."[27]

This combines two ideas. The first is that the felon, by his actings, has broken the law, and so has forfeited his right to be protected by it. More crudely, he set out to attack somebody, and so laid himself open to counter-attack. The second idea is that the citizen who kills a felon in self-defence is acting as an officer of the law; he is not just defending himself, he is administering "extreme and summary justice".[28] This accounts for Hume's apparent enthusiasm for the defence. The law has scant sympathy for the felon and sheds no tears over his death. Even if the felon was not committing a capital offence, there is still the feeling that society is well-rid of the miscreant, and that it would be churlish and hypocritical to be too severe on the accused.[29]

Hume also speaks of the indignation and resentment a woman is entitled to feel at an attempt to rape her, and suggests that the right of third parties to kill the intending ravisher rests on their right to partake of this resentment.[30] But if this were the basis of the right, whether the killing was justifiable would depend on whether in fact the accused acted under the influence of resentment, and the plea of self-defence would in effect become a plea of justifiable provocation. Nor would it be possible to distinguish between a resentment which operated to prevent rape, and one which operated to kill the ravisher after the rape had been completed. If a man is entitled to defend himself or a third party he is entitled to do so whether in indignation or cold blood, and conversely, if he is not entitled to do so, he does not become so entitled because he feels indignant. What is important is not the indignation, but whether the accused was *entitled* to feel indignant; for if he was not, the indignation can only mitigate his punishment, it cannot exculpate him.

Self-defence in a quarrel

Hume's treatment of this type of situation blurs the distinction **24.06** between it and self-defence against a felon, although he makes the distinction explicitly both at the outset of his whole treatment of self-

---

[25] Hume, i, 217.

[26] Hume, i, 218.

[27] *ibid.*

[28] *ibid.* It should of course be remembered that when Hume wrote, rape and aggravated theft were capital offences.

[29] *cf.* Donnedieu de Vabres, 230 where he points out that a person who acts in self-defence "*a rendu service à la société*".

[30] Hume, i, 218.

defence,[31] and at the outset of his treatment of the quarrel cases.[32] Indeed, the practical result of the application of Hume's views is to negate any right of self-defence in a quarrel. He talks of "self-defence on a sudden quarrel"[33] but adds that "wherever it appears that either in the origin or progress of the quarrel, or in the ultimate strife, there was any thing faulty or excessive on the part of the survivor; here for the sake of correction and example, the judge inflicts a suitable punishment, though it be true that he did not kill out of wickedness or malice, but only to save his own life, and really believing that he could not otherwise escape."[34]

This means that a plea of self-defence cannot succeed where the accused started the quarrel, and also makes it impossible to justify the application of different rules to quarrels from those applied to self-defence against a felon. If the accused must have remained blameless throughout, the only difference between the two is that in the latter the deceased's first assault was in itself sufficiently violent to endanger the accused's life, while in the former there was no danger to life at the outset and so no immediate need to kill in self-defence. But if the accused's conduct remains exemplary throughout, once the situation reaches the stage of danger to his life it will be indistinguishable from defence against a felon. It may be said that in the quarrel cases the accused has a chance to escape at an early stage before the danger to his life develops, but in that event the distinction between the two types is not one of kind based on the felonious nature of the attack, but simply one of degree, depending on the degree of actual necessity, so that both types of self-defence require to be justified by necessity. Moreover, the requirement of exemplary conduct on the part of an accused means that if he does not retreat when he can he is not entitled to succeed in his plea of self-defence at all, so that if he is entitled to succeed the situation must have been indistinguishable from that in the felon cases.

If these two types are indistinguishable, which rules are to apply — the rules of strict necessity said to apply to self-defence in a quarrel, or the less strict rules said to apply to self-defence against a felon? It appears from the examples given by Hume that the strict rules are to be applied in all cases. It seems as if in talking of defence against a felon Hume was carried away by his sympathy for the innocent man who when attacked by felons stands up and defends himself, but that when he came to actual cases and examples he fell back on the principle of necessity. He gives the following example when discussing the rule that a man may not kill in self-defence unless escape is impossible — one of the requirements of necessity — "One, for instance, is assaulted at mid-day, on the street, where he may easily retire, and find shelter among the bystanders; but instead of doing so, he deliberately waits to receive the onset, and will not give back",[35] and says that such a man is not acting in justifiable self-defence. It seems, therefore, that the man surprised on the highway by

---

[31] Hume, i, 217.

[32] *ibid.* 222.

[33] *ibid.*

[34] *ibid.* 223. Hume seems to regard this type of self-defence more in the nature of a mitigatory excuse than a justification; for example, he does not allow that third parties have a right to kill to prevent the death of one of the parties to a quarrel although they have such a right where there is a felonious attack: Hume, i, 218.

[35] Hume, i, 226.

night is entitled to stand on his defence, not because of any natural right to kill a foul criminal, but simply because he has no reasonable chance of escaping.

Hume's insistence on the complete innocence of the accused thus means that he does not recognise any right of defence where the accused started the quarrel, and means in effect that he does not allow self-defence in a quarrel despite the fact that this is the title he gives to a section of his treatment of self-defence. Hume takes his rejection of self-defence in a quarrel so far as to hold that a man who tweaks the nose of another is not entitled to defend himself if that other retaliates by running at him with a drawn sword.[36]

A Humean theory

From the above critique of Hume's treatment of self-defence there **24.07** emerges a simple and consistent theory. A man is entitled to kill an assailant in order to save life or chastity, when he reasonably apprehends that these are in danger, where there is no other way of averting the danger, and where the person whose life is endangered is in no way to blame for the situation. The plea thus becomes one of necessity, and the only problem, a problem not discussed by Hume, is whether a legal system (as envisaged by him[37]) which refuses to allow the plea of necessity in circumstances of physical necessity can allow it in circumstances of self-defence. The answer which Hume would have given would be that it can, and that self-defence is accepted by the law as a defence because of the innocence of the accused and, conversely, the guilt of the victim. As Hall says, "In self-defense, the defender injures the creator and embodiment of the evil situation; in necessity, he harms a person who was in no way responsible for the imminent danger, one who, indeed, might himself have been imperilled by it."[38] One of the principal difficulties in the case of physical necessity is that of determining which of a number of innocent lives is to be sacrificed.[39] In self-defence this problem does not arise since one of the persons involved is to blame for the situation. The point is not that anyone who commits a crime forfeits his right to the protection of the law but that, once the stage of necessity has been reached, and only then, the law is able to resolve the impasse by reference to the legal guilt or innocence of the parties involved.

---

[36] Hume, i, 233. In *Lieutenant Robinson* (1758) Maclaurin's Cases, 181, No. 68, R. twisted a fellow-officer's nose after having suffered a prolonged course of verbal provocation from him. The latter aimed a blow with a poker, and then ran at R. with a sword, and R. killed him. R. was acquitted on a combined defence of accident, absence of malice and self-defence. Hume concedes that on the whole there was not much injustice done, but takes the view that this was not a case of justifiable self-defence, because R. started the fight: Hume, i, 233.

[37] See Vol. I, para. 13.20. Modern Scots law recognises a limited necessity defence which shares many of the rules for self-defence and which may be a species of a wider genus of necessity (see Vol. I, paras 13.21–13.22). It is not clear, however, if that recently recognised limited defence is applicable to murder charges (see Vol. I, p.516, n.94): if it is not so applicable, that would form at least one distinct difference in law between it and self-defence albeit that both defences are branches of the genus of necessity.

[38] Hall, pp. 435–436.

[39] See Vol. I, para. 13.11.

THE LAW SINCE HUME

Self-defence against a felon

24.08	Hume himself recognised the absence of authority for his distinction between the two types of defence and said of his favourable treatment of defence against a felon, "These observations I only offer as my own sentiments which are not indeed contradicted by anything on record, but do not rest on any judgment of our Supreme Court."[40] He notes also that lawyers in Scotland and abroad deal mostly with quarrel situations.[41]

Burnett[42] and Alison[43] both retain Hume's distinction between defence against a felon and defence in a quarrel but offer no examples of the former other than *Symons*[44] of which they both disapprove. Burnett says in terms at one point that the rules of necessity apply to all cases of self-defence,[45] and Alison stresses the difficulty of succeeding in a plea of self-defence in any situation at all.[46]

In *John Forrest*[47] the accused was a foreman in charge of some buildings which housed women servants. He killed one of a group of intruders who were trying to break into the women's quarters, and pleaded both self-defence and accident. This was a case of defence against a felonious attack, but Lord Moncreiff directed the jury in general terms applicable to any form of self-defence, telling them that "if you think . . . he fired *intentionally*, you will then consider whether he had reason to fear immediate danger to his own life, or to the safety of those in his house."[48]

In *Robert McAnally*[49] the accused killed his father, and the jury were directed that in order to succeed in his plea of self-defence he must show that what he did was absolutely necessary and that escape was impossible, although there was no suggestion that the accused was to blame for the initial situation which arose out of an attack by the father on the accused's mother and then on the accused himself.[50]

Macdonald disregards defence against a felon entirely, and sets out the quarrel rules as applicable to all cases of self-defence,[51] and this almost certainly is the modern law.

---

[40] Hume, i, 218.

[41] *ibid*. He does, however, refer in a note to the case of *John Symons* (1810) Hume, i, 228; Burnett, p.43. Symons was attacked in the street by the deceased who struck him with his fists and feet. Symons drew his sword and the deceased ran off, but Symons pursued and killed him. Hume explains Symons' acquittal on the ground that this was a case of defence against a felon. The case is not, however, clear authority for this view. Symons pleaded self-defence, provocation, the right to pursue and apprehend the deceased, and that he acted under such great perturbation of mind as to be almost insensible of what he did; and his acquittal proceeded on both the first and last of these pleas: Burnett, p.45. Burnett himself doubts whether self-defence was justifiable in the circumstances.

[42] At pp. 39 *et seq.*

[43] Alison, i, 133 *et seq.*

[44] *supra.*

[45] Burnett, p.42.

[46] Alison, i, 100.

[47] (1837) 1 Swin. 404.

[48] At 418.

[49] (1836) 1 Swin. 210.

[50] Lord Mackenzie at 217–218.

[51] Macdonald, p.106.

Self-defence in a quarrel

It is impossible to trace the development of the law on this matter in **24.09**
view of the almost complete absence of reported cases prior to 1938.[52]

In *H.M. Advocate v. Kizileviczius*[53] the evidence was that the accused
had punched his father after picking a quarrel with him about an alleged
prior assault by the father on the accused's mother, and that when the
father made to pick up a poker the accused hit him several times with an
iron instead of trying to keep the poker from him. After a little the
father approached the accused with a flat-iron in his hand and threatened him, and the accused took the iron from his father and beat him to
death with it. This can be seen as a case of self-defence in a quarrel
initiated by the accused (and in fact the accused was convicted of
culpable homicide), but Lord Jamieson directed the jury that if they
thought the accused had acted in necessary self-defence they could
acquit him.[54] There was no suggestion that the accused was not entitled
to plead self-defence at all because of his part in the events leading up to
the death.

In *Robertson and Donoghue*[55] a plea of self-defence was advanced by a **24.10**
man charged with robbing and killing a café proprietor. He failed in his
plea, but on appeal Lord Justice-General Normand said:

> "[A]lthough an accused person may commit the first assault and
> may be, in general, the assailant, he is not thereby necessarily
> excluded from a plea of self-defence. If the victim, in protecting
> himself or his property, uses violence altogether disproportionate to
> the need, and employs savage excess, then the assailant is in his turn
> entitled to defend himself against the assault by his victim . . . in a
> case in which there is a struggle, the right of self-defence may be
> invoked by the original assailant as well as by a man who was at the
> outset his victim . . . [but] the victim of an assault who in resisting
> the assailant begins to overpower him does not become merely by
> the success of his resistance an assailant in his turn."[56]

Lord Moncrieff said that "such an intruder has only a duty to withdraw
and can rarely have occasion for self-defence".[57] But whatever the
qualifications — "savage" excess is probably not a higher standard than
the "cruel" excess standard applied in other cases of self-defence, in
which there is also a duty to withdraw[58] — the case is authority for the
view that a plea of self-defence may succeed in such situations. Macdonald's repetition of Hume's requirement that the accused should not
have started the trouble[59] cannot stand with either *Kizileviczius*[60] or

---

[52] In 1826, however, in *David Landale* (1826) Shaw 163 it was held that in some
circumstances the reluctant partner in a duel might succeed in a plea of self-defence,
despite Hume's outright refusal to countenance the plea in cases of duelling: Hume,
i, 230–232.

[53] 1938 J.C. 60.

[54] At 62.

[55] High Court at Edinburgh, Aug. 1945; High Court of Justiciary on Appeal, Oct. 1945,
unrep'd.

[56] Transcript of Opinions of Court, 10.

[57] *ibid.* 21.

[58] *H.M. Advocate v. Doherty*, 1954 J.C. 1; *Fenning v. H.M. Advocate*, 1985 S.C.C.R. 219,
Lord Cameron at 225; *Low v. H.M. Advocate*, 1993 S.C.C.R. 493, L.J.C. Ross at 507B.

[59] Macdonald, p.106.

[60] 1938 J.C. 60, *supra* para. 24.09.

Robertson,[61] and it is now clear that it is the latter two authorities which represent the modern law.[62] It is not, therefore, necessarily destructive of a plea of self-defence that the accused started or provoked the trouble which ended in the death of the victim at the accused's hands; and as Lord Justice-General Hope stated in *Burns v. H.M. Advocate*[63]:

> "The question whether the plea of self-defence is available depends, in a case of this kind [*i.e.*, where the accused starts or provokes the trouble], on whether the retaliation is such that the accused is entitled then to defend himself. That depends on whether the violence offered by the victim was so out of proportion to the accused's own actings as to give rise to the reasonable apprehension that he was in immediate danger from which he had no means of escape, and whether the violence which he used was no more than was necessary to preserve his own life or protect himself from serious injury."

If, therefore, the accused was in danger of his life by reason of an unjustified assault — however much provoked — at the time of the fatal blow and could save himself only by killing the "assailant", he is entitled to succeed in his plea of self-defence; and where there is a single incident during which blows are exchanged and which concludes with the accused inflicting a fatal injury on the deceased, the incident should be treated as a whole for the purpose of determining whether the accused acted in self-defence.[64] Consequently, all that is left of the distinction between self-defence against a felon and self-defence in a quarrel is that a jury will no doubt regard the plea most favourably if the accused was defending himself against a felon, and least favourably if he himself was a robber who killed his victim.

The rules

24.11   Homicide in self-defence is justifiable only in the following circumstances:

(1) The danger must be imminent.[65] It is not self-defence for A to kill B now because he is sure that if he does not, B will kill him in a day or even in an hour. B's attack must have already begun, or at least be on the point of beginning, before A is entitled to retaliate in self-defence.

---

[61] *supra.*

[62] See *Boyle v. H.M. Advocate*, 1992 S.C.C.R. 824, where the opinions of Lord Jamieson in *Kizileviczius* (*supra*) and the Lord Justice-General in *Robertson and Donoghue* (*supra*) were followed, and *Burns v. H.M. Advocate*, 1995 S.C.C.R. 532, which confirmed the correctness of the law as set out in *Boyle* and expressly disapproved the contrary statements in Macdonald at p.106, and Hume at i, 223.

[63] 1995 S.C.C.R. 532, at 536C.

[64] *Surman v. H.M. Advocate*, 1988 S.L.T. 371. In practice, an accused's defence is often a mixture of self-defence and accident, in the sense that the victim hit the accused and the accused defended himself but never meant to inflict the injury which killed the victim; the two defences of self-defence and accident are theoretically contradictory, but are not necessarily mutually exclusive in practice: see *Surman*, *supra*; *cf. McKenzie v. H.M. Advocate*, 1983 S.L.T. 220; *H.M. Advocate v. Woods*, 1972 S.L.T. (Notes) 77.

[65] Hume, i, 224; Alison, i, 132; *H.M. Advocate v. Kizileviczius*, 1938 J.C. 60, Lord Jamieson at 62; *Owens v. H.M. Advocate*, 1946 J.C. 119, L.J.-G. Normand at 125; *H.M. Advocate v. Doherty*, 1954 J.C. 1, Lord Keith at 4.

(2) A must have no means of escape or retreat.[66] This rule probably **24.12** applies in all cases today except perhaps in that of an officer of law executing his duty.[67] A person attacked by a felon is probably therefore not now entitled to stand his ground and defend himself if escape is open. Self-defence in a duel is probably excluded by this requirement.[68] The means of escape or retreat must be of a kind the accused can reasonably be expected to adopt. He cannot be deprived of the right of self-defence because he declined to jump out of a high window even if the ground below was soft.

They must be such as not themselves to increase his danger[69] — a man is not bound to expose himself to a stab in the back, for example, and it is submitted that Lord Keith's suggestion in *H.M. Advocate v. Doherty*[70] that an accused should retreat down a stair rather than stand and defend himself is too broadly expressed in that the circumstances (for example, the narrowness, steepness, and state of lighting of the staircase) would have to be weighed before self-defence was excluded by virtue of the accused's failure to take such a route of escape. As Hume says, "though the party ought to retire from the assault, yet this is always said under provision, that he can do so without materially increasing his own danger, or putting himself to an evident disadvantage with respect to his defence: As if he have to retire down a dark or steep staircase, or by passages better known to the invader than to him."[71] It is interesting in this connection to note the judgement of Edmund Davies L.J. in *R. v. McInnes*[72]:

> "We prefer the view expressed by the full court of Australia that a failure to retreat is only an *element* in the consideration upon which the reasonableness of an accused's conduct is to be judged (see *Palmer v. The Queen* [1971] 2 W.L.R. 831, 840) or, as it is put in *Smith and Hogan Criminal Law*, 2nd ed. (1969), p. 231[73]: '. . . simply a factor to be taken into account in deciding whether it was necessary to use force, and whether the force used was reasonable.'
>
> The modern law on the topic was, in our respectful view, accurately set out in *Reg. v. Julien* [1969] 1 W.L.R. 839, 843 by Widgery L.J. in the following terms:
>
> > 'It is not, as we understand it, the law that a person threatened must take to his heels and run in the dramatic way suggested by Mr. McHale; but what is necessary is that he should demonstrate by his actions that he does not want to fight. He must demonstrate that he is prepared to temporise and disengage and

---

[66] *Robt McAnally* (1836) 1 Swin. 210, Lord Mackenzie at 217; *H.M. Advocate v. Kizileviczius*, 1938 J.C. 60, Lord Jamieson at 62; *H.M. Advocate v. Doherty*, 1954 J.C., Lord Keith at 5; Macdonald, p.106.

[67] See *supra*, para. 23.35.

[68] *H.M. Advocate v. Doherty*, *supra*; Hume, i, 230. It is also excluded on policy grounds: *Smart v. H.M. Advocate*, 1975 J.C. 30, *infra*, para. 29.39.

[69] See E.M. Burchell and P.M.A. Hunt, *South African Criminal Law and Procedure* (3rd ed., 1997), Vol. I, *General Principles of Criminal Law* (by J.M. Burchell), p.77; *cf.* J. Burchell and J. Milton, *Principles of Criminal Law* (2nd ed., 1997, Juta and Co.), pp. 139–141.

[70] 1954 J.C. 1, at p. 4.

[71] Hume, i, 229.

[72] [1971] 1 W.L.R. 1600, 1607F-H.

[73] The same statement appears in the current (9th) edition of 1999, at p.257.

perhaps to make some physical withdrawal; and that that is necessary as a feature of the justification of self-defence is true, in our opinion, whether the charge is a homicide charge or something less serious.' "

24.13   (3) The retaliation must not be excessive, that is to say the accused is entitled to use only such force as is necessary to preserve his own life.[74] The measure of retaliation is not an exact one.[75] Lord Keith said in *H.M. Advocate v. Doherty*[76]: "You do not need an exact proportion of injury and retaliation; it is not a matter that you weigh in too fine scales . . . Some allowance must be made for the excitement or the state of fear or the heat of blood".[77] An assault with fists will not justify retaliation with weapons unless in exceptional circumstances, but an assault with a hammer, for example, may well justify retaliation with a bayonet. It is a question of degree to be decided on the facts of each case. For example, "if A see B on the ground at some distance off, and C with his knife uplifted to stab him, A is justified in shooting C, although he might not be so were he close enough to grasp C's hand and stop the blow."[78]

There can be very few cases in which it is necessary to kill an assailant rather than render him harmless in some less drastic way, but what is at issue is not so much the fatal result of the accused's actings as the seriousness of the actual assault made by him on the deceased. The "test case" for self-defence, and the one in the light of which the right to kill in self-defence must be considered, is that in which B endangers A's life, or any other value he is entitled to defend, and A deliberately kills B in order to preserve that value. Self-defence is a defence to a charge of intentional homicide,[79] and if A decides that it is necessary to kill B he will be entitled to succeed in a plea of self-defence if his decision was at all reasonable.[80]

24.14   In most cases, however, A does not make up his mind to kill B; he merely assaults B in order to defend himself from an assault by B which itself may not be homicidal in intent. In such a case the important question is not whether the death of B was justifiable, but whether A's assault itself was justifiable. What is measured is not B's death against A's danger, but the violence used by A against the violence threatened or used by B.[81] It is sometimes said that A may be entitled to kill to defend himself against serious injury, such as demembration,[82] but this is

---

[74] Macdonald, p.106; *H.M. Advocate v. Kizileviczius*, 1938 J.C. 60; *H.M. Advocate v. Doherty*, 1954 J.C. 1; Hume, i, 227; Alison, i, 134. In *Burns v. H.M. Advocate*, 1995 S.C.C.R. 532, at 536C, L.J.-G. Hope included the alternative of protecting oneself from serious injury: on the question whether this amounts to a lower standard, see para. 24.14, *infra*.

[75] *Kizileviczius, supra; Doherty, supra*.

[76] *Doherty, supra*, at 4.

[77] At 4–5. *Cf. Palmer v. R.* [1971] A.C. 814, PC, 832B: "If a jury thought that in a moment of unexpected anguish a person attacked had only done what he honestly and instinctively thought was necessary that would be most potent evidence that only reasonable defensive action had been taken."

[78] Macdonald, pp. 106–107.

[79] *Robt McAnally* (1836) 1 Swin 210, Lord Mackenzie at 217; *Drury v. H.M. Advocate*, Feb. 2, 2001, High Court of Justiciary on Appeal (five judges), unrep'd, L.J.G. Rodger at para. 10 of the transcript of his opinion.

[80] *cf. Owens v. H.M. Advocate*, 1946 J.C. 119.

[81] See *Brady v. H.M. Advocate*, 1986 S.C.C.R. 191, L.J.-C. Ross at 199.

[82] *Crawford v. H.M. Advocate*, 1950 J.C. 67, Lord Keith at 71; *cf. Burns v. H.M. Advocate*, 1995 S.C.C.R. 532, L.J.-G. Hope at 536C.

not quite accurate. Threat of serious injury is regarded as justifying homicide because if B's attack is so serious as to involve such harm A will be entitled to retaliate to the same degree, and that being so will be entitled to use force to a degree which may prove fatal, particularly as he is given the benefit of the rule that his retaliation need not balance B's violence exactly.[83]

If A's assault on B is justified by B's assault or by his apprehension of B's assault on him, A is not guilty of homicide if B dies as a result. If, for example, B punches A, and A retaliates by punching B, A is not guilty of homicide if his punch kills B who has a weak heart or falls and breaks his skull: in such a case A has caused B's death in the course of a "lawful" act, and provided his retaliation was reasonable no question of "criminal negligence" can arise, so that A is guilty neither of murder nor of culpable homicide.

The requirement that retaliation must not be excessive means also that A must not continue his attack on B after the danger to himself has passed, again giving due allowance for the heat of the moment.[84] Modern authority suggests, however, that the measure of excessive retaliation is whether or not the accused's retaliation exhibits "cruel excess"; consequently, references to "the heat of the moment" are merely illustrative and need not be included in a charge to a jury.[85]

If A does exceed the due measure of retaliation because of the violence or duration of his attack on B his behaviour ceases to be justifiable and B is in turn entitled to retaliate in self-defence.[86]

Error. If A believes that he is endangered by B he is entitled to defend **24.15** himself against B, and he does not lose his right of self-defence if in fact he was not in danger, provided that his belief was not unreasonable.[87]

What may be defended

The modern tendency to concentrate on necessity and on the passages **24.16** in Hume which deal with self-defence in a quarrel encourages the view that homicide is justifiable only in defence of life. The present position is not altogether clear, but it is probably the law that homicide is justifiable only to save life or to prevent rape. It is true that in *Crawford*[88] Lord Keith included resistance to a housebreaker as one of the classic instances of self-defence,[89] but it is extremely unlikely that homicide in defence of property would be considered justifiable in modern times, and it is submitted that Macdonald is correct in saying that, "It is personal danger, not patrimonial loss, which justifies homicide."[90]

---

[83] *cf.* the assault case of *Whyte v. H.M. Advocate*, 1996 S.C.C.R. 575, where it was held that the accused's later admission, that he had hit the victim with excessive force, was not considered fatal *per se* to a plea of self-defence, since allowance should be made for errors of judgment at the time — it being difficult in the heat of the moment to determine what degree of retaliation would have been sufficient in the circumstances.

[84] Hume, i, 228; *cf. H.M. Advocate v. Graham*, 1958 S.L.T. 167; *R. v. Clegg* [1995] A.C. 482, HL.

[85] *Fenning v. H.M. Advocate*, 1985 J.C. 76.

[86] *Robertson and Donoghue*, High Court at Edinburgh, Aug. 1945, High Court of Justiciary on Appeal, Oct, 1945, unrep'd.

[87] *Owens v. H.M. Advocate*, 1946 J.C. 119, see Vol. I, para. 9.30; *Jones v. H.M. Advocate*, 1989 S.C.C.R. 726.

[88] 1950 J.C. 67.

[89] At 71.

[90] Macdonald, p.107.

24.17   This view is supported by the case of *McCluskey v. H.M. Advocate*.[91] The accused was charged with murder and pleaded self-defence. He said that he had assaulted the deceased while resisting an attempt by the latter to commit sodomy upon him. The trial judge refused to direct the jury that if they accepted the accused's story they could acquit him on the ground of self-defence. The accused was convicted of culpable homicide and appealed, but the Appeal Court upheld the trial judge. Lord Russell set out danger to life as a necessary condition for a successful plea of self-defence, and Lord Justice-General Clyde quoted Hume's remarks on the necessity of danger to life, made with reference to self-defence in a quarrel, as applying to the instant case which was clearly a case of resistance to a felony. In the course of his opinion Lord Clyde said:

> "Murder is still one of the most serious crimes in this country, for no man has a right at his own hand deliberately to take the life of another. Indeed it is because of this principle of the sanctity of human life that the plea of self-defence arises. Just because life is so precious to all of us, so our law recognises that an accused man may be found not guilty, even of the serious crime of murder, if his own life has been endangered by an assailant . . . But I can see no justification at all for extending this defence to a case where there is no apprehension of danger to the accused's life, and indeed, very little evidence of any real physical injury done to the accused himself, but merely a threat, pushed no doubt quite far, but none the less still only a threat, of an attack on the appellant's virtue . . ."[92]

> ". . . where an attack by an accused person on another man has taken place and where the object of the attack has been to ward off an assault upon him it is essential that the attack should be made to save the accused's life before the plea of self-defence can succeed."[93]

It is true that the existence of a right to kill in defence of property is not inconsistent with the last sentence quoted, and that the court did not refer in their judgments to the authorities quoted to them in support of the view that homicide can be justified if committed in defence of property, or, more generally, in the prevention of a felony,[94] but it seems implicit in Lord Clyde's language that self-defence can be justified only by danger to life. In any event, it seems impossible that a twentieth-century legal system should allow a man to kill to defend his property but not to defend himself against sodomy.[95]

Lord Clyde specifically allowed for the continued operation of the plea of self-defence by a woman resisting rape, saying that rape, unlike sodomy, required a complete absence of consent on the part of the woman, and it appears that the exception for rape was thought of as being a corollary of the classic definition of rape with its requirement of resistance to the utmost by the victim.

---

[91] 1959 J.C. 39. *McCluskey* was followed in *Elliott v. H.M. Advocate*, 1987 S.C.C.R. 278.
[92] At 42.
[93] At 43.
[94] Hume, i, 218–222; Alison, i, 136; *Crawford v. H.M. Advocate*, 1950 J.C. 67, Lord Keith at 71.
[95] Self-defence against sodomy is recognised in South Africa: E.M. Burchell and P.M.A. Hunt, *South African Criminal Law and Procedure* (3rd ed. 1997), Vol. I, *General Principles of Criminal Law* (by J.M. Burchell), p.75.

If, then, rape is put on one side as a unique exception, the result of **24.18**
McCluskey,[96] is that homicide can be justified only by the necessity of
saving life from an unlawful attack. If this is so, then Scots law is
probably in line with Article 2[97] of the European Convention on Human
Rights which, as incorporated into domestic law by Schedule 1, Part I of
the Human Rights Act 1998, provides:

> "(1) Everyone's right to life shall be protected by law. No one shall
> be deprived of his life intentionally save in the execution of a
> sentence of a court following his conviction of a crime for which this
> penalty is provided by law.
>
> (2) Deprivation of life shall not be regarded as inflicted in
> contravention of this Article when it results from the use of force
> which is no more than absolutely necessary—
> (a) in defence of any person from unlawful violence:
> (b) in order to effect a lawful arrest or to prevent the escape of a
>   person lawfully detained:
> (c) in action lawfully taken for the purpose of quelling a riot or
>   insurrection."

The phrase "defence of any person from unlawful violence" could be
read to include the case of a man resisting sodomy or a woman resisting
rape, but it clearly excludes the defence of property.

---

[96] 1959 J.C. 39.
[97] See, *e.g.*, the interpretation of the Article and the exceptions in Art. 2(2) offered by
the European Court of Human Rights in *McCann and Ors v. United Kingdom*, 1996 221
E.H.R.R. 97.

CHAPTER 25

VOLUNTARY CULPABLE HOMICIDE

Burnett, primarily reflecting views prior to the nineteenth century, **25.01** observes: "*Culpable Homicide* is properly that which is committed through some blame, negligence, or want of due precaution on the part of the slayer, but without any intention to kill, and is contradistinguished from a homicide *preceded by that intent*, or by a purpose of *great bodily harm*."[1] He also refers to a judicial observation[2] by Lord Justice-Clerk McQueen in 1791 to the effect that culpable homicide "means homicide *culpa lata commissum*; instances of which he gave of one riding violently through a public street, or carelessly throwing a stone from a height, and thereby killing; but that a slaughter committed *animo occidendi*, or on provocation, was a *felonious*, not a *culpable* killing — was the effect properly of *dole*, not of CULPA."[3] Burnett continues: "Notwithstanding of this opinion, the Jury, in that case, returned a verdict of Culpable Homicide; and the practice . . . for some years preceding, and in many cases since, while it has acknowledged the term *culpable* applied to homicide, as a proper *nomen juris*, has sustained its application to cases of slaughter in heat of passion, and in sudden provocation."[4] In this way, it seems that the position was attained whereby the crime of culpable, that is to say negligent, homicide was enlarged in scope to include some intentional killings which should not be regarded as murders. It is proposed to refer to such killings as "voluntary culpable homicides".[5]

---

[1] Burnett, p.26.

[2] Case of *McGhie*, 1791: Burnett, pp. 26–27.

[3] Burnett, p.27.

[4] *ibid.*

[5] This title may also be used to cover recklessly caused killings where there is an absence of the wickedness which would enable them to be classed as murders; but the title is then less apt, and its use in such circumstances may be rendered doubtful by the decision in *Drury, infra.* "Involuntary culpable homicide" would thus be a convenient way of classifying any killings which fall more appropriately within Burnett's account of "proper" culpable homicide: see, *e.g.*, *Morton v. H.M. Advocate*, 1986 S.L.T. 622 (Note), where in a murder case, the jury, having returned a verdict of "culpable homicide without evil intent", clarified their verdict as meaning "although the accused struck the blow he did not mean to kill". For involuntary culpable homicide, see Chap. 26, *infra*.

The recent case of *Drury v. H.M. Advocate*, 2001 S.L.T. 1013 (five judges), may be thought to have cast doubts on the validity of the distinction between voluntary and involuntary culpable homicide, by providing (see opinion of L.J.-G. Rodger, at para. [13]) that culpable homicide covers the killing of human beings in all circumstances short of murder "where the criminal law attaches a relevant measure of blame to the person who kills." That measure of blame may be obvious in cases of negligent (or reckless) killing, or in killings which result from an assault which was not homicidal in intent; but in killings where death was intended — as in most cases of provoked killings — additional argument is necessary (and is provided in *Drury*: see, *e.g.*, L.J.-G.'s opinion, at paras [31] and [32]) to explain why, if murder is ruled out, there should be sufficient blame to make culpable homicide applicable (*cf.*, *e.g.*, intentional killing in self-defence, which is not criminal at all). In short, *Drury* itself can provide justification for a distinction to be drawn between types of culpable homicide, according as the killings in question were intended or non-intended. In any event, the distinction, it is submitted, remains a useful analytical tool.

The initial recognition of "voluntary culpable homicide" in relation to provoked killings was probably the result of the fact that murder at the time carried the fixed penalty of death and of the sentiment that the man who killed under provocation did not merit such a severe penalty as the deliberate cold-blooded murderer. But during the nineteenth century, the approach to voluntary culpable homicide became a much more general one. Murder was thought of as a crime requiring a particular degree of wickedness or "malice", and where this was absent killing, even if done intentionally, was not murder but culpable homicide. Diminished responsibility and intoxication, for example, were not so much independent "defences", as examples of factors which negatived murderous malice, and so reduced the crime to culpable homicide.[6]

During the twentieth century, however, the conceptual analysis of voluntary culpable homicide altered significantly, probably due to the development of the idea of *mens rea* as a specific intent rather than a general wickedness of disposition. In particular, the *mens rea* of murder became settled in the form set out by Macdonald as follows: "Murder is constituted by any wilful act causing the destruction of life, whether intended to kill, or displaying such wicked recklessness as to imply a disposition depraved enough to be regardless of consequences."[7] This having become the accepted definition, it was plain that those who killed intentionally would have to be convicted of murder unless, for example, provocation or diminished responsibility was involved and could be used to "reduce the quality of the crime" from murder to culpable homicide.[8] Thus, provocation and diminished responsibility were taken to be partial defences, in the sense that they did not, if successfully established, lead to acquittal but rather achieved mitigation of sentence — which would be impossible in the case of a charge of murder unless a verdict of guilty of culpable homicide were to be returned.[9]

---

[6] see *Alex. Dingwall* (1867) 5 Irv. 466, Lord Deas at 479–480; *John Middleby* or *Tierney* (1875) 3 Couper 152, Lord Ardmillan at 166; *H.M. Advocate v. McDonald* (1890) 2 White 517, L.J.-C. Macdonald at 524; *H.M. Advocate v. Kane* (1892) 3 White 386, L.J.-C. Macdonald at 388–390. But see now *Brennan v. H.M. Advocate*, 1977 J.C. 38: Vol. I, para. 12.12 *et seq*.

[7] Macdonald, p.89.

[8] This was almost invariably the way in which the effect of such pleas was described: see, *e.g.*, *Hillan v. H.M. Advocate*, 1937 J.C. 53 (a case of assault — but see L.J.-C. Aitchison at 57, "Provocation is frequently a plea in reduction of the quality of the crime, as where it is sufficient to reduce the crime of murder to culpable homicide."); *H.M. Advocate v. Hill*, 1941 J.C. 59, Lord Patrick (to the jury) at 61; *Crawford v. H.M. Advocate*, 1950 J.C. 67, L.J.-G. Cooper at 69; *Stobbs v. H.M. Advocate*, 1983 S.C.C.R. 190, Lord Cowie (to the jury) at 199; *Thomson v. H.M. Advocate*, 1985 S.C.C.R. 448, L.J.-C. Wheatley at 457; *Graham v. H.M. Advocate*, 1987 S.C.C.R. 20, Lord Cullen (to the jury) at 22; *Lennon v. H.M. Advocate*, 1991 S.C.C.R. 611, L.J.-G. Hope at 614F; *Low v. H.M. Advocate*, 1993 S.C.C.R. 493, Lord Abernethy (to the jury) at 495G; *H.M. Advocate v. McKean*, 1996 S.C.C.R. 402, Lord MacLean (to the jury) at 403D. See also Report of the Select Committee on Murder and Life Imprisonment, H.L. Paper 78 (Sess. 1988–89), Vol. III, p.385, "Memorandum by the Scottish Law Commission", para. 6 (2nd text para., p.386, there being no extant para. 7); p.405, "Memorandum by the Crown Office" at para. 6, p.466; "Memorandum by the Lord Justice General and the Lord Justice Clerk", at para. 2. *Cf.*, however, Lord Mayfield's charge to the jury in *Fenning v. H.M. Advocate*, 1985 S.C.C.R. 219, at 220, where he indicates that if the deceased's conduct was so violent and threatening as to cause the accused to lose his self-control, there would be an absence of wicked intent or wicked recklessness, and that provocation would thus deprive the accused's acts of the element of murderous intent.

[9] Murder carried a capital sentence in all cases until 1957: see the Homicide Act 1957, s.1. Since 1965 (see the Murder (Abolition of Death Penalty) Act 1965) the fixed penalty for murder has been life imprisonment: see now the 1995 Act, s.205.

In the recent case of *Drury v. H.M. Advocate*,[10] a return to nineteenth century analysis is evident. One of the essentials which a jury must determine in a murder case is that the Crown has established the necessary *mens rea*, which, *pace* Macdonald,[11] is now either a *wicked* intention to kill or wicked recklessness. Provocation is a factor to which, in an appropriate case, a jury must have regard in deciding if the *mens rea* has been established, in the sense that provocation is inconsistent with that wickedness which murder requires. The Court in *Drury* appears to suggest that there are other factors which may show an absence of wickedness, and states that it is incorrect analysis to consider that provocation or such other factors operate only once all the elements of murder have been established and then in order to reduce that crime to culpable homicide.[12] The Court in *Drury* mentions diminished responsibility as a factor similar in function to provocation,[13] but does not enlarge upon what other factors may relevantly be pled. It is uncertain, therefore, whether there is a finite number of these, or whether, since the matter is at basis concerned with the determination of wickedness in intentional killing,[14] any factor which may be inconsistent with the establishment of wickedness will suffice.

If the latter is correct, then self-induced intoxication, for example, may be considered to have a bearing on the matter, as indeed was stated in 1890 by Lord Justice-Clerk Macdonald: "while drunkenness is no excuse, yet if the means adopted were not of themselves likely to lead to bad results, and if there was no malice aforethought here, then the fact that the man was in a drunken state may be considered in determining the question between murder and culpable homicide."[15] To admit self-induced intoxication as a relevant factor would, however, be inconsistent with the reasoning of, and public policy considerations discussed in, the seven judge decision of *Brennan v. H.M. Advocate*[16]; it would also sit uneasily with the treatment of self-induced intoxication in the five judge decision of *Ross v. H.M. Advocate*.[17]

The state of the law at the close of the twentieth century was generally accepted as being of this order: that there were factors which, as a matter of Crown Office discretion rather than *ius scriptum*, were

---

[10] 2001 S.L.T. 1013 (five judges).

[11] See passage from Macdonald, p.89, quoted above.

[12] 2001 S.L.T. 1013 (five judges) opinion of L.J.-G. Rodger, at paras [10], [11], [17] and [18]; opinion of Lord Johnston, at para. [18]: *cf.* para [17]; opinion of Lord Nimmo Smith, at paras [2], [3] and [7]; opinion of Lord Mackay of Drumadoon, at paras [8] and [9]; opinion of Lord Cameron of Lochbroom, at para. [6]: *cf.*, para. [9]. The analysis criticised in *Drury* appears to be the one favoured by the English Law Commission in its Draft Code: see "A Criminal Code for England and Wales" (L.C. No. 177), H.C. No. 299 (1989), Vol. 1, Draft Code, cl. 58 (Provocation).

[13] No detailed analysis of diminished responsibility is, however, provided by the Court, since to do so would have been to proceed well beyond the scope of the instant appeal. See now, however, *Galbraith v. H.M. Advocate*, 2001 S.L.T. 953.

[14] Perhaps this is also so of the wickedness in "wicked recklessness", since *Drury* holds that there has to be wickedness in either branch of Macdonald's definition of murder: see opinion of L.J.-G. Rodger, at para. [11].

[15] *H.M. Advocate v. Macdonald* (1890) 2 White 517, at 523–524. See also L.J.-C. Macdonald in *H.M. Advocate v. Kane* (1892) 3 White 386, at 388–389: "where it comes to be a question of extent of the malice under which he was actuated in what he did — that is to say, whether the thing which he did and which cannot be excused, falls into a very bad category, or into a less bad category — that his state of intoxication might be taken into consideration."

[16] 1977 J.C. 38: see Vol. I, paras 12.12 *et seq.*

[17] 1991 J.C. 210: see Vol. I, paras 3.18 *et seq.*

considered to justify a charge of culpable homicide rather than murder in a case of intentional killing[18]; and there were also factors which as a matter of law would, if established, require the return of a culpable homicide verdict on a murder charge. The current position may be similar to that which pertained at the close of last century — although the theory by which the various factors operate to achieve a culpable homicide verdict will or may have changed as a result of *Drury*.[19]

The factors

25.02 A. *The unofficial factors*. There were, and probably still are, certain circumstances in which as a matter of practice only culpable homicide would be charged, although a charge of murder could properly have been brought, at least under the pre-*Drury*[20] law. These were:

(1) INFANTICIDE. Where a mother killed her child in circumstances which would in England have amounted to infanticide — that is to say, where the child was not more than a year old and the mother was suffering from the after-effects of birth or lactation.[21] In such cases, under the Macdonald definition of murder,[22] the crime would have been strictly murder unless the mother could have been shown to be of diminished responsibility; in fact it was always presumed by the Crown that she was of diminished responsibility, and such a presumption might have applied also in cases which did not fall strictly within the limits of the English legislation.[23] Presumably this factor is still a matter for Crown discretion, although the view might now be taken, under the post-*Drury* law, that the mother's acts could not show the wickedness which the *mens rea* of murder requires.

25.03 (2) EUTHANASIA. There are no reported cases of this. Lord Cooper's view was that it would be charged as culpable homicide,[24] Lord Keith's that there was no reason why it should not be charged as murder.[25]

---

[18] These are referred to below as "unofficial factors", and may be what the Home Advocate Depute, Mr G.W. Penrose, as he then was, had in mind when, in reply to a question whether an intentional killing for a merciful motive might be murder in Scotland, he said that that might be so but, "what one would do would be to take account of the full circumstances and ask questions under well-known categories": see Report of the Select Committee on Murder and Life Imprisonment, H.L. Paper 78, Sess. 1988–89, Vol. III, p.419, Q. 1696. Such factors are certainly what the Crown Office had in mind in its Memorandum, where it refers to the Lord Advocate's discretionary power to charge culpable homicide rather than murder in cases of mercy killing and suicide pacts — these being advanced simply as illustrations: *ibid.*, p.404.

[19] *Drury v. H.M. Advocate*, 2001 S.L.T. 1013 (five judges).

[20] *ibid.*

[21] Infanticide Act 1938.

[22] See para. 25.01, *supra*.

[23] R.C. Evid of Lord Cooper, Q. 5428.

[24] R.C. Evid. Q. 5428.

[25] *ibid.* Q. 5186. In *Dryden Alexander Brown*, High Court at Edinburgh, Dec. 1961, *unrepd.* the accused killed his wife, who had long been mentally ill and to whom he was said to be devoted, when she was due to return to a mental hospital, a prospect which she feared. He was charged only with culpable homicide, and pleaded guilty. Although the charge was based on diminished responsibility, the diminished responsibility was itself largely the result of concern over his wife's illness and the strain of looking after her, and the circumstances are comparable with those of euthanasia. He was sentenced to 15 months' imprisonment. That case is referred to in the Report of the Select Committee of the House of Lords on "Murder and Life Imprisonment", H.L. Paper 78 (Sess. 1988–89),

(3) SUICIDE PACTS. Lord Cooper expressed the view before the Royal **25.04** Commission on Capital Punishment that the survivor of a suicide pact would be charged only with culpable homicide[26] and the Crown Agent agreed.[27] It can therefore be accepted that that was (and probably still is) the position in practice, although in law the Royal Commission were correct when they said in their report that such a person would be guilty of murder if he had killed his partner.[28]

(4) NECESSITY. It is still open for the court to treat cases of murder **25.05** committed in circumstances of necessity or coercion as only culpable homicide, and it is likely that the Crown would have restricted, and will restrict, the charge in such cases.[29]

(5) IN EXCESS OF DUTY. If a soldier kills while on duty, or in what he **25.06** reasonably believes to be his duty, but the circumstances are not such as to justify his action because, for example, he acted hastily, or used more violence than was justifiable, he may be treated as guilty only of culpable homicide, unless the excess was gross.[30] The position of such an accused is comparable to that of someone who kills in circumstances of unjustifiable self-defence and who may be entitled to plead provocation.[31] Soldiers who kill in the execution of an unlawful order from a superior would probably also be charged only with culpable homicide.[32]

(6) OMISSIONS. There was a tendency to treat homicide by pure **25.07** omission as only culpable homicide. In *H.M. Advocate v. McPhee*[33] the victim was brutally assaulted and then left to die, but although the crime was charged as murder the jury convicted only of culpable homicide. Cases of child neglect or ill-treatment and desertion which result in death were, and probably still are, regarded as culpable homicide.[34]

B. *The legal factors*: **25.08**
    (1) *Diminished responsibility.*[35]

Vol. III, p.404, in the Memorandum by the Crown Office; the Memorandum notes, however, that the "circumstances of the Brown case fall to be contrasted with the situation where a person, who, in pursuance of his belief that euthanasia is justified, brings about or facilitates the death of a person suffering from terminal illness."

[26] R.C. Evid. Q. 5428.

[27] *ibid.* Q. 1888.

[28] R.C. para. 167.

[29] See Vol. I, paras 13.20–13.22, and 13.29.

[30] *cf. R. v. Clegg* [1995] 1 A.C. 482, HL.

[31] See *infra.* Examples of this type of homicide by soldiers are *Wm Dreghorn* (1807) Burnett 82; *Wm Inglis* (1810) Burnett 79; *Thos Whyte* (1814) Hume, i, 210.

[32] See *H.M. Advocate v. Sheppard*, 1941 J.C. 67; and see Vol. I, para. 13.34.

[33] 1935 J.C. 46.

[34] R.C. Evid., Crown Agent's memo., App. (a), para. 14; such homicides are, however, often involuntary.

[35] The account of diminished responsibility set out in Vol I, Chap. 11 has been significantly altered by the recent full-bench decision in *Galbraith v. H.M. Advocate (No. 2)*, 2001 S.L.T. 953. L.J.-G. Rodger, giving the opinion of the Court, confirmed that what has come to be referred to as "diminished responsibility" is a legal rather than a medical or psychological concept, and concluded that developments in (*e.g.*) psychiatric or psychological knowledge do not necessarily affect the law's view of that concept: see his Lordship's opinion at paras [22] and [43]. The Court re-examined the historical evolution of that concept and the terminology used to describe it, and concluded that L.J.-C. Alness in *H.M. Advocate v. Savage*, 1923 J.C. 49, at 50 (see Vol. I, para. 11.19) had not given to the jury in

(2) *Intoxication.*[36]
(3) *Provocation.*

PROVOCATION

25.09   Provocation is a plea in respect of which an intentional killer is convicted of culpable homicide and not murder since someone who kills under provocation does not kill out of wickedness, but "from sudden passion involving loss of self-control by reason of provocation."[37]

The provocation must be recent

25.10   To succeed in a plea of provocation A must have acted in hot blood, and while suffering from a loss of self-control caused by the provocation. The plea of provocation is not open where A acts out of deliberate revenge after he has had time to think things over. If B attacks A, and A

---

that case any definitive general account of the concept, but rather had furnished them with a number of specific examples of mental states which had been found sufficient for diminished responsibility by courts prior to 1923: see the opinion of the Court, at paras [25]–[28] and [29]–[32]; it followed, therefore, that the court in *Connelly v. H.M. Advocate*, 1990 J.C. 349, had been wrong to regard L.J.-C. Alness's directions to the jury in *Savage* as setting out rigid conditions which had to be met if a plea of diminished responsibility was to be successful: see *Galbraith*, opinion of the Court at para. [32]. The Court in *Galbraith* also concluded, after examining the prior case authorities, that it is not essential to the success of such a plea that the accused's mental state should be found to have been "bordering upon insanity" or that he should be found to have been suffering from "mental disease": see opinion of the Court at para. [39]; accordingly, the decision of the court in *Williamson v. H.M. Advocate*, 1994 J.C. 149, was incorrect on this point.

The Court in *Galbraith* (at para. [41]) also set out definitively the principle on which diminished responsibility is based when it is pled in answer to a murder charge: "In our law diminished responsibility applies in cases where, because the accused's ability to determine and control his actings [or omissions] is impaired as a result of some mental abnormality, his responsibility for any killing can properly be regarded as correspondingly reduced. The accused should, accordingly, be convicted of culpable homicide rather than of murder." It is clear, therefore, that a person found to be, or to have been at the material time, suffering from such impairment is entitled to mitigation of the penalty which would otherwise have been imposed on a normal offender, and that this dictates that a conviction for murder, with its fixed penalty, must give way to one for culpable homicide (see the opinion of the Court at paras [45] and [51]). It is also clear that the cause of the mental abnormality (which must be one recognised by medical science: see the summary of the Court's opinion, at para. [54]) is generally not material — save where the law for policy reasons dictates othewise (as it already does in relation to self-induced intoxication and psychopathic personality disorder: see *Brennan v. H.M. Advocate*, 1977 J.C. 38; *Carraher v. H.M. Advocate*, 1946 J.C. 108) — and that the degree of impairment effected by that abnormality must be substantial: see the opinion of the Court at para. [44]; *cf.* para [46].

The Court's opinion is confined to the effect of diminished responsibility on a charge of murder, and the views of the Court are expressed to be "tentative" and of the nature of "observations" which may need to be modified or refined in subsequent cases: see the Court's opinion at para. [40]; but the opinion makes it impossible to maintain that diminished responsibility is not a doctrine about responsibility (*cf.* Vol. I, paras 11.01, 11.02): mitigation is the eventual practical effect of a successful plea of diminished responsibility; but mitigation is achieved because of impaired responsibility.

[36] This category is now of very limited application: *Brennan v. H.M. Advocate;* Vol. I, paras 12.12 *et seq.*, esp. 12.21.
[37] *Att.-Gen. for Ceylon v. Perera* [1953] A.C. 200. Lord Goddard C.J. at 206. This is also now the plain view of Scots law: see *Drury v. H.M. Advocate*, 2001 S.L.T. 1013 (five judges). See also *Lee Chun-Chuen v. The Queen* [1963] A.C. 220; *Cmwth v. Webster* (1850) 5 Cush. 295, Sayre, 785, Shaw C.J. at 786–787; *Parker v. The Queen* [1964] A.C. 1369.

retaliates immediately, the plea may be open: it will not be open if A goes home and then returns and attacks B.[38]

Cumulative provocation. It is doubtful whether a long course of provoca- **25.11** tive conduct can found a successful plea of provocation, unless there is also some final act of provocation which, albeit because it follows on the earlier provocation and is the last straw, actually provokes a loss of control — it is not sufficient that it should merely provide an occasion for A to exact revenge for the deceased's prior provocation. The fact that the deceased had indulged in a course of provocative conduct may indeed in some circumstances militate against the plea of provocation, as showing that A had become so used to this type of behaviour that it no longer affected his self-control.[39] In *H.M. Advocate v. Hill*[40] the accused was a soldier who had obtained compassionate leave because he suspected his wife was committing adultery; he came home and met his wife and the suspected paramour; they confessed their adultery and he killed them. Lord Patrick directed the jury that he was entitled to succeed in his plea of provocation if he had not previously known of the adultery.[41] In *H.M. Advocate v. Callander*[42] the accused assaulted his wife and her lesbian paramour when he found them together, but he had known of the association for some time, and Lord Guthrie told the jury that if they thought "that the accused here was not acting under the influence of the discovery of his wife in a compromising situation . . ., but was merely acting under the influence of what he had known for a long time, then that would not amount to provocation."[43]

---

[38] Hume, i, 252; Burnett, pp. 17–18; Alison, i, 8; Anderson, p.150; Macdonald, p.94; *David Peter* (1807) Hume, i, 253; *Walter Redpath* (1810) Hume, i, 252; *James Macara* (1811) *ibid.; Francis Cockburn* (1828) Alison, i, 9 and 16; *Joseph and Maxwell Allison* (1838) 2 Swin. 167; *H.M. Advocate v. Hill*, 1941 J.C. 59, Lord Patrick (to the jury) at 62; *Drury v. H.M. Advocate*, 2001 S.L.T. 1013 (five judges) opinion of L.J.-G. Rodger, at para. [21].

[39] The comment has been made, under reference to *Thomson v. H.M. Advocate*, 1985 S.C.C.R. 448, that "a history of provocative acts, so far permitting a successful plea of provocation, may simply provide a motive for murder": Report of the Select Committee of the House of Lords on "Murder and Life Imprisonment", H.L. Paper 78, Vol. III, p.386, Memorandum of the Scottish Law Commission, at para. [7]. See also *Parr v. H.M. Advocate*, 1991 S.C.C.R. 180, L.J.-G. Hope at 187C.

[40] 1941 J.C. 59.

[41] At 61–62. It may be different where the deceased on two different occasions discloses his infidelity, but reveals much more on the second occasion: see *Rutherford v. H.M. Advocate*, 1997 S.C.C.R. 711, L.J.-G. Rodger, at 719E-F. In that case, the first, limited, revelation was made on a Friday, and the second on the following Sunday: it was considered that the accused could in the circumstances advance the argument that he had not known the full nature and extent of the infidelity prior to the Sunday, the second revelation and the subsequent fatal killing.

[42] 1958 S.L.T. 24.

[43] At 25. In *Crawford v. H.M. Advocate*, 1950 J.C. 67, 71 L.J.-G. Cooper referred to "the provocation which the jury may have been entitled to infer from his unhappy home life," but this was *obiter*, and there was evidence of a threatened attack by the deceased immediately before his death: see *infra*, para. 25.28. In cases where (*e.g.*) a wife is subjected to a long course of violence and abuse by her husband, and kills him without there being a sufficient final provoking act on his part, it would seem that provocation is not an available plea: Lord Dunpark nevertheless allowed a plea of provocation to be considered by the jury in such circumstances in *H.M. Advocate v. Greig*, High Court, May 1978, unrep'd (see C.H.W. Gane and C.N. Stoddart, *A Casebook on Scottish Criminal Law* (3rd ed., 2001), at pp. 423–424), and a verdict of culpable homicide was returned; but his decision to leave that plea to the jury was criticised by L.J.-C. Ross in *Thomson v. H.M. Advocate*, 1985 S.C.C.R. 448, at 457. The modern emphasis on the wickedness element in the *mens rea* of murder may, however, suggest that such criticism may be less compelling than was once the case: see *Drury v. H.M. Advocate*, 2001 S.L.T. 1013 (five judges).

Types of provocation

25.12   In dealing with the law of provocation it is convenient to distinguish three types of situation, although there may be little practical difference between the first two.

These are:

(1) Cases in which A is in danger of his life and acts in self-defence, but does so in such a way that his killing of the deceased is not justifiable.

(2) Cases in which A is defending himself against an attack which, although serious, does not place his life in danger.

(3) Cases in which there is no serious attack on A, but he acts while deprived of self-control as a result of the provocative behaviour of the deceased or of someone else. This group really comprises three types of situation: (i) a minor assault by the deceased, (ii) provocation by insulting words or gestures or other insulting behaviour on the part of the deceased, and (iii) provocation by such behaviour on the part of someone other than the deceased.

(1) *Provocation and self-defence*

25.13   *The law in Hume and Alison.* Hume states that where a man acts in defence of his life in circumstances where his action is not justifiable — because he acted excessively or because he started the quarrel[44] — he is guilty of culpable homicide. Hume deals with such cases under the head of self-defence and not in his section on provocation,[45] although he talks of provocation in connection with some of the cases he mentions.[46] In dealing with cases in which the accused started the quarrel, he does not go on to ask if the deceased's retaliation led to loss of control by the accused.[47] It is not altogether clear whether Hume's line of argument is, "He could have escaped — or he started the trouble — and his action is therefore not altogether justifiable, so we convict him of culpable homicide," or, "He was attacked and acted under provocation, being excited and agitated, and so is guilty only of culpable homicide." Hume's use of phrases like "absolute and entire justification" in talking of cases of excessive retaliation[48] suggests the former approach, as if there were a full justification leading to acquittal where the accused's retaliation was not excessive, and a less full one leading to conviction for culpable homicide where it was excessive. But Hume also talks in terms of "provocation" and "resentment" in dealing with cases of unjustifiable self-defence.[49]

Alison at one point classes together persons who are "provoked, or placed in circumstance of real or supposed danger", as having a duty to exercise self-control, and as guilty of culpable homicide, "where that control has not been exerted, or the belief of danger was not real."[50] But he later enunciates a separate proposition that "Culpable homicide is

---

[44] Hume, i, 223, 232. *Cf. Edward Lane* (1830) Bell's Notes 77; *Wm Wright* (1835) 1 Swin. 6; *Mungo Campbell* (1769) Hume, i, 249; *John Forrest* (1837) 1 Swin. 404.

[45] According to Burnett provocation only began to be recognised as a plea in about 1760: Burnett, p.14.

[46] For example, *Ensign Hardie* (1701) Hume, i, 223.

[47] Hume, i, 232.

[48] Hume, i, 227.

[49] Hume, i, 223 *et seq.*

[50] Alison, i, 92.

committed by an undue precipitance, or the unjustifiable use of lethal weapons, in defence of life or property."[51] For Alison the culpable homicide conviction comes about because a prima facie case of self-defence is partially defeated by the accused's excessive reaction[52] and not because the accused acted while deprived of self-control. A certain degree of excess reduces the effect of the plea of self-defence from acquittal to conviction for culpable homicide; a greater degree of excess destroys its effect altogether and results in a conviction for murder. This approach views the plea of "provocation" as a plea of "unjustifiable self-defence in mitigation", and appears to have led to a terminological confusion between self-defence and provocation such that self-defence was considered capable of being a plea in mitigation, and provocation (at least in assault) as being an exculpatory plea.[53]

It would be feasible to make unjustifiable self-defence a valid plea in mitigation whether or not the accused lost control as a result of the attack made on him.[54] A man can stand his ground and fight instead of taking advantage of an opportunity to escape whether or not he is so provoked by the attack as to have lost self-control. If escape were impossible, he would be acquitted, and would not have to show that he lost control; and it may be said that if escape were possible he should be convicted only of culpable homicide, even if he did not lose self-control.

---

[51] Alison, i, 100.

[52] Alison, i, 93, 103.

[53] See *Hillan v. H.M. Advocate*, 1937 J.C. 37, L.J.-C. Aitchison at 57: "Provocation is frequently a plea in reduction of the quality of the crime, as where it is sufficient to reduce the crime of murder to culpable homicide. But also in certain cases it may amount to a complete defence to the crime libelled, so that, on its being satisfactorily established, the proper verdict is one of acquittal. Again, it may neither reduce the quality of the crime nor afford a complete defence, but only be effectual to establish mitigating circumstances that go to the sentence to be imposed . . . Where the provocation is of such a kind as to justify the retaliation, the panel is entitled to be acquitted; where it is substantial and yet falls short of justifying the retaliation so as not to amount to a complete defence, the panel is guilty under provocation." At 58 of the report, Lord Aitchison indicated that self-defence could be "a complete justification for what the panel has done, or it may reduce the quality of the crime, as, for example, from murder to culpable homicide, where the panel has struck in his own defence but with a measure of violence that cannot be justified, or it may simply be an element in palliation of the offence of the panel which is relevant to the matter of sentence." There may be something to be said in favour of such statements in assault (see Chap. 29, *infra*) — and *Hillan* was a case of assault. The later cases which criticised *Hillan*, on the ground that the functions of self-defence and provocation were entirely separate, only self-defence being a justificatory plea, were cases of murder: see *Crawford v. H.M. Advocate*, 1950 J.C. 67, L.J.-G. Cooper at 70 (*cf.* Lord Keith at 71, who said that in *Hillan*, "Provocation seems to me to have been the relevant plea either in exculpation or mitigation, and it may be that some day the case will have to be reconsidered."); and *Fenning v. H.M. Advocate*, 1985 S.C.C.R. 219. It seems, however, that provocation, at least in assault, was considered correctly (as following Hume and Alison) in *Hillan* to be capable of justifying an assault "of a suitable level" on the person whose conduct had provoked the accused, in order to deter as well as punish the initial assailant — although such an approach has become no longer acceptable: *Drury v. H.M. Advocate*, 2001 S.L.T. 1013 (five judges), opinion of L.J.-G. Rodger, at para. [17]. Nevertheless, the modern approach to provocation is based closely on loss of control on the part of the accused: see *infra*.

[54] See, *e.g.*, "A Criminal Code for England and Wales" (L.C. No. 177), H.C. No. 299: Vol. I, Draft Code, cl. 59. The Report of the Select Committee of the House of Lords on "Murder and Life Imprisonment" (H.L. Paper 78, Sess. 1988–89), Vol. I (Report) at Pt 6 (Defences) p.28, para. 86, considered that excessive self-defence *was* a factor in Scots law which would enable the return of a culpable homicide verdict on a murder charge, and that the introduction of such a 'defence' in England would bring English law into line with Scots law: *cf. Fenning v. H.M. Advocate*, 1985 S.C.C.R. 219, where Lord Cameron at 224 denied that there was any such defence: see para. 25.15, *infra*.

25.14 *The modern law.* The modern law allows the plea of provocation only where the accused has lost control; but the idea that provocation is a form of unjustifiable self-defence continued for a considerable part of the twentieth century. The passage in which Macdonald deals with provocation in homicide is very confused, and the only clear points that he makes are that excessive retaliation in the face of real danger amounts only to culpable homicide if done in heat and without thought, and that "provocation such as would deprive a reasonable man of the power of self-control" may reduce the charge from murder to culpable homicide where a plea of self-defence would fail because the accused started the trouble, or his retaliation was excessive, or he did not escape when this was possible.[55] Macdonald seems to be saying that the plea of provocation will apply only where the accused acts in defence, either against a murderous attack or against an attack which is serious but not murderous.

In *H.M. Advocate v. Kizileviczius*,[56] in which the evidence was that the accused had killed his father after disarming him of a weapon with which the father was threatening him, Lord Jamieson distinguished three pleas open to the accused — self-defence leading to acquittal; self-defence leading to a conviction of culpable homicide; provocation leading to a conviction of culpable homicide. Lord Jamieson said that the third was very like the second, and that the second — which is the plea of unjustifiable self-defence — required both danger to the accused's life and that he should have acted in heat without thought, but he did treat the second and third as distinct.

25.15 *Kizileviczius*[57] is an example of the confusion between self-defence and provocation which is expressed in the idea of a plea of self-defence in mitigation and which was criticised in *Crawford v. H.M. Advocate*,[58] where it was said that self-defence could operate only in exculpation, and that the plea in mitigation was one of provocation. But although *Crawford* makes it clear that provocation is a plea in mitigation only and self-defence one in exculpation only, Scots law in practice probably achieves something close to the former Australian concept of "excessive self-defence" as a plea reducing murder to manslaughter.[59] This is because in cases of excessive self-defence it is in practice assumed that the accused was still acting under the influence of the provocation of the original assault, or at least that the circumstances were such as to prevent the Crown from establishing the necessary wicked intent or wicked recklessness. Excessive self-defence may, therefore, be one of the factors which the Court had in mind in the recent case of *Drury v. H.M. Advocate*.[60]

---

[55] Macdonald, pp. 93–94.

[56] 1938 J.C. 60.

[57] 1938 J.C. 60.

[58] 1950 J.C. 67.

[59] *R. v. Howe* (1958) 100 C.L.R. 448; C. Howard, "Two Problems in Excessive Defence" (1968) 84 L.Q.R. 343. *R. v. Howe* was overruled by the High Court of Australia in *D.P.P. v. Zekevic* (1987) 61 A.L.J.R. 375 in view of the difficulty in charging juries under *Howe* (rather than because the Court disagreed with *Howe* in principle), and the law reverted to what was decided in *Palmer v. The Queen* [1971] A.C. 814, a Privy Council case from Jamaica; thus, in Australia, as in current English law, the use of unjustified force in self-defence results in a conviction for murder rather than manslaughter: see "A Criminal Code for England and Wales" (L.C. No. 177), H.C. 299 (1989), Vol. 2, at para. 14.19.

[60] *Drury v. H.M. Advocate*, 2001 S.L.T. 1013 (five judges); and see *McCluskey v. H.M. Advocate*, 1959 J.C. 39, which in effect arrived at the same result as *Howe, supra*.

It is, of course, possible to figure a case in which it was clearly proved that the accused acted excessively and in cold blood, and in that case he would be guilty of murder, but such a case is likely to be found only rarely. *Kizileviczius* is itself a fairly typical case in which there can be little doubt that the result would have been the same even if the jury had been directed as required by *Crawford*. An example of the twentieth century practice is the following extract from Lord Thomson's charge to the jury in *H.M. Advocate v. Byfield and Ors*[61] where, after giving the jury the usual definition of murder in terms of wicked recklessness, Lord Thomson said:

> "If you get a situation where you think that the Crown has failed to prove — and the onus is on the Crown — such a high degree of wicked recklessness but, nonetheless, has established to your satisfaction that the accused acted in an unjustifiable way, that would be enough to reduce the charge from one of murder to one of culpable homicide. Moreover, ladies and gentlemen, and this is perhaps closer to the facts of this case, if you took the view that the defence of self-defence was not established either because, for instance, the force used in retaliation was excessive or because although the man was petrified, as he says, nonetheless, he really ought to have been able to see there was a way of escape, and should have taken it: in both those cases the self-defence would fail but in both those cases it would be open to you to say 'Well, he shouldn't have done what he did but it is not murder' and in circumstances of that kind the verdict would be culpable homicide. It is sometimes said that this arises from an application of the principle of provocation and you can apply that to this case too. It comes, in a way, to the same thing. If you take the view, upon the whole evidence, that there was provocation by the man Ewart — provocation in the sense of threat of an immediate attack in the way in which it was done — if you take that view and you take the view that the accused's reaction was not such as to constitute self-defence you could nonetheless take the view that although he shouldn't have retaliated at all so as to exculpate himself, nonetheless he was provoked in such a way as to make it understandable why he did react in the way he did and if he simply used too much force or didn't try to escape when he should have done, or the like, then you could bring in a verdict of culpable homicide."

The modern law is probably therefore that whether or not the accused's life was in danger the appropriate verdict will probably be one of culpable homicide if he acted under loss of self-control induced by provocation; although where there is danger to life the law more or less assumes that the accused acted under provocation. Accordingly it becomes unnecessary to have a special category for cases in which the accused's life was endangered, and such cases can be treated as similar to cases where the accused was subjected to a substantial attack or threat of force.

---

[61] High Court at Glasgow, Jan 1976, unrep'd, at 16–17. Following the decision in *Drury v. H.M. Advocate*, 2001 S.L.T. 1013 (five judges), it would be necessary in modern practice to avoid directing juries in terms of "reducing murder to culpable homicide" and to refer instead to the factors which the jury may take into account in determining whether the *mens rea* of murder was established or not.

(2) *Provocation by serious assault*

25.16 *Its nature.* In his section on provocation Hume deals only with provocation by serious assault, and seems to consider this a different question from that of unjustifiable self-defence. Where the accused's life is not in danger it is essential that he should have lost control. Culpable homicide under provocation arises where the accused "is not actuated by wickedness of heart, or hatred of the deceased, but by the sudden impulse of resentment, excited by high and real injuries, and accompanied with terror and agitation of spirits."[62]

This type of provocation is described by Macdonald[63] in a passage adopted in *H.M. Advocate v. Kizileviczius*[64] as follows: "Being agitated and excited, and alarmed by violence, I lost control over myself, and took life, when my presence of mind had left me, and without thought of what I was doing." This passage is regarded as an authoritative expression of the law,[65] and is frequently quoted by judges in directing juries. But it may be questioned if it accurately represents the law; in particular one can conceive of cases in which an accused might well succeed in a plea of provocation although he could not say that he acted without thought of what he was doing. The description given by Macdonald takes no account of the fact that provocation is a defence to intentional killing. The plea is designed not for someone who kills automatically, but for someone who is so provoked by the deceased that he sees red, and determines on the spot that he will "swing for the bastard", like the husband who kills his wife's paramour on hearing of their adultery.[66]

25.17 *Its rules.* The rules regarding this sort of provocation show that it is very much influenced by ideas of self-defence. Indeed, it is still often thought of as a form of unjustifiable self-defence, self-defence against serious

---

[62] Hume, i, 239, quoted with approval in *Drury v. H.M. Advocate*, 2001 S.L.T. 1013 (five judges), by L.J.-G. Rodger, at paras [13] and [19]. *Cf.* Burnett, pp.13–14; Alison, i, 12.

[63] Macdonald, p.94.

[64] 1938 J.C. 60, 63.

[65] See, *e.g.*, *Cosgrove v. H.M. Advocate*, 1990 S.C.C.R. 358, Lord Cowie at 360E and 361, where the passage from Macdonald is referred to as "the classic" and "proper" definition of provocation. In *Drury v. H.M. Advocate*, 2001 S.L.T. 1013 (five judges), the Court did not suggest that this passage from Macdonald was not authoritative; but L.J.-G. Rodger, at paras [22]–[24], in examining the appellant's contention that "loss of control" in the passage meant total loss of control such that the accused might be considered to have been acting involuntarily at the relevant time and thus in a state where a test of proportionality between his response and the degree of the provocation made no sense, concluded (with reference to the decision of the Privy Council in *Phillips v. The Queen* [1969] 2 A.C. 130) that the passage should be read as if "loss of control" meant that the accused occupied the middle ground between "icy detachment" and "going berserk" (which would be more appropriate for a finding of temporary insanity than provocation). Lord Rodger also pointed out that Hume, i, 239 emphasises that there is no question of the person acting under provocation being in a state of involuntariness; rather he is in a state where he failed to master his emotions or passions — that failure constituting the element of blame which justifies a conviction for culpable homicide.

[66] Macdonald, following Hume, holds that provocation can never apply to poisoning even if the accused "were immediately to place poison in food or drink in retaliation", because "the resolution, although sudden, is deliberate and malignant in character": Macdonald, p.94. *Cf.* Hume, i, 252; Alison, i, 9, although it is not absolutely clear that the older writers would exclude an *immediate* retaliation. Although cases of poisoning on provocation are likely to be rare indeed, there is no reason in principle for the restriction of provocation to certain forms of homicide.

assault and not against danger to life itself. The position is this: the accused was grossly assaulted, he retaliated in order to defend himself from bodily harm; but he killed his assailant, and therefore, since the accused's life was not in danger, he must have exceeded the limits of justifiable self-defence; but if he acted under the provocation of the attack, he may be convicted of culpable homicide.

That this is the position can be seen by considering some of the rules regarding provocation. These rules are: (a) the provocation must be by "real" injury, (b) the retaliation must not have been grossly excessive, (c) it is important to consider who started the quarrel, (d) A is entitled to plead provocation if he kills B because of an attack by B on C.

(a) The provocation must be by "real" injury — "real" meaning **25.18** "physical".[67] It must be physical because without physical attack there can be no question of self-defence at all; it must be substantial because otherwise there would be no need for any defensive action. So Hume, Burnett, Alison, Anderson and Macdonald, all exclude insulting words or disgusting behaviour, and even minor assaults,[68] and Hume specifically rejects the then current English view that *any* assault might amount to provocation.[69]

(b) There must be some equivalence between the mode of retaliation **25.19** or resentment and the provocation given.[70] Exact equivalence cannot be demanded, because if the accused killed the deceased while retaliating exactly to the deceased's assault on him the deceased's assault must have been murderous, and so the accused would be entitled to acquittal on a plea of self-defence.[71]

This approach cannot be justified if the only important element in provocation is loss of control, for then the relation of retaliation to provocation would be important only as a guide to credibility — a jury would be unlikely to believe that a slap on the face so provoked the accused that he could not stop himself cleaving the victim's head with a hatchet. But if loss of control is what matters, and they do believe the unlikely story, they should then be able to sustain the plea. If, however, the analogy with self-defence is important they would have to reject the plea because of the obvious gross in equivalence of the retaliation.[72] In *Smith v. H.M. Advocate*,[73] Lord Cooper told the jury: "it takes a

---

[67] R.C. Evid. of Faculty of Advocates, Q. 5662–5663.

[68] Hume, i, 247–248; Burnett, pp. 17, 31; Alison, i, 12; Anderson, p.150; Macdonald, p.93.

[69] Hume, i, 247–248. Cases of provocation by trespassing or theft are also excluded: Hume, i, 247; Macdonald, p.94. See also *Mungo Campbell* (1769) Hume, i, 249; *James Craw* (1826) Syme 188, 210. In *Andrew Ewart* (1828) Syme 315 it was held that the sight of someone robbing a grave was not sufficient to found a plea of provocation.

[70] Burnett, p.17; *Mrs Mackinnon* (1823) Alison, i, 14; *Edward Armstrong* (1826) Alison, i, 15; *Peter Scott* (1823) *ibid.*; Macdonald, p.93; *cf. Mancini v. D.P.P.* [1942] A.C. 1, Lord Chancellor Simon at 9; *R. v. Brown* [1972] 2 Q.B. 229.

[71] *cf.* Kenny, para. 119. The requirement depends on the idea of unjustifiable self-defence to assault; if the accused's retaliation was grossly excessive he is guilty of murder, if it was excessive but not grossly so then if he was provoked he is entitled to a verdict of culpable homicide. And from this it follows that the assault on the accused must have been substantial since otherwise his retaliation must have been excessive.

[72] *cf. R. v. Davies (Peter)* [1975] Q.B. 691. Macdonald seems to have realised this when he said that a "murderous purpose" is unlikely to be presumed where the retaliation is roughly equivalent: Macdonald, p.93.

[73] High Court at Glasgow, Feb. 1952, unrep'd, reported on another point, 1952 J.C. 66.

tremendous amount of provocation to palliate stabbing a man to death. Words, however abusive or insulting are of no avail. A blow with the fist is no justification for the use of a lethal weapon. Provocation, in short, must bear a reasonable retaliation to the resentment which it excites."[74]

In recent years, the courts in Scotland have accepted, it seems, that the plea entails an excessive response to the provocation offered — that being consistent with the ideas of loss of control and acting in the heat of the moment, in anger or excitement[75]; thus the focus of attention has rather been on the allowable extent of that excess. In *Lennon v. H.M. Advocate*,[76] for example, Lord Justice-General Hope considered that a cruel excess[77] would bar the plea if that meant that there was a gross disproportion between the provocation and the accused's reaction to it; and in *Robertson v. H.M. Advocate*,[78] Lord Justice-Clerk Ross was firmly of the view that loss of control was not the sole criterion for the plea, and that there had to be a reasonable proportion between the violence offered and the response of the accused. In the recent case of *Drury v. H.M. Advocate*, the court ruled that there was no way in which discovery of sexual infidelity could sensibly be related proportionately to the accused's response to that discovery; but it is clear that the court also regarded provocation by such discovery as an exceptional type of provocation, and thus reserved its opinion on the question of proportionality in cases of violent provocative acts.[79]

25.20   (c) It was at one time the law that a person who had started a quarrel could not succeed in a plea of provocation, any more than in a plea of self-defence.[80] This is probably no longer the law.[81]

25.21   (d) The rule that A may plead provocation where he has killed B under the provocation of the latter's attack on C,[82] can be explained by the analogy with the similar rule that A may kill B in order to save C's life.

---

[74] Transcript of Judge's charge, 22. This passage is quoted in full in *Drury v. H.M. Advocate*, 2001 S.L.T. 1013 (five judges), L.J.-G. Rodger's opinion, at para. [33].

[75] See *Low v. H.M. Advocate*, 1993 S.C.C.R. 493, L.J.-C. Ross at 507B; *Drury v. H.M. Advocate*, 2001 S.L.T. 1013 (five judges), opinion of L.J.-G. Rodger, at para. [32].

[76] 1991 S.C.C.R. 611, at 614F. The case involves assault, however, rather than homicide.

[77] *cf. Hillan v. H.M. Advocate*, 1937 J.C. 53, at 64, where Lord Wark said that a cruel excess meant "out of all proportion to the provocation received"; something that was grossly excessive. In *Low v. H.M. Advocate*, 1993 S.C.C.R. 493, at 506F–507A and 507B, L.J.-C. Ross declared that the use of the term "cruel excess" was inappropriate, since it was better suited to self-defence than to provocation: instead the term "gross disproportion" was to be preferred. See also *Parr v. H.M. Advocate*, 1991 S.C.C.R. 180, L.J.-G. Hope at 187E, who also refers to the test of "gross disproportion".

[78] 1994 S.C.C.R. 589, at 593E-F. (The accused there had inflicted 99 stab wounds on the victim, who had allegedly made homosexual advances to and presented a knife at the accused.)

[79] 2001 S.L.T. 1013 (five judges), opinion of L.J.-G. Rodger, at paras [28] and [35]; opinion of Lord Nimmo Smith, at para. [5]; opinion of Lord Cameron, at para. [7]: *cf.* opinion of Lord Johnston, at paras [18]–[19].

[80] Hume, i, 248; *cf. Edward Armstrong* (1826) Alison, i, 15.

[81] *cf. supra*, paras 24.06, 24.09–24.10. It is not the law in England: *Edwards v. R.* [1973] A.C. 648, PC.

[82] *James McGhie* (1791) Hume, i, 246; *Gray v. H.M. Advocate*, 1994 S.C.C.R. 225; *cf. R. v. Harrington* (1866) 10 Cox C.C. 370.

(3) Provocation and loss of self-control

It is possible to adopt a rule that wherever an accused is provoked so **25.22** as to lose his capacity for self-control he is guilty only of culpable homicide. If such a rule is recognised, the fact that in any particular case the provocation took the form of a serious assault will be irrelevant (since the more general category includes the less general one), and the rules set out above will give way to the more general rules applying to provocation leading to loss of control, whatever the nature of the provocation. The special rules applied because of the self-defence analogy could then be disregarded whether or not the facts were analogous to self-defence.

Should such a rule be recognised? The law of provocation has to balance **25.23** two conflicting considerations. It must allow for the fact that it is not in accord with ordinary moral attitudes to brand the person who kills under extreme provocation as a murderer, a consideration perhaps weakened by the abolition of capital punishment,[83] but still strong since it will continue to be felt that the law should recognise the inappropriateness of classing such a person with deliberate murderers. Failure to make allowance for this and for the sympathy naturally felt with a man who gives way to violence under the pressure of provocation will bring the law into disrepute and may also, as Hume points out, lead to juries acquitting altogether in cases of provocation.[84] There is much to be said, from the point of view of the individual accused, for the argument that a man who acts when he is unable to control himself cannot be regarded as guilty of killing at all. This was the view taken by Lord Justice-Clerk Aitchison in *H.M. Advocate v. Gilmour*[85] when he said that if the accused "acted in the first transport of his passion without appreciating to the full extent what he was doing" the jury would not "hold him criminally responsible for the death that occurred", but would convict him only of assault.[86] Presumably, on this view, if he did not appreciate what he was doing at all, he would be entitled to complete acquittal. For some time after *Gilmour* the law was unsettled,[87] but it has now been decided that where the accused has caused death and the only defence is provocation, it is not open to the jury to convict of assault: they must convict of culpable homicide.[88]

---

[83] Murder (Abolition of Death Penalty) Act 1965: see now 1995 Act, s.205.

[84] Hume, i, 240. Hume's point here is stressed by L.J.-G. Rodger in *Drury v. H.M. Advocate*, 2001 S.L.T. 1013 (five judges), of his opinion at paras [19]–[32].

[85] 1938 J.C. 1. (The jury there returned a verdict of guilty of assault.)

[86] At 3.

[87] *Gilmour* was strongly criticised in *H.M. Advocate v. Delaney*, 1945 J.C. 138, at 140, by Lord Moncrieff, and was not followed in *H.M. Advocate v. Hill*, 1941 J.C. 59. But in *McCluskey v. H.M. Advocate*, 1959 J.C. 39, in a charge of murder to which the defence was that the killing had been occasioned by an attempt of the deceased to commit sodomy on the accused, Lord Strachan, at 40, directed the jury that they could bring in a verdict of guilty of assault if they found adequate reason for disregarding the fact that the accused had killed the deceased. The other cases were cases of husbands killing their wives and/or their paramours.

[88] *McDermott v. H.M. Advocate*, 1973 J.C. 8; see L.J.-G. Emslie at 13: "where death is brought about by an unlawful act, including an assault upon the victim, it is always homicide and it is always culpable." (The jury could convict of assault only if satisfied that the acts of the accused did not cause the death.)

On the other hand, the law cannot deal as leniently with the person who acts without full appreciation of his deeds by reason of provocation as it can with someone who is in such a condition by reason of error or mental disease. It is generally recognised that there is a duty to retain one's self-control and to endeavour not to give way to passion. Any undue extension of the plea of provocation will weaken the strength of this duty, and it is important for the law to discourage people from giving way to passion by imposing some punishment on those who do give way to it. It was for this reason that Hume felt that it would be wrong to allow all assaults to rank as provocation, and felt that the law as set out by himself was "more suitable to the fervent temper of the Scottish people".[89] Hume thus recognises that "what is 'provocation' sufficiently 'gross' to transform murder into manslaughter . . . cannot be satisfactorily dealt with by the Courts by means of purely legal analysis, i.e. without taking into account the attitudes and needs of contemporary society and of the different groups within it."[90]

If, then, contemporary attitudes in Scotland recognise that provocation should not be restricted to cases of serious assault, the law should accept this and modify or develop its concept of provocation accordingly. English law has now developed to the extent that provocation may be constituted by anything done or said,[91] and it seems unlikely that Scottish attitudes today are different from English ones.[92] The circumstances in which the ordinary man would feel that loss of self-control was partially excusable (and thus not wicked for the purposes of murder) are clearly not restricted to cases of serious assault. Many situations can be

---

[89] Hume, i, 249.

[90] H. Mannheim, *Group Problems in Crime and Punishment*, (London, 1955), p.268.

[91] See Homicide Act 1957, s.3.

[92] An opportunity for judicial reconsideration of the rules on provocation might have been taken in *Drury v. H.M. Advocate*, 2001 S.L.T. 1013 (five judges), the larger court having been assembled with that in mind; but since the appeal in the case was concerned with a particular aspect of an exceptional type of provocation (discovery of sexual infidelity), the judges took the view either that they had heard insufficient argument on the general rules affecting provocation or that reform was better conducted by the legislature: see, *e.g.*, opinion of L.J.-G. Rodger, at para. [35]; opinion of Lord Nimmo Smith, at para. [9]; and opinion of Lord Mackay of Drumadoon, at para. [3]. The following passage from the opinion of the Lord Justice-General (para. [25]) may be noted: "In matters of homicide Scots law admits the plea of provocation only within certain bounds which are considerably narrower than those within which it operates in English law. In Scots law it applies only where the accused has been assaulted and there has been substantial provocation. In English law, by contrast, even a slight blow or mere jostling may be sufficient to admit the plea. In Scots law, no mere verbal provocation can palliate killing. The same applied in England until the law was changed by Section 3 of the Homicide Act 1957. The difference in scope of the doctrine of provocation in the two systems does not arise, it should be stressed, because Hume and the Scottish judges are unaware that people may react violently to minor physical provocations or to insults. Rather, as a matter of policy, the law has taken the view that in such cases the person assaulted or the person insulted should be expected to control himself, at least to the extent of not killing his tormentor. To this policy Scots law admits only one exception: the law recognises that when an accused discovers that his or her partner, who owes a duty of sexual fidelity, has been unfaithful, the accused may be swept with sudden and overwhelming indignation which may lead to a violent reaction resulting in death. In such cases the law provides that, where the jury are satisfied that this is in fact what happened, they should return a verdict of culpable homicide on the ground that, because of the effect of the provocation, the accused did not act with the wicked state of mind required for murder." (*Cf.* L.J.-G. Rodger's view at para. [27] in relation to a comment by Lord Hoffmann in *R. v. Smith (Morgan)* [2000] 3 W.L.R. 654, HL, at 674F-G that the law of provocation should no longer make allowances for male obsessiveness and jealousy on the discovery of sexual infidelity.)

imagined which would illustrate this, but it will be sufficient to notice the one mentioned to the Royal Commission on Capital Punishment by the Faculty of Advocates: the situation of the victim of a blackmailer who is exasperated into killing his oppressor. The provocation of blackmail, as the Faculty pointed out, may be much more extreme than that of blows.[93]

In considering the conflict between the plea of provocation and the deterrent purpose of the law it is also important to remember a fact so obvious that it is sometimes forgotten — the accused who succeeds in a plea of provocation is not acquitted, he is convicted of culpable homicide, a crime for which he can receive a very severe sentence. To insist on the principle of deterrence being given full weight twice over — in deciding what amounts to provocation as well as in restricting the effect of a successful plea of provocation — may well be to tip the balance too far against the accused.

Acceptance of the general rule that any provocation causing loss of self-control should operate as provocation in law would be in accord with the general tendency of Scots law to give weight to any feature which shows that the accused did not act out of wickedness or malice.[94] The view that a killing may be intentional yet not murder because of "the extent of the malice under which [the accused] was actuated",[95] and the idea that there are different categories of homicide, run through the nineteenth-century homicide cases, and influenced Scots attitudes to diminished responsibility and intoxication.[96] It seems reasonable to adopt the same broad approach to the question of provocation, but it must be admitted that in fact provocation, like intoxication and (until very recently)[96a] diminished responsibility, has come to be hedged round with legal technicalities.

Does Scots law recognise the rule?

(1) *The special case of infidelity.* Hume, Burnett, Alison, Anderson and **25.24** Macdonald all recognise one exception to the rule that only provocation of the nature of serious assault is relevant. They all recognise that a husband who kills his wife or her paramour under the provocation of finding them in adultery is guilty of only culpable homicide.[97] Hume calls this a "peculiar case", and it is still regarded as special.[98]

---

[93] R.C. Evid. of Faculty of Advocates, Q. 5664.
[94] See *Drury v. H.M. Advocate*, 2001 S.L.T. 1013 (five judges).
[95] *H.M. Advocate v. Kane* (1892) 3 White 386, L.J.-C. Macdonald at 388.
[96] *cf.* Vol. I, paras 11.13, 12.08–12.10.
[96a] See *Galbraith v. H.M. Advocate,* 2001 S.L.T. 953, supra. n.35.
[97] Hume, i, 245; Burnett, p.53; Alison, i, 113; Anderson, p.153; Macdonald, p.97; *James Christie* (1731) Hume, i, 245.
[98] It is indeed highly peculiar in the scheme of law laid down by these authors. For it lacks any element of physical assault, and does not permit of any measurement of the equivalence between provocation and retaliation: see *Drury v. H.M. Advocate*, 2001 S.L.T. 1013 (five judges), esp. the opinion of L.J.-G. Rodger, at para. [28]. There is no suggestion for example, that discovery of adultery in some circumstances may palliate assault but not homicide, but simply an independent rule that a husband discovering his wife in adultery is guilty only of culpable homicide if he kills her or her paramour forthwith and under the influence of loss of control induced by the discovery.

The scope of this "peculiar case" has been somewhat extended in the twentieth century,[99] but no inference can be drawn from the extension which would be applicable to the law of provocation in general. It is the law today that, for example, a husband provoked by hearing a confession of adultery is in the same position as one who finds his wife committing or about to commit adultery,[1] but that does not mean that Scots law recognises any other form of verbal provocation.[2] The extension for adultery confessions was effected by treating "discovery of adultery" as equivalent to "finding in adultery", and by pointing out that adultery might be discovered through confession. As Professor Smith remarks, this verbal provocation is therefore at best restricted to provocation by giving information, and does not include provocation by words of insult.[3] It is probably restricted further to confessions of sexual infidelity, and the courts would be loth to extend it, for example, to a confession that the deceased had just assaulted, or even killed, the accused's wife or any other relation or friend, or to information given otherwise than in the form of a confession.

25.25   (2) *Provocation by minor assault.* Macdonald follows Hume in saying that minor blows will not palliate homicide,[4] but the Royal Commission on Capital Punishment were of opinion that Hume's strict views might not be followed today,[5] and Professor Smith agrees with them.[6] If

---

[99] See *H.M. Advocate v. Hill*, 1941 J.C. 59 (discovery of adultery by way of confession is sufficient); *H.M. Advocate v. Callander*, 1958 S.L.T. 24 (lesbianism considered by Lord Guthrie to be as much a breach of the marital obligation of sexual fidelity as adultery); *McDermott v. H.M. Advocate*, 1973 J.C. 8 (discovery of illicit association between accused's common law wife and the victim, the victim having approached the "wife" with affectionate gestures which were reciprocated immediately prior to the assault, considered sufficient by Lord Cameron); *MacKay v. H.M. Advocate*, 1991 S.C.C.R. 364, and *Rutherford v. H.M. Advocate*, 1997 S.C.C.R. 711 (discovery of the sexual infidelity of one's partner in a non-marital relationship, where fidelity is expected on the part of each partner by the other, is sufficient); *H.M. Advocate v. McKean*, 1992 S.C.C.R. 402 (the exception extends to homosexual relationships, where again sexual fidelity is expected on the part of each partner by the other).

[1] *H.M. Advocate v. Hill*, 1941 J.C. 59; *H.M. Advocate v. Delaney*, 1945 J.C. 138 — both single judge decisions. It was suggested to the Royal Commission on Capital Punishment that the Scots courts might follow the contrary decision of the House of Lords in *Holmes v. D.P.P.* [1946] A.C. 588, but that this was unlikely: *cf.* R.C. Evid. of Lord Cooper, Supp. Memo., para. 13. It can now be regarded as impossible since *Holmes* is no longer law in England: Homicide Act, 1957, s.3.

[2] See *Drury v. H.M. Advocate*, 2001 S.L.T. 1013 (five judges), opinion of L.J.-G. Rodger at para [25], set out as part of n.92, *supra*.

[3] T.B. Smith, "Capital Punishment", 1953 S.L.T. (News) 197, 199. See *McKay v. H.M. Advocate*, 1991 S.C.C.R. 364, and *McCormack v. H.M. Advocate*, 1993 S.C.C.R. 581, where in each case the distinction was drawn between words which were, or which the accused might believe to be, informative of sexual infidelity and those which were merely insulting or humiliating: *Cf. Berry v. H.M. Advocate* (1976) S.C.C.R. (Supp.) 156, where insults were left to the jury by Lord Keith, but the Appeal Court expressed grave doubts as to the correctness of his having done so. See also the doubts expressed by L.J.-C. Wheatley in *Thomson v. H.M. Advocate*, 1985 S.C.C.R. 448, at 457.

[4] Macdonald, p.93. See also *Harris and Ors*, High Court at Glasgow, Sept. 1950, unrep'd, where L.J.-C. Thomson said, "There must be provocation in a substantial sense. No light or trivial provocation can justify the taking of life": Transcript of proceedings, 388.

[5] R.C. para. 131.

[6] T.B. Smith, *op. cit., loc. cit.* Hume himself noted that the indulgence of juries had led to an extension of the benefit of provocation: Hume, i, 248; *Wm Goldie* (1804) Hume, i, 249. Burnett, too, comments on a recent mitigation in the law of provocation, but he goes on to say that the mitigation had not gone the length of including resentment on slight injury: Burnett, p.17.

Hume's strict views have been relaxed, then any assault, although of a minor nature, may constitute provocation; and if that is so, the element of self-defence in provocation will be greatly diminished and it will then be easier to extend provocation to cover words or gestures. If killing may be palliated by a minor assault on the accused this will be because of the accused's consequent loss of control rather than because he has been defending himself from attack, and it will no longer be plausible to exclude the plea of provocation on the ground that the accused's retaliation is grossly excessive, since such an exclusion will mean a return to the Humean position. An emphasis on loss of control in provocation would also make the question of who started the quarrel much less important. Juries would doubtless still be less inclined to sustain a plea of provocation on the part of someone who initiated the quarrel even if, at the time of the killing, he was deprived of self-control as the result of provocation, but they would not be barred from sustaining the plea on that ground.[7]

The modern view, that "evidence relating to provocation is simply one of the factors which the jury should take into account in performing their general task of determining the accused's state of mind at the time when he killed his victim",[8] that is to say the jury question is whether "he had acted with the wickedness of a murderer"[9] rather than whether what would otherwise be murder is palliated or mitigated by provocation, might suggest a weakening of the strict rules within which Hume allowed the plea to operate; it is perhaps easier to think of a person who has reacted with fatal violence to a minor assault or an insult as not necessarily being wicked in doing so than it is to consider that minor assaults or insults can palliate what has already been proved to be sufficient for murder in law; but no such weakening is apparently envisaged by the court in *Drury v. H.M. Advocate*.[10] There may well be, and certainly has been,[11] a view that relaxation of the strict rules of provocation in Scotland is overdue; but the modern approach of the courts seems to be that reform of the plea is better left to the Scottish Parliament.[12] In any event, the scope for the operation of minor violence as provocation is limited by the requirement that any retaliation must bear a reasonable relation to the provocation offered.[13]

(3) *Provocation other than by blows.* The question here is whether loss **25.26** of control caused by provocative words, gestures, or other actings not amounting to assault or the threat of assault, can be the basis of a successful plea of provocation. Any argument from the infidelity cases is

---

[7] *H.M. Advocate v. McGuinness*, 1937 J.C. 37. *Cf. Robertson and Donoghue*, High Court at Edinburgh, August 1945, unrep'd; *Forbes*, High Court at Edinburgh, Sept. 1958, unrep'd, both cases where a plea of provocation by a robber or thief was left to the jury.

[8] *Drury v. H.M. Advocate*, 2001 S.L.T. 1013 (five judges), opinion of L.J.-G. Rodger, at para. [17].

[9] *ibid.*, at para. [33].

[10] 2001 S.L.T. 1013 (five judges): see esp. the opinion of L.J.-G. Rodger, at para. [25] (set out as part of n.92, *supra*).

[11] See Report of the Select Committee of the House of Lords on "Murder and Life Imprisonment" (H.L. Paper 78, Sess. 1988–89), Vol. III, pp. 474–475, Q. 2072, opinions of L.J.-G. Emslie and L.J.-C. Ross.

[12] See *Drury v. H.M. Advocate*, 2001 S.L.T. 1013 (five judges), opinion of Lord Nimmo Smith, at para. [9], and opinion of Lord Mackay of Drumadoon, at para. [3].

[13] See, *e.g.*, *Thomson v. H.M. Advocate*, 1985 S.C.C.R. 448; P.W. Ferguson, *Crimes Against the Person* (2nd ed., 1998) at para. 10.05. See also para. 25.19, *supra*.

circular — if the law does not generally recognise provocation other than by assault, they are exceptions[14]; if they are not exceptions this can only be because the law does recognise provocation by words, etc., in cases other than the adultery ones. In any event, as has been noted, they concern words as a source of information, and not as insults.

Although the advisability of extending provocation beyond cases of physical assault has been widely recognised in other countries,[15] Scots law has traditionally set its face against allowing insulting words or disgusting conduct to operate as provocation.[16] Macdonald repeats Hume's example of throwing the contents of a chamber pot in a man's face[17] as being insufficient to amount to provocation, and the rejection of mere words follows *a fortiori* from this. The Scots attitude seems based on the view that "Sticks and stanes may break your banes, but words will never hurt you."[18]

Despite this, the then Lord Advocate (thereafter Lord Milligan) somewhat surprisingly opposed the application to Scotland of section 3 of the Homicide Act 1957 which allows a jury to take into account "things done or said" when considering a plea of provocation, on the ground that the section expressed what was already the law of Scotland. He told the House of Commons that, "There is nothing that I have been able to find which would indicate that a judge in Scotland would be precluded from leaving provocation by words to a jury."[19] He added that, "It is quite conceivable that a person might lose all reason by seeing something," in which case he said that the question of provocation might be left to a jury. The discussion of this question before the Royal Commission on Capital Punishment and in Parliament seems to have been bedevilled by an undue concentration on the cases involving confessions of adultery. Even on the limited question of confessions of adultery the Commission recommended legislation to clarify the position in Scotland,[20] but the Lord Advocate may have been right in regarding such legislation as unnecessary although it would have done no harm, especially as Lord Cooper expressed doubts as to the applicability or otherwise of *Holmes v. D.P.P.*[21] in Scotland.[22] So far as the general law is concerned, the Lord Advocate's statement leaves Hume, Burnett, Alison, Anderson and Macdonald out of account. His Lordship offered the House no authority for his view of the law, and there is no conclusive authority for it. What little authority there is rests on five cases, none of which is satisfactory as authority for the wide proposition that provocation may be constituted by words or actings other than assaults.

---

[14] And this is now unquestionably the law's approach: see *Drury v. H.M. Advocate*, 2001 S.L.T. 1013 (five judges), esp. the opinion of L.J.-G. Rodger, at para. [25], quoted in full as part of n.92, *supra*.

[15] *cf.* R.C. App. 11 (*f*), and so far as insulting acts are concerned, the Fourth Report of the Criminal Law Commissioners, p. xxxviii, Parl. Papers, 1839, xix, Digest, Art. 41; and Report of Commission on Draft Code of 1879, C.-2345. 24–25, Draft Code, s.176.

[16] Hume, i, 248; Alison, i, 18; Anderson, p.150; Macdonald, p.93; *H.M. Advocate v. Robert Smith* (1893) 1 Adam 34, Lord McLaren at 49. Mackenzie, however, indicates a contrary view: Mackenzie, I, 11, 3.

[17] *Wm Aird* (1693) Hume, i, 248.

[18] See *Drury v. H.M. Advocate*, 2001 S.L.T. 1013 (five judges), opinion of L.J.-G. Rodger, at para. [25], quoted in full as part of n.92, *supra*.

[19] *Hansard*, H.C., Jan. 28, 1957, Vol. 563, Col. 784.

[20] R.C. para. 153; see also Recommendation 6.

[21] [1946] A.C. 588.

[22] See R.C. para. 132.

The first is *H.M. Advocate v. McGuinness*[23] which in fact contained an **25.27** element of assault. The deceased had entered a house occupied by the four accused, had used language calculated to lead to violence, and had threatened them with a baton. He was disarmed and put out of the house. He then created a disturbance and challenged one of the accused to fight, whereupon all four came out and attacked him. He was killed by a combination of stab, poker and hatchet wounds. Lord Justice-Clerk Aitchison told the jury that the best direction he could give them was a "perfectly general" one, and he directed them that if they found that the accused "were provoked in a real and substantial sense, so that it was only natural and human that they should retaliate,"[24] they should bring in a verdict of culpable homicide. This dictum is wide enough to cover any form of provocation, but it should be read, it is submitted, in its context which was, or could be regarded as, one of threatened violence. It must also, it is submitted, be read in its historical context, the context of High Court at Glasgow in the 1930s when judges and juries were extremely loth to convict anyone of murder.[25] Such a wide statement, in any event, can probably not be regarded as expressing Lord Aitchison's considered views on the whole question of provocation, especially as apparently no authorities were cited to him. His Lordship clearly felt that the facts in *McGuinness* could amount to provocation, but it cannot be assumed that he thought that any other facts which fitted his "perfectly general" direction would also amount to provocation.

The second case is an unreported case referred to by Professor Smith in his article on "Capital Punishment" in 1953 *Scots Law Times*.[26] It was a case in 1940 in which the accused was a Dunkirk survivor whom the victim had called a "bloody Dunkirk harrier", and a "sympathetic - if self-willed - jury refused to convict,"[27] which suggests that they were directed to disregard the verbal provocation but refused to do so. In any event the facts are exceptional, and even if the jury were directed that they might take the provocation into account it is unlikely that the courts would follow such an exceptional unreported case, or treat it as authority for the general principle that words of abuse can constitute provocation.

The third case is *Crawford v. H.M. Advocate*.[28] Crawford killed his **25.28** father after what he believed to be a threat by the latter. The accused had frequently quarrelled with his father but had only once been assaulted by him, and that had been many years previously when he was only 16. His plea of self-defence was withdrawn from the jury, but Lord Mackay, the trial judge, left to them a plea of provocation caused by many years of domestic unhappiness. His Lordship had his doubts about whether this could amount to provocation, but took the view that as provocation was not a special defence he should leave it to the jury; he seems also to have thought that it might be possible to regard the facts as amounting to a "constant terrification" lasting up to the time of the fatal assault.[29]

---

[23] 1937 J.C. 37.

[24] At 40.

[25] So far did this unwillingness go that in the first murder trial of the notorious Patrick Carraher the jury were directed that the absence of provocation by the victim might lead them to take the view that the accused had not acted deliberately in killing him, and so entitle them to reduce the charge to one of culpable homicide: see Blake (ed.), *Trials of Patick Carraher* (London and Edinburgh, 1951), pp. 117–118.

[26] 1953 S.L.T. (News) 197, 199.

[27] *ibid.*

[28] 1950 J.C. 67.

[29] See Extract of Proceedings, High Court at Glasgow, May 1950.

The appeal in *Crawford* was directed against the trial judge's refusal to leave the special defence of self-defence to the jury, and so was not directly concerned with the sufficiency of the provocation; in any event there was evidence of diminished responsibility to support the jury's verdict of culpable homicide. But Lord Justice-General Cooper in the course of his opinion said, "I assume in the appellant's favour that the culpability of his action falls to be reduced because of his physical and mental state, coupled with the provocation which the jury may have been entitled to infer from his unhappy home life."[30] This does suggest a much broader view of provocation than that taken by the Institutional writers, but it is *obiter*, and is not even expressed as a definite dictum. It is submitted that it is unlikely that it represented Lord Cooper's considered views on the matter, especially as his Lordship did not consider the relation of such a defence to the rule that where provocation is pled in response to a charge of murder the assault must be shown to have followed immediately on the provocation.[31] A long course even of persecution, and *a fortiori* of unhappiness, would probably not be enough unless coupled with a final provocative act.

25.29   The fourth case is *Jas Berry*,[32] in which Lord Keith left provocation to the jury, although the only provocation alleged was verbal. The accused was convicted of murder, and in dismissing his appeal on another point the Lord Justice-General, giving the opinion of the court,[33] said:

> "The murder was the murder of a lady with whom the applicant had been having a sexual encounter without great success.
> . . . the provocation alleged here was that in the course of the sexual encounter the lady taunted the applicant with his inadequate prowess, compared him unfavourably to his uncle in that regard and made some critical observations about whether or not he might be the father of his children. This the judge left to the jury on the basis that the jury would be entitled to decide whether the taunts in all the circumstances could amount to sufficient provocation which in law would justify the jury in reducing the quality of the crime from murder to culpable homicide. Whether the judge was right to leave that matter to the jury is a matter on which we entertain grave doubt".

The final case is *Stobbs v. H.M. Advocate*,[34] where Lord Cowie left to the jury as provocation the accused's story that the girl he had killed and with whom he was having an affair had threatened to tell his wife of that affair if he, in accordance with the intentions he expressed to the girl, brought the affair to an end. His Lordship told the jury that words were normally not sufficient, but that there might be cases where the type of words used could result in loss of self-control. The subsequent appeal was not, however, concerned with this issue.

Section 3 of the Homicide Act 1957 does not apply to Scotland, and the mere fact of its non-application may, if anything, tell against its acceptance in Scotland. The obvious approach would be to read the Act as meaning that Parliament did not intend to interfere with Scots law on

---

[30] 1950 J.C. at 71.
[31] Macdonald, p.94.
[32] (1976) S.C.C.R. (Supp.) 156.
[33] *ibid*., at 158.
[34] 1983 S.C.C.R. 190.

this matter by amending it in the same way as it amended the law of England.[35] In any event, *McGuiness, Crawford, Berry,* and *Stobbs* were criticised in *Thomson v. H.M. Advocate*[36] as being "difficult to reconcile with the statements of Hume, Alison and Macdonald", although it did not prove necessary to reach any concluded view on the soundness of what was said by the trial judges in these cases.

(4) *Third party provocation.* If loss of control was to be taken as the **25.30** only important element in provocation, and the question of who started the trouble was regarded as unimportant, there would be no reason to confine provocation to provocation by the deceased. Provocation by A which caused B to lose control and kill C could then operate to convict B of culpable homicide, just as provocation by C could have done. Thus, as Professor Smith suggests,[37] Iago's statements to Othello could rank as provocation, since they gave him information regarding Desdemona's adultery which led him to kill her while suffering from loss of control as a result of discovering her adultery. Provocation does not justify homicide,[38] it only operates to show that in acting as he did, the accused was not doing so with the wickedness that murder requires. That being so, it should be concerned solely with the accused's state of mind, should look at the situation solely from the accused's point of view; and from Othello's point of view Iago's lies were just as provocative as a true confession from Desdemona would have been.[39]

One can figure other situations in which an accused may be taunted into killing someone in circumstances in which the taunter cannot be charged with murder because the accused must be regarded as a free agent, but in which at the same time it would be unfair not to allow the taunts to rank as provocation. Suppose A meets B, who many years earlier killed A's mother, and C, who has a grudge of his own against B. Suppose C reveals B's guilt to A and expresses the view that A should now kill B: so far, if A kills B he is guilty of murder. But suppose C

---

[35] The Lord Advocate's reason for not applying the section to Scotland even "for the removal of doubt", so to speak, was that to do so would mean that "it might be said that a judge, in circumstances in which he felt that there was an opportunity for a verdict of culpable homicide rather than a verdict of murder, but there did not exist either provocation by words or provocation by actions, would be bound to withdraw the possibility of culpable homicide from the jury": *Hansard,* H.C., Jan. 28, 1957, Vol. 563, cols 782–783, which is difficult to understand. If there is provocation neither by words nor actings there is no provocation, and no alteration of the law of provocation is going to affect the matter. Nor is the law of provocation going to affect any other ground on which culpable homicide might be returned on a murder charge. Professor Smith's view in 1953 was that words of insult, as against verbal information, had always been regarded as insufficient to constitute provocation: T.B. Smith, "Capital Punishment", 1953 S.L.T. (News) 197, at 199. In 1957 he said of s.3 that "In the English law of murder now, as in Scotland already, rigid categories of provocation have been discarded": "Malice in Murderland", 1957 S.L.T. (News) 129, 130, but this remark follows on a discussion of *Holmes v. D.P.P.* [1946] A.C. 588, and may be restricted to adultery cases. Professor Smith's view in 1955 was that "verbal provocation of the nature of mere vulgar abuse . . . will generally not be accepted as sufficient": see his volume on Scotland in *The British Commonwealth* series, at 732. His latest view is that section 3 was not made applicable to Scotland because Parliament considered it was already law here: T.B. Smith, p.144.

[36] 1985 S.C.C.R. 448, Lord Cameron at 457; Lord Hunter, at 459–460, referred to these cases as being of "doubtful authority".

[37] "Malice in Murderland", 1957 S.L.T. (News) 129, 130.

[38] As Donnedieu de Vabres points out, if A kills a husband in order to prevent the latter killing him, A's action is justifiable: Donnedieu de Vabres, 232.

[39] cf. *H.M. Advocate v. McKean*, 1996 S.C.C.R. 402, where the information as to the infidelity came not from the deceased but from the deceased's child.

expresses contempt for A's reluctance to kill B, casts scorn on A's devotion to his mother, taunts A with cowardice, and so on, until A gives way under the pressure and kills B. Surely, in such circumstances, if the law recognises provocation by words at all, it should sustain a plea of provocation by A.[40]

Similarly A would be entitled to plead provocation where he had lost his self-control because of what the deceased B said to C, whether or not the situation was analogous to a plea of justifiable homicide in defence of C's life. Hume recognises that A is entitled to plead provocation where he kills B in excessive retaliation in defence of C. If loss of self-control were the only criterion, A may be entitled to plead provocation where, for example, he sees B insulting his wife or ill-treating his dog.

The degree of provocation

25.31   Whatever the law is regarding the nature of the provocation it will recognise, it must also decide what degree of provocation it will recognise as sufficient to justify the return of a culpable homicide verdict on a murder charge. In particular it must decide whether provocation is to be measured by reference to the particular accused, or by reference to the reasonable man. Need the accused show only that he was in fact provoked to loss of control by the actings of the deceased, or must he show in addition that a reasonable man would have been so provoked? Is the test subjective or objective?

It is rather paradoxical to talk of the reasonable man in this connection, and to ask "Would the reasonable man have been provoked to the extent of losing control of himself?" This is because it is strange to talk of the provoked reasonable man, of the extent to which a reasonable man is likely to lose his reason, and of what constitutes reasonable action on the part of a man who is *ex hypothesi* suffering from an inability to control his actions by the use of his reason. The question really is "Would the average man have lost control?" or rather "Was it to be expected that a normal average man would lose control as a result of the provocation offered?"

25.32   *The test of the reasonable man.* The arguments for and against the reasonable man test can best be appreciated in the light of examples. In the following two examples the reasonable man test excludes a plea of provocation, whether or not the provocation in question is of a nature recognised by the law.

In *Bedder v. D.P.P.*,[41] the accused was an impotent man who had unsuccessfully tried to have intercourse with a prostitute. She jeered at him for his failure, hit him, and kicked him; he lost control and stabbed her to death. The House of Lords held that as the prostitute's conduct would not have provoked the reasonable man into killing her, the accused's conviction of murder must stand, since the fact of his impotence could not be taken into account.

The second example was given by Mr A. Greenwood, M.P., in one of the debates on the Homicide Act 1957.[42] Two Yugoslavs were working

---

[40] This may sound fantastic, but such a situation might arise if *e.g.* B was a former concentration-camp guard who had tortured A's mother to death and escaped punishment.
[41] [1954] 1 W.L.R. 1119. *Cf. D.P.P. v. Camplin* [1978] A.C. 705, and see now *R. v. Smith (Morgan)* [2000] 3 W.L.R. 654, HL.
[42] *Hansard*, H.C., Nov. 15, 1956, Vol. 560, col. 1164.

on a farm in England; one had fought with the partisans and all his family had been killed by the Germans; the other had been a Quisling. One day the partisan broke down and wept over the fate of his family, and the Quisling jeered at him for this. The partisan picked up an axe and killed the Quisling. The partisan was convicted of murder and hanged, perhaps partly because of the verbal nature of the provocation offered. But even if verbal provocation is admitted, as it now is in England, he would still be guilty of murder if the degree of provocation were tested by reference to a similar situation involving two Englishmen. It is clear that justice requires that the peculiar relationship of the two men to each other, one a partisan and one a Quisling, should be taken into account in considering the defence of provocation.[43]

The arguments in favour of the reasonable man test. The reason given for **25.33** the adoption of the test is that "if it were not so there might be circumstances in which a bad-tempered man would be acquitted and a good-tempered man would be hanged, which, of course, is neither law nor sense."[44] It is submitted, with the greatest respect, that this argument is itself neither law nor sense. There is no question of acquitting anyone, but merely of convicting him of culpable homicide and not of murder. And, as is pointed out in *Russell on Crime*,[45] there can never be any question of hanging the good-tempered man. If the good- and bad-tempered man are thought of as being the two extremes on either side of the reasonable man, the good-tempered man will never need to invoke the plea of provocation, because he will never be provoked into killing anyone.

If the good-tempered man *is* the reasonable man he will be provoked only by what would provoke the reasonable man and so will never be hanged. The good-tempered man cannot be hanged on the objective test, and no man, good- or bad-tempered, can be hanged on the subjective test if he was in fact provoked so as to lose control. The good-tempered man cannot be affected by the extension of a rule of law which at its narrowest is sufficient to protect him.

The real objection is to allowing the bad-tempered man to use his bad temper as an excuse. But to refuse to allow this "may be in effect to inflict punishment not so much in respect of the particular act of deliberate malice, as of a want of habitual control over a mind naturally impetuous and ready to break forth on slight occasions."[46] It would be as illogical as punishing a drunk man for his drunkenness by convicting him of murder, which, of course, is what the law now does.[47]

Even if it is accepted that the law has a duty to curb the bad-tempered man, and that a man cannot plead his "want of habitual control over a mind . . . ready to break forth on slight occasions", it by no means

---

[43] See now *R. v. Smith (Morgan)* [2000] 3 W.L.R. 654, HL.

[44] R.C. Evid. of Lord Cooper, Q. 5367. In *Smith v. H.M. Advocate*, High Court at Glasgow, Feb. 1952, reported on another point, 1952 J.C. 66, Lord Cooper directed the jury that it was "not the provocation which might produce consequences in a pugnacious and excitable man under the influence of a good many drinks", which was relevant; it had to be "such as would induce an ordinary reasonable man to act as this man did." (Lord Cooper's directions, in so far as relevant, were quoted by L.J.-G. Rodger in *Drury v. H.M. Advocate*, 2001 S.L.T. 1013 (five judges), opinion at para. [33].)

[45] At 546.

[46] Fourth Report of the Criminal Law Commissioners, p. xxxviii, Parl. Papers, 1839, xix, Digest, Art. 43, note (*i*).

[47] *Brennan v. H.M. Advocate*, 1977 J.C. 38; Vol. I, paras 12.12 *et seq.*

follows that the law must adopt the test of the reasonable man in its
entirety. There is a great difference between merely giving way to
temper, and losing control in circumstances in which it would be unfair
wholly to blame one for doing so. The scope of the plea of provocation
can be restricted, and the principle of deterrence sufficiently satisfied, it
is submitted, by asking if the accused made reasonable efforts to control
himself.[48] He would have to satisfy the jury that he did not just "fly off
the handle" and indulge his temper because that was the easiest way of
reacting to the situation: he would have to show that he was provoked
beyond his endurance. It seems unfair to ask that he should go further
and show that he was provoked beyond the endurance of the reasonable
man, that is to say, in practice, show that he was provoked beyond what
the judge or jury, sitting in the calm atmosphere of the court, think
would have been the extent of their own endurance.

25.34 *The arguments against the reasonable man test.* (i) As Mr. J.W.C. Turner
points out, the use of the reasonable man in the law of provocation is
"one more illustration of the way in which a point of evidence has been
allowed to slide into a point of law, and of the inevitable mischief which
thereby results."[49] Instead of being used as a way of testing the truth of
the accused's statement that he lost self-control, the reasonable man has
been turned into an objective standard of self-control. Even if the jury
believe that the accused, in fact, lost control to an extreme degree, and
that he killed because of this, they must probably convict him of murder
unless they think that the reasonable man would have lost control to that
degree, a result which, it is submitted, is clearly unjust, especially when
what is in question is not the objective rightness of what was done but
whether the accused showed the degree of wickedness which murder
requires. If the accused's alleged loss of self-control was something
which the jury feel was quite unusual and unexpected in the circumstances this may properly lead them to refuse to believe that he did lose
control, but if they do believe it, its unexpectedness seems unimportant
— even the law must recognise that the unexpected can happen.

25.35   (ii) The objective test is also open to the criticism that it refuses to
recognise that certain groups of people are more susceptible to certain
types of provocation than are others. Even within the principle of
disfacilitation,[50] so to speak, its standard is too impersonal — it deals
always with "the reasonable man", the man on top of a "bus in
Sauchiehall Street", instead of dealing with, for example, the reasonable
Yugoslav in a case in which the accused is a Yugoslav, or the reasonable
impotent man in a case in which the accused is impotent. Any
reasonable man — in the non-legal meaning of the word — would
consider the accused in the two examples given as being more deserving
of sympathy than a normal man like Kizileviczius who disarmed and
killed his father,[51] or the four accused in *McGuinness*[52] who wantonly
slaughtered the deceased because he had challenged one of them to a

---

[48] This requirement, incidentally, might result in the conviction for murder of indignant,
e.g., husbands who as the law now stands are likely to be convicted of culpable homicide.
Cf. Drury v. H.M. Advocate, 2001 S.L.T. 1013.
[49] *Russell on Crime*, p.534.
[50] Vol. I, para. 7.56.
[51] *H.M. Advocate v. Kizileviczius*, 1938 J.C. 60.
[52] *H.M. Advocate v. McGuinness*, 1937 J.C. 37.

fight. It is, with respect, wrong to say, as did the House of Lords in *Bedder v. D.P.P.*,[53] that, "It would be plainly illogical not to recognise an unusually excitable or pugnacious temperament in the accused as a matter to be taken into account but yet to recognise for that purpose some unusual physical characteristic, be it impotence or another." But, even if it is assumed that the standard is the even-tempered man, why must it be the even-tempered potent healthy average Scotsman? Of course such a person is not going to kill someone who says, "You're the scum of the earth, you dirty Jew", but that is no reason for refusing *a priori* to accept that such a remark might in some circumstances provoke a survivor of Belsen into killing the person who said it; conversely the fact that a Glaswegian might be provoked into doing violence by being called a "f. . .g Billyboy"[54] does not mean that a black African who reacts violently to such a remark is entitled to claim the same degree of loss of self-control through provocation just because he happens to stand trial for murder in Glasgow.

(iii) The purpose of the plea of provocation is to enable the law to **25.36** take cognisance of the plight of the individual accused and to override to some extent the principle of deterrence. This purpose will be defeated by the laying down of general rules *ab ante* as to the circumstances in which a plea of provocation can be accepted. It is the purpose of the law "to curb and repress a jealous, choleric, or quarrelsome humour, so far as this can be done without injustice in the particular case",[55] and justice in each particular case requires an investigation of the circumstances of that case, and an assessment of the position of the particular accused; it cannot be done by ignoring the particular case and concentrating on a hypothetical case in which the particular accused is replaced by a legal fiction. Just as the trivial nature of the provocation offered, or the unexpectedness of the accused's loss of control, may help the jury to disbelieve his story, so the fact that he was impotent or a black African, or the fact that the deceased was a prostitute or a member of the Ku Klux Klan, may help them to understand why the accused reacted as he did, and lead them to believe his story.

Scots law

The position in Scots law has recently been clarified by the full bench **25.37** appeal of *Drury v. H.M. Advocate*.[56] The primary issue in the appeal was whether the trial judge had been correct to direct the jury, in a case where the accused allegedly lost self-control as a result of his discovery of the sexual infidelity of his partner (from whom he was entitled to expect fidelity), that the violent reaction of the accused immediately following such discovery should not have been grossly disproportionate to the provocation. The court had no difficulty in disposing of that issue: since the time of Hume, discovery of sexual infidelity had been regarded as an exceptional type of provocation wherein the rules might differ from those applicable to "ordinary" provocation; in particular, if there was a rule requiring some measure of proportionality in "ordinary"

---

[53] [1954] 1 W.L.R. 1119. Lord Simmonds L.C. at 1123.
[54] *cf. McGuinness, supra.*
[55] Hume, i, 249.
[56] 2001 S.L.T. 1013 (five judges).

provocation (that is to say, provocation by violence),[57] it did not and could not apply in the exceptional sort of provocation involved in the appeal, where the provoking events and the reaction to them were not commensurable.[58]

The Advocate Depute, however, argued[59] that if the law did not demand proportionality in relation to cases of "sexual infidelity" provocation, the Appeal Court should introduce such a requirement, since otherwise all killings carried out in the aftermath of the discovery of infidelity would have to be regarded as culpable homicides; in short, that the accused's own evidence that he had made such a discovery, had lost control and had at once killed his unfaithful partner would be all that would be necessary to establish provocation (provided that he was believed, and that he and his partner had in fact been the sole parties to a relationship in which each was entitled to demand fidelity from the other).

That there should be no test of the "reasonableness" of, for example, the nature and extent of the accused's response to the provocation in all the relevant circumstances would scarcely have accorded well with the general preference for objectivity in Scots criminal law; Lord Justice General Rodger, therefore, favoured the suggestion put forward by the appellant's counsel that the accused's reaction should be tested not by resort to the fiction of the reasonable man (since that was objectionable for the sort of reasons discussed above[60]), but rather by use of the concept of the ordinary man or woman.[61] But of what is the ordinary man or woman to be the measure? There are at least two possibilities.[62]

---

[57] The court noted that an absence of gross disproportion between the provoking violence and the accused's reaction to it had been required in many cases involving ordinary provocation; but it declined to rule on the correctness of such requirement in the absence of having heard sufficient argument on the issue. See *ibid.*, opinion of L.J.-G. Rodger, at para. [35]; opinion of Lord Johnston, at paras [18]–[19]; opinion of Lord Nimmo Smith, at para. [5]: *cf.* opinion of Lord Cameron of Lochbroom, at para. [7].

[58] See, *ibid.*, opinion of L.J.-G. Rodger, at para. [28]; opinion of Lord Johnston, at para. [20]; opinion of Lord Nimmo Smith, at para. [7]; opinion of Lord Cameron of Lochbroom, at paras [8] and [10]. (Lord Mackay of Drumadoon agreed in general with the opinion of the Lord Justice General; see Lord Mackay's opinion, at para. [1].)

[59] See opinion of L.J.-G. Rodger, *ibid.*, at para. [29], and opinion of Lord Nimmo Smith, *ibid.*, at para. [9].

[60] See paras 25.34–25.36, *supra.*

[61] *Drury v. H.M. Advocate*, 2001 S.L.T. 1013 (five judges), opinion of L.J.-G. Rodger, at paras [29] and [30].

[62] In *Drury, supra*, of course, the concept of the ordinary man or woman is to be applied as a test in relation to the exceptional type of provocation which featured in the appeal, and it seems to have been accepted that in "ordinary" cases of provocation a proportionality test would be applied to preserve a measure of objectivity: thus, if the provocation involved violence, or sufficient threats of violence, a gross disproportion between that provocation and the accused's reaction to it would bar the plea. It is submitted, however, that the ordinary man or woman test is suitable and preferable for both types of provocation: once it is accepted that the plea of provocation entails disproportionate reaction to provocative conduct and involves a concession by the law to human weakness, it is arguably more just to ask whether the accused reacted as an ordinary man or woman might have done in the precise circumstances of the individual case, rather than attempt to enquire, and rely solely upon, whether the accused's reaction was overly disproportionate to the provocation offered. As L.J.-G. Rodger pointed out in *Drury* (see his opinion, at para. [24]), Scots law is not bound by any statutory formula relative to this issue; and the law is entitled to, and should, discard any lingering reliance upon the notion of the reasonable man. (*Cf.*, the terms of the Homicide Act 1957, s.3, which applies exclusively to England and Wales: "Where on a charge of murder there is evidence on which the jury can find that the person charged was provoked (whether by things done or by things said or by

The first possibility concerns the loss of control itself. In provocation, the accused must have lost his self-control because of the provocative conduct of another. The question lies, however, whether it was "reasonable" for him to have lost control. If it is enough that the accused is believed when he declares that he *did* lose control, then to that extent the plea of provocation involves a subjective element. Put another way, the question concerns how provoking the provocative acts were or might have been in relation to the particular accused. As long as Scots law continues to discount insulting or humiliating words or behaviour, it will probably manage to avoid the problems faced in other jurisdictions where no such restrictions apply. As was pointed out above,[63] the extent to which particular words are insulting or humiliating will depend upon the characteristics (for example, ethnic background, physical disabilities, mental infirmities, prior history) of the recipient. In current Scots law, words are probably relevant only to the exceptional plea of provocation which involves the discovery of sexual infidelity, where there is almost a rule that an ordinary person may be expected to lose self-control at the moment he or she discovers a breach of the fidelity he or she was entitled to expect of another.

The second possible issue is concerned with the nature and extent of the accused's reaction to the provocation. As has been pointed out in *Drury*,[64] the person who is provoked does not lose all control, and is indeed blameable for the purposes of culpable homicide because he fails to exert control over his emotions — just as ordinary people regrettably, but understandably, tend to do from time to time. It follows that if the accused over-reacts, beyond what might be understandable in the case of an ordinary man or woman, he or she will lose the benefit of the plea. Lord Justice-General Rodger makes it plain in *Drury* that the test of the ordinary man or woman is applicable to the nature and extent of the accused's reactions, but not to the loss of control — at least in a case of "sexual infidelity" provocation. As he puts the matter[65]:

> "If there is evidence of a relationship entitling the accused to expect sexual fidelity on the part of the deceased, the jury should be directed to consider two matters. First, they should consider whether, at the time when he killed the deceased, the accused had in fact lost his self-control as a result of the preceding provocation. If they conclude that he had not lost his self-control, then the plea of provocation must fail and the jury will have to consider, on the basis of all the rest of the evidence, whether the appropriate verdict is one of murder or culpable homicide. If, on the other hand, the jury come to the conclusion that he had indeed lost his self-control due to the provocation, then they should ask themselves whether an ordinary man, having been thus provoked, would have been liable to react as he did. The nature and degree of the violence perpetrated

---

both together) to lose his self-control, the question whether the provocation was enough to make a reasonable man do as he did shall be left to be determined by the jury; and in determining that question the jury shall take into account everything both done and said according to the effect which, in their opinion, it would have on a reasonable man." It is not the case, however, that the expression "reasonable man" is to be taken quite literally: see, in particular, the recent case of *R. v. Smith (Morgan)* [2000] 3 W.L.R. 654, HL.)

[63] See para. 25.35, *supra*.

[64] *Drury v. H.M. Advocate*, 2001 S.L.T. 1013 (five judges), opinion of L.J.-G. Rodger, at paras [19], and [22]–[24].

[65] *ibid.*, at para. [34].

by the accused will, of course, be relevant to the jury's consideration of that issue. If they conclude that the accused's reaction was more extreme than was to be expected of the ordinary man, then again the plea of provocation will fail and the jury will have to consider, on the basis of all the rest of the evidence, whether the appropriate verdict is one of murder or culpable homicide. If, however, they conclude that the accused reacted in the way in which an ordinary man would have been liable to react in the same circumstances, or the evidence on provocation leaves them in reasonable doubt as to whether he acted wickedly, the jury will return a verdict of culpable homicide."[66]

Where the test is one relating to the ordinary man or woman, it seems impossible to avoid consideration of some of the same problems which beset the reasonable man notion, save that there is a semantic advantage in that one is not forced to think in terms of, for example, the "reasonable glue sniffer"[67] or the "reasonable man suffering from brain damage".[68] The main problem relates to the special characteristics of particular accused, and whether the ordinary man or woman is to be considered as a 'person' sharing such characteristics. In *R. v. Smith (Morgan)*,[69] the House of Lords decided by a narrow majority that the construct of the ordinary man or woman is to be considered as having all the characteristics of the defendant, both mental and physical; but Lord Hoffmann, who gave one of the two leading judgments for the majority, was forced into an unsatisfactory compromise, in that juries — although to be directed primarily that all characteristics of the accused are to be weighed — will also have to be dissuaded by trial judges from upholding provocation pleas on "inappropriate" grounds, such as the defendant's propensity for violent rages or childish tantrums.[70] In *Drury*, the Appeal Court did not find that there were any special characteristics of the appellant to take into account, and thus reserved its opinion on what

---

[66] Lord Mackay of Drumadoon broadly agrees with this approach (see, *ibid.*, his opinion at para. [14]); but Lord Johnston (*ibid.*, his opinion at para. [20]) and Lord Nimmo Smith (*ibid.*, of his opinion at para. [7]) would both apply the ordinary man or woman test also to the loss of control element.

[67] *cf. R. v. Morhall* [1996] 1 A.C. 90, HL.

[68] *cf. Luc Thiet Thuan v. The Queen* [1997] A.C. 131, PC.

[69] [2000] 3 W.L.R. 654, HL: this case reviews the extensive English (and foreign) case law built up (or referred to) by the House of Lords, the Privy Council and the Court of Appeal in determining the interpretation of s.3 of the Homicide Act 1957. The problem for English law, as to whether the characteristics of the accused are to be attributed to the ordinary person and if so to what extent and in relation to which issue(s), is probably solved by the majority decision in *Smith*, where there are strong hints that the problem was in part caused by over-zealous attention to certain New Zealand cases by English courts, which failed to note that such cases were concerned with the peculiar statutory rule contained in s.169(2) of the New Zealand Crimes Act 1961, which attempts to isolate the accused's capacity for self-control from his other characteristics, and reads:

"Anything done or said may be provocation if—
(a) In the circumstances of the case it was sufficient to deprive a person having the power of self-control of an ordinary person but otherwise having the characteristics of the offender, of the power of self-control; and
(b) It did in fact deprive the offender of the power of self-control and thereby induced him to commit the act of homicide."

[70] *ibid.*, at pp. 674–679: *cf.* the opinion of Lord Clyde at p. 684G-H, where he would except from individual characteristics conditions which are self-induced, and traits of exceptional pugnacity or excitability.

relevance such characteristics might have relative to the ordinary man or woman test.[70a]

Provocation and diminished responsibility. Where an accused is subjected **25.38** to a course of provocation which so affects his mind as to render him insane he will be entitled to succeed in a plea of insanity, in the same way as if his condition had been caused by alcohol, whether or not the provocation is of a kind recognised by the law. Where the result of the provocation is to produce a state of diminished responsibility he should similarly be treated like any other person of diminished responsibility. In *H.M. Advocate v. Robert Smith*,[71] the accused was subjected to a course of taunting by his fellow-workmen which so affected him that he eventually killed one of his tormentors. The taunts were described as "altogether insufficient" to cause such a reaction in an ordinary man, and this was regarded by Lord McLaren as indicating that his mind was "displaced from its balance by the long course of provocation"[72] and he was convicted of culpable homicide on the ground of diminished responsibility. Lord McLaren referred to the analogy of intoxication, and although the law regarding the relationship between intoxication and diminished responsibility is now that a man who is not of diminished responsibility when sober cannot avail himself of the doctrine when his mind is affected by drink,[73] it is submitted that this should not affect the approach of the law to the relationship between provocation and diminished responsibility.[74]

[70a] In the recent case of *Cochrane v. H.M. Advocate*, High Court on Appeal, June 13, 2001, unrep'd, it was decided that coercion, being an exculpatory defence, required to be tested objectively by reference to the ordinary sober person of reasonable firmness, in the accused's situation and sharing his characteristics. The characteristics which could be taken into account, however, were limited to those which did not destroy the essential characteristic of the hypothetical ordinary person — *i.e.*, his reasonable firmness: see opinion of L.J.-G. Rodger at paras [20]–[22]. At para. [23] of his opinion, the Lord Justice-General noted that in *Drury v. H.M. Advocate*, 2001 S.L.T. 1013, the court had left open the extent to which a wider range of characteristics might be taken into account for the purposes of provocation, and indeed whether the majority view of the House of Lords in *R. v. Smith (Morgan)*, *supra*, was to be adopted in Scotland. His Lordship decided, however, that there was a distinction to be made between defences which exculpated, such as coercion or necessity, and those, such as provocation, which were concerned not with exculpation but with the basis for punishment: see Lord Rodger's opinion at para. [25]. (*Smith* was also distinguished on other grounds: see *ibid*., at paras [26]–[28]). The implication is that consideration of a wider range of the accused's characteristics might be allowed in provocation.

[71] (1893) 1 Adam 34.

[72] At 50.

[73] *H.M. Advocate v. Macleod*, 1956 J.C. 20. See also *Galbraith v. H.M. Advocate, (No. 2)* 2001 S.L.T. 953.

[74] If that is so, it is only reasonable to hold that where an accused is already of diminished responsibility his condition should be taken into account in assessing his reaction to provocation; but such a situation cannot arise in practice since the pre-existing diminished responsibility will itself result in a conviction for culpable homicide without any reference to provocation.

CHAPTER 26

INVOLUNTARY CULPABLE HOMICIDE

Introduction

Involuntary culpable homicide[1] is the causing of death unintentionally **26.01** but either with a degree of negligence which is regarded as sufficient to make the homicide culpable but not murderous, or in circumstances in which the law regards the causing of death as criminal even in the absence of any negligence.

Causation in involuntary culpable homicide. For the purposes of the **26.02** crime of involuntary culpable homicide A will be held to have caused B's death where B's death results directly from an act or omission by A, and whether or not it was a foreseeable result of that act or omission.[2] There are some kinds of culpable homicide which require negligence on A's part and for that reason are confined to circumstances where B's death was foreseeable, but that is a question of *mens rea*; so far as the *actus reus* of the crime is concerned the criterion is that of directness and not that of foreseeability.[3]

Types of involuntary homicide. Involuntary homicides may be classed in **26.03** three groups:

(1) Where the death is accidental, as where A accidentally falls off a roof on to a pedestrian who dies as a result. In such cases it can barely be said that death was caused by A's act at all, and no question of culpability arises.

(2) Where the death is caused by A's act but is not a foreseeable result of that act, as where A slaps B who falls and dies because he suffers from an unusual physical condition unknown to A. In such a case there is no question of negligence and A's responsibility for the death must rest in the culpability of his act — here his assault on B — by way of a form of constructive *mens rea*.

(3) Where the death is a foreseeable result of A's conduct. This type includes all those cases in which A is negligent and can be subdivided according to the number of degrees of negligence recognised by the legal system in question. Modern Scots law appears to recognise two main degrees of negligence — gross negligence, and negligence, which is not gross. The second degree is measured by the same standard as is used in civil claims for reparation, by reference to the care exercised by the

---

[1] When the term "culpable homicide" is used in this chapter, it is used to mean involuntary culpable homicide.

[2] See, *e.g., Lord Advocate's Ref. (No. 1 of 1994)*, 1995 S.C.C.R. 177; *Paxton v. H.M. Advocate*, 2000 S.L.T. 771.

[3] This paragraph was considered to be a correct statement of the law by the Appeal Court in *Lord Advocate's Reference (No. 1 of 1994)*, 1995 S.C.C.R. 177, at 185F to 186A. See also Vol. I, para. 4.13.

reasonable man. The first degree cannot be measured by reference to any standard at all. It is usually described as gross, palpable, or wicked, or even just as criminal.[4] Into which degree a particular case falls is a question of fact, a question for the jury, and the only help they are given by the judge is by way of the epithets just mentioned, which are hardly more than vituperative and have no definite meaning. Presumably the jury simply look at the facts, and then look again, and come to a decision. The simplest way for them to decide would probably be to imagine they were witnessing the situation under examination, for example a situation in which the accused drove his car into a group of people. If their imagined reaction is "What a careless way to drive", then they will find that the accused's negligence was of the less gross variety. If their reaction is "What a damn stupid way to drive", they will find that the accused was grossly negligent. This second type of negligence is often referred to as recklessness, but it must be distinguished from that "wicked and deliberate" recklessness whose presence may make even unintentional homicide murder.[5]

It was at one time the law of Scotland that to cause death by negligence was always culpable homicide, however slight the degree of negligence and however lawful the conduct in the course of which the negligence occurred. In the modern law, however, homicide in the course of lawful conduct is culpable homicide only where the negligence is gross. Homicide in the course of assault is still, as it always was, culpable even in the absence of negligence, but it is not clear whether there are any circumstances today in which culpable homicide is constituted by ordinary negligence in the absence of any assault.

Culpable homicide must be considered separately with reference to homicide in the course of lawful conduct, homicide in the course of assault, and homicide in the course of other forms of unlawful conduct.

HOMICIDE IN THE COURSE OF LAWFUL CONDUCT

The old law

26.04   Hume states that, "it is culpable homicide, where slaughter follows on the doing even of a lawful act; if it is done without that caution and circumspection which may serve to prevent harm to others",[6] which means that any negligent homicide is criminal. Hume gives the following as examples of culpable homicide: "if a man leave his fowling-piece loaded, and afterwards kill in trying the lock, having forgot the condition in which he left the piece[7]: Or if in driving any carriage through the streets of a town, the driver quit his horses and they run off with the carriage, and a passenger is killed[8]: Or if workmen on the roof of a building by the side of a highway throw down slates or rubbish, without timely warning to the passenger." "In all these instances," Hume says, "there is a want of that serious and considerate regard to the safety of

---

[4] *Paton v. H.M. Advocate*, 1936 J.C. 19; *H.M. Advocate v. Sheppard*, 1941 J.C. 67.
[5] *cf. supra*, para. 23.19.
[6] Hume, i, 233.
[7] *David Buchanan* (1817) Hume, i, 192.
[8] *Robt Jackson* (1810) *ibid.*

one's neighbour, which justly makes one answerable for the consequences, and punishable to such an extent as may serve to correct so faulty a habit of mind, in one's self or others."[9]

Alison follows Hume, and states that, "It is culpable homicide if death ensue in the performance even of an act not in itself criminal, if due care of others is not taken in the performance of it."[10] He refers to *Peter Scott*[11] where it was held that a gamekeeper who picked up his gun at a party and held it in a dangerous manner was guilty of culpable homicide when the gun went off and the shot went through a hole in a partition and killed someone in the passage outside, because "even though the gun was discharged by accident, he was blameable, for putting it in such a situation that it *could go off*, and injure the inmates of the house, while in his hands",[12] and also to *Bernard Johnston and John Webster*,[13] a case of careless blasting of rocks as a result of which stone fell and killed a passer-by, as well as to a number of cases of bad driving,[14] and bad management of ships.[15]

The development of this type of culpable homicide can be traced **26.05** through the later nineteenth century cases, in which there is a great number and variety of charges. They include carelessness by persons lawfully using guns[16]; by chemists[17]; by builders[18]; by persons conducting blasting operations,[19] or storing explosives[20]; by pit managers, miners and

---

[9] Hume, i, 192–193. *Cf.* Burnett, p.26: "Culpable homicide is properly that which is committed through some blame, negligence, or want of due precaution on the part of the slayer but without any intention to kill." Hume, i, 192–193 refers to a number of cases of culpable homicide by reckless driving, including *Robert Jackson* (1810) Hume, i, 192, where the driver of a cartload of logs of wood went for a drink leaving the horses to proceed, in consequence of which a deaf and almost blind old woman was struck by a log and killed. Burnett refers to the similar case of *Spiers* (1810) Burnett 28, where a horse left on the street by the accused took fright and ran off, killing a child, but the jury acquitted because the horse had been left tied to a rail and the cause of its fright was unforeseen. Hume also refers to *Mathew Graham* (1813) Hume, i, 192, who was charged with culpable homicide but acquitted, for felling a tree carelessly which fell on and killed a passer-by. See also two cases of careless navigation of ships: *Duncan McInnes* (1825) and *Ezekiel McHaffie* (1827) both Hume, i, 193.

[10] Alison, i, 113.

[11] (1830) Alison, i, 115.

[12] *ibid. per* Lord Gillies: the jury acquitted the accused, apparently because of unsatisfactory evidence.

[13] (1827) Alison, i, 116.

[14] Alison, i, 116–122.

[15] *ibid.*, 122–126.

[16] *John Kilgour* (1827) Alison, i, 144, who was acquitted because of the unforeseeability of death in the particular case; *Geo. Barbier and Ors* (1867) 5 Irv. 483.

[17] *Robt Henderson and Wm Lawson* (1842) 1 Broun 360 where a chemist was charged with allowing an unqualified person to dispense drugs, and that person with dispensing carelessly; *Edmund F. Wheatley* (1853) 1 Irv. 225: prescribing an excessive dose; *Geo. Armitage* (1885) 5 Couper 675: selling poison by mistake for medicine; *H.M. Advocate v. Wood* (1903) 4 Adam 150: dispensing poison as a result of failure to read a label on a bottle.

[18] *Jas Kirkpatrick and Robt Stewart* (1840) Bell's Notes 71, where a contractor and foreman were charged with failure to employ the normal precautions in the course of building operations; *Alex. Dickson* (1847) Ark. 352 and *John Wilson* (1852) 1 Irv. 84, where buildings collapsed because of faults in their structure; *Hugh McLure and Ors* (1848) Ark. 448, where a railway and a bridge were badly built.

[19] *Jas Finney* (1848) Ark. 432; *John Drysdale and Ors* (1848) *ibid.* 440; *Jas Auld* (1856) 2 Irv. 459; *John Faill and Ors* (1877) 3 Couper 497.

[20] *Jas Donald Clark* (1877) 3 Couper 472, 504.

persons in charge of machinery[21]; by coachmen or horsemen[22]; by persons in charge of boats[23]; by engine drivers,[24] railway signalmen,[25] and other persons responsible for the proper running of railways.[26] The standard of care required was simply due care and circumspection. In *James Donald Clark*,[27] a charge of causing death by leaving explosives in a dangerous place, Lord Justice-Clerk Moncreiff said that if it was the accused's duty to keep the explosives in a store and not where he in fact had left them, then "[i]f that was his duty, and if he neglected it, he was guilty."[28]

26.06   The *locus classicus* of the nineteenth-century law of culpable homicide is the charge to the jury in *Wm Paton and Richd McNab*.[29] The accused were a railway superintendent and driver respectively, and were charged with culpable homicide after an accident caused by their use of a defective railway engine to carry a passenger, who had missed the ordinary train, from Glasgow to Edinburgh by a special train. Lord Justice-Clerk Hope said:

> "The degree of blame, which will constitute this crime, varies with the circumstances of each case. It is not necessary, in order to substantiate a charge of Culpable Homicide, either that there should be any intention to do to another the injury which has occurred, or that the party should even know that another is actually exposed to risk, as in the case of a carter who neglects his duty and runs down a child, though he may not know that any child actually is near him. The general rule is, that every person, placed in a situation in which his acts may affect the safety of others, must take all precautions to guard against the risk to them arising from what he is doing . . . and if that has been omitted, which common sense,

---

[21] *Robt Young* (1839) 2 Swin. 376: a diving bell; *Robt Rouatt* (1852) 1 Irv. 79, and *Geo. Seton Stenhouse and Arch. McKay* (1852) 1 Irv. 94; *Thos Hamilton and Anr* (1874) 3 Couper 19: all cases of pit machinery.

[22] *Adam Stoddart* (1836) Bell's Notes 73; *Jas Matheson* (1837) 1 Swin. 593; *Will Messon* (1841) 2 Swin. 548; *John Macarthur* (1841) Bell's Notes 74; *Wm Trotter* (1842) Bell's Notes 74; *Alex. Smith* (1842) 1 Broun 220; *John Ross and Ors* (1847) Ark. 258; *Robt Lonie* (1862) 4 Irv. 204.

[23] *John Sutherland* (1838) Bell's Notes 74; *Wm McAlister and Ors* (1837) 1 Swin. 587; *Robt Maclean* (1842) 1 Broun 416; *Thos Henderson and Ors* (1850) J. Shaw 394; *Angus MacPherson and John Stewart* (1861) 4 Irv. 85.

[24] *Jas Boyd* (1842) 1 Broun 7; *Wm Paton and Richd McNab* (1845) 2 Broun 525; *Alex. Robertson* (1859) 3 Irv. 328; *Wm Dudley* (1864) 4 Irv. 468; *H.M. Advocate v. Gourlay* (1907) 5 Adam 295.

[25] *John McDonald and Ors* (1853) 1 Irv. 164; *Alex. Currie and Anr* (1873) 2 Couper 380.

[26] *Jas Cooper* (1842) 1 Broun 389: pointsman not having switches in order; *Wm Paton and Richd McNab, supra*: superintendent allowing faulty engine to be used; *Chas Ormond and Wm Wylie* (1848) Ark. 483: careless coupling; *Wm Lyall and Alex. Ramsay* (1853) 1 Irv. 189: improper starting of train; *Thos K. Rowbotham and Ors* (1855) 2 Irv. 89: neglect to issue proper regulations for working signals and improper signalling; *Wm Baillie and Jas McCurrach* (1870) 1 Couper 442: improper starting and leaving unqualified person in charge of a station; *Alex. Currie and Anr, supra*: improper shunting by stationmaster; *Geo. Little and Ors* (1883) 5 Couper 259: improper starting. *Wm Gray* (1836) 1 Swin. 328 left undecided the question whether it is culpable homicide to allow an unauthorised person to ride on the tender of an engine which is involved in a collision which kills him.

[27] (1877) 3 Couper 472 and 504.

[28] At 507.

[29] (1845) 2 Broun 525.

and ordinary reflection as to the situation of others required, which
. . . duty to the law required for the safety of others, the guilt is
clear".[30]

The standard there set out is the same as the present-day standard in
civil law, and indeed, Lord Hope's statement of the duty of care sounds
very like Lord Atkin's famous statement of the law in *Donoghue v.
Stevenson.*[31]

The only difficulty in the nineteenth century cases was that although **26.07**
culpable homicide consisted merely of the negligent causing of death it
was common to libel as a lesser alternative charge either culpable and
reckless neglect or merely culpable neglect, and often both were libelled.
This was done even when the act involved was not strictly lawful. In one
case a nursemaid who killed a child by giving it laudanum, for the
purpose of keeping it quiet; was charged with culpable homicide, and
also with "culpable and negligent or culpable and reckless" administration of laudanum to a child to the injury of the health or danger of the
life of the child, and her plea to culpable and negligent administration
was accepted by the Crown.[32] The position of the alternative charges was
discussed in *Thos Henderson and Ors*,[33] where the charges were of
culpable homicide, and culpable and reckless neglect of duty by a ship's
officer causing the wreck of the ship and loss of life. Lord Justice-Clerk
Hope told the jury that there was no difference between the charges, and
described the introduction of the two charges as "inexpedient, as tending
to distract and confuse the minds of the Jury."[34] The jury, however,
remained determinedly confused, and convicted one accused of culpable
and reckless neglect and another of culpable but not reckless neglect,
and the court took those distinctions into account in passing sentence.

The "confusion" shown in *Henderson*[35] has persisted in the law of
culpable homicide, and foreshadowed the former distinction between
culpable homicide and the statutory crime of causing death by reckless
driving.[36] The two crimes of which the accused were convicted in
Henderson were both considered less serious than culpable homicide, so
that "reckless" conduct was regarded as something less than the type of
conduct necessary for a conviction of culpable homicide, although the
latter was said to be committed "whenever a person unintentionally
committed an act whereby the life of another was lost, or where he failed
to perform his duty when charged with the preservation of life, without

---

[30] At 533–534.
[31] 1932 S.C. (H.L.) 31, 44.
[32] *Jean Crawford* (1847) Ark. 394: it was not libelled in the alternative charge that death
had resulted from the dangerous act. In *Eliz. Hamilton* (1857) 2 Irv. 738, in similar
circumstances, only a charge of culpable homicide was brought.
[33] (1850) J. Shaw 394.
[34] At 437.
[35] (1850) J. Shaw 394.
[36] Road Traffic Act 1988, s.1. This statutory offence was replaced by the offence of
causing death by driving dangerously: see Road Traffic Act 1991, s.1, which, by adding
s.2A to the 1988 Act, provides a definition of "dangerously" in terms similar to those used
by the Scottish courts in their interpretation of "recklessly" under the older law; see
Allan v. Patterson, 1980 J.C. 57; *Mitchell v. Lockhart*, 1993 S.C.C.R. 1070, L.J.-C. Ross (op.
of the court) at 1074C–1075A; and para. 26.13, *infra. Cf. Paton v. H.M. Advocate*, 1936 J.C.
19; *Andrews v. D.P.P.* [1937] A.C. 576.

having a sufficient excuse for such neglect, and life was lost in consequence",[37] *i.e.* when culpable neglect results in death.

26.08   In two subsequent cases it was argued that it was incompetent to libel
the crime of causing death by culpable neglect as an alternative to
culpable homicide since both crimes were the same. The court rejected
the arguments, holding that although they might be right in principle
there were conclusive authorities against them.[38] In one case the Crown
stated specifically that, "the charge might have been culpable homicide
only, but in practice it has been found convenient to state the charge in
the alternative and less serious form."[39] In other words, the Crown found
it convenient to offer the jury an opportunity of convicting the accused
of something less than culpable homicide, in order to obviate the chance
of their acquitting him altogether because of their dislike of convicting of
culpable homicide where death was caused by the accused while acting
lawfully. The alternative form of charge does not seem to have been
used after 1887, but its place is now taken by statutory charges in road
traffic cases, which are the most frequent modern examples of "lawful-
act" culpable homicide.

The law does not appear to have changed throughout the nineteenth
century but, apart from traffic cases, this type of culpable homicide
became less common, perhaps because of a number of unsuccessful
prosecutions.[40] In 1903, however, Lord McLaren said in a case in which
the charge was one of culpable homicide by negligently dispensing
poison that, "it would be a very dangerous doctrine to lay down that a
man who by mistake caused the death of another was free from all
blame, and from liability to punishment merely because he was able to
say that he meant no harm, and only neglected all the precautions that
experience has shown to be necessary in the handling of poisons."[41] But
it is clear that Lord McLaren encouraged the jury to acquit the accused,
and so to avoid acting on his definition of the crime of culpable
homicide.

The modern law

26.09   "Lawful-act" culpable homicide is almost entirely confined to traffic
cases.[42] The reasons for this are mainly extra-legal. It is true that the use
of explosives, and the management of factories and mines, are now
governed by statute so that it is possible to deal with them without

---

[37] *Henderson, supra*, at 437.
[38] *Robt Lonie* (1862) 4 Irv. 204; *Jos. Calder* (1877) 3 Couper 494.
[39] *Jos. Calder, supra,* at 495.
[40] For example, *Thos Hamilton and Anr* (1874) 3 Couper 19; *Geo. Armitage* (1885) 5
Couper 675; *James Donald Clark* (1877) 3 Couper 472 and 504; *John Faill and Ors* (1877) 3
Couper 497.
[41] *H.M. Advocate v. Wood* (1903) 4 Adam 150, 160.
[42] But see the unusual case of *Sutherland (No. 1) v. H.M. Advocate*, 1994 S.C.C.R. 80,
where the accused set fire to his own house, thus destroying it whilst also unintentionally
causing the death of the man who had assisted him; the view was taken that the fire-raising
was a lawful act for the purposes of culpable homicide, the fact that there was a known
crime of setting fire to one's own property with intent to defraud insurers and that the
fire-raising in the case had been done with such an intent not being sufficient to convert
the case to one of 'unlawful act' culpable homicide (on the basis that the sole
'criminalising' factor — fraud — did not carry the necessary connotation of personal
injury). See also the very unusual case of *Fredk G. Thomsett*, High Court at Edinburgh,
Feb. 1939, unrep'd; see *infra*, para. 26.16.

reference to the common law, and fatal accidents caused by carelessness are normally followed at most only by statutory prosecutions[43]; but road traffic is also regulated by statute, and common law prosecutions for culpable homicide caused by grossly negligent driving still occur.[44] No one would be taken seriously who suggested that whenever a fatal factory or mine accident was caused by gross negligence the manager or foreman or other person responsible should be charged with culpable homicide. But on principle and on nineteenth-century authority such a charge would be quite proper, and could be brought even where an employer merely failed to employ competent staff or to instruct his staff properly,[45] or where he allowed the use of dangerous machinery.[46]

One reason for the absence of such prosecutions during the twentieth-century is the complex nature of modern factories and mines, which makes it very difficult to single out the negligent party.[47] The negligence may also be far removed in time and place from the death — the immediacy of the traffic accident is lacking, and the feeling of indignation aroused by that immediacy is dissipated by the complexity of the situation in a factory.

Another reason is probably the reluctance of the authorities to brand a respectable factory owner or senior employee as a common law criminal, especially where the circumstances are not such as to arouse any immediate indignation which might counter-balance this reluctance. It is accordingly the present practice, if not the present law, that an employer who causes the death of a workman by gross carelessness, for example, by leaving a dangerous machine unfenced, or by allowing the use of a system of working so bad that its use is "obvious folly",[48] is not guilty of culpable homicide, or indeed of any common law crime. No doubt if such a charge were brought the standard of negligence necessary for conviction would be that gross, palpable and wicked negligence required in traffic cases, and it would be very difficult to establish this degree of negligence in the absence of anything akin to the situation of the driver recklessly careering down the road at speed and running into his victim.

Traffic cases. In the nineteenth century the standard of care imposed by **26.10** the criminal law was the same as that imposed by the civil law — reasonable care. Signs of modern developments can, however, be seen in the case of *Drever and Tyre*[49] which arose out of a shipping collision. The accused were charged with culpable homicide, and alternatively with "culpable and reckless neglect of duty" by members of a ship's crew in failing to keep a proper lookout. Lord Young directed the jury that:

---

[43] For example, *Wilson v. McFadyean*, 1954 J.C. 107.

[44] Although they are in process of disappearing now that causing death by "dangerous driving" is a statutory offence which carries a maximum penalty of 10 years in prison: *infra*, para. 26.13.

[45] For example, *Thos Rowbotham and Ors* (1855) 2 Irv. 89; *Wm Baillie and Jas McCurrach* (1870) 1 Couper 442.

[46] *cf. Wm Paton and Richd McNab* (1845) 2 Broun 525, L.J.-C. Hope at 534.

[47] This problem is exacerbated by the approach which the law adopts to the problem of corporate criminal liability: see Vol. I, Chap. 8, paras 8.89 *et seq.; cf. Att.-Gen.'s Ref. (No. 2 of 1999)* [2000] 3 W.L.R. 195, CA, which affirms that under modern English law, in cases alleging corporate manslaughter, it remains essential to identify the human individual responsible for the death in question.

[48] *cf. Morton v. Wm Dixon Ltd*, 1909 S.C. 807.

[49] (1885) 5 Couper 680.

"[L]aw upon this subject undoubtedly is, that any person who is in a situation or charged with a duty which involves the safety of human life, must observe care and caution in the discharge of his duty, or at least an absence of gross negligence and recklessness. I put it to you in that way, gentlemen, because it is not any slight fault or neglect which will make a man a criminal; it must be a notable and serious fault or neglect by a man upon whose care and caution the safety of human life depends."[50]

Lord Young here requires more than ordinary negligence, he requires "gross negligence". The reason for this development was clearly a feeling of sympathy with the sailors, a feeling that "it is hard to impute crime, and it will require exceptional circumstances to impute crime, to a man who is present at his post, on the spot where his duty requires him to be, attending to his duty to the best of his ability and to nothing else."[51] The benefit of this attitude has now, however, been extended to motor drivers driving in a manner contrary to the criminal provisions of the Road Traffic Acts.

Denver and Tyre[52] did not establish any definite change in the law. In 1907, for example, an engine driver who failed to adhere to the proper method of driving in a snowstorm and as a result ran into a station and killed twenty-two people was charged simply with failing to take the necessary precautions and killing the victims. The words "reckless" and "negligent" do not appear in the indictment, and the report of the judge's charge is unhelpful.[53]

26.11   The next case of interest is *Waugh v Campbell*[54] which did not involve homicide. The accused was charged with driving "recklessly and negligently", contrary to section 1 of the Motor Car Act of 1903; he had taken a blind corner on the wrong side of the road, without sounding his horn, and had collided with a car coming in the opposite direction. The sheriff-substitute acquitted him, holding that there was nothing to show either recklessness or negligence, but the High Court reversed this decision and held that there had been negligence within the meaning of the Act. They took the opportunity to observe that the statutory negligence differed from common law negligence, and that the sheriff had erred in applying the common law requirement of moral blame. This case sets the tone for the modern law in that it states clearly that there are at least two types of road traffic negligence — one, a minor degree of negligence, constitutes a statutory offence; the other, a gross degree of negligence, constitutes a common law offence. Lord Salveson pointed out that "the statutory offence may be constituted merely by negligence, although the judge who tries the case thinks the negligence was not gross negligence and involved no moral blame",[55] although it is not clear what sort of blame Lord Salvesen thought attached to common law negligence. He also specifically distinguished the civil and criminal standards,

---

[50] At 686.

[51] *ibid.* at 687.

[52] (1885) 5 Couper 680.

[53] *H.M. Advocate v. Gourlay* (1907) 5 Adam 295. But in 1889 in *H.M. Advocate v. Donald Campbell* (1889) 2 White 313, where the accused was charged with causing a fatal collision by bad navigation, the Crown accepted that the collision was due to the accused's mistaking a white light for a green light and invited a verdict of Not Guilty.

[54] 1920 J.C. 1.

[55] At 6.

saying "We are quite familiar with cases in which drivers are found liable by a jury for negligence involving loss of life or injury to person, and yet the public prosecutor would never dream of bringing a complaint."[56]

Although there was no citation of common law authorities in *Waugh v. Campbell*,[57] the dicta are in accord with the twentieth century attitude to traffic cases. There may, however, have been some doubt on the matter in the 1920s, as in 1931 a short extract from a charge to a jury by Lord Justice-Clerk Alness in a culpable homicide case was reported. Lord Alness said, "at one time in our law it was quite sufficient to establish a charge of culpable homicide that any fault on the part of the accused resulting in the death of a fellow human being had been established. I do not think that this is the law today . . . the carelessness which the Crown must prove, according to our conception of the law today, in a case of this kind, must be gross and palpable carelessness."[58]

This standard was approved by the Criminal Appeal Court in the case **26.12** of *Paton v. H.M. Advocate*,[59] where it was said that there must be "gross or wicked, or criminal negligence, something amounting, or at any rate analogous, to a criminal indifference to consequences."[60] The court were rather reluctant to set such a high standard, and Lord Aitchison went so far as to suggest that this "unfortunate" modification of the old law should perhaps be reconsidered. Yet the only authority quoted to the court was *Cranston*[61] and there seems to have been nothing to prevent them reconsidering the matter there and then. It can only be surmised that the high standard had become very generally accepted, perhaps because of the refusal of juries to convict drivers except in extreme cases.

The standard in *Paton* is not only extreme, it is also rather vague. It is clear that recklessness sufficient to entail conviction for the former offences of reckless driving, under the now repealed section 2 of the Road Traffic Act 1972, or causing death by reckless driving, under the now repealed section 1 of that Act, is not necessarily sufficient to entail conviction for culpable homicide, but that is all that is clear.[62] But to say that there must be criminal negligence before there can be a conviction for culpable homicide is tautologous, unless the word "criminal" is used emotively; to say there must be gross, or wicked, or palpable, negligence, is just to say that there must be negligence, and to add an expletive. The assessment of negligence is very much a jury question, and therefore there can be no definite categories of negligence. All that *Paton*[63] means is that the jury ought not to convict of culpable homicide unless they feel the accused has been very careless indeed. Juries are, of course, only too willing not to convict drivers of culpable homicide, and the modern

---

[56] At 5. Lord Salvesen also showed a remarkable lack of prescience when he said that the best way to remedy the apparent contradiction between the common and statutory law would be to alter the statute to conform with the common law, since "It may have been that, when the statute was framed, a motor car was looked upon as an instrument of greater danger to the public than we are now accustomed to consider it, and I think it would be better if legislation with regard to motor cars were brought more up to date."

[57] 1920 J.C. 1.

[58] *H.M. Advocate v. Cranston*, 1931 J.C. 28.

[59] 1936 J.C. 19.

[60] L.J.-C. Aitchison at 22.

[61] 1931 J.C. 28, *supra*, para. 26.11.

[62] *Paton, supra; Dunn v. H.M. Advocate*, 1960 J.C. 55. *Cf. Andrews v. D.P.P.* [1937] A.C. 576; *Allan v. Patterson*, 1980 J.C. 57.

[63] 1936 J.C. 19.

development of the law probably owes a great deal to the fact that whereas nineteenth-century judges and juries did not drive railway engines but were on the contrary passengers, modern judges and juries do drive cars, and are easily moved by arguments of the "There but for the grace . . ." kind. Before they will convict they must be convinced that the accused behaved in a way in which they would not behave, that he behaved "wickedly" and "criminally".[64]

26.13   ROAD TRAFFIC ACT 1988. Sections 1, 2 and 2A, as substituted/inserted by the Road Traffic Act 1991 provide:

"**1.** A person who causes the death of another person by driving a mechanically propelled vehicle dangerously on a road or other public place is guilty of an offence.[65]

2. A person who drives a mechanically propelled vehicle dangerously on a road or other public place is guilty of an offence.[66]

2A.—(1) For the purposes of sections 1 and 2 above a person is to be regarded as driving dangerously if (and subject to subsection (2) below, only if)—
(a) the way he drives falls far below what would be expected of a competent and careful driver, and
(b) it would be obvious to a competent and careful driver that driving in that way would be dangerous.
(2) A person is also to be regarded as driving dangerously for the purposes of sections 1 and 2 above if it would be obvious to a competent and careful driver that driving the vehicle in its current state would be dangerous.
(3) In subsections (1) and (2) above 'dangerous' refers to danger either of injury to any person or of serious damage to property; and in determining for the purposes of these subsections what would be expected of, or obvious to, a competent and careful driver in a particular case, regard shall be had not only to the circumstances of which he could be expected to be aware but also to any circumstances shown to have been within the knowledge of the accused.
(4) In determining for the purposes of subsection (2) above the state of a vehicle, regard may be had to anything attached to or carried on or in it and to the manner in which it is attached or carried."

The standard of driving which qualifies for conviction under either section 1 or section 2 is, of course, the same, as was the case with the

---

[64] In practice convictions of motorists for culpable homicide during the 20th century since *Paton* were normally obtained only where the driver was drunk, and were usually not sought except in such cases: see, however, now paras 26.13 and 26.14 *infra*. More recent cases, involving motorists (and non-motorists), seem to imply that the test may not be as high as *Paton* would tend to suggest: see, *e.g.*, *Sutherland (No. 1) v. H.M. Advocate*, 1994 S.C.C.R. 80; *McDowall v. H.M. Advocate*, 1998 S.C.C.R. 343; and see Vol. I, para. 7.59.

[65] Maximum penalty, 10 years' imprisonment: Road Traffic Offenders Act 1988, Sched. 2, as substituted by the Criminal Justice Act 1993, s.67(1).

[66] Maximum penalty, on indictment two years' imprisonment and a fine, or on summary conviction, six months and a fine of the statutory maximum: Road Traffic Offenders Act 1988, Sched. 2.

now repealed offences of "causing death by driving recklessly" and "driving recklessly" prior to 1991. Those previous offences had been enacted in 1977,[67] and the use of the adverb "recklessly" had probably been intended to introduce a measure of subjectivity to these most serious of traffic offences;[68] but the "recklessness" required at that time was left entirely undefined, and courts at the highest level in both Scotland and England subsequently interpreted the offences quite objectively.[69] In Scotland in particular, the Appeal Court considered that in order to convict a person of driving recklessly it was not necessary to enquire as to his state of mind at all. Indeed, in words now echoed in section 2A(1) of the Road Traffic Act 1988, the Court stated:

> "[B]efore the adverb 'recklessly' [can be applied to the driving in question by a jury] they must find that it fell far below the standard of driving to be expected of the competent and careful driver and that it occurred either in the face of obvious and material dangers which were or should have been observed, appreciated and guarded against, or in circumstances which showed a complete disregard for any potential dangers which might result from the way in which the vehicle was being driven."[70]

The reference there, in the alternative, to "a complete disregard for any potential dangers" might suggest the "indifference to consequences" which in turn is suggestive of something more than negligence, however gross: but the current offences involving dangerous driving do not refer to indifference to consequences at all. What those offences require is driving which falls far below[71] the standard to be expected of a competent and careful driver and which would carry, in the estimation of such a driver, risk of personal injury or serious damage to property — a purely objective standard of negligence. As the offence of causing death by dangerous driving now carries a maximum penalty of 10 years' imprisonment,[72] there seems little reason to invoke culpable homicide in the case of drivers who kill (unintentionally) in consequence of the manner of their driving — and this will be especially so if *Paton*[73]

---

[67] Criminal Law Act 1977, s.50, which substituted new provisions for ss. 1 and 2 of the Road Traffic Act 1972; these provisions were re-enacted by the Road Traffic Act 1988, prior to the amendments introduced by the Road Traffic Act 1991.

[68] See, *e.g.*, Road Traffic Law Review Report (Dr P. North, Chairman), Dept of Transport, 1988, para. 4.9.

[69] See *Allan v. Patterson*, 1980 J.C. 57; *R. v. Lawrence* [1982] A.C. 510, HL.

[70] *Allan v. Patterson*, 1980 J.C. 57, at 60. The debt which the new offences involving "driving dangerously" owed to the opinion of the court in that case was acknowledged in *Mitchell v. Lockhart*, 1993 S.C.C.R. 1070. See also *H.M. Advocate v. Campbell*, 1993 S.C.C.R. 765, a case of causing death by reckless driving under the old law, where it was held that the interpretation of "recklessness" given in *Allan v. Patterson* was sufficiently wide to cover mechanical defects which were within the knowledge of the driver and which adversely and significantly affected the safety of his vehicle: it will be noted that *Campbell* introduced thus far a subjective element of knowledge — an element which is conspicuously absent from the detailed account of "dangerousness" given in the modern statutory law.

[71] This enables a distinction to be drawn between them and careless driving contrary to s.3 of the Road Traffic Act 1988.

[72] It is relatively rare for penalties of more than 10 years' to be imposed for culpable homicide: see Sheriff N.M.P. Morrison (ed.), *Sentencing Practice* (Edinburgh, 2000, W. Green/Sweet & Maxwell,), paras C8.0001 *et seq.*

[73] *Paton v. H.M. Advocate*, 1936 J.C. 19: see para. 26.12, *supra*.

continues to rule the common law offence and to demand a standard higher[74] than that required under section 1 of the 1988 Act. In addition, modern statutory law has also created the offence of causing death by careless driving where the accused was under the influence of drink or drugs at the relevant time.[75]

26.14 *Causing death by careless driving when under the influence of drink or drugs.* Section 3A of the 1988 Act[76] provides:

> "(1) If a person causes the death of another person by driving a mechanically propelled vehicle on a road or other public place without due care and attention, or without reasonable consideration for other persons using the road or place, and—
> (a) he is, at the time when he is driving, unfit to drive through drink or drugs, or
> (b) he has consumed so much alcohol that the proportion of it in his breath, blood or urine at that time exceeds the prescribed limit[77], or
> (c) he is, within 18 hours after that time, required to provide a specimen in pursuance of section 7 of this Act, but without reasonable excuse fails to provide it,
> he is guilty of an offence.

> (2) For the purposes of this section a person shall be taken to be unfit to drive at any time when his ability to drive properly is impaired.
> (3) Subsection (1)(b) and (c) above shall not apply in relation to a person driving a mechanically propelled vehicle other than a motor vehicle."[78]

26.15 CAUSE. It was not necessary under the prior law to show that the reckless driving was the sole cause of death but only that it was a material rather than a minimal one,[79] and there is no reason to suppose that the same rule does not apply to the current law. Thus where an accident resulting in fatality is caused by the dangerous or, where appropriate, careless, driving of two persons one, or both, may be convicted under section 1 or 3A, as the case may be.[80]

---

[74] See *McDowall v. H.M. Advocate*, 1998 S.C.C.R. 343, Lord Abernethy to the jury at 345G–346A.

[75] See para. 26.14, *infra*. It is open to a jury to convict under s.2 (or of careless driving under s.3) on a charge under s.1; Road Traffic Offenders Act 1988, s.24(1), as substituted by the Road Traffic Act 1991, s.24; where culpable homicide has been charged, it is open to a jury to find the accused not guilty of that crime but guilty of an offence under s.2: Road Traffic Offenders Act 1988, s.23(1), as amended by the Road Traffic Act 1991, Sched. 4, para. 90.

[76] Inserted by the Road Traffic Act 1991, s.3.

[77] See Road Traffic Act 1988, s.11(2).

[78] Maximum penalty, 10 years' imprisonment: Road Traffic Offenders Act 1988, Sched. 2, as substituted by the Criminal Justice Act 1993, s.67(1).

[79] *Watson v. H.M. Advocate* (1978) S.C.C.R. (Supp.) 192, at 193–4, where it was also stated that it was a misdirection for the trial judge to have told the jury that they could acquit the accused driver only if they found that the other person involved was wholly to blame; see also *R. v. Hennigan* [1971] 3 All E.R. 133, CA.

[80] *R. v. Gould* [1964] 1 W.L.R. 145.

Other cases. The standard of gross negligence was applied in the unusual **26.16** case of *Fredk G. Thomsett*.[81] The accused was the master of a trawler which was sheltering in a bay off Stornoway. Five young fishermen came aboard to beg for fish without the master's consent but with that of the mate. The master ordered the men off the trawler and back to their boat, and started to tow them to the shore. On the way the boat was swamped and some of the men killed. The master was convicted of culpable homicide.[82] The jury were directed, to quote the paraphrase of Lord Justice-Clerk Aitchison's charge set out in the opinion of Lord Justice General Normand in the appeal court: "that want of consideration or want of understanding of the situation or loss of temper were not issues they were trying; that the question was whether the accused was guilty of such wicked and criminal recklessness in ordering the men back into their boat . . . that made it just that he should be held answerable as for a crime."[83]

ERRONEOUS PERFORMANCE OF A DUTY.[84] In *H.M. Advocate v. Macpher-* **26.17** *son*[85] a drunk soldier on leave shot at a car which was showing lights in the blackout and killed its occupant. He was charged with culpable homicide, and Lord Justice-Clerk Aitchison directed the jury that they should acquit if they found that he had acted out of a mistaken sense of duty, or that he had, "looking at it broadly, some kind of just excuse for what he did", and should convict only if it were proved that he had acted "with criminal recklessness". This suggests that an error of law as to one's duty may entitle one to acquittal, but leaving that aside, it appears from *Macpherson* that where a soldier acts unjustifiably he is to be treated as if he had caused death by a lawful act, and not as someone who has caused death by an unlawful assault. Similar directions were given in *H.M. Advocate v. Sheppard*[86] — passages from the judge's charge in *Macpherson* were read to the jury — where a soldier escorting a prisoner shot him in order to prevent his escape. The accused was acquitted on a plea of justification based on the defence of military duty and obedience to superior orders, but the jury were directed that even if they did not accept that plea they could convict of culpable homicide only if they found that there had been gross negligence.

Macdonald cites these cases as authority for the proposition that "mere negligence in carrying out a duty does not now infer criminal consequences; there must be gross and wicked recklessness in its performance",[87] a proposition which is *a fortiori* of the cases themselves in which the accused were mistaken in believing they were performing a

---

[81] High Court at Edinburgh, Feb. 1939; High Court at Edinburgh, June 1939, unrep'd.

[82] The indictment averred that the five men "having been allowed to go on board the said trawler, [the accused] did order [them] to re-enter [their] boat and did insist upon their doing so against their protests at a time when, owing to the heavy sea . . . it was manifestly dangerous to their lives to be in said boat, and did thereafter proceed with said trawler culpably and recklessly to tow said boat . . . so that the said boat was manifestly in imminent danger of being swamped . . . and did culpably and recklessly continue so to tow said boat until it filled with water and overturned, whereby [the men] were thrown into the sea and [four of them] were drowned . . . and you did kill [them]."

[83] L.J.-G's Opn, 3. See also *Sutherland (No. 1) v. H.M. Advocate*, 1994 S.C.C.R. 80, L.J.-G. Hope at 92C–93F: the case involved lawful fire-raising of the accused's own house.

[84] See Vol. I, paras 13.33 and 13.34.

[85] High Court at Edinburgh, Sept. 1940, unrep'd; see 1941 J.C. 69–70.

[86] 1941 J.C. 67.

[87] Macdonald, p.101.

duty. *Sheppard* indicates further that the law is the same where a duty is performed with excessive zeal. It might be argued that *Macpherson* and *Sheppard* should not be applied except in the same circumstances as were constituted by their own facts, and that they are to be explained by reference to the national situation in the early 1940s, but it is more likely that they will be extended to include other public officers, such as policemen, acting in the purported exercise of their duty. They may even apply to excess or error in any performance of what is or is believed to be a right, as where a parent kills a child by excessive chastisement or where someone kills a thief in order to protect his property.

Where the situation involves an error of law the initial act will still be unlawful but the doctrine of the irrelevance of error of law will not operate to create criminal liability for culpable homicide in the absence of the *mens rea* which would be required had the initial act been lawful.[88]

HOMICIDE IN THE COURSE OF ASSAULT[89]

26.18 *"Taking the victim as you find him"*. There is one general rule which applies to all cases of culpable homicide caused by assault, and that is that the assailant "takes his victim as he finds him". This means that the likelihood of a fatal result is estimated according to the actual physical condition of the victim, so that an assault which would not be remotely likely to be fatal in the case of an ordinary man will be regarded as the cause of death if the particular victim was suffering from a physical condition which rendered him peculiarly susceptible to fatal injury. For example, a slap is not likely to be fatal in the case of an ordinary person but it may be foreseeably fatal in the case of an extremely highly-strung person with a very weak heart. If someone slaps and kills such a person the death is regarded as a probable result of the slap, and so the assault is regarded as the cause of death. And this is so whether or not the assailant knows of the heart condition.

There is ample authority for this rule,[90] but it rests on a paralogism. In *Robertson and Donoghue*[91] an elderly cafe proprietor who, unknown to his assailant and indeed to himself, suffered from a weak heart was attacked, robbed and killed. Lord Justice-Clerk Cooper told the jury, "Now, it cannot be sufficiently emphasised . . . that if an intruder or aggressor, acting from some criminal intent and in pursuance of some criminal purpose, makes a violent attack upon any man or woman he

---

[88] *cf.* P.J. Fitzgerald, "Crime, Sin and Negligence" (1963) 79 L.Q.R. 351, 357–358.

[89] Cases of this kind are very numerous, *e.g. Andrew Burt* (1804) Burnett 34; *John Macfarlane* (1804) Hume, i, 234; *Richd Hamilton* (1815) Hume, i, 256; *Angus Cameron* (1811) Hume, i, 234; *Jas Irving* (1815) *ibid.*; *Colin Telfer* (1815) Hume, i, 257; *Thos Wood* (1821) Hume, i, 235; *John Neal* (1821) *ibid.*; *Wm Stewart* (1824) Alison, i, 95; *Wm Mailler* (1824) Alison, i, 98; *John Tod* (1825) Alison, i, 98; *John Macdonald* (1826) Alison, i, 99; *Jas Gallagher* (1826) Alison, i, 98; *John Campbell and Wm Helm* (1827) Hume, i, 237; *A. McKenzie* (1827) Syme 158; *Wm Macewan* (1830) Alison, i, 99; *Jas Grace* (1835) 1 Swin. 14; *David Patterson* (1838) 2 Swin. 175; *John Jones and Ed Malone* (1841) 2 Swin. 509; *Dundas McRiner* (1844) 2 Broun 262; *Margt Shiells or Fletcher* (1846) Ark 171; *Margt McMillan or Shearer* (1851) J. Shaw 468; *Peter Jafferson and Geo. Forbes* (1848) Ark 464; *Isabella Brodie* (1846) Ark. 45; *Robt Bruce* (1855) 2 Irv. 65.

[90] For example, *Angus Cameron* (1811) Hume, i, 234; *Wm Brown* (1879) 4 Couper 225; *Robertson and Donoghue*, High Court at Edinburgh, Aug. 1945, unrep'd, see C.H.W. Gane and C.N. Stoddart, *A Casebook on Scottish Criminal Law* (3rd ed., 2001), at para. 4.05; *H.M. Advocate v. Rutherford*, 1947 J.C. 1; *Bird v. H.M. Advocate,* 1952 J.C. 23.

[91] High Court at Edinburgh, Aug. 1945, unrep'd, see n. 90, *supra*.

must take his victim as he finds him. It is every whit as criminal to kill a feeble and infirm old man, or a newborn infant as it is to kill an adult in the prime of life."[92] In *H.M. Advocate v. Rutherford*,[93] where a young man was charged with strangling his girlfriend, there was a suggestion that she was of an excitable nature, and might die very quickly or easily, but Lord Justice-Clerk Cooper said, "[I]t is no answer for an assailant who causes death by violence to say that his victim had a weak heart or was excitable or emotional, or anything of that kind. He must take his victim as he finds her. It is just as criminal to kill an invalid as it is to kill a hale and hearty man in the prime of life."[94]

The last sentence of each of these quotations is indisputable, just as it is indisputable that "that may be criminal violence in the case of a frail person, which would not be such in the case of a person in good health."[95] But it is a *non sequitur* to say that therefore "you must take your victim as you find him", with respect to any kind of physical condition. There is a great difference between a patent weakness such as infancy or old age, which the accused must have known of and ought to have taken into account, and a latent condition which he cannot be expected to have known of or even suspected. Responsibility for a latent condition cannot rest on negligence. But the effect of this rule is that the law is enabled to pretend to be proceeding on the ground of negligence, and to pretend that the victim's death was reasonably foreseeable, since it is reasonably foreseeable that a slight injury may kill someone with a weak heart — what the law conveniently forgets is that it is foreseeable only to someone who knows about the weak heart.

The "real" reason for the rule, is, again, the principle of disfacilitation.[96] As Lord Cooper said in *Robertson and Donoghue*, "It would never do for it to go forth from this court that housebreakers or robbers, or others of that character should be entitled to lay violent hands on very old or very sick or very young people, and if their victim died as a result, to turn round and say that they would never have died if they had not been very weak or very old or very young."[97] This is excellent oratory, since it combines the emotive fear of robbers with the admitted responsibility towards the very old or very young. But in *H.M. Advocate v. Rutherford* the accused was not a robber or a housebreaker, and his victim was to all appearances a normal young girl; in *Bird v. H.M. Advocate*[98] the accused was not a robber or a housebreaker, and the victim died from trivial injuries because of her weak heart; and the rule was applied in both these cases.[99]

Casual homicide. The textbook writers divided involuntary homicide into **26.19** casual and culpable, and treated all homicide as culpable except where it fell into the category of casual homicide. Casual homicide was defined as homicide occurring "when a person kills unintentionally, who is lawfully

---

[92] Transcript of Judge's charge, 17; see C.H.W. Gane and C.N. Stoddart, *A Casebook on Scottish Criminal Law* (3rd ed., 2001), at para. 4.05.

[93] 1947 J.C. 1.

[94] At 3.

[95] Macdonald, p.88; *cf.* Hume, i, 238; *Thos Breckinridge* (1836) 1 Swin. 153.

[96] See Vol. I, para. 7.56.

[97] Transcript of Judge's charge, 17–18; see C.H.W. Gane and C.N. Stoddart, *A Casebook on Scottish Criminal Law* (3rd ed., 2001), at para. 4.05.

[98] 1952 J.C. 23.

[99] See also *Mamote-Kulang v. R.* (1946) 111 C.L.R. 62; *R. v. John*, 1969 (2) S.A. 560 (R.,A.D.).

employed, and neither means bodily harm to any one, nor has failed in
the due degree of care for preventing danger to his neighbour."[1] The
dichotomy of casual and culpable homicide no longer applies as a
general principle. The drunk motorist who carelessly kills a pedestrian is
not lawfully employed, and one would not ordinarily describe the killing
as "casual", but it is not necessarily culpable.[2] It would, therefore have
been open to the courts to reject this dichotomy in relation to assault
cases, but in fact they have not done so, but have on the contrary
reasserted the proposition that any homicide caused by assault is
culpable.[3]

26.20 *Assault cases in modern law.* There are three ways in which the liability of
an assailant for culpable homicide could be limited within the general
framework of current law.

First, liability for death in the absence of negligence could be limited
to cases of assault and robbery, and perhaps assault and rape, by analogy
with the law of murder.[4]

Secondly, the law could have taken up the position that in assault
cases ordinary negligence was sufficient for culpable homicide, and that
it was not necessary to prove gross negligence. In that event the law
would have been as stated by Lord Moncrieff in *H.M. Advocate v.
Delaney*[5] where he said:

> "It may be that those who offer violence, especially violence which
> is subject to be followed by death, have not had in view the taking of
> life. They, however, are not accidental in their use of violence. They
> are responsible for the violence they use so far as the violence is
> concerned; and, if consequences follow which they did not antici-
> pate or apprehend, they are also responsible for these con-
> sequences. One cannot say 'I chose to exercise violence against a
> person against whom I thought I had a grievance, and it was
> merely accidental that a probable consequence of that violence
> followed.' "[6]

Lastly, it would be possible to hold that culpable homicide was always
present where death was caused in the course of an assault and robbery

---

[1] Hume, i, 194; *cf.* Burnett, p.35; Alison, i, 139; Anderson, p.147.

[2] This is perhaps evidenced by the creation of the statutory offence set out at
para. 26.14, *supra*.

[3] *H.M. Advocate v. Rutherford*, 1947 J.C. 1; *Bird v. H.M. Advocate*, 1952 J.C. 23. But
Prof. T.B. Smith refers to an unreported case in 1951: *Cameron*, High Court, Feb. 1951,
where the accused inflicted slight injuries on his mistress under provocation and she died
because of a lymphatic condition, in which Lord Cooper indicated that it might be argued
that in view of the development of the law in "lawful act" cases, a comparable
development would be appropriate in the case of a minor assault not intended or
calculated to cause serious injury. No such argument was proffered, however, and the
accused pled guilty: T.B. Smith, pp. 186–187. Much as one agrees with Prof. Smith's views
on what the law should be and how it may yet develop, one feels that Lord Cooper's own
recorded pronouncements indicate that he would not have accepted the suggested
argument.

[4] *cf. supra*, para. 23.33. An example of robbery-culpable homicide is *Wm Brown* (1879)
4 Couper 225, where the accused tried to steal a woman's handbag, and in pulling at the
bag swung the woman round so that she fell on to the pavement, and died a fortnight later
from "nervous shock acting on a weak, diseased heart" and from the slight injuries she had
received.

[5] 1945 J.C. 138.

[6] At 139.

or rape, and also when it was caused negligently in the course of an ordinary assault. This would involve constructive *mens rea*, but would be preferable to holding that every death caused by an assault was *ipso facto* culpable homicide. The latter is a very extreme position — it means that A may be punished for causing the death of B in circumstances in which he would not be civilly liable for that death because of the absence of negligence — but there are two twentieth century cases which indicate that it is still the law of Scotland. These two cases are *H.M. Advocate v. Rutherford*[7] and *Bird v. H.M. Advocate*.[8]

(1) *H.M. Advocate v. Rutherford.* This is a most unusual and difficult **26.21** case, but one of great importance because of the charge of the presiding judge, Lord Justice-Clerk Cooper. The facts given in evidence were these: R and his girl friend went into a park in the early hours of the morning; the girl pestered R with requests to kill her; eventually he put his tie round her throat in order to humour her and, in his own words, "only meant to give her a fright and see if it would put a finish to her nonsense of wanting to be strangled."[9] In fact R may have been grossly reckless, and he said in evidence that he had given no thought to the risk when he put the tie round the girl's neck, and could not remember how tightly he had pulled it,[10] but Lord Cooper's charge proceeded on the view that the degree of negligence was important only in deciding if the crime was murder or culpable homicide, and that R could not be acquitted altogether. He directed the jury that "on no view of the evidence . . . would you be entitled to accept . . . that this is a case of misadventure or pure accident or casual homicide as known to the law".[11] This was presumably on the view that death had been caused by an assault, and that it was therefore necessarily a case of culpable homicide.[12]

Rutherford presents a further complication in that the deceased had, according to the accused, asked him to kill her. Lord Cooper dealt with this by pointing out that "if life is taken under circumstances which would otherwise infer guilt of murder, . . . [t]he attitude of the victim is irrelevant."[13] It does not, however, follow that consent can never be an answer to a charge of culpable homicide. The facts in *Rutherford* were very special — it may be said that death is always a foreseeable result of choking, and also that to commit an assault in answer to a request by the victim that she be killed is never justifiable or lawful. But if A inflicts a minor injury on B with B's consent in circumstances which do not render him guilty of assault and B dies as an unforeseeable result, it is submitted that this is casual homicide, since A has behaved lawfully and

---

[7] 1947 J.C. 1.

[8] 1952 J.C. 23.

[9] Accused's evidence, Transcript of Proceedings, High Court at Edinburgh, Oct. 1946, 93.

[10] *ibid.*, 96.

[11] 1947 J.C. at 5.

[12] *ibid.*, 6. See also *H.M. Advocate v. Morris* (1966) 30 J.C.L. 201; *cf. Mamote-Kulang v. The Queen* (1964) 111 C.L.R. 62; *R. v. Senekal* 1969 (4) S.A. 478 (R., A.D.); *R. v. Church* [1966] 1 Q.B. 59 which limits the rule to cases where "the unlawful act must be such as all sober and reasonable people would inevitably recognise must subject the other person to, at least, the risk of some harm resulting therefrom, albeit not serious harm." See also *D.P.P. v. Newbury* [1977] A.C. 500, HL, where *R. v. Church* was affirmed and applied.

[13] At 5–6.

without negligence.[14] If this were not so, there would be culpable homicide if A killed his opponent by a fair blow in a boxing match or a fair tackle on a rugby field which unexpectedly caused death, and it is submitted that that is not the law.[15]

26.22   (2) *Bird v. H.M. Advocate*.[16] B was a drunken sailor who believed that his victim had gone off with his money. He pursued her for about half a mile and made such a nuisance of himself and caused her such apprehension that her husband and her daughter sent for the police. Eventually the victim tried to get into a passing car, B pulled her out, and she fell down dead.[17] Her injuries were trivial but she had a bad heart, and it was likely that a slight shock might kill her if she was in a state of physical exhaustion and fear. B was charged with culpable homicide, and convicted. In his charge to the jury Lord Jamieson stated that any death following on an assault was culpable homicide, and emphasised that an assault did not need to be anything involving great violence, but might be just a threatening gesture. The degree of violence, he said, was not a question for the jury, but was something to be taken into account in assessing sentence.[18] The conviction was upheld on appeal, although the matter seems to have been dealt with rather summarily. The main authority quoted was *Wm Brown*[19] which can be distinguished on the ground that B was not bent on robbing his victim but on recovering what he believed was his own.[20] It was argued for B that the jury should have been specifically directed that in order to convict they must find that he killed the woman in the course of unlawful conduct. The Appeal Court held that such a direction was unnecessary because no "conceivable justification in law or in fact or in common sense could be assigned to the conduct proved against the appellant",[21] a phrase which raises many difficulties about what constitutes justification, and whether it need be in law or only in fact or in common sense, none of which difficulties was considered by the court.

The other factor, which weighed with the court, was that death followed on a course of conduct "well calculated to induce great apprehension in the mind of any reasonable woman."[22] That is to say, they held that apprehension was foreseeable, or perhaps that the accused must be deemed to have intended to cause great apprehension, and so

---

[14] It is, however, homicide to cause someone's death by injecting him with a dangerous drug, given the necessary degree of recklessness, even where the injection was with the consent, or at the request, of the victim: *Finlayson v. H.M. Advocate*, 1979 J.C. 33.

[15] See *infra*, para. 29.42. There are a number of nineteenth century cases of culpable homicide in fair fight: *e.g. Jas Irving* (1815) Hume, i, 234; *John Tod* (1825) Alison, i, 98; *Jas Grace* (1835) 1 Swin. 14, but these were not organised Queensbury Rules contests; but see *Dobbs and Macdonald v. Neilson* (1899) 3 Adam 10. In one old case; *Wm Bathgate* (1710) Hume, i, 194, the deceased sustained injuries in a fall inflicted in the course of a wrestling bout "in sport" with the accused which proved fatal because of his weak health, and a defence of casual homicide was held relevant.

[16] 1952 J.C. 23.

[17] There was evidence that B struck the woman several times before she tried to get into the car but the Appeal Court did not rely on this.

[18] At 25.

[19] (1879) 4 Couper 225.

[20] That L.J.-G. Cooper regarded this belief as being without any justification does not matter unless the belief is to be characterised as unreasonable and therefore irrelevant, but this was not done.

[21] 1952 J.C. at 27.

[22] *ibid.*

upheld the conviction of homicide, presumably on the ground that where an accused intends some harm and causes death he is guilty of culpable homicide.[23]

Indeed, the law seems to go further than this, and holds that any assault, however technical, which results in death constitutes the crime of culpable homicide.[24] To take an extreme case, if A spits at B who is so surprised that he loses his balance, falls, cracks his skull on the pavement, and dies, A is guilty of culpable homicide.[25] It is true that culpable homicide is a crime which varies enormously in seriousness from case to case,[26] and the punishment for which has ranged from life imprisonment to a fine of 1s. (5p)[27] and even an absolute discharge,[28] but it is still unsatisfactory that persons should be convicted of such a crime in the absence of any fault at all so far as death is concerned and solely because of the operation of a doctrine of constructive guilt.[29]

WICKEDNESS. A comparison of the law of involuntary culpable homi- **26.23** cide with that of involuntary murder prompts the suggestion that there should be some rule in culpable homicide analogous to the requirement of wickedness in murder. The suggestion would be that the necessary wickedness is found in the grossness or "wickedness" of the negligence in lawful act cases, in the intent to rob or rape or commit abortion in that class of case, and in the intention to inflict harm of a not altogether

---

[23] *cf.* Hume, i, 234.

[24] *Bird, supra,* Lord Jamieson at 24–25; *Rutherford, supra,* L.J.-C. Cooper at 6. Where a weapon, such as a knife, is produced merely to deter a potential aggressor, and is not actively brandished at him, there may be no assault by the holder of the weapon, and therefore no culpable homicide if the aggressor runs on to the weapon and is fatally injured — quite apart from any question of self-defence: see *Mackenzie v. H.M. Advocate,* 1983 S.L.T. 220.

[25] See *H.M. Advocate v. Hartley,* 1989 S.L.T. 135 (Note), where at 136D Lord Sutherland gave the jury this particular example.

[26] *cf. McKendrick v. Sinclair,* 1972 S.C. (H.L.) 25, at 24: "But culpable homicide covers a very wide variety of cases from something not far short of murder, to cases deserving little punishment. In my own experience it was not very uncommon to direct that a charge of culpable homicide should be tried summarily."

[27] *Robt Bruce* (1855) 2 Irv. 65.

[28] *Shaw,* High Court at Edinburgh, Jan. 1959, unrep'd. And see *H.M. Advocate v. A.B.* (1887) 1 White 532 where no sentence at all was imposed — the accused pointed a revolver at someone, forgetting it was loaded, and the weapon went off. In that case, however, as L.J.-C. Macdonald suggested, after the accused pleaded guilty, there may have been no crime at all, since there was no intention to injure, and even the technical assault involved in presenting the gun was probably not truly an assault having been done apparently in jest. *Cf. Fullerton* (1966) 30 J.C.L. 201, at 204, where the accused was less fortunate. See also *Burns v. H.M. Advocate,* 1998 S.C.C.R. 281, and *Docherty v. H.M. Advocate,* 2000 S.C.C.R. 106, where sentences of community service were imposed.

[29] Thus in *Burns v. H.M. Advocate,* 1998 S.C.C.R. 281, the fatal blow was delivered with little force, and the resulting death was caused not only in a way which was quite unforeseeable but also as something of a mischance: the accused, however, pled guilty; similarly in *Docherty v. H.M. Advocate,* 2000 S.C.C.R. 106, the accused's blow which proved fatal was a matter of ill luck, although he again pled guilty. Such pleas were probably inevitable in the present state of the law. But it is thought that there should be no crime where two friends are playing at pointing a gun at each other and one of them without gross negligence fires the gun at and kills the other: *R. v. Lamb* [1967] 2 Q.B. 981: where, as in *Fullerton* (1966) 30 J.C.L. 201, at 204, the victim is not party to the jest the position may, however, be different.

insubstantial kind in the simple assault cases.[30] Such a requirement would at least remove technical assaults, such as threatening gestures or playful pushes, from the operation of the rule that any assault resulting in death is culpable homicide.[31]

HOMICIDE IN THE COURSE OF OTHER UNLAWFUL EMPLOYMENT

26.24   The law regarding death caused without gross negligence in the course of unlawful employment has rarely been considered in modern law outside the case of assault on the one hand and the unlawful driving of motor-cars on the other. It is clear that it is no longer the law that even any negligent homicide committed by someone unlawfully employed is culpable, but the effects of this change in the law have not been worked out.

26.25   *"Unlawful employment" and "unlawful act".* The classic definition of casual homicide speaks of the accused being "lawfully employed"[32] but this is an unsatisfactory criterion. It can hardly be the law that a housebreaker who inadvertently slips on a roof and falls to the ground on top of a passer-by is guilty of culpable homicide just because he fell while employed as a housebreaker and not as a chimney sweep or slater: in both cases death is caused by accident, and not by any "act" of the killer at all. Alison states that, "if a person's gun burst in his hand, and kill his neighbour", that is casual homicide[33]; it is submitted that it cannot become culpable homicide if the person did not have a licence for the gun, or was carrying it for the purpose of poaching. To make such an incident culpable homicide would be "To pronounce [someone] guilty of one offence because a misfortune befell him while he was

---

[30] *cf. R. v. Church* [1966] 1 Q.B. 59, 70; *R. v. Sharmpal Singh* [1962] A.C. 188. The law in England is that it is manslaughter to do intentionally an act which is unlawful and such that all sober and reasonable persons would regard as likely to cause some harm where that act causes death; it is unnecessary to prove that the accused knew the act was dangerous: *D.P.P. v. Newbury; R. v. Jones* [1977] A.C. 500; *R. v. Larkin* (1942) 29 Cr.App.R. 18; *R v. Church, supra; R. v. Cato* [1976] 1 W.L.R. 110. See also *R. v. D.P.P., ex p. Manning and Anr* [2000] 3 W.L.R. 463, Lord Bingham of Cornhill at 470C-E. It has been held in South Africa that even where death is caused by assault, culpable homicide is committed only where death is reasonably foreseeable: *S. v. Bernardus*, 1965 (3) S.A. 287 (A.D.); see J. Burchell and J. Milton, *Principles of Criminal Law* (2nd ed., 1997), pp. 474–5.

[31] There is a hint of it in the remarks about lack of justification in *Bird, supra,* and in Lord Jamieson's reference to persons with "a grievance": at 24, and it is true that the circumstances of *Bird* might be regarded as displaying at least some ill will by the accused to the deceased. A comparison of the two old cases of *Isabella Livingstone* (1842) 1 Broun 247, and *Isabella Brodie* (1846) Ark. 45 also supports the suggestion. In each case the accused pushed an old woman who fell and died unexpectedly as a result. In *Livingstone* the jury were directed to acquit because death appeared to have been caused by a single push "which might, under the circumstances, have been given without any intent to injure", although it was not suggested that the push itself was accidental. In *Brodie* they were directed to convict, "If . . . the panel gave a push to the deceased, an old woman of seventy, which caused her to fall, and which led to her death . . . although she may not have contemplated inflicting on her any serious injury": L.J.-C. Hope at 48. It is difficult to reconcile the cases, except that Livingstone pushed the deceased after the latter had got into a quarrel with her because of L's brandy drinking and had thrown some water over her, while Brodie killed her landlady after a quarrel about money and a demand that she leave the house, which suggests an element of spite absent in the earlier case.

[32] Hume, i, 194; Alison, i, 139.

[33] Alison, i, 140.

committing another offence", and "is surely to confound all the boundaries of crime".[34]

The criterion of "unlawful employment" should be replaced by that of
"unlawful act", and "unlawful act" should, it is submitted, be defined as
"criminal act".[35] In *Geo. Broadley*[36] Lord Moncreiff spoke of "a person
. . . engaged in an unlawful act, or in the discharge of a lawful act in an
unlawful way",[37] but in that case death was caused by one sailor pushing
another overboard in a fight, so that the meaning of discharging a lawful
act in an unlawful way did not arise. It is not clear what that meaning is,
unless it is performing an unlawful act for some ultimately lawful
purpose, which is just performing an unlawful act.[38]

In *Patrick McCarron*[39] on one version of the facts the accused had
gone after his wife with a gun with the intention of frightening her and
the gun had gone off accidentally. Lord Wheatley directed the jury that
if they accepted that version they should acquit. It was not suggested that
as the accused was "unlawfully employed", being on his way to frighten
his wife, perhaps by assaulting her, he must be guilty of culpable
homicide.

Criminal acts may be divided into those which involve an intention to
cause physical harm and those which do not.

Acts intended to cause harm. The law regarding death caused by an act **26.26**
which involves unlawful personal injury, or at least which involves the
intentional infliction of such injury, is probably the same as the law
regarding death caused by assault. It is culpable homicide to give A a
drug intended to make him sick but which in fact kills him.[40] It may be
doubted whether it is still the law that it is culpable homicide if the
intention is only to make him drunk.[41] It is culpable homicide to desert
or expose a child who dies as a result,[42] or to deprive a child or invalid of
necessary sustenance or neglect it in any other way which proves fatal.[43]
It is unlikely that an official of the Department of Social Security who

---

[34] Macaulay, p.508, where he gives the following example: "A heaps fuel on a fire, not
in an imprudent manner, but in such a manner that the chance of harm is not worth
considering. Unhappily the flame bursts out more violently than there was reason to
expect. At the same moment a sudden puff of wind blows Z's light dress towards the
hearth. The dress catches fire, and Z is burned to death." Would that be murder, Macaulay
asks, if "the fuel which caused the flame to burst forth was a will, which A was fraudulently
destroying?"

[35] cf. *H.M. Advocate v. Hartley*, 1989 S.L.T. 135, at 136 where Lord Sutherland directed
the jury that: "Culpable homicide is simply the causing of death by any unlawful act. The
unlawful act must be intentional, but it is quite immaterial whether death was the
foreseeable result of that act." The circumstances were, however, that the deceased had
been assaulted by the accused who were convicted of murder.

[36] (1884) 5 Couper 490.

[37] At 492.

[38] One might say that a drunk driver was performing a lawful act in an unlawful way but
he is in fact committing a crime, and paradoxically is not liable for culpable homicide
unless he acts with gross negligence. (*Cf.* the statutory crime set out at para. 26.14, *supra*.)

[39] High Court at Perth, Feb. 1964; High Court of Justiciary on Appeal, March 1964,
unrep'd.

[40] *Henry Inglis and Others* (1784) Hume, i, 237. Given such an intention it does not
matter that the motive was one of practical joking: Hume, i, 237; Macdonald, p.99.

[41] In *Adam Philip* (1818) Hume, i, 237, a 10-year-old boy was given seven large whiskies
in 10 minutes which indicates a degree of fault. See also *Alex. Forbes* (1828) Alison, i, 99.

[42] *Eliz. Kerr* (1860) 3 Irv. 645; *Catherine McGavin* (1846) Ark. 67.

[43] Macdonald, p.99; *R. v. Instan* [1893] Q.B. 450; *Barbara Gray or McIntosh* (1881) 4
Couper 389; *R. v. Stone* [1977] Q.B. 354.

deliberately deprived an applicant of necessary help would be charged with culpable homicide, but not impossible. Mere neglect to look after an applicant would not today be culpable homicide.[44] In one case a charge of culpable homicide was brought for giving a child an overdose of laudanum to make it sleep,[45] although in an earlier case a plea of guilty to culpable and reckless administration of laudanum was accepted,[46] and it is unlikely that the giving of an overdose of sedatives would be treated as a common law crime at all today if the only purpose was to help the child to sleep.

Although abortion does not strictly speaking involve an intention to injure it is regarded as a crime against the person, and there can be little doubt that any death caused by a criminal abortion would be regarded as culpable homicide.[47] If a skilled surgeon carried out an abortion with every possible precaution he would be guilty of culpable homicide if the mother died as a result unless he could show that the abortion itself was legally justifiable.

26.27 *Other crimes.* There are few reported cases of non-negligent culpable homicide where death was caused by a criminal act in the absence of any intent to cause some physical harm. It was submitted in the second edition of this work that constructive culpable homicide of the type found in the assault cases should not be extended beyond cases involving such an intent.[48] It was argued that if it were extended further, it would be difficult to draw any line between crimes of different kinds, and it would be necessary to hold that culpable homicide was present in every case in which death was caused by a criminal act. This would mean that if in opening a door a housebreaker set off a booby trap erected by someone else, or knocked over and fired a gun which had been left at the other side of the door, and killed someone, he would be guilty of culpable homicide, while if the same thing had happened when a member of the household opened the door the homicide would be casual. Although it is considered that such argument remains persuasive, the courts have not always been persuaded by it.

In *Finnigan*[49] the accused was charged with wrenching a gas meter from a shelf and with stealing it, thus breaking the supply pipe, and causing the death of persons in an adjoining house. He was convicted of culpable homicide, but the case can be regarded as one of gross negligence since what he did was obviously dangerous.[50]

In *Lourie v. H.M. Advocate*,[51] however, it was alleged (omitting the conspiracy charges which were withdrawn by the Crown) that the

---

[44] *cf. Wm Hardie* (1847) Ark. 247.

[45] *Eliz. Hamilton* (1857) 2 Irv. 738.

[46] *Jean Crawford* (1847) Ark. 394.

[47] *R. v. Creamer* [1966] 1 Q.B. 72.

[48] See 2nd ed., para. 26–26. *Cf. Die Staat v. Van der Mescht*, 1962 (1) S.A. 521 (A.D.), Hoexter J.A. at 538.

[49] High Court at Glasgow, March 1958, unrep'd.

[50] *cf. Wm O'Neil*, High Court at Glasgow, Sept. 1961, unrep'd, where O'N was charged with murder by assaulting a man, wrenching his gas meter from its installation, forcing the meter open and stealing its contents, and, "knowing that coal gas was escaping from said inlet pipe" leaving his victim lying unconscious so that he died from gas poisoning; a plea of guilty to culpable homicide was accepted by the Crown for a number of reasons. In *R. v. Cunningham* [1957] 2 Q.B. 396 it was held that actual foresight was necessary in a charge of endangering life in circumstances similar to those in *Finnigan*, but *Cunningham* proceeded on the interpretation of "maliciously" in s.23 of the Offences against the Person Act 1861.

[51] 1988 S.C.C.R. 634.

accused had called at the house of the victim (an elderly woman), entered her house uninvited and then in her presence stolen a handbag: it was further alleged that the victim had died in consequence of the effect on her diseased heart of the alarm and distress she had experienced. Lord Morison in charging the jury said that some improper or illegal conduct was required for culpable homicide, and agreed with counsel for the accused that the Crown carried the burden of showing that the illegal conduct of the accused was likely to have had some physical effect on the victim. The accused were convicted of culpable homicide. At the subsequent appeal, the court noted that the question had been raised whether an assault, in its ordinary sense, was a necessary ingredient for the particular type of culpable homicide involved in the case; but the court considered that it was not necessary to answer that question, the Crown having conceded that the essential factual elements in the charge had not been satisfactorily proved at the trial. There was no proof, however, that there had ever been any intention to harm the victim; and neither entering a house uninvited nor theft bears any such necessary connotation.

In *Sutherland (No. 1) v. H.M. Advocate*,[52] the accused set fire to his own house, his motive being to perpetrate a fraud on the insurers of the building. He was assisted by a friend, who was killed during their fire-raising operations; one of the charges against the accused was thus the culpable homicide of his friend. On the assumption that the fire-raising had been a lawful act, the case could be, and was, disposed of by determining whether or not the accused had shown sufficient negligence in relation to the death[53]; but Lord Sutherland directed the jury that even if they were persuaded that the accused had committed the crime of fire-raising with intent to defraud insurers, that would not be sufficient unlawfulness to make him guilty of culpable homicide. As his Lordship stated: "If the setting fire in itself was a lawful act but performed for an unlawful motive which converts it into a crime, it still remains a lawful act as far as the actual setting fire is concerned and therefore, if death results from that, that would not be culpable homicide. It is a bit complicated but what it amounts to is simply this, because the only illegality is the intent to defraud the insurers, that is not an unlawful act for the purpose of the law relating to culpable homicide *which deals with offences against the person*."[54] Although this might be thought to provide some support for the above submission, the following case may go some way to undermine it.

In the *Lord Advocate's Reference (No. 1 of 1994)*[55] the accused was charged with culpable homicide of the victim by unlawfully supplying her with a controlled "and potentially lethal" drug "in a lethal quantity", she having then ingested that drug to the danger of her health, safety and life. There was no question of his having administered the drug to the

---

[52] 1994 S.C.C.R. 80.

[53] Similarly, any fire-raiser who caused death would probably be charged with culpable homicide because of the dangerous nature of the crime and the consequent very high duty to take care not to injure anyone. It may still be the law that in such cases any degree of negligence is sufficient to constitute culpable homicide. In *Mathieson v. H.M. Advocate*, 1981 S.C.C.R. 196, however, where death was caused by reckless fire-raising, the High Court upheld a direction to the jury that if death results directly from the commission of an unlawful act, that is culpable homicide.

[54] *ibid.*, at 83D, emphasis added.

[55] 1995 S.C.C.R. 177.

victim[56]; there was no allegation of his having had any intent to harm her[57]; and the supply was not described as having been reckless. Nor was the prosecution predicated on the fact that the supply of such a drug was unlawful under the Misuse of Drugs Act 1971. Lord Coulsfield, the trial judge, acquitted the accused of the charge of culpable homicide on the basis that the causal link between supply and death had been broken by the voluntary conduct of the victim, and most of the subsequent Lord Advocate's Reference is concerned with the correctness or otherwise of his having done so. But, in response to the argument that the offence of supply of noxious and dangerous substances could not have been the foundation of the homicide charge, since such an offence required averments of recklessness[58] which had been absent from the indictment, the Court said:

> "Of course we recognise that . . . there is in [the] charge . . . no express averment of culpable and reckless conduct. However, in [the] charge . . . it is libelled that the supply was unlawful and that the supply was of a controlled and potentially lethal drug. It is also libelled that the drug was supplied in a lethal quantity. It is clear from what is said in the reference and in the trial judge's report that X supplied a quantity of the controlled drug to a number of people, including the deceased, and that the purpose of that supply was so that the deceased and others could take doses of the drug. In our opinion such conduct on the part of X is the equivalent of culpable and reckless conduct. No doubt the extent of any injurious consequences would depend upon the quantity of the drug which the deceased ingested, but since the purpose of the supply was obviously for the drug to be ingested by those to whom it was given by X, it does not appear to us that this affects the matter."

It seems clear from this that culpable homicide can be based upon the supply of harmful substances to another, where that supply is considered unlawful in terms of the principle laid down in *Khaliq v. H.M. Advocate*[59]: as recklessness was not libelled in the homicide charge itself,[60] it seems that there is now a rule that the supply of controlled drugs to another is *ipso facto* sufficient for culpable homicide if the person supplied ingests a quantity of the drug and dies in consequence.[61] It may be that the rule is limited to controlled drugs; but the principle in *Khaliq*, on which the rule is predicated, is not thus limited. It was also argued that the rule should be limited as in the English case of *R. v. Dalby*,[62] in terms that the unlawful act causally linked to the death of the victim should be shown to have been directed at that victim and to have been

---

[56] Indeed, she not only sought the drug from the accused but also determined for herself when, how and in what quantity to ingest it. *Cf. Finlayson v. H.M. Advocate,* 1978 S.L.T. (Notes) 18 and 60.

[57] Although this may be thought to be furnished by use of the word "lethal". Supply of 100 aspirin tablets in a standard commercial transaction could, however, equally be described as supply of a drug in a lethal quantity.

[58] See *Khaliq v. H.M. Advocate*, 1984 J.C. 23; *Ulhaq v. H.M. Advocate*, 1990 S.C.C.R. 593.

[59] 1984 J.C. 23.

[60] And gross negligence in respect of the death would perhaps have been difficult to establish in the case, unless the existence of such negligence were always to be presumed in such cases.

[61] See, *e.g., Paxton v. H.M. Advocate*, 2000 S.L.T. 771.

[62] [1982] 1 All E.R. 916.

likely to have caused her immediate injury; but this argument for limitation was rejected by the court. In point of fact, the decision of the court is plainly influenced by the moral standing of trafficking in controlled drugs; but the generality of the decision, as stated above, cannot be limited to such considerations.[63]

Where, however, death is caused by a criminal act which does not involve any moral obloquy, but is only a statutory offence of a more or less technical kind, it should be necessary to prove not merely negligence but negligence of the *Paton*[64] standard in respect of the death. If A shoots at a bird and by some unforeseeable chance kills a man, his guilt of culpable homicide cannot depend on whether the incident happened on a Sunday and so contravened the Wildlife and Countryside Act 1981, or happened on a Saturday and so was lawful; and equally it would be unfair to convict A for being negligent on a Sunday, but only for being grossly negligent on a Saturday.[65]

---

[63] There is thus much to be said in favour of the principles which the Law Commission adopted as a basis for reform of the English law of involuntary manslaughter. These are that a person should be responsible for causing death unintentionally only if he unreasonably and advertently took a risk of causing death or serious injury, or if he unreasonably but inadvertently took such a risk where his failure to advert to that risk was blameworthy in the sense that the risk was obviously foreseeable and he had the capacity to advert to it: see Law Commission No. 237, "Legislating the Criminal Code: Involuntary Manslaughter" (1996), para. 4.43.

[64] 1936 J.C. 19, *supra*.

[65] *cf.* the South African case of *Die Staat v. Van der Mescht* 1962 (1) S.A. 521 (A.D.) where death was caused by poisonous fumes given off by some gold amalgam which the accused was melting illegally; it was held that culpable homicide was not committed in the absence of proof of negligence, and in particular that it was not committed merely because death had been caused by an unlawful act.

CHAPTER 27

CONCEALMENT OF PREGNANCY[1]

Concealment and child murder

It appears that during the 1680s there was a large number of cases of **27.01**
murder of newly born children by their mothers and that the Crown
experienced great difficulty in bringing home guilt because of the
difficulty of proving what had happened at the birth.[2] An Act was
therefore passed in 1690[3] which provided that "if any woman shall
conceale her being with child dureing the whole space and shall not call
for and make use of help and assistance in the birth, the child being
found dead or amissing, the mother shall be holden and repute the
murderer of her own childe." This Act was regarded as raising a
presumption of murder from the fact of concealment. By the late
eighteenth century its operation was regarded as unduly harsh and it was
repealed in 1809 by an Act[4] which provided that:

> "If . . . any woman in . . . Scotland shall conceal her being with child
> during the whole period of her pregnancy, and shall not call for and
> make use of help or assistance in the birth, and if the child be found
> dead or be amissing, the mother . . . shall be imprisoned for a
> period not exceeding two years".[5]

The similarity with the Act of 1690 is obvious, and Hume took the view
that what the Act of 1809 did was to substitute a presumption of
culpable homicide for the presumption of murder.[6] It is also possible to
treat the Act as creating a self-contained crime, that of concealing
pregnancy, and this is the modern view.[7] The interpretation of the Act,
and particularly of "concealment", may depend on which of these views
is adopted.

Concealment and revelation

Concealment consists in a failure to reveal. It is not necessary for the **27.02**
Crown to show that the accused actively disguised her condition or hid

---

[1] See also the *Stair Memorial Encyclopaedia*, Vol. 7, "Criminal Law" (Edinburgh, 1995),
paras 290–293; P.W. Ferguson, *Crimes Against the Person* (2nd ed., Edinburgh, 1998),
paras 5.02–5.08.

[2] Hume, i, 291.

[3] Ch. 50. A.P.S. IX, 195.

[4] Now called, somewhat misleadingly, the Concealment of Birth (Scotland) Act: Short
Titles Act 1896.

[5] Despite the terms of the Act it is probably a defence to show that the accused herself
was unaware of her condition; *cf. Harding v. Price* [1948] 1 K.B. 695; see Vol. I, para. 8.24.

[6] Hume, i, 293.

[7] *cf.* Burnett, p.572.

herself away[8]; a person may be guilty of the crime although her condition was known to others.[9] The law requires the woman to make some active revelation of her condition, but it does not demand that she actually tell someone about it: it will be sufficient for example if she makes open preparations for the birth, or makes an oblique admission of her condition.[10]

A disclosure to one person is sufficient to avoid conviction under the Act[11] even where that person is a confidant of the mother, or the father of the child.[12]

The disclosure need not be voluntary. An admission extorted by pressure is sufficient to elide the Act.[13] The position of an accidental disclosure has not been considered.

27.03 *The purpose of the revelation.* It is still undecided whether a revelation made for the purpose of obtaining assistance in keeping the mother's condition secret, or even in preventing the child's survival, is sufficient to negative a charge of concealment.[14] The question was debated by a Full Bench in *Ann Gall*[15] where disclosure had been made to the father of the child, but the *ratio* of the acquittal in that case was that there was no finding as to the purpose of the revelation which was accordingly presumed to be an innocent one.[16] All the judges indicated, however, that a disclosure made for the purpose of obtaining assistance in concealing the pregnancy would not be a defence to the statutory charge, on the ground that to treat it as a defence would be contrary to the purpose of the statute. Macdonald's view is that such a disclosure is a defence, and he argues for a literal interpretation of the Act.[17] In practice charges of concealment are brought only with some reluctance, and evidence of any form of revelation is accepted gratefully as a reason for not proceeding, so that it is likely that even where the revelation was made for an improper purpose it would be regarded as a bar to proceedings. Such an approach is in line with the principle that criminal statutes should be interpreted literally and strictly.

27.04 *Art and part.* Macdonald argues also that revelation for any purpose must be sufficient,[18] on the ground that it is the law that there can be no art and part guilt in the offence. As an argument this is sound — it would be inequitable to convict the mother of concealment of pregnancy where she had invoked the father's aid in her deception, and to acquit him on the ground that the law does not recognise guilt by accession (or presumably conspiracy to conceal). But if the judges in *Gall*[19] were

---

[8] Hume, i, 294.

[9] *Ann Gall* (1856) 2 Irv. 266, Lord Ardmillan at 381.

[10] Hume, i, 294–295; Macdonald, p.111; *Jane Skinner* (1841) Bell's Notes 80, where the Crown dropped the charge after a witness said the accused had laughed and denied being pregnant when he asked her, and that his "impression from her laughing, as also from her appearance, and the talk of the country, was that the panel was pregnant."

[11] Hume, i, 295; Alison, i, 155; Macdonald, p.111.

[12] *Jean Kiellor* (1850) J. Shaw 576; 2 Irv. 376n; *Ann Gall* (1856) 2 Irv. 366.

[13] Hume, i, 296; Alison, i, 156; Macdonald, p.110.

[14] Macdonald, p.111; *Ann Gall, supra.*

[15] (1856) 2 Irv. 366.

[16] Lord Ivory at 375, Lord Handyside at 379.

[17] At p.112. See also Anderson, p.157.

[18] Macdonald, p.112; he is followed by Anderson at p.157.

[19] (1856) 2 Irv. 366.

correct, it would follow that the authorities which held that there was no art and part in the crime were wrong[20] so that to argue by reference to art and part is to beg the question.

"The whole period". The Crown must show that the pregnancy was **27.05** concealed throughout its period.[21] Where a pregnancy is terminated at an early stage there can be no charge of concealment, since the mother could claim that she had intended to reveal her condition at a later time. It is, however, enough for the Crown to show that the pregnancy lasted long enough to make a live birth possible,[22] but where the birth is premature this will operate as a mitigation of the offence.[23]

Help at birth. In addition to proving concealment throughout the **27.06** pregnancy the Crown must also show that the mother did not call for and make use of help in the birth. The Act suggests that the mother must both call for and use help, and Hume's view is that it is no defence to call for help "in such a way as shows that the message was a mere device to get rid of this troublesome witness."[24] But unless the pregnancy is said to end when labour begins, merely to call for assistance will amount to disclosure,[25] and the only question remaining will be whether the purpose of the disclosure is relevant. Alison's view is that it is sufficient merely to call for help, even where it does not arrive until after the child has died.[26] It may also be a defence to make use of help provided by someone else on his own initiative.

Found dead or missing. A mother who conceals her condition and **27.07** successfully delivers herself of a live child is not guilty of an offence under the statute. The offence is completed only when the child dies, and this may be proved either by evidence of death, or by the failure of the mother to produce the child, by its being "amissing". There is a presumption that but for the concealment the child would have been born alive, and also that a missing child died as a result of the concealment. It is a defence for the mother to prove that the child was not properly describable as such, but was "an abortion, or a *foetus*, which, from some accident, was in such a condition that . . . it could not have been in any reasonable sense called 'a child' ",[27] since the Act requires birth of a child. It is not clear whether it is a defence that the child was stillborn,[28] but it is submitted that the spirit if not the letter of the Act requires that an accused who can show that even with assistance the child, although not a monstrous birth, would not have been born alive or survived birth, should not be convicted.

---

[20] These are Hume, i, 299; Alison, i, 158; *Alison Punton* (1841) 2 Swin. 572.

[21] Hume, i, 296; Alison, i, 155; Macdonald, p.112.

[22] Macdonald, p.112; Hume, i, 297; Alison, i, 154; Anderson, p.158; *Eliz. Brown* (1837) 1 Swin. 482; *Alison Punton* (1841) 2 Swin. 572. Macdonald explains *Margt Fallon* (1867) 5 Irv. 367 as depending on the failure of the Crown to show how long the pregnancy had lasted.

[23] See Macdonald, 3rd ed., p.151; *Mary Sinclair* (1847) and *Margt Murdoch* (1859) both *supra*.

[24] Hume, i, 297.

[25] See Alison, i, 157.

[26] Alison, i, 157; *Stirling* (1726) *supra*.

[27] Macdonald, p.113; *cf.* Hume, i, 297.

[28] Hume, i, 298.

According to Hume, if the child is born alive and is acknowledged by the mother, and then dies, there is no crime, because it is not then "dead or missing *on the birth*": this is on the ground that the child has by then survived the birth and is a known person whose disappearance will provoke inquiry.[29]

It is hardly likely that a child will survive any length of time without its existence becoming known, but if it did it is unlikely that its subsequent death or disappearance would be sufficient to render the mother guilty of concealment, if only because of the difficulty of connecting the death clearly with the failure to disclose the pregnancy and obtain help in the birth.

---

[29] Hume, i, 296. *Cf.* Macdonald, p.113, and Alison, i, 157, who regard late revelation as an atonement for the prior concealment.

CHAPTER 28

ABORTION

Prior to the passing of the Abortion Act 1967 all abortions were **28.01** criminal, subject to an ill-defined exception for abortions necessary to preserve the mother's life or health. As a result of the Act it is no longer criminal to carry out abortions for the purposes and under the rules set out in the Act. The Act specifically provides that anything done with intent to procure a miscarriage is illegal unless authorised by section 1 of the Act,[1] thus apparently excluding the common law defence of necessity, and ensuring that any abortion carried out by someone who is not a registered medical practitioner,[2] even if she is the mother acting alone, is unlawful.[3]

It is proposed to consider first the common law rules and then the provisions of the Act.

Abortion at common law

The first recorded charge of abortion in Scotland is *John Fenton* in **28.02** 1763,[4] and both Burnett and Hume refer to abortion only in passing in order to distinguish it from murder.[5] Alison includes "Administering drugs to procure abortion" among his list of innominate offences,[6] and refers to one case of this kind[7] and to two which involved the use of instruments.[8] The books and cases deal only with the use of drugs or

---

[1] Section 5(2), as amended by the Human Fertilisation and Embryology Act 1990, s.37(5).

[2] It has been held by a narrow majority of the House of Lords that the protection of the Act extends to "junior doctors, nurses, para-medical and other members of hospital staff involved in the treatment, in accordance with accepted medical practice" provided that a registered medical practitioner takes responsibility for all stages of the treatment: *Royal College of Nursing v. D.H.S.S.* [1981] A.C. 800, *per* Lord Diplock at 828B–E.

[3] In Smith and Hogan at pp. 396–7, it is argued that s.5(2) cannot, or should not, be read literally so as to eliminate all general defences, such as nonage and insanity; and, if that be conceded, it is further submitted that coercion and necessity should also be available. Their hypothetical example, of a non-registered but qualified medical practitioner who, finding himself in a remote location with a pregnant woman, "forms the opinion in good faith that immediate termination of [the] pregnancy in order to save the life of the mother" is essential, is certainly compelling; but it does not follow from the availability of nonage and insanity that "excuses" or even justifications, such as coercion and necessity, are not excluded. See also s.1(4) of the Act, *infra* para. 28.05.

[4] Burnett, p.6. But see *Patrick Robertson and Marion Kempt* (1627) Hume, i, 186, a trial for adultery "and the administering and taking of a *poisonable draught* . . . wherewith she destroyed her child in the womb", which may or may not have been treated as a murder charge.

[5] Burnett, pp. 5–6. Hume, i, 186–187.

[6] At i, 628.

[7] *Charles Munn* (1824) Alison, i, 629.

[8] Alison, i, 628–629; *Catharine Robertson and Geo. Batchelor* (1806) Hume, i, 187; *Alex. Aitken* (1823) Alison, i, 628.

instruments,[9] but the crime is not the use of drugs or instruments to procure abortion, but the procuring of abortion. Macdonald states that it is a crime to "cause or procure abortion whether by drugs or by instruments or violence",[10] and it would be equally criminal to use other means, such as manual manipulation, or giving the mother a fright.

Abortion may be committed at any stage between conception and birth. It is probably not necessary for the Crown to show that the aborted foetus was capable of normal development and birth, but it is a defence to show that the foetus was dead before any attempt was made to clear the womb.

28.03 *Can the mother be guilty of abortion?* A woman who permits someone to carry out an operation on her or takes drugs supplied to her for the purpose of abortion is art and part guilty of the crime.[11] There are no modern reported cases in which the mother has been charged, partly because it is usually impossible to convict the abortionist without her evidence.[12] It is submitted that Macdonald is correct in stating that it is also a crime for a pregnant woman to take drugs in order to procure her abortion, even where she is unsuccessful.[13] The only case which directly raised the question was *Jessie Webster*[14]; the charge was of taking and using drugs by a pregnant woman for the purpose of causing herself to abort, but it was dropped by the Crown after a number of objections had been taken to its relevancy, and no opinions are reported.

28.04 *Attempted abortion.* It is not an objection to a charge of attempted abortion that the woman was not pregnant at the time of the attempt[15]: but there is probably no independent crime of administering abortifacients to a non-pregnant woman with intent to cause an abortion.[16]

The Abortion Act

28.05 This Act, while not conferring any right to an abortion, may be said to confer a privilege on doctors who carry out abortions for one of the

---

[9] Hume, i, 186–187; Burnett, pp. 5-6; Alison, i, 628; *Wm Reid* (1858) 3 Irv. 235; *H.M. Advocate v. Chas Rae* (1888) 2 White 62; *H.M. Advocate v. Grahan* (1897) 2 Adam 412; *Jessie Webster* (1858) 3 Irv. 95; *H.M. Advocate v. Baxter* (1905) 5 Adam 609; *H.M. Advocate v. Anderson* 1928 J.C. 1; *H.M. Advocate v. Semple*, 1937 J.C. 41.

[10] Macdonald, p.114.

[11] Alison, i, 628; *Patrick Robertson and Marion Kempt* (1806) Hume, i, 186; Macdonald, p.114. This was accepted without argument in *H.M. Advocate v. Chas Rae* (1888) 2 White 62.

[12] If a mother were charged along with the abortionist, she would be punished much less severely: Alison, i, 628.

[13] Macdonald, p.114. Macdonald suggests that this follows from *H.M. Advocate v. Semple*, 1937 J.C. 41, where a man instigated a woman to take abortifacients. But (a) he was charged with attempted abortion and not with instigating the woman to commit abortion, and (b) it is logically possible for A to be art and part guilty of a crime or guilty of instigating a crime of which the actual offender cannot be convicted: *cf. R. v. Whitchurch* (1890) 24 Q.B.D. 420; *R. v. Bourne* (1952) 36 Cr.App.R. 125.

[14] (1858) 3 Irv. 95.

[15] *Docherty v. Brown*, 1996 J.C. 48, which overruled *H.M. Advocate v. Anderson*, 1928 J.C. 1, as also *H.M. Advocate v. Semple*, 1937 J.C. 41, to the extent that it supported *Anderson*: see Vol. I, para. 6.56.

[16] See Vol. I, para. 1-28.

somewhat heterogeneous grounds set out in the Act, at a place authorised, and in accordance with procedures laid down, by the Act.[17]

Section 1 of the Act provides a defence for persons charged with abortion, and is as follows[18]:

"(1) Subject to the provisions of this section, a person shall not be guilty of an offence under the law relating to abortion when a pregnancy is terminated by a registered medical practitioner if two registered medical practitioners are of the opinion, formed in good faith—

    (a) that the pregnancy has not exceeded its twenty-fourth week and that the continuance of the pregnancy would involve risk, greater than if the pregnancy were terminated, of injury to the physical or mental health of the pregnant woman or any existing children of her family; or

    (b) that the termination is necessary to prevent grave permanent injury to the physical or mental health of the pregnant woman; or

    (c) that the continuance of the pregnancy would involve risk to the life of the pregnant woman, greater than if the pregnancy were terminated; or

    (d) that there is a substantial risk that if the child were born it would suffer from such physical or mental abnormalities as to be seriously handicapped.

(2) In determining whether the continuance of a pregnancy would involve such risk of injury to health as is mentioned in paragraph (a) or (b) of subsection (1) of this section, account may be taken of the pregnant woman's actual or reasonably foreseeable environment.

(3) Except as provided by subsection (4) of this section, any treatment for the termination of pregnancy must be carried out in a hospital vested in the Secretary of State for the purposes of his functions under the National Health Service Act 1977 or the National Health Service (Scotland) Act 1978 or in a hospital vested in a Primary Care Trust or a National Health Service Trust or in a place approved for the purposes of this section by the Secretary of State.

(3A) The power under subsection (3) of this section to approve a place includes power, in relation to treatment consisting primarily in the use of such medicines as may be specified in the approval and

---

[17] See Brian Davis, "The Legalization of Therapeutic Abortion", 1968 S.L.T. (News) 205; Kenneth McK. Norrie, "British Abortion Rules Altered: Or are They?", 1992 S.L.T. (News) 41. Abortions which are lawful under the provisions of the Act probably do not contravene Art. 2 ("Right to life") of the European Convention on Human Rights (as applied to domestic law under the terms of the Human Rights Act 1998); but the European Court of Human Rights has not yet had to rule "whether a right to abortion is guaranteed under the Convention or whether the foetus is encompassed by the right to life as contained in Article 2": see *Open Door Counselling and Dublin Well Woman v. Ireland* (1993) 15 E.H.R.R. 244, at 264. See also D. Gomien, D. Harris and L. Zwaak, *Law and Practice of the European Convention on Human Rights and the European Social Charter* (Council of Europe, 1996), pp. 102–103, and especially at p.103 where the authors conclude that in such a sensitive area where there are such differing opinions it is right to show restraint and leave "a rather broad discretion to the legislature to set the norms."

[18] As amended by the Health Services Act 1980, Sched. 1; the National Health Service and Community Care Act 1990, Sched. 9, para. 8; the Human Fertilisation and Embryology Act 1990, s.37; and the Health Act 1999 (Supplementary, Consequential, etc. Provisions) Order 2000 (S.I. 2000 No.90), Sched. 1, para. 6.

carried out in such manner as may be so specified, to approve a class of places.

(4) Subsection (3) of this section, and so much of subsection (1) as relates to the opinion of two registered medical practitioners, shall not apply to the termination of a pregnancy by a registered medical practitioner in a case where he is of the opinion, formed in good faith, that the termination is immediately necessary to save the life or to prevent grave permanent injury to the physical or mental health of the pregnant woman."

The Act is so framed that anyone, whether or not a doctor, is free from guilt if he or she participates in a permitted abortion, but only a registered practitioner is permitted to carry out an abortion.[19]

It will be noted, too, that provided the two certifying practitioners[20] opine in good faith the abortion is not criminal, however unreasonable their opinion is.[21]

28.06 *Duty to save life.* Section 4 of the Act, which relieves persons with a conscientious objection to abortion from any legal duty to participate[22] in permitted abortions, has a proviso that this relief: "shall [not] affect any duty to participate in treatment which is necessary to save the life or to prevent grave permanent injury to the physical or mental health of a pregnant woman."

28.07 *Offences in relation to embryos.* Contraventions of the following provisions of the Human Fertilisation and Embryology Act 1990 are made offences under section 41 of the Act[23]:

"**3.**—(1) No person shall—
(a) bring about the creation of an embryo, or
(b) keep or use an embryo,
   except in pursuance of a licence.[24]
(2) No person shall place in a woman—
(a) a live embryo other than a human embryo, or

---

[19] It seems that it is lawful for a registered doctor to authorise a nurse or other member of the hospital medical staff to administer an abortifacient drug provided that the doctor remains responsible for all stages of the procedure: *Royal College of Nursing v. D.H.S.S.* [1981] A.C. 800, HL, Lords Wilberforce and Edmund-Davies diss.

[20] One of whom may be, for aught the Act says, the abortionist.

[21] *cf. R. v. Smith (John)* [1973] 1 W.L.R. 1510.

[22] It has been held that "participate" is not intended to carry a criminal law meaning in the sense of invoking any doctrine of accession (or art and part); instead it is to be given its ordinary meaning, such that it refers only to those who take part in the abortion treatment in a hospital or approved place; a secretary in a health centre who was asked to type a letter of referral to a consultant in a hospital was not, therefore, able to justify her refusal to do so on the basis of s.4: see *Janaway v. Salford Area Health Authority* [1988] 3 W.L.R. 1350, HL.

[23] Maximum penalty for contravention of ss. 3(2), 3(3), 3A or 4(1)(c): on indictment, 10 years' and a fine (see s.41(1)); maximum penalties for contravention of s.3(1) — provided no breach of s.3(3) is involved, ss. 4(1)(a), 4(1)(b), or 4(3): on indictment, two years' and a fine; on summary conviction, six months' and a fine of the statutory maximum (see s.41(2)).

[24] Under s.1(1) of the Act, embryo means "a live human embryo where fertilisation is complete, and . . . includes an egg in the process of fertilisation", fertilisation not being considered "complete until the appearance of a two cell zygote." Creation of an embryo, under s.1(2) means creation outside the human body; and, under s.1(3), keeping or using applies only to the keeping or using of an embryo outside the human body: see also s.2(2). "Licence" means a licence granted under the provisions of the Act: see s.2(1).

(b) any live gametes other than human gametes."

"**3A**.[25]—(1) No person shall, for the purpose of providing fertility services for any woman, use female germ cells taken or derived from an embryo or a foetus or use embryos created by using such cells.

(2) In this section—

'female germ cells' means cells of the female germ line and includes such cells at any stage of maturity and accordingly includes eggs; and

'fertility services' means medical, surgical or obstetric services provided for the purpose of assisting women to carry children.

4.—(1) No person shall—

(a) store any gametes, or

(b) in the course of providing treatment services for any woman, use the sperm of any man unless the services are being provided for the woman and the man together or use the eggs of any other woman, or

(c) mix gametes with the live gametes of any animal, except in pursuance of a licence. . . .

(3) No person shall place sperm and eggs in a woman in any circumstances specified in regulations except in pursuance of a licence."[26]

---

[25] Added by s.156(2) of the Criminal Justice and Public Order Act 1994.

[26] Under s.41(10), a person charged with an offence under ss. 3(1) or 4(1) has a defence if he was acting under the direction of another, and believed on reasonable grounds (i) that that other person was licensed (or was a person to whom certain directions had been given by virtue of s.24(9) of the Act) and (ii) that he was authorised by virtue of the licence or directions to do the thing in question. Under s.41(11) there is a general "due diligence" defence.

CHAPTER 29

ASSAULT AND REAL INJURY

ASSAULT

Any attack upon the person of another is an assault.[1] The requirement **29.01** of an attack distinguishes assault from other forms of real injury, but "attack" has a very wide meaning. It covers more than a forcible attack, and it does not necessarily connote that the accused had to overcome resistance by the victim. It is an assault to injure a person by placing a piece of paper in his hand while he is asleep and setting it alight,[2] or to have intercourse with a sleeping woman,[3] or, it is submitted, to pour poison down a sleeping man's throat.

There need not be substantial violence,[4] and indeed an extremely trivial attack is sufficient. It is an assault to slap someone on the back, even perhaps to tap him on the shoulder, and to spit on someone "is an assault in the eye of the law".[5] Injury to the victim is unnecessary: it is an assault to kiss a girl without her consent. In practice, however, prosecutions are not brought where the assault does not involve any significant violence or injury, unless the circumstances are special. The deliberate use of threatening gestures in order to place a person in a state of fear and alarm for his safety, even for a jocular ulterior motive, is, however, sufficient for assault.[6]

The attack may be indirect. It is assault for A to injure B by setting a dog on him,[7] by whipping or forcibly stopping the horse he is riding so that it injures him[8] or setting off a squib which frightens the horse into

---

[1] Macdonald, p.115. On the civil law of assault see D.M. Walker, *The Law of Delict in Scotland* (2nd ed., 1981), pp. 488 *et seq.*; J. Thomson, *Delictual Liability* (2nd ed., 1999), pp. 12–15.

[2] *Lachlan Brown* (1842) 1 Broun 230.

[3] *Chas Sweenie* (1858) 3 Irv. 109; *Wm Thomson* (1872) 2 Couper 346; *H.M. Advocate v. Logan*, 1936 J.C. 100.

[4] In *Atkinson v. H.M. Advocate*, 1987 S.C.C.R. 534, *e.g.*, it was held that to enter a shop with one's face masked and to jump over the counter towards the cashier can be an assault: the motive, however, was robbery. See also *Lord Advocate's Ref. (No.2 of 1992)*, 1992 S.C.C.R. 960.

[5] *Jas Cairns and Ors* (1837) 1 Swin. 597, L.J.-C. Boyle at 610; *cf. Tullis v. Glenday* (1834) 13 S. 698; *Ewing v. Earl of Mar* (1851) 14 D. 314.

[6] See para. 29.03, *infra*, and *Lord Advocate's Ref. (No.2 of 1992)*, 1992 S.C.C.R. 960, where, *e.g.*, at 970A, Lord Sutherland said: "The pointing of a gun at a shop assistant accompanied by words such as those used by the panel [*i.e.*, 'Get the money out of the till and lay on the floor'] would undoubtedly constitute the *actus reus* of the crime of assault".

[7] Macdonald, p.115; it seems, however, that the accused must cause the dog to move at another person with the intention that the movement will at least frighten that person: *Kay v. Allan* (1978) S.C.C.R. (Supp.) 188. See also *Quinn v. Lees*, 1994 S.C.C.R. 159.

[8] *David Keay* (1837) 1 Swin. 543; *cf. Kennedy v. Young* (1854) 1 Irv. 533.

running away with him,[9] by running him down with a car or horse,[10] driving a car across the path of another car in which B is a passenger,[11] or driving on while B is clinging to A's car,[12] by pulling away the chair on which B is sitting, or by pursuing B over a precipice.[13]

29.02 *Assault and attempted assault.* The distinction between assault and attempted assault is very indistinct, if, indeed, attempted assault exists at all.[14] It is assault to aim a blow at B with the intention of striking him although the blow misses its aim.[15] This is so whether or not the "attempted assault" is made with weapons — to aim a kick or punch at B and miss him is as much an assault as to aim a blow with an axe or to shoot at him. According to Alison it is necessary that B should have "incurred alarm and apprehension",[16] but it may be that where a blow is actually aimed or a shot fired it does not matter whether or not B is alarmed.

29.03 *Menaces.* It is also assault to menace B by a threatening gesture or by presenting or brandishing a weapon at him even if the weapon is not capable of being fired, unless the victim knows this.[17] Converse it is an assault to menace B with a toy gun if he believes it real and loaded.[18] The production of a gun may constitute presentation even without its being actually pointed at someone, if it is produced as a threat.[19] Where the assault consists only of a threatening gesture it is necessary that B should have been alarmed and put in fear of actual injury.[20] The

---

[9] *cf. Geo. Wood Jr and Alex. King* (1842) 1 Broun 262. See D.W. Elliott, "Frightening a Person into Injuring Himself" [1974] Crim.L.R. 15.

[10] *Donald v. Hart* (1892) 3 White 274; *cf. McMillan v. H.M. Advocate,* 1987 S.C.C.R. 491.

[11] *cf. John Currie and Ors,* High Court at Glasgow, Dec. 1962, unrep'd, Vol. I, para 7.80.

[12] *cf. D.P.P. v. Smith* [1961] A.C. 290.

[13] *cf. Patrick Slaven and Ors* (1885) 5 Couper 694; *R. v. Roberts* (1971) 56 Cr.App.R. 95. It may even be an assault not to remove an object, such as a car wheel, which one has accidentally placed on the victim: *Fagan v. Metropolitan Police Commissioner* [1969] 1 Q.B. 439.

[14] See P.W. Ferguson, *Crimes Against the Person* (2nd ed., 1998), para. 1.03; *cf.* T.H. Jones and M.G.A. Christie, *Criminal Law* (2nd ed., 1996), para. 9-11.

[15] Alison, i, 175–176; Macdonald, p.115; *C. & A. Stewarts v. P.F. Forfarshire* (1829) 2 S.J. 32; *Earl of Mar* (1831) Bell's Notes 89. Hume's statement of this principle, i, 329, is restricted to cases of assault with intent to kill, but the principle is now of general application.

[16] Alison, i, 175.

[17] *Brown v. Alexander* (1757) Hume, i, 443; *P.F. Edinburgh v. Hog* (1831) Alison, i, 175; *Robt Charlton* (1831) Bell's Notes 89; *Walter Morison* (1842) 1 Broun 394; *Lord Advocate's Ref. (No. 2 of 1992),* 1992 S.C.C.R. 960.

[18] See *Gilmour v. McGlennan,* 1993 S.C.C.R. 837.

[19] *Walter Morison, supra.* It appears, however, that "it is always a question of fact, circumstances and degree, whether the presentation of a weapon such as a knife to another as a deterrent through fear or otherwise in order to prevent further violence is an assault in law": *Mackenzie v. H.M. Advocate,* 1983 S.L.T. 220, at 223, L.J.-C. Wheatley. The accused in the case, which was one of murder, stated that he had taken a knife from his pocket and held it at about waist height to discourage the victim from resuming hostilities against him: this was quite apart from any question of self-defence.

[20] Alison, i, 175; Macdonald, p.115. The accuracy of this rule was assumed in *Lord Advocate's Ref. (No. 2 of 1992),* 1992 S.C.C.R. 960; and *Gilmour v. McGlennan,* 1993 S.C.C.R. 837. *Cf Ewing v. Earl of Mar* (1851) 14 D. 314, in which the defender rode his horse at the pursuer so as to endanger him. There has been recorded a conviction for "assault by chasing": *Francis Cassidy,* High Court at Glasgow, Dec. 1965, unrep'd.

menacing gesture must be of a kind which would induce fear in the ordinary man,[21] but it does not matter that B's fear was erroneous. Verbal threats, unaccompanied by menacing gestures, do not constitute assault, although they may be criminal.[22]

Aggravated assaults

The punishment for assault is not fixed by law, and therefore ranges **29.04** from life imprisonment to absolute discharge, and the judge may take into account any circumstance of the offence or of its background in passing sentence in any case; as Macdonald says, "The seriousness of an assault depends on its own general circumstances".[23] But there are certain circumstances which are recognised as specific aggravations of assault. Prior to the Criminal Procedure (Scotland) Act 1887 these were set out in the major proposition of the indictment, which libelled not just "assault", but, for example, "Assault especially when committed to the effusion of blood and serious injury of the person, and more especially still when committed upon a clergyman within his manse or dwelling-house, and by a person who went . . . with the premeditated purpose of seeking [him] . . . therein to assault him",[24] or "Assault . . . especially . . . upon . . . officers of the law . . . while in the execution of their duty, and for the purpose of preventing or obstructing them".[25] Today the matter is only one of specification, and there are certain recognised aggravations which must be specified in the charge if the Crown wish to lead evidence of them,[26] and which the jury are usually asked to deny or affirm.[27] There are also certain statutory forms of aggravated assault which constitute specific offences.

The most important ways in which assault may be aggravated are: **29.05**

(1) *By the weapon used.* The use of any form of weapon constitutes an aggravation of assault, but certain types of assault are regarded as specially aggravated. These are assaults by firearms,[28] by stabbing or cutting,[29] and by throwing corrosive substances.[30] These assaults are not normally charged summarily,[31] and are often dealt with in the High Court.

(2) *By the injury caused.* Any injury constitutes an aggravating circum- **29.06** stance in the sense that an assault causing injury is likely to be more severely punished than one which does not cause injury. It is not now the

---

[21] D.M. Walker, *Delict* (2nd ed., 1981), pp. 490–491; *Glegg on Reparation,* (4th ed., Edinburgh, 1955), p.129; Macdonald, p.115.

[22] Macdonald, p.115; *cf.* Anderson pp. 158–159. See *infra*, para. 29.62 *et seq.*

[23] Macdonald, p.118.

[24] *David Robertson Williamson* (1853) 1 Irv. 244.

[25] *Falconer and Ors* (1847) Ark. 242.

[26] *Brown v. Hilson*, 1924 J.C. 1, L.J.-G. Clyde at 4.

[27] Alison, i, 181.

[28] Alison, i, 179–181 and cases cited there; Macdonald, p.118; *Walter Morison* (1842) 1 Broun 394; *Robt Dewar and Ors* (1842) 1 Broun 233.

[29] Macdonald, p.118; *Jas Affleck* (1842) 1 Broun 354; *Edward and Patrick Hagan* (1853) 1 Irv. 342.

[30] Macdonald, p.118; *Mary Fitzherbert* (1858) 3 Irv. 63; *Wm Fitchie* (1856) 2 Irv. 485.

[31] Assaults by stabbing cannot be dealt with in district courts: 1995 Act, s.7(8)(b)(iv).

practice to libel the injuries sustained by the victim in detail, nor any longer to aver injury "to the effusion of blood",[32] but it is still the practice to libel that the victim was assaulted "to his severe injury"[33] in which case the jury may convict either of "assault as libelled" or of assault without the aggravation. What constitutes severe injury is a question of fact. Generally, injuries will be regarded as severe when they are extensive, as in the case of multiple lacerations, or involve injury to an important organ, or fracture of an important bone. It is no longer the practice to treat demembration as a specific crime,[34] but injuries involving demembration would be "severe". Cases of assault to severe injury may be dealt with by the High Court, but are more likely now to be prosecuted in the sheriff court.[35]

It is also still the practice to aver that an assault was "to the danger of life", and this is regarded as a very serious aggravation, almost always involving trial in the High Court.[36]

An assault may be to the danger of life even though no actual injury was caused: in *Jane Smith or Thom*[37] the accused was charged with throwing a child out of a railway train, and although the child was uninjured it was held relevant to libel that the assault had been to the danger of its life.

29.07   MENS REA. This type of aggravation is objective. It is not necessary to show that the accused intended to inflict severe injury or to endanger life in order to prove the aggravation. In practice, however, the accused's intention would be taken into account in passing sentence.

29.08   (3) *By the place of the assault.* Every assault charge contains a specification of the *locus* of the offence and it is unusual for any special reference to be made to it in modern practice. At one time assaults in the presence of the Sovereign or in her palaces,[38] or in the Supreme Courts,[39] were statutory crimes; this is no longer the case, although such assaults might still be regarded as aggravated by the place of their commission.[40]

29.09   HAMESUCKEN. Prior to the Criminal Procedure (Scotland) Act 1887, to assault a man in his own house after having invaded the house for that purpose[41] constituted the capital crime of hamesucken. Now that hamesucken is no longer capital it is not charged as a specific crime, but

---

[32] For example, among older cases *Lachlan Brown* (1842) 1 Broun 230; *David Robertson Williamson* (1853) 1 Irv. 244.

[33] The older cases use the phrase "serious injury", *e.g. Jas Cairns and Ors* (1837) 1 Swin. 597; *Peter Leys* (1839) 2 Swin. 337.

[34] See Hume, i, 330; Alison, i, 195 *et seq.*

[35] See P.W. Ferguson, *Crimes Against the Person* (1st ed., 1990), at para. 1.05. Cases involving fracture of a limb cannot be dealt with in district courts: 1995 Act, s.7(8)(b)(iv).

[36] Macdonald, p.118.

[37] (1876) 3 Couper 332; see also *Kerr (Stephen) v. H.M. Advocate*, 1986 S.C.C.R. 91.

[38] Macdonald, p.118; Hume, i, 326–327.

[39] Macdonald, p.118; Hume, i, 405.

[40] Hume, i, 327; Macdonald, p.118.

[41] Hume, i, 312; Alison, i, 199.

an assault on a man in his own house is still regarded as an aggravated form of assault,[42] especially where the house has been broken into.[43]

(4) *By the character of the victim.* Where this is relied on as an **29.10** aggravation it must be specifically libelled.[44] Assault may be aggravated by the "absolute" character of the victim, or by the relationship between the victim and the accused.

(a) ABSOLUTE CHARACTER. (i) Officers of law. Assault is aggravated by **29.11** being committed on officers of law in the execution of their duty, or with the intention of deterring them from carrying out their duty, or in revenge for their having done their duty.[45] "Officer of law" includes police officers, sheriff-officers and messengers-at-arms,[46] revenue officers,[47] and any other persons charged with the enforcement of statutory provisions for the regulation of trade,[48] or indeed of any statutory provisions.[49]

It also includes assaults on magistrates engaged in dealing with a riot,[50] or in connection with other magisterial duty.[51] The aggravation extends to assaults on persons assisting officers of law in the execution of their duty.[52]

An assault committed with the purpose of preventing officers of law from carrying out a judicial warrant constitutes the specific crime of deforcement,[53] but such cases are now dealt with as aggravated assaults.[54]

Statutory Provisions: (1) Police (Scotland) Act 1967, s.41. This section **29.12** provides:

"(1) Any person who—

---

[42] Alison, i, 197; *Alex. Macdonald and John Fraser* (1818) Hume, i, 318.

[43] Charges of such aggravated assaults had been brought before 1887 as alternatives to hamesucken: *e.g. David Robertson Williamson* (1853) 1 Irv. 244, and Alison refers to a practice of libelling a charge of breaking into a man's house and assaulting him there as an alternative to hamesucken to provide for the eventuality of failure to prove that the housebreaking was committed with intent to assault: i, 197. In *H.M. Advocate v. Patrick Jas Deighan*, Edinburgh Sheriff Court, Feb. 24, 1961, unrep'd, there were averments of housebreaking, and assault and robbery; the robbery was not proved and the jury convicted of housebreaking and assault, their verdict being recorded as "assault aggravated by housebreaking". See also Alison, i, 633.

[44] *Brown v. Hilson*, 1924 J.C. 1, L.J.-G. Clyde at 4; Hume, ii, 197; Macdonald (3rd ed.), pp. 333, 405–406.

[45] Alison, i, 194; Hume, i, 329; Macdonald, pp. 118–119.

[46] *cf. Beattie v. P.F. Dumfries* (1842) 1 Broun 463.

[47] Hume, i, 329; *David Barnet and John Brown* (1820) *supra.; Alex. and Jas Alexander* (1842) 1 Broun 28.

[48] Hume, i, 329.

[49] For example, *Jas Affleck and Jas Rodgers* (1842) 1 Broun 207; *Alex. Smith and John Milne* (1859) 3 Irv. 506; *Mays v. Brown*, 1988 S.C.C.R. 549: all cases of water-bailiffs.

[50] For example, *Falconer and Ors* (1847) Ark. 242.

[51] *Robert Laughlan* (1821) Shaw 65; *Robt Duncan* (1827) Syme 280, where the accused assaulted a bailie who had previously sent him to prison; *John Irving* (1833) Bell's Notes 88.

[52] For example, *Nicholson and Shearer* (1847) Ark. 264; *Margt Stewart and Ors* (1856) 2 Irv. 416.

[53] Hume, i, 386 *et seq.*; Alison, i, 491 *et seq.*; Macdonald, p.168. See *Alex. McLean and Malcolm Macgillivray* (1838) 2 Swin. 185; *Andrew Young and Ors* (1842) 1 Broun 213; *Margt Stewart and Ors* (1856) 2 Irv. 416; *Cunningham and Ors v. Wilson* (1900) 3 Adam 243.

[54] Macdonald, p.168.

    (a) assaults, resists, obstructs, molests or hinders a constable in the execution of his duty or a person assisting a constable in the execution of his duty, or

    (b) rescues or attempts to rescue, or assists or attempts to assist the escape of, any person in custody,

shall be guilty of an offence and on summary conviction shall be liable [to imprisonment not exceeding 9 months or to a fine not exceeding the prescribed sum or to both.][55]

(2) The reference in subsection (1) of this section to a person in custody shall be construed as a reference to a person—

    (a) who is in the lawful custody of a constable or any person assisting a constable in the execution of his duty, or

    (b) who is in the act of eluding or escaping from such custody, whether or not he has actually been arrested.

(3)[56] This section also applies to a constable who is a member of a police force maintained in England and Wales or in Northern Ireland when he is executing a warrant or otherwise acting in Scotland by virtue of any enactment conferring powers on him in Scotland."

This section enables a sheriff in the summary court to impose a sentence of up to nine months' imprisonment for police assault[56a]: when assaults on the police are dealt with on indictment they are charged as aggravated common law assaults; alternatively, a charge under the section can be included as part of an indictment in terms of section 292(6) of the 1995 Act, although the maximum penalty in the event of conviction is then restricted to what would have applied had prosecution been before a summary court.

Under an earlier but similarly worded statutory provision, it was held that 'obstruction' involved an element of physical obstruction since the juxtaposition of 'obstruction' and 'assault' required such an interpretation[57]: the position is probably the same today under the 1967 Act, although it has been emphasised that the more modern provision's incorporation of 'hinders' demonstrates how little is required in order to satisfy such a physical element.[58] The provisions relating to escapes and rescues probably also require some element of physical intervention on the part of the accused.

29.13   (2) Customs and Excise Management Act 1979, section 16. This section provides:

---

[55] Different maximum penalties were originally provided, depending upon whether the accused had a prior conviction under the section; the same penalties are now applicable whether or not there is such a prior conviction: Criminal Procedure (Consequential Provisions) (Scotland) Act 1995, Sched. 1, para. 4(5).

[56] Added by the Criminal Justice and Public Order Act 1994, Sched. 10, para. 18.

[56a] A district court may try this offence, but with restricted powers of punishment: 1995 Act, s.7(7).

[57] *Curlett v. McKechnie*, 1938 J.C. 176, where the giving of false information to police officers was considered insufficient for conviction under the Prevention of Crime Act 1871, s.12 which (as extended by the Prevention of Crime (Amendment) Act 1885) applied to assaulting, resisting or wilfully obstructing a constable in the execution of his duty.

[58] *Skeen v. Shaw and Anr*, 1979 S.L.T. (Notes) 58. *Cf. Carmichael v. Brannan*, 1986 S.L.T. 5, where the interpretation of the offence of obstruction under the Misuse of Drugs Act 1971, s.23(4)(a), was held not to be governed by *Curlett v. McKechnie, supra*, but by the general rules of statutory construction.

"(1) Any person who—
    (a) obstructs, hinders, molests or assaults any person duly
        engaged in the performance of any duty or the exercise of any
        power imposed or conferred on him by or under any enact-
        ment relating to an assigned matter, or any person acting in
        his aid:
        or . . .
    (d) prevents the detention of any person by a person duly
        engaged or acting as aforesaid or rescues any person so
        detained,
    or who attempts to do any of the aforementioned things shall be
    guilty of an offence."[59]

In charges of assault against officers of law the Crown must show that
the victim was an officer of law duly qualified to carry out the duty on
which he was engaged,[60] and that he was acting within the proper limits
of that duty and in accordance with any warrant he was engaged in
carrying out.[61] It is not enough that the victim is an officer of law by
profession, he must be shown to have been actually engaged in duty at
the time of the offence.[62]

(ii) Judges, etc. It may still be an aggravation of assault that it is **29.14**
committed upon a member of the College of Justice while engaged as
such,[63] or on any judge so engaged, but such assaults would probably
mow be regarded as aggravated only when they involve an attempt to
pervert the course of justice.[64]

(iii) Clergymen. It is unlikely that the victim's being a clergyman **29.15**
would now be regarded as a specific aggravation.[65]

---

[59] Maximum penalty: on indictment, two years' and a fine; on summary conviction, three
months' and fine of the prescribed sum (s.16(2)(a), (b)). See also s.85 of the Act, *infra*,
para. 29.27. There are also numerous statutory provisions making it an offence to obstruct
persons carrying out their duties under the statute, particularly when these duties include
the exercise of rights of entry, search or seizure.

[60] *Gunn and Ors v. P.F. Caithness* (1845) 2 Broun 554.

[61] *Margt Stewart and Ors* (1856) 2 Irv. 416 where the accused was acquitted of assault on
revenue officers who were attempting to force a lockfast place on a warrant which did not
entitle them to do so. *Cf. Stirton v. MacPhail*, 1982 S.C.C.R. 301, where it was pointed out
by L.J.-C. Wheatley (at 305) that the offence in question (contravention of s.41(1)(a) of
the Police (Scotland) Act 1967) did not depend on whether or not there was a valid
warrant but rather on whether a constable had been acting in the execution of his duty at
the relevant time. See also *Smith v. Hawkes* (1980) S.C.C.R. (Supp.) 261; *Stocks v.
Hamilton*, 1991 S.C.C.R. 190; *Gillespie v. Hamilton*, 1994 S.L.T. 761.

[62] *Monk v. Strathern*, 1921 J.C. 4 where it was held that an assault on a policeman who,
when on his way home in uniform at 11.20 p.m. asked the accused who were standing on a
street corner, "Are you not away to bed yet, boys?" was not an assault on a police officer
in the execution of his duty.

[63] This was at one time a statutory offence: Hume, i, 405.

[64] In *John McDonald and Wm Dustan* (1872) 2 Couper 174 the fact that the assault was
on an advocate about to go into court was libelled only as narrative and not as a
substantive aggravation.

[65] It was at one time a statutory offence to assault a clergyman of the established
Church: Hume, i, 326.

29.16   (iv) The Sovereign. Assaults on the Sovereign may constitute high
treason or treason felony.[66] In addition the Treason Act 1842, section 2,
provides:

> "If any person shall wilfully discharge or attempt to discharge or
> point, aim, or present at or near to the person of the Queen, any
> gun, pistol, or any other description of firearms or of other arms
> whatsoever, whether the same shall or shall not contain any
> explosive or destructive material, or shall discharge or cause to be
> discharged, or attempt to discharge or cause to be discharged, any
> explosive substance or material near to the person of the Queen, or
> if any person shall wilfully strike or strike at, or attempt to strike or
> to strike at, the person of the Queen, with any offensive weapon, or
> in any other manner whatsoever, or if any person shall wilfully
> throw or attempt to throw any substance, matter, or thing what-
> soever at or upon the person of the Queen, with intent in any of the
> cases aforesaid to injure the person of the Queen, or . . . to break
> the public peace, or whereby the public peace may be endangered,
> or with intent . . . to alarm her Majesty, or if any person shall, near
> to the person of the Queen, wilfully produce or have any gun, pistol,
> [etc.] with intent to use the same to injure the person of the Queen,
> or to alarm her Majesty [he shall be liable to seven years'
> imprisonment]."

29.17   (v) Children. In *John and Mary Craw*[67] there was a charge of "assault,
especially when committed on a child." In that case the accused either
had parental responsibilities in relation to the two-year-old child in
question or were in charge of him and would today be charged under the
Children and Young Persons (Scotland) Act 1937,[68] but any assault on a
child is probably aggravated by the defencelessness of the victim. It is the
practice to insert the age of the victim when it is under 17.

29.18   (vi) Assault by poachers. Statutory Provisions: (1) Night Poaching Act
1828, section 2. This section empowers the occupier of land, or his
gamekeeper or other servant, or any person assisting any of those
persons, to seize anyone found on the land committing an offence
against the Act, or to pursue such a person and seize him in any place to
which he has escaped, and provides that if the offender assaults any
person authorised to seize him, he shall be liable to six months'
imprisonment and a fine of level 4 on the standard scale. The section
also applies to offenders under the Night Poaching Act 1844.

29.19   (2) Game (Scotland) Act 1832, section 6. This section, which deals
with day poaching, makes it an offence for any person "being in the
commission of a trespass" to assault or obstruct any person acting in the
execution or in virtue of the powers and provisions of the Act for the
apprehension of trespassers.[69]

---

[66] See *infra,* paras 37.04, 37.24.

[67] (1939) 2 Swin. 449.

[68] Section 12, as amended by the Children (Scotland) Act 1995, Sched. 4, para. 7; under
s.110 of the 1937 Act, a child for the purposes of s.12 means a person under the age of 14
years. See *infra,* para. 31.02.

[69] The maximum penalty is a fine of level 3 on the standard scale: see Criminal Justice
and Public Order Act 1994, Sched. 9, para. 1(6).

(b) RELATIVE CHARACTER. Cursing and beating of parents was at one **29.20** time a statutory offence,[70] and an assault by a child on his parent might still be regarded as aggravated by the relationship.[71] An assault may also be aggravated by being committed by a husband on his wife.[72]

There are a number of cases of assault or cruel and barbarous usage which have been libelled as aggravated by being committed by an asylum keeper on an inmate,[73] or by a parent or guardian on a child or weak-minded person,[74] and an assault by such a person on his ward would similarly be aggravated by the relationship. Assault is also aggravated by being committed by an officer of law on his prisoner.[75]

MENS REA. Where the Crown seek to establish an aggravation which **29.21** depends on the character of the victim, it is necessary for them to show that the accused was aware of that character. There is authority for this proposition so far as common law aggravations are concerned,[76] and in practice the same rule is applied in the most common of the statutory assaults of this kind, contraventions of the Police (Scotland) Act 1967.[77] In *Myles Martin and Ors*,[78] and *John Nicolson and Ors*[79] there were charges of assaulting persons who, it was alleged, the accused well knew or had reason to know were officers of law, which suggests that recklessness may be a sufficient *mens rea*, but the point was not taken in these cases, and it may be that proof that the accused had "reason to know" will be relevant only as objective evidence of actual knowledge. On the other hand it is still open to the courts to hold that it is sufficient that the accused knew or ought to have known of the character of the victim.[80]

(5) *By the accused's intention.* Assault is aggravated by being com- **29.22** mitted with intent to commit another crime. Macdonald says of this type of aggravation that "Formerly it was also the practice to treat assaults as being aggravated by intent to commit more serious crime, but the

---

[70] Hume, i, 324. See *James Alves* (1830) 5 D. & A. 147.

[71] Alison, i, 196.

[72] Alison, i, 196; *Benjamin Ross* (1824) *supra.*, 197; *John Shaw* (1823) *supra. Cf. Geo. Fay* (1847) Ark. 397, a case of cruel and barbarous usage.

[73] *cf. Adam Coupland and Wm Beattie* (1863) 4 Irv. 370.

[74] *John and Mary Craw* (1839) 2 Swin. 449; *David and Janet Gemmell* (1841) 2 Swin. 552; *Wm Fairweather* (1842) 1 Broun 309; *Barbara Gray or McIntosh* (1881) 4 Couper 389.

[75] *Alex. Findlater and Jas McDougall* (1841) 2 Swin. 527.

[76] *Alex. and Jas Alexander* (1842) 1 Broun 28; *Geo. McLellan and Ors* (1842) *supra.* 478; *Beattie v. P.F. Dumfries* (1842) *supra.* 463.

[77] The need to prove the accused's knowledge of the character of the complainer in a charge under s.41 of the 1967 Act was in effect upheld by the sheriff in *Annan v. Tait*, 1982 S.L.T. (Sh.Ct.) 108.

[78] (1886) 1 White 297.

[79] (1887) *ibid.* 307.

[80] In *O'Brien v. McPhee* (1880) 4 Couper 375, 386, Lord Young suggested that it was for the accused to show he did not know the victim was a policeman, but it is submitted that that goes too far — it is for the Crown to prove facts from which such knowledge can be inferred, at which stage the evidential burden will shift to the accused. Where, for example, A assaults a plain-clothes policeman who has exhibited his warrant card to him it is unlikely that A will be heard to say that he thought the card was a fake and did not believe the victim was a policeman at all. In any event wilful blindness will probably be accepted as equivalent to knowledge: see Vol. I, para. 7.64; *cf. Annan v. Tait*, 1982 S.L.T. (Sh.Ct.) 108, Sheriff Poole at 109.

present practice is to charge assault and attempt to commit the more serious crime"[81]; but there are situations in which an assault has been committed with the intention of proceeding to the commission of another crime only the stage of attempt has not been reached, and in such cases assault with intent to commit the other crime will still be charged. Suppose it can be proved that A intended to rape B but that he only went the length of kissing her or pushing her onto a bed against her will: in such a case there has been no attempted rape, but there has been an assault with intent to ravish.[82] "Assaults with intent" are confined in practice mainly to assaults with intent to ravish[83] and assaults with intent to rob,[84] but charges of these crimes are still quite common.

29.23   (i) INTENT TO KILL, ETC. It is not now common to charge assault with intent to kill or do grievous bodily harm,[85] although these charges are still competent and do occasionally occur.[86] Where an accused is charged with homicide, or assault to serious injury, it is competent for the jury to convict him of assault with intent to kill, or with intent to do serious injury,[87] but there is no reported instance of such a case.

29.24   (ii) INDECENT ASSAULT. It was formerly the practice to charge assaults as aggravated by lewdness or an intent "to gratify lewdness"[88] but this form of charge is not now used. Where there has been actual lewdness committed against the will of the other party, the lewd acts are specified in the charge and aggravate the assault. "Indecent assault" is not a specific crime, it is simply an assault accompanied by circumstances of indecency.[89] Such assaults are further aggravated where the victim is a child,[90] or where venereal disease is communicated.[91]

29.25   (iii) EXTORTION. An assault may be aggravated by being committed with the intention of extorting something from the victim, such as a confession.[92]

---

[81] Macdonald, p.117.

[82] See, *e.g.*, *McGill v. H.M. Advocate*, 2001 S.C.C.R. 28.

[83] See Hume, i, 329; Alison, i, 184.

[84] See Alison, i, 188; Hume, i, 329.

[85] See Hume, i, 328; *Mysie Brown* (1827) Syme, 152; *Geo. Lougton* (1831) Bell's Notes 88; Anderson, p.159, for the earlier practice.

[86] For example, *Mary Desson*, High Court at Edinburgh, Jan. 1939, unrep'd, a charge of assault with intent to murder; but see *Somervilles*, High Court at Edinburgh, Sept. 1964, High Court of Justiciary on Appeal, Nov. 1964, unrep'd, where a jury convicted of assault with intent to do grievous bodily harm on a charge of attempted murder, and the Appeal Court deleted the aggravation.

[87] 1995 Act, Sched. 3, para. 10 (3); Macdonald, p.255.

[88] For example, *Peter Borrowman* (1837) Bell's Notes 86; *Wm Galloway* (1838) Bell's Notes 85; *David Brown* (1844) 2 Broun 261; *Andrew Lyall* (1853) 1 Irv. 218; *Robt Philip* (1855) 2 Irv. 243.

[89] Certain cases of obtaining sexual intercourse with a woman without her consent are not rape but indecent assault: see para. 33.19, *infra*.

[90] See n.88, *supra*.

[91] *Jas Mack* (1858) 3 Irv. 310: it is submitted that the communication must be intentional or at least reckless. In *H.M. Advocate v. Kelly*, High Court at Glasgow, Feb. 2001, unrep'd, the accused was convicted of a charge which read: "knowing or believing that you were infected with the Human Immunodeficiency Virus and knowing that said Virus could be transmitted to another during sexual intercourse, on various occasions . . . you did pretend to A.C. . . . that you were not infected with said Virus and did culpably and recklessly and with total disregard for the consequences repeatedly engage in sexual intercourse with her whereby she became infected with said Virus to her permanent impairment, to the danger of her health and to the danger of her life."

[92] *Alex. Findlater and Jas McDougall* (1841) 2 Swin. 527.

(iv) PERVERSION OF THE COURSE OF JUSTICE. There are some reported **29.26**
cases of threats aggravated by being made to deter a person from giving
evidence,[93] or in revenge for giving evidence or information to the
authorities,[94] and an assault would similarly be aggravated by such
circumstances.

(v) IN CONNECTION WITH SMUGGLING. Section 85(2) of the Customs and **29.27**
Excise Management Act 1979 provides:

> "Any person who fires upon any vessel, aircraft or vehicle in the
> service of Her Majesty while that vessel, aircraft or vehicle is
> engaged in the prevention of smuggling shall be liable on conviction
> on indictment to imprisonment for a term not exceeding five years."

(vi) TRADE DISPUTES. At one time an assault was aggravated by being **29.28**
committed with intent to further a trade dispute.[95] This is almost
certainly no longer the case.

Section 241 of the Trade Union and Labour Relations (Consolidation)
Act 1992, however, provides:

> "(1) A person commits an offence who, with a view to compelling
> another person to abstain from doing or to do any act which that
> person has a legal right to do or abstain from doing, wrongfully and
> without legal authority—
>> (a) uses violence to or intimidates that person or his wife or
>> children, or injures his property,
>
> . . .
>
> (2) A person guilty of an offence under this section is liable on
> summary conviction to imprisonment for a term not exceeding six
> months or a fine not exceeding level 5 on the standard scale, or
> both."[96]

An offence is completed when violence is used or threats made for the
prohibited purpose whether or not the purpose is achieved.[97]

(vii) ELECTIONS. An assault is aggravated by being committed with **29.29**
intent to interfere with the victim's political rights.[98] Cases of assault in
connection with elections could now be dealt with under the Representation of the People Act 1983, section 115(2)(a).[99]

---

[93] *Margt McDaniel and Anr* (1876) 3 Couper 271.
[94] *Chas Ross* (1844) 2 Broun 271.
[95] Hume, i, 329; Alison, i, 188; *Wm Ewing and Ors* (1821), and *Jas Steel* (1826), both
Hume, i, 329; *Jas Thomson and Ors* (1837) 1 Swin. 532.
[96] The remaining provisions of this section are considered *infra*, para. 39.32 *et seq.*
[97] *Agnew v. Munro* (1891) 2 White 611, interpreting s.7 of the Conspiracy and Protection
of Property Act 1875 which is consolidated in the 1992 Act.
[98] *cf. Alex. Mitchell* (1833) Bell's Notes 90.
[99] See *infra*, para. 38.32.

Mens rea in assault generally

29.30   Assault is a crime of intent and cannot be committed recklessly or
negligently.[1] Unintentional infliction of personal injury is in certain
circumstances criminal, but it is not assault.[2] It seems, however, that the
doctrine of transferred intent[3] applies in assault so that if A intends to
strike B, and in fact strikes C who is standing nearby, A is guilty of
assaulting C[4]: whether A is also guilty of assaulting B, or of an attempted
assault on B,[5] is undecided; but it is clearly necessary that A should have
had an intent to assault someone.[6]

Perhaps the sole unresolved issue in connection with the *mens rea* of
assault in Scotland concerns whether it is necessary to show that the
required intent was also "evil". Macdonald states that "evil intention" is
of the essence of assault[7] but seeks, in doing so, to distinguish assault
from the causing of injury by carelessness "however culpable". In *Lord
Advocate's Reference (No. 2 of 1992)*[8] Lord Justice-Clerk Ross opined as
follows: "It has often been said that evil intention is of the essence of
assault . . . But what that means is that assault cannot be committed
accidentally or recklessly or negligently."

Lord Sutherland in the same case stated that the "words 'evil intent'
have an eminently respectable pedigree, being used by Hume when he
describes dole or *mens rea* as 'that corrupt and evil intention which is
essential to the guilt of any crime' "; but his Lordship went on to
conclude that the *mens rea* of assault was the intention to perform the
relevant acts "without necessarily intending evil consequences from
those acts".[9] Use of the epithet "evil" in the context of intention in
assault suggests that the accused's motive determines whether the *mens
rea* element is satisfied or not; but the decision of the Court in the *Lord
Advocate's Reference (No. 2 of 1992)* expressly denies that motive has any
such role to play in the crime. In the recent case of *Drury v. H.M.
Advocate*,[10] where it was decided that in murder "wickedness" was an

---

[1] *Lord Advocate's Ref. (No. 2 of 1992)*, 1992 S.C.C.R. 960, L.J.-C. Ross at 965D, Lord
Cowie at 968B, Lord Sutherland at 969D; *H.M. Advocate v. Harris*, 1993 S.C.C.R. 559
(Court of five judges), L.J.-C. Ross at 564F, Lord Murray at 566D-E, Lord Morison at
571C; *cf.* Lord Prosser at 576A-B: Lord McCluskey's dissent does not extend to this point.
Suggestions in the earlier cases of *Connor v. Jessop*, 1988 S.C.C.R. 624, and *Roberts v.
Hamilton*, 1989 S.L.T. 399, that assault may be committed recklessly must now be
considered wrong. Scots law does not, therefore, follow English law in this matter: see *R. v.
Venna* [1976] Q.B. 421. See also, Macdonald, p.115; *John Roy* (1839) Bell's Notes 88; *H.M.
Advocate v. Phipps* (1905) 4 Adam 616. *Cf. David Keay* (1837) 1 Swin. 543, Lord Moncreiff
at 545.
[2] This is implicit from the concession made by the respondent in *H.M. Advocate v.
Harris*, 1993 S.C.C.R. 559 — a concession accepted as correct by all five judges in the
Appeal Court. (Lord McCluskey's dissent does not extend to this point.)
[3] See Vol. I, para. 9.10.
[4] *Roberts v. Hamilton*, 1989 S.L.T. 399. The earlier case of *Connor v. Jessop*, 1988
S.C.C.R. 624, must probably now be read in the same way, in spite of the suggestions there
that what happened was so likely to happen that liability could not be avoided: see Vol. I,
para. 9.10.
[5] Assuming that attempted assault exists: see para. 29.02, *supra*.
[6] See Macdonald, pp. 115–116, who, citing the case of *John Roy* (1839), Bell's Notes 88,
and the opinion of Lord Moncrieff in *David Keay* (1837) 1 Swin. 543 at 545, says that it is
not assault "if some act of mischief, not directed against the person of anyone, causes
injury to another of whose presence the perpetrator of the mischief was not aware."
[7] At p.115.
[8] 1992 S.C.C.R. 960, at 965D.
[9] *ibid.*, at 969F.
[10] 2001 S.L.T. 1013 (five judges).

essential part of the *mens rea* element in intentional murder, it was also acknowledged that the standard definition of assault includes "evil intent". Lord Justice General Rodger,[11] however, agreed with Lord Mackay of Drumadoon that in murder cases, where it is alleged that the accused had assaulted the victim, it will often be confusing for the trial judge to provide the jury with the standard definition of assault as part of his charge, since that will then present them with the "evil intent" for assault together with the "wickedness" necessary for murder. As Lord MacKay put it[12]:

> "If such a direction is given, it becomes necessary to make it clear to a jury that the crime of murder requires more than evil intent. Murder requires a wickedness, over and above the evil intent that may suffice for an assault. . . . Therein lies a possible difficulty. Depending upon the circumstances of a particular case, explaining to a jury the difference between 'wickedness' and 'evil intent' may not be straightforward. Reference to the standard definition of assault may therefore introduce a complication".

This is itself all rather confusing, and, it is respectfully suggested, unnecessarily so. In keeping with the ethos of the more modern decisions on assault[13] (as opposed to homicide), it is submitted that the *mens rea* for assault is simply an intent to cause another bodily harm or an intent to put him in fear of such harm, and that use of epithets such as 'evil' is both unnecessary and misleading, as well as being in itself the source of much confusion. It would be preferable for the standard definition of assault, therefore, to refer simply to intention as the *mens rea* of the crime.

The intention need not be to cause the injury which actually results: if A cuts B with a knife with the intention of scratching him and in fact cuts a vital organ he will be guilty of cutting that organ and so of assault to severe injury or danger of life as the case may be. But suppose A shoots at B intending only to frighten him, and in fact causes him injury, is he guilty of injuring B? The only case which raised this point was *H.M. Advocate v. Phipps*[14] in which the accused shot at some poachers and the jury were directed that if their intention had been only to frighten them away they were not guilty of assault, but that proceeded at least in part on the view that they were entitled to frighten them away by shooting[15] so that what they intended to do was not an assault. It is submitted that if A shoots at B intending unlawfully to frighten him and in fact injures him he is guilty of assaulting and injuring him, since his intention to shoot at and frighten is itself an intent to assault. Where, however, A points a gun at B with the intention of frightening him and the gun accidentally goes off,[16] or he pulls the trigger in the belief that the gun is empty, it may be argued that he is not guilty of the resultant injury which was not caused by an intentional act of his, but only of the assault constituted by the pointing of the gun itself.

---

[11] See his opinion, at para. [10].
[12] *ibid.*
[13] See in particular, *Lord Advcate's Ref. (No.2 of 1992)*, 1992 S.C.C.R. 960; *H.M. Advocate v. Harris*, 1993 S.C.C.R. 559.
[14] (1905) 4 Adam 616.
[15] Lord Ardwall at 634.
[16] *cf. Patrick McCarron, supra*, para. 26.25.

Justified assaults

29.31   Assault is justified in the following circumstances:
(1) *In the furtherance of public justice.* Officers of law are entitled to use reasonable force in the execution of their duty, for example in arresting or detaining prisoners.[17] Private persons exercising their lawful powers of arrest, or assisting officers of law are in the same position as such officers.[18] So, also, are persons, such as railway officials, exercising statutory powers of detention.[19]

29.32   (2) *In military duty.* Persons subject to military law who act in accordance with and within the limits allowed by that law are not guilty of assault in respect of any violence they may inflict in the course of their duty.[20]

29.33   (3) *In obedience to a lawful order.*[21]

29.34   (4) *In self-defence.* Where A assaults B in order to protect his life from B's attack there can be no doubt that A commits no crime. But the principle that a conviction for an assault committed in self-defence is a contradiction in terms[22] extends to cases in which something less than life is being defended. A is entitled to use force where necessary in order to ward off any unjustified personal attack made on him. The rules regarding necessity and the due measure of retaliation are the same in assault as in homicide[23]: only 'cruel excess' will defeat the plea.[24] Hume refers to this defence as a defence of provocation which justifies assault,[25] which in turn prompted the response in the second edition of this work that this was a terminological error, due, perhaps to Hume's equation of the term "self-defence" with "defence of life".[26] The modern

---

[17] An erroneous but reasonable belief in the need to use force is sufficient: *McLean v. Jessop*, 1989 S.C.C.R. 13; but the use of excessive force will amount to an assault: see, *e.g.*, *Bonar v. McLeod*, 1983 S.C.C.R. 161; *Marchbank v. Annan*, 1987 S.C.C.R. 718. If the officer acts illegally, *e.g.* in detaining a person, the use of force by the officer is unjustifiable and may lawfully be resisted: *cf. Stocks v. Hamilton*, 1991 S.C.C.R. 190; *Kinnaird v. Higson*, 2001 S.C.C.R. 427.

[18] *cf.* the position in homicide, *supra*, para. 23.35. Powers of a private citizen to arrest a person B are probably confined, however, to situations where he witnesses the commission of a serious crime by B, or perhaps where, being the victim of a crime, he has had B pointed out to him (as the fleeing perpetrator) by an eye witness: see *Bryans v. Guild*, 1990 J.C. 51; *Codona v. Cardle*, 1989 S.L.T. 791.

[19] For example, *Highland Ry. v. Menzies* (1878) 5 R. 887.

[20] *cf.* the position in homicide, *supra*, para. 23.38.

[21] *cf.* the position in homicide, *supra*, para. 23.38.

[22] *Mackenzie v. Gray* (1898) 2 Adam 625, L.J.-C. Macdonald at 627.

[23] Hume, i, 335; Alison. i, 177; *Alex. Haliburton* (1705) Hume, i, 335; *Captain Charteris* (1707) *ibid.; Jas Brown* (1829) Alison, i, 178. Hume seems to suggest at one stage that a greater excess is permissible in assault than in homicide, saying that "the retaliation is intended to deter the assailant, as well as to punish him for the violence he has already done; and this effect it can only have, if it bear evidence of resentment as well as resolution": Hume, i, 335, but this attitude is unlikely to be adopted today: See *Drury v. H.M. Advocate*, 2001 S.L.T. 1013 (five judges), L.J.-G. Rodger's opinion at para. [16], where he accepts that such an attitude is no longer acceptable.

[24] *Fraser v. Skinner*, 1975 S.L.T (Notes) 84. What amounts to cruel excess is a matter of fact: *Moore v. MacDougall*, 1989 S.C.C.R. 659, and is not to be weighed in too fine a balance but may take into account any genuine error of judgment made by the accused: *Whyte v. H.M. Advocate*, 1996 S.C.C.R. 575

[25] Hume, i, 334.

[26] See 2nd ed., at para. 29–34.

view, however, is that Hume had fallen into no such error, but was simply expressing the law as it was in the 18th and 19th centuries, and as it continued to be until at least 1937[27]: thus a plea of self-defence or provocation could result in an acquittal on an assault charge until fairly modern times. Hume's justification for allowing provocation as an exculpatory plea equivalent to self-defence was based on the need to deter as well as to punish the initial aggressor[28]; but it is now accepted that "with an organised police force throughout the land, an individual can never be justified in resorting to violence to deter and punish his assailant."[29] Unlike self-defence, therefore, provocation is not now a plea which can normally result in an acquittal on a charge of assault; but where an accused has acted excessively in self-defence, he will be entitled to plead provocation in the same way as in cases of homicide.[30] As in homicide A is entitled to attack B in order to protect C.[31]

DEFENCE OF PROPERTY. There is little or no authority regarding assaults **29.35** committed in defence of proprietary rights. Alison comments that where A fires at B "in consequence of an erroneous opinion in point of law as to the right to fire on intruders or suspected thieves, a more lenient course has been adopted by the Court."[32]

But the leniency related only to sentence in the two cases he quotes.[33]

In *Kennedy v. Young*[34] the accused was a toll-keeper at a bridge who was charged with assaulting a cart driver who refused to pay the toll, and also with breach of the peace, and obstructing the streets to the danger of the lives of a crowd which gathered there. The charge of assault was held relevant, and Lord Justice-Clerk Hope said that even if the accused had a civil right to exact a toll charge he was not entitled to enforce it as he did.[35] But the general *ratio* of the case was that "For the sake of fourpence, the [accused] was not entitled to cause such a disturbance",[36] and that the case should never have been brought. The case does not help in considering the case, for example, of a man who knocks down someone he sees running off with his watch without at the same time creating a disturbance which endangers the safety of passers-by.

Assault by firearms in defence of property is not justifiable, but the infliction of minor violence for that purpose may be permissible.[37] A man is, however, entitled to use reasonable force to seize and detain someone who is committing a crime, in the exercise of the citizen's right of arrest, and prosecution is unlikely in such cases unless excessive force is used.

---

[27] See *Drury v. H.M. Advocate*, 2001 S.L.T. 1013 (five judges), L.J.-G. Rodger's opinion at para. [16]. Hume's view of the law had been upheld by L.J.-C. Aitchison in *Hillan v. H.M. Advocate*, 1937 J.C. 53, but had fallen out of favour at some point during the ensuing time period.

[28] Hume, i, 335.

[29] *Drury v. H.M. Advocate*, 2001 S.L.T. 1013 (five judges), L.J.-G. Rodger's opinion at para. [16].

[30] *Hillan v. H.M. Advocate*, 1937 J.C. 53.

[31] *H.M. Advocate v. Carson and Anr*, 1964 S.L.T. 21.

[32] Alison, i, 180.

[33] *Jas Corbet* (1828) Alison, i, 181; *Lieut. Robertson* (1829) Alison, i. 180.

[34] (1854) 1 Irv. 533.

[35] At 539–540.

[36] L.J.-C. at 538.

[37] *Donald Kennedy* (1838) 2 Swin. 213, Lord Meadowbank at 231–232; Bell's *Principles*, para. 2032; *Glegg On Reparation* (4th ed., Edinburgh, 1955), p.131; D.M. Walker, *Delict* (2nd ed., 1981), pp. 495 and 496, where the learned author refers only to the prevention of malicious damage to property.

It may be that even if it is not permissible to injure another in defence of one's property it is lawful to threaten him or frighten him away.[38] It may be too that where A wounds B while defending his property he will be charged with culpable and reckless injury and not with assault.[39]

29.36 POACHERS. The Night Poaching Act 1828, section 2, and the Game (Scotland) Act 1832, also section 2, give landowners and their agents specific powers to detain poachers.

29.37 TRESPASS. There is some civil authority to the effect that the occupier of premises is entitled to remove unwanted persons, provided he does not use unnecessary or excessive force, but the extent of his rights is not very clear[40]: there is no criminal authority on the matter.[41]

In his *Principles of Scottish Private Law*[42] Professor Walker says:

> "The proprietor may prevent trespass by warning trespassers off his lands but may not eject them forcibly unless the trespasser uses or threatens violence to the proprietor or is doing actual damage to property and even then may use only the force reasonably necessary in the circumstances. An intruder into a private house may more readily be forcibly ejected."

29.38 (5) *In chastising children.* Parents, guardians, and other persons[43] (excluding members of staff in privately, or state, run schools, but including members of staff in some privately run nursery schools[44]) in

---

[38] Macdonald, p.142, citing *H.M. Advocate v. Phipps* (1905) 4 Adam 616, although that case may be regarded as special because it involved poaching.

[39] *H.M. Advocate v. Phipps* (1905) 4 Adam 616, especially Lord Ardwall at 631.

[40] See D.M. Walker, *Delict* (2nd ed., 1981), p.496; *Glegg on Reparation* (4th ed., Edinburgh, 1955), 131; *Bell v. Shand* (1870) 7 S.L.R. 267, which involved trespass on land in breach of the Game (Scotland) Act 1832; *Wood v. North-British Ry.* (1899) 2 F. 1, where railway constables removed a cabman who refused to leave a railway station, and where L.J.-C. Macdonald said (at 1) they were entitled at common law to remove him forcibly and Lord Trayner observed (at 2) in the course of counsel's argument that "The notion, often expressed, that . . . if a man is, contrary to the desire of the proprietor, on private property he cannot be removed, seems to be a loose and inaccurate one"; *Cook v. Paxton* (1910) 48 S.L.R., where L.J.-C. Macdonald said (at 8) that a hotelkeeper had the privilege and right of any householder to remove a person who was misbehaving himself on the premises or had no right to be there.

[41] *H.M. Advocate v. Phipps, supra; Donald Kennedy* (1838) 2 Swin. 213; *John Reid* (1837) *ibid.* 236n. are all prosecutions for shooting poachers.

[42] (4th ed., Oxford, 1989), Vol. III, pp. 99–100.

[43] *cf. Skinner v. Robertson*, 1980 S.L.T. (Sh.Ct.) 43, where a nurse in a mental hospital was acquitted of assaulting mentally handicapped children by throwing water over them and slapping them in order to maintain control over them; although the sheriff decided that the nurse was protected by the provisions of s.107 of the Mental Health (Scotland) Act 1960 (now s.122 of the Mental Health (Scotland) Act 1984) — no civil or criminal liability for what is done in pursuance of the Act unless done in bad faith or without reasonable care — it seems clear that a wider justificatory plea was applicable since the sheriff accepted that such a nurse will sometimes be required to use reasonable measures of force in order to control patients, a justification which must also extend to adult mental patients: *cf. Norman v. Smith*, 1983 S.C.C.R. 100, where the accused's actions were held to have gone well beyond reasonable measures of control.

[44] See the Standards in Scotland's Schools, etc. Act 2000, s.16; members of staff include teachers, and any other persons who work or otherwise provide services (for payment or not) at the school or other place at which education is provided for pupils and who have lawful control or charge of pupils: s.16(5); nursery schools are schools which provide activities for children below school age: see Eduction (Scotland) Act 1980, s.1(5)(a)(i).

charge of children are entitled to use force for the purpose of disciplining their charges.[45] The force must be moderate, and not inspired by vindictiveness.[46]

(6) *By the consent of the victim.* It is submitted that the simplest **29.39** approach to this problem is to distinguish between assaults which involve the commission of another crime, and assaults which do not. So far as the first class is concerned the question is not whether the assault can be justified by consent, but whether the other crime can be so justified. In such cases the element of assault is little more than part of the narrative of the other crime; even if the assault were negatived by the consent of the party assaulted, that would not affect the accused's guilt of the other crime. If A commits lewd practices against a girl of 15, her consent to his behaviour will not prevent his being charged with a contravention of section 6 of the Criminal Law Consolidation (Scotland) Act 1995,

---

This statutory removal of the former common law entitlement of members of staff in most schools to administer corporal punishment to pupils (*i.e.* to do anything "for the purpose of punishing the pupil concerned (whether or not there are other reasons for doing it) which, apart from any justification, would constitute physical assault upon the pupil": 2000 Act, s.16(3)) may go further than what is required under Art. 3 of the European Convention on Human Rights: see *Costello-Roberts v. U.K.* [1993] 19 E.H.R.R. 112; *cf. Campbell and Cosans v. U.K.* [1982] 4 E.H.R.R. 293. Under s.16(4) of the 2000 Act, it is provided that "corporal punishment shall not be taken to be given to a pupil by virtue of anything done for reasons which include averting — (a) an immediate danger of personal injury to; or (b) an immediate danger to the property of, any person (including the pupil concerned)." Under s.16(2), a member of staff is not entitled to give corporal punishment "at any time and whether or not [it is] given at the place where education is provided": this provision probably deals with the situation in the odd case of *Stewart v. Thain*, 1981 J.C.13, where a teacher outwith school premises appears to have acted as the specifically appointed agent of the child's parent who later complained about the propriety of the form of chastisement used — inducing a 15-year-old boy to remove his trousers and bend over some furniture, and then lifting the waistband of his pants and smacking him on the upper part of his buttocks: the accused was charged with indecent assault, although there was no suggestion of any sexual element, and was acquitted, it having been said that humiliation might form part of a legitimate punishment.

[45] For a discussion of the view that the chastisement of children by parents and others may not be in accordance with current U.K. convention obligations, see R.K. Smith, "Spare the Rod and Spoil the Child?", 1999 S.L.T. (News) 139.

[46] See, *e.g.*, *Guest v. Annan*, 1988 S.C.C.R. 275 (not excessive chastisement for a father to strike his eight-year-old daughter on the buttocks in response to her staying out late and telling lies as to where she had been); *Peebles v. McPhail*, 1989 S.C.C.R. 410 (unreasonable chastisement, and therefore assault, for a mother to slap her two-year-old son in the face, knocking him over); *Byrd v. Wither*, 1991 S.L.T. 206 (person acting as father to a four-year-old child, striking that child on the buttocks with great force, drawing blood and causing abrasions, held guilty of assault since the sheriff was entitled to draw an inference of the "evil intent" necessary for assault): *cf. B. v. Harris*, 1990 S.L.T. 208 (referral of children to children's hearing, on ground that their mother had assaulted one of them, held not to be justified since what the mother had done to that child (slapping following by striking once on the thigh with a belt) was not done out of vindictiveness or with intent to injure but instead was a response to a situation where the child "richly deserved punishment" and "the mere fact that a parent is angry when punishing a child, using moderate force, cannot by itself demonstrate the existence of the evil intent which is an essential ingredient of the crime of assault" (see pp. 209 and 210)). It is not possible to derive any general rules from such examples as to the precise standards to be met; but it seems clear that the standards to be applied are those accepted in Scotland and not in the country of origin of the accused's family: see *R. v. Derriviere* (1969) 53 Cr.App.R. 637.

whether or not it may prevent his being charged with assault[47]; but if A is charged with assaulting B and committing rape upon her, B's consent will elide both charges, because in law consent is a defence to the crime of rape.

Where the assault does not involve another crime the position appears to be that consent is a good defence, provided the accused did not act with intent to cause any bodily harm. In *Smart v. H.M. Advocate*[48] the accused was charged with injuring the victim by assaulting him during a "square go", a duel without weapons. The court rejected a defence of consent, and rejected the distinction made in the first edition of this book[49] between major and minor injuries. The court held that evil intention to injure was of the essence of assault, and that the attitude of the victim was irrelevant where such evil intention was present.[50]

The court accepted nonetheless that "touching" a consenting person in a sexual context was not assault, holding that the necessary intent was absent in such a case. It seems, therefore, that where there is no intention to do bodily harm, consent may still be a defence to assault.[51]

---

[47] It is interesting in this connection that the statutory provision which applies to England (Sexual Offences Act 1956, s.14(2)) says that consent shall not be a defence to a charge of indecent assault, while the Scots provision merely extends the age at which a consenting girl may be the subject of a charge of lewd practices. Where the girl is under 12 it seems that her consent would be inoperative both in relation to the assault and to the lewd practices (*cf. C. v. H.M. Advocate*, 1987 S.C.C.R. 104), although in practice it is more usual to charge such cases as lewd practices and not as assault where the child offers no resistance.

[48] 1975 J.C. 30.

[49] At 774.

[50] The English Court of Appeal declined to follow the *ratio* of *Smart* in *Attorney-General's Ref. (No.6 of 1980)* [1981] Q.B. 715, but held that consent was not a defence to assault where there was an intention to do actual bodily harm or such harm was actually caused in the course of a consensual fight. "Minor struggles" were said to be another matter. It was held to be irrelevant whether the assault took place in public or private. The court noted that this meant that most fights other than sporting events were illegal, but expressed the hope that their decision would not lead to unnecessary prosecutions. The position in England thus appears to be that consent is an element of assault such that the Crown must show absence of the victim's consent in order to secure a conviction (see *Faulkner v. Talbot* [1981] 1 W.L.R. 1528, Lord Lane C.J. at 1534C) unless, exceptionally in particular situations, the public interest requires the consent of the victim to be disregarded — as it does, for example, in sado-masochistic encounters, where the degree of violence involved is extreme (*e.g.*, to the point where blood is drawn or there is a risk of infection): *R. v. Brown (Anthony)* [1994] 1 A.C. 212, HL; or in fighting to settle differences which causes bodily harm and where (it seems) there is an intent to cause such harm: *Attorney-General's Ref. (No. 6 of 1980), supra*; but there are also exceptions to the exceptions. Where, *e.g.*, bodily harm is caused with intent to cause it but without the defendant's having acted aggressively or dangerously, there is no assault if the victim consented: see *R. v. Wilson* [1997] Q.B. 47, CA where a husband branded his wife on the buttocks at her request as a decorative adornment and an expression of love; see also *R. v. Jones* [1986] 83 Cr.App.R. 375, CA, where schoolboys threw other schoolboys in the air for a joke, without intent to do any very serious harm, and where there had been (or was believed to have been) consent to rough and undisciplined play: nevertheless, although one of the two victims had his arm broken whilst the other sustained injuries which led to the surgical removal of his spleen, there was considered to have been no assault. It is very difficult to draw general principles or rules from these cases, as was conceded by Russell L.J. in *R. v. Wilson, supra*, at 50H, where, in giving the opinion of the Court of Appeal, he said: "In this field, in our judgment, the law should develop upon a case by case basis rather than upon general propositions to which, in the changing times in which we live, exceptions may arise from time to time not expressly covered by authority."

[51] See G.H. Gordon, "Consent in Assault" (1976) 21 J.L.S. 168. In *Wm Fraser* (1847) Ark. 280, Lord Mackenzie observed *obiter* that "In some circumstances, a beating may be consented to, as in a case of rheumatism, or in a case of a father confessor ordering

SURGICAL OPERATIONS.[52] In the case of surgical operations consent is a **29.40** defence even where the injuries are likely to cause danger to life. This is probably because the injuries are inflicted in such cases not for their own sake or in order to cause pain or gratify an intention to harm, but for the benefit of the patient. Even in the absence of consent a surgeon may be justified and perhaps even obliged to operate in an emergency: his failure to do so indeed might in some circumstances constitute culpable homicide should the patient die as a result.[53] To be lawful the operation must, of course, be one which is recognised by the profession as appropriate and be carried out in accordance with proper professional standards. Professor Glanville Williams refers to ritual circumcision and plastic surgery as difficult cases in this connection.[54] He explains ritual circumcision on the basis of religious toleration[55]; it is probably better explained by reference to the minor nature of the injury involved, but this explanation may be precluded by *Smart v. H.M. Advocate*.[56] It might be argued that evil intention is absent because of the religious motive involved, but religious toleration would not extend to the practice of burning widows alive, or to the infliction of injuries likely to cause death. Plastic surgery is intended to benefit the patient but it does involve some injury, and would have to be excused by treating the surgeon's motive as precluding the existence of any evil intent. But would it be justifiable to amputate a limb or endanger the patient's life in order to carry out a cosmetic operation? In practice, however, there is a very wide umbrella which covers all surgical operations performed by recognised doctors in accordance with accepted medical procedures, and the plastic surgery cases would simply be classed as surgical operations and justified accordingly without any further inquiry into the relationship between the injury and the benefit in any case.[57]

ILLEGAL OPERATIONS. The only exception in practice to the protection **29.41** afforded to surgical operations is where the operation itself is illegal, and the only example of such an operation which has so far been considered by the common law is abortion. Even here the practice prior to the Abortion Act 1967[58] was to regard abortion carried out by qualified

---

flagellation; but this is not violence or assault, because there is consent": at 302. In *Dobbs and Macdonald v. Neilson* (1899) 3 Adam 10, two boxers fighting with gloves and under Queensberry rules were convicted of assault, but this matter was not raised on appeal. See also T.B. Smith, "Law, Professional Ethics and the Human Body", 1959 S.L.T. (News) 245; Gl. Williams, "Consent and Public Policy" [1962] Crim.L.R. 74; Kenny, para. 156; Smith and Hogan, pp. 408–412; G. Hughes, "Consent in Sexual Offences" (1962) 25 M.L.R. 672; "Two Views on Consent in the Criminal Law" (1963) 26 M.L.R. 233; M. Gunn and D. Ormerod, "The Legality of Boxing" (1995) 15 L.S. 181.

[52] See G. Hughes, "Two Views on Consent in the Criminal Law", *supra*; T.B. Smith, *op.cit.*

[53] *cf. R. v. Bourne* [1939] 1 K.B. 687.

[54] [1962] Crim.L.R. at 156–157.

[55] *ibid.* 157.

[56] 1975 J.C. 30.

[57] As Lord Mustill (dissenting in the decision) said in *R. v. Brown (Anthony)* [1994] 1 A.C. 212, at 266F-G: "Many of the acts done by surgeons would be very serious crimes if done by anyone else, and yet the surgeons incur no liability. Actual consent, or the substitute for consent deemed by the law to exist where an emergency creates a need for action, is an essential element in this immunity: but it cannot be a direct explanation for it, since much of the bodily invasion involved in surgery lies well above the point at which consent should even arguably be regarded as furnishing a defence. Why is this so? The answer must in my opinion be that proper medical treatment, for which actual or deemed consent is a prerequisite, is in a category of its own."

[58] See *supra*, para. 28.05.

doctors under normal operating conditions as therapeutic abortion, and so as justifiable, or at any rate as an operation which would not be made the subject of criminal prosecution.

Questions have been raised in England as to the legality of operations for sterilisation or castration,[59] but the matter has not arisen in Scotland. It is unlikely that the courts would today create new crimes of this kind, so that unless and until they are made illegal by statute operations for sterilisation or castration will be treated in the same way as other surgical operations, although the court could rely on *Smart*[60] if it wished to characterise the operation as evil and therefore as an assault.

Under the statutory law, ritual female circumcision is prohibited by the Prohibition of Female Circumcision Act 1985, even when performed by a recognised medical practitioner, and thus qualifies as an "illegal operation".[61]

29.42 SPORT. Injuries inflicted in the course of sport are regarded in England as justified by reference to the public policy of encouraging manly exercises which "may fit people for defence, public as well as personal, in time of need", and so as distinguishable from similar injuries inflicted, say, for the sake of erotic satisfaction.[62] So far as Scots law is concerned, it appears that where the prime intention is not to injure but to engage in a sporting contest with recognised rules, presumably for reward or prestige, there is no evil intent to injure and so no assault.[63] This concession does not extend to duelling whether with weapons or with fists, at any rate where the prime purpose is to inflict injury in pursuance of a personal quarrel. The exception for sporting injuries presumably extends to all acts done under the rules of the game, and also to "an application of force that is in breach of the rules of the game, if it is the sort of thing that may be expected to happen during the game."[64]

29.43 THE NATURE OF THE CONSENT. In order to be valid, consent must be freely given. Where it is obtained by fraud or extortion there is probably no assault, but the crime of fraud or extortion will have been committed.[65]

Where the victim is incapable of giving a true consent any apparent consent will be inoperative. The position of children and persons of

---

[59] Gl. Williams, *op.cit.*; *Bravery v. Bravery* [1954] 1 W.L.R. 1169. See also Report of Departmental Committee on Sterilisation (1933), Cmd 4485.

[60] 1975 J.C. 30.

[61] Maximum penalty: on indictment, five years' and a fine; on summary conviction, six months' and fine of the statutory maximum (s.1(2)(a), (b)). Exceptions are created by s.2 for surgery which is necessary for the physical or mental health of the woman, provided it is performed by a registered medical practitioner or, in connection with labour or the giving of birth, by such a practitioner or a registered midwife or a person who is in training with a view to qualifying as such a practitioner or midwife.

[62] See *R. v. Donovan* [1934] 2 K.B. 498, 508.

[63] *Smart v. H.M. Advocate*, 1975 J.C. 30.

[64] Gl. Williams, "Consent and Public Policy" [1962] Crim.L.R. 74, at 81. See *R. v. Billinghurst* [1978] Crim.L.R. 553 for an example of an assault between rugby players; *cf. Butcher v. Jessop*, 1989 S.L.T. 593.

[65] *cf. R. v. Richardson* (1998) 2 Cr.App.R. 200, CA, where convictions for assault occasioning actual bodily harm (contrary to s.47 of the Offences Against the Person Act 1861) were quashed on the basis that dental patients, who had continued to be treated by R, a dentist who, unknown to them, had been suspended from practice by the General Dental Council, had been defrauded only to the extent of R's holding herself out as not being so suspended — a fraud which did not negative their consent to be treated by her.

weak intellect has, however, been greatly clarified by modern legislation: a child, that is to say a person under 16 years of age, has for example legal capacity to consent to his own medical or dental treatment if the medical practitioner attending him is of opinion that that child is capable of understanding the nature and possible consequences of the treatment[66]; alternatively, where a child is too young to have such capacity, those with parental rights over him have the right to act as his representative, which includes the giving of consent to medical or dental treatment provided it promotes the child's health, development and welfare.[67] Where an adult (that is to say a person over 16 years of age) is incapable of making, communicating, understanding, or retaining the memory of, decisions due to mental disorder or physical disability, and the medical practitioner primarily responsible for his medical treatment has certified in the approved form that such incapacity exists, that practitioner generally has authority to do what is reasonable in relation to medical treatment to promote that adult's physical or mental health within the limits laid down by the Adults with Incapacity (Scotland) Act 2000.[68]

Provocation in assault

The effect of provocation in assault. Hume begins his discussion of **29.44** provocation in assault by saying that provocation by words can mitigate but never justify assault,[69] and then goes on to say that, "the defence of provocation by real injuries suffered in the person is subject to a different construction, and may not only mitigate the sentence, but amount to an entire justification."[70] He then discusses the requirement that there must be "due measure" in retaliation in terms which are reminiscent of self-defence.[71] Alison is not as forthright as Hume, but does not suggest that Hume incorrectly sets out the law.[72] In the assault case of *Hillan v. H.M. Advocate*[73] the Appeal Court followed Hume by making it clear that provocation, as distinct from self-defence, could operate in justification of assault. Indeed Lord Justice-Clerk Aitchison distinguished four possibilities in *Hillan*: self-defence leading to acquittal; self-defence leading to mitigation; provocation leading to acquittal; and provocation leading to mitigation.[74] The essential feature of self-defence was said to be that the accused acts for his own protection to ward off danger[75]; the essential feature of provocation was not defined. The difference between the two types of provocation was not defined either, although Lord Aitchison's opinion gives the impression that the nature of the provocation, the extent of the retaliation, and whether or not the accused had started the quarrel, were all factors to be taken into account in deciding which type of provocation was present. *Hillan* was

---

[66] Age of Legal Capacity (Scotland) Act 1991, s.2(4).
[67] Children (Scotland) Act 1995; see ss. 2(1)(d) and 5(1).
[68] See ss. 47–52, and s.1(6) of the Act.
[69] Hume, i, 333.
[70] *ibid.* 334.
[71] It seems that "cruel excess" in retaliation will be the "due measure" which excludes provocation: see *Lennon v. H.M. Advocate*, 1991 S.C.C.R. 611. Hume does not deal with self-defence as such at all in his treatment of assault, perhaps because he regarded the term as confined to defence of life or chastity or some other equivalent value.
[72] Alison, i, 176–178.
[73] 1937 J.C. 53.
[74] *ibid.*, at 57 and 58.
[75] *ibid.*, L.J.-C. Aitchison at 58.

strongly criticised in *Crawford v. H.M. Advocate*,[76] a homicide case, where it was said that self-defence was always a plea in exculpation and provocation always a plea in mitigation[77]: and this generally was the view taken by the courts[78] and textbooks[79] until the full-bench decision of *Drury v. H.M. Advocate*.[80] There Lord Justice General Rodger accepts that the law was indeed as Hume represented it to be, that is to say that, whatever might have been the case with self-defence, provocation could result in an acquittal on a charge of assault; that this remained the law until some little time after *Hillan*; and that the justification for acquittal was based upon society's desire to deter and punish the original aggressor. Lord Rodger also accepts, however, that the practice since *Hillan* has changed and that the function of provocation in assault is now restricted to the mitigation of penalty.[81]

Hillan would not now be followed, therefore; and if it is accepted that provocation is only a plea in mitigation, it becomes in the last resort a question for the judge who will in any event take all the circumstances of the case into account in passing sentence. But it is the practice to leave provocation to the jury and to ask them to indicate in their verdict whether they find the accused guilty as libelled or guilty under provocation, and the judge will abide by the jury's finding on this point in passing sentence.

29.45 *The nature of provocation in assault.* The law regarding provocation in assault is similar to that regarding provocation in homicide, but the rules are somewhat less strictly applied in assault.

The most important difference between homicide and assault is that provocation by words is relevant to mitigate assault.[82] There are no reported cases of verbal provocation in assault cases subsequent to 1837, and it is not clear what requirements must be fulfilled before words will be regarded as sufficient to mitigate assault. In *MacIntosh v. Cameron*[83] the jury were directed that they could find provocation in an offensive letter written by the victim to the accused. It is unlikely that this would be accepted today as provocation, but there would of course be nothing to prevent its being taken into account in assessing sentence. Modern law would probably require immediate inflammatory abuse leading to a loss of self-control, and not merely words leading to irritation and a desire for revenge.

29.46   PROVOCATION MUST BE RECENT. There is some old authority that the requirement of recency does not apply strictly in assault cases. Macdonald states that verbal provocation must be "very recent",[84] but refers

---

[76] 1950 J.C. 67.

[77] For a defence of *Hillan* see R.J.D. Scott, "The Defence of Provocation", 1965 S.L.T. (News) 193.

[78] See, *e.g.*, *Fenning v. H.M. Advocate*, 1985 S.C.C.R. 219; *Thomson v. H.M. Advocate*, 1985 S.C.C.R. 448.

[79] See, *e.g.*, T.B. Smith, at p.142; R.A.A. McCall Smith and D. Sheldon, *Scots Criminal Law* (2nd ed., 1997), at pp. 145 and 164; P.W. Ferguson, *Crimes Against the Person* (2nd ed., 1998), paras 9.04 to 9.07. *Cf.* Macdonald, at p.116, where the confusing pre-*Crawford* statement is made as follows: "Provocation by blows will justify retaliation in self-defence if not excessive."

[80] 2001 S.L.T. 1013 (five judges).

[81] *ibid.*, the L.J.-G.'s opinion at para. [16].

[82] Hume, i, 333; Alison, i, 176–177; Anderson, p.159; Macdonald, p.116.

[83] (1832) 5 D. & A. 257.

[84] Macdonald, pp. 116–117.

to *MacIntosh v. Cameron*[85] where there was an interval of four days between the provocation and the assault. In *Donald Stewart and Ors*[86] where a charge of mobbing and assault was brought in connection with a riot that took place after an election, the defence were not allowed to lead evidence of provocation on the morning of the day of the assault, on the ground that the charge related only to what happened after the election. Anderson deals with these two cases by saying that where the provocation is spoken the assault must take place within a few hours, but where it is written it should be no longer than a few days after.[87] It is very difficult to justify any such distinction, particularly as the effect of written words is likely to be less violent than that of spoken ones, and indeed it is difficult to accept the former as constituting provocation at all.

Where there has been a course of provocation it may still be relevant to lead evidence of incidents at any rate in the two or three days preceding the assault, but it is necessary to prove some final incident which led to a loss of self-control, and to show that the accused was not just acting in revenge for what had happened earlier.[88]

Generally speaking, it is probably the law today that provocation in assault must satisfy much the same requirements regarding recency as provocation in homicide, although in practice the rules will not be applied as stringently as they are in homicide cases, if only because provocation which is not recent may be taken into account in passing sentence, although not perhaps under the head of provocation as defined by law.

OTHER FORMS OF REAL INJURY

All intentional infliction of physical injury is criminal. Hume opens his **29.47** treatment of common law assault as follows:

> "Let us now attend to those offences against the person, which remain on the footing of the common law . . . These are various in kind and degree; and the law is provided with sundry corresponding terms for them, more or less comprehensive, and commonly employed in libels, such as assault, invasion . . . But although the injury do not come under any of those terms of style, not be such as can be announced in a single phrase, this circumstance in nowise affects the competency of a prosecution. Let the libel, in the *major* proposition, give an intelligible account of it in terms at large; and, if it amount to a real injury, it shall be sustained to infer punishment, less or more, *pro modo admissi*; no matter how new or how strange the wrong. We have besides, in our law, the general term of *stellionate,* borrowed from the Roman practice, which may be employed in such a case, along with the full description of the injury."[89]

---

[85] (1832) 5 D. & A. 257, *supra*, para. 29.45.
[86] (1837) 1 Swin. 540.
[87] Anderson, p.159.
[88] *cf. John Ross* (1823) Alison, i, 179; *H.M. Advocate v. Callander,* 1958 S.L.T. 24.
[89] Hume, i, 327–328. See also Alison, i, 633–634.

The term "stellionate" is no longer in use, but it is still the case that a charge of causing physical injury by any means whatever is relevant.

29.48 *Drugging.* One well-recognised form of real injury is by the administration of drugs or other deleterious substances. The circumstances of such administration may often involve fraud, but the crime would normally be libelled as one of drugging rather than as fraud.[90] The mere administration of a drug, for example whisky or a purgative, which causes injury is not a crime in the absence of some intent to injure[91] or, where the injury is libelled as having been inflicted recklessly, of recklessness.[92]

There are no reported cases in which the victim has merely been rendered unconscious without any ulterior purpose such as an intent to steal from him, but Alison, Macdonald and Anderson[93] all consider that such an act would constitute a crime, and there seems no reason for excluding stupefaction from the category of injury.[94]

Drugging may be aggravated in the same way as asault.[95]

29.49 *Cruel and unnatural treatment.* Where injury is caused by omission, or by a combination of acts and omissions, the crime is usually called cruel and unnatural treatment. The cases mainly concern neglect of children by their parents[96] or other person in charge of them[97] and many cases would today be treated as offences against the Children and Young Persons (Scotland) Act 1937.[98]

The crime can also be committed by persons in charge of invalids[99] or weak-minded persons,[1] and by husbands on their wives.[2]

---

[90] For a 20th century example of a charge of drugging see *Grant v. H.M. Advocate*, 1938 J.C. 7 where the accused was alleged to have "put a liquid . . . containing carbolic, into a bottle containing milk to be consumed by [M.W.] aged one year . . . in order that the said [M.W.] might partake of said milk containing carbolic with intent to do her grievous bodily harm, and the said milk containing carbolic was duly taken by said [M.W.] to her grievous bodily harm."

[91] *Peter Milne and John Barry* (1868) 1 Couper 28.

[92] But it is probably always criminal to give a child a quantity of whisky which injures its health: *Robt Brown and John Lawson* (1842) 1 Broun 415; and see Children and Young Persons (Scotland) Act 1937, s.16. It has been held that drugging may in some circumstances be committed by supplying persons with drugs in the knowledge that they are to be used by the persons supplied to the danger of their health and lives: *Khaliq v. H.M. Advocate*, 1984 J.C. 23; *Ulhaq v. H.M. Advocate*, 1991 S.L.T. 614: see Vol. I, para. 4.06, n. 16.

[93] Alison, i, 629; Macdonald, p.126; Anderson, p.172.

[94] The 2nd Sched. to the Firearms Act 1968 refers to the crime of "Administration of drugs with intent to enable or assist the commission of a crime", perhaps under the influence of the Offences against the Person Act 1861, s.22.

[95] For example, *David Wilson and Ors* (1828) Bell's Notes 22; *John and Catherine Stuart* (1829) *ibid.*: intent to steal; *Alex. Mitchell* (1833) Bell's Notes 90: intent to prevent the exercise of lawful business or political rights.

[96] For example, *John Robertson* (1841) Bell's Notes 82; *David and Janet Gemmell* (1841) 2 Swin. 552; *John and Mary Craw* (1839) 2 Swin. 449; *Jean Stewart and John Wallace, Jr.* (1845) 2 Broun 544; *Catherine McGavin* (1846) Ark. 67; *Wm Fairweather* (1842) 1 Broun 309.

[97] For example, *Barbara Gray or McIntosh* (1881) 4 Couper 389.

[98] *infra*, para. 31.02.

[99] For example, *Fairweather, supra.* In *McManimy and Higgans* (1847) Ark. 321, a lodging-house keeper who carried an invalid out of his house and left him in the street where he lay until a policeman took him to hospital was charged *inter alia* with cruel treatment. See also the charges in *Lambert v. H.M. Advocate*, 1993 S.L.T. 339.

[1] *John and Catherine McRae* (1842) 1 Broun 395.

[2] *Geo. Fay* (1847) Ark. 397, where the wife was locked in a dirty closet without adequate clothing.

The offence usually consists in failure to provide proper food, clothing or accommodation, and is usually charged as having been committed recklessly (or, formerly, negligently), but can, of course, be committed with intent to injure. The cruel treatment must be specific, and the charge must set forth particular acts of criminal conduct; the law cannot look to those "various modes of unkindness, ingratitude, treachery and oppression, by which, in too many instances, the heart and health are broken."[3]

MENTAL HEALTH (SCOTLAND) ACT 1984. Section 105 of this Act provides: **29.50**

"(1) It shall be an offence for any person being an officer on the staff or otherwise employed in a hospital or nursing home, or being a manager of a hospital or a person carrying on a nursing home—
  (a) to ill-treat or wilfully neglect a patient for the time being receiving treatment for mental disorder as an in-patient in that hospital or nursing home; or
  (b) to ill-treat or wilfully neglect, on the premises of which the hospital or nursing home forms part, a patient for the time being receiving such treatment there as an out-patient.

(2) It shall be an offence for any individual to ill-treat or wilfully neglect a patient who is for the time being in his custody or care.

(2A) It shall be an offence for any individual to ill-treat or wilfully neglect a patient in respect of whom a community care order is for the time being in force."[4]

ADULTS WITH INCAPACITY (SCOTLAND) ACT 2000. Section 83 of this Act **29.51** provides:

"(1) It shall be an offence for any person exercising powers under this Act relating to the personal welfare of an adult to ill-treat or wilfully neglect that adult."[5]

Abduction. Hume deals with abduction only in connection with forcible **29.52** abduction and marriage,[6] but abduction for any purpose is criminal whether or not it is accompanied by behaviour which can be categorised

---

[3] Hume, i, 189, and see *Robt Watt and Jas Kerr* (1868) 1 Couper 123 where the cruel treatment libelled was that of a master of a ship against boys in the crew by compelling them to leave the ship and make their way with insufficient provisions across an area of ice. See also W. Roughead, "The Boys on the Ice" (1939) 51 J.R. 28.

[4] As amended by the Mental Health (Patients in the Community) Act 1995, Sched. 2, para. 6, and the Adults With Incapacity (Scotland) Act 2000, Sched. 6. For a "community care order", see the 1984 Act, s.35A, as inserted by the Mental Health (Patients in the Community) Act 1995, s.4(1). The maximum penalties are six months' imprisonment and a fine of the statutory maximum, on summary conviction; and two years' imprisonment and a fine on indictment.

[5] An adult for the purposes of this legislation is a person of 16 years of age or over (s.1(6)); maximum penalties are, on summary conviction, six months' and a fine of the statutory maximum; and on indictment, two years' and a fine (see s.83(2).) (The Act establishes a detailed scheme to provide for (*inter alia*) the personal welfare (including medical treatment) of adults who are incapable of acting (or of making, communicating, understanding, or retaining the memory of, decisions) because of mental disorder (which includes personality disorder or mental handicap however caused or manifested), or physical disability which prevents communication (provided that such disability cannot be overcome by human or mechanical intervention). Amongst those exercising personal welfare powers in respect of such adults are welfare attorneys, managers of establishments, and medical practitioners: see esp. ss. 1(5) and (6), 16, 47 and 87(1).)

[6] Hume, i, 310.

as assault or fraud.[7] The essential feature of the crime is the deprivation of the victim's personal freedom, and unlawful detention without any element of carrying off would also, it is submitted, be criminal.[8]

The carrying off of children under the age of puberty is dealt with as theft.[9]

Section 6[10] of the Child Abduction Act 1984 provides:

"(1) Subject to subsections (4) and (5) below, a person connected with a child under the age of sixteen years commits an offence if he takes or sends the child out of the United Kingdom—
(a) without the appropriate consent if there is in respect of the child—
(i) an order of a court in the United Kingdom awarding custody of the child to any person or naming any person as the person with whom the child is to live; or
(ii) an order of a court in England, Wales or Northern Ireland making the child a ward of court;
(b) if there is in respect of the child an order of a court in the United Kingdom prohibiting the removal of the child from the United Kingdom or any part of it.

(2) A person is connected with a child for the purposes of this section if—
(a) he is a parent or guardian of the child; or
(b) there is in force an order of a court in the United Kingdom awarding custody of the child to him or naming him as the person with whom the child is to live (whether solely or jointly with any other person); or
(c) in the case of a child whose parents are not and have never been married to one another, there are reasonable grounds for believing that he is the father of the child.

(3) In this section, the 'appropriate consent' means—
(a) in relation to a child to whom subsection (1)(a)(i) above applies—
(i) the consent of each person

---

[7] Macdonald, p.124. *Cf.* Burnett, p.109 where he says: "When the abduction is neither with a view to marriage, nor rape, it is punishable *tanquam crimen in suo genere*, as an unjust oppression, and restraint": *Coppinger* (1720) *ibid.* and *John Lindsay* (1791) *ibid.* 110, both cases involving forcible carrying off, the former to prevent the victim appearing as a witness, the latter to prevent him voting in a local election. In *Jas MacLean*, High Court at Glasgow, May 1980, unrep'd, where there was a charge of abducting a little girl and also a charge of raping her, Lord Kincraig directed the jury on the abduction charge that (transcript of the judge's charge, p.7): "it is a crime to carry off or confine any person forcibly against their will without lawful authority. In the case of a child of six 'forcibly' is not a necessary element in the proof. It would be sufficient to constitute the crime of abducting a child if there was evidence of her being led away by the accused or inducing her to follow. That would be sufficient to establish proof that she was taken away against her will. So far as any proper authority is concerned, a stranger has no proper authority to lead away a child." See also *Elliot v. Tudhope*, 1987 S.C.C.R. 85, a charge of wrongful detention against a police officer.

[8] For the law relating to carrying off for sexual purposes, see *infra*, paras 36.33, 36.34. In *Stevenson v. Rankin*, Oban Police Court, June 1962 (see *The Guardian*, June 26, 1962), a plea of guilty was offered to a charge of assault by stopping a chairlift containing the victim in a place where he could not alight, the charge being one of "depriving him of his liberty and causing him inconvenience and discomfort".

[9] *supra*, para. 14.26.

[10] As amended by the Law Reform (Parent and Child) (Scotland) Act 1986, Sched. 1, para. 20(a), and the Children (Scotland) Act 1995, Sched. 4, para. 34 (a), (b) and (c).

> (a) who is a parent or guardian of the child; or
> (b) to whom custody of the child has been awarded or who is named as the person with whom the child is to live (whether the award is made, or the person so named is named solely or jointly with any other person) by an order of a court in the United Kingdom; or
> (ii) the leave of that court;
> (b) in relation to a child to whom subsection (1)(a)(ii) above applies, the leave of the court which made the child a ward of court; . . .[11]
> (4) In relation to a child to whom subsection (1)(a)(i) above applies, a person does not commit an offence by doing anything without the appropriate consent if—
> (a) he does it in the belief that each person referred to in subsection (3)(a)(i) above —
> (i) has consented; or
> (ii) would consent if he was aware of all the relevant circumstances; or
> (b) he has taken all reasonable steps to communicate with such other person but has been unable to communicate with him.
> (5) In proceedings against any person for an offence under this section it shall be a defence for that person to show that at the time of the alleged offence he had no reason to believe that there was in existence an order referred to in subsection (1) above.
> (6) For the purposes of this section—
> (a) a person shall be regarded as taking a child if he causes or induces the child to accompany him or any other person, or causes the child to be taken; and
> (b) a person shall be regarded as sending a child if he causes the child to be sent. . . ."[12]

Abduction in connection with elections is now dealt with by the Representation of the People Act 1983, section 115(1) and (2)(b)[13] but is also recognised as a common law crime.[14]

INTERNATIONAL OFFENCES

Genocide. Section 1 of the Genocide Act 1969 makes it an offence to **29.53** commit any of the acts specified in the Schedule to that Act, being acts prohibited by the Genocide Convention 1948. The schedule reads as follows:

> "In the present Convention, genocide means any of the following acts committed with intent to destroy, in whole or in part, a national, ethnical, racial or religious group, as such:
> (a) Killing members of the group;
> (b) Causing serious bodily or mental harm to members of the group;

---

[11] Omitted text refers to the situation where there is more than one applicable order.

[12] Maximum penalties, on summary conviction, three months' imprisonment and a fine not exceeding the statutory maximum; on indictment, two years' and a fine: see s.8.

[13] *infra*, para. 38.32.

[14] Alison, i, 642; *J. Taylor* (1826) Alison, i, 643; *Maclachlan and Ors* (1831) *ibid.*

(c) Deliberately inflicting on the group conditions of life calculated to bring about its physical destruction in whole or in part;
(d) Imposing measures intended to prevent births within the group;
(e) Forcibly transferring children of the group to another group."[15]

29.54 *Geneva Conventions*. The Geneva Conventions Act 1957, as amended by the Geneva Conventions (Amendments) Act 1995, gives effect to the Geneva Conventions 1949 and Protocols of 1977 which are set out in the six schedules to the Act.[16]

Section 1 of the Act penalises grave breaches of any of the scheduled conventions or of the First Protocol.[17] Such breaches are defined in the respective conventions in broadly similar terms. That in the Fourth Schedule which deals with the protection of civilians is as follows:

"Grave breaches to which the preceding Article relates shall be those involving any of the following acts, if committed against persons or property protected by the present Convention: wilful killing, torture or inhuman treatment, including biological experiments, wilfully causing great suffering or serious injury to body or health, unlawful deportation or transfer or unlawful confinement of a protected person, compelling a protected person to serve in the forces of a hostile Power, or wilfully depriving a protected person of the rights of fair and regular trial prescribed in the present Convention, taking of hostages and extensive destruction and appropriation of property, not justified by military necessity and carried out unlawfully and wantonly."[18]

29.55 *Hostages*. The Taking of Hostages Act 1982, implementing the International Convention against the Taking of Hostages, provides by section 1:

"(1) A person, whatever his nationality, who, in the United Kingdom or elsewhere—
(a) detains any other person ("the hostage"), and
(b) in order to compel a State, international governmental organisation or person to do or abstain from doing any act, threatens to kill, injure or continue to detain the hostage, commits an offence."[19]

29.56 *Terrorism*. The Terrorism Act 2000 provides by section 61:

"(1) A person commits an offence if—

---

[15] Maximum penalty, life imprisonment: where the offence consists of the killing of any person, otherwise 14 years: s.1(2)(a), (b).

[16] They deal with the amelioration of the condition of the wounded and sick in armed forces in the field; and of wounded, sick and shipwrecked members of armed forces at sea; the treatment of prisoners of war; and the protection of civilians in time of war.

[17] Maximum penalty, life imprisonment where the breach involves the wilful killing of a person protected by the Convention or Protocol, otherwise 14 years: s.1(1)(i) and (ii).

[18] Article 147.

[19] Maximum penalty, life imprisonment: s.1(2). See also the Internationally Protected Persons Act 1978, s.1(3): para. 29.66, *infra*.

(a) he incites another person to commit an act[20] of terrorism[21] wholly or partly outside the United Kingdom, and

(b) the act would, if committed in Scotland, constitute one of the offences listed in subsection (2).

(2) Those offences are—

(a) murder,

(b) assault to severe injury, and

(c) reckless conduct which causes actual injury.

(3) A person guilty of an offence under this section shall be liable to any penalty to which he would be liable on conviction of the offence listed in subsection (2) which corresponds to the act which he incites.

(4) For the purposes of subsection (1) it is immaterial whether or not the person incited is in the United Kingdom at the time of the incitement.
 . . .".

UNINTENTIONAL INJURY

It is a crime at common law to cause injury to the person by **29.57** negligence of the requisite degree. There are quite a number of reported cases which are authority for this proposition; for example, in the early twentieth century there is the case of *H.M. Advocate v. Phipps*,[22] where the accused was charged with assault, and alternatively with the infliction of injury by the reckless discharge of loaded guns. Lord Ardwall rejected the argument that the alternative charge disclosed no crime, and told the jury:

"[T]here have been several cases where a verdict of reckless discharge of firearms was found justified in our law where the result was quite outwith the expectation of the accused, . . . on an occasion when crime was the last thing present in the accused's mind, at a wedding festivity, the accused had fired off a gun loaded blank by way of a salute, and injured a member of the public passing by, who was struck by the cotton wad. Conviction followed."[23]

---

[20] Under s.121, "act" includes omission.

[21] Section 1 provides:

"(1) In this Act 'terrorism' means the use or threat of action where—

   (a) the action falls within subsection (2),

   (b) the use or threat is designed to influence the government or to intimidate the public or a section of the public, and

   (c) the use or threat is made for the purpose of advancing a political, religious or ideological cause.

(2) Action falls within this subsection if it—

   (a) involves serious violence against a person,

   (b) involves serious damage to property,

   (c) endangers a person's life, other than that of the person committing the action,

   (d) creates a serious risk to the health or safety of the public or a section of the public, or

   (e) is designed seriously to interfere with or seriously to disrupt an electronic system.

(3) The use or threat of action falling within subsection (2) which involves the use of firearms or explosives is terrorism whether or not subsection (1)(b) is satisfied.
 . . .".

[22] (1905) 4 Adam 616.

[23] At 631.

The cases prior to *Phipps* are by no means restricted to firearms, and include cases of negligent driving of horses[24] and railway engines,[25] the negligent navigation of vessels,[26] the negligent use of explosives[27] and negligence in erecting buildings.[28] It was recognised as a general rule in the nineteenth century that culpable neglect of duty resulting in injury to the person was a crime; and this is still the law, although the standard of culpability necessary for conviction is now much higher.

One of the most recent cases to discuss these issues is *H.M. Advocate v. Harris*[29] in which it was established beyond doubt by a court of five judges[30] that at common law there are two relevant but separate offences of culpable negligence, which is now usually referred to as "recklessness", which does not result in death: these are recklessly causing injury, and recklessly causing danger to others.[31] In so far as the earlier case of *Quinn v. Cunningham*[32] decided that a charge of causing injury by culpable negligence was not a relevant charge without an express (or perhaps clearly implied[33]) averment that the accused's conduct was productive of danger to the public, that case was overruled as wrongly decided.[34] The court in *Harris* were also of the opinion that the degree of negligence to be shown by the Crown in such a charge was the high degree referred to by Lord Justice-Clerk Aitchison in *Paton v. H.M. Advocate*,[35] such that mere carelessness or negligence was insufficient, whatever might have been the case in the nineteenth century.[36] Lord Prosser, it is respectfully submitted, correctly stated that there is no offence of reckless conduct *per se* in the absence of actual injury to another or danger of injury to others[37]; and his Lordship was surely also correct to state that the crime of recklessly causing injury is not necessarily confined to "high-risk" activities (such as the handling of explosives or inflammable substances, the navigation of ships or the driving of motor vehicles) since the circumstances rather than categories should dictate when that crime might appropriately be charged. Lord Murray was of the view that the reckless causing of injury was not an

---

[24] *Jas Bartholomew and Ors* (1825) Hume, i, 193.

[25] *David Balfour* (1850) J. Shaw 377; *Thos Smith* (1853) 1 Irv. 271.

[26] *Houston and Ewing* (1847) Ark. 252; *Thos Henderson and Ors* (1850) J. Shaw 394; Arch. *Grassom and Jas Drummond* (1884) 5 Couper 483.

[27] For example, *Jas Finney* (1848) Ark 432.

[28] *Alex. Dickson* (1847) Ark. 352.

[29] 1993 S.C.C.R. 599.

[30] Lord McCluskey dissented on the issue whether the two alternative charges in the indictment in the case were distinct; his view was that both charges were in fact identical charges of assault: see his opinion, at 570G to 571A.

[31] *supra.*, especially L.J.-C. Ross at 563B and 564B; and Lord Prosser at 573C and 573D-F.

[32] 1956 J.C. 22.

[33] See, *e.g.*, *W. v. H.M. Advocate*, 1982 S.C.C.R. 152.

[34] *Harris v. H.M. Advocate*, 1993 S.C.C.R. 559, L.J.-C. Ross at 564A; Lord Murray at 566C and 566F; Lord Morison at 572A; Lord McCluskey at 568E; and, Lord Prosser at 575D-E. See also Lord Prosser at 574B-C, where his Lordship is at pains to point out that Macdonald, at p.142, should not be read as if the causing of injury was merely evidence of "danger to others", as if in turn such danger were the true essential requirement of such offences.

[35] 1936 J.C. 19, at 22; see, *supra*, para. 26.12.

[36] *H.M. Advocate v. Harris*, 1993 S.C.C.R. 559, Lord Murray at 566B; Lord Morison at 571F-G; Lord Prosser at 577E.

[37] *supra.*, at 573C-D, 574D-E, and 577D.

offence unless the injury suffered by the victim was "substantial" or "severe"[38]; but the issue is whether the conduct of the accused was reckless, in the sense of showing complete indifference to the safety of the person injured, and not whether the ensuing injury was itself of a certain degree of severity; in any event, it may be noted that the charge of reckless injury in *Harris* was aggravated rather than substantiated by being to the victim's severe injury and permanent disfigurement.[39]

Endangering the lieges

It is a crime in certain circumstances to cause danger to the lieges by culpable recklessness.[40] Several instances of such a charge occur in modern cases,[41] although the limits of the offence have still not been precisely determined. It seems that exposure to danger of a particular individual or particular individuals, or exposure to danger of the public in a wider sense, will be sufficient, where the danger relates to a significant risk to life or health: and it seems reasonably clear that the negligence requires to be of the *Paton*[42] standard. Macdonald divides the cases under this head into three groups: traffic cases; cases involving firearms; and other cases,[43] and this classification is a useful one. **29.58**

Traffic cases. Alison states that, "Furious or improper driving along the high road is in itself a police offence; and if it leads to injury to the persons or property of others, becomes the fit object of higher criminal punishment."[44] It is now accepted, however, that no common law offence is committed by "furious" or reckless driving unless there is danger to the lieges,[45] mere danger or even injury to property being insufficient.[46] **29.59**

It is not enough that the lieges should in fact be endangered or even injured; there must be driving which can be properly characterised as "reckless". The latest case on this point, which may well also be the last,[47] *Quinn v. Cunningham*,[48] recognises this clearly, although it does so by treating the phrase "to the danger of the lieges" as describing a degree of negligence, rather than as describing the result of negligence. In that case a pedal cyclist was charged with riding his cycle "in a

---

[38] *supra.*, at 566B and 566E.

[39] These same aggravations were added to the alternative charge of assault.

[40] *H.M. Advocate v. Harris*, 1993 S.C.C.R. 559, which confirms what had been accepted for some time; see *e.g. John Elder Murdoch* (1849) J. Shaw 229.

[41] See, *e.g.*, *MacPhail v. Clark*, 1982 S.C.C.R. 395 (Sh.Ct); *Khaliq v. H.M. Advocate*, 1983 S.C.C.R. 483; *Ulhaq v. H.M. Advocate*, 1990 S.C.C.R. 593; *Normand v. Morrison*, 1993 S.C.C.R. 207 (Sh.Ct); *Kimmins v. Normand*, 1993 S.C.C.R. 476; *Normand v. Robinson*, 1994 S.L.T. 558; *Donaldson v. Normand*, 1997 S.C.C.R. 351; *Cameron v. Maguire*, 1999 S.C.C.R. 44.

[42] 1936 J.C. 19, *supra*, para. 26.12.

[43] Macdonald, pp.141–142.

[44] Alison, i, 625. *Cf. John Barr* (1839) 2 Swin. 282, Lord Medwyn at 315, and *David Smith and William McNeil* (1842) 1 Broun 240, where, at 242, L.J.-C. Hope observed *obiter*, the case being one of reckless discharge of firearms, that "Furious driving upon a public road, even when no passengers are to be seen upon it, is an offence, although it may not be worth while to try the case in the Court of Justiciary, unless some person has been injured."

[45] *McAllister v. Abercrombie* (1907) 5 Adam 366.

[46] *ibid.*

[47] Traffic cases today are mostly dealt with under the Road Traffic Act 1988, which extends to pedal cyclists. Shipping falls under the Merchant Shipping Act 1995.

[48] 1956 J.C. 22. The decision is not overruled on this point by *H.M. Advocate v. Harris*, 1993 S.C.C.R. 559.

reckless manner and [causing it to] collide with and knock down [F.C.]
... whereby [the accused and F.C.] sustained slight injuries." This
charge was held to be irrelevant because it did not specify that the
recklessness was "to the danger of the lieges".[49] Lord Justice General
Clyde said, "There is all the difference in the world between a reckless
act which in fact happens to result in injury, and a reckless disregard of
the safety of the public which in fact does injure someone."[50] The double
use of "reckless" makes this a little confusing, but in its context the
meaning is fairly clear — mere carelessness is not criminal even if it
causes injury, but carelessness of the degree characterised as reckless
disregard of public safety is criminal if it injures someone.[51]

29.60 *Firearms.* The reckless discharge of firearms to the danger of the lieges is
criminal, and danger means merely danger to safety.[52] In *David Smith
and Wm McNeil*[53] the charge was of discharging firearms into an
inhabited house to the danger of the lives of the inhabitants, but Lord
Justice-Clerk Hope stated that the firing into an inhabited house was in
itself an offence, and that it was unnecessary to prove actual danger. He
went on to say that the offence was committed even if the inhabitants of
the house had "accidentally" left the room when the shot was fired into
it.[54]

29.61 *Other cases.* Macdonald's treatment of these is short and confusing. After
talking of the traffic cases, he says: "But although acts of rashness such
as those above described are punishable even where no accident follows,
they are only held to be so because of their manifest wilfulness, and of
the general danger caused by such wanton proceedings. In other cases, in
order to make a relevant charge of danger to the lieges, it may be
necessary to specify that injury resulted to some of them."[55] If this means
that a charge of reckless conduct to the danger of the lieges requires
"wantonness" in the sense of criminal recklessness as defined in *Paton v.
H.M. Advocate*[56] it is correct, but applies equally to traffic cases. But if it
means that no charge of causing danger is relevant unless actual injury is
caused, it is clearly wrong. There are a number of cases where charges of
acting recklessly to the injury or to the danger of the lives of specified

---

[49] This exposition was held to be wrong, see now *H.M. Advocate v. Harris*, 1993 S.C.C.R.
559; *supra*, para. 29.57.
[50] At 26.
[51] This also seems clear on the authority of *McAllister v. Abercombie*, *supra*, and the
form of charge given in the 1995 Act, Sched. 5, which reads simply, "You did drive a horse
and cart recklessly to the danger of the lieges." It was this form of charge which may have
been responsible for the confusing nomenclature used in *Quinn v. Cunningham*. The court
wished to make use of it in order to show that the actual charge was irrelevant because it
contained no averment of danger, and as the charge there did aver injury the court treated
"danger to the lieges" as describing the degree of recklessness and not its result.
[52] Macdonald, p.142; *Temple Annesley* (1831) Bell's Notes 76; *David Johnston and Wm
McQueen* (1842) 1 Broun 214; *David Smith and Wm McNeil* (1842) *ibid.* 240; *Cameron v.
Maguire*, 1999 S.C.C.R. 44, disapproving *Gizzi and Anr v. Tudhope*, 1982 S.C.C.R. 442,
where the inappropriate road-traffic recklessness standard of *Allan v. Patterson*, 1980 J.C.
57, had been applied.
[53] *supra.*
[54] At 243–244.
[55] Macdonald, p.142.
[56] 1936 J.C. 19, *supra*, para. 26.12.

persons have been sustained, and it follows that a charge of acting to the danger of life would be relevant in itself.[57]

The only cases in which this question is discussed at any length are old. In *Robert Young*[58] the accused was in charge of a diving-bell which was faulty, as a result of which certain persons were killed. He was charged with culpable homicide, and also with culpable neglect of duty "whereby lives are lost, or bodily injuries suffered, or the safety of the lieges put in danger." It was argued that the last alternative was irrelevant, an argument which was opposed by the Crown, who asked the court to decide the matter on relevancy. The court, however, declined to do so, since they regarded the last alternative as unnecessary and the matter as speculative. In *David Smith and Wm McNeil*[59] Lord Justice-Clerk Hope referred to *Young* and said — after talking about furious driving — "If by the argument which was stated in the case of *Young*, it is meant that in order to constitute an indictable offence, there must be injury to the person, this is clearly erroneous." In the same case Lord Hope gave as an example of criminal conduct the situation where someone throws a heavy substance over a wall, having heard a crowd there, even though the crowd had moved back before the stone was thrown.[60] In *Jas Finney*[61] alternative charges of injuring the lieges or putting them in danger of their lives went unchallenged. On the other hand, a charge of putting lives in danger was rejected as irrelevant in *Thos Simpson*,[62] a case of failure to make a coal mine secure. The court in *Simpson* gave no reason for their decision which is difficult to reconcile with the earlier cases.

There is no reason in principle for distinguishing the reckless use of firearms from any other form of recklessness. If A does behave recklessly so as to cause danger he is guilty of a crime whether or not he actually injures someone.[63] Some of the old cases talked of acts being to the "great terror and alarm, or to the danger of the lives of" certain persons,[64] but the main element in the charge is that of danger: the crime is endangering life and not creating a breach of the peace.[65]

So far as the authorities go, however, it may be that except in traffic and firearms cases it is necessary to specify danger to particular persons,

---

[57] See *Jas Finney* (1848) Ark. 432; *John Drysdale and Ors* (1848) Ark. 440; *John Elder Murdoch* (1849) J. Shaw 229, where there was no averment of injury. See also *Robt Watt and Jas Kerr* (1868) 1 Couper 123, a charge of recklessly compelling boys to leave a ship and proceed 12 miles over ice without food or clothing whereby they were put in danger of their lives: cf. *Kahliq v. H.M. Advocate*, 1984 J.C. 23, and *Ulhaq v. H.M. Advocate*, 1991 S.L.T. 614, both of which are authority for an offence of recklessly endangering the health of particular persons, by supplying and thus (by treating supplying as equivalent to administering) causing them to inhale toxic substances.

[58] (1839) 2 Swin. 376.

[59] (1842) 1 Broun 240.

[60] At 244.

[61] (1848) Ark. 432.

[62] (1864) 4 Irv. 490.

[63] This seems to be the import of *H.M. Advocate v. Harris*, 1993 S.C.C.R. 559; see esp. the opinion of Lord Prosser, at pp. 573C–575A: but the case was primarily concerned with whether recklessly caused injury was criminal in the absence of any averment of danger to the lieges.

[64] *Jas Finney, supra*; *John Drysdale, supra*.

[65] In a case in Glasgow where railway sleepers were placed on railway lines and struck by trains, charges were brought of maliciously placing the sleepers on the lines whereby trains struck them, and of causing damage to the trains and endangering the lives of the crews and passengers: *John Brand and Ors*, Glasgow Sheriff Court, May 1965, unrep'd. It is true that the charges included the crime of malicious mischief but the serious allegation was that of endangering life.

and also necessary to show that their lives, and not merely their safety, were endangered.[66]

THREATS

29.62 Threats are divided into two classes: those which are criminal in themselves and those which are criminal only when made with a certain motive or intention. Threats of either class may be oral or written.[67]

The first class includes threats "to burn a man's house . . . to put him to death, or to do him any grievous bodily harm, or to do any serious injury to his property, his fortune, or his reputation."[68] In the case of such threats there is a completed crime as soon as the threat is uttered,

---

[66] *Dalzell v. Dickie and Murray* (1905) 4 Adam 693 in which it was held not to be a crime to allow a savage dog to go at large to the danger of the lieges whereby a girl was injured, may be regarded as very special. It seems to have proceeded on the absence of any positive duty or any act calculated of its nature to be harmful. L.J.-G. Dunedin, at 696, said it was not expedient to discuss the general question of whether there could be criminal recklessness in the absence of loss of life. In *Reynolds v. Lockhart* (Edinburgh Sheriff Court, March 1976, conviction upheld on appeal, Oct. 1976) the accused was convicted of recklessly disregarding the lives and safety of the public by releasing or allowing to be released a pet puma kept by him in a cage in a public house, whereupon the puma attacked two customers. The sheriff distinguished *Dalzell* on the ground: (a) that a puma was a wild animal, and (b) its release was evidence of recklessness for the safety of others.

It is an offence under s.2 of the Dangerous Wild Animals Act 1976 to keep a dangerous wild animal except under a licence granted by the local authority. Animals in zoos, circuses, licensed pet shops and places registered for experiments under the Animals (Scientific Procedures) Act 1986 are exempt (see s.5). Maximum penalty, a fine of level 5 on the standard scale.

See also s.1 of the Guard Dogs Act 1975, which provides:

"(1) A person shall not use or permit the use of a guard dog at any premises unless a person ('the handler') who is capable of controlling the dog is present on the premises and the dog is under the control of the handler at all times while it is being so used except while it is secured so that it is not at liberty to go freely about the premises.

(2) The handler of a guard dog shall keep the dog under his control at all times while it is being used as a guard dog at any premises except —

(a) while another handler has control over the dog; or

(b) while the dog is secured so that it is not at liberty to go freely about the premises.

(3) A person shall not use or permit the use of a guard dog at any premises unless a notice containing a warning that a guard dog is present is clearly exhibited at each entrance to the premises."

No offence is committed under s.1(1) by the user of the dog where the handler is absent, provided the dog has been secured: *Rafferty v. Smith* (1978) S.C.C.R. (Supp.) 200, following *Hobson v. Gleldhill* [1978] 1 W.L.R. 215.

The breeding or sale of fighting dogs (the underlying assumption being that they are dangerous to the public) is made an offence by s.1(7) of the Dangerous Dogs Act 1991: maximum penalty, six months' and a fine of level 5 on the standard scale; and under s.3 of that Act, the owner and the person in charge of a dog which is "dangerously out of control" in "a public place" (both being defined in s.10(2)) are guilty of an offence, there being a defence for the owner if he was not in charge of the dog at the material time, and can prove it was in the charge of someone he reasonably believed to be a fit and proper person: maximum penalty, six months' and a fine of level 5 on the standard scale on summary conviction; but if someone is injured by the dog (an aggravated offence), two years' and a fine on indictment, and six months' and a fine of the statutory maximum on summary conviction.

[67] Although the classical instance of the crime, so to speak, is the sending of threatening letters, oral threats are equally criminal: *Jas Miller* (1862) 4 Irv. 238, L.J.-C. Inglis at 245; *Margt McDaniel and Anr* (1876) 3 Couper 271.

[68] *Jas Miller, supra*, at 244. See *MacKellar v. Dickson* (1898) 2 Adam 504.

for example, by posting a threatening letter. The motive or intent with which the threat is made is irrelevant except in so far as it may be an aggravation of the offence[69]; it is a crime to utter a threat of this kind even as a joke.[70]

The second class comprises all other threats, including threats of **29.63** violence not amounting to grievous harm.[71] It has been held that a charge merely of "threatening violence" made without any specification from which one can infer "grievous bodily harm or sinister intent" is irrelevant,[72] but a charge of threatening violence with intent to deter the victim from giving evidence,[73] or threatening a judge in reference to his judicial capacity,[74] would be relevant.[75] Where the purpose of the threat is to induce the victim to pay money to the accused, the crime would today be charged as extortion or attempted extortion, as the case may be.[76] Indeed, attempted extortion can probably be charged wherever the intention is to induce the victim to act to his prejudice, that phrase being defined as it is in the law of fraud,[77] but where something other than money is involved the charge might well be made as one of threats, particularly if the victim resists the threat.[78]

Where the purpose of the threat is to persuade a witness not to give evidence the charge will probably be one of attempt to pervert the course of justice.

Breach of the peace. Although "threatening violence" is not criminal **29.64** unless the violence is serious, conduct of a kind which puts the lieges into a state of fear and alarm is a recognised form of breach of the

---

[69] For example, to prevent the victim giving evidence: *Margt McDaniel and Anr, supra*, or in revenge for the giving of information by the victim to the authorities: *Chas Ross* (1844) 2 Broun 271.

[70] *Eliz. Edmiston* (1866) 5 Irv. 219.

[71] *Kenny v. H.M. Advocate*, 1951 J.C. 104. *Cf. Gray v. Mackenzie* (1862) 4 Irv. 166; *Anderson v. McFarlane* (1899) 2 Adam 644; *Hill v. McGrogan*, 1945 S.L.T.(Sh.Ct.) 18.

[72] *Kenny, supra.*

[73] *ibid.*

[74] *Alex. Carr* (1854) 1 Irv. 464; *Peter Porteous* (1832) 5 D. & A. 53, a charge under the Judges Act 1540.

[75] The most recent example of a charge of this kind was *Walter Scott Ellis*, High Court at Edinburgh, Feb. 1965, where the charge was described as "slandering and threatening Judge and Prosecutor." The indictment narrated that the accused had been convicted by a particular sheriff-substitute at a trial conducted by a particular procurator fiscal depute and that having thereafter been sentenced in the High Court he had been committed to prison. The charge then alleged that he had sent letters to the sheriff-substitute "in each of which letters you used slanderous and insulting language towards said [sheriff-substitute and procurator fiscal depute] and threatened to do them serious bodily injury or cause such to be done to them . . . with intent to slander and insult [them] in reference to their conduct and capacities as Sheriff-Substitute and Procurator Fiscal Depute respectively, and to menace and intimidate them in the lawful discharge of their functions, and to place them in fear and alarm for their safety." The accused was acquitted but no challenge was made to the charge.

[76] For a discussion of extortion, see *supra*, Chap. 21. Alison classes the use of threats of death or attempting or pretending to carry them out in order to compel a confession of a real or supposed crime as an innominate offence, on the basis of *Andrew Macgregor* (1828) Alison, i, 631. Schedule 2 to the Firearms Act 1968 refers to the crime of "[u]se of threats with intent to extort money or property."

[77] See *supra*, para, 18.21 *et seq.*

[78] In one old case, *Robt Sprot and Ors* (1844) 2 Broun 179, the charge was of threatening certain persons "with intent to compel them . . . to put out of their houses individuals lodging or residing therein, or to compel . . . any of the lieges to quit the place of abode, or the employment and service chosen by them."

peace, and to threaten minor violence to the lieges, or to a particular person or persons, whether in public or private,[79] may constitute breach of the peace if alarm is caused or reasonably to be apprehended.[80]

29.65 *Statutory threats.* A number of statutes create specific offences in connection with threats made for particular purposes, *e.g.* Representation of the People Act 1983, section 115,[81] Criminal Law (Consolidation) (Scotland) Act 1995, section 7(2)(a).[82]

29.66 *Threats to internationally protected persons.* Section 1 of the Internationally Protected Persons Act 1978 provides, *inter alia*:

"(3) If a person in the United Kingdom or elsewhere, whether a citizen of the United Kingdom and Colonies or not—
    (a) makes to another person a threat that any person will do an act which is an offence mentioned in paragraph (a) of the preceding subsection[83]; or
    (b) attempts to make or aids, abets, counsels or procures or is art and part in the making of such a threat to another person,
with the intention that the other person shall fear that the threat will be carried out, the person who makes the threat or, as the case may be, who attempts to make it or aids, abets, counsels or procures or is art and part in the making of it, shall in any part of the United Kingdom be guilty of an offence and liable on conviction on indictment to imprisonment for a term not exceeding ten years and not exceeding the term of imprisonment to which a person would be liable for the offence constituted by doing the act threatened at the place where the conviction occurs and at the time of the offence to which the conviction relates.

(4) For the purposes of the preceding subsections it is immaterial whether a person knows that another person is a protected person.

(5) In this section—
    'act' includes omission;
    'a protected person' means, in relation to an alleged offence, any of the following, namely—
        (a) a person who at the time of the alleged offence is a Head of State, a member of a body which performs the functions of a Head of State under the constitution of the State, a Head of Government or a Minister for Foreign Affairs and is outside the territory of the State in which he holds office.
        (b) a person who at the time of the alleged offence is a representative or an official of a State or an official or agent of an international organisation of an inter-governmental character, is entitled under international

---

[79] *cf. Young v. Heatly*, 1959 J.C. 66 for the proposition that breach of the peace can be committed privately: *infra*, para. 41.10.

[80] *cf.* the charge in Sched. 5 of the 1995 Act: "You did threaten violence to the lieges and commit a breach of the peace", which suggests that alarm is at least to be presumed from any such threat.

[81] *infra*, para. 38.32.

[82] *infra*, para. 33.11.

[83] Offences mentioned in s.1(1)(a) include: murder, culpable homicide, rape, assault causing injury, abduction, false imprisonment or plagium, or a contravention of s.2 of the Explosive Substances Act 1883.

law to special protection from attack on his person, freedom or dignity and does not fall within the preceding paragraph;

    (c) a person who at the time of the alleged offence is a member of the family of another person mentioned in either of the preceding paragraphs and—

        (i) if the other person is mentioned in paragraph (a) above is accompanying him,

        (ii) if the other person is mentioned in paragraph (b) above, is a member of his household;

'relevant premises' means premises at which a protected person resides or is staying or which a protected person uses for the purpose of carrying out his functions as such a person; and

'vehicle' includes any means of conveyance;

and if in any proceedings a question arises as to whether a person is or was a protected person, a certificate issued by or under the authority of the Secretary of State and stating any fact relating to the question shall be conclusive evidence of that fact."

Threats of attacks on UN workers. Section 3 of the United Nations **29.67** Personnel Act 1997 provides:

"(1) If a person in the United Kingdom or elsewhere contravenes subsection (2) he shall be guilty of an offence.

    (2) A person contravenes this subsection if, in order to compel a person to do or abstain from doing any act, he—

    (a) makes to a person a threat that any person will do an act which is—

        (i) an offence mentioned in section 1(2)[84] against a UN worker,[85] or

        (ii) an offence mentioned in subsection (2) of section 2 in connection with such an attack as is mentioned in subsection (1) of that section, and

    (b) intends that the person to whom he makes the threat shall fear that it will be carried out.

    (3) A person guilty of an offence under this section shall be liable on conviction on indictment to imprisonment for a term—

    (a) not exceeding ten years, and

    (b) not exceeding the term of imprisonment to which a person would be liable for the offence constituted by doing the act threatened at the place where the conviction occurs and at the time of the offence to which the conviction relates."

Taking hostages. Section 1 of the Taking of Hostages Act 1982 makes it **29.68** an offence to detain any other person ("the hostage") and threaten to kill, injure or detain him in order to compel a State, international governmental organisation or person to do or abstain from doing any act.[86]

---

[84] Under s.1(2), offences include: murder, culpable homicide, rape, assault causing injury, abduction and false imprisonment, and an offence under s.2 of the Explosive Substances Act 1883.

[85] Defined in s.4(1).

[86] See, *supra*, para. 29.55.

29.69 *Torture.* Section 134 of the Criminal Justice Act 1988 provides:

> "(1) A public official or person acting in an official capacity, whatever his nationality, commits the offence of torture if in the United Kingdom or elsewhere he intentionally inflicts severe pain or suffering on another in the performance or purported performance of his official duties.
>
> (2) A person not falling within subsection (1) above commits the offence of torture, whatever his nationality, if—
>
> > (a) in the United Kingdom or elsewhere he intentionally inflicts severe pain or suffering on another at the instigation or with the consent or acquiescence—
> >
> > > (i) of a public official; or
> > >
> > > (ii) of a person acting in an official capacity; and
> >
> > (b) the official or other person is performing or purporting to perform his official duties when he instigates the commission of the offence or consents to or acquiesces in it.
>
> (3) It is immaterial whether the pain or suffering is physical or mental and whether it is caused by an act or an omission.
>
> (4) it shall be a defence for a person charged with an offence under this section in respect of any conduct of his to prove that he had lawful authority, justification or excuse for that conduct.
>
> (5) For the purposes of this section 'lawful authority, justification or excuse' means—
>
> > (a) in relation to pain or suffering inflicted in the United Kingdom, lawful authority, justification or excuse under the law of the part of the United Kingdom where it was inflicted;
> >
> > (b) in relation to pain or suffering inflicted outside the United Kingdom—
> >
> > > (i) if it was inflicted by a United Kingdom official acting under the law of the United Kingdom or by a person acting in an official capacity under that law, lawful authority, justification or excuse under that law;
> > >
> > > (ii) if it was inflicted by a United Kingdom official acting under the law of any part of the United Kingdom or by a person acting in an official capacity under such law, lawful authority, justification or excuse under the law of the part of the United Kingdom under whose law he was acting; and
> > >
> > > (iii) in any other case, lawful authority, justification or excuse under the law of the place where it was inflicted.
>
> (6) A person who commits the offence of torture shall be liable on conviction on indictment to imprisonment for life."

This provision must now be read subject to Article 3 of the European Convention on Human Rights, which provides as follows: "No one shall be subjected to torture or to inhuman or degrading treatment or punishment."[87]

---

[87] This part of the Convention is incorporated within Scots law by virtue of the Human Rights Act 1998, Sched. 1. It appears that the prohibition of torture under Art. 3 is an absolute one and that there never can be justification for acts done in breach of it: *Ireland v. U.K.* (1978) 2 E.H.R.R. 25, at 79 (para. 163).

CHAPTER 30

STATUTORY OFFENCES CONCERNED WITH PERSONAL INJURY

There are a number of statutory offences which have as their primary **30.01** object the prevention of personal injury, although some are also directed to the prevention of injury to property.[1] A number of Acts, such as the Factories Act 1961, the Mines and Quarries Act 1954, and the various regulations made under them, are (or were) used mainly to provide grounds of liability in actions for damages, but they also create (or created) criminal offences consisting in the failure to take certain specified precautions against accidents.[1a] Others, however, such as the Road Traffic Act 1988 and the Firearms Act 1968, are directed principally to the creation of criminal offences, and require more detailed consideration.

TRAFFIC OFFENCES

Road Traffic Act 1988

This Act, as supplemented by the Road Traffic Offenders Act 1988 **30.02** and as amended (principally by the Road Traffic Act 1991), contains a large number of provisions, most of which may be said to be directed at the prevention of road accidents, and the same can be said of the Road Vehicles (Construction and Use) Regulations 1986[2] and the Road Vehicles Lighting Regulations 1989,[3] which have effect by virtue of section 41 of the Act, and provide, for example, that all vehicles should have efficient steering, brakes and lights. But there are some sections of the Act which are intended to strike directly at conduct of the same kind although not necessarily of the same degree as common law furious or reckless driving. These are sections 2, 3, 4, 5, and 35; and the same is true of regulation 25 of the Zebra, Pelican and Puffin Pedestrian Crossings Regulations and General Directions 1997,[4] having effect under section 25 of the Road Traffic Regulation Act 1984.

Bad Driving. Sections 2, 2A and 3 (as substituted or inserted by the Road **30.03** Traffic Act 1991)[5] of the Road Traffic Act 1988 provide as follows:

---

[1] For international offences and torture, see paras 29.53–29.56 and 29.66–29.69, *supra*.

[1a] Much of the two Acts mentioned in the text is now spent, following repeals of a great part of their respective contents; see now, therefore, the Health and Safety etc. at Work Act 1974, *infra*, para. 30.54.

[2] S.I. 1986 No. 1078.

[3] S.I. 1989 No. 1796.

[4] S.I. 1997 No. 2400.

[5] Section 2 is substituted by s.1 of the 1991 Act; s.2A is added by s.1 of that Act; and s.3 is substituted by s.2 of that Act.

"**2.** A person who drives a mechanically propelled vehicle dangerously on a road or other public place is guilty of an offence.[6]

2A.—(1) For the purposes of sections 1[7] and 2 above a person is to be regarded as driving dangerously if (and, subject to subsection (2) below, only if)—
(a) the way he drives falls far below what would be expected of a competent and careful driver, and
(b) it would be obvious to a competent and careful driver that driving in that way would be dangerous.
(2) A person is also to be regarded as driving dangerously for the purposes of sections 1 and 2 above if it would be obvious to a competent and careful driver that driving the vehicle in its current state would be dangerous.
(3) In subsections (1) and (2) above "dangerous" refers to danger either of injury to any person or of serious damage to property; and in determining for the purposes of those subsections what would be expected of, or obvious to, a competent and careful driver in a particular case, regard shall be had not only to the circumstances of which he could be expected to be aware but also to any circumstances shown to have been within the knowledge of the accused.
(4) In determining for the purposes of subsection (2) above the state of a vehicle, regard may be had to anything attached to or carried on or in it and to the manner in which it is attached or carried.

3.—(1) If a person drives a mechanically propelled vehicle on a road or other public place without due care and attention, or without reasonable consideration for other persons using the road or place,[8] he is guilty of an offence."[9]

Driving in public places other than roads is not penalised by sections 1 to 3 of the Road Traffic Act 1988 where it is in accordance with an authorisation for a motoring event given under regulations made by the Secretary of State.[10]

Sections 28[11] and 29 of the Road Traffic Act 1988 apply provisions similar to those in sections 2, 2A and 3 to the dangerous or careless riding of pedal cycles, but restrict the offences to such riding "on roads".

---

[6] Maximum penalty, under the Road Traffic Offenders Act 1988, Sched. 2, Pt I, on indictment — two years' and a fine; and on summary conviction, 6 months' and a fine of the statutory maximum. In both cases, disqualification is obligatory as is endorsement (with 3–11 penalty points). (For disqualification and endorsement, see Road Traffic Offenders Act 1988, ss. 27–50, and Sched. 2.)

[7] For instance, the offence of causing death by dangerous driving.

[8] These are two separate offences normally charged cumulatively. It has been suggested that "other persons" does not include passengers in the accused's vehicle — see *MacDonald v. Thomson* (1954) 70 Sh.Ct.Rep. 228, but there seems no reason for this restriction which has been rejected in England: *Pawley v. Wharldall* [1966] 1 Q.B. 373, and is in practice not applied in Scotland either.

[9] Maximum penalty under the Road Traffic Offenders Act 1988, Sched. 2, Pt I, on summary conviction, a fine of level 4 on the standard scale. Disqualification is discretionary, but endorsement (with 3–9 penalty points) is obligatory. (For disqualification and endorsement, see Road Traffic Offenders Act 1988, ss. 27–50, and Sched. 2.)

[10] See s.13A, as inserted by the Road Traffic Act 1991, s.5.

[11] As substituted by s.7 of the Road Traffic Act 1991.

"DRIVES". The word "drives" (including any of its correlatives, such as **30.04** "driving" or "driver") occurs frequently in road traffic legislation but is not itself statutorily defined. In seeking to define the word, the Scottish courts have expressed the views that its meaning should be sufficiently general to be applicable throughout such legislation, and that that meaning should be the same in both Scotland and England[12]: the former of these views has been realised, but not, it seems, the latter. In *Ames v. MacLeod*,[13] the question arose whether a person, who was standing outside a vehicle (which had run out of fuel and which was being run or pushed backwards down a slope) and who was steering it by grasping the steering wheel through an open window, was the driver of the vehicle at the time of these manoeuvres: it was held that he was, the test being "whether he was in a substantial sense controlling the movement and direction of the [vehicle]."[14]

This test was approved by the five judge court in *McArthur v. Valentine*,[15] where it was said: "[T]he question is not simply whether some control is being exercised over the movement and direction of the [vehicle], but rather whether this is being done in a substantial sense so as to show, on the facts of the case and as a matter of extent and degree, that the accused was driving the [vehicle]."[16] This enables the issue to be dealt with broadly as "one of extent and degree"[17] or of fact and degree[18]; but the court in *McArthur v. Valentine* expressly disapproved[19] of the English test evolved in *R. v. MacDonagh*.[20]

In *MacDonagh*, the Court of Appeal considered the Scottish test in *Ames v. MacLeod* but declared that test to be "not exhaustive".[21] The view taken was that although the essence of driving was the use of a vehicle's controls to direct the movement of that vehicle (however such movement was produced — for example, by the power of its engine, or by towing or pushing),[22] the net was not to be cast so wide as to include activities which could not be said to be "driving" in any ordinary sense of the word in the English language[23]: there was, for example, a difference between pushing a vehicle and driving it, although the dividing line was not an easy one to draw.[24] The Court of Appeal also expressed the

---

[12] See *McArthur v. Valentine*, 1990 J.C. 146 (full bench), L.J.-G. Hope (opinion of the court) at 153.

[13] 1989 J.C. 1.

[14] *ibid.*, L.J.-G. Clyde at 3.

[15] 1990 J.C. 146.

[16] *ibid.*, L.J.-G. Hope (opinion of the court) at 153.

[17] *ibid.* In the unusual case of *Hoy v. McFadyen*, 2000 S.C.C.R. 875, the accused was held to have been driving when he was sitting in the driving seat of a vehicle with his foot pressed on the brake pedal; the engine was running at the time, and it was necessary to depress the footbrake to prevent the vehicle moving off down a slope since the handbrake was defective. As Lord Sutherland (delivering the opinion of the court) said at 877F: "movement of the car is not essential if the driver's activities have got beyond the stage of mere preparation for driving but have got to the stage where there is active intervention on his part to prevent movement and direction of the vehicle."

[18] See, *e.g.*, *Whitfield v. D.P.P.* [1998] Crim.L.R. 349; *McKoen v Ellis* [1987] R.T.R. 26.

[19] *ibid.*, at 152.

[20] [1974] 1 Q.B. 448.

[21] *ibid.*, Lord Widgery, C.J., at 452E-H.

[22] *ibid.*, Lord Widgery, C.J. at 451D.

[23] *ibid.*, Lord Widgery, C.J. at 451E. The English test is thus considered to be a dual stage one, consisting of first the enquiry whether the defendant was exercising control over the movements of the vehicle, and second (following an affirmative response to the enquiry) whether his doing so amounted to "driving" in the ordinary sense of the word.

[24] *ibid.*, Lord Widgery, C.J., at 452H.

opinion that a person's walking beside a motor vehicle, which was being pushed by another or moving under the force of gravity, was not sufficient to make that person the driver of the vehicle even if he had his hand on the steering wheel at the time,[25] and that pushing a broken down motor cycle by manhandling it by the handlebars was not to be equated with driving it.[26]

Notwithstanding the differences of approach adopted by the Scottish and English courts in construing the word "drives", similar solutions are in fact likely to be arrived at in both jurisdictions: if there was substantial control of a vehicle's movement and direction, there should be "driving" in any ordinary sense of the word. It is of no moment whether the person alleged to have been driving was in the driver's seat at the relevant time or whether he was outside the vehicle,[27] whether the engine was running or even capable of being run at the time,[28] or whether the vehicle was being pushed or towed.[29] Where the vehicle was moved forward by accidental contact with the accelerator, the selector lever of the automatic gearbox having been left in the "drive" position, it was held that there had been no driving by the defendant.[30] Where the defendant was a passenger in a vehicle driven by another and that passenger suddenly seized the steering wheel in order momentarily to alter the direction of the vehicle, it was held in two English cases that the passenger had not been driving on the basis either that the assumption of control had been too fleeting[31] or that his act had been one of interfering with the driving of the vehicle rather than an act of driving itself[32]: in any event, however, the matter is clearly a question of fact and degree.[33]

As a rule only one person can drive a motor-vehicle at a time,[34] but in exceptional cases two persons may be simultaneously in sufficient control of a vehicle for both to be driving. In *Langman v. Valentine and Anr*[35] the owner of the vehicle who was supervising a learner driver was sitting in the passenger seat with one hand on the brake and the other on the steering wheel, and in a position to switch off the engine as well as to steer and start the car, while the learner in the driving seat was using the footbrake and accelerator, and both were held to be driving. In *Tyler v. Whatmore*[36] a girl sat in the passenger seat with both hands on the steering wheel and having the ignition switch and handbrake within reach, while the man in the driving seat could not see ahead and had no hands on the wheel. Both were held to be driving, she having control of the steering and he of the gears and foot controls. Where a separate

---

[25] *ibid.*, Lord Widgery, C.J., at 452H–453A.

[26] *ibid.*, Lord Widgery, C.J., at 453B-C: *cf. McKoen v. Ellis* [1987] R.T.R. 26, and *Gunnell v. D.P.P.* [1994] R.T.R. 151, where it was held that sitting astride a motor cycle and pushing it along by use of feet placed on the ground constituted "driving".

[27] *Ames v. MacLeod*, 1969 J.C. 1; *McArthur v. Valentine*, 1990 J.C. 146; *McQuaid v. Anderton* [1981] 1 W.L.R. 154; *R. v. MacDonagh* [1974] 1 Q.B. 448; *Whitfield v. D.P.P.* [1998] Crim.L.R. 340: *cf. Cawthorn v. D.P.P.* [2000] R.T.R. 45.

[28] *Saycell v. Bool* [1948] 2 All E.R. 83; *R. v. Kitson* (1955) 39 Crim. App.R. 66; *Burgoyne v. Phillips* [1983] R.T.R. 49.

[29] *R. v. Spindley* [1961] Crim. L.R. 486

[30] *Blaney v. Knight* [1975] R.T.R. 279.

[31] *Jones v. Pratt* [1983] R.T.R. 54.

[32] *D.P.P. v. Hastings* [1993] R.T.R. 205.

[33] *ibid.*, Buckley J. at 208C.

[34] Although others may be art and part in the driving: see Vol. I, para. 5.04.

[35] [1952] 2 All E.R. 803.

[36] [1976] R.T.R. 83.

person acts as steersman of a motor-vehicle both that steersman and any other person driving the vehicle are regarded as "driving" the vehicle.[37]

INVOLUNTARY DRIVING. Before A can be convicted of a driving offence **30.05** it seems reasonable that he should be shown to have been voluntarily driving the vehicle in question. A may be convicted of an offence of dangerous, of careless, or even of drunken driving whether or not he knew of the factors which made his driving criminal, but he cannot be convicted unless he was driving. Automatism should, therefore, be a defence to a driving offence. Now, however, that automatism has been recognised as a general defence,[38] it is plain that it operates where a person has been rendered incapable of forming *mens rea* by reason of some external factor which was not self-induced and which he was not bound to foresee in relation to the relevant situation which arose; and it is equally plain that such a defence is not easily applicable to driving offences which are regarded as being of strict liability. Yet, in *Hill v. Baxter*[39] Lord Goddard C.J. said:

> "[T]here may be cases where the circumstances are such that the accused could not really be said to be driving at all. Suppose he had a stroke or an epileptic fit, both instances of what may properly be called acts of God; he might well be in the driver's seat even with his hands on the wheel, but in such a state of unconsciousness that he could not be said to be driving. A blow from a stone or an attack by a swarm of bees I think introduces some conception akin to *novus actus interveniens.*"[40]

Pearson J. indicated in the same case that all these conditions, including the blow from a stone and the attack by bees, would create a situation in which the accused could not be said to be driving. This may seem clear common sense; but in *Ross v. H.M. Advocate*,[41] a distinction was made between external and internal factors, only the former being sufficient for the defence. A blow by a stone or an attack by a swarm of bees should meet the "external factor" criterion for the availability of automatism, but the same cannot necessarily be said of a stroke or an epileptic fit. Still less can it confidently be said of conditions such as diabetic-induced hypoglycaemia that they amount to external factors. In the sheriff court, however, it has been assumed that automatism applies to driving offences in general and that unconsciousness induced by diabetes may qualify for the defence — provided that the other criteria for the defence can be met.[42] Thus, if a diabetic is aware of his propensity to become unconscious without warning signs which he would recognise, automatism will be denied if he succumbs to hypoglycaemia whilst driving alone.[43] Similarly, where a plea of automatism in response

---

[37] 1988 Act, s.192(1). (This provision does not apply to s.1 of the Act.) For an example of what the provision covers, see *Wallace v. Major* [1946] K.B. 473, Lord Goddard C.J. at 477.

[38] *Ross v. H.M. Advocate*, 1991 J.C. 210: see Vol. I, para. 3.18 *et seq.*

[39] [1958] 1 Q.B. 277.

[40] At 283.

[41] 1991 J.C. 210.

[42] See *Farrell v. Stirling*, 1975 S.L.T. (Sh.Ct.) 71 (which pre-dates the decision in *Ross v. H.M. Advocate*, 1991 J.C. 210); *MacLeod v. Mathieson*, 1993 S.C.C.R. 488, Sh.Ct. See also *MacLeod v. Napier*, 1993 S.C.C.R. 303: *cf. Finnegan v. Heywood*, 2000 S.C.C.R. 460.

[43] *MacLeod v. Mathieson*, 1993 S.C.C.R. 488, Sh.Ct.: that such hypoglycaemia may be an internal factor was not considered.

to a driving offence was based on parasomnia, the defence was denied since the accused had voluntarily consumed alcohol knowing that alcohol triggered the condition.[44] The way in which, and the extent to which, the defence of automatism applies to statutory driving offences remain, therefore, to be authoritatively resolved by the courts in Scotland.

If, however, the accused was aware, for example, that he was subject to fits, his driving at all might be regarded as careless; and the man who falls asleep at the wheel may be guilty of careless driving in not stopping to rest, although not by reason of anything that happened while he was asleep.[45]

It may also be argued that the accused is not responsible for any behaviour of his car which is due to a sudden unforeseeable mechanical defect so far as a driving offence is concerned, although such unforeseeability is no defence to a charge of using a defective vehicle contrary to the Construction and Use Regulations. If a car turns to its right because of an unforeseeable mechanical defect and hits another car the accident has not been caused by the manner of the accused's driving nor by a defect which would have made driving the vehicle obviously dangerous to a competent and careful driver, and the accused is not therefore guilty of dangerous or careless driving in such a situation. But if the defect was known to him he is almost certainly guilty of dangerous driving,[46] and may be guilty of careless driving in the same way as the driver who knows he is subject to fits may be guilty of such driving.[47]

30.06   "MECHANICALLY PROPELLED VEHICLE". Sections 2 and 3 of the Road Traffic Act 1988 (as substituted/amended by the Road Traffic Act 1991, sections 1 and 2 relate to "mechanically propelled vehicles", but no definition of such vehicles is offered by the legislation. Other offences,[48] however, are committed only in respect of "motor vehicles" which are defined as "mechanically propelled vehicle[s] intended or adapted for use on roads."[49] Consequently, dangerous or careless driving offences may be committed in respect of any vehicle provided it is mechanically propelled, which must mean that it has a means of propulsion other than muscle power, wind power, or gravity. If a vital part of the mechanical means of propulsion has been removed from a vehicle, it has been held that it may cease to be a mechanically propelled vehicle if the accused has no intention of replacing that part.[50] Conversely, if a vehicle retains its means of mechanical propulsion but there is some defect therein which prevents that vehicle being driven by virtue of that means of

---

[44] *Finnegan v. Heywood*, 2000 S.C.C.R. 460: that parasomnia may be an internal factor was not discussed. *Cf.* the Canadian case of *R. v. Parks* [1992] 1 S.C.R. 876.

[45] *Hill v. Baxter* [1958] 1 Q.B. 277, Pearson J. at 286. *Cf. Higgins v. Bernard* [1972] 1 W.L.R. 455.

[46] See s.2A of the Road Traffic Act 1988, set out at para. 30.03, *supra*.

[47] *R. v. Spurge* [1961] 2 Q.B. 205.

[48] See, *e.g.*, s.5 of the Road Traffic Act 1988 — driving or being in charge of a motor vehicle with excess alcohol: see para. 30.15, *supra*.

[49] 1988 Road Traffic Act, s.185(1). Thus, *e.g.*, a "go-kart" is a mechanically propelled vehicle but not one intended or adapted for use on roads: *Carstairs v. Hamilton*, 1997 S.C.C.R. 311.

[50] *MacLean v. Hall*, 1962 S.L.T. (Sh.Ct.) 30 (van, from which the engine and gear box had been removed with the intention of scrapping both these items and the van, not a mechanically propelled vehicle: *Newberry v. Simmonds* [1961] 2 W.L.R. 675, distinguished); *McNeill v. Ritchie*, 1967 S.L.T. (Sh.Ct.) 68 (vehicle, from which gear box removed and scrapped — vehicle itself being retained only as a source of spare parts, not a mechanically propelled vehicle).

propulsion, it seems that it will continue to have the status of a mechanically propelled vehicle unless the defect amounts to something beyond repair or renewal: but the issue is essentially one of fact, circumstances and degree.[51]

"The relevant tests are objective and must be related to the actual condition of the vehicle itself and to the extent of its decrepitude or disrepair, or the extent to which it has permanently lost parts essential to its propulsion or capacity for propulsion on a road."[52]

It has been held in England, surely correctly, that the test is one of construction of the vehicle rather than user.[53]

"ROAD OR OTHER PUBLIC PLACE". The driving in relation to offences **30.07** under sections 2 and 3 of the Road Traffic Act 1988 must take place "on a road or other public place". According to section 192(1) of that Act, "road" for the purposes of Scots law means[54] "any road within the meaning of the Roads (Scotland) Act 1984 and any other way to which the public has access and includes bridges over which a road passes." Consequently, the definition includes what appears in that 1984 Act at section 151, which provides[55]:

"(1) "road" means, subject to subsection (3) below,[56] any way (other than a waterway) over which there is a public right of passage (by whatever means and whether subject to a toll or not) and includes the road's verge, and any bridge (whether permanent or temporary) over which, or tunnel through which, the road passes; and any reference to a road includes a part thereof.

(1A)[57] A way to which the public has access (by whatever means and whether subject to a toll or not) which passes over a bridge constructed in pursuance of powers conferred by, or by an order made under or confirmed by, a private Act shall, for the purposes of the definition of "road" in subsection (1) above, be treated as if there were a public right of passage over it."[58]

---

[51] *Tudhope v. Every*, 1976 J.C. 42, L.J.-G. Emslie (opinion of the court) at 46.

[52] *ibid.*, at 45. It was held there (at 46) that the personal intention of the owner or user not to repair the vehicle's means of propulsion was not conclusive, a better test being this: "although repair was mechanically practicable [whether] the cost thereof in relation to the value of the vehicle would be so prohibitive as to justify the conclusion that no reasonable owner would contemplate repair, and that accordingly the vehicle could be viewed objectively as virtually fit for nothing but scrap."

[53] *McEachran v. Hurst* [1978] R.T.R. 462, where the defendant was using a moped as if it were a bicycle, *i.e.* propelling it by its pedals since the engine was not in working order. As he was taking the moped to be repaired, the court had no difficulty in finding that it retained its constructional status as a mechanically propelled vehicle.

[54] As substituted by the Road Traffic Act 1991, Sched. 4, para. 78(2)(b).

[55] As amended by the New Roads and Street Works Act 1991, Sched. 8, para. 94(b).

[56] Subsection (3) excludes a footpath which is a public path created by agreement between a local authority and a landowner under s.30 of the Countryside (Scotland) Act 1967; a footpath which forms part of a long-distance route approved under s.40 of that Act of 1967; and, a road forming part of land owned or managed by a local authority and used for recreational, sporting, cultural or social activities relative to the authority's duties under s.14 of the Local Government and Planning (Scotland) Act 1982.

[57] Added by the Local Government (Scotland) Act 1994, s.146: the Forth, Tay and Skye road bridges would appear to fall within this subsection.

[58] Under subs. (2), it is clear that "footways", "footpaths" (other than those referred to in subs. (3) — see n.56, *supra*) and "cycletracks" are "roads", as indeed are "carriageways".

In essence, therefore, relevant driving must take place either on a way (over which there is a public right of passage, or to which the public has access) or on a public place.

Whether the *locus* for the offence was a "way" or not is essentially a question of fact.[59]

It has been held, for example, that a local authority car park, which was restricted to the authority's employees in possession of permits during the working day, was a "way" during the evenings and at weekends when the authority permitted unrestricted parking[60]: a "way" need not, therefore, have that status at all times[61]; nor need it connect with more than one other "way".[62] It seems that a car park can be considered to be a "way" if there is a definable way into and out of it from and to another "way", as also across it.[63] A "way" has been described as "an area in which some form of travel takes place",[64] and this seems a reasonable description to adopt provided that the "travel" which is to be considered includes that by pedestrians as well as by vehicles, since it has been repeatedly emphasised that most driving offences were created as such for the protection of the public in general.[65]

In assessing whether there is in fact *public* access in relation to a particular "way", or whether a particular *locus* is a *public* place, it is necessary to look beyond the presence of any special public group, such as the group which is expressly or impliedly invited to be there for social or business reasons.[66] As Lord Justice General Hope put it in *Rodger v. Normand*[67]:

> "The distinction . . . is between persons who are there in response to an invitation, permission or requirement not issued to the public generally, and those members of the public who choose to go to the place because it is open to the public or because the public was permitted access to it."

---

[59] *Aird v. Vannet*, 1999 J.C. 205, at 206I.

[60] *Aird v. Vannet*, *supra*. *Cf.* the civil case of *Clarke v. Kato* [1998] 1 W.L.R. 1647, where the House of Lords (reversing the decision of the Court of Appeal in *Cutter v. Eagle Star Insurance Co. Ltd.* [1998] R.T.R. 309) held that a multi-storey car park was not a road for the purposes of s.145 of the Road Traffic Act 1988; see especially the opinion of Lord Clyde at 1653 C-D, where it was stated that only rarely could a car park ever be considered to be a road; but this simply underlines the different statutory definition of "road" which pertains in England: see Road Traffic Act 1988, s.192(1) (as amended by the Road Traffic Act 1991, Sched. 4, para. 78) — meaning of "road" at (a).

[61] See also *Dick v. Walkingshaw*, 1995 S.C.C.R. 307 (car deck of a ferry held to be a "way" only at times when connected to the dockside by a ramp).

[62] *ibid.*, at 309E-G, where Sheriff J.R. Smith, with whose opinion the Appeal Court concurred, gave the examples of a cul-de-sac and a street signposted (and de facto) "No through road", both of which nevertheless being "ways".

[63] *Beattie v. Scott*, 1990 S.C.C.R. 435, L.J.-G. Hope at 437E-G, upholding the sheriff on this issue.

[64] *Aird v. Vannet*, 1999 J.C. 205, Lord Weir (opinion of the court) at 206I, approving this particular definition of "way" from the *Shorter Oxford English Dictionary*.

[65] See, *e.g.*, *Harrison v. Hill*, 1932 J.C. 13, L.J.-G. Clyde at 16; *Cheyne v. MacNeill*, 1973 S.L.T. 27, opinion of the court at 29; *Brown v. Braid*, 1984 S.C.C.R. 286, L.J.-G. Emslie at 289; *Rodger v. Normand*, 1994 S.C.C.R. 861, L.J.-G. Hope at 865C.

[66] *Harrison v. Hill*, 1932 J.C. 13, L.J.-G. Clyde at 16, approved in *Young v. Carmichael*, 1990 S.C.C.R. 332; *Alston v. O'Brien*, 1992 S.C.C.R. 238; and *Rodger v. Normand*, 1994 S.C.C.R. 361.

[67] 1994 S.C.C.R. 861, at 865E-F.

It has been stated, however, that "a way may be a road without every single member of the public having unrestricted access to it and right of passage over it at all times and by every means imaginable."[68] If, therefore, entry to the car-deck of a ferry is restricted to drivers of vehicles in possession of valid tickets,[69] or entry to a car park is restricted to those willing to pay the required fee[70] or patronise a particular public house,[71] such restriction will not normally prevent a finding of public access, public place or public right of passage, as the case may be.[72]

Whether or not there is a public right of passage depends on facts and circumstances.

There is a general right of passage, for example, over roadways maintained at public expense — a right which extends to areas connected to such roadways and maintained by the same authority.[73] It is not necessary, however, for there to be a right of public passage, since it suffices if the public simply has access to the "way" in question.[74] Whether such access exists is a pure question of fact based on actual user rather than the existence of signs forbidding entry or designating the "way" as "private", or the absence of physical barriers to entry: the matter is resolved, then, by considering the actual (or perhaps expected) use made of the "way" by members of the public in conjuction with evidence as to what is permitted or tolerated by the owner, or other person with the right to exclude others.[75] It is also, of course, sufficient in relation to sections 2 and 3 of the Road Traffic Act 1998 if the *locus* is a "public place" rather than a "road". Places which are clearly private, such as driveways to, or parking areas within the grounds of, private houses do not qualify, since permitted use of such places by tradesmen, delivery men or the police is insufficient to make them "public".[76]

---

[68] *Dick v. Walkingshaw*, 1995 S.C.C.R. 307, Sheriff J.R. Smith at 310A, approved by the Appeal Court at 312A-B.

[69] As in *Dick v. Walkingshaw*, *supra*, itself.

[70] *Paterson v. Ogilvy*, 1957 J.C. 42, L.J.-C. Thomson at 44–45.

[71] *Vannet v. Burns*, 1998 S.C.C.R. 414, L.J.-G. Rodger at 416B-D (where *Paterson v. Ogilvy*, *supra*, is quoted as authority).

[72] It may be noted, however, that in *Paterson v. Ogilvy*, 1957 J.C. 42, where entry to a field used as a temporary car park for the duration of an agricultural show was restricted to those willing to pay a 10s. (50p.) parking fee, L.J.-C. Thomson (at 44) remarked that whilst only drivers of vehicles had to pay, passengers from these vehicles would also be likely to be found there as would attendants and police officers; as he put it (at 45): "I cannot see that it was any the less a public place because it was frequented by a special section of the public . . . On the facts here there was a sufficiently wide invitation to the public and a sufficiently wide use of the place by the public to come under the words 'other public place' in the sense of the statute."

[73] See, *e.g.*, *Beattie v. Scott*, 1990 S.C.C.R. 435, where an offence was alleged to have taken place in a parking area which was maintained by the same local authority which was responsible for the maintenance of the main road, and the access from that road to the parking area, and L.J.-G. Hope (at 438A) thus considered it to be quite clear that there was a public right of passage over that area.

[74] See s.191(1) of the Road Traffic Act 1988, as amended by the Road Traffic Act 1991, Sched. 4, para. 78.

[75] See *Harrison v. Hill*, 1932 J.C. 13, L.J.-G. Clyde at 16; *Cheyne v. MacNeill*, 1973 S.L.T. 27; *Dunn v. Keane*, 1976 J.C. 39; *Thomson v. MacPhail*, 1992 S.C.C.R. 466.

[76] See, *e.g.*, *Young v. Carmichael*, 1990 S.C.C.R. 332 (car park and lawn within the grounds of a private house considered not to be "public", where "private property" and "no entry" signs were displayed, and actual user restricted to those with express or implied social or business invitations); *Alston v. O'Brien*, 1992 S.C.C.R. 238 (farmyard and driveway from it to farmhouse considered not "public", notwithstanding that visitors' and delivery vehicles were to be found parked in the farmyard from time to time). *Cf. Rodger v. Normand*, 1994 S.C.C.R. 861 (school playground considered to be a public place, since

30.08   "DANGEROUSLY". What "driving dangerously" means is set out definitively in section 2A.[77] There are two possibilities: the first of these[78] requires the Crown to show that the way the accused was driving fell far below what would be expected of a competent and careful driver[79] and that it would be obvious[80] to such a driver that driving in that way would be dangerous[81]: there is thus a two part test for such driving and both parts must be satisfied before conviction can be justified.[82] The English courts have taken the view that *mens rea* plays no part in dangerous

---

children and adults often to be found disporting themselves there after school hours — there being no physical barriers to entry and no other steps taken to impede entry — notwithstanding the local authority's policy to forbid access to such places after school hours); *Brown v. Braid*, 1984 S.C.C.R. 286 (forecourt of disused filling-station held to be a public place, since it provided a convenient pedestrian short-cut from one pavement to another — although, under the current legislation, the same decision could be reached by considering the forecourt, thus used, to be a "way" to which the public had access); and *McPhee v. P.F., Oban*, High Court on Appeal, July 5, 2001, (tarmac area — part driveway and part car park — providing access to a block of flats, but also to two other dwellings in private ownership, considered to be a public place, there being no physical obstruction to entry and no signs suggesting that it was private: the case was regarded by the Appeal Court as a marginal one, but they appear to have endorsed the sheriff's view that *Young v. Carmichael, supra*, was distinguishable since the proprietors of the two other dwellings could be regarded as members of the public having access over the tarmac area which pertained to the block of flats; the Court opined, however, at para. [5], that if "all the persons having an interest, as joint proprietors or co-occupants or beneficiaries of a right of access, choose to make it clear that a car park or common access relating to a number of properties is being kept private, then that may be an important factor, as it was in *Young v. Carmichael*").

[77] See para. 30.03, *supra*. The offence under s.2 is to be interpreted in a common sense way, since it is clearly designed to promote public safety: *McQueen v. Buchanan*, 1996 S.C.C.R. 826, L.J.-G. Hope at 829B.

[78] See s.2A(1).

[79] The statutory language here is based upon the test evolved by the Scottish courts for the bad driving offence known as reckless driving, for which dangerous driving was substituted in 1991: see Road Traffic Act 1972, s.2; Criminal Law Act 1977, s.50(1); *Allan v. Patterson*, 1980 J.C. 57; Road Traffic Act 1988, s.2; and the Road Traffic Act 1991, s.1. Consequently, what was said in *Allan v. Patterson* has remained influential in the Scottish courts' approach to the current offence of dangerous driving: see, *e.g.*, *Mitchell v. Lockhart*, 1993 S.C.C.R. 1070, L.J.-C. Ross at 1074C.

[80] In determining what would be "obvious" to the competent and careful driver, such a driver is to be deemed to have any particular knowledge as to circumstances which the accused actually had (s.2A(3)); thus the English courts have considered relevant here the defendant's knowledge that he had consumed alcohol (assuming that he was adversely affected by it): *R. v. Woodward* [1995] 2 Cr.App.R. 388, CA, as also the defendant's knowledge that he was susceptible to hypoglycaemia: *R. v. Marison* [1997] R.T.R. 457, CA, McCowan L.J. at 461B-D; see also *R. v. Ash* [1999] R.T.R. 347, CA. It is moot whether the knowledge which a professional driver ought to have is to be attributed to the accused and thus deemed to be within the knowledge of the competent and careful driver for the purposes of s.2A(3): see *R. v. Roberts (David)* [1997] R.T.R. 462, CA, at 469. Apart from deemed special knowledge, the circumstances of which the competent and careful driver could be expected to be aware include not only actual but also potential hazards: see *McQueen v. Buchanan*, 1996 S.C.C.R. 826, L.J.-G. Hope at 829B; *Mitchell v. Lockhart*, 1993 S.C.C.R. 1070, L.J.-C. Ross at 1074E-F; *Howdle v. O'Connor*, 1998 S.L.T. 94, L.J.-G. Rodger at 95J-K: and an obvious circumstance (or defect, see s.2A(2)) is something which "could be seen and realised at first glance": see *R. v. Strong* [1995] Crim.L.R. 428 (where serious corrosion underneath a vehicle was held not to be something obvious to an ordinary motorist).

[81] "Dangerous" means that there is a danger of injury to any person (including the driver himself: *Carstairs v. Hamilton*, 1997 S.C.C.R. 311, where the accused drove a "go-kart" on a road which was busy with pedestrian and vehicular traffic — the go-kart being too small to be seen easily by others, and lacking safety and protective devices and equipment found on motor vehicles intended for use on roads) or of serious damage to property: s.2A(3).

[82] *Aitken v. Lees*, 1993 S.C.C.R. 845.

driving[83]; but this is based on the opinion that negligence is not a matter of *mens rea*. As the way the accused was driving has to fall far below the standard expected of a competent and careful driver, a form of negligence is clearly involved, and thus the contrast between dangerous driving (of this type at least) and driving without due care[84] depends upon the degree of departure from that expected standard.[85] Driving in excess of the permitted maximum speed, for example, which is a statutory offence in its own right,[86] may amount to either careless or dangerous driving — the latter if the speed was grossly excessive. But driving at excessive speed is not *per se* driving dangerously[87]; there must be evidence of actual or potential hazards which would make it obvious to a competent and careful driver that driving at such speed was indeed dangerous in the circumstances.[88]

The second possibility[89] for driving dangerously arises if it would be obvious[90] to a competent and careful driver that driving the vehicle in its current state would be dangerous.[91] If the accused knows of the state of his vehicle which in fact makes driving it dangerous, then that state will be treated as obvious to the competent and careful driver.[92] It has been suggested in some cases that the relevant state of his vehicle should always[93] be shown to have been within the knowledge of the accused[93]; but that, it is submitted, goes beyond what the statutory description of the offence requires.

---

[83] See, *e.g.*, *R. v. Loukes* [1996] R.T.R. 164, where Auld L.J. at 169K-L described it as a "wholly objective offence" and as an "absolute offence", and considered that the driver's state of mind is relevant only in relation to such special knowledge he has which is to be attributed to the competent and careful driver in terms of s.2A(3): see n.80, *supra*. This also seems to have been the view of the Scottish Appeal Court in *Allan v. Patterson*, 1980 J.C. 57, L.J.-G. Emslie (opinion of the court) at 60.

[84] Under s.3 of the Road Traffic Act 1988: see para. 30.09, *infra*.

[85] See, *e.g.*, *McCallum v. Hamilton*, 1985 S.C.C.R. 368, L.J.-C. Ross at 370, where what is to be shown for careless driving is said to be a falling below the required standard.

[86] Road Traffic Regulation Act 1984, ss. 88, 89.

[87] *Howdle v. O'Connor*, 1998 S.L.T. 94, L.J.-G. Rodger at 95J-K.

[88] Actual hazards might include the state of the road; weather and light conditions; and the amount of traffic (both vehicular and pedestrian) in the vicinity of the driving in question: potential hazards (borrowed from the account of the former offence of reckless driving given in *Allan v. Patterson*, 1980 J.C. 57, by L.J.-G. Emslie at 60) might include the possibility of traffic emerging at road junctions, field entrances and lay-bys in the vicinity of the accused's driving; and the possibility of deer, intoxicated persons or debris being suddenly encountered on the carriageway of the road in question: see *Abbas v. Houston*, 1993 S.C.C.R. 1019; *Mitchell v. Lockhart*, 1993 S.C.C.R. 1070; *Trippick v. Orr*, 1994 S.C.C.R. 736; *McQueen v. Buchanan*, 1996 S.C.C.R. 826; *Howdle v. O'Connor*, 1998 S.L.T. 94. Overtaking vehicles on motorways or dual carriageway roads at grossly excessive speed is thought to be especially dangerous in this context, since drivers of vehicles about to be overtaken will not be aware of the excessive speed at which the overtaking vehicle is in fact approaching: see *Howdle v. O'Connor*, *supra*, L.J.-G. Rodger at 95J-K; see also *Jansch v. Orr*, Appeal Court, March 31, 1994, unrep'd: the opinion of the Court in *Jansch* appears, however, as part of the Commentary to the report of *Trippick v. Orr*, 1994 S.C.C.R. 736, at 742. *cf. Brown v. Orr*, 1994 S.C.C.R. 668, where the Appeal Court seems to have taken the view that the trial court's account of potential hazards was too speculative: this case has, however, been distinguished rather than followed in later decisions.

[89] Section 2A(2): see also s.2A(4), as to things attached to or carried in a vehicle which make the driving of that vehicle dangerous.

[90] See n.80, *supra*.

[91] See n.81, *supra*.

[92] See s.2A(2).

[93] See *Carstairs v. Hamilton*, 1997 S.C.C.R. 311, Lord Sutherland (opinion of the court) at 313F; *H.M. Advocate v. Campbell*, 1993 S.C.C.R. 765, Lord Murray at 770G–771A (although this case concerned the former offence of reckless driving, where "reckless" was not statutorily defined).

The defence of necessity appears to apply to road traffic offences in general[94] and thus to driving dangerously, as is the case in England.[95] Where driving is objectively dangerous, the accused's erroneous belief that his driving was not dangerous in the circumstances is an irrelevant element. Thus, in pursuing a suspected stolen vehicle, an experienced police driver drove his vehicle at excessive speed across a road junction against a red traffic light in the genuine, but erroneous belief that another police vehicle which he saw there was controlling the entry of traffic to that junction; but it was held that he had no sufficient defence to a charge of causing death by dangerous driving, since the offence was one of strict liability.[96]

In English law, provocation has (properly, it is submitted) been ruled out as a possible defence to driving dangerously.[97]

30.09   "DUE CARE". The offence of driving without due care seems of its very nature to require negligence. The standard is an objective one. To convict of careless driving it is necessary to show that the accused failed to exercise "the degree of care and attention which a reasonably prudent driver would exercise",[98] and such a failure may consist in an "error of judgment".[99] Carelessness may arise in actual driving, as by turning right without giving a proper signal or without taking steps to see that one's signal is observed,[1] or by driving with a defective car or while overtired,

---

[94] *Moss v. Howdle*, 1997 S.C.C.R. 215: see Vol. I, para. 13.21.

[95] See, *e.g.*, *R. v. Cairns* [2000] R.T.R. 15, CA; *R. v. Backshall* [1999] 1 Cr.App.R. 35.

[96] *R. v. Collins* [1997] R.T.R. 439, CA; *cf. Sigournay v. Douglas*, 1981 S.C.C.R. 303 (a case involving a s.3 offence of careless driving).

[97] *R. v. Dickinson* [1998] R.T.R. 469, Nelson J. at 475B-C.

[98] *Simpson v. Peat* [1952] 2 Q.B. 24, Lord Goddard C.J. at 28. In *McCallum v. Hamilton*, 1985 S.C.C.R. 368, at 370, L.J.-C. Ross implied that the test was whether the driving fell below the standard to be expected of a careful and competent driver — which makes clear that the difference between this offence and driving dangerously is simply a matter of degree: and a conviction under s.3 is always an implied alternative under a s.2 charge — Road Traffic Act 1988, s.24, as substituted by the Road Traffic Act 1991, s.24; see, *e.g.*, *Murray v. H.M. Advocate*, 2001 S.L.T. 435. In *Brunton v. Lees*, 1993 S.C.C.R. 98, L.J.-G. Hope at 100E said this: "The essential question is whether the appellant was exercising the degree of care which a reasonable, competent and prudent driver would be expected to exercise in the circumstances." These two tests are essentially the same, and the Scottish courts treat them as interchangeable: see *Wilson v. MacPhail*, 1991 S.C.C.R. 170, L.J.-G. Hope at 172E-F; *Farquhar v. MacKinnon*, 1986 S.C.C.R. 524, L.J.-C. Ross at 526; *Rae v. Friel*, 1992 S.C.C.R. 688, L.J.-C. Ross at 693E.

[99] *Simpson v. Peat* [1952] 2 Q.B. 24, Lord Goddard C.J., at 28.

[1] *Sorrie v. Robertson*, 1944 J.C. 95, where a lorry driver turned to the right after signalling his intention to do so, even though he was aware that a motor cycle had begun to overtake him. See also, *McCrone v. Normand*, 1989 S.L.T. 332, and *Farquhar v. MacKinnon*, 1986 S.C.C.R. 524, both cases where drivers reversed large vehicles without being able to see what was immediately behind those vehicles — in contravention of the Highway Code, r.178 (in the current edition of 1998), which requires drivers to obtain assistance prior to undertaking such manoeuvres. Breach of a rule of the Highway Code is a relevant consideration as to whether an offence contrary to s.3 has been committed, but is not conclusive thereof: thus breach of r.127 as to the use by drivers of mobile telephones may or may not amount to driving without due care, depending upon the circumstances: see *Rae v. Friel*, 1992 S.C.C.R. 688, especially L.J.-C. Ross at 693D; *MacPhail v. Haddow*, 1990 S.C.C.R. 339 (Sh.Ct); *Stock v. Carmichael*, 1993 S.C.C.R. 136. "Speeding" may be sufficient for conviction of driving without due care: see, *e.g.*, *Brunton v. Lees*, 1993 S.C.C.R. 98, where driving at 60–70 mph at 3 a.m. on a road where the limit was 40 mph was sufficient for conviction under s.3 in view of the potential dangers represented by the proximity of four all-night filling stations, two roundabouts, and several road junctions and pedestrian crossings.

although in the latter type of case prosecution is unlikely in the absence of objective bad driving.[2]

In assessing the manner of driving it is necessary to take into account the whole circumstances, including any prior incident which leads to the accused driving in what is objectively a careless manner. This introduces an element of subjectivity into the matter, but is necessary in order to deal with the situation described by Lord Goddard C.J. in *Simpson v. Peat*[3]:

> "Suppose a driver is confronted with a sudden emergency through no fault of his own; in an endeavour to avert a collision he swerves to his right — it is shown that had he swerved to the left the accident would not have happened: that is being wise after the event and, if the driver was in fact exercising the degree of care and attention which a reasonably prudent driver would exercise, he ought not to be convicted [of dangerous or careless driving], even though another and perhaps more highly skilled driver would have acted differently."

When therefore a driver turns right at a road junction with which she is unfamiliar and which has no sign indicating that such a turn is prohibited, so that she finds herself driving on the wrong side of a dual carriageway, she is probably not guilty of careless driving. The offence can be committed only where there is some fault in the sense of "a falling below the care or skill of a competent and experienced driver, in relation to the manner of the driving and to the relevant circumstances of the case."[4] Necessity may be a defence, although it has been opined in England that "due" care enables such necessity as there may be to be taken into consideration in the determination whether the offence has been committed.[5]

"REASONABLE CONSIDERATION". The offence of driving without reason- **30.10** able consideration for other road users has not been defined, and is rarely charged on its own. Such a charge might, however, be appropriate for a driver who emerges from a side road in such a way as to make the main road drivers stop to allow him through, where a charge of careless driving might not be brought because there was in fact time for them to do so. It would also be the appropriate charge to bring against someone who drove with undipped headlights so as to cause inconvenience to oncoming traffic.[6]

In *Wilson v. MacPhail*,[7] the accused, a taxi driver, pulled out to overtake a line of traffic which was halted at a set of temporary traffic lights: there were only two lanes in the road at that point, and the accused's object in pulling out into the "wrong" lane was to gain access to a side road situated about 300 to 400 yards to the right, just in front of the traffic lights. In carrying out this manoeuvre at a speed of about 20 mph, he began to

---

[2] See *R. v. Spurge* [1961] 2 Q.B. 205.

[3] [1952] 2 Q.B. 24, 28.

[4] *R. v. Gosney* [1971] 2 Q.B. 674, Megaw L.J. at 680B-C.

[5] *D.P.P. v. Harris* [1995] 1 Cr.App.R. 170, McCowan L.J. at 179–180; *cf. R. v. Backshall* [1999] 1 Cr.App.R. 35, CA, Evans L.J. at 42B. In *Harris*, the actual decision to deny the defence of duress of circumstances (see Vol. 1, paras 13.18 and 13.19) was based on regulations relating to traffic lights and the precise duty incumbent on police proceeding past a traffic light "at red".

[6] See also the list of suggestions contained in J. Wheatley, *Road Traffic Law in Scotland* (3rd ed., 2000), at p.55.

[7] 1991 S.C.C.R. 170.

encounter oncoming vehicles, the lights having changed in favour of such traffic. Four of those vehicles had to slow in order to pass the accused's taxi, and one vehicle had to stop to allow the accused to execute the right turn which had been his objective. The charge against the accused was in the usual Scottish form, which narrates both driving without due care and driving without reasonable consideration for other road users, although the facts suggest that the latter was the more appropriate. The Appeal Court seems to have accepted, however, the suggestion of counsel for the appellant that the appropriate test was whether the appellant had "exercised the degree of care to be expected of a reasonable, competent and prudent driver in all the circumstances"[8]: and this suggests that the test for each part of section 3 is the same.[9]

30.11 *Driving while unfit.* Section 4[10] provides:

> "(1) A person who, when driving[11] or attempting to drive a mechanically propelled vehicle[12] on a road or other public place,[13] is unfit to drive through drink or drugs shall be guilty of an offence.[14]
>
> (2) Without prejudice to subsection (1) above, a person who, when in charge of a mechanically propelled vehicle[15] which is on a road[16] or other public place, is unfit to drive through drink or drugs shall be guilty of an offence."[17]

A person is unfit to drive through drink or drugs if "his ability to drive properly is for the time being impaired."[18] "Drink" is usually understood as meaning intoxicating liquor.

A drug has been held to include "a medicament or medicine, something given to cure, alleviate or assist an ailing body,"[19] but in fact extends to any substance which when "taken into the human body by whatever means, for example, by inhalation, or by injection, or by mouth

---

[8] *ibid.*, at 172E-F. The Court said that there was force in counsel's submission, and that (at 172F) "the primary question in all these cases must be whether the required degree of care has been exercised."

[9] *cf. Price v. D.P.P.* [1990] R.T.R. 413, where an English divisional court (at 416C-D) raised the issue (but without deciding it) whether proof of actual inconvenience or failure to consider other road users is required or whether "it is sufficient to show that a notional road user would have been inconvenienced by inconsiderate behaviour by a motorist."

[10] As amended by the Road Traffic Act 1991, s.4.

[11] *supra*, paras 30.04, 30.05.

[12] *supra*, para. 30.06.

[13] *supra*, para. 30.07.

[14] Maximum penalty, on summary conviction, six months' and a fine of level 5 on the standard scale, and obligatory disqualification and endorsement (3–11 penalty points): Road Traffic Offenders Act 1988, Sched. 2, Pt I.

[15] *supra*, para. 30.06.

[16] *supra*, para. 30.07.

[17] Maximum penalty three months' and a fine of level 4 on the standard scale, on summary conviction; disqualification is discretionary but endorsement is obligatory (10 penalty points): Road Traffic Offenders Act 1988, Sched. 2, Pt I. Section 30 (as amended by the Road Traffic Act 1991, Sched. 8) makes it an offence to ride a pedal cycle while unfit to do so through drink or drugs, the maximum penalty being, on summary conviction, a fine of level 3 on the standard scale.

[18] Road Traffic Act 1988, s.4(5).

[19] *Armstrong v. Clark* [1957] 2 Q.B. 391, Lord Goddard C.J., at 394; in this case, a diabetic whose driving was affected by the insulin he had taken was convicted of driving under the influence of drugs.

. . . affect[s] the control of the human body".[20] The subsections each create only one offence, that of being unfit to drive, which can be committed either as a result of drink or of drugs, or of a combination of both, and the Crown are not bound to show which caused the unfitness in any case.[21]

"IN CHARGE". This phrase has caused much difficulty, and although in **30.12** practice the special defence which is available under section 4(3) of the 1988 Act avoids most of the problems raised by the phrase, it is still necessary for the Crown to show that the accused was "in charge" of the vehicle before the onus shifts to him to set up his defence, and the meaning of the phrase has not been altered.

A person is in charge of a vehicle when he is in *de facto* charge, and is responsible for the control or driving of the car. Where the accused is not "the driver of the car for the time being" he is not in charge of it. These propositions were laid down in *Crichton v. Burrell*[22]: the accused there had arranged for his chauffeur to drive him home; he was arrested by the police as he stood by the vehicle waiting for the chauffeur to arrive, and it was held that although he had the keys of the vehicle in his possession he was not "in charge" of the car. This decision rests partly on the view that at any given time only one person can be in charge of a car[23]; had the owner been intending to drive it himself he would have been in charge. That is to say, a person can be the driver of a car for the time being although he is not actually driving it. If A takes his car to a party and parks it he remains "in charge" unless the circumstances come to be such that someone else can be described as "the driver". The person, on this view, in charge of any car is the person who would come forward if someone asked, "Who is the driver of this car?" So in *Winter v. Morrison*[24] where the owner of a car was sitting in the passenger seat beside his wife a learner-driver who was about to drive it, it was held that the owner was not in charge. The situation of a person who is supervising a learner driver is, however, a special one in that that person is performing a role which is more than merely sitting in the vehicle as a passenger. Depending probably upon the circumstances and the abilities of the driver being supervised, it may be necessary for the supervisor to exercise control over the vehicle in order to avoid an accident. The question then becomes whether it is possible in such a situation for more than one person to be in charge of the vehicle at the same time, or whether the supervisor is in charge of the vehicle only when he or she is compelled by circumstances actually to assume control. The more modern authorities tend to assume

---

[20] *Bradford v. Wilson* (1984) 78 Cr.App.R. 77, Robert Goff L.J. at 82, who declared that he was adopting a common sense approach to, rather than attempting any general definition of, the term "drugs". The drug in question in that case was toluene, a narcotic found in glue. It is not at all necessary that the drug which has been taken should appear in the schedules to the Misuse of Drugs Act 1971. See also *Duffy v. Tudhope*, 1983 S.C.C.R. 440. Under s.11 of the Road Traffic Act 1988, it is simply stated that "drug" includes any intoxicant other than alcohol.

[21] *Thomson v. Knights* [1947] K.B. 336. *Cf.* "Drink *And* a Drug", 1953 S.L.T. (News) 129.

[22] 1951 J.C. 107.

[23] Two people can drive a car at once: see *Langman v. Valentine* [1952] 2 All E.R. 803, but at times when they are not driving or attempting to drive probably only one of them is in charge although there may be exceptional cases involving, for example, joint owners or supervisors of those learning to drive.

[24] 1954 J.C. 7.

that a supervisor is a person in charge of the vehicle throughout the period of supervision,[25] and it is submitted that they are correct to do so. *Winter v. Morrison*[26] has not been overruled; but the decision there, it is submitted, is neither sensible nor defensible given the background of road-safety promotion which underlies the offence: and to this extent at least, the propositions in *Crichton v. Burrell*[27] cannot be supported.

The accused's presence in the vehicle must be voluntary. Where A was placed in the back of his car by friends in order that he might there sleep off the effects of alcohol he was held not to be in charge of the car.[28]

30.13   STATUTORY DEFENCE. Section 4(3) and (4) provide further:

> "(3)[29] . . . a person shall be deemed not to have been in charge of a mechanically propelled vehicle if he proves that at the material time the circumstances were such that there was no likelihood of his driving it so long as he remained unfit through drink or drugs.
>
> (4) The court may, in determining whether there was such a likelihood as is mentioned in subsection (3) above, disregard any injury to him and any damage[30] to the vehicle."

That there was "no likelihood" of the accused's driving is a question for the court to decide according to the circumstances of each case, there being no statutory definition of the phrase. It should be noted, however, that the accused's intentions or normal arrangements for alternative transportation are not conclusive of the matter.[31] If the burden on the accused is a persuasive one, it will be met if he proves on the balance of probabilities that there was no likelihood of his driving during the relevant period[32]; but to impose a persuasive burden on the accused is probably incompatible with Article 6 (presumption of innocence) of the European Convention on Human Rights. Under section 3 of the Human Rights Act 1998, legislation must, in so far as it is possible to do so, be read and given effect in a way which is compatible with Convention rights; and the majority of the House of Lords in *R. v. Lambert*[32a] (a case

---

[25] See *Clark v. A.Y. Clark*, 1950 S.L.T. (Sh.Ct.) 68; *Lees v. Lawrie*, 1993 S.C.C.R. 1, Sh.Ct.; *Williamson v. Crowe*, 1995 S.L.T. 959.

[26] 1954 J.C. 7.

[27] 1951 J.C. 107, *supra*.

[28] *Dean v. Wishart*, 1952 J.C. 9. The accused's friends had also immobilised the car, which would provide a defence under the present law. Other examples are *Adair v. McKenna*, 1951 S.L.T. (Sh.Ct.) 40 where a mechanic found beside a car he was repairing but which he had no authority to drive and to which he had no ignition key was held not to be in charge, and *Macdonald v. Crawford*, 1952 S.L.T. (Sh.Ct.) 92 where a taxi driver whose taxi had broken down and who had sent for a friend to tow him and then had a drink and returned to his taxi to sit in the back and wait for the friend was held to be in charge, the sheriff-substitute distinguishing *Crichton v. Burrell*, *supra*, on the ground that the accused had not succeeded in divesting himself of control of the car, the friend being unaware of the situation at the time in question. See also *MacDonald v. Kubirdas*, 1955 S.L.T.(Sh.Ct.) 50 and *Macdonald v. Bain*, 1954 S.L.T. (Sh.Ct.) 30.

[29] As amended by the Road Traffic Act 1991, s.4.

[30] In *Drake v. D.P.P.* [1994] R.T.R. 411, it was held that a car immobilised by a wheel clamp could not be considered to be damaged thereby; for "damage" (see 418c) there had to be evidence of some intrusion into the integrity of the vehicle.

[31] See *Cartmill v. Heywood*, 2000 S.L.T. 799; *Williamson v. Crowe*, 1995 S.L.T. 959. Cf., *Brown v. Higson*, 2000 S.L.T. 994.

[32] *Brown v. Higson*, 2000 S.L.T. 994; *Drake v. D.P.P.* [1994] R.T.R. 411.

[32a] [2001] 3 W.L.R. 206, HL; see Lord Slynn of Hadley at 212D–G; Lord Steyn at 220H–224B; Lord Hope of Craighead at 237F–H and 238C–D; and Lord Clyde at 258H–259C; *cf.* Lord Hutton at 274D–G.

concerned with the burden of proof imposed by section 28 of the Misuse of Drugs Act 1971[32b]) was strongly of the view that such a burden on an accused should, to avoid incompatibility with the Convention, wherever possible be construed as an evidential rather than a persuasive one. It is likely, therefore, that the defence under section 4(3) will now be construed in accordance with the majority view in *Lambert*.

General defences. Automatism is probably a defence to a section 4 **30.14** charge[33]; and necessity, which appears to be a defence to road traffic offences in general,[34] has certainly been held in the sheriff court to be a defence to driving or attempting to drive after having consumed excess alcohol.[35]

Section 5. This provides as follows: **30.15**

"(1) If a person—
> (a) drives or attempts to drive a motor vehicle on a road or other public place; or
> (b) is in charge of a motor vehicle on a road or other public place;

after consuming so much alcohol that the proportion of it in his breath, blood or urine exceeds the prescribed limit he is guilty of an offence.[36]

(2) It is a defence for a person charged with an offence under subsection (1)(b) above to prove that at the time he is alleged to have committed the offence the circumstances were such that there was no likelihood of his driving the vehicle whilst the proportion of alcohol in his breath, blood or urine remained likely to exceed the prescribed limit.

(3) The court may, in determining whether there was such a likelihood as is mentioned in subsection (2) above, disregard any injury to him and any damage to the vehicle."[37]

This offence can be committed only in respect of a "motor vehicle", which is defined in section 185(1) of the Road Traffic Act 1988 as meaning "subject to section 20 of the Chronically Sick and Disabled Persons Act 1970 (which makes special provision about invalid carriages,

---

[32b] See para. 43.17, *infra*.

[33] See para. 30.05, *supra*.

[34] See *Moss v. Howdle*, 1997 J.C. 123; the rules for the defence must be satisfied, however: see *Ruxton v. Lang*, 1998 S.C.C.R. 1 Sh.Ct,; *Dawson v. Dickson*, 1999 S.C.C.R. 698; *Dolan v. McLeod*, 1999 J.C. 32. If those rules are not satisfied, it may still be possible to plead necessity in mitigation of sentence: see, *e.g.*, *McLeod v. MacDougall*, 1988 S.C.C.R. 519. See generally, Vol. I, para. 13.21.

[35] Contrary to s.5 of the Road Traffic Act 1988: see *Tudhope v. Grubb*, 1983 S.C.C.R. 350, Sh.Ct.

[36] Maximum penalty, for s.5(1)(a), on summary conviction, six months' and a fine of level 5 on the standard scale, obligatory disqualification and obligatory endorsement (3–11 penalty points); and for s.5(1)(b), on summary conviction, three months' and a fine of level 4 on the standard scale, discretionary disqualification and obligatory endorsement (10 penalty points): Road Traffic Offenders Act 1988, Sched. 2, Pt I.

[37] For the current prescribed limits, procedural matters relative to the offence, police powers, and general interpretation, all of which being beyond the scope of this work, see ss.6–11 of the Road Traffic Act 1988; and for discussion of these provisions, as also an indication of the evolution of, and the extensive case law relative to, the offence, see the *Encyclopaedia of Road Traffic Law* (Sweet and Maxwell).

within the meaning of that Act)[38] a mechanically propelled vehicle[39] intended or adapted for use on roads." Mere use on the road on an isolated occasion does not make a vehicle a motor vehicle in terms of the Act; it must be a vehicle of a kind intended or adapted for ordinary road purposes. A diesel dumper which although capable of being driven on a road is really a piece of building plant wholly unsuitable for ordinary road transport is not a motor vehicle even when it is being driven on a road.[40] But, on the other hand, a tractor of a kind normally used for drawing agricultural implements both on farms and on roads is a motor vehicle even when it is being used by road-making contractors.[41]

"Intended" has been given an objective meaning: a vehicle is intended for use on roads if a reasonable person looking at the vehicle would say that one of its users was a road user.[42] It is not settled whether "adapted" means "fit and apt", or "altered". In *MacDonald v. Carmichael*[43] Lord Justice-Clerk Aitchison preferred the former meaning but Lord Mackay and Lord Jamieson disagreed with him. The question did not, however, fall to be decided in that case, nor in *Burns v. Currell*[44] where it was left open. It is submitted that Lord Aitchison's view is correct. There are other sections of the Act where "adapted" is used as an alternative to "constructed"[45] and clearly means "altered", but in the context of section 185 "fit or apt" seems a more suitable reading.

30.16 *Sections 35 and 36.* Section 35 makes it an offence to fail to comply with a direction given by a police constable or traffic warden on traffic duty, whilst section 36 makes it an offence to fail to comply with an authorised traffic sign such as a "Stop" sign or traffic lights.[46]

It is probably no defence to a charge under these sections that the accused did not see the sign.[47]

---

[38] Invalid carriages, if mechanically propelled, are not motor vehicles for the purposes of (*inter alia*) the Road Traffic Act 1988, and are also not subject to ss. 1–4, 163, 170 and 181 of that Act which would otherwise apply to them as mechanically propelled vehicles: see Road Traffic Act 1991, Sched. 4, para. 3.

[39] See para. 30.06, *supra*.

[40] *MacDonald v. Carmichael*, 1941 J.C. 27; *MacLean v. McCabe*, 1964 S.L.T. (Sh.Ct.) 39.

[41] *Woodward v. Jas Young (Contractors) Ltd*, 1958 J.C. 28.

[42] *D.P.P. v. Saddington* [2001] R.T.R. 227, approving and applying the test laid down in *Burns v. Currell* [1963] 2 Q.B. 433, which decided that a mechanically propelled "Go-Kart" was not a motor vehicle in terms of the Act. See also *Chalgray Ltd and Anr v. Aspley* [1965] Crim.L.R. 440; *cf. Chief Constable of Avon and Somerset Constabulary v. F.* [1987] R.T.R. 378.

[43] 1941 J.C. 27.

[44] [1963] 2 Q.B. 433.

[45] For example, s.189(2).

[46] Maximum penalty for each offence, on summary conviction, a fine of level 3 on the standard scale, and, in the case of police or traffic warden directions and of certain signs, discretionary disqualification and obligatory endorsement (three penalty points): see Road Traffic Offenders Act 1988, Sched. 2, Pt I; Traffic Signs Regulations and General Directions 1994 (S.I. 1994 No. 1519).

[47] *Brooks v. Jeffries* [1936] 3 All E.R. 232. *Cf. Keane v. McSkimming*, 1983 S.C.C.R. 220, where the sheriff's opinion that he had found sufficient evidence from the evidence led for the Crown that the accused had not seen a constable's signal to stop, was upheld by the Appeal Court: but that Court (at 223) also stated as follows: "It is not of course for the Crown in a case such as this to establish that a driver did see a signal to halt. It is quite sufficient that the Crown leads evidence that a signal was given at a time and in circumstances which ought to make it obvious to an approaching driver. If such evidence is led then in the absence of explanation the case for the Crown is made out upon a prima facie basis and if the driver in question fails to react to the signal and that is established the court is entitled to proceed to convict, and the Crown prosecution of a motorist in these circumstances is entitled to succeed."

Pedestrian crossings. Regulations 25 and 26 of the Zebra, Pelican and **30.17**
Puffin Pedestrian Crossings Regulations and General Directions 1997[48]
provide:

"**25.**—(1) Every pedestrian, if he is on the carriageway within the
limits of a zebra crossing, which is not for the time being controlled
by a constable in uniform or a traffic warden, before any part of a
vehicle has entered those limits, shall have precedence within those
limits over that vehicle and the driver of the vehicle shall accord
precedence to any such pedestrian.[49]

(2) Where there is a refuge for pedestrians or central reservation
on a zebra crossing, the parts of the crossing situated on each side
of the refuge for pedestrians or central reservation shall, for the
purposes of this regulation, be treated as separate crossings.

26. Where the vehicular light signals at a pelican crossing are
showing the flashing amber signal,[50] every pedestrian, if he is on the
carriageway or a central reservation within the limits of the crossing
(but not if he is on a central reservation which forms part of a
system of staggered crossings) before any part of a vehicle has
entered those limits, shall have precedence within those limits over
that vehicle and the driver of the vehicle shall accord such precedence to any such pedestrian."[51]

With respect to zebra crossings, there is no traffic light control and the
duty upon the driver of a vehicle to accord precedence is dependent on
observation of pedestrian movement relative to the limits of the crossing
— which means relative to the striped part of that crossing.[52] Each such
crossing incorporates a "give way line" which signifies the position "at or
before which a vehicle should be stopped for the purposes of complying
with regulation 25".[53] It would seem, therefore, that a driver is obliged to
accord precedence to a pedestrian who steps onto the striped part of the
crossing before that driver's vehicle has passed the give way line; but
regulations 14 and 25 are not entirely consistent with one another, and
the matter is not entirely clear.[54]

---

[48] S.I. 1997 No. 2400: zebra crossings are not controlled by traffic lights; pelican and
puffin crossings have associated traffic lights — the former crossings, unlike the latter,
having (for drivers of vehicles) a flashing amber signal during the lights sequence.

[49] Failure to accord precedence is a contravention of the regulations which is an offence
under s.25(5) of the Road Traffic Regulation Act 1984: maximum penalty on summary
conviction, a fine of level 3 on the standard scale, with discretionary disqualification and
obligatory endorsement (three penalty points) where the contravention is committed with
a motor vehicle (Road Traffic Offenders Act 1988, Sched. 2, Pt I).

[50] See reg.12 for the sequence of vehicular traffic lights at these crossings: see in
particular reg.12(1)(f).

[51] See n.49, *supra*. Failure to obey a traffic sign, including a traffic light signal, is an
offence under s.36(1) of the Road Traffic Act 1988; maximum penalty, on summary
conviction, a fine of level 3 on the standard scale, with discretionary disqualification and
obligatory endorsement (three penalty points): Road Traffic Offenders Act 1988, Sched. 2,
Pt I.

[52] This usually consists of a series of alternate black and white stripes (S.I. 1997 No.
2400, Sched. 1, Pt II, paras 6–8). Some zebra crossings also have a row of studs on either
side of the striped part of the crossing; but these are optional (*ibid.*, para. 9(1)) and do not
therefore delineate any part of the limits of the crossing (see *ibid.*, Sched. 1, Pt II,
Diagram).

[53] See reg. 14, and Sched. 1, Pt II, para. 6(b) and Diagram.

[54] *cf. Hughes v. Hall* [1960] 1 W.L.R. 733; *Moulder v. Neville* [1974] R.T.R. 53: these
cases deal with previous forms of the relevant regulations.

It is the duty of a driver who is approaching such a crossing to be driving in such a way as to be able to stop if necessary: where his view of the crossing is masked by other vehicles so that he cannot see if anyone is on the crossing he must be able to stop at the crossing.[55] There is some authority, however, that although there is a duty of care on a driver approaching the crossing which is greater than the ordinary duty of driving carefully, the duty to accord precedence is not absolute. That was the view taken in *Watson v. Wright*,[56] but the then current regulations spoke of a duty on "approaching" vehicles to give precedence, and the case proceeded to a considerable extent on the interpretation of "approach". The present regulations give a right to precedence over "a vehicle" and appear absolute in their terms. But in *Leicester v. Pearson*[57] the regulation under consideration[58] was similar to the current regulation 25, and it was held that the obligation to give precedence was not absolute. This case was described in *Gibbons v. Kahl*[59] as special, and in *Lockie v. Lawton*[60] Lord Parker C.J. treated *Leicester v. Pearson* as exceptional and regarded *Gibbons v. Kahl* as authority for the existence of an unqualified duty. Lord Parker referred to the facts of the two cases — in *Leicester* the accused was driving slowly and could have stopped but failed to see the pedestrian because of darkness and shadows, his failure not being negligent, while in *Gibbons* he was not driving slowly and failed to see the pedestrian because the latter was masked by another vehicle — and said that it did not matter whether the duty was expressed as absolute or as requiring only reasonable steps, because "reasonable" had to be read "in the light of the clear duty which arises from regulation 4".[61] In *Hughes v. Hall*,[62] however, which was concerned with the meaning of "limits of an uncontrolled crossing", Lord Parker C.J. observed that, "It is, I think, clear on the latest decisions of this court, that regulation 4 imposes an absolute duty, and that it is quite immaterial whether there is any evidence of negligence or failure to take reasonable care."[63]

The matter may now be regarded as settled by *Burns v. Bidder*,[64] where a defence of sudden brake failure due to latent defect was held relevant. *Leicester v. Pearson*[65] was described as an example of a very rare occurrence of a driver having a full view of the crossing, keeping a proper lookout, and yet not seeing a pedestrian because of circumstances for which he was in no way responsible. According to *Burns v. Bidder* it is a defence to show that "Some circumstances over which the driver had no reasonable or possible control brought about the collision."[66] The defence seems to be limited to cases where there can be said to be no *actus reus*: as where the driver is stung by a swarm of bees, or is pushed into the crossing by a following vehicle, or where there is a sudden

---

[55] *Gibbons v. Kahl* [1956] 1 Q.B. 59.
[56] 1940 J.C. 32.
[57] [1952] 2 Q.B. 668.
[58] The Pedestrian Crossings (London) Regulations 1951, (S.I. 1951 No. 1193), reg. 4.
[59] [1956] 1 Q.B. 59.
[60] (1959) 57 Loc.Gov.Rep. 329.
[61] At 331.
[62] [1960] 1 W.L.R. 733, approved in *Neal v. Bedford* [1966] 1 Q.B. 505.
[63] At 736.
[64] [1967] 2 Q.B. 227; but see Gl. Williams, "'Absolute Liability' in Traffic Offences" [1967] Crim.L.R. 142.
[65] [1952] 2 Q.B. 668.
[66] [1967] 2 Q.B. 227, James J. at 240E.

removal of control for which the driver is not to blame: *i.e.* due to automatism, the act of another, or situations in the *R. v. Spurge*[67] category.[68] Beyond these limited cases the obligation is absolute, which suggests that *Leicester v. Pearson* has been virtually overruled. It remains to be seen whether it can ever be a defence that the pedestrian suddenly ran out into the path of the car.[69]

It was held in *McKerrell v. Robertson*[70] that where a woman was about to cross a road pushing a go-chair in front of her, and had placed the go-chair on the crossing before the accused's car reached it, the accused was guilty of failing to accord precedence to the woman although she had not herself left the pavement, the woman and the chair being regarded as one entity.[71] It has also been held that a cyclist who was wheeling his cycle on a zebra crossing qualified as a "foot-passenger",[72] as the then current regulations referred to a pedestrian.

No special consideration is given to the police or any other emergency service in relation to zebra crossings.[73]

In relation to puffin crossings, which are controlled by vehicular traffic lights, there is no light signal in the sequence of those lights which raises any question of precedence[74]: but pelican crossings, which are also controlled by traffic lights, incorporate a flashing amber light signal to vehicles; this signal follows a red signal light, and signifies that traffic may proceed in anticipation of a green signal to follow, provided that precedence is accorded to any pedestrian who is on the carriageway within the limits of the crossing at the time. The limits of a pelican crossing are denoted by two parallel rows of studs set into the carriageway, at right angles to that carriageway.[75] Failure to accord such precedence to a pedestrian is subject to the same considerations, *mututis mutandis*, as apply to zebra crossings.

PRECEDENCE. The duty is to "accord precedence" and this means, it is **30.18** submitted, that once a pedestrian has stepped on to a zebra crossing[76] no vehicle is entitled to cross until the pedestrian has proceeded beyond its line of travel. The decision in *Wishart v. MacDonald*[77] that it is not an

---

[67] [1961] 2 Q.B. 205: sudden mechanical failure.

[68] Jones J. in *Burns v. Bidder, supra*, at 240G, also mentions the suffering by the driver of "a sudden epileptic fit"; but it may be that such fits are now subject to different considerations: see Vol. I, para. 3.22.

[69] *cf.* the careless driving case of *Sigournay v. Douglas*, 1981 S.C.C.R. 302, where, on appeal, the accused was acquitted of a charge under s.3 of the Road Traffic Act 1988, the situation having been that a pedestrian suddenly broke free from the person who was restraining her and ran into the path of the accused's vehicle.

[70] 1956 J.C. 50.

[71] There was a baby in the go-chair, but there could be no charge of failing to allow him precedence because he was not a "pedestrian", and the *ratio* of *McKerrell* would probably apply if there were only laundry in the chair.

[72] *Crank v. Brooks* [1980] R.T.R. 441: Waller L.J. also raised the issue of what the decision might be if the cyclist had been using the cycle as a scooter on the crossing.

[73] See *Lockie v. Soppett* [1956] Crim.L.R. 487.

[74] But see reg. 13, S.I. 1997 No. 2400, under which there is specific exemption from "stop" light signals for vehicles being used for fire brigade, ambulance, national blood service or police purposes; but the exemption is subject to conditions which include the according of precedence to pedestrians who are on the part of the carriageway which lies within the limits of the crossing at the time: see reg. 13(1)(f)(ii).

[75] See S.I. 1997 No. 2400, Sched. 4 and relative Diagrams.

[76] Precedence in relation to pelican crossings is a much clearer concept: see para. 30.17, *supra*.

[77] 1962 S.L.T. (Sh.Ct.) 29.

offence to drive across a zebra crossing in front of a pedestrian unless his progress is impeded or he is apprehensive of danger from the vehicle reads words into the regulations which are not there, and is clearly wrong.[78] The regulations apply to all vehicles and not merely to motor-vehicles.

Other statutes relating to traffic

30.19 *Merchant Shipping.* Section 58 of the Merchant Shipping Act 1995 provides:

"(1) This section applies—
  (a) to the master of, or any seaman employed in, a United Kingdom ship; and
  (b) to the master of, or any seaman employed in, a ship which—
    (i) is registered under the law of any country outside the United Kingdom; and
    (ii) is in a port in the United Kingdom or within United Kingdom waters while proceeding to or from any such port.
(2) If a person to whom this section applies, while on board his ship or in its immediate vicinity—
  (a) does any act which causes or is likely to cause —
    (i) the loss or destruction of or serious damage to his ship or its machinery, navigational equipment or safety equipment, or
    (ii) the loss or destruction of or serious damage to any other ship or any structure, or
    (iii) the death of or serious injury to any person, or
  (b)[79] omits to do anything required—
    (i) to preserve his ship or its machinery, navigational equipment or safety equipment from being lost, destroyed or seriously damaged, or
    (ii) to preserve any person on board his ship from death or serious injury, or
    (iii) to prevent his ship from causing the loss or destruction of or serious damage to any other ship or any structure, or the death of or serious injury to any person not on board his ship,
and either of the conditions specified in subsection (3) below is satisfied with respect to that act or omission, he shall (subject to subsections (6) and (7) below) be guilty of an offence.
(3) Those conditions are—
  (a) that the act or omission was deliberate or amounted to a breach or neglect of duty;
  (b) that the master or seaman in question was under the influence of drink or a drug at the time of the act or omission.
(4) If a person to whom this section applies—

---

[78] The further suggestion that since a blind person cannot see the car no offence is committed is such a case unless he is actually impeded, is even more clearly wrong.

[79] Actual damage is not necessary for an offence under this para. of subs. (2): *Foreman v. MacNeill* (1978) S.C.C.R. (Supp.) 210.

(a) discharges any of his duties, or performs any other function in relation to the operation of his ship or its machinery or equipment, in such a manner as to cause, or to be likely to cause, any such loss, destruction, death or injury as is mentioned in subsection (2)(a) above, or

(b) fails to discharge any of his duties, or to perform any such function, properly to such an extent as to cause, or to be likely to cause, any of those things,

he shall (subject to subsections (6) and (7) below) be guilty of an offence.

(5) A person guilty of an offence under this section shall be liable—

(a) on summary conviction, to a fine not exceeding the statutory maximum;

(b) on conviction on indictment, to imprisonment for a term not exceeding two years or a fine, or both.

(6) In proceedings for an offence under this section it shall be a defence to prove—

(a) in the case of an offence under subsection (2) above where the act or omission alleged against the accused constituted a breach or neglect of duty, that the accused took all reasonable steps to discharge that duty;

(b) in the case of an offence under subsection (2) above, that at the time of the act or omission alleged against the accused he was under the influence of a drug taken by him for medical purposes and either that he took it on medical advice and complied with any directions given as part of that advice or that he had no reason to believe that the drug might have the influence it had;

(c) in the case of an offence under subsection (4) above, that the accused took all reasonable precautions and exercised all due diligence to avoid committing the offence; or

(d) in the case of an offence under either of those subsections—

    (i) that he could have avoided committing the offence only by disobeying a lawful command, or

    (ii) that in all the circumstances the loss, destruction, damage, death or injury in question, or (as the case may be) the likelihood of its being caused, either could not reasonably have been foreseen by the accused or could not reasonably have been avoided by him.

(7) In the application of this section to any person falling within subsection (1)(b) above, subsections (2) and (4) above shall have effect as if subsection (2)(a)(i) and (b)(i) above were omitted; . . .

(8) In this section—

    "breach or neglect of duty", except in relation to a master, includes any disobedience to a lawful command;

    "duty"—

        (a) in relation to a master of seaman, means any duty falling to be discharged by him in his capacity as such; and

        (b) in relation to a master, includes his duty with respect to the good management of his ship and his duty with respect to the safety of operation of his ship, its machinery and equipment; and "structure" means any fixed or moveable structure (of whatever description) other than a ship."[80]

Section 98 of the Act provides:

"(1) If a ship which—

(a) is in a port in the United Kingdom, or

(b) is a United Kingdom ship and is in any other port,

is dangerously unsafe,[81] then subject to subsections (4) and (5) below, the master and the owner of the ship shall each be guilty of an offence.

(2) Where, at the time when a ship is dangerously unsafe, any responsibilities of the owner with respect to the matters relevant to its safety have been assumed (whether wholly or in part) by any person or persons other than the owner, and have been so assumed by that person or (as the case may be) by each of those persons either—

(a) directly, under the terms of a charter-party or management agreement made with the owner, or

(b) indirectly, under the terms of a series of charter-parties or management agreements,

the reference to the owner in subsection (1) above shall be construed as a reference to that other person or (as the case may be) to each of those other persons.

(3) A person guilty of an offence under this section shall be liable—

(a) on summary conviction, to a fine not exceeding £50,000;

(b) on conviction on indictment, to imprisonment for a term not exceeding two years or a fine or both.

(4) It shall be a defence in proceedings for an offence under this section to prove that at the time of the alleged offence—

(a) arrangements had been made which were appropriate to ensure that before the ship went to sea it was made fit to do so without serious danger to human life by reason of the matters relevant to its safety which are specified in the charge (or, in Scotland, which are libelled in the complaint, petition or indictment); or

(b) it was reasonable for such arrangements not to have been made".

Section 98(5) and (6) provide additional defences where the relevant responsibilities had been assumed by other persons and the defender

---

[80] See also s.59 (concerted disobedience and neglect of duty): maximum penalty, as for s.58, *supra*.

[81] Under s.94 of the Act (as amended by the Merchant Shipping and Maritime Security Act 1997, Sched. 1, para. 1),

"(1) . . . a ship in port is 'dangerously unsafe' if, having regard to the nature of the service for which it is intended, the ship is, by reason of the matters mentioned in subsection (2) below, unfit to go to sea without serious danger to human life.

(1A) . . .

(2) Those matters are —

(a) the condition, or the unsuitability for its purpose, of —

(i) the ship or its machinery or equipment, or

(ii) any part of the ship or its machinery or equipment;

(b) undermanning;

(c) overloading or unsafe or improper loading;

(d) any other matter relevant to the safety of the ship;

and are referred to in [s.98], in relation to any ship, as 'the matters relevant to its safety'."

had exercised reasonable diligence to secure their proper discharge, having regard in particular to whether the defender should have been aware of any deficiency in the discharge of these responsibilities and to what he could have done to terminate a charter or intervene in the management of the ship. This section does not apply to ships on rivers or inland waterways.[82]

Section 100 of the Act also places a general duty on shipowners to take all reasonable steps to secure that the ship is operated in a safe manner.[83]

Railways. The Railway Regulation Act 1842, s.17, entitles railway officers **30.20** or constables to apprehend any servants of the railway who "wilfully, maliciously, or negligently" do or omit "any act whereby the life or limb of any person passing along or being upon such railway or the works thereof . . . shall be or might be injured or endangered", and provides that any person so detained if convicted in the sheriff summary court is liable to two months' imprisonment or a fine of level 1 on the standard scale.[84]

Aircraft. The Air Navigation Order 1995[85] contains the following **30.21** provisions:

> "Article 55. A person shall not recklessly or negligently act in a manner likely to endanger an aircraft, or any person therein.
>
> Article 56. A person shall not recklessly or negligently cause or permit an aircraft to endanger any person or property.
>
> Article 57(2). A person shall not, when acting as a member of the crew . . . be under the influence of drink or a drug to such an extent as to impair his capacity so to act."

Section 81(1) of the Civil Aviation Act 1982 provides:

> "Where an aircraft is flown in such a manner as to be the cause of unnecessary danger to any person or property on land or water, the pilot or the person in charge of the aircraft, and also the owner thereof unless he proves to the satisfaction of the court that the aircraft was so flown without his actual fault or privity, shall be liable on summary conviction to [six months' imprisonment and/or a fine of level 4 on the standard scale]."

---

[82] But see s.99 of the Act, which makes it an offence to use or cause to be used or permit to be used in navigation any lighter, barge or similar vessel which is so unsafe that human life is endangered by it: maximum penalty, on summary conviction, a fine of statutory maximum; and on conviction on indictment, a fine (s.99(1)); this offence does not affect the liability of the owner in respect of loss of life or personal injury caused to persons carried in such a vessel (s.99(3)).

[83] Maximum penalty, on summary conviction, a fine not exceeding £50,000; and on conviction on indictment, two years' and a fine: see s.100(3).

[84] In order to obtain a conviction under s.17, the Crown must show that a potential danger to persons passing along the railway existed as the result of the accused's negligence: *Rodger v. Smith*, 1981 S.L.T. (Notes) 31. (Although this is unlikely to trouble Scottish courts, for the purposes of the Channel Tunnel Rail Link Act 1996, the maximum penalty is raised to a fine of level 3 on the standard scale: Sched. 9, para. 8.)

[85] S.I. 1995 No. 1038. Maximum penalty a fine of the statutory maximum on summary conviction, two years' imprisonment and a fine on indictment.

30.22 AVIATION SECURITY ACT 1982. This Act empowers the Secretary of State to impose restrictions and direct the carrying out of searches and the taking of other measures for the purpose of protecting aircraft and aerodromes against acts of violence as defined in section 10 of the Act.[86] Failure without reasonable excuse to comply with such requirements or directions is an offence.[87]

Section 4 of the Act makes it an offence to have with one on an aircraft or aerodrome without lawful authority or reasonable excuse, firearms or explosives, or any other article made or adapted for use for causing injury to or incapacitating a person or for destroying or damaging property, or intended for such use by the possessor or by any other person.[88]

Section 3 creates the offence of destroying or damaging any property used to provide air navigation facilities, or to interfere with the operating of such property, if the destruction, damage or interference is likely to endanger the safety of aircraft in flight.[89]

30.23   Section 2 provides:

"(1) It shall, subject to subsection (4) below,[90] be an offence for any person unlawfully and intentionally—
  (a) to destroy an aircraft in service or so to damage such an aircraft as to render it incapable of flight or as to be likely to endanger its safety in flight, or
  (b) to commit on board an aircraft in flight any act of violence which is likely to endanger the safety of the aircraft.

(2) It shall also, subject to subsection (4) of this section, be an offence for any person unlawfully and intentionally to place, or cause to be placed, on an aircraft in service any device or substance which is likely to destroy the aircraft, or is likely so to damage it as to render it incapable of flight or as to be likely to endanger its safety in flight; but nothing in this subsection shall be construed as limiting the circumstances in which the commission of any act—
  (a) may constitute an offence under subsection (1)(a) above, or
  (b) may constitute attempting or conspiring to commit, or aiding, abetting, counselling or procuring, or being art and part in, the commission of such an offence.

(3) Except as provided by subsection (4) below, subsections (1) and (2) above shall apply whether any such act as is therein mentioned is committed in the United Kingdom or elsewhere,

---

[86] Acts of violence are similar to those narrated in s.2(7), *infra*, save that in s.10, the acts in question may be actual or potential, and also include malicious mischief.

[87] Maximum penalty a fine of the statutory maximum on summary conviction, two years' imprisonment and fine on indictment: ss. 12(9), 13(4) and 14(7), as amended by the Aviation and Maritime Security Act 1990, s.34, Sched. 4, paras 4, 5 and 6. (If the failure to comply continues after a conviction has been obtained, the person concerned is guilty of a further offence, which, on summary conviction, carries a maximum penalty of a fine of one-tenth of level 5 on the standard scale for each day during which the failure continues.)

[88] Maximum penalty three months' imprisonment and a fine of the statutory maximum, on summary conviction; five years and a fine on indictment.

[89] Maximum penalty life imprisonment: s.3(3).

[90] Which deals with acts committed in relation to military, customs or police service by foreigners outside the U.K.

whatever the nationality of the person committing the act and whatever the State in which the aircraft is registered . . .

(6) In this section "unlawfully"—

(a) in relation to the commission of an act in the United Kingdom, means so as (apart from this Act) to constitute an offence under the law of the part of the United Kingdom in which the act is committed, and

(b) in relation to the commission of an act outside the United Kingdom, means so that the commission of the act would (apart from this Act) have been an offence under the law of England and Wales if it had been committed in England and Wales or of Scotland if it had been committed in Scotland.

(7) In this section "act of violence" means—

(a) any act done in the United Kingdom which constitutes the offence of murder, attempted murder, manslaughter, culpable homicide or assault or an offence under section 18, 20, 21, 22, 23, 24, 28 or 29 of the Offences against the Person Act 1861 or under section 2 of the Explosive Substances Act 1883, and

(b) any act done outside the United Kingdom which, if done in the United Kingdom would constitute such an offence as is mentioned in paragraph (a) above."

Wrecks. Section 2 of the Protection of Wrecks Act 1973 empowers the **30.24** Secretary of State to designate a prohibited area round a dangerous wreck, entry on which is an offence.[91]

OFFENCES IN CONNECTION WITH WEAPONS

I — Firearms

A firearm is defined by section 57(1) of the Firearms Act 1968 as **30.25** meaning:

"a lethal[92] barrelled weapon of any description[93] from which any shot, bullet or other missile can be discharged and includes—

(a) any prohibited weapon,[94] whether it is such a lethal weapon as aforesaid or not; and

(b) any component part of such a lethal or prohibited weapon; and

(c) any accessory to any such weapon designed or adapted to diminish the noise or flash caused by firing the weapon."

---

[91] Maximum penalty a fine of level 5 on the standard scale on summary conviction and a fine on indictment: s.3(4).

[92] "A lethal weapon is a weapon which when misused is capable of causing injury from which death might result": *R. v. Thorpe* [1987] 1 W.L.R. 383, CA, Kenneth Jones J. at 388G, following Lord Parker C.J. in *Moore v. Gooderham* [1960] 1 W.L.R. 1308, at 1311.

[93] A speargun, where the mode of propulsion consisted of rubber bands and the barrel was in two parts, was considered to be a firearm within the meaning of s.57(1) in *Boyd v. McGlennan*, 1994 S.L.T. 1148: provided the two parts of the barrel performed the task of a barrel — *i.e.*, "to control and guide the harpoon when it is fired" (see 1149L) — it did not matter that a harpoon did not pass along either part for its entire length when fired.

[94] See s.5, *infra*, para. 30.30.

In *Muir v. Cassidy*[95] a two-barrelled pistol with holes pierced in the side of its barrels so that it could only fire blanks was held to be a firearm since if the holes were blocked up it would be capable of firing live ammunition. This decision was overruled, however, by *Kelly v. MacKinnon*,[96] where two revolvers, which could not fire live ammunition by virtue of the way they had been manufactured or altered, were nevertheless capable of being converted to fire such ammunition; the Appeal Court was firmly of the persuasion that such revolvers were neither firearms nor component parts of such, within the meaning of section 57(1), and that the fact that they were convertible to be firearms within the meaning of the 1968 Act was irrelevant: but this is no longer an irrelevant consideration; and the factual situations in both cases would now be subject to the provisions of the Firearms Act 1982. Section 1 of that Act applies the Firearms Act 1968 to any imitation firearm which has the appearance of being a firearm to which section 1 of the 1968 Act applies, if it is so constructed or adapted as to be readily convertible into a firearm to which that section does apply — that is to say, if it can be so converted without any special skill on the part of the person converting it in the construction or adaptation of any kind of firearm, and the conversion work involved does not require equipment or tools other than such as are in common use by persons carrying on works of construction and maintenance in their own homes.[97]

Section 58(2) of the Act excludes from the operation of the Act any "antique firearm which is sold, transferred, purchased, acquired or possessed as a curiosity or ornament."[98]

30.26 *Firearm certificates.* Under section 1(1) of the Firearms Act 1968, it is an offence to possess, purchase or acquire a firearm and/or ammunition unless either a valid firearm certificate is held which covers the firearm and/or ammunition in question, or a specific relevant exception applies

---

[95] 1953 S.L.T. (Sh.Ct.) 4; appr'd. *R. v. Freeman* [1970] 1 W.L.R. 788.

[96] 1982 J.C. 94.

[97] Section 1(6) of the 1982 Act. In the application of that Act (see s.1(4)(b)), s.57(1) of the 1968 Act is to be read without paras (b) and (c); and the provisions of s.4(3) and (4) of the 1968 Act (see para. 30.32, *infra*) do not apply to imitation firearms to which the 1982 Act applies (see s.2(2)(a) of the 1982 Act). Also, under s.2(2)(b) of the 1982 Act, that Act does not operate to apply to imitation firearms the provisions of the 1968 Act relating to, or to the enforcement of control over, the manner in which a firearm is used or the circumstances in which it is carried, but this is without prejudice to the application of these provisions to imitation firearms independently of the 1982 Act. (Section 2(3) of the 1982 Act indicates that the provisions of the 1968 Act thus referred to are ss. 16–20 and 47: of these provisions, ss. 16A (inserted by the Firearms (Amendment) Act 1994, ss. 1(1)), 17 and 18 include references to imitation firearms by virtue of the wording of the 1968 Act itself; and under s.57(4) of the 1968 Act, an imitation firearm means "any thing which has the appearance of being a firearm (other than such a weapon as is mentioned in section 5(1)(b) of this Act) whether or not it is capable of discharging any shot, bullet or other missile.")

[98] Antiquity is a question of fact: *Richards v. Curwen* [1977] 1 W.L.R. 747; *R. v. Burke* [1978] 67 Cr.App.R. 220, CA; *Bennett v. Brown* (1980) 71 Cr.App.R. 109, where the view was expressed that it was unlikely that a firearm manufactured during the 20th century would be regarded as an antique: see Eveleigh L.J. at 112, Watkins L. also at 112. It is not a defence to a charge of possessing a firearm that one wrongly believed it was an antique: *R. v. Howells* [1977] Q.B. 614; *Walkingshaw v. Wallace*, 1990 S.C.C.R. 203, Sh.Ct. Provision is now made for licensing museums to possess firearms: Firearms (Amendment) Act 1988, s.19, Sched., as amended by the Firearms (Amendment) Act 1997, s.47, and the Scotland Act 1998 (Transfer of Functions to the Scottish Ministers etc.) Order 1999 (S.I. 1999 No. 1750), Art. 6(1), Sched. 5, para. 7(3).

under the Act.[99] It is also an offence to fail to comply with any of the conditions imposed by such a certificate.[1]

Section 1(1) applies to any firearm, except those firearms specified in subsection (3), which covers:

> "(a)[2] a shot gun within the meaning of this Act, that is to say a smooth-bore gun (not being an air gun) which—
>> (i) has a barrel not less than 24 inches in length and does not have any barrel with a bore exceeding 2 inches in diameter;
>> (ii) either has no magazine or has a non-detachable magazine incapable of holding more than two cartridges[3]; and
>> (iii) is not a revolver gun[4]; and
> (b) an air weapon (that is to say, an air rifle, air gun or air pistol[5]

---

[99] Maximum penalty, on indictment (as amended by the Criminal Justice and Public Order Act 1994, Sched. 8), five years' and a fine (save where the offence is committed in aggravated form, see s.4(4) of the 1968 Act (para. 30.31, *infra*), when the maximum prison sentence is increased to seven years); on summary conviction, six months' and fine of level 5 on the standard scale. For exceptions, see *infra*. Under s.32 of the Firearms (Amendment) Act 1997, the transfer of a firearm or ammunition (within the meaning of s.1 of the 1968 Act) by way of sale, letting on hire, loan or gift must be made in person by the transferor to the transferee; the transferee must produce to the transferor the certificate or permit entitling him to purchase or acquire the firearm or ammunition; and the transferor must comply with any instructions contained in that certificate or permit. Any failure to comply with these requirements is an offence: maximum penalty, on indictment, five years' and a fine; and on summary conviction, six months' and a fine of the statutory maximum (s.36(a)). Such transfer must also be notified within seven days by any party to it who is the holder of a firearms certificate (or visitors' firearm permit: see Firearms (Amendment) Act 1988, s.17) to the chief constable of police who granted the certificate or permit: failure to comply with such notification requirement is an offence (s.33(4)), with maximum penalty as above under s.36(a).

[1] Section 1(2): maximum penalty, on summary conviction, six months' and fine of level 5 on the standard scale.

[2] As substituted by the Firearms (Amendment) Act 1988, s.2(2), the purpose of the substitution being to bring within the requirement of a firearms certificate certain shot guns which were at one time exempted (see 1988 Act, s.2(1)). Regard should also be had to s.7(2) of the 1988 Act, which (subject to s.7(3) — shortening of barrels by a registered firearms' dealer for the sole purpose of replacing parts) provides:

> "Any weapon which—
>> (a) has at any time since the coming into force of section 2 above been a weapon to which section 1 of the principal Act [i.e., the 1968 Act] applies; or
>> (b) would at any previous time have been such a weapon if those sections had then been in force,
> shall, if it has, or at any time has had, a rifled barrel less than 24 inches in length, be treated as a weapon to which section 1 of the Principal Act applies notwithstanding anything done for the purpose of converting it into a shot gun or an air weapon."

Cf. Creaser v. Tunnifcliffe [1977] 1 W.L.R. 1493, and the case of *R. v. Hucklebridge* [1980] 1 W.L.R. 1284, CA which overruled it.

[3] A gun which has been adapted to have such a magazine is not considered to comply with this sub-paragraph unless the magazine bears an approved mark and the adaptation has been carried out by an approved person: s.1(3A), added by the Firearms (Amendment) Act 1988, s.2(3).

[4] See s.57(2B), as added by the Firearms (Amendment) Act 1988, s.25(2), which provides: "'revolver' in relation to a smooth-bore gun, means a gun containing a series of chambers which revolve when the gun is fired."

[5] Air guns, air rifles and air pistols all include guns, rifles and pistols powered by compressed carbon dioxide gas: Firearms (Amendment) Act 1997, s.48. (That provision reverses *R. v. Thorpe* [1987] 1 W.L.R. 383, CA and *Peat (t/a Paintball Consortium) v. Lees*, 1993 S.C.C.R. 256.)

not of a type declared by rules[6] made by the Secretary of State under section 53 of this Act to be specially dangerous)."

Section 1(1) also applies to any ammunition for a firearm except, under section 1(4):

> "(a) cartridges containing five or more shot, none of which exceeds .36 inch in diameter;
> (b) ammunition for an air gun, air rifle or air pistol; and
> (c) blank cartridges not more than one inch in diameter measured immediately in front of the rim or cannelure of the base of the cartridge."

The offence under section 1(1) is of strict liability, to the extent that it is immaterial that the accused does not know that what he has in his possession is a firearm[7]; but possession itself requires, of course, knowledge and control.[8]

30.27 *Licences.* The requirements of the Game Licences Act 1860 relating to licences to kill game are unaffected by the Firearms Acts.[9]

30.28 *Shotguns.* Section 2 of the Firearms Act 1968 makes it an offence to possess or purchase or acquire a shotgun without a shotgun certificate[10] or to fail to comply with the conditions of any such certificate one holds.[11]

Under the Firearms (Amendment) Act 1997,[12] the transfer of a shotgun by way of sale, letting on hire, gift or gratuitous loan for a period of more than 72 hours, must be made in person by the transferor to the transferee; the transferee must produce to the transferor the certificate or permit entitling him to purchase or acquire[13] the shotgun; and the transferor must comply with any instructions entered in that certificate or permit. Any failure to comply with these requirements is an offence.[14] Such transfer must also be notified[15] within seven days by any

---

[6] See the Firearms (Dangerous Air Weapons) (Scotland) Rules 1969 (S.I. 1969 No. 270), as amended by the Firearms (Dangerous Air Weapons) (Scotland) (Amendment) Rules 1993 (S.I. 1993 No. 1541), which relate to air weapons (including those disguised as another object) capable of discharging missiles in excess of a stated kinetic energy.

[7] *Smith v. H.M. Advocate*, 1996 S.C.C.R. 49, following *R. v. Hussain* [1981] 1 W.L.R. 416.

[8] See Vol. I, para. 3.40. In *Argo v. Carmichael*, 1990 J.C. 210, it was held that the appellant, who kept his brother's firearm in a locked cupboard and the bolt and firing pin thereof in a locked safe elsewhere in his house, had sufficient knowledge and control to be guilty of an offence under s.1(1). His brother had allowed his own firearm certificate to lapse; but more than "mere custody" was involved, since his brother would not have been able to gain physical possession of the weapon, or its bolt and firing pin, save on application to the appellant.

[9] Firearms Act 1968, s.58(5).

[10] Section 2(1). Maximum penalty, on indictment, five years' and a fine; on summary conviction, six months' and a fine of the statutory maximum: Sched. 6, Pt I, as amended by the Criminal Justice Act 1988, s.44(2), and the Criminal Justice and Public Order Act 1994, Sched. 8, Pt III.

[11] Section 2(2): maximum penalty six months' and a fine of the statutory maximum.

[12] Section 32.

[13] Under s.57(4) of the 1968 Act, "acquire" means hire, accept as a gift or borrow.

[14] Maximum penalty, on summary conviction, six months' and a fine of level 5 on the standard scale: s.36 of the 1997 Act.

[15] See s.33 of the 1997 Act.

party to it who is the holder of a shotgun certificate or visitors' shotgun permit[16] to the chief officer of police who granted the certificate or permit: failure to comply with such notification requirement is an offence.[17]

Pawning. Under Part I of the 1968 Act, business dealings in firearms and **30.29** ammunition are generally restricted to those registered as firearms dealers[18]; and it is a specific offence for "a pawnbroker to take in pawn any firearm or ammunition to which section 1 of [the Act] applies, or a shot gun."[19]

Prohibited weapons. Section 5 of the Firearms Act 1968, which deals with **30.30** prohibited weapons, provides:

> "(1) A person commits an offence if, without the authority of the Secretary of State or the Scottish Ministers (by virtue of provision made under section 63 of the Scotland Act 1998)[20] he has in his possession, or purchases or acquires, or manufactures, sells or transfers—
>
> (a)[21] any firearm which is so designed or adapted that two or more missiles can be successively discharged without repeated pressure on the trigger;
>
> (ab)[22] any self-loading or pump-action[23] rifled gun other than one which is chambered for .22 rim-fire cartridges;
>
> (aba)[24] any firearm which either has a barrel less than 30 centimetres in length or is less than 60 centimetres in length overall, other than an air weapon, a muzzle-loading gun[25] or a firearm designed as signalling apparatus[26];

---

[16] Firearms (Amendment) Act 1988, s.17.

[17] Maximum penalty, on summary conviction, six months' and a fine of level 5 on the standard scale: s.36 of the 1997 Act.

[18] See Pt II of the Act, ss. 33–39, 40–45, and Sched. 4, for registration of dealers.

[19] Section 3(6). Maximum penalty three months' and a fine of level 3 on the standard scale.

[20] Amended from "Defence Council" by the Transfer of Functions (Prohibited Weapons) Order 1968. (S.I. 1968 No. 1200). Under s.63 of the Scotland Act, such functions may be exercised by the Scottish Ministers, if an appropriate Order in Council is passed: see the Scotland Act 1998 (Transfer of Functions etc.) Order 1999 (S.I. 1999 No. 1750), Art. 6(1), Sched. 5, para. 3(2). The authority required must be in writing, and conditions may be attached: s.5(3),(4). It is an offence for a person to fail to comply with such conditions (s.5(5)): maximum penalty, on summary conviction, six months' and fine of level 5 on the standard scale.

[21] Substituted by s.1(2) of the Firearms (Amendment) Act 1988.

[22] Inserted by s.1(2) of the Firearms (Amendment) Act 1982, and amended by the Firearms (Amendment) Act 1997, s.1(3).

[23] For "self-loading" and "pump-action", see the Firearms Act 1968, s.57(2A), as inserted by the Firearms (Amendment) Act 1988, s.25(2).

[24] Inserted by the Firearms (Amendment) Act 1997, s.1(2), and amended by the Firearms Amendment (No. 2) Act 1997, s.1.

[25] For "muzzle-loading gun", see s.5(9) of the Firearms Act 1968, as inserted by the Firearms (Amendment) Act 1997, s.1(6).

[26] In this paragraph, and in paragraph (ac) *infra*, any detachable, folding, retractable or other moveable butt-stock is to be disregarded in measuring the length of the firearm: s.5(8) of the Firearms Act 1968, as inserted by s.1(6) of the Firearms (Amendment) Act 1997.

    (ac)[27] any self-loading or pump-action smooth-bore gun which is not an air weapon or chambered for .22 rim fire cartridges and either has a barrel less than 24 inches in length or is less than 40 inches in length overall[28];

    (ad)[29] any smooth-bore revolver[30] gun other than one which is chambered for 9 mm. rim-fire cartridges or a muzzle-loading gun;

    (ae)[31] any rocket launcher, or any mortar, for projecting a stabilised missile, other than a launcher or mortar designed for line-throwing or pyrotechnic purposes or as a signalling apparatus;

    (b) any weapon of whatever description designed or adapted[32] for the discharge of any noxious liquid, gas or other thing[33]; and

    (c)[34] any cartridge with a bullet designed to explode on or immediately before impact, any ammunition containing or designed or adapted to contain any such noxious thing as is mentioned in paragraph (b) above and, if capable of being used with a firearm of any description, any grenade, bomb (or other like missile), or rocket or shell designed to explode as aforesaid.[35]

(1A)[36] Subject to section 5A[37] of this Act, a person commits an offence if, without the authority of the Secretary of State or the Scottish Ministers (by virtue of provision made under section 63 of the Scotland Act 1998), he has in his possession, or purchases or acquires, or sells or transfers—

    (a) any firearm which is disguised as another object;

    (b) any rocket or ammunition not falling within paragraph (c) of subsection (1) of this section which consists in or incorporates

---

[27] Inserted by s.1(2) of the Firearms (Amendment) Act 1988 and amended by s.1(4) and Sched. 3 of the Firearms (Amendment) Act 1997.

[28] *cf. Peat (t/a Paintball Consortium) v. Lees*, 1993 S.C.C.R. 256: the weapons discussed in that case would now be classified as air guns — see the Firearms (Amendment) Act 1997, s.48.

[29] Inserted by the Firearms (Amendment) Act 1988, s.1(2), and amended by s.1(5) of the Firearms (Amendment) Act 1997.

[30] For "revolver", see s.57(2B) of the Firearms Act 1968, inserted by s.25(2) of the Firearms (Amendment) Act 1988.

[31] Inserted by s.1(2) of the Firearms (Amendment) Act 1988.

[32] A harmless container is not "adapted" for the discharge of a noxious liquid merely by being filled with that liquid: *R. v. Formosa* [1991] 2 Q.B. 1 (where a washing-up liquid bottle, filled with hydrochloric acid, was found in the defendant's inside jacket-pocket).

[33] It was held by the House of Lords that an electric stunning device was a prohibited weapon, since it emitted electricity at a very high voltage and was therefore within the terms of this paragraph, although no physical object or substance was ejected from the device: *Flack v. Baldry* [1988] 1 W.L.R. 393.

[34] Substituted by s.1(3) of the Firearms (Amendment) Act 1988.

[35] Maximum penalty 10 years' and a fine on indictment, six months' and a fine of level 5 on the standard scale on summary conviction: Firearms Act 1968, Sched. 6, Pt I, as amended by the Criminal Justice and Public Order Act 1994, Sched. 8.

[36] Inserted by the Firearms Acts (Amendment) Regulations 1992 (S.I. 1992 No. 2823), reg. 3(1), and amended by the Scotland Act 1998 (Transfer of Functions to the Scottish Ministers etc.) Order 1999 (S.I. 1999 No. 1750), Art. 6(1), Sched. 5, para. 3(2).

[37] Section 5A contains various exemptions from the requirement to have the authority of the Secretary of State or the Scottish Ministers relative to the prohibited weapons and ammunition specified in this subsection: s.5A of the Firearms Act 1968 was inserted by the Firearms Acts (Amendment) Regulations 1992 (S.I. 1992 No. 2823), reg. 3(4), and amended by the Scotland Act 1998 (Transfer of Functions to the Scottish Ministers etc.) Order 1999 (S.I. 1999 No. 1750), Art. 6(1), Sched. 5, para. 3(3).

a missile designed to explode on or immediately before impact and is for military use;

(c) any launcher or other projecting apparatus not falling within paragraph (ae) of that subsection which is designed to be used with any rocket or ammunition falling within paragraph (b) above or with ammunition which would fall within that paragraph but for its being ammunition falling within paragraph (c) of that subsection;

(d) any ammunition for military use which consists in or incorporates a missile designed so that a substance contained in the missile will ignite on or immediately before impact;

(e) any ammunition for military use which consists in or incorporates a missile designed, on account of its having a jacket and hard-core, to penetrate armour plating, armour screening or body armour;

(f)[38] any ammunition which incorporates a missile designed or adapted to expand on impact;

(g) anything which is designed to be projected as a missile from any weapon and is designed to be, or has been, incorporated, in—

    (i) any ammunition falling within any of the preceding paragraphs; or

    (ii) any ammunition which would fall within any of those paragraphs but for its being specified in subsection (1) of this section.[39]

(2)[40] The weapons and ammunition specified in subsections (1) and (1A) of this section (including, in the case of ammunition, and missiles falling within subsection (1A)(g) of this section) are referred to in this Act as 'prohibited weapons' and 'prohibited ammunition' respectively".

In addition, section 1(4) of the Firearms (Amendment) Act 1988 empowers the Secretary of State to apply the provisions of the Firearms Act 1968 relating to prohibited weapons and ammunition to any other firearm (other than an air weapon) not lawfully on sale in Great Britain in substantial numbers before 1988 which appears to him to be especially dangerous or wholly or partly composed of material making it not readily detectable by a metal detector, as well as to any ammunition which appears to him to be specially dangerous.

Further, section 7(1) of the Firearms (Amendment) Act 1988[41] provides:

"Any weapon which—

(a) has at any time (whether before or after the passing of the Firearms (Amendment) Act 1997) been a weapon of a kind described in section 5(1) or (1A) of the principal Act (including any amendments to section 5(1) made under section 1(4) of this Act); and

---

[38] Substituted by s.9 of the Firearms (Amendment) Act 1997.

[39] Maximum penalty, on indictment, 10 years' and a fine; and on summary conviction, six months' and a fine of the statutory maximum (the Firearms Acts (Amendment) Regulations 1998 (S.I. 1998 No. 2823), reg. 3(6), as amended by the Criminal Justice and Public Order Act 1994, Sched. 8).

[40] As amended by the Firearms Acts (Amendment) Regulations 1992 (S.I. 1992 No. 2823), reg. 3(2).

[41] As amended by the Firearms (Amendment) Act 1997, Sched. 2, para. 16.

(b) is not a self-loading or pump-action smooth-bore gun which has at any such time been such a weapon by reason only of having had a barrel less than 24 inches in length,

shall be treated as a prohibited weapon notwithstanding anything done for the purpose of converting it into a weapon of a different kind".

If a weapon, prohibited under section 5(1), is modified in such a way that, for example, it is capable of firing single shots only, it has been held to remain within a prohibited category, since "the language [of section 5(1)(a)] is descriptive of the kind of firearm which is to be subject to the general proposition and not descriptive of any individual weapon at the time it is found to be in the possession of a member of the public. If a firearm is one designed or adapted to achieve continuous fire this establishes its kind or character for the purposes of the general prohibition."[42]

It has also been held that section 5 creates an offence of strict liability, and that it is not a defence to a charge of possessing a CS gas canister that one was reasonably ignorant of the fact that it contained gas.[43]

30.31 *Converting guns.* Section 4 of the Firearms Act 1968 provides:

"(1) Subject to this section, it is an offence to shorten the barrel of a shotgun to a length less than 24 inches.

(2) It is not an offence under subsection (1) above for a registered firearms dealer to shorten the barrel of a shot gun for the sole purpose of replacing a defective part of the barrel so as to produce a barrel not less than 24 inches in length.

(3) It is an offence for a person other than a registered firearms dealer to convert into a firearm anything which, though having the appearance of being a firearm, is so constructed as to be incapable of discharging any missile through its barrel.

(4)[44] A person who commits an offence under section 1 of this Act by having in his possession, or purchasing or acquiring, a shotgun which has been shortened contrary to subsection (1) above or a firearm which has been converted as mentioned in subsection (3) above (whether by a registered firearms dealer or not), without

---

[42] *Jessop v. Stevenson*, 1988 S.L.T. 223, opinion of the court at 225G. In this case, a bren gun had been modified to fire single shots, but the modification would have taken but a few minutes work to reverse — thus restoring the ability of the gun to fire bullets in bursts, as it was designed to do. The court in *Jessop v. Stevenson* followed the English cases of *R. v. Pannell* (1983) 76 Cr.App.R. 53, CA, where it was also held that possession of all the parts of a stripped down prohibited weapon amounted to possession of a prohibited weapon, and, *R. v. Clarke* [1986] 1 W.L.R. 209, CA, where it was held that possession of a prohibited weapon included possession of the component parts of such a weapon by virtue of s.57(1)(b) of the Firearms Act 1968.

[43] *R. v. Bradish* [1990] 1 Q.B. 981, CA. In that case, the defendant was found to have had an aerosol of CS gas about his person. It was accepted that such gas was noxious and that, together with its container, the gas formed a prohibited weapon within the meaning of s.5(1)(b) of the 1968 Act. Auld J., in giving the opinion of the Court, said (at 992G) that s.5 created an absolute offence, and that it was no defence that the defendant did not know, and could not reasonably have been expected to know, that the container was filled with CS gas. (The defendant's case was somewhat weakened, however, by the fact that the canister was clearly marked with a description of its contents.)

[44] As amended by the Firearms (Amendment) Act 1988, s.23(1).

holding a firearm certificate authorising him to have it in his possession, or to purchase or acquire it, shall be treated for the purposes of the provisions of this Act relating to the punishment of offences as committing that offence in an aggravated form."[45]

Section 6 of the Firearms (Amendment) Act 1988 provides:

"(1) Subject to subsection (2) below, it is an offence to shorten to a length less than 24 inches the barrel of any smooth-bore gun to which section 1 of the principal Act [*i.e.*, the Firearms Act 1968] applies other than one which has a barrel with a bore exceeding 2 inches in diameter; and that offence shall be punishable—
  (a) on summary conviction, with imprisonment for a term not exceeding six months or a fine not exceeding the statutory maximum or both;
  (b) on indictment, with imprisonment for a term not exceeding five years or a fine or both.
(2) It is not an offence under this section for a registered firearms dealer to shorten the barrel of a gun for the sole purpose of replacing a defective part of the barrel so as to produce a barrel not less than 24 inches in length."

Sale to drunk or insane persons. Section 25 of the Firearms Act 1968 **30.32** provides:

"It is an offence for a person to sell or transfer any firearm or ammunition to, or to repair, prove or test any firearm or ammunition for, another person whom he knows or has reasonable cause for believing to be drunk or of unsound mind."[46]

Children. Section 22 of the Firearms Act 1968 provides: **30.33**

"(1) It is an offence for a person under the age of seventeen to purchase or hire any firearm or ammunition.[47]
  (1A)[48] Where a person under the age of eighteen is entitled, as the holder of a certificate under this Act, to have a firearm in his possession, it is an offence for that person to use that firearm for a purpose not authorised by the European weapons directive.[49]
  (2)[50] It is an offence for a person under the age of fourteen to have in his possession any firearm or ammunition to which section 1 of this Act applies, except in circumstances where under section 11

---

[45] Maximum penalty under both ss. 4(1) and 4(3), seven years' and a fine on indictment, six months' and a fine of level 5 on the standard scale on summary conviction: 1968 Act, Sched. 6, Pt I, as amended by the Criminal Justice and Public Order Act 1994, Sched. 8.

[46] Maximum penalty three months' and a fine of level 3 on the standard scale.

[47] Maximum penalty on summary conviction, six months' and a fine of level 5 on the standard scale: 1968 Act, Sched. 6, Pt I.

[48] Inserted by the Firearms Acts (Amendment) Regulations 1992 (S.I. 1992 No. 2823), reg. 4(1).

[49] Maximum penalty on summary conviction, three months' and a fine of level 5 on the standard scale: 1968 Act, Sched. 6, Pt I, added by the Firearms Acts (Amendment) Regulations 1992 (S.I. 1992 No. 2823), reg. 4(4). The "European weapons directive" means the directive of the Council of the European Communities, No. 91/477 EEC (O.J., £256, 12.09.91, P.51): 1968 Act, s.57(4), added by S.I. 1992 No. 2823, *supra*, reg. 5(2)(c).

[50] As amended by the Firearms (Amendment) Act 1988, s.23(4).

(1), (3) or (4) of this Act or section 15 of the Firearms (Amendment) Act 1988 he is entitled to have possession of it without holding a firearm certificate.[51]

(3) It is an offence for a person under the age of fifteen to have with him an assembled shotgun except while under the supervision of a person of or over the age of twenty-one, or while the shotgun is so covered with a securely fastened gun cover that it cannot be fired."[52]

Section 24 provides:

"(1) It is an offence to sell or let on hire any firearm or ammunition to a person under the age of seventeen.

(2) It is an offence—

(a) to make a gift of or lend any firearm or ammunition to which section 1 of this Act applies to a person under the age of fourteen; or

(b)[53] to part with the possession of any such firearm or ammunition to a person under that age, except in circumstances where that person is entitled under section 11(1), (3) or (4) of this Act or section 15 of the Firearms (Amendment) Act 1988 to have possession thereof without holding a firearm certificate.

(3) It is an offence to make a gift of a shotgun or ammunition for a shotgun to a person under the age of fifteen

. . .

(5) In proceedings for an offence under any provision of this section it is a defence to prove that the person charged with the offence believed the other person to be of or over the age mentioned in that provision and had reasonable ground for the belief."[54]

30.34 *Unlawful Possession of Firearms.* POSSESSION WITH INTENT TO COMMIT OFFENCES OR RESIST ARREST. Section 18 of the Firearms Act 1968 provides:

"(1) It is an offence for a person to have with him[55] a firearm or imitation firearm with intent to commit [any offence specified in

---

[51] Maximum penalty, as for s.22(1A): see n.49, *supra*.

[52] Maximum penalty on summary conviction, a fine of level 3 on the standard scale: 1968 Act, Sched. 6, Pt I.

[53] As amended by the Firearms (Amendment) Act 1988, s.23(4).

[54] Maximum penalty for a s.24(1) or (2) offence, on summary conviction, six months' and a fine of level 5 on the standard scale; and for a s.24(3) offence, on summary conviction, a fine of level 3 on the standard scale: 1968 Act, Sched. 6, Pt I.

[55] *cf. infra*, para. 30.46. It has been held that it is not necessary to prove that at some time before its actual use the firearm was being carried with the intention of using it, and that the ratio of such cases as *R. v. Jura* [1954] 1 Q.B. 503 (see para. 30.46, *infra*) does not apply to s.18: *R. v. Houghton (Andrew)* [1982] Crim.L.R. 112. The English courts also take the view that "have with him" is wider than "carry", and extends to all situations where there was a close physical link between the defendant and the firearm and a degree of immediate control by him over it: see *R. v. Kelt* [1977] 1 W.L.R. 1365, CA; *cf. R. v. Jones (Keith)* [1987] 1 W.L.R. 692, CA; *R. v. Pawlicki; R. v. Swindell* [1992] 1 W.L.R. 827.

paragraphs 1 to 18 of Schedule 2 to this Act],[56] or to resist arrest or to prevent the arrest of another, in either case while he has the fircarm or imitation firearm with him.[57]

(2) In proceedings for an offence under this section proof that the accused had a firearm or imitation firearm with him and intended to commit an offence, or to resist or prevent arrest, is evidence that he intended to have it with him while doing so."

POSSESSION IN PUBLIC. Section 19 of the Firearms Act 1968 provides: **30.35**

"A person commits an offence if without lawful authority[58] or reasonable excuse (the proof whereof lies on him) he has with him[59] in a public place[60] a loaded shotgun or loaded air weapon, or any other firearm (whether loaded or not) together with ammunition suitable for use in that firearm."[61]

TRESPASSING. Section 20 of the Firearms Act 1968, as amended by the **30.36** Firearms (Amendment) Act 1994, section 2(1), provides:

"(1) A person commits an offence if while he has a firearm or imitation firearm with him, he enters or is in any building or part of

---

[56] It has been held in England that the ingredients of this offence are, that the defendant had a firearm with him, that he intended to have it with him (owing to the form of s.18(2), *infra*), and that at the same time as he had it with him he intended to commit one of the specified offences; and that consequently it is not necessary to show that he intended to use or carry the firearm in furtherance of the intended offence: *R. v. Stoddart (John)* (1998) 2 Cr.App.R. 25, CA. In that case, the defendant's contention, that he had the firearm with him not to use in furtherance of a robbery on a security guard but rather to sell it, was considered irrelevant.

The offences listed in this Schedule are as follows: abduction, administration of drugs with intent to enable or assist the commission of a crime, assault, housebreaking with intent to steal, malicious mischief, mobbing and rioting, perverting the course of justice, prison-breaking and breaking into prison to rescue prisoners, rape, robbery, theft, use of threats with intent to extort money or property, wilful fire raising and culpable and reckless fire raising, and (as amended by the Civic Government (Scotland) Act 1982, Sched. 3, para. 2) contraventions of the following statutory provisions: Explosive Substances Act 1883, ss. 2 to 4; Police (Scotland) Act 1967, s.41; Civic Government (Scotland) Act 1982, s.57; Road Traffic Act 1988, s.178. Paragraph 19 of the Schedule refers to attempts to commit any of these offences.

[57] Maximum penalty life imprisonment and a fine: 1968 Act, Sched. 6, Pt I, as amended by the Criminal Justice Act 1988, s.44(3)(b).

[58] The possession of a shotgun certificate is not lawful authority within the meaning of this section: *Ross v. Collins* [1982] Crim. L.R. 368; but it has been held that the exercise of a public right of recreation on the foreshore is: *McLeod v. McLeod*, 1982 S.C.C.R. 130, Sh.Ct.

[59] *cf.* n. 55, *supra*; also *cf. McVey v. Friel*, 1996 S.C.C.R. 768.

[60] In *Anderson v. Miller* (1977) 64 Cr.App.R. 178 it was held to be an offence to keep a firearm behind the counter of a shop, although the public were not allowed into that part of the shop: *cf. Cawley v. Frost* [1976] 1 W.L.R. 1207.

[61] There is no requirement that the defendant or accused should be shown to have known that the shotgun he was carrying was loaded: *R. v. Harrison* (1996) 1 Cr.App.R. 138, Rougier J., at 141D-G; *Smith v. H.M. Advocate*, 1996 S.C.C.R. 49, Sheriff Mitchell at 50D. Maximum penalty six months' and a fine of level 5 on the standard scale on summary conviction, seven years' and a fine on indictment (but not if an air weapon); 1968 Act, Sched. 6, Pt I, as amended by the Criminal Justice and Public Order Act 1994, Sched. 8.

a building as a trespasser and without reasonable excuse (the proof whereof lies on him).[62]

(2) A person commits an offence if while he has a firearm or imitation firearm with him he enters or is on any land[63] as a trespasser and without reasonable excuse (the proof whereof lies on him)."[64]

30.37 POSSESSING FIREARMS WITH INTENT TO INJURE. Section 16 of the Firearms Act 1968 provides:

"It is an offence for a person to have in his possession any firearm or ammunition with intent by means thereof to endanger life[65] or cause serious injury to property, or to enable another person by means thereof to endanger life or cause serious injury to property, whether any injury to person or property has been caused or not."[66]

30.38 POSSESSING FIREARMS WITH INTENT TO CAUSE FEAR OF VIOLENCE. Section 16A[67] of the Firearms Act 1968 provides:

"It is an offence for a person to have in his possession any firearm or imitation firearm with intent—
(a) by means thereof to cause, or
(b) to enable another person by means thereof to cause,
any person to believe that unlawful violence will be used against him or another person."[68]

---

[62] Maximum penalty on indictment (but not if the weapon was an imitation firearm or an air weapon), seven years' and a fine; on summary conviction, six months' and a fine of level 5 on the standard scale: 1968 Act, Sched. 6, Pt I, as amended by the Criminal Justice and Public Order Act 1994, Sched. 8.

[63] Including land covered with water: s.20(3).

[64] A person who has authority to be on land for one purpose (*e.g.* shooting vermin) may become a trespasser if he enters that land for another purpose (*e.g.* shooting deer): see *Ferguson v. MacPhail*, 1987 S.C.C.R. 52. Maximum penalty for an offence under s.19(2), on summary conviction, three months' and a fine of level 4 on the standard scale: 1968 Act, Sched. 6, Pt I.

[65] In *R. v. Norton* [1977] Crim.L.R. 478 this was held not to include the accused's own life: *cf. Bryan v. Mott* (1976) 62 Cr.App.R. 71; *infra*, para. 30.45.

[66] Maximum penalty on indictment, life imprisonment: 1968 Act, Sched. 6, Pt I, as amended by the Criminal Justice Act 1972, s.28(2), which is applicable to Scotland by virtue of s.66(7)(a). The intention need not be to use the weapons immediately or unconditionally: *R. v. Bentham* [1973] 1 Q.B. 357, CA; nor to use them in Scotland or even the U.K.: *R. v. El-Hakkaoui* [1975] 1 W.L.R. 396, CA. It has been held in England that the intention to endanger life must be for an unlawful purpose, so that where the purpose is self-defence, s.16 has not been contravened: *R. v. Georgiades* [1989] 1 W.L.R. 759, CA; but the court expressed the view that cases where such a defence could be raised would be rare: *cf.* the offensive weapons cases of *Grieve v. MacLeod*, 1967 J.C. 32, and *Evans v. Hughes* [1972] 1 W.L.R. 1452. It has been held in England that "with intent to enable another person by means thereof to endanger life" means more than giving another the opportunity to endanger life, since that would be to make this part of the offence one of (almost) strict liability; certainly it would then allow the offence to encapsulate the giving of the firearm to an irresponsible person: for conviction, therefore, it would have to be shown that the defendant possessed (since the offence is not concerned with supply) the firearm with intention that another person would then be enabled to endanger life: *R. v. Jones (Ivor)* [1997] Q.B. 798, CA.

[67] Inserted by the Firearms (Amendment) Act 1994, s.1(1).

[68] Maximum penalty, on indictment, 10 years' and a fine: 1968 Act, Sched. 6, Pt I, as inserted by the Firearms (Amendment) Act 1994, s.1(2).

POSSESSION BY EX-PRISONERS. Section 21[69] of the Firearms Act 1968 **30.39**
prohibits a person who has been sentenced to more than three months'
detention from possessing[70] a firearm or ammunition for five years after
his release, without special permission.[71] Where the sentence is for more
than three years the duration of the prohibition is unlimited.[72] Contravention of these provisions is an offence.[73] It is also an offence to sell or
transfer a firearm or ammunition or to test or repair a firearm or
ammunition for a person one knows or has reasonable ground for
believing to be such a person.[74]

Use of firearms in connection with arrest. Section 17 of the Firearms Act **30.40**
1968 provides:

> "(1) It is an offence for a person to make or attempt to make any
> use whatsoever of a firearm[75] or imitation firearm with intent to
> resist or prevent the lawful arrest or detention of himself or another
> person.[76]
> (2) If a person, at the time of his committing or being arrested for
> an offence specified in Schedule 2[77] to this Act, has in his possession
> a firearm or imitation firearm, he shall be guilty of an offence under
> this subsection unless he shows that he had it in his possession for a
> lawful object."[78]

Air guns. Section 22 of the Firearms Act 1968 provides: **30.41**

---

[69] As amended by the Criminal Justice Act 1972, ss. 29 and 66(7)(a), the Criminal Law
Act 1977, Sched. 9, para. 9, the Criminal Justice Act 1982, Sched. 14, para. 24(a),(b), the
Criminal Justice and Public Order Act 1994, Sched. 10, para. 24, and the Crime and
Disorder Act 1998, s.121(6)(g) and Sched. 8, para. 14.

[70] Possession requires knowledge and control beyond mere reluctant picking up and
handing to the police (at their request) a firearm which belonged to the accused's brother,
and which happened to be present in a house which the accused was visiting: *Davis v.
Buchanan*, 1994 S.C.C.R. 369.

[71] See s.21(2); see also subss. (2A), (3) and (3A).

[72] Firearms Act 1968, s.21(1). Where consecutive sentences are imposed, the relevant
period for the purposes of s.21 is that of their aggregate: *Davis v. Tomlinson* (1980) 71
Cr.App.R. 279.

[73] Section 21(4). Maximum penalty, on indictment, five years' and a fine, on summary
conviction, six months' and a fine of level 5 on the standard scale: 1968 Act, Sched. 6, Pt 1,
as amended by the Criminal Justice and Public Order Act 1994, Sched. 8, Pt III.

[74] Section 21(5). Maximum penalty, as above for s.21(4): see n.73, *supra*. For removal of
the prohibition, see s.21(6), as amended by the Criminal Justice Act 1972, s.29.

[75] As defined in s.57(1) without paragraphs (b) and (c) thereof: s.17(4).

[76] Responsibility is strict and it is not necessary for the Crown to prove that the accused
knew that the weapon he had was a "firearm": *R v. Pierre* [1963] Crim.L.R. 513 (a decision
under s.23 of the Firearms Act 1937). Maximum penalty life imprisonment: 1968 Act,
Sched. 6, Pt I, as amended by the Criminal Justice Act 1972, s.28(2) which is applicable to
Scotland under s.66(7).

[77] Relative to Scotland, Sched. 2 is substituted for Sched. 1 by virtue of s.17(5). For the
offences referred to in Sched. 2, see n.56, *supra*.

[78] Maximum penalty life in prison and a fine: 1968 Act, Sched. 6, Pt I, as amended by
the Criminal Justice Act 1988, s.44(3). Penalties under s.17 are in addition to any penalty
imposed for the offence in connection with which the contravention occurred. It is not
necessary for a conviction under s.17(2) that it be proved in respect of an arrest for a
scheduled offence that the accused committed the scheduled offence for which he was
arrested: *R. v. Nelson* [2001] 1 Q.B. 55, CA, distinguishing the apparently contrary reading
of the offence in *R. v. Baker* [1962] 2 Q.B. 530 (a decision in terms of s.23(2) of the
Firearms Act 1937).

"(4) Subject to section 23 below, it is an offence for a person under the age of fourteen to have with him an air weapon[79] or ammunition for an air weapon.[80]

(5) Subject to section 23 below, it is an offence for a person under the age of seventeen to have an air weapon with him in a public place, except an air gun or air rifle which is so covered with a securely fastened gun cover that it cannot be fired."[81]

Section 22(4) does not apply where the person under 14 is under the supervision of a person of or over 21.[82] Nor is it an offence under either subsection for a person to have an air weapon or ammunition when engaged as a member of an approved rifle club in connection with shooting practice, or when using the weapon or ammunition at a shooting gallery where only air weapons or miniature rifles are used.[83]

Section 24(4) makes it an offence to give an air weapon or ammunition for an air weapon to a person under 14 or to part with possession of such a weapon or ammunition to a person under 14 except where he is permitted to have them under section 23.[84]

30.42 *Crossbows.* Crossbows may or may not be firearms within the meaning of the Firearms Act 1968 depending upon their design[85]; but, under section 3 of the Crossbows Act 1987, it is an offence for a person under the age of 17 to have with him a crossbow which is capable of discharging a missile[86] or parts of a crossbow which can (without any other parts) be assembled to form a crossbow capable of such discharge, unless he is under the supervision of a person of at least 21 years of age.[87] It is also an offence for a person under 17 years of age to buy or hire a crossbow or any part of same[88]: conversely, it is an offence for A to sell or let on hire a crossbow or a part thereof to a person under the age of 17, unless A believes on reasonable grounds that that person is of the age of 17 years or above.[89] Crossbows may, however, be offensive weapons.[90]

---

[79] As defined in s.1(3)(b) of the 1968 Act, an air weapon is an air rifle, air gun or air pistol not of a type declared by rules made by the Secretary of State to be specially dangerous.

[80] Maximum penalty, on summary conviction, a fine of level 3 on the standard scale: 1968 Act, Sched. 6, Pt I.

[81] Maximum penalty, as for s.22(4): *supra* at n.80.

[82] Section 23(1). It is, however, an offence for such a person under 14 who is under supervision on any premises to use the air weapon to fire any missile beyond those premises, and also an offence for his supervisor to allow him to so use it (s.23(1)(a), (b)): maximum penalty for either offence, on summary conviction, a fine of level 3 on the standard scale: 1968 Act, Sched. 6, Pt I.

[83] Section 23(2), as amended by the Firearms (Amendment) Act 1988, s.23(4) and the Firearms (Amendment) Act 1997, Sched. 2, para. 3, and Sched. 3.

[84] Maximum penalty a fine of level 3 on the standard scale: 1968 Act, Sched. 6, Pt I. Section 24(5) applies: *supra*, para. 30.33.

[85] *cf. Boyd v. McGlennan*, 1994 S.L.T. 1148 (speargun considered to be a firearm within the meaning of s.57(1) of the 1968 Act).

[86] There is an exception under s.5 for crossbows with a draw weight of less than 1.4 kg.

[87] Maximum penalty, on summary conviction, a fine of level 3 on the standard scale: s.6(2).

[88] Section 2. Maximum penalty as for s.3: see n.87, *supra*.

[89] Section 1. Maximum penalty, on summary conviction, six months' and a fine of level 5 on the standard scale: s.6(1).

[90] See paras 30.43 *et seq.*, *infra*.

II — Offensive weapons

Section 47 of the Criminal Law (Consolidation) (Scotland) Act 1995 **30.43** which applies both to firearms and to any other "offensive weapon" provides as follows:

"(1) Any person who without lawful authority or reasonable excuse, the proof whereof shall lie on him, has with him in any public place any offensive weapon shall be guilty of an offence . . ."[91]

(4)[92] . . . 'public place' includes any road within the meaning of the Roads (Scotland) Act 1984 and any other premises or place to which at the material time the public have or are permitted to have access whether on payment or otherwise; and 'offensive weapon' means any article made or adapted for use for causing injury to the person, or intended by the person having it with him for such use by him or by some other person."[93]

Offensive weapons fall into three classes — those made for use for **30.44** causing personal injury, those adapted for such use, and those not so made or adapted but intended by the accused for such use.

(i) *Weapons made for use for causing personal injury.* This class probably includes guns (other than airguns,[94] shotguns[95] and other guns used for killing game), flick knives,[96] nunchucka sticks,[97] flails,[98] shuriken (Chinese throwing stars),[99] swordsticks,[1] knuckledusters, coshes,[2] bayonets and daggers[3] (except, perhaps, where the latter are worn as part

---

[91] Maximum penalty on indictment four years' and a fine, and on summary conviction six months' and a fine of the statutory maximum: s.47(1)(a), (b), as amended by the Offensive Weapons Act 1996, s.2. The court may also make an order for forfeiture of the weapon: s.47(2). The burden of proof on the accused is probably an evidential one: see para. 30.13, *supra.*

[92] As amended by the Offensive Weapons Act 1996, s.5.

[93] Under s.49A(2) of the Act, inserted by the Offensive Weapons Act 1996, s.4(3), it is an offence for a person to have with him on school premises an offensive weapon within the meaning of s.47: maximum penalty, on indictment, four years' and a fine; on summary conviction, six months' and a fine of the statutory maximum: s.49A(5)(b). "School premises" mean land used for the purposes of a school but excluding any land occupied solely as a dwelling by a person employed at the school: "school" has the same meaning as in s.135(1) of the Education (Scotland) Act 1980, and includes schools for primary and secondary education, nursery schools, special schools, grant-aided schools and independent schools; defences are set out in s.49A(3) and (4).

[94] *R. v. Jura* [1954] 1 Q.B. 503.

[95] *R. v. Hodgson* [1954] Crim.L.R. 379.

[96] See *Tudhope v. O'Neill*, 1982 S.C.C.R. 45, where the inclusion of such knives in s.1(1)(a) of the Restriction of Offensive Weapons Act 1959 (see para. 30.48, *infra*) was held sufficient to make them offensive weapons *per se.* See also *Gibson v. Wales* [1983] 1 W.L.R. 393; *R. v. Simpson (Calvin)* [1983] 1 W.L.R. 1494.

[97] See *Hemming v. Annan*, 1982 S.C.C.R. 432; *Kincaid v. Tudhope*, 1983 S.C.C.R. 389.

[98] See *Glendinning v. Guild*, 1988 S.L.T. 252 (Notes).

[99] See *McGlennan v. Clark*, 1993 S.C.C.R. 334, which was based on the inclusion of such items (as weapons not to be manufactured, sold or hired, offered for sale or hire, exposed for sale, or possessed for sale or hire, or lent or given to any other person) — in terms of s.141 of the Criminal Justice Act 1988 in the list set out in the Schedule to the Criminal Justice Act 1988 (Offensive Weapons) Order 1988 (S.I. 1988 No. 2019).

[1] *Davis v. Alexander* (1971) 54 Cr.App.R. 398.

[2] See *Latham v. Vannet*, 1999 S.C.C.R. 119; *cf. McKee v. MacDonald*, 1995 S.C.C.R. 512.

[3] See *Houston v. Snape*, 1993 S.C.C.R. 995; see also I. Brownlie, "The Prevention of Crime Act, 1953" [1961] Crim.L.R. 19, at 28.

of ceremonial, fancy or Highland dress[4]). In the case of these weapons the Crown need prove only that the accused had one with him, and it is then for him to show that he had it "with lawful authority or reasonable excuse".[5] Where an article has both an offensive and an innocent use, it is not a weapon of this class.[6]

(ii) Weapons adapted for use for causing personal injury. This class includes weapons like broken bottles, razor blades stuck in potatoes, severed pieces of bicycle chain, webbed belts with metal studs placed in them, and domestic or industrial tools or cutlery which have been filed or sharpened for use as weapons.[7] In these cases, too, the Crown need prove only that the accused had with him a weapon of this kind.

(iii) All other weapons, such as razors,[8] shotguns, dirks, skeandhus,[9] air rifles,[10] or sheath knives.[11] In such cases it is for the Crown to show that the accused had the weapon with the intention of using it to cause personal injury,[12] and this means both that the *onus* remains on the Crown throughout, for the Crown must always prove that the weapon was an "offensive weapon" in terms of the section, and that in many cases once the intention has been proved there is an end to the case. An intention to cause injury is enough, whether the use is defensive or offensive,[13] unless the accused can invoke the defence of lawful authority or reasonable excuse.[14] The intention must, in England, be shown to exist at the time of the charge, an earlier intention subsequently abandoned (or carried out?) is irrelevant.[15]

In order to prove that a weapon in class (iii) is an offensive weapon the Crown must prove that it was intended to be used to cause personal injury, so that if it appears that the weapon was intended for use to cause injury to property the charge will fall.[16] Whether or not there is intention to cause personal injury is a question of fact and circumstances[17]: thus, for example, where the accused went to the door of a house and attempted to strike the occupant with a spanner when the occupant answered to the accused's knocking, and where the accused also used aggressive language which seemed to challenge the occupant to fight, the

---

[4] See *infra*, n.8.

[5] *R. v. Petrie* [1961] 1 W.L.R. 358, Salmon J. at 361.

[6] See *Woods v. Heywood*, 1988 S.L.T. 849 (machete, both a tool and a weapon); *Coull v. Guild*, 1986 S.L.T. 184 (Notes) (sheath knife).

[7] I. Brownlie, *op. cit.* at 29. It was held in *McLaughlin v. Tudhope*, 1987 S.C.C.R. 456, that an article consisting of a knife at one end and a potato peeler at the other had not been "adapted" simply because the potato peeling blade was missing, as was the cover for the knife: there was also, it seems, no evidence that the accused had performed these "modifications" (although this is not a requirement of the statutory provision).

[8] *R. v. Petrie* [1961] 1 W.L.R. 358.

[9] *Macleod v. Green* [1954] C.L.Y. 3670; see (1954) 66 J.R. 165.

[10] *R. v. Jura* [1954] 1 Q.B. 503.

[11] *Woodward v. Koessler* [1958] 1 W.L.R. 1255; *Farrell v. Rennicks*, 1959 S.L.T. (Sh.Ct.) 71; *R. v. Williamson* (1978) 67 Cr.App.R. 35; *Coull v. Guild*, 1986 S.L.T. 184.

[12] *R. v. Petrie* [1961] 1 W.L.R. 358; *Coull v. Guild*, 1986 S.L.T. 184; *Ralston v. Lockhart*, 1986 S.C.C.R. 400; *Kane v. H.M. Advocate*, 1988 S.C.C.R. 585.

[13] *Miller v. Douglas*, 1988 S.C.C.R. 565; *Evans v. Hughes* [1972] 1 W.L.R. 1452; *cf. Skeen v. Gemmell; Skeen v. Smith* (1974) 38 J.C.L. 80.

[14] Which he cannot easily do: see *Geraghty v. Skeen* (1974) 38 J.C.L. 79.

[15] *R. v. Allamby* [1974] 1 W.L.R. 1494.

[16] *Farrell v. Renicks*, 1959 S.L.T. (Sh.Ct.) 71; *Ralston v. Lockhart*, 1986 S.C.C.R. 400.

[17] *Murdoch v. Carmichael*, 1993 S.C.C.R. 494.

necessary intent was found to exist.[18] It appears that an intention to frighten is relevant only where the fright intended is of a kind likely to cause actual injury by shock.[19] But where the weapon falls into class (i) or (ii) the accused must show that he had it with "lawful authority or reasonable excuse", and it would presumably not be a defence in such a case that he intended to use the weapon only to cause injury to property, or for any other unlawful purpose.

"Lawful authority or reasonable excuse".[20] These words have not been **30.45** defined. It may be that a possessor of a class (i) weapon would be entitled to plead "lawful authority" if he had the weapon in the course of his duty as a soldier or policeman or, in the case of a firearm, if he had a licence. It is unlikely, however, that the holder of a firearms licence would be entitled to an acquittal if he had the gun with him at the time for the purpose of causing unlawful personal injury. It is unlikely that anyone can have a class (ii) or class (iii) weapon with lawful authority.

"Reasonable excuse" is a very wide concept. Whether there is such an excuse is a question of fact for the trial court.[21] It may include some forms of self-defence, but to allow a person to carry a weapon "in case" he should become involved in a fight, or because he was going to attend a dance hall where he had been previously assaulted, would be to encourage the type of situation whose occurrence the Act is intended to avoid.[22] But if A carried a weapon in order to protect himself from robbery while he was carrying a large sum of money that might be a reasonable excuse.[23]

In *Grieve v. Macleod*[24] the accused was a taxi-driver who carried a two feet length of rubber hose with a piece of metal in the end of it, which he produced one night during an argument with a customer. His defence was that Edinburgh taxi-drivers are at risk of attack at nights and that it

---

[18] *Wallace v. Ruxton*, 1998 S.C.C.R. 701. *Cf. Orme v. Ruxton*, 1999 S.C.C.R. 344, where the accused's waving a large piece of wood (similar to a table leg) above his head was held not to show the required intent, since there were no persons in the vicinity at the time against whom the accused could have manifested hostility; his act of throwing the wood away when the police approached was considered to be neutral relative to that intent: his conduct prior to that act was considered to have been consistent with mere showing-off. See also *Owens v. Crowe*, 1994 S.C.C.R. 310 (where the fact that a lock knife was taken by the accused to a crowded disco at 11.30 p.m. was considered sufficient to allow an inference of intent to cause personal injury to be drawn), and *Brown v. Kennedy*, 1999 S.C.C.R. 574 (where the fact that a small kitchen knife had been concealed by the accused in his hat prior to his entering a public house, enabled the court to find that the evidence was sufficient for there to be a case for him to answer, in the sense that an intent to cause personal injury was one possible inference to be drawn from the facts and circumstances).

[19] *Woodward v. Koessler* [1958] 1 W.L.R. 1255, as explained by *R. v. Edmonds* [1963] 2 Q.B. 142.

[20] See Vol. I, para. 9.22. R.E.I. Card, "Authority and Excuse as Defences to Crime" [1969] Crim.L.R. 359.

[21] *cf., e.g., Hemming v. Annan*, 1982 S.C.C.R. 432; *Kincaid v. Tudhope*, 1983 S.C.C.R. 389; and *Glendinning.v Guild*, 1988 S.L.T. 252 — all concerned with offensive weapons *per se* used by persons who practised martial arts: a reasonable excuse was denied in the first two cases, but held to have been proved in the third.

[22] See *Miller v. Douglas*, 1988 S.C.C.R. 565. See also I. Brownlie, *op. cit.* at n.33. It has been held that a dance-hall "bouncer" is not entitled to carry a truncheon as part of his uniform: *R. v. Spanner, Poulter and Ward* [1973] Crim.L.R. 704.

[23] In *Evans v. Wright* [1964] Crim.L.R. 466 a wages collector who carried a truncheon to protect himself was convicted of having it in his car on an occasion when he was not carrying wages, the court suggesting that had he been carrying wages his possession would have been lawful.

[24] 1967 J.C. 32.

was customary to carry some object such as a torch which might be used for defence. The sheriff held the article in question was made or adapted for use for causing personal injury, and convicted. The accused's appeal, which was based on "reasonable excuse", failed. Lord Justice-Clerk Grant said:

> "I think that the only general proposition which can be laid down in regard to 'reasonable excuse' is that each individual case must be judged on its own particular facts and circumstances. I do not think it is possible to lay down *ab ante* general rules applicable to classes of persons, whether they be taxi-cab drivers, bank messengers, security guards or vulnerable shopkeepers with a cosh below the counter. Thus, as the appellant's counsel frankly admitted, one must, for example, have regard to the nature of the offensive weapon. There may be circumstances where there is reasonable excuse for carrying a wooden truncheon, but none for carrying a sawn-off shotgun or a butcher's knife. Equally one must keep in mind that quite apart from dealing with what one might call the 'professional' weapon-carrier, one object of [section 47] as I read it, is to ensure that ordinary citizens do not, unless in exceptional and justifiable circumstances, take the law into their own hands."[25]

In *Evans v. Hughes*[26] the excuse offered was that the accused had himself been attacked by three men a week earlier, and was carrying the weapon, a short metal bar, for his own protection. Lord Widgery C.J. said that:

> "[I]t may be a reasonable excuse . . . that the carrier is in anticipation of imminent attack and is carrying it for his own personal defence, but what is abundantly clear to my mind is that [section 47] never intended to sanction the permanent or constant carriage of an offensive weapon because of some constant or enduring supposed or actual threat or danger to the carrier"[27]

The fact that the purpose for which the weapon is carried is not illegal does not of itself provide a reasonable excuse.[28] The test may be whether a reasonable man would think it excusable to have the weapon for that purpose.[29] However, under section 49 of the Criminal Law (Consolidation) (Scotland) Act 1995, which defines the offence of having with one in a public place an article which has a blade or which is sharply pointed, there is a defence that there was "good reason" for having it with one in that place[30]: and in *Lister v. Lees*,[31] Lord Justice-Clerk Ross said that although "good reason" was different from "reasonable excuse", the same approach was applicable to both concepts.[32] The approach

---

[25] At 36.

[26] [1972] 1 W.L.R. 1452.

[27] At 1455F. The court treated the facts of the case as borderline, in view of the length of time for which the weapon had been carried, but did not interfere with the justices' decision to uphold the defence. See also *R. v. Peacock* [1973] Crim.L.R. 639; *Bradley v. Moss* [1974] Crim.L.R.430; *Pittard v. Mahoney* [1977] Crim.L.R. 169.

[28] *cf. Brown v. Farrel*, 1997 S.C.C.R. 356, a case concerned with "good reason" under s.49 of the Criminal Law (Consolidation) (Scotland) Act 1995: see para. 30.48, *infra*.

[29] *Bryan v. Mott* (1976) 62 Crim.App.R. 71: carrying a broken bottle in order to commit suicide not a reasonable excuse, the whole purpose of the section being "to discourage people from being in public places 'tooled up' with weapons of this kind": Lord Widgery C.J. at 73.

[30] See s.49(1), (2) and (4): see para. 30.48, *infra*.

[31] 1994 S.C.C.R. 548.

[32] *ibid.*, at 553A-B.

favoured in that case[33] was based on the purpose of the statutory provision. The purpose of section 49 (or, it is submitted, of section 47) which contains a general prohibition "must be to protect the public from persons who may use such articles to cause injury or to threaten others",[34] and, therefore "the court must determine whether the reason advanced[35] appears to constitute a justifiable exception to the general prohibition contained in the legislation."[36] In short, the reason (or excuse) may be good (or reasonable) provided it is not inconsistent with the purpose of the statutory offence.

In *Glendinning v. Guild*,[37] it was emphasised that what is now section 47 of the Criminal Law (Consolidation) (Scotland) Act 1995 is concerned with the possession and not the use of the weapon in question, such that the sheriff at the trial in that case had been wrong to consider that the accused's reasonable excuse for carrying a flail in public (that is, that he required it for a martial arts training class to which he had been then proceeding) was to be set aside on account of the accused's unreasonable use of the weapon (that is, waving it about in a public place).

"Reasonable excuse" would probably include carrying a weapon in order to surrender it to a policeman.[38]

"Has with him". This is a non-technical phrase and should be read in its **30.46** ordinary meaning, free of the technicalities of "possession". This might suggest that the accused should actually be shown to have been carrying the weapon on or about his person at the material time: but it is not necessary for him to be carrying it in that sense in order that he should "have it with him". In *Smith v. Vannet*,[39] the accused's car was found to contain a cosh under the passenger seat and a knife under the driver's mat. The accused had the keys of the car in his pocket and was standing some six feet from the vehicle at the material time. The question thus arose as to whether he could be said to have these weapons with him at that time and in those circumstances. Lord Justice General Rodger (giving the opinion of the court) was of the opinion that a purposive approach should be taken to the statutory offences involved in the case.[40] His view was that both sections 47 and 49 of the Criminal Law (Consolidation) (Scotland) Act 1995 were "designed to prevent people in a public place having offensive weapons and knives available to them which they may be liable to use."[41] Thus, in the case itself, the facts and circumstances demonstrated that the weapons were readily available for use by the accused, bearing particularly in mind his propinquity to the

---

[33] Subsequently applied in later cases: see *Brown v. Friel*, 1997 S.C.C.R. 356; *Crowe v. Waugh*, 1999 S.C.C.R. 610.

[34] 1994 S.C.C.R., at 552E.

[35] Or, perhaps, in the case of s.47, 'excuse tendered'.

[36] 1994 S.C.C.R., at 553A–B. At 552F, L.J.-C. Ross counselled that, in making the determination, the court should avoid making any moral judgment. Lord Ross declined, however, to provide further guidance, since each case must ultimately depend on its own facts and circumstances.

[37] 1988 S.L.T. 252 (Note).

[38] *cf. Wong Pooh Yin v. Public Prosecutor* [1955] A.C. 93.

[39] 1998 S.C.C.R. 410 (following, thus far, *R. v. Kelt* [1977] 1 W.L.R. 1365, CA), where the accused was charged with contraventions of ss. 47 and 49 of the Criminal Law (Consolidation) (Scotland) Act 1995. For s.49, see para. 30.48, *infra*.

[40] Following, thus far, *R. v. Pawlicki; R. v. Swindell* [1992] 1 W.L.R. 827, a case dealing with s.18 of the Firearms Act 1968.

[41] 1998 S.C.C.R., at 413B-C.

vehicle which contained them. It seems, therefore, that the test for "having it with him" is predicated upon the extent to which the weapons are readily available to the accused; and that this test is easily satisfied when the weapon in question is on or about his person, and depends on the precise facts and circumstances when the weapon is not so situated.

In *R. v. Jura*[42] A had an air rifle at a shooting gallery, and in a moment of anger he shot a girl with it. He was charged under what is now section 47 of the Act, but it was held that the statutory provision struck at possession and not at use, and that as he had not had the gun in his possession with any unlawful intent he should be acquitted. This suggests that section 47 requires that at any rate so far as class (iii) weapons are concerned A must take the weapon out with him with the intention of causing injury with it, or at least form that intention some time before he puts it into effect. As Mr Brownlie puts it, "having with one" is "a state of affairs".[43] In *Woodward v. Koessler,*[44] where A threatened someone with a weapon he had with him for housebreaking purposes, it was said that his intention must be ascertained from his use of the weapon,[45] but this is inconsistent with *Jura*, and *Jura* was adopted, albeit *obiter*, in *R. v. Dayle*.[46] In that case Kilner Brown J., giving the opinion of the Court of Appeal (Criminal Division), said:

> "The terms of section 1(1) of the Prevention of Crimes Act 1953[47] are apt to cover the case of a person who goes out with an offensive weapon without lawful authority or reasonable excuse and also the person who deliberately selects an article, such as the stone in *Harrison v. Thornton* [1966] Crim.L.R. 388, with the intention of using it as a weapon without such authority or excuse. But, if an article, already possessed lawfully and for good reason, is used offensively to cause injury, such use does not necessarily prove the intent which the Crown must establish in respect of articles which are not offensive weapons per se. Each case must depend on its own facts."[48]

Jura was given further support in *Ohlson v Hylton*.[49] A carpenter carrying his tools home got into a quarrel with a man and took a hammer out of his briefcase and assaulted the man. It was held that there was no contravention of section 1 of the Act, because "no offence is committed under the Act of 1953 where an assailant seizes a weapon for instant use on his victim . . . the prosecution must show that the defendant was carrying or otherwise equipped with the weapon, and had the intent to use it offensively before any occasion for its actual use had arisen."[50]

So far as Scots law is concerned the question is probably academic, since where the weapon is used the accused will be charged with the offence involved in its use, and not with a contravention of section 47 of the current Act.[51]

---

[42] [1954] 1 Q.B. 503.

[43] I. Brownlie *op.cit.* at 27.

[44] [1958] 1 W.L.R. 1255.

[45] Donovan J. at 1257.

[46] [1974] 1 W.L.R. 181.

[47] Now s.47(1) of the Criminal Law (Consolidation) (Scotland) Act 1995.

[48] At 184H.

[49] [1975] 1 W.L.R. 724. See also *R. v. Humphreys* [1977] Crim.L.R. 225.

[50] Lord Widgery C.J. at 730–731. *Ohlson* was applied in *Bates v. Bulman* [1979] 1 W.L.R. 1190, where the accused, after punching a man, requested and received from a friend a clasp knife which he opened and held against the victim's head. But *cf. Skeen v. Gemmell*; *Skeen v. Smith* (1974) 38 J.C.L. 79.

[51] See 1954 S.L.T. (News) 67.

The accused must, of course, have the weapon with him "in a public place", and, if he is arrested in a non-public place, it may be possible to infer from the facts and circumstances that he must have passed through a public place on his way to the place of his apprehension.[52] It seems to have been accepted that a weapon which is in a vehicle is in a public place if that vehicle is itself in or on a public place, as defined in section 47(4).[53]

Obstructing search for weapons. Section 48 of the Criminal Law (Consol- **30.47** idation) (Scotland) Act 1995 gives a police constable power to search persons he has reasonable cause to suspect of having offensive weapons,[54] and subsection (2) provides:

> "Any person who—
> (a) intentionally obstructs a constable in the exercise of the constable's powers under subsection (1) above; or
> (b) conceals from a constable acting in the exercise of the said powers an offensive weapon,
> shall be guilty of an offence and liable on summary conviction to a fine not exceeding level 4 on the standard scale."

It is not an offence under section 48(2)(b) for a person in possession of an offensive weapon to hand it to a friend on the approach of the police.[55]

Articles with blades or sharp points. Knives, and other instruments with **30.48** blades or sharp points, may or may not be offensive weapons within the meaning of section 47 of the Criminal Law (Consolidation) (Scotland) Act 1995, but are separately addressed by section 49 of that Act, which provides:

> "(1) Subject to subsections (4) and (5) below, any person who has an article to which this section applies with him[56] in a public place[57] shall be guilty of an offence . . .[58]
> (2) Subject to subsection (3) below, this section applies to any article which has a blade or is sharply pointed.

---

[52] See, *e.g.*, *Normand v. Donnelly*, 1993 S.C.C.R. 639; *Wallace v. Ruxton*, 1998 S.C.C.R. 701.

[53] See, *e.g.*, *Murdoch v. Carmichael*, 1993 S.C.C.R. 444; *Smith v. Vannet*, 1989 S.C.C.R. 410.

[54] Which have the same meaning as they are given under s.47: s.48(4).

[55] *Burke v. Mackinnon*, 1983 S.C.C.R. 23, where L.J.-G. Emslie said at 25: "So far as section 4(2)(b) [of the Criminal Justice (Scotland) Act 1980, now re-enacted as s.48(2)(b) of the Criminal Law (Consolidation) (Scotland) Act 1995] is concerned there must, in order to support a relevant charge, be an active step of concealment to prevent discovery of the offensive weapon by the searching officer."

[56] 'has with him' is subject to the same considerations which apply in relation to offences under s.47 of the Act: see para. 30.46, *supra*.

[57] The question whether it may be inferred that an accused person, found with (*e.g.*) a knife in a non-public place, must have had that knife with him in a public place, is subject to the same considerations which apply to offences under s.47 of the Act: see *Wilson v. Vannet*, 1999 S.C.C.R. 722 (applying *Wallace v. Ruxton*, 1998 S.C.C.R. 701, but distinguishing *McKernon v. McGlennan*, 1999 S.C.C.R. 255), and para. 30.46, *supra*.

[58] Maximum penalty, on indictment, two years' and a fine; and on summary conviction, six months' and a fine of the statutory maximum: s.49(1)(a), (b).

(3) This section does not apply to a folding pocket knife if the cutting edge of its blade does not exceed three inches (7.62 centimetres).[59]

(4) It shall be a defence for a person charged with an offence under subsection (1) above to prove that he had good reason or lawful authority for having the article with him in the public place.[60]

(5) Without prejudice to the generality of subsection (4) above, it shall be a defence for a person charged with an offence under subsection (1) above to prove that he had the article with him—

    (a) for use at work[61];

    (b) for religious reasons;

    (c) as part of any national costume . . .

(7) In this section 'public place' includes any place to which at the material time the public have or are permitted access, whether on payment or otherwise."

Under section 49A(1) of the same Act (which section is inserted by virtue of section 4(3) of the Offensive Weapons Act 1996), it is an offence for any person to have an article to which section 49 of the Act applies with him on any school premises.[62]

30.49 *Other Statutes.* The possession of weapons is made an offence or an aggravation of another offence by the Customs and Excise Management Act 1979, section 86,[63] and also by the Night Poaching Act 1828, section 9, which provides:

---

[59] The length of the blade may be established by use of a measuring instrument in common use without the need to prove that instrument's accuracy: *Normand v. Walker*, 1994 S.C.C.R. 875 (plastic ruler obtained from the clerk of court considered sufficient for the measurement required). A knife, the blade of which can be folded, is not within the exception in subs. (3) if "it has a device which is designed, until it has been overcome, to prevent its blade being folded": *Stewart v. Friel*, 1995 S.C.C.R. 492, L.J.-G. Hope at 495D (knife, the blade of which was locked in place when opened).

[60] Whilst "good reason" is linguistically different from the "reasonable excuse" referred to in s.47 of the Act, the two concepts are subject to the same approach: *Lister v. Lees*, 1994 S.C.C.R. 548, L.J.-C. Ross at 553A-B. See, therefore, para. 30.45, *supra*. For "lawful authority", also see para. 30.45, *supra*. It is not necessary to show "good reason" or "lawful authority" if one of the specific defences in subs. (5), *infra*, applies: *Douglas v. McFadyen*, 1999 S.C.C.R. 884, Lord Coulsfield at 887F. The burden of proof on the accused is probably an evidential one: see para. 30.13, *supra*.

[61] Whether or not this defence applies will depend on the facts and circumstances of each case: thus, *e.g.*, a gardener, who was found to have an axe at the side of the driver's seat of his car with the axe-handle so positioned as to make it readily available to the driver, was denied the defence, the remainder of his gardening tools being in the boot of the vehicle. His explanation that, after use, the axe had simply been thrown by him into the vehicle such that its resting place was a mere matter of chance, was disbelieved by the trial judge: *Mackenzie v. Vannet*, 1999 J.C. 44. In that case, a purposive approach to the offence is again evident in the determination of the issue at stake: see the opinion of Lord Kirkwood at 46E, where the purpose of the offence is stated to be the prevention of such articles being readily available to those who might use them to injure or threaten others. "For use at work" covers the person in question both in his going to and coming from his work: *Douglas v. McFadyen*, 1999 S.C.C.R. 884, Lord Coulsfield at 887F.

[62] Maximum penalty, on indictment, two years' and a fine; on summary conviction, six months' and a fine of the statutory maximum: s.49A(5)(a). For "school premises", see para 30.43, n.93, *supra*. It is a defence under s.49A(3) for the accused to prove that he had good reason or lawful authority for having the article with him on the premises; and it is a separate defence (under subs. (4)), for him to prove that he had the article with him "(a) for use at work; (b) for educational purposes; (c) for religious reasons, or (d) as part of any national costume."

[63] *infra*, para. 38.06.

"If any persons, to the number of three of more together, shall by night unlawfully enter or be in any land, whether open or enclosed, for the purpose of taking or destroying game or rabbits, any of the persons being armed with any gun, crossbow, fire arms, bludgeon, or any other offensive weapon, each and every of such persons shall be guilty of [an offence]."[64]

It is clear from this section that if even one of the group is armed, all are guilty of the offence.

In *Jas. Mitchell and Ors*[65] Lord Young directed the jury that "A walking stick is an offensive weapon within the meaning of the ninth section; even the wooden pegs about 2 feet long and 1 inch in thickness, which are used for keeping the poacher's net in position . . . are offensive weapons . . . and it is not necessary . . . that the pegs should have been taken with the intention, if necessary, of using them as arms."[66] It may be doubted, however, whether implements such as pegs would today be regarded as weapons, unless used as such. It has been held that the section may be contravened by picking up stones lying on the ground, although the accused were unarmed when they entered the ground.[67]

Sale of knives. The Restriction of Offensive Weapons Act 1959, section 1 **30.50** (as amended by the Restriction of Offensive Weapons Act 1961 and the Criminal Justice Act 1988, section 46(3)) provides:

"(1) Any person who manufactures, sells or hires or offers for sale or hire or exposes or has in his possession for the purpose of sale or hire, or lends or gives to any other person—

(a) any knife which has a blade which opens automatically by hand pressure applied to a button, spring or other device in or attached to the handle of the knife, sometimes known as a 'flick-knife' or 'flick-gun'; or

(b) any knife which has a blade which is released from the handle or sheath thereof by the force of gravity or the application of centrifugal force and which, when released, is locked in place by means of a button, spring, lever, or other device, sometimes known as a 'gravity knife'

shall be guilty of an offence . . ."[68]

Section 1(2) of the Act prohibits the importation of any such knives.

Marketing knives. Under section 1 of the Knives Act 1997 it is an offence **30.51** for a person to market[69] a knife[70] in a way which indicates or suggests that it is suitable for combat[71] or is otherwise likely to stimulate or

---

[64] Maximum penalty on summary conviction, six months' and a fine of level 4 on the standard scale: Criminal Law Act 1977, Sched. 12, para. 2.

[65] (1887) 1 White 321.

[66] At 326.

[67] *John McNab and Ors* (1845) 2 Broun 416, at 424. Section 2 of the Act makes it an offence for a poacher to assault a gamekeeper, etc: see *supra*, para. 29.18.

[68] Maximum penalty six months' and a fine of level 5 on the standard scale on summary conviction.

[69] Under s.1(4) of the Act, marketing means selling or hiring, offering or exposing for sale or hire, or having in one's possession for sale or hire.

[70] Under s.10 of the Act, "knife" means "an instrument which has a blade or is sharply pointed."

[71] Under s.10 of the Act, "suitable for combat" means "suitable for use as a weapon for inflicting injury on a person or causing a person to fear injury."

encourage violent behaviour[72] involving the use of the knife as a weapon.[73] Under section 2, it is an offence for a person to publish any written, pictorial or other material in connection with the marketing of any knife if that material indicates or suggests that the knife is suitable for combat or is otherwise likely to stimulate or encourage violent behaviour involving the use of the knife as a weapon.[74] It is a defence to either offence that the person charged took all reasonable precautions and exercised all due diligence to avoid committing it.[75]

30.52 *Selling etc. particular weapons.* It is an offence under section 141 of the Criminal Justice Act 1988 to manufacture, sell or hire or offer for sale or hire, expose or possess for sale or hire, or lend or give to anyone else, any weapon of a kind specified by the Secretary of State by order,[76] other than a weapon subject to the Firearms Act 1968 or a crossbow. The importation of such weapons is also prohibited.[77] It is a defence for the accused to prove that any conduct with which he is charged was only for the purposes of functions carried out on behalf of the Crown or of a visiting force,[78] or of making the weapon available to a non-profit making museum or gallery.[79] It is also a defence for someone acting on behalf of such a museum or gallery who is charged with hiring or lending a weapon to prove that he had reasonable grounds for believing that the hirer or lessee would use it only for cultural, artistic or educational purposes.[80]

It is an offence under section 141A[81] of the Act for a person to sell to a person under the age of 16 any knife, knife blade, razor blade, axe, and any other article which has a blade or which is sharply pointed and which is made or adapted for causing personal injury.[82] It is a defence for a person charged with such an offence to prove that he took all reasonable precautions and exercised all due diligence to avoid committing it.[83]

Explosives

30.53   The manufacture of explosives is regulated in the interests of public safety by the Explosives Act 1875. The use of explosives in a way likely to cause danger and the making or possessing of explosives in suspicious circumstances are penalised by the Explosive Substances Act 1883.[84]

---

[72] Under s.10 of the Act, "violent behaviour" means "an unlawful act inflicting injury on a person or causing a person to fear injury."

[73] Maximum penalty, on indictment, two years' and a fine; and on summary conviction, six months' and a fine of the statutory maximum: s.1(5). See s.4(1) for defences to this offence.

[74] Maximum penalty, as for s.1: see s.2(2), and n.73, *supra*. See s.4(2) of the Act for defences to this offence.

[75] Section 4(3).

[76] See the Criminal Justice Act 1988 (Offensive Weapons) Order 1988 (S.I. 1988 No. 2019), Schedule, for a list of proscribed weapons for the purposes of s.141 of the Act.

[77] Section 1(4) of the Act.

[78] Section 1(5).

[79] Section 1(8) and (11).

[80] Section 1(9).

[81] Added by the Offensive Weapons Act 1996, s.6(1). Maximum penalty, on summary conviction, six months' and a fine of level 5 on the standard scale.

[82] This provision does not apply to any article described in the Restriction of Offensive Weapons Act 1959, in an order made under s.141 of the 1988 Act, or an order made by the Secretary of State under the instant section.

[83] Section 141A(5).

[84] *supra*, paras 22.21, 22.22. See also Health and Safety etc. at Work Act 1974, s.33(4).

Safety at work

A number of statutes, such as the Factories Act 1961 and the Mines **30.54** and Quarries Act 1954, contain (or contained)[85] provisions or empower the making of regulations containing provisions for regulating the way in which industrial undertakings are to be conducted for the protection of employees. Breach of such provisions is usually a criminal offence.

In addition the Health and Safety etc. at Work Act 1974 places general duties on employers, self-employed persons and employees, breaches of which are criminal offences.[86] The following are among the provisions of the Act:

"**3.**—(1) It shall be the duty of every employer to conduct his undertaking in such a way as to ensure, so far as is reasonably practicable, that persons not in his employment who may be affected thereby are not thereby exposed to risks to their health or safety.

(2) It shall be the duty of every self-employed person to conduct his undertaking in such a way as to ensure, so far as is reasonably practicable, that he and other persons (not being his employees) who may be affected thereby are not thereby exposed to risks to their health or safety.

(3) In such cases as may be prescribed, it shall be the duty of every employer and every self-employed person, in the prescribed circumstances and in the prescribed manner, to give to persons (not being his employees) who may be affected by the way in which he conducts his undertaking the prescribed information about such aspects of the way in which he conducts his undertaking as might affect their health or safety.[87]

4.[88] —(1) This section has effect for imposing on persons duties in relation to those who—

(a) are not their employees; but
(b) use non-domestic premises made available to them as a place of work or as a place where they may use plant or substances provided for their use there,

and applies to premises so made available and other non-domestic premises used in connection with them.

(2) It shall be the duty of each person who has, to any extent, control of premises to which this section applies or of the means of access thereto or egress therefrom or of any plant or substance in such premises to take such measures as it is reasonable for a person in his position to take to ensure, so far as is reasonably practicable, that the premises, all means of access thereto or egress therefrom available for use by persons using the premises, and any plant or

---

[85] Since most of these two Acts are spent after successive repeal of their contents.

[86] Section 33, which also provides penalties, ranging from a fine of level 5 on the standard scale on summary conviction for some offences, to two years' imprisonment and a fine on indictment in other cases such as offences consisting of the acquisition, possession or use of explosives, s.33(3) and (4). See *Armour v. Skeen,* 1977 S.L.T. 71.

[87] Even where no cases or information have been prescribed under s.3(3), failure to give information may be an offence under s.3(1) where the information is necessary to prevent exposure to risk to health or safety: see, *e.g., Carmichael v. Rosehall Engineering Works Ltd,* 1983 S.C.C.R. 353; *R. v. Swan Hunter Shipbuilders Ltd* [1981] I.C.R. 831.

[88] On the relationship between ss.3 and 4, see *Aitchison v. Howard Doris Ltd,* 1979 S.L.T. (Notes) 22.

substance in the premises, or, as the case may be, provided for use there, is or are safe and without risks to health . . .

> **7.** It shall be the duty of every employee while at work—
> (a) to take reasonable care for the health and safety of himself and of other persons who may be affected by his acts or omissions at work; and
> (b) as regards any duty or requirement imposed on his employer or any other person by or under any of the relevant statutory provisions, to co-operate with him so far as is necessary to enable that duty or requirement to be performed or complied with.

> **8.** No person shall intentionally or recklessly interfere with or misuse anything provided in the interests of health, safety or welfare in the pursuance of any of the relevant statutory provisions."

A duty is also placed on persons who design, manufacture, import or supply any article or substance for use at work, to ensure so far as reasonably practicable (by *inter alia* carrying out tests) that the article or substance is safe.[89]

Dangerous Animals

30.55 Dangerous wild animals, as described in the Schedule to the Dangerous Wild Animals Act 1976, may not lawfully be kept unless the person keeping them holds a local authority licence to do so.[90] Licences are not granted to those who are disqualified from holding them or who are under 18 years of age.[91] It is an offence to keep such an animal without a licence entitling one to do so[92] or to fail to comply with the conditions attached to a licence which has been granted.[93] There are, however, exemptions for qualifying zoos, circuses, pet shops and scientific establishments.[94]

30.56 *Dangerous Dogs Act 1991.* Apart from the prohibition on the keeping of certain types of dog in section 1, the Dangerous Dogs Act 1991 enacts that the owner, or the person for the time being in charge, of a dog is guilty of an offence if that dog is dangerously out of control in a public place.[95] Under section 10(3), a dog is dangerously out of control if on

---

[89] Section 6.

[90] Dangerous Wild Animals Act 1976, s.1(1).

[91] *ibid.*, s.1(2)(d).

[92] *ibid.*, s.2(5).

[93] *ibid.*, s.2(6). It is a defence to this offence that the accused took all reasonable precautions and exercised all due diligence to avoid committing it (s.2(7)). Maximum penalty for any offence under the Act is a fine of level 5 on the standard scale, and the person who has been convicted may be disqualified from holding a licence or may have his existing licence cancelled (s.6).

[94] See s.5.

[95] Section 3(1). Maximum penalty, on summary conviction, six months' and a fine of level 5 on the standard scale; but if the dog, whilst dangerously out of control, injures anyone, the offence becomes an aggravated one, and may be tried on indictment, in which case the maximum penalty is two years' and a fine: s.3(4). There is a defence to this offence, where the owner is charged and he is able to prove that the dog was at the material time in the charge of some other person whom he reasonably believed to be a fit and proper person to be in charge of the animal (s.3(2)): see *Swinlay v. Crowe*, 1994 S.C.C.R. 851.

any occasion[96] there are grounds for reasonable apprehension that the dog will injure any person, whether or not it actually does so. "Public place" is defined, also in section 10(3), as meaning "any street, road or other place (whether or not enclosed) to which the public have or are permitted to have access whether for payment or otherwise and includes the common parts of a building containing two or more separate dwellings": as this definition refers to the common parts "of a building", it is uncertain whether or not common areas such as drying greens and garden ground outside a flatted building are intended to be included.[97] It is an offence under section 3(3) of the Act if the owner of a dog, or the person meantime in charge of it, allows the animal to enter a non-public place where it is not permitted to be, and whilst there the dog injures someone or there are reasonable grounds for apprehension that it may do so.[98] If both offences, under sections 3(1) and 3(2), are charged in the alternative, but it is not established that the locus was a public or a non-public place, no conviction can be justified under either subsection; for a finding of "public place" is as essential to the one as a finding of "not a public place" is to the other.[99]

---

[96] If a dog has no history of aggression, but bites two persons unexpectedly and in rapid succession, there is but one "occasion" and no grounds for the reasonable apprehension required: *Tierney v. Valentine*, 1994 S.C.C.R. 697. If, however, there is an interval between a dog's biting two persons, there may be two separate "occasions", the interval between them giving time for reflection that there are grounds for reasonable apprehension that it will injure someone: see *Normand v. Lucas*, Appeal Court, Feb. 16, 1993, unrep'd; see, however, the note following the report of *Tierney v. Valentine*, 1994 S.C.C.R. 700.

[97] cf. *McGeachy v. Normand*, 1993 S.C.C.R. 951.

[98] Maximum penalty is the same as that for an offence under s.3(1): see n.95, *supra*. Again, the offence is aggravated if actual injury is caused; but the defence available under a s.3(1) charge (see s.3(2)) is not applicable here.

[99] *Walton v. Miller*, 1999 S.L.T. 1137.

CHAPTER 31

OFFENCES AGAINST CHILDREN

At common law

The exposure and desertion of infants by their parents or guardians is **31.01**
a common law crime.[1] Hume appears to require that the child's life must
be endangered before the exposure is criminal,[2] but Alison cites two
cases of simple exposure,[3] and *Rachel Gibson*[4] contained two separate
charges: one of "Exposing and Deserting an Infant Child" and one of
"Placing an Infant Child in a Situation of Danger to its Life, by the
mother of such child".

It is also a common law crime to neglect a child to the injury of its
health in ways other than by exposing and deserting it.[5] In *Barbara Gray
or McIntosh*[6] the charge was of "culpable and wilful neglect and bad
treatment of a child of tender age by a person who has the custody and
keeping of it, whereby such child is injured in its health", and the
negligence consisted in failing to supply "wholesome and sufficient food
and clothing", allowing the child to be kept in dirty and damp conditions
exposed to cold, and failing to give it the care and attention necessary to
preserve its health.

Under the Children and Young Persons (Scotland) Act 1937

Cases of neglect of and cruelty to children and young persons are now **31.02**
dealt with under the Children and Young Persons (Scotland) Act 1937.[7]
Section 12(1)[8] of the Act provides:

"If any person who has attained the age of sixteen years and who
has parental responsibilities[9] in relation to a child[10] or young person

---

[1] For example, *Rachel Gibson* (1845) 2 Broun 366.

[2] Hume, i, 299.

[3] *David Buchanan* (1824) and *Janet and Wm Craig* (1827), both Alison, i, 162.

[4] *supra*, n.1.

[5] This is sometimes called "Cruel and Unnatural Treatment": *John and Mary Craw*
(1839) 2 Swin. 449; *David and Janet Gemmell* (1841) 2 Swin. 552; *Alex. Watson* (1875) 3
Couper 150. See *supra*, para. 29.49.

[6] (1880) 4 Couper 389.

[7] Which replaced the Children Act 1908 and the Children and Young Persons
(Scotland) Act 1932.

[8] As amended by the Children (Scotland) Act 1995, Sched. 4, para. 7(2)(a).

[9] Persons having parental responsibilities under the Children (Scotland) Act 1995
include the child's genetic father and mother (s.15(1)), but not the father if he was not
married to the mother at the time of the child's conception or at a time subsequent to that
(see s.3(1)(b)) unless there is an agreement between him and the mother under s.4; his
guardian (s.7); or someone having such responsibilities by court order (see s.11). The
parental responsibilities themselves are listed at s.1(1), paras (a) to (d).

[10] Under s.110(1), a child is a person under the age of 14 years.

under that age[11] or has charge or care of a child or such a young person wilfully assaults, ill-treats, neglects, abandons, or exposes him, or causes or procures him to be assaulted, ill-treated, neglected abandoned, or exposed, in a manner likely to cause him unnecessary suffering or injury to health (including injury to or loss of sight, or hearing, or limb, or organ of the body, and any mental derangement), that person shall be guilty of an offence,[12] and shall be liable [on conviction on indictment to ten years' imprisonment[13] and a fine, and on summary conviction to six months' imprisonment and/ or a fine of the prescribed sum]."

31.03 *"Charge or care"*. Whether or not a person has parental responsibilities in respect of a child or young person is determined as a matter of law by the provisions of the Children (Scotland) Act 1995[14]; but whether a person has "charge or care" of a child or young person is a question of fact: whoever in fact has such charge or care is subject to section 12(1) of the Act irrespective of his legal relationship, if any, to the child. In *Liverpool Society for the Prevention of Cruelty to Children v. Jones*[15] it was held that the father of an illegitimate child who lived in family with the child and its mother could be a person having custody, charge or care of the child.[16] In *R. v. Drury*[17] a husband was held to have custody, charge or care of a 14-year-old baby-sitter who was looking after the children while his wife was in hospital, for the purposes of the English provisions corresponding to section 13 of the Act.[18] More than one person may be guilty of an offence under the section in relation to a particular child at a particular time; and normally both parents of a child will be subject to the obligations of the section,[19] either because each has parental responsibilities as a matter of law or because each has the charge or care of the child.

In addition to actual charge or care, the Act provides that certain persons shall be presumed to have charge or care of a child in certain circumstances. Section 27[20] of the Act provides that for the purposes of Part II of the Act, which includes section 12:

"Any person to whose charge a child or young person is committed by any person who has parental responsibilities in relation to him shall be presumed to have charge of the child or young person;

---

[11] Under s.110(1), a young person is a person who has attained the age of 14 but is under the age of 17 years, unless the context of the statutory provision (as is true of s.12(1)) dictates otherwise.

[12] The section has been said to create one compendious offence of cruelty which may be committed in a number of ways: *R. v. Hayles* [1969] 1 Q.B. 364.

[13] As increased from the original two years' by the Criminal Justice Act 1988, s.45.

[14] See n.9, *supra*.

[15] [1914] 3 K.B. 813.

[16] Prior to 1995, the Children and Young Persons (Scotland) Act 1937, s.12(1), referred to a person having the "custody, charge or care" of a child or young person, as did the English equivalent Act (*i.e.*, the Children Act 1908 with which the court was concerned in *Liverpool Society for the Prevention of Cruelty to Children v. Jones, supra*); but any decision as to the interpretation of "custody, charge or care" is likely to be no less valid relative to "charge or care".

[17] (1975) 60 Cr.App.R. 195.

[18] Section 13 was repealed by the Sexual Offences (Scotland) Act 1976, Sched. 2: the current corresponding provision is found in s.10 of the Criminal Law (Consolidation) (Scotland) Act 1995, although it refers to persons having "parental responsibilities" in relation to, or the "charge or care" of, a girl under the age of 16, rather than the "custody, charge or care" of the older legislation.

[19] For example, *R. v. Watson and Watson* (1959) 43 Cr.App.R. 111.

[20] As amended by the Children (Scotland) Act 1995, Sched. 4, para. 5(a).

Any other person having actual possession or control of a child or young person shall be presumed to have the care of him."

Wilfully. This term means that the acts or omissions must be deliberate **31.04** and intentional, "not by accident or inadvertence, but so that the mind of the person who does the act goes with it".[21] It does not involve any intention to cause suffering to the child. If A fails to provide his child with medical attention because he has a religious objection to medicine he is guilty of an offence if his behaviour otherwise amounts to neglect.[22]

It is not a defence in Scotland that the accused was unaware that what he was doing was likely to cause suffering.[23]

Neglects. Neglect is a failure to bestow proper care and attention on a **31.05** child[24]; it must amount to something more than trivial, but it is not necessary that a child should show outward signs of neglect.[25] A person fails to bestow proper care and attention[26] when his behaviour shows "want of reasonable care — that is, the omission of such steps as a reasonable parent would take, such as are usually taken in the ordinary experience of mankind."[27] In the relatively modern case of *H. v. Lees; D v. Orr*,[28] Lord Justice General Hope said that the appropriate standard was "what a reasonable parent, in all the circumstances, would regard as necessary to provide proper care and attention to the child." In addition section 12(2)[29] of the Act provides:

---

[21] *R. v. Senior* [1899] 1 Q.B. 283, Lord Russell C.J. at 290–291. See *H. v. Lees; D. v. Orr*, 1993 S.C.C.R. 900, L.J.-G. Hope at 907C-D, where Lord Russell's opinion is quoted without hint of disapproval.

[22] *R. v. Senior, supra*, n. 21.

[23] *Clark v. H.M. Advocate*, 1968 J.C. 53. *Cf. R. v. Sheppard* [1981] A.C. 394, HL, which interpreted the similarly worded English equivalent offence in s.1 of the Children and Young Persons Act 1933, and where a bare majority of the House of Lords (Lords Fraser of Tullybelton and Scarman diss.) favoured the view that "wilfulness" applies not only to the (*e.g.*) neglect but also to the consequences thereof as specified in the section. The case concerned neglect by failure on the part of the parents of a 16-month-old child to obtain medical aid for him when he was suffering from gastroenteritis. According to Lord Diplock (at 404H–405A): "Such a failure . . . could not be properly described as 'wilful' unless the parent *either* (1) had directed his mind to the question whether there was some risk (though it might fall far short of a possibility) that the child's health might suffer unless he were examined by a doctor and provided with such curative treatment as the examination might reveal as necessary, and had made a conscious decision, for whatever reason, to refrain from arranging for such medical examination; *or* (2) had so refrained because he did not care whether the child might be in need of medical treatment." Consequently, it had been wrong of the trial judge to rule that the parents' possible unawareness of the likelihood of unnecessary suffering or injury to health was irrelevant; and thus, the fact that the parents were of low intelligence was a matter of potential importance. The decision in *Sheppard* and the difference of opinion amongst the judges in the House were noted by L.J.-G. Hope in *H. v. Lees; D. v. Orr*, 1993 S.C.C.R. 900 at 908D-F; but "wilfulness" was not an issue in the appeals there; and the law thus remains as stated in *Clark v. H.M. Advocate, supra*.

[24] *H. v. Lees; D. v. Orr*, 1993 S.C.C.R. 900, L.J.-G. Hope at 908C-D, quoting Lord Keith of Kinkel in *R. v. Sheppard* [1981] A.C. 394, at 417D.

[25] In *Kennedy v. S.*, 1986 S.C. 43, at 49–50, L.J.-C. Ross held that a sheriff had been in error in confining "neglect" to what could be seen: "Children may have the appearance of being clean and well fed and yet may have been the victims of neglect within the meaning of the statutes."

[26] In the deeming provision of s.12(2), *infra*, the standard is that of failure to provide *adequate* food, etc.

[27] *Clark v. H.M. Advocate*, 1968 J.C. 53, L.J.-C. Grant at 56, quoting from *R. v. Senior* [1899] 1 Q.B. 283, Lord Russell of Killowen at 291.

[28] 1993 S.C.C.R. 900, at 909A-B.

[29] As amended by the Children (Scotland) Act 1995, Sched. 4, para. 7(2)(b).

"For the purposes of this section—

(a) a parent or other person legally liable to maintain[30] a child or young person, or the legal guardian of a child or young person, shall be deemed to have neglected him in a manner likely to cause injury to his health if he has failed to provide adequate food, clothing, medical aid or lodging for him, or if, having been unable otherwise to provide such food, clothing, medical aid or lodging, he has failed to take steps to procure it to be provided under the enactments applicable in that behalf[31];

(b) where it is proved that the death of a child under three years of age was caused by suffocation (not being suffocation caused by disease or the presence of any foreign body in the throat or air passages of the child) while the child was in bed with some other person who has attained the age of sixteen years, that other person shall, if he was, when he went to bed, under the influence of drink, be deemed to have neglected the child in a manner likely to cause injury to his health."

31.06 *Abandons.* A abandons a child when he "leaves it to its fate" intending to go away and wash his hands of it.[32] It is abandonment to leave children in a juvenile court,[33] or to walk out of a house and leave them after asking a Society for the Prevention of Cruelty to take care of them but without waiting to see if they are taken care of,[34] or, it is submitted, to take them along to a Children's Shelter or Cruelty Society Office and just leave them there.[35] It appears, however, that it can never be abandonment to leave a child with the person who has parental responsibilities in respect of it, even if the accused is aware that the person does not want the child and is unable to provide for it. If a mother takes her child to its father in the street and just puts it in his arms and walks off, she may be guilty of neglecting it, but her action does not amount to abandonment, provided the father has parental responsibilities in respect of the child.[36] Ultimately, however, abandonment is a question of fact, circumstances and degree.[37] A parent, for example, who leaves his young children to fend for themselves for a prolonged and indefinite period and without having made any definite arrangements for them to be looked after during his absence, may well

---

[30] See Family Law (Scotland) Act 1985, s.1; Wilkinson & Norrie, *Parent and Child* (2nd ed., by K.McK. Norrie, 1999), Ch. 13.
[31] See National Assistance (Adaption of Enactments) Regulations 1951 (S.I. 1951 No.174), Sched.
[32] *Mitchell v. Wright* (1905) 7 F. 568; *R. v. Boulden* (1957) 41 Cr.App.R. 105.
[33] *cf. R. v. Whibley* (1938) 26 Cr.App.R. 184.
[34] *R. v. Boulden, supra.*
[35] *cf. New Monkland Parish Council v. Erskine,* 1926 S.C. 835 where it was held that a mental defective whose parent had placed her in a poorhouse and declined to pay for her keep although able to so do, was a person found "abandoned" in the poorhouse, for the purposes of the Mental Deficiency and Lunacy (Scotland) Act 1913.
[36] *cf. McLean v. Hardie* 1927 S.C. 344, which dealt with the concept of "legal custody" found in the former, as opposed to the concept of "parental responsibilities" favoured by the new (or amended) legislation.
[37] *McD. v. Orr,* 1994 S.C.C.R. 645, at 649E.

be considered to have abandoned them wilfully,[38] even if it was plain that he would at some time return.[39] It may be that a person who has parental responsibilities in respect of, or who has charge or care of, a very young child may be considered to have abandoned the child if that person is very drunk at the material time: thus, in *H. v. Lees; D. v. Orr*,[40] where the mother of a nine-month-old child was so drunk as to be incapable of looking after the child, Lord Justice General opined that she might as well not have been there at all and might "indeed be said to have abandoned the child and [might] also be liable to create risks for the child which would not arise if . . . she were sober."[41] A finding of wilful abandonment (or indeed, *e.g.*, wilful neglect) is not, however, conclusive of the commission of the offence: the abandonment must be "in a manner likely to cause [the child or young person] unnecessary suffering or injury to health."[42]

In a manner likely to cause unnecessary suffering or injury to health. **31.07** Before an assault on a child, or the ill-treatment, neglect, abandonment or exposure of a child can be a statutory offence, it must be shown to have been done "in a manner likely to cause him unnecessary suffering or injury to health".[43] An assault, or other ill-treatment, of a lesser degree is not struck at by the Act. And the suffering or injury involved must be substantial — minor injury, fright, or "slight mental suffering" is insufficient.[44] The risks of unnecessary suffering or injury to health must

---

[38] *ibid*. The children in that case were aged 12, 11, 9 and 6 years respectively; apart from telling them to go to their grandmother's house or to school, the accused (their father) simply left them in the street and then departed by bus with no indication when he might return. *Cf. H. v. Lees; D. v. Orr*, 1993 S.C.C.R. 900, where, in the case of "D", the child in question was aged 13 and one half years, had refused to accompany her father on a visit to a neighbouring town, was capable of looking after herself to a reasonable degree, and had some reasonably clear indication when her father would be likely to return: the charge was in fact one of neglect; but the quashing of the conviction for neglect was surely *a fortiori* of any question of abandonment.

[39] In *McD. v. Orr*, 1994 S.C.C.R. 645, *e.g.*, the accused father had taken his eldest child (aged 14) with him when he left his other children to their own devices; but there was no suggestion that the two of them did not at some time mean to return home: he was nevertheless convicted of wilful abandonment. The duration of the relevant person's absence obviously bears some relationship to the age of the child left on its own: see, *e.g.*, *McF. v. Normand*, 1995 S.C.C.R. 380, where a child of 18 months was left alone in a locked car in Bath Street, Glasgow, whilst his parents pursued Christmas shopping. The age of the child is also related to the circumstances: see, *e.g.*, *W. v. Clark*, 1999 S.C.C.R. 775, where children of eight, five and two years of age were left alone in a flat which was secure and warm — but without food they could manage without cooking, and in the company of a dog of the "pit bull" variety; it was not disputed that the children had in these circumstances been abandoned.

[40] 1993 S.C.C.R. 900.

[41] *ibid.*, at 910A-B.

[42] See para. 31.07, *infra*.

[43] In the case of wilful neglect or abandonment there requires to be evidence of a specific and substantial risk of such suffering or injury: see, *e.g.*, *H. v. Lees; D. v. Orr*, 1993 S.C.C.R. 900.

[44] *R. v. Whibley* (1938) 26 Cr.App.R. 184 where the child was left in a juvenile court. Also see *R. v. Hatton* [1925] 2 K.B. 322 where a parent who committed an act of indecency in the child's presence and put his hand over her mouth when she screamed was held not to have assaulted the child in contravention of the then applicable statute, having caused only "agitation of mind, astonishment and disgust".

also flow from, the neglect or abandonment,[45] and must not be entirely speculative.[46]

The statute is concerned with "likely" and not with actual suffering, and section 12(3) specifically provides:

"A person may be convicted of an offence under this section—
 (a) notwithstanding that actual suffering or injury to health, or the likelihood of actual suffering or injury to health, was obviated by the action of another person; . . ."

This provision has not been authoritatively construed, and it leads to difficulties, particularly in abandonment cases such as *R. v. Whibley*,[47] where the abandonment took place in a juvenile court. In that case the accused was acquitted on the ground that his actions only involved some fright on the part of the child, but it does not appear to have been argued that but for the intervention of others a child who is abandoned is likely to suffer total neglect. The section can be read in two ways. One can say that an offence is committed wherever A behaves towards the child in a way that is likely to cause the requisite suffering unless the child is in fact cared for by others, and whether or not such care is likely: or one can say that an offence is committed only where suffering is likely in the sense both that it would be the normal result of A's behaviour in the absence of intervention by others and in the sense that the intervention of others is unlikely, and that subsection 3(a) is concerned only to prevent the accused taking advantage of some unexpected event which prevents actual harm. In *R. v. Boulden*[48] the accused was convicted of neglect and abandonment where he telephoned the Society for the Prevention of Cruelty to Children and told them he had to leave his children, and where they were, although he gave a false reason for leaving them, and then went off without waiting to see if anyone came to look after the children. It could be said there at least that the accused did not care whether or not the children were looked after as he did not wait to see if any arrangements were in fact going to be made for them, and it does not follow from *Boulden* that it is an offence to take one's children along to a Cruelty Prevention Society or Children's Officer and there abandon them. The distinction between these two situations can perhaps not be justified on a strict reading of the statute, but it is one the courts might well be tempted to make.

---

[45] *H. v. Lees*; *D. v. Orr*, 1993 S.C.C.R. 900, L.J.-G. Hope at 910F.

[46] *ibid*. See also *McF. v. Normand*, 1995 S.C.C.R. 380 where, in respect of an 18-month-old child left alone in a locked car in Bath Street, Glasgow, whilst its parents were Christmas shopping, the sheriff had considered what might have happened if the child had become suddenly ill, or someone had broken into the car, or the car had been involved in a collision with another vehicle, or the child had been taken from the car by some evily disposed or perverted person — but the Appeal Court dismissed such considerations as speculative and not created by the parents' period of absence: see L.J.-G. Hope's opinion at 394E. Lord Hope did, however, consider there to be some force in the Crown's argument that the longer such a young child was left alone, the more likely it was that he would become distressed and that such distress might amount to "unnecessary suffering". *Cf. W. v. Clark*, 1999 S.C.C.R. 775, where the manner of abandonment (in a flat where there was no readily usable food, and in the company of a dog of doubtful temperament) was considered likely to cause unnecessary suffering and injury to health within the meaning of the offence.

[47] (1938) 26 Cr.App.R. 184.

[48] (1957) 41 Cr.App.R. 105.

Chastisement. Section 12(7) specifically reserves the right of parents, **31.08** teachers and other persons having "lawful control or charge" of a child or young person to administer punishment to him; but the modern law prevents teachers from exercising any such right.[49]

Other Offences. The 1937 Act[50] also contains a number of other offences **31.09** against children. These include the following:

1. It is an offence for any person having parental responsibilities in relation to, or having charge or care of, a child or young person under 16 to allow him to be used for begging.[51] A person who has parental responsibilities in relation to, or charge or care of, a person under 16 who allows him to be in any place where he is in fact used for begging will be presumed to have allowed him to be there for that purpose,[52] and if any person who is performing or offering anything for sale in a street or public place has a child with him who has been "lent or hired out to him" the child is deemed to be there for the purpose of inducing the giving of alms.[53]

2. It is an offence to give excisable liquor to a child under five years **31.10** old except in case of sickness or emergency, or on medical advice.[54]

3. Section 22[55] of the Act provides: **31.11**

"If any person who has attained the age of sixteen years, and who has parental responsibilities in relation to a child under the age of seven years or charge or care of such a child allows the child to be in any room containing an open fire grate not sufficiently protected to guard against the risk of his being burnt or scalded without taking reasonable precautions against that risk, and by reason thereof the child is killed or suffers serious injury, he shall on summary conviction be liable to a fine [of level 2 on the standard scale]:

Provided that neither this section, nor any proceedings taken thereunder, shall affect any liability of any such person to be proceeded against by indictment for any indictable offence."

Criminal Law (Consolidation) (Scotland) Act 1995. This Act contains a **31.12** number of sexual offences in connection with persons under 16 years of age. These include the following which replace sections 13 and 14 of the 1937 Act:

"**4.** It is an offence for any person having parental responsibilities (within the meaning of the Children (Scotland) Act 1995) in relation to, or having charge or care of, a girl under 16 to cause or encourage her seduction, or unlawful sexual intercourse with or

---

[49] See *supra*, para. 29.38.

[50] As amended by the Children (Scotland) Act 1995, Sched. 4, para. 7(3).

[51] Section 15(1). Maximum penalty three months' and a fine of level 3 on the standard scale.

[52] Section 15(2).

[53] Section 15(3). This subsection does not apply to young persons — *i.e.* persons over 14 years old.

[54] Section 16. Maximum penalty a fine of level 1 on the standard scale. Section 18, as amended and extended by the Protection of Children (Tobacco) Act 1986 and the Children and Young Persons (Protection from Tobacco) Act 1991, deals with the selling of tobacco to persons under sixteen.

[55] As amended by the Children (Scotland) Act 1995, Sched. 4, para. 7(4).

prostitution of her, or the commission upon her of an indecent assault or an offence against section 6 of the Criminal Law (Consolidation) (Scotland) Act 1995.[56] As the latter section deals with lewd practices committed upon consenting girls aged between 12 and 16, 'indecent assault' in relation to girls under 12 is probably meant to include lewd practices whether or not any actual assault is involved.

A person is deemed to have caused or encouraged the seduction, etc. of a girl 'if he has knowingly allowed her to consort with, or to enter or continue in the employment of, any prostitute or person of known immoral character.'[57] 'Knowingly allows' refers to 'such a permission as can be deemed to be causing or encouraging,' and mere negligence in controlling the child's activities is not sufficient."[58]

31.13   "**5.** It is an offence for any person having parental responsibilities (within the meaning of the Children (Scotland) Act 1995) in relation to or having charge or care of a child or young person between four and 16 to allow him or her 'to reside in or frequent a brothel.' "[59]

31.14 *Indecent photographs.* It is an offence to take or permit to be taken or possess any indecent photograph of a person under the age of 16.[60]

---

[56] Section 10(1) and (3): maximum penalty two years' on indictment, three months' on summary conviction. In *R. v. Drury* (1975) 60 Cr.App.R. 195 the accused allowed a baby-sitter in his charge to become drunk and behave indiscreetly with a visitor he had brought to the house: he was convicted of encouraging an indecent assault by the visitor because of his failure to intervene.

[57] Section 10(2).

[58] *cf. R. v. Chainey* [1914] 1 K.B. 137 where a father was acquitted, the girl having been allowed out late by others when he was on night shift, and there being evidence that he had once ordered her indoors on seeing her out late but did not know of any immoral intercourse involving her.

[59] Section 12(1). Maximum penalty six months' and a fine of level 2 on the standard scale. The section does not affect the accused's liability under s.9 of the Criminal Law (Consolidation) (Scotland) Act 1995: *infra*, para. 36.36.

[60] Civic Government (Scotland) Act 1982, ss. 52 and 52A: see, *infra*, paras 41.23 and 41.22.

PART IV

INJURY TO ANIMALS

CHAPTER 32

CRUELTY TO ANIMALS

Protection of Animals (Scotland) Act 1912

Sections 1, 1A and 1B of this Act provide: **32.01**

"**1.**—(1) If any person—
  (a) shall cruelly beat, kick, ill-treat, over-ride, over-drive, over-
      load, torture, infuriate or terrify any animal, or shall cause or
      procure, or, being the owner, permit any animal to be so
      used, or shall, by wantonly or unreasonably doing or omitting
      to do any act, or causing or procuring the commission or
      omission of any act, cause any unnecessary suffering, or,
      being the owner, permit any unnecessary suffering to be so
      caused to any animal; or
  (b) shall convey or carry, or cause or procure, or, being the
      owner, permit to be conveyed or carried, any animal in such
      manner or position as to cause that animal any unnecessary
      suffering; or
  (c) shall cause, procure, or assist at the fighting or baiting of any
      animal[1]; or shall keep, use, manage, or act or assist in the
      management of, any premises or place for the purpose, or
      partly for the purpose, of fighting or baiting any animal, or
      shall permit any premises or place to be so kept, managed, or
      used, or shall receive, or cause or procure any person to
      receive, money for the admission of any person to such
      premises or place[2]; or
  (d) shall wilfully, without any reasonable cause or excuse, admin-
      ister, or cause or procure, or being the owner permit, such
      administration of, any poisonous or injurious drug or sub-
      stance to any animal, or shall wilfully, without any reasonable
      cause or excuse, cause any such substance to be taken by any
      animal; or

---

[1] *cf. Johnstone and Ors v. Abercrombie* (1892) 3 White 432, a decision, by a court of
seven judges, relative to s.1 of the now repealed Cruelty to Animals (Scotland) Act 1850,
which section was similar in its terms to s.1(1) of the 1912 Act: the case dealt with
cock-fighting, and it was held that cocks were not included in the term "animal" given the
then limited meaning of that term in s.11 of the 1850 Act. (See now s.13(a), (b) of the 1912
Act, and ss.1A and 1B, *infra*.)
[2] The Cockfighting Act 1952 penalises the possession of instruments or appliances
designed or adapted for use in the fighting of domestic fowl for the purpose of using or
permitting such use — maximum penalty on summary conviction three months' and a fine
of level 3 on the standard scale (s.1(1) as amended by the Criminal Procedure
(Consequential Provisions) (Scotland) Act 1995, Sched. 2, Pt II).

(e) shall subject, or cause or procure, or being the owner permit to be subjected, any animal to any operation which is performed without due care and humanity[3];

such person shall be guilty of an offence of cruelty within the meaning of this Act . . .[4]

1A.[5]—(1) A person who is present when animals are placed together for the purpose of their fighting each other shall be guilty of an offence and liable on summary conviction to a penalty not exceeding level 4 on the standard scale.

(2) It shall be a defence for a person charged with an offence under subsection (1) above to prove that he had a reasonable excuse for being so present.

1B.—If a person who publishes or causes to be published an advertisement for a fight between animals knows that it is such an advertisement he shall be guilty of an offence and liable on summary conviction to a penalty not exceeding level 4 on the standard scale."

The Abandonment of Animals Act 1960 provides that it shall be an offence of cruelty within the meaning of section 1(1) of the 1912 Act if the owner or person in charge or control of any animal abandons it without reasonable cause or excuse, whether permanently or not, in circumstances likely to cause it unnecessary suffering. It is also an offence to cause or procure such abandonment, or for the owner of the animal to permit it.[6]

---

[3] The Protection of Animals (Anaesthetics) Act 1954 (as amended by the Protection of Animals (Anaesthetics) Act 1964, the Animals (Scientific Procedures) Act 1986, Sched. 3, para. 3, and the Protection of Animals (Anaesthetics) Order 1982 (S.I. 1982 No. 1626), Art. 2), which does not apply to fowls, birds, fish or reptiles, provides that the performance of certain operations without anaesthetics is deemed to be a performance without due care and humanity. See, *e.g.*, *Braid v. Brown*, 1990 S.C.C.R. 33 (stitching of wound to dog, caused by a dog groomer, by that groomer without the administration of an effective anaesthetic, held not to fall within the minor operations excepted under Sched. 1 from the deeming provision of the 1954 Act).

[4] Maximum penalty on summary conviction a fine of level 5 (if the amendment proferred by the Protection of Animals (Scotland) Act 1993, s.1 is followed) or level 4 (if the amendment stated in the Criminal Procedure (Consequential Provisions) (Scotland) Act 1995, Sched. 2, Pt II, is accepted) on the standard scale and six months' imprisonment: Sheriff N.M.P. Morrison (ed.), *Sentencing Practice* (W. Green, Edinburgh, 2000), at para. L3.0002 (Note), suggests that the later of the two statutes should be accepted as setting the correct fine level. The court may also order the animal to be destroyed under certain circumstances: s.2, or deprive the owner of his ownership and "make such order as to the disposal of the animal as they think fit" if the animal is likely to be exposed to further cruelty: s.3. A person who is convicted of an offence may be disqualified from keeping an animal: see Protection of Animals (Amendment) Act 1954, s.1 (as amended by the Protection of Animals (Amendment) Act 1988, s.1), and if so is disqualified from applying for a licence to keep a riding establishment: Riding Establishments Act 1964, s.1(2)(e), or an animal boarding establishment, s.1(2)(e): Animal Boarding Establishments Act 1963, or a breeding establishment for dogs: Breeding of Dogs Act 1973. Where a defendant was disqualified from keeping cattle, it was held by a divisional court in England that the disqualification extended to the keeping of sheep: *Wastie v. Phillips* [1972] 1 W.L.R. 1293.

[5] This section, and s.1B, *infra*, inserted by the Protection of Animals (Amendment) Act 1988, s.2(3).

[6] The maximum penalties are the same as those for a contravention of s.1(1) of the 1912 Act: see n.4, *supra*.

The 1912 Act, unlike its predecessor the Cruelty to Animals **32.02** (Scotland) Act 1850, is not limited to cases of "wanton" cruelty, and cases decided under the earlier Act[7] cannot be relied on in dealing with charges under the 1912 Act.[8] It is not necessary to show that there was any intention to cause pain to the animal: it is enough if "the accused actually knew that he was inflicting unnecessary pain and suffering on a dumb animal, or at least that he ought to have known that, because the proved circumstances would have conveyed such knowledge to any normal and reasonable person."[9] It would, however, still be a defence that the accused was unaware of the circumstances which caused the suffering.[10]

The accused's motive is irrelevant, but where what is done is a customary operation done in the belief that it is necessary for the well-being of the beast, there may be no *mens rea*.[11] It is a defence that the suffering was inflicted on the animal in self-defence, or in defence of another animal,[12] but it is an offence to injure a trespassing animal.[13] It may also be doubted whether it can still be said that it is not an offence to kill or injure an animal provided only that the killing or injuring is not done "cruelly".[14]

If the Crown is unable to prove that any suffering at all was caused to an animal as a result of the accused's conduct, no offence can have been committed under section 1 of the Act which, indeed, requires not only suffering[15] but unnecessary suffering.[16]

---

[7] Such as *Cornelius v. Grant* (1880) 4 Couper 327, and *Jack v. Campbell* (1880) 4 Couper 351.

[8] *Easton v. Anderson*, 1949 J.C. 1.

[9] *ibid.*, L.J.-G. Cooper at 6.

[10] *cf. Sharp v. Mitchell* (1872) 2 Couper 273; *Downie and Anr v. Fraser* (1893) 1 Adam 80; *Wright and Wade v. Rowan* (1890) 2 White 426, cases of ill-treatment by servants where that ill-treatment was unknown to the accused.

[11] *Renton v. Wilson* (1888) 2 White 43; *Todrick v. Wilson* (1891) 2 White 636; both cases of dishorning cattle.

[12] *Farrell v. Marshall*, 1962 S.L.T. (Sh.Ct.) 65.

[13] *cf. Clark v. Syme*, 1957 J.C. 1: a conviction for malicious mischief for shooting a sheep.

[14] See *Cornelius v. Grant* (1880) 4 Couper 327 where it was held not to be wanton cruelty to kill a dog with a knife in order to protect one's own dog, there being no intent to injure or inflict pain needlessly, which is best regarded as a case of self-defence, and *Jack v. Campbell* (1880) 4 Couper 351 where it was held not to be wanton cruelty to shoot at and injure a trespassing dog where the shooting was without any cruel purpose.

[15] See *Patchett v. MacDougall*, 1983 J.C. 63, where the accused deliberately and unreasonably shot and killed a dog with a semi-automatic shotgun. Since there was no evidence that the unfortunate animal had suffered any pain at all prior to its demise, and on the assumption that loss of life was not "suffering" within the meaning of the statutory provision, the Appeal Court considered that no offence under s.1 of the Act had been committed. As L.J.-C. Wheatley put it, at 65: "The onus was on the prosecution to establish the constituent elements of the charge, and in the absence of a finding that the dog underwent any suffering or that a reasonable inference can be drawn from the findings that the dog underwent suffering ... I do not consider that the charge against the appellant was established or that the conviction recorded against him can stand." The Court did opine, however, that the prosecution might have had greater success if the charge had been one of malicious mischief at common law (see opinion of L.J.-C. Wheatley at 64 and 65).

[16] Where the accused caused suffering to a dog, but had done so out of a desire to render the animal unconscious and thus release it from the pain and distress of distemper, it was held that such suffering had not been "unnecessary": *Tudhope v. Ross*, 1986 S.C.C.R. 467, Sh.Ct.

32.03 *Omissions.* Cruelty may be committed by omission of or neglect in a duty to take care of animals. In *Anderson v. Wood*[17] it was held to be cruelty to leave a horse out in the cold without food, and in *Wilson v. Johnstone*[18] it was held to be cruelty to leave oxen in a slaughterhouse for 77 hours without food. In *Easton v. Anderson*[19] a carter who allowed his horse to draw a cart while suffering from saddle sores was convicted of cruelty although he had used a chambered saddle in an effort to relieve the horse of pain, the effort having been clearly unsuccessful. A master may be guilty of an offence where his servant ill-treats an animal if the master has conducted his affairs so carelessly as to make such ill-treatment likely.[20]

The Act provides that "an owner shall be deemed to have permitted cruelty . . . if he shall have failed to exercise reasonable care and supervision in respect of the protection of the animal therefrom."[21]

32.04 The Act does not apply to any act which would be lawful under the Animals (Scientific Procedures) Act 1986,[22] or to anything done or omitted "in the course of the destruction, or the preparation for destruction, of any animal as food for mankind, unless . . . accompanied by the infliction of unnecessary suffering", or, under certain circumstances, to coursing or hunting.[23]

32.05 The Act applies to any domestic or captive animal,[24] whether a quadruped or not. A domestic animal is any animal including any fowl which is tame or has been, or is being, sufficiently tamed to serve some purpose for the use of man. A captive animal is any non-domestic animal, including any bird, fish or reptile, "which is in captivity, or confinement, or which is maimed, pinioned, or subjected to any appliance or contrivance for the purpose of hindering or preventing its escape from captivity or confinement."[25]

Other statutes

32.06 Under section 3 of the Animals (Scientific Procedures) Act 1986, the application of any experimental or other scientific procedure to a living vertebrate animal is prohibited if that procedure may have the effect of causing the animal pain, suffering, distress or lasting harm, except where the procedure is carried out by persons licensed to do so and as part of an approved project in an approved place.[26] Also, the public exhibition of such procedures is prohibited, as is the showing of them live on television for general reception.[27]

---

[17] (1881) 4 Couper 543.

[18] (1874) 3 Couper 8.

[19] 1949 J.C. 1.

[20] *Wright and Wade v. Rowan* (1890) 2 White 426, L.J.-C. Macdonald and Lord Shand at 433.

[21] Section 1(2). Where an owner is convicted only by virtue of this provision he is not liable to imprisonment without the option of a fine.

[22] *infra*. This Act, by s.27(1) and Sched. 3, para. 2, amends s.1(3) of the 1912 Act.

[23] Section 1(3).

[24] See *Rowley v. Murphy* [1964] 2 Q.B. 43: a wounded stag taken into an enclosure and there killed not a captive animal, there being no exercise of dominion over it apart from mere confinement.

[25] Section 13(a)–(c).

[26] Maximum penalty, on indictment, two years' and a fine; on summary conviction, six months' and a fine of the statutory maximum (s.22(1)).

[27] Section 16(1). Maximum penalty, on summary conviction, three months' and a fine of level 4 on the standard scale (s.22(3)). It is also an offence, under s.16(2), to advertise the carrying out of any such procedure as would contravene s.16(1); the maximum penalty is the same as that for a contravention of s.16(1).

The Performing Animals (Regulation) Act 1925 provides for the **32.07** registration of exhibitors and trainers of animals and for the prohibition of exhibitions involving cruelty. The Act does not apply to training or exhibiting animals trained for military, police, agricultural or sporting purposes.[28] A person convicted under the Protection of Animals (Scotland) Act 1912 may be disqualified from training or exhibiting animals.[29] The Protection of Animals Act 1934 prohibits public performances involving the throwing or casting of unbroken horses or bulls, the wrestling, fighting or struggling with untrained bulls, and riding bulls or horses stimulated by the use of appliances or treatment involving cruelty with the intention of making them buck.[30]

The slaughter of animals is regulated by the Slaughter of Animals **32.08** (Scotland) Act 1980; provisions to avoid the suffering of pain by animals when being slaughtered are contained in sections 10 and 12 of that Act.[31] Similarly, the slaughter of poultry is regulated by the Slaughter of Poultry Act 1967.[32]

The Wildlife and Countryside Act 1981 makes general provision for **32.09** safeguarding the lives of, and preventing disturbance to, certain birds and animals.[33] Also, under the Wild Mammals (Protection) Act 1996, it is an offence[34] for any person to mutilate, kick, beat, hit, nail or otherwise impale, stab, burn, stone, crush, drown, drag or asphyxiate any wild mammal with intent to inflict unnecessary suffering; and under the Protection of Badgers Act 1992, it is an offence for a person cruelly to ill-treat a badger,[35] to use badger tongs in the course of killing or taking (or attempting to kill or take) a badger, to dig for a badger or to use for

---

[28] See s.7.

[29] 1925 Act, s.4(2) read with s.6(b).

[30] Maximum penalty on summary conviction, three months' and a fine of level 4 on the standard scale (s.2, as amended by the Criminal Procedure (Consequential Provisions) (Scotland) Act 1995, Sched. 2, Pt II).

[31] It is an offence to contravene these provisions; maximum penalty, on summary conviction, six months' and a fine of level 3 on the standard scale (s.18(1)): in addition, if the convicted person is licensed under s.6, the court may cancel his licence (s.18(3)). (Cancellation of registration under s.4 is no longer a possible penalty, since s.4 was repealed by the Deregulation (Slaughterhouses Act 1974 and the Slaughter of Animals (Scotland) Act 1980) Order 1996 (S.I. 1996 No. 2235), reg. 6, Sched.) It is a defence if the accused proves that a contravention was necessary to prevent physical injury or suffering to any person or animal due to an accident or other emergency (s.18(2)). The provisions of s.10 (methods of slaughtering animals in slaughterhouses) do not apply where an animal is slaughtered for the food of Jews or Muslims by methods appropriate to the Jewish or Muslim faiths, provided no unnecessary suffering is inflicted (s.11).

[32] See s.1(1) as amended by the Animal Health and Welfare Act 1984, s.5; Sched. 1, para. 1(2). Maximum penalty, on summary conviction, three months' and a fine of level 3 on the standard scale (s.1(3), as amended by the 1984 Act, *supra*, Sched. 1, para. 1(3)). See also s.2 of the 1967 Act.

[33] See, in particular, ss. 1, 3, 5 (as amended by the Wildlife and Countryside (Amendment) Act 1991, s.1), 8, 9, 11 (as amended by the last mentioned Act, s.2) and 12 — together with the Schedules to which these sections refer. For specific exceptions, see ss. 2 and 10: for maximum penalties, see s.21. See, *e.g.*, *Hawthorn v. Cramb*, 1960 J.C. 97 (interpreting s.5(3) of the now repealed Protection of Birds Act 1954, the current equivalent of that subsection being s.5(1)(e) of the Wildlife and Countryside Act 1981).

[34] Subject to the exceptions contained in s.2. Maximum penalty, on summary conviction, six months' and a fine of level 5 on the standard scale, or, if more than one wild mammal was involved, a fine determined as if the accused had been convicted of a separate offence in respect of each such mammal (s.5). "Wild mammal" is defined in s.3.

[35] Defined in s.14 as any animal of the species "Meles meles".

the purpose of taking or killing a badger any firearm other than a smooth bore weapon as statutorily defined.[36]

A number of game statutes also contain provisions designed to protect certain kinds of animals.[37]

---

[36] Section 2(1). Under s.3, it is an offence (*inter alia*) intentionally or recklessly to disturb a badger when it is occupying a badger sett (as defined in s.14: see *D.P.P. v. Green* [2001] 1 W.L.R. 505). General exceptions are provided by s.6, and exceptions specific to the provisions of s.3 by s.8. Maximum penalty, on summary conviction, six months' and fine of level 5 on the standard scale (s.12(1)): under s.12(2), if an offence is committed in respect of more than one badger, the maximum fine is to be determined as if the person convicted had been convicted of a separate offence in respect of each badger.

[37] See, *e.g.*, The Ground Game Act 1880, s.1, proviso — para. (3) — which (as amended by the Agriculture (Scotland) Act 1948, s.48(1)) restricts the killing by firearms of ground game in the exercise of rights under that Act on moorland and unenclosed lands to the period between July 1 and March 31, an exception being made for detached portions of moorlands or unenclosed lands of less than 25 acres which adjoin arable lands; and the Agriculture (Scotland) Act 1948, s.50(1)(a), as substituted by the Pests Act 1954, s.10 — which prohibits the use of a firearm for killing hares or rabbits at night (maximum penalty, on summary conviction, a fine of level 3 on the standard scale: s.50(2), as amended by the Criminal Procedure (Consequential Provisions) (Scotland) Act 1995, Sched. 2, Pt II). See also the Animals (Cruel Poisons) Act 1962.

PART V

SEXUAL OFFENCES

CHAPTER 33

RAPE[1]

Rape is the carnal knowledge of a female by a male person obtained **33.01** by overcoming her will.[2] An essential element is the absence of an honest belief on the part of the male that the female is consenting.[3] Mistaken but genuine belief that the woman was a consenting party, even if not based on reasonable grounds, is therefore a defence.[4] It is not a defence that at the material time the female person was the male person's wife.[5]

---

[1] For a general discussion of this crime, see C.H.W. Gane, *Sexual Offences* (Butterworths' Scottish Criminal Law and Practice Series, 1992), Ch. 2.

[2] *cf. Jamieson v. H.M. Advocate (No. 1)*, 1994 S.C.C.R. 181, L.J.-G. Hope (opinion of the court) at 186A; Hume, i, 301–302; Burnett, p.101; Alison, i, 209; Macdonald, p.119 — all of whom require the carnal knowledge to be obtained by force: contrast the English definition contained in s.1 of the Sexual Offences Act 1956 (as substituted by the Criminal Justice and Public Order Act 1994, s.142), which provides:
"(1) It is an offence for a man to rape a woman or another man.
(2) A man commits rape if —
(a) he has sexual intercourse with a person (whether vaginal or anal) who at the time of the intercourse does not consent to it; and
(b) at the time he knows that the person does not consent to the intercouse or is reckless as to whether that person consents to it . . ."

[3] *Meek v. H.M. Advocate*, 1982 S.C.C.R. 613, L.J.-G. Emslie at 618; *Jamieson v. H.M. Advocate (No. 1)*, 1994 S.C.C.R. 181, L.J.-G. Hope at 186A.

[4] *Meek v. H.M. Advocate*, 1982 S.C.C.R. 613; *Jamieson v. H.M. Advocate (No. 1)*, 1994 S.C.C.R. 181. The decision in *Meek* emphasises that it is unnecessary for the judge to direct the jury on the matter of honest belief in consent where the defence case is that the woman actively co-operated and the Crown case is that she struggled: see also *Quinn v. H.M. Advocate*, 1990 S.L.T. 877, and *cf.* the factual situation in *Jamieson*. Both *Meek* and *Jamieson* apparently apply the law laid down for England in *R. v. Morgan* [1976] A.C. 182, HL; and under the modern English law (see n.2, above), which stems from *Morgan*, it is enough for conviction that the defendant knew that the victim did not consent or was reckless as to that matter; and, further, where recklessness as to consent is in issue, what is meant in England is subjective recklessness (*R. v. Satnam* (1984) 78 Cr.App.R. 149; *cf. R. v. Pigg* [1983] 1 W.L.R. 6): it remains to be decided whether subjective or objective recklessness will be applied to this aspect of rape under Scots law. See Vol. I, paras 7.45, 7.49–7.51, 7.58 *et seq.*; 9.26, 9.27 and 9.32.
It has been held in New Zealand that if the accused initially believes the woman is consenting, but realises after penetration that this is not the case and carries on nonetheless, he is guilty of rape: *Kaitamaki v. The Queen* [1985] A.C. 147; and it has been held in both England and Canada that an error as to consent resulting from the defendant's self-induced intoxication is an irrelevant error as far as recklessness is concerned: *R. v. Woods* (1981) 74 Cr.App.R. 312; *Leary v. The Queen* [1978] 1 S.C.R. 29; see also Vol. I, para. 12.25.

[5] *S. v. H.M. Advocate*, 1989 S.L.T. 469. See also *H.M. Advocate v. Duffy*, 1983 S.L.T. 7; *H.M. Advocate v. Paxton*, 1985 S.L.T. 96. This is also the law in England: *R. v. R.* [1992] 1 A.C. 599, HL, where the rejection of the "marital exemption" as a defence to rape was subsequently held not to have contravened Art. 7(1) of the European Convention on Human Rights: *S.W. v. U.K.* (1996) 21 E.H.R.R. 363.

Carnal knowledge

33.02   Rape is completed by penetration of the woman's body: emission of semen into the body is unnecessary. Penetration must be intended to be *per vaginam*. Other forms of intercourse, such as buggery, do not constitute rape even when obtained forcibly, but only indecent assault. It was at one time thought that it was only *proof* of emission which was unnecessary,[6] but it is now settled that rape can be committed even where there is proof that there was no emission.[7] Penetration to any extent is sufficient, even if it is not complete, and Macdonald refers to an unreported case in which a plea of guilty to rape was tendered although the woman's hymen was unbroken.[8] In practice, however, it will be very difficult to obtain a conviction for rape where the hymen is unbroken.

It follows from the definition of rape in terms of penetration that a eunuch may be guilty of rape.[9] Nor is there any presumption in Scots law that a boy under puberty cannot commit rape[10]; in *Robt Fulton, Jun.*[11] a boy aged 13 years and 10 months was convicted of the rape of a girl aged five.

33.03   *"Of a female person"*. The crime of rape may be committed upon any female, whatever her age or condition. A prostitute is entitled to the same protection as any other woman.[12] Under Scots law, a male person cannot be raped.[13]

33.04   *"By a male person"*. It is not rape for a woman to force a man or boy to have intercourse with her.[14] Nor is it rape for a woman to force another woman to indulge in penetrative sexual relations with her. A woman can, however, be art and part guilty of a rape committed by a man.[15]

---

[6] See Alison, i, 209. *Cf. Duncan Macmillan* (1833) Bell's Notes 82.

[7] *Arch. Robertson* (1836) 1 Swin. 93; Macdonald, p.120.

[8] *Frank McCann* (1891) Macdonald 120. There are suggestions in earlier cases that at any rate where the victim is adult penetration must be complete: *Arch. Robertson, supra,* Lord Meadowbank at 102; *cf. Richd Jennings* (1850) Macdonald 120, a conviction for raping a child without complete penetration. *Robertson Edney* (1833) Bell's Notes 83 was a case where the hymen was unruptured and the labia only slightly irritated and the jury convicted of assault with intent to ravish only, but the case is not of value as an authority and only the verdict is reported. In *Alex. Macrae* (1841) Bell's Notes 83, on the other hand, it was said that so long as there was penetration its extent was unimportant and it was not necessary to prove that the vagina had been entered.

[9] *Arch. Robertson, supra,* Lord Meadowbank at 102, Lord Medwyn at 105–106.

[10] Burnett, p.102; Macdonald, p.121. (The presumption in English law that a boy under the age of 14 was not capable of sexual intercourse and thus not capable of committing rape was abolished under the Sexual Offences Act 1993.)

[11] (1841) 2 Swin. 564.

[12] Hume, i, 304–305; Macdonald, p.121; *Ed. Yates and Henry Parkes* (1851) J. Shaw 528. *Dub.* Burnett, p.104 and Alison, i, 214–215.

[13] It has been held in England that a person who was born male and remained biologically of that sex was a man for the purpose of criminal charges which required the defendant to be a male, notwithstanding that the actual defendant had had gender reassignment surgery and hormone treatment to alter his physical characteristics so that they approximated to those of a woman; and it was considered to be of no consequence that the defendant had become philosophically, psychologically and socially a female: *R. v. Tan and Ors* [1983] Q.B. 1053, CA. Other cases also support this view: see, *e.g., Re. P. and G. (Transsexuals)* [1996] 2 F.L.R. 90; *Cossey v. U.K.* (1990) 13 E.H.R.R. 622; *cf. B. v. France* (1992) 16 E.H.R.R. 1.

[14] Mackenzie suggests that a woman can commit rape: Mackenzie, I.16.5, but he may be thinking of the crime of *"raptus"* which consisted in forcible abduction: Burnett, p.102.

[15] See *Chas Matthews and Margt Goldsmith*, High Court at Glasgow, Dec. 1910, unrep'd; *Walker and McPherson*, High Court at Dundee, March 1976, unrep'd.

"Overcoming her will"

Macdonald follows Hume and Alison and speaks of rape as committed **33.05** "forcibly" as well as "against the will of the victim",[16] but this aspect of the law of rape has developed since the time of Hume and Alison. The modern law depends mainly on two nineteenth-century cases: *Wm Fraser*[17] and *Chas Sweenie*.[18]

(i) *Wm Fraser*. F. had intercourse with a married woman by pretending to be her husband. He was charged with rape, and also with the innominate crime of "Fraudulently and Deceitfully obtaining Access to and having Carnal Knowledge of a Married Woman, by pretending to be her husband, or otherwise conducting himself, and behaving towards her so as to deceive her into the belief that he was her husband." The court were agreed that the innominate offence constituted a crime, as being a species of fraud,[19] but the majority held that the circumstances did not constitute rape. The ground of decision was that the intercourse had been obtained with the woman's consent, albeit a consent impetrated by fraud. It was argued that the fraud was of such a nature as to vitiate any apparent consent, but this argument was rejected by the majority of the court.

To have intercourse with a married woman by pretending to be her husband was declared to be rape by section 4 of the Criminal Law Amendment Act 1885[20] (now section 7(3) of the Criminal Law (Consolidation) (Scotland) Act 1995, but other forms of "fraudulent intercourse" fall to be dealt with at common law, except that it is an offence under section 7(2)(b) of the 1995 Act to procure a woman to have intercourse with oneself or others by fraud.[21] It is clear from *Fraser*[22] that it is not rape for A to induce B to have intercourse with him by pretending that he is X,[23] but the law regarding other types of fraud is unsettled. In *R. v. Flattery*[24] it was held in England that it was rape for A to have intercourse with B by pretending that he was giving her medical treatment, but there is no Scots reported case of this kind. The error induced in such a case is distinguishable from that in *Fraser* since it is an error as to subject-matter, so to speak, and not as to person. The woman in *Fraser* did consent to have sexual intercourse, the woman in *Flattery* did not. But in each case intercourse is obtained by fraud, and the *Flattery* type case might well be charged as fraud in Scotland, if only because such a charge would be clearly relevant and avoid the difficulties which a rape charge would present. Again, there is much force in the

---

[16] Macdonald, 119; see Hume, i. 302; Alison, i. 209.
[17] (1847) Ark. 280.
[18] (1858) 3 Irv. 109.
[19] Lord Cockburn at Ark. 312; *cf. supra*, para. 18.15.
[20] See *infra,* para. 33.18.
[21] See *infra*, para. 36.29.
[22] (1847) Ark. 280.
[23] Lord Cockburn at Ark. 310–311.
[24] (1877) 2 Q.B.D. 410; see also *R. v. Williams* [1923] 1 K.B. 340.

argument that if an error as fundamental as that in *Fraser* does not vitiate consent, no other form of error would be regarded as vitiating it.[25]

33.06   (ii) *Chas Sweenie*.[26] Lord Cockburn said in *Fraser*[27] that the essence of rape was that intercourse was obtained "without the woman's consent",[28] but *Fraser* can also be explained by reference to the absence of the use of any force by the accused. These two interpretations of *Fraser* were before the court in *Sweenie* and the majority preferred the latter, holding that an element of force was necessary to constitute rape. The accused in *Sweenie* had intercourse with a sleeping woman, and was charged with rape, and with "having carnal knowledge of a woman when asleep, and without her consent, by a man not her husband." It was accepted by the court that Sweenie was guilty of a crime, and most of the judges regarded it as a form of indecent assault.[29] There is much force in the view that an indecent assault which involves penetration is rape, and it may well be that the only reason the majority of the court did not accept this was because of a disinclination to extend the scope of what was technically a capital crime,[30] but whatever the reason, *Sweenie* is authority that this view is wrong.[31] It follows that rape requires a greater degree of force than does indecent assault, and that at least it requires more force than is involved in the act of intercourse itself.[32]

The majority of the court in *Sweenie* were faced with two difficulties: they had to decide what degree of force was necessary for rape; and they had to reconcile their decision with the accepted law that it is rape to have intercourse with a woman who has been drugged by the accused so that she becomes insensible or otherwise incapable of giving or withholding consent.[33] The best solution offered was that of Lord Ardmillan,

---

[25] It is now plain that, in English law, fraud vitiates consent of the victim not only where that fraud induces error as to the nature of the act itself but also, and independently, where it deceives the victim as to the identity of the person with whom sexual intercourse is to be had, whether that person is the husband, cohabitee or lover of the complainer: *R. v. Linekar* [1995] 2 Cr.App.R. 49, CA, Morland J. (opinion of the court) at 53. In *Linekar*, it was held that a prostitute who had allowed the defendant to have sexual intercourse with her following his promise to pay her £25 was not raped by him, although he refused to honour that promise and had had no intention of honouring it from the outset: although there had been fraud, it did not deceive her either as to the nature of the act involved or as to the identity of the person with whom the act was to be performed.

In Scotland, error of the *Fraser* type has been held to vitiate consent in the law of contract, *supra*, para. 14.43, and should logically have the same result in rape. Lord Cockburn in *Fraser* did not seem to appreciate that there is a difference between pretending to be Mr B., the victim's husband, and pretending that one has gone through a valid marriage ceremony with her. The latter situation is clearly not rape (see *Gray v. Criminal Injuries Compensation Board*, 1993 S.L.T. 28, OH, Lord Weir at 21B; 1999 S.C.L.R. 191, IH, Lord Coulsfield at 197B–198A) but it does not follow that the former is not rape either. *Cf. Papadimitropoulos v. The Queen* (1957) 98 C.L.R. 249; *R. v. K.,* 1966 (1) S.A. 366 (S.R.,A.D.); *Bolduc and Bird v. R.* [1967] S.C.R. 678. See "Absence of Consent in Rape", 1958 S.L.T. (News) 181.

[26] (1858) 3 Irv. 109.

[27] (1847) Ark. 280.

[28] *ibid.*, at 308.

[29] 3 Irv., Lord Ardmillan at 138, Lord Cowan at 145, Lord Deas at 146, Lord Neaves at 154.

[30] Lord Cowan at 143, Lord Deas at 149–150, Lord Neaves at 151–152. *Cf. H.M. Advocate v. Logan*, 1936 J.C. 100, L.J.-C. Aitchison at 102; T.B. Smith, p.189.

[31] That it is wrong is supported by the more modern case of *Sweeney and Anr v. X.*, 1982 S.C.C.R. 509: see esp. L.J.-G. Emslie's opinion at 522–523 (Thomson's Appeal); *cf.* his Lordship's opinion at 524 (Sweeney's Appeal).

[32] Lord Ardmillan at 3 Irv. 137.

[33] The court were also concerned about the question of rape committed on children and idiots, but these cases are special: see *infra*, paras 33.12, 33.14.

who said that "any mode of overpowering the will, without actual personal violence, such as the use of threats, or drugs, is force in the estimation of the law — and . . . any degree of force is sufficient in law to constitute the crime of rape, if it is sufficient in fact to overcome the opposing will of the woman."[34] It is simpler, however, to discard the concept of force altogether, and to define rape in terms of overpowering or overcoming the will of the victim. It is this element which was absent in *Fraser* and *Sweenie* and which is present in the drugging cases, and it offers a satisfactory way of reconciling them.

Drugging. It is accepted that rape can be committed by drugging a **33.07** woman so that she becomes incapable of resisting the accused.[35]

The only relatively modern case which deals with drugging as a mode of rape is *H.M. Advocate v. Logan*.[36] The charge there was that the accused raped a woman "while she was in a state of insensibility from the effects of intoxicating liquor supplied to her by you for the purpose of rendering her incapable of resistance." The jury were directed that if the woman took the drink voluntarily there was no rape but only indecent assault, even if she had been "invited or coaxed" to drink, but that if she "was plied with drink, and drink of a deadly kind, the nature of which was concealed from her, in order to overcome her resistance" there was rape.[37]

These directions raise two points:

(1) The woman must have been drugged by the accused so that he might rape her. It is not rape to have intercourse with a woman who has drugged herself or been drugged by a third party any more than it is rape to have intercourse with a sleeping woman.[38] It is submitted further that it is not rape to drug a woman for the purpose, for example, of robbing her, and thereafter to form and carry out an intention to have intercourse with her. *A fortiori* it is not rape to drug a woman for a lawful purpose, such as the administration of an anaesthetic for an operation, and then to form and carry out an intention to have intercourse with her.[39]

(2) The directions in *Logan*[40] indicate that the woman must be unaware of the nature of the drug administered. It is possible, however, to figure cases in which there is no question of concealing or disguising what the woman is given, but in which it seems reasonable to regard the crime as rape. If A knows that B will not consent to have intercourse with him, and deliberately sets out to ply her with whisky so that she will become incapable of resisting him, he has overcome her will and should, it is thought, be guilty of rape. It is difficult in practice to distinguish this situation from that where A merely spends a night drinking with B and then takes advantage of her, but the two situations are different.[41]

---

[34] 3 Irv. at 137.

[35] *Fraser, supra,* Lord Moncreiff at 303, Lord Medwyn at 304, Lord Cockburn at 308; *Sweenie, supra,* Lord Ardmillan at 137, Lord Ivory at 141, Lord Deas at 148, L.J.-G. McNeill at 157; *H.M. Advocate v. Logan,* 1936 J.C. 100; Alison, i, 211; Macdonald, p.120; *dub.* Burnett, p.103. *Duncan Macmillan* (1833) Bell's Notes 83 is inconclusive.

[36] 1936 J.C. 100.

[37] L.J.-C. Aitchison at 101–102.

[38] *H.M. Advocate v. Grainger and Rae,* 1932 J.C. 40.

[39] L.J.-G. McNeill was of the view that this was rape: *Sweenie, supra,* at 157.

[40] 1936 J.C. 100.

[41] Alison suggests that whether or not it is rape depends on whether the prior conduct of the parties indicates that the woman would have been willing to have intercourse with the man, but this is not a satisfactory criterion: Alison, i, 213.

Where the woman is given doped drink or induced to take a drug by some other fraud, it might be argued that intercourse is obtained by fraud and so does not constitute rape.

But a distinction can be drawn between the *Fraser*[42] type of case, where the woman is induced by fraud to consent to intercourse, and the drugging cases, where she is induced by fraud to take something which deprives her of the ability to consent or refuse consent to intercourse. In the latter case her will is overcome by fraud, so there is rape; in the former she consents to intercourse so there can be no rape

33.08   CRIMINAL LAW (CONSOLIDATION) (SCOTLAND) ACT. Section 7(2)(c) of the Criminal Law (Consolidation) (Scotland) Act 1995 provides a maximum penalty of two years' imprisonment for anyone who:

> "[A]pplies or administers to, or causes to be taken by, any woman or girl any drug, matter or thing, with intent to stupefy or overpower so as thereby to enable any person to have unlawful sexual intercourse with such woman or girl."[43]

This section applies to a person drugging a girl in order to have intercourse with her himself.[44]

33.09   *The degree of violence necessary.* In the ordinary case of forcible rape it must be shown that the woman's resistance was overcome by violence and that she did not consent to intercourse. In practice this usually means that the Crown must show that the accused used violence of a kind which the "reasonable woman" would not have been able to resist, and it is sometimes said that they must also show that the particular woman "resisted to the utmost", or "to the last".[45] The degree of violence required, however, is a question of fact in each case. Where a woman is drunk, a lesser degree may be necessary than in the case of a sober woman,[46] and there may even be cases where hardly any violence is necessary at all because although the woman is capable of refusing consent she is not capable of putting up any resistance as in Hume's example of "a poor cripple lame lass of sixteen years old, lying bedfast . . . and unable to make any resistance."[47] All that is necessary in any case is to show that the woman's will to resist was overcome — the important matter is not the amount of resistance put up, but whether the woman remained an unwilling party throughout, and the degree of violence or resistance is important only as evidence of this.[48] If the woman remains unwilling, and not merely coy, the fact that she is a weak vessel who gives up the struggle as hopeless at a time when she might have continued to struggle should not prevent the man being guilty of rape.

---

[42] *Wm Fraser* (1847) Ark. 280.

[43] One adminstration constitutes one offence, however many men have intercourse with the drugged girl: *R. v. Shillingford; R. v. Vanderwall* [1968] 1 W.L.R. 566, CA.

[44] *cf. R. v. Williams* (1898) 62 J.P. 310; see *infra*, para. 36.29.

[45] *cf.* Hume, i, 302; Anderson, p.161.

[46] *Duncan Macmillan* (1833) Bell's Notes 83; *Sweeney and Anr v. X*, 1982 S.C.C.R. 509.

[47] *Jas Mackie* (1650) Hume, i, 303.

[48] *Barbour v. H.M. Advocate*, 1982 S.C.C.R. 195, Lord Stewart, charge to the jury, at 198. *Cf. R. v. Olugboja* [1982] 1 Q.B. 321, CA; *R. v. Malone (Thomas Patrick)* (1998) 2 Cr.App.R. 447, CA, esp. opinion of L.J. Roch (opinion of the court) at 457A–458A.

THREATS. Rape, like robbery, may be committed by threats of immi- **33.10** nent harm.[49] To obtain intercourse by threat of future action is extortion and not rape.[50] Again, it may not be rape to wear a woman's resistance down by persuasion, or even perhaps by ill-treatment, such as kidnapping and imprisoning her, if in the end she consents to intercourse, provided that that consent was obtained "without any use of threats or violence at the time or recently before."[51] As in cases involving violence, it is a question of fact whether the woman's will to resist was overcome by the threats used.[52] The threats may be directed to a third party, such as the woman's baby.[53]

CRIMINAL LAW (CONSOLIDATION) (SCOTLAND) ACT 1995. It is an offence **33.11** under section 7(2)(a) of the Criminal Law (Consolidation) (Scotland) Act 1995 to procure or attempt to procure by threats a woman "to have unlawful sexual intercourse", including connection with the procurer.[54]

Constructive rape

There are three types of case in which rape can be committed without **33.12** any overcoming of the victim's will.

(1) *Where the female is under 12 years old.* It is rape for a man to have sexual intercourse with a girl below the age of puberty, that is to say with a girl less than 12 years old.[55] This is said to be because such a child is incapable of consenting or of having a proper will in the matter at all,[56] or because there is a legal presumption in such cases that there was no consent,[57] but it is simpler to accept that there is a rule of law that such intercourse is always rape.

MENS REA. On principle it should be a defence to constructive rape of **33.13** this kind that A believed the girl to be over the age of 12 since it is a defence to any rape that A believed the woman was a consenting party.[58] The question has never been raised in a Scots case, and could be avoided by charging the accused under section 5(1) of the Criminal Law

---

[49] Hume, i, 302; Alison, i, 211; *John Murray* (1826) Alison, i, 212; Macdonald, p.121.

[50] *cf. Martin v. H.M. Advocate*, 1993 S.C.C.R. 803, where the appellant's threats to go to the 14-year-old complainer's mother and make trouble, and to batter the complainer, were left to the jury as evidence of the overcoming of the complainer's unwillingness to allow the appellant to have sexual intercourse with her.

[51] Hume, i, 302.

[52] See, *e.g.*, *Martin v. H.M. Advocate*, 1993 S.C.C.R. 803. In one unusual South African case a policeman was convicted of rape where the girl put up no resistance at all, but was frightened of being shot as she knew he was a European policeman and carried a gun: it seems that the rape was committed by the accused's use of his position of authority to frighten the girl: *S. v. S.*, 1971 (2) S.A. 591 (A.D.). In *McKenzie v. Strang*, High Court at Glasgow, Jan. 1976, unrep'd, where the Crown averred a threat to strike with a bottle, and the victim was described as a "rather pathetic person", who could not put up a very great resistance, Lord Wylie told the jury to look at the whole circumstances "and if the threats were serious enough to induce her to believe they might be carried out unless she yielded then he who threatened her in that way and induced her to yield in that way commits the crime of rape" (Transcript of Judge's charge, p.15).

[53] *Paul Macdonald*, High Court at Glasgow, June 1969, unrep'd. In *Martin v. H.M. Advocate*, 1993 S.C.C.R. 803, some of the threats were made against the complainer's mother.

[54] See *infra*, para. 36.29.

[55] Hume, i. 303; Alison, i, 213; Macdonald, p.119; *Jas Burtnay* (1822) Alison, i, 214.

[56] Hume, i, 303; Alison, i, 213.

[57] *Chas Sweenie* (1858) 3 Irv. 109, Lord Ardmillan at 138, Lord Deas at 147.

[58] *cf. R. v. Z.* 1960 S.A. 739 (A.D.).

(Consolidation) (Scotland) Act 1995,[59] either as the sole charge or as an alternative to a charge of rape.[60] Section 5(1) does not require *mens rea* for the offence it creates, that is to say the offence of having sexual intercourse with a girl under the age of 13. If the question were to arise the court would doubtless have scant sympathy with the accused and might well hold that *mens rea* as to age was unnecessary.[61] At best for the accused the court would, it is thought, hold that only recklessness was required.

33.14   (2) *Where the female is mentally abnormal.* The fact that the woman was of weak intellect seems at one time to have been regarded mainly as an adminicle of evidence which entitled the court to hold that there had been rape although the other evidence in the case did not indicate either the use of any considerable force by the accused or any considerable resistance by the woman.[62] In *Chas Sweenie,*[63] however, although the question did not fall to be decided the judges were prepared to accept that an idiot, and in some cases a lunatic, was probably in the same position as a child, and their opinions suggest that it is always rape to have intercourse with a person incapable through mental abnormality of giving a proper consent, although no force is used and the woman offers no resistance.[64] *Sweenie* also suggests that idiots, like children, are deemed incapable of consent,[65] while in the case of other mentally abnormal persons their ability to consent is a question of fact in each case.

The matter has never been decided at common law, but the statutory provisions regarding sexual intercourse with mentally abnormal women appear to assume that such intercourse is not necessarily rape, even where the woman is seriously impaired mentally. The Criminal Law Amendment Act 1885, hs.5(2), made carnal knowledge of "any female idiot or imbecile woman or girl, under circumstances which do not amount to rape" a specific statutory offence, and section 46 of the Mental Deficiency and Lunacy (Scotland) Act 1913 and section 96 of the Mental Health (Scotland) Act 1960[66] both provided that a person might be acquitted of rape and convicted of the statutory offence of having intercourse with a defective. In practice, persons who have sexual

---

[59] Section 5(1) provides: "Any person who has unlawful sexual intercourse with any girl under the age of 13 years shall be liable on conviction on indictment to imprisonment for life."

[60] Formerly, under the Sexual Offences (Scotland) Act 1976, s.15 (now repealed by the Crime and Punishment (Scotland) Act 1997, Sched. 3), it was possible for a person accused of the rape of a girl under 12 years of age to be convicted of (*inter alia*) a contravention of s.3(1) of that Act — the then equivalent of s.5(1) of the Criminal Law (Consolidation) (Scotland) Act 1995: but the terms of s.14 of the 1995 Act mean that an alternative verdict of guilty of a s.5(1) offence cannot now be returned by the jury unless a specific charge under that subsection has been inserted as an alternative in the indictment.

[61] *cf. R. v. Prince* (1875) L.R. 2 C.C.R. 154, which admittedly dealt with a statutory offence; *cf.* also, *B. (A Minor) v. D.P.P.* [2000] 2 W.L.R. 452, HL, where it was held that the offence under s.1(1) of the (English) Indecency with Children Act 1960 required *mens rea*, *i.e.* an absence of belief that the victim was aged 14 years or above.

[62] *Hugh McNamara* (1848) Ark. 521.

[63] (1858) 3 Irv. 109.

[64] *ibid.*, Lord Ardmillan at 137, Lord Ivory at 140, Lord Cowan at 144, Lord Deas at 147, Lord Neaves at 153.

[65] *ibid. Cf.* Anderson, 161; *H.M. Advocate v. Grainger and Rae*, 1932 J.C. 40, Lord Anderson at 41.

[66] The last Act repealed the 1913 Act and s.5(2) of the 1885 Act.

intercourse with "consenting defectives"[67] have since 1885 been dealt with for a statutory offence and not at common law.[68]

The current provision,[69] however, does not refer to defectives, idiots or imbeciles but rather to women protected by the section, that is to say any woman or girl "who is suffering from a state of arrested or incomplete development of mind which includes significant impairment of intelligence and social functioning",[70] and again assumes that a person may be acquitted of rape but convicted of the offence of having unlawful sexual intercourse with such a woman or girl.[71]

The present position regarding women who suffer from mental disorder as distinguished from mental impairment is not clear. The Mental Deficiency and Lunacy (Scotland) Act 1913 applied to certified lunatics in the same way as it applied to defectives,[72] but the Mental Health (Scotland) Act 1984 contains no provisions regarding intercourse with mentally ill persons except where the accused is in one of the special "fiduciary" relationships to the woman set out in section 107 of the Act. It is submitted that it must be a crime to have intercourse with a woman incapable through mental disorder of giving a valid consent and the only question is whether it is rape or a form of "clandestine injury" analogous to having intercourse with a sleeping woman. The opinions of the judges in *Sweenie*[73] suggest that it can be rape, and the only authority to the contrary is an *obiter dictum* of Lord Thomson in *Mack v. H.M. Advocate*[74] to the effect that it is not a crime at common law to have intercourse with a certified lunatic. The position may well be that if such a case were charged as rape the charge would be held relevant, but that it is more likely to be charged as a form of indecent assault.

MENS REA. The statutory crime of having intercourse with a mentally **33.15** impaired woman requires recklessness as to the woman's condition,[75] and at least the same *mens rea* would be required for a common law charge of constructive rape of or clandestine injury to a mentally abnormal person. The common law might, however, require knowledge of the condition as did the earlier Mental Deficiency and Lunacy (Scotland) Act 1913.[76]

MENTAL HEALTH (SCOTLAND) ACT 1984. Section 106 of this Act provides **33.16** that:

"(1) It shall be an offence, subject to the exception mentioned in this section,—

---

[67] The term "defective" is not now encountered in modern legislation: see *infra*.

[68] The statutes applied (and the current provision, *infra*, applies) only to "unlawful" intercourse, so that it was (and is) probably not an offence at all for a man to have intercourse with his defective (or, now, "mentally impaired") wife.

[69] Mental Health (Scotland) Act 1984, s.106.

[70] *ibid.*, s.106(6), (7). The threshold is thus one of "mental impairment" rather than mental disorder which (see s.1(2) of the 1984 Act as amended by the Mental Health (Public Safety and Appeals (Scotland) Act 1999 (asp 1), s.3) means mental illness including personality disorder.

[71] 1984 Act, s.106 (1)(a), (5).

[72] Section 56. See *D.P.P. v. Head* [1959] A.C. 83.

[73] (1858) 3 Irv. 109.

[74] 1959 S.L.T. 288, at 289, where the question was not argued at all.

[75] Mental Health (Scotland) Act 1984, s.106(2).

[76] Section 46, which applied only to certified lunatics or defectives and required knowledge of their condition.

(a) for a man to have unlawful sexual intercourse with a woman who is protected by the provisions of this section;

. . .

(2) A person shall not be guilty of an offence against this section if he did not know and had no reason to suspect that the woman in respect of whom he is charged was protected by the provisions of this section.

(3) Any person guilty of an offence under this section shall be liable on conviction on indictment to imprisonment for a term not exceeding 2 years or to a fine.

. . .

(6) A woman is protected by the provisions of this section if she is suffering from a state of arrested or incomplete development of mind which includes significant impairment of intelligence and social functioning.

(7) In this section 'woman' includes girl."

"Unlawful intercourse" means intercourse outside marriage.[77]

33.17   Section 107 of the Act[78] makes it an offence for a male member of a hospital or nursing home staff or of the board of management of a hospital or a man carrying on a nursing home, to have unlawful intercourse with a woman receiving in-patient treatment in that hospital or nursing home for mental disorder, or to have intercourse in the hospital or nursing home with a person receiving treatment for mental disorder as an out-patient of the hospital or nursing home. The section also makes it an offence for a man to have unlawful intercourse with a woman suffering from mental disorder who is under his care. The same requirement as to knowledge applies as in cases under section 106.[79]

33.18   (3) *By impersonating the woman's husband.* Section 4 of the Criminal Law Amendment Act 1885 (now section 7(3) of the Criminal Law (Consolidation) (Scotland) Act 1995) virtually overruled *Wm Fraser*,[80] and provided that it was rape for A to induce a married woman to permit him to have intercourse with her by impersonating her husband. In *H.M. Advocate v. Montgomery*[81] the woman was at the time married to her second husband, her first being dead, and the accused pretended to be her first husband. This was held to be rape in terms of the section, on the view that if he were indeed her first husband her second marriage would be invalid and the first husband be in law still her husband. The woman was, of course, a married woman, but the *ratio* of the case suggests that "married woman" in the section should be interpreted to include widows.

---

[77] *Henry Watson* (1885) 5 Couper 696.
[78] As amended by the Adults with Incapacity (Scotland) Act 2000 (asp 4), Sched. 6.
[79] The maximum penalty under s.107 is also two years' imprisonment. Under s.107(3), any reference to having unlawful sexual intercourse with a woman is to include a reference to committing a homosexual act under s.13(4) of the Criminal Law (Consolidation) (Scotland) Act 1995 (see also s.13(3)); thus the protection of s.107 is extended to males who might otherwise be subjected to sexual exploitation.
[80] (1847) Ark. 280.
[81] 1926 J.C. 2.

The effect on the section of the provision that a marriage may be dissolved on the ground of the husband's presumed death[82] has not been considered, but as such a dissolution is unconditional, at any rate unless it is reduced,[83] an accused who pretended that he was a husband in respect of whose presumed death the marriage had been dissolved would not, it is submitted, be guilty of this form of constructive rape.

The section is limited to the single case of impersonation of a particular person, the woman's husband. It does not apply where A merely pretends to be married to the woman, for example, by going through a bigamous form of marriage, or by concealing from the woman that their "marriage" is void for any other reason.

Clandestine injury to women

The innominate offence of having intercourse with a sleeping woman **33.19** is a form of assault[84] but may also be charged as a specific offence, which has been called "clandestine injury to women",[85] and it is not necessary to aver that the woman was "assaulted".[86] The woman in *Sweenie*,[87] was both married and asleep, but the offence can be committed against an unmarried woman,[88] and also against a woman who has been rendered unconscious by drink either self-administered or given by a third party,[89] by a faint, or from any other cause. It may apply also where the woman has been rendered incapable of giving or refusing consent to intercourse from any temporary cause, as distinguished from the case where the incapacity arises from some constitutional condition such as mental defect, or some long-standing disease such as insanity.

---

[82] Presumption of Death (Scotland) Act 1977, s.3.

[83] See E.M. Clive, *The Law of Husband and Wife in Scotland* (4th ed., 1997), para. 29.008.

[84] *Chas Sweenie* (1858) 3 Irv. 109; *Wm Thomson* (1872) 2 Couper 346; Macdonald, p.120; *Sweeney and Anr v. X.*, 1982 S.C.C.R. 509; *Quinn v. H.M.Advocate.*, 1990 S.L.T. 877.

[85] Macdonald, p.120; *H.M. Advocate v. Grainger and Rae*, 1932 J.C. 40; *Rodgers v. Hamilton*, 1994 S.L.T. 822, where L.J-C. Ross at 823C treats indecent assault and clandestine injury as interchangeable. It has also achieved statutory recognition: see, *e.g.*, the Criminal Procedure (Scotland) Act 1995, s.274(2)(c).

[86] *Wm Thomson, supra; Wm McEwan or Palmer* (1862) 4 Irv. 227, where the offence was libelled as having been committed "stealthily".

[87] (1858) 3 Irv. 109.

[88] *Wm Thomson, supra.*

[89] *H.M. Advocate v. Grainger and Rae, supra.*

CHAPTER 34

SODOMY AND BESTIALITY

SODOMY

Sodomy, as a crime at common law, is defined as unnatural carnal **34.01** connection between male persons.[1] It consists in and is limited to penetration of the anus of one male by the penis of another, the degree of penetration required being the same as that in rape.[2] Both parties are guilty of the offence.[3]

The crime in Scots law is sodomy, rather than buggery,[4] and it is submitted that it is not sodomy, or indeed a crime at all as such, to have anal intercourse with a consenting adult woman.[5]

Other forms of unnatural connection such as oral intercourse do not **34.02** constitute sodomy, nor is there any classification in Scotland corresponding to what the American Law Institute's Model Penal Code calls "deviate sexual intercourse" and which it defines as "sexual intercourse per os or per anum between human beings who are not husband and wife, and any form of sexual intercourse with an animal",[6] although conduct of this kind may constitute shameless indecency.[7]

---

[1] Alison, i, 566; Macdonald, p.149; Anderson, p.97; Mackenzie, I.15.3 says it "is when a man lyes with a man." The scope of this common law crime has been much reduced by statutory provisions: see para. 34.03, *infra*.

[2] Alison, i, 556. *Cf. Wm Simpson and Ralph Dodds* (1845) 2 Broun 671.

[3] There is no authority or ground for Alison's statement that a catamite under 14 cannot be guilty of sodomy: Alison bases his opinion on English authority: Alison, i, 566; *cf.* Smith and Hogan, p.481. But since a consenting child is not guilty in a case of lewd practices it would be reasonable to treat the child in sodomy in the same way, and in practice a charge would never be brought against a catamite under 16, or even against someone under that age taking an active part if, in either case, the other partner was significantly older.

[4] Although in *John Swan and John Litster* (1570) Hume, i, 469 it was described as "sodomy, otherwise named bougarie."

[5] *cf. R. v. H.*, 1962 (1) S.A. 278 (S.R.). Where the woman does not consent the question is academic since the facts constitute indecent assault, and it is no longer necessary to specify a *nomen juris*, the "label" on the backing of the indictment being solely for convenience, although it may find its way into a schedule of previous convictions. In *Donaldson and Ors*, High Court at Glasgow, Sept. 1975, unrep'd, a charge of appalling depravity, which included the averment that the accused assaulted a woman, and did "place private members in her mouth, repeatedly ravish her, repeatedly with your private members penetrate her naked hinder parts and have unnatural connexion with her," was described on the backing as "assault, rape and sodomy". The accused were found not guilty. In *J.P. Deavy*, High Court at Glasgow, Feb. 1969, a charge of shameless indecency was brought for buggery with the accused's 14-year-old daughter.

[6] Model Penal Code, O.D. s.213.2 (1); an earlier draft did not exclude spouses: T.D. 4, s.207.5(6). Such intercourse is criminal in the code only where one person causes another to carry it out "by force or its equivalent".

[7] *infra.*, para. 36–20.

34.03   An act of sodomy between two male persons is no longer criminal if both parties consent, both are aged 16 years or above, and the act takes place in private.[8] For the act to be "in private", the locus must not be a lavatory to which the public have or are permitted to have access.[9] A male person ("the other person") who suffers from a mental deficiency of a nature or degree which precludes his living an independent life or guarding himself against serious exploitation is deemed incapable of giving consent to such an act,[10] although the person who commits sodomy with him will have a defence if that person proves that he did not know and had no reason to suspect that the other person was suffering from such a deficiency.[11]

Where the qualifying conditions mentioned above cannot be met in relation to an act of sodomy, the common law offence of sodomy is available; but section 13(5)[12] of the Criminal Law (Consolidation) (Scotland) Act 1995 provides: "[I]t shall be an offence to commit or to be party to the commission of, or to procure or attempt to procure the commission of [an act of sodomy] — (a) otherwise than in private; (b) without the consent of both parties to the act; or (c) with a person under the age of sixteen years."[13] (Since this offence carries a maximum penalty of two years' imprisonment, it may be thought unfair to proceed in such a case with a common law charge where the penalty would be unlimited.[14]) It is also a statutory offence under section 13(6) to procure or attempt to procure the commission of (*inter alia*) an act of sodomy between two other male persons.[15]

Where one of the parties to an act of sodomy is under the age of 16 whilst the other has attained that age, the person under 16 is to be considered as not having committed an offence contrary to section

---

[8] Criminal Law (Consolidation) (Scotland) Act 1995, s.13(1), as amended by the Sexual Offences (Amendment) Act 2000, s.1(3)(a). "Homosexual act" in s.13(1) includes sodomy: s.13(4).

[9] Criminal Law (Consolidation) (Scotland) Act 1995, s.13(2), as amended by the Convention Rights (Compliance) (Scotland) Act 2001 (asp 7), s.1.

[10] *ibid.*, s.13(3).

[11] *ibid.*

[12] As amended by the Sexual Offences (Amendment) Act 2000, s.1(3)(a).

[13] It is a defence to a charge under s.13(5)(c) that the person charged "being under the age of 24 years [and having] not previously been charged with a like offence, had reasonable cause to believe that the other person was of or over the age of 16 years": s.13(8), as amended by the Sexual Offences (Amendment) Act 2000, s.1(3)(b). On this defence, see the similar defence under s.5(5) of the Criminal Law (Consolidation) (Scotland) Act 1995 considered at paras 36.03 *et seq., infra*.

[14] The use of the common law in such a situation is, however, not without support from the Appeal Court: see *Batty v. H.M. Advocate*, 1995 S.C.C.R. 525; *cf. Cartwright v. H.M. Advocate*, High Court Appeal against sentence, June 27, 2001, unrep'd, where the Court invited counsel for the appellant to address them on the competency of the Crown's having prosecuted the appellant for a common law crime where the appropriate statutory offence had become time-barred — an invitation which was not taken up; the Court did consider, however, that the maximum penalty for the common law crime in such circumstances should not exceed the maximum which would have been allowed had the statutory offence been prosecuted within the prescribed period after that offence's alleged commission.

[15] Maximum penalty, for this offence, or an offence under s.13(5), is, on indictment, two years' and a fine, and on summary conviction, three months' or a fine of the prescribed sum: s.13(7). Under s.13(11) there is a time limit on the commencement of proceedings for a s.13(5) or s.13(6) offence of 12 months from the date on which the alleged offence was committed; should this limit be permitted to expire, there appears to be no statutory bar to commencement of proceedings for the common law offence of sodomy; *cf. Cartwright, supra*.

13(5)(a) or (c),[16] apparently in accordance with the view that those who are underage are to be protected rather than prosecuted.[17]

BESTIALITY

It is a crime to have "Unnatural carnal connection with a beast",[18] the **34.04** intercourse being "after the manner and in the place where that crime is usually committed."[19] In England bestiality (buggery) may be committed *per anum* or *per vaginam*[20] and there is no reason for supposing that the same is not the case in Scotland.

In England a woman may be guilty of bestiality,[21] but the position is not clear in Scotland. In *Jas McGivern*[22] the major proposition of the indictment referred only to "carnal connection with a beast", but Alison described bestiality as the connection of a man with an animal.[23] There are no reported cases of bestiality by a woman and it is unlikely that any such charge would now be brought.

---

[16] Section 13(8A), inserted by the Sexual Offences (Amendment) Act 2000.

[17] See J.P. Burnside, "The Sexual Offences (Amendment) Act 2000: The head of a 'kiddy-libber' and the torso of a 'child-saver'?" [2001] Crim.L.R. 425.

[18] *Jas. McGivern* (1845) 2 Broun 444; Hume, i, 469; Alison, i, 566; Macdonald, p.149.

[19] Alison, i, 566.

[20] Smith and Hogan, at p. 479; *R. v. Bourne* (1952) 36 Cr.App.R. 125.

[21] Smith and Hogan, *op. cit., loc. cit.*

[22] (1845) 2 Broun 444.

[23] Alison, i, 566. *Contra.* Lev. xviii, 23.

CHAPTER 35

INCEST

The law of incest is contained in the first four sections of the Criminal **35.01** Law (Consolidation) (Scotland) Act 1995.[1] In terms of section 1, sexual intercourse[2] between the following persons is incestuous and thus criminal: parent and child, grandparent and grandchild, siblings, aunt and nephew, uncle and niece, great-grandparents and great-grandchildren, where in each case the parties are of different sexes. Incest is committed whether the relationship is of the full blood or the half blood and whether or not it is traced through or to any person whose parents were not married to each other. The relationship must, however, be consanguineous, except in the case of adoptive or former adoptive parents and children. Consent is not an issue which is relevant to incest, save that "[i]f it is alleged that the woman concerned did not consent, the proper approach is to charge rape".[3]

It is a defence for the accused to prove that he or she did not know and had no reason to suspect that his or her partner was related to him or her in one of the degrees specified, or that he or she did not consent to the intercourse, or that he or she was married to his or her partner by virtue of a marriage entered into abroad but recognised as valid in Scotland.

Section 1(3) specifically provides that incest is limited to the relationships listed above.

Intercourse between step-parent and step-child. Under the former law, **35.02** intercourse between step-parents and step-children was included within the crime of incest.[4] This is no longer so; but section 2 of the Criminal Law (Consolidation) (Scotland) Act 1995 makes it an offence for a step-parent or former step-parent to have intercourse with a step-child who is either under the age of 21 or who, although of or over that age, has at any time before becoming 18, lived in the same household and been treated as a child of the step-parent's family. The same defences are available as in the case of incest,[5] with an additional defence of reasonable belief that the child was of or over the age of 21. Although

---

[1] The original law was defined by the Incest Act 1567 (A.P.S. iii, 26, c.15). That Act was repealed by the Incest and Related Offences (Scotland) Act 1986, Sched. 2, and new provisions substituted by the device of adding ss. 2A-2D to the Sexual Offences (Scotland) Act 1976: that Act of 1976 was repealed retrospectively by the Crime and Punishment (Scotland) Act 1997, Sched. 1, para. 6, and by Sched. 3. (For an account of the former law, see Chap. 35 in the 2nd ed. of the present work.)

[2] Sexual intercourse is not defined in the Act but, as under the former law, must have the same meaning as in the Scots law of rape: Al. i, 566. *Cf.* the Sexual Offences (Amendment) Act 2000, s.3: see para. 35.04, *infra*.

[3] *McDade (R.C.) v. H.M. Advocate*, 1997 S.C.C.R. 731, Lord Sutherland at 733E.

[4] See the 2nd ed. of this work at para. 35.05.

[5] See para. 35.01, *supra*.

that defence appears as an independent alternative defence in section 2(b), it will of course be irrelevant where the basis of the charge is that the child lived in family with the accused when the child was under 18.

Intercourse between a foster-child and foster-parent is not struck at by the above statutory offence; but such intercourse may be a contravention of section 3 of the Act[6] or an example of the common law crime of shamelessly indecent conduct.[7]

35.03 *Breach of position of trust or authority.* Section 3 of the Criminal Law (Consolidation) (Scotland) Act 1995 also makes it an offence for a person over the age of 16 to have intercourse with a child under that age who is a member of the same household as the accused and in relation to whom the accused is in a position of trust or authority. It is a defence for the accused to prove: (a) that he believed on reasonable grounds that the other person was 16 or over; or (b) that he, the accused, did not consent to the intercourse; or (c) that the parties were married by a foreign marriage recognised as valid in Scotland.[8]

35.04 *Abuse of position of trust.* Further, under section 3 of the Sexual Offences (Amendment) Act 2000 it is an offence[9] for a person of at least 18 years of age ("A") to have sexual intercourse (whether vaginal or anal) with a person ("B") under that age or "to engage in any other sexual activity with or directed towards such a person"[10] if A is in a position of trust in relation to B. It is a defence for A to prove: (a) that he did not know, and could not reasonably have been expected to know, that B was under 18 or that B was a person in relation to whom he was in a position of trust, or (b) that he was lawfully married to B.[11] A is in a position of trust in relation to B if he looks after[12] persons under the age of 18 — (1) who are detained in an institution under a court order or any enactment, and B is detained there; (2) who are resident in a home or other place where accommodation is provided by an authority under section 26(1) of the Children (Scotland) Act 1995, and B is resident there; (3) who are accommodated and cared for "in an institution which is — (a) a hospital;

---

[6] If the conditions of that offence are met: see para. 35.03, *infra*.

[7] *cf. H.M. Advocate v. K.*, 1994 S.C.C.R. 499: see paras 36.20 *et seq.*, *infra*.

[8] The maximum penalty for an offence under ss. 1, 2 or 3 is, on summary conviction, three months'; and on indictment, life imprisonment (see s.4(5)).

[9] For a critical analysis of this offence, see J.P. Burnside, "The Sexual Offences (Amendment) Act 2000: The head of a 'kiddy-libber' and the torso of a 'child-saver'?" [2001] Crim.L.R. 425, at 428 *et seq.*

[10] Under s.3(5), "sexual activity": "(a) does not include any activity which a reasonable person would regard as sexual only with knowledge of the intentions, motives or feelings of the parties; but (b) subject to that, means any activity which such a person would regard as sexual in all the circumstances." This inevitably entails that the meaning of the concept will be dependent on the individual views of judge or jury in each particular case.

[11] Section 3(2). It is also declared that no offence will be committed (under s.3) if prior to the commencement of the Act a sexual relationship already existed between A and B (s.3(3)). Maximum penalty for an offence under s.3, on indictment, five years' and a fine; and on summary conviction, six months' and a fine of the statutory maximum.

[12] As defined under s.4(7), *i.e.*: "A person looks after persons under 18 for the purposes of this section [and thus of s.3] if he is regularly involved in caring for, training, supervising or being in sole charge of such persons." It is obvious, therefore, that those who are involved in such caring, training or supervision, but not on a regular basis, cannot be brought within the offence; they may, however, be within the reach of the common law offence of shameless indecency: *cf. Batty v. H.M. Advocate*, 1995 S.C.C.R. 525: see para. 36.20 *et seq.*, *infra*.

(b) a residential care home, nursing home, mental nursing home or private hospital; (c) a community home, voluntary home, children's home or residential establishment", and B is accommodated and cared for there; (4) who are receiving full-time education at an educational institution, and B is receiving such education there.[13]

---

[13] "Educational institution" is not defined, although it is stated that a person receives full-time education at such an institution if he is enrolled or registered there as a full-time pupil or student, or if he receives education there under arrangements with another educational institution where he is so enrolled or registered. Many of the other institutions etc. referred to in s.4(2)–(5) are given further meaning by reference to various enactments in s.4(9). Under s.4(1), situations further to those set out in s.4(2)–(5) under which a person is considered to be in a position of trust may be specified by statutory instrument.

CHAPTER 36

OTHER SEXUAL OFFENCES

INDECENT BEHAVIOUR

Offences involving indecent behaviour may be dealt with under three **36.01** headings — offences involving children and the mentally impaired, indecent exposure, and other forms of shameless indecency including homosexual offences.

Offences involving children and young persons

Sexual intercourse with girls under 16. Prior to 1885 it was not an offence **36.02** to have intercourse with a consenting girl who had reached the age of 12, that being the common law age of puberty. Section 5(1) and (2) of the Criminal Law (Consolidation) (Scotland) Act 1995[1] makes it an offence, punishable with life imprisonment, to have intercourse with any girl under the age of 13, and an offence punishable with ten years' imprisonment to attempt to do so.[2] Section 5(3) of the 1995 Act makes it an offence punishable with two years' imprisonment to have or attempt to have sexual intercourse with a girl of or above the age of 13 and under the age of 16.[3] Only the man is guilty of the offence[4]; and sentence must proceed on the basis that the girl consented, since if she did not the prosecution should probably have been for rape.[5]

ERROR AS TO MARRIAGE AND AGE IN SECTION 5. Section 5(5) of the 1995 **36.03** Act provides:

"It shall be a defence to a charge under subsection (3) above that the person so charged—

---

[1] Originally s.4 of the Criminal Law Amendment Act 1885.

[2] This section applies equally to girls under 12, but the practice is to charge common law rape where the girl is under 12 and to use the Act only for girls between 12 and 13. (The penalty for an offence under s.5(2) was increased from two years to 10 years by the Crime and Punishment (Scotland) Act 1997, s.14(1)(a).)

[3] These subsections speak of "unlawful" intercourse, but that has been defined as extra-marital intercourse: *Henry Watson* (1885) 5 Couper 696, and marriage with a girl under 16 is now itself unlawful: Marriage (Scotland) Act 1977, s.1(1). Difficulties may, however, arise where a girl under 16 has been lawfully married abroad: *Alhaji Mohammed v. Knott* [1969] 1 Q.B. 1. (The penalty for an offence under s.5(3) was increased from two years to 10 years by the Crime and Punishment (Scotland) Act 1997, s.14(1)(b).)

[4] See Vol. I, para. 5.05.

[5] *Thomas v. H.M. Advocate*, 1977 S.C.C.R. 77, L.J.-C. Ross at 81B-D: it may, however, be an element in mitigation "if the complainer had not merely consented but encouraged [the accused] to have intercourse with her" (at 81F).

(a) had reasonable cause to believe[6] that the girl was his wife; or
(b) being a man under the age of 24 years who had not previously been charged with a like offence,[7] had reasonable cause to believe[8] that the girl was of or over the age of 16 years."

36.04 MARRIAGE. Where A believes, with reasonable cause, that he has gone through a valid marriage with a girl who, unknown to him, is under 16 he is entitled to an acquittal whatever his age and previous history.[9]

36.05 "REASONABLE CAUSE". It has been held that the mere appearance of the girl is not sufficient to amount to "reasonable cause", at any rate unless her physical and mental development are extraordinary, and it appears that the accused must show that his belief was based on some particular information which it was reasonable for him to accept, such as a statement by her family, or the production to him of an inaccurate birth certificate[10]: that at any rate is the law in theory; in practice juries take a more lenient view, and tend to acquit when the girl was a willing partner, at any rate when she is of bad character.

36.06 "PREVIOUSLY CHARGED". These words have not generally been judicially defined in Scotland. They could refer to a charge by the police, an appearance on petition or complaint at the instance of the procurator fiscal, or an appearance on indictment. In England it has been held that where a man appears before a magistrate in committal proceedings that

---

[6] And, presumably, did believe: *cf. R. v. Banks* [1916] 2 K.B. 621 and *R. v. Harrison* (1938) 26 Cr.App.R. 166, in which it was held that the accused must in fact believe the girl to be of full age. Section 6(3) of the Sexual Offences Act 1956 makes the requirement of actual belief explicit in England.

[7] For instance an offence under s.5(3) of the Criminal Law (Consolidation) (Scotland) Act 1995, or ss. 4(1) or 10(1) of the Sexual Offences (Scotland) Act 1976, or an offence or an attempt to commit an offence under s.6 of the Sexual Offences Act 1956, which is the English equivalent of s.5(3) of the 1995 Act: 1995 Act, s.5(6). See para. 36.06, *infra*.

[8] See n.6, *supra*.

[9] Although presumably a belief that he had married a girl he knew to be under 16 would not be reasonable unless the marriage took place in a country where the age of marriage is under 16, and neither party was domiciled in Scotland or England: see *Pugh v. Pugh* [1951] P.482; *cf. Alhaji Mohamed v. Knott* [1969] 1 Q.B. 1.

[10] *H.M. Advocate v. Hoggan* (1893) 1 Adam 1, L.J.-C. Macdonald at 3–4; *H.M. Advocate v. Macdonald* (1900) 3 Adam 180, Lord McLaren at 182. *Cf. Mair v. Russell*, 1996 S.C.C.R. 453, where the complainer (who was 13) initially told the accused that she was 18, then that she was 16 — a statement endorsed by the complainer's friends: the conviction of the accused was quashed on appeal by consent of the Crown, on the ground that the sheriff at the trial had been wrong to determine the issue by reference to the complainer's appearance whilst she had been giving evidence; but the Appeal Court stated (at 456E) that had the evidence at the trial been more equivocal, it might well be that "the court [would] be able to decide this issue by having regard to the appearance of the complainer in the witness box." *(Cf.* The rebuttable presumption (pertaining to whether a person in respect of whom certain offences have been committed is under a specified age or not) provided by s.46(3) of the Criminal Procedure (Scotland) Act 1995. This presumption applies to any offence under the Children and Young Persons (Scotland) Act 1937, to offences under ss. 1, 10(1)–(3), and 12 of the Criminal Law (Consolidation) (Scotland) Act 1995, and to offences referred to in Sched. 1, paras 3 and 4 of the Criminal Procedure (Scotland) Act 1995. Other than the above specified offences in the Criminal Law (Consolidation) (Scotland) Act 1995, offences under Part I of that Act appear to be excluded from the ambit of the presumption, unless they can be brought within the terms of para. 4 of the Criminal Procedure (Scotland) Act 1995.)

is a previous charge, being an appearance before a competent court, except where he is committed for trial, in which case the trial itself is his first charge.[11] The nearest Scots equivalent to committal proceedings is an appearance on petition, but it is unlikely that such an appearance would be regarded as a "previous charge" for the purposes of the subsection, particularly as it does not nowadays involve any adjudication on the case by the court. In practice, therefore, a man may not be regarded as having been "previously charged" with an offence unless he has previously stood trial for it. Where a man appears on trial for having intercourse with more than one girl then, even if he was separately "charged" at an earlier stage in respect of each girl, he is entitled to the defence in respect of all the girls, provided he would have been entitled to it had be been tried only in respect of one girl.[12]

It has recently been decided that a man charged with raping a girl between the ages of 13 and 16 is *ipso facto* put on notice that he may alternatively be convicted of a section 5(3) offence in respect of her, since such an alternative is permitted by section 14 of the Criminal Law (Consolidation) (Scotland) Act 1995: thus, in any subsequent trial of such a man for having committed a section 5(3) offence, he is considered to be a person previously charged with such an offence, and unable to benefit from the statutory defence. (In the case in question, however, the man had stood trial for rape, although he had been acquitted of that, and any other lawful alternative, charge.)[12a]

ERROR AS TO AGE IN SECTION 5(1). The special provision of a defence of **36.07** error regarding age in section 5(5) of the 1995 Act suggests that no such defence is available in a charge under section 5(1).[13] This leads to the paradoxical result that even if it is a defence to a common law charge of rape of a girl of 11 for A to show that he had reasonable cause to believe the girl to be 14, if he is charged with the same crime as a contravention of section 5(1) this defence is not available to him.

---

[11] *R. v. Rider* [1954] 1 W.L.R. 463.

[12] *R. v. Rider, supra.* If A has intercourse with B in July and with C in August, and is tried in September and acquitted in respect of B it is doubtful if the defence would be open to him on a trial in November in respect of C. If, however, he were tried in September in respect of C, and then in November in respect of B, it might be felt that he should be entitled to the defence in both trials, although strictly speaking this would not be the case.

[12a] See *McMaster v. H.M. Advocate*, 2001 S.C.C.R. 517. It was argued in the appeal that the accused's rights under Art. 6(3)(a) of the European Convention on Human Rights had been infringed, because the original indictment for rape had contained no express mention of any alternative charge of which he might be convicted; but the Appeal Court applied the decision of the European Court of Human Rights in *De Salvador Torres v. Spain*, (1996) 23 E.H.R.R. 601, and held that there had been no infringement.

[13] *cf. B (A Minor) v. D.P.P.* [2000] 2 W.L.R. 452, HL, where the main argument of the House (that the offences within the Sexual Offences Act 1956 did not form a coherent code but were simply consolidated from a number of different statutes and, therefore, that in general legislative intent as to *mens rea* could not be gleaned by comparing the wording of one offence with another) does not apply to the offences in s.5(1)–(3) of the Criminal Law (Consolidation) (Scotland) Act 1995, since these were originally enacted together as ss.4 and 5 of the Criminal Law Amendment Act 1885 and since the forerunner of the current defence to s.5(3) of the 1995 Act was applied only to a s.5 offence under the 1885 Act: see also the amendment to the original defence under s.2 of the Criminal Law Amendment Act 1922. (This is also, in fact, the view taken of the English equivalent offences in ss. 5 and 6 of the Sexual Offences Act 1956: *see R. v. K* [2001] 3 W.L.R. 471, HL, Lord Bingham of Cornhill at 481H–482A.)

36.08 *Sexual intercourse with the mentally impaired.* Section 106(1)(a) of the Mental Health (Scotland) Act 1984 makes it an offence for a man to have unlawful intercourse with a woman (or girl) who is protected by the provisions of the section, unless the accused "did not know and had no reason to suspect that she was so protected."[14]

36.09 *Lewd practices.* COMMON LAW. It is a crime at common law to indulge in indecent practices towards children under the age of puberty,[15] with or without their consent.[16] Such practices may include performing sexual acts in presence of a child.[17] A woman may be convicted of using lewd practices towards a girl,[18] and presumably also towards a boy.

There is some authority for the view that lewd practices towards consenting boys "about" the age of puberty may constitute the crime of "lewd, indecent and libidinous practices and behaviour" at common law,[19] but the question is unlikely to arise now, since indecent behaviour by one male person with another male person who is under the age of 16 years is a statutory offence,[20] and is probably also punishable at common law as an example of "shamelessly indecent conduct".[21]

36.10   CRIMINAL LAW (CONSOLIDATION) (SCOTLAND) ACT 1995. Section 6 of the Criminal Law (Consolidation) (Scotland) Act 1995 provides:

---

[14] She is protected in terms of s.106(6), "if she is suffering from a state of arrested or incomplete development of mind which includes significant impairment of intelligence and social functioning." See *supra*, para. 33.16.

[15] The crime is known as "lewd, indecent and libidinous practices and behaviour."

[16] The cases cited by Bell in support of the proposition that it may be a crime to indulge in lewd practices with consenting girls over the age of puberty, *e.g. Wm Galloway* (1838) Bell's Notes 85; *Malcolm Maclean* (1838) Bell's Notes 86, are inconclusive, and would not have been followed in the later 19th and early 20th centuries: *Robert Philip* (1855) 2 Irv. 243; *Lockwood v. Walker* (1909) 6 Adam 124, L.J.-C. Macdonald at 127; Macdonald pp. 149–150; but the Appeal Court has stated (*obiter*) in *Batty v. H.M. Advocate*, 1995 S.C.C.R. 525 (a case of common law shamelessly indecent conduct involving female complainers between the ages of 13 and 16), at 528F, that "the balance of authority is now in favour of the view that the age of the complainer is not of the essence of the crime of lewd, libidinous and indecent practices and behaviour" (see also 528F–529E), and that the enactment of the statutory offence (now contained in s.6 of the Criminal Law (Consolidation) (Scotland) Act 1995) pertaining to indecent behaviour towards girls aged between 12 and 16 makes no difference. It seems that the availability of the common law offence of shamelessly indecent conduct in such cases will obviate the need for any final decision on the matter.

[17] *Samuel Innes*, High Court at Perth, Feb. 1968, unrep'd, a charge under s.4 of the Criminal Law Amendment Act 1922 which included an averment that the accused had intercourse with his wife in the girl's presence, as well as a charge of buggering the girl.

[18] *Walker and McPherson*, High Court at Dundee, March 1976, unrep'd, again a charge under s.4 of the 1922 Act.

[19] *David Brown* (1844) 2 Broun 261; *Andrew Lyall* (1853) 1 Irv. 218 — both pleas of guilty.

[20] Criminal Law (Consolidation) (Scotland) Act 1995, s.13(5), subject to the defence in s.13(8), both as amended by the Sexual Offences (Amendment) Act 2000, s.1(3)(a). There is, however, a time limit on prosecuting the statutory offence: see s.13(11).

[21] *McLaughlan v. Boyd*, 1934 J.C. 19. The question has arisen, but not been decided, whether it is competent for the Crown to charge common law shameless indecency where the appropriate statutory offence has become time-barred: see *Cartwright v. H.M. Advocate*, 2001 S.L.T. 1163, where it was held that (on the assumption of such competency) the maximum penalty for shameless indecency in those circumstances should not exceed the maximum which would have pertained under the statutory offence at the time when it could competently have been charged against the accused. Any such charge of shameless indecency must, of course, be a relevant one: *cf. H.M. Advocate v. Roose*, 1999 S.C.C.R. 259.

"Any person who uses towards a girl of or above the age of 12 years and under the age of 16 years, any lewd, indecent or libidinous practice or behaviour which, if used towards a girl under the age of 12 years, would have constituted an offence at common law shall, whether the girl consented . . . or not, be [guilty of an offence]."[22]

The Act is silent about any defence of error as to the girl's age, and it appears therefore that such a defence can never be open.[23]

MENTALLY IMPAIRED WOMEN. Indecent behaviour with a mentally **36.11** impaired woman may constitute the crime of lewd practices at common law,[24] but there are no reported examples of such a charge. Where, however, the woman is so mentally impaired as to be incapable of properly understanding, and so of properly consenting to, the behaviour involved, the man may be guilty of an indecent assault where the behaviour includes some physical contact between the parties.[25]

Indecent exposure

"Indecent exposure" is not a *nomen juris*,[26] but "the exposure of those **36.12** parts of the person that are usually concealed" may be a crime in certain circumstances.[27]
Indecent exposure is criminal in two sets of circumstances, apart from cases in which it is an element in the offence of lewd practices.

---

[22] Maximum penalty on summary conviction three months' imprisonment, on indictment ten years' imprisonment: see the Crime and Punishment (Scotland) Act 1997, s.14(2).

[23] (*cf.*, however, the general attitude of the House of Lords to such statutory offences: *B. (A Minor) v. D.P.P.* [2000] 2 W.L.R. 452, HL, which was concerned with the interpretation of the English Indecency with Children Act 1960, s.1(1)); see also *R. v. K.* [2001] 3 W.L.R. 471, HL. Section 15 of the Criminal Law (Consolidation) (Scotland) Act 1995 makes belief with reasonable cause that the girl is one's wife a defence to a charge of indecent assault (apparently whether or not the girl consented!), but a charge under s.6 is not a charge of indecent assault. The English Sexual Offences Act 1956, s.14, provides that a girl under 16 cannot consent to what would be an indecent assault but for her consent, so that in England the crime of "lewd practices" towards a girl under 16 is indecent assault. In Scotland, however, it is just lewd practices, a distinction which seems to have been ignored by the framers of the now repealed Age of Marriage Act 1929, the proviso to s.1(1) of which was the origin of s.15 of the 1995 Act. Whatever the strict construction of the section, however, it is unlikely that a charge would be brought under s.6 where the accused believed with reasonable cause that he was married to the girl and that she was over 16.

[24] *cf.* Hume, i, 310, where he explains that the crime is intended to protect children against corruption "before they have attained to sufficient intelligence or discretion, to defend themselves against such pollution": *Robert Philip* (1855) 2 Irv. 243, L.J.-C. Hope at 252; Macdonald, p.150.

[25] In England neither a child nor a mentally impaired woman can give a valid consent to an indecent assault: Sexual Offences Act 1956, s.14.

[26] *McKenzie v. Whyte* (1864) 4 Irv. 570, L.J.-C. Inglis at 575–6; *Lees, Petitioner*, 1998 S.C.C.R. 401, L.J.-G. Rodger at 404F-G.

[27] *McKenzie v. Whyte* (1864) 4 Irv. 570. It has therefore been held that merely to charge "wilfully, indecently and in a shameless manner expose" is irrelevant: *Carlin v. Malloch* (1896) 2 Adam 98; *cf. Harper v. Neilson* (1898) 2 Adam 582. Schedule 5 to the Criminal Procedure (Scotland) Act 1995 authorises a charge in the form "publicly expose your person in a shameless and indecent manner in presence of the lieges." The modern view is that indecent exposure falls within the category or description of "shameless indecency": *Lees, Petitioner*, 1998 S.C.C.R. 401, L.J.-G. Rodger at 405A-B; and it has been said to be correct to treat charges of "shamelessly indecent conduct" as charges of indecent exposure in appropriate cases: see *Usai v. Russell*, 2000 S.C.C.R. 57, Lord McCluskey (opinion of the Court) at 62B.

36.13 (1) Where the exposure is made to a particular person or persons in such a way as to indicate an improper motive on the part of the accused,[28] that is to say, where the exposure is a form of sexual gesture or invitation, and is something from which the exposer derives gratification, something which is for him a sexual act. This form of indecent exposure is really an example of lewd practices although it may be committed against adults, as where A exposes himself to women in the street.[29] It is not clear whether exposure in a private place to a particular female is a crime where the female is above the age of puberty, even where the woman is not a consenting party, but it probably is, the crime consisting in an "outrage" to her sense of decency. In *McKenzie v. Whyte*[30] Lord Justice-Clerk Inglis spoke of exposure "with the view and with the effect of corrupting the morals of others",[31] but this is too narrow a definition. The man who stands under a lamp-post and exposes himself to passing women may not be trying to debauch them, and may not in fact do more than annoy them, but he is guilty of indecent exposure because he is exposing himself *to* them, and his exposure is for him a sexual act. An indecent stage or night club performance would not constitute this form of criminal exposure, since it is not directed at any particular person, and is not regarded by the performer as a sexual act, but it might be shameless indecency.[32]

36.14 (2) Where the exposure is made in, or into,[33] a public place in a "shameless and indecent" manner, but is not made with any sexual overtones, as where an eccentric runs naked through the streets from his hotel to the beach. This form of indecent exposure is really an example of breach of the peace, and its criminality depends on whether the circumstances are such as to be likely to cause public commotion. In *McKenzie v. Whyte*[34] a charge of exposure "in an indecent and unbecoming manner" on the banks of a river "to the annoyance of the lieges" was held to be irrelevant because it did not set out that the accused, who were bathing, were doing so in a public place, or in what manner the

---

[28] See, *e.g.*, *Lees, Petitioner*, 1998 S.C.C.R. 401; *cf. McKenzie v. Whyte* (1864) 4 Irv. 570, Lord Neaves at 573.

[29] Such behaviour could also be treated as a breach of the peace, but is in practice often charged as indecent exposure.

[30] (1864) 4 Irv. 570.

[31] At 575.

[32] In the famous "happening" at the Edinburgh Festival of 1963 a woman who was wheeled across a gallery of a hall while nude during a drama conference was acquitted on a charge of shameless indecency brought in the Burgh Court: *Heatly v. Kesselaar*: see *Scotsman*, December 4, 1963. See also *Herron v, MacDonald, infra*, para. 36.23; *Smith v. Brown, infra*, n.38. *Cf. Geddes v. Dickson*, 2000 S.C.C.R. 1007.

[33] *cf. Usai v. Russell*, 2000 S.C.C.R. 57, where the accused stood naked at a window of his house where he could clearly be seen by any person outside in a public place, as also by persons in their own houses which faced the accused's window: the charges against him were in form charges of shamelessly indecent conduct, but the Appeal Court upheld the sheriff's decision to treat them as charges of indecent exposure. Although the accused was seen to be handling his penis, there was insufficient evidence that he was actuated by any improper sexual motive — he was severely myopic and was not wearing his contact lenses at the material times.

[34] (1864) 4 Irv. 570.

public were annoyed.[35] Recklessness, in the sense of indifference, is sufficient *mens rea* for this type of indecent exposure: thus where the accused stood naked at a window of his house where he was likely to be, and was, seen by others, he was held properly to have been convicted of indecent exposure since (although in fact unaware of his being observed by others owing to myopia) he had chosen to stand where he did, indifferent in the circumstances to the risk of such observation.[36]

THE MEANING OF EXPOSURE. What constitutes "exposure" will neces- **36.15** sarily vary from place to place and from time to time. In practice, however, the crime is normally restricted to exposure of the male member. Female exposure could, no doubt, be charged as such but would more likely be charged as lewd practices, or in a case like an obscene striptease act as shameless indecency.[37] Cases of this kind in which convictions have been obtained have related to "professional" performances including sexual acts of at least a masturbatory nature, or the touching of the woman's private parts by a member of the audience.[38]

Homosexual offences

It is not clear whether homosexual practices between adults short of **36.16** sodomy were regarded as common law crimes prior to *McLaughlan v. Boyd*.[39] There are two cases in which an accused pleaded guilty to using "lewd and abominable or indecent practices towards [boys] under or about the age of puberty"[40] and it may have been accepted that the crime of lewd practice could be committed upon young boys even if they

---

[35] It would not be necessary to specify the latter today, but it would be necessary, it is thought, to prove it. It is sufficient to libel "did publicly expose yourself in a shameless and indecent manner in presence of the lieges": Criminal Procedure (Scotland) Act 1995, Sched. 5; *Poli v. Thomson* (1910) 6 Adam 261. *Cf. S. v. B.* 1968 S.A. (2) 649 (T.P.D.) where a couple copulating in a field near a road were held not to be "wilfully and openly" exposing themselves in an indecent dress or manner. The judge pointed out that no part of their bodies was exposed until the witness pulled them apart and that in any event there was no evidence of any intention to be seen: they had no need or urge to exhibit themselves or their conduct to others: they were satisfying their instincts in a more normal manner without being even aware of the presence of witnesses. Such conduct might in Scotland constitute a breach of the peace or shameless indecency, but that is true of a great variety of behaviour. The English Law Commission at one time recommended the creation of a statutory offence of engaging in sexual intercourse or any other sexual behaviour in circumstances where one knows or ought to know one's conduct is likely to be seen by others to whom it is likely to cause serious offence: Report on Conspiracy and Criminal Law Reform (L.C. No. 76), 1976, Draft Bill, cl. 21; but this has never been enacted (*cf.* the Public Order Act 1986, s.4A, inserted by the Criminal Justice and Public Order Act 1994, s.154, and s.5 which depend for their relevance to the matter discussed above upon the interpretation of "insulting" or "disorderly" behaviour); nor does it appear as part of the English draft Code of 1989 (L.C. No. 177, "A Criminal Code for England and Wales", Vol. 1 (1989), draft Code Bill, H.C. No. 299.).

[36] *Usai v. Russell*, 2000 S.C.C.R. 57, Lord McCluskey (opinion of the Court) at 64D-E. See also *McKenzie v. Whyte* (1864) 4 Irv. 570, L.J.-C. Inglis at 577; *McDonald v. Cardle*, 1985 S.C.C.R. 195. *Cf. Niven v. Tudhope*, 1982 S.C.C.R. 365, opinion of the Court at 366.

[37] *cf. Geddes v. Dickson*, 2000 S.C.C.R. 1007, where the accused was alleged to have encouraged male and female patrons of a public house to show their private members or breasts, as appropriate, for the amusement of other patrons and in return for free drinks; and *Heatly v. Kesselaar, supra*, n.32.

[38] *Smith v. Brown*, Edinburgh Sheriff Court, June 1976 unrep'd: *cf. Herron v. Macdonald, infra.*, para. 36.23.

[39] 1934 J.C. 19, see *infra*.

[40] *David Brown* (1844) 2 Broun 261; *Andrew Lyall* (1853) 1 Irv. 218.

were a little over fourteen,[41] but there was nothing to indicate that homosexual behaviour short of sodomy between adults was a distinct crime as such.

36.17   THE CRIMINAL LAW (CONSOLIDATION) (SCOTLAND) ACT 1995. Homosexual offences are now governed by section 13 of the Criminal Law (Consolidation) (Scotland) Act 1995, whose general effect[42] is that homosexual conduct between consenting males over the age of 16 in private is not criminal. Section 13 of the Act provides, *inter alia*:

> "(1) Subject to the provisions of this section, a homosexual act in private shall not be an offence provided that the parties consent thereto and have attained the age of sixteen years.
> (2) An act which would otherwise be treated for the purposes of this Act as being done in private shall not be so treated if done—
>   . . .
>   (b) in a lavatory to which the public have, or are permitted to have, access whether on payment or otherwise. . . .
> (4) In this section, a 'homosexual act' means sodomy or an act of gross indecency or shameless indecency by one male person with another male person."

The effect of these provisions is that homosexual behaviour which is not protected by them remains a crime at common law, whether it is sodomy[43] or some lesser form of gross indecency between males which would be prosecuted as shamelessly indecent conduct[44] or, in cases involving young boys, as lewd practices.[45] ("Gross indecency" has not been judicially defined. In practice the most common form which it takes is the handling by one male of the private member of another, but it has been held in England that actual physical contact is unnecessary, a "grossly indecent exhibition" is enough.[46])

It is also an offence, under section 13(5),[47] to commit or be party to, or to procure or attempt to procure, the commission of a homosexual act in any of the following cases: (a) otherwise than in private; (b) without the consent of the parties to the act; or (c) with a person under the age of sixteen years"; and under section 13(6), it is an offence to procure or attempt to procure the commission of a homosexual act between two other male persons.[48] It is a defence to a charge under section 13(5)(c), where the accused is under 24 years of age and has not been previously charged with a like offence, that he had reasonable grounds to believe the other person was aged 16 or over[49]; and it is also stated under section

---

[41] *cf. Robert Philip* (1855) 2 Irv. 243.
[42] As amended by the Sexual Offences (Amendment) Act 2000, s.1(3) and by the Convention Rights (Compliance) (Scotland) Act 2001 (asp 7), s.10.
[43] See Chap. 34, *supra*.
[44] See para. 36.20, *et seq.*, *infra*.
[45] See para. 36.09, *supra*.
[46] *R. v. Hunt and Badsey* (1950) 34 Cr.App.R. 135. *Cf. R. v. Hornby and Peaple* (1946) 32 Cr.App.R. 1.
[47] As amended by the Sexual Offences (Amendment) Act 2000, s.1(3) and by the Convention Rights (Compliance) (Scotland) Act 2001 (asp 7), s.10.
[48] Maximum penalty for any of these offences is, on indictment, two years' and a fine, and on summary conviction, three months' or a fine of the prescribed sum. Proceedings must be commenced not later than 12 months after the date on which the offence was committed.
[49] Section 13(8), as amended by the Sexual Offences (Amendment) Act 2000, s.1(3)(b). *Cf.* paras 36.03, 36.05 and 36.06, *supra*.

13(8A)[50] that, "A person under the age of sixteen years does not commit an offence under subsection (5)(a) or (c) above if he commits or is party to the commission of a homosexual act with a person who has attained that age."

Male persons who are mentally handicapped are protected by section 13(3) which provides:

"A male person who is suffering from mental deficiency which is of such a nature or degree that he is incapable of living an independent life or of guarding himself against serious exploitation cannot in law give any consent which, by virtue of subsection (1) above, would prevent a homosexual act from being an offence; but a person shall not be convicted on account of the incapacity of such a male person to consent, of an offence consisting of such an act if he proves that he did not know and had no reason to suspect that male person to be suffering from such mental deficiency."

THE MENTAL HEALTH (SCOTLAND) ACT 1984. Section 107 of the Mental **36.18** Health (Scotland) Act 1984, read subject to subsection (3),[51] and as amended by the Adults with Incapacity (Scotland) Act 2000 (asp 4), Schedule 6, provides:

"(1) . . . it shall be an offence, subject to the exception mentioned in this section,—
   (a) for a man who is an officer on the staff or is otherwise employed in a hospital or nursing home, or who is a manager of a hospital or who is a person carrying on a nursing home to commit a homosexual act with a male person who is for the time being receiving treatment for mental disorder as an in-patient in that hospital or nursing home, or to commit such an act on the premises of which the hospital or nursing home forms part with a male person who is for the time being receiving such treatment there as an outpatient;
   (b) for a man to commit a homosexual act with a male person suffering from mental disorder who is in his custody or care under this Act or in the care of a local authority under the Social Work (Scotland) Act 1968 or resident in a house provided by a local authority under that Act.[52]
(2) It shall not be an offence under this section for a man to commit a homosexual act with a male person if he does not know and has no reason to suspect him to be a person suffering from mental disorder."

SEXUAL OFFENCES (AMENDMENT) ACT 2000. It is an offence under section **36.19** 3 of the Sexual Offences (Amendment) Act 2000 for a person of at least 18 years of age ("A") to have (*inter alia*) anal intercourse with a person under that age ("B") or "to engage in any other sexual activity with or directed towards such a person" if A is in a position of trust in relation to B.[53]

---

[50] Inserted by the Sexual Offences (Amendment) Act 2000, s.2(4).

[51] Section 107(3) provides: "In this section any reference to having unlawful sexual intercourse with a woman shall include a reference to committing a homosexual act as defined in s.13(4) of the Criminal Law (Consolidation) (Scotland) Act 1995."

[52] Maximum penalty on indictment, two years' and a fine (s.107(4)).

[53] For a more detailed account of this offence, see para. 35.04, *supra*.

Shameless indecency

36.20   Macdonald stated that "All shamelessly indecent conduct is criminal",[54] but offered no authority for this wide and vague proposition. In *McLaughlan v. Boyd*[55] the proposition was adopted by the High Court.

The accused in *McLaughlan* was a publican who had behaved indecently to persons who came into his bar in course of their work. For aught that appears in the report the offences were committed when no one else was present. For some reason the charges were brought at common law and not under what was then section 11 of the Criminal Law Amendment 1885,[56] and read "in your licensed premises . . . did use lewd, indecent and libidinous practices towards . . . by seizing his hand and placing it on your private parts." There were a number of charges of this kind, and also a number of charges of assaulting men "by placing your hand upon [their] private parts." The accused was convicted on some charges of each kind. The assault charges were doubtless relevant, but the charges of lewd practices were attacked on the ground that that crime was restricted to practices with persons under the age of puberty. The court held the charges relevant, relying on *David Brown*,[57] *Andrew Lyall*[58] and *Robert Philip*,[59] and some cases in Bell's Notes to Hume,[60] none of which is authority for the proposition that any shamelessly indecent conduct is criminal. At most they indicate that the crime of lewd practices may be committed with boys who are a little over the age of puberty.

There are at least three grounds on which Macdonald's proposition might have been challenged.

(i) It is so vague as to offend against the principle *nullum crimen sine lege*.[61]

(ii) It is not necessary to the decision in *McLaughlan*. The case could have been decided on the narrower ground that such homosexual practices were criminal. Indeed, it appears from the opinions of the judges in *McLaughlan* that they regarded the charges of lewd practices as involving an element of assault, and Lord Justice General Clyde at one point observed that the findings in fact were inconsistent with there having been any consent by the persons towards whom the practices were used,[62] and all that was required in *McLaughlan* was to hold that a charge of lewd practices is relevant even where the practices are tantamount to an assault.[63]

(iii) There is no prior authority for the proposition except Macdonald's own statement. The earlier cases all concerned the recognised and specific crime of lewd practices towards children, and at most extended that crime to protect youths.

---

[54] 3rd ed., p.206; 1st ed. p.202.

[55] 1934 J.C. 19.

[56] Perhaps because had they been taken under the Act the case would have had to be dealt with in the sheriff court.

[57] (1844) 2 Broun 261.

[58] (1853) 1 Irv. 218.

[59] (1855) 2 Irv. 243.

[60] Bell's Notes 85–86.

[61] See Vol. I, para. 1.16. And see Lord Reid's dissenting speech in the English case of *Shaw v. D.P.P.* [1962] A.C. 221.

[62] At 23.

[63] See especially Lord Morison at 23.

Far from rejecting Macdonald's proposition, however, the courts in Scotland have consistently upheld its correctness,[64] and have affirmed that there is a generic crime, "shamelessly indecent conduct", of which lewd practices towards children is only one example.[65]

The crime of shamelessly indecent conduct. McLaughlan v. Boyd[66] and the **36.21** proposition from Macdonald which it approved were of little practical importance prior to the decision of the Appeal Court in *Watt v. Annan*,[67] where the accused was charged in terms that he conducted himself in a shamelessly indecent manner, and did exhibit or cause to be exhibited to a number of consenting adult men in a locked lounge bar a film of an obscene or indecent nature, the film being described as liable to create depraved, inordinate or lustful desires in those watching it, and to corrupt the morals of the lieges. The accused was convicted and appealed on the grounds that such a charge did not disclose a crime known to the law of Scotland. Lord Cameron, with whom Lord Justice General Emslie and Lord Johnston agreed, found the charge relevant, since Macdonald's proposition that "all shamelessly indecent conduct is criminal" had not been challenged or criticised in any decided case, and indeed had been specifically approved by Lord Clyde in *McLaughlan v. Boyd* in a passage which had also stood unchallenged in subsequent case law.

The task in *Watt v. Annan*, therefore, was to give shape to the offence. Indecent conduct was essential but not sufficient; and Lord Cameron set out the framework of the offence as follows[68]:

> "It is clear that . . . it is not the indecency of the conduct itself which makes it criminal but it is the quality of 'shamelessness' and the question is what is the content of this qualification? It was accepted, and rightly so, in the submission for the Crown that the conduct to be criminal, in such circumstances as the facts in the present case disclose,[69] must be directed towards some person or

---

[64] See *Watt v. Annan*, 1978 S.L.T. 198, Lord Cameron (with whom L.J.-G. Emslie and Lord Johnston agreed) at 201; *R. v. H.M. Advocate*, 1988 S.C.C.R. 254, L.J.-G. Emslie at 259 (where it is described as a "fundamental proposition"); *Paterson v. Lees*, 1999 S.C.C.R. 231, L.J.-G. Rodger at 233E-F (*cf.* Lord Coulsfield's opinion at 236F–238A).

[65] On *McLaughlan v. Boyd* and the declaratory power, see Vol. I, para. 1.31.

[66] 1934 J.C. 19.

[67] 1978 S.L.T. 198.

[68] 1978 S.L.T., at 201.

[69] This qualification suggests that the account given by Lord Cameron is perhaps not the sole method of describing the crime; but the courts have tended to take the view, not always without reluctance, that his opinion in *Watt v. Annan* is definitive: see, *e.g.*, *Geddes v. Dickson*, 2000 S.C.C.R. 1007, Lord Milligan (opinion of the Court) at 1015F. (In this case, the issue of the compatibility of shamelessly indecent conduct with Art.7 of the European Convention on Human Rights was raised; but the appeal was decided without the need to consider that issue.) *Cf. Paterson v. Lees*, 1999 S.C.C.R. 231, Lord Sutherland at 235D: "It is in my view impossible to produce a definition of shamelessly indecent conduct which encompasses all forms of such conduct. Indeed, one of the criticisms of the whole concept of shameless indecency is that it is an amorphous offence which can gradually expand its boundaries and thus become an offence which can only be defined by reference to what the courts may class at any time as being shameless." For contemporary, or near contemporary, criticism of the step taken by the Appeal Court in *Watt v. Annan*, see G.H. Gordon, "Shameless Indecency and Obscenity" (1980) 25 J.L.S. 262; G. Maher, "The Enforcement of Morals Continued", 1978 S.L.T. (News) 281; J.B. Stewart, "Obscenity Prosecutions", 1982 S.L.T. (News) 93; I.D. Willock, "Shameless Indecency — How Far has the Crown Office Reached?" (1981) 52 SCOLAG Bul. 199. See generally C. Gane, *Sexual Offences* (Edinburgh, 1992), Chap. 8.

persons with an intention or knowledge that it should corrupt or be calculated or liable to corrupt or deprave those towards whom the indecent or obscene conduct was directed."

It would appear from the above account of the crime that the *actus reus* consists of conduct which is indecent or obscene.[70] It has also been held that the conduct must amount to something positive rather than take the form of an omission,[71] possibly since this accords better with the requirement that the conduct should be directed towards at least one other person.[72] Such direction has to be intentional; although reckless-ness, in the sense of indifference, may sometimes be sufficient.[73] The critical *mens rea* requirement is, however, "shamelessness", which Lord Cameron treats as objective, in that knowledge on the part of the accused that his conduct is likely to corrupt or deprave those to whom it is directed is considered sufficient irrespective of what he describes as "moral obloquy" on the part of the accused[74]: but the *mens rea*, at least

---

[70] This sits uneasily, however, with cases of shameless indecency where the conduct was considered to be "repugnant to society" in view of the relationship between the accused and complainer rather than because of some intrinsic indecency of the conduct itself: see, *e.g.*, *R. v. H.M. Advocate*, 1988 S.L.T. 623 (sexual activity, short of intercourse, between a man and his 16-year-old lawful daughter considered to be incestuous in quality and thus repugnant to society); *H.M. Advocate v. K.*, 1994 S.C.C.R. 499 (sexual intercourse between a man and his foster daughter, she being at least between 16 and 18 years old at the relevant times, considered to be in breach of a relationship of trust similar to that between a father and his lawful daughter): *cf. H.M. Advocate v. Roose*, 1999 S.C.C.R. 259 (sexual intercourse between a man and a girl of between 13 and 14 years of age, where he was some 20 years older than the girl, charged as shamelessly indecent conduct on account of the age disparity, but held not criminal at common law).

Judges or juries are, it seems, to make up their own minds as to the propensity of the conduct to deprave or corrupt those at whom it is directed, unaided by evidence from psychiatrists or psychologists: *Ingram v. Macari*, 1982 S.C.C.R. 372, Lord Dunpark (opinion of the Court) at 375.

In terms of the facts in *Watt v. Annan* itself, of course, it was not the accused's conduct which was indecent or obscene *per se*; his conduct consisted in showing to others something which itself depicted prior acts which might have been indecent or obscene when they had been filmed, and thus the case is closer to offences concerned with the dissemination of "obscene publications" than, for example, lewd live performances or offences of or akin to indecent exposure. It is no surprise, therefore, that shamelessly indecent conduct was quickly extended to conduct consisting of the selling or exposing for sale of indecent magazines, films and similar items: see, *e.g.*, *Skeen v. Murdoch* (1978) S.C.C.R. (Supp.) 227, Sh.Ct; *Robertson v. Smith*, 1980 J.C. 1; *Tudhope v. Taylor*, 1980 S.L.T. (Notes) 54; *Ingram v. Macari*, 1982 J.C. 1; *Dean v. John Menzies (Holdings) Ltd*, 1981 J.C. 23; *Tudhope v. Barlow*, 1981 S.L.T. (Sh.Ct.) 94; *Tudhope v. Sommerville*; *Sommerville v. Tudhope*, 1981 J.C. 58.

[71] *Paterson v. Lees*, 1999 S.C.C.R. 231 (failure to prevent a child from watching an indecent videotape programme considered not to fulfil the requirements of shamelessly indecent conduct).

[72] But, more likely out of a desire to limit the ambit of the offence: see the views of all three judges in *Paterson v. Lees, supra. Cf. Tudhope v. Sommerville; Sommerville v. Tudhope*, 1981 J.C. 58.

[73] This was conceded in general by the appellant in *Usai v. Russell*, 2000 S.C.C.R. 57, although the case was concerned with indecent exposure charged as shamelessly indecent conduct. It cannot, therefore, necessarily be taken as a general rule that recklessness is a sufficient form of *mens rea* for all types of shameless indecency.

[74] If this is not sufficiently clear in *Watt v. Annan* itself, it is made plain in Lord Cameron's dissenting opinion in *Dean v. John Menzies (Holdings) Ltd*, 1981 J.C. 23, at 32. If no such knowledge is proved or inferred, then the accused is entitled to be acquitted: *Tudhope v. Barlow*, 1981 S.L.T. (Sh.Ct.) 94; but efforts made by the accused to conceal indecent material he has for sale from all but those adults who seek it out can provide evidence that the accused had the necessary knowledge: see *Robertson v. Smith*, 1980 J.C. 1, Lord Cameron at 5; *Tudhope v. Taylor*, 1980 S.L.T. (Sh.Ct.) 54.

in relation to the selling or exposing for sale of indecent material, was treated subjectively by Lords Stott and Maxwell who formed the majority of the Appeal Court in *Dean v. John Menzies (Holdings) Ltd.*[75] In that case, they held that an accused must be shown to be so lost to any sense of shame as to authorise or permit the sale of such material in his retail shop in order to be convicted of shamelessly indecent conduct,[76] and that a corporation as opposed to a human being could not be shown to possess any such character trait.

It is usually necessary to libel in the indictment or complaint both the requisite conduct and the facts and circumstances from which the required 'shamelessness' can be inferred[77]; but, at least in the form of the offence where the sale or exposure for sale of indecent or obscene material is concerned, it is not necessary to libel expressly that the conduct was liable to raise inordinate and lustful desires in the minds of those to whom it was directed, or to corrupt or deprave the lieges, since such consequences are implied from the indecency or obscenity of the material itself.[78] The consent of those to whom the conduct is directed is not a relevant issue in relation to guilt or innocence[79]; nor is it relevant that the conduct is directed to another with sufficient "shamelessness" in a private as opposed to a public place.[80]

Given the confused and confusing state of the authorities relative to this crime, it is difficult to do other than sympathise with those who consider that shamelessly indecent conduct has no clear ambit, no defensible underpinning principle, and no, or virtually no, settled definition.[81] In the second edition of this work, it was stated that in theory the approval of Macdonald's proposition that "All shamelessly indecent conduct is criminal" opened the way to prosecution for all kinds of sexual behaviour, including lesbian practices which Macdonald himself regarded as non-criminal,[82] buggery with a consenting woman, fornication in the back of a car in a deserted street, and any other behaviour which struck the particular court as "shamelessly indecent". The way in which the crime has been developed since *Watt v. Annan* was decided has done much to suggest that the way has indeed been opened for such prosecutions, although the most recent case decisions have shown a reluctance on the part of the Appeal Court to entertain further expansion of the crime.[83] Its amorphous nature does, nevertheless, raise the issue of its compatibility with the articles of the European Convention on Human Rights.

---

[75] 1981 J.C. 23, at 36, 38 and 45.

[76] See especially the opinion of Lord Stott at 36.

[77] *Robertson v. Smith*, 1980 J.C. 1, Lord Cameron at 4; *Geddes v. Dickson*, 2000 S.C.C.R. 1007.

[78] *Ingram v. Macari*, 1982 J.C. 1, opinion of the Court at 2.

[79] *Watt v. Annan*, 1978 S.L.T. 198, Lord Cameron at 201. It was not suggested in the cases concerning sexual activity between the accused and their lawful or foster daughters that those daughters did not consent to what was done to them, and it must have been accepted that they did consent, and that that consent was in a sense necessary for a charge of shamelessly indecent conduct to be appropriate in the circumstances: see *R. v. H.M. Advocate*, 1988 S.L.T. 623; *H.M. Advocate v. K.*, 1994 S.C.C.R. 499.

[80] *Watt v. Annan*, 1978 S.L.T. 198, Lord Cameron at 201 and 202.

[81] See, *e.g.*, P.W. Ferguson, *Crimes Against the Person* (2nd ed., Edinburgh, 1998), at para. 8.11.

[82] Macdonald, p.150.

[83] See, *e.g.*, *Paterson v. Lees*, 1999 S.C.C.R. 231, comments of L.J.-G. Rodger at 233F-G; *H.M. Advocate v. Roose*, 1999 S.C.C.R. 259, comments of Lord Marnoch at 260; *Geddes v. Dickson*, 2000 S.C.C.R. 1007. See also para. 36.22, *infra*.

36.22 *Shameless indecency and the European Convention on Human Rights.* As Lord Coulsfield said in *Paterson v. Lees*[84] (of Macdonald's assertion that "All shamelessly indecent conduct is criminal", and the limited range of illustrative examples given by that author[85]):

> "In the absence of other authority, I might have been inclined to the view that Macdonald was concerned only with a limited crime, namely indecent exposure or lewd and libidinous practices involving indecent handling of children . . . However, the decisions in *McLaughlan v. Boyd* and *Watt v. Annan*[86] have taken Macdonald's proposition as a free-standing definition of a crime."

And, in the same case, Lord Justice General Rodger said this[87]:

> "In some of the cases . . . the term 'shamelessly' has been glossed in ways which take it beyond its normal meaning and hence beyond the meaning which, one might suppose, Macdonald would have intended it to bear when he framed his proposition in 1866. As a result, the crime which the adverb is meant to define has become amorphous, with any limits being hard to discern."

The crime is certainly too broadly based, and it is difficult to imagine that any reasonable person, having read Macdonald's proposition in the context of the examples Macdonald produces, would be able to anticipate that the courts could decide that exposure for sale of indecent magazines,[88] indecent exposure,[89] and sexual behaviour between a man and his 16-year-old foster child[90] (this not being behaviour criminalised by any relevant statute[91]), were all examples of some general offence of "shamelessly indecent conduct" based upon that proposition.

Development of common law crimes by the courts is not prohibited[92] by Article 7.1 of the European Convention on Human Rights which provides:

> "No one shall be held guilty of any criminal offence on account of any act or omission which did not constitute a criminal offence under national or international law at the time when it was committed. Nor shall a heavier penalty be imposed than the one that was applicable at the time the criminal offence was committed."[93]

Indeed, the European Court of Human Rights has stated that:

---

[84] 1999 S.C.C.R. 231, at 237B-C.
[85] Macdonald, pp. 150–151.
[86] 1934 J.C. 19, and 1978 S.L.T. 198 respectively.
[87] *ibid.*, at p. 233F.
[88] See, *e.g.*, *Robertson v. Smith*, 1980 J.C. 1; *Tudhope v. Taylor*, 1980 S.L.T. (Notes) 54; *Ingram v. Macari*, 1982 J.C. 1. Further expansion, into the field of corporate crime, was halted, however, by the decision of the majority of the Appeal Court in *Dean v. John Menzies (Holdings) Ltd*, 1981 J.C. 23.
[89] See, *e.g.*, *Usai v. Russell*, 2000 S.C.C.R. 57.
[90] *H.M. Advocate v. K.*, 1994 S.C.C.R. 499; see also *R. v. H.M. Advocate*, 1988 S.L.T. 623: *cf. H.M. Advocate v. Roose*, 1999 S.C.C.R. 259; *Batty v. H.M. Advocate*, 1995 S.C.C.R. 525 (the substance of which might now be criminal under statute: see Sexual Offences (Amendment) Act 2000, ss. 3, 4).
[91] *cf.* the offences under the Criminal Law (Consolidation) (Scotland) Act 1995, s.3, and the Sexual Offences (Amendment) Act 2000, ss. 3, 4.
[92] See, *e.g.*, *S.W. v. United Kingdom*; *C.R. v. United Kingdom* (1996) 21 E.H.R.R. 363.
[93] Human Rights Act 1998, Sched. 1, Convention Articles, Pt I.

"[I]n the United Kingdom, as in the other Convention States, the progressive development of the criminal law through judicial law-making is a well entrenched and necessary part of legal tradition. Article 7 of the Convention cannot be read as outlawing the gradual clarification of the rules of criminal liability through judicial interpretation from case to case, provided that the resultant development is consistent with the essence of the offence and could reasonably be foreseen."[94]

It would seem, therefore, that shamelessly indecent conduct must be confined to such instances of it as have already been granted recognition by the Scottish courts. To introduce novel forms of "shameless indecency" will now be to invite challenge under Article 7 of the Convention; and there seems little doubt that had the Convention been in force at the time when the more extreme cases were brought by the Crown under the Macdonald proposition, it is unlikely that they could have survived the mandatory scrutiny which Article 7 now requires.[95]

Keeping places of lewdness. Hume, in a section on fornication, states that, **36.23** "The keeping of an open and notorious house of lewdness, for the reception of loose and dissolute visitors" is an offence against public decency and the quiet of the neighbourhood.[96] This passage is usually thought of as applying to brothels,[97] but in the unreported sheriff court case of *Herron v. MacDonald*[98] the presentation of an indecent performance was charged as keeping an open and notorious place of lewdness for the reception of loose and dissolute persons. The details were that persons were charged for entrance to the premises, and that the accused therein caused and permitted acts of shameless indecency to take place in their presence, by exhibiting pornographic films depicting fornication and sodomy, and causing and permitting a woman to perform "lewd libidinous and obscene" dances in the course of which she undressed publicly, "exposed her naked person in a shameless, lewd and indecent manner", committed various solitary sexual acts, and also handled and fornicated with a spectator. Such a charge would now presumably be brought as one of shamelessly indecent conduct — provided that it could survive Convention scrutiny.[99]

---

[94] *S.W. v. U.K.; C.R. v. U.K.* (1996) 21 E.H.R.R. 363, at 399. See also the opinion of the (then) Commission of Human Rights, in the same case at 390, paras 46–50, where, at para. 46, it is emphasised by quoting from the case law of the Court that "a norm cannot be regarded as a law unless it is formulated with sufficient precision to enable the citizen to regulate his conduct: he must be able — if need be with appropriate advice — to foresee, to a degree that is reasonable in the circumstances, the consequences which a given action may entail."

[95] See P.R. Ferguson, "Breach of the Peace and the European Convention on Human Rights" (2001) 5 E.L.R. 145, which, though concerned principally with the equally amorphous crime of breach of the peace, includes much critical discussion also relevant to shamelessly indecent conduct.

[96] Hume, i, 468–469.

[97] *infra*, para. 36.25.

[98] Glasgow Sheriff Court; complaint dated Dec. 1973.

[99] See para. 36.22, *supra*.

BROTHEL-KEEPING, PROCURING AND PROSTITUTION

Brothel-keeping

36.24   Section 11(5) of the Criminal Law (Consolidation) (Scotland) Act 1995 provides:

"Any person who—
  (a) keeps or manages or acts or assists in the management of a brothel, or
  (b) being the tenant, lessee, occupier or person in charge of any premises, knowingly permits such premises or any part thereof to be used as a brothel or for the purposes of habitual prostitution, or
  (c) being the lessor or landlord of any premises, or the agent of such lessor or landlord, lets the same or any part thereof with the knowledge that such premises or some part thereof are or is to be used as a brothel, or is wilfully a party to the continued use of such premises or any part thereof as a brothel,
shall be guilty of an offence."[1]

"Managing" and "assisting in managing" are not mutually exclusive alternatives, and two accused may both be convicted of "managing or assisting in the management of" a brothel where they assist each other in management.[2]

36.25   *Brothel.*[3] A brothel has been defined in England as a "bawdy house", a house resorted to by persons of both sexes for the purpose of prostitution.[4] In *Milne v. McNicol,*[5] Sheriff-substitute Aikman Smith adopted the English definition, and went on to say that the Scottish conception of a bawdy house is embodied in Hume's statement that, "It is not, however, to be doubted that the keeping of an open and notorious house of lewdness, for the reception of loose and dissolute visitors, is of itself such an offence against public decency, and the quiet of the neighbourhood, as is punishable at common law".[6] The High Court did not find it necessary to consider this definition but contented themselves with holding that the sheriff-substitute was justified on the facts in holding that the accused had managed the premises as a brothel.[7] A house occupied by a single prostitute who uses it for her trade is not a brothel,[8]

---

[1] Maximum penalty, on summary conviction, in the sheriff court, three months' and a fine of level 4 on the standard scale, and in the district court, three months' and a fine of level 3 on the said scale. For an example of brothel-keeping, see *Milne v. McNicol* (1965) S.C.C.R. (Supp.) 8.

[2] *Vaughan v. Smith*, 1919 J.C. 9.

[3] See generally Leno, "De Lustris", 1979 S.L.T. (News) 73.

[4] *Singleton v. Ellison* [1895] 1 Q.B. 607, Wills J. at 608.

[5] (1965) S.C.C.R. (Supp.) 8.

[6] Hume, i, 468–469.

[7] The facts were that the accused was the keeper of a respectable boarding house to which prostitutes began to bring their clients during the typhoid epidemic in Aberdeen in June 1964, until, as the sheriff-substitute found, it became notoriously a place to which loose and dissolute visitors resorted for purposes of lewd behaviour to the reasonable annoyance of other residents in the neighbourhood. The main point at issue in the case appears to have been whether the accused, whose part in the matter seems to have been wholly passive, and who charged the prostitutes only her normal rates, knew of the use being made of her premises.

[8] *Singleton v. Ellison* [1895] 1 Q.B. 607.

although it may be a place used for habitual prostitution. But a house to which the occupier and one other woman bring men for prostitution is a brothel.[9] The question whether premises are or are not a brothel, however, is ultimately one of fact and degree, such that it has been held that a house where a number of prostitutes plied their trade (but never more than one particular prostitute per day) was nevertheless a brothel.[10] The fact that a number of rooms in a house are separately let to individual prostitutes does not necessarily prevent the house being a brothel, the test being whether the premises constitute in fact a "nest" of prostitutes.[11] If the individual prostitutes carry on their trade wholly independently of each other there is probably not a brothel unless the landlord takes an active part in managing the premises as a brothel.[12] It has been held in England that for premises to be considered as a brothel, "it is not essential that there be evidence that normal sexual intercourse is provided in those premises. It is sufficient to prove that more than one woman offers herself as a participant in physical acts of indecency for the sexual gratification of men."[13] It was also stated in the same case that, "A brothel is also constituted where the women (for there must be more than one woman) do not charge for sexual intercourse."[14]

Habitual prostitution. It is not an offence under section 11(5)(b) for a **36.26** prostitute to use a house she occupies herself for her own habitual prostitution, since she cannot be said to "permit" such use.[15] Similarly, it

---

[9] *Gorman v. Standen* [1964] 1 Q.B. 294. The apparent restriction in the text of the present para. to heterosexual practices is compelled as a result of erroneous consolidation of earlier statutory provisions: under the Criminal Justice (Scotland) Act 1980, s.80(13), premises were to be treated as a brothel for the purposes of ss. 13 (brothel-keeping) and 14 (allowing a child to be in a brothel) of the Sexual Offences (Scotland) Act 1976 if persons resorted there for the purpose of homosexual acts (within the meaning of s.80(6)) in circumstances in which resort thereto for heterosexual practices would have led to the premises being treated as a brothel under the said ss. 13 and 14. Under s.13(10) of the Criminal Law (Consolidation) (Scotland) Act 1995, which is intended to be a consolidation of s.80(13) of the 1980 Act, premises are to be treated as a brothel relative to homosexual acts "for the purposes of sections 11(1) and 12 of this Act." But s.11(1) of the 1995 Act relates to the offence of male persons living wholly or in part on the earnings of prostitution and contains no reference to "a brothel", and it seems clear that s.13(10) should have referred to s.11(5) of the 1995 Act — which is the direct equivalent of s.13 of the 1976 Act. It may be that the error is rectifiable simply by application of the "rule" that "an error made in transcribing an enactment for inclusion in a consolidation Act . . . [raises] an irresistible inference that the original wording should be followed" (F. Bennion, *Statutory Interpretation* (1984), p.340, 'Example 5'): but since the provision in question here is one which extends the reach of an offence, the matter is not free from difficulty. (The Sexual Offences (Scotland) Act 1976 was repealed in its entirety by the Crime and Punishment (Scotland) Act 1997, Sched. 3; and s.80 of the Criminal Justice (Scotland) Act 1980 was repealed by the Criminal Procedure (Consequential Provisions) (Scotland) Act 1995, Sched. 5.)

[10] *Stevens and Stevens v. Christy* (1987) 85 Cr.App.R. 249, in which *Gorman v. Standen* (*supra*) was applied, and *Singleton v. Ellison* (*supra*) distinguished.

[11] *Donovan v. Gavin* [1965] 2 Q.B. 648, Sachs J., at 659D-F; *Abbott v. Smith* [1964] 3 All E.R. 762.

[12] *Donovan v. Gavin* [1965] 2 Q.B. 648, Lord Parker C.J. at 661.

[13] *Kelly v. Purvis* [1983] Q.B. 663, Ackner L.J., at 671B: the facts were that women working at a licensed massage parlour offered masturbation to male customers as extra services at extra cost; but there was insufficient evidence that sexual intercourse was offered or performed there.

[14] *Kelly v. Purvis* [1983] Q.B. 663, Ackner L.J. at 670A, under reference to *Winter v. Woolfe* [1931] 1 K.B. 549.

[15] *Mattison v. Johnson* (1916) 25 Cox C.C. 373; *Girgawy v. Strathern* 1925 J.C. 31.

is not an offence for the male occupier or joint occupiers of a house to use it habitually to entertain prostitutes, but it is an offence for them to allow other men to take prostitutes there habitually, whether or not the occupiers derive any profit from them.[16] It is an offence under section 11(5)(b) to allow a single prostitute to use premises of which one is the tenant, etc., to ply her trade.[17]

36.27 *Other offences connected with brothels.* It is an offence for any person having parental responsibilies[18] in relation to, or having charge or care of, a child between four and 16 years of age to allow him or her "to reside in or frequent a brothel".[19]

It is an offence to detain a woman in a brothel.[20]

Procuring and allied offences

36.28 *Procuring women under 21.* It is an offence under section 7(1) of the Criminal Law (Consolidation) (Scotland) Act 1995 to procure or attempt to procure any female under 21 years old to have unlawful sexual intercourse "with any other person or persons in any part of the world."[21]

There are no reported Scots cases on this section, but the English cases which deal with its meaning would probably be followed. It was held in *R. v. Christian and Anr*[22] that "procuring" involves some active step and that the section "is not aimed at brothel-keepers who give girls an opportunity, if they come in there, of carrying on that trade. It is aimed at people who get girls by some fraud or persuasion, or by inviting them to it if they cannot get money in any other way — turning them on to the streets".[23]

It is not an offence under this subsection for A to procure a girl for the purpose of himself having intercourse with her, but it has been held that where A procures a girl for B, B may be convicted of aiding and abetting him in the procuring.[24] It was also held in the same case that if A procures a girl in Scotland to have intercourse with B in England, A is

---

[16] *Girgawy v. Strathern, supra.*

[17] For the meaning of "prostitution", see *infra.*

[18] Within the meaning of the Children (Scotland) Act 1995, s.1(3).

[19] Criminal Law (Consolidation) (Scotland) Act 1995, s.12(1), *supra*, para. 31.13. "Brothel" here includes a male brothel: see s.13(10) of the 1995 Act.

[20] Criminal Law (Consolidation) (Scotland) Act 1995, s.(3)(b): maximum penalty, on indictment, two years', and on summary conviction, three months'.

[21] Maximum penalty two years' imprisonment on indictment, three months' on summary conviction. The terms of the English Sexual Offences Act 1956, s.23, are that it is an offence "to procure a girl under the age of twenty-one to have unlawful sexual intercourse in any part of the world with a third person." The English draft code (L.C. No. 177, "A Criminal Code for England and Wales", H. of C. 299, 1989, Vol. 1, Draft Code Bill), Cl. 132, would add a defence of belief that the woman was of or over 21 years of age; but this may already be the law in England: see *B. (A Minor) v. D.P.P.* [2000] 2 W.L.R. 452, HL; *R. v. K.* [2001] 3 W.L.R. 472, HL.

[22] (1913) 23 Cox C.C. 541.

[23] Bosanquet, Common Serjt. at 542. In that case one accused had taken the girl to a brothel after which the girl went there of her own free will, and was neither persuaded nor solicited to remain. She shared her earnings with the brothel-keeper who was also charged. Both accused were acquitted. See also *R. v. Broadfoot* [1976] 3 All E.R. 753; and see Vol. I, para. 5.04.

[24] *R. v. Mackenzie and Higginson* (1910) 6 Cr.App.R. 64.

guilty of procuring in England, since the offence is a continuing one committed where intercourse occurs.

Error as to the girl's age is probably no defence.[25]

Procuring any woman or girl. It is an offence to procure or attempt to **36.29** procure any woman or girl to have any unlawful sexual intercourse in any part of the world by threats or intimidation,[26] or to procure any woman or girl for such a purpose by false pretences or false representations.[27]

These offences are committed if A uses such means to procure a woman to have unlawful intercourse with himself.[28]

Procuring mentally handicapped females. It is an offence under section **36.30** 106(1)(b) of the Mental Health (Scotland) Act 1984 for a man or woman "to procure or encourage any woman who is protected by the provisions of this section[29] to have unlawful sexual intercourse."[30] It is a defence that the accused "did not know and had no reason to suspect" the woman's condition.[31]

"Encourage" has presumably a wider meaning than "procure", and would probably cover the case of a brothel-keeper who allows his premises to be used by a woman protected under the section, although he has not "procured" her, or even of a person who verbally encourages such a woman to fulfil her own desire to have unlawful intercourse. It is probably also the case that A may be guilty of this offence by unsuccessfully encouraging such a woman to have intercourse with himself, although the circumstances do not amount even to an attempt to commit the offence of having intercourse with such a woman.

INTERCOURSE NECESSARY. An offence of procuring contrary to any of **36.31** the above statutory provisions is not committed unless intercourse actually takes place, although there might be a criminal attempt at an earlier stage.[32] Since section 7(2)(a) of the 1995 Act refers specifically to attempt and section 7(2)(b) does not, it may be that there is no offence of attempting to contravene section 7(2)(b).

Procuring males.[33] It is an offence contrary to section 13(5) of the **36.32** Criminal Law (Consolidation) (Scotland) Act 1995[34] to procure or attempt to procure the commission of a homosexual act.[35]

---

[25] *cf.* n. 21, *supra*.

[26] Criminal Law (Consolidation) (Scotland) Act 1995, s.7(2)(a). Maximum penalty two years' on indictment, three months on summary conviction.

[27] *ibid.*, s.7(2)(b). Maximum penalty as above.

[28] *R. v. Williams* (1898) 62 J.P. 310. *Cf. R. v. Jones* [1896] 1 Q.B. 4.

[29] Under s.106(6) "A woman is protected under the provisions of this section if she is suffering from a state of arrested or incomplete development of mind which includes significant impairment of intelligence and social functioning."

[30] Maximum penalty two years' imprisonment (s.106(3)). See also *supra*, paras 33.14, 33.16.

[31] Under s.106(7), "woman" includes "girl".

[32] *R. v. Johnson (Gerald)* [1964] 2 Q.B. 404.

[33] See also para. 36.17, *supra*.

[34] Maximum penalty, on indictment, two years' and a fine; and, on summary conviction, three months' or a fine of the prescribed sum: s.13(7).

[35] See s.13(4) for the meaning of "homosexual act".

It is also an offence contrary to section 13(6) of that Act to procure or attempt to procure the commission of a homosexual act between two other male persons.[36]

36.33 *Abduction.* It is an offence at common law to abduct a woman for the purpose of marrying her, where the abduction is carried out by violence,[37] and perhaps also where it is carried out by trickery.[38] There are no recent cases of this kind, and any which did arise could be dealt with as assault or simple kidnapping or even, in appropriate cases, as fraud. There is no authority at common law for the proposition that it is an offence to take a girl over the age of 12 away from her home with her consent in the absence of any fraud.

36.34 The Criminal Law (Consolidation) (Scotland) Act 1995, section 8, provides:

> "(1) Any person who, with intent that any unmarried girl under the age of 18 years should have unlawful sexual intercourse with men or with a particular man, takes or causes to be taken such girl out of the possession and against the will of her father or mother, or any other person having the lawful care and charge of her,[39] shall be [guilty of an offence].[40]
>
> (2) It shall be a defence to any charge under subsection (1) above that the person so charged had reasonable cause to believe that the girl was of or over the age of 18 years."[41]

This section deals with a type of offence more familiar to the law of England than to that of Scotland.[42] There are no reported Scots cases dealing with it,[43] but the English decisions on this and other similar statutory provisions would probably be followed. The girl must be "taken" from her parents, and it is not an offence to fail to return a girl who has herself left her parents and come to the accused of her own accord.[44] The fact that the girl consented to leave is not in itself a defence to a charge of taking her.[45] The accused must, however, be shown to have taken some active part in the girl's leaving — he is not guilty of an offence if he merely passively consents to the girl's own suggestion that she should leave.[46] It is an offence under the section for A to take a girl with intent to have intercourse with her himself. A charge can be brought whether or not intercourse has actually taken place.

---

[36] Maximum penalty as set out in n. 34, *supra*.
[37] Hume, i, 310; Alison, i, 226; Anderson, p.167; Macdonald, p.124.
[38] Hume, i, 310; *Thos. Gray* (1751) Maclaurin's Cases, No 59.
[39] *cf. supra*, para. 31.03.
[40] Maximum penalty two years' on indictment, three months' on summary conviction.
[41] *cf. supra*, para. 36.05.
[42] *cf.* Sexual Offences Act 1956, ss. 17–20.
[43] Except the civil case of *Albinet v. Fleck* (1894) 2 S.L.T. 30 in which was affirmed the self-evident proposition that no offence is committed unless the purpose of the taking is unlawful sexual intercourse.
[44] *R. v. Olifier* (1866) 10 Cox C.C. 402.
[45] See P. Rook and R. Wood, *Rook & Ward on Sexual Offences* (2nd ed., 1997), paras 11.40 and 11.41; *R. v. Manktelow* (1853) 6 Cox C.C. 143; *R. v. Jones (J.W.)* [1973] Crim L.R. 621.
[46] *R. v. Jarvis* (1903) 20 Cox C.C. 249.

It is a defence that A did not know that the girl was at the time in the possession of her parents or in anyone's lawful charge.[47]

"Unlawfully" refers to intercourse outwith marriage, so that it is not an offence under this section to remove a girl in order that she may marry the remover or any other person.[48]

Unlawful detention. It is an offence under section 8(3) of the Criminal **36.35** Law (Consolidation) (Scotland) Act 1995 to detain any female against her will, (a) "in or upon any premises with intent that she may have unlawful sexual intercourse with men or with a particular man, or (b) in any brothel."[49] Where a woman is in premises for the purpose of unlawful intercourse or in a brothel, anyone who withholds her clothes or other property or threatens to take legal proceedings against her should she take away any clothes provided by him, with the intention, in either case, of keeping her there, is deemed to be detaining her there.[50] And a woman who takes away any clothes she needs to enable her to leave or is found with any clothes taken for that purpose, is not liable to any civil or criminal proceedings in respect of her taking possession thereof.[51]

Suffering children or mentally impaired women to be on premises for **36.36** *intercourse.* Section 9(1) of the Criminal Law (Consolidation) (Scotland) Act 1995 provides that an offence is committed where:

> "Any person who, being the owner or occupier of any premises, or having or acting or assisting in, the management or control of any premises, induces or knowingly suffers any girl [under 16 years of age] to resort to or to be in or upon such premises for the purpose of having unlawful sexual intercourse with men or with a particular man".[52]

It is a defence for a person under 24 charged with an offence under this section for the first time and who has not been previously charged under it or section 5(3) of the 1995 Act to show that he believed with reasonable cause that the girl was 16 or over.[53]

It is an offence under this section for A to allow a girl to be on his premises for the purpose of having intercourse with himself.

An offence may be committed under this section even where the premises are the girl's home. In *R. v. Webster*[54] the accused knew that her daughter had come home with a man and had intercourse with him in the house, and was convicted of suffering her to be in the premises for unlawful intercourse.

---

[47] *R. v. Hibbert* (1869) L.R. 1 C.C.R. 184.

[48] *R. v. Chapman* [1959] 1 Q.B. 100.

[49] Maximum penalty two years' imprisonment on indictment, three months' on summary conviction.

[50] Section 8(4).

[51] Section 8(5).

[52] Maximum penalty, where the girl is under 13, life imprisonment, where she is between 13 and 16, two years' on indictment, three months' on summary conviction (s.9(1)(a),(b)).

[53] Section 9(2); see *supra*, para. 36.06. *Quaere* the appropriate penalty where A believes a 12-year-old girl to be 13.

[54] (1885) 16 Q.B.D. 134.

36.37   It is an offence under section 106(1)(c) of the Mental Health (Scotland) Act 1984:

> "[F]or the owner or occupier of any premises or any person having or assisting in the management or control of premises to induce any woman who is protected by the provisions of this section[55] to resort to or be upon such premises for the purpose of unlawful sexual intercourse with any man."[56]

It is a defence that the accused did not know and had no reason to suspect the woman's condition.[57]

36.38 *Procuring for prostitution.* It is an offence under section 7 of the Criminal Law (Consolidation) (Scotland) Act 1995 to procure or attempt to procure any woman or girl:

(i) to become a common prostitute anywhere in the world,[58]

(ii) to leave the United Kingdom with intent that she may become an inmate of or frequent a brothel elsewhere,[59]

(iii) to leave her usual place of abode in the United Kingdom with intent that she may become an inmate of or frequent a brothel in any part of the world for the purpose of prostitution.[60]

Offences in connection with prostitution

36.39 *Prostitute.* A prostitute is a person who commonly offers[61] her body for lewdness in return for payment.[62] The lewdness is not limited to normal

---

[55] Under s.106(6), a woman is protected "if she is suffering from a state of incomplete development of mind which includes significant impairment of intelligence and social functioning"; and under s.106(7), "woman" includes "girl".

[56] Maximum penalty two years' imprisonment or a fine (s.106(3)). See also *supra*, paras 33.14 to 33.16.

[57] Section 106(2).

[58] Section 7(1)(b). In England, it has been held that, to procure a woman for a single act of lewdness with oneself is not to procure her to become a common prostitute: *R. v. Morris-Lowe* [1985] 1 W.L.R. 29. A common prostitute is a "woman who offers herself commonly for lewdness for reward", one "who is prepared for reward to engage in acts of lewdness with all and sundry, or with anyone who may hire her for that purpose": *R. v. Morris-Lowe, supra cit.*, Lord Lane C.J. at 32C and 32D-E, following the definition offered by Darling J. in *R. v. De Munck* [1918] 1 K.B. 635, at 637–8. Darling J.'s definition has been accepted in Scotland — see *Smith v. Sellars*, 1978 J.C. 79; but *cf. White v. Allan*, 1985 S.C.C.R. 85, at 87, where L.J.-C. Wheatley suggests that the epithet "common" is now tautological. (This contrasts with the opinion of Lord Lane C.J. in the above cited case of *R. v. Morris-Lowe*, where, at 32C-D, he stated that the word "common" was neither meaningless nor mere surplusage.) See also, para. 36.39, *infra*.

It has also been held in England that an accused who genuinely believes on reasonable grounds that the woman allegedly procured or attempted to be procured is already a prostitute does not have the *mens rea* for this offence: *R. v. Brown (Raymond)* [1984] 1 W.L.R. 1211, CA. *Quaere* if he would be entitled to be acquitted if he believed her to be a prostitute, but not a common prostitute.

[59] Section 7(1)(c).

[60] Section 7(1)(d). The maximum penalty for any offence under s.7(1) is two years' imprisonment on indictment, three months' on summary conviction.

[61] In England, it has been held that it is sufficient to offer such services, such that a woman who offers appropriate services and takes money for them in advance but without any intent to provide them is nevertheless a prostitute: *R. v. McFarlane* (1994) 99 Cr.App.R. 8, CA.

[62] It seems that a single act of lewdness with a man on one occasion for payment may be sufficient, since the term "prostitute" is to be contrasted with "common prostitute": *R. v. Morris-Lowe* [1985] 1 W.L.R. 29; see n. 58, above. See also P. Rook and R. Wood, *Rook & Wood on Sexual Offences* (2nd ed., 1997) para. 8.13.

sexual intercourse but includes all forms of carnal connection and also other forms of sexual behaviour, such as active or passive participation in masturbation or in sadistic or masochistic practices, where the woman offers herself as a participant in physical acts of indecency for the sexual gratification of men.[63]

Prostitution. A male or female prostitute is not guilty of any common-law **36.40** crime for carrying on his or her trade.

Soliciting and importuning by either male or female prostitutes is, however, an offence under the Civic Government (Scotland) Act 1982, section 46, which provides:

"(1) A prostitute (whether male or female) who for the purposes of prostitution—
(a) loiters in a public place;
(b) solicits in a public place or in any other place so as to be seen from a public place; or
(c) importunes any person who is in a public place,
shall be guilty of an offence and liable, on summary conviction, to a fine not exceeding [level 2 on the standard scale].
(2) In subsection (1) above, 'public place' has the same meaning as in section 133[64] of this Act but includes—
(a) any place to which at the material time the public are permitted to have access, whether on payment or otherwise; and
(b) any public conveyance other than a taxi or hire car within the meaning of section 23[65] of this Act."

A prostitute cannot be convicted of importuning without evidence of his or her "status" as a prostitute independent of, and prior to, the occasion of importuning which is the subject of the charge.[66]

Section 11(1)(b) of the Criminal Law (Consolidation) (Scotland) Act 1995 penalises "every male person who in any public place persistently solicits[67] or importunes for immoral purposes."[68] This provision was

---

[63] *R. v. Webb* [1964] 1 Q.B. 357, Lord Parker C.J. at 366; Widgery J. suggested in the course of argument that an obscene strip-tease act might amount to prostitution: at 360; *R. v. de Munck* [1918] 1 K.B. 635. For the term "common prostitute", see n. 58, *supra*. The English draft code (L.C. No. 177, "A Criminal Code for England and Wales", H.C. 299, 1989, Vol. 1, Cl. 122) defines "prostitute" as meaning "a person who, for gain, offers his body for sexual purposes to others or offers to do sexual acts to their bodies, whether or not he selects those to whom he makes his services available": the absence of selection may make a person a "common" prostitute, as against just a prostitute, but the definition seems very wide; *cf.*, however, *R. v. McFarlane* (1994) 99 Cr.App.R. 8, CA (n. 61, *supra*).

[64] Section 133 provides: " 'public place' means any place (whether a thoroughfare or not) to which the public have unrestricted access and includes — (a) the doorways or entrances of premises abutting on any such place; and (b) any common passage, close, court, stair, garden or yard pertinent to any tenement or group of separately owned houses."

[65] Section 23 provides, no far as relevant, "(1) . . . 'taxi' means a hire car which is engaged, by arrangements made in a public place between the person to be conveyed in it (or a person acting on his behalf) and its driver for a journey beginning there and then; and 'private hire car' means a hire car other than a taxi within the meaning of this subsection. (2) In subsection (1) above, "hire car" means a motor vehicle with a driver (other than a vehicle being a public service vehicle within the meaning of the Public Passenger Vehicles Act 1981) which is, with a view to profit, available for hire by the public for personal conveyance."

[66] *White v. Allan*, 1985 S.L.T. 396.

[67] The soliciting must be personal and not, *e.g.* by advertising in a shop: *Burge v. D.P.P.* [1962] 1 W.L.R. 265.

[68] Maximum penalty two years' on indictment, six months' on summary conviction.

probably intended to apply to males importuning on behalf of female prostitutes, but may well apply to a man soliciting a woman to have intercourse with himself, or even to soliciting another male to commit an act of gross indecency with himself or other men.[69] The corresponding English provision has been held not to apply to a man soliciting a woman for himself, as in kerb-crawling.[70] "Persistently" requires at least two acts.

There is a separate offence under section 13(9) of the Criminal Law (Consolidation) (Scotland) Act 1995 of soliciting or importuning any male person for the purpose of procuring the commission of a homosexual act (which means[71] sodomy, an act of gross indecency or shameless indecency by one male person with another male person).[72]

36.41 *Procuring and brothel-keeping.* The Criminal Law (Consolidation) (Scotland) Act 1995, section 7(1), deals with procuring for prostitution, and sections 8(1)–(5) and 9 make provisions regarding brothels and other premises used for habitual prostitution.[73]

36.42 *Living on the earnings of prostitution.* Section 11(1)(a) of the Criminal Law (Consolidation) (Scotland) Act 1995 penalises "every male person who knowingly lives wholly or in part on the earnings of prostitution." It is unlikely that a man who lived on the earnings of male prostitution would be charged under section 11(1)(a), since the prostitution with whose earnings that section is concerned is female prostitution,[74] and section 13(9) specifically provides that a person who knowingly lives wholly or in part on the earnings of another from male prostitution is guilty of an offence.[75]

36.43   EXERCISING CONTROL OVER PROSTITUTES. Section 11(3) of the Criminal Law (Consolidation) (Scotland) Act 1995 provides:

> "Where a male person is proved to live with or to be habitually in the company of a prostitute, or is proved to have exercised control, direction or influence over the movements of a prostitute in such a manner as to show that he is aiding, abetting or compelling her prostitution with any other person, or generally, he shall, unless he can satisfy the court to the contrary, be deemed to be knowingly living on the earnings of prostitution."[76]

36.44   OFFENCES BY WOMEN. Section 11(4) of the Criminal Law (Consolidation) (Scotland) Act 1995 provides that any female "who is proved to have, for the purposes of gain, exercised control, direction or influence over the movements of a prostitute" in the manner described in section

---

[69] *Dale v. Smith* [1967] 1 W.L.R. 700; *R. v. Ford (Graham)* [1977] 1 W.L.R. 1083.

[70] *Crook v. Edmonson* [1966] 2 Q.B. 81.

[71] See s.13(4). See also C. Gane, "Soliciting for Immoral Purposes", 1978 S.L.T. (News) 181.

[72] Maximum penalty, on indictment, two years', and on summary conviction, six months'.

[73] *supra.* See also, *supra,* paras 31.12, 31.13.

[74] And here as elsewhere the law presumably ignores the existence of lesbianism.

[75] Maximum penalty, under s.11(1)(a) as also under s.13(9), is, on indictment, two years', and, on summary conviction, six months'.

[76] See *R. v. Clarke* (1976) 63 Cr.App.R. 16.

11(3) of the Act, is liable to the penalties set out in section 11(1). A woman may also be guilty art and part of an offence under section 11(1)(a) of the Act.[76a]

LIVING ON EARNINGS. In *Calvert v. Mayes*[77] the accused was a driver **36.45** whose car was hired to take airmen and prostitutes from a public-house to places where they could have intercourse, and also on journeys back to the airmen's base during which intercourse took place in the back of the car. He was convicted of living on the prostitutes' earnings (although they were not paid in money, but in entertainment, etc.) on the ground that although he could have charged the men the same fare for an ordinary journey they would not in fact have been using his vehicle at all but for the prostitutes: he was therefore earning money he would not have earned but for the girls' prostitution. It does not make any difference whether the money is paid to the accused by the prostitutes out of their earnings, or, as was the case in *Calvert v. Mayes*, is paid direct to him by their clients as part of the price of the prostitution. This case shows that in certain circumstances a man may be living on immoral earnings although he is himself providing what is prima facie a legitimate service, but it should be stressed that there was a finding in *Calvert v. Mayes* that the defendant did exercise direction and influence over the prostitutes' movements, and generally aided and abetted their prostitution. In *R. v. Ansell*,[78] where the accused received a fee for providing prospective clients with a list of prostitutes without the knowledge of the women, and where the fee was paid before the clients met the women, he was held not to be guilty of the offence, since there was a total absence of any direction or influence. On the other hand, in *R. v. Farrugia (Francis)*[79] taxi drivers waited at an escort agency where they also collected prostitutes and took them to hotels and there introduced them to the agency's clients. They were paid only their normal fare, but collected an agency fee from the client which they delivered to the agency, £5 of which was received by some of the girls. The girls did not pay any of their own earnings to the agency. The drivers, as well as the persons running the agency, were convicted of living on the earnings of prostitution.

There remains the problem of differentiating between those persons **36.46** whose provision of a service to prostitutes is innocent and those whose provision of a service constitutes living on immoral earnings.

In *Shaw v. D.P.P.*,[80] Lord Reid suggested that "living on" connoted parasitic living, and gave as an example of this the prostitute's tout or bully.[81] But a tout provides a service, as so, perhaps, does a bully. In the same case, the majority of the House of Lords accepted Viscount Simonds' statement that:

"[A] person does not necessarily escape [conviction] by receiving payment for the goods or services that he supplies to a prostitute.

[76a] *Reid v. H.M. Advocate*, 199 S.C.C.R. 19; see para. 36.42, *supra*.
[77] [1954] 1 Q.B. 342.
[78] [1975] Q.B. 215; *cf.* Vol. I, para. 5.29.
[79] (1979) 69 Cr.App.R. 108.
[80] [1962] A.C. 220.
[81] At 269–270.

The argument that such a person lives on his own earnings, not on hers, is inconclusive. To give effect to it would be to exclude from the operation of the Act the very persons, the tout, the bully or protector, whom it was designed to catch. For they would surely claim that they served the prostitute, however despicable their service might seem to others. Somewhere the line must be drawn and I do not find it easy to draw it . . .

[A] person may fairly be said to be living in whole or in part on the earnings of prostitution if he is paid by prostitutes for goods or services supplied by him to them for the purpose of their prostitution which he would not supply but for the fact that they were prostitutes. I emphasise the negative part of this proposition, for I wish to distinguish beyond all misconception such a case from that in which the service supplied could be supplied to a woman whether a prostitute or not."[82]

Shaw itself was a simple case. The accused was the publisher of a periodical called *The Ladies' Directory* in which prostitutes advertised themselves for a fee paid to the accused. This was clearly a service which would not have been supplied but for the fact that they were prostitutes and, as Lord Reid pointed out, the accused was in the same position as a tout.[83] But once one leaves the sphere of touting it is difficult to think of any goods or services which would not be supplied to a woman but for the fact that she was a prostitute. For example, women who are not prostitutes make use of contraceptives although prostitutes who buy them do so for the purpose of prostitution; a landlord who supplies a prostitute with a base for her professional operations is often thought of as living on her earnings, since a prostitute would have difficulty in carrying on her trade without a room in which to work; but she would not have a body to prostitute at all if she did not eat and drink, yet her grocer and her vintner are not normally thought of as living on her earnings.[84]

36.47 The question is usually raised in relation to the letting of accommodation to prostitutes. In *R v. Thomas*,[85] Pilcher J. held that where a prostitute was charged a grossly inflated rent "for the express purpose of allowing her to ply her immoral trade" it was for the jury to say whether an offence had been committed. Pilcher J. told them that in his view anyone who acts in that fashion is "acting as it were as a coadjutor of the prostitute, and is in quite a different position to the shopkeeper, doctor or anyone else who performs services or sells goods in the ordinary way to a prostitute." This statement was approved by the Court of Criminal Appeal, as also was Pilcher J.'s disapproval of an earlier case, *R. v. Silver*,[86] in which it had been held that a landlord was in the same position as a doctor even although he charged an exorbitant price. In *Shaw v. D.P.P.*,[87] Viscount Simonds deprecated the stress laid on the amount of rent, and rested his approval of *Thomas* on the fact that the

---

[82] At 263–264.
[83] At 270.
[84] See Viscount Simonds at 266.
[85] [1957] 1 W.L.R. 747.
[86] [1956] 1 W.L.R. 281.
[87] [1962] A.C. 220.

room in that case had been rented to the prostitute solely for use in her trade, while in *Silver* the room had been let for her "occupation" as well, that is to say, as the place where she lived as well as worked. Lord Simonds referred to the *Silver* type of case as very difficult and suggested that a conviction could occur in such a case on the basis of an exorbitant rent only on the view that "to the extent to which the rent is in excess of normal, he extorts it from the prostitute upon no other ground than that she is a prostitute."[88] He also disapproved the common view that where the premises are let for occupation the landlord is guilty "merely because he knows that his tenant is a prostitute and must be assumed to know that she will there ply her trade."[89]

These cases were considered in *Soni v. H.M. Advocate*,[90] the only Scottish authority on the subject. The accused was a landlord who owned a number of houses, some of which he let to prostitutes. He appealed unsuccessfully against conviction on the ground that the jury were wrongly directed that he could be convicted even if the rents he charged were reasonable, provided he was shown to have participated and assisted in the prostitution. It was accepted that the requirements of (what is now) section 11(3) of the Criminal Law (Consolidation) (Scotland) Act 1995 had not been met. The only evidence of participation and assistance was that he gave priority to prospective tenants who were prostitutes, that he gave some of them a change of accommodation to premises more suitable for their trade, discussed with them the installation of a telephone for the purposes of their trade, and gave them advice "and counselled them against conduct which might get them involved with the police and a possible cutting off of their income", and that he "witnessed the prostitutes in their immoral operations and encouraged them to get on with it".[91] The court held that these facts could be regarded as showing "a personal involvement with their immoral activities designed to secure and advance his own financial interests."[92]

On the general question of the need to prove an exorbitant rent, the court said that there could be a conviction without such proof, without proof that the room was let exclusively and specifically for prostitution and without proof of the provisions of (what is now) section 11(3) of the Criminal Law (Consolidation) (Scotland) Act 1995. The question was always whether in any given case the accused was living on immoral earnings. It was accepted that more was needed than knowledge that the tenant was trading as a prostitute, but the court was not prepared to restrict any additional requirement to the one case of exorbitant rent. They held that, "While proof of payment of an exorbitant rent may be a factor, and possibly a telling factor, in the issue, it is not an essential one. In its absence, proof that the accused was living on the immoral earnings of prostitution might be difficult, but that is not to say it is impossible."[93]

It is submitted that the test in every case of services should be whether, as Lord Justice-Clerk Grant said in *Soni*, the accused is

---

[88] *ibid.*, at 265–266.
[89] *ibid.*
[90] 1970 S.L.T. 275.
[91] *ibid.* 277–278.
[92] At 278.
[93] At 277.

"participating and assisting", or, as Pilcher J. put it in *Thomas*,[94] the accused is "as it were, a coadjutor," or, as Lord Reid said in *Shaw*,[95] "he is making her engage in a joint adventure with him which will bring to him a part of her immoral earnings over and above rent", or, as Sellers J. put it in *Calvert v. Mayes*,[96] he is "trading in prostitution". The *Thomas* type of case is comparatively simple — a lease of premises solely for use in prostitution is analogous to touting for clients, and like touting it indicates that the accused is art and part in the prostitution. In other cases the evidence may not indicate this so clearly, but the question is always whether the goods or services supplied are supplied in circumstances which in common law terms would render the accused art and part in prostitution by their supply, and this is so whatever the form of service provided.

SADO-MASOCHISTIC PRACTICES

36.48   Those who indulge in sado-masochistic practices intend to obtain sexual gratification thereby. Such practices, obviously, involve the participation of at least two persons, and (usually) the infliction of pain by one person upon another.[97] The methods used to achieve sexual gratification may be such as to bring the participants' conduct within the ambit of assault; and, unless there is plainly no consent on the part of the submissive participant, the question for the criminal law then concerns the degree to which consent by B is acceptable as a defence to an assault by A upon B. In *Smart v. H.M. Advocate*,[98] the Appeal Court accepted that "touching" a consenting person in a sexual context was not assault, provided there was no intention to do bodily harm to that person.[99] Since, therefore, and to the extent to which, consensual sado-masochistic encounters involve the deliberate infliction of bodily harm, the parties involved in such encounters may be prosecuted in Scotland for assault.

In England, the House of Lords decided by a narrow majority in *R. v. Brown*[1] that participants in private consensual sado-masochistic practices which involved the infliction of significant, though non-permanent, injury were guilty of either assault occasioning actual bodily harm[2] or unlawful wounding[3] on policy and public interest grounds.[4] Those convicted alleged that their rights under the European Convention on Human Rights had been violated by the House's decision; but the European

---

[94] [1957] 1 W.L.R. 747.

[95] [1962] A.C. at 271.

[96] [1954] 1 Q.B. at 349.

[97] Where only humiliation is involved, there is probably no issue which is of interest to the criminal law, although it is conceivable that charges of breach of the peace or shamelessly indecent conduct might be brought.

[98] 1975 J.C. 30.

[99] See para. 29.39, *supra*.

[1] [1994] 1 A.C. 212.

[2] Contrary to s.47 of the Offences Against the Person Act 1861.

[3] Contrary to s.20 of the Offences Against the Person Act 1861.

[4] The majority of the House referred to such matters as the degrading and unpredictably dangerous nature of the conduct of the appellants, the entitlement of society to protect itself against a culture of violence, and the sense that the toleration of cruelty would be uncivilised.

Court on Human Rights upheld the decision and declared that in the circumstances any interference with the applicants' rights under Article 8 had been justified.[5]

---

[5] See *Laskey, Jaggard and Brown v. United Kingdom* (1997) 24 E.H.R.R. 39. Article 8 (see the Human Rights Act 1998, Sched. 1, Pt 1) provides: "1. Everyone has the right to respect for his private and family life, his home and his correspondence. 2. There shall be no interference by a public authority with the exercise of this right except such as is in accordance with the law and is necessary in a democratic society in the interests of national security, public safety or the economic well-being of the country, for the prevention of disorder or crime, for the protection of health or morals, or for the protection of the rights and freedoms of others." The conclusion of the European Court on Human Rights (at 60) was that there had been interference with the applicants' right to private life under Art. 8(1), but that that could be justified as follows: "50. In sum, the Court finds that the national authorities were entitled to consider that the prosecution and conviction of the applicants were necessary in a democratic society for the protection of health within the meaning of Article 8(2) of the Convention." (The Court did not find it necessary to decide whether the interference with the applicant's right to respect for private life could also be justified on the ground of protection of morals.)

PART VI

OFFENCES AGAINST THE STATE

CHAPTER 37

TREASON AND ALLIED OFFENCES

TREASON

The old Scots law of treason was abolished by the Treason Act 1708 **37.01** which provided that "such crimes and offences which are high treason or misprision of high treason within England shall be construed adjudged and taken to be high treason and misprision of high treason within Scotland and that . . . no crimes or offences shall be high treason or misprision of high treason within Scotland but those that are high treason or misprision of high treason in England."[1] The Scots law of treason is therefore entirely and wholly English law; it rests on the English Treason Act 1351 together with a few later statutes, and the general rules of English law apply to treason in such matters as accession and attempt. For that reason and because there have been no prosecutions for treason in Scotland for well over a century, it is proposed to deal only briefly with the law.[2]

The ways of committing treason

Treason may be committed in a number of ways which can be **37.02** collected under seven heads, and no act can be treason unless it falls under one of these heads.

The Act of 1351. The basis of the law of treason is the Treason Act 1351 **37.03** which sets out a number of types of treason, of which the following are still applicable:

(1) Compassing or imagining the death of the sovereign, or of his Queen, or of their eldest son and heir;
(2) Violating the King's consort, or his eldest daughter unmarried, or the wife of his eldest son and heir;
(3) Levying war against the sovereign in the realm;
(4) Being adherent to the sovereign's enemies in the realm, giving them aid and comfort in the realm, or elsewhere.

---

[1] Section 1. "High" treason is so called to distinguish it from "petit" treason, high treason being treason against the King and petit treason, treason against a lesser feudal superior. The law of petit treason, which was assimilated to murder in 1828, was never applied to Scotland: see Kenny, para. 400.

[2] *cf.* Hume, i, 513: "To be acquainted with this part of the system, the Scottish lawyer has therefore to resort to the books of the law of England. Now, as these are patent to all the world, and treat very fully of the subject, and with much ability; so all that is here proposed is to compile a summary from them (in many places exhibiting their very words) of those leading and settled points of doctrine, wherein all the best authorities are agreed." Treason is no longer a capital offence: see the Crime and Disorder Act 1998, s.36.

37.04   (1) *Compassing the death of the sovereign.* The Treason Act 1351 was intended to stabilise the law of treason, and prevent the courts from extending its scope.[3] In practice, however, the courts continued to create constructive treasons, especially under the head of "compassing or imagining the death" of the sovereign. The scope of this type of treason was extended in two ways: it was held to include the compassing or imagining of some personal harm to the sovereign other than death, such as deposition or restraint[4]; and it was also extended so as to transfer the feudal idea of treason as a breach of a duty to a person into the modern idea of it as "armed resistance, made on political grounds, to the public order of the realm."[5] So, although it is not treason to compass to levy war on the Sovereign as such, it was held to be constructive compassing of the death of the Sovereign to do so, and the actual levying of war might be charged either as such, or as a form of compassing the death of the Sovereign.[6] This may be so even if the "war" levied involves no personal danger at all to the sovereign, as where an attempt was made to raise a rebellion in a remote colony.[7] The levying of war, however, must be actual and not constructive.[8] It is also a compassing of the death of the sovereign to incite foreigners to invade the country.[9]

37.05   OVERT ACT. The Treason Act 1351 provided in reference to the treason of adhering to the sovereign's enemies that the accused must "thereof be provably attainted of open deed", and the courts have applied this requirement to all forms of treason.[10] This interpretation is of most importance in reference to the treason of compassing or imagining the death of the sovereign which read literally would not require any action at all on the part of the accused.

In a trial for treason the question of fact at issue is whether the Crown have proved the overt acts charged; it then becomes a question of law whether the overt act constitutes treason of the type charged. It is not treason to kill the sovereign, but such killing may be an overt act of compassing her death.[11] An overt act is "any act manifesting the criminal intention, and tending towards the accomplishment of the criminal object".[12] The following are examples of overt acts of compassing the death of the sovereign: lying in wait to kill him, providing arms for killing him, marching in force in array of war against him, fortifying a place to resist him, enlisting men to depose him, inviting foreigners to invade the realm.[13]

---

[3] Kenny, para. 401.

[4] Hume, i, 514, 516, 520; Alison, i, 598, 605; Macdonald, pp. 172–173.

[5] Kenny, para. 413, quoting Stephen's *General View of the Criminal law* (1st ed.), p.36.

[6] Hume, i, 515; Alison, i, 598; *The Laws of Scotland: Stair Memorial Encyclopaedia*, (Edinburgh, 1995), Vol. 7, para. 571. *Cf. Jas Wilson*, Trials for Treason in Scotland, (1820) ii., 28 at 332, *per* Lord Hope: "it is impossible to conceive there can be a levying of war against the King which does not necessarily include the compassing and imagining the King's death."

[7] *R. v. Maclane* (1797) 26 St.Tr. 721, 784.

[8] *cf. Halsbury's Laws of England* (4th ed.), Vol. 11(1), reissue 1990, para. 81; for the distinction between actual and constructive levying of war, see *infra*, paras 37.09, 37.10.

[9] Hume, i, 517; *Halsbury's Laws of England, supra*, para. 81.

[10] Kenny, paras 403, 410; Alison, i, 597; Hume, i, 513; Macdonald, p.172.

[11] Kenny, para. 402; *R. v. Twenty-nine Regicides* (1660) 5 St.Tr. 947, 982.

[12] *R. v. Thistlewood* (1820) 33 St.Tr. 681, Lord Tenterden at 684, quoted in Kenny, para. 403.

[13] Hume, i, 514–515; *cf.* Kenny, para. 403.

WORDS. Any words spoken or written in pursuance of an existing **37.06** treasonable conspiracy constitute overt acts.[14] It is an overt act of treason to incite someone to treason by words of advice or persuasion spoken or written, to send letters in course of and for the furtherance of a treasonable conspiracy, to arrange, or even to attend, a meeting at which a treasonable conspiracy is discussed although nothing is decided on. It is also an overt act to publish a proclamation inviting people in general to join in a treasonable conspiracy.[15] Speculative writings advocating the overthrow of monarchs and established governments in general are not treasonable, but writings advocating the violent overthrow of the Queen or her Government may be treasonable even if unconnected with any actual conspiracy,[16] although it is extremely unlikely that a charge would be brought in such a case. Mere loose spoken words of abuse at Crown or Government, unconnected with any treasonable conspiracy, are not treasonable.[17]

It is not clear whether unpublished writings can ever be treasonable.[18] Hume takes the view that unpublished writings are treasonable if connected with an actual conspiracy,[19] but it is probably correct to state that unpublished writings cannot be charged as an overt act, although they may be proved as evidence of other overt acts.[20] It is in any event unlikely that any attempt would be made to base a charge of treason on unpublished writings alone.

QUEEN AND HEIR. This type of treason extends not only to the King but **37.07** to "our lady his Queen, or . . . their eldest son and heir". Read literally, this does not include the consort of a Queen regnant, or indeed her son, and Alison expressly excludes the former.[21] The heir to the throne is included only when he is the son of the sovereign.

In the case of these persons there can be no constructive treason, and treason is committed only where their actual death is compassed or imagined.[22]

(2) *Violating the King's consort, etc.* "Violating" does not require force, **37.08** and it is treason to have unlawful sexual intercourse with any of the persons mentioned even if they consent. Indeed, if they do consent, they are equally guilty of treason, as in the cases of Anne Boleyn and Catherine Howard.[23] It appears however that a Queen consort, for example, is not guilty of treason if she commits adultery with a foreigner abroad who, because he does not owe allegiance, cannot himself be guilty of treason, since her guilt in any case is only by accession to that of the man.[24]

---

[14] *Halsbury's Laws of England* (4th ed.), Vol. 11(1) (reissue 1990), para. 81; Hume, i, 517–518; Alison, i, 602; Macdonald, p.172.
[15] *Jas Spiers* (1820) Hume, i, 515; *Robt Munroe* (1820) Hume, i, 516.
[16] Hume, i, 518; Macdonald, p.172.
[17] Hume, i, 519.
[18] Kenny, para. 404.
[19] Hume, i, 517–518. See also Alison, i, 602–603; Macdonald, p.172.
[20] See, *e.g.*, *Archbold's Criminal Pleading, Evidence and Practice (2001)*, para. 25–15.
[21] Alison, i, 605.
[22] Hume, i, 521; Alison, i, 605; Macdonald, p.173.
[23] Kenny, para. 405.
[24] Kenny, para. 411.

37.09   (3) *Levying war in the realm.* DIRECT LEVYING OF WAR. It is treason to raise an army against the sovereign to depose or imprison her, or to force her to change her Government.[25] War may be levied by a small number of persons, and without any military assembly. Any attack on the Queen's forces, or any fortifying of a place against them is levying war, as also is the mere raising of a band with warlike weapons, without any actual fighting.[26] In *John Baird*[27] a group of about 40 persons who engaged in a skirmish with some troops were convicted of treason by levying war.[28] It is not even necessary that the accused should be armed with warlike weapons, although Hume holds that where no arms are carried but only picks or axes or the like, there is no levying of war unless there is actual fighting.[29] Where military weapons are carried, war may be levied by the mere assembling without any fighting. In *Jas Wilson*[30] about 20 people armed with guns and pikes set out to join an insurrection and then turned back on hearing that the insurrection had not taken place: they were convicted of treason and Lord Hope said that, "the smallest body which rises in arms to effectuate a general purpose . . . constitutes a levying of war."[31]

37.10   CONSTRUCTIVE LEVYING OF WAR. Any riot or insurrection which has as its purpose a general redress of grievances or alteration of the law is a levying of war although there is no question of any conflict with the armed forces of the Crown. It is a levying of war to raise an insurrection to open all prisons, or destroy all the meeting houses of a particular religious sect.[32] Where the grievance is local or particular the crime is only rioting or mobbing and not treason.[33] It is treason to raise a riot to free all prisoners, or execute all reprieved persons, but not to rescue a particular prisoner or hang a particular person.[34]

Treasonable levying of war can be committed only within the realm, and it is not treason of this kind to enlist men to fight abroad against the sovereign, but such enlistment would be a treasonable compassing of the Queen's death, and might also be an adhering to her enemies.

---

[25] *Halsbury's Law of England* (4th ed.), Vol. 11(1) (reissue, 1999), para. 79.

[26] Alison, i, 608; Hume, i, 522; *Jas Wilson* (1820), *supra*, L.P. Hope at 334: "it is not necessary there should be battles — it is not necessary that the troops should be in regular battalions, or that they should be clothed like regular soldiers."

[27] (1820) Hume, i, 522.

[28] See also *Andrew Hardie* (1820) 1 St.Tr. (N.S.) 609.

[29] Hume, i, 523.

[30] *Trials for Treason in Scotland* (1820), ii, 28.

[31] The accused had also taken part in a strike a few days earlier, and had forced a number of people to join them on the preceding day.

[32] *R. v. Dammaree* (1710) 15 St.Tr. 521; Kenny, para. 385; Hume, i, 525; Alison, i, 611. Cf. *Jas Wilson* (1820), *supra*, L.P. Hope at 336: "any persons who take the law into their hands, and pull down these places, are guilty of levying war against the King; because they are usurping the public authority of the land." It may even be treason to combine to destroy all brothels!: see Hume, i, 525; *R. v. Dammaree, supra* at 607.

[33] *R. v. Andrew Hardie* (1820) 1 St.Tr. (N.S.) 609, L.P. Hope at 623, 766. See also *John Duncan and Ors* (1843) 1 Broun 512 where a plea of guilty to breach of the peace was accepted on a charge of mobbing.

[34] So the Porteous mob were charged only with riot and not with treason: Hume, i, 526; *R. v. Maclauchlan* (1737) 17 St.Tr. 993. Alison makes a distinction between riot and treason depend on whether the tumult is directed against Parliament or a court of justice: Alison, i, 611; but Hume's distinction between general and particular purposes is preferable.

(4) *Adhering to the Queen's enemies.* It is treason to adhere to the **37.11** Queen's enemies by giving them aid and comfort anywhere. A man may be guilty of this treason by giving aid and comfort in the realm to enemies in the realm or by giving aid and comfort elsewhere to enemies elsewhere.[35] Any act which tends to strengthen the Queen's enemies or to weaken the Queen's power to resist or attack the enemy constitutes giving aid and comfort.[36] In *R. v. Casement*[37] the prisoner endeavoured to persuade British prisoners of war in Germany to join an Irish Brigade to fight against Britain; in *Joyce v. D.P.P.*,[38] the prisoner broadcast propaganda to Britain from Germany. It is a treasonable adherence to the Queen's enemies for a British subject to become the naturalised subject of an enemy during a war.[39]

It is treason to commit acts against the Queen's allies in order to aid the common enemy.[40]

MENS REA. It appears that in some circumstances it is a defence to a **37.12** charge of adherence that the accused did not act with the intention of giving aid to the Queen's enemies. In *R. v. Ahlers*[41] the conviction of the German consul in Sunderland for assisting German subjects to return home after the declaration of war was quashed on the ground that the judge had wrongly directed the jury that it was no defence to show that the prisoner had acted as he believed he was lawfully entitled to do. It was held that the question at issue was whether he had acted with intent to assist the King's enemies, or in the belief that he was only carrying out his duty as consul.[42]

ENEMY. The Queen's enemies are those states or the subjects of those **37.13** states which are in a state of hostility to this country, whether or not war has been declared,[43] and also any foreigners who invade the country whether or not their state is at war with the Queen.[44] A British subject, however, can never be an enemy under the Treason Act.[45]

Other forms of treason. Some later statutes have added to the treasons set **37.14** out in the Treason Act 1351. These additional treasons are as follows:

(5) *Disputing or Hindering the Succession.* The Treason Act 1702, section 3, makes it treason to attempt by overt acts to hinder the succession as limited by the Act of Settlement 1700.

(6) *Killing Judges.* The Treason Act 1708, section 11 makes it treason **37.15** to kill any of the Lords of Session or Justiciary "sitting in Judgement in the Exercise of their Office within Scotland."[46]

---

[35] Kenny, para. 407. *R. v. Casement* [1917] 1 K.B. 98; *Joyce v. D.P.P.* [1946] A.C. 347.

[36] *R. v. Casement, supra,* Lord Reading C.J. at 133.

[37] *supra.*

[38] *supra.*

[39] *R. v. Lynch* [1903] 1 K.B. 444.

[40] Hume, i, 529; Alison, i, 613; Macdonald, p.175.

[41] [1915] 1 K.B. 616. *Cf.,* Vol. I, para. 7.19.

[42] See also *R. v. Purdy* (1946) 10 J.C.L. 182.

[43] Hume, i, 529; *Halsbury's Laws of England* (4th ed.), Vol. 11(1) (reissue, 1990), para. 80, n.1.

[44] *Halsbury, supra.*

[45] See, *Archbold's Criminal Pleading, Evidence and Practice* (2001) para. 25–31.

[46] Killing English judges in similar circumstances is treason under the Treason Act 1351.

37.16 (7) *Counterfeiting Seals.* Section 12 of the Treason Act 1708 makes it treason to counterfeit any seals appointed to be kept, used and continued in Scotland under the twenty-fourth Article of Union. The Forgery Act 1913 made such counterfeiting whether of English or Scottish seals felony only,[47] but that Act did not extend to Scotland and did not repeal section 12 of the Treason Act 1708 which was repealed as to England by the Forgery Act 1830, so that it is technically treason to counterfeit Scots seals in Scotland.[48]

Treason and allegiance

37.17 Treason is essentially a breach of allegiance and can be committed only as between persons united by a bond of allegiance. This raises difficulty in respect of aliens and of usurpers.

37.18 *Aliens.* An alien owes allegiance to the Queen while he remains in this country, and can accordingly be guilty of treason in this country.[49] An alien enemy, however, will probably be dealt with as a spy rather than a traitor, although technically he may be guilty of treason if he accepts the protection of the Queen. An alien resident who remains in British territory while it is occupied by enemy forces may be guilty of treason committed there during that occupation, the theory being that the Queen's protection is not removed by the occupation since after the occupation her courts have power to deal with wrongs done during the occupation.[50] Normally an alien cannot commit treason outside British territory, but an alien who leaves Britain on a British passport and retains that passport owes allegiance by virtue of the protection afforded him by the passport, even if he is in an enemy country, and may be convicted of treason by adhering to the enemy in their country.[51]

An alien who serves in the armed forces of the Crown owes allegiance as being under the Queen's protection.[52]

37.19 *British Subjects.* A British subject who is a citizen of the United Kingdom and colonies[53] owes allegiance wherever he may be, and is guilty of treason if he abandons his nationality for that of an enemy country.[54]

37.20 *Usurpers.* Whether it is treason to support a King *de facto* against a King *de jure* or vice versa is a question more likely to be decided by political considerations and according to whether a man is tried in the courts of the King he supported or of the King he opposed than by any considerations of the law of allegiance. The Treason Act 1495 did,

---

[47] Section 5(1).
[48] The Forgery Act 1913 was repealed by the Forgery and Counterfeiting Act 1981, Sched., Pt I.
[49] *Halsbury's Laws of England* (4th ed.), Vol. 11(1) (reissue, 1990), para. 77.
[50] *De Jager v. Att-Gen. Natal* [1907] A.C. 326.
[51] *Joyce v. D.P.P.* [1946] A.C. 347.
[52] *R. v. Arrowsmith* [1975] Q.B. 678, 688B.
[53] British Nationality Act 1948, s.3: A British subject or citizen of Eire who is not such a citizen is not guilty of any offence against the laws of the U.K. by reason of anything done or omitted in any commonwealth or foreign country or Eire unless the act or omission would be an offence if committed by an alien or in relation to conduct in a commonwealth country or Eire would be an offence if committed in a foreign country.
[54] *R. v. Lynch* [1903] 1 K.B. 444.

however, attempt to protect those persons who had served a King *de facto* against the vengeance of a restored King *de jure* by providing that no one serving "the King and sovereign lord of this lande for the tyme being" should be guilty of treason in respect of such service.[55] Hume supports the principle behind this Act by remarking that allegiance is owed to such a King in return for his protection, and that no allegiance can be owed to an absent King who has never possessed his throne.[56]

Compulsion

Compulsion is in certain circumstances a defence to treason. A person **37.21** who takes part in a levying of war or who adheres to the Queen's enemies through force and fear and continued apprehension for his life, is not guilty of treason. The force must, however, be shown to have continued throughout the period of his treason, and the fear must be for his life, and not merely for his property.[57]

Accession

In treason, unlike other offences in English law, accession before the **37.22** fact, by incitement or in any other way, makes the accessory guilty as a principal.[58]

MISPRISION OF TREASON

Misprision of treason consists in the failure by anyone who has **37.23** any information that might lead to the arrest of a traitor to give the information to the authorities.[59] It may also be misprision to fail to give information about a projected treason.[60]

TREASON FELONY

Section 3 of the Treason Felony Act 1848 provides: **37.24**

"If any person whatsoever shall, within the United Kingdom or without, compass, imagine, invent, devise, or intend to deprive or depose . . . the Queen, from the style, honour, or royal name of the imperial crown of the United Kingdom, or of any other of her

---

[55] Provided, the Act goes on to say, he does not "hereafter declyne" from his allegiance.
[56] Hume, i, 520. Hume is undecided as to the position of a deposed King who still maintains his claim to the throne, considering that a distinction should be drawn between bearing arms against him under compulsion, and killing him voluntarily or for reward.
[57] *R. v. MacGrowther* (1746) 18 St.Tr. 391. *Cf. R. v. Purdy* (1946) 10 J.C.L. 182; *R. v. Steane* [1947] 1 K.B. 997. See Vol. I, paras 7.19, 13.20 *et seq.*
[58] *Halsbury's Laws of England* (4th ed.), Vol. 11(1) (reissue, 1990), para. 82.
[59] Hume, i, 551; Kenny, para. 421.
[60] Kenny, para. 421. On the concept of "misprision" see *R. v. Aberg* [1948] 2 K.B. 173; *Sykes v. D.P.P.* [1962] A.C. 528; C.K. Allen, "Misprision" (1962) 78 L.Q.R. 40. Misprision of treason is punishable by imprisonment for life and forfeiture of the offender's goods absolutely and of his lands for life; Kenny, para. 421.

Majesty's dominions and countries, or to levy war against her Majesty, within any part of the United Kingdom, in order by force or constraint to compel her to change her measures or counsels, or in order to put any force or constraint upon or in order to intimidate or overawe both Houses or either House of Parliament, or to move or stir any foreigner or stranger with force to invade the United Kingdom or any other of her Majesty's dominions or countries under the obeisance of her Majesty, and such compassings, imaginations, inventions, devices, or intentions, or any of them, shall express, utter, or declare, by publishing any printing or writing, or by any overt act or deed,[61] every person so offending shall . . . be liable [to life imprisonment]."

The Act of 1848 preserves the Treason Act of 1351 on the one hand, and does not alter the common law of sedition and conspiracy on the other, so that the same act may be charged as treason, treason felony, sedition or a conspiracy to alter the constitution by force.[62]

Assaults on the Queen

37.25   Assaults on the person of the Queen are aggravated assaults at common law, and are also punishable with seven years' imprisonment under the Treason Act 1842.[63]

CONSPIRACY TO ALTER THE CONSTITUTION BY FORCE

37.26   To conspire to alter the constitution or the laws of the country by force of arms is arguably a constructive compassing of the death of the Queen under the Treason Act 1351, and probably a compassing to levy war under the Treason Felony Act 1848, but it is also a common law crime similar to, if not indistinguishable from, sedition.[64] The modern practice appears to be to charge conspiracy only. In *H.M. Advocate v. Walsh*[65] and many other trials of Sinn Feiners in the period after 1918 the charge was of conspiracy to further the purposes of Sinn Fein "by the unlawful use of force and violence". In *H.M. Advocate v. MacAlister and Ors*[66] the resemblance of the charge to one of treason was very marked, since what was libelled was a common law conspiracy to further by criminal means the purposes of the "Scottish Republican Army", "with the intention of coercing Her Majesty's Government in Great Britain into the setting up of a separate Government in Scotland, or with the intention of overthrowing Her Majesty's Government in Scotland."

---

[61] An averment of conspiring, combining, confederating, and agreeing is a sufficient averment of an overt act: *Mulcahy v. The Queen* (1868) L.R. 3 H.L. 306.

[62] *Jas Cumming, John Grant and Ors* (1848) J. Shaw 17. *Cf. H.M. Advocate v. MacAlister and Ors*, High Court, Nov. 1953, unrep'd; see *MacAlister v. Associated Newspapers Ltd*, 1954 S.L.T. 14; see also Vol. I, paras 6.64, 6.65.

[63] *supra*, para. 29.16.

[64] See *Jas Cumming, John Grant and Ors* (1848) J. Shaw 17, Lord Cockburn at 49, Lord Wood at 50.

[65] 1922 J.C. 82.

[66] High Court at Edinburgh, Nov. 1953, unrep'd; see *MacAlister v. Associated Newspapers Ltd*, 1954 S.L.T. 14; also see Vol. I, para. 6.64.

OFFENCES IN CONNECTION WITH WAR AND THE ARMED SERVICES

Incitement to disafffection

It is a crime at common law to persuade members of the armed forces **37.27** of the Crown to desert,[67] but this would nowadays be dealt with under the Incitement to Disaffection Act 1934, which provides:

"**1.** If any person maliciously and advisedly endeavours to seduce any member of Her Majesty's forces from his duty or allegiance to Her Majesty, he shall be guilty of an offence under this Act.

2.—(1) If any person, with intent to commit or to aid, abet, counsel, or procure the commission of an offence under section one of this Act, has in his possession or under his control any document of such a nature that the dissemination of copies thereof among members of Her Majesty's forces would constitute such an offence, he shall be guilty of an offence".[68]

Interference with duty. It is an offence under sections 193 of the Army **37.28** Act 1955 and of the Air Force Act 1955 to obstruct or otherwise interfere with a member of the respective services in the exercise of his duty.[69] Section 94 of the Naval Discipline Act 1957[70] makes it an offence punishable by court martial with imprisonment for a person in a ship or on a naval establishment to seduce naval personnel from their duty.

Desertion. It is an offence under sections 192 of the Army Act 1955 and **37.29** of the Air Force Act 1955, and under section 97 of the Naval Discipline Act 1957, to procure, persuade or assist any act of desertion or absence without leave of a member of the respective services or knowingly to assist a deserter or person absent without leave.[71]

It is also an offence under sections 191 of the Army Act 1955 and of the Air Force Act 1955, section 96 of the Naval Discipline Act 1957, and section 99 of the Reserve Forces Act 1996, to pretend to be a deserter.[72]

Malingering. It is an offence under sections 194 of the Army Act 1955 **37.30** and of the Air Force Act 1955 to induce illness or provide drugs in order to aid servicemen to malinger.[73]

---

[67] Hume, i, 528; *Wilson and Hopper* (1799), *ibid.*

[68] The maximum penalty for offences under the Act is four months' imprisonment on summary conviction and a fine of the prescribed sum, and two years' imprisonment and a fine on indictment. See also Aliens Restriction (Amendment) Act 1919, s.3; Police (Scotland) Act 1967, s.42 (as amended by s.63(8) of the Police and Magistrates' Courts Act 1994) *infra*. The 1934 Act has been little used; but see *R. v. Arrowsmith* [1975] Q.B. 678, CA.

[69] Maximum penalty three months' imprisonment and a fine of level 3 on the standard scale.

[70] As amended by the Armed Forces Act 1976, s.15.

[71] As amended by the Armed Forces Act 1966, s.18, and, in the case of the Naval Discipline Act 1957, by the Armed Forces Act 1976, s.15: the Army Act is also amended by the Visiting Forces and International Headquarters (Application of Law) Order 1999 (S.I. 1999 No. 1736), art. 18 (which applies s.192 to visiting forces): see also the Reserve Forces Act 1996, s.101. Maximum penalty on indictment two years' imprisonment and a fine, on summary conviction three months' imprisonment and a fine of the prescribed sum.

[72] Maximum penalty three months' imprisonment and a fine of level 3 (level 4 relative to the Reserve Forces Act 1996, s.99) on the standard scale.

[73] Maximum penalty, on indictment, two years' and a fine, and, on summary conviction, three months' and fine of the prescribed sum.

Foreign Enlistment Act 1870

37.31　　This Act, which applies in all the Queen's dominions and to British subjects everywhere,[74] creates a number of offences in connection with foreign wars.

(1) *Enlistment in foreign services.* Section 4 of the Act provides:

> "If any person, without the licence of Her Majesty, being a British subject, within or without Her Majesty's dominions, accepts or agrees to accept any commission or engagement in the military or naval service of any foreign state at war with any foreign state at peace with Her Majesty, and in this Act referred to as a friendly state, or whether a British subject or not within Her Majesty's dominions, induces any other person to accept or agree to accept any commission or engagement in the military or naval service of any such foreign state as aforesaid, [he shall be guilty of an offence . . . and . . . punishable by fine and/or imprisonment]."

This section penalises the enlistment of a British subject in the service of a foreign state, and also forbids any person to recruit in Britain on behalf of a foreign state, whether or not the persons he seeks to recruit are British subjects.

"Foreign state" includes "any person . . . exercising or assuming to exercise the powers of government in or over any foreign country, colony, province, or part of any province or people."[75]

Section 5 makes it an offence for a British subject to leave or to board a ship with a view to leaving the Queen's dominions with the intention of accepting service with a foreign state which is at war with a friendly state, and for any person to induce any other person to do so. Section 6 makes it an offence to induce any person to leave or board a ship with a view to leaving the Queen's dominions "under a misrepresentation or false representation of the service in which such person is to be engaged" with intent that he should accept service of a kind forbidden by section 4. Section 7 makes it an offence for a shipmaster or shipowner knowingly to take on board any ship within the Queen's dominions any British subject who has accepted a forbidden foreign commission or is about to leave the country with intent to do so, or any person who has been induced to embark under a misrepresentation of the kind set out in section 6.[76]

37.32　　(2) *Fitting out expeditions.* Section 11 provides:

> "[I]f any person within the limits of her Majesty's dominions, and without the licence of Her Majesty,—
>
> Prepares or fits out any naval or military expedition to proceed against the dominions of any friendly state, the following consequences shall ensue:
>
> (1) Every person engaged in such preparation or fitting out, or assisting therein, or employed in any capacity in such expedition, shall be guilty of an offence . . . [and punishable by fine and/or imprisonment] . . .
>
> (2) All ships, and their equipment, and all arms and munitions of war, used in or forming part of such expedition, shall be forfeited".

---

[74] Sections 2 and 4; *R. v. Jameson* [1896] 2 Q.B. 425.
[75] Section 30.
[76] All these offences are punishable by fine and imprisonment.

It is an offence under this section for a British subject who is outside the Queen's dominions to assist in the preparation of a forbidden expedition which is raised in her dominions.[77]

(3) *Illegal shipbuilding, etc.* It is an offence under section 8 of the Act **37.33** for any person in the Queen's dominions without licence to build, or agree to build, or cause to be built, or issue or deliver any commission for, or equip, or despatch or cause or allow to be despatched, any ship, "with intent or knowledge, or having reasonable cause to believe that the same shall or will be employed in the service of any foreign state at war with any friendly state."[78]

It is an offence under section 10 of the Act for any person in the Queen's dominions without licence to "increase or augment" or procure or be knowingly concerned in the increase or augmentation of the "warlike force" of any ship which while it is in the Queen's dominions is in the military or naval service of a foreign state at war with a friendly state.[79]

Unlawful drilling

Section 1 of the Unlawful Drilling Act 1819[80] prohibits all **37.34** unauthorised meetings for military training or drilling without lawful authority, as being "dangerous to the peace and security of Her Majesty's liege subjects and of Her government", and provides that any person who attends such a meeting, for the purpose of training persons to use arms, or the practice of military exercises, or who trains or drills any person in the use of arms or in military exercises, shall be liable to seven years' imprisonment, while any person who attends such a meeting for the purpose of being trained to the use of arms or military exercise, is liable to two years' imprisonment.[81]

OFFENCES IN CONNECTION WITH OFFICIAL SECRETS

Under the Official Secrets Acts

(1) *Spying and being in prohibited places.* Section 1 of the Official **37.35** Secrets Act 1911 (as amended by the Official Secrets Act 1920) provides:

"(1) If any person for any purpose prejudicial to the safety or interests of the State—
  (a) approaches, inspects, passes over, or is in the neighbourhood of, or enters any prohibited place within the meaning of this Act; or
  (b) makes any sketch, plan, model, or note which is calculated to be or might be or is intended to be directly or indirectly useful to an enemy; or
  (c) obtains, collects, records, or publishes, or communicates to any other person any secret official code word, or pass word

---

[77] *R. v. Jameson* [1896] 2 Q.B. 425.
[78] Maximum penalty fine and imprisonment and forfeiture of ship.
[79] Maximum penalty fine and imprisonment.
[80] As amended by the Firearms Act 1920, s.16, and by the Statute Law (Repeals) Act 1995, Sched. 1, Pt v, Gp 1; Sched. 2, para. 1.
[81] See also Public Order Act, 1936, s.2; *infra*, para. 39.17.

or any sketch, plan, model, article, or note, or other document or information which is calculated to be or might be or
is intended to be directly or indirectly useful to an enemy;
he shall be guilty of [an offence].[82]

(2) On a prosecution under this section, it shall not be necessary
to show that the accused person was guilty of any particular act
tending to show a purpose prejudicial to the safety or interests of
the State, and, notwithstanding that no such act is proved against
him, he may be convicted if, from the circumstances of the case, or
his conduct, or his known character as proved, it appears that his
purpose was a purpose prejudicial to the safety or interests of the
State; and if any sketch, plan, model, article, note, document, or
information relating to or used in any prohibited place . . ., or
anything in such a place or any secret official code word or pass
word, is made, obtained, collected, recorded, published, or communicated by any person other than a person acting under lawful
authority, it shall be deemed to have been made, obtained, collected, recorded, published or communicated for a purpose prejudicial to the safety or interests of the State unless the contrary is
proved."

37.36 COMMUNICATION WITH FOREIGN AGENTS. Section 2 of the Official
Secrets Act 1920 provides that the fact that a person charged under
section 1 of the 1911 Act has been in communication with a foreign
agent or has attempted such communication, within or outside the
United Kingdom, shall be evidence that he has obtained or attempted to
obtain information calculated to be useful to an enemy, for a purpose
prejudicial to the safety or interests of the state.[83]

37.37 *Purpose prejudicial to the safety or interests of the state*: *Chandler v.
D.P.P.*[84] In *Chandler v. D.P.P.* a group of nuclear disarmers planned a
demonstration at an air base, a prohibited place, which was to consist in
entering the base and immobilising it for a few hours: the base was one
in use by the American Air Force for aircraft which were on continuous
"combat alert", and the proposed demonstration would have prevented
the use of the base had an emergency arisen during it. The accused were
tried for conspiring to enter the base for a purpose prejudicial to the
safety and interests of the state. They sought unsuccessfully to lead
evidence that their purpose was the prevention of nuclear war by
effecting nuclear disarmament and that such a purpose was beneficial to
the people of this country since it would avert the dangers to which they
would be subjected by the use of nuclear weapons. The House of Lords
held that whatever the motive or ultimate purpose of the accused, one of
their purposes was the obstruction of the base. They held further that
"the interests of the state" were to be determined by reference to the
actual policy of the Government of the time being, and that it was not
proper to ask a jury to determine whether that policy was beneficial to

---

[82] Maximum penalty 14 years' imprisonment: Official Secrets Act 1920, s.8; offences
under the Official Secrets Act can be tried only in the High Court: 1911 Act, s.10(3).

[83] The section goes on to set out certain circumstances which constitute such communication and to define "foreign agent" as including a person employed by a foreign power or
acting in the interests of a foreign power for a purpose prejudicial to the safety or interests
of the state.

[84] [1964] A.C. 763. For an attack on the decision see D. Thomson, "The Committee of
100 and the Official Secrets Act 1911" [1963] *Public Law* 201.

the people of the country. It was held further that any interference with the disposition of the armed forces of the state was prejudicial to the interests of the state, and that the disposition of these forces was within the royal prerogative, and could not be inquired into by the court.[85] Since evidence had been given that the demonstration would interfere with the forces on the base it was necessarily prejudicial to the interests of the state.[86]

SPYING. Although the sidenote to section 1 of the 1911 Act refers only **37.38** to spying, the section extends to any prejudicial conduct, including conduct of the kind discussed in *Chandler v. D.P.P.*[87]

FAILURE TO INFORM. Section 6 of the Official Secrets Act 1920, as **37.39** substituted by the Official Secrets Act 1939, provides:

"(1) Where a chief officer of police is satisfied that there is reasonable ground for suspecting that an offence under section one of the [Official Secrets Act 1911] has been committed and for believing that any person is able to furnish information as to the offence or suspected offence, he may apply to a Secretary of State for permission to exercise the powers conferred by this subsection and, if such permission is granted, he may authorise a superintendent of police or any police officer not below the rank of inspector, to require the person believed to be able to furnish information to give any information in his power relating to the offence or suspected offence, and, if so required and on tender of his reasonable expenses, to attend at such reasonable time and place as may be specified . . .; and if a person [so] required . . . fails to comply with any such requirement or knowingly gives false information, he shall be guilty of [an offence].[88]

(2) Where a chief officer of police has reasonable grounds to believe that the case is one of great emergency and that in the interests of the State immediate action is necessary, he may exercise the powers conferred by the last foregoing subsection without applying for or being granted the permission of a Secretary of State, but if he does so shall forthwith report the circumstances to the Secretary of State.

(3) Reference in this section to a chief officer of police shall be construed as including references to any other officer of police expressly authorised by a chief officer of police to act on his behalf

---

[85] Lord Devlin, however, at 803–804, took the view that the question of prejudice was one of fact and could not be wholly removed from a jury, since the courts could intervene to correct abuses or excesses in the exercise of the prerogative, but he agreed that there was no question but that the accused had acted to the prejudice of the interests of the state.

[86] There was some discussion in the case of the meaning of "purpose", and the question was raised of the person who invaded an airfield in order to stop the flight of an aeroplane carrying a time bomb; the view of the majority was that in that case the purpose was to prevent the bomb exploding, and the obstruction of the aircraft only incidental or at most the means of effecting the purpose, while in *Chandler* obstruction was the direct purpose of the demonstration, and nuclear disarmament its motive or indirect purpose: see Viscount Radcliffe at 794–795 and, to a different effect, Lord Devlin at 804–805. Lord Reid thought that "purpose" involved both intention and desire: at 790.

[87] [1964] A.C. 763; *supra*, para. 37.37.

[88] Maximum penalty on indictment, two years' imprisonment, on summary conviction three months' and a fine of the prescribed sum: 1920 Act, s.8.

for the purposes of this section when by reason of illness, absence or other cause he is unable to do so."

37.40 *Prohibited place.* A "prohibited place" is defined by section 3 of the Official Secrets Act 1911 (as amended by the Official Secrets Act 1920) as:

> "(a) any work of defence, arsenal, naval or air force establishment or station, factory, dockyard, mine, minefield, camp, ship, or aircraft belonging to or occupied by or on behalf of Her Majesty, or any telegraph, telephone, wireless or signal station, or office so belonging or occupied, and any place belonging to or occupied by or on behalf of Her Majesty and used for the purpose of building, repairing, making, or storing any munitions of war, or any sketches, plans, models or documents relating thereto, or for the purpose of getting any metals, oil, or minerals of use in time of war:
>
> (b) any place not belonging to Her Majesty where any munitions of war, or any sketches, models, plans or documents relating thereto, are being made, repaired, gotten or stored under contract with, or with any person on behalf of, Her Majesty, or otherwise on behalf of Her Majesty; and
>
> (c) any place belonging to or used for the purposes of Her Majesty which is for the time being declared by order of a Secretary of State to be a prohibited place for the purposes of this section on the ground that information with respect thereto, or damage thereto, would be useful to an enemy; and
>
> (d) any railway, road, way, or channel, or other means of communication by land or water (including any works or structures being part thereof or connected therewith), or any place used for gas, water, or electricity works or other works for purposes of a public character, or any place where any munitions of war, or any sketches, models, plans or documents relating thereto, are being made, repaired, or stored otherwise than on behalf of Her Majesty, which is for the time being declared by order of a Secretary of State to be a prohibited place for the purposes of this section, on the ground that information with respect thereto, or the destruction or obstruction thereof, or interference therewith, would be useful to an enemy."

37.41 ATOMIC ENERGY. Section 6(3) of the Atomic Energy Authority Act 1954[89] provides that places used or belonging to the Authority are to be deemed to be places used or belonging to Her Majesty for the purposes of section 3(c) of the Official Secrets Act 1911. Section 6(3) also provides that no one shall be entitled to exercise any right of entry to such places without the consent of the Authority, except police and revenue officers on duty, inspectors of the International Atomic Energy

---

[89] As amended by the Nuclear Safeguards and Electricity (Finance) Act 1978, s.2(3), as also by the Nuclear Safeguards Act 2000, s.11(1).

Agency, and specially authorised officers of other government departments.[90]

PHOTOGRAPHS. The word "sketch" includes photographs or any other **37.42** form of representing any place or thing.[91]

"ENEMY". The word "enemy" is not restricted to states with whom the **37.43** Queen is at war, or to time of war, but includes any state which is potentially an enemy in that the Queen might at some future date be at war with it.[92]

(2) *Frauds, etc.* Section 1 (1) of the Official Secrets Act 1920 provides: **37.44**

"If any person for the purpose of gaining admission, or of assisting any other person to gain admission, to a prohibited place, within the meaning of the Official Secrets Act 1911 . . ., or for any other purpose prejudicial to the safety or interests of the State within the meaning of the said Act—

(a) uses or wears, without lawful authority, any naval, military, air-force, police, or other official uniform, or any uniform so nearly resembling the same as to be calculated to deceive, or falsely represents himself to be a person who is or has been entitled to use or wear any such uniform: or

(b) orally, or in writing in any declaration or application, or in any document signed by him or on his behalf, knowingly makes or connives at the making of any false statement or any omission: or

(c) forges, alters, or tampers with any passport or any naval, military, air-force, police, or official pass, permit, certificate, licence, or other document of a similar character (hereinafter in this section referred to as an official document), or uses or has in his possession any such forged, altered, or irregular official document; or

(d) personates, or falsely represents himself to be a person holding, or in the employment of a person holding, office under Her Majesty, or to be or not to be a person to whom an official document or secret official code word or pass word has been duly issued or communicated, or with intent to obtain an official document, secret official code word or pass word, whether for himself or any other person, knowingly makes any false statement; or

(e) uses, or has in his possession or under his control, without the authority of the Government Department or the authority

---

[90] The list includes members of staff of the Scottish Administration specially authorised in that behalf by the Scottish Ministers: see the Scotland Act 1998 (Consequential Modifications) (No. 2) Order 1999 (S.I. 1999 No. 1820), art. 4, Sched. 2, para. 28. See also the Nuclear Installations Act 1965, Sched. 1, para. 3, as inserted by the Atomic Energy Authority Act 1971, s.17(6) and amended by the Nuclear Safeguards and Electricity (Finance) Act 1978, s.2(3), the S.I. 1999 No. 1820 (referred to above), art. 4, Sched. 2, para. 38, and the Nuclear Safeguards Act 2000, s.11(2). Similar provisions are made for the Civil Aviation Authority: Civil Aviation Act 1982, s.18(2),(3) as amended by the S.I. 1999 No. 1820 referred to above, art. 4, Sched. 2, para. 69.

[91] Official Secrets Act 1911, s.12.

[92] *R. v. Parrott* (1913) 8 Cr.App.R. 186, Phillimore J., 192.

concerned, any die, seal, or stamp of or belonging to, or used, made or provided by any Government Department, or by any diplomatic, naval, military, or air-force authority appointed by or acting under the authority of Her Majesty, or any die, seal or stamp so nearly resembling any such die, seal or stamp as to be calculated to deceive, or counterfeits any such die, seal or stamp, or uses, or has in his possession, or under his control, any such counterfeited die, seal or stamp:

he shall be guilty of [an offence]."[93]

37.45   (3) *Obstruction*. Section 3 of the Official Secrets Act 1920 provides:

"No person in the vicinity of any prohibited place[94] shall obstruct, knowingly mislead or otherwise interfere with or impede, the chief officer or a superintendent or other officer of police, or any member of Her Majesty's forces engaged on guard, sentry, patrol, or other similar duty in relation to the prohibited place, and, if any person acts in contravention of, or fails to comply with, this provision, he shall be guilty of [an offence]."[95]

37.46   (4) *Harbouring*. Section 7 of the Official Secrets Act 1911 (as amended by the Official Secrets Act 1920) provides:

"If any person knowingly harbours any person whom he knows, or has reasonable grounds for supposing, to be a person who is about to commit or who has committed an offence under this Act, or knowingly permits to meet or assemble in any premises in his occupation or under his control any such persons, or if any person having harboured any such person, or permitted to meet or assemble in any premises in his occupation or under his control any such persons, wilfully omits or refuses to disclose to a superintendent of police any information which it is in his power to give in relation to any such person he shall be guilty of [an offence]."[96]

37.47   (5) *The Official Secrets Act 1989: Disclosing or retaining confidential information*. Sections 1 to 4 of the Official Secrets Act 1989 create a number of offences consisting in the disclosure (or in some cases the damaging disclosure) without lawful authority by persons who are or have been Crown servants or government contractors, of information, documents or other articles which have come into their possession by virtue of their positions as such. In the case of sections 1 to 3 it is a defence for the accused to prove that he did not know and had no reasonable cause to believe that the information was covered by the section or, where relevant, that its disclosure would be damaging.[97]

---

[93] Maximum penalty on indictment two years' imprisonment, on summary conviction three months' and a fine of the prescribed sum: 1920 Act, s.8.

[94] This includes persons inside the place itself: *Adler v. George* [1964] 2 Q.B. 7.

[95] Maximum penalty as for s.1(1): see n.93, *supra*.

[96] Maximum penalty as for s.1(1) of the Official Secrets Act 1920: see n.93, *supra*.

[97] Maximum penalty for any offence under ss. 1–4 is, on indictment, two years' and a fine, or, on summary conviction, six months' and a fine of the statutory maximum: s.10(1).

Disclosure of information relating to security and intelligence. Section 1(1) **37.48** of the 1989 Act relates to disclosure by a present or former member of the security and intelligence services, or a person whose work is connected with those services and who has received written notification that he is subject to section 1(1), of information, any document or other article "relating to security or intelligence[98] which is or has been in his possession by virtue of his position as a member of those services or in the course of his work while the notification is or was in force."

Section 1(3) of the Act relates to damaging disclosure by a present or former Crown servant or government contractor of information, a document or other article "relating to security or intelligence which is or has been in his possession by virtue of his position as such but otherwise than as mentioned in [s.1(1)]." A disclosure is damaging[99] if it damages, or is such that its unauthorised disclosure is likely to damage, the security and intelligence services, or if it "falls within a class or description of information, documents or articles the unauthorised disclosure of which would be likely to have that effect."

Disclosure of information relating to matters of defence. Section 2(1) of the **37.49** 1989 Act provides:

> "A person who is or has been a Crown servant or government contractor is guilty of an offence if without lawful authority he makes a damaging disclosure of any information, document or other article relating to defence[1] which is or has been in his possession by virtue of his position as such."

Disclosure is damaging if it: (a) damages the capability of the armed forces, or leads to loss of life or injury to their members or serious damage to their equipment or installations, or (b) endangers the interests of the United Kingdom abroad, or seriously obstructs the promotion or protection of these interests by the United Kingdom or endangers the safety of British citizens abroad, or (c) is likely to have any of these effects.[2]

Disclosure of information relating to international relations. Section 3(1) of **37.50** the 1989 Act provides:

> "A person who is or has been a Crown servant or government contractor is guilty of an offence if without lawful authority he makes a damaging disclosure of—
> (a) any information, document or other article relating to inter-national relations[3]; or
> (b) any confidential[4] information, document or other article which was obtained from a State other than the United Kingdom or an international organisation,
> being information or a document or article which is or has been in his possession by virtue of his position as a Crown servant or government contractor."

---

[98] See s.1(9).
[99] See s.1(4).
[1] See s.2(4).
[2] See s.2(2).
[3] "International relations" are defined in s.3(5).
[4] See s.3(6).

A disclosure is damaging if it endangers the interests of the United Kingdom abroad, seriously obstructs the promotion or protection of these interests or endangers the safety of British citizens abroad, or is likely to have any of these effects.[5]

37.51 *Disclosure of other specified information.* Section 4 of the 1989 Act provides:

"(1) A person who is or has been a Crown servant or government contractor is guilty of an offence if without lawful authority he discloses any information, document or other article to which this section applies and which is or has been in his possession by virtue of his position as such.

(2) This section applies to any information, document or other article—

(a) the disclosure of which—

(i) results in the commission of an offence; or

(ii) facilitates an escape from legal custody[6] or the doing of any other act prejudicial to the safekeeping of persons in legal custody; or

(iii) impedes the prevention or detection of offences or the apprehension or prosecution of suspected offenders; or

(b) which is such that its unauthorised disclosure would be likely to have any of these effects.

(3) This section also applies to—

(a)[7] any information obtained by reason of the interception of any communication in obedience to a warrant issued under section 2 of the Interception of Communications Act 1985 or under the authority of an interception warrant under section 5 of the Regulation of Investigatory Powers Act 2000, any information relating to the obtaining of information by reason of any such interception and any document or other article which is or has been used or held for use in, or has been obtained by reason of, any such interception; and

(b)[8] any information obtained by reason of action authorised by a warrant issued under section 3 of the Security Service Act 1989 or under section 5 of the Intelligence Services Act 1994 or by an authorisation given under section 7 of that Act, any information relating to the obtaining of information by reason of any such action and any document or other article which is or has been used or held for use in, or has been obtained by reason of, any such action."

It is a defence for the accused to prove, in the case of disclosure under subsection (2)(a), that he did not know and had no reasonable cause to believe that the disclosure would have any of the effects listed there[9]; and it is a defence for him to prove, in respect of any other disclosure, that he did not know and had no reasonable cause to believe that the information, document or article in question was information or a document or article to which section 4 applied.[10]

---

[5] See s.3(2) and (3).
[6] See s.4(6).
[7] As amended by the Regulation of Investigatory Powers Act 2000, Sched. 4, para. 5.
[8] As amended by the Intelligence Services Act 1994, Sched. 4, para. 4.
[9] See s.4(4).
[10] See s.4(5).

Disclosure by other persons. Section 5 of the 1989 Act provides: **37.52**

"(1) Subsection (2) below applies where—
  (a) any information, document or other article protected against disclosure by the foregoing provisions of this Act has come into a person's possession as a result of having been—
    (i) disclosed (whether to him or another) by a Crown servant or government contractor without lawful authority; or
    (ii) entrusted to him by a Crown servant or government contractor on terms requiring it to be held in confidence or in circumstances in which the Crown servant or government contractor could reasonably expect that it would be so held; or
    (iii) disclosed (whether to him or another) without lawful authority by a person to whom it was entrusted as mentioned in sub-paragraph (ii) above; and
  (b) the disclosure without lawful authority of the information, document or article by the person into whose possession it has come is not an offence under any of those provisions.

(2) Subject to subsections (3) and (4) below, the person into whose possession the information, document or article has come is guilty of an offence if he discloses it without lawful authority knowing, or having reasonable cause to believe, that it is protected against disclosure by the foregoing provisions of this Act and that it has come into his possession as mentioned in subsection (1) above.

(3) In the case of information or a document or article protected against disclosure by sections 1 to 3 above, a person does not commit an offence under subsection (2) above unless—
  (a) the disclosure by him is damaging; and
  (b) he makes it knowing, or having reasonable cause to believe, that it would be damaging;
and the question whether a disclosure is damaging shall be determined for the purposes of this subsection as it would be in relation to a disclosure of that information, document or article by a Crown servant in contravention of section 1(3), 2(1) or 3(1) above.

(4) A person does not commit an offence under subsection (2) above in respect of information or a document or other article which has come into his possession as a result of having been disclosed—
  (a) as mentioned in subsection (1)(a)(i) above by a government contractor; or
  (b) as mentioned in subsection (1)(a)(iii) above,
unless that disclosure was by a British citizen or took place in the United Kingdom, in any of the Channel Islands or in the Isle of Man or a colony.

(5) For the purposes of this section information or a document or article is protected against disclosure by the foregoing provisions of this Act if—
  (a) it relates to security or intelligence, defence or international relations within the meaning of section 1, 2 or 3 above or is such as is mentioned in section 3(1)(b) above; or
  (b) it is information or a document or article to which section 4 above applies;
and information or a document or article is protected against disclosure by sections 1 to 3 above if it falls within paragraph (a) above.

(6) A person is guilty of an offence if without lawful authority he discloses any information, document or other article which he knows, or has reasonable cause to believe, to have come into his possession as a result of a contravention of section 1 of the Official Secrets Act 1911."

37.53 *Information entrusted in confidence to other States or international organisations.* Section 6 of the 1989 Act provides:

"(1) This section applies where—
   (a) any information, document or other article which —
      (i) relates to security or intelligence, defence or international relations; and
      (ii) has been communicated in confidence by or on behalf of the United Kingdom to another State or to an international organisation,
   has come into a person's possession as a result of having been disclosed (whether to him or another) without the authority of that State or organisation or, in the case of an organisation, of a member of it; and
   (b) the disclosure without lawful authority of the information, document or article by the person into whose possession it has come is not an offence under any of the foregoing provisions of this Act.
(2) Subject to subsection (3) below, the person into whose possession the information, document or article has come is guilty of an offence if he makes a damaging disclosure of it knowing, or having reasonable cause to believe, that it is such as is mentioned in subsection (1) above, that it has come into his possession as there mentioned and that its disclosure would be damaging.
(3) A person does not commit an offence under subsection (2) above if the information, document or article is disclosed by him with lawful authority or has previously been made available to the public with the authority of the State or organisation concerned or, in the case of an organisation, of a member of it.
(4) For the purposes of this section 'security or intelligence', 'defence' and 'international relations' have the same meaning as in sections 1, 2 and 3 above and the question whether a disclosure is damaging shall be determined as it would be in relation to a disclosure of the information, document or article in question by a Crown servant in contravention of sections 1(3), 2(1) and 3(1) above.
(5) For the purposes of this section information or a document or article is communicated in confidence if it is communicated on terms requiring it to be held in confidence or in circumstances in which the person communicating it could reasonably expect that it would be so held."

37.54 *Safeguarding information.* Section 8 of the 1989 Act provides:

"(1) Where a Crown servant or government contractor, by virtue of his position as such, has in his possession or under his control any document or other article which it would be an offence under any of the foregoing provisions of this Act for him to disclose without lawful authority he is guilty of an offence if—
   (a) being a Crown servant, he retains the document or article contrary to his official duty; or

(b) being a government contractor, he fails to comply with an official direction for the return or disposal of the document or article,

or if he fails to take such care to prevent the unauthorised disclosure of the document or article as a person in his position may reasonably be expected to take.

(2) It is a defence for a Crown servant charged with an offence under subsection (1)(a) above to prove that at the time of the alleged offence he believed that he was acting in accordance with his official duty and had no reasonable cause to believe otherwise.

(3) In subsections (1) and (2) above references to a Crown servant include any person, not being a Crown servant or government contractor, in whose case a notification for the purposes of section 1(1) above is in force.

(4) Where a person has in his possession or under his control any document or other article which it would be an offence under section 5 above for him to disclose without lawful authority, he is guilty of an offence if—

(a) he fails to comply with an official direction for its return or disposal; or

(b) where he obtained it from a Crown servant or government contractor on terms requiring it to be held in confidence or in circumstances in which that servant or contractor could reasonably expect that it would be so held, he fails to take such care to prevent its unauthorised disclosure as a person in his position may reasonably be expected to take.

(5) Where a person has in his possession or under his control any document or other article which it would be an offence under section 6 above for him to disclose without lawful authority, he is guilty of an offence if he fails to comply with an official direction for its return or disposal.

(6) A person is guilty of an offence if he discloses any official information, document or other article which can be used for the purpose of obtaining access to any information, document or other article protected against disclosure by the foregoing provisions of this Act and the circumstances in which it is disclosed are such that it would be reasonable to expect that it might be used for that purpose without authority.

(7) For the purposes of subsection (6) above a person discloses information or a document or article which is official if—

(a) he has or has had it in his possession by virtue of his position as a Crown servant or government contractor; or

(b) he knows or has reasonable cause to believe that a Crown servant or government contractor has or has had it in his possession by virtue of his position as such.

(8) Subsection (5) of section 5 above applies for the purposes of subsection (6) above as it applies for the purposes of that section.

(9) In this section 'official direction' means a direction duly given by a Crown servant or government contractor or by or on behalf of a prescribed[11] body or a body of a prescribed class."

---

[11] See, *e.g.*, the Official Secrets Act 1989 (Prescription) Order 1990 (S.I. 1990 No. 200), art. 4, Sched. 3.

37.55   Section 1(2) of the Official Secrets Act 1920 makes provision similar
to that of section 8 of the 1989 Act[12] with regard to official documents
which are in or have come into the possession of, or are found by, any
persons whether or not they are in any confidential relationship to the
Crown. The section provides:

> "If any person—
> (a) retains for any purpose prejudicial to the safety or interests of
>   the State any official document, whether or not completed or
>   issued for use, when he has no right to retain it, or when it is
>   contrary to his duty to retain it, or fails to comply with any
>   directions issued by any Government Department or any
>   person authorised by such department with regard to the
>   return or disposal thereof; or
> (b) allows any other person to have possession of any official
>   document issued for his use alone, or communicates any
>   secret official code word or pass word so issued, or, without
>   lawful authority or excuse, has in his possession any official
>   document or secret official code word or pass word issued for
>   the use of some person other than himself, or on obtaining
>   possession of any official document by finding or otherwise,
>   neglects or fails to restore it to the person or authority by
>   whom or for whose use it was issued, or to a police constable;
>   or
> (c) without lawful authority or excuse, manufactures or sells, or
>   has in his possession for sale any such die, seal or stamp as
>   aforesaid;
> he shall be guilty of [an offence]."[13]

37.56   Section 11 (2) of the European Communities Act 1972 provides:

> "Where a person (whether a British subject or not) owing either—
> (a) to his duties as a member of any Euratom institution or
>   committee, or as an officer or servant of Euratom; or
> (b) to his dealings in any capacity (official or unofficial) with any
>   Euratom institution or installation or with any Euratom joint
>   enterprise;
> has occasion to acquire, or obtain cognisance of, any classified
> information, he shall be guilty of a misdemeanour if, knowing or
> having reason to believe that it is classified information, he commu-
> nicates it to any unauthorised person or makes any public disclosure
> of it, whether in the United Kingdom or elsewhere and whether
> before or after the termination of those duties or dealings; and for
> this purpose "classified information" means any facts, information,
> knowledge, documents or objects that are subject to the security
> rules of a member State or of any Euratom institution.
>   This subsection shall be construed, and the Official Secrets Acts
> 1911 to 1939 shall have effect, as if this subsection were contained
> in the Official Secrets Act 1911, but so that in that Act sections 10
> and 11, except section 10 (4), shall not apply."

---

[12] See para. 37.54, *supra*.
[13] Maximum penalty, on indictment, two years', and, on summary conviction, three
months' and a fine of the prescribed sum.

(7) *Attempts, etc.* Section 7 of the Official Secrets Act 1920 provides **37.57** that attempts or incitements to commit an offence under the Official Secrets Acts, and also acts preparatory to the commission of such offences and aiding and abetting their commission, are punishable in the same way as the appropriate completed offence.[14]

Section 7 requires *mens rea*, but it is sufficient that the accused must have realised that the transmission of prejudicial information was a possible result of his action. In *R. v. Bingham*[15] where the defence was that the accused "believed and intended and thought that her control over her husband" who actually passed the information would be such that only harmless information would be passed and the recipients gulled into paying for it, the court said:

> "The act preparatory to the commission of an offence mentioned in the section is an act which is . . . an act done by the accused with the commission of an offence under the principal Act in mind; in other words, unless, when the act complained of is done, the accused has the subsequent commission of an offence under the principal Act in mind, then there can be no question of the presence of the mens rea required for the present purposes.
>
> But what is meant by 'in mind'? One must somewhat further refine the true effect of that phrase, and in the end as it seems to us the controversy in this case turns on this: is it sufficient to convict the appellant that, when she did the act complained of by approaching the Soviet Embassy, she must have realised that the transmission of prejudicial material might follow, in other words, is it suffcient that she recognised as a possibility that the transmission of prejudicial information might follow, or is it necessary to show that the transmission of prejudicial information was probably to follow? The difference is an extremely narrow one when one comes to the final analysis, but it is on narrow distinctions of that kind that many of the most important decisions in the criminal law have depended . . . one must bear in mind . . . that this is a very special kind of offence based on a section which was passed no doubt by Parliament to fill what was otherwise a gap in the law. It contemplates something which is even more remote from the substantive offence than an attempt to commit it; it contemplates doing an act when the commission or the non-commission of the substantive offence is something entirely in the future, and as the judge put it in the summing-up no one can be a prophet in that regard. It is clearly not necessary, to establish the offence, that any substantive offence should actually follow. It is clearly sufficient by the terms of this argument that, if the commission of a substantive offence is likely, a conviction can be sustained, and we see no reason why the construction of the section should be given such a narrow scope as to provide that the possibility of the passing of prejudicial information should be insufficient to support the charge."[16]

---

[14] See *R. v. Oakes* [1959] 2 Q.B. 350.
[15] [1973] 1 Q.B. 870, CA.
[16] At 875B–876A.

Under other Acts

37.58 *Naval Discipline Act 1957.* Section 93[17] of this Act makes it an offence triable by court martial and punishable by imprisonment for any person not subject to the Act to act on board a naval vessel or in a naval establishment outside the United Kingdom and colonies, "as a spy for the enemy".

37.59 *Atomic Energy Act 1946.* Section 11 of this Act provides:

"(1) Subject to the provisions of this section, any person who without the consent of the Minister communicates to any other person except an authorised person any document, drawing, photograph, plan, model, or other information whatsoever which to his knowledge describes, represents or illustrates—

(a) any existing or proposed plant used or proposed to be used for the purpose of producing or using atomic energy:

(b) the purpose or method of operation of any such existing or proposed plant; or

(c) any process operated or proposed to be operated in any such existing or proposed plant;

shall be guilty of an offence under this Act[18]:

Provided that it shall not be such an offence to communicate information with respect to any plant of a type in use for purposes other than the production or use of atomic energy, unless the information discloses that plant of that type is used or proposed to be used for the production or use of atomic energy . . .

(4) Where any information has been made available to the general public otherwise than in contravention of this section, any subsequent communication of that information shall not constitute an offence under this Act."[19]

37.60 *Radioactive Substances Act 1993.* Section 34 (1) of this Act provides:

"If any person discloses any information relating to any [process applied for the purposes of, or in connection with, the production or use of radioactive material] or trade secret used in carrying on any particular undertaking which has been given to or obtained by him under this Act or in connection with the execution of this Act he shall be guilty of an offence unless the disclosure is made—

(a) with the consent of the person carrying on that undertaking, or

(b) in accordance with any general or special directions given by the Secretary of State, or

(bb)[20] under or by virtue of section 113 of the Environment Act 1995, or

---

[17] As amended by the Armed Forces Act 1976, s.15(1), and the Armed Forces Act 1981, Sched. 5, Pt II.

[18] Maximum penalty on summary conviction a fine of the prescribed sum and three months' imprisonment, on indictment a fine and five years' imprisonment: s.14. The section does not apply to anything done by or to the Atomic Energy Authority: Atomic Energy Authority Act 1954, Sched. 3.

[19] See also Atomic Energy Authority Act 1954, *supra*. *Cf.* the Nuclear Safeguards Act 2000, s.2.

[20] Added by the Environment Act 1995, Sched. 22, para. 220. Section 113 of the 1995 Act has been amended by the Pollution Prevention and Control Act 1999, Sched. 12, para. 18, as also by the S.I. 2000 No. 1973, Sched. 10, para. 17.

(c) in connection with the execution of this Act, or

(d) for the purposes of any legal proceedings arising out of this Act or of any report of any such proceedings."[21]

Registered Designs Act 1949. The Registrar of Designs is empowered by **37.61** section 5(1) of the Act to give directions prohibiting or restricting the publication of information regarding any design which appears to him to be one of a class notified to him by the Secretary of State as relevant for defence purposes, and anyone who fails to comply with such a direction is guilty of an offence.[22]

Legal Aid (Scotland) Act 1986. Section 34 of this Act provides: **37.62**

"(1) Subject to subsection (2) below, no information furnished for the purposes of this Act to the [Scottish Legal Aid] Board or to any person on its behalf shall be disclosed—

(a) in the case of such information furnished by, or by any person acting for, a person seeking or receiving legal aid or advice and assistance, without the consent of the person seeking or receiving legal aid or advice and assistance; or

(b) in the case of such information furnished otherwise than as mentioned in paragraph (a) above, without the consent of the person who furnished it,

and any person who, in contravention of this subsection, discloses any information obtained by him when employed by, or acting on behalf of, the Board shall be guilty of an offence and liable, on summary conviction, to a fine not exceeding level 4 on the standard scale.

(2) Subsection (1) above shall not apply to the disclosure of information—

(a) for the purpose of the proper performance or facilitating the proper performance by the Secretary of State, the Board, any court or tribunal or by any other person or body of duties or functions under this Act;

(b) for the purpose of investigating, prosecuting or determining any complaint of professional misconduct—

(i) against a solicitor, by the Law Society or the Scottish Solicitors' Discipline Tribunal;

(ii) against an advocate, by the Faculty of Advocates;

(c) for the purpose of investigating or prosecuting any offence or for the report of any proceedings in relation to such an offence.

(3) For the purposes of this section, information furnished to any person in his capacity as counsel or a solicitor by or on behalf of a person seeking or receiving legal aid or advice and assistance is not information furnished to the Board or to a person acting on its behalf."

The section is restricted to information given to the Scottish Legal Aid Board, and an offence under it can be committed only by someone who

---

[21] Maximum penalty on summary conviction a fine of the prescribed sum and three months', on indictment, a fine and two years': s.34(2).

[22] Section 33. Maximum penalty on summary conviction six months' and a fine of the statutory maximum, and, on indictment, two years' and a fine: s.33(1).

has received the information while employed by the Board or acting on its behalf. It would not, for example, be an offence under the section for someone not so employed or acting to disclose information which had come into his hands.

37.63 *Criminal Procedure (Scotland) Act 1995.* Section 194J. Under section 194J[23] of this Act, it is an offence for a person who is or has been a member or employee of the Scottish Criminal Cases Review Commission[24] to disclose any information obtained by the Commission in the exercise of their functions except as permitted in the circumstances stated in section 194K.[25]

37.64 *Statutes in connection with trade.* A number of statutes dealing with trade regulations and statistics contain provisions penalising the unauthorised disclosure of information obtained under them.[26]

ASSISTING PRISONERS OF WAR TO ESCAPE

37.65 To assist prisoners of war to escape is a crime at common law[27] and may constitute treason as an adherence to the Queen's enemies.[28]

---

[23] Inserted by s.25 of the Crime and Punishment (Scotland) Act 1997.

[24] See s.194A of the 1995 Act, inserted as narrated in n.23, *supra*.

[25] Maximum penalty, on summary conviction, a fine of level 5 on the standard scale.

[26] See *e.g.* Supply Powers Act 1975, ss. 5 and 6(1), as amended by the Visiting Forces and International Headquarters (Application of Law) Order 1999 (S.I. 1999 No. 1736), art. 4; Statistics of Trade Act 1947, s.9 (excluded for the purposes of s.27 of the Health and Safety at Work etc., Act 1974; and subject to the exceptions described in s.9A, as inserted by the Environment Act 1995, Sched. 22, para. 2), as amended by the Coal Industry Act 1994, Sched. 9, para. 3, the Gas Act 1995, Sched. 4, para. 4; Industrial Organisation and Development Act 1947, s.5; Agricultural Statistics Act 1979, ss. 3 (as amended by the Feeding Standards Act 1999, Sched. 5, para. 5, and by the Scotland Act 1998 (Consequential Modifications) (No. 2) Order 1999 (S.I. 1999 No. 1820), Sched. 2, para. 61) and 4; Sea Fish Industry Act 1970, s.14 (as amended by the Scotland Act 1998 (Consequential Modifications) (No. 2) Order 1999 (S.I. 1999 No. 1820), Sched. 2, para. 49); Control of Pollution Act 1974, s.94.

[27] Hume, i, 527, n.3; Macdonald, p.182; *Wm Fitzsymons* (1799) Hume, i, 527; *John Armour* (1799) Hume, i, 528; *Jas and Jessie Hyslop* (1813) *ibid*.

[28] *cf.* Hume, i, 527.

CHAPTER 38

OFFENCES OF DISHONESTY AGAINST THE STATE

I — REVENUE OFFENCES

Customs and Excise Management Act 1979

The Customs and Excise Management Act 1979[1] contains a large **38.01** number of sections dealing with various offences connected with smuggling and with the evasion of customs duties and of various prohibitions and licensing provisions relating to the import and export of goods, and to the manufacture and sale of, and other dealings in, liquor and tobacco. The 1979 Act is applied to European Community customs duties by section 1(7); and section 6(5)(a) of the European Communities Act 1972 (as amended by Schedule 4, Table, Part I of the 1979 Act) applies the 1979 Act to Community agricultural levies. The following are some of the more important provisions of the 1979 Act.

Evasion of duty. The most general section of the 1979 Act is section 170 **38.02** which[2] deals with the fraudulent evasion of duty, and provides:

"(1) Without prejudice to any other provision of the Customs and Excise Acts 1979,[3] if any person—
  (a) knowingly acquires possession of any of the following goods, that is to say—
    (i) goods which have been unlawfully removed from a warehouse or Queen's warehouse[4];
    (ii) goods which are chargeable with a duty which has not been paid;
    (iii) goods with respect to the importation or exportation of which any prohibition or restriction is for the time being in force under or by virtue of any enactment[5]; or

---

[1] Hereinafter referred to as "the 1979 Act".
[2] As amended by s.23 of the Forgery and Counterfeiting Act 1981 and s.12(1)(a) of the Finance Act 1988.
[3] The phrase "Customs and Excise Acts 1979" refers to the 1979 Act itself, the Customs and Excise Duties (General Reliefs) Act 1979, the Alcoholic Liquor Duties Act 1979, the Hydrocarbon Oil Duties Act 1979, the Matches and Mechanical Lighters Duties Act 1979, and the Tobacco Products Duty Act 1979: the 1979 Act, s.1(1).
[4] See para. 38.18, *infra,* for these terms.
[5] "Any enactment" includes relevant European Union legislation having direct effect: see *R. v. Sissen* [2001] 1 W.L.R. 902, CA.

(b) is in any way knowingly concerned in carrying, removing, depositing, harbouring, keeping or concealing or in any manner dealing[6] with any such goods

and does so with intent to defraud Her Majesty of any duty payable on the goods or to evade[7] any such prohibition or restriction with respect to the goods he shall be guilty of an offence under this section and may be arrested.[8]

(2) Without prejudice to any other provision of the Customs and Excise Acts 1979,[9] if any person is, in relation to any goods, in any way knowingly concerned in any fraudulent evasion or attempt at evasion—

(a) of any duty chargeable on the goods;

(b) of any prohibition or restriction for the time being in force with respect to the goods under or by virtue of any enactment; or

(c) of any provision of the Customs and Excise Acts 1979[10] applicable to the goods,

he shall be guilty of an offence under this section and may be arrested.[11]

(3) Subject to subsection (4), (4A) or (4B) below, a person guilty of an offence under this section shall be liable—

(a) on summary conviction, to a penalty of the prescribed sum or of three times the value of the goods, whichever is the greater, or to imprisonment for a term not exceeding 6 months, or to both; or

(b) on conviction on indictment, to a penalty of any amount, or to imprisonment for a term not exceeding 7 years, or to both.

(4) In the case of an offence under this section in connection with a prohibition or restriction on importation or exportation having effect by virtue of section 3 of the Misuse of Drugs Act 1971, subsection (3) above shall have effect subject to the modifications specified in Schedule 1 to this Act.[12]

---

[6] Merely to deal in prohibited goods, such as drugs, which must at some time have been illegally imported, does not in itself show an intent to evade the prohibition: see *R. v. Watts and Stack* (1979) 70 Cr.App.R. 187, CA; nor is an insurance company which pays out on a policy for the theft of goods where the goods are known to be uncustomed guilty of a breach of s.170, since the company would have no intent thereby to defraud the Crown; but such a payment would be *contra bonos mores* and there is, therefore, no obligation on the company to make it: *Geismar v. Sun Alliance & London Insurance Ltd.* [1978] 1 Q.B. 187, CA.

[7] "Evade" means only "avoid or get round" (when not used, as here, in conjunction with "avoid"), and a person who believes he is acting legally can act with intent to evade a prohibition: see *R. v. Hurford-Jones* (1977) 65 Cr.App.R. 263, a case under what is now s.68(2) of the 1979 Act — being knowingly concerned in the export of goods with intent to evade a prohibition.

[8] The original wording of s.1 stated that such a person was liable to be "detained"; but s.114(1), applied to Scotland by s.120(5) of the Police and Criminal Evidence Act 1984, substitutes "arrested" for "detained" throughout the customs and excise Acts (which, under s.1(1) of the 1979 Act, mean the 1979 Act "and any other enactment for the time being in force relating to customs and excise").

[9] See n.3, *supra*.

[10] See n.3, *supra*.

[11] See n.7, *supra*.

[12] The effect of the modifications, as amended by the Controlled Drugs (Penalties) Act 1985, is that the maximum penalty on conviction on indictment is life imprisonment where a Class A drug is involved, and 14 years' in the case of a Class B drug. The offence of evading the prohibition imposed by s.3 of the Misuse of Drugs Act 1971 is created by the combined effects of s.3 of that Act and s.170 of the 1979 Act: see *R. v. Whitehead* [1982] Q.B. 1272, CA.

(4A) In the case of an offence under this section in connection with the prohibitions contained in sections 20 and 21 of the Forgery and Counterfeiting Act 1981,[13] subsection (3)(b) above shall have effect as if for the words '2 years' there were substituted the words '10 years'.

(4B)[14] In the case of an offence under subsection (1) or (2) above in connection with the prohibition contained in regulation 2 of the Import of Seal Skins Regulations 1996,[15] subsection (3) above shall have effect as if—

(a) for paragraph (a) there were substituted the following —
   '(a) on summary conviction, to a fine not exceeding the statutory maximum or to imprisonment for a term not exceeding three months, or to both'; and

(b) in paragraph (b) for the words '7 years' there were substituted the words '2 years'.

(5) In any case where a person would, apart from this subsection, be guilty of—

(a) an offence under this section in connection with a prohibition or restriction; and

(b) a corresponding offence under the enactment or other instrument imposing the prohibition or restriction, being an offence for which a fine or other penalty is expressly provided by that enactment or other instrument,

he shall not be guilty of the offence mentioned in paragraph (a) of this subsection."

Goods which are allowed to enter the country free of duty for any special purpose, such as use by privileged persons like U.S. servicemen, become liable to duty when they pass into the hands of an unprivileged person, and the latter may be convicted of keeping them with intent to defraud the Crown of the duty due thereon.[16]

Importing includes unloading, and transhipment within the customs area at an international airport.[17] A person may be knowingly concerned in evasion if he is a party to the importation of goods into the United Kingdom as a staging post, even if he himself does nothing in the United Kingdom.[18] He may also be guilty if his part in the enterprise is not carried out until after the goods have arrived in the United Kingdom or even been seized by customs officers unknown to him: the offence is a continuing one, ending only when the goods cease to be prohibited or, perhaps, are re-exported.[19]

---

[13] Section 20 of the 1981 Act prohibits (*inter alia*) the importation (and s.21(1) the exportation) of a counterfeit of a currency note or of a protected coin without the consent of the Treasury.

[14] This subsection added by S.I. 1996 No. 2686, reg. 4(2).

[15] S.I. 1996 No. 2686.

[16] *McQueen v. McCann*, 1945 J.C. 151; *Schneider v. Dawson* [1960] 2 Q.B. 106; *R. v. Berry* [1969] 2 Q.B. 73, CA.

[17] *R. v. Smith (Donald)* [1973] Q.B. 924, CA.

[18] *ibid. cf. R. v. Doot* [1973] A.C. 807.

[19] *R. v. Green (Harry)* [1976] Q.B. 985. See also *R. v. Sisson* [2001] 1 W.L.R. 902, CA, where the defendant was discovered to have parrots of an endangered species in his possesion in England, the importation of such parrots being prohibited without a permit under European Community regulations (which are "enactments" for the purposes of s.170(2)(b) of the 1979 Act); the conviction of the defendant was considered proper notwithstanding that the birds' entry point to the European Union was a Member State other than the United Kingdom: see especially the opinion of Ouseley J., at 915–916, paras 40–43.

In order to be guilty of an offence under section 170(2) the accused must know that what he is involved in is the evasion of a prohibition on importation, but he need not know what kind of prohibited goods are being imported,[20] provided he knows or believes them to be what they are — *i.e.*, prohibited goods: thus in *R. v. Hennessey*[21] the defendant believed that the concealed compartment in his vehicle contained "blue movies" rather than the cannabis actually found there, but was convicted since both such "movies" and controlled drugs are prohibited goods[22]; but in *R. v. Taaffe*[23] the defendant's belief that the goods in question were currency rather than (as it turned out) cannabis was sufficient to acquit him, currency not being a prohibited import.[24] In England it has been held that this offence is one involving a specific intent — *i.e.*, the intent dishonestly to evade the prohibition or restriction — and that neither recklessness nor negligence can supply the lack of such intent.[25] Also, it has been stated by the House of Lords that the offence under section 170(2) is widely drawn, and that there is no justification for restricting it by construing it as if it read: "if any person is, in relation to any goods, in any way *fraudulently and* knowingly concerned in any fraudulent evasion", even though, under the subsection as it stands, a drugs enforcement officer who carried a large quantity of heroin from Pakistan to the United Kingdom as part of a scheme to trap drug traffickers must himself have been guilty of such an offence.[26]

A person may be convicted under section 170 in relation to dutiable or prohibited goods even if the circumstances of the offence occurred at a time and place far distant from those of the importation.[27]

Although the section requires knowledge and intent to defraud,[28] in any proceedings brought under it or under any other section of the 1979 Act the burden of proof lies on the accused in any question which arises as to whether or not any duty has been paid, or whether any goods have been lawfully imported or exported or are subject to any prohibition or restriction.[29]

---

[20] *R. v. Hussain* [1969] 2 Q.B. 576.

[21] (1978) 68 Cr.App.R. 419.

[22] See Customs Consolidation Act 1876, s.42; Misuse of Drugs Act 1971, s.3.

[23] [1984] A.C. 539.

[24] *cf. R. v. Shivpuri* [1987] A.C. 1, HL, — attempt in relation to s.170(1)(b).

[25] *R. v. Panayi* [1989] 1 W.L.R. 187, CA, where the defendants claimed that they had imported cannabis into the United Kingdom not by design but as a result of wind, tide and navigational error, their intention having been to sail their yacht from Spain to Holland at the material time.

[26] *R. v. Latif* [1996] 1 W.L.R. 104, HL, opinion of Lord Steyn (with whom all other law lords agreed) at 112B-D.

[27] *R. v. Ardalen* [1972] 1 W.L.R. 463; *R. v. Caippara* (1988) 87 Cr.App.R. 316, CA. It seems from *Caippara*, as also from the case of *R. v. Mitchell* [1992] Crim.L.R. 594, CA, that the unsolicited receipt of controlled drugs followed by their retention in the knowledge of their nature is sufficient to convict the recipient of an offence contrary to s.170(2).

[28] For example, *McQueen v. McCann*, 1945 J.C. 151; but see *R. v. Cohen* [1951] 1 K.B. 505. "Fraudulently" in s.170(2) requires proof of dishonest conduct deliberately intended to evade the prohibition, restriction or duty, but does not require proof of an act of deceit in presence of a customs officer; a failure to stop a car when signalled to do so by a police officer is therefore sufficient if done with the necessary intent: *Att-Gen.'s Reference (No. 1 of 1981)* [1982] Q.B. 848, CA. If a deliberate act with *mens rea* is performed which will have, and has, the effect of importing prohibited goods into the United Kingdom from a foreign country, then the offence is committed notwithstanding any change of mind by the defendant while the goods are in transit: see *R. v. Jakeman (Susan Lesley)* (1982) 76 Cr.App.R. 223, CA, which involved the importation of cannabis.

[29] Section 154(2). But it is not an offence to pay the duty demanded even when it has been calculated on what the accused knew to be an undervaluation, provided he did not induce the customs officer's mistake: *R. v. Tan* [1977] A.C. 650, HL.

Smuggling. The 1979 Act includes the following provisions against **38.03**
smuggling.

BREAKING SEALS. Section 83[30]:

"(1) Where, in pursuance of any power conferred by the customs
and excise Acts[31] or of any requirement imposed by or under those
Acts, a seal, lock or mark is used to secure or identify any goods for
any of the purposes of those Acts and—

(a) at any time while the goods are in the United Kingdom or
within the limits of any port or on passage between ports in
the United Kingdom or between a port in the United
Kingdom and a port in the Isle of Man, the seal, lock or mark
is wilfully and prematurely removed or tampered with by any
person; or

(b) at any time before the seal, lock or mark is lawfully removed,
any of the goods are wilfully removed by any person,

that person and the person then in charge of the goods shall each be
liable on summary conviction to a penalty of [level 5 on the
standard scale].

(2) For the purposes of subsection (1) above, goods in a ship or
aircraft shall be deemed to be in the charge of the master of the
ship or commander of the aircraft.

(3) Where, in pursuance of any Community requirement or
practice which relates to the movement of goods between countries
or of any international agreement to which the United Kingdom is a
party and which so relates,—

(a) a seal, lock or mark is used (whether in the United Kingdom
or elsewhere) to secure or identify any goods for customs or
excise purposes; and

(b) at any time while the goods are in the United Kingdom, the
seal, lock or mark is wilfully and prematurely removed or
tampered with by any person,

that person and the person then in charge of the goods shall each be
liable on summary conviction to a penalty of [level 5 on the
standard scale]."

SIGNALLING. Section 84 of the 1979 Act provides: **38.04**

"(1) In this section references to a 'prohibited signal' or a 'prohibited message' are references to a signal or message connected
with the smuggling or intended smuggling of goods into or out of
the United Kingdom.

(2) Any person who by any means makes any prohibited signal or
transmits any prohibited message from any part of the United
Kingdom or from any ship or aircraft for the information of a
person in any ship or aircraft or across the boundary shall be liable
on summary conviction to a penalty of [level 3 on the standard
scale], or to imprisonment for a term not exceeding 6 months, or to
both, and may be arrested; and any equipment or apparatus used
for sending the signal or message shall be liable to forfeiture.

---

[30] As amended by the Isle of Man Act 1979, Sched. 1, para. 19.
[31] The phrase "the customs and excise Acts" means the Customs and Excise Acts 1979
(see n.3, *supra*) and any other enactment for the time being in force relating to customs
and excise: s.1(1) of the 1979 Act.

(3) Subsection (2) above applies whether or not the person for whom the signal or message is intended is in a position to receive it or is actually engaged at the time in smuggling goods.

(4) If, in any proceedings under subsection (2) above, any question arises as to whether any signal or message was a prohibited signal or message, the burden of proof shall lie upon the defendant or claimant . . .''

38.05   INTERFERENCE WITH REVENUE VESSELS. Section 85 of the 1979 Act provides:

"(1) Any person who save for just and sufficient cause interferes in any way with any ship, aircraft, vehicle, buoy, anchor, chain, rope or mark which is being used for the purposes of any functions of the Commissioners[32] under Parts III to VII of this Act shall be liable on summary conviction [to a fine of level 2 on the standard scale].

(2) Any person who fires upon any vessel, aircraft or vehicle in the service of Her Majesty while that vessel, aircraft or vehicle is engaged in the prevention of smuggling shall be liable on conviction on indictment to imprisonment for a term not exceeding 5 years."

38.06   ARMED OR DISGUISED SMUGGLERS. Section 86 of the 1979 Act provides:

"Any person concerned in the movement, carriage or concealment of goods—
    (a) contrary to or for the purpose of contravening any prohibition or restriction for the time being in force under or by virtue of any enactment with respect to the importation thereof; or
    (b) without payment having been made of or security given for any duty payable thereon,
who, while so concerned, is armed with any offensive weapon or disguised in any way, and any person so armed or disguised found in the United Kingdom in possession of any goods liable to forfeiture under any provision of the customs and excise Acts[33] relating to imported goods or prohibited or restricted goods, shall be liable on conviction on indictment to imprisonment for a term not exceeding 3 years and may be arrested."

It has been held in *R. v. Jones (Keith)*[34] that a person can be "armed" even when he is not carrying a weapon, provided that he has arms "readily available for use".

38.07   OFFERING GOODS FOR SALE AS SMUGGLED. Section 87 of the 1979 Act provides:

"If any person offers any goods for sale as having been imported without payment of duty, or as having been otherwise unlawfully imported, then, whether or not the goods were so imported or were in fact chargeable with duty, the goods shall be liable to forfeiture

---

[32] That is to say, the Commissioners of Customs and Excise: s.1(1).
[33] See n.31, *supra*.
[34] [1987] 1 W.L.R. 692, CA: the facts of the case were that the defendant had the arms in a locker in the wheelhouse of a boat of which he was the captain.

and the person so offering them for sale shall be liable on summary conviction to a penalty of three times the value of the goods or [a fine of level 3 on the standard scale] whichever is the greater and may be arrested."

Falsehood and fraud. The 1979 Act contains a number of provisions **38.08** dealing with false statements and fraud, the most important being contained in sections 167–169, which provide as follows.

UNTRUE DECLARATIONS. Section 167: **38.09**

"(1) If any person either knowingly or recklessly—
> (a) makes or signs, or causes to be made or signed, or delivers or causes to be delivered to the Commissioners or an officer,[35] any declaration, notice, certificate or other document whatsoever; or
> (b) makes any statement in answer to any question put to him by an officer which he is required by or under any enactment to answer,

being a document or statement produced or made for any purpose of any assigned matter,[36] which is untrue in any material particular, he shall be guilty of an offence under this subsection and may be arrested; and any goods in relation to which the document or statement was made shall be liable to forfeiture.

(2) Without prejudice to subsection (4) below, a person who commits an offence under subsection (1) above shall be liable—
> (a) on summary conviction, to a penalty of the prescribed sum, or to imprisonment for a term not exceeding 6 months, or to both; or
> (b) on conviction on indictment, to a penalty of any amount, or to imprisonment for a term not exceeding 2 years, or to both.

(3) If any person—
> (a) makes or signs, or causes to be made or signed, or delivers or causes to be delivered to the Commissioners or an officer, any declaration, notice, certificate or other document whatsoever; or
> (b) makes any statement in answer to any question put to him by an officer which he is required by or under any enactment to answer,

being a document or statement produced or made for any purpose of any assigned matter, which is untrue in any material particular, then, without prejudice to subsection (4) below, he shall be liable on summary conviction to a penalty of [level 4 on the standard scale].

(4) Where by reason of any such document or statement as is mentioned in subsection (1) or (3) above the full amount of any duty payable is not paid or any overpayment is made in respect of any drawback, allowance, rebate or repayment of duty, the amount of the duty unpaid or of the overpayment shall be recoverable as a debt due to the Crown or may be recovered as a civil debt."

---

[35] That is to say, a person commissioned by the Commissioners of Customs and Excise: s.1(1) of the 1979 Act.

[36] That is to say, "any matter, in relation to which the Commissioners are for the time being required in pursuance of any enactment to perform any duties": s.1(1) of the 1979 Act. See, *e.g., Napier v. H.M. Advocate*, 1988 S.L.T. 271 (Note).

(5)[37] An amount of excise duty, or the amount of an overpayment in respect of any drawback, allowance, rebate or repayment of any excise duty, shall not be recoverable as mentioned in subsection (4) above unless the Commissioners have assessed the amount of the duty or of the overpayment as being excise duty due from the person mentioned in subsections (1) and (3) above and notified him or his representative accordingly."

38.10   COUNTERFEITING. Section 168 (1):

"If any person—
  (a) counterfeits or falsifies any document which is required by or under any enactment relating to an assigned matter or which is used in the transaction of any business relating to an assigned matter[38]; or
  (b) knowingly accepts, receives or uses any such document so counterfeited or falsified; or
  (c) alters any such document after it is officially issued; or
  (d) counterfeits any seal, signature, initials or other mark of, or used by, any officer for the verification of such a document or for the security of goods or for any other purpose relating to an assigned matter,
he shall be guilty of an offence."[39]

38.11   FALSE SCALES. Section 169:

"(1) If any person required by or under the customs and excise Acts[40] to provide scales for any purpose of those Acts provides, uses or permits to be used any scales which are false or unjust he shall be guilty of an offence under this section.

(2) Where any article is or is to be weighed, counted, gauged or measured for the purposes of the taking of an account or the making of an examination by an officer, then if—
  (a) any such person as is mentioned in subsection (1) above; or
  (b) any person by whom or on whose behalf the article is weighed, counted, gauged or measured,
does anything whereby the officer is or might be prevented from, or hindered or deceived in, taking a true and just account or making a due examination, he shall be guilty of an offence under this section.

This subsection applies whether the thing is done before, during or after the weighing, counting, guaging or measuring of the article in question.

(3) Any person committing an offence under this section shall be liable on summary conviction to a penalty of [level 4 on the standard scale] and any false or unjust scales, and any article in connection with which the offence was committed, shall be liable to forfeiture.

(4) In this section 'scales' includes weights, measures and weighing or measuring machines or instruments."[41]

---

[37] Added by the Finance Act 1997, Sched. 6, para. 5.

[38] See n.36, *supra*.

[39] Maximum penalty, on indictment, two years' and a fine, and, on summary conviction, six months' and a fine of the prescribed sum: s.168(2).

[40] See n.31, *supra*.

[41] The 1979 Act also penalises fraudulent claims for drawbacks, allowances, remissions or repayments of, or any rebate from, duty: s.136, as amended by the Finance Act 1982, s.11(3) and the Finance Act 1988, s.12(3).

Import and export. The 1979 Act contains a number of provisions relating **38.12**
to import and export, and provides for the forfeiture of goods
improperly imported.[42]

IMPROPER AND FRAUDULENT IMPORTATION. Section 50[43]: **38.13**

"(1) Subsection (2) below applies to goods of the following descriptions, that is to say—
   (a) goods chargeable with a duty which has not been paid; and
   (b) goods the importation, landing or unloading of which is for
       the time being prohibited or restricted by or under any
       enactment.
(2) If any person with intent to defraud Her Majesty of any such
duty or to evade any such prohibition or restriction as is mentioned
in subsection (1) above—
   (a) unships or lands in any port or unloads from any aircraft in
       the United Kingdom . . . any goods to which this subsection
       applies, or assists or is otherwise concerned in such unship-
       ping, landing or unloading; or
   (b) removes from their place of importation or from any
       approved wharf, examination station, transit shed or customs
       and excise station any goods to which this subsection applies
       or assists or is otherwise concerned in such removal,
he shall be guilty of an offence under this subsection and may be
arrested.
   (3) If any person imports or is concerned in importing any goods
contrary to any prohibition or restriction for the time being in force
under or by virtue of any enactment with respect to those goods,
whether or not the goods are unloaded, and does so with intent to
evade the prohibition or restriction, he shall be guilty of an offence
under this subsection and may be arrested.
   (4) Subject to subsection (5), (5A) or (5B) below, a person guilty
of an offence under subsection (2) or (3) above shall be liable—
   (a) on summary conviction, to a penalty of the prescribed sum or
       three times the value of the goods, whichever is the greater,
       or to imprisonment for a term not exceeding 6 months, or to
       both; or
   (b) on conviction on indictment, to a penalty of any amount, or
       to imprisonment for a term not exceeding 7 years, or to both.
   (5) In the case of an offence under subsection (2) or (3) above in
connection with a prohibition or restriction on importation having
effect by virtue of section 8 of the Misuse of Drugs Act 1971,
subsection (4) above shall have effect subject to the modifications
specified in Schedule 1 to this Act.[44]
   (5A)[45] In the case of an offence under subsection (2) or (3) above
in connection with the prohibition contained in section 20 [prohibi-
tion of importation of counterfeit currency notes and coins without
the consent of the Treasury] of the Forgery and Counterfeiting Act

---

[42] Section 49.
[43] As amended by the Finance Act 1988, s.12(1). See also s.170, *supra*, para. 38.02; *R. v.
Smith (Donald)* [1973] Q.B. 924.
[44] Maximum penalty, life imprisonment for a Class A drug; 14 years' for a Class B drug:
Controlled Drugs (Penalties) Act 1985, s.1(2).
[45] Inserted by the Forgery and Counterfeiting Act 1981, s.23(1).

1981, subsection (4)(b) above shall have effect as if for the words '7 years' there were substituted the words '10 years'.

(5B)[46] In the case of an offence under subsection (2) or (3) above in connection with the prohibition contained in regulation 2 of the Import of Seal Skins Regulations 1996, subsection (4) above shall have effect as if—

(a) for paragraph (a) there were substituted the following—

'(a) on summary conviction, to a fine not exceeding the statutory maximum or to imprisonment for a term not exceeding three months, or to both'; and

(b) in paragraph (b) for the words '7 years' there were substituted the words '2 years'.

(6) If any person—

(a) imports or causes to be imported any goods concealed in a container holding goods of a different description; or

(b) directly or indirectly imports or causes to be imported or entered any goods found, whether before or after delivery, not to correspond with the entry made thereof,

he shall be liable on summary conviction to a penalty of three times the value of the goods or [level 3 on the standard scale], whichever is the greater.

(7) In any case where a person would, apart from this subsection, be guilty of—

(a) an offence under this section in connection with the importation of goods contrary to a prohibition or restriction; and

(b) a corresponding offence under the enactment or other instrument imposing the prohibition or restriction, being an offence for which a fine or other penalty is expressly provided by that enactment or other instrument,

he shall not be guilty of the offences mentioned in paragraph (a) of this subsection."

Importation is not limited to the first port entered, but occurs at the port where the goods are discovered and at any port in the United Kingdom entered en route thereto. The only *mens rea* required is the knowledge that one is engaged in importing prohibited goods.[47] It has been held that where goods are intercepted by customs and replaced by harmless substances before being left to go to the originally intended recipient, the latter is guilty of being concerned in their unlawful importation even if he took no part in the enterprise prior to the replacement.[48]

38.14 UNAUTHORISED UNLOADING OF EXPORT GOODS. Section 67:

"(1) If any goods which have been loaded or retained on board any ship or aircraft for exportation are not exported to and discharged at a place outside the United Kingdom but are unloaded in the United Kingdom, then, unless—

---

[46] Inserted by the Import of Seal Skins Regulations 1996 (S.I. 1996 No. 2686), reg. 4(1)(b).

[47] See *MacNeil v. H.M. Advocate*, 1986 S.C.C.R. 288, L.J.-G. Emslie at p. 310. On the meaning of "being concerned in", see *MacNeil, supra,* and para. 43.07, *infra*.

[48] *R. v. Ciappara* (1988) 87 Cr.App.R. 316, CA. *Cf. R. v. Whitehead* [1892] Q.B. 1272 (a case involving s.304 of the Customs and Excise Act 1952).

(a) the unloading was authorised by the proper officer; and
(b) except where that officer otherwise permits, any duty chargeable and unpaid on the goods is paid and any drawback or
allowance paid in respect thereof is repaid,

the master of the ship or the commander of the aircraft and any
person concerned in the unshipping, relanding, landing, unloading
or carrying of the goods from the ship or aircraft without such
authority, payment or repayment shall each be guilty of an offence
under this section.

(2) The Commissioners[49] may impose such conditions as they see
fit with respect to any goods loaded or retained as mentioned in
subsection (1) above which are permitted to be unloaded in the
United Kingdom. (3) If any person contravenes or fails to comply
with, or is concerned in any contravention of or failure to comply
with, any condition imposed under subsection (2) above he shall be
guilty of an offence under this section.

. . .

(4) Where any goods loaded or retained as mentioned in
subsection (1) above or brought to a customs and excise station for
exportation by land are—

(a) goods from a warehouse, other than goods which have been
kept, without being warehoused, in a warehouse by virtue of
section 92(4) [which, *inter alia,* refers to goods originating or
in free circulation in European Union member States] below;
(b) transit goods;
(c) other goods chargeable with a duty which has not been paid;
or
(d) drawback goods,

then if any container in which the goods are held is without the
authority of the proper officer opened, or any mark, letter or device
on any such container or on any lot of the goods is without that
authority cancelled, obliterated or altered, every person concerned
in the opening, cancellation, obliteration or alteration shall be guilty
of an offence under this section.

(5) Any goods in respect of which an offence under this section is
committed shall be liable to forfeiture and any person guilty of an
offence under this section shall be liable on summary conviction to a
penalty of three times the value of the goods or [level 3 on the
standard scale], whichever is the greater."

Offences in connection with customs officers. The 1979 Act creates the **38.15**
following offences in connection with officers of the customs and excise
department.

PERSONATION OF OFFICERS. Section 13:

"If, for the purpose of obtaining admission to any house or other
place, or of doing or procuring to be done any act which he would
not be entitled to do or procure to be done of his own authority, or
for any other unlawful purpose, any person falsely assumes the
name, designation or character of a Commissioner[50] or officer[51] or

---

[49] That is to say, the Commissioners of Customs and Excise: s.1(1).
[50] See n.49, *supra.*
[51] See n.35, *supra.*

of a person appointed by the Commissioners, he may be arrested and shall, in addition to any other punishment to which he may have rendered himself liable, be liable—

    (a) on summary conviction to a penalty of the prescribed sum, or to imprisonment for a term not exceeding 3 months, or to both; or

    (b) on conviction on indictment, to a penalty of any amount, or to imprisonment for a term not exceeding 2 years, or to both."

38.16   BRIBERY AND COLLUSION. Section 15:

"(1) If any Commissioner[52] or officer[53] or any person appointed or authorised by the Commissioners to discharge any duty relating to an assigned matter[54]—

    (a) directly or indirectly asks for or takes in connection with any of his duties any payment or other reward whatsoever, whether pecuniary or other, or any promise or security for any such payment or reward, not being a payment or reward which he is lawfully entitled to claim or receive; or

    (b) enters into or acquiesces in any agreement to do, abstain from doing, permit, conceal or connive at any act or thing whereby Her Majesty is or may be defrauded or which is otherwise unlawful, being an act or thing relating to an assigned matter,

he shall be guilty of an offence under this section.

(2) If any person—

    (a) directly or indirectly offers or gives to any Commissioner[55] or officer[56] or to any person appointed or authorised by the Commissioners as aforesaid any payment or other reward whatsoever, whether pecuniary or other, or any promise or security for any such payment or reward; or

    (b) proposes or enters into any agreement with any Commissioner, officer or person appointed or authorised as aforesaid,

in order to induce him to do, abstain from doing, permit, conceal or connive at any act or thing whereby Her Majesty is or may be defrauded or which is otherwise unlawful, being an act or thing relating to an assigned matter,[57] or otherwise to take any course contrary to his duty, he shall be guilty of an offence under this section.

(3) Any person committing an offence under this section shall be liable on summary conviction to a penalty of [level 5 on the standard scale] and may be arrested."

This section is so widely phrased that if A gave or offered a bribe to an officer in order to trap him into an illegal agreement so that he might expose him, he would be guilty of offering money to influence him to act contrary to his duty.[58]

---

[52] See n.49, *supra*.
[53] See n.35, *supra*.
[54] See n.36, *supra*.
[55] See n.49, *supra*.
[56] See n.35, *supra*.
[57] See n.36, *supra*.
[58] *cf. R. v. Smith* [1960] 2 Q.B. 423 where such a person was convicted under a statute which required the offer to be "corrupt": see *infra*. para. 44.08. Even if *Smith* is not accepted, the terms of the Customs and Excise Act themselves lead to this result: see *R. v. Latif* [1996] 1 W.L.R. 104, HL, Lord Steyn (with whom all the Law Lords agreed) at 112B-D (a case concerning s.170 of the 1979 Act).

OBSTRUCTION. Section 16: **38.17**

"(1) Any person who—

(a) obstructs, hinders, molests or assaults any person duly engaged in the performance of any duty or the exercise of any power imposed or conferred on him by or under any enactment relating to an assigned matter,[59] or any person acting in his aid; or

(b) does anything which impedes or is calculated to impede the carrying out of any search for any thing liable to forfeiture under any such enactment or the detention, seizure or removal of any such thing; or

(c) rescues, damages or destroys any thing so liable to forfeiture or does anything calculated to prevent the procuring or giving of evidence as to whether or not any thing is so liable to forfeiture; or

(d) prevents the arrest of any person by a person duly engaged or acting as aforesaid or rescues any person so arrested,

or who attempts to do any of the aforementioned things, shall be guilty of an offence under this section."[60]

Removal, etc., of warehoused goods. Customs authorities are empowered **38.18** to approve places of security for the keeping without payment of duty of certain goods chargeable to duty, and these places are referred to in the Act as "excise warehouses" and "victualling warehouses".[61] The 1979 Act prohibits the removal of such goods without payment of duty except in certain circumstances specially permitted under the Act. The corresponding penal provisions are as follows:

Section 100. "(1) Any person who, except with the authority of the proper officer or for just and sufficient cause, opens any of the doors or locks of a warehouse or Queen's warehouse[62] or makes or obtains access to any such warehouse or to any goods warehoused therein shall be liable on summary conviction to a penalty of [level 5 on the standard scale] and may be arrested.

(2) Where—

(a)[63] any goods which have been entered for warehousing or are otherwise required to be deposited in a warehouse are taken into the warehouse without the authority of, or otherwise

---

[59] See n.36, *supra*.

[60] Maximum penalty, on indictment, a penalty of any amount and two years', and, on summary conviction, a penalty of the prescribed sum and three months': s.16(2). Under s.16(3), a person committing, or any person aiding or abetting the commission of, an offence under the section may be arrested. One of the powers exercisable by an officer (and to which s.16 would then apply) is contained in s.162 of the 1979 Act — *i.e.*, the power to proceed to and from a pipe-line in which anything conveyed is chargeable with a duty of customs or excise where that duty has not been paid.

[61] Section 92, as amended by the Customs Warehouses Regulations 1991 (S.I. 1991 No. 2725), reg. 3(4), and by the Finance Act 1994, Sched. 4, para. 2(1), (2).

[62] This is a warehouse to which goods may be removed if an approved warehouse ceases to be approved or if approval of an occupier as an authorised warehousekeeper is revoked: see ss. 98 and 99 of the 1979 Act, as amended by the Warehousekeepers and Owners of Warehoused Goods Regulations 1999 (S.I. 1999 No. 1278), reg. 10; the Customs Warehousing Regulations 1991 (S.I. 1991 No. 2725), and the Finance Act 1981, Sched. 8, para. 4. (Warehousing is now very largely regulated by European law: see *The Laws of Scotland: The Stair Memorial Encyclopaedia*, (Edinburgh, 1995), Vol. 7, paras 1174 *et seq*.)

[63] As amended by the Finance (No. 2) Act 1992, Sched. 2, para. 3(a).

than in accordance with any directions given by, the proper officer; or

(b)[64] save as permitted by the Customs and Excise Acts 1979[65] or by or under warehousing regulations, any goods which have been entered for warehousing or are otherwise required to be deposited in a warehouse are removed without being duly warehoused or are otherwise not duly warehoused; or

(c) any goods which have been deposited in a warehouse or Queen's warehouse are unlawfully removed therefrom or are unlawfully loaded into any ship, aircraft or vehicle for removal or for exportation or use as stores; or

(d)[66] any goods are concealed at a time before they are warehoused when they have been entered for warehousing or are otherwise required to be deposited in a warehouse or when they are required to be in the custody or under the control of the occupier of a warehouse; or

(e) any goods which have been lawfully permitted to be removed from a warehouse or Queen's warehouse without payment of duty for any purpose are not duly delivered at the destination to which they should have been taken in accordance with that permission,

those goods shall be liable to forfeiture.

(3) If any person who took, removed, loaded or concealed any goods as mentioned in subsection (2) above did so with intent to defraud Her Majesty of any duty chargeable thereon or to evade any prohibition of restriction for the time being in force with respect thereto under or by virtue of any enactment, he shall be guilty of an offence under this section and may be arrested.

(4) A person guilty of an offence under subsection (3) above shall be liable—

(a) on summary conviction, to a penalty of the prescribed sum or of three times the value of the goods, whichever is the greater, or to imprisonment for a term not exceeding 6 months, or to both; or

(b) on conviction on indictment, to a penalty of any amount, or to imprisonment for a term not exceeding 7[67] years, or to both."

38.19 *Unlawful removal of spirits from distilleries, etc.* Section 17 of the Alcoholic Liquor Duties Act 1979 provides as follows:

"(1) If any person—

(a) conceals in or without the consent of the proper office removes from a distillery any wort, wash, low wines, feints or spirits; or

(b) knowingly buys or receives any wort [etc.] so concealed or removed; or

(c) knowingly buys or receives or has in his possession any spirits which have been removed from the place where they ought to have been charged with duty before the duty payable thereon has been charged and either paid or secured, not being spirits

---

[64] See n.63, *supra*.
[65] See n.3, *supra*.
[66] Substituted by the Finance (No. 2) Act 1992, Sched. 2, para. 3(b).
[67] As amended by the Finance Act 1988, s.12(1).

which have been condemned or are deemed to have been condemned as forfeited,

he shall be guilty of an offence under this section and may be arrested.[68]

(2) A person guilty of an offence under this section shall be liable—

(a) on summary conviction, to a penalty of the prescribed sum or three times the value of the goods, whichever is the greater, or to imprisonment for a term not exceeding 6 months, or to both; or

(b) on conviction on indictment, to a penalty of any amount, or to imprisonment for a term not exceeding 2 years, or to both."

Taxes Management Act 1970

Section 107(2) of this Act provides: **38.20**

"If any person, for the purpose of obtaining any allowance, reduction, rebate or repayment in respect of tax, either for himself or for any other person, or, in any return made with reference to tax, knowingly makes any false statement or false representation, he shall be liable, on summary conviction, to [six months' imprisonment]."

Value Added Tax

Section 72 of the Value Added Tax Act 1994 provides: **38.21**

"(1) If any person is knowingly concerned in, or in the taking of steps with a view to, the fraudulent evasion of VAT by him or any other person, he shall be liable—

(a) on summary conviction, to a penalty of the statutory maximum or of three times the amount of the VAT, whichever is the greater, or to imprisonment for a term not exceeding 6 months, or to both; or

(b) on conviction on indictment, to a penalty of any amount or to imprisonment for a term not exceeding 7 years or to both.

(2) Any reference in subsection (1) above or subsection (8) below to the evasion of VAT includes a reference to the obtaining of—

(a) the payment of a VAT credit; or

(b) a refund under section 35,[69] 36[70] or 40[71] of this Act or section 22 of the 1983 Act[72]; or

---

[68] "Arrested" substituted for the original "detained" by virtue of the Police and Criminal Evidence Act 1984, s.114(1), applied to Scotland by s.120(5).

[69] That is to say, to persons constructing or converting certain buildings; s.35 is amended by the Finance Act 1995, s.33(2), and by the Finance Act 1996, s.30.

[70] That is to say, relative to bad debts: s.36 is amended by the Finance Act 1997, s.39 and Sched. 18, Pt IV; the Finance Act 1998, s.23, Sched. 27, Pt II; and the Finance Act 1999, s.15.

[71] That is to say, relative to, in certain circumstances, the supplying of "new means of transport".

[72] That is to say, the Value Added Tax Act 1983. Section 22 of that Act is equivalent to s.36 of the present Act.

      (c) a refund under any regulations made by virtue of section 13(5)[73]; or

      (d) a repayment under section 39[74];

and any reference in those subsections to the amount of VAT shall be construed—

      (i) in relation to VAT itself or a VAT credit, as a reference to the aggregate of the amount (if any) falsely claimed by way of credit for input tax and the amount (if any) by which output tax was falsely understated, and

      (ii) in relation to a refund or repayment falling within paragraph (b), (c) or (d) above, as a reference to the amount falsely claimed by way of refund or repayment.

    (3) If any person—

    (a) with intent to deceive produces, furnishes or sends for the purposes of this Act or otherwise makes use for those purposes of any document which is false in a material particular; or

    (b) in furnishing any information for the purposes of this Act makes any statement which he knows to be false in a material particular or recklessly makes a statement which is false in a material particular,

he shall be liable—

      (i) on summary conviction, to a penalty of the statutory maximum or, where subsection (4) or (5) applies, to the alternative penalty specified in that subsection if it is greater, or to imprisonment for a term not exceeding 6 months or to both; or

      (ii) on conviction on indictment, to a penalty of any amount or to imprisonment for a term not exceeding 7 years or to both.

    (4) In any case where—

    (a) the document referred to in subsection (3)(a) above is a return required under this Act, or

    (b) the information referred to in subsection (3)(b) above is contained in or otherwise relevant to such a return,

the alternative penalty referred to in subsection (3)(i) above is a penalty equal to three times the aggregate of the amount (if any) falsely claimed by way of credit for input tax and the amount (if any) by which output tax was falsely understated.

    (5) In any case where—

    (a) the document referred to in subsection (3)(a) above is a claim for a refund under section 35, 36 or 40 of this Act or section 22 of the 1983 Act, for a refund under any regulations made by virtue of section 13(5) or for a repayment under section 39, or

    (b) the information referred to in subsection (3)(b) above is contained in or otherwise relevant to such a claim,

the alternative penalty referred to in subsection (3)(i) above is a penalty equal to 3 times the amount falsely claimed.

---

[73] That is to say, relative to goods deemed not to be acquired in the United Kingdom since VAT has been paid on them in another Member State of the European Union.

[74] That is to say, relative to those in business other than in the United Kingdom.

(6) The reference in subsection (3)(a) above to funrishing, sending or otherwise making use of a document which is false in a material particular, with intent to deceive, includes a reference to furnishing, sending or otherwise making use of such a document, with intent to secure that a machine will respond to the document as if it were a true document.

(7) Any reference in subsection (3)(a) or (6) above to producing, furnishing or sending a document includes a reference to causing a document to be produced, furnished or sent.

(8) Where a person's conduct during any specified period must have involved the commission by him of one or more offences under the preceding provisions of this section, then, whether or not the particulars of that offence or those offences are known, he shall, by virtue of this subsection, be guilty of an offence and liable—

(a) on summary conviction, to a penalty of the statutory maximum or, if greater, three times the amount of any VAT that was or was intended to be evaded by his conduct, or to imprisonment for a term not exceeding 6 months or to both, or

(b) on conviction on indictment to a penalty of any amount or to imprisonment for a term not exceeding 7 years or both.

(9) Where an authorised person has reasonable grounds for suspecting that an offence has been committed under the preceding provisions of this section, he may arrest anyone whom he has reasonable grounds for suspecting to be guilty of the offence.

(10) If any person acquires possession of or deals with any goods, or accepts the supply of any services, having reason to believe that VAT on the supply of the goods or services, on the acquisition of the goods from another member State or on the importation of the goods from a place outside the member States has been or will be evaded, he shall be liable on summary conviction to a penalty of level 5 on the standard scale or three times the amount of VAT, whichever is the greater.

(11) If any person supplies goods or services in contravention of paragraph 4(2) of Schedule 11,[75] he shall be liable on summary conviction to a penalty of level 5 on the standard scale . . ."

II — Election Offences

The main enactment, the Representation of the People Act 1983,[76] **38.22** contains a number of penal provisions: these are divided into three classes — corrupt practices, illegal practices, and offences.[77]

---

[75] That is to say, supplying goods or services under a taxable supply without giving security for payment of VAT where the Commissioners have required such security as a condition of such supplying by a taxable person.

[76] The provisions of this Act are extensively amended and extended by a considerable body of legislation, foremost among which being the Representation of the People Act 1985, the Representation of the People Act 2000 and the Political Parties, Elections and Referendums Act 2000. In general, the statutory provisions set out or described in the paragraphs below apply not only to Parliamentary, General and Local Government elections but also, with modifications, to elections to the Scottish and European Parliaments: see, in particular, the Scottish Parliament (Elections etc.) Order 1999 (S.I. 1999 No. 787), the European Parliamentary Elections Regulations 1999 (S.I. 1999 No. 1214), the Scottish Parliament (Elections etc.) (Amendment) Order 2001 (S.S.I. 2001 No. 1399), and the European Parliamentary Elections (Franchise of Relevant Citizens of the Union)

Corrupt practices

38.23   Section 168(1)[78] of the Representation of the People Act 1983[79] provides:

> "A person who is guilty of a corrupt practice shall be liable—
>> (a) on conviction on indictment—
>>> (i)   in the case of a corrupt practice under section 60[80] above, to imprisonment for a term not exceeding two years, or to a fine, or to both,
>>> (ii) in any other case, to imprisonment for a term not exceeding one year or to a fine, or to both;
>> (b) on summary conviction, to imprisonment for a term not exceeding six months, or to a fine not exceeding the statutory maximum, or to both."[81]

38.24 *Incapacity.* Subsections (4), (4A), (5) and (5A)[82] of section 160 provide that a candidate or other person who is reported by an election court personally guilty of a corrupt practice shall for five years from the date of the report be incapable of being registered as an elector or voting at any Parliamentary election in the United Kingdom or at any local government election in Great Britain,[83] or of being elected to the House of Commons (or the Scottish Parliament)[84]: if already so elected, he must vacate the seat as from the date of the report.[85] In addition, a candidate or other person so reported personally guilty of such a practice shall for five years from the date of the report be incapable of holding a public[86] or judicial[87] office in Scotland and, if already holding such an office, must

---

Regulations 2001 (S.I. 2001 No. 1184).

[77] Alison refers to some old convictions at common law for forcibly carrying off and detaining, and intimidating, voters, and procuring an election by fraud or violence, the latest being *Maclachlan and Ors* in 1831: Alison, i, 642–643, but any election offence today would be dealt with under the relevant Acts.

[78] As substituted by the Representation of the People Act 1985 (hereinafter referred to as "the 1985 Act"), Sched 3, para. 8. The substituted subsection (1) replaces subsections (1)-(4) of the original s.168.

[79] Hereinafter referred to as "the 1983 Act".

[80] Section 60 describes the corrupt practice of personation: see para. 38.26, *infra*.

[81] With reference to corrupt practices in relation to Scottish Parliamentary elections, the maximum penalty on summary conviction is three months' and a fine of level 5 on the standard scale: the Scottish Parliament (Elections etc.) Order 1999 (S.I. 1999 No. 787), art. 85, Sched. 6, Pt I, entry for s.168.

[82] As substituted or added by the Political Parties, Elections and Referendums Act 2000, Sched. 17, para. 8. The provisions are made subject to s.174 of the 1983 Act which provides that if a person disqualified by reason of a report of an election court is subsequently acquitted in a prosecution for the matter in question the court may order the incapacity to cease, and if he is convicted the court shall have the same power of remission or mitigation of any incapacity as if it had been imposed on conviction. A person incapacitated by a report of an election court cannot be further incapacitated on conviction.

[83] The specified incapacities relative to registration and voting are confined by subs. (4A) to the reporting of personal guilt of a corrupt practice under s.60 (Personation) of the 1983 Act.

[84] The reference to the Scottish Parliament was added to s.160(4) of the 1983 Act by the Scottish Parliament (Elections etc.) Order 1999 (S.I. 1999 No. 787), art 85, Sched. 6, Pt I, and impliedly confirmed by the Scottish Parliament (Elections etc.) (Amendment) Order 2001 (S.I. 2001 No. 1399), art. 21(2)(d).

[85] Section 160(4)(b).

[86] Under s.185, as amended by the Political Parties, Elections and Referendums Act 2000, Sched. 17, para. 10(b), "public office" in Scotland means any office held under the Crown, under the charter of a city or under the Acts relating to local government, public health or public education.

[87] This includes the office of justice of the peace: 1983 Act, s.185.

vacate it as from that date.[88] The same incapacities follow on conviction of a corrupt practice,[89] save that a seat already held in the House of Commons is to be vacated at the end of the prescribed period within which notice of appeal may be given or an application for leave to appeal may be made[90]; during that prescribed period (or any lawful extension of it), the holder of the seat is, however, suspended from exercising any of his functions as a member of Parliament.[91]

In addition, section 159(1) provides that the election of any candidate reported by an election court personally guilty or guilty by his agents of any corrupt practice shall be void; and section 159(3)[92] provides:

> "A candidate at a local government election in Scotland who is reported personally guilty or guilty by his agents of any corrupt . . . practice shall also be incapable from the date of the report of holding the office of councillor of any local authority in Scotland—
>   (a) for ten years, if reported personally guilty of a corrupt practice,
>   (b) for three years, if reported guilty by his agents of a corrupt practice . . .
>   and if at the date of the report he holds any such office, then the office shall be vacated as from that date . . ."[93]

PROFESSIONS. Where a justice of the peace is reported by an election **38.25** court guilty of a corrupt practice the matter is reported to the Secretary of State by the court,[94] and where an advocate or solicitor, or any member of a profession admission to which is regulated by law, is so reported by an election court, the court reports this to the appropriate disciplinary body who may deal with him as if the corrupt practice were professional misconduct.[95]

Types of corrupt practice. The following are corrupt practices.   **38.26**

PERSONATION. Section 60 of the 1983 Act provides:

---

[88] Section 160 (5A).

[89] The 1983 Act, s.173 and 173A, as substituted/added by the Political Parties, Elections and Referendums Act 2000, s.136.

[90] Section 173(4)(a). If the prescribed period is prospectively extended, then the appropriate date is the end of that extended period or the end of a period of three months beginning with the date of the conviction, whichever is earlier: s.173(4)(b); see also s.173(5). If before the appropriate date notice of appeal is given or an application for leave to appeal made, the seat is to be vacated three months after the date of the conviction, unless the appeal is dismissed or abandoned within that time (when the date of abandonment or dismissal will be the date for vacation of the seat) or, again within that time, the appeal court determines that the conviction should not be upheld, in which case the seat is retained: but once a seat is vacated, under the provisions of s.173 "no subsequent determination of a court that the conviction should not be upheld shall entitle him to resume the seat": s.173(6). This last mentioned provision supersedes the decision of the Divisional Court, given under the pre-amended form of s.173, in *Att.-Gen. v. Jones* [2000] Q.B. 66.

[91] Section 173(7), (8).

[92] As substituted by the Political Parties, Elections and Referendums Act 2000, Sched. 17, para 7(b): para 7(a) of that Sched. declares that subs. (2) of s.59 is to be omitted.

[93] Section 159(3)(c) applies only to illegal practices.

[94] Section 161 of the 1983 Act, as amended by the 1985 Act, Sched. 4, para. 53.

[95] Section 162, as amended by the 1985 Act, Sched. 4, para. 54.

"(1) A person shall be guilty of a corrupt practice if he commits, or aids, abets, counsels or procures the commission of, the offence of personation.

(2) A person shall be deemed to be guilty of personation at a parliamentary or local government election if he—

(a) votes in person or by post as some other person, whether as an elector or as proxy, and whether that other person is living or dead or is a fictitious person; or

(b) votes in person or by post as proxy —

(i) for a person whom he knows or has reasonable grounds for supposing to be dead or to be a fictitious person; or

(ii) when he knows or has reasonable grounds for supposing that his appointment as proxy is no longer in force.

(3) For the purposes of this section, a person who has applied for a ballot paper for the purpose of voting in person or who has marked, whether validly or not, and returned a ballot paper issued for the purpose of voting by post, shall be deemed to have voted."

38.27 FALSE PARTICULARS OR SIGNATURES. Section 65A[96] of the 1983 Act provides:

"(1) A person is guilty of a corrupt practice if, in the case of any relevant election, he causes or permits to be included in a document delivered or otherwise furnished to a returning officer for use in connection with the election—

(a) a statement of the name or home address of a candidate at the election which he knows to be false in any particular; or

(b) anything which purports to be the signature of an elector who proposes, seconds or assents to, the nomination of such a candidate but which he knows—

(i) was not written by the elector by whom it purports to have been written, or

(ii) if written by that elector, was not written by him for the purpose of signifying that he was proposing, seconding or (as the case may be) assenting to, that candidate's nomination.

(2) In this section 'relevant election' means—

(a) any parliamentary election . . ."[97]

38.28 UNAUTHORISED INCURRING OF EXPENSES. Section 75 of the 1983 Act provides:

"(1) No expenses shall, with a view to promoting or procuring the election of a candidate at an election, be incurred by any person other than the candidate, his election agent and persons authorised in writing by the election agent on account—

(a) of holding public meetings or organising any public display; or

(b) of issuing advertisements, circulars or publications; or

(c) of otherwise presenting to the electors the candidate or his views or the extent or nature of his backing or disparaging another candidate,

---

[96] Inserted by the Representation of the People Act 2000, Sched. 6, para. 5.

[97] This section does not apply to local government elections in Scotland: s.65A(2)(b).

but paragraph (c) of this subsection shall not—

(i)[98] restrict the publication of any matter relating to the election in a newspaper or other periodical or in a broadcast made by the British Broadcasting Corporation or by Sianel Pedwar Cymru or in a programme included in any service licensed under Part I or III of the Broadcasting Act 1990 or Part 1 or II of the Broadcasting Act 1996; or

(ii)[99] apply to any expenses incurred by any person which do not exceed in the aggregate the permitted sum (and are not incurred by that person as part of a concerted plan of action), or to expenses incurred by any person in travelling or in living away from home or similar personal expenses . . .

(1ZA)[1] For the purposes of subsection (1)(ii) above, 'the permitted sum'[2] means—

(a) in respect of a candidate at a parliamentary election, £500;

(b) in respect of a candidate at a local election, £50 together with an additional 0.5p for every entry in the register of local government electors for the electoral area in question as it has effect on the last day for publication of notice of the election;

and expenses shall be regarded as incurred by a person 'as part of a concerted plan of action' if they are incurred by that person in pursuance of any plan or other arrangement whereby that person and one or more other persons are to incur, with a view to promoting or procuring the election of the same candidate, expenses which (disregarding subsection (1)(ii)) fall within subsection (1) above.

. . .

(5) If a person—

(a) incurs, or aids, abets, counsels or procures any other person to incur, any expense in contravention of this section, or

(b) knowingly makes the declaration required by subsection (2) [relating to expenses] falsely,

he shall be guilty of a corrupt practice; . . ."

Section 75(5) contains a proviso permitting a court to remit any incapacity to which a person is liable by virtue of conviction under it and provides that a candidate shall not be liable for any corrupt (or illegal) practice under it committed by an agent without his consent or connivance.

Section 75 is directed at the unauthorised incurring of expenses of a kind which if authorised by an agent would form part of a candidate's election expenses. It does not, therefore, apply to expenditure incurred

---

[98] As amended by the Broadcasting Act 1990, Sched. 20, para. 35(2), and by the Broadcasting Act 1996, Sched. 10, Pt III, para. 28 (which relates to digital services).

[99] As amended by the Political Parties, Elections and Referendums Act 2000, s.131(2).

[1] Inserted by s.131(3) of the Political Parties, Elections and Referendums Act 2000. (These recent amendments to s.75 are presumably designed to bring the law into conformity with Art. 10 of the European Convention on Human Rights: see *Bowman v. United Kingdom* (1998) 26 E.H.R.R. 1.)

[2] Under s.76A, as substituted by the Political Parties, Elections and Referendums Act 2000, s.133(1), the Secretary of State may vary by statutory instrument the monetary limits set out in, *inter alia*, s.75(1ZA).

in general political propaganda,[3] although the effect of such expenditure is to facilitate the election of a particular candidate.[4]

The section only strikes at expenses incurred "with a view" to promoting the election of a candidate, and whether or not expenses are incurred with this view depends on the intention of the person incurring them.[5] An intention to prevent the election of a particular candidate is sufficient; it is not necessary to show an intention to secure the election of a particular candidate.[6]

38.29   FALSE DECLARATION OF EXPENSES. Section 82 of the 1983 Act provides for the submission of a declaration respecting election expenses in parliamentary elections and provides that it is a corrupt practice for a candidate or agent knowingly[7] to make a false declaration.[8]

38.30   BRIBERY. Section 113 of the 1983 Act provides:

"(1) A person shall be guilty of a corrupt practice if he is guilty of bribery.

(2) A person shall be guilty of bribery if he, directly or indirectly, by himself or by any other person on his behalf—

    (a) gives any money or procures any office to or for any voter or to or for any other person on behalf of any voter or to or for any other person in order to induce any voter to vote or refrain from voting; or

    (b) corruptly does any such act as mentioned above on account of any voter having voted or refrained from voting; or

    (c) makes any such gift or procurement as mentioned above to or for any person in order to induce that person to procure, or endeavour to procure, the return of any person at an election or the vote of any voter,

or if upon or in consequence of any such gift or procurement as mentioned above he procures or engages, promises or endeavours to procure the return of any person at an election or the vote of any voter.

---

[3] *cf.* the Political Parties, Elections and Referendums Act 2000, Pt IV — esp. Chap. II (restriction on donations to registered [political] parties), Chap. III (reporting of donations to registered [political] parties) and Sched. 7; and Pts V (control of campaign expenditure) — esp. s.9 and Sched. 9 — and VI (controls relating to third party national election campaigns): for provisions relating to the registration of political parties, see the Representation of the People Act 2000, Pt II. For controls in relation to referendums, see the Representation of the People Act 2000, Pt VII.

[4] *R. v. Tronoh Mines Ltd and The Times Publishing Co.* (1952) 35 Cr.App.R. 196; *Walker and Anr v. Unison*, 1995 S.C.L.R. 786, OH.

[5] *Grieve v. Douglas-Hume*, 1968 S.C. 315 where it was held that the expenses incurred by the B.B.C. and I.T.A. in promoting party political broadcasts by the outgoing Prime Minister during an election campaign were incurred for the purpose of informing the public and not with a view to promoting his election.

[6] *D.P.P. v. Luft* [1977] A.C. 962, HL, applying *R. v. Hailwood and Ackroyd Ltd* [1928] 2 K.B. 277, and disapproving reasoning to the contrary in *R. v. Tronoh Mines Ltd*, *supra*.

[7] In *R. v. Jones and Whicher* [1999] 2 Cr.App.R. 253, CA, it was held that an honest belief in the truth of the declaration, as to the accuracy of the figures disclosed, was a complete defence, and that it was for the Crown to show the lack of such an honest belief: "The nub of the offence is the declaration of an honest belief in the accuracy of a disclosure which is known to be incomplete or inaccurate" (opinion of the Court, delivered by Lord Bingham, C.J., at 259B-D).

[8] Section 82(6). Section 85(1) provides that a candidate who does not make a declaration in time may not sit or vote until the declaration is delivered.

For the purposes of this subsection—

    (i) references to giving money shall include references to giving, lending, agreeing to give or lend, offering, promising, or promising to procure or endeavour to procure any money or valuable consideration; and

    (ii) references to procuring any office shall include references to giving, procuring, agreeing to give or procure, offering, promising, or promising to procure or to endeavour to procure any office, place or employment.

(3) A person shall be guilty of bribery if he advances or pays or causes to be paid any money to or for the use of any other person with the intent that that money or any part of it shall be expended in bribery at any election or knowingly pays or causes to be paid any money to any person in discharge or repayment of any money wholly or in part expended in bribery at any election.

(4) The foregoing provisions of this section shall not extend or be construed to extend to any money paid or agreed to be paid for or on account of any legal expenses incurred in good faith at or concerning an election.

(5) A voter shall be guilty of bribery if before or during an election he directly or indirectly by himself or by any other person on his behalf receives, agrees, or contracts for any money, gift, loan or valuable consideration, office, place or employment for himself or for any other person for voting or agreeing to vote or for refraining or agreeing to refrain from voting.

(6) A person shall be guilty of bribery if after an election he directly or indirectly by himself or by any other person on his behalf receives any money or valuable consideration on account of any person having voted or refrained from voting or having induced any other person to vote or refrain from voting.

(7) In this section the expression 'voter' includes any person who has or claims to have a right to vote."

In *Cooper v. Slade*[9] it was held that any money paid in pursuance of a promise forbidden by the Act then in force[10] was "corruptly" paid, although the person making the promise or payment — in that case a candidate paying the travelling expenses of voters — believed it to be permitted by law.[11] It is unsettled whether a payment made after an election is bribery if it is not made in pursuance of a corrupt promise to pay made before polling.[12]

In *Britt v. Robinson*[13] money was paid to voters for voting at a "test ballot" held to decide which of three Liberal candidates should stand as Liberal at the election in a constituency which it was expected would return a Liberal candidate unless the Liberal vote was split. The payments were held to constitute bribery, as being given for the purpose of procuring the election of the person who succeeded in the test ballot.

---

[9] (1858) 6 H.L.C. 746.

[10] The Corrupt Practices Prevention Act 1854 (repealed by the Representation of the People Act 1949, Sched. 9).

[11] (1856) 6 H.L.C., Willes J. at 773–774.

[12] See *Halsbury's Laws of England* (4th ed.), Vol. 15 (reissue, 1990); *Cooper v. Slade, supra,* Lord Wensleydale at 797; *The Harwich Borough Case* (1880) 3 O'M. & H. 61, Lush J. at 70.

[13] (1870) L.R. 5 C.P. 503.

38.31   TREATING. Section 114 of the 1983 Act provides:

"(1) A person shall be guilty of a corrupt practice if he is guilty of treating.

(2) A person shall be guilty of treating if he corruptly, by himself or by any other person, either before, during or after an election, directly or indirectly gives or provides, or pays wholly or in part the expense of giving or providing any meat, drink, entertainment or provision to or for any person—

(a) for the purpose of corruptly influencing that person or any other person to vote or refrain from voting; or

(b) on account of that person or any other person having voted or refrained from voting, or being about to vote or refrain from voting.

(3) Every elector or his proxy who corruptly accepts or takes any such meat, drink, entertainment or provision shall also be guilty of treating."

It is a question of circumstance whether the provision of entertainment or refreshments at political meetings amounts to treating.[14] The provision of entertainment or refreshment after an election, for example in a celebration party, does not constitute treating unless it is given in pursuance of a promise corruptly made prior to polling.[15]

38.32   UNDUE INFLUENCE. Section 115 of the 1983 Act provides:

"(1) A person shall be guilty of a corrupt practice if he is guilty of undue influence.

(2) A person shall be guilty of undue influence—

(a) if he, directly or indirectly, by himself or by any other person on his behalf, makes use of or threatens to make use of any force, violence or restraint, or inflicts or threatens to inflict, by himself or by any other person, any temporal or spiritual injury, damage, harm or loss upon or against any person in order to induce or compel that person to vote or refrain from voting, or on account of that person having voted or refrained from voting; or

(b) if, by abduction, duress or any fraudulent device or contrivance, he impedes or prevents the free exercise of the franchise of an elector or proxy for an elector, or so compels, induces or prevails upon an elector or proxy for an elector either to vote or to refrain from voting."

Section 158(3) provides that if a candidate reported by an election court guilty of treating or undue influence is also reported to have proved that the offences concerned were committed without his sanction or consent, that he and his agent took all reasonable means to prevent the commission of corrupt (and illegal) practices, that the offences were trivial, and that the election was in all other respects free from any corrupt (or illegal) practice by the candidate or his agent, then the candidate shall not be treated as having been reported guilty by his agents for the purposes of the imposition of incapacities under section 159.

---

[14] See *The St. George's Division Case* (1895) 5 O'M. & H. 89, 98 *et seq.*
[15] *The Harwich Borough Case* (1880) 3 O'M. & H. 61, Lush J. at 70.

Illegal practices

Offences which are classified as illegal practices are punishable **38.33** summarily by a maximum fine of level 5 on the standard scale.[16]

Incapacity. Subsections (4), (4A), and (5)[17] of section 160 provide that a **38.34** candidate or other person who is reported by an election court personally guilty of an illegal practice shall for three years from the date of the report be incapable of being registered as an elector or voting at any Parliamentary election in the United Kingdom or at any local government election in Great Britain,[18] or of being elected to the House of Commons (or the Scottish Parliament)[19]: if already so elected, he must vacate the seat as from the date of the report.[20] The same incapacities follow on conviction of an illegal practice,[21] save that a seat already held in the House of Commons is to be vacated at the end of the prescribed period within which notice of appeal may be given or an application for leave to appeal may be made[22]; during that prescribed period (or any lawful extension of it), the holder of the seat is, however, suspended from exercising any of his functions as a member of Parliament.[23]

In addition, section 159(1) provides that the election of any candidate reported by an election court personally guilty or guilty by his agents of any illegal practice shall be void; and section 159(3)[24] provides:

"A candidate at a local government election in Scotland who is reported personally guilty or guilty by his agents of any . . . illegal

---

[16] Section 169 of the 1983 Act, as amended by the 1985 Act, Sched. 3, para. 9.

[17] As substituted or added by the Political Parties, Elections and Referendums Act 2000, Sched. 17, para. 8. The provisions are made subject to s.174 of the 1983 Act which provides that if a person disqualified by reason of a report of an election court is subsequently acquitted in a prosecution for the matter in question the court may order the incapacity to cease, and if he is convicted the court shall have the same power of remission or mitigation of any incapacity as if it had been imposed on conviction. A person incapacitated by a report of an election court cannot be further incapacitated on conviction. Section 167 of the 1983 Act empowers the court to excuse any innocent act which would otherwise constitute an illegal practice.

[18] The specified incapacities relative to registration and voting are confined by subs. (4A) to the reporting of personal guilt of an illegal practice under s.61 (see para. 38.37, *infra*) of the 1983 Act.

[19] The reference to the Scottish Parliament was added to s.160(4) of the 1983 Act by the Scottish Parliament (Elections etc.) Order 1999 (S.I. 1999 No. 787), art. 85, Sched. 6, Pt I, and impliedly confirmed by the Scottish Parliament (Elections etc.) (Amendment) Order 2001 (S.S.I. 2001 No. 1399), art. 21(2)(d).

[20] Section 160(4)(b).

[21] The 1983 Act, ss. 173 and 173A, as substituted/added by the Political Parties, Elections and Referendums Act 2000, s.136.

[22] Section 173(4)(a). If the prescribed period is prospectively extended, then the appropriate date is the end of that extended period or the end of a period of three months beginning with the date of the conviction, whichever is earlier: s.173(4)(b); see also s.173(5). If before the appropriate date notice of appeal is given or an application for leave to appeal made, the seat is to be vacated three months after the date of the conviction, unless the appeal is dismissed or abandoned within that time (when the date of abandonment or dismissal will be the date for vacation of the seat) or, again within that time, the appeal court determines that the conviction should not be upheld, in which case the seat is retained: but once a seat is vacated, under the provisions of s.173 "no subsequent determination of a court that the conviction should not be upheld shall entitle him to resume the seat": s.173(6). *Cf. Att.-Gen. v. Jones* [2000] Q.B. 66.

[23] Section 173(7), (8).

[24] As substituted by the Political Parties, Elections and Referendums Act 2000, Sched. 17, para 7(b): para 7(a) of that Sched. declares that subs. (2) of s.159 is to be omitted.

practice shall also be incapable from the date of the report of holding the office of councillor of any local authority in Scotland—

. . .

    (c) during the period for which the candidate was elected to serve or for which if elected he might have served, if reported personally guilty or guilty by his agents of an illegal practice,

and if at the date of the report he holds any such office, then the office shall be vacated as from that date. . . ."[25]

38.35 *Types of illegal practices.* There is a large number of illegal practices which include the following.

BROADCASTING. Section 93 of the 1983 Act provides[26]:

"(1)[27] In relation to a parliamentary or local government election—
    (a) pending such an election it shall not be lawful for any item about the constituency or electoral area to be
        (i) broadcast by the British Broadcasting Corporation or Sianel Pedwar Cymru; or
        (ii) included in any service licensed under Part I or III of the Broadcasting Act 1990 or Part I or II of the Broadcasting Act 1996,

if any of the persons who are for the time being candidates at the election takes part in the item and the broadcast is not made with his consent; and

    (b) where an item about a constituency or electoral area is so broadcast pending such an election there, then if the broadcast either is made before the latest time for delivery of nomination papers, or is made after that time but without the consent of any candidate remaining validly nominated, any person taking part in the item for the purpose of promoting or procuring his election shall be guilty of an illegal practice, unless the broadcast is so made without his consent.

(2) For the purposes of subsection (1) above—
    (a) a parliamentary election shall be deemed to be pending during the period ending with the close of the poll and beginning—
        (i) at a general election, with the date of the dissolution of Parliament or any earlier time at which Her Majesty's intention to dissolve Parliament is announced; or
        (ii) at a by-election, with the date of the issue of the writ for the election or any earlier date on which a certificate of the vacancy is notified in the London Gazette in accordance with the Recess Elections Act 1975; and
    (b) a local government election shall be deemed to be pending during the period ending with the close of the poll and beginning with the last date on which notice of the election may be published in accordance with rules made under . . . in Scotland, section 42, above."

---

[25] Section 159(3)(a) and (b) apply only to corrupt practices.
[26] As amended by the 1985 Act, Sched. 4, para. 35.
[27] As amended by the Broadcasting Act 1990, Sched. 20, para. 35(4), and the Broadcasting Act 1996, Sched. 10, para. 29.

EXPENSES. Many breaches of the comprehensive and complicated rules **38.36** laid down by the 1983 Act regarding expenses are classed as illegal practices. They include the contraction of expenses otherwise than through an election agent[28]; provision of money or other property, for the purposes of meeting election expenses, other than to the candidate or his election agent[29]; and the failure to make proper returns and declarations under sections 81 and 82.[30] It is also an illegal practice for an election agent to fail to pay election expenses timeously, or to pay expenses which have not been claimed timeously.[31]

VOTING. Section 61[32] of the 1983 Act sets out a number of voting **38.37** offences which are declared[33] to be illegal practices. These include voting while under a legal incapacity, and voting twice at any election, and the offence may be committed by voting personally, or by proxy, or as proxy for an incapable person, or voting twice as proxy for any person. Section 61(5) makes it an offence for anyone knowingly to induce or procure another person "to do an act which is, or but for that other person's want of knowledge would be, an offence by that other person under . . . this section."[34]

ILLEGAL PAYMENTS, EMPLOYMENTS AND HIRINGS. Section 175(2) of the **38.38** 1983 Act provides that a candidate or election agent who is personally guilty of an illegal payment, employment or hiring shall be guilty of an illegal practice.

The employment of paid canvassers is an illegal employment.[35]

In relation to local government elections in Scotland, the hiring of licensed premises or of schools other than independent schools as committee rooms is an illegal hiring.[36]

---

[28] Section 73(6) of the 1983 Act, as amended by the Political Parties, Elections and Referendums Act 2000, Sched. 18, para. 3. (The amendments effected by Sched. 18 do not apply to local government elections in Scotland: the 2000 Act, above, s.138(2).)

[29] Section 71A(3), inserted by the Political Parties, Elections and Referendums Act 2000, s.130(2). Rules controlling donations to candidates are to be found in Sched. 2A to the 1983 Act, Sched. 2A being Sched. 16 to the Act of 2000, above: see s.71A(4) of the 1983 Act, inserted as above, and s.130(3) of the Act of 2000. (Amendments to the 1983 Act effected by s.130 of the 2000 Act do not apply to local government elections in Scotland: s.130(4).)

[30] Section 84. A candidate who sits in the House of Commons without making timeous return and declaration regarding expenses is liable to a fine of £100 for every day he takes his seat after the declaration and return should have been made: s.85(1).

[31] Section 78(3) of the 1983 Act. See also s.92: using wireless stations outside the United Kingdom; s.109(2): giving or accepting payment for exhibiting election notices; s.110(12), as substituted by Sched. 18, para. 14 (for parliamentary elections — see s.138(2)) of the Political Parties, Elections and Referendums Act 2000: candidate or election agent publishing documents or advertisements not bearing the name and address of the printer, promoter and the person on whose behalf they are published.

[32] As amended by the 1985 Act, Sched. 2, para. 3.

[33] See s.61(7).

[34] A candidate is not liable for an illegal practice by any agent under this section other than an offence under subsection (5): s.61(7).

[35] Section 111 of the 1983 Act.

[36] See s.108 of the 1983 Act (which is to be omitted relative to parliamentary elections: the Political Parties, Elections and Referendums Act 2000, s.138 and Sched. 18, para. 13). Persons other than candidates and election agents who are convicted of illegal payments, employments or hirings are liable on summary conviction to a fine of level 3 on the standard scale: s.175(1).

38.39   FALSEHOODS AND FRAUDS. Section 106 of the 1983 Act provides:

> "(1) A person who, or any director of any body or association
> corporate which—
> (a) before or during an election,
> (b) for the purpose of affecting the return of any candidate at the
>   election,
> makes or publishes any false statement of fact in relation to the
> candidate's personal character or conduct of the candidate shall be guilty
> of an illegal practice, unless he can show that he has reasonable grounds
> for believing, and did believe, the statement to be true.
> (2) A candidate shall not be liable nor shall his election be avoided
> for any illegal practice under subsection (1) above committed by his
> agent other than his election agent unless—
> (a) it can be shown that the candidate or his election agent has
>   authorised or consented to the committing of the illegal
>   practice by the other agent or has paid for the circulation of
>   the false statement constituting the illegal practice; or
> (b) an election court find and report that the election of the
>   candidate was procured or materially assisted in consequence
>   of the making or publishing of such false statements.
>   . . .
> (5) Any person who, before or during an election, knowingly
> publishes a false statement of a candidate's at the election for the
> purpose of promoting or procuring the election of another candi-
> date shall be guilty of an illegal practice.
> (6) A candidate shall not be liable, nor shall his election be
> avoided, for any illegal practice under subsection (5) above com-
> mitted by his agent other than his election agent."[37]

Section 94 of the 1983 Act provides that it is an illegal practice to issue
"any poll card or document so closely resembling an official poll card as
to be calculated to deceive" in order to promote or procure the election
of any parliamentary candidate.[38]

38.40   CORRUPT WITHDRAWAL. Section 107 of the 1983 Act provides:

> "Any person who corruptly induces or procures any other person to
> withdraw from being a candidate at an election, in consideration of
> any payment or promise of payment, and any person withdrawing in
> pursuance of the inducement or procurement, shall be guilty of an
> illegal payment."

38.41   DISTURBANCES. Section 97 of the 1983 Act provides:

> "(1) A person who at a lawful public meeting to which this section
> applies acts, or incites others to act, in a disorderly manner for the
> purposes of preventing the transaction of the business for which the
> meeting was called together shall be guilty of an illegal practice.
> (2) This section applies to—

---

[37] Subsection (4) disapplied subss. (1), (2) and (3) to an election of councillors in
Scotland: but subs. (4) was deleted by the 1985 Act, Sched. 4, para. 41.
[38] This provision also applies to local government elections: 1985 Act, Sched. 4,
para. 36.

(a) a political meeting held in any constituency between the date of the issue of a writ for the return of a member of Parliament for the constituency and the date at which a return to the writ is made;

(b)[39] a meeting held with reference to a local government election in the electoral area for that election in the period beginning with the last date on which notice of the election may be published in accordance with rules made under section 36 or, in Scotland, section 42 above and ending with the day of election.

(3) If a constable reasonably suspects any person of committing an offence under subsection (1) above, he may if requested so to do by the chairman of the meeting require that person to declare to him immediately his name and address and, if that person refuses or fails so to declare his name and address or gives a false name and address, he shall be liable on summary conviction to a fine not exceeding level 1 on the standard scale, and—

(a) if he refuses or fails so to declare his name and address or

(b) if the constable reasonably suspects him of giving a false name and address,
the constable may without warrant arrest him . . ."

Other offences

FRAUDS AT ELECTIONS. Section 65 of the 1983 Act provides: **38.42**

"(1) A person shall be guilty of an offence, if, at a parliamentary or local government election he—

(a) fraudulently defaces or fraudulently destroys any nomination paper; or

(b) fraudulently defaces or fraudulently destroys any ballot paper, or the official mark on any ballot paper, or any declaration of identity or official envelope used in connection with voting by post; or

(c) without due authority supplies any ballot paper to any person; or

(d) fraudulently puts into any ballot box any paper other than the ballot paper which he is authorised by law to put in; or

(e) fraudulently takes out of the polling station any ballot paper; or

(f) without due authority destroys, takes, opens or otherwise interferes with any ballot box or packet of ballot papers then in use for the purposes of the election; or

(g) fraudulently or without due authority, as the case may be, attempts to do any of the foregoing acts.

(2) In Scotland, a person shall be guilty of an offence if—

(a) at a parliamentary or local government election, he forges any nomination paper, delivers to the returning officer any nomination paper knowing it to be forged, or forges or counterfeits any ballot paper or the official mark on any ballot paper; or

(b) at a local government election, he signs any nomination paper as candidate or in any other capacity certifies the truth

---

[39] As amended by the 1985 Act, Sched. 4, para. 39.

of any statement contained in it, knowing such statement to be false; or

(c) he fraudulently or without due authority, as the case may be, attempts to do any of the foregoing acts.

(3)[40] If a returning officer, a presiding officer or a clerk appointed to assist in taking the poll, counting the votes or assisting at the proceedings in connection with the issue or receipt of postal ballot papers is guilty of an offence under this section, he shall be liable—

(a) on conviction on indictment to a fine, or to imprisonment for a term not exceeding 2 years, or to both;

(b) on summary conviction, to a fine not exceeding the statutory maximum, or to imprisonment for a term not exceeding 6 months, or to both.

(4) If any other person is guilty of an offence under this section, he shall be liable on summary conviction to a fine not exceeding level 5 on the standard scale, or to imprisonment for a term not exceeding 6 months or to both."

38.43   SERVICE DECLARATIONS and DECLARATIONS OF LOCAL CONNECTION. Section 62(1) of the 1983 Act, as substituted by the Representation of the People Act 2000,[41] makes it an offence for a person to make a service declaration or a declaration of local connection when he is not authorised to do so,[42] or when he knows that the declaration contains a false statement as to any of the particulars required by regulations made under section 16: it is also an offence for a person to attest a service declaration when he knows that he is not authorised to do so or that the declaration contains such a false statement as is referred to above.[43]

38.44   BREACHES OF DUTY. Section 63 of the 1983 Act[44] provides that any sheriff clerk, registration officer, returning officer, presiding officer, any person whose duty is to be responsible for used ballot papers and other documents after a local government election, or any postmaster, and any deputy or assistant of the foregoing persons who is without reasonable cause guilty of any act or omission in breach of his official duty is liable on summary conviction to a fine not exceeding level 5 on the standard scale. Section 63(2) provides, however, that no person to whom that section applies shall be liable to any common law penalty or to an action of damages in respect of the breach of his official duty.

Section 66 of the 1983 Act makes various provisions designed to maintain the secrecy of voting at elections.[45]

Section 99 of the 1983 Act makes it an offence for any returning officer at a parliamentary or local government election or any officer or clerk appointed under the parliamentary election rules to act as an agent of a candidate.[46]

---

[40] Subsections (3)–(5) are replaced by subsections (3) and (4) of the 1985 Act, Sched. 3, para. 2.

[41] See Sched. 1, para. 17 of that 2000 Act.

[42] Under ss.7B(1), as inserted by s.6 of the Representation of the People Act 2000, or 15(1) of the 1983 Act.

[43] Maximum penalty on summary conviction a fine of level 5 on the standard scale.

[44] As substituted by the 1985 Act, Sched. 4, para. 19.

[45] Maximum penalty (as substituted by the 1985 Act, Sched. 3, para 3), on summary conviction, a fine of level 5 on the standard scale.

[46] Maximum penalty on summary conviction, a fine of level 4 on the standard scale: 1985 Act, Sched. 3, para. 4.

Section 100 of the 1983 Act prohibits canvassing by police officers.[47]

PUBLICATION OF EXIT POLLS. Section 66A[48] of the 1983 Act provides: **38.45**

"(1) No person shall, in the case of an election to which this section applies, publish before the poll is closed—
  (a) any statement relating to the way in which voters have voted at the election where that statement is (or might reasonably be taken to be) based on information given by voters after they have voted, or
  (b) any forecast as to the result of the election which is (or might reasonably be taken to be) based on information so given.
(2) This section applies to—
  (a) any parliamentary election; and
  (b) any local government election in England or Wales.[49]
(3) If a person acts in contravention of subsection (1) above, he shall be liable on summary conviction to a fine not exceeding level 5 on the standard scale or to imprisonment for a term not exceeding 6 months.
(4) In this section—
"forecast" includes estimate;
"publish" means make available to the public at large, or any section of the public, in whatever form and by whatever means;
and any reference to the result of an election is a reference to the result of the election either as a whole or so far as any particular candidate or candidates at the election is or are concerned."

CORRUPT WITHDRAWAL OF ELECTION PETITION. Section 149 of the 1983 **38.46** Act provides:

"If a person makes any agreement or terms, or enters into any undertaking, in relation to the withdrawal of an election petition, and such agreement, terms or undertaking—
  (a) is or are for the withdrawal of the election petition in consideration of any payment, or in consideration that the seat or office should at any time be vacated, or in consideration of the withdrawal of any other election petition, or
  (b) is or are (whether lawful or unlawful) not mentioned in the affidavits referred to in section 148 above,
he shall be liable[50]—
    (i) on conviction on indictment, to imprisonment for a term not exceeding one year, or to a fine, or to both;
    (ii) on summary conviction, to imprisonment for a term not exceeding 6 months, or to a fine not exceeding the statutory maximum, or to both."

---

[47] Maximum penalty, on summary conviction, a fine of level 3 on the standard scale: 1985 Act, Sched. 3, para. 5.

[48] Inserted by the Representation of the People Act 2000, Sched. 6, para. 6.

[49] *cf.* the Scotland Act 1998, Sched. 5 (reserved matters), Pt II, Head B — Home Affairs, Section B3 (elections).

[50] As substituted by the 1985 Act, Sched. 3, para. 7.

Jurisdiction

38.47   OFFENCES ABROAD. Section 178[51] of the 1983 Act provides:

"Proceedings in respect of an offence under this Act alleged to have
been committed outside the United Kingdom by a Commonwealth
citizen[52] or citizen of the Republic of Ireland may be taken, and the
offence may for all incidental purposes be treated as having been
committed, in any place in the United Kingdom."

38.48   OFFENCES BY ASSOCIATIONS. Section 179 of the 1983 Act provides:

"Where—
  (a) any corrupt or illegal practice or any illegal payment, employ-
       ment or hiring, or
  (b) any offence under section 110 above,
is committed by any association or body of persons, corporate or
unincorporate, the members of the association or body who have
taken part in the commission of the offence shall be liable to any
fine or punishment imposed for that offence by this Act."[53]

---

[51] As substituted by the 1985 Act, Sched. 4, para. 62.
[52] See the British Nationality Act 1981, s.37.
[53] See also ss.75(6), 106 and 92(3).

PART VII

OFFENCES AGAINST PUBLIC ORDER AND WELFARE

CHAPTER 39

SEDITION AND ALLIED OFFENCES

SEDITION

The law of sedition as discussed by Hume and Alison rests mainly on **39.01** the notorious series of sedition trials held in the 1790s under the presidency of Lord Justice-Clerk Braxfield.[1] Neither the political outlook which governed these trials nor Lord Braxfield's modes of expression would commend themselves at the present day, and the statements of the law made by the court at that time cannot be regarded as authoritative today. The only other reported discussion of sedition is in *Jas Cumming, John Grant and Ors*[2] in which a group of Chartists were charged with treason felony, "Conspiring to Effect an Alteration of the Laws and Constitution of the Realm by force and violence, or by armed resistance to lawful authority", and sedition, as a result of their efforts to recruit a "National Guard" in support of the Charter, and it is in the judgments in that case that the law must be sought.[3]

Real and verbal sedition. Hume and Alison make a distinction between **39.02** real and verbal sedition. Hume confines verbal sedition to writings of a generally inflammatory kind which do not propose any plan of active operation, and uses the term real sedition for writings which go on to recommend measures for altering the law.[4] Alison describes verbal sedition as including words which prompt men to attempt to subvert established institutions illegally, and real sedition as consisting in acts calculated to disturb the peace, and as the carrying into effect and beginning to execute a course of action of the kind recommended by verbal sedition.[5] The distinction is probably of little importance, and if

---

[1] For example, *Jas Tytler* (1793) 23 St.Tr. 1; *John Morton and Ors* (1793) *ibid.* 7; *Berry and Robertson* (1793) *ibid.* 81; *Thos Muir* (1973) *ibid.* 117; *Thos Fyshe Palmer* (1793) 23 St.Tr. 237; *Wm Skirving* (1794) *ibid.* 391; *Maurice Margarot* (1794) *ibid.* 603; *Chas Sinclair* (1974) *ibid.* 777.

[2] (1848) J. Shaw 17.

[3] There was a trial for sedition in 1921 but it was not reported. The indictment related to the publication of a communist newspaper urging, *inter alia*, the overthrow of capitalist society and parliamentary government. Large parts of the paper were quoted in the indictment which concluded, "which newspaper, articles and words above libelled are calculated to excite popular disaffection, commotion, and violence and resistance to lawful authority." There was also libelled a previous conviction for seditious libel, described as "an offence inferring breach of public order", which indicates that that was regarded as the nature of sedition: *Guy Aldred*, High Court at Glasgow, June 1921, unrep'd; see 1922 J.C. 13.

[4] Hume, i, 559.

[5] Alison, i, 582.

anyone is ever again prosecuted for sedition it is likely to be for verbal sedition as described by Alison, which may amount to much the same thing as Hume called real sedition.[6]

39.03 SEDITION, MOBBING AND TREASON. It is not easy to distinguish Alison's real sedition from mobbing or treason, and Alison himself regards it as forming a half-way house between the two. It is said to be distinguished from mobbing because its purpose is a general reformation of the state and not the redress of local grievances. It is more difficult to distinguish it from treason, and it seems that if a seditious assembly progresses far enough in its purpose it will become treasonable.[7] It may be that real sedition is, so to speak, a form of common law treason felony in that it enables treasonable behaviour to be prosecuted by way of a lesser charge than high treason.

39.04 *Public disorder.* The essence of the crime of sedition is the tendency of what is done to cause public disorder in relation to government policy or the constitution. Criticism of the government or the sovereign, however violent, is not seditious unless it has this inflammatory character, and inflammatory words are not seditious unless they are directed against the state.[8] It has been said that language calculated to bring the laws and constitution into contempt is seditious[9] but it is unlikely that that would be enough today. Sedition was defined by Lord Justice-Clerk Hope in *John Grant and Ors*[10] as follows:

> "The crime of sedition consists in wilfully, unlawfully, and mis-
> chievously, and in violation of the party's allegiance, and in breach
> of the peace, and to the public danger, uttering language calculated
> to produce popular disaffection, disloyalty, resistance to lawful
> authority, or, in more aggravated cases, violence and insurrection.
> The party must be made out not to be exercising his right of free
> discussion for legitimate objects, but to be purposely, mischievously,
> without regard to his allegiance, and to the public danger, scattering
> burning firebrands, calculated to stimulate and excite such effects as
> I have mentioned — reckless of all consequences."

39.05 SEDITION IS VARIABLE. What particular language constitutes sedition varies according to the time, place and circumstances in which it is

---

[6] In two 20th century cases: *H.M. Advocate v. Walsh*, 1922 J.C. 82, and *MacAlister and Ors,* High Court at Edinburgh, Nov. 1953, unrep'd, see *MacAlister and Ors v. Associated Newspapers Ltd*, 1954 S.L.T. 14, charges were brought of conspiracy to further the objects of the Irish and Scottish Republican organisations respectively, and in the latter of conspiring to alter the constitution by criminal means, but they were not described as sedition.

[7] Alison, i, 582. *Cf. Chas Sinclair* (1794) 23 St.Tr. 777, L.J.-C. Braxfield at 800.

[8] *cf. Guy Aldred, supra. Pace* Lord Thomson who in an address given when Lord Advocate said that the scope of the crime was in general terms "activities directed against the State which either are likely to result in violence or advocate the subversion of the constitution by non-constitutional means": "The Lord Advocate's Address to the Muir Society", 1946 S.L.T. (News) 83.

[9] *John Grant and Ors* (1848) J. Shaw 51, Lord Moncreiff at 103.

[10] *supra*, at 80.

used.[11] Words which were seditious in 1793 or 1848 may be harmless in the early 21st century, words which are seditious in Glasgow may not be seditious in Edinburgh, words which might be seditious if used at a public meeting or published in the popular press may be harmless if used in a university lecture or published in a thesis.

The object of sedition. As has been indicated, it appears that language is **39.06** seditious by the law of Scotland only when it is directed against the laws and the constitution. In England sedition may be committed by any conduct calculated to disturb the tranquillity of the state by creating ill-will towards the sovereign or established institutions, or by exciting ill-will between different classes of the lieges, or by any conduct encouraging any class to subvert the laws by disobedience or to resist their execution, or to do any violence to the danger of public peace.[12]

Actual disturbance unnecessary. The crime of sedition is completed as **39.07** soon as the words are spoken or published whether or not any actual disturbance results. If A publishes a seditious libel because he has been bribed to do so or for any other reason, and immediately repents and successfully endeavours to counteract its effects, he is still guilty of sedition.[13]

Mens rea. In *John Grant and Ors*[14] the jury convicted some of the accused **39.08** of "sedition, in so far as [they] used language calculated to excite popular disaffection and resistance to lawful authority", and deliberately negatived any intention to produce such a result. It was argued that this rendered their verdict bad. The majority of the court rejected this argument and held that the use of words plainly calculated to cause disaffection constituted sedition whatever the accused's intention, motive or purpose. The Crown must show that the use of the words was intentional, in the sense that it was voluntary and deliberate, but it is no defence that the words so used were not intended to provoke disaffection.[15]

It appears also from *John Grant and Ors.* that sedition is a crime which may be committed either intentionally or recklessly, the use of words plainly calculated to lead to disaffection being usually reckless, since the accused in such a situation ought, as an ordinary man, to have realised the obvious results of his actions. Where the words are not plainly seditious in their tenor the accused's intention may be relevant, and an innocent motive a defence.[16]

---

[11] *cf. R. v. Sullivan* (1868) 11 Cox C.C. 44, 50; "The Lord Advocate's Address to the Muir Society", *supra.*

[12] See *Halsbury's Laws of England* (4th ed.), Vol. 11(1) (reissue, 1990), para. 89. See also the Public Order Act 1986, ss. 17–23; *infra*, para. 39.22 *et seq.*

[13] *cf. John Grant and Ors* (1848) J. Shaw 51, Lord Mackenzie at 97.

[14] *supra.*

[15] L.J.-C. Hope at 70 and 80, Lord Mackenzie at 96, Lord Moncreiff at 103–104.

[16] L.J.-C. Hope at 69–70, Lord Medwyn at 109.

ALLIED OFFENCES

The Terrorism Act 2000

39.09 Terrorism offences are now governed by the Terrorism Act 2000,[17] and
the more important of these offences are set out, or described, in the
paragraphs below. Unlike previous terrorism legislation,[18] the present
Act is a permanent enactment of a wide-ranging nature. Section 1 of the
2000 Act provides:

> "(1) In this Act "terrorism" means the use or threat of action
> where—
>   (a) the action falls within subsection (2),
>   (b) the use or threat is designed to influence the government or
>   to intimidate the public or a section of the public, and
>   (c) the use or threat is made for the purpose of advancing a
>   political, religious or ideological cause.
> (2) Action falls within this subsection if it—
>   (a) involves serious violence against a person,
>   (b) involves serious damage to property,
>   (c) endangers a person's life, other than that of the person
>   committing the action,
>   (d) creates a serious risk to the health or safety of the public or a
>   section of the public, or
>   (e) is designed seriously to interfere with or seriously to disrupt
>   an electronic system.
> (3) The use or threat of action falling within subsection (2) which
> involves the use of firearms or explosives is terrorism whether or not
> subsection (1)(b) is satisfied.
> (4) In this section—
>   (a) 'action' includes action outside the United Kingdom,
>   (b) a reference to any person or to property is a reference to any
>   person, or to property, wherever situated,
>   (c) a reference to the public includes a reference to the public of
>   a country other than the United Kingdom, and
>   (d) 'the government' means the government of the United King-
>   dom, or a Part of the United Kingdom or of a country other
>   than the United Kingdom.
> (5) In this Act a reference to action taken for the purposes of
> terrorism includes a reference to action taken for the benefit of a
> proscribed organisation."[19]

39.10   PROSCRIBED ORGANISATIONS: MEMBERSHIP OR SUPPORT. It is an offence
to belong or profess to belong to a proscribed organisation,[20] but a
person charged with such an offence has a defence if he proves[21] "that

---

[17] Hereinafter referred to as "the 2000 Act".

[18] For example, the Prevention of Terrorism (Temporary Provisions) Act 1989.

[19] An organisation is proscribed if it is listed in Sched. 2 to the 2000 Act or operates
under the same name as an organisation so listed: s.3(1). The Secretary of State may add
an organisation to, or remove one from, the list in Sched. 2: s.3(3)(a),(b); but under s.3(4),
he may add an organisation only if he believes it to be concerned in terrorism, as defined
in s.3(5), *i.e.* if it "(a) commits or participates in acts of terrorism, (b) prepares for
terrorism, (c) promotes or encourages terrorism, or (d) is otherwise concerned in
terrorism."

[20] See s.11 of the 2000 Act.

[21] See s.118 of the 2000 Act.

the organisation was not proscribed on the last (or only) occasion on which he became a member or began to profess to be a member" and that he has not participated in the activities of the organisation at any time since it became proscribed.[22] It is also an offence to invite support for a proscribed organisation, if that support is not confined to the provision of money or other property[23]; to arrange or manage, or assist in arranging or managing, a meeting[24] knowing that the function of that meeting is to support or further the activities of a proscribed organisation,[25] or that the meeting is to be addressed by a person who belongs or professes to belong to a proscribed organisation[26]; or, to address a meeting if the purpose of the address is "to encourage support for a proscribed organisation or to further its activities".[27]

Under section 13 of the 2000 Act, it is an offence for a person to wear an item of clothing, or wear, carry or display an article "in such a way or in such circumstances as to arouse reasonable suspicion that he is a member or supporter of a proscribed organisation".[28]

OFFENCES IN CONNECTION WITH MONEY OR PROPERTY. It is an offence **39.11** under the 2000 Act for a person to invite another to provide[29] money or other property where that person intends it to be used for the purposes of terrorism[30] or has reasonable cause to suspect that it may be so used; to receive money or other property where he intends it to be so used or has reasonable cause to suspect that it may be so used; or, to provide money or other property where he knows or has reasonable cause to suspect that it will or may be so used.[31]

It is also an offence for a person to use money or other property for the purposes of terrorism, or to possess money or other property intending it to be, or having reasonable cause to suspect that it may be, so used.[32] Entering into or becoming concerned in an arrangement, whereby money or other property is made or to be made available to another, knowing or having reasonable cause to suspect that it will or

---

[22] Section 11(2). Maximum penalty, on indictment, 10 years' and a fine; on summary conviction, six months' and a fine of the statutory maximum: s.11(3).

[23] Section 12(1). *Cf.* s.15, para. 39.11, *infra.*

[24] That is to say, a meeting of at least three persons, whether the public are admitted or not: s.12(5)(a).

[25] Section 12(2)(a), (b).

[26] Section 12(2)(c): there is a defence under s.12(4) if the meeting is one to which the public are not admitted (s.12(2)(5)(b)) and the accused proves (see s.118) that he had no reasonable cause to believe that the address would support or further the activities of a proscribed organisation.

[27] Section 12(3). Maximum penalty for any offence under s.12, on indictment, 10 years' and a fine, and, on summary conviction, six months' and a fine of the statutory maximum: s.12(6).

[28] Section 13(1). "Article" is not defined. An express power of arrest without warrant is conferred on the police in Scotland: s.13(2); and the maximum penalty on summary conviction is six months' and a fine of level 5 on the standard scale: s.13(3).

[29] "Provide" means give, lend or otherwise make available, whether for consideration or not: s.15(4).

[30] See s.1 of the 2000 Act: para. 39.09, *supra.*

[31] Section 15(1)–(3). Maximum penalty, on indictment, 14 years' and a fine, and, on summary conviction, six months' and a fine of the statutory maximum: s.22. There may also be forfeiture of the relevant money or other property: s.23.

[32] Section 16. Maximum penalty, as for offences under s.15: see n.31, *supra.*

may be used for the purposes of terrorism is made an offence under section 17[33] of the 2000 Act.

Section 18 of the 2000 Act provides:

"(1) A person commits an offence if he enters into or becomes concerned in an arrangement which facilitates the retention or control by or on behalf of another person of terrorist property[34]—

    (a) by concealment,

    (b) by removal from the jurisdiction,

    (c) by transfer to nominees, or

    (d) in any other way.

(2) It is a defence for a person charged with an offence under subsection (1) to prove[35] that he did not know and had no reasonable cause to suspect that the arrangement related to terrorist property."[36]

Under section 21 of the 2000 Act, a person does not commit an offence under sections 15 to 18 if he is acting with the express consent of a police constable, or he discloses on his own initiative and as soon as reasonably practicable to the police[37] his suspicions or belief (together with the information on which such suspicion or belief is based) that the money or property pertaining to a transaction or arrangement in which he was involved is terrorist property: it is also a defence under this section to any offence under sections 15 to 18[38] for the accused to prove[39] that he intended to make a disclosure of the kind set out above but had reasonable excuse for his failure to do so.[40]

Where a person in the course of a trade, profession, business or employment comes by information whereby he believes or suspects that another person has committed an offence[41] under sections 15 to 18 of the 2000 Act, and he fails to disclose that belief or suspicion and the

---

[33] Maximum penalty as for offences under s.15: see n.31, *supra*.

[34] "Terrorist property" is defined in s.14 of the 2000 Act as follows: "(1) . . . (a) money or other property which is likely to be used for the purposes of terrorism (including any resources of a proscribed organisation), (b) proceeds of the commission of acts of terrorism, and (c) proceeds of acts carried out for the purposes of terrorism. (2) In subsection (1) — (a) a reference to proceeds of an act includes a reference to any property which wholly or partly, and directly or indirectly, represents the proceeds of the act (including payments or other rewards in connection with its commission), and (b) the reference to an organisation's resources includes a reference to any money or other property which is applied or made available, or is to be applied or made available, for use by the organisation."

[35] See s.118.

[36] Maximum penalty as for offences under s.15: see n.31, *supra*.

[37] Or makes the disclosure in accordance with a disclosure procedure established by his employer: s.21(6).

[38] With the exception of an offence under s.15(1), *i.e.* inviting another to provide money or other property intending or having reasonable cause to suspect that it may be used for terrorism.

[39] See s.118.

[40] See s.21(5).

[41] Under s.19(7) of the 2000 Act, a person is to be treated as having committed such an offence if — "(a) he has taken an action [which includes making an omission: s.121] or been in possession of a thing, and (b) he would have committed an offence under one of those sections [*i.e.* ss. 15–18] if he had been in the United Kingdom at the time when he took the action or was in possession of the thing."

information on which it is based to a police constable as soon as reasonably practicable, he is guilty of an offence.[42]

OFFENCES IN CONNECTION WITH TERRORIST INVESTIGATIONS. Section 39 **39.12** of the 2000 Act provides:

"(1) Subsection (2) applies where a person knows or has reasonable cause to suspect that a constable is conducting or proposes to conduct a terrorist investigation.[43]

(2) The person commits an offence if he—

(a) discloses to another anything which is likely to prejudice the investigation, or

(b) interferes with material which is likely to be relevant to the investigation.

(3) Subsection (4) applies where a person knows or has reasonable cause to suspect that a disclosure has been or will be made under any of sections 19 to 21.[44]

(4) The person commits an offence if he—

(a) discloses to another anything which is likely to prejudice an investigation resulting from the disclosure under that section, or

(b) interferes with material which is likely to be relevant to an investigation resulting from the disclosure under that section.

(5) It is a defence for a person charged with an offence under subsection (2) or (4) to prove[45]—

(a) that he did not know and had no reasonable cause to suspect that the disclosure or interference was likely to affect a terrorist investigation, or

(b) that he had a reasonable excuse for the disclosure or interference.

(6) Subsections (2) and (4) do not apply to a disclosure which is made by a professional legal adviser—

(a) to his client or to his client's representative in connection with the provision of legal advice by the adviser to the client and not with a view to furthering a criminal purpose, or

(b) to any person for the purpose of actual or contemplated legal proceedings and not with a view to furthering a criminal purpose.

---

[42] Section 19(2); maximum penalty, on indictment, five years' and a fine, and, on summary conviction, six months' and a fine of the statutory maximum: s.19(8). Under s.19(3), there is a defence if the accused proves (see. s.118) that he had reasonable excuse for his failure; and under s.19(4) there is also a defence if the accused proves (see s.118) that he made the required disclosure under a procedure for doing so established by his employer. Where privilege attaches to information obtained by a professional legal adviser, there is no duty to disclose that information or the belief or suspicion to which it gives rise: s.19(5), (6).

[43] Under s.32 of the 2000 Act, "terrorist investigation" means an investigation of "(a) the commission, preparation or instigation of acts of terrorism [see s.1(1), above at n. 39.09], (b) an act which appears to have been done for the purposes of terrorism, (c) the resources of a proscribed organisation, (d) the possibility of making an order under s.3(3) [*i.e.*, adding to, removing from or otherwise amending the list of proscribed organisations], or (e) the commission, preparation or instigation of an offence under this Act." For "conducting" such an investigation, see subs. (8)(a), *infra*.

[44] Section 19 creates a duty to disclose relevant information; s.20 permits relevant disclosures to be made, notwithstanding rules of law to the contrary; and, s.21 provides defences to particular offences created under the Act where a person co-operates with the police or makes relevant disclosures: see generally para. 39.11, *supra*.

[45] See s.118.

(7) A person guilty of an offence under this section shall be liable—

(a) on conviction on indictment, to imprisonment for a term not exceeding five years, to a fine or to both, or

(b) on summary conviction, to imprisonment for a term not exceeding six months, to a fine not exceeding the statutory maximum or to both.

(8) For the purposes of this section—

(a) a reference to conducting a terrorist investigation includes a reference to taking part in the conduct of, or assisting, a terrorist investigation, and

(b) a person interferes with material if he falsifies it, conceals it, destroys it or disposes of it, or if he causes or permits another to do any of thoses things."

39.13   TERRORIST OFFENCES. It is an offence to provide (generally or to one or more specific persons[46]) or receive instruction or training in the making or use of firearms, explosives, or chemical, biological or nuclear weapons[47]: it is also an offence to invite[48] another to receive instruction or training where the receiving of such would be an offence or would be but for the fact that it is to take place abroad.[49] An accused who can prove[50] that his involvement is wholly for a purpose other than "assisting, preparing for or participating in terrorism" has a defence.[51]

Section 56 of the 2000 Act provides:

"(1) A person commits an offence if he directs, at any level, the activities of an organisation which is concerned in the commission of acts of terrorism.

(2) A person guilty of an offence under this section is liable on conviction on indictment to imprisonment for life."

Under section 57 of the 2000 Act, it is an offence to possess[52] an article[53] in circumstances which give rise to reasonable suspicion that it is possessed "for a purpose connected with the commission, preparation or instigation of an act of terrorism."[54]

It is an offence to collect or make a record of information of a kind likely to be of use to a person committing or preparing for an act of terrorism,[55] and also an offence to possess a document or record[56]

---

[46] Section 54(4)(a).

[47] Section 54(1),(2): biological, chemical and nuclear weapons are defined in s.55.

[48] See s.54(4)(b).

[49] Section 54(3). Maximum penalty for an offence under s.54 is, on indictment, 10 years' and a fine, or, on summary conviction, six months' and a fine of the statutory maximum: s.54(6); forfeiture may be ordered of anything which the court considers to have been in the accused's possession for purposes connected with the offence: s.54(7)–(9).

[50] See s.118.

[51] Section 54(5).

[52] Under s.57(3), "if it is proved that an article — (a) was on any premises at the same time as the accused, or (b) was on premises of which the accused was the occupier or which he habitually used otherwise than as a member of the public, the court may assume that the accused possessed the article, unless he proves [see s.118] that he did not know of its presence on the premises or that he had no control over it."

[53] This includes a substance: s.121.

[54] Section 57. Maximum penalty, on indictment, 10 years' and a fine, or, on summary conviction, six months' and a fine of the statutory maximum: s.57(4).

[55] Section 58(1)(a). For "terrorism", see s.1(1) of the 2000 Act, *supra* para. 39.09.

[56] This includes a photographic or electronic record: s.58(2).

containing such information.[57] An accused who proves[58] that he had reasonable excuse for what he did or what he possessed will have a defence.[59] In addition, a person commits an offence[60] if he incites another[61] to commit an act of terrorism[62] wholly or partly outside the United Kingdom, and the act if committed in Scotland would constitute one of a number of listed offences.[63]

Relative to terrorist bombing (according to the marginal note[64]), section 62 of the 2000 Act provides:

"(1) if—
  (a) a person does anything outside the United Kingdom as an act of terrorism or for the purposes of terrorism,[65] and
  (b) his action would have constituted the commission of one of the offences listed in subsection (2) if it had been done in the United Kingdom,
he shall be guilty of the offence.
(2) The offences referred to in subsection (1)(b) are—
  (a) an offence under section 2, 3 or 5 of the Explosive Substances Act 1883 (causing explosions, etc.),
  (b) an offence under section 1 of the Biological Weapons Act 1974 (biological weapons), and
  (c) an offence under section 2 of the Chemical Weapons Act 1996 (chemical weapons)."

Public meetings, processions and assemblies

Public meetings, processions and assemblies are lawful at common **39.14** law, provided they do not constitute a breach of the peace.

Public Meeting Act 1908. Section 1 of this Act[66] provides: **39.15**

"1.—(1) Any person who at a lawful public meeting acts in a disorderly manner for the purpose of preventing the transaction of the business for which the meeting was called together shall be guilty of an offence[67] . . .
(2) Any person who incites others to commit an offence under this section shall be guilty of a like offence."

The Act empowers a constable at the request of the chairman to take the name and address of any person causing a disturbance at a meeting, and

---

[57] Section 58(1)(b). Maximum penalty for either offence, on indictment, 10 years' and a fine, or, on summary conviction, six months' and a fine of the statutory maximum: s.58(4); forfeiture may also be ordered: s.58(5)–(7).

[58] See s.118.

[59] Section 58(3).

[60] Under s.61(1).

[61] Whether or not that other person is in the United Kingdom at the time of the incitement: s.61(4).

[62] See s.1(1) of the 2000 Act, *supra*, para. 39.09.

[63] That is to say, murder, assault to severe injury and reckless conduct causing actual injury: s.61(2). Under s.61(3), the maximum penalty for the statutory offence is the same as that for the corresponding common law listed offence.

[64] And see s.64(2), (3) and (6) which refer to the [United Nations] Convention for the Suppression of Terrorist Bombings of January 12, 1998.

[65] For "terrorism", see s.1(1), *supra*, para. 39.09.

[66] As amended by the Public Order Act 1936, s.6 and the Representation of the People Acts 1949 (Sched. 9) and 1983 (Sched. 8, para. 1).

[67] Maximum penalty on summary conviction six months' and a fine of level 5 on the standard scale: Criminal Procedure (Consequential Provisions) (Scotland) Act 1995, Sched. 2, Pt I.

makes it an offence to refuse to give one's name and address or to give them falsely.[68]

The Act does not apply to disturbances at election meetings which are dealt with in section 97 of the Representation of the People Act 1983.[69]

39.16 It is an offence under section 12(2) of the Terrorism Act 2000 for a person to arrange or manage, or assist in arranging or managing, a meeting if he knows that the function of the meeting is to support or further the activities of a proscribed organisation or that it is to be addressed by a person who belongs to or professes to belong to such an organisation. It is also an offence for a person to address a meeting when the purpose of his address is to encourage support for such an organisation or further its activities.[70]

39.17 *Public Order Act 1936.* POLITICAL ORGANISATIONS. This Act, as applied to Scotland, provides:

> "**1.**—(1) Subject as hereinafter provided, any person who in any public place or at any public meeting wears uniform signifying his association with any political organisation or with the promotion of any political object shall be guilty of an offence[71]:
>
> Provided that, if the chief officer of police is satisfied that the wearing of any such uniform as aforesaid on any ceremonial, anniversary, or other special occasion will not be likely to involve risk of public disorder, he may, with the consent of a Secretary of State, by order permit the wearing of such uniform on that occasion either absolutely or subject to such conditions as may be specified in the order . . .
>
> **2.**—(1) If the members or adherents of any association of persons, whether incorporated or not, are—
>
> (a) organised or trained or equipped for the purpose of enabling them to be employed in usurping the functions of the police or of the armed forces of the Crown; or
>
> (b) organised and trained or organised and equipped either for the purpose of enabling them to be employed for the use or display of physical force in promoting any political object, or in such manner as to arouse reasonable apprehension that they are organised and either trained or equipped for that purpose;
>
> then any person who takes part in the control or management of the association, or in so organising or training as aforesaid any members or adherents thereof, shall be guilty of an offence under this section[72]
>
> Provided that in any proceedings against a person charged with the offence of taking part in the control or management of such an association as aforesaid it shall be a defence to that charge to prove that he neither consented to nor connived at the organisation,

---

[68] Section 1(3); punishable by a fine of level 1 on the standard scale.

[69] *supra*, para 38.41.

[70] Section 12(3). See para. 39.10, *supra*.

[71] Maximum penalty three months' imprisonment and a fine of level 4 on the standard scale: s.7(2), as amended by Criminal Procedure (Consequential Provisions) (Scotland) Act 1995, Sched. 2, Pt II.

[72] Maximum penalty on indictment two years' and a fine, or, on summary conviction six months' and a fine of the prescribed sum: s.7(1).

training, or equipment of members or adherents of the association in contravention of the provisions of this section . . .

(6) Nothing in this section shall be construed as prohibiting the employment of a reasonable number of persons as stewards to assist in the preservation of order at any public meeting held upon private premises, or the making of arrangements for that purpose or the instruction of the persons to be so employed in their lawful duties as such stewards, or their being furnished with badges or other distinguishing signs."

It would appear that any article of clothing may constitute a uniform, if, (a) although worn by a single person, it is recognised as the uniform of some particular organisation, or (b) it is used to indicate that a group of men are together and in association, even if there is no proof that it has been previously so used. The fact that the uniform signifies a political association may be proved either from past use, or from the events to be seen on the occasion when the alleged uniform was worn.[73]

It is an offence under section 13 (1) of the Terrorism Act 2000 for a person in a public place to wear any item of clothing or wear, carry or display any article so as to arouse reasonable suspicion that he is a member or supporter of a proscribed organisation.[74]

Public Order Act 1986. CONTROL OF PROCESSIONS. Under section 12 of the **39.18** Public Order Act 1986,[75] where a public procession[76] is being held or persons are assembling to take part in an intended public procession,[77] the most senior-ranking police officer present at the scene (having had regard to the time, place, circumstances and route or proposed route) may (where he reasonably believes that the procession may result in serious public disorder, serious damage to property or serious disruption to the life of the community, or that the purpose of the organisers is the intimidation of others with a view to compelling them to refrain from doing what they have a right to do (or to do an act they have a right not to do)) give directions which impose such conditions[78] on the organisers

---

[73] *O'Moran v. D.P.P.* [1975] 1 Q.B. 864, Lord Widgery, C.J. at 873–874: dark berets, worn with dark glasses and dark pullover at I.R.A. funeral procession held to be a uniform signifying association with a political organisation.

[74] See *supra*, para. 39.10. Maximum penalty, on summary conviction, six months' and a fine of level 5 on the standard scale.

[75] Hereinafter referred to as "the 1986 Act".

[76] Defined in s.16 as a procession in a public place, *i.e.*, one in a road, within the meaning of the Roads (Scotland) Act 1984 (see ss. 151(1) and (3) thereof), or in any place to which the public has access at the material time, on payment or otherwise and whether as of right or by virtue of express or implied permission.

[77] In its application to Scotland, s.12 (see s.12(11)) does not extend to a situation where a procession is proposed to be held on a future occasion. Notification of most proposed public processions must be submitted (in accordance with ss. 62–64 of the Civic Government (Scotland) Act 1982, as amended by the Public Order Act 1986, Sched. 2, paras 3 and 4, the Local Government etc. (Scotland) Act 1994, Sched. 13, para. 129(4)–(6), and the National Parks (Scotland) Act 2000 (asp 10), Sched. 5, para. 9) to the relevant local authority, which, after consultation with the chief constable and (where applicable) the National Parks Authority, may prohibit the procession or allow it to proceed subject to conditions: it is an offence to hold, or refuse to desist from participating in, a procession where such notification has not been given (unless an exemption applies under s.62), or in contravention of an order prohibiting, or imposing conditions on, its being held: s.65(1), (2) of the 1982 Act, as amended by the enactments referred to above in relation to ss. 62–64.

[78] As to the route of the procession, or prohibiting it from entering any specified public place.

or participants which appear to him necessary to prevent such disorder, damage, disruption or intimidation. It is an offence under section 12(4) for an organiser of the procession,[79] or, under section 12(5), for a participant,[80] knowingly to fail to comply with such a condition, although it is a defence for him to prove that the failure arose from circumstances beyond his control. It is also an offence to incite another to commit an offence under section 12(5).[81]

39.19   CONTROL OF PUBLIC ASSEMBLIES. Under section 14 of the 1986 Act, where a public assembly[82] is being held or is intended to be held, and a senior police officer[83] reasonably believes that it may result in serious public disorder, serious damage to property or serious disruption to the life of the community, or that the purpose of the organisers is to intimidate[84] others with a view to compelling them to refrain from doing what they have a right to do, or to do what they have a right not to do, he may issue directions imposing on the organisers and participants such conditions as to the place where the assembly may be held (or continue to be held), its maximum duration, or the maximum number of persons who may constitute it,[85] as appear to him to be necessary to prevent such disorder, damage, disruption or intimidation. It is an offence under section 14(4) for an organiser[86] of such an assembly, or, under section 14(5), a participant[87] in such an assembly, knowingly to fail to comply with any condition so imposed; it is a defence, however, for him to prove that the failure arose from circumstances beyond his control. It is also an offence to incite another to commit an offence under section 14(5).[88]

39.20   PROHIBITION OF TRESPASSORY ASSEMBLIES. Under section 14A of the 1986 Act,[89] if a chief officer of police reasonably believes that an assembly[90] is intended to be held on land[91] to which the public[92] has no

---

[79] Maximum penalty, on summary conviction, three months' and fine of level 4 on the standard scale: s.12(8).

[80] Maximum penalty, on summary conviction, a fine of level 3 on the standard scale: s.12(9).

[81] Section 12(6), maximum penalty, on summary conviction, three months' and a fine of level 4 on the standard scale: s.12(10).

[82] That is to say, an assembly of 20 or more persons in a public place (see n.76, *supra*) which is wholly or partly open to the air: s.16. Where a person breaks away from such an assembly, at least in order to continue to prosecute its aims by entering a public place to which the assembly has been denied access by virtue of a direction given under the authority of s.14, he does not thereby form an "assembly" of fewer than 20 persons to which s.14 does not apply: *Broadwich v. Chief Constable of Thames Valley Police Authority* [2000] Crim. L.R. 924, Div. Ct.

[83] That is to say, the most senior police officer present where the assembly is being held, or the chief officer of police relative to an assembly intended to be held: s.14(2)(a), (b).

[84] It has been held in England that "intimidate" meant more than causing (conscious) discomfort to persons entering a foreign embassy to attend a reception there; for the concept of "intimidate" to be satisfied, there would require to have been shown an intention on the part of the accused to compel such persons not to enter the embassy at all: *Police v. Reid (Lorna)* [1987] Crim. L.R. 702.

[85] *Quaere*, if the maximum number permitted were to be fewer than 20.

[86] Maximum penalty, on summary conviction, three months' and fine of level 4 on the standard scale: s.12(8).

[87] Maximum penalty, on summary conviction, a fine of level 3 on the standard scale: s.12(9).

[88] Maximum penalty, on summary conviction, three months' and a fine of level 4 n the standard scale: s.12(8).

[89] Inserted by s.70 of the Criminal Justice and Public Order Act 1994.

[90] That is to say, an assembly of 20 or more persons: s.14A(9).

[91] That is to say, land in the open air: s.14A(9).

[92] Or a section of the public: s.14A(9).

right, or only a limited right,[93] of access, or that an assembly is likely to be held without the permission of the occupier[94] or to conduct itself in such a manner as to exceed the limits of any permission granted by him or of the public's right of access, and that that assembly may result in serious disruption to the life of the community, or, where the land or a building or monument on it is of historical, architectural, archaeological or scientific importance, in significant damage to the land, building or monument, he may apply to the council of the local government area of which the land in question forms part for an order prohibiting for a specified period the holding of all trespassory assemblies in the local government area or the part of it specified in the order. If the council in question makes the order, the effect will be to prohibit the holding of such an assembly on land to which the public has no right of access, or only a limited right, without the permission of the occupier, or so as to exceed any permission granted by him or the limits of the public's right of access: but no order may be made for a period greater than four days, or in an area exceeding the area of a circle with a radius of five miles from a specified centre.

It is an offence under section 14B[95] for a person to organise or take part in an assembly which he knows to be prohibited by an order made under section 14A.[96]

PLAYS. Section 6(1) of the Theatres Act 1968 provides: **39.21**

"Subject to section 7 [exceptions for certain performances] of this Act, if there is given a public performance of a play involving the use of threatening, abusive or insulting words or behaviour, any person who (whether for gain or not) presented or directed that performance shall be guilty of an offence under this section if—
(a) he did so with intent to provoke a breach of the peace; or
(b) the performance, taken as a whole, was likely to occasion a breach of the peace."[97]

Public Order Act 1986: Incitement of racial hatred

Racial hatred is dealt with in the Public Order Act 1986, section 17 of **39.22** which defines "racial hatred" as "hatred against a group of persons in Great Britain defined by reference to colour, race, nationality (including citizenship) or ethnic or national origins." Sections 18 to 23, as amended by section 164 of the Broadcasting Act 1990, create a number of offences

---

[93] That is to say, where access is restricted to use for a particular purpose (as, possibly, in the case of a highway or road; *cf. D.P.P. v. Jones* [1999] 2 A.C. 240, HL, *infra*, n.96): s.14A(9).

[94] That is to say, the person entitled to natural possession of the land: s.14A(9).

[95] Inserted by s.70 of the Criminal Justice and Public Order Act 1994: maximum penalty, on summary conviction, for organising such an assembly, three months' and a fine of level 4 on the standard scale, and, for taking part in such an assembly, a fine of level 3 on the standard scale: s.14B(5), (6).

[96] *cf. D.P.P. v. Jones* [1999] 2 A.C. 240, HL, where it was held (Lords Slynn of Hadley and Hope of Craighead diss.) that it was not a breach of a s.14A order for a peaceful assembly to be held on a highway adjacent to Stonehenge, since such conduct was within the public's right to use and enjoy a highway at common law, or, alternatively, that such conduct was protected by Art. 11 of the European Convention on Human Rights: see in particular, Lord Irvine of Lairg, L.C., at 257D, and 259B-G.

[97] Maximum penalty, on summary conviction, six months' and a fine of level 5 on the standard scale: s.6(2), as amended by the Criminal Procedure (Consequential Provisions) (Scotland) Act 1995, Sched. 2.

dealing with different ways of using or publishing "threatening, abusive or insulting words or behaviour intended or likely to stir up racial hatred" ("racial incitement").[98] Where a "programme service" is referred to in those sections, what is meant is a television or sound broadcasting service (including a satellite television service[99] and any digital sound programming service[1]) and includes advertisements and any item included in the service.[2]

39.23 USE OF WORDS OR BEHAVIOUR. Section 18 of the 1986 Act provides:

"(1) A person who uses threatening, abusive or insulting words or behaviour, or displays any written material which is threatening, abusive or insulting, is guilty of an offence if—
(a) he intends thereby to stir up racial hatred, or
(b) having regard to all the circumstances racial hatred is likely to be stirred up thereby.

(2) An offence under this section may be committed in a public or a private place, except that no offence is committed where the words or behaviour are used, or the written material is displayed, by a person inside a dwelling and are not heard or seen except by other persons in that or another dwelling.

(3) A constable may arrest without warrant anyone he reasonably suspects is committing an offence under this section.

(4) In proceedings for an offence under this section it is a defence for the accused to prove that he was inside a dwelling and had no reason to believe that the words or behaviour used, or the written material displayed, would be heard or seen by a person outside that or any other dwelling.

(5) A person who is not shown to have intended to stir up racial hatred is not guilty of an offence under this section if he did not intend his words or behaviour, or the written material, to be, and was not aware that it might be, threatening, abusive or insulting.

(6) This section does not apply to words or behaviour used, or written material displayed, solely for the purpose of being included in a programme included in a programme service."[3]

39.24 PUBLISHING OR DISTRIBUTING WRITTEN MATERIAL. Section 19 of the 1986 Act provides:

"(1) A person who publishes or distributes written material which is threatening, abusive or insulting is guilty of an offence if—
(a) he intends thereby to stir up racial hatred, or
(b) having regard to all the circumstances racial hatred is likely to be stirred up thereby.

---

[98] Maximum penalty for any offence under ss. 18–23 is, on indictment, two years' and a fine, or, on summary conviction, six months' and a fine of the statutory maximum: s.27(3).
[99] See the Broadcasting Act 1990, s.43, as substituted by the Television Broadcasting Regulations 1998 (S.I. 1998 No. 3196), Sched., para. 2.
[1] Within the meaning of Pt II of the Broadcasting Act 1996.
[2] See the Broadcasting Act 1990, ss. 2(5) (as amended by the Broadcasting Act 1996, Sched. 10, Pt I, para. 1(5)), 71(1) (as amended by the Broadcasting Act 1996, Sched. 10, para. 17 and the Satellite Television Service Regulations 1997 (S.I. 1997 No.1682), Sched. para. 10), 126(1) (as amended by the Broadcasting Act 1996, Sched. 10, para. 9), 201 (as amended by the Broadcasting Act 1996, Sched. 10, para. 11), and 202(1).
[3] For maximum penalty, see n.98, *supra*.

(2) In proceedings for an offence under this section it is a defence for an accused who is not shown to have intended to stir up racial hatred to prove that he was not aware of the content of the material and did not suspect, and had no reason to suspect, that it was threatening, abusive or insulting.

(3) References in this Part [*i.e.*, Part III] to the publication or distribution of written material are to its publication or distribution to the public or a section of the public."[4]

PUBLIC PERFORMANCE OF PLAYS. Section 20 of the 1986 Act penalises **39.25** the presenter or director of a play which is publicly performed and which contains threatening, abusive or insulting words or behaviour if he intends to stir up racial hatred thereby or in all the circumstances racial hatred is likely to be so stirred up. Performances given solely or primarily for the purposes of rehearsal, making recordings or enabling their inclusion in a programme service are excluded unless these are attended by persons not directly connected with the rehearsal, recording or enabling. A performer is not a director unless he performs other than as directed without reasonable excuse. It is a defence for a presenter or director who is shown not to have intended to stir up racial hatred to prove that he did not know and had no reason to suspect that the performance would involve the use of the offending words or behaviour, or that they were threatening, abusive or insulting, or that the circumstances of the performance would be such as were likely to stir up racial hatred.[5]

DISTRIBUTING OR PLAYING RECORDINGS. Section 21 penalises the dis- **39.26** tribution, showing or playing of a recording of visual images or sounds which are threatening, abusive or insulting, where they are intended or likely to stir up racial hatred. The section does not apply "to the showing or playing of a recording solely for the purposes of enabling the recording to be included in a programme service."[6] A defence, in similar terms to that contained in section 18(5),[7] is provided.[8]

PROGRAMMES INCLUDED IN PROGRAMME SERVICES. Section 22 of the **39.27** 1986 Act provides:

"(1) If a programme involving threatening, abusive or insulting visual images or sounds is included in a programme service, each of the persons mentioned in subsection (2) is guilty of an offence if—
(a) he intends thereby to stir up racial hatred, or
(b) having regard to all the circumstances racial hatred is likely to be stirred up thereby.
(2) The persons are—
(a) the person providing the programme service,
(b) any person by whom the programme is produced or directed, and
(c) any person by whom offending words or behaviour are used.

---

[4] For maximum penalty, see n.98, *supra*.
[5] For maximum penalty, see n.98, *supra*.
[6] See s.21(4).
[7] See para. 39.23, *supra*.
[8] Section 21(3). For maximum penalty, see n.98, *supra*.

(3) If the person providing the service, or a person by whom the programme was produced or directed, is not shown to have intended to stir up racial hatred, it is a defence for him to prove that—

(a) he did not know and had no reason to suspect that the programme would involve the offending material, and

(b) having regard to the circumstances in which the programme was included in a programme service, it was not reasonably practicable for him to secure the removal of the material.

(4) It is a defence for a person by whom the programme was produced or directed who is not shown to have intended to stir up racial hatred to prove that he did not know and had no reason to suspect—

(a) that the programme would be included in a programme service, or

(b) that the circumstances in which the programme would be so included would be such that racial hatred would be likely to be stirred up.

(5) It is a defence for a person by whom offending words or behaviour were used and who is not shown to have intended to stir up racial hatred to prove that he did not know and had no reason to suspect—

(a) that a programme involving the use of the offending material would be included in a programme service, or

(b) that the circumstances in which a programme involving the use of the offending material would be so included, or in which a programme so included would involve the use of the offending material, would be such that racial hatred would be likely to be stirred up.

(6) A person who is not shown to have intended to stir up racial hatred is not guilty of an offence under this section if he did not know, and had no reason to suspect, that the offending material was threatening, abusive or insulting."[9]

39.28   POSSESSION OF RACIALLY INFLAMMATORY WRITTEN MATERIAL OR RECORDINGS. The possession of racially inflammatory material is dealt with by section 23 of the 1986 Act which provides:

"(1) A person who has in his possession written material which is threatening, abusive or insulting, or a recording of visual images or sounds which are threatening, abusive or insulting, with a view to—

(a) in the case of written material, its being displayed, published, distributed, or included in a programme service, whether by himself or another, or

(b) in the case of a recording, its being distributed, shown, played, or included in a programme service, whether by himself or another,

is guilty of an offence if he intends racial hatred to be stirred up thereby or, having regard to all the circumstances, racial hatred is likely to be stirred up thereby.

---

[9] Subsections (7) and (8) are repealed by the Broadcasting Act 1990, s.164(3). For maximum penalty, see n.98, *supra*.

(2) For this purpose regard shall be had to such display, publication, distribution, showing, playing, or inclusion in a programme service as he has, or it may reasonably be inferred that he has, in view.

(3) In proceedings for an offence under this section it is a defence for an accused who is not shown to have intended to stir up racial hatred to prove that he was not aware of the content of the written material or recording and did not suspect, and had no reason to suspect, that it was threatening, abusive or insulting."[10]

Causing disaffection[11]

Aliens Restriction (Amendment) Act 1919. Section 3 of this Act provides: **39.29**

"(1) If any alien attempts or does any act calculated or likely to cause sedition or disaffection amongst any of Her Majesty's Forces or the Forces of Her Majesty's allies, or amongst the civilian population, he shall be liable on conviction on indictment to [ten years' imprisonment], or on summary conviction to [three months' imprisonment]."

Trade disputes

Trade Union and Labour Relations (Consolidation) Act 1992.[12] This Act **39.30** contains the modern law regarding trade unions and industrial disputes. At common law combinations of workmen, and perhaps also of employers, to alter wages were illegal,[13] but they were made lawful by a series of Acts beginning with the Combinations of Workmen Act 1825 and culminating in the Trade Disputes Act 1906. The 1992 Act still, however, makes certain actings in the course of trade disputes criminal.

BREACH OF CONTRACT INVOLVING INJURY. Section 240 of the 1992 Act **39.31** provides:

"(1) A person commits an offence who wilfully and maliciously breaks a contract of service or hiring, knowing or having reasonable cause to believe that the probable consequences of his so doing, either alone or in combination with others, will be—
  (a) to endanger human life or cause serious bodily injury, or
  (b) to expose valuable property, whether real or personal, to destruction or serious injury.

(2) Subsection (1) applies equally whether the offence is committed from malice conceived against the person endangered or injured or, as the case may be, the owner of the property destroyed or injured, or otherwise.

(3) A person guilty of an offence under this section is liable on summary conviction to imprisonment for a term not exceeding three months or to a fine not exceeding level 2 on the standard scale or both.

---

[10] For maximum penalty, see n.98, *supra*. (Subsection (4) of s.23 was repealed by the Broadcasting Act 1990, s.164(4)(c).)

[11] See also *supra*, para. 37.27, and for causing disaffection in the police, *infra*, para. 49.03.

[12] Hereinafter referred to as "the 1992 Act".

[13] Hume, i, 496; Burnett, Chap. XII.

(4) This section does not apply to seamen."

39.32   INTIMIDATION. Section 241 of the 1992 Act provides:

"(1) A person commits an offence who, with a view to compelling another person to abstain from doing or to do any act which that other person has a legal right to do or abstain from doing, wrongfully and without legal authority—

(a) uses violence to or intimidates that person or his wife or children, or injures his property, or

(b) persistently follows that person about from place to place,

(c) hides any tools, clothes, or other property owned or used by that person, or deprives him of or hinders him in the use thereof,

(d) watches or besets the house or other place where that person resides, works, carries on business or happens to be, or the approach to any such house or place, or

(e) follows that person with two or more other persons in a disorderly manner in or through any street or road.

(2) A person guilty of an offence under this section is liable on summary conviction to imprisonment for a term not exceeding six months or a fine not exceeding level 5 on the standard scale, or both.

(3) A constable may arrest without warrant anyone he reasonably suspects is committing an offence under this section."

This section, derived from section 7 of the Conspiracy and Protection of Property Act 1875, creates one offence, the various paragraphs merely setting out different ways in which that offence may be committed.[14]

The meanings of "persistently follows" and following "in a disorderly manner" in paragraphs (b) and (e) above were discussed in *Elsey v. Smith*,[15] where the "following" was done by a car on a motorway "in order to follow somebody else, and . . . in order to achieve that object . . . persistently [driving] near to that other person, in company with two other vehicles similarly engaged, and on occasions [altering] one's speed so as to require that other person to overtake."[16] One determined effort to follow over a substantial distance may constitute persistent following.[17] Following of a kind which is calculated to, and does, distress and harass, and which could have been restrained by interdict, is wrongful.[18] "Wrongful" means contrary to law, and an act which is protected from civil proceedings because it is carried out in an industrial dispute does not thereby cease to be wrongful for the purposes of a prosecution under section 241.[19]

---

[14] *Clarkson, etc. v. Stuart* (1894) 1 Adam 466; *Wilson and Ors v. Renton* (1909) 6 Adam 166.

[15] 1982 S.C.C.R. 218.

[16] *ibid.*, at 229.

[17] *ibid.*

[18] *ibid.*, L.J.-G. Emslie at 240.

[19] *Galt v. Philp*, 1983 J.C. 51, where it was also accepted that "watching and besetting" may be carried out from inside the premises in question. In *D.P.P. v. Fidler* [1992] 1 W.L.R. 91, it was held by a divisional court that since s.7 of the 1875 Act, as amended by the Trade Disputes Act 1906, used the word "compel" rather than the original term "persuade", the defendants' conduct (in attempting to dissuade women from entering an abortion clinic) fell outwith the section, there having been no evidence that any person had been or had been likely to be prevented from having an abortion there in consequence of such conduct.

INTIMIDATION. The threats employed must be serious, and cause in the **39.33** victim reasonable apprehension of violence to himself or his family.[20] The offence is completed when the threats are uttered, whether or not they succeed in their object.[21]

STRIKE THREATS. Threats to strike do not constitute intimidation under **39.34** this section.[22]

PICKETING. Section 220 of the 1992 Act makes peaceful picketing **39.35** lawful. It provides:

"(1) It is lawful for a person in contemplation or furtherance of a trade dispute to attend—
   (a) at or near his own place of work, or
   (b) if he is an official of a trade union, at or near the place of work of a member of the union whom he is accompanying and whom he represents,
for the purpose only of peacefully obtaining or communicating information, or peacefully persuading any person to work or abstain from working.[23]
(2) If a person works or normally works—
   (a) otherwise than at any one place, or
   (b) at a place the location of which is such that attendance there for a purpose mentioned in subsection (1) is impracticable,
his place of work for the purposes of that subsection shall be any premises of his employer from which he works or from which his work is administered.
(3) In the case of a worker not in employment where—
   (a) his last employment was terminated in connection with a trade dispute, or
   (b) the termination of his employment was one of the circumstances giving rise to a trade dispute,
in relation to that dispute his former place of work shall be treated for the purposes of subsection (1) as being his place of work.
(4) A person who is an official of a trade union by virtue only of having been elected or appointed to be a representative of some of the members of the union shall be regarded for the purposes of subsection (1) as representing only those members; but otherwise an official of a union shall be regarded for those purposes as representing all its members."

Conspiracy. Section 243 of the 1992 Act provides that in Scotland a **39.36** conspiracy by two or more persons to do an act "in contemplation or furtherance of a trade dispute" should not be indictable if the act would

---

[20] *Agnew v. Munro* (1891) 2 White 611; *R. v. Jones* [1974] I.C.R. 310.

[21] *ibid.*

[22] *Gibson v. Lawson, Curran v. Treleaven* (1891) 2 Q.B. 545 which involved threats to strike unless a workman joined a particular Union.

[23] *cf.* "To summarise, a mass picket ceases to be legal when collectively it becomes a riotous or threatening mob, and individual pickets are criminally liable for any conduct amounting to a breach of the peace. In addition the police may in the execution of their duty clear any obstruction of the street and take such steps as are necessary, including dispersal of the pickets, to prevent a (reasonably apprehended) breach of the peace. Physical obstruction of the police in such circumstances is also an offence": P.J. Wallington, "The Case of the Longannet Miners and the Criminal Liability of Pickets" (1972) 1 I.L.J. 219, 225.

not be criminal if done by one person, but this is probably only declaratory of the common law.[24]

39.37   TRADE DISPUTE. Section 244 of the 1992 Act provides:

"(1) In this Part [Part V] 'trade dispute' means a dispute between workers and their employer which relates wholly or mainly to one or more of the following—

(a) terms and conditions of employment, or the physical conditions in which any workers are required to work;

(b) engagement or non-engagement, or termination or suspension of employment or the duties of employment, of one or more workers;

(c) allocation of work or the duties of employment between workers or groups of workers;

(d) matters of discipline;

(e) a worker's membership or non-membership of a trade union;

(f) facilities for officials of trade unions; and

(g) machinery for negotiation or consultation, and other procedures, relating to any of the above matters, including the recognition by employers or employers' associations of the right of a trade union to represent workers in any such negotiation or consultation or in the carrying out of such procedures.

(2) A dispute between a Minister of the Crown and any workers shall, notwithstanding that he is not the employer of those workers, be treated as a dispute between those workers and their employer if the dispute relates to matters which—

(a) have been referred for consideration by a joint body on which, by virtue of provision made by or under any enactment, he is represented, or

(b) cannot be settled without him exercising a power conferred on him by or under an enactment.

(3) There is a trade dispute even though it relates to matters occurring outside the United Kingdom, so long as the person or persons whose actions in the United Kingdom are said to be in contemplation or furtherance of a trade dispute relating to matters occurring outside the United Kingdom are likely to be affected in respect of one or more of the matters specified in subsection (1) by the outcome of the dispute.

(4) An act, threat or demand done or made by one person or organisation against another which, if resisted, would have led to a trade dispute with that other, shall be treated as being done or made in contemplation of a trade dispute with that other, notwithstanding that because that other submits to the act or threat or accedes to the demand no dispute arises.

(5) In this section—

'employment' includes any relationship whereby one person personally does work or performs services for another; and

'worker', in relation to a dispute with an employer, means—

(a) a worker employed by that employer; or

(b) a person who has ceased to be so employed if his employment was terminated in connection with the

---

[24] See Vol. I, para. 6.65.

dispute or if the termination of his employment was one of the circumstances giving rise to the dispute."

Aliens Restriction (Amendment) Act 1919. Section 3(2) of this Act **39.38** provides:

"If any alien promotes or attempts to promote industrial unrest in any industry in which he has not been bona fide engaged for at least two years immediately preceding in the United Kingdom, he shall be liable on summary conviction to [three months' imprisonment]."

CHAPTER 40

MOBBING

A mob is a group of persons acting together for a common illegal **40.01**
purpose, which they effect or attempt to effect by violence, intimidation,
or a demonstration of force, and in breach of the peace and to the alarm
of the lieges,[1] and it is a crime to form part of a mob. In *Coleman v.
H.M. Advocate*,[2] Lord Coulsfield remarked that mobbing "far from
providing a simple means of dealing with cases of group violence . . .
involves embarking on an area of law which is full of uncertainties and
narrow distinctions."[3] He did not think, however, that the limited
discussion of the older authorities by counsel had provided a sufficient
basis upon which the court might embark on a reconsideration of the
extent and limits of the crime.[4]

Numbers. No fixed number is necessary to constitute a mob.[5] Whether **40.02**
the group is large enough in any case to constitute a mob is a question of
fact depending on circumstances, and in particular on the nature of the
group's behaviour.[6] In one case in which there was no actual outbreak of
violence but only intimidation, 17 people were held to be sufficient to
constitute a mob, and it was suggested that five would be too few.[7]

Purpose. The most important distinction between mobbing and breach of **40.03**
the peace is that the former requires a common purpose.[8] The purpose
need not, however, be preconceived or planned; it can arise in the course
of an originally spontaneous and unorganised commotion.[9] Again, the
purpose need not be articulate or clearly present in the minds of the
members of the mob — provided they act with a sense of common
purpose they are guilty of mobbing. In *Michael Hart and Ors*[10] the charge
was of forming part of a mob assembled for the purpose of assaulting
Orangemen, "or for some other unlawful purpose to the prosecutor
unknown". The anti-Orange purpose was not proved, and the accused

---

[1] *Sloan v. Macmillan*, 1922 J.C. 1; *Myles Martin and Ors (Borniskitaig Crofters)* (1886) 1
White 297, Lord Muir at 303; *John Gordon Robertson and Ors* (1842) 1 Broun 152, L.J.-C.
Hope at 192–193; *Hancock v. H.M. Advocate*, 1981 J.C. 74, Lord Cameron at 81–82, and
L.J.-G. Emslie at 86.
[2] 1999 S.C.C.R. 87.
[3] *ibid.*, at 111C.
[4] *ibid.*, at 109F-G. Apart from what is said in *Coleman* itself and in the case of
Hancock v. H.M. Advocate, 1981 J.C. 74, there is little modern authority on mobbing.
[5] Hume, i, 416; Alison, i, 510; Macdonald, p.132.
[6] *Sloan v. Macmillan*, *supra*, L.J.-C. Scott Dickson at 6.
[7] *ibid.*, Lord Salvesen at 6–7.
[8] Hume, i, 418; Alison, i, 513; Macdonald, p.132; *Francis Docherty and Ors* (1841) 2
Swin. 635, L.J.-C. Hope at 638. See also *Hancock v. H.M. Advocate*, 1981 J.C. 74.
[9] Hume, i, 418; Alison, i, 513; Macdonald, p.132; *Alex. Orr and Ors* (1856) 2 Irv. 502,
L.J.-C. Hope at 506; *Hancock v. H.M. Advocate*, 1981 J.C. 74, Lord Cameron at 84.
[10] (1854) 1 Irv. 574.

were convicted on the alternative averment. Lord Justice-Clerk Hope directed the jury that they might be convicted on that averment although, "If any of the people here engaged had been asked what was their purpose, they would probably have been much surprised. They were only transporting to this country some of those practices to which they were accustomed at Donnybrook fair."[11]

40.04   THE NATURE OF THE PURPOSE. *Michael Hart and Ors*[12] is authority for the proposition that any unlawful behaviour is sufficient to found a charge of mobbing.[13] In practice, however, cases of mobbing have often included a specific ulterior purpose, such as interference with courts or their officers[14]; furthering trade[15] or religious disputes,[16] asserting what are believed to be local rights[17]; or engaging in election riots,[18] but a common purpose to do violence to person or property, for no ulterior purpose, is sufficient.[19] It is probably enough simply to form a common purpose to create a disturbance sufficiently severe to amount to mobbing.[20] In the absence of any antecedent agreement amongst those alleged to form part of a mob, however, where there is but a series "of unrelated events and episodes arising out of entirely accidental encounters which themselves form no part of a recognisable pattern",[21] it may be impossible to infer that there is any common purpose at all.[22]

Where there is a common purpose it may shift, however, during the course of the mob's activities, as, for example, where an initial purpose limited to the attacking and injuring of particular persons develops to the stage where one of those persons is murdered.[23]

40.05   ILLEGAL. The purpose must be illegal, but this refers to what the mob do, and not to their ulterior purpose. It is mobbing to use violence and intimidation of sufficient proportions in order to achieve a lawful object, such as the removal of an illegal toll or barrier,[24] or perhaps even to

---

[11] At 577–578.

[12] (1854) 1 Irv. 574.

[13] See also *Geo. Smith and Ors* (1848) Ark. 473.

[14] *Myles Martin and Ors (Borniskitaig Crofters)* (1886) 1 White 297; *McLean and Ors (Tiree Crofters)* (1886) 1 White 232; *John Nicolson and Ors (Garralpin Crofters)* (1887) 1 White 307; *John McDonald and Ors (Herbusta Crofters)* (1887) 1 White 315: attacks on sheriff officers by crofters; *John Gordon Robertson and Ors* (1842) 1 Broun 152: obstructing a Presbytery; *Nicholson and Shearer* (1847) Ark. 264; *Geo. McLellan and Ors* (1842) 1 Broun 478; *John Harper and Ors* (1842) 1 Broun 441; *John Urquhart and Ors* (1844) 2 Broun 13: rescuing prisoners.

[15] *Sloan v. Macmillan*, 1922 J.C. 1; *Wm Gibson and Ors* (1842) 1 Broun 485; *Wm Roy and Ors* (1834) and *John McNaught and Ors, John Logue and Ors* (1834) all Bell's Notes.

[16] *Alex. Orr and Ors* (1856) 2 Irv. 502; *Alex. Gollan and Ors* (1883) 5 Couper 317: objection to Sabbath-breaking.

[17] *Daniel Blair, Henry Scott and John Fraser* (1868) 1 Couper 168; *Thos Wild and Ors* (1854) 1 Irv. 552: attacking toll gates.

[18] *Jas Farquhar and Ors* (1861) 4 Irv. 28; *Jas Cairns and Ors* (1837) 1 Swin. 597.

[19] *Michael Hart and Ors, supra.*

[20] See *infra.*

[21] *Hancock v. H.M. Advocate*, 1981 J.C. 74, Lord Cameron at 84.

[22] *ibid.*, Lord Cameron at 84–85.

[23] See *Coleman v. H.M. Advocate*, 1999 S.C.C.R. 87, esp. L.J.-C. Cullen at 101C–D.

[24] Macdonald, p.132; *Alex. Macphie and Ors* (1823) Alison, i, 512; *McDonald and Ors v. Mackay* (1842) 1 Broun 435. *Daniel Blair, Henry Scott and John Fraser* (1868) 1 Couper 168, was a decision on the particular wording of the charge; in so far as it may purport to require an illegal ulterior purpose for mobbing it is wrong. See also *Hugh Macdonald and Ors* (1823) Alison, i, 512: an attempt to prevent a minister entering his church because his appointment was believed to be wrongful.

carry out an order of court as where a messenger-at-arms unnecessarily seeks assistance from a group of people who behave riotously.[25]

BREACH OF THE PEACE. Mobbing is usually thought of as involving an **40.06** actual and tumultuous disturbance of the public peace,[26] but this is not a necessary element in the crime. It has been held to be mobbing merely to bar the entry to a church "by dense numbers, and by refusing to move, though there were no noise nor other acts."[27] In *Sloan v. Macmillan*[28] 17 men went during a coal strike to a mine in order to stop some volunteers working there; five of the 17 went into the pit and told the volunteers that the pit was surrounded by hundreds of desperate men whom they were having difficulty in controlling; as a result the volunteers were overawed and the strikers were able to draw the fires and prevent further work. This was held to be mobbing, since it consisted in intimidation by numbers for an illegal purpose.

Mobbing may also be committed before the mob have begun to carry out their purpose of tumult or intimidation. The crime is completed once the mob have assembled in order to carry out their illegal purpose, or at least as soon as they have begun to make their way to the place where they intend to carry it out, even if they are intercepted and prevented from creating any disturbance, or give up their purpose on finding unexpected difficulties in the way of its fulfilment.[29]

INTIMIDATION. Conversely, not every breach of the peace even by a **40.07** numerous group who might be said to have a common aim is mobbing. The essence of mobbing is violence and/or intimidation. A noisy crowd at a football match, or even at an election, is not a mob unless and until it begins to behave in an intimidating fashion.[30] Where there is no ulterior purpose which the mob seek to achieve by intimidation, their actings must probably be such as to intimidate and alarm the lieges in general. A street fight between rival gangs, for example, or an attack by a gang on one or two victims would not normally be treated as mobbing unless it was accompanied by such general tumult as to alarm or terrorise the neighbourhood, but there have been a number of late twentieth century cases where gang fights have been of such a kind as to cause alarm to the lieges and a charge of mobbing has been sustained.[31]

Mobbing and sedition. Hume distinguishes mobbing from sedition by **40.08** reference to the general public nature of the latter as against the private nature of the former.[32] A riot aimed at electing a particular Member of Parliament would probably be treated as mobbing,[33] while a riot for the purpose of effecting a general reform, such as the extension or restriction of the suffrage, would be sedition. It is, however, probably open to

[25] Hume, i, 417; Alison, i, 511.
[26] *cf.* the indictments in most of the cases.
[27] *John Gordon Robertson and Ors* (1842) 1 Broun 152, L.J.-C. Hope at 192.
[28] 1922 J.C. 1.
[29] Hume, i, 419–420; Alison, i. 517; *John Fraser* (1784) Hume, i, 420.
[30] Hume, i, 416–417; Alison, i, 511; *Jas Farquhar and Ors* (1861) 4 Irv. 28.
[31] *cf. Coleman v. H.M. Advocate*, 1999 S.C.C.R. 87, where Lord Coulsfield (at 111D) was critical of the use of mobbing by the Crown in the circumstances of the case, his view being that "there was no necessity to do so and in which, as the event shows, to do so risked nothing but an increase in confusion and possible prejudice to the outcome of the trial."
[32] Hume, i, 418.
[33] Alison, i, 515–516.

the Crown to proffer the lesser charge of mobbing even in circumstances which would justify a conviction for sedition.[34]

40.09 *Mobbing and picketing.* Section 220 of the Trade Union and Labour Relations (Consolidation) Act 1992 does not legalise any behaviour which constitutes mobbing.[35]

Art and part in mobbing

40.10   Most pre-1887 indictments for mobbing contain two charges in the major proposition — a charge of mobbing and a separate charge of assault or fire-raising or whatever particular crime is involved; there was usually only one minor proposition but it covered both charges and concluded by alleging that the accused, for example, did "form part of the said mob . . . and were actively engaged with, and did aid and abet the said mob . . . in the commission of the foresaid unlawful acts of mobbing and rioting and of assault."[36] In such indictments the acts of assault or fire-raising are in effect libelled in two ways — as aggravations of or incidents in the mobbing charge, and as separate crimes, and although convictions for the specific crime alone were rare, convictions for mobbing only, or for both mobbing and the specific crime, were frequent. In considering the responsibility of any member of a mob for any criminal act which occurs in the course of the riot this distinction must be kept in mind. Unfortunately, the style of charge adopted in modern cases of mobbing (*i.e.*, that the accused formed part of a riotous mob of evilly disposed persons and did various criminal acts such as assault, breach of the peace and even murder)[37] lends itself to the obfuscation of the distinction such that where, for example, the accused are convicted "as libelled", it is uncertain whether they have been convicted of mobbing alone (to which the various criminal acts are aggravations) or of mobbing *and* those various acts as separate crimes. Where the verdict of the jury discriminates amongst the accused, such that all are convicted of mobbing but individual accused are found guilty or acquitted of different combinations of libelled criminal acts, the confusion is exacerbated and may (at least in cases where the adoption of a common purpose is dependent on what can be inferred from the criminal acts libelled) lead to the quashing of the convictions on appeal.[38]

40.11 *The substantive crime.* Responsibility for a substantive charge of assault or fire-raising, or any other crime, should depend on the ordinary law of art and part, and should be judged in the same way as if the substantive

---

[34] *cf. John Duncan and Ors* (1843) 1 Broun 512, where a plea of guilty to breach of the peace was accepted.

[35] See *supra*, para. 39.35.

[36] *Myles Martin and Ors (Borniskitaig Crofters)* (1868) 1 White, 297. *Cf. Alex. Orr and Ors* (1856) 2 Irv. 502; *Jas Thomson and Ors* (1837) 1 Swin. 532; *Jas Cairns and Ors* (1837) *ibid.* 597; and see *Thos Wild and Ors* (1854) 1 Irv. 552 where the assault charge was withdrawn after an objection that the minor set forth no acts of assault as committed by the accused, and *John Harper and Ors* (1842) 1 Broun 441, where an averment of theft in the minor was struck out because the major did not libel theft. See also *Jas Gavin and Ors* (1865) 5 Irv. 82; *Michael Currie and Ors* (1864) 4 Irv. 578; *Wm Gibson and Ors* (1842) 1 Broun 485.

[37] See, *e.g.*, *Hancock v. H.M. Advocate*, 1981 J.C. 74; *Coleman v. H.M. Advocate*, 1999 S.C.C.R. 87.

[38] See *Hancock v. H.M. Advocate*, 1981 J.C. 74.

charge stood on its own and was not allied to a charge of mobbing. A might therefore be acquitted of assault, but be convicted of forming part of a mob whose actings are alleged to have included acts of assault[39]: his responsibility for these acts would then be limited to responsibility as a person forming part of an illegal mob which indulged in them, and would not extend to responsibility for them as substantive crimes.[40] Where, however, A's participation in the assault is such as to satisfy the ordinary rules of art and part, he might be convicted both of mobbing and of assault.[41]

Mobbing. The ordinary rules of art and part apply to mobbing, in **40.12** addition to the special rules regarding mobbing.[42] A person who organises or arranges for a riot, or provides supplies for rioters, may be guilty of mobbing although he was not himself present at the time of the riot.[43] And a person who is the leader of a mob may be guilty of acts committed by the mob after he has left them.[44]

PRESENCE. Prior to *Coleman v. H.M. Advocate*,[45] the view was taken **40.13** (based on various dicta[46]) that a person might also be held responsible for everything done by a mob, including any assault or other criminal conduct, and guilty of mobbing in respect thereof, on account of his presence in the mob although such presence would not necessarily have been sufficient to make him art and part guilty of a specific crime in relation to any assault or other crime committed by the mob.

Thus in *Myles Martin and Ors*[47] Lord Mure concluded his charge to the jury in a case of mobbing and rioting and assault on a sheriff in the execution of his duty by saying:

> "If you are satisfied that the prisoners formed part of a mob, whose object was to intercept, and even attack the officers of the law in the discharge of their duty and were aware of that object, you will be entitled in law to find they were art and part guilty of the acts of the mob, whether by mobbing and rioting, or of assault, although they may not be proved to your satisfaction to have been actual participators in the assault. If, on the other hand, you should have doubts whether the accused or any of them, though among the mob and engaged with them generally in their illegal rioting, were aware of the intention of the mob to assault the Sheriff, and are of opinion

---

[39] *Alex. Orr and Ors* (1856) 2 Irv. 503; *Martin, supra*; *Thos Marshall and Ors* (1824) Alison, i, 525; *Robert McCallum and Ors* (1825) and *Ralph Forrester* (1831) both Alison, i, 521.

[40] It would now be competent to convict a person of assault on an indictment which charged only mobbing but averred acts of assault by the mob: see Vol. I, paras 6.60–6.62.

[41] *cf.* Hume, i, 427; *Jas, Cairns and Ors* (1837) 1 Swin. 597, Lord Mackenzie at 605. *Lawtie and Ors*, High Court at Aberdeen, Feb. 1975, unrep'd suggests that there should be a conviction for the specific crime only when the mobbing is not established — Transcript of Judge's charge, 53. In the same case Lord Stott held that a conviction for breach of the peace was not competent on a charge of mobbing which averred conduct "in breach of the public peace", including shouting and swearing, but this seems to be contrary to the view taken in conspiracy cases: Vol. I, paras 6.60–6.62.

[42] *cf. Coleman v. H.M. Advocate*, 1999 S.C.C.R. 87, Lord Coulsfield at 111B–C.

[43] Hume, i, 420–421; Alison, i, 518–519; Macdonald, p.135.

[44] Macdonald, p.135; *Nicholson and Shearer* (1847) Ark. 264.

[45] 1999 S.C.C.R. 87.

[46] See *infra*.

[47] (1886) 1 White 297, at 305–306.

they were not actual participators in that assault, you may, while finding them guilty of mobbing and rioting as charged, consider yourselves justified in finding them not guilty of the assault."

Again, in *Lawtie and Ors*[48] Lord Stott put it as follows:

"Now, if the Crown can bring home a Charge of mobbing and rioting, it has this peculiar and quite serious consequence, that anyone who knowingly forms part of the rioting mob is held responsible in law for everything the mob does as a mob while he is a member of it. Once it is proved against you that you formed part of a riotous mob, you will be responsible in law, not only for what you do yourself, but also for any assault on persons or property which is committed at the time you are part of the mob by any others in the mob as members of the rioting mob."

Thus, the question of whether anyone present with a mob was liable for criminal acts committed not by himself but by other persons who were members of that mob was to be answered solely, it appeared, by determining whether by his presence he "knowingly" formed part of it. If he did thus form part of it, he was apparently liable for each and every crime committed by the mob or any particular member of it. The basis for this rule was not entirely clear.

It is true, of course, that the essence of mobbing is the coming together of a large group of people who endeavour to carry out their purpose by force of numbers, and everyone who swells their numbers helps them to effect their purpose. As Alison says:

"The circumstance which renders a mob so dangerous is, that it implies a large convocation of disorderly persons, and of course not only accumulates a force generally irresistible and always formidable to individuals, but puts them in a situation where the passions are most strongly excited, and the contagion of violence becomes most difficult to be withstood. For this reason all are held to be art and part in the enterprise, who, by their mere presence, add to the terror and intimidation which the acts of the more violent are calculated to inspire."[49]

The rule may also have been predicated on the difficulty of distinguishing one member of the group from another. As Lord Stott put it:

"You see, when you have a riot going on and damage is done to person or property it may be almost impossible, may it not, to say who precisely in the mob is responsible for what particular item of injury or damage is done, and the theory of the law as I understand it is that it is a good citizen's duty — if he knows there is a riot going on — to keep out of it and if he chooses not to keep out of it then he must just take the consequences."[50]

Presence, however, must be presence as one of the mob, and not as a mere spectator or by being accidentally caught up in the mob.[51] The

---

[48] High Court at Aberdeen, Feb. 1975, unrep'd, Transcript of Judge's charge, 4. See also the trial judge's charge to the jury in *Coleman v. H.M. Advocate*, 1999 S.C.C.R. 87, at 90–92.

[49] Alison, i, 518; *cf. Murison and Ors* (1813) Alison, i, 521; *Robt McCallum and Ors* (1852) *ibid.*; *Thos Kettle and Ors* (1831) *ibid.*

[50] *Lawtie and Ors, supra*, 5.

[51] Hume, i, 422; *Samuel McLachlan* (1831) Bell's Notes 108.

question is always *"Quo animo* was this man there?"[52] It has been said that what is required is "Presence . . . in order to countenance what is done",[53] and this appears to accord with the modern law. As Lord Justice-General Emslie said in *Hancock v. H.M. Advocate*[54]:

> "A mob is essentially a combination of persons, sharing a common criminal purpose, which proceeds to carry out that purpose by violence, or by intimidation by sheer force of numbers. A mob has, therefore, a will and a purpose of its own, and all members of the mob contribute by their presence to the achievement of the mob's purpose, and to the terror of its victims, even where only a few directly engage in the commission of the specific unlawful acts which it is the mob's common purpose to commit. Where there has assembled a mob which proceeds to behave as a mob a question may arise whether all those present when it acts to achieve its common purpose are truly members of the mob or mere spectators. Membership of a mob is not to be inferred from proof of mere presence at the scene of its activities. The inference of membership is, however, legitimate if there is evidence that an individual's presence is a 'countenancing' or contributory presence, *i.e.*, if his presence is for the purpose of countenancing or contributing to the achievement of the mob's unlawful objectives."

In practice, almost any prolonged presence in a mob will be regarded as a "countenancing" or "contributory" presence in the mobbing. Every citizen has a duty to assist the authorities to keep the peace, or at least to withdraw himself from any mob, and his failure to do so raises a strong inference that he is a participant in the mob.[55] This does not explain, however, why a person who is present in such a "countenancing" capacity should thus be made liable for *all* criminal acts perpetrated by members of the mob other than himself, and indeed the modern law does not provide unqualified support for such a rule.[56]

PRESENCE AND LIABILITY FOR PARTICULAR ACTS OF A MOB. It appears **40.14** now to be accepted that qualifying presence in a mob[57] leads to guilt not only of mobbing but also of "such outrages as are the natural results of the common enterprize, and which all who engaged in it must have made up their minds to be indifferent to, when they once concurred in its adoption."[58] As Alison proceeds to say, by way of illustration:

> "Thus, if a mob repair to a warehouse of grain, with intent to compel the dealer to sell at their own price, certainly all the measures calculated to constrain or intimidate his will are chargeable upon all those present, as throwing stones, breaking open his doors, threatening or molesting his own or his servants' persons, or the like".[59]

---

[52] *ibid. Cf.* Macdonald, p.133; *Alex. Orr and Ors* (1856) 2 Irv. 502, L.J.-C. Hope at 506; *Thos Wild and Ors* (1854) 1 Irv. 552, Lord Cowan at 559.

[53] *John Gordon Robertson and Ors* (1842) 1 Broun 152, L.J.-C. Hope at 194.

[54] 1981 J.C. 74, at 86.

[55] *Lawtie and Ors, supra; cf. Jas Cairns and Ors* (1837) 1 Swin. 597, L.J.-C. Boyle at 609–610.

[56] See para. 40.14, *infra*.

[57] See para. 40.13, *supra*.

[58] Alison, i, 524, quoted with approval by L.J.-C. Cullen in *Coleman v. H.M. Advocate*, 1999 S.C.C.R. 87, at 100D.

[59] Alison, i, 524.

A fortiori, if the mob's purpose is "a declared intention to burn a certain house, or kill a certain person, and they carry their design into effect, all are guilty of the fire-raising or murder, though they are not the very persons who inflicted the wounds or applied the torch."[60]

Where, however, as in *Coleman v. H.M. Advocate*,[61] the "declared intention" of the mob is to assault a particular individual or family and the mob arms itself with weapons which include knives and swords, and where one of the mob's victims is murdered by stab wounds inflicted by particular members of that mob, whether a person other than those particular members can be convicted of that murder because of his presence with the mob depends not only on whether his presence was a "countenancing" one but also on whether it can be shown that he adopted the enhanced common purpose when it became a murderous purpose: if that cannot be shown (and it must be difficult to show it in the absence on his part of any active participation in the killing), he is not guilty of the murder, although he may be guilty of mobbing.[62] As Lord Justice-Clerk Cullen said in *Coleman*[63]:

> "I consider that [counsel for Coleman] was well founded in his submission . . . that the trial judge had failed to give the jury accurate or adequate directions in relation to the distinction between guilt on the part of a participant in respect of events naturally occurring in the course of the mob's activities, and those actings which might properly be regarded as special to one or more members of the mob."

The distinction to be observed is, therefore, that between criminal acts of the mob which are the natural consequence of its common purpose and criminal acts which are "special", in the sense that they lie outwith the original purpose. As Alison remarked,[64] in relation to the rule that all in a mob are guilty of criminal acts which are the natural result of the common purpose:

> "It will not hold, therefore, with separate and independent acts of violence, as are not so much the object or natural and usual

---

[60] *ibid.*, Alison proceeds to cite the example of the Porteous Mob, in respect of which "the guilt of the murder was not peculiar to him who put the rope about the neck of the unfortunate victim, but extended to all who were active in breaking open the jail, or attending in arms at the place of execution, or in any other way co-operating in the enterprize."

[61] 1999 S.C.C.R. 87.

[62] *Coleman v. H.M. Advocate*, 1999 S.C.C.R. 87. The decision of the Appeal Court there depends to a large extent upon the soundness of what was decided in *Brown v. H.M. Advocate*, 1993 S.C.C.R. 382, namely, that knowledge on the part of A that a person B, with whom A acts in concert, is carrying lethal weapons and is prepared to use them in the course of a joint enterprise is not sufficient to make A art and part guilty of murder if those weapons are used to fatal effect by B, unless A can be shown to have foreseen that B was prepared to use them with (at least) that wicked recklessness which satisfies the *mens rea* of murder: see Vol. I, paras 5.37–5.42. The Crown in *Coleman* submitted that that decision in *Brown* had been contrary to prior authority and should, therefore, be overruled; but the Appeal Court was not prepared, or indeed in a position, to reconsider the soundness of the approach taken in *Brown*.

[63] 1999 S.C.C.R. 87, at 104E–F. At 105B there, Lord Cullen also accepted that, depending on the circumstances, it might be possible to convict some members of the mob of murder whilst convicting others of culpable homicide: see also the opinion of Lord Coulsfield, at 111D–F.

[64] Alison, i, 524, in a passage quoted with approval in *Coleman v. H.M. Advocate*, 1999 S.C.C.R. 87, by L.J.-C. Cullen at 100D, and by Lord Coulsfield at 110F: *cf.* Alison, i, 526, referred to by Lord Cullen, *ibid.*

consequence of the undertaking, as the result of an accidental and casual ebullition of wickedness on the part of some of the actors, which went much beyond the common purpose of the assembly."

Similarly, it may be said that the responsibility of a person present in a mob is limited to things done "in the course and for the purposes of" the mob. He accepts the purposes of the mob by joining them and is liable for things done in order to carry out that purpose in much the same way as a party to a criminal enterprise is responsible generally for things done in the course of the enterprise and for things which occur as foreseeable consequences of it.[65] But just as a person who organises a housebreaking is not responsible if one of the housebreakers kills someone during the housebreaking in order to satisfy a private grudge, so the members of a mob are not responsible for something done by one of their number who takes advantage of the riot in order to satisfy a private grudge.[66]

[65] Vol. I, para. 5.38 *et seq.*
[66] *Wm Gibson* (1842) 1 Broun 485, Lord Medwyn at 491; *John Gordon Robertson and Ors* (1842) 1 Broun 152, L.J.-C. Hope at 196.

CHAPTER 41

BREACH OF THE PEACE, OBSCENE PUBLICATIONS AND BLASPHEMY

BREACH OF THE PEACE[1]

Breach of the peace as an indictable offence appears to have been **41.01** regarded originally as a lesser form of mobbing and rioting,[2] and the term "breach of the peace" may still have this connotation in ordinary language. Typically, a breach of the peace was, and still includes, a public disturbance, such as brawling or fighting in public,[3] shouting and swearing in the street,[4] or any general tumult or interference with the peace of a neighbourhood. Whether or not any particular acts amount to such a disturbance is a question of fact depending on the circumstances of each case.[5] It is not a breach of the peace, however, or any other

---

[1] For a detailed discussion of the 19th and 20th century authorities, see M. Christie, *Breach of the Peace* (Edinburgh, 1990).

[2] Hume, i, 439. Hume deals with breach of the peace in two sentences: "In familiar discourse, and sometimes, but rather improperly in the proceedings of the inferior courts, which have the ordinary cognisance of such disturbances, the name of riot is also given to a mere brawl, or occasional quarrel and strife, among persons who were not assembled with any mischievous purpose. If, however, a contest of this sort happens in such a place, or is carried to such a length, as to disturb and alarm the neighbourhood, this seems to be cognisable at the instance of the public prosecutor, as a breach of the public peace; to the effect at least of inflicting a fine and imprisonment, and exacting caution from the offenders, for their good behaviour for the future." And see *John Duncan and Ors* (1843) 1 Broun 512; *John McCabe and Ors* (1838) 2 Swin. 20.

[3] For example, *Jas Bower Burn and Ors* (1842) 1 Broun 1, which concerned a duel; *Dobbs and Macdonald v. Neilson* (1899) 3 Adam 10, which concerned a boxing match; *Derret v. Lockhart*, 1991 S.C.C.R. 109, fighting in the street; *Butcher v. Jessop*, 1989 S.L.T. 593, fighting between rival players at a football match.

[4] For example, *Glen v. Neilson* (1899) 3 Adam 79, but *cf. Hutton v. Main* (1891) 3 White 41, and see para. 41.05, *infra*.

[5] For example, it has been held not to be a breach of the peace merely to use insulting or threatening language: *Banks v. McLennan* (1876) 3 Couper 359; *Buist v Linton* (1865) 5 Irv. 210; *Galbraith v. Muirhead* (1856) 2 Irv. 520, but such language might constitute a breach of the peace in certain circumstances: see para. 41.05, *infra*. It may or may not be a breach of the peace to proclaim someone publicly as a coward, but such an action would fall into the category of conduct likely to provoke a breach of the peace rather than a breach in itself: *Jas McKechnie* (1832) Bell's Notes 111. It depends on the circumstances whether or not it is a breach of the peace to play music in the street: *Marr v. McArthur* (1878) 4 Couper 53; *Whitchurch v. Millar* (1895) 2 Adam 9; *McAvoy v. Jessop*, 1989 S.C.C.R. 301 (Orange Order band ordered to keep playing as the procession to which it was attached passed a catholic church where worshippers were about to enter); to hold a prayer meeting there: *Hutton v. Main* (1891) 3 White 41; *Deakin and Ors v. Milne* (1882) 5 Couper 174; to shout: *Glen v. Neilson* (1899) 3 Adam 80; *Hendry v. Ferguson* (1883) 5 Couper 278; *Ritchie v. McPhee* (1882) 5 Couper 147; or to disturb a public meeting: *Sleigh and Russell v. Moxey* (1850) J. Shaw 369; *Armour v. Macrae* (1886) 1 White 58 (but these cases would now be subject to Art. 10 of the European Convention on Human Rights under which there is a right to freedom of expression: see the Human Rights Act 1998,

crime at common law merely to form part of a disorderly crowd in circumstances not amounting to mobbing[6]; it would be necessary to aver that the accused himself behaved in a disorderly manner, either directly, or impliedly, by averring that each member of the crowd so behaved.[7]

41.02 *Disorderly conduct.* The Glasgow Police Act 1866 made it an offence to be "disorderly" in one's behaviour, and in *Campbell v. Adair*[8] it was held that "disorderly" connoted something less than breach of the peace, and that an omnibus inspector who had bullied a passenger while investigating a complaint made by her was guilty of disorderly behaviour.[9] In practice, however, no distinction is made at common law between breach of the peace and behaviour which is merely disorderly. The statutory form of charge in breach of the peace cases avers only that the accused conducted himself "in a disorderly manner and did commit a breach of the peace",[10] and these words form the basis of almost every modern complaint.[11]

Conduct calculated to provoke a breach of the peace

41.03   In addition to its position as a lesser form of riot the offence of breach of the peace has been used as a way of maintaining order and decency, and of enabling the police to carry out their duty of preserving public order. The way in which this has been done is by regarding any conduct which appears calculated to provoke an actual breach of the peace as itself constituting the crime of breach of the peace. This aspect of breach of the peace has been of considerable importance, and has been much developed in the second half of the twentieth century, so that actings which are in themselves very far removed from the creation of a public disturbance have been treated as breach of the peace,[12] but the origins of this development are in the nineteenth century. In *Jas McKechnie*[13] the

---

Sched. 10, Art. 10(1) and (2)). In *Jackson v. Linton* (1860) 3 Irv. 563, it was said to be a breach of the peace to attempt to pick a pocket; in *Stevenson v. Lang* (1878) 4 Couper 76, it was said not to be a breach of the peace to throw soot into the air; in *Macbeath v. Fraser* (1886) 1 White 286, a group of people who trespassed on a field in order to listen to a speaker were held guilty of breach of the peace; in *Docherty v. Thaw*, High Court on appeal, Jan 1962, unrep'd, a person taking part in a sit-down demonstration in the street was convicted of breach of the peace on a complaint which libelled obstruction of traffic on the road on which she sat.

[6] *MacNeill v. Robertson and Ors*, 1982 S.C.C.R. 468.

[7] *Tudhope v. Morrison*, 1983 S.C.C.R. 262, Sh.Ct.; *cf. Tudhope v. O'Neill*, 1984 S.L.T. 424.

[8] 1945 J.C. 29.

[9] *cf. Stevenson v. Lang* (1878) 4 Couper 76.

[10] See the 1995 Act, Sched. 5.

[11] The bare statutory style of charge in the 1995 Act was at one time thought sufficiently specific to meet the test of relevancy: see, *e.g.*, *Anderson v. Allan*, 1985 S.C.C.R. 399; *Butcher v. Jessop*, 1989 S.C.C.R. 119: but in *Smith v. Donnelly*, 2001 S.L.T. 1007, at 1012J–K, Lord Coulsfield, said: "We would add that it seems to us that, notwithstanding the decision in *Butcher v. Jessop* that a charge of breach of the peace in statutory form is sufficient to meet the requirements of notice, it will normally be proper, now that regard must be had to the Convention, to specify the conduct said to form the breach of the peace in a charge, as indeed is common practice already." (See the Human Rights Act 1998, Sched. 1, Art. 6(3): "Everyone charged with a criminal offence has the following minimum rights: (a) to be informed promptly, in a language which he understands and in detail, of the nature and cause of the accusation against him.")

[12] For example, *Young v. Heatly*, 1959 J.C. 66.

[13] (1832) Bell's Notes 111.

court suggested that to proclaim a man a coward might be a crime as being an endeavour to provoke to a breach of the peace, or as itself a constructive breach of the peace. In *Hugh Fraser*[14] it was held to be a breach of the peace to insist on attending communion after having been suspended by the Kirk Session, and in *Dougall v. Dykes*[15] persistently to walk out of church during the service was held to be a breach of the peace because it was "calculated to give rise to great irritation, and to a determination to suppress it."[16] The most extreme nineteenth century case is *Jackson v. Linton*[17] in which a police court charge of attempted pick-pocketing was upheld on the ground that it disclosed a police offence and was a breach of the peace, although attempted theft was not then a crime as such.

Causing alarm and annoyance. Conduct calculated to provoke a breach **41.04** of the peace usually bears this character because it is likely to create alarm and annoyance and so lead to a disturbance by the person alarmed and annoyed. So, although it has been held not to be a breach of the peace merely to annoy someone[18] such annoyance could amount to a criminal breach of the peace if the circumstances were such that it was calculated to lead to actual disturbance.[19] Thus, it has been held to be a breach of the peace to shout pro-I.R.A. slogans outside Celtic Football Park, on the ground that many spectators would have found them highly provocative and inflammatory.[20] It has also been held to be a breach of the peace to direct offensive remarks and gestures towards rival supporters inside a football ground.[21] But other twentieth century cases have gone much further: it was held, for example, that it could be a breach of the peace merely to cause embarrassment,[22] or cause "concern" on

---

[14] (1839) 2 Swin. 436. See S.S.R., "The Delinquent Dominie" (1977) 22 J.L.S. 125.

[15] (1861) 4 Irv. 101.

[16] *ibid.*, Lord Neaves at 105. See also *Mackie v. MacLeod*, High Court on Appeal, March 1961, unrep'd, and perhaps also *Young v. Heatly*, 1959 J.C. 66. One of the features of *Docherty v. Thaw*, High Court on Appeal, Jan. 1962, unrep'd, was that the accused was one of a number of people sitting on the road. On the sufficiency of "irritation" for breach of the peace, see para. 41.05, *infra*.

[17] (1860) 3 Irv. 563.

[18] *Buist v. Linton* (1865) 5 Irv. 210.

[19] Or perhaps even if it was regarded by the court as particularly offensive: *Young v. Heatly*, 1959 J.C. 66; but grounding a conviction for breach of the peace solely on the disgusting or offensive nature of the conduct is now frowned upon: *Smith v. Donnelly*, 2001 S.L.T. 1007, Lord Coulsfield at 1012I. Conduct which might not constitute a breach of the peace if committed once can, however, become such a breach if persisted in, since the longer it goes on the more likely it is that other persons will be provoked into a disorderly protest: see *Dougall v. Dykes* (1861) 4 Irv. 101; *Raffaelli v. Heatly*, 1949 J.C. 101; *Colquhoun v. Friel*, 1996 S.C.C.R. 497; *McAlpine v. Friel*, 1997 S.C.C.R. 453: cf. *Monson v. Higson*, 2000 S.C.C.R. 751.

[20] *Duffield and Anr v. Skeen*, 1981 S.C.C.R. 66; cf. *Alexander v. Smith*, 1984 S.L.T. 176.

[21] *Wilson v. Brown*, 1982 S.C.C.R. 49, where, at 51, Lord Dunpark offered the following general statement: "It is well established that a test which may be applied in charges of breach of the peace is whether the proved conduct may reasonably be expected to cause any person to be alarmed, upset or annoyed or to provoke a disturbance of the peace. Positive evidence of actual alarm, upset, annoyance or disturbance created by reprisals is not a prerequisite of conviction."

[22] *Sinclair v. Annan*, 1980 S.L.T. (Notes) 55, where the accused addressed indecent remarks to a woman.

account of the accused's language.[23] On the other hand, it was held not to be a breach of the peace merely to sniff glue when in a state of apparent oblivion to one's surroundings[24]; whilst in another case, glue sniffing in the sight of someone who became sufficiently apprehensive to call the police was considered to be a breach of the peace.[25] It has even been held that it is a breach of the peace for a transvestite to go about the red light area of a Scottish city whilst attired as a woman.[26]

41.05 *The essence of the offence*: Smith v. Donnelly.[27] In *Smith v. Donnelly*, the point at issue was the compatibility of breach of the peace with Article 7 of the European Convention on Human Rights.[28] The jurisprudence of the European Court of Human Rights relative to that article indicates that offences must be clearly defined in law, whether the law is written or unwritten, but that the gradual clarification of the rules of criminal law is not incompatible with Article 7 "provided the resultant development is consistent with the essence of the offence and could reasonably be foreseen."[29] The accused in *Smith* had argued before the district court firstly that breach of the peace was too vaguely defined to comply with Article 7, and, secondly, that the offence had been developed to the point where any conduct deemed to be "inappropriate" would be sufficient for conviction. It was necessary in this case, therefore, for the Appeal Court to explore the essence of breach of the peace, which was done by identifying the "leading cases" or "principal authorities" containing the "central statements as to the nature of the crime".[30] These cases were considered to be *Ferguson v. Carnochan*,[31] *Raffaelli v. Heatly*[32] and, to a lesser extent, *Young v. Heatly*.[33]

---

[23] *McMillan v. Normand*, 1989 S.C.C.R. 269, in which a man's conviction of breach of the peace for swearing at police officers in his own house was upheld on the basis that the officers "were concerned by his language": this is probably, however, one of the cases indirectly criticised in *Smith v. Donnelly*, 2001 S.L.T. 1007, by Lord Coulsfield, at 10121H-J, in that bad language or refusal to co-operate with the police "even if forcefully or even truculently stated, is not likely to be sufficient in itself to justify a conviction" since it proceeds beyond the "essential character of the crime". (See para. 41.05, *infra*.)

[24] *Fisher v. Keane*, 1981 J.C. 50.

[25] *Taylor v. Hamilton*, 1984 S.C.C.R. 393.

[26] *Stewart v. Lockhart*, 1990 S.C.C.R. 390.

[27] 2001 S.L.T. 1007.

[28] Article 7 states: "(1) No one shall be held guilty of any criminal offence on account of any act or omission which did not constitute a criminal offence under national or international law at the time when it was committed . . ." (see the Human Rights Act 1998, Sched. 1). The compatibility of what was averred in the complaint (lying down in the roadway outside a naval base, disrupting the free flow of traffic and refusing to desist when requested to do so — which was part of a protest against nuclear weapons) with Art. 10 (freedom of expression) of the Convention was considered by the district court (see 2001 S.L.T. 1009C–D) but not by the Appeal Court. (On the compatibility of Arts 10 and 11 (freedom of assembly and association) with this offence, see P.R. Ferguson, "Breach of the Peace and the European Convention on Human Rights" (2001) 5 E.L.R. 145, esp. at 147 and 161–2.)

[29] *S.W. v. U.K.*; *C.R. v. U.K.* (1995) 21 E.H.R.R. 363, at 398–399.

[30] 2001 S.L.T. at 1012A and 1012E.

[31] (1889) 16 R (J) 93, esp. the opinions of L.J.-C. Macdonald at 94, and Lord McLaren at 94–95.

[32] 1949 J.C. 101, esp. the opinions of L.J.-C. Thomson at 104, and Lord Mackay at 105.

[33] 1959 J.C. 66, L.J.-G. Clyde at 70. The case of *Wilson v. Brown*, 1982 S.C.C.R. 49, and the account of the offence given there by Lord Dunpark at 51 (see n.21, *supra*), were not mentioned, possibly because they add nothing to the other identified authorities.

From dicta in these cases,[34] and especially passages from the opinion of Lord Justice-Clerk Macdonald[35] in *Ferguson v. Carnochan*, the Appeal Court considered that "what is required to commit the crime is conduct severe enough to cause alarm to ordinary people and threaten serious disturbance to the community."[36] Conduct which caused (or might reasonably cause) mere "annoyance" or "upset", or which could be described merely as a "breach of decorum", would not be sufficient since otherwise something minor such as "inappropriate" behaviour or conduct likely to produce "irritation" could result in conviction — which would be contrary to the central statements of the offence in the leading authorities, provided the relevant dicta in these authorities are read as a whole.[37] "What is required, therefore, . . . is conduct which does present as genuinely alarming and disturbing, in its context, to any reasonable person."[38] The Court concluded that, thus interpreted, the definition of breach of the peace was sufficiently clear to comply with Article 7 of the Convention. This interpretation, therefore, must be borne in mind by courts in all cases of breach of the peace which come before them.

With respect to the appellant's second line of argument, the Appeal Court considered that breach of the peace applies to a wide variety of circumstances, but conceded that "there are cases in which a breach of the peace has been held established on grounds which might charitably be described as tenuous."[39] There are, therefore, some cases in which convictions for breach of the peace have been returned which are difficult to support in terms of the essence of the offence as clarified in *Smith v. Donnelly*. What these case are is not clear from *Smith v. Donnelly* itself, since the Appeal Court was not in a position to review prior decisions of the High Court on appeal; nor did the Court see the need to convene a larger number of judges in order to review them. As the Court stated[40]:

---

[34] Set out at 2001 S.L.T. 1010L–1011H.

[35] Whose words are referred to as the "starting point" (*Smith v. Donnelly*, 2001 S.L.T. 1007, at 1011K).

[36] *Smith v. Donnelly*, 2001 S.L.T. 1007, at 1011K-L.

[37] *ibid.*, at 1011K–1012A. *Cf.* the opinion of Lord McCluskey in *MacDougall v. Dochrie*, 1992 S.L.T. 624, at 628E, where he refers to the required conduct as that which could be expected to have an impact upon persons not taking part in the accused's conduct by causing them "disgust, fear, horror, humiliation, revulsion, or other such serious reaction."

[38] *Smith v. Donnelly*, 2001 S.L.T. 1007, at 1012B. At 1012C, it is opined that this is what L.J.-G. Clyde meant in *Young v. Heatly*, 1959 J.C. 66, at 70 when he said that it was not necessary in breach of the peace cases to have evidence that particular persons were actually alarmed or [*sic*] annoyed; but where there was no such evidence "then the nature of the conduct giving rise to the offence must be so flagrant as to entitle the court to draw the necessary inference from the conduct itself." Other cases specifically mentioned by the Court as supporting this interpretation of the leading authorities are *Buist v. Linton* (1865) 5 Irv. 210 and *Banks v. McLennan* (1876) 3 Couper 359 (see n.5, *supra*); and also, *Kinnaird v. Higson*, 2001 S.C.C.R. 427 (where the use of swearing by way of impolite conversation with the police was held not to amount to breach of the peace, there being no evidence of the hurling of abuse or shouting on the part of the accused, and no finding in fact that anyone was, or was likely to be, alarmed or disturbed). Each of these cases, in which breach of the peace was held to be an inappropriate charge, no doubt meet with the remark in *Smith v. Donnelly* (at 1012H) that "there are both old and recent authorities which support which might be called a robust approach to cases involving the use of bad language."

[39] *Smith v. Donnelly*, 2001 S.L.T. 1007, at 1012F.

[40] *ibid.*, at 1012F-H.

"Given the nature of the charge, and the need to apply it in a wide variety of circumstances, it is inevitable that there will be cases which are at or near the borderline and decisions will have to be taken upon those cases as they arise. That is, however, not an uncommon situation in dealing with criminal law which is not statutory, and, provided that the central statements of the nature of the crime are kept in mind, we do not see any need for a comprehensive re-examination of the authorities which have ensued since *Young v. Heatly* ... [W]e would not favour any attempt to derive a definition or redefinition of breach of the peace from close analysis of the facts of particular marginal decisions."

The conclusion was that breach of the peace cases since *Young v. Heatly*[41] had not "attempted to redefine or modify in any way the central statements of the nature of the crime found in *Ferguson* and the other cases cited"[42] by the Court, and that, therefore, as none of those breach of the peace cases was of general authority in relation to the definition of the offence, there had been no development of breach of the peace inconsistent with the essence of that offence: there was thus no question of incompatibility between breach of the peace and Article 7 of the European Convention on Human Rights.

The Court in *Smith v. Donnelly* also proceeded to offer some guidance to courts and prosecutors under the title "comments on some recurrent themes".[43] Included there is the advice that where a person refuses to co-operate with the police or other officials "even if forcefully or truculently stated",[44] this is not *per se* sufficient for conviction of breach of the peace: the same applies where a person merely uses "bad language".[45] The Court also referred to cases "in which actions done or words spoken in private have been held to amount to breach of the peace, or conduct likely to provoke such a breach more because of some perceived unpleasant or disgusting character than because of any real

---

[41] 1959 J.C. 66.

[42] *Smith v. Donnelly*, 2001 S.L.T. 1007, at 1012F.

[43] *ibid.*, at 1012H.

[44] *ibid.*, at 1012H-I.

[45] *ibid.*, at 1012H. In terms of the more recent cases involving swearing at the police, it may be that the use of repeated bad language in the presence only of police officers who are not alarmed or have no reasonable cause to be alarmed, or who are merely "concerned" or "annoyed" thereby, cannot justify convictions for (or arrest on the basis of) breach of the peace: see *Logan v. Jessop*, 1987 S.C.C.R. 604; *Cardle v. Murray*, 1993 S.C.C.R. 170; *Cavanagh v. Wilson*, 1995 S.C.C.R. 693; *Grogan v. Heywood*, 1999 S.C.C.R. 705 (although the decision there was partly based on the district court's having applied the test of the possibility of alarm rather than the correct test of reasonable expectation of such). Cf. *Boyle v. Wilson*, 1988 S.C.C.R. 485 (where swearing was accompanied by a challenge to fight); *Stewart v. Jessop*, 1988 S.C.C.R. 492 (where there had also been long-standing public complaints over the accuseds' behaviour); *Norris v. McLeod*, 1988 S.C.C.R. 572 (where there was also personal provocative abuse directed at the police); *Saltman v. Allan*, 1989 S.L.T. 262 (where the bad language was delivered in circumstances of urgency and tension); *McMillan v. Normand*, 1989 S.C.C.R. 210 (where the conviction — now doubtful as to its correctness — was based on the "concern" of police officers over swearing addressed to them by a man in his own house); *Lochrie v. Jessop*, 1992 S.L.T. 556 (swearing at the police in the vicinity of blocks of flats); *Woods v. Normand*, 1992 S.C.C.R. 805 (where there were also threats of violence to the police); and, *Mackay v. Heywood*, 1998 S.C.C.R. 210 (which is possibly a marginal case, given that the police considered the accused's repeated swearing to be "unacceptable", one of the officers being "upset" thereby).

risk of disturbance",[46] and advises that in such cases "it is perhaps particularly necessary to bear in mind what the essential character of the crime is."[47]

Threats

The crime of making threats is at common law restricted to threats of **41.06** certain grave kinds,[48] and it has been held that the use of threatening language is not necessarily a breach of the peace,[49] but almost any threat may be prosecuted as a breach of the peace if it can reasonably be said to place the threatened person "in a state of fear and alarm". The fifth Schedule to the 1995 Act gives the style "threaten violence to the lieges and commit a breach of the peace", but it is common to charge the putting of a particular person in a state of fear and alarm as a breach of the peace.

Actual alarm unnecessary

It is unnecessary, however, to prove actual alarm, at any rate where **41.07** the accused's conduct can in the circumstances reasonably[50] be said to be calculated to provoke a breach of the peace. In *Rafaelli v. Heatly*[51] the accused was a peeping Tom who was charged that he "did conduct [him]self in a disorderly manner, peer in at a lighted window of [a] dwelling house . . . put residents in [the] street in a state of fear and alarm and commit a breach of the peace." There was a finding in fact that one woman was afraid to tell her husband about the accused's activities in case he would take the law into his own hands and assault him, but no evidence that anyone was alarmed. The accused was held to have committed a breach of the peace, and Lord Justice-Clerk Thomson said that "where something is done in breach of public order or decorum which might reasonably be expected to lead to the lieges being alarmed or upset or tempted to make reprisals at their own hand, the circumstances are such as to amount to breach of the peace."[52] Conversely, if the complainer provides evidence of his or her actual alarm, this must be tested objectively: the court is required to consider not just that the complainer was alarmed, but also whether it was reasonable in the circumstances for such alarm to have been caused. If this were not so,

---

[46] 2001 S.L.T. at 1012I. *Cf. Young v. Heatly*, 1959 J.C. 66 (disgusting remarks made to adolescent boys by a headmaster in the privacy of his own room at a technical college); *Thomson v. H.M. Advocate*, 1989 S.L.T. 637 (injecting oneself with drugs inside a locked toilet cubicle); and, *MacDougall v. Dochrie*, 1992 S.L.T. 624 (spying on naked women in an adjoining solarium from the "privacy" of a locked toilet cubicle, where the conduct was reasonably likely to be discovered).

[47] *ibid*.

[48] *supra*, para. 29.62.

[49] *Galbraith v. Muirhead* (1856) 2 Irv. 520.

[50] See *Donaldson v. Vannet*, 1998 S.C.C.R. 422, which distinguished *Wyness v. Lockhart*, 1992 S.C.C.R. 808 (both cases of begging in the street charged as breach of the peace).

[51] 1949 J.C. 101. See also *MacDougall v. Dochrie*, 1992 S.L.T. 624 (accused spying upon naked women in a solarium adjacent to the locked toilet cubicle he was occupying): *cf. Bryce v. Normand*, 1997 S.L.T. 1351 (accused spying upon, and taking video-recording of, a 15-year-old girl while she was partly undressed within her own bedroom).

[52] At 104. This passage was quoted with approval by the Appeal Court in *Smith v. Donnelly*, 2001 S.L.T. 1007, at 1011E: see para. 41.05, *supra*. For an assertion of the contrary view — *viz.* that A's conduct cannot be made criminal solely on the ground that it may provoke B to disturbance — see the Canadian case of *Fey v. Fedoruk*, 1950 S.C.R. 517 where it was held that conduct of the "peeping Tom" type was not criminal.

then breach of the peace would be dependent in many cases upon the subjective temperament of the individual complainer.[53]

41.08   In *Mackie v. MacLeod*[54] the High Court upheld a conviction of breach of the peace on a charge which libelled that the accused "did conduct [him]self in a disorderly manner, follow C.P. . . . and J.R.F. . . . , put the said C.P. in a state of fear and alarm and commit a breach of the peace." The circumstances were that the accused had become infatuated with C.P., a young woman whom he hardly knew, and had formed a habit of waiting outside her place of employment, looking at her, and following her and her fiancé, J.R.F. On the occasion in question no words had been spoken and no gestures made by the accused; he had merely followed the couple on to a 'bus. As a result the girl was said to be alarmed and agitated, and her fiancé angry and indignant. But the latter gave evidence that he did not intend to create a disturbance, but merely to make a complaint to the police. The sheriff-substitute found in fact that "Although there was no overt disturbance of the peace . . . and the incidents on the date in question were not in themselves of much significance, the circumstances were such that . . . a breach of the peace might well have occurred if it had not been for the self-restraint displayed by [the girl and fiancé]."[55]

Mens rea

41.09   Very few authorities have ever mentioned let alone discussed in any detail the *mens rea* requirement for breach of the peace. It is clear that it is not necessary to show that the accused intended to provoke a disturbance; it is enough that his conduct was such that the court regarded it as objectively likely to do so.[56] In *H.M. Advocate v. Forbes*[57] Lord Justice-General Hope stated: "[In breach of the peace] the effect of [the accused's] conduct must be judged by what he did or by what he said, not by reference to his state of mind or his intention",[58] which suggests that if *mens rea* is a relevant issue in the offence, it is determined entirely objectively. On the other hand, in *Hughes v. Crowe*[59] the court agreed that the quality of the accused's acts must be such as to enable an inference of *mens rea* to be drawn. The quality of the accused's acts there was considered to show a gross lack of consideration for others, which suggests that some degree of negligence may be sufficient: but that was perhaps peculiar to the special circumstances of the offence in that case.

---

[53] As was stated in *Donaldson v. Vannet*, 1998 S.C.C.R. 422, Lord Johnston (opinion of the court) at 424B. See also *Farrell v. Normand*, 1992 S.C.C.R. 859; *Cameron v. Normand*, 1992 S.C.C.R. 866; *Colquhoun v. Friel*, 1996 S.C.C.R. 497; and *Biggins v. Stott*, 1999 S.C.C.R. 595.

[54] High Court, Mar. 1961, unrep'd; contrast *Shannon v. Skeen*, High Court on Appeal, Nov. 1977, unrep'd.

[55] See also *McAlpine v. Friel*, 1996 S.C.C.R. 497, where two years of unwanted following of, staring at and presenting gifts and verbal statements of affection to the victim were followed by a conviction for breach of the peace. (There was no appeal against conviction, the appeal being concerned with sentence.)

[56] *McKenzie v. Normand*, 1992 S.C.C.R. 14.

[57] 1994 S.C.C.R. 163.

[58] *ibid.*, at 168B-C.

[59] 1993 S.C.C.R. 320.

The accused's motive for causing a breach of the peace seems to be irrelevant, such as the desire of the accused in *Ralston v. H.M. Advocate*[60] to draw attention to prison conditions by means of a "roof-top" protest; but it has been opined that it would be a defence to a possible breach of the peace that one was engaged in the investigation of suspected criminal activities at the time.[61]

Breach of the peace in private

Breach of the peace is typically a crime which is committed in public. **41.10** But it is reasonable that conduct which takes place in private but whose effects are public should be regarded as breach of the peace. To have a noisy party in one's house which results in a disturbance of one's neighbour's peace, or the peace of the street, is to commit a breach of the peace.[62]

In *Young v. Heatly*,[63] the further step was taken of holding that conduct occurring in private could constitute a breach of the peace if it was calculated to result in public disturbance. The accused was a master at a technical school who was charged on a complaint relating to four offences all committed on the same afternoon and each consisting of an indecent conversation in his study with a male pupil of the school aged about 16. There was no evidence that anyone was annoyed or alarmed, or that anyone but the respective pupils even knew what had happened. Despite this the High Court held that in the special circumstances of the case the magistrate was entitled to draw the "necessary inference" and convict of breach of the peace in respect of each charge. The reason for the court's decision seems to have been the disgusting nature of the accused's behaviour,[64] and it is difficult to resist the conclusion that "breach of the peace" was used in order to penalise the accused for behaving immorally. Following the opinion of the Appeal Court in *Smith v. Donnelly*,[65] however, it appears that the decision in *Young v. Heatly* would now be found wanting on application of the "central statements" of the offence.[66]

Justification

There may be assault-type situations in which the charge is only one of **41.11** breach of the peace, *e.g.* by brandishing a weapon. In such situations a plea of self defence is open.[67] But it is not a defence to a charge of

---

[60] 1989 S.L.T. 474.

[61] *MacDougall v. Dochrie*, 1992 S.L.T. 624, L.J.-C. Ross at 627J–K.

[62] *Ferguson v. Carnochan* (1889) 2 White 278; *Matthews and Rodden v. Linton* (1860) 3 Irv. 570; *Hughes v. Crowe*, 1993 S.C.C.R. 320.

[63] 1959 J.C. 66.

[64] L.J.-G. Clyde at 70.

[65] 2001 S.L.T. 1007: see para. 41.05, *supra*.

[66] In *Smith v. Donnelly, supra cit.*, at 1012I, the Appeal Court states: "there have been cases in which actions done or words spoken in private have been held to amount to breach of the peace, or conduct likely to provoke such a breach, more because of some perceived unpleasant or disgusting character than because of any real risk of disturbance. In such cases, it is perhaps particularly necessary to bear in mind what the essential character of the crime is." Although no specific cases are referred to by the Court, *Young v. Heatly* must impliedly be comprehended within the above caveat. (For the "essential character" of breach of the peace, see para. 41.05, *supra*.)

[67] *Derret v. Lockhart*, 1991 S.C.C.R. 109. It may be a defence that the accused was engaged in playing a sport with rules at the time of the alleged offence, if his conduct was within those rules or, at least, within the normal incidents of the game: *Butcher v. Jessop*, 1989 S.L.T. 593.

breach of the peace that one acted in order to stop a breach of the peace. In *Palazzo v. Copeland*[68] the accused fired a gun in the air in order to put an end to a disturbance being created by a group of youths in the early hours of the morning. His conviction for breach of the peace was upheld. The court said that firing a gun at such an hour in an urban area was calculated to be likely to cause fear and alarm to the general public although the only persons actually alarmed were the obstreperous youths.

Statutory Offences

41.12 *Civic Government (Scotland) Act 1982.* This Act creates a number of offences which are somewhat analogous to common law breach of the peace. In particular, section 54 provides:

"(1) Any person who—
   (a) sounds or plays any musical intrument;
   (b) sings or performs; or
   (c) operates any radio or television receiver, record player, tape-recorder or other sound-producing device,
so as to give any other person reasonable cause for annoyance and fails to desist on being required to do so by a constable in uniform, shall be guilty of an offence and liable, on summary conviction, to a fine not exceeding level 2 on the standard scale."[69]

Sections 55 and 56 also provide:

"**55.**—(1) Any person who—
   (a) in a public place—
      (i) touts for the purpose of selling or advertising anything or otherwise obtaining custom so as to give any other person reasonable cause for annoyance; or
     (ii) importunes any other person for that purpose so as to give that, or any other, person reasonable cause for annoyance; and
   (b) fails to desist when required to do so by a constable in uniform, shall be guilty of an offence and liable, on summary conviction, to a fine not exceeding level 2 on the standard scale.

56. — Any person who lays or lights a fire in a public place so as to endanger any other person or give him reasonable cause for alarm or annoyance or so as to endanger any property shall be guilty of an offence and liable, on summary conviction, to a fine not exceeding level 3 on the standard scale."[70]

---

[68] 1976 J.C. 52.

[69] Various exceptions are set out in subs. (2), and in subs. (3) as amended by the Roads (Scotland) Act 1984, Sched. 9, para. 87(4). Subsections (2A)–(2C) have been added by the Crime and Disorder Act 1998, s.24(2), under which a police constable may enter premises, where he reasonably suspects in relation to a musical instrument or other sound-producing device that an offence under s.54 is being committed, and seize any such instrument or device he finds there: Sched. 2A, added by the Crime and Disorder Act 1998 s.24(4), Sched. 1, provides rules relating to the retention and disposal of items so seized.

[70] For the meaning of "public place", see s.133 of the Act.

Telecommunications Act 1984. Section 43 of this Act provides: **41.13**

"(1) A person who—
(a) sends, by means of a public telecommunication system, a message or other matter that is grossly offensive or of an indecent, obscene or menacing character; or
(b) sends by those means, for the purpose of causing annoyance, inconvenience or needless anxiety to another, a message that he knows to be false or persistently makes use for that purpose of a public telecommunication system,
shall be guilty of an offence and liable on summary conviction to imprisonment for a term not exceeding 6 months or a fine not exceeding level 5 on the standard scale.[71]
(2)[72] Subsection (1) above does not apply to anything done in the course of providing a programming service (within the meaning of the Broadcasting Act 1990)."

False reports. Section 31(1)[73] of the Fire Services Act 1947 provides: **41.14**

"Any person who knowingly gives or causes to be given a false alarm of fire to any fire brigade maintained in pursuance of this Act or to any member of such a brigade shall be liable on summary conviction to a fine [of level 4 on the standard scale and/or three months' imprisonment]."

Other false reports could be dealt with as breaches of the peace.[74] Bomb hoaxes are now punishable under the Criminal Law Act 1977.[75]

OBSCENE PUBLICATIONS

At common law

The general common law offence. It is an offence at common law to **41.15** publish an obscene work which is intended to corrupt public morals.[76] The last reported common law prosecution for this offence was in 1843 where the charge was of "Publishing, Vending, or Circulating, or Causing to be Published, Vended or Circulated, any lewd, impure, gross or obscene book, or printed work, devised, contrived, and intended to vitiate and corrupt the morals of the lieges, particularly of the youth or young persons of both sexes, and to raise and create in their minds inordinate and lustful desires; as also . . . Exposing for Sale, or Causing to be Exposed for Sale, any such book or printed work."[77]

---

[71] Maximum penalty increased to these levels by the Criminal Justice and Public Order Act 1994, s.92(1). The offence does not extend to things done in the course of providing a programme service within the meaning of the Broadcasting Act 1990, these being dealt with under s.51(2A) of the Civic Government (Scotland) Act 1982: see para. 41.18, *infra*.

[72] As amended by the Cable and Broadcasting Act 1984, Sched. 5, para. 45(4), and the Broadcasting Act 1990, Sched. 20, para. 38(4).

[73] As amended by the Criminal Procedure (Consequential Provisions) (Scotland) Act 1995, Sched. 2, Pt II.

[74] *cf. R. v. Madden* [1975] 1 W.L.R. 1379, CA, which deals with the English offence of public nuisance.

[75] Section 51, as amended by the Criminal Justice Act 1991, s.26(4); maximum penalty a fine of the prescribed sum and six months' on summary conviction, seven years' on indictment.

[76] Macdonald, p.152.

[77] *Henry Robinson* (1843) 1 Broun 643.

This common law offence my be restricted to works intended to corrupt morals, and it has also been suggested that this offence is not committed at common law by merely keeping works for sale, but that they must be actually disseminated or sold, or at least exposed or exhibited for sale.[78]

41.16 *Shameless indecency.* It has been held in a number of cases that the common law crime of shameless indecency (usually now referred to as "shamelessly indecent conduct")[79] is committed by selling or exposing for sale (and perhaps even having for sale where there is also a charge of exposing for sale) articles which are obscene and "likely to deprave and corrupt the morals of the lieges and to create in their minds inordinate and lustful desires".[80]

It is necessary for the Crown to show that the accused was aware of the obscene character of the article, and that his conduct was directed towards some person or persons with an intention or in the knowledge that it should corrupt or be calculated to corrupt them.[81] Nevertheless, the fact that the exposure is restricted to persons not under 18 years of age, far from being a defence, is evidence of the accused's awareness of the obscene character of the material.[82]

Material or articles held as reserve stock in a back shop or kept in drawers are "exposed for sale" if they are kept in immediate readiness for sale.[83]

An averment that an article is "indecent and obscene" is tantamount to an averment that it is liable to deprave and corrupt, that being the common law meaning of "indecent and obscene".[84] Its tendency to corrupt and deprave is a matter of fact for the court, and not a matter for expert evidence.[85]

41.17 *Other offences.* In *Sommerville v. Tudhope*,[86] it was held not to be an offence at common law for a wholesaler to have obscene articles in his possession for circulation to retailers; the premises in which the articles were kept in that case were not premises to which the public were invited to resort, and there was therefore "no affront to public decency or morals nor any action which of itself is designed or calculated to corrupt the morals of the lieges."[87]

It may, however, be a crime to distribute obscene material to retailers with intent that it be sold to the public, the crime being describable as "trafficking in obscene publications", although there is no example of such a crime save a reference by Lord Cooper in *Galletly v. Laird*[88] to

---

[78] *McGowan v. Langmuir*, 1931 J.C. 10, L.J.-G. Clyde at 18.
[79] See, *supra*, para. 36.20, and also paras 36.21–36.22 for shameless indecency and shamelessly indecent conduct. See also Vol. I, para. 1.31.
[80] *Robertson v. Smith*, 1980 J.C. 1.
[81] *Dean v. John Menzies (Holdings) Ltd*, 1981 J.C. 23, Lord Cameron at 32; *Tudhope v. Barlow*, 1981 S.L.T. (Sh.Ct.) 94.
[82] *Robertson v. Smith*, 1980 J.C. 1; *Tudhope v. Taylor*, 1980 S.L.T. (Notes) 54; *Centrewall Ltd. v. MacNeill*, 1983 S.L.T. 326; *Smith v. Downie*, 1982 S.L.T. (Sh.Ct.) 23.
[83] *Scott v. Smith*, 1981 J.C. 46.
[84] *Ingram v. Macari*, 1982 J.C. 1.
[85] *Ingram v. Macari*, 1983 J.C. 1.
[86] 1981 J.C. 58.
[87] *ibid.*, Lord Cameron at 63.
[88] 1953 J.C. 16.

traffic in pornography as an evil which obscenity legislation is designed to prevent.[89] Such distribution might constitute a conspiracy to commit shameless indecency, or make the wholesaler art and part in the retailer's shameless indecency once the latter had exposed the articles for sale.[90]

Under statute

The Civic Government (Scotland) Act 1982. Section 51 of this Act **41.18** provides (*inter alia*)[91]:

> "(2) Subject to subsection (4) below, any person who publishes, sells,[92] or distributes or, with a view to its eventual sale or distribution, makes, prints, or keeps any obscene material shall be guilty of an offence under this section.
>
> (2A)[93] Subject to subsection (4) below, any person who—
>> (a) is responsible for the inclusion of any obscene material in a programme included in a programme service; or
>> (b) with a view to its eventual inclusion in a programme so included, makes, prints, has or keeps any obscene material,
>> shall be guilty of an offence under this section.
>
> (3)[94] A person guilty of an offence under this section shall be liable, on summary conviction, to a fine not exceeding the prescribed sum or to imprisonment for a period not exceeding 6 months or to both or, on conviction on indictment, to a fine or to imprisonment for a period not exceeding three years or to both.
>
> (4) A person shall not be convicted of an offence under this section if he proves that he had used all due diligence to avoid committing the offence.
> . . .
> (6) Nothing in this section applies in relation to any matter—
> . . .

---

[89] See *Sommerville v. Tudhope*, 1981 J.C. 58.

[90] Section 45 of the Civic Government (Scotland) Act 1982 allows local authorities to apply Sched. 2 to the Act, which empowers them to license sex shops, *i.e.* premises used for dealing in, or displaying or demonstrating, what are called sex articles: Sched. 2, para. 2(1). Such articles specifically include reading matter and vision or sound recordings portraying sexual activity or genital organs, or intended to stimulate or encourage sexual activity: Sched. 2, para. 2(4). Local authorities are thus empowered to license the sale of pornography, but such licences are of no avail in a prosecution for shameless indecency or obscenity, since para. 1 of Sched. 2 provides that nothing in the Schedule shall afford a defence to any charge except one under the Schedule itself (*e.g.*, for breach of the licensing conditions) or be taken into account in any way in the trial of any such charge. Under Sched. 2, para. 19(1)(a), it is an offence to use, or knowingly cause or permit the use of, premises as a sex shop without a licence: maximum penalty on summary conviction a fine of £20,000 (Sched. 2, para. 19(3)). *Cf. Rees v. Lees*, 1996 S.C.C.R. 601, where the first charge in the complaint erroneously alleged a contravention of s.7(1) of the Civic Government (Scotland) Act 1982.

[91] For a discussion of the law, see Keith Ewing, "Obscene Publications. Effect of the Civic Government (Scotland) Bill", 1982 S.L.T. (News) 55.

[92] "Sells" includes "offers for sale": see *Rees v. Lees*, 1996 S.C.C.R. 601, L.J.-C. Ross at 605D.

[93] Inserted by the Broadcasting Act 1990, s.163(2).

[94] As amended by the Criminal Justice and Public Order Act 1994, s.87.

(b) included in a performance of a play (within the meaning of the Theatres Act 1968).[95]

. . .

(8) In this section—

'material' includes any book, magazine, bill, paper, print, film, tape, disc or other kind of recording (whether of sound or visual images or both), photograph, drawing, painting, representation, model or figure;

'photograph' includes the negative as well as the positive version; . . .

'programme' and 'programming service' have the same meanings as in the Broadcasting Act 1990 [as extended by the Broadcasting Act 1996];[96]

and the reference to publishing includes a reference to playing, projecting or otherwise reproducing, or, where the material is data stored electronically, transmitting that data."[97]

41.19 *Theatres.* The Theatres Act 1968, which replaces the former system of censorship by the Lord Chamberlain and all other offences of indecency or obscenity in theatres, applies to Scotland, and is very similar to the English Obscene Publications Act 1959, with the result that the authorities on the latter will have to be considered if a prosecution is ever brought in Scotland under the former.[98] The relevant provisions of the Act are as follows:

"**2.**—(1) For the purposes of this section a performance of a play shall be deemed to be obscene if, taken as a whole, its effect was such as to tend to deprave and corrupt persons who were likely, having regard to all relevant circumstances, to attend it.

(2) Subject to sections 3 and 7 of this Act, if an obscene performance of a play is given, whether in public or private, any person who (whether for gain or not) presented or directed that performance shall be liable—

(a) on summary conviction, to a fine not exceeding the prescribed sum or to imprisonment for a term not exceeding six months;

(b) on conviction on indictment to a fine or to imprisonment for a term not exceeding three years, or both.

(3) A prosecution on indictment for an offence under this section shall not be commenced more than two years after the commission of the offence.

---

[95] For theatres, see para. 41.19, *infra.* (Subparagraph (a) of s.51(6) was deleted by the Broadcasting Act 1990, s.163(3).)

[96] Definition inserted by the Broadcasting Act 1990, s.163(4)(b), as amended by the Broadcasting Act 1996, in particular by Sched. 10, para. 11 thereof (which adds digital programming services to the meaning).

[97] The inclusion of "data stored electronically" is made by the Criminal Justice and Public Order Act 1994, Sched. 9, para. 20.

[98] There was such a prosecution in *Herron v. MacDonald, supra,* para. 36.23, but it was as an alternative to the common law charge, and it is understood that it was later accepted that in fact the premises were not a theatre, so no questions arose under the Act. (For an account of the way in which the English Obscene Publications Acts are interpreted, see Smith and Hogan, pp. 720–735.)

(4) No person shall be proceeded against in respect of a performance of a play or anything said or done in the course of such a performance—

    (a) for an offence at common law where it is of the essence of the offence that the performance or, as the case may be, what was said or done was obscene, indecent, offensive, disgusting or injurious to morality; . . .[99]

and no person shall be proceeded against for an offence at common law of conspiring to corrupt public morals, or to do any act contrary to public morals or decency, in respect of an agreement to present or give a performance of a play, or to cause anything to be said or done in the course of such a performance.

    3.—(1) A person shall not be convicted of an offence under section 2 of this Act if it is proved that the giving of the performance in question was justified as being for the public good on the ground that it was in the interests of drama, opera, ballet or any other art, or of literature or learning.

    (2) It is hereby declared that the opinion of experts as to the artistic, literary or other merits of a performance of a play may be admitted in any proceedings for an offence under section 2 of this Act either to establish or negative the said ground."

Section 7(1) provides that the above sections shall not apply to a performance of a play given on a domestic occasion in a private dwelling.

Section 7(2)[1] provides that sections 2 and 3 shall not apply to rehearsals, or to performances given in order to make a record or film or broadcast thereof, or for inclusion in a programme service within the meaning of the Broadcasting Act 1990.

Films. The presentation of obscene or indecent films may be an offence **41.20** of shameless indecency at common law.[2] The display of obscene films is also an offence under section 51(1) of the Civic Government (Scotland) Act 1982.[3] It is also the case that section 1 of the Cinemas Act 1985 prohibits the use of premises for film exhibition[4] unless those premises are licensed for that purpose under the Act[5]: the use of unlicensed premises for such a purpose is an offence.[6]

---

[99] Section 2(4)(b) is repealed by the Schedule to, and now replaced by provisions of, the Indecent Displays (Control) Act 1981; see para. 41.25, *infra*. Section 2(4)(c) is repealed by the Civic Government (Scotland) Act 1982, with the result that the Theatres Act 1968 does not expressly exclude proceedings for an offence under s.51 of the Civic Government (Scotland) Act 1982.

[1] As amended by the Broadcasting Act 1990, Sched. 20, para. 13.

[2] *Watt v. Annan*, 1978 J.C. 84. *Cf. R. v. G.L.C., ex p. Blackburn* [1976] 1 W.L.R. 550, CA; see also *Attorney-General's Reference No. 2 of 1975* [1976] 1 W.L.R. 710, CA.

[3] See para. 41.25, *infra*.

[4] This means any exhibition of moving pictures which is produced otherwise than by the simultaneous reception and exhibition of a programme included in a programme service within the meaning of the Broadcasting Act 1990: s.21(1) of the Cinemas Act 1985, as amended by the Broadcasting Act 1990, Sched. 20, para. 40.

[5] See s.1 of the Cinemas Act 1985.

[6] See s.10(1)(a) of the above Act. Maximum penalty on summary conviction, a fine of £20,000: s.11(1)(a).

41.21 *Indecent photographs of children.* Section 52 of the Civic Government (Scotland) Act 1982 provides[7]:

> "(1) Any person who—
>
> (a) takes, or permits to be taken, or makes any indecent photograph or pseudo-photograph of a child (meaning in this section a person under the age of 16);
>
> (b) distributes or shows such an indecent photograph or pseudo-photograph;
>
> (c) has in his possession such an indecent photograph or pseudo-photograph with a view to its being distributed or shown by himself or others; or
>
> (d) publishes or causes to be published any advertisement likely to be understood as conveying that the advertiser distributes or shows such an indecent photograph or pseudo-photograph, or intends to do so
>
> shall be guilty of an offence under this section.
>
> (2) In subsection (1) above 'child' means, subject to subsection (2B) below, a person under the age of 16; and in proceedings under this section a person is to be taken as having been a child at any material time if it appears from the evidence as a whole that he was then under the age of 16.
>
> (2A) In this section, 'pseudo-photograph' means an image, whether produced by computer-graphics or otherwise howsoever, which appears to be a photograph.
>
> (2B) If the impression conveyed by a pseudo-photograph is that the person shown is a child, the pseudo-photograph shall be treated for all purposes of this Act as showing a child and so shall a pseudo-photograph where the predominant impression conveyed is that the person shown is a child notwithstanding that some of the physical characteristics shown are those of an adult.
>
> (2C) In this section, references to an indecent pseudo-photograph include—
>
> (a) a copy of an indecent pseudo-photograph;
>
> (b) data stored on a computer disc or by other electronic means which is capable of conversion into a pseudo-photograph.
>
> . . .
>
> (4) For the purposes of this section, a person is to be regarded as distributing an indecent photograph or pseudo-photograph if he parts with possession of it to, or exposes or offers it for acquisition by, another person.
>
> (5) Where a person is charged with an offence under subsection (1)(b) or (c) above, it shall be a defence for him to prove—
>
> (a) that he had a legitimate reason for distributing or showing the photograph or pseudo-photograph or (as the case may be) having it in his possession; or
>
> (b) that he had not himself seen the photograph or pseudo-photograph and did not know, nor had any cause to suspect, it to be indecent.
>
> . . .

---

[7] As amended by the Criminal Justice and Public Order Act 1994, s.84(6).

(8) In this section—

(a) references to an indecent photograph include an indecent film, a copy of an indecent photograph or film and an indecent photograph comprised in a film;

(b) a photograph (including one comprised in a film) shall, if it shows a child and is indecent, be treated for all purposes of this section as an indecent photograph of a child;

(c) references to a photograph include —

　(i) the negative as well as the positive version; and

　(ii) data stored on a computer disc or by other electronic means which is capable of conversion into a photograph;

(d) 'film' includes any form of video-recording."[8]

It has been held that the context in which a photograph was taken is relevant to a charge of taking an indecent photograph under section 52(1)(a), since it may show that the accused did not take it in a sufficiently deliberate sense, but that such context is not relevant to the assessment whether the photograph is indecent.[9] It has also been held that a person "makes" an indecent photograph or pseudo-photograph where he downloads relevant data from an external source of such and stores it on his computer, since "makes" was not intended to be limited to "create".[10] It has also been held that it is not necessary for the Crown to prove that the defendant knew the age of the persons depicted in an indecent video-recording of a child.[11]

Section 52A[12] of the Civic Government (Scotland) Act 1982 provides: **41.22**

"(1) It is an offence for a person to have any indecent photograph or pseudo-photograph of a child in his possession.

(2) Where a person is charged with an offence under subsection (1), it shall be a defence for him to prove—

(a) that he had a legitimate reason for having the photograph or pseudo-photograph in his possession; or

(b) that he had not himself seen the photograph or pseudo-photograph and did not know, nor had any cause to suspect, it to be indecent; or

---

[8] Maximum penalty, on indictment, three years' and a fine, and, on summary conviction, six months' and a fine of the prescribed sum: s.52(3), as amended by the Criminal Justice and Public Order Act 1994, s.84(6)(e).

[9] *Bruce v. McLeod*, 1998 S.C.C.R. 733, applying *R. v. Graham-Kerr* [1988] 1 W.L.R. 1098, CA — a decision on the English equivalent legislation. It has been held in England that the age of the child may be relevant in considering whether the photograph is indecent: *R. v. Owen (Charles)* [1988] 1 W.L.R. 134, CA.

[10] *Longmuir v. H.M. Advocate*, 2000 S.C.C.R. 447, applying *R. v. Bowden* [2000] 2 W.L.R. 1083, CA. See also *Atkins v. D.P.P.* [2000] 1 W.L.R. 1427, Div.Ct, where it was held *inter alia* that making an indecent photograph included intentional copying or storing of an image on a computer but did not include an unintended storage of the image by virtue of what was done automatically by a particular computer programme, unknown to the accused. Cf. *Kirk v. Kennedy*, 2001 S.C.C.R. 31 an appeal in which the accused's submission of ignorance as to the illegality of downloading indecent photographs or pseudo-photographs of children from the internet was considered relevant to the question of sentence. (Current guidelines for sentencing in such cases will be found in *Ogilvie v. H.M. Advocate*, High Court Sentencing Appeal, July 27, 2001, unrep'd.

[11] *R. v. Land* [1999] Q.B. 65, CA.

[12] Inserted by s.161 of the Criminal Justice Act 1988, and as amended by the Criminal Justice and Public Order Act 1994, s.84(7).

(c) that the photograph or pseudo-photograph was sent to him without any prior request made by him or on his behalf and that he did not keep it for an unreasonable time.

(3) A person shall be liable on summary conviction of an offence under this section to imprisonment for a period not exceeding 6 months or to a fine not exceeding level 5 on the standard scale or to both.

(4) Subsections (2) to (2C) and (8) of section 52 of this Act shall have effect for the purposes of this section as they have for the purpose of that section."

In England, it has been held relative to the equivalent English legislation that "academic research" may be a legitimate reason for the possession of an indecent photograph of a child, but that the matter is a pure matter of fact for judge or jury who are entitled to be sceptical when such a defence is put forward.[13]

41.23 *Obscenity a question of fact.* Whether or not material is indecent and/or obscene at common law is determined by enquiring whether the material is likely to deprave or corrupt; and that enquiry is to be conducted as a question of fact by the tribunal on a perusal of the material under attack.[14] Consideration of other similar works which are alleged to be regarded as acceptable is irrelevant.[15]

41.24 *Non-sexual obscenity.* Obscenity in Scots criminal law has so far been confined to sexual obscenity. But in *John Calder (Publications) Ltd v. Powell*[16] a novel dealing with drug addiction was held to be obscene as having a tendency to deprave, since it might encourage drug-taking.

41.25 *Indecent displays.* The Indecent Displays (Control) Act 1981 provides[17]:

"(1) If any indecent matter is publicly displayed the person making the display and any person causing or permitting the display to be made shall be guilty of an offence.[18]

(2) Any matter which is displayed in or so as to be visible from any public place shall, for the purposes of this section, be deemed to be publicly displayed.

(3) In subsection (2) above, 'public place', in relation to the display of any matter, means any place to which the public have or are permitted to have access (whether on payment or otherwise) while that matter is displayed except—

(a) a place to which the public are permitted to have access only on payment which is or includes payment for that display; or

(b) a shop or any part of a shop to which the public can only gain access by passing beyond an adequate warning notice;

---

[13] *Atkins v. D.P.P.* [2000] 1 W.L.R. 1427, Div. Ct, where it was also held that an indecent image prepared by taping two separate photographs together was not a photograph for the purposes of the equivalent English legislation, although a photocopy of an image so prepared might fall within the wording of the offence as a pseudo-photograph.

[14] See *Ingram v. Macari*, 1982 S.C.C.R. 372.

[15] *Galletly v. Laird*, 1953 J.C. 16.

[16] [1965] 1 Q.B. 509.

[17] As amended by the Cinemas Act 1985, Sched. 2 and the Broadcasting Act 1990, Sched. 20.

[18] Maximum penalty, on indictment, two years' and a fine, and, on summary conviction, a fine of the prescribed sum in the sheriff court and a fine of level 3 on the standard scale in the district court: s.4(2) and (3).

but the exclusions contained in paragraphs (a) and (b) above shall only apply where persons under the age of 18 years are not permitted to enter while the display in question is continuing.

(4) Nothing in this section applies in relation to any matter—

(a) included by any person in a television broadcasting service or other television programme service (within the meaning of Part I of the Broadcasting Act 1990); or

(b) included in the display of an art gallery or museum and visible only from within the gallery or museum; or

(c) displayed by or with the authority of, and visible only from within a building occupied by, the Crown or any local authority; or

(d) included in a performance of a play (within the meaning of the Theatres Act 1968); or

(e) included in a film exhibition as defined in the Cinemas Act 1985—

    (i) given in a place which as regards that exhibition is required to be licensed under section 1 of that Act or by virtue only of section 5, 7 or 8 of that Act, is not required to be so licensed; or

    (ii) which is an exhibition to which section 6 of that Act applies, given by an exempted organisation as defined in subsection (6) of that section.

(5) In this section 'matter' includes anything capable of being displayed, except that it does not include an actual human body or any part thereof; and in determining for the purpose of this section whether any displayed matter is indecent—

(a) there shall be disregarded any part of that matter which is not exposed to view; and

(b) account may be taken of the effect of juxtaposing one thing with another.

(6) A warning notice shall not be adequate for the purposes of this section unless it complies with the following requirements—

(a) The warning notice must contain the following words, and no others—

'WARNING

Persons passing beyond this notice will find material on display which they may consider indecent. No admittance to persons under 18 years of age.'

(b) The word 'WARNING' must appear as a heading.

(c) The notice must be so situated that no one could reasonably gain access to the shop or part of the shop in question without being aware of the notice and it must be easily legible by any person gaining such access."

Nothing in this Act (except to the extent provided for by it) affects the law relating to shameless indecency or obscenity at common law or under section 51 of the Civic Government (Scotland) Act 1982.[19]

It is also an offence under section 51(1) of the Civic Government (Scotland) Act 1982 to display any obscene material in any public place or in any other place where it can be seen by the public.[20] It is a defence

---

[19] Indecent Displays (Control) Act 1981, s.5(4).

[20] Maximum penalty, on indictment, three years' and a fine, and, on summary conviction, six months' and a fine of the prescribed sum: s.51(3), as amended by the Criminal Justice and Public Order Act 1994, s.87.

for the accused to show that he had used all due diligence to avoid committing the offence.[21] It remains to be seen whether publishing warnings or restricting entry to premises will constitute due diligence, or simply be seen as evidence of the accused's knowledge that the material is obscene.[22] It should be noted that any place to which the public are permitted to have access, whether on payment or otherwise, is a public place for the purposes of section 51(1), so that that subsection can be contravened in circumstances which would not contravene the Indecent Displays (Control) Act 1981.[23]

The Indecent Displays (Control) Act 1981 does not affect section 51 of the Civic Government (Scoland) Act 1982,[24] but a person charged under section 51(1) may be convicted of a breach of the Indecent Displays (Control) Act 1981.[25]

Section 51(1) does not apply to any matter included in a performance of a play within the meaning of the Theatres Act 1968.[26]

"Material" has the same meaning in relation to offences under section 51(1) as it has in relation to offences under section 51(2).[27]

Postal Services Act

41.26   Section 85 of the Postal Services Act 2000 provides:

> "(3) A person commits an offence if he sends by post a postal packet which encloses—
>
> (a) any indecent or obscene print, painting, photograph, lithograph, engraving, cinematograph film or other record of a picture or pictures, book, card or written communication, or
>
> (b) any other indecent or obscene article (whether or not of a similar kind to those mentioned in paragraph (a)).
>
> (4) A person commits an offence if he sends by post a postal packet which has on the packet, or on the cover of the packet, any words, marks or designs which are of an indecent or obscene character."[28]

Unsolicited Goods

41.27   Section 4 of the Unsolicited Goods and Services Act 1971 provides:

> "(1) A person shall be guilty of an offence if he sends or causes to be sent to another person any book, magazine or leaflet (or advertising material for any such publication) which he knows or ought reasonably to know is unsolicited and which describes or illustrates human sexual techniques.
>
> (2) A person found guilty of an offence under this section shall be liable on summary conviction to a fine not exceeding [level 5 on the standard scale]."

---

[21] Section 51(4).

[22] *cf.* P.W. Ferguson, "The Limits of Statutory Obscenity", 1983 S.L.T. (News) 249; *Centrewall Ltd v. MacNeill*, 1983 S.L.T. 326.

[23] Civic Government (Scotland) Act 1982, s.51(8): *cf.* s.133, *supra*, para. 36.40.

[24] Indecent Displays (Control) Act 1981, s.5(4)(b), as substituted by the Civic Government (Scotland) Act 1982, s.51(7).

[25] Civic Government (Scotland) Act 1982, s.51(5).

[26] *ibid.*, s.51(6).

[27] See para. 41.18, *supra*.

[28] Maximum penalty for an offence under either of these subsections, on indictment, 12 months and a fine, and, on summary conviction, a fine of the statutory maximum: s.85(5).

BLASPHEMY

The last reported prosecutions for blasphemy were in 1843. In *Thos* **41.28**
Paterson[29] the charge was of publishing, vending or circulating or
exposing for sale, a "profane, impious, or blasphemous book, or any
book . . . containing a denial of the truth and authority of the Holy
Scriptures, or of the Christian Religion, and devised, contrived, and
intended to asperse, vilify, ridicule, or bring into contempt the Holy
Scriptures or the Christian Religion."[30] Lord Justice-Clerk Hope held
that it was no defence to show that the Bible deserved the character
attributed to it, saying that the Bible and the Christian religion were part
of the law of the land, and that whatever vilified them was an
infringement of the law. His Lordship reserved the question whether it
was a crime to deny their truth in a manner not designed to vilify, but
told the jury that before they could convict they must be satisfied that the
"character of the books was not that of fair and serious speculation . . .
or argument but such as indicated an obvious intention to bring [the
Bible and the Christian religion] into ridicule and contempt."[31] In
passing sentence his Lordship said that the law was intended to protect
"a class of persons . . . whose education is imperfect, and their reading
misdirected",[32] and it may be that had the law of blasphemy developed it
would have done so in the same way as the law of obscenity so that the
crime would consist in publishing or disseminating blasphemous material
of an aspersive character to those likely to be corrupted thereby.

It is extremely unlikely that any prosecution will now be brought for
blasphemy, and it may be said that blasphemy is no longer a crime.
Blasphemous publications which are indecent in their terms may be dealt
with as indecent publications, and blasphemous statements made in
circumstances likely to provoke a breach of the peace may be dealt with
as breaches of the peace.[33]

---

[29] (1843) 1 Broun 629.
[30] A similar charge was brought in *Henry Robinson* (1843) 1 Broun 643.
[31] Broun at 637–638.
[32] At 642.
[33] Macdonald, p.153. See G. Maher, "Blasphemy in Scots Law", 1977 S.L.T. (News)
257. For a modern English case of blasphemy, see *R. v. Lemon* [1979] A.C. 617. See also
Wingrove v. U.K. (1996) 24 E.H.R.R. 1 (where it was held that refusal to grant a film a
certificate on the grounds that it contravened the English law of blasphemy was not a
contravention of Art. 10 of the Convention).

CHAPTER 42

VIOLATION OF SEPULCHRES

It is a crime at common law to interfere with a corpse, the crime **42.01**
known as violation of sepulchres.[1] The crime can be committed only
where the corpse has been buried or entombed[2] or otherwise removed
from the protection of the law of theft, and put in a place of safe
keeping.[3]

The crime is completed once the body is moved from its resting place,
however slightly.[4]

The essence of the crime is the disturbance of a body without the
authority of the relatives or executors of the deceased or other lawful
authority such as, for example, a warrant for exhumation. The offence is
committed whatever the purpose of the accused.[5]

There is some authority for the proposition that the crime cannot be
committed by the owner of the ground where the body lies,[6] but it is
difficult to see why this should be so since the essence of the crime is not
dishonesty or trespass but irreverence. A reverent removal followed by
some other reverent disposal of the remains, on the other hand, would
probably not constitute violation of sepulchres even if the removal were
unauthorised.

The crime can be committed only in respect of a body which is in a
condition to be regarded as an object of reverential treatment, so that
there comes a time when a body is so far gone in dissolution that its
removal no longer constitutes violating sepulchres.[7]

---

[1] Hume, i, 85; Alison, i, 461; Macdonald, p.52.

[2] *Chas Soutar* (1882) 5 Couper 65.

[3] *cf. Dewar v. H.M. Advocate,* 1945 J.C. 5, *supra*, para. 14.27.

[4] Macdonald, p.52.

[5] The best known examples of the crime were, of course, those committed by the
"body-snatchers" who removed corpses for use as anatomical specimens. In *H.M.
Advocate v. Coutts* (1899) 3 Adam 50, the purpose was to make use of the grave for fresh
remains.

[6] *Sir Geo. Weir of Blackwood and Ors* (1710): see 3 Adam 55n., and Lord McLaren at 60.

[7] *H.M. Advocate v. Coutts, supra*, Lord McLaren at 54–55.

CHAPTER 43

DANGEROUS DRUGS

Dangerous drugs are controlled by the Misuse of Drugs Act 1971.[1]   **43.01**

General provisions

Offences. Section 18 of the Act provides that anyone who acts in contravention of or fails to comply[2] with any regulation made under the Act, or contravenes, or fails to comply with the conditions of, a licence or authority granted under or in pursuance of the Act, shall be guilty of an offence.

FRAUD. The making of false statements in order to obtain a licence or **43.02** authority constitutes an offence against the Act.[3]

FOREIGN OFFENCES. Section 20 of the Act provides: **43.03**

"A person commits an offence if in the United Kingdom he assists in or induces the commission in any place outside the United Kingdom of an offence punishable under the provisions of a corresponding law in force in that place."[4]

A corresponding law is

"[A] law stated in a certificate purporting to be issued by or on behalf of the government of a country outside the United Kingdom to be a law providing for the control and regulation in that country of the production, supply, use, export and import of drugs and other substances in accordance with the provisions of the Single

---

[1] In this chapter "the Act" means the Misuse of Drugs Act 1971. For an account of the law more detailed than that which can be essayed in the present work, see R.S. Shiels, *Controlled Drugs* (2nd ed., 1997); and for the most up to date version of the legislation, see *Renton & Brown's Statutory Offences* (Edinburgh, 1999), Div. A, "Controlled Substances". It should be noted that the penalties for offences dealt with in this chapter must be read subject to s.41 of the Criminal Law (Consolidation) (Scotland) Act 1995, which provides (*inter alia*) that where a person convicted on indictment of a contravention of a drug trafficking offence (which includes by virtue of s.49(5) of the Proceeds of Crime (Scotland) Act 1995 contraventions of ss. 4(2), 4(3) or 5(3) of the Misuse of Drugs Act 1971) is sentenced to imprisonment but no confiscation order is made against him, he must also be fined an amount determined by reference to his likely profits unless the court is satisfied that a fine is inappropriate. The court is also empowered to impose both a confiscation order and a fine as well as imprisonment. See also ss. 33–36 of the Criminal Justice and Police Act 2001, which authorise the making of a travel restriction order on a person convicted of drug trafficking offences for which a prison sentence of at least four years is imposed.
[2] Under s.37(1) of the Act, "contravention" includes "failure to comply".
[3] Section 18(4).
[4] See *R. v. Vickers* [1975] 1 W.L.R. 811: conviction for agreeing in England to transport containers to Italy for use there to ship drugs to U.S. in contravention of U.S. law.

675

Convention on Narcotic Drugs signed at New York on 30th March 1961[5] or a law providing for the control and regulation in that country of the production, supply, use, export and import of dangerous or otherwise harmful drugs in pursuance of any treaty, convention or other agreement or arrangement to which the government of that country and Her Majesty's Government in the United Kingdom are for the time being parties."[6]

43.04 ATTEMPTS AND INCITEMENTS. Section 19 of the Act provides:

"It is an offence for a person to attempt to commit an offence under any other provision of this Act or to incite or attempt to incite another to commit such an offence."

43.05 CONTROL. The Act controls the importation, exportation, production, supply and possession of controlled drugs. A controlled drug is any substance or product specified in Schedule 2 to the Act, which Schedule is subject to amendment by way of addition or subtraction by Order in Council.[7] The drugs in the Schedule are divided into three classes, A, B and C, for the purpose of differentiation of penalty, as provided in Schedule 4. Class A drugs include cocaine, lysergamide, lysergide and other N-alkyl derivatives of lysergamide, methadone, morphine, opium and pethidine.[8] Class B drugs include amphetamine, cannabis,[9] cannabis resin[10] and codeine. Class C drugs include benzphetamine. The descriptions in the Schedule are generic terms and include derivative forms of the drug named, so that, for example, "cocaine" includes both the direct extracts of the coca-leaf and whatever results from a chemical transformation thereof,[11] and "amphetamine" includes salt of amphetamine.[12] The Schedule has been much amended since 1971, some of the more recent additions being etryptamine (Class A), methcathinene and zipeprol (Class B), and aminorex, brotizolem and mesocarb (Class C).[13] Where the prohibited drug is defined as a preparation or product containing a drug, the prohibition does not extend to material which is in its natural state, although it contains the drug when it is in that state.[14]

---

[5] See J.J. Paust, *et al.* (eds.), *International Criminal Law; Cases and Materials* (Durham, N. Carolina, 1996), pp. 1254 and 1257. The Convention was amended by the Geneva Protocol of 1972.

[6] Section 36(1).

[7] See s.2 of the Act.

[8] Included in the drugs added to Class A since 1971 are the phenethylamine derivatives commonly known as "Ecstasy": see the Misuse of Drugs Act 1971 (Modification) Order 1977 (S.I. 1977 No. 1243), art. 3(c). See *Glennie v. H.M. Advocate*, 2001 S.C.C.R. 423.

[9] That is to say, any part of any plant of the genus *Cannabis* except cannabis resin, and except (a) mature stalk, (b) fibre produced from mature stock, and (c) seed, all of any such plant after separation from the rest of the plant: s.37(1) of the Act, definition of "cannabis", as substituted by the Criminal Law Act 1977, s.52.

[10] Cannabis and cannabis resin are treated as distinct substances in the interpretation section of the Act (s.37(1)), and, therefore, evidence of possession of cannabis resin does not establish a contravention of a charge of possessing cannabis: *Arnott v. MacFarlane*, 1976 S.L.T. (Notes) 39. Synthetically produced cannabis resin is not included in the prohibition, but the Crown do not have to prove that any cannabis resin produced was not synthetically produced: *Guild v. Ogilvie*, 1986 S.L.T. 343 (Note).

[11] *R. v. Greensmith* [1983] 1 W.L.R. 1124, CA.

[12] *Heywood v. Macrae*, 1988 S.L.T. 218, in which *Arnott v. MacFarlane*, 1976 S.L.T. (Notes) 39 (see n.10, *supra*), was distinguished.

[13] Misuse of Drugs Act 1971 (Modification) Order 1998 (S.I. 1998 No. 50), art. 2.

[14] *Murray v. MacNaughton*, 1985 J.C. 3.

Section 7 of the Act empowers the Secretary of State to exempt any controlled drug from the provisions of sections 3, 4 or 5 of the Act,[15] or to make other provisions enabling persons to do things which would otherwise be unlawful under sections 4, 5 or 6 of the Act,[16] and in particular to license the doing of things which would otherwise contravene these provisions. "Doing things" in this context includes having things in one's possession.[17]

The Secretary of State may also by regulation exclude the application of any offence-creating section of the Act in prescribed cases[18]; poppystraw is excluded from sections 4(1) and 5(1).[19]

Import and export

The importation and exportation of controlled drugs are prohibited by **43.06** section 3, unless the drug is exempted by regulations made under section 7, or the import or export is licensed by the Secretary of State. This section does not create an offence but enables the provisions of sections 50(1), 68(2) and 170 of the Customs and Excise Management Act 1979[20] to be invoked.[21]

Production and supply

Section 4 provides: **43.07**

"(1) Subject to any regulations under section 7 of this Act for the time being in force, it shall not be lawful for a person—
    (a) to produce a controlled drug; or
    (b) to supply or offer to supply a controlled drug to another.
(2) Subject to section 28 of this Act, it is an offence for a person—
    (a) to produce a controlled drug in contravention of subsection (1) above; or
    (b) to be concerned in the production of such a drug in contravention of that subsection by another.
(3) Subject to section 28 of this Act, it is an offence for a person—
    (a) to supply or offer to supply a controlled drug to another in contravention of subsection (1) above; or
    (b) to be concerned in the supplying of such a drug to another in contravention of that subsection; or

---

[15] Which prohibit export and import, production and supply, and possession, respectively. *Cf. R. v. Hunt* [1987] A.C. 352, where it was held that the burden of proving that the drug found in the possession of the defendant was in the prohibited form lay on the Crown, *i.e.* that it was not for the defendant to prove that what he possessed fell into an exempted category.

[16] Section 6 prohibits the cultivation of cannabis plant.

[17] Section 7(8).

[18] Section 22(a)(i).

[19] Misuse of Drugs Regulations 1985 (S.I. 1985 No. 2066), reg. 4(3).

[20] *supra*, para. 38.02.

[21] Section 22 of the Misuse of Drugs Act empowers the Secretary of State to exclude, in such cases as may be prescribed by regulation, the application of these sections of the Customs and Excise Management Act 1979 to prohibitions under s.3 of the Misuse of Drugs Act 1971, s.22 (a)(ii). See Misuse of Drugs Regulations 1985 (S.I. 1985 No. 2066) reg. 4. *Cf. R. v. Whitehead* [1982] Q.B. 1272, CA; *R. v. Keyes, Edjedewe and Chapman* (2000) 2 Cr.App.R. 181, CA.

(c) to be concerned in the making to another in contravention of that subsection of an offer to supply such a drug."[22]

It has been held at a High Court trial that a person who is in possession of controlled drugs with intent to supply them to another (in contravention of section 5(3) of the Act) is also a person concerned in supplying those drugs to another, and that the Crown may choose under which section they wish to charge him.[23]

Being concerned in the supply of drugs covers more than art and part guilt in supply, and extends to a great variety of activities both at the centre and at the fringes of drug-dealing, including the activities of couriers, go-betweens, lookouts, financiers, advertisers, and any person who was a link in a chain of distribution or took part in breaking up or adulterating quantities of drugs and weighing and packing drug deals.[24] A person may be convicted of being concerned in the supply of drugs before the supply has been completed[25] or even if no actual supply takes place,[26] and the offence can relate to drugs supplied or to be supplied by the accused himself.

"Supply" means "transfer physical control".[27] Where, therefore, X gives Y a drug to keep for him, Y supplies the drug to X when he returns it to him, although it has remained in X's ownership throughout.[28]

It has been held that merely to assist a person to take a drug he has already obtained, *e.g.* by injecting it into him, is not to "supply" him.[29]

A person may be convicted of offering to supply a controlled drug where he and the offeree wrongly believe the substance in question to be a controlled drug.[30]

---

[22] Maximum penalty for Class A and B drugs 12 months' and a fine of the prescribed sum on summary conviction, life in prison and a fine on indictment (see the Controlled Drugs (Penalties) Act 1985, s.1). For class C drugs three months' and £2,500, and five years' and a fine, respectively; see Criminal Law Act 1977, Sched. 5.

[23] *H.M. Advocate v. Kiernan*, 2001 S.C.C.R. 129; *cf. Dickson v. H.M. Advocate*, 1994 S.C.C.R. 478.

[24] *Kerr (D.A.) v. H.M. Advocate*, 1986 S.C.C.R. 81, Lord Hunter at 87. See also *Clements v. H.M. Advocate*, 1991 S.C.C.R. 266, L.J.-G. Hope at 274A-B, and, *H.M. Advocate v. Hamill*, 1998 S.C.C.R. 164, Lord Marnoch at 166C, where doubts were expressed as to the need to employ or consider art and part liability given the width of the offence contained in s.4(3)(b) of the Act: these doubts voiced by Lords Hope and Marnoch were endorsed by L.J.-G. Rodger in *Salmon v. H.M. Advocate; Moore v. H.M. Advocate*, 1998 S.C.C.R. 740, at 760B; see also Lord Rodger's opinion at 763B.

For a discussion of the *mens rea* required for the offence of being concerned in supply (*i.e.*, knowledge of being concerned in the supply of something, which is found to have been a controlled drug), see *Salmon v. H.M. Advocate; Moore v. H.M. Advocate*, *supra cit.*, L.J.-G. Rodger at 756F-763D; *cf. Glancy v. H.M. Advocate*, 2001 S.C.C.R. 385; for jurisdictional questions as they relate to this offence, see *Clements v. H.M. Advocate*, 1991 S.C.C.R. 266: Vol. I, para. 3.47.

[25] See *Douglas v. Boyd*, 1996 S.C.C.R. 44.

[26] *Kerr (D.A.) v. H.M. Advocate*, 1986 S.C.C.R. 81, Lord Hunter at 88.

[27] *Donnelly v. H.M. Advocate*, 1985 S.L.T. 243; *R. v. Maginnis* [1987] A.C. 303, HL.

[28] *R. v. Delgado* [1984] 1 W.L.R. 89; *Murray v. MacPhail*, 1991 S.C.C.R. 245.

[29] *R. v. Harris (Janet)* [1968] 1 W.L.R. 769, a case under reg. 8 of the Dangerous Drugs (No. 2) Regulations 1964 (S.I. 1964 No. 1811), which made it an offence "to supply or procure."

[30] *Haggard v. Manson* [1976] 1 W.L.R. 187.

Possession

Section 5 provides: **43.08**

"(1) Subject to any regulations under section 7 of this Act for the time being in force, it shall not be lawful for a person to have a controlled drug in his possession.

(2) Subject to section 28 of this Act and to subsection (4) below, it is an offence for a person to have a controlled drug in his possession in contravention of subsection (1) above.

(3) Subject to section 28 of this Act, it is an offence for a person to have a controlled drug in his possession, whether lawfully or not, with intent to supply it to another in contravention of section 4(1) of this Act.

(4) In any proceedings for an offence under subsection (2) above in which it is proved that the accused had a controlled drug in his possession, it shall be a defence for him to prove—

(a) that, knowing or suspecting it to be a controlled drug, he took possession of it for the purpose of preventing another from committing or continuing to commit an offence in connection with that drug and that as soon as possible after taking possession of it he took all such steps as were reasonably open to him to destroy the drug or to deliver it into the custody of a person lawfully entitled to take custody of it; or

(b) that, knowing or suspecting it to be a controlled drug, he took possession of it for the purpose of delivering it into the custody of a person lawfully entitled to take custody of it and that as soon as possible after taking possession of it he took all such steps as were reasonably open to him to deliver it into the custody of such a person.

(5) Subsection (4) above shall apply in the case of proceedings for an offence under subsection 19(1) of this Act consisting of an attempt to commit an offence under subsection (2) above as it applies in the case of proceedings for an offence under subsection (2), subject to the following modifications, that is to say—

(a) for the references to the accused having in his possession, and to his taking possession of, a controlled drug there shall be substituted respectively references to his attempting to get, and to his attempting to take, possession of such a drug; and

(b) in paragraphs (a) and (b) the words from 'and that as soon as possible' onwards shall be omitted.

(6) Nothing in subsection (4) or (5) above shall prejudice any defence which it is open to a person charged with an offence under this section to raise apart from that subsection."[31]

Regulation 6 of the Misuse of Drugs Regulations 1985 gives general authority to possess drugs to constables, carriers, persons engaged in

---

[31] Maximum penalty under s.5(2) for Class A drugs 12 months' and a fine of the prescribed sum on summary conviction, seven years' and a fine on indictment; for Class B drugs three months' and £2,500, and five years' and a fine respectively; for Class C drugs three months' and £1000, and two years and a fine, respectively. Maximum penalty under s.5(3) is as for s.4(3). Section 5(6) does not come into operation until the Crown have proved the elements of the offence: *R. v. Wright (Brian)* (1975) 62 Cr.App.R. 169; *McKenzie v. Skeen,* 1983 S.L.T. 121; Vol. I, paras 3.39–3.40. Coercion may be an example of a possible defence to an offence relative to this offence: *cf. Trotter v. H.M. Advocate,* 2000 S.C.C.R. 968.

Postal services, customs officers and persons working in laboratories to which drugs have been sent for forensic examination, all while acting in the course of such duty or business, and to persons engaged in conveying the drugs to an authorised person.

43.09 *"Possession"*. This includes possession art and part.[32] Most of the problems relating to *mens rea* in possession cases[33] are now superseded by sections 5(4) and 28 of the Act.[34]

There is no quantitative limitation on the amount of a controlled drug which the accused can be convicted of possessing: provided the amount in question is sufficient to be identifiable as a controlled drug, it is of no moment that that amount was too minute to be usable.[35]

A may be in possession of goods which are in the custody of another, provided they are subject to his control.[36] He may also be in possession of drugs which are in the hands of an innocent agent, provided that he was responsible for the agent having them, or must have known that his dealing with them would involve their being in the agent's hands.[37]

A person does not possess a drug which is present in his urine, since such drugs have been "literally consumed and changed in character", unlike a swallowed diamond. But the presence of traces of a drug in urine is evidence of possession at an earlier time.[38]

In *R. v. Buswell*[39] the accused obtained controlled drugs on prescription. He mislaid them and, believing them to have been dissolved when the jeans in which he thought they were had to be washed, obtained more from his doctor. He later found the original drugs in a drawer, by which time he had completed his medical treatment: he used some and was found with the remainder. It was held that he had remained in possession of the drugs throughout, and that such possession was lawful since the drugs were obtained on prescription.

43.10 *"Intent to supply"*. Whether or not the possession of controlled drugs involves an intent to supply them to another is a matter of inference from the facts and circumstances[40]; but it is not necessary for the Crown to prove that the accused intended to make an immediate supply at the moment he was found in possession of them: "[I]ntent to supply denotes supplying taking place sometime in the future".[41] It is no defence to a charge of attempt to possess with intent to supply that the accused

---

[32] *cf. McAttee v. Hogg* (1903) 4 Adam 190; *McRae v. H.M. Advocate*, 1975 J.C. 34; on the difficulty of proving possession against the individual members of a commune or household in whose premises drugs are found, see *Lustmann v. Stewart*, 1971 S.L.T. (Notes) 58; *Allan v. Milne*, 1974 S.L.T. (Notes) 76; *Balloch and Ors*, High Court on appeal, Jan. 1977, unrep'd; *Mingay v. MacKinnon*, 1980 J.C. 33; *cf. White v. H.M. Advocate*, 1991 S.C.C.R. 555, and *Bath v. H.M. Advocate*, 1995 S.C.C.R. 323; *cf.* also *R. v. Hussain* [1969] 2 Q.B. 567. See also *Sullivan v. Earl of Caithness* [1976] Q.B. 966, a case on the Firearms Act 1968.

[33] For example, *R. v. Warner* [1969] 2 A.C. 256; *Lockyer v. Gibb* [1967] 2 Q.B. 243; *R. v. Marriott* [1971] 1 W.L.R. 187.

[34] *infra*, para. 43.17.

[35] *Keane v. Gallacher*, 1980 J.C. 77; *R. v. Boyesen* [1982] A.C. 768, HL.

[36] Section 37(3) of the Act.

[37] *Amato v. Walkingshaw*, 1990 J.C. 45.

[38] *Hambleton v. Callinan* [1968] 2 Q.B. 427, Lord Parker C.J., at 432.

[39] [1972] 1 W.L.R. 64, CA.

[40] See, *e.g.*, *Donnelly v. H.M. Advocate*, 1984 S.C.C.R. 419; *Lockhart v. Hardie*, 1994 S.C.C.R. 722.

[41] *Lockhart v. Hardie*, 1994 S.C.C.R. 722, L.J.-C. Ross at 724F.

believed erroneously that the substance or product in question was a controlled drug.[42]

Cultivation of cannabis

It is an offence to cultivate any plant of the genus cannabis, except as **43.11** allowed by regulations under section 7.[43] A plant is cultivated when it is grown, and the term "cultivate" does not require that any particular care or labour be bestowed on it.[44] The evidence of cultivation in *Tudhope v. Robertson*[45] was "the positioning of the plants to secure the light necessary to growth, the condition of the plants, the presence of the seeds, and the objective which the respondents had in mind in having the plants in their house at all."[46]

Offences by occupiers

Section 8 provides: **43.12**

"A person commits an offence if, being the occupier or concerned in the management of any premises, he knowingly[47] permits or suffers any of the following activities to take place on those premises. That is to say—
(a) producing[48] or attempting to produce a controlled drug in contravention of section 4(1) of this Act;
(b) supplying or attempting to supply a controlled drug to another in contravention of section 4(1) of this Act, or offering to supply a controlled drug to another in contravention of section 4(1)[49];
(c) preparing opium for smoking;
(d) administering or using a controlled drug which is unlawfully in any person's possession at or immediately before the time when it is administered or used."[50]

A co-tenant may be convicted of allowing another co-tenant to use the premises in contravention of the section.[51]

---

[42] *Docherty v. Brown*, 1996 S.C.C.R. 136.

[43] Section 6. Maximum penalty 12 months' and a fine of the prescribed sum on summary conviction; 14 years' and a fine on indictment.

[44] *Tudhope v. Robertson*, 1980 J.C. 62.

[45] *supra*.

[46] *ibid.*, L.J.-G. Emslie at 65–66.

[47] See *R. v. Thomas* (1976) 63 Cr.App.R. 65; *R. v. Brock and Anr* [2001] 1 W.L.R. 1159, CA.

[48] It has been held in England that in view of the definition of cannabis as any part of any plant of the genus cannabis (see para. 43.05, *supra*), to grow a cannabis plant is to produce the drug cannabis: *Taylor v. Chief Constable of Kent* [1981] 1 W.L.R. 606.

[49] It has been held sufficient for the Crown to prove that the defendant knew that supplying of a controlled drug was taking place on the premises; the Crown does not require to prove knowledge of a particular drug having been so supplied, even if the charge specifies a particular drug: *R. v. Bett* [1999] 1 W.L.R. 2109, CA.

[50] Paragraph (d) is substituted by s.38 of the Criminal Justice and Police Act 2001. Maximum penalty for an offence under s.8, on summary conviction — Class A or B drug, 12 months' and a fine of the prescribed sum; Class C drug, three months' and a fine of £2500; on conviction on indictment — Class A or B drug, 14 years' and a fine; Class C drug, five years' and a fine. See also Licensing (Scotland) Act 1976, s.80 (a): permitting persons convicted under s.4 or s.5 of the 1971 Act to be on licensed premises: Maximum penalty a fine of level 3 on the standard scale.

[51] *R. v. Ashdown* (1974) 59 Cr.App.R. 193, CA.

An occupier is a person who has possession of the premises in a substantial sense involving some degree of permanence, and who as a matter of fact exercises control of the premises and dictates their use. He need not have any legal right or title to possession, but may be a squatter.[52] But someone whose possession is transient or accidental, such as a daughter left in charge of her parents' house while they are on holiday, is not an occupier for the purposes of the section.[53] On the other hand, a student living in a room in a college hostel is an occupier of that room.[54]

43.13 *Manufacture and supply of substances used to produce drugs.* Section 12 of the Criminal Justice (International Co-operation) Act 1990[55] makes it an offence to manufacture or supply to another, without the express approval of a constable, a substance listed in Schedule 2 to that Act, knowing or suspecting that it is to be used for the unlawful production of a controlled drug.[56]

43.14 *Concealing or dealing in the proceeds of drug trafficking.* Section 14 of the Criminal Justice (International Co-operation) Act 1990 provides:

"(1) A person is guilty of an offence if he—
  (a) conceals or disguises any property which is, or in whole or in part directly or indirectly represents, his proceeds of drug trafficking; or
  (b) converts or transfers that property or removes it from the jurisdiction,
for the purpose of avoiding prosecution for a drug trafficking offence[57] or the making or enforcement in his case of a confiscation order.

(2) A person is guilty of an offence if, knowing or having reasonable grounds to suspect that any property is, or in whole or in part directly or indirectly represents, another person's proceeds of drug trafficking, he—
  (a) conceals or disguises that property; or
  (b) converts or transfers that property or removes it from the jurisdiction,
for the purpose of assisting any person to avoid prosecution for a drug trafficking offence or the making or enforcement of a confiscation order.
. . .[58]

---

[52] *Christison v. Hogg*, 1974 S.L.T. (Notes) 33; *R. v. Josephs and Christie* (1977) 65 Cr.App.R. 253.

[53] *R. v. Mogford* [1970] 1 W.L.R. 988.

[54] *R. v. Tao* [1977] Q.B. 141.

[55] As amended by the Criminal Justice (International Co-operation) (Amendment) Act 1998, s.1.

[56] Maximum penalty, on indictment, 14 years' and fine; on summary conviction, six months': s.12(2).

[57] A "drug trafficking offence" is defined in s.24(3) of the 1990 Act as an offence to which s.1 of the Criminal Justice (Scotland) Act 1987 relates: but s.1 of the Criminal Justice (Scotland) Act 1987 was repealed by the Criminal Procedure (Consequential Provisions) (Scotland) Act 1995, Sched. 5, without formal amendment of s.24(3) of the 1990 Act. It is probably now the case that such an offence has the meaning given by s.49(5) of the Proceeds of Crime (Scotland) Act 1995: see n.1, *supra*.

[58] Subsections (3) and (5) were repealed by the Criminal Justice Act 1993, Sched. 6, Pt I.

(4) In subsections (1)(a) and (2)(a) above the references to concealing or disguising any property include references to concealing or disguising its nature, source, location, disposition, movement or ownership or any rights with respect to it.

. . .

(6) A person guilty of an offence under this section is liable—

(a) on summary conviction, to imprisonment for a term not exceeding 6 months or a fine not exceeding the statutory maximum or both;

(b) on conviction on indictment, to imprisonment for a term not exceeding 14 years or a fine or both."

It is also an offence to do anything to prejudice an investigation into drug trafficking which one knows or suspects is taking place, subject to a defence of lack of knowledge or suspicion, or of reasonable grounds for suspicion that one's actings were likely to prejudice the investigation, and to a defence of lawful authority or reasonable excuse for one's actings.[59]

It is also an offence to acquire or use or have possession of any property which one knows is, or in whole or in part represents, the proceeds of drug trafficking, subject to a defence that one gave "adequate consideration" for it.[60] No offence is committed if the accused discloses to a constable or a person commissioned by the Commissioners of Customs and Excise or to his employer his suspicions or belief that any property is the proceeds of drug trafficking, provided that that disclosure is made before he does any act[61] in relation to that property in contravention of section 37(1) and such an act is then done with the consent of the constable or person commissioned, or, provided that if the disclosure is made after he has done, such an act it is made on his own initiative and as soon as it is reasonable for him to make it.[62] It is a defence that the accused intended to make such a disclosure as is mentioned above, but there was reasonable excuse for his failure to do so.[63]

It is also an offence to enter into an arrangement with a person one knows or suspects to be a drug trafficker whereby that person is helped to retain control of the proceeds of drug trafficking.[64] It is a defence for the accused to prove that he did not know or suspect that the arrangement related to the proceeds of drug trafficking, or that the arrangement had the prohibited effect.[65] No offence is committed if

---

[59] Criminal Law (Consolidation) (Scotland) Act 1995, s.36. Maximum penalty, on indictment, five years' and a fine, and, on summary conviction, six months' and a fine of the statutory maximum: s.36(5) By virtue of subsections (3) and (4) of s.36, it is not an offence for a professional legal adviser to disclose information or any other matter to his client (or a representative of that client) in connection with the giving of legal advice, or to any person in contemplation of or in connection with and for the purpose of legal proceedings, provided there is no view thereby to further any criminal purpose.

[60] Criminal Law (Consolidation) (Scotland) Act 1995, s.37. Maximum penalty, on indictment, 14 years' and a fine, and, on summary conviction, six months' and a fine of the statutory maximum: s.37(9).

[61] Which includes having possession of the property: s.37(6).

[62] Section 37(5), (8).

[63] Section 37(7); see also s.37(10).

[64] Criminal Law (Consolidation) (Scotland) Act 1995, s.38. Maximum penalty, on indictment, 14 years' and a fine, and, on summary conviction, six months' and fine of the statutory maximum: s.38(6).

[65] Section 38(4)(a), (b).

the accused discloses the arrangement to the authorities (or to his employer)[66] before it is entered into, or as soon as reasonable thereafter if the disclosure is made on his own initiative, or if he proves that he intended to make such disclosure but there is reasonable excuse for his failure to have done so.[67]

43.15 *Concealing drug money laundering.* Section 39 of the Criminal Law (Consolidation) (Scotland) Act 1995 provides:

> "(1) A person is guilty of an offence if—
> (a) he knows, or suspects, that another person is engaged in drug money laundering,[68]
> (b) the information, or other matter, on which that knowledge or suspicion is based came to his attention in the course of his trade, profession, business or employment, and
> (c) he does not disclose the information or other matter to a constable or to a person commissioned by the Commissioners of Customs and Excise as soon as is reasonably practicable after it comes to his attention.[69]
> (2) Subsection (1) above does not make it an offence for a professional legal adviser to fail to disclose any information or other matter which has come to him in privileged circumstances.[70]
> (3) It is a defence to a charge of committing an offence under this section that the person charged had a reasonable excuse for not disclosing the information or other matter in question. . . ."[71]

It is also an offence for a person to disclose information to another when he knows or suspects that a constable or a person commissioned by the Commissioners of Customs and Excise is conducting or proposing to conduct an investigation into drug money laundering, and that information is likely to prejudice that investigation or proposed investigation.[72] It is a defence for such a person to prove that he did not know or suspect that the disclosure was likely to prejudice such an investigation.[73]

Opium

43.16 Section 9 of the Act provides:

> "Subject to section 28 of this Act, it is an offence for a person—

---

[66] See s.38(3).

[67] Section 38(3)(b), (4)(c).

[68] "Drug money laundering" means doing any act which constitutes an offence under ss. 37 or 38 of the Criminal Law (Consolidation) (Scotland) Act 1995, or under s.14 of the Criminal Justice (International Co-operation) Act 1990, or which, if the act is done outside Scotland, would constitute such an offence if done in Scotland: s.39(7); "having possession of any property" is taken to be "doing an act" in respect of it: s.39(8).

[69] Disclosure may also be made to an employer: s.39(5).

[70] For what is meant by "privileged circumstances", see s.39(9), (10).

[71] Maximum penalty, on indictment, five years' and a fine, and, on summary conviction, six months' and a fine of the statutory maximum: s.39(11).

[72] See s.39(1) of the Criminal Law (Consolidation) (Scotland) Act 1995. Maximum penalty, on indictment, five years' and a fine, and, on summary conviction, six months' and a fine of the statutory maximum: s.40(7). See also the offences under s.40(2) and (3) of the Criminal Law (Consolidation) (Scotland) Act 1995. There are the usual exceptions for disclosures made by professional legal advisers: see s.40(4), (5).

[73] Section 40(6).

(a) to smoke or otherwise use prepared opium; or
(b) to frequent a place used for the purpose of opium smoking; or
(c) to have in his possession—
>   (i) any pipes or other utensils made or adapted for use in connection with the smoking of opium, being pipes or utensils which have been used by him or with his knowledge and permission in that connection or which he intends to use or permit others to use in that connection; or
>   (ii) any utensils which have been used by him or with his knowledge and permission in connection with the preparation of opium for smoking."[74]

Defences under the Misuse of Drugs Act 1971

In addition to provisions such as section 5(4) of the Act, a general **43.17** defence is provided under section 28 in the following terms:

"(1) This section applies to offences under any of the following provisions of this Act, that is to say section 4(2) and (3), section 5(2) and (3), section 6(2) and section 9.

(2) Subject to subsection (3) below, in any proceedings for an offence to which this section applies it shall be a defence for the accused to prove that he neither knew of nor suspected nor had reason to suspect the existence of some fact alleged by the prosecution which it is necessary for the prosecution to prove if he is to be convicted of the offence charged.

(3) Where in any proceedings for an offence to which this section applies it is necessary, if the accused is to be convicted of the offence charged, for the prosecution to prove that some substance or product involved in the alleged offence was the controlled drug which the prosecution alleges it to have been, and it is proved that the substance or product in question was that controlled drug, the accused—

(a) shall not be acquitted of the offence charged by reason only of proving that he neither knew nor suspected nor had reason to suspect that the substance or product in question was the particular controlled drug alleged; but
(b) shall be acquitted thereof—
>   (i) if he proves that he neither believed nor suspected nor had reason to suspect that the substance or product in question was a controlled drug; or
>   (ii) if he proves that he believed the substance or product in question to be a controlled drug, or a controlled drug of a description, such that, if it had in fact been that controlled drug or a controlled drug of that description, he would not at the material time have been committing any offence to which this section applies.

---

[74] Maximum penalty, on indictment, 14 years' and a fine, and, on summary conviction, 12 months' and a fine of the prescribed sum.

(4) Nothing in this section shall prejudice any defence which it is open to a person charged with an offence to which this section applies to raise apart from this section."[75]

The leading Scottish authority on the interpretation and application of section 28 is *Salmon v. H.M. Advocate; Moore v. H.M. Advocate*[76] which was concerned with appeals relating to offences under sections 5(3) and 4(3)(b) of the Act. The opinion of Lord Justice General Rodger[77] makes the following points clear. The defences created by section 28 do not alter the burden of proof on the Crown.[78] In relation to section 4(3)(b), that burden is discharged if the Crown prove that the accused knew he was concerned in the supply of something to another, that something being in fact a controlled drug: the Crown do not have to prove that the accused knew that that something was a controlled drug.[79] Relative to a section 5(3) charge, the Crown must show that the accused had the necessary knowledge and control which possession requires[80]; but if, as is often the case, the accused is shown to have had possession of a container which he knew contained something, and that something is in fact a controlled drug, the Crown will have discharged their burden of proof (there being no requirement on the Crown to prove that the accused knew the contents to be a controlled drug).[81] If the Crown fail to establish that the accused had the necessary knowledge, acquittal must follow, and reference to section 28 is unnecessary.[82] If, however, the Crown discharge their burden of proof and the accused alleges that he thought the "something" in question was not of the nature of a drug at all — for example, neither powder nor tablets — then he may avail himself of the defence offered by section 28(2).[83] But if he did know that the "something" was of the form which drugs usually take — for example, powder or tablets — his defence then lies with section 28(3), that is to say that he believed the "something" to be, for example, tablets of aspirin or some non-controlled life-style drug[84]: it would not be open to him to assert by way of defence that he believed the "something" to have been a controlled drug of a different description to that expressed in the charge.[85]

The above account of the operation of section 28, and especially of subsection (2) thereof, depends to a large extent on there being a clear distinction between substances or products which on the one hand have the nature of drugs and on the other do not[86]; and it is not clear that the

---

[75] See, *e.g.*, *Trotter v. H.M. Advocate*, 2000 S.C.C.R. 968 (coercion pled in response to a charge of a contravention of s.5(3) of the Act; the defence failed since the essential requirements of coercion were not met).

[76] 1998 S.C.C.R. 740.

[77] With whom Lord Johnston agreed.

[78] *Salmon v. H.M. Advocate; Moore v. H.M. Advocate*, 1998 S.C.C.R. 740, opinion of L.J.-G. Rodger at 751E and 757B-D.

[79] *ibid.*, p. 757A-B.

[80] See Vol. I, paras 3.39–3.40.

[81] *Salmon v. H.M. Advocate; Moore v. H.M. Advocate*, 1998 S.C.C.R. 740, L.J.-G. Rodger at 754A-D. See also *R. v. Lambert* [2001] 3 W.L.R. 206, HL, Lord Hope of Craighead at 229A-C; Lord Clyde at 246G–249C.

[82] *ibid.*, 757D–E.

[83] *ibid.*, 757E–758A.

[84] *ibid.*, see, *e.g.*, 758A–C.

[85] Since, of course, s.28(3)(a) forbids such a line of defence.

[86] Pornographic video-tapes are thus not of the nature of drugs: see *R. v. McNamara* (1987) 87 Cr.App.R. 246.

account will be applicable over the generality of possible situations as opposed to the specific examples presented by the Lord Justice-General.[87]

Section 28 does, however, purport to place a persuasive burden of proof on the accused, and the question must be asked whether such a burden contravenes article 6 of the European Convention on Human Rights.[88] This question arose in the recent English appeal of *R. v. Lambert*.[89] The major issue at stake was whether the Convention as set out in the Human Rights Act 1998 could apply retrospectively to the case before the House of Lords, and, although the majority of the House decided that it could not so apply, the opportunity was taken to consider whether the burden imposed upon an accused by section 28 of the Misuse of Drugs Act 1971 contravened Article 6. The majority of the House were clearly of the view that although prima facie section 28 imposed a persuasive rather than an evidential burden, section 3 of the Human Rights Act 1998 required legislation to be read and given effect in a way which was compatible with the Convention, and that no great harm would be caused to the objectives of the Misuse of Drugs Act by construing section 28 as imposing an evidential burden on an accused who no more than wished to avail himself of the defences it contains.[90] There is, therefore, highly persuasive authority for construing as evidential the burden imposed on an accused by section 28; and it is understood that the Crown in Scotland accept the correctness of the majority view expressed on this matter in *Lambert*.

Offences by doctors, etc.

Section 7(3) obliges the Secretary of State to make regulations to **43.18** secure that doctors, dentists, veterinary practitioners and surgeons, should be able to prescribe, administer, manufacture, compound and supply controlled drugs, and pharmacists be able to manufacture, compound and supply such drugs.[91]

Section 7(4) empowers the Secretary of State, if of opinion that it is in the public interest to do so, to remove the rights of practitioners and pharmacists to do these things, except under licence, in the case of any drug designated by order as one whose production, supply and possession is either wholly unlawful, or unlawful except for research or other special purposes. The Misuse of Drugs (Designation) Order 1986[92] designates a number of drugs "as drugs to which section 7(4) . . . applies." They include cannabis, cannabis resin, lysergamide, lysergide and other N-alkyl derivatives of lysergamide, and raw opium.

---

[87] It does, however, represent a considerable advance over prior authorities, where it was opined that s.28(2) was without intelligible meaning: see, *e.g.*, *McKenzie v. Skeen*, 1983 S.L.T. 121, L.J.-G. Emslie at 121.

[88] Article 6(2) provides: "Everyone charged with a criminal offence shall be presumed innocent until proved guilty according to law": see the Human Rights Act 1998, Sched. 1.

[89] [2001] 3 W.L.R. 206, HL.

[90] See *R. v. Lambert* [2001] 3 W.L.R. 206, Lord Slynn of Hadley at 212D-G; Lord Hope of Craighead at 237F-H and 238C-D; Lord Clyde at 258H–259C: *cf.* Lord Hutton at 274D-G, who decided that the burden imposed by s.28 was a justifiable contravention of Art. 6. *Cf.* also *Salmon v. H.M. Advocate; Moore v. H.M. Advocate*, 1998 S.C.C.R. 740, L.J.-G. Rodger at 750F.

[91] The regulations are the Misuse of Drugs Regulations 1985 (S.I. 1985 No. 2066), regs 6–11, which also cover various classes of nurses, analysts and sampling officers.

[92] S.I. 1986 No. 2331.

43.19   ADDICTS. The act also controls the right to prescribe drugs to addicts. Section 10(2)(h) empowers the Secretary of State by regulation to require any doctor who attends an addict to notify such particulars with respect to the addict as may be prescribed, and section 10(2)(i) empowers the Secretary of State by regulation to prohibit any doctors from prescribing for or supplying or administering to addicts such drugs as may be prescribed, except under licence.

Section 12[93] empowers the Secretary of State by direction to prohibit practitioners or pharmacists from possessing or otherwise dealing with drugs, where the prohibited person has been convicted of certain offences including an offence under the Act or its predecessors, or of a customs offence connected with drugs.

Section 13 gives power to make a similar direction in the case of doctors who contravene regulations made under section 10(2)(h) or (i). It also provides that where the Secretary of State is of the opinion that a practitioner is "prescribing, administering or supplying or authorising the administration or supply of any controlled drugs in an irresponsible manner", he may on the recommendation of a tribunal, and subject to the consideration of representations by an advisory body, make a direction prohibiting the practitioner from prescribing, etc., such controlled drugs as may be specified. A contravention of regulations made under section 10(2)(h) or (i) is not in itself an offence, but it is an offence to contravene any direction made under section 12 or 13.[94]

43.20   INFORMATION. Section 17 empowers the Secretary of State to obtain information from pharmacists and doctors in any area in which it appears to him that there exists "a social problem caused by the extensive misuse of dangerous or otherwise harmful drugs." Failure to provide information and the provision of false information known to be so or recklessly given are offences.[95]

Custody of drugs

43.21   Regulation 3 of the Misuse of Drugs (Safe Custody) Regulations 1973,[96] which applies to retail premises, nursing homes, residential establishments under the Social Work (Scotland) Act 1968, and private hospitals, requires the occupier and every person concerned in the management of such premises to ensure that all controlled drugs not exempted under Schedule 1 to the regulations are kept, so far as circumstances permit, "in a locked safe, cabinet or room which is so constructed and maintained as to prevent unauthorised access to the drugs."[97] This requirement does not apply where the drug is under the direct supervision of the pharmacist or the person in charge of the nursing home, etc., or of a member of his staff designated for the

---

[93] As amended by the Customs and Excise Management Act 1979, Sched. 4, para. 8, and the Criminal Justice (International Co-operation) Act 1990, s.23(2).

[94] Maximum penalty, on indictment, Class A or B drug, 14 years' and a fine; Class C drug, five years' and a fine; and, on summary conviction, Class A or B drug, 12 months' and a fine of the prescribed sum; Class C drug, three months' and a fine of £2,500.

[95] Section 17(3), (4). Maximum penalty for failure to provide, a fine of level 3 on the standard scale; for false information, six months' and a fine of the prescribed sum, on summary conviction, and two years' and a fine on indictment.

[96] S.I. 1973 No. 798. Maximum penalty for contravention: six months' and a fine of the prescribed sum on summary conviction, two years' and a fine on indictment.

[97] Regulation 3(2).

purpose. It is possible for a retail pharmacist to obtain from a chief constable a certificate in relation to a safe, cabinet or room on his premises.[98] Unless such a certificate exists, any person to whom regulation 3 applies must comply with the structural requirements of Schedule 2 to the regulations in relation to every safe, cabinet or room in which drugs are kept.

Where any controlled drug is not kept as aforesaid, any person (other than a person engaged in Postal services) who has possession of the drug must ensure that so far as circumstances permit it is kept in a locked receptacle[99] which can be opened only by him or a person authorised by him.[1]

In addition, section 11 of the Act empowers the Secretary of State to serve notice on the occupier of any premises to give directions to take precautions for the safe custody of drugs.[2]

---

[98] Regulation 4.
[99] This does not include a car: *Kameswara Rao v. Wyles* [1949] 2 All E.R. 685.
[1] Regulation 5.
[2] Contravention of a direction is an offence punishable as above.

CHAPTER 44

OFFENCES IN CONNECTION WITH OFFICIALS

Breach of duty

It is a crime at common law for a public official, a person entrusted **44.01** with an official situation of trust, wilfully to neglect his duty, even where no question of danger to the public or to any person is involved.[1] There are a number of cases in which postal officials were charged at common law with breach of duty by opening or detaining letters entrusted to them,[2] and one charge is reported against a post office superintendent for absenting himself from duty.[3]

In modern times common law prosecutions against officials for breach of duty are almost unknown except in the case of bribery of judicial officials.[4] Offences by officials are usually dealt with under the appropriate statute dealing with their duties, either under provisions relating specially to officials,[5] or under general penal provisions.[6] The last reported case of a breach of duty by a non-judicial official[7] is *Thos Black Webster*,[8] in which a doctor was convicted of fabricating a false certificate for the purposes of the Vaccination (Scotland) Act 1863. What he did

---

[1] Hume, i, 411; Alison, i, 634–635; Macdonald, p.141; *Archibald Stewart* (1747) Hume, i, 411: a charge against a Lord Provost for failing to make proper arrangements to defend Edinburgh against the rebels in 1745. Where danger or injury is involved the breach of duty may become a criminal omission of another kind, *e.g. Wm Hardie* (1847) Ark. 247: a charge of culpable homicide against an inspector of poor for failing to look after a pauper: see Vol. I, para. 3.36.

[2] *Donald Smith* (1827) Syme 185; *Wm Cunningham* (1820), *John Graham* (1830), both Alison, i, 635.

[3] *Henry Frederick Adie* (1843) 1 Broun 601. A case is also reported against a customs official for making false entries in his books with intent to defraud: *Chas Macculloch* (1828) Bell's Notes 106.

[4] *infra*, para. 49.04. The fairly recent sheriff court case of *Wilson v. Smith*, 1997 S.L.T. (Sh.Ct.) 91, suggests, however, that the common law offence is still available for breaches of duty of a more general nature; there, a police officer was prosecuted at common law for failure in her duty to submit timeously to the procurator fiscal reports on alleged offenders: see A. Brown, "Wilful Neglect of Duty by Public Officials" (1996) 64 Sc. Law Gaz. 130.

[5] For example, Customs and Excise Management Act 1979, s.15, *supra*, para. 38.16; Postal Services Act 2000, s.83, *infra* para. 44.02; Representation of the People Act 1983, ss. 63 (as substituted by the Representation of the People Act 1985, Sched. 4, para. 19), 64, 65 (as amended by the said Act of 1985, Sched. 3, para. 2), 66 (as amended by the said Act of 1985, Sched. 3, para. 3), 99 (as amended by the said Act of 1985, Sched. 3, para. 4) and 100 (as amended by the said Act of 1985, Sched. 4, para. 5): see *supra*, para. 38.44; Police (Scotland) Act 1967, s.44, *infra*, para. 49.06.

[6] For example, Registration of Births, Deaths and Marriages (Scotland) Act 1965, s.53 (as amended by the Children (Scotland) Act 1995, Sched. 4, para. 12(4)); *Jas Kinnison* (1870) 1 Couper 457.

[7] Where "judicial official" includes the police: *cf., Wilson v. Smith*, 1997 S.L.T. (Sh.Ct.) 91.

[8] (1872) 2 Couper 339.

was not made an offence by the Act, but was held by Lord Neaves to be "a serious violation of public duty, involving punishment".[9]

44.02   *Postal Services Act 2000.* Section 83 of the Postal Services Act 2000 provides:

"(1) A person who is engaged in the business of a postal operator[10] commits an offence if, contrary to his duty and without reasonable excuse, he—

(a)   intentionally delays or opens a postal packet[11] in the course of its transmission by post,[12] or

(b)   intentionally opens a mail-bag.[13]

(2) Subsection (1) does not apply to the delaying or opening of a postal packet or the opening of a mail-bag under the authority of—

(a)   this Act or any other enactment (including, in particular, in pursuance of a warrant issued under any other enactment), or

(b)   any directly applicable Community provision.

(3) Subsection (1) does not apply to the delaying or opening of a postal packet in accordance with any terms and conditions applicable to its transmission by post . . ."[14]

An exception is made for the delaying of a postal packet due to industrial action "in contemplation or furtherance of a trade dispute".[15]

Bribery and corruption

44.03   Bribery of judicial officials is a recognised common law crime,[16] and there is some authority for the view that bribery of or the taking of bribes by any public servant to act contrary to his duty is criminal.[17] But there are no reported cases dealing with other than judicial matters; and it is unthinkable that the High Court would now purport to declare bribery of non-judicial officials criminal standing. Article 7 of the European Convention on Human Rights.[18] In practice, and in any event, most cases of such bribery can now be dealt with under statute.

---

[9] At 344.

[10] Under s.125(1), a " 'postal operator' means a person who provides the service of conveying postal packets from one place to another by post or any of the incidental services of receiving, collecting, sorting and delivering such packets".

[11] Under s.125(1), a " 'postal packet' means a letter, parcel, packet or other article transmissible by post".

[12] Under s.125(3)(a), "a postal packet shall be taken to be in course of transmission by post from the time of its being delivered to any post office or post office letter box to the time of its being delivered to the addressee".

[13] Under s.125(1), a " 'mail-bag' includes any form of container or covering in which postal packets in the course of transmission by post are enclosed by a postal operator in the United Kingdom or a foreign postal administration for the purposes of conveyance by post, whether or not it contains any such packets".

[14] Maximum penalty, on indictment, two years' and a fine, and, on summary conviction, six months' and a fine of the statutory maximum.

[15] Section 83(4); "trade dispute" is defined by subs.(5).

[16] See *infra*, para. 49.04; Hume, i, 408; *H.M. Advocate v. Logue*, 1932 J.C. 1.

[17] Hume, i, 408; *H.M. Advocate v. Logue, supra*, L.J.-G. Clyde at 3. But see *H.M. Advocate v. Dick* (1901) 3 Adam 344, where Lord Young held and indeed the Crown conceded that it was not an offence at common law for a town councillor who was not a magistrate and had no concern with the granting of licences to receive money from an applicant for a licence as consideration for using his influence to procure him a licence: at 350. Such conduct by a concillor, even in respect of a matter with which he is not directly concerned, might, it is submitted, be regarded as a breach of his duty as a councillor, and a criminal abuse of his position.

[18] See Vol. I, para. 1.43.

Public Bodies Corrupt Practices Act 1889. Section 1 of this Act[19] provides: **44.04**

"(1) Every person who shall by himself or by or in conjunction with any other person, corruptly solicit or receive, or agree to receive for himself, or for any other person, any gift, loan, fee, reward,[20] or advantage whatever as an inducement to, or reward for, or otherwise on account of any member, officer, or servant of a public body as in this Act defined, doing or forbearing to do anything in respect of any matter or transaction whatsoever, actual or proposed, in which the said public body is concerned, shall be guilty of [an offence].

(2) Every person who shall by himself or by or in conjunction with any other person corruptly give, promise, or offer any gift, loan, fee, reward, or advantage whatsoever to any person whether for the benefit of that person or of another person, as an inducement to or reward for or otherwise on account of any member, officer or servant of any public body as in this Act defined, doing or forbearing to do anything in respect of any matter or transaction whatsoever, actual or proposed, in which such public body as aforesaid is concerned, shall be guilty of [an offence]."

PENALTY. The maximum penalty for an offence under the Act is seven **44.05** years' imprisonment and a fine.[21] In addition a convicted person is liable to pay to the public body in question the value of anything corruptly received by him, and is liable to be adjudged incapable of holding any public office for five years from the date of his conviction and to forfeit any office held by him at the date of his conviction (on a second or subsequent offence he is liable to be adjudged incapable for ever of holding public office, and incapable for five years of voting at any parliamentary election or election for any public body), and to forfeit any claim he may have to a pension as an employee of a public body.[22]

PUBLIC BODY. The Act originally applied only to local authorities and **44.06** other bodies administering money raised by rates, but it was extended by the Prevention of Corruption Act 1916 to include "local and public authorities of all descriptions."[23]

A "public office" is "any office or employment of a person as a member, officer, or servant" of a public body,[24] and included, for

---

[19] As applied to Scotland by s.8.
[20] Including the receipt of money for a past favour without any antecedent agreement: *R. v. Andrews-Weatherfoil Ltd* [1972] 1 W.L.R. 118; *R. v. Parker (Leslie Charles)* (1985) 82 Cr.App.R. 69, CA.
[21] Section 2(a) of the 1889 Act, as substituted by the Criminal Justice Act 1988, s.47(1). On summary conviction, the maximum penalty, is six months' and a fine of the statutory maximum.
[22] Section 2 as amended by Representation of the People Act 1948, s.52(7).
[23] Section 4(2). In *R. v. Newbould* [1962] 2 Q.B. 102, Winn J., held that the Act did not apply to the National Coal Board but was restricted to local and public authorities of the kind set out in the 1889 Act. But in *R. v. Joy and Emmony* (1974) 60 Cr.App.R. 132, Judge Rigg, disagreeing with Winn J., applied the Act to the Gas Council. *R. v. Newbould* was overruled by *R. v. Manners* [1978] A.C. 43, HL which applied the Act to the Gas Board. The Act applies only to public bodies in the United Kingdom: 1889 Act, s.7.
[24] 1889 Act, s.7.

example, a member of a licensing court, since such a court had an administrative function.[25]

44.07   ADVANTAGE. This is defined as including:

> "[A]ny office or dignity, and any forbearance to demand any money or money's worth or valuable thing, and includes any aid, vote, consent, or influence, or pretended aid, vote, consent, or influence, and also includes any promise or procurement of or agreement or endeavour to procure, or the holding out of any expectation of any gift, loan, fee, reward, or advantage, as before defined."[26]

44.08   CORRUPTLY. In *R. v. Smith*[27] the accused was charged with a contravention of section 1(2) of the Act of 1889 by offering a gift to a mayor in order to help himself to acquire some land belonging to the council. His defence was that he had not offered the money corruptly but in order to expose corruption, and that his intention was to bring the matter to light if his offer were accepted. This defence was rejected by the Court of Criminal Appeal on the ground that the accused's motive was irrelevant. "Corruptly" was held to mean only deliberately offering a person money with intent that he should enter into a corrupt bargain. Lord Parker C.J. pointed out[28] that the mere agreement by the mayor to accept the gift offered would in itself be an offence, and that therefore what the accused had intended to induce the mayor to do was something prohibited by the Act.

The court in *Smith* relied on the authority of *Cooper v. Slade*[29] and on Willes J.'s dictum that "corruptly" did not involve dishonesty, but only "purposely doing an act which the law forbids as tending to corrupt".[30] *Cooper v. Slade* was a case of bribery at an election by paying voters' travelling expenses, and the defence of a bona fide belief that such payments were lawful was rejected. This is altogether different from the situation in *Smith*, and it is submitted that *Cooper* has no bearing on the issue in *Smith*. It is submitted further that *Smith* was wrongly decided and should not be followed in Scotland. In the well-known case of *Campbell v. H.M. Advocate*[31] the police arranged a trap whereby a respectable citizen handed the accused, a Glasgow bailie, a bribe under the eyes of police officers.[32] The accused pleaded guilty so that the question whether the evidence of the citizen and the police should be regarded as that of *socii criminis* did not arise,[33] but it is submitted that

---

[25] *Campbell v. H.M. Advocate*, 1941 J.C. 86. But it has been held to be irrelevant to charge a member of a licensing court as an "agent" of the court for the purposes of the Prevention of Corruption Act 1906: *Copeland v. Johnston*, 1967 S.L.T. (Sh.Ct.) 28. See now Licensing (Scotland) Act 1976, s.1.

[26] 1889 Act, s.7.

[27] [1960] 2 Q.B. 423.

[28] At 428.

[29] (1858) 6 H.L.C. 746.

[30] At 773.

[31] 1941 J.C. 86.

[32] See Sir P. Silitoe, *Cloak without Dagger* (London, 1955), Chap. 13.

[33] This could have been a live issue at the time — *i.e.* that the evidence of a *socius criminis* should be received *cum nota*: for the current position, see *Docherty v. H.M. Advocate*, 1987 J.C. 81 (Court of nine judges); Walker and Walker, *The Law of Evidence in Scotland* (2nd ed., by M.L. Ross with J. Chalmers, 2000), para. 13.18.2 (pp. 216–217).

the court would not have so regarded it.[34] It is true that in *Campbell* the bribe had been initially solicited by the accused but that does not, it is submitted, affect the guilt or innocence of a subsequent offer of money, although Lord Parker in *Smith* seems to have been influenced by a desire to preserve public officials from temptation. The Act does not distinguish between giving solicited and giving unsolicited bribes.

In *R. v. Calland*[35] it was held not to be corruption for an insurance agent to pay a government official for a list of newborn children, since he had no intention of dishonestly trying to wheedle him away from his loyalty to his employer.

Where it is proved that any money, gift or other consideration has been paid or given to or received by a person in public employment by or from a person seeking a contract from the public body concerned, there is a presumption of corruption for the purposes of an offence under the Public Bodies Corrupt Practices Act 1889.[36]

It is no defence that while the accused knew that what he was given was intended as a bribe he did not accept it as such but as a reward for work done in the past.[37]

Other statutes

Customs and Excise Management Act 1979. Bribery in connection with **44.09** customs and excise officers is dealt with by section 15 of this Act.[38]

Prevention of Corruption Act 1906.[39] A public officer who is an agent as **44.10** defined by this Act is liable to prosecution under it, whether or not he is also liable to be prosecuted under the Public Bodies Corrupt Practices Act 1889.[40]

Local Government (Scotland) Act 1973. Section 68(2) of this Act **44.11** provides:

> "An officer of a local authority shall not, under colour of his office or employment, accept any fee or reward whatsover other than his proper remuneration."[41]

The section also requires local authority officers to declare any interest they may have in any contract entered into or proposed to be entered into by the authority.

Representation of the People Act 1983. Corruption in connection with **44.12** elections is dealt with under this Act.[42]

---

[34] It was said *obiter* in *R. v. Mills* (1978) 68 Cr.App.R. 154, at 159 by Geoffrey Lane L.J. that, "if the money is received in order to entrap the defendant or in order to provide evidence for a policeman who is listening and may be taking a recording on tape of the conversation, then the man does not intend to keep the money and it would plainly not be corrupt."

[35] [1967] Crim.L.R. 236.

[36] Prevention of Corruption Act 1916, s.2 (which also applies to an offence under the Prevention of Corruption Act 1906): see, *e.g.*, *R. v. Braithwaite* [1983] 1 W.L.R. 385, CA; *Beaton v. H.M. Advocate*, 1993 S.C.C.R. 48.

[37] *R. v. Mills* (1978) 68 Cr.App.R. 154, CA.

[38] *supra*, para. 38.16.

[39] *supra*, para. 21.23.

[40] *Graham v. Hart* (1908) 5 Adam 457.

[41] Maximum penalty, on summary conviction, a fine of level 4 on the standard scale.

[42] *supra*, para. 38.22, *et seq.*

Obstruction of officials

44.13   Violent obstruction of officers of law is a recognised common law crime,[43] but there is no authority on whether it is a common law crime to obstruct other state officials in the exercise of their duty.

A large number of statutes which give power to officials to do certain acts, particularly to enter premises or obtain information, contain clauses making it an offence to obstruct these officials or to fail to give the required information.

44.14 *Inland Revenue Regulation Act 1890.* Section 11 of this Act makes it an offence to obstruct Inland Revenue officers and employees acting in the execution of their duty or of their legal power and authority, or to obstruct any person "acting in the aid of an officer or any person so employed."[44]

Sale of offices and honours

44.15 *Sale of offices.* The Sale of Offices Act 1551, applied to Scotland by section 1 of the Sale of Offices Act 1809, prohibited the sale or purchase of judicial offices, revenue offices and offices concerned with the maintenance of fortresses, and provided that the seller of such offices should forfeit any right he had in the office, and the buyer be disabled from holding the office.[45]

Section 1 of the Sale of Offices Act 1809 extended the 1551 Act to all offices in the gift of the Crown, and all commissions, civil, naval or military,[46] and to all places and employments in any public departments.[47]

The 1809 Act makes it an offence to sell or bargain to sell, or receive any reward or profit for, any office as defined by the Act, or for the appointment, or nomination to, or the resignation thereof, or for the consent or voice of any person in any such appointment or resignation.[48] It is also an offence for any person to receive any money for any interest, recommendation or negotiation to be made or pretended to be made in connection with any such nomination, appointment or resignation, or with the obtaining of anyone's voice or consent thereto, or to recommend or negotiate on behalf of anyone in any prohibited matter in expectation of reward.[49] Offences under the Act are punishable by fine and imprisonment[50] in addition to the forfeiture and disability provided for by the 1551 Act.[51]

---

[43] Macdonald, p.169; *Jas Hunter and Thos Peacock* (1860) 3 Irv. 518. *Cf.* Police (Scotland) Act 1967, s.41, *supra*, para. 29.12.

[44] Maximum penalty a fine of level 3 on the standard scale: see *Tighe v. Wilson* (1912) 7 Adam 46.

[45] According to Alison, buying and selling offices of public trust and importance is a crime at common law, but he cites no Scots authority: Alison, i, 635–636.

[46] Extended to the Air Force by S.R. & O. 1918 No. 548 Rev. I, 896, as amended by the Defence (Transfer of Functions) (No. 1) Order 1964 (S.I. 1964 No. 488), Sched. 2 (list).

[47] Except such offices as were excepted by the 1551 Act, and except any offices legally saleable prior to 1809 and in the gift of any person by virtue of any office held by him under any patent or appointment for life: 1809 Act, s.9.

[48] Section 3.

[49] Section 4.

[50] Section 13.

[51] The 1809 Act also prohibits the use of premises in connection with the purchase of appointments: s.5, and the advertising of any such place or the name of any broker or agent for such a purpose: s.6. The penalty under s.6 as amended by the Common Informers Act 1951 is a fine of level 3 on the standard scale.

The Act does not prohibit an agreement for the payment out of the fees of an office of a salary to a lawfully appointed deputy.[52]

Sale of honours. The Honours (Prevention of Abuses) Act 1925 **44.16** provides as follows:

"**1.**—(1) If any person accepts or obtains or agrees to accept or attempts to obtain from any person, for himself or for any other person, or for any purpose, any gift, money or valuable consideration as an inducement or reward for procuring or assisting or endeavouring to procure the grant of a dignity or title of honour to any person, or otherwise in connection with such a grant, he shall be guilty of [an offence].

(2) If any person gives, or agrees or proposes to give, or offers to any person any gift, money or valuable consideration as an inducement or reward for procuring or assisting or endeavouring to procure the grant of a dignity or title of honour to any person, or otherwise in connection with such a grant, he shall be guilty of [an offence]."[53]

---

[52] Section 10.

[53] Maximum penalty on indictment two years' imprisonment and a fine, on summary conviction three months' imprisonment and a fine of the prescribed sum; and forfeiture of any gift, etc., received: s.1(3).

CHAPTER 45

BIGAMY

Bigamy is a very difficult crime to classify. It appears at first glance to **45.01**
be a sexual offence, and Hume regards it as being similar to adultery.[1]
But adultery is no longer regarded as criminal, and although it appears
to be an invariable practice to libel that cohabitation followed upon the
bigamous marriage,[2] the crime consists in the marriage and not in the
subsequent adultery.[3] Bigamy was at one time prosecuted as perjury
under the now repealed Act 1551, c.19,[4] as involving a breach of
marriage vows,[5] but it is now always prosecuted as an independent
common law crime. Where only one of the parties to the bigamous
marriage is married and the other is unaware of the fact, the married
partner is guilty of fraud, and this is regarded as an aggravation of the
bigamy, but bigamy may be committed although both parties know the
true situation, and the unmarried party is then art and part in the other's
bigamy.[6] Bigamy may also be regarded as an offence against the
provisions regarding the registration of marriages,[7] but making false
entries in the register is itself a statutory offence[8] and bigamy may be
committed by a "marriage" which is irregular. Hume describes it as "a
flagrant breach" of "laudable discipline and economy",[9] and the crime is
perhaps best regarded as an offence against public order and decency.[10]

The requisites of bigamy

Bigamy consists in the contraction of a formally valid second marriage **45.02**
by a person who is a party to a prior subsisting valid marriage.

Prior marriage. The prior marriage may be either regular or irregular.[11] **45.03**
In practice most cases of bigamy based on irregular first marriages have

---

[1] Hume, i, 459.

[2] See all the reported indictments in the cases referred to *infra*; Criminal Procedure
(Scotland) Act 1995, Sched. 2.

[3] Mackenzie, I,18,5, Macdonald, p.145; *cf*. Hume, i, 462.

[4] See A.P.S. Vol. II, p.486, c.11.

[5] Mackenzie, I,18,1.

[6] Hume, i, 462; Alison, i, 539.

[7] *cf*. Gl. Williams, "Language and the Law" (1945) 61 L.Q.R. 71, at 76–78.

[8] *supra*, para. 19.13.

[9] Hume, i, 459.

[10] This is the approach adopted in the *Stair Memorial Encyclopaedia* (Edinburgh, 1995),
Vol. 7, "Criminal Law", para. 477 *et seq*. *Cf*. J. Burchell and J. Milton, *Principles of* [South
African] *Criminal Law* (2nd ed., 1997), p.522, where it is classed as an offence against
family life. (But see also the criticism of the offence, offered *ibid*., at pp. 528–529.) *Cf*. also
Gray v. Criminal Injuries Compensation Board, 1993 S.L.T. 28.

[11] Macdonald, p.146; E. Clive, *Husband and Wife* (Edinburgh, 4th ed., 1997), para. 18.027;
contra Hume, i, 459; Alison, i, 536.

been where the first marriage was a marriage by declaration.[12] In principle the same rule applies to marriage by promise *subsequente copula*,[13] and marriages by habit and repute, but in practice the difficulties of proving the date and place of such irregular marriages make it difficult to succeed in a charge of bigamy based on a first marriage which was contracted in these ways.[14] There is also the further difficulty of meeting the defence in a habit and repute case that the accused was not aware that he was married.[15] Where, however, the second marriage takes place after the first has been established by decree of declarator these difficulties disappear and a conviction for bigamy will follow.[16]

45.04 *Valid.* The prior marriage must have been valid and in the case of a foreign marriage this may involve consideration of the foreign law as deponed to by expert witnesses.[17] There are no reported bigamy cases which turn on the distinction between void and voidable marriages, and the position of voidable marriages is not clear. Doubts have been expressed particularly in connection with marriages voidable for impotence.[18]

Where the first marriage was void, as for example for non-age or for being itself bigamous,[19] the second marriage is valid and there is no bigamy. Where, however, the first marriage was voidable only, as is the case with impotence,[20] it subsists until dissolved, and if either spouse contracts a second marriage before the first is dissolved by decree of nullity, the second marriage may well be bigamous.

---

[12] *Wm Brown* (1846) Ark. 205; *Jas Purves* (1848) J. Shaw 124; *Abraham Langley* (1862) 4 Irv. 190. Irregular marriages of this kind have not been competent since July 1, 1940: Marriage (Scotland) Act 1939, s.5, and relative commencement order: S.R. & O. 1940, No 859, Rev. XIX, 970.

[13] Also abolished from July 1, 1940, *ibid.*

[14] Macdonald, p.146; *John Armstrong* (1844) 2 Broun 251; *Abraham Langley* (1862) 4 Irv. 190, Lord Cowan and Lord Deas at 193; *Reid v. H.M. Advocate*, 1934 J.C. 7, L.J.G. Clyde at 8. But such a charge was sustained in *Waugh v. Davidson and Robertson*, 1946 S.L.T. (Sh.Ct.) 9.

[15] *cf.* Hume, i, 460, commenting on *John Roger* (1813) where the accused was acquitted, the first marriage being allegedly by habit and repute. But see *Waugh v. Davidson and Robertson, supra.*

[16] *Reid v. H.M. Advocate, supra.*

[17] *Wm Bennison* (1850) J. Shaw 453; *Patrick Quillichan* (1852) J. Shaw 537.

[18] Mackenzie, I.18.5, and Hume, i, 456, thought impotence should not be a defence; Macdonald thinks that impotence in the first marriage is a defence to bigamy: at p.147. In *Wm Masterton* (1837) 1 Swin. 427, the Crown declined to proceed further after a defence of impotence had been lodged: see Macdonald, p.147.

[19] *cf.* Kenny, para. 171, where he points out that if X marries A, and then B while A is alive, and later marries C after A's death but during B's life, his marriage with C is not bigamous. An even odder situation arose in *Risi v. R.*, Court of Session, March 26, 1964, unrep'd, where R married A who divorced him. R then married B while he was unaware of the divorce. B obtained decree of declarator that her marriage was void since R did not intend to marry her but to commit bigamy. R, however, could not be convicted of bigamy since he was in fact free to marry B. (Under the current Scots law, he would probably have been guilty of attempted bigamy: see Vol. I, para. 6.56.) And it would appear that R could have contracted any number of void marriages after his divorce from A and while his marriage to B was still unreduced without committing bigamy, provided his intention was to commit bigamy on each occasion. And, conversely, a belief by a man that his earlier marriage is bigamous is a good defence to a charge of bigamy during its subsistence: see *Balshaw v. B.*, 1967 S.C. 63; *R. v. King* [1964] 1 Q.B. 285.

[20] *S.G. v. W.G.*, 1933 S.C. 728.

Subsisting. A marriage may cease to subsist by reason of the death of one **45.05** spouse or by reason of divorce or dissolution. If either spouse remarries before such divorce or dissolution the second marriage is bigamous, whether or not the parties to the first marriage have been judicially separated, and whether or not divorce proceedings are pending.[21] Generally speaking, once a final decree of divorce has been pronounced the spouses are free to remarry, and the fact that the divorce decree is itself subsequently declared invalid will not make any intervening marriage criminally bigamous, not because at the time it took place there was not a prior subsisting marriage, but because the accused will be entitled to say be believed he was free to remarry.[22] Where, however, the divorce decree is invalid because of some fraud or other improper actings by the accused, he may not be entitled to plead the decree as a defence to a charge of bigamy.[23]

A second formal marriage. The second marriage must be in the form of a **45.06** legally recognised ceremony, but it does not matter that in addition to being void as bigamous it is also void on any other ground such as relationship.[24]

If the marriage is *ex facie* formally valid it does not matter that the requirements as to notice have not been obtempered.[25] It is no defence that either of the parties did not regard the marriage as religiously binding, as for example where a Roman Catholic goes through a marriage by declaration[26] or before a registrar, or where a Christian goes through a regular Jewish or Quaker marriage.[27]

Mens rea

The ordinary common law requirements of *mens rea* apply to bigamy **45.07** as to any other common law crime.[28] The position of error in bigamy is, however, complicated.

Error. Problems regarding error may arise in respect of a belief that the **45.08** first spouse is dead, that the first marriage was invalid, that the first marriage was dissolved, or that the second ceremony was not in fact a marriage ceremony at all.

---

[21] *Janet Henderson* (1829) Alison, i. 539.

[22] Mackenzie, I.18.6; Hume, i, 461.

[23] The matter is unsettled. Mackenzie inclines to the view that in such a case the accused is to be deemed to have known that the divorce was bad and that the earlier marriage still subsisted: I,18,6, and Hume and Alison accept this view: Hume, i, 461; Alison, i, 538.

[24] Hume, i, 462; Alison, i, 539; Macdonald, p.147. The idea seems to be that the marriage is void anyway as being bigamous so that there is no point in taking any other voiding feature into account; *ibid*. It would perhaps be better to base the rule on the view that the important feature is the pretended *ceremony* of marriage.

[25] Macdonald, p.146; *John McLean* (1836) 1 Swin. 278.

[26] *Septimus Thorburn* (1844) 2 Broun 4.

[27] Kenny, para. 172.

[28] See *e.g. Thos More and Christina Coupar* (1865) 5 Irv. 73; *cf. Catherine Potter and David Inglis* (1852) 1 Irv. 73.

45.09   DEATH OF FIRST SPOUSE. There is common law authority that a belief that one's first spouse was dead is a defence to a charge of bigamy, and such a defence is clearly relevant on general principles, although proof of the belief would rest on the accused[29] who might have to show that he has made "due inquiry"[30] or at least that he had reasonable grounds for his belief.[31] The position is not affected by section 13 of the Presumption of Death (Scotland) Act 1977 which provides:

> "It shall be a defence against a charge of bigamy for the accused to prove[32] that at no time within the period of seven years immediately preceding the date of the purported marriage forming the substance of the charge had he any reason to believe that his spouse was alive."

45.10   INVALIDITY OF FIRST MARRIAGE. Such a belief would constitute an error of law, and might therefore be irrelevant,[33] if only because the courts are likely to have scant sympathy for an accused who pleads this defence but has taken no step to have the first marriage declared void. The defence might, however, be sustained in extreme cases as where A believed that the first marriage was "only a play or charade", which would amount to an error of fact.

45.11   DISSOLUTION OF FIRST MARRIAGE. If A believes that he has been divorced when in fact he has only obtained a separation decree that belief will be relevant, but if he believes that a separation decree dissolves the marriage so as to entitle him to remarry that might be regarded as an error of law and so as irrelevant.[34]

45.12   SECOND CEREMONY. If A goes through a formal ceremony of marriage in the belief that he is acting a charade he is not guilty of bigamy. If, however, he goes through what he knows to be a marriage ceremony but which he believes for some reason to be lacking in some formal requirement or to be invalid for any other reason, he will be guilty of bigamy.

Art and part in bigamy

45.13   All persons who take part knowingly in a bigamous marriage whether as party, celebrant or witness, are guilty of bigamy,[35] and the same would be the position of anyone else who assisted in the bigamy, for example, by telling the innocent spouse that the accused was free to marry, or by making arrangements for the ceremony.

---

[29] Hume, i, 461; Alison, i, 539; *Norman Macdonald* (1842) 1 Broun 238, in which the Crown dropped their case on the suggestion of the court after the defence had been set up. See also *Mackenzie v. Macfarlane* (1891) 5 S.L.T. 292; *Sharp v. S.* (1898) *ibid.* 291. The burden on the accused is presumably only an evidential one: see G.H. Gordon, "The Burden of Proof on the Accused", 1968 S.L.T. (News) 29, 40.

[30] *Wm Bennison* (1850) J. Shaw 453, L.J.-C. Hope at 458.

[31] If A suffers from amnesia and as a result has forgotten that he ever was married it would appear on general principles that he cannot be guilty of bigamy since he is completely lacking in *mens rea*.

[32] That is to say, the persuasive burden is on him.

[33] See Vol. I, para. 9.17.

[34] *cf. Thomas v. R.* (1937) 59 C.L.R. 279; *R. v. Gould* [1968] 2 Q.B. 65. See also Vol. I, para. 9.17.

[35] Hume, i, 462.

CHAPTER 46

POLLUTION

Disposal of waste on land

Part II of the Environmental Protection Act 1990 makes provision for **46.01** the proper collection and disposal of controlled waste, *i.e.* household, industrial and commercial or any such waste,[1] and for the disposal of other waste.

Section 33[2] provides:

"(1) Subject to subsections (2) and (3) below, a person shall not—
   (a) deposit controlled waste, or knowingly[3] cause or knowingly permit controlled waste to be deposited in or on any land unless a waste management licence[4] authorising the deposit is in force and the deposit is in accordance with the licence;
   (b) treat, keep or dispose of controlled waste, or knowingly cause or knowingly permit controlled waste to be treated, kept or disposed of—
      (i) in or on any land, or
      (ii) by means of any mobile plant,[5]
   except under and in accordance with a waste management licence;
   (c) treat, keep or dispose of controlled waste in a manner likely to cause pollution of the environment[6] or harm to human health.

---

[1] Section 75(4). Definitions of "household", "industrial" and "commercial" wastes are provided by s.75(5), (6), and (7) respectively.

[2] As amended by the Environment Act 1995, Sched. 22, para. 64, and Sched. 24.

[3] It has been held that "knowledge" relates only to the causing or permitting the deposit of waste, and not to whether or not a waste management licence existed or whether or not the deposit was in accordance with the terms of any such licence: *Shanks v. McEwan (Teesside) Ltd v. Environment Agency* [1999] Q.B. 333.

[4] See s.35 (as amended by the Environment Act 1995, Sched. 22, para. 66). It has been held that the word "land" (in the equivalent provision of the Control of Pollution Act 1974) includes buildings and other structures: *Gotech Industrial and Env. Services Ltd v. Friel*, 1995 S.C.C.R. 22.

[5] See s.29(9).

[6] " 'Environment' consists of all, or any of the following media, namely land, water and the air", and " 'pollution of the environment' means pollution of the environment due to the release or escape (into any environmental medium) from—
   (a) the land on which controlled waste is treated,
   (b) the land on which controlled waste is kept,
   (c) the land in or on which controlled waste is deposited,
   (d) fixed plant by means of which controlled waste is treated, kept or disposed of, substances or articles constituting or resulting from the waste and capable (by reason of the quantity or concentrations involved) of causing harm to man or any other living organisms supported by the environment.": s.29(2), (3).

(2) Subsection (1) above does not apply in relation to household waste[7] from a domestic property which is treated, kept or disposed of within the curtilage of the dwelling by or with the permission of the occupier of the dwelling.

(3) Subsection (1)(a), (b) or (c) above do not apply in cases prescribed in regulations made by the Secretary of State and the regulations may make different exceptions for different areas.

(4) The Secretary of State, in exercising his power under subsection (3) above, shall have regard in particular to the expediency of excluding from the controls imposed by waste management licences—

(a) any deposits which are small enough or of such a temporary nature that they may be so excluded;

(b) any means of treatment or disposal which are innocuous enough to be so excluded;

(c) cases for which adequate controls are provided by another enactment than this section.

(5) Where controlled waste is carried in and deposited from a motor vehicle, the person who controls or is in a position to control the use of the vehicle shall, for the purposes of subsection (1)(a) above, be treated as knowingly causing the waste to be deposited whether or not he gave any instructions for this to be done.

(6) A person who contravenes subsection (1) above or any condition of a waste management licence commits an offence.

(7) It shall be a defence for a person charged with an offence under this section to prove—

(a) that he took all reasonable precautions and exercised all due diligence to avoid the commission of the offence; or

(b) that he acted under instructions from his employer and neither knew nor had reason to suppose that the acts done by him constituted a contravention of subsection (1) above; or

(c) that the acts alleged to constitute the contravention were done in an emergency in order to avoid danger to human health in a case where—

(i) he took all such steps as were reasonably practicable in the circumstances for minimising pollution of the environment and harm to human health; and

(ii) particulars of the acts were furnished to the waste regulation authority as soon as reasonably practicable after they were done.

(8) Except in a case falling within subsection (9) below, a person who commits an offence under this section shall be liable—

(a) on summary conviction, to imprisonment for a term not exceeding six months or a fine not exceeding £20,000 or both; and

(b) on conviction on indictment, to imprisonment for a term not exceeding two years or a fine or both.

---

[7] "Household waste" includes waste from domestic property, a caravan, a residential home, premises forming part of a university or school or other educational establishment, and premises forming part of a hospital or nursing home: s.75(5).

(9) A person who commits an offence under this section in relation to special waste[8] shall be liable—

(a) on summary conviction, to imprisonment for a term not exceeding six months or a fine not exceeding £20,000 or both; and

(b) on conviction on indictment, to imprisonment for a term not exceeding five years or a fine or both."

Section 63(1) of the Environmental Protection Act 1990 empowers the **46.02** Secretary of State to provide by regulation that prescribed provisions of Part II of the Act shall apply in a prescribed area as if references to controlled waste included references to waste from mines, quarries or agricultural premises.

Section 63(2)[9] and (3) provide:

"(2) A person who deposits, or knowingly causes or knowingly permits the deposit of any waste—

(a) which is not controlled waste, but

(b) which, if it were controlled waste, would be special waste,

in a case where he would be guilty of an offence under section 33 above if the waste were special waste and any waste management licence were not in force, shall, subject to subsection (3) below, be guilty of that offence and punishable as if the waste were special waste.

(3) No offence is committed by virtue of subsection (2) above if the act charged was done under and in accordance with any consent, licence, approval or authority granted under any enactment (excluding any planning permission under the enactments relating to town and country planning)."

Transporting controlled waste. Section 1 of the Control of Pollution **46.03** (Amendment) Act 1989[10] makes it an offence for a person other than a registered carrier of controlled waste to transport such waste in the course of anyone's business or with a view to profit.[11]

Pollution of coastal, inland and ground waters

Section 30F[12] of the Control of Pollution Act 1974 provides: **46.04**

---

[8] "Special waste" means controlled waste in respect of which regulations are in force under s.62 (as amended by the Environment Act 1995, Sched. 22, para. 80), which relates to waste which is dangerous or difficult to treat: s.75(9).

[9] As substituted by the Environment Act 1995, Sched. 22, para. 81.

[10] As amended by the Environmental Protection Act 1990, Sched. 15.

[11] Maximum penalty, on summary conviction, a fine of level 5 on the standard scale: s.1(5). Exceptions are provided, or referred to, in subss. (2) and (3); and defences are set out in subs. (4) read with subs. (6).

[12] As inserted by the Environment Act 1995, Sched. 16, para. 2. (Section 30F replaces the former ss. 31 and 32 of the 1974 Act, which were repealed by the Environment Act 1995, Sched. 16, para. 3.) Section 30F has been amended by the Groundwater Regulations 1998 (S.I. 1998 No. 2746), reg. 14, such that a person is to be treated as contravening that section if (a) he causes or knowingly permits disposal or tipping of any listed substance (otherwise than in accordance with an authorisation under reg. 18) in circumstances which might lead to an indirect discharge of that substance into groundwater, or any activity which contravenes a prohibition imposed (or an authorisation granted) under reg. 19; or (b) he contravenes the conditions of any authorisation under regs 18 or 19.

"(1) A person contravenes this section if he causes or knowingly permits any poisonous, noxious or polluting matter or any solid waste matter to enter any controlled waters.

(2) A person contravenes this section if he causes or knowingly permits any matter, other than trade effluent or sewage effluent,[13] to enter controlled waters by being discharged from a sewer or from a drain[14] in contravention of a prohibition imposed under section 30G below.

(3) A person contravenes this section if he causes or knowingly permits any trade effluent or sewage effluent to be discharged—

(a) into any controlled waters; or

(b) from land in Scotland, through a pipe, into the sea outside the seaward limits of controlled waters.

(4) A person contravenes this section if he causes or knowingly permits any trade effluent or sewage effluent to be discharged, in contravention of any prohibition imposed under section 30G below, from a building or any plant—

(a) on to or into any land; or

(b) into any waters of a loch or pond which are not inland waters.

(5) A person contravenes this section if he causes or knowingly permits any matter whatever to enter any inland waters so as to tend (either directly or in combination with other matter which he or another person causes or permits to enter those waters) to impede the proper flow of the waters in a manner leading, or likely to lead, to a substantial aggravation of—

(a) pollution due to other causes; or

(b) the consequences of such pollution.

(6) Subject to the following provisions of this Part, a person who contravenes this section shall be guilty of an offence and liable—

(a) on summary conviction, to imprisonment for a term not exceeding three months or to a fine not exceeding £20,000 or to both;

(b) on conviction on indictment, to imprisonment for a term not exceeding two years or to a fine or to both."[15]

"Controlled waters" are defined in section 30A[16] of the Act as follows:

---

[13] " 'Sewage effluent' includes any effluent from the sewage disposal or sewerage works of a local authority within the meaning of the Sewerage (Scotland) Act 1968"; " 'trade effluent' includes any effluent which is discharged from premises used for carrying on any trade or industry, other than surface water and domestic sewage" (and, under s.56(3), any premises (whether on land or not) which are wholly or mainly used for fish farming, or scientific research or experiment are deemed to be (and in the case of a fish farm, always to have been) premises used for carrying on a trade); and " 'effluent' means any liquid, including particles of matter and other substances in suspension in the liquid": s.56(1) of the 1974 Act, as substituted by the Water Act 1989, Sched. 23, para. 6. (Section 56(1) also contains definitions of "underground strata", "water authority" and "watercourse".)

[14] "Drain" and "sewer" have the same meaning as they do in s.59(1) of the Sewage (Scotland) Act 1968: s.56(1) of the 1974 Act, as amended by the Environment Act 1995, Sched. 16, para. 8.

[15] Under s.30I (inserted by the Environment Act 1995, Sched. 16, para. 2; and as amended by the Pollution Prevention and Control (Scotland) Regulations 2000 (S.S.I. 2000 No. 323), reg. 1), no offence is committed under s.30F if the discharge was made under and in accordance with any described consent, authorisation, licence or statutory provision.

[16] Added by the Water Act 1989, Sched. 23, para. 4 (which, *inter alia*, adds ss. 30A–30E to the 1974 Act).

"(1) This part [*i.e.* Part II of the 1974 Act] applies to any waters (in this Part referred to as "controlled waters") of any of the following classes—

(a) relevant territorial waters, that is to say, subject to subsection (5)[17] below, the waters which extend seaward for three miles[18] from the baselines from which the breadth of the territorial sea adjacent to Scotland is measured;

(b) coastal waters, that is to say, any waters which are within the area which extends landward from those baselines as far as the limit of the highest tide or, in the case of the waters of any relevant river or watercourse, as far as the fresh-water limit of the river or watercourse, together with the waters of any enclosed dock which adjoins waters within that area;

(c) inland waters, that is to say, the waters of any relevant loch or pond[19] or of so much of any relevant river or watercourse[20] as is above the fresh-water limit[21];

(d) ground waters, that is to say, any waters contained in underground strata, or in—

   (i) a well, borehole or similar work sunk into underground strata, including any adit or passage constructed in connection with the well, borehole or work for facilitating the collection of water in the well, borehole or work; or

   (ii) any excavation into underground strata where the level of water in the excavation depends wholly or mainly on water entering it from the strata."

Under section 30J,[22] it is a defence to a contravention of section 30F that a discharge was made in an emergency in order to avoid danger to life or health, provided that all steps as were reasonably practicable in the circumstances to minimise the extent of the discharge and its polluting effects were taken and that particulars of the discharge were furnished to the Scottish Environmental Protection Agency as soon as reasonably practicable thereafter.[23] It is also a defence under that section (to a contravention of section 30F) that water from an abandoned mine was permitted to enter controlled waters, provided that the mine was abandoned on or before December 31, 1999.[24]

---

[17] Subsection (5) states that the Secretary of State may by order provide that any area of the territorial sea adjacent to Scotland may be treated as an area of territorial waters, and that "any loch or pond which does not discharge into a relevant river or watercourse or into a relevant loch or pond is to be treated . . . as a relevant loch or pond."

[18] "miles" means "international nautical miles of 1,852 metres": s.30A(4).

[19] "Loch or pond" includes a reservoir; and "relevant loch or pond" means (subject to subs. (5)) "any loch or pond which (whether it is natural or artificial or above or below the ground) discharges into a relevant river or watercourse or into another loch or pond which is itself a relevant loch or pond": s.30A(4).

[20] "Relevant river or watercourse" means "any river or watercourse (including an underground river or watercourse and an artificial river or watercourse) which is neither a public sewer nor a sewer or drain which drains into a public sewer": s.30A(4).

[21] This paragraph is to have effect as if "inland waters" included all waters which need to be classified under the Surface Waters (Abstraction for Drinking Water) (Classification) (Scotland) Regulations 1996 (S.I. 1996 No. 3047), reg. 15(1).

[22] Inserted by the Environment Act 1995, Sched. 16, para. 2.

[23] Section 30J(1).

[24] Section 30J(3), (4); see also subss. (5) and (6). Other defences are contained in subss. (7) and (8). No offence is committed under s.30F where a person causes or permits a discharge of trade or sewage effluent from a vessel: s.30J(2).

Dumping at sea

46.05   Part II of the Food and Environment Protection Act 1985 sets up a
licensing system for the depositing of substances and articles in the sea
or under the sea-bed. Sections 5 and 6[25] of that Act provide:

> "**5.**—Subject to the following provisions of this Part of this Act, a
> licence under this Part of this Act is needed—
> > (a) for the deposit of substances or articles within United
> > Kingdom waters[26] or United Kingdom controlled waters[27]
> > either in the sea or under the sea-bed—
> > > (i) from a vehicle, vessel,[28] aircraft, hovercraft or marine
> > > structure[29];
> > > (ii) from a container floating in the sea; or
> > > (iii) from a structure on land constructed or adapted wholly
> > > or mainly for the purpose of depositing solids in the
> > > sea;
> > (b) for the deposit of substances or articles anywhere in the sea
> > or under the sea-bed—
> > > (i) from a British Vessel, British aircraft, British hovercraft
> > > or British marine structure[30]; or
> > > (ii) from a container floating in the sea, if the deposit is
> > > controlled from a British vessel, British aircraft, British
> > > hovercraft or British marine structure;
> > . . .
> > (e) for the scuttling of vessels—
> >
> > > (i) in United Kingdom waters or United Kingdom con-
> > > trolled waters;
> > > (ii) anywhere at sea, if the scuttling is controlled from a
> > > British vessel, British aircraft, British hovercraft or
> > > British marine structure.
> > (f) for the loading of a vessel, aircraft, hovercraft, marine
> > structure or floating container in the United Kingdom or
> > United Kingdom waters with substances or articles for
> > deposit anywhere in the sea or under the sea-bed;
> > (g) for the loading of a vehicle in the United Kingdom with
> > substances or articles for deposit from that vehicle as men-
> > tioned in paragraph (a) above; and

---

[25] As amended by the Environmental Protection Act 1990, s.146. Exemptions may be
provided for by statutory instrument made under s.7.

[26] "'United Kingdom waters' means any part of the sea within the seaward limits of
United Kingdom territorial waters": s.24(1).

[27] "United Kingdom controlled waters" refers to any part of the sea within limits
designated by s.1(7) of the Continental Shelf Act 1964: s.24(1); definition added by the
Environmental Protection Act 1990, s.146(7).

[28] "Vessel" has the meaning assigned to "ship" by the Merchant Shipping Act 1995:
s.24(1), as amended by the Merchant Shipping Act 1995, Sched. 13, para. 75(b).

[29] "'Marine structure' means a platform or man-made structure at sea other than a
pipe-line": s.24(1).

[30] Definitions of "British" aircraft, hovercraft and marine structure are provided by
s.24(1). A "British vessel" means a vessel registered in the United Kingdom, or a vessel
exempted from such registration under the Merchant Shipping Act 1995: s.24(1), as
amended by the Merchant Shipping Act 1995, Sched. 13, para. 75(a).

(h) for the towing or propelling from the United Kingdom or United Kingdom waters of a vessel for scuttling anywhere at sea.

6.—(1) Subject to the following provisions of this Part of this Act, a licence is needed—

(a) for the incineration of substances or articles on a vessel or marine structure—

    (i) in United Kingdom waters or United Kingdom controlled waters; or

    (ii) anywhere at sea, if the incineration takes place on a British vessel or British marine structure; [and]

(b) for the loading of a vessel or marine structure in the United Kingdom or United Kingdom waters with substances or articles for incineration anywhere at sea.

(2) In this Act 'incineration' means any combustion of substances and materials for the purpose of their thermal destruction.''

It is an offence under section 9 of the 1985 Act for a person to do anything for which a licence is needed, or to cause or permit any other person to do any such thing, except in pursuance of a licence and in accordance with that licence's terms.[31] It is a defence for a person charged with such an offence to prove that what he did was for the purpose of "securing the safety of a vessel, aircraft, hovercraft or marine structure or of saving life" and that he took steps to effect official notification of what had been done within a reasonable time.[32] The defence will be denied, however, if the court is satisfied that what was done was not necessary for such a purpose and was not a reasonable step to take in the circumstances.[33]

Oil pollution

(1) *From places on land.* This is dealt with by the Prevention of Oil **46.06** Pollution Act 1971. Section 2[34] provides as follows:

"(1) If any oil[35] or mixture containing oil is discharged as mentioned in the following paragraphs into waters to which this section applies, then, subject to the provisions of this Act, the following shall be guilty of an offence, that is to say—

. . .

---

[31] Maximum penalty, on summary conviction, a fine of £50,000, and, on indictment, two years' and a fine: s.21(2A), as inserted by the Environmental Protection Act 1990, s.146(6). See also the Petroleum Act 1998, Pt IV, which contains provisions relative to the abandonment of offshore installations.

[32] Section 9(3).

[33] Section 9(4). See also the defences set out in subs. (5) which (as amended by the Environmental Protection Act 1990, s.146(4)) refers to subss. (6) and (7). There is a general "due diligence" defence to any offence under the 1985 Act in s.22.

[34] Paragraphs (a) and (b) of subs. (1) were repealed by the Merchant Shipping (Prevention of Oil Pollution) Order 1983 (S.I. 1983 No. 1106), art. 2, Sched.

[35] Defined as crude oil, fuel oil, lubricating oil, and heavy diesel oil as defined by regulation: s.1(2).

(c) if the discharge is from a place on land, the occupier of that place, unless he proves that the discharge was caused as mentioned in paragraph (d) of this subsection;

(d) if the discharge is from a place on land and is caused by the act of a person who is in that place without the permission (express or implied) of the occupier, that person;

(e) if the discharge takes place otherwise than as mentioned in the preceding paragraphs and is the result of any operations for the exploration of the sea-bed and sub-soil or the exploitation of their natural resources, the person carrying on the operations.

(2) This section applies to the following waters, that is to say—

(a) the whole of the sea within the seaward limits of the territorial waters of the United Kingdom; and

(b) all other waters (including inland waters) which are within those limits and are navigable by sea-going ships.

(3) In this Act 'place on land' includes anything resting on the bed or shore of the sea, or of any other waters to which this section applies, and also includes anything afloat (other than a vessel) if it is anchored or attached to the bed or shore of the sea or of any such waters; and 'occupier', in relation to any such thing as is mentioned in the preceding provisions of this subsection, if it has no occupier means the owner thereof, and, in relation to a railway wagon or road vehicle, means the person in charge of the wagon or vehicle and not the occupier of the land on which the wagon or vehicle stands.

(4) A person guilty of an offence under this section shall be liable on summary conviction to a fine not exceeding £50,000 or on conviction on indictment to a fine."

46.07 (2) *From oil pipe-lines or exploration activities.* Section 3 of the Prevention of Oil Pollution Act 1971 provides:

"(1) If any oil to which section 1 of this Act applies, or any mixture containing such oil, is discharged into any part of the sea—

(a) from a pipe-line; or

(b) (otherwise than from a ship) as the result of any operation for the exploration of the sea-bed and subsoil or the exploitation of their natural resources in a designated area,

then, subject to the following provisions of this Act, the owner of the pipe-line or, as the case may be, the person carrying on the operations shall be guilty of an offence unless the discharge was from a place in his occupation and he proves that it was due to the act of a person who was there without his permission (express or implied).

(2) In this section 'designated area' means an area for the time being designated by an Order made under section 1 of the Continental Shelf Act 1964.

(3) A person guilty of an offence under this section shall be liable on summary conviction to a fine not exceeding £50,000 or on conviction on indictment to a fine."

DEFENCES. The Prevention of Oil Pollution Act 1971 provides the **46.08** following defences by section 6:

"(1) Where a person is charged, in respect of the escape of any oil or mixture containing oil, with an offence under section 2 or 3 of this Act—
  (a) as the occupier of a place on land; or
  (b) as a person carrying on operations for the exploration of the sea-bed and subsoil or the exploitation of their natural resources; or
  (c) as the owner of a pipe-line,
it shall be a defence to prove that neither the escape not any delay in discovering it was due to any want of reasonable care and that as soon as practicable after it was discovered all reasonable steps were taken for stopping or reducing it.

(2) Where a person is charged with an offence under section 2 of this Act in respect of the discharge of a mixture containing oil from a place on land, it shall also, subject to subsection (3) of this section, be a defence to prove—
  (a) that the oil was contained in an effluent produced by operations for the refining of oil;
  (b) that it was not reasonably practicable to dispose of the effluent otherwise than by discharging it into waters to which that section applies; and
  (c) that all reasonably practical steps had been taken for eliminating oil from the effluent.

(3) If it is proved that, at a time to which the charge relates, the surface of the waters into which the mixture was discharged from the place on land, or land adjacent to those waters, was fouled by oil, subsection (2) of this section shall not apply unless the court is satisfied that the fouling was not caused, or contributed to, by oil contained in any effluent discharged at or before that time from that place."

(3) *From ships into United Kingdom national waters.* The Merchant **46.09** Shipping Act 1995 provides as follows:

"**131.**—(1) If any oil or mixture containing oil is discharged as mentioned in the following paragraphs into United Kingdom national waters[36] which are navigable by sea-going ships, then, subject to the following provisions of this Chapter, the following shall be guilty of an offence, that is to say—
  (a) if the discharge is from a ship, the owner or[37] master of the ship, unless he proves that the discharge took place and was caused as mentioned in paragraph (b) below;

---

[36] Under s.313(2), "(a) 'United Kingdom waters' means the sea or other waters within the seaward limits of the territorial sea of the United Kingdom; and (b) 'national waters', in relation to the United Kingdom, means United Kingdom waters landward of the baselines for measuring the breadth of its territorial sea."

[37] "Or" has to be read conjunctively, such that both the owner and master may be liable: *R. v. Federal Steam Navigation Co. and Moran* [1974] 1 W.L.R. 505; *Davies v. Smith*, 1983 S.C.C.R. 232.

(b) if the discharge is from a ship but takes place in the course of a transfer of oil to or from another ship or a place on land and is caused by the act or omission of any person in charge of any apparatus in that other ship or that place, the owner or master of that other ship or, as the case may be, the occupier of that place.[38]

(2) Subsection (1) above does not apply to any discharge which—

(a) is made into the sea; and

(b) is of a kind or is made in circumstances for the time being prescribed by regulations made by the Secretary of State.

(3) A person guilty of an offence under this section shall be liable—

(a) on summary conviction, to a fine not exceeding £250,000[39];

(b) on conviction on indictment, to a fine.

(4) In this section 'sea' includes any estuary or arm of the sea.

(5) In this section 'place on land' includes anything resting on the bed or shore of the sea, or of any other waters included in United Kingdom national waters, and also includes anything afloat (other than a ship) if it is anchored or attached to the bed or shore of the sea or any such waters.

(6) In this section 'occupier', in relation to any such thing as is mentioned in subsection (5) above, if it has no occupier, means the owner thereof."

It is a defence for the owner or master of a ship charged with an offence under section 131 to prove that the discharge of oil or mixture was necessary (and a reasonable step to take in the circumstances) to secure the safety of any ship, to prevent damage to any ship or cargo, or to save life.[40] It is also a defence for such an owner or master to prove that an escape of oil was due to damage to the ship (and that all reasonable steps were taken for preventing, stopping or reducing that escape), or to leakage (provided that neither the leakage nor any delay in discovering it was due to want of reasonable care, and that as soon as reasonably practicable after the discovery of the leakage all reasonable steps were taken to stop or reduce it).[41] Where an occupier is so charged in respect of an escape of any oil or mixture, he has a defence if he proves that neither the escape nor any delay in discovering it was due to lack of reasonable care and that, once it was discovered, all reasonable steps were taken for stopping or reducing it.[42]

---

[38] See also s.135 of the Act, which prohibits the transfer of oil to or from a ship in any U.K. harbour between sunset and sunrise unless notice has been given in accordance with the provisions of the section: maximum penalty for a contravention of the prohibition, on summary conviction, a fine of level 3 on the standard scale (s.131(5)). It is also an offence under s.136 of the Act to fail to report discharges or leakages of oil from a ship into the waters of a U.K. harbour: maximum penalty, on summary conviction, a fine of level 5 on the standard scale (s.136(3)).

[39] Increased from £50,000 by the Merchant Shipping and Maritime Security Act 1997, s.7(1).

[40] Section 132(1).

[41] Section 132(2).

[42] Section 133.

(4) *From ships into the sea.* Regulation 12 of the Merchant Shipping **46.10** (Prevention of Oil Pollution) Regulations 1996[43] prohibits (subject to certain exceptions) United Kingdom ships other than oil tankers from discharging, and United Kingdom oil tankers from discharging from specified bilges, oil or oily mixture into any part of the sea, wherever these ships or tankers happen to be.[44] Regulation 13 of these Regulations prohibits (subject to certain exceptions)[45] United Kingdom oil tankers and (subject to regulation 38) all other oil tankers from discharging oil or oily mixture (except those for which provision is made in regulation 12) into any part of the sea.[46] Neither prohibition applies to discharges which occur "landward of the line which for the time being is the baseline for measuring the breadth of the territorial waters of the United Kingdom",[47] save that discharges "prohibited by paragraph (4) shall continue to be prohibited when made in the sea on the landward side of the line referred to in paragraph (6)."[48] Both regulations are subject to regulation 11 which specifies general exceptions including that the discharge was necessary for the purpose of saving life at sea or securing the safety of a ship at sea, or that the discharge was the result of damage to a ship or its equipment (provided that all reasonable precautions were taken to prevent or minimise the discharge and the owner or master did not act recklessly, knowing that damage would probably result, or with intent to cause that damage).[49]

If any ship fails to comply with the requirements of regulations 12 or 13, "the owner and the master shall each be guilty of an offence and section 131(3) of the Merchant Shipping Act 1995 shall apply as it applies under that section, so that each of the owner and the master shall be liable on summary conviction to a fine not exceeding £250,000 or on conviction on indictment to a fine."[50]

(5) *Following shipping accidents.* Under section 137 of the Merchant **46.11** Shipping Act 1995,[51] where an accident[52] has occurred to or in a ship[53]

---

[43] S.I. 1996 No. 2154.

[44] Regulation 12(1)–(3).

[45] Which include that the tanker is not within a special area and that it is more than 50 miles from the nearest land. "Special areas" are defined in reg. 16, as amended by the Merchant Shipping (Prevention of Pollution) (Amendment) Regulations 2000 (S.I. 2000 No. 483), reg. 3.

[46] Regulation 13(1)–(3).

[47] See reg. 12(6) and reg. 13(6).

[48] Paragraph (4), of both regs 12 and 13, states: "No discharge into the sea shall contain chemicals or other substances in quantities or concentrations which are hazardous to the marine environment or contain chemicals or other substances introduced for the purposes of circumventing the conditions of discharge prescribed by this regulation."

[49] Regulation 11(c) also provides an exception for any approved discharge into the sea of substances containing oil "for the purpose of combating specific pollution incidents in order to minimise the damage from pollution."

[50] Regulation 36(2), as amended by the Merchant Shipping (Prevention of Oil Pollution) (Amendment) Regulations 1997 (S.I. 1997 No. 1910), reg. 8.

[51] As amended by the Merchant Shipping and Maritime Security Act 1997, s.2.

[52] " 'Accident' means a collision of ships, stranding or other incident of navigation, or other occurrence on board a ship or external to it resulting in material damage or imminent threat of material damage to a ship or cargo": s.137(9) as substituted by the Merchant Shipping and Maritime Security Act 1997, s.2(4)(a).

[53] Section 137 and its associated provisions (*i.e.*, ss. 138–140) may be made applicable, by Order in Council, to ships which are not United Kingdom ships and to ships which are outside U.K. waters: s.141. Provisions relative to offshore installations but similar to ss.137–140 may be made by regulations: Pollution Prevention and Control Act 1999, s.3.

and the Secretary of State is of opinion that oil[54] from that ship will or may cause significant pollution in the United Kingdom, in United Kingdom waters, or in a specified part of the sea, he may give directions to the owner or master or salvor or pilot of that ship (or where appropriate the harbour master or harbour authority) as to what should or should not be done in respect of it or its cargo, for the purpose of preventing or reducing the pollution or the risk thereof. It is an offence under section 139 to contravene or fail to comply with any requirement of such a direction.[55]

Radioactive waste

46.12   The unauthorised disposal and accumulation of radioactive waste is penalised by sections 13, 14 and 32 of the Radioactive Substances Act 1993.[56]

Atmospheric pollution

46.13   The emission of dark smoke from a chimney of a building or from a chimney serving the furnace of any fixed boiler or industrial plant is prohibited (subject to exceptions for lighting furnaces from cold, and certain failures of apparatus or unavailability of fuel) by section 1 of the Clean Air Act 1993.[57]

The emission of dark smoke from industrial or trade premises, otherwise than from a chimney is penalised by section 2 of the Clean Air Act 1993.[58]

The Act also provides for the control by regulation of the emission of grit, dust and fumes from furnace chimneys[59] and the creation of smoke control areas.[60]

Part IV of the Clean Air Act 1993 empowers the Secretary of State to make regulations in order to limit or reduce air pollution, by controlling the composition of motor fuel, and limiting the sulphur content of furnace or engine fuel.[61]

---

[54] Under s.138A of the Act (as inserted by the Merchant Shipping and Maritime Security Act 1997, s.3(1)), the application of s.137 is extended to pollution by any prescribed substance, or any other substance which is "liable to create hazards to human health, to harm living resources and marine life, to damage amenities or to interfere with other legitimate uses of the sea."

[55] Maximum penalty, on summary conviction, a fine of £50,000, and, on indictment, a fine of any amount: s.139(4). There is a defence of due diligence, as also a defence of reasonable belief that compliance would have involved serious risk to human life: s.139(3).

[56] Maximum penalty £20,000 and six months' on summary conviction, five years' and a fine on indictment: s.32(2).

[57] Maximum penalty a fine of level 5 (level 3 where the chimney is that of a private dwelling) on the standard scale: s.1(5).

[58] Maximum penalty a fine of level 5 on the standard scale: s.2(5). Industrial or trade premises include any premises used to burn matter in connection with an industrial or trade process: s.2(6).

[59] See Pt II of the Clean Air Act 1993.

[60] See Pt III of the Clean Air Act 1993.

[61] Maximum penalty for contravention of regulations a fine of the statutory maximum on summary conviction, and an unlimited fine on indictment: s.32(2).

Noise pollution

Section 62[62] of the Control of Pollution Act 1974, which replaces section **46.14**
2 of the Noise Abatement Act 1960, controls noise in streets, and is as
follows:

"(1) Subject to the provisions of this section, a loudspeaker in a
road shall not be operated—
   (a) between the hours of nine in the evening and eight in the
       following morning, for any purpose;
   (b) at any other time, for the purpose of advertising any enter-
       tainment, trade or business;
and any person who operates or permits the operation of a
loudspeaker in contravention of this subsection shall be guilty of an
offence against this Part of this Act.

(1A) Subject to subsection (1B) of this section, the Secretary of
State may by order amend the times specified in subsection (1)(a) of
this section.

(1B) An order under subsection (1A) of this section shall not
amend the times so as to permit the operation of a loudspeaker in a
street at any time between the hours of nine in the evening and
eight in the following morning.

(2) Subsection (1) of this section shall not apply to the operation
of a loudspeaker—
   (a) for police, fire brigade or ambulance purposes, by a water
       authority ('water authority' being construed in accordance
       with the Local Government (etc.) (Scotland) Act 1994) in the
       exercise of any of its functions, or by a local authority within
       its area;
   (b) for communicating with persons on a vessel for the purpose
       of directing the movement of that or any other vesel;
   (c) if the loudspeaker forms part of a public telephone system;
   (d) if the loudspeaker—
       (i) is in or fixed to a vehicle, and
       (ii) is operated solely for the entertainment of or for
            communicating with the driver or a passenger of the
            vehicle or, where the loudspeaker is or forms part of the
            horn or similar warning instrument of the vehicle, solely
            for giving warning to other traffic, and
       (iii) is so operated as not to give reasonable cause for
             annoyance to persons in the vicinity;
   (e) otherwise than on a public road (within the meaning of the
       Roads (Scotland) Act 1984) by persons employed in connec-
       tion with a transport undertaking used by the public in a case
       where the loudspeaker is operated solely for making
       announcements to passengers or prospective passengers or to
       other persons so employed;
   (f) by a travelling showman on land which is being used for the
       purposes of a pleasure fair;
   (g) in case of emergency.

---

[62] As amended by the Roads (Scotland) Act 1984, Sched. 9, para. 74(5); the Noise and
Statutory Nuisance Act 1993, s.7; and the Local Government (etc.) (Scotland) Act 1994,
Sched. 13, para. 95(6).

(3) Subsection (1)(b) of this section shall not apply to the operation of a loudspeaker between the hours of noon and seven in the evening on the same day if the loudspeaker—

(a) is fixed to a vehicle which is being used for the conveyance of a perishable commodity for human consumption; and

(b) is operated solely for informing members of the public (otherwise than by means of words) that the commodity is on sale from the vehicle; and

(c) is so operated as not to give reasonable cause for annoyance to persons in the vicinity.

(3A) Subsection (1) of this section shall not apply to the operation of a loudspeaker in accordance with a consent granted by a local authority under Schedule 2 to the Noise and Statutory Nuisance Act 1993."

Noise on construction sites may be regulated by local authorities.[63]

Section 63 also empowers local authorities to create noise abatement zones in which they may control the permissible level of noise. It is an offence to exceed that level.[64] Noise from plant or machinery may be controlled by regulations.[65]

The maximum penalty for all the above offences[66] is a fine of level five on the standard scale together in each case with a further £50 for each day on which the offence continues after conviction.[67]

---

[63] Sections 60 and 61. See also s.58 (as amended by the Noise and Statutory Nuisance Act 1993, Sched. 1, para. 2), and 58A and 59A (which are added by the Noise and Statutory Nuisance Act 1993, Sched. 1, para. 3).

[64] Section 65(5).

[65] Section 68.

[66] Except for offences under ss. 58A(7) and 59A(9), see n. 63, *supra*, where the maximum penalty is a fine of level 3 on the standard scale.

[67] Section 74, as amended by the Noise and Statutory Nuisance Act 1993, Sched. 1, para. 8. For cognate offences dealing directly or indirectly with noise pollution, see, *e.g.*, the Civic Government (Scotland) Act 1982, s.54, as amended by the Roads (Scotland) Act 1984, Sched. 9, para. 87(4) and the Crime and Disorder Act 1998, s.24(2) (offence of sounding or playing any musical instrument, singing or performing, or operating any sound producing device so as to give any other person reasonable cause for annoyance), and the Criminal Justice and Public Order Act 1994, s.63 (which relates to persons gathering on land in the open air at which amplified music is played during the night "and is such as, by reason of its loudness and duration and the time at which it is played" likely to cause serious distress to inhabitants of the locality: the offence is committed by failing to leave the land in question when so directed by the police).

PART VIII

OFFENCES AGAINST THE COURSE OF JUSTICE

CHAPTER 47

PERJURY AND ALLIED OFFENCES

THE CONCEPT OF OFFENCES AGAINST THE COURSE OF JUSTICE

The term "offences against the course of justice" used to be regarded **47.01** as a collective term for a number of offences such as perjury, subornation of perjury, deforcement and prison breaking, in the same way as "offences against property" is a collective term for such offences as theft, fraud, reset and so on. The common feature which distinguished the group of offences against the course of justice was that they all constituted attempts to defeat or pervert the course of justice. It does not follow logically from that that any attempt to defeat or pervert the course of justice is necessarily a crime — an offence against the course of justice, like any other type of offence, was criminal only if the circumstances of the offence corresponded to the *actus reus* and *mens rea* of a particular crime, either a known crime or an innominate offence declared criminal by the High Court. Over the last half century, however, attempt to pervert or defeat the course of justice has come to be regarded as a particular known crime and the tendency is to regard any such attempt as an example of that crime, irrespective of whether the facts fall within the scope of any of the particular crimes such as perjury or prison breaking.[1]

This development has not yet fully crystallised, and the cases which display it may yet be regarded as atypical. It is still the practice to charge specific crimes such as perjury when the facts appear to fall within their definition, and in such cases it is still necessary for the Crown to satisfy the requirements of the particular crime charged.[2] Perjury and the like have not yet been entirely relegated to the status of being only modes of the crime of attempting to defeat the course of justice, and must still be considered as separate crimes.

PERJURY

Perjury is committed by wilfully giving false evidence on oath or **47.02** affirmation in any judicial proceeding.[3] Perjury was at one time dealt

---

[1] *Scott (A.T.) v. H.M. Advocate*, 1946 J.C. 90, Lord Carmont at 93; *Dalton v. H.M. Advocate*, 1951 J.C. 76; *H.M. Advocate v. Martin*, 1956 J.C. 1; *H.M. Advocate v. Mannion*, 1961, J.C. 79, see *infra*, para. 47.41. For a criticism of the current approach see Vol. I, para. 1.36. Schedule 2 to the Firearms Act 1968 lists both "perverting the course of justice" and prison breaking as crimes. For a rare example of a charge of perverting the course of justice, see *Raymond Murphy*, Criminal Appeal Court, Oct. 1977, unrep'd.

[2] See *Scott (A.T.) v. H.M. Advocate*, 1946 J.C. 90.

[3] *Angus v. H.M. Advocate,* 1935 J.C. 1, Lord Morison at 6. *Cf.* Hume, i, 366; Alison, i, 465; Burnett, p.203; Macdonald, p.164.

with in a number of now repealed Scots statutes, and it can today be prosecuted under particular provisions of the Criminal Law (Consolidation) (Scotland) Act 1995,[4] but in practice it is always dealt with at common law.[5]

Judicial proceedings

47.03 The evidence must be given in judicial proceedings, These include proceedings before any court of law, and before any tribunal which is empowered to take evidence on oath.[6] According to Alison, perjury can be committed "in all cases . . . where an oath is required and imposed by law, either as a safeguard to the revenue, or for the protection of the interest of a number of other persons, or as a necessary step towards making effective a legal right,"[7] and refers to oaths made in revenue matters, and in giving up inventories of property in the Commissary Court. But in *John Speirs and Ors*[8] and *Nathan McLachlan*[9] the Crown dropped charges of perjury in relation to false affidavits to a statutory Board of Trustees, and an oath of qualification as a voter under the Reform Act 1832, respectively. "Judicial proceedings" includes matters preliminary or incidental to proceedings in court[10] and includes affidavits sworn by creditors in a sequestration, as well as evidence given by the bankrupt himself in a private or public examination.[11] It would also include oaths of calumny, or oaths required to be made before a magistrate issues a warrant.

47.04 *Irregular proceedings*. It is not a defence to a charge of perjury that the action in which the evidence was given was incompetent because of a technicality, such as a failure to call an underage child's legal representative as a defender in an action against that child.[12] The proceedings must, however, be before a competent court[13] — perjury could not be committed, it is submitted, in a trial for rape in the sheriff court, or in a trial for an offence outwith the territorial jurisdiction of the court.

---

[4] *infra.* Sections 44–46 of the Criminal Law (Consolidation) (Scotland) 1995 Act consolidate most provisions of the False Oaths (Scotland) Act 1933.

[5] *cf. Styr v. H.M. Advocate*, 1993 S.C.C.R. 278, where charges were brought under s.1 of the False Oaths (Scotland) Act 1933 in respect of false statements made during interviews conducted under oath by inspectors investigating insider dealing offences.

[6] For example, an inquiry set up under s.6 of the Explosive Substances Act 1883; the Special Commissioners of Income Tax: *R. v. Hood-Barrs* [1943] K.B. 455; and any tribunal set up under s.1 of the Tribunals of Inquiry (Evidence) Act 1921 (as amended by the Statute Law Repeals Act 1995, Sched. 1, Pt. VI, Gp. 1). It is not clear whether perjury can be committed in giving evidence before a church court: Hume, i, 370; Alison i, 471; Burnett, p.206; *J. and W. Wilson* (1803) Burnett, 206. Alison suggests (at i, 371) that the old case of *Wm Barclay* (1601) cited by Hume as an example of perjury before a church court proceeded on a waiver by the accused of any objections to the competency of the proceedings.

[7] Alison, i, 472.

[8] (1836) 1 Swin. 163.

[9] (1837) 1 Swin. 528.

[10] *cf. Logue v. H.M. Advocate*, 1932 J.C. 1, L.J.-G. Clyde at 4.

[11] See the Bankruptcy (Scotland) Act 1985, ss. 44 and 47; Alison, i, 472; *Mathew Steele* (1823); *John Baillie* (1823); *Wm Hay* (1824) all Hume, i, 374. *cf. H.M. Advocate v. Nicholson*, 1958 S.L.T. (Sh.Ct.) 17; *William Hutchson and John Carter* (1831) Bell's Notes 96; *Dawson v. McLennan* (1863) 4 Irv. 357; *Jas Henderson* (1862) 4 Irv. 208.

[12] *Wm Richardson* (1872) 2 Couper 321.

[13] *ibid*. Lord Ardmillan at 322.

The oath must also have been taken before a person qualified to receive it, but it is not necessary for the Crown to prove his qualifications by, for example, producing a sheriff's commission.[14]

Voluntary oaths. The oath which is the subject of a perjury charge must **47.05** be one which the accused was required to make, either absolutely, as in the case of a witness at a trial, or as a condition of exercising a right or obtaining any privilege. If A merely presents himself before a magistrate and offers to make a statement on oath, he is not guilty of perjury if he swears falsely.[15]

Perjury by a party. A party to an action who swears falsely in giving **47.06** evidence, or an accused who gives false evidence at his trial, may be guilty of perjury in the same way as any other witness.[16]

Oath. Historically, the distinctive feature of perjury is that it involves a **47.07** false appeal to a Diety. It is therefore restricted to statements made on oath[17] or in a form which is regarded by the law as equivalent to an oath for the purposes of perjury.

STATEMENTS ON OATH. Section 46(1)(a) of the Criminal Law (Consol- **47.08** idation) (Scotland) Act 1995 provides that for the purposes of proceedings for perjury,

> "[T]he forms and ceremonies used in administering an oath shall be immaterial if the court or person before whom the oath is taken has power to administer an oath for the purpose of verifying the statement in question, and if the oath has been administered in a form and with ceremonies which the person taking the oath has accepted without objection or has declared to be binding on him."[18]

AFFIRMATION. Section 46(1)(b) of the Criminal Law (Consolidation) **47.09** (Scotland) Act 1995 provides that an affirmation or declaration made in place of an oath is of the same effect as if it had been made on oath. Section 5 of the Oaths Act 1978 provides:

> "(1) Any person who objects to being sworn shall be permitted to make his solemn affirmation instead of taking an oath.
>
> (2) Subsection (1) above shall apply in relation to a person to whom it is not reasonably practicable without inconvenience or delay to administer an oath in the manner appropriate to his

---

[14] In *Wm Hastie* (1863) 4 Irv. 389, where a bankrupt was charged with perjury during his public examination, and pleaded that the sheriff had not been present throughout the examination, the case was left to the jury to decide whether the evidence given in the absence of the sheriff had been properly recorded.

[15] Hume, i, 370; Alison, i, 471.

[16] Hume, i, 373; Alison, i, 473. Accused persons frequently commit perjury but are in practice rarely if ever prosecuted unless there is some question of falsifying documents or of a conspiracy to mislead the court otherwise than by simply giving false evidence; such a charge was, however, held relevant in a case of "simple perjury" in *H.M. Advocate v. Cairns*, 1967 J.C. 37, but the accused, who had been acquitted of murder, died before the perjury trial began.

[17] Hume, i, 369; *John Barr* (1839) 2 Swin. 282.

[18] For the forms of oath and affirmation see the Act of Adjournal (Criminal Procedure Rules) 1996 (S.I. 1996 No. 513), Sched. 2, r.14.5, and App., Forms 14.5–A and 14.5–B. The forms are directive and not mandatory, and it is sufficient that the witness acknowledges his obligation to tell the truth: *McAvoy v. H.M. Advocate*, 1991 S.C.C.R. 123.

religious belief as it applies in relation to a person objecting to be sworn.

(3) A person who may be permitted under subsection (2) above to make his solemn affirmation may also be required to do so.

(4) A solemn affirmation shall be of the same force and effect as an oath."[19]

It is the practice in Scotland to allow anyone to affirm who wishes to do so, without requiring any statement from him as to his religious beliefs.[20]

47.10 *Equivocal statements.* The false statement must be definite and unequivocal. If it is capable of two meanings, one of which is true and the other false, it cannot constitute perjury.[21] Prevarication in giving evidence may amount to contempt of court,[22] but is not perjury.

Again, if a witness depones that he cannot remember something, or is not sure of it, or is speaking only to the best of his recollection, this will not normally constitute perjury.

Where, however, it is clear that his claim to ignorance or lack of memory is false, he may be convicted of perjury — a statement that one does not remember may be as much a lie as any other false statement.[23] It will, however, be very difficult to prove perjury in such cases.[24]

47.11   OMISSIONS. Hume states that it is very difficult to ground a charge of perjury on an omission,[25] and it is probably the case that a mere failure to tell "the whole truth" cannot constitute perjury, if only because such a failure can hardly constitute an unequivocal false statement. Where therefore an accused gives only a partial answer to a question, or conceals some explanation which would alter the tenor of his evidence, he will probably not be guilty of perjury. Similarly, if he is asked to enumerate the persons present at a particular occasion, and omits to name one, that omission will probably not constitute perjury. For perjury to be committed he would have to be asked specifically if the person in question had been present, and to deny it. An omission to identify an accused, if the witness is specifically asked if he sees the person he saw at the scene of the crime, might amount to perjury if the witness in fact was in a position to pick out the accused. Generally speaking it may be said that an omission cannot be perjury unless it is equivalent to an unequivocal false denial.[26]

---

[19] Subsection (2) and (3) are intended to avoid the difficulty caused by *R. v. Singh* (1958) 42 Cr.App.R. 44 which held that a person holding religious beliefs could not affirm.

[20] An oath is not affected by the fact that the person taking it has no religious belief.

[21] Hume, i, 366; Alison, i, 465–466.

[22] *infra*, para. 50.04. So, too, may perjury: *Manson, Petr* (1977) S.C.C.R. (Supp.) 176.

[23] *Wolf v. R.* [1975] 2 S.C.R. 107; *cf. Simpson v. Tudhope*, 1988 S.L.T. 297.

[24] Hume, i, 368; Alison, i, 467; Burnett, pp. 203–204; Macdonald, p.164; *Geo. Montgomery* (1716) Hume, i, 368.

[25] Hume, i, 367.

[26] But see *Angus v. H.M. Advocate*, 1935 J.C. 1, *infra* para. 48.16, where the court did not deal with this aspect of the case. See also *Simpson v. Tudhope*, 1988 S.L.T. 297, where it was held to be perjury for a witness to state that he had been with A at the material time "the truth being as you well knew that you did not know if you were accompanied by [A]."

OPINION EVIDENCE. Normally the expression of an opinion cannot **47.12** constitute perjury, if only because of the difficulty of proving that the witness did not hold the opinion he gave.[27] But where the opinion can clearly be shown to have been given dishonestly, for example by showing that the witness was bribed to give it, or that it was clearly an untenable opinion, perjury may be committed.[28]

Relevant and competent evidence. The false statement in perjury must **47.13** constitute evidence, and this has been held to mean that it must be relevant (or pertinent) to the issues involved, and be competent evidence.[29] In the words of Alison: "The falsehood must be in a matter pertinent to the issue, and competent to be asked of the witness; but if this be the case, it matters not in how trivial a matter the falsehood may consist, or how far from the original relevant matter the witness may have been led before he makes the false affirmation."[30]

RELEVANCY. Any false statement which is relevant to the issue of the **47.14** case, or to the credibility of the witness, may constitute perjury.[31] In *Eliz. Muir*[32] the accused had deponed falsely as a witness in a trial that the policeman who had arrested the accused at that trial was drunk and had behaved improperly, a matter which had nothing to do with the original accused's guilt, but was important in assessing her own credibility, and she was convicted of perjury.[33] Perjury may be committed by swearing falsely to one's own character as well as to the facts of the case.

In *Hall v. H.M. Advocate*[34] the witness had deponed falsely that he had not made a particular statement to the police, a matter relevant only to credibility and competently elicited only to enable the Crown to use the provisions of the Evidence (Scotland) Act 1852, section 3,[35] in order to attack his credibility. At the perjury trial this evidence was held to be relevant, and that is now accepted as correct.

---

[27] Hume, i, 368–369; Alison, i, 468; Macdonald, p.164.

[28] Hume, i, 375; Alison, i, 468; Macdonald, p.164. Hume and Macdonald think that a false oath of calumny cannot constitute perjury — Hume, i, 369, Macdonald, p.164 — but if a pursuer who knows the meaning of the oath and knows that there has been collusion nonetheless takes the oath, this would appear clearly to be perjury. The oath of calumny in divorce proceedings was abolished by the Divorce (Scotland) Act 1976, s.9.

[29] See *Lord Advocate's Ref. (No. 1 of 1985)*, 1987 S.L.T. 187, esp. L.J.-G. Clyde at 192D and 192G–L; see also 193E-H where Lord Clyde disapproved what was stated in para. 48–14 of the 2nd ed. of this work.

[30] Alison, i, 469, approved by L.J.-G. Clyde in *Lord Advocate's Ref. (No. 1 of 1985)*, 1987 S.L.T. 187, at 192J. It is, of course, the Crown's privilege not to prosecute instances of perjury in relation to very trivial matters: *cf. ibid.*, Lord Clyde at 192H.

[31] Alison, i, 469; Burnett, p.206; *David Brown* (1843) 1 Broun 525; *Angus v. H.M. Advocate, infra*, para. 47.15. *Contra* Hume, i, 369; *H.M. Advocate v. Smith, infra*, para. 47.15.

[32] (1830) Alison, i, 469–470.

[33] See also *David Brown* (1843) 1 Broun 525, where the accused had sworn in the original trial of some friends of his for theft that the police had threatened to assault them if they did not confess, and he was convicted of perjury; and *Aitchison v. Simon*, 1976 S.L.T. (Sh.Ct.) 73.

[34] 1968 S.L.T. 275.

[35] See now the Criminal Procedure (Scotland) Act 1995, s.263(4).

47.15   COMPETENCY. The question of competency has given rise to some difficulty.[36]

It is not clear whether competency is a question of law for the original trial judge or for the judge in the perjury trial.[37] In *H.M. Advocate v. Smith*[38] a charge of perjury against S. was held by Lord Justice-Clerk Aitchison to be irrelevant. The allegedly perjured evidence had been given at the trial of T. and O. for soliciting bribes, and S. had there sworn that the person allegedly solicited by T. and O. had not told him, S., about this. Lord Aitchison's view was that evidence of what that person said to S. outwith the presence of T. and O. was incompetent, and that questions about it should not have been put to S. even to test his credibility.

In *Angus v. H.M. Advocate*[39] A was charged with attempted subornation of perjury. The circumstances were that A. had given S., whom he knew to be seeking an abortion, the name of someone who had in turn directed her to an abortionist R., and that A. had then asked S. to omit all reference to himself in giving her evidence at R.'s trial. It was argued that this charge was bad since what A. had told S. about R. was not competent in R.'s trial. The argument was rejected on the ground that such evidence *was* competent evidence in a charge of abortion. The court in *Angus*[40] did not have the full judgment in *Smith*[41] before them, and so were unable to pronounce formally on it, but they suggested that it showed too narrow an approach to the problem, and that it was inconsistent with *David Brown*.[42]

Smith and *Angus* agree that incompetent evidence cannot constitute perjury — incompetent evidence is regarded as if it had not been given at all[43]; the conflict between the two cases is as to what type of evidence is to be regarded as incompetent. *Smith* is a single judge decision, albeit one by Lord Justice-Clerk Aitchison, and *Angus* technically does not decide any more than that evidence about how the "victim" of an abortion got in touch with the abortionist is relevant in a trial for abortion. The general question of what is meant by "competent evidence" in a perjury charge may therefore still be technically open, but it is now clear that evidence touching on the credibility of a witness will be regarded as a proper subject of a perjury charge unless it is strictly incompetent, and should not have been allowed to be given at all.

47.16   *Competency may be of three kinds.* (1) Evidence may be incompetent in the sense that it is of a kind which could never competently be led in the process in question. Parole evidence of a matter which (prior to the commencement of section 11 of the Requirements of Writing (Scotland) Act 1995) required to be proved by writ or oath would have been incompetent in this sense,[44] and evidence given by a witness as to what

---

[36] *Angus v. H.M. Advocate*, 1935 J.C. 1. *Cf. Strathern v. Burns*, 1921 J.C. 92; *Hall v. H.M. Advocate*, 1968 S.L.T. 275.

[37] *Graham v. H.M. Advocate*, 1969 S.L.T. 116; *H.M. Advocate v. Smith*, 1934 J.C. 66.

[38] 1934 J.C. 66.

[39] 1935 J.C. 1.

[40] 1935 J.C. 1.

[41] 1934 J.C. 66.

[42] (1843) 1 Broun 525. Lord Morison's statement in *Angus*, at 6, that any false evidence is perjury if the jury at the perjury trial regard it as having been material, has been held to be incorrect: *Lord Advocate's Ref. (No. 1 of 1985)*, 1987 S.L.T 187, L.J.-G. Emslie at 193D.

[43] *Smith, supra*, L.J.-C. Aitchison at 69.

[44] See *Angus, supra*, Lord Morison at 6.

he said when being precognosced on behalf of any party to the case is probably in the same position.[45] Evidence of this kind can never form the basis of a charge of perjury.

(2) Evidence may be incompetent in the sense of being inadmissible against an accused person or a party. It is about this type of evidence that *Smith*[46] and *Angus*[47] appear to disagree, and the law as laid down in *Angus* and *Hall*[48] is that evidence of this kind can constitute perjury. What a witness said on a prior occasion is not evidence against an accused, but it is something which may properly be put to a witness to test his credibility, and as such is competent evidence in the sense that questions directed to it are unobjectionable.[49] If A and B are charged by the police with a crime and A is later used as a witness against B, A's reply to the police charge is not evidence against B, but it is competent to put it to A at B's trial if A goes back on it, in order to attack his credibility. And if A lies about it he is guilty of perjury.[50]

The basis of Lord Aitchison's opinion in *Smith*[51] was that the alleged perjured evidence was evidence which should not have been allowed to be given, since it related to statements by the complainers in the original trial. Although the court in *Angus*[52] may have disagreed with Lord Aitchison's assessment of competency, both cases accept that the test is whether the evidence should have been disallowed by the trial judge.[53]

(3) Evidence may be incompetent in the sense that it cannot properly be elicited from the particular witness. If a wife is called as a witness against her husband who is being tried on two charges, and she is a competent witness against him on only one of them, her false answers to any questions directed to the charge on which she is not a competent witness will not constitute perjury, being answers to questions which were not in Alison's phrase, "competent to be asked of the witness".[54]

Where the witness gives false evidence in response to a question which he could have declined to answer on the ground that his answer would be self-incriminatory he is guilty of perjury, even if he was not warned of his right to refuse to answer, at least if the answer he gave was not in fact incriminatory.[55]

Contradictory oaths. The mere fact that A swears on one occasion that *x* **47.17** is the case, and on another that *x* is not the case, is not sufficient to found a charge of perjury. The Crown must be able to prove that either *x*

---

[45] The question whether a statement was a statement or a precognition will normally be decided by the trial judge; but where that question is truly an open one, it may be left by him for decision by the jury: *Low v. H.M. Advocate*, 1988 S.L.T. 97, opinion of the court (L.J.-C. Ross) at 100F. Whether a statement made to the police is of the nature of a precognition need not depend upon the precise stage which an investigation has reached at the time it was made, nor upon whose instructions the police were acting on at that time: *H.M. Advocate v. McGachy*, 1991 S.C.C.R. 884.

[46] 1934 J.C. 66.

[47] 1935 J.C. 1.

[48] *Hall v. H.M. Advocate*, 1968 S.L.T. 275.

[49] See *Aitchison v. Simon*, 1976 S.L.T. (Sh.Ct.) 73.

[50] *cf.* Alison, i, 469; *Angus, supra; Hall, supra.*

[51] 1934 J.C. 66.

[52] 1935 J.C. 1.

[53] It may be doubted whether Lord Morison was correct in saying in *Angus* that the court in the perjury trial cannot review the decision of the original court that the evidence in question was admissible.

[54] Alison, i, 469; *Patrick Maccurly* (1777) Hume, i, 369.

[55] *Graham v. H.M. Advocate*, 1969 S.L.T. 116.

or not-*x* is the case, they cannot merely show that A must have committed perjury on one or other occasion.[56]

47.18 *Oaths de fideli, etc.* Perjury consists in the making of a false statement. To make a false promise is not perjury. If, therefore, A takes an oath that he will do something, for example faithfully carry out the duties of an office, and fails to do so he is not guilty of perjury.[57] This is said to be because perjury requires that the falsehood be contemporaneous with the oath, so that technically it might be perjury to take such an oath intending all along to break it,[58] but a prosecution for perjury would almost certainly never be brought in such a case.

47.19 *Mens rea.* Hume states that perjury must be committed wilfully and out of malice by one who knows the truth.[59] It is undecided whether he must also know that he is on oath or has made an affirmation rendering him liable to the pains of perjury.

Subornation of perjury

47.20   Subornation of perjury consists in inducing a person to give perjured evidence.[60] The same requirements as to competency, etc., which apply in a charge of perjury apply in a charge of subornation.[61] The means adopted to induce the witness to swear falsely do not matter — subornation may be effected by bribery, by threats or merely by persuasion.[62] It is also immaterial whether the suborner and perjurer agree a story between them, or the suborner merely induces the perjurer to give evidence according to a statement which he provides.[63] Subornation may take place before an indictment has been served,[64] and indeed at any time prior to the witness's giving evidence.

47.21 *Attempted subornation.* The crime of subornation is not completed until the suborned witness actually gives his false evidence as a result of the subornation.[65] Now that an attempt to commit any crime is itself criminal[66] attempted subornation does not require special treatment. Hume and Alison regarded it as in itself a substantive offence, completed

---

[56] Hume, i, 372; Alison, i. 476; Macdonald, p.164. *Cf. Thomas Bauchop* (1840) 2 Swin. 513. In *Tsang Ping-Nam v. The Queen* [1981] 1 W.L.R. 1462, PC, the Crown admitted that it was unable to prove either that the defendant's written statements (not made on oath) had been false or that he had committed perjury by giving evidence contrary to those statements, and thus had charged him with attempting to pervert the course of justice, on the basis that one or other of his statements or his evidence had to be true but not both: the Judicial Committee, however (at 1466F), held that "it was wholly illegitimate for the Crown to seek to overcome their difficulties of proof" by so charging him.

[57] Hume, i, 371–372; Alison, i, 475–476; Macdonald, p.166.

[58] See Hume and Alison, *loc. cit.*

[59] Hume, i, 368; Alison, i, 467; Macdonald, p.164. *Cf. Felix Monaghan* (1844) 2 Broun 131.

[60] Hume, i, 381; Alison, i, 486; Macdonald, p.166.

[61] *cf. Angus. v. H.M. Advocate*, 1935 J.C. 1.

[62] To threaten injury to a person if he does not give false evidence can also be charged as a criminal threat: *Margt McDaniel and Anr* (1876) 3 Couper 271.

[63] Hume, i, 381.

[64] *Angus v. H.M. Advocate, supra.*

[65] Hume, i, 381; Alison, i, 486; Macdonald, p.166.

[66] Criminal Procedure (Scotland) Act 1995, s.294, re-enacting earlier provisions.

as soon as the witness was solicited, provided the solicitation was made "in an ouvert and palpable shape, such as testifies an earnest and serious determination to seduce."[67]

A may be guilty of attempted subornation although B subsequently informs on him, before the trial, or at the trial,[68] or gives true evidence at the trial,[69] or resists the solicitations throughout and never gives any indication of agreement.[70]

Attempted subornation is not restricted to cases where the trial diet has been fixed, but may be committed in reference to a trial which is only in prospect as a possibility, and which in fact never takes place.[71]

Interference with witnesses may also be dealt with as a contempt of court in certain circumstances.[72]

CRIMINAL LAW (CONSOLIDATION) (SCOTLAND) ACT 1995

Sections 44 to 46 of the Criminal Law (Consolidation) (Scotland) Act **47.22** 1995 make general provision for offences in connection with false oaths and statutory declarations. Where an offence under the provisions of these sections is also an offence at common law or under another Act it may be prosecuted either under the 1995 Act, or under that other Act or at common law, as the case may be.[73] Where there is a statutory provision applying to the particular facts of an offence it is the practice to bring the charge under that provision and not under the above mentioned Act of 1995, and where the facts constitute common law perjury the charge is always brought at common law. Consequently, comparatively few prosecutions are brought under the above numbered sections of the 1995 Act.

False oaths and declarations. Section 44 of the Act provides: **47.23**

"(1) Any person who—
  (a) is required or authorised by law to make a statement on oath for any purpose; and
  (b) being lawfully sworn wilfully makes a statement which is material for that purpose and which he knows to be false or does not believe to be true,
shall be guilty of an offence and liable [to a fine and/or five years' imprisonment].

(2) Any person who knowingly and wilfully makes, otherwise than on oath, a statement false in a material particular, and the statement is made—

---

[67] Hume, i, 382; Alison, i, 487.
[68] *Robert Stirling* (1821) Alison, i. 487.
[69] *Angus v. H.M. Advocate*, 1935 J.C. 1.
[70] Alison, i, 487; Hume, i, 382.
[71] Hume, i, 383; Macdonald, p.167.
[72] *infra*, para 50.13.
[73] Section 45(3)–(5). Where the other Act, whether passed before or after the Criminal Law (Consolidation) (Scotland) Act 1995, authorises only summary proceedings, it seems that proceedings under the 1995 Act are to be taken only summarily: s.45(5). Where the other Act provides that the offence is a corrupt practice, or provides for penalties other than fine and imprisonment, such as forfeiture or disqualification, the offender is liable both to punishment under the above mentioned Act of 1995 and to those other penalties: s.45(4).

    (a) in a statutory declaration; or

    (b) in an abstract, account, balance sheet, book, certificate, declaration, entry, estimate, inventory, notice, report, return or other document, which he is authorised or required to make, attest, or verify by, under, or in pursuance of any public general Act of Parliament for the time being in force; or

    (c) in any oral declaration or oral answer which he is authorised to make by, under or in pursuance of any public general Act of Parliament for the time being in force; or

    (d) in any declaration not falling within paragraph (a), (b) or (c) above, which he is required to make by an order under section 2 of the Evidence (Proceedings in Other Jurisdictions) Act 1975,

shall be guilty of an offence and shall be liable [to a fine and/or two years' imprisonment]."

47.24   EUROPEAN COURT. Section 11(1)[74] of the European Communities Act 1972 provides:

> "A person who, in sworn evidence before the European Court, or any court attached thereto, makes any statement which he knows to be false or does not believe to be true shall, whether he is a British subject or not, be guilty of an offence and may be proceeded against and punished—
>
> . . .
>
>   (b) in Scotland as for an offence against section 44(1) of the Criminal Law (Consolidation) (Scotland) Act 1995 . . ."

47.25   AIDING AND ABETTING, ETC. Section 45(1)[75] provides that any person who "aids, abets, counsels, procures, or suborns another person to commit an offence against section 44 of this act" shall be liable to be dealt with as a principal offender, so that a person may be convicted of perjury or falsehood under the Act in respect of a false statement sworn or made by someone else. Section 45(2) provides for punishment by fine and/or two years' imprisonment for inciting or attempting to procure or suborn another person to commit an offence against section 44 of the Act.

47.26 *Lawfully sworn.* The Act does not lay down any specific form of oath, but provides by section 46(1) that in proceedings under section 44(1):

> "(a) the forms and ceremonies used in administering an oath shall be immaterial if the court or person before whom the oath is taken has power to administer an oath for the purpose of verifying the statement in question, and if the oath has been administered in a form and with ceremonies which the person taking the oath has accepted without objection or has declared to be binding on him:
>
> (b) an affirmation or declaration made in lieu of an oath shall be of the like effect in all respects as if it had been made on oath."[76]

---

[74] As amended by the European Communities (Amendment) Act 1986, s.2(b).

[75] As amended by the Crime and Punishment (Scotland) Act 1997, Sched. 1, para. 18(8).

[76] See *supra*, para. 47.09.

STATUTORY DECLARATION. Section 46(4) of the Criminal Law (Consol- **47.27** idation) (Scotland) Act 1995 defines "statutory declaration" as "a declaration made by virtue of the Statutory Declarations Act 1835, or of any enactment (including subordinate legislation) applying or extending the provisions of that Act." The 1835 Act provides that certain statements in regard mainly to revenue matters which had formerly required to be made on oath may instead be made by declaration.

MENS REA. So far as section 44(1) is concerned an offence is committed **47.28** by a person who makes a statement on oath which he does not believe to be true. Where, however, the statement is not made on oath and so falls under subsection (2) an offence is committed only if the statement is made in the knowledge of its falsity.[77]

False statements in connection with registration. Section 44(4) of the **47.29** Criminal Law (Consolidation) (Scotland) Act 1995 provides that subsection (2) of that section "applies . . . to any oral statement made for the purpose of any entry in a register kept in pursuance of any Act of Parliament . . .". This means that such statements are struck at by subsection (2) whether or not the accused was "authorised or required" to make them.

A statement made "for the purpose" of an entry probably refers only to statements made directly to the person responsible for the entry, giving him false information for entry in the register, or inducing him to make an entry, for example, by representing oneself as in some way authorised to request the entry to be made.

PROFESSIONAL REGISTERS.[78] Section 44(3) of the Criminal Law (Consol- **47.30** idation) (Scotland) Act 1995 provides:

"Any person who—

(a) procures or attempts to procure himself to be registered on any register or roll kept under or in pursuance of any Act of Parliament for the time being in force of persons qualified by law to practise any vocation or calling; or

(b) procures or attempts to procure a certificate of the registration of any person on any such register or roll,

by wilfully making or producing or causing to be made or produced either verbally [*sic*] or in writing, any declaration, certificate, or representation, which he knows to be false or fraudulent, shall be guilty of an offence and [liable to a fine and/or twelve months' imprisonment]."[79]

So far as oral statements are concerned, the offences described in section 44(3) and 44(2), the latter as made applicable by subsection (4), somewhat overlap, with the strange result that an oral statement made to procure a false registration in a register of the type described in subsection (4) may be more severely punishable than a written statement

---

[77] *cf. Waugh v. Mentiplay*, 1938 J.C. 117, L.J.-G. Normand at 120. To say that it is an offence to make any statement which is in fact false, whether or not it is known to be false, is to deprive "knowingly" of any meaning in the phrase "knowingly and wilfully".

[78] For specific statutory offences, see *supra,* paras 19.100 *et seq.*

[79] Section 45, *supra,* applies also to offences against s.44(3).

made for the same purpose. Subsection (3), however, may strike at statements made at some remove from the act of registration itself to which subsection (2), by virtue of subsection (4), might not apply. On the other hand, subsection (3) strikes at the use of fraudulent certificates, which may not be struck at by subsection (2). It seems also that while a written statement intended to procure oneself to be registered, or to obtain a certificate of anyone's registration, may be an offence under subsection (3), a written statement intended to procure someone else to be registered may not, unless it can be brought under subsection (2) by showing that the accused was "authorised" to make such a statement.

Common law

47.31   It is a crime at common law to make a false declaration where the declaration is one required by Act of Parliament even where the form of declaration does not involve an appeal to the Deity and so does not constitute perjury,[80] but offences of this kind would today be prosecuted under the Criminal Law (Consolidation) (Scotland) Act 1995.

Other statutes

47.32   Many statutes require the giving of information and penalise false statements in varying degrees. These, however, are more properly regarded as statutory frauds or as offences analogous to fraud, and are dealt with under that heading.[81]

OTHER CRIMES INVOLVING FALSEHOOD IN JUDICIAL MATTERS

Frauds against the course of justice

47.33   *Conspiracy to defraud.* It is now accepted that it is a substantive crime to conspire to commit any crime,[82] but even before this was generally accepted it was recognised that it was criminal to conspire to commit a fraud on a court of justice.[83] This crime may be committed by conspiring to procure false evidence to be given even where no charge of subornation could be brought[84] as, for example, where a crime is simulated in front of innocent witnesses with intent that they should later give evidence that it was committed.[85] Another example is a conspiracy to substitute A for the true accused B at the latter's trial.[86] Even apart from conspiracy, probably any fraud directed at the course of justice is criminal whether or not it achieves any practical result.[87]

---

[80] *John Barr* (1839) 2 Swin. 282, which related to an "oath" required as a preliminary to exercising a right of voting at a parliamentary election.

[81] *supra*, Chap. 19.

[82] Vol. I, para. 6.67.

[83] Hume, i, 383.

[84] Alison, i, 488.

[85] *Nicol Muschet and Jas Campbell* (1721) Hume, i, 170, 383: *Margt Gallocher or Boyle and Ors* (1859) 3 Irv. 440.

[86] *John Rae and Thos Little* (1845) 2 Broun 476.

[87] Macdonald, p.58; *Elliot Millar* (1847) Ark. 355. It has been held in England that to give a person one knows to be a suspected criminal the registration numbers of unmarked police cars in order to assist his escape is an attempt to pervert the course of justice even where the giver does not know of the suspect's guilt, and does not act corruptly, dishonestly or threateningly: *R. v. Thomas (Derek)* [1979] Q.B. 326, CA.

Fraudulent obstruction. Interference with the execution of a court order **47.34** by fraudulent means is also criminal.[88]

Destruction of real evidence. It is a crime, and in certain circumstances **47.35** also a contempt of court, to destroy an article or document in order to prevent its use as evidence.[89] Most of the cases deal with concealment or other frauds by bankrupts[90] but the crime is not confined to such cases. In *Walter Murray and Margt Scott*[91] the charge was of destroying a bill of exchange "with intent to destroy the evidence of debt . . . and thereby to defraud the holder thereof."[92] It is also a crime to dispose of evidence to another person in order to defeat the ends of justice, and this may be dealt with as a contempt of court.[93]

False information

False accusation. It is a crime falsely to accuse someone else of a crime.[94] **47.36**

False evidence. According to Alison, "All practices tending to procure **47.37** false evidence, are punishable, though not falling exactly under the description of subornation or attempt at subornation."[95] The examples he gives are of conspiracies to produce false evidence,[96] and the destruction of evidence,[97] and this crime seems to have been limited to situations constituting fraudulent conspiracy or fraudulent destruction of evidence. Misleading or corrupting witnesses or destroying, suppressing or altering evidence during a trial or precognition is punishable as a contempt of court. The tendering of evidence of a forged certificate authorised by the Documentary Evidence Act 1868 or the Documentary Evidence Act 1882 is an offence under these Acts.[98]

It is an offence of perverting the course of justice to induce one's solicitor to provide a court with false information in a plea in mitigation.[99]

---

[88] *Geo. Kippen* (1849) J. Shaw 276, where K. tried to prevent the execution of a poinding by raising a fictitious summons against his creditor and arresting in his own hands on the dependence of the fictitious action the goods liable to poinding.

[89] Hume, ii, 140; Alison, i, 488.

[90] *supra*, paras 19.01, 19.07.

[91] Bell's Notes 66.

[92] *cf. John and David Reid* (1835) Bell's Notes 66; *Alexander Murray* (1830) Alison, i, 631.

[93] *Lord Advocate v. Alex. Galloway* (1839) 2 Swin. 465 where a witness after being cited to attend for precognition and produce an allegedly forged bill gave it to a third party on payment of the contents.

Interference short of destruction may in certain circumstances be sufficient: it has been held in England, for example, to be an attempt to pervert the course of justice for an accused to interfere with his portion of a blood specimen before sending it for analysis, with intent to pervert the course of justice, but without doing anything further; this was on the view that the resultant false analysis would be bound to be communicated to the accused's solicitor or the police, so that there was risk of injustice, and that that risk was sufficient to constitute the offence: *R. v Murray (Gordon)* [1982] 1 W.L.R. 475, CA.

[94] Hume, i, 341–342; Macdonald, 130; *Margt Gallocher or Boyle and Ors* (1859) 3 Irv. 440; *Elliot Millar* (1847) Ark. 355, where the facts were also charged as fraud with intent to subject an innocent person to accusation.

[95] Alison, i, 488.

[96] *Nicol Muschet and Jas Campbell* (1721) Hume, i, 170, 383; *Chas Isaackson and Ors* (1710) Hume, i, 383.

[97] *Jas Dun* (1793) Hume, i, 384.

[98] *supra*, para 19.93. These Acts are amended by the Scotland Act 1998 (Consequential Modifications) (No. 1) Order 1999 (S.I. 1999 No. 1042), Sched. 1, paras 1 and 3 respectively.

[99] *Murphy v. H.M. Advocate*, 1978 J.C. 1.

47.38 *Misleading the police*. In *Kerr v. Hill*[1] the accused was charged with falsely representing to police officers that an omnibus belonging to a particular company had knocked someone down and that he did "cause officers . . . maintained at the public expense for the public benefit to devote their time and service in the investigation of said false story told by you, and did temporarily deprive the public of [their] services and did render the lieges and particularly drivers [of the company in question] liable to suspicion and to accusations of driving recklessly." This charge represents a considerable extension of the crime of false accusation,[2] since no particular persons were accused, and even the employees of the company were at most rendered "liable" to suspicion and accusation. The gravamen of the charge indeed appears to be wasting the time of the police by telling them lies.[3] This view is supported by the later case of *Gray v. Morrison*[4] where the charge was similar to that in *Kerr*[5] except that it ended "did render the lieges liable to suspicion and to accusations of theft", and where Lord Justice-General Cooper said that "the gravamen of the charge is . . . the deliberate setting in motion of the police authorities by an invented story."[6]

47.39 *Inducing persons to give false information to the police*. In *Dalton v. H.M. Advocate*[7] the accused was charged with pretending to S. that if she refrained from picking out a man at an identification parade it would be of assistance to a friend of the accused, who had been charged with a crime in which this man was said to be involved, and with thus attempting to pervert the course of justice. He was also charged with threatening harm to S. if she did not do as he wished and with intimidating her, but that part of the charge was not proved. It was objected that the facts proved did not constitute a crime, but this objection was summarily dismissed by the Criminal Appeal Court. Lord Justice-Clerk Thomson said, "I have not the slightest hesitation in saying that these facts do constitute a crime . . . taking steps to destroy in advance evidence which might lead to the detection of a serious crime and the conviction of those responsible for it."[8] This ignores the obvious distinction between real evidence and oral evidence. Fraudulent destruction of real evidence is clearly criminal, but oral evidence cannot be

---

[1] 1936 J.C. 71.

[2] And is a copy of the charge in an English case of "public mischief": *R. v. Manley* [1933] 1 K.B. 529. It has since been held that conspiracy to effect a public mischief is not a crime in England: *R. v. Withers* [1975] A.C. 842, HL, but conduct of the kind described is probably criminal: see Law Commission Report on Conspiracy and Criminal Law Reform 1976 (Law Com. No. 76) 127; Smith and Hogan, pp. 287–289. The offence is regarded in Northern Ireland as indictable as being prejudicial to the administration of justice on the view that that administration cannot be confined to the judicial process but extends to police investigations: *R. v. Bailey* [1956] N.I. 15.

[3] 1936 J.C. 71, L.J.-G. Normand at 75.

[4] 1954 J.C. 31. It is also supported by *Bowers v. Tudhope*, 1987 S.L.T. 748 (making a false report to the police of the loss of an article, without any element of accusation) and *Robertson v. Hamilton*, 1987 S.C.C.R. 477 (making a false complaint to the police about the behaviour of a police dog). It seems to be a clear requirement of the offence, however, that the statement or report or complaint to the police was known by the accused to be false when it was made: *Walkingshaw v. Coid*, 1988 S.C.C.R. 454 (Sh.Ct).

[5] 1936 J.C. 71.

[6] At 34. The facts in these two cases could be said to constitute a fraud; *cf. Elliot Millar* (1847) Ark 355: inducing the police to take action they would not otherwise have taken, and this was argued by the Crown in *Kerr* but not referred to by the court. For a criticism of these cases as an extension of the criminal law, see Vol. I, para. 1.37.

[7] 1951 J.C. 76.

[8] At 79. See also Lord Patrick at 81.

destroyed or tampered with. Oral evidence is protected by the crimes of perjury and subornation of perjury, and it is not subornation of perjury to induce someone to give a false statement to the police.[9]

The charge in *Dalton*[10] was expressed to be "attempt to pervert the course of justice", and *Dalton* should perhaps be regarded as an example of this crime,[11] rather than of the old crimes of subornation or destruction of evidence.[12] The precise scope of this crime in relation to false information is unsettled,[13] but in *Scott (A.T.) v. H.M. Advocate*[14] where subornation of perjury was charged as an attempt to pervert the course of justice, Lord Carmont observed that "attempts to pervert the course of justice, as a crime", might be constituted "by inducing persons to make false statements outwith the witness box — to the police or even in certain circumstances to others",[15] which is very wide indeed.

Dalton[16] is not authority for the proposition that it is a crime to refrain from giving information to the police. Failure to identify someone is tantamount to a false denial of his presence at the place in question, and could amount to perjury if done in evidence in court. There is no authority for saying that Scotland is a police state in which every man is bound to inform on his neighbour. There is, on the contrary, some authority that it is not a crime merely to tell lies to the police[17] and this in turn suggests that, on general principles, it should not be a crime to induce someone else to do so, since there is no authority for saying that A may be convicted of inducing B to do something which is not in itself a crime.[18] *A fortiori* it is not an offence for an accused falsely to deny his guilt, even where the result is to throw suspicion on others. The position where the true criminal accuses another to the police or lodges a defence of incrimination is more difficult but is unsettled.[19]

---

[9] *cf. Scott (A.T.) v. H.M. Advocate*, 1946 J.C. 90.

[10] 1951 J.C. 76.

[11] *cf. R. v. Panayiotou and Antoniades* [1973] 1 W.L.R. 1032, CA: conspiracy to pervert the course of justice by dissuading a witness from giving evidence. Despite its name "attempt to pervert the course of justice" is a substantive crime rather than an attempt to commit the more rarely charged crime of perversion of the course of justice, for an example of which see *Raymond Murphy*, Criminal Appeal Court, Oct. 1977, unrep'd.

[12] See *supra*.

[13] *Dalton* has not been followed in any reported case, and might not itself have been brought but for the element of intimidation which the Crown failed to prove.

[14] 1946 J.C. 90.

[15] At 93.

[16] 1951 J.C. 76.

[17] *Curlett v. McKechnie*, 1938 J.C. 176, Lord Fleming, *obiter*, at 179; *cf. Waddell v. MacPhail*, 1986 S.C.C.R. 593, *infra* at para. 48.45. In *Dean v. Stewart*, 1980 S.L.T. (Notes) 86, the driver of a car (which had failed to stop after an accident) and another man pretended that the other man had been driving the car at the material time: the charge brought was one of attempting to pervert the course of justice, and it seems, therefore, that to tell lies to the police when interviewed by them in the course of criminal investigations is a crime.

[18] It remains the case, however, that giving or inducing the giving of false information might in some cases be contempt of court. It may be, however, that once investigations have begun with a view to identifying the culprit in an offence which is known to have been committed, the giving of any false information to the police may constitute an attempt to pervert the course of justice: *Dean v. Sewart*, 1980 S.L.T. (Notes) 85. (In England it has been held that it is not an attempt to pervert the course of justice to have endorsements removed from DVLC records where this is not done with intent to interfere with any pending or imminent proceedings, or any investigations which might lead to proceedings: *R. v. Selvage* [1982] Q.B. 372, CA; *cf. R. v. Rafique* [1993] Q.B. 843, CA, in which *Selvage* was distinguished.)

[19] It has been held in New Zealand that while a suspect is not bound to incriminate himself it is an attempt to defeat the ends of justice to name someone else as the culprit: *Cane v. The Queen* [1968] N.Z.L.R. 787.

47.40 *Failure to attend as a witness.* It is contempt of court for a duly cited witness wilfully to fail to attend.[20] But failure to be available for citation may constitute an attempt to pervert the course of justice.

In *H.M. Advocate v. Mannion*[21] the accused were charged on an indictment which read:

> "[Y]ou did form a criminal purpose to hinder and frustrate the course of justice, in pursuance of which you, knowing that you were required to give evidence for the prosecution in the trial of S. McK. . . . did leave your . . . house and go into hiding somewhere to the Prosecutor unknown for the purpose of avoiding giving evidence as aforesaid, and the diet of said trial having been deserted *pro loco et tempore*, and a new diet appointed for trial . . . you, again knowing that you were required to give evidence as aforesaid, continued to hide for the purpose aforesaid until said S. McK. had been tried . . . all with intent that your evidence would not be available to the prosecution and with intent to hinder and frustrate the course of justice, and you remained in hiding until . . . you were apprehended by officers of police, and you did attempt to defeat the ends of justice."

This indictment goes far beyond any precedent, since Mannion was never cited as a witness — the crime consisted in going away from home to somewhere where the police could not trace him.[22] An objection to the relevancy of the charge was described as "ingenious", and Lord Justice-Clerk Thomson said of it:

> "[It] really comes to this . . . : — that, until a man has actually received a citation to come to a criminal court, it is open to him to take any steps he likes to remove himself from the possibility of being called upon to give evidence, and that, while this may be socially reprehensible, it is not criminal. I find myself unable to agree with this proposition, and I do not think that I am doing anything revolutionary in failing to agree with it. It seems to me to be clear that if a man, with the evil intention of defeating the ends of justice, takes steps to prevent evidence being available, that is a crime by the law of Scotland. Evil intention, of course, is of the essence of the matter and must be established. This indictment clearly narrates the evil intention of the accused to avoid being called upon to give evidence, and that is sufficient to make the indictment relevant."[23]

If this represents the law, and it must be conceded that it is in line with current trends, it is probably the case that any conduct carried on with intent to defeat the ends of justice is a crime made up almost entirely of *mens rea*. And it is not even clear what that *mens rea* was in

---

[20] *infra*, para. 50.06. For an example of wilfulness, see *Orr v. Annan*, 1988 S.L.T. 251 (where the accused knew that he had been cited to attend court, was unsure of the date of the court hearing, but took no steps whatsoever to ascertain that date).

[21] 1961 J.C. 79.

[22] *cf. R. v. Rafique* [1993] Q.B. 843, CA, where witnesses to a fatal shooting concealed the weapon and lay low for some 12 days: in justifying their conviction for acting with intent to pervert the course of public justice, Lord Taylor of Gosforth, C.J., at 850H–851A, said that the facts were such that the defendants must have had in contemplation the likelihood of investigations and judicial proceedings — at the very least, an inquest.

[23] At 80.

Mannion.[24] Lord Thomson spoke of "evil intention", which is a throwback to Humean ideas of dole. If any intention to avoid being called to give evidence is sufficient, then *Mannion* creates the crime of avoiding the giving of evidence, but the indictment alleged a purpose to defeat the ends of justice, and probably an intention of that nature is necessary. *Mannion* goes very far, but it would be going even farther to suggest that it was a crime to leave home for the purpose of being on holiday at the time of the trial.

Statutory offences involving failure to give information to the police

Road Traffic Act 1988. This Act makes it an offence to fail to give **47.41** information to the police in certain circumstances.[25]

SECTION 170. Section 170[26] imposes a duty on a driver through the presence of whose vehicle on the road damage has been caused to another person or vehicle or to certain animals to give his particulars to interested parties, and in the event of his not doing so to report the accident to the police.[27]

SECTIONS 164 AND 165. Sections 164 and 165[28] of the Act empower police **47.42** constables, and in some cases vehicle examiners, to require production of driving licences and counterparts, insurance certificates and test certificates, and the names and addresses of the persons involved and the owner of the vehicle, in certain cases of persons driving or believed with reasonable cause to have been driving motor-vehicles or to have committed offences in relation to the use of such vehicles on roads.[29]

SECTIONS 168 AND 169. Section 168[30] provides that if the driver of a **47.43** mechanically propelled vehicle alleged to have committed an offence of dangerous or careless driving refuses to give his name and address or gives a false name or address on being required "by any person having reasonable ground for so requiring" he shall be guilty of an offence.[31] Section 169 empowers a constable to require a pedestrian who fails to comply with a direction by a police officer to stop, in contravention of section 37 of the Act, to give his name and address.[32]

SECTIONS 171 AND 172. Sections 171 and 172 of the Act provide as **47.44** follows:

---

[24] 1961 J.C. 79.

[25] For definitions of road traffic terms see *supra*, paras 30.04 *et seq.*

[26] As amended principally by the Road Traffic Act 1991, Sched. 4, para. 72. (For the most modern version of this, and all other sections of the 1988 Act referred to in this and the following paragraphs, see Sweet and Maxwell's *Encyclopaedia of Road Traffic Law*.)

[27] Maximum penalty, for failure to report is six months' and a fine of level 5 on the standard scale. There is also a duty on the driver to stop at the time of the accident; and if he does not produce his insurance certificate at the time he must report the accident and produce the certificate to the police. On the *mens rea* required for these offences, see *Harding v. Price* [1948] 1 K.B. 695: Vol. I, para 8.24.

[28] As amended principally by the Road Traffic Act 1991, Sched. 4, paras 68 and 69.

[29] Failure to produce the documents or give the required information is an offence punishable by a fine of level 3 on the standard scale. A similar power exists in relation to persons accompanying or believed to have been accompanying learner drivers, except in relation to the production of insurance or test certificates.

[30] As amended by the Road Traffic Act 1991, Sched. 4, para. 71.

[31] Maximum penalty a fine of level 3 on the standard scale.

[32] Failure to do so is punishable by a fine of level 1 on the standard scale.

"**171.**—(1) For the purpose of determining whether a motor vehicle was or was not being driven in contravention of section 143[33] of this Act on any occasion when the driver was required under section 165(1) or 170 of this Act to produce such a certificate of insurance or security, or other evidence as is mentioned in section 165(2)(a) of this Act, the owner of the vehicle must give such information as he may be required, by or on behalf of a chief officer of police, to give.[34] . . .

(3) In this section 'owner' in relation to a vehicle which is the subject of a hiring agreement, includes each party to the agreement.

172.[35]—(1) This section applies—

    (a) to any offence under the preceding provisions of this Act except—
        (i) an offence under part V,[36] or
        (ii) an offence under section 13, 16, 51(2), 61(4), 67(9), 68(4), 96 or 120,
        and to an offence under section 178[37] of this Act,
    (b) to any offence under sections 25, 26 or 27 of the Road Traffic Offenders Act 1988,
    (c) to any offence against any other enactment relating to the use of vehicles on roads, except an offence under paragraph 8 of Schedule 1 to the Road Traffic (Driver Licensing and Information Systems) Act 1989, and
    (d) to manslaughter, or in Scotland culpable homicide, by the driver of a motor vehicle.

(2) Where the driver of a vehicle is alleged to be guilty of an offence to which this section applies—

    (a) the person keeping the vehicle shall give such information as to the identity of the driver as he may be required to give by or on behalf of a chief officer of police, and
    (b) any other person shall if required as stated above give any information which it is in his power to give and may lead to identification of the driver.[38]

(3) Subject to the following provision, a person who fails to comply with a requirement under subsection (2) above shall be guilty of an offence.[39]

(4) A person shall not be guilty of an offence by virtue of paragraph (a) of subsection (2) above if he shows that he did not know and could not with reasonable diligence have ascertained who the driver of the vehicle was.

(5) Where a body corporate is guilty of an offence under this section and the offence is proved to have been committed with the consent or connivance of, or to be attributable to neglect on the part of, a director, manager, secretary or other similar officer of the

---

[33] Which deals with driving while uninsured.
[34] Failure to comply with the requirement is an offence (subs. (2)), maximum penalty a fine of level 4 on the standard scale.
[35] As amended by the Vehicle Excise and Registration Act 1994.
[36] Part V relates to driving instruction.
[37] Taking and driving away in Scotland.
[38] The right to require information depends on the officer being in possession of information which supports an allegation made by him of an offence which is ultimately charged: *Hingston v. Pollock*, 1990 J.C. 138; *Galt v. Goodsir*, 1982 J.C. 4.
[39] Maximum penalty, a fine of level 3 on the standard scale.

body corporate, or a person who was purporting to act in any such capacity, he, as well as the body corporate, is guilty of that offence and liable to be proceeded against and punished accordingly.

(6) Where the alleged offender is a body corporate, or in Scotland a partnership or an unincorporated association, or the proceedings are brought against him by virtue of subsection (5) above or subsection (11) below, subsection (4) above shall not apply unless, in addition to the matters there mentioned, the alleged offender shows that no record was kept of the persons who drove the vehicle and that the failure to keep a record was reasonable.

(7) A requirement under subsection (2) may be made by written notice served by post; and where it is so made—

    (a) it shall have effect as a requirement to give the information within the period of 28 days beginning with the day on which the notice is served, and

    (b) the person on whom the notice is served shall not be guilty of an offence under this section if he shows either that he gave the information as soon as reasonably practicable after the end of that period or that it has not been reasonably practicable for him to give it.

(8) Where the person on whom a notice under subsection (7) above is to be served is a body corporate, the notice is duly served if it is served on the secretary or clerk of that body.

(9) For the purposes of section 7 of the Interpretation Act 1978 as it applies for the purposes of this section the proper address of any person in relation to the service on him of a notice under subsection (7) above is—

    (a) in the case of the secretary or clerk of a body corporate, that of the registered or principal office of that body or (if the body corporate is the registered keeper of the vehicle concerned) the registered address, and

    (b) in any other case, his last known address at the time of service.

    (10) In this section—

    'registered address', in relation to the registered keeper of a vehicle, means the address recorded in the record kept under the Vehicle Excise and Registration Act 1994 with respect to that vehicle as being that person's address, and

    'registered keeper', in relation to a vehicle, means the person in whose name the vehicle is registered under that Act;

and references to the driver of a vehicle include references to the rider of a cycle.

(11) Where, in Scotland, an offence under this section is committed by a partnership or by an unincorporated association other than a partnership and is proved to have been committed with the consent or connivance or in consequence of the negligence of a partner in the partnership or, as the case may be, a person concerned in the management or control of the association, he (as well as the partnership or association) shall be guilty of the offence."

Section 172 applies to a person falling within a category described in subsection (1) whether or not he is himself the driver the police are seeking, and whether or not his answer would incriminate him.[40] The obligation to give information is limited, however, to information required by someone acting specifically on behalf of a chief constable.

A police officer is not acting in that behalf merely because he is acting in the course of his duty, he must be specially authorised in relation to section 172.[41] But a general authorisation to act under the section is sufficient, and no specific or separate authority is required in relation to each incident which is the subject of inquiry,[42] although the opinions of the judges in *Foster v. Farrell*[43] suggested that because of the unusual nature of a power to require a person to incriminate himself the latter was the case.

It is not open to a doctor to refuse to give information obtained by him from a patient.[44]

47.45 *Vehicle Excise and Registration Act* 1994. Section 46[45] of the Vehicle Excise and Registration Act 1994 contains provisions similar to those of section 172 of the Road Traffic Act in relation to the offences of using or keeping a vehicle without a licence under the Act, the misuse of trade licences, and failure to have a nil licence for an exempt vehicle.[46]

47.46 *Official Secrets Acts*. Section 6 of the Official Secrets Act 1920 gives the police restricted powers to require information in connection with offences against section 1 of the Official Secrets Act 1911, powers normally exercisable only with the permission of a Secretary of State.[47]

---

[40] *Foster v. Farrell*, 1963 J.C. 46; *Bingham v. Bruce* [1962] 1 W.L.R. 70. Contrast s.81 of the Weights and Measures Act 1985 which requires the giving of information to inspectors acting under the Act and specifically reserves the right not to incriminate oneself, and s.6 of the Explosive Substances Act 1883 which obliges a witness on oath in an inquiry before a sheriff to answer incriminating questions but provides that his answers cannot be used against him in any proceedings except proceedings for perjury.

It might have been thought that the requirements to give information laid down by s.172 would contravene the implied privilege against self-incrimination contained in Art. 6 of the European Convention on Human Rights; but in *Brown v. Stott*, 2001 S.C. 43, PC, the Judicial Committee decided that such a privilege was not an absolute right and that the requirement provisions of s.172(2) were not incompatible with Convention rights. As Lord Bingham of Cornhill stated, at 80E: "The jurisprudence of the European Court very clearly establishes that while the overall fairness of a criminal trial cannot be compromised, the constituent rights comprised, whether expressly or implicitly, within article 6 are not themselves absolute. Limited qualification of these rights is acceptable if reasonably directed by national authorities towards a clear and proper public objective and if representing no greater qualification than the situation calls for."

[41] *Foster v. Farrell*, 1963 J.C. 46.

[42] *Gray v. Farrell*, 1969 S.L.T. 250.

[43] *supra*.

[44] *Hunter v. Mann* [1974] Q.B. 767.

[45] As amended by the Finance Act 1997, Sched. 3, para. 7(1).

[46] Maximum penalty a fine of level 3 on the standard scale. See also s.46A, added by the Finance Act 1996, Sched. 2, para. 12.

[47] See *supra*, para. 37.39.

CHAPTER 48

ESCAPES FROM LAWFUL CUSTODY

Prison breaking

Prison breaking is recognised as a specific offence at common law[1] and **48.01** consists in the escape from a prison of a person lawfully confined there.[2]

Prison. Prison breaking may be committed by escaping from any public **48.02** prison, whether it is a national prison or only a local gaol. It is not prison breaking to escape from police cells, or any other place of temporary custody.[3] "Prison" includes all the buildings and precincts of a gaol, and it is prison breaking to escape from a prison yard.[4] It may not be prison breaking to escape from a working party outside the prison grounds.[5] It would not be prison breaking to fail to return from leave or parole, or from a place to which the prisoner was sent as part of his training without being accompanied by a prison officer. But all these things might be criminal attempts to defeat the ends of justice.[6]

Lawful confinement. A person is lawfully confined in a prison when he is **48.03** confined in pursuance of an *ex facie* valid warrant applicable to him.[7] Provided the warrant appears valid it is not vitiated for this purpose by any extrinsic fault such as an irregularity in the trial or application as a result of which it was granted. The test is probably whether the fault in the warrant is one into which the prison authorities were bound to inquire: if it is not, then the detention is lawful, and an escape constitutes prison breaking.[8] Where a person is placed in prison by a police officer on suspicion and without a warrant, he is not guilty of prison breaking if he escapes.[9]

Where a person unlawfully confined escapes from prison he may also be guilty of any crime committed in the course of his escape, such as assault or malicious mischief. Similarly, if a mob break into a prison to rescue someone unlawfully confined, they may be guilty of mobbing.[10]

---

[1] Hume, i, 401; Alison, i, 555; Macdonald, p.169.
[2] *ibid.*
[3] Hume, i, 404; Alison, i, 557; Macdonald, p.170.
[4] *Andrew Otto* (1833) Bell's Notes 104.
[5] *H.M. Advocate v. Martin*, 1956 J.C. 1; see Vol. I, para 1.36.
[6] *supra,* para 47.01.
[7] Hume, i, 402; Alison, i, 556; Macdonald, p.169.
[8] Hume, i, 403; Alison, i, 556.
[9] *Jas Inglis* (1720) Hume, i, 403.
[10] *cf. John and Geo. Sinclairs* (1699) Hume, i, 404.

48.04 FORM OF CONFINEMENT. It is equally prison breaking whether the prisoner is serving a sentence, or has been committed to prison to await trial or for further examination, or is undergoing civil imprisonment.[11]

48.05 *Breaking.* Prison breaking is committed by escaping from prison, whatever means are used to effect the escape[12]: violence to warders, effraction of the building, fire-raising,[13] using false keys, corrupting warders, forging bail bonds or other documents which induce the authorities to release the prisoner,[14] or merely walking out of a door carelessly left open.[15] It is also prison breaking to take advantage of the actions of a mob breaking into the prison from outside, in order to escape.[16]

48.06 AGGRAVATIONS. Prison breaking may be aggravated by the mode employed, as for example by setting fire to a cell door.[17]

48.07 *Breaking into prison.* To break into a prison to rescue prisoners seems to be regarded as a specific crime,[18] although it is usually connected with mobbing.[19] It would probably be dealt with today as the crime of effecting the escape of a prisoner.

48.08 *Effecting someone else's escape.* There is no reason why the ordinary principles of art and part guilt should not apply to prison breaking so that anyone who assisted another prisoner to escape would be guilty of prison breaking whether or not he himself was a prisoner or he himself escaped as well. In *Turnbull v. H.M. Advocate*[20] however, where the accused was charged with assisting the escape of a prisoner by means of a forged bail bond, the indictment libelled that he entered into a conspiracy to effect the escape of a prisoner, and "by fraud and the uttering of forged documents [did] effect the escape of said . . . from lawful custody to the hindrance of the course of justice." The crime was described by Lord Cooper as "effecting the escape of a prisoner from lawful custody."[21] In *H.M. Advocate v. Martin*[22] the prisoner's accomplices were said to have aided and abetted him to abscond but he and they were all charged with attempting to defeat the ends of justice; and in *Fletcher v. Tudhope*[23] it was held to be an attempt to pervert the course of justice to warn a person that he was about to be arrested, where the intention was to enable him to escape the police who were looking for him. It has also been held to be perverting the course of

---

[11] Hume, i, 401; Alison, i, 555. The lawful application of civil imprisonment, other than for contempt of court, is now very limited: see *The Laws of Scotland: The Stair Memorial Encyclopaedia*, (1992), Vol. 8, paras 347–349.

[12] Hume, i, 401; Alison, i, 555; Macdonald, p.170.

[13] *Jean Bryan* (1841) 2 Swin. 545.

[14] cf. *Turnbull v. H.M. Advocate*, 1953 J.C. 59, *infra*.

[15] *Wm Hutton* (1837) 1 Swin. 497.

[16] Hume, i, 402; Alison, i, 555; Macdonald, p.170; *Jas Ratcliff or Walker* (1739) Hume, i, 402.

[17] *Jean Bryan, supra*; *Neil Macqueen* (1840) Bell's Notes 181.

[18] Macdonald, p.170; *John Urquhart* (1844) 2 Broun 13; Firearms Act 1968, Sched.2.

[19] *John Urquhart, supra*; *John and Geo. Sinclairs* (1699) Hume, i, 404.

[20] 1953 J.C. 59.

[21] At 59–60.

[22] 1956 J.C. 1.

[23] 1984 S.C.C.R. 267.

justice to assist a person to evade lawful arrest by allowing him to enter and make off in a vehicle driven by the accused.[24]

Escaping from lawful custody

There are a number of situations in which a person who escapes from **48.09** lawful custody cannot be charged with prison breaking such as, for example, where a prisoner is taken from prison to give evidence at court, to attend a funeral, or to attend a hospital for treatment[25] accompanied by prison officers. It appears, however, that any escape from lawful custody is a crime, whether or not it can be said to be analogous to prison breaking, and the crime is treated as an example of the crime of attempting to defeat the ends of justice, rather than as an extension of the crime of prison breaking.[26]

In *H.M. Advocate v. Martin and Ors*[27] a prisoner who escaped from a working party outside prison was charged with absconding from lawful custody and attempting to defeat the ends of justice. And there have been several cases in which persons escaping from police vans conveying them from court to prison have been similarly charged.[28]

Lawful custody. Section 13 of the Prisons (Scotland) Act 1989 provides: **48.10**

"A person shall be deemed to be in legal custody—
   (a) while he is confined in or being taken to or from any prison in which he may lawfully be confined; or
   (b) while he is working or is, for any other reason, outside the prison in the custody or under the control of an officer of the prison [or prisoner custody officer[29] performing custodial duties at the prison or a prison officer temporarily attached to the prison][30]; or
   (c) while he is being taken to any place to which he is required or authorised by or under this Act to be taken; or
   (d) while he is kept in custody in pursuance of such requirement or authorisation."[31]

Other institutions. It is an attempt to defeat the ends of justice to escape **48.11** from a young offenders institution, place of detention or a remand home. It appears not to be an offence for a child to abscond from a place of safety or residential establishment in which he has been placed under the Children (Scotland) Act 1995, or from the control of a person under

---

[24] *McElhinney v. Normand*, 1996 S.C.C.R. 86: the accused knew at the material time that the police were pursuing that person in order to arrest him.

[25] See *McAllister v. H.M. Advocate*, 1987 S.L.T. 552.

[26] See, *e.g. Allan James Cairns Peden*, Criminal Appeal Court, March 1978, unrep'd, where someone who was under arrest tried to run away from the arresting officer; he was convicted of attempting to pervert the course of justice.

[27] 1956 J.C. 1.

[28] For example, *William Melvin*, High Court, July 11, 1962, on remit after a plea of guilty in Edinburgh Sheriff Court, where the indictment charged simply that the accused "while being conveyed in lawful custody in a police van [from Edinburgh Sheriff Court to Her Majesty's Prison, Edinburgh], force[d] open the rear doors of said van and escape[d] from said vehicle and from lawful custody and did attempt to defeat the ends of justice."

[29] Relative to a contracted out prison: see n.30, *infra*.

[30] Words in square brackets apply to contracted out prisons: see the Criminal Justice and Public Order Act 1994, s.110(4). For "prisoner custody officer", see *ibid.*, s.107(1).

[31] See also Extradition Act 1989, s.17, and Mental Health (Scotland) Act 1984, s.120(1), *infra*. See also the Criminal Procedure (Scotland) Act 1995, s.295.

whose supervision he has been so placed, but such a child may be arrested without warrant and brought back to that place or establishment.[32]

48.12 *Mental Hospitals, etc.* Section 120 of the Mental Health (Scotland) Act 1984 provides:

> "(1) Any person required or authorised by or by virtue of this Act to be conveyed to any place or to be kept in custody or detained in a place of safety or at any place to which he is taken under section 68(5) of this Act[33] shall, while being so conveyed, detained or kept as the case may be, be deemed to be in legal custody."

48.13 MENTAL HOSPITALS. The Mental Health (Scotland) Act 1984 does not contain any provisions making it an offence for a patient to escape from a mental hospital in which he has been confined by virtue of a court order whether or not that order restricts his discharge.[34]

48.14 AIDING PATIENTS TO ESCAPE. Section 108 of the Mental Health (Scotland) Act 1984 provides:

> "(1) Any person who induces or knowingly assists any other person—
> (a)[35] being liable to be detained in a hospital under this Act, to absent himself without leave; or
> (b) being in legal custody by virtue of section 120 of this Act, to escape from such custody,
> shall be guilty of an offence"[36]

48.15 *Rescuing from police custody.* Section 41(1)(b) of the Police (Scotland) Act 1967 makes it an offence to rescue or attempt to rescue, or assist or attempt to assist the escape of, any person in custody.[37] A person in custody is a person:

---

[32] Children (Scotland) Act 1995, s.82. It is an offence under s.83 of that Act for a person knowingly (*inter alia*) to assist or induce a child to abscond in circumstances which would render the child liable to arrest under s.82: see para. 48.17, *infra*.

[33] Section 68(5) authorises the Secretary of State to direct the attendance of a patient subject to a restriction order at any place at which his attendance is desirable in the interests of justice or for the purpose of any public inquiry.

[34] A patient in respect of whom there is such a restriction (or a hospital direction) may, however, be apprehended and returned to hospital at any time, while if no such restriction exists he may not be apprehended after a certain period at large: Mental Health (Scotland) Act 1984, s.28 (as amended by the Mental Health (Detention) (Scotland) Act 1991, s.3, and the Mental Health (Patients in the Community) Act 1995, s.5(1)), s.62(1)(c) (as amended by the Criminal Procedure (Consequential Provisions) (Scotland) Act 1995, Sched. 4, para. 50(4), and the Mental Health (Patients in the Community) Act 1995, Sched. 2, para. 4), and s.62A(5)(c) (added to the Mental Health (Scotland) Act by the Crime and Punishment (Scotland) Act 1997, s.7(1)).

[35] As amended by the Adults with Incapacity (Scotland) Act 2000 (asp 4), Sched. 6.

[36] Maximum penalty on summary conviction six months' and a fine of the statutory maximum, on indictment two years' and a fine. For s.120 of the Mental Health (Scotland) Act 1984, see para. 48.12, *supra*.

[37] Maximum penalty on summary conviction a fine of level 4 on the standard scale and three months', or, on a subsequent offence within two years, nine months' and a fine of the prescribed sum.

"(a) who is in the lawful custody of a constable[38] or any person assisting a constable to execute his duty, or

(b) who is in the act of eluding or escaping from such custody, whether or not he has actually been arrested."[39]

The section applies only to persons assisting others to escape. It is not an offence under the Act, and is perhaps not an offence at all[40] to run away from a policeman, even after arrest.

An offence against section 41 can be committed only where the rescue or escape is effected by an assault or by some direct action against a constable akin to assault.[41]

According to Anderson[42] it is a common law offence to rescue a person from an officer of law who is lawfully detaining him, but such an offence would now be prosecuted either under the Police (Scotland) Act or as the effecting of an escape from lawful custody.

Harbouring escapees

Except in the case of the armed forces and merchant navy and **48.16** absconders from mental hospitals or under the Children (Scotland) Act 1995, there is no specific provision penalising the harbouring of escaped prisoners. Such harbouring would, however, constitute an attempt to defeat the course of justice, and would be prosecuted as such in appropriate cases. It is not the practice to bring such charges against a prisoner's family.

Thus, in *Miln v. Stirton*[43] it was held that a charge against a wife, of attempting to defeat the ends of justice by harbouring her husband against whom (as she knew) there was an outstanding extract conviction warrant for his arrest, was incompetent.[44]

Residential establishments. Section 83 of the Children (Scotland) Act **48.17** 1995 provides in relation to children liable to be arrested under section 82[45] of the Act that:

---

[38] A constable includes "a member of a police force maintained in England and Wales or in Northern Ireland when he is executing a warrant or otherwise acting in Scotland by virtue of any enactment conferring powers on him in Scotland": Criminal Justice and Public Order Act 1994, Sched. 10, para. 18 (which adds subs. (3) to s.41 of the 1967 Act).

[39] s.41(2).

[40] Except perhaps as a form of the protean crime of attempting to defeat the ends of justice.

[41] cf. *Curlett v. McKechnie*, 1938 J.C. 176.

[42] Anderson, p.85. In the sheriff court case of *Annan v. Tait*, 1981 S.C.C.R. 326, it was held that because the offence under s.41(1)(b) was an enactment in statutory form of the old common law offence referred to by Anderson, *mens rea* was required, such that if the accused had had an honest belief, based on reasonable grounds, that the person rescued was not in lawful custody (since the arresting officer had been in plain clothes and the accused was thus arguably in ignorance of that officer's status), he was entitled to be acquitted.

[43] 1982 S.L.T. (Sh.Ct.) 11.

[44] The sheriff followed Hume, i, 49 and Alison, i, 669. But cf. *Smith v. Watson*, 1982 J.C. 34: see *supra.*, para. 20.05.

[45] Which deals with absconding from a place of safety or the control of a supervisor, and with absconding from residential establishments.

"A person who—
  (a) knowingly assists or induces a child to abscond in circumstances which render the child liable to arrest under subsection (1) or (3) of section 82 of this Act;
  (b) knowingly and persistently attempts to induce a child so to abscond;
  (c) knowingly harbours or conceals a child who has so absconded; or
  (d) knowingly prevents a child from returning—
      (i) to a place mentioned in paragraph (a) or (b) of the said subsection (1);
      (ii) to a person mentioned in paragraph (c) of that subsection, or in the said subsection (3),

shall, subject to section 38(3) and (4) of this Act, to section 51(5) and (6) of the Children Act 1989 and to Article 70(5) and (6) of the Children (Northern Ireland) Order 1995 (analogous provision for England and Wales and for Northern Ireland), be guilty of an offence and liable on summary conviction to a fine not exceeding level 5 on the standard scale or to imprisonment for a term not exceeding six months or to both such fine and such imprisonment."

48.18 *Mental Patients.* Section 108(2) of the Mental Health (Scotland) Act 1984 provides:

"Any person who knowingly harbours a patient who is absent without leave or is otherwise at large and liable to be retaken under this Act, or gives him any assistance with intent to prevent, hinder or interfere with his being taken into custody or returned to the hospital or other place where he ought to be, shall be guilty of an offence."[46]

48.19 *Forces, etc.* Harbouring deserters and unlawful absentees is punishable under section 192 of the Army Act 1955 and of the Air Force Act 1955, and section 97 of the Naval Discipline Act 1957.[47]

---

[46] Maximum penalty on summary conviction six months' and a fine of the statutory maximum, and, on indictment, two years' and a fine.

[47] Maximum penalty on summary conviction three months' and a fine of the prescribed sum, and, on indictment, two years' and a fine.

CHAPTER 49

OFFENCES IN CONNECTION WITH JUDICIAL OFFICIALS

OFFENCES AGAINST JUDICIAL OFFICIALS

Deforcement

Deforcement consists in resisting an officer of law, such as a mes- **49.01** senger, in order to prevent him carrying out his duty.[1] It is not now prosecuted as such, but as an aggravated assault.[2]

Obstructing the Police

The Police (Scotland) Act 1967, s.41(1)(a), provides: **49.02**

> "Any person who assaults, resists, obstructs, molests or hinders a constable in the execution of his duty or a person assisting such a constable . . . shall be guilty of an offence."[3]

The words "resists . . . hinders" are *ejusdem generis* with assault and require an element of physical obstruction.[4]

Seducing the Police

The Police (Scotland) Act 1967, s.42(1), provides[5]: **49.03**

> "Any person who causes, or attempts to cause, or does any act calculated to cause, disaffection amongst [any constables], or who induces, or attempts to induce, or does any act calculated to induce, any constable to withhold his services shall be guilty of an offence."[6]

---

[1] Hume, i, Chap. 13; Alison, i, Chap. 22.

[2] Macdonald, p.168; *supra*, para 29.11.

[3] Maximum penalty, nine months' and a fine of the prescribed sum on summary conviction: s.41, as amended by the Criminal Law Act 1977, s.31 and Sched. 6; the Criminal Justice (Scotland) Act 1980, s.57; and the Criminal Procedure (Consequential Provisions) (Scotland) Act 1995, Sched. 1, para. 4 and Sched. 2. "Constable" includes a member of a police force maintained in England and Wales or Northern Ireland when executing a warrant in Scotland or acting in Scotland by virtue of statutory powers: s.41(3), as inserted by the Criminal Justice and Public Order Act 1994, Sched. 10, para. 18.

[4] *Curlett v. McKechnie*, 1938 J.C. 176. *Cf. Skeen v. Shaw and Anr*, 1979 S.L.T. (Notes) 58, where the Appeal Court queried, but did not decide, whether "hinders" requires a physical element of obstruction.

[5] As amended by the Police and Magistrates' Courts Act 1994, s.63(8).

[6] Maximum penalty on indictment two years', or on summary conviction three months' and a fine of the prescribed sum. Conviction carries permanent disqualification from becoming or remaining a constable: s.42(2).

OFFENCES BY JUDICIAL OFFICIALS

Bribery

49.04   It is a crime at common law for a judicial officer to take a bribe, or for anyone to offer a bribe to such an officer. "Judicial officer" includes clerks of court, procurators fiscal, macers and messengers as well as judges.[7] The crime extends to any attempt by bribery to interfere with "those proceedings . . . which take place in a court of law, or are the incidents of or preliminaries to judicial procedure."[8]

The crime extends to bribery in connection with any "holder of a public office which charges him with the duty of seeing that some system of legal regulation is enforced equally against all offending members of the public at large, or of a particular class of members of the public to which the system specially applies"[9] such as a sanitary inspector or a member of a licensing board.[10] This crime may not extend to bribery of officials whose function is purely administrative, unconnected with enforcing any system of legal regulation.[11]

Oppression and neglect of duty

49.05   Oppression by judicial officials is a recognised crime at common law[12] although it is unknown in recent times. It may consist in partiality or refusal of justice by a judge, in the persistent bringing of groundless charges by an official prosecutor, or in any abuse of official judicial position to gratify personal desires.[13]

Neglect or breach of duty by judicial officers may be criminal in the same way as neglect or breach of duty by other public officials.[14]

49.06 *Police*. Section 44 of the Police (Scotland) Act 1967 provides:

"(1) Any constable who wilfully absents himself from duty otherwise than in accordance with regulations made under . . . this Act shall be guilty of an offence.

(2) Any constable who neglects or violates his duty shall be guilty of an offence."

The maximum penalty under the 1967 Act is 60 days' imprisonment,[15] and more serious cases would still be dealt with at common law.[16] Where

---

[7] Hume, i, 408; *Logue v. H.M. Advocate,* 1932 J.C. 1, L.J.-G. Clyde at 4; *H.M. Advocate v. Stewart and Mulholland*, High Court at Edinburgh, July 1976, unrep'd: the indictment seems to combine a charge of corruption with one of "interference with the course of justice", on an averment of showing favour by imposing a light sentence after receiving offers of money. The accused were acquitted.

[8] *Logue v. H.M. Advocate*, 1932 J.C. 1, L.J.-G. Clyde at 4.

[9] *ibid.*

[10] See *Maxwell v. H.M. Advocate*, 1980 J.C. 40, Lord Cameron at 43–44.

[11] *Logue v. H.M. Advocate*, 1932 J.C. 1, L.J.-G. Clyde at 4.

[12] Hume, i, 408 and ii, 141; Alison, i, 632; Macdonald, p.127.

[13] *cf. Alex. Waddell* (1829) Bell's Notes 92, a charge of "violence and oppression by messengers-at-arms . . . and incarcerating and detaining one of the lieges, more especially when committed under the colour of law."

[14] Hume, i, 410–411; Alison, i, 634; Macdonald, p.141; *supra*, para. 44.01.

[15] The alternative being a fine of level 3 on the standard scale: s.44(5) as amended by the Criminal Justice Act 1982, Sched. 6 (now Sched. 2, Pt III, of the Criminal Procedure (Consequential Provisions) (Scotland) Act 1995).

[16] See *Wilson v. Smith*, 1997 S.L.T. (Sh.Ct.) 91; A. Brown, "Wilful Neglect of Duty by Public Officials" (1996) 64 Sc. Law Gaz. 130.

a policeman obtains money on a promise to release a prisoner or refrain from reporting an offence he may be charged with extortion,[17] and a constable who takes bribes may be charged under the Prevention of Corruption Acts.[18] Common law crimes committed by police in the course of their duty, such as theft or assault, are prosecuted as such, the accused's official position being an aggravation.

---

[17] *Geo. Jeffrey* (1842) Bell's Notes 92.
[18] *supra*, paras 21.23 and 44.04.

CHAPTER 50

CONTEMPT OF COURT[1]

Contempt of court is not a crime and is in many ways *sui generis*,[2] but **50.01** since it is punishable by fine and imprisonment it may be regarded as virtually a crime, at least where the court in question is a criminal one.[3] It has been described as "conduct which challenges or affronts the authority of the court or the supremacy of the law itself."[4] Where conduct which constitutes contempt is also a criminal offence, for example an attempt to pervert the course of justice, it may, of course, be prosecuted as such, in cases in which the court has not dealt with it as contempt.[5] The rules of criminal procedure do not apply to proceedings for contempt.[6]

Every court has an inherent power to punish persons who are in contempt of it; but where a person is committed to prison for contempt, the committal must be for a fixed term, although this does not prevent the court from authorising his discharge prior to the completion of that term.[7] The maximum penalty which can be imposed by a Scottish court for contempt is two years in prison and a fine of any amount, save that in the sheriff court, where the contempt is dealt with otherwise than in connection with criminal proceedings on indictment, the maximum is restricted to three months' imprisonment and a fine of level 4 on the standard scale: in the district court, the maximum penalty for contempt is further restricted to 60 days' imprisonment and a fine of level 4 on the standard scale.[8]

Where the contempt occurs in the court itself it may be dealt with on the spot without any formal charge,[9] but where it is committed outside

---

[1] There is an old crime called "obstruction of courts" which consists in obstructing the proceedings of a court, for example, by preventing the judges or officials from entering the court-room. The crime extends to obstructing a Presbytery meeting: *John G. Robertson and Ors* (1842) 1 Broun 152; *Andrew Holm and Alex. Fraser* (1844) 2 Broun 18. For an account of the modern law, see R.M.M. McInnes (with J. D. Fairley), *Contempt of Court in Scotland* (CLT Professional Publishing, 2000).

[2] *H.M. Advocate v. Airs*, 1975 J.C. 64.

[3] Appeals against sentences for contempt of a civil court are heard in the Court of Session; those against sentences in a criminal court by the High Court: *Cordiner, Petr*, 1973 J.C. 16.

[4] *H.M. Advocate v. Airs, supra*, at 69.

[5] *ibid.*; *Manson Petr*, High Court, May 1977 unrep'd.

[6] *ibid.*

[7] Contempt of Court Act 1981 (hereinafter referred to as "the 1981 Act"), s.15(1). The provisions of s.15 have applied to contempt proceedings from August 27, 1981 — which must be borne in mind relative to contempt cases decided prior to that date.

[8] The 1981 Act, s.15(2), as amended by the Criminal Procedure (Consequential Provisions) (Scotland) Act 1995, Sched. 4, para. 36(2): see also the 1981 Act, s.15(3) (as substituted by the 1995 Act, Sched. 4, para. 36(3), which replaces the former subsections (3) and (4) of s.15 of the 1981 Act) and s.15(5) (as amended by the 1995 Act, Sched. 4, para. 36(4)) which deals with the disposal of young and mentally disordered persons found in contempt. See also s.155 of the 1995 Act, *infra* para. 50.07.

[9] For example, *Wylie and Anr v. H.M. Advocate*, 1966 S.L.T. 149; *Morris v. Crown Office* [1970] 2 Q.B. 114.

the court the person in contempt may be brought before the court by petition and complaint at the instance of the Lord Advocate[10] or on the motion of a party to the cause, or on an indictment or complaint where the contempt is also an ordinary crime.[11] He may also, in appropriate circumstances, be charged on summary complaint under section 155(3) of the 1995 Act.[12]

50.02 *Improper behaviour in court.*[13] Any improper or disorderly behaviour in court, which wilfully challenges or affronts the authority of that court or defies its orders,[14] may constitute contempt.[15] It is contempt of court for a party, an accused,[16] a witness,[17] a juryman[18] or anyone else, to appear drunk in court. The court should exercise its power to punish on the spot with great discretion, and should always allow the "accused" an opportunity to explain his behaviour.[19] It is common practice for judges to order persons guilty of contempt, *e.g.* by prevarication, to be detained until the end of a day or of the trial, and then to deal with them, thus giving them a chance to explain or purge their contempt.[20]

50.03 *Slandering judges.* Slandering judges, which is sometimes called "murmuring judges" is a crime at common law.[21] The last reported prosecution for slandering judges was *Alex Robertson*[22] where the accused was charged in 1870 and sentenced to one month's imprisonment and a fine of £50 on pleading guilty to two common law charges of writing a

---

[10] For example, *H.M. Advocate v. Bell*, 1936 J.C. 89; *H.M. Advocate v. Airs*, 1975 J.C. 64.

[11] *cf. Petrie v. Angus* (1889) 2 White 358.

[12] *infra*, para. 50.07.

[13] It has been said that contempt of court is restricted to behaviour which offends the dignity of the court, and does not include acts such as refusal to obey a court order, or publishing material prejudicial to a pending litigation, which latter are properly charged as interference with the course of justice: *Johnson v. Grant*, 1923 S.C. 789, L.P. Clyde at 790, but that was said in order to point out that imprisonment for breach of interdict could not be avoided by an apology for offending the court's dignity. In practice certain forms of interference with the administration of justice are prosecuted as contempt, particularly where they are not committed with intent to pervert the course of justice: see *infra*.

[14] *McMillan v. Carmichael*, 1993 S.C.C.R. 943, where it is affirmed that such contempt cannot be committed recklessly. See also *Aitken v. Carmichael*, 1993 S.C.C.R. 889, where a person's act of putting on headphones as he left the public benches after a case had been adjourned was considered not to constitute contempt. *Cf. William v. Clark*, 2001 S.C.C.R. 505.

[15] Hume, ii, 138; *e.g. Robert Clark or Williamson* (1829) Shaw 215: insulting a judge after being sentenced; *Young v. Lees*, 1998 S.C.C.R. 558: returning to court and insulting the sheriff after having been ejected from the public gallery for causing a disturbance; *Gallagher, Petr*, 1996 S.C.C.R. 833: staring menacingly at a jury which had just returned a guilty verdict. *Cf., Mowbray v. Valentine*, 1991 S.C.C.R. 494: a party litigant to be allowed sufficient latitude relative to the conduct of his case and any possible misunderstandings of judicial rulings during the proceedings; *cf.* also *McMillan v. Carmichael*, 1993 S.C.C.R. 943: yawning "openly and unrestrainedly" in a warm and stuffy court not contempt, unless intended to challenge or affront the authority of the court.

[16] *Alex. McLean* (1838) 2 Swin. 185, 187.

[17] *John Allan* (1826) Shaw 172; *Jas Wemyss* (1840) Bell's Notes 165.

[18] *Wilson v. John Angus and Sons*, 1921 2 S.L.T. 139.

[19] *Royle v. Gray*, 1973 S.L.T. 31.

[20] *cf. Wylie and Anr v. H.M. Advocate*, 1966 S.L.T. 149; *Young v. Lees*, 1998 S.C.C.R. 558.

[21] Hume, i, 406. The Judges Act 1540 (A.P.S. II, p. 374, c.22), which provided "giff ony maner of persoun murmuris ony Juge temporale or spirituale als weill lordis of the sessioune as vtheris and previs nocht the samin sufficientlie he salbe pvnst", is now repealed: Statute Law (Repeals) Act 1973, Sched. 1.

[22] (1870) 1 Couper 404. But see *Walter Scott Ellis*, High Court, Feb. 1965, unrep'd; *supra*, para. 29.63.

slanderous complaint to the Lord Chancellor about a sheriff-substitute. It was argued that such a complaint was privileged but the court held that although a complaint made to the authorities in good faith and setting forth specific charges which could be investigated would not constitute murmuring, the mere fact that the complaint had been made to an authority did not excuse it if it was done out of private malice.

It is not contempt of court merely to criticise a judge's decision or to urge that the law as decided by him is unjust or immoral and in need of amendment.[23] Generally speaking, the courts are unwilling to treat criticisms of judges or courts as contempt unless they are clearly disrespectful in their terms or are likely to interfere with the proper administration of justice, recognising that "disappointed litigants sometimes feel aggrieved and that some of them are ill-tempered, and that they may say or write things which are foolish and reprehensible", and that there is a danger that the process of contempt of court might "degenerate into an oppressive or vindictive abuse of the Court's powers."[24] A statement, however, that a judge had not merely come to a wrong decision but had acted unfairly or unjudicially would be treated as a contempt. General abusive statements about judges unrelated to any particular case might also be treated as contempts of court, but would more likely be ignored. It is contempt to write an abusive letter to a judge about the exercise of his judicial functions.[25] To write a threatening letter would also constitute contempt, but may be prosecuted as an aggravated charge of making threats.[26]

Contempt by witnesses. PREVARICATION. At common law, prevarication by **50.04** witnesses constitutes contempt of court,[27] as does perjury.[28] It is also contempt of court at common law for a witness to refuse to answer competent and relevant questions,[29] or to refuse to take an oath or

---

[23] However vigorous, rumbustious, or wide of the mark the criticism is, and whether it is expressed in good taste or bad taste, provided it keeps within the limits of reasonable courtesy and good faith: *R. v. Comm. of Metropolitan Police, ex p. Blackburn* [1968] 2 Q.B. 150. The non-contemptuous article in question was written by Mr Quentin Hogg, as he then was; *Milburn*, 1946 S.C. 301; *Glasgow Corporation v. Hedderwick and Sons*, 1918 S.C. 639.

[24] *Milburn, supra*, L.P. Normand at 315. *Cf. Lawrie v. Roberts and Linton* (1882) 4 Couper 606.

[25] *Lord Advocate v. John Hay* (1822) 1 S. 288; *Lord Advocate v. Jamieson* (1822) 1 S. 285.

[26] *Alex. Carr* (1854) 1 Irv. 464; *Walter Scott Ellis*, High Court, Feb. 1965, unrep'd, *supra*, para. 29.63.

[27] Hume, i, 380; Alison, i, 484; Burnett, p.209; *Robt Dewar and Ors* (1842) 1 Broun 233; *cf. Wm Smith* (1854) 1 Irv. 378; *Adam Baxter and Ors* (1867) 5 Irv. 351; *MacLeod v. Speirs*, (1884) 5 Couper 387; *David McEwan and Daniel McLeod* (1829) Shaw 213. In *McNeilage, Petr*, 1999 S.C.C.R. 471, at 475B, L.J.-C. Cullen quoted with approval the following account of prevarication from Lord Young in *MacLeod v. Spiers, supra*, at 405: "It is a loose and indefinite term, which may mean many different things short of perjury; the general idea which it conveys is manifest unwillingness candidly to tell the whole truth, fencing with questions in such manner as to show reluctance to disclose the truth, and a disposition to conceal or withhold it." For a witness to be guilty of prevarication he must be shown to be deliberately refusing to give evidence it is proved he was able to give: *Childs v. McLeod*, 1981 S.L.T. (Notes) 27; *Sze v. Wilson*, 1992 S.C.C.R. 54; *Mustard v. Colley*, 1997 S.L.T. 1123; *McInally, Petr*, 1993 S.C.C.R. 212. See also *Bacon, Petr*, 1986 S.C.C.R. 265; *Smith, Petr*, 1987 S.C.C.R. 726. For the procedure in dealing with such a witness, see *Hutchison v. H.M. Advocate*, 1984 S.L.T. 233; *Omond v. Lees*, 1994 S.C.C.R. 389.

[28] *Manson, Petr*, High Court, May 1977, unrep'd.

[29] *A. Kerr* (1822) Shaw 68; *McLauchlin v. Douglas and Kidston* (1863) 4 Irv, 273; *H.M. Advocate v. Airs* 1975 J.C. 64 (but see para. 50.05, *infra*).

affirmation.[30] The court has a discretion to permit a witness to refuse to answer on grounds of conscience, but in the absence of such permission (or of a legally recognised privilege) it is no answer at common law to a charge of contempt that the witness was bound to secrecy by a professional code, such as that observed by doctors or journalists.[31]

50.05   CONTEMPT OF COURT ACT 1981. The common law position of a witness who refuses to disclose the source of his information is now subject to section 10 of the 1981 Act which provides:

> "No court may require a person to disclose, nor is any person guilty of contempt of court for refusing to disclose, the source of information contained in a publication[32] for which he is responsible, unless it be established to the satisfaction of the court that disclosure is necessary in the interests of justice or national security or for the prevention of disorder or crime."

In the petition and complaint presented to the High Court in *H.M. Advocate v. Airs*,[33] the finding of contempt was based on the common law position that a witness at a criminal trial, who repeatedly refused to answer questions which were competent and relevant as to the identity of a person who had provided that witness with particular information, was guilty of contempt. No such finding can now be made where section 10 applies unless the court is satisfied by the person seeking disclosure that the disclosure was necessary in the interests of one or other of the matters specified in that section. There is, therefore, no longer an unqualified "legal duty to answer any question which is both competent and relevant"[34]; nor, however, is there an absolute protection for journalistic sources.[35]

50.06   FAILURE TO ATTEND. It is contempt of court for a witness or an accused wilfully to fail to answer a citation, this being really a form of the contempt of failing to obey an order of court.[36] The test is whether, in failing to answer the citation or being late in attending court, the accused or witness was wilfully defying the court or was intending disrespect to the court or was acting in any way against the court or was attempting to pervert the course of justice.[37] Where a witness was well aware of the citation and the time for appearance, but did nothing to enable herself to

---

[30] *Christian Tweedie or Laidlaw (John Turnbull)* (1829) Shaw 222; *Wylie and Anr v. H.M. Advocate*, 1966 S.L.T. 149.

[31] *Airs, supra*; but see para. 50.05, *infra*.

[32] "Publication" is defined in s.2(1) of the 1981 Act: see para. 50.16, *infra*.

[33] 1975 J.C. 64.

[34] *ibid.*, L.J.-G. Emslie at 70. On the interpretation of s.10, and its compatibility with article 10 (freedom of expression) of the European Convention on Human Rights, *cf. Ashworth Hospital Authority v. MGN Ltd* [2001] 1 W.L.R. 515, CA, Lord Phillips of Worth Matravers, at 531A *et seq.*; *cf.* also *X Ltd v. Morgan-Grampian Plc.* [1990] 2 W.L.R. 1000, HL, Lord Bridge of Harwich, at 1006D *et seq.*

[35] *cf. Camelot Group Plc. v. Centaur Ltd* [1999] Q.B. 124, CA, Schiemann L.J. at 134E.

[36] *Chappell v. Friel*, 1997 S.L.T. 1325; *H.M. Advocate v. Bell*, 1936 J.C. 89; *Pirie v. Hawthorne*, 1962 J.C. 69; *Petrie v. Angus* (1889) 2 White 358. In *Thos Innes and John McEwan* (1831) Shaw 238, a witness who broke out of and escaped from a witness room in which he had been confined was convicted of contempt.

[37] *Caldwell v. Normand*, 1993 S.C.C.R. 624, L.J.-G. Hope at 625F–626A, quoting from *Kane v. Carmichael*, High Court on appeal, January 20, 1993, unrep'd (but see 1993 S.C.C.R. 626C–627D for the opinion of L.J.-C. Ross in that case). See also *Cameron v. Orr*, 1995 S.C.C.R. 365; *Chappell Friel*, 1997 S.L.T. 1325.

attend and tendered no explanation, it was considered that the necessary wilfulness had been established.[38] The same test would apply where a solicitor is late for his client's appearance in court.[39]

An accused who refuses to appear in court and insists on remaining in the court cells is in contempt of court.[40]

Section 155 of the 1995 Act provides: **50.07**

"(1) If a witness in a summary prosecution—
   (a) wilfully fails to attend after being duly cited; or
   (b) unlawfully refuses to be sworn; or
   (c) after the oath has been administered to him refuses to answer any question which the court may allow; or
   (d) prevaricates in his evidence,

he shall be deemed guilty of contempt of court and be liable to be summarily punished forthwith for such contempt by a fine not exceeding level 3 on the standard scale or by imprisonment for any period not exceeding 21 days.[41]

. . .

(3) Subsections (1) and (2)[42] above are without prejudice to the right of the prosecutor to proceed by way of formal complaint for any such contempt where a summary punishment, as mentioned in the said subsection (1), is not imposed.

(4) Any witness who, after being duly cited . . .
   (a) fails without reasonable excuse, . . . to attend for precognition by a prosecutor . . . or
   (b) refuses when so cited to give information within his knowledge regarding any matter relative to the commission of the offence in relation to which such precognition is taken,

shall be liable to the like punishment as is provided in subsection (1) above."

CHILDREN (SCOTLAND) ACT 1995. It is an offence for a relevant person as **50.08** respects a child[43] whose case is being considered by a children's hearing to fail to attend all stages of the hearing unless the hearing are satisfied that it would be unreasonable to require his attendance or that his attendance is unnecessary for the proper consideration of the case.[44]

---

[38] *Chappell v. Friel*, 1997 S.L.T. 1325.

[39] See *Ferguson v. Normand*, 1994 S.C.C.R. 812, where a solicitor accepted instructions to represent a person in a district court at a time when he was also due to appear for a client at a three day trial in a sheriff court. His error of judgment, in considering that the district court appearance would be concluded in time for the de facto start of the resumed sheriff court trial and in remaining at the district court when it was clear that the business there would overrun the commencement of the relevant sheriff court business, was not considered sufficient to show the necessary wilfulness on his part for contempt.

[40] *Dawes v. Cardle*, 1987 S.C.C.R. 135.

[41] See *Logan v. McGlennan*, 1999 S.C.C.R. 584.

[42] This subsection deals with the record to be kept where summary punishment is imposed under subs.(1): see *Logan v. McGlennan*, 1999 S.C.C.R. 584; *cf. Riaviz v. Howdle*, 1996 S.C.C.R. 20.

[43] See s.93(2)(b) for the meaning of "child" and "relevant person".

[44] Section 45(8), (9). Maximum penalty, a fine of level 3 on the standard scale.

50.09 *Failure to obey.* Failure by any person to obtemper an interlocutor of a court is contempt of that court.[45] It is also contempt of court for a party to fail to honour an undertaking given on his behalf,[46] or to fail to co-operate with officers in the provision of reports required by the court.[47] It is not contempt, however, to fail to pay a fine.[48] A legal representative has a duty to obey any clear ruling made by a judge during the case in which he appears, and it might well be contempt to refuse to do so; it is not for a judge, however, to dictate the way in which a legal representative conducts his client's case in court.[49]

50.10 *Interference with the course of justice.* Interference with the course of justice or with judicial proceedings always in a sense constitutes contempt of court.[50] In practice only certain forms of interference are treated as contempt, the remainder being dealt with as attempts to pervert or defeat the ends of justice, if done with that purpose.[51]

50.11 TAMPERING WITH PROCESS. It is contempt of court for a person to dispose of a production which he has been cited to produce at precognition,[52] or to abstract or retain unlawfully anything which has been lodged in court as a production.[53]

50.12 *Prejudicing a fair trial.* At common law,[54] the publication of statements regarding matters which were *sub judice* constituted contempt of court where the statements were prejudicial to any party or were in any way likely to impede a fair trial, for example, by influencing potential jurors, or creating an unfavourable climate of public opinion.[55] To publish a

---

[45] For example, *Leys v. Leys* (1886) 13R. 1223; *Muir v. Milligan* (1868) 6M. 1125: failure to deliver child in custody action. Cf. *Att.-Gen. v. Punch Ltd* [2001] 2 W.L.R. 1713, CA, which was concerned with the circumstances under which an interlocutory injunction obtained against one party was available against a third party.

[46] *Graham v. Robert Younger Ltd*, 1955 J.C. 28.

[47] See, *e.g.*, *Urquhart v. Hamilton*, 1996 S.C.C.R. 217 (supplementary social work report required in connection with a deferred sentence hearing).

[48] *Anderson v. Douglas*, 1997 S.C.C.R. 632.

[49] *Blair-Wilson, Petr*, 1997 S.L.T. 621. A greater latitude is allowed to party-litigants, especially if it is thought they may not fully have understood the rulings which have been made: *Mowbray v. Valentine*, 1991 S.C.C.R. 494.

[50] But see *Johnson v. Grant*, 1923 S.C. 789.

[51] Intimidation of witnesses, for example, would normally be treated as subornation or attempting to defeat the ends of justice, although it has been said to constitute contempt of court: *Forkes v. Weir* (1897) 5 S.L.T. 194.

[52] *Lord Advocate v. Alexander Galloway* (1839) 2 Swin. 465.

[53] *Watt v. Ligertwood and Anr* (1874) 1 R. (H.L.) 21, 24; *Levison v. Jewish Chronicle Ltd*, 1924 S.L.T. 755. It has been held in England that where documents are made available by a party under an order to produce them in proceedings, it is a contempt of court for them to be made publicly available by the other party: *Home Office v. Harman* [1983] 1 A.C. 280, HL.

[54] The common law position in relation to prejudicial publications is now significantly altered (if strict liability is to apply) by the provisions of the Contempt of Court Act 1981. See para. 50.16 *et seq.*, *infra*.

[55] Hume, i, 384; *Lord Advocate v. John Hay* (1822) 1 S. 288; *Henderson v. Laing* (1824) 2 S. 384; *Robt Emond* (1829) Shaw 229; *The St. Mungo Manufacturing Co. v. Hutchison Main and Co. Ltd* (1908) 15 S.L.T. 893; *Smith v. John Ritchie and Co.* (1892) 3 White 408; *John Gilkie* (1777) Hume, i, 384; *Ewan Macewan* (1785) Hume, i, 385; *MacAlister v. Associated Newspapers Ltd*, 1954 S.L.T. 14; *Stirling v. Associated Newspapers Ltd and Anr*, 1960 J.C. 5. This is not the approach of the modern law, which favours a more liberal approach; as Lord Coulsfield states in *Montgomery v. H.M. Advocate*, 2000 S.C.C.R. 1044, at

statement of known facts was not contempt merely because they had some connection with a pending trial if they were not calculated to cause prejudice,[56] but in practice, the courts interpreted "calculated to cause prejudice" very widely in order to protect accused persons. The unauthorised publication of an accused or suspected person's photograph was contempt of court at common law,[57] as was the publication of statements made about the case by potential witnesses,[58] or of a statement that the police believed that an organisation to which the accused were alleged to belong was a body of violent criminals.[59] Indeed, the publication of any information relating to a projected criminal trial other than the bare fact of an accused's arrest and committal on a particular charge might well have been treated as contempt at common law.

The prohibition of the publication of such statements was not confined at common law to the duration of the actual proceedings. It was contempt to publish prejudicial statements after the arrest of a person by the police and before he had appeared before a court at all[60]; and there may even have been circumstances in which the publication of information about a suspect before arrest could have been treated as contempt at common law.[61] To introduce references to an immediately pending trial (for assaulting a patient with severe brain damage by trying to block her air supply) into a television programme dealing with the issue of maintaining life-support systems for such patients might well have been a contempt of court at common law, and would certainly have been so if the references were such as to suggest that the accused was carrying out a policy of withdrawing such support.[62]

1080F—1081A: "At one time, a very strict view was taken in Scotland about the permissible limits of comment in and publicity about an ongoing prosecution. The law of contempt has been very substantially liberalised, a development with which I wholly agree. One of the factors which have had to be borne in mind in the process of liberalisation is the extent to which juries can be trusted to ignore potentially prejudicial comments, act in accordance with their oath and follow the directions of the trial judge. Again I wholly agree that experience supports the view that juries can be relied upon to deserve such trust." At the core of the current approach is, therefore, a test close to that favoured in *Stuurman v. H.M. Advocate*, 1980 J.C. 111, whereby the question is whether the risk of prejudice from what was published is so serious that no direction to the jury by a trial judge can be expected to reduce or eliminate it. See also in *Montgomery* the opinions of L.J.-G. Rodger at pp. 1074D–1075F and 1078D, and Lord Hope of Craighead at pp. 1105C–1107E. (See also the opinion of Lord Clyde, *ibid.*, at p. 1109E–F, where he opines that in modern law, which must take account of the various rights established under the European Convention on Human Rights, an important factor with which to balance the right of the accused to a fair trial (under Art. 6(1) of the Convention) following what has been published is the right of freedom of expression safeguarded by Art. 10.)

[56] *Cowie v. Outram and Co. Ltd* (1912) 6 Adam 556.

[57] *Stirling v. Associated Newspapers Ltd and Anr*, 1960 J.C. 5.

[58] *ibid.*

[59] *MacAlister v. Associated Newspapers Ltd*, 1954 S.L.T. 14.

[60] *Stirling v. Associated Newspapers Ltd and Anr*, 1960 J.C. 5, upheld on this point (but for different reasons) by the full bench decision in *Hall v. Associated Newspapers Ltd*, 1979 J.C. 1.

[61] *cf.* A.L. Goodhart, "Contempt of Court when Proceedings Imminent" (1964) 80 L.Q.R. 166; *R. v. Beaverbrook Newspapers Ltd and Ors* [1962] N.I. 15. Where the Contempt of Court Act 1981 applies, the criterion is whether proceedings are "active" as determined by the provisions of Sched. 1 of that Act: see para. 50.16, *infra*.

[62] *Atkins v. London Weekend Television Ltd*, 1978 J.C. 48, a rare case where the prosecution was abandoned because of the contempt. Where prosecutions have been continued after contempt by prejudicial publicity they have been held to be competent on the ground that the contempt occurred some time before the trial so that its continuing

The court in *Atkins v. London Weekend Television Ltd*[63] recognised it as part of the common law that prejudice which is an incidental and unintended by-product of a discussion of public affairs is not contempt, and section 5 of the Contempt of Court Act 1981 now provides that a publication made as part of a discussion in good faith of public affairs or other matters of general public interest is not to be treated as contempt under the strict liability rule if the risk of impediment or prejudice to particular legal proceedings is merely incidental to the discussion. This defence would not have succeeded in *Atkins*, since the reference to the particular case was specific and deliberate. The court might also have held that in any event in the circumstances responsibility did not depend on the strict liability rule but on recklessness since they described the respondents as having "undoubtedly chose[n] to sail very close to the wind and [taken] what they must have recognised was a calculated risk".[64]

Merely to report that a witness has been given police protection and is being kept during a trial at a secret address, where this is in fact so, is not a contempt.[65]

It was not clear at common law whether a case under appeal was still *sub judice* so as to prevent the publication of comment or of any facts other than those disclosed in court.[66]

50.13   INTERFERING WITH THE INVESTIGATION OF CRIME. In *Stirling v. Associated Newspapers Ltd*[67] in which a newspaper had interviewed persons who were potential witnesses against a man who had been arrested on a murder charge, and then published their statements, Lord Justice-General Clyde said that the investigation of crime in Scotland was exclusively the province of the procurator fiscal,[68] and suggested that any private person who conducted an investigation might be acting unlawfully. Theoretically the police act as the agents of the procurator fiscal in investigating crime, and historically the fiscal himself acts as the agent of the sheriff in the latter's capacity as examining magistrate,[69] so that it might be said that an interference with the fiscal's investigations constituted an interference with the administration of justice. But in practice the sheriff no longer even purports to act as examining magistrate, and the fiscal exercises only a general supervision over the police,[70] most of whose investigations in any event precede the stage of

---

effect, if any, could be countered by appropriate directions to the jury: *Stuurman v. H.M. Advocate*, 1980 J.C. 111; *X v. Sweeney*, 1982 J.C. 70; see also *Al Megrahi v. Times Newspapers Ltd*, 1999 S.C.C.R. 824; *Montgomery v. H.M. Advocate*, 2000 S.C.C.R. 1044, PC. For cases in summary procedure, see *Tudhope v. Glass*, 1981 S.C.C.R. 336; *Aitchison v. Bernardi*, 1984 S.L.T. 343.

[63] 1978 J.C. 48.

[64] *ibid.*, at 56. Section 5 of the Contempt of Court Act 1981 is at least in part a consequence of the decision of the European Court of Human Rights in *Sunday Times Ltd v. United Kingdom* [1979] 2 E.H.R.R. 245, in which the decision of the House of Lords in *Att.-Gen. v. Times Newspapers Ltd* [1974] A.C. 273, was criticised. On the interpretation of s.5, see, *e.g.*, *Att.-Gen. v. English* [1983] 1 A.C. 116, HL.

[65] *Kemp and Ors, Petrs*, 1982 J.C. 29.

[66] In *Glasgow Corporation v. Hedderwick and Sons*, 1918 S.C.639 the statements complained of which attacked the decision and urged an appeal were published within the reclaiming days but before any appeal was marked, and the case was treated as not being then *sub judice*.

[67] 1960 J.C. 5.

[68] *cf. Smith v. H.M. Advocate*, 1952 J.C. 66, L.J.-C. Thomson at 71.

[69] *County Council of Dumfries v. Phyn* (1895) 22 R. 538.

[70] Police (Scotland) Act 1967, s.17(3); *Smith v. H.M. Advocate*, 1952 J.C. 66; *Stirling v. Associated Newspapers and Anr*, 1960 J.C. 5.

committal by the sheriff. Lord Clyde was concerned in *Stirling*[71] with the publication of information before the commencement of any form of judicial proceedings,[72] and he said that, "Any independent interviewing of possible witnesses by representatives of the Press, while the investigations by the Crown authorities are in progress, constitutes interference with the authorities' public duty and, usually, will impede their investigations. . . . If the result of these interviews is published in the Press before the trial is over, this may well constitute contempt of Court."[73]

Whilst it remains possible that any private investigation which hindered the official investigation might be dealt with as contempt even although its purpose was to advance the cause of justice, it is submitted that it is not a crime or a contempt of court for a private person merely to pursue an investigation or interview potential witnesses. It is arguable that only persons with a recognised interest such as those acting on behalf of an accused person are entitled to investigate crime,[74] but there is much to be said for the view that the Press as well as the Crown represent the public interest, and that it would be constitutionally dangerous to prevent their acting as watchdogs in a matter which is being dealt with by the police.[75] The value of private investigation by someone with no interest in the matter other than curiosity may be outweighed by its almost inevitable nuisance value to the police, but here, as elsewhere in the law of contempt, the courts must be careful "lest a process, the purpose of which is to prevent interference with the administration of justice, should degenerate into an oppressive or vindictive abuse of the Court's powers."[76] *Stirling*[77] is authority only for treating the publication of the result of an investigation as contempt, there is no authority for treating the investigation in this way; where it actually impedes the course of justice it should be dealt with as an offence against the administration of justice, although this might mean that if it was not done with intent to defeat or pervert the course of justice it would go unpunished; where it does not impede the course of

---

[71] 1960 J.C. 5.

[72] It was held in the Full Bench case of *Hall v. Associated Newspapers Ltd*, 1979 J.C. 1 (see A.M. MacLean, "Contempt in Criminal Process", 1978 S.L.T. (News) 257) that the court's jurisdiction in contempt begins when the accused is arrested or when a warrant for his arrest is granted, or (in summary proceedings) from the service of the complaint, whichever is earliest. The statement in *Stirling v. Associated Newspapers Ltd and Anr*, 1960 J.C. 5, that jurisdiction arises the moment a crime is committed was rejected by the court in *Hall*. They held, however, that it was not a defence that the offenders were unaware that there had been an arrest or that an arrest warrant had been issued; but that statement must now be read subject to the Contempt of Court Act 1981: see, *infra*, para. 50.17. Where the statement complained of is made with the intention of creating prejudice it may, of course, be punishable as a contempt or as an attempt to pervert the course of justice, at whatever stage of the investigation it is made, or even if it is made before any investigation has begun: see, *supra*, para. 47.39; *Hall, supra*, L.J.-G. Emslie at 15; *Skeen v. Farmer*, 1980 S.L.T. (Sh.Ct.) 133; Contempt of Court Act 1981, s.6(c).

[73] At 11. In *Peter Graham* (1876) 3 Couper 217 it was said to be an interference with criminal procedure to offer money to a prisoner charged with theft in return for information as to the whereabouts of the stolen property. L.J.-C. Moncreiff said, "To tamper with a man while in custody for the purpose not of obtaining evidence which would lead to the ends of public justice, but to the ends of private interests — and not only so, but substantially to offer a reward for a confession of guilt — is wholly inconsistent with the principles of our criminal procedure." at 221.

[74] *cf. Connolly v. Dale* [1996] Q.B. 120.

[75] Their investigation in *Stirling v. Associated Newspapers Ltd and Anr*, 1960 J.C. 5, was regarded by the court (at 11) as "a search for sensation".

[76] *Milburn*, 1946 S.C. 301, L.P. Normand at 315.

[77] 1960 J.C. 5.

justice there is no good reason for treating it as a crime or a contempt merely in order to maintain a police monopoly in the investigation of crime.[78]

50.14   VICTIMISATION OF WITNESSES. Intimidation of or other interference with witnesses prior to a trial may be subornation, contempt or an attempt to pervert the course of justice.[79] To assault or threaten a person in revenge for his having given evidence is an aggravated form of assault or of the crime of making threats.[80] It has been held in England that victimisation of a witness after a trial because of the evidence he gave, as where a union dismisses an official or a landlord terminates the lease of a tenant who has given evidence against the victimiser, is a contempt of court.[81] It has also been held in England that "the concept of interference with witnesses extends to interference with proper and reasonable attempts by a party's legal advisers to identify and thereafter interview potential witnesses."[82]

50.15   *Mens rea.* There is no reported authority on *mens rea* in contempt of court. Where the contempt is a direct personal one, so to speak, as where A creates a disturbance in court, or fails to attend when cited, the ordinary common law rules apply and the contempt must be wilful and in deliberate defiance of the court.[83] But where the case concerned newspaper publication of evidence or of contemptuous comment, responsibility at common law appears to have been strict, and to have extended to the editor, owners and publishers of the paper.[84]

---

[78] See [Anon.] "Contempt of Court by Newspapers", 1960 S.L.T. (News) 29. In England, it has been held that police efforts to frustrate the investigation of a defence for the defendant in order to maintain the efficacy of the police's own investigations amounted to a contempt: *Connolly v. Dale* [1996] Q.B. 120.

[79] *cf. R. v. Kellett* [1976] Q.B. 372: attempt to pervert by threatening to sue potential witness for slander. See also *R. v. Toney* [1993] 2 All E.R. 419, CA.

[80] *cf. Chas Ross* (1844) 2 Broun 271.

[81] *Attorney General v. Butterworth* [1963] 1 Q.B. 696; *cf. Chapman v. Honig* [1963] 2 Q.B. 502.

[82] *Connolly v. Dale* [1996] Q.B. 120, Balcombe L.J. (opinion of the court) at 125F: in arriving at their decision, the divisional court applied *Att.-Gen. v. Butterworth* [1963] 1 Q.B. 696, CA, and *R. v. Kellett* [1976] Q.B. 372, CA.

[83] Almost all modern cases stress the need for the contempt to be deliberate: see, *e.g.*, *Muirhead v. Douglas*, 1979 S.L.T. (Notes) 17; *Macaraa v. MacFarlane*, 1980 S.L.T. (Notes) 26; *McKinnon v. Douglas*, 1982 S.C.C.R. 80; *Mowbray v. Valentine*, 1991 S.C.C.R. 494; *McMillan v. Carmichael*, 1993 S.C.C.R. 943; *Caldwell v. Normand*, 1993 S.C.C.R. 624; *Ferguson v. Normand*, 1994 S.C.C.R. 812; *Cameron v. Orr*, 1995 S.C.C.R. 365; *Chappell v. Friel*, 1997 S.L.T. 1325; *cf. Pirie v. Hawthorn*, 1962 J.C. 69. In *Anderson v. Douglas*, 1997 S.C.C.R. 632, at 635D, the court stressed that neither gross neglect or carelessness was sufficient for contempt. (In *Williams v. Clark*, 2001 S.C.C.R. 505, however, the accused's mobile telephone had begun to ring in court when he was being addressed by the sheriff; although the accused had been unaware that the device had been switched on, he was held to have been in contempt of court. At the subsequent appeal, Lord Cameron of Lochbroom (giving the opinion of the court), said (at 507F): "we do not accept that the sheriff was not entitled to regard as a contempt of court the ringing of a mobile telephone within court, particularly in the circumstances where the person is the accused and he is in the dock, and with the added advantage of there being clear notices at various points within the court building to the effect that mobile telephones should be switched off." This suggests that the accused's negligence would have been sufficient for contempt; but Lord Cameron also affirmed the appropriateness of a test of "intentional disrespect or action against the authority of the court"; in any event, the appeal was allowed on the grounds that the sheriff had taken into account matters extraneous to the ringing of the phone and on which she had not invited the accused to address her.)

[84] *cf. MacAlister v. Associated Newspapers Ltd*, 1954 S.L.T. 14, L.J.-G. Cooper at 16. *Cf.* also the English case of *Att.-Gen. v. Punch Ltd* [2001] 2 W.L.R. 1713, CA.

CONTEMPT OF COURT ACT 1981. Sections 1 to 6 of this Act limit the **50.16**
application of the assumed common law rule that *mens rea* is unnecessary in relation to conduct which constitutes contempt as tending to
interfere with the course of justice in particular legal proceedings, which
the Act calls the "strict liability rule".[85]

Section 2, as amended by the Broadcasting Act 1990,[86] provides:

"(1) The strict liability rule applies only in relation to publications,
and for this purpose 'publication' includes any speech, writing,
programme included in a programme service or other communication in whatever form, which is addressed to the public at large or
any section of the public.

(2) The strict liability rule applies only to a publication which
creates a substantial risk that the course of justice in the proceedings in question will be seriously impeded or prejudiced.[87]

(3) The strict liability rule applies to a publication only if the
proceedings in question are active within the meaning of this section
at the time of publication.

(4) Schedule 1 applies for determining the times at which
proceedings are to be treated as active within the meaning of this
section.

(5) In this section 'programme service' has the same meaning as
in the Broadcasting Act 1990."

---

[85] Contempt of Court Act 1981 (hereafter referred to as "the 1981 Act"), s.1.

[86] Sched. 20, para. 31(1)(a), (b).

[87] In *H.M. Advocate v. News Group Newspapers Ltd*, 1989 S.C.C.R. 156, at 161E-F,
L.J.-G. Emslie took the view that a "substantial risk" is one which is more than a minimal
one. He also opined, at 162D, that it was not enough for an accused to have tried to avoid
committing a contempt of court; it was necessary for him to have succeeded in doing so in
order to avoid conviction under the strict liability rule. (Efforts made to avoid a contempt
are, of course, relevant from the point of view of sentence.) That the publication caused
some risk of serious prejudice will thus not be enough unless that risk is substantial, which
has been taken to mean, following L.J.-G. Emslie's view above and the opinion of Lord
Diplock in *Att.-Gen. v. English* [1983] A.C. 116 at 142, that only a remote risk will be
excluded: see *H.M. Advocate v. Caledonian Newspapers Ltd; H.M. Advocate v. Scottish Daily
Record and Sunday Mail Ltd*, 1995 S.C.C.R. 330, L.J.-G. Hope at 344B-D; Lord Hope, at
341E, also stated that the degree of the risk was to be determined at the time of
publication, without regard to what may happen or may have happened thereafter, and
that "prejudice will be regarded as serious if it may affect the outcome of the trial in
regard to such matters as the evidence of witnesses or the evaluation by the jury of the
evidence"; for an example of a case where the court considered the risk to be slight, see
Att.-Gen. v. Unger [1998] 1 Cr.App.R. 308. A finding of contempt may be avoided if the
risk of prejudice created by a particular publication is considered to have contributed little
or nothing to a risk of prejudice which already existed by virtue of material published by
others prior to proceedings having become active: see *Att.-Gen. v. MGN Ltd* [1997] 1 All
E.R. 456, although the circumstances there were very special. The most recent Scottish
decisions in this field of law strongly support, however, a much more liberal attitude
towards the interpretation of what constitutes contempt: see, *e.g.*, *Montgomery v. H.M.
Advocate*, 2000 S.C.C.R. 1044, PC; *Galbraith v. H.M. Advocate*, 2001 S.L.T. 465; *B.B.C.,
Petrs*, 2001 S.C.C.R. 440.

See also *H.M. Advocate v. Scottish Media Newspapers Ltd*, 1999 S.C.C.R. 599, which *inter
alia* emphasises that the 1981 Act was enacted to bring certain aspects of the law of
contempt into line with article 10 of the European Convention on Human Rights, and that
strict attention to the terms of s.2 of the Act should ensure compatibility with that article
("freedom of expression"). It was also held in the case that prejudicial material, published
when proceedings were active, may not present a substantial risk of serious prejudice if it is
clear at the time of publication that no trial will take place until a significant period of time
has elapsed; *cf. H.M. Advocate v. The Scotsman Publications Ltd*, 1999 S.C.C.R. 163. See
too *Cox and Griffiths, Petrs*, 1998 S.C.C.R. 561; *H.M. Advocate v. Danskin*, 2000 S.C.C.R.
101.

"Proceedings" include proceedings in any tribunal or body exercising the judicial power of the State[88]; proceedings before United Kingdom courts sitting in Scotland, as well as before the House of Lords in appeals from any court sitting in Scotland are treated as Scottish proceedings.[89]

Criminal proceedings (*i.e.* proceedings against a person in respect of an offence, other than appellate proceedings)[90] are active from the stage of arrest or the grant of a warrant of arrest, or from the grant of a warrant to cite, or from the service of an indictment or other document specifying a charge, whichever is the earliest, until they are concluded by acquittal or sentence, or by any other order putting an end to the proceedings, or by discontinuance or operation of law.[91] "Sentence" includes a deferred sentence under section 202 of the Criminal Procedure (Scotland) Act 1995, so that the strict liability rule may cease to apply before the accused is actually disposed of.[92] The Act specifically provides that express abandonment by the prosecutor or desertion simpliciter constitutes a discontinuance[93]; it would appear, therefore, that desertion *pro loco et tempore* is not considered to be such a discontinuance.[94] A finding of insanity in bar of trial constitutes a discontinuance of the proceedings, but they become active again if they are resumed.[95]

Where proceedings begin with the grant of an arrest warrant, they cease to be active after twelve months if there has been no arrest, but revive with a subsequent arrest.[96]

Appellate proceedings are active from the time they are begun by application for leave to appeal, notice of appeal or application for a stated case until they are "disposed of or abandoned, discontinued or withdrawn."[97] When the appeal court remits the case to the lower court or grants authority for a new prosecution, any further or new proceedings become active from the conclusion of the appeal proceedings.[98]

50.17 Section 3 of the 1981 Act provides a specific defence of reasonable care which limits the application of the strict liability rule even in those cases where it applies by reason of section 2 of the Act. It provides:

> "(1) A person is not guilty of contempt of court under the strict liability rule as the publisher of any matter to which that rule applies if at the time of the publication (having taken all reasonable care)

---

[88] The Professional Conduct Committee of the General Medical Council was considered not to be a court for the purposes of the 1981 Act since, although it did exercise a judicial function in the public interest and had procedural rules similar to those applicable to courts of law, it was in effect a body exercising self-regulatory powers of a particular profession rather than exercising the judicial power of the State: *General Medical Council v. B.B.C.* [1998] 1 W.L.R. 1573, CA, Stuart-Smith L.J. at 1580E-F. An industrial tribunal does, however, fulfil the definition: *Peach Grey and Co. v. Sommers* [1995] 2 All E.R. 513, as does a mental health review tribunal: *Pickering v. Liverpool Daily Post and Echo* [1991] 2 W.L.R. 513, HL.
[89] Section 19.
[90] Sched. 1, para. 1.
[91] Sched. 1, paras 3–5.
[92] *ibid.*, para. 6.
[93] *ibid.*, para 7(*b*).
[94] See *H.M. Advocate v. Express Newspapers Plc*, 1998 S.C.C.R. 471.
[95] Sched. 1, para. 10(a).
[96] *ibid.*, para. 11.
[97] *ibid.*, para. 15.
[98] *ibid.*, para. 16.

he does not know and has no reason to suspect that relevant proceedings are active.

(2) A person is not guilty of contempt of court under the strict liability rule as the distributor of a publication containing any such matter if at the time of distribution (having taken all reasonable care) he does not know that it contains such matter and has no reason to suspect that it is likely to do so.

(3) The burden of proof of any fact tending to establish a defence afforded by this section to any person lies upon that person."

The strict liability rule does not apply to publication as part of a bona **50.18** fide discussion of matters of public interest if the risk of prejudice is merely incidental.[99]

Section 6 of the 1981 Act specifically provides that the preceding **50.19** sections of the Act will not: (a) prejudice any common law defence to strict liability contempt, (b) make any publication a contempt which would not otherwise have been so, or (c) restrict liability for contempt in respect of conduct intended to impede or prejudice the administration of justice.

The 1981 Act provides the same maximum penalty for all contempts **50.20** of court, whether under the Act itself or at common law, and makes it no longer competent to order a person to be committed to prison until such time as he purges his contempt.[1]

PRESS PUBLICATION OF JUDICIAL PROCEEDINGS

At common law the publication of anything said in open court is both **50.21** lawful and privileged. The publication of confidential matter such as statements in an open record[2] is contempt. The publication by Crown officials of their precognitions would constitute a breach of duty and a contravention of the Official Secrets Acts, and their publication by anyone else might constitute contempt as being prejudicial to a fair trial.

Section 9 of the 1981 Act prohibits the use of sound recording devices in court without leave, except for the purpose of official transcripts. There is apparently no prohibition on making silent films. Section 9 provides:

"(1) Subject to subsection (4) below, it is a contempt of court—
    (a) to use in court, or bring into court for use, any tape recorder or other instrument for recording sound, except with the leave of the court;
    (b) to publish a recording of legal proceedings made by means of any such instrument, or any recording derived directly or indirectly from it, by playing it in the hearing of the public or any section of the public, or to dispose of it or any recording so derived, with a view to publication;
    (c) to use any such recording in contravention of any conditions of leave granted under paragraph (a).

---

[99] The 1981 Act, s.5. See, *supra*, para. 50.12.
[1] The 1981 Act, s.15. The maximum penalties are set out in para. 50.01, *supra*.
[2] *Young v. Armour* (1921) 1 S.L.T. 211.

(2) Leave under paragraph (a) of subsection (1) may be granted or refused at the discretion of the court, and if granted may be granted subject to such conditions as the court thinks proper with respect to the use of any recording made pursuant to the leave; and where leave has been granted the court may at the like discretion withdraw or amend it either generally or in relation to any particular of the proceedings.

(3) Without prejudice to any other power to deal with an act of contempt under paragraph (a) of subsection (1), the court may order the instrument, or any recording made with it, or both, to be forfeited; and any object so forfeited shall (unless the court otherwise determines on application by a person appearing to be the owner) be sold or otherwise disposed of in such manner as the court may direct.

(4) This section does not apply to the making or use of sound recordings for purposes of official transcripts of proceedings."

50.22   CONTEMPT OF COURT ACT 1981. The common law rule set out in the preceding paragraph is preserved by section 4(1) of the 1981 Act, which provides:

"(1) Subject to this section a person is not guilty of contempt of court under the strict liability rule in respect of a fair and accurate report of legal proceedings held in public, published contemporaneously and in good faith."

Publication may, however, be restricted by the court in terms of section 4(2) which provides:

"In any such proceedings the court may, where it appears to be necessary for avoiding a substantial risk of prejudice to the administration of justice in those proceedings, or in any other proceedings pending or imminent, order that the publication of any report of the proceedings, be postponed for such period as the court thinks necessary for that purpose."[3]

It is uncertain what is meant by other proceedings which are "pending or imminent", but it has been suggested that the statutory phrase may tend to cover subsequent proceedings which may possibly (rather than inevitably) follow as a result of current proceedings, as, for example, where the Crown might be granted the opportunity to have a new prosecution as the result of an appeal.[3a]

Section 4(2) presupposes that fair and accurate reports of public legal proceedings might nevertheless carry a risk of prejudice to a particular accused either in those proceedings or in proceedings "pending or imminent"; thus, if the risk of such prejudice is substantial, the court has discretion to postpone reports of the whole or particular parts of those proceedings. Prejudice is, however, unlikely to be regarded as sufficiently substantial unless jurors, suitably directed, would be unable to dismiss the prejudicial material from their minds and arrive at their verdict

---

[3] See *R. v. Horsham JJ., ex p. Farquharson* [1982] Q.B. 762; *Keane v. H.M. Advocate,* 1987 S.L.T. 220; *R. v. Beck* (1992) 94 Cr.App.R. 376, CA, Farquharson L.J., at p. 381.

[3a] *Galbraith v. H.M. Advocate,* 2001 S.L.T. 465, opinion of the court at 468K. Nevertheless, the court in *Galbraith,* and in *B.B.C., Petrs,* 2001 S.C.C.R. 440, reserved their opinion on the precise significance of the phrase "pending or imminent".

solely on the basis of the evidence advanced during the proceedings in question. Recent cases suggest that the Scottish courts retain considerable faith in the ability of properly directed juries to ignore prior published material of a prejudicial nature, and thus it is likely that section 4(2) orders will be granted sparingly in future.[3b] Also, it has been determined that in considering whether an application for a section 4(2) order should be granted, a court should bear in mind that the right of an accused to a fair trial (under Article 6(1) of the European Convention on Human Rights) is to be weighed against "the interests of the wider public" in having the ability to scrutinise the judicial process through publication of fair and accurate reports of legal proceedings.[3c] Where a court is persuaded to grant such an order, it must ensure that the order is no wider in scope than is necessary to avoid risk of prejudice.[3d]

Publication of a report which is postponed by an order under section 4(2) is contemporaneous if it is published as soon as practicable after the expiry of the order.[4]

Where a court allows a name or other matter to be withheld from the **50.23** public in court proceedings it may give such directions prohibiting its publication in connection with the proceedings as appear necessary for the purpose for which it was withheld.[5]

Section 8 of the 1981 Act renders jury deliberations confidential. It **50.24** provides:

"(1) Subject to subsection (2) below, it is a contempt of court to obtain, disclose[6] or solicit any particulars of statements made, opinions expressed, arguments advanced or votes cast by members of a jury in the course of their deliberations in any legal proceedings.

(2) This section does not apply to any disclosure of any particulars—

(a) in the proceedings in question for the purpose of enabling the jury to arrive at their verdict, or in connection with the delivery of that verdict, or

---

[3b] See *Galbraith v. H.M. Advocate*, 2001 S.L.T. 465; *B.B.C., Petrs*, 2001 S.C.C.R. 440.

[3c] See *B.B.C., Petrs*, 2001 S.C.C.R. 440, opinion of the court at paras [12]–[14], where the importance of Art. 10 (freedom of expression) of the Convention is discussed. (It is clear from this case that since *Galbraith v. H.M. Advocate*, 2001 S.L.T. 465, the practice has been to make an order under s.4(2) temporary until 5 p.m. on the second working day after the order was granted, so that interested parties may have time to make representations to the court that the order should be recalled or limited: copies of the order are also emailed to certain organisations, and the order is noted on the Scottish Court Service's web site.)

[3d] *Galbraith v. H.M. Advocate*, 2001 S.L.T. 465, opinion of the court at 469B.

[4] Section 4(3)(a).

[5] The 1981 Act, s.11. In *R. v. Legal Aid Board, ex. p. Kaim Todner* [1999] Q.B. 966, CA, it was held that if there is no statutory rule sanctioning the withholding of, *e.g.*, a name, a court should not make an order withholding it and prohibiting publication, save where that is necessary for the proper administration of justice. It was also held that there was no justification for according the legal profession special treatment in relation to the granting of such an order, and, that persons initiating proceedings in court could reasonably be considered to have accepted the normal incidents of such — including the public nature of such proceedings.

[6] It is disclosure under this section for a person to publish disclosures already made by an individual juror to that person directly or indirectly: *Att.-Gen. v. Associated Newspapers Ltd* [1994] 2 W.L.R. 277, HL, where it was held that there was no reason to give "disclosure" a restrictive meaning.

(b) in evidence in any subsequent proceedings for an offence
alleged to have been committed in relation to the jury in the
first mentioned proceedings,

or to the publication of any particulars so disclosed."

"In the course of their deliberations" refers only to "what passes among
the jurors while they are considering their verdict after the judge has
directed them to retire to do so."[7]

50.25 *Publication of indecent matter.* The Judicial Proceedings (Regulation of
Reports) Act 1926 (as applied to Scotland)[8] provides:

"**1.**—(1) It shall not be lawful to print or publish,[9] or cause or
procure to be printed or published—
  (a) in relation to any judicial proceedings any indecent medical,
      surgical or physiological details being matters or details the
      publication of which would be calculated to injure public
      morals;
  (b) in relation to any proceedings under Part II of the Family
      Law Act 1996 or otherwise in relation to any judicial
      proceedings for dissolution of marriage, for nullity of mar-
      riage, or for judicial separation, or an action of adherence or
      of adherence and aliment, any particulars other than the
      following, that is to say—
      (i) the names, addresses and occupations of the parties and
          witnesses;
      (ii) a concise statement of the charges, defences and coun-
           tercharges in support of which evidence has been given;
      (iii) submissions on any point of law arising in the course of
            the proceedings, and the decision of the court thereon;
      (iv) the summing-up of the judge and the finding of the jury
           (if any) and the judgment of the court and observations
           made by the judge in giving judgment:
      Provided that nothing in this part of this subsection shall be
      held to permit the publication of anything contrary to the
      provisions of paragraph (a) of this subsection.[10]
  (2) . . . Provided that no person, other than a proprietor, editor,
master printer or publisher, shall be liable to be convicted under
this Act."

50.26 *Persons under 16.* Section 47 of the Criminal Procedure (Scotland) Act
1995 provides:

---

[7] *Scottish Criminal Cases Review Commission, Petrs*, High Court, July 25, 2001, unrep'd,
opinion of the court at para. [7]. It was also held there that the Crown (and the Scottish
Criminal Cases Review Commission) are bound by s.8, but the Court reserved their
opinion on the question whether the Appeal Court was so bound when exercising powers
under s.104 of the Criminal Procedure (Scotland) Act 1995.

[8] And as amended by the Family Law Act 1996, Sched. 8, para. 2 (which applies to
Scotland by virtue of s.67(4)(a)(ii)).

[9] For the meaning of "publish" in the context of this section, see *Gilchrist v. Scott*, 2000
S.C.C.R. 28.

[10] Maximum penalty on summary conviction four months' and a fine of level 5 on the
standard scale. For a discussion of the Act from the journalists' point of view see A.
Bonnington, R. McInnes and B. McKain, *Scots Law for Journalists* (7th ed., 2000),
Chap. 12.

"(1) Subject to subsection (3) below, no newspaper report of any proceedings in a court shall reveal the name, address or school, or include any particulars calculated to lead to the identification, of any person under the age of 16 years concerned in the proceedings, either—

(a) as being a person against or in respect of whom the proceedings are taken; or

(b) as being a witness in the proceedings.

(2) Subject to subsection (3) below, no picture which is, or includes, a picture of a person under the age of 16 years concerned in proceedings as mentioned in subsection (1) above shall be published in any newspaper in a context relevant to the proceedings.

(3) The requirements of subsections (1) and (2) above shall be applied in any case mentioned in any of the following paragraphs to the extent specified in that paragraph—

(a) where a person under the age of 16 years is concerned in the proceedings as a witness only and no one against whom the proceedings are taken is under the age of 16 years, the requirements shall not apply unless the court so directs;

(b) where, at any stage of the proceedings, the court, if it is satisfied that it is in the public interest to do so, directs that the requirements (including the requirements as applied by a direction under paragraph (a) above) shall be dispensed with to such extent as the court may specify; and

(c) where the Secretary of State, after completion of the proceedings, if satisfied as mentioned in paragraph (b) above, by order dispenses with the requirements to such extent as may be specified in the order.

(4) This section shall, with the necessary modifications, apply in relation to sound and television programmes included in a programme service (within the meaning of the Broadcasting Act 1990) as it applies in relation to newspapers.

(5) A person who publishes matter in contravention of this section shall be guilty of an offence and liable on summary conviction to a fine not exceeding level 4 on the standard scale.

(6) In this section, references to a court shall not include a court in England, Wales or Northern Ireland."[11]

Proceedings at children's hearings. Section 44 of the Children (Scotland) **50.27** Act 1995 provides:

"(1) No person shall publish any matter in respect of proceedings at a children's hearing, or before a sheriff on an application under section 57, section 60(7), section 65(7) or (9), section 76(1) or section 85(1) of this Act, or on any appeal under this Part of this Act, which is intended to, or is likely to, identify—

(a) any child[12] concerned in the proceedings or appeal;

---

[11] See also the Fatal Accident and Sudden Deaths Inquiry (Scotland) Act 1976, s.4(4), which makes similar provision for the protection of persons under 17 "involved" in an inquiry under the Act: maximum penalty a fine of level 4 on the standard scale: s.4(5).

[12] "child" means a child under the age of 16; a child over the age of 16 but under the age of 18 in respect of whom a supervision requirement is in force; a child whose case has been referred to a children's hearing under s.33 of the Act; or, in the case of a person who has failed to attend school regularly, child includes a person over 16 who is not over school age: s.93(2)(b).

(b) an address or school as being that of any such child.

(2) Any person who contravenes subsection (1) above shall be guilty of an offence and shall be liable on summary conviction to a fine not exceeding level 4 on the standard scale in respect of each such contravention.

(3) It shall be a defence in proceedings for an offence under this section for the accused to prove that he did not know, and had no reason to suspect, that the published matter was intended, or was likely, to identify the child or, as the case may be, the address or school.

(4) In this section 'to publish' includes, without prejudice to the generality of that expression—

(a) to publish matter in a programme service, as defined by section 201 of the Broadcasting Act 1990 (definition of programme service); and

(b) to cause matter to be published.

(5) The requirements of subsection (1) above may, in the interests of justice, be dispensed with by—

(a) the sheriff in any proceedings before him;

(b) the Court of Session in any appeal under section 51 (11) of this Act; or

(c) the Secretary of State in relation to any proceedings at a children's hearing,

to such an extent as the sheriff, Court of Session or the Secretary of State as the case may be considers appropriate."

50.28 *Committal proceedings.* It is an offence to publish anywhere in Britain any details of committal proceedings in England and Wales which result in the committal of anyone for trial until after the trial unless the magistrates' court on application by an accused permits publication.[13] The prohibition does not extend to the publication of the names of those concerned, the place of committal and the charges involved.[14]

---

[13] Magistrates' Courts Act 1980, s.8. Maximum penalty, a fine of level 3 on the standard scale: s.8(5).

[14] *ibid.*, s.8(4). See also the offences of reporting in Scotland certain preliminary proceedings in English proceedings: ss. 38, 42 and 60 of the Criminal Procedure and Investigations Act 1996.

INDEX